THE ROUTLEDGE HANDBOOK OF AFRICAN DEMOGRAPHY

This handbook provides an authoritative and comprehensive overview of African population dynamics, variations, causes and consequences, demonstrating the real-world applications of research in policies and programmes.

African demography has come of age. Over 50 years, the discipline has grown exponentially in the number of training and research institutions, specialist experts and academic output, all with an aim of addressing the enormous demographic challenges faced by the continent. The book draws on old and emerging analytical tools to explore the relationships between population dynamics and social, economic, cultural and political environments from African perspectives. Key topics include fertility, sexual behaviours, healthcare, ageing, mortality, migration, displacement, the causes and consequences of demographic changes and teaching and research developments in African demography.

The Routledge Handbook of African Demography will be an essential resource for students and researchers of African demography, sociology, development and cultural studies.

Clifford O. Odimegwu is a Professor of Demography, Social Statistics and Population Health at the University of the Witwatersrand, South Africa.

Yemi Adewoyin is a Lecturer at the University of Nigeria and a Research Fellow in Population Health and Spatial Demography at the University of the Witwatersrand, Johannesburg, South Africa.

THE ROUTLEDGE HANDBOOK OF AFRICAN DEMOGRAPHY

Edited by
Clifford O. Odimegwu and Yemi Adewoyin

Routledge
Taylor & Francis Group
LONDON AND NEW YORK

Cover image: © Getty Images

First published 2022
by Routledge
2 Park Square, Milton Park, Abingdon, Oxon OX14 4RN

and by Routledge
605 Third Avenue, New York, NY 10158

Routledge is an imprint of the Taylor & Francis Group, an informa business

British Library Cataloguing-in-Publication Data
A catalogue record for this book is available from the British Library

Library of Congress Cataloging-in-Publication Data
Names: Odimegwu, C. O., editor. | Adewoyin, Yemi, editor.
Title: The Routledge handbook of african demography / edited by Clifford O. Odimegwu and Yemi Adewoyin.
Description: New York, NY : Routledge, 2022. | Series: Routledge international handbooks | Includes bibliographical references and index.
Identifiers: LCCN 2021034960 (print) | LCCN 2021034961 (ebook) | ISBN 9780367253288 (hardback) | ISBN 9781032183107 (paperback) | ISBN 9780429287213 (ebook)
Subjects: LCSH: Africa—Population. | Demography—Africa.
Classification: LCC HB3661.A3 R68 2022 (print) | LCC HB3661.A3 (ebook) | DDC 304.6096—dc23
LC record available at https://lccn.loc.gov/2021034960
LC ebook record available at https://lccn.loc.gov/2021034961

ISBN: 978-0-367-25328-8 (hbk)
ISBN: 978-1-032-18310-7 (pbk)
ISBN: 978-0-429-28721-3 (ebk)

DOI: 10.4324/9780429287213

Typeset in Bembo
by Apex CoVantage, LLC

This Handbook is dedicated to all African and Africanist scholars who are dedicated to changing the African narratives.

CONTENTS

FIGURES

TABLES

CONTRIBUTORS

Manikandan AD, International Institute for Population Sciences, Mumbai, India

Olukemi Adebola, Federal University of Technology, Akure, Nigeria

Ayo S. Adebowale, University of Ibadan, Nigeria, and University of Calabar, Nigeria

Sunday A. Adedini, Federal University, Oye-Ekiti, Nigeria, and University of the Witwatersrand, Johannesburg, South Africa

Aderanti Adepoju, World Economic Forum Global Agenda Council on Migration, Lagos, Nigeria

Jacob A. Adetunji, Office of Population and Reproductive Health, Bureau for Global Health, USAID, Washington, DC

David A. Adewole, University of Ibadan, Nigeria

Yemi Adewoyin, University of Nigeria and University of the Witwatersrand, Johannesburg, South Africa

Milton Adieri, University of Nairobi, Kenya

Rotimi F. Afolabi, University of Ibadan, Nigeria

Sam Agbahoungba, Consortium Régional pour la Recherche en Economie Générationnelle and Université de Thiès-Sénégal, Senegal

Patricia Agupusi, American University, Washington, DC, USA

Khandaker Jafor Ahmed, The University of Adelaide, Australia

Joshua O. Akinyemi, University of Ibadan, Nigeria, and University of the Witwatersrand, Johannesburg, South Africa

Edem Akpo, Consortium Régional pour la Recherche en Economie Générationnelle and Université de Thiès-Sénégal, Senegal

Oluwatosin Ariyo, East Tennessee State University, Tennessee, USA

Carlos Arnaldo, Universidade Eduardo Mondlane, Mozambique

Mark A. Aviisah, University of Groningen, The Netherlands, and University of Health and Allied Sciences, Ghana

Bernard Baffour, Australian National University, Canberra, Australia

Dalomi Bahan, Consortium Régional pour la Recherche en Economie Générationnelle and Université de Thiès-Sénégal, Senegal

Boladé Hamed Banougnin, National Institute for Statistics and Economic Analysis, Cotonou, Benin Republic

Segun Bello, University of Ibadan, Nigeria

Obasanjo Afolabi Bolarinwa, University of KwaZulu-Natal, South Africa

Pamela Chirwa-Banda, Ministry of General Education, Lusaka, Zambia

Giuseppe T. Cirella, University of Gdansk, Poland

Fidelia A. A. Dake, University of Ghana, Ghana

Justin Dansou, University of Parakou, Benin Republic

Gabriela Narcizo de Lima, College of the Northern Border, Mexico

Nicole De Wet, University of the Witwatersrand, Johannesburg, South Africa

Robert Y. Djogbenou, University of Montreal, Canada

Henry Victor Doctor, Regional Office for the Eastern Mediterranean, World Health Organization, Cairo, Egypt

Latif Dramani, Consortium Régional pour la Recherche en Economie Générationnelle and Université de Thiès-Sénégal, Senegal

Adeniyi F. Fagbamigbe, University of Ibadan, Nigeria

Arlette Simo Fotso, Institut de recherche pour le développement (IRD) et Université de Paris, Inserm ERL, Paris, France

Sasha Frade, University of the Witwatersrand, Johannesburg, South Africa

Michel Garenne, University of the Witwatersrand, Johannesburg, South Africa; Institut Pasteur, Epidémiologie des Maladies Emergentes, Paris, France; Institut de Recherche pour le Développement (IRD), UMI Résiliences, Bondy, France; and Université d'Auvergne, Clermont-Ferrand, France

Babatunde M. Gbadebo, University of Ibadan, Nigeria

Francis Gendreau, retired from Institut de recherche pour le développement, France

Anne Goujon, Austrian Academy of Sciences, University of Vienna, and European Commission Joint Research Centre, Ispra, Italy

Françoise Gubry, retired from Institut de recherche pour le développement, France

Camille Guidimé, Consortium Régional pour la Recherche en Economie Générationnelle and Université de Parakou, Bénin Republic

Razak M Gyasi, African Population and Health Research Center (APHRC), Nairobi, Kenya

Hinke H. Haisma, University of Groningen, The Netherlands

Rogers Hansine, Universidade Eduardo Mondlane, Mozambique

Lawrence Ikamari, University of Nairobi, Kenya

Chimaraoke Izugbara, International Center for Research on Women, Washington, DC, USA

Vinod Joseph Kannankeril Joseph, International Institute for Population Sciences, Mumbai, India

Samir K.C., Austrian Academy of Sciences, University of Vienna, and Shanghai University, Shanghai, People's Republic of China

Caroline W. Kabiru, African Population and Health Research Center, Kenya, and University of the Witwatersrand, South Africa

Jacob Kazungu, KEMRI Welcome Trust, Kenya

Mpho Keetile, University of Botswana, Gaborone, Botswana

Silvère Konan, Consortium Régional pour la Recherche en Economie Générationnelle and Université de Cocody, Cote d'Ivoire

Gobopamang Letamo, University of Botswana, Gaborone, Botswana

Crispin Mabika, Consortium Régional pour la Recherche en Economie Générationnelle and Université de Kinshasa, Democratic Republic of Congo

Beatrice W. Maina, African Population and Health Research Center, Kenya and University of the Witwatersrand, South Africa

K. Mangombe, University of Zimbabwe, Harare, Zimbabwe

Blessing U Mberu, African Population and Health Research Center (APHRC), Nairobi, Kenya

Lungile F. Motsa, University of the Witwatersrand, Johannesburg, South Africa

Marifa Muchemwa, University of the Witwatersrand, Johannesburg, South Africa

Mary Muyonga, University of Nairobi, Kenya

Ivy Nandongwa, African Population and Health Research Center, Kenya

Kannan Navaneetham, University of Botswana, Gaborone, Botswana

Larissa Nawo, University of Dschang, Cameroon

Cheikh Tidiane Ndiaye, Consortium Régional pour la Recherche en Economie Générationnelle and Gestion Université Gaston Berger, Sénégal

Alex Njeru, KEMRI Welcome Trust, Kenya

Lorretta Favour Chizomam Ntoimo, Federal University Oye-Ekiti, Nigeria

Vollan O. Ochieng, African Population and Health Research Center (APHRC), Nairobi, Kenya

Clifford O. Odimegwu, University of the Witwatersrand, Johannesburg, South Africa

George Odipo, University of Nairobi, Kenya

Jean Baptiste Oga, Consortium Régional pour la Recherche en Economie Générationnelle and Université de Parakou, Bénin Republic

David I. Ojakaa, BRIM Research Ltd., Nairobi, Kenya

Tubosun Olowolafe, University of Ibadan, Nigeria

Dorothy N. Ononokpono, University of Uyo, Nigeria

Obiageli Onwusaka, University of Ibadan, Nigeria

Morné Oosthuizen, University of Cape Town, South Africa

Alfred Agwanda Otieno, University of Nairobi, Kenya

Daniel Esteban Quiroga, National University of Catamarca, Argentina

Claudia Reiter, Austrian Academy of Sciences, University of Vienna, Austria

Mobolaji M. Salawu, University of Ibadan, Nigeria

David A. Sánchez-Páez, Université Catholique de Louvain, Belgium.

Bruno Schoumaker, Université Catholique de Louvain, Belgium.

Yandisa Sikweyiya, University of the Witwatersrand, South Africa, and South Africa Medical Research Council, Pretoria, South Africa

Daniel Jordan Smith, Brown University, Rhode Island, USA

Yan Tan, The University of Adelaide, Australia

Nsidibe Usoro, University of Uyo, Nigeria

Tobias C. Vogt, University of Groningen, The Netherlands; Manipal Academy of Higher Education, India; and Max Planck Institute for Demographic Research, Rostock, Germany

Samuel Mwangi Wanjiku, Tübingen University, Germany

N.N. Wekwete, University of Zimbabwe, Harare, Zimbabwe

Sanni Yaya, University of Ottawa, Canada

Helena Yeboah, University of Ottawa, Canada

Nelson C. Zavale, Universidade Eduardo Mondlane, Mozambique

Timalizge Zgambo, University of the Western Cape, South Africa

Roberto Ariel Abeldaño Zuñiga, University of Sierra Sur, Mexico

FOREWORD

Since the advent of the massive trans-Atlantic slave trade, which was followed by colonialism, post-colonial Africa has been on a journey in search of development solutions to its perennial social, economic and political challenges. These have been characterized by the often raw strife of human life against nature and fed into an unrelenting and deafening sound of guns. Many argue that the effects of COVID-19 have not been as devastating in claiming life in Africa as in other parts of the world because of its young population. This, if it is so, is a dividend acquired by accident. Africa should cease to be prone to accidents, be they humanmade or natural. This makes the study of the economic, social and political evolution of human populations extremely relevant, in particular regarding changes in reproduction, migration and death. The determinants and correlates of these changes are central to population development trajectories. In the context of Agenda 2063 (the Africa we want, with its seven aspirations) and Agenda 2030 (and its attendant 17 Sustainable Development Goals [SDGs]), this seminal contribution, *Handbook of African Demography*, edited by Professor Clifford O. Odimegwu and Dr Yemi Adewoyin, is an apt effort by African scholars to, among other aims, open up spaces to link with works undertaken in particular by the National Statistics Offices.

We touch on that in relation to Chapters 6, 7, 8 and 44. In 45 chapters, the scholars have created a unique potpourri of transdisciplinary contributions covering a broad range of determinants and correlates of demographic states and changes on the African continent. I pick out a few of these chapters only to illustrate how the mosaic of information is brought together in a symphony. In Chapter 1 of what is his fourth book, Clifford O. Odimegwu, one not short of ambition, and his co-editor have set the bar even higher. In this prelude, they provide a glimpse of things to come: "Themes covered in this 45-chapter book include demographic training and research in Africa, marriage, fertility and reproductive health, gender issues, demographic crises emanating from and attributable to environment and health, migration, ageing, mortality, and demographic transition and dividend." With their intellectual compatriots who authored chapters in this volume, these themes traverse the entire value chain of development challenges facing Africa. For instance, in Chapter 2, Yemi Adewoyin and Clifford O. Odimegwu introduce the cause-consequences interplay between the spatial dimensions of economy and demography. They cast their intellectual net into the emergent implications of conflict on the demography of Africa, thereby whetting the readers' appetite for understanding the stubborn changes and challenges of the demographics of the space economy. The title sets the importance of practice in regional science: "Spatiotemporal Patterns and Development Linkages."

Chapter 3, "Demographic Training in African Institutions: Past, Present and Future" (Alfred Agwanda Otieno and Lawrence Ikamari) shows the ubiquitous value of demographic techniques in areas of insurance and risk management. In this regard, this chapter on training connects naturally with the challenges of our times covered in Chapter 28, "Climate Change and Population Displacement in Africa" (Roberto Ariel Abeldaño Zuñiga, Gabriela Narcizo de Lima and Daniel Esteban Quiroga). Seized with the worst pandemic in a century, Chapter 4 raises the question of "African Demographic Research: Progress and Challenges" (Michel Garenne). By focusing on diseases and pandemics, this chapter provides pathways through which Africa's experiences with the HIV and AIDS and Ebola pandemics may have to contend with COVID-19. Never has the world focused on the science of modelling as it has in the world of COVID-19. Chapter 5, "Indirect Estimation Techniques and Statistical Modeling in African Demographic Research" (Joshua O. Akinyemi and Sunday A. Adedini), will definitely raise for the reader the question of whether there is convergence in the science of modelling and estimation maths, statistics and demography. This chapter should find resonance in the context of COVID-19, and thus, it catapults demography to the centre.

Parts of the continent have not been well studied, or new stressful phenomena have emerged. Chapters 6, 7, 8 and 44 pose important questions that are country specific by colonial master. Bringing Lusophone Africa on board through Chapter 6, "The Demographic Research in Lusophone Africa: What Is Known and What Needs to Be Done?" (Carlos Arnaldo, Rogers Hansine and Nelson C. Zavale) raises important questions which the national statistics offices should address. In particular, it has to address the advent of the likes of the African Census Analysis Project (ACAP), Africa Symposium Statistical Development (ASSD) and the Strategies for Harmonisation of Statistics in Africa (SHaSA). These initiatives are now waning, ironically, at the time they need to scale up the contribution of the population database. In this vein, Chapter 7 looks into "Old, Contemporary and Emerging Sources of Demographic Data in Africa" (Babatunde M. Gbadebo), which was the main mission of the efforts of the ASSD. Chapter 8, "Demographic Operations in Distress? The Case of French-Speaking African Countries South of the Sahara" (Françoise Gubry and Francis Gendreau), draws similar attention to events in Francophone Africa.

Perhaps the central question on impact is by what measure Africa will know that it has succeeded in removing the safety net of luck from its lexicon and life. Chapters 34, 35 and 45 address this question. Chapter 34, "The Economic Lifecycle and Africa's Demographic Dividend" (Morné Oosthuizen), and Chapter 35, "Demographic Dividend Monitoring Index Conceptual Framework and Case Studies in Africa" (Latif Dramani, Crispin Mabika, Camille Guidimé, Jean Baptiste Oga, Cheikh Tidiane Ndiaye, Dalomi Bahan, Edem Akpo, Sam Agbahoungba and Silvère Konan), should be a wakeup call to Africa that it shall not survive on luck and potential but by transforming the potential of youthfulness into a real dividend. Otherwise, the sad 400-year journey is going to be easily repeated.

In conclusion, a foreword can hardly do justice to the complexity of the subject so well addressed in the 45 chapters by African scholars. Suffice it to point out that the context of SDGs and Agenda 2063 could have not been better served by these experts. If not now, then when, and if not by African intellectuals, then by whom?

Pali Lehohla
Former Statistician-General, South Africa
Professor of Practice, University of Johannesburg and
Research Associate, Oxford Poverty and Human Development Initiative,
University of Oxford

PREFACE

African demography has been in transition since 1994. There has been a significant increase in the number of training and research institutions and a commensurate growth in the number of specialists in the field. These have resulted in an increasing number of African contributions to global demographic research and a massive increase in African demographic research outputs. The most recent work on African demography is *Continuity and Change in Sub-Saharan Africa*, edited by Clifford O. Odimegwu and John Kekovole. This work, though seminal, does not capture all the different studies done on Africa. Its data source was mainly census data archived across many platforms. The need to extend this work and also systematically capture the increasing contributions by African and Africanist scholars to global demographic research in a compendium as an authoritative and comprehensive reference resource for the current, emerging and next generations of researchers and the general public inform this Handbook of African demography.

Although an analysis of the list of contributors to this edited volume will reveal a blend of old, not-so-old and emerging demographers, population scientists and allied professionals whose works speak to the eclectic nature of the discipline of demography, this handbook is also a parting gift from the golden generation of African demographers and population scientists tending to retirement from training and research scenes. The urgency of documenting the body of work by these scholars, and others, in the past 50 years and defining future demographic research agenda in Africa necessitated working with very strict timelines to bring this handbook to light. For this "inconvenience," we sincerely appreciate all contributors and reviewers for prioritizing our very exacting demands while still sticking to the quality and scientific rigour that informed their selection as contributors in the first place.

With broad objectives of comprehensively reviewing demographic research findings in Africa by African and Africanist scholars working in the field of African demography; providing a comprehensive collection of methodological, theoretical and practical issues on the determinants and consequences of population change on the African continent; providing exhaustive bibliographies of African demographic research; and defining future demographic research agenda for the next generation of African demographers and population scientists, the handbook is presented in 45 chapters. Themes covered include demographic training and research in Africa, marriage, fertility, sexual and reproductive health, gender issues, environment, health and development, migration, ageing, mortality and demographic transition. In their various contributions, all the authors have ensured that the broad objectives of the handbook are adequately addressed.

Clifford O. Odimegwu and Yemi Adewoyin

ACKNOWLEDGEMENTS

Given the ongoing demographic transitions on the African continent and their implications for global sustainable development, the idea of a *Handbook of African Demography* to document these transitions is not only essential but also timely. For mooting this idea over a series of discussions with the editors, the Routledge team is gratefully acknowledged. We also would like to express our appreciation to all the contributors for their painstaking efforts in making their chapters worth the space in this compendium. The details that went into the final versions of their manuscripts amplify the quality and depth of the discourse contained in this edited volume. Regarding the latter, we extend our sincere gratitude to the team of reviewers for their efforts and wonderful assistance. For graciously providing the copyright permissions for some of the materials used in this handbook, the editors are also grateful to the *African Population Studies* journal and the *African Journal of Reproductive Health*. We equally thank the teams behind the libraries and electronic platforms that provided resource access to our chapter contributors. Last, but by no means least, we thank our families for tolerating the inconveniences associated with this massive intellectual engagement.

PART 1

Introductory chapters

1 INTRODUCTION

Clifford O. Odimegwu and Yemi Adewoyin

Introduction

The world's population is set to reach 9.7 billion by 2050, with over 50% of growth occurring in sub-Saharan Africa (SSA). Interestingly, the world has experienced tremendous demographic changes evident in declines in fertility and mortality – both of which have been associated with rapid economic growth in many developed countries (Lee & Mason, 2010). Sub-Saharan Africa alike has witnessed some slow-paced changes in its demographic profile consisting of changes in the patterns of fertility, mortality, and migration. Compared with the experience of other world regions, sub-Saharan Africa stands out not only in terms of fertility levels and its indices such as the onset of marriage and childbearing, longer birth intervals, persistence of high ideal family size, and low level of contraceptive use but also with regard to mortality and migration (Bongaarts & Casterline, 2013; A. C. Ezeh, Mberu, & Emina, 2009; Hertrich, 2017; Timaeus & Moultrie, 2008).

While declines in fertility levels have been slow paced in many sub-Saharan African countries, the fertility level is still substantially higher in Africa than elsewhere (Bongaarts & Casterline, 2013). The level of fertility in sub-Saharan Africa is about 5.1 births per woman, a level much lower now than expected (Bongaarts & Casterline, 2013), with wide variations among the regions. For example, the total fertility level in Southern Africa is lower and about half the fertility level of other regions (Gerland, Biddlecom, & Kantorová, 2017). Even across countries, there are wide variations, ranging from less than two births per woman in Mauritius to about eight births per woman in the republic of Niger (Gerland et al., 2017).

Multiple factors have contributed to the observed patterns in fertility decline. For example, the increased use of modern contraceptives, delayed age at first marriage, education, and female labour-force participation are some of the key drivers of fertility decline in SSA (Bongaarts & Casterline, 2013; A. C. Ezeh et al., 2009; Mensch, Grant, & Blanc, 2006; Ndagurwa & Odimegwu, 2019; Osili & Long, 2008; Shapiro, 2012; Shapiro & Gebreselassie, 2013). Although the African region has the lowest modern contraceptive use, evidence suggests that the use of modern methods of contraception has accelerated steadily throughout the region since 2005. Some authors have also noted an association between contraception use and fertility

 DOI: 10.4324/9780429287213-2

in sub-Saharan Africa (Casterline & El-Zeini, 2014). Aside from the numbers, resolving the uncertainty of the timing of the fertility decline in sub-Saharan Africa is also essential to evaluate the feasibility and magnitude of demographic dividend – a golden opportunity to attain economic growth in sub-Saharan Africa.

Nonetheless, sub-Saharan Africa has also witnessed a decline in the under-five mortality rate by less than 30%, from 180 deaths per 1000 live births in 1990 to 129 deaths per 1000 live births in 2009 (You, Jones, Hill, Wardlaw, & Chopra, 2010) and 83 deaths per 1000 live births in 2015 (You et al., 2015). Compared to other regions, sub-Saharan Africa is reported to have the highest rate of under-five mortality, with nearly double the average of developing regions (You et al., 2010). Consistent with the demographic transition theory (Lee, 2003; Reher, 2004), the significant declines in infant and child mortality have been vital drivers of fertility decline in the region. While the reductions in under-five mortality have been lower in sub-Saharan Africa than elsewhere, the robust expansion of rudimentary public health and nutrition interventions, such as immunization, breastfeeding, vitamin A supplementation, and safe drinking water, has contributed to the rapid gains in the countries with the most significant progress (You et al., 2010).

Additionally, sub-Saharan Africa is characterized by a high level of skilled and unskilled emigration. Estimates suggest that about 30 million Africans have migrated internationally outside and within Africa (Ratha et al., 2011). The patterns of migration in sub-Saharan Africa also vary quite greatly. About two-thirds of migrants from sub-Saharan Africa, mainly poorer migrants, go to other countries in the region, while the bulk of migrants remain within their subregion's countries (Ratha et al., 2011). More importantly, the migration of health workers from sub-Saharan Africa to more developed countries has gained prominence and increased significantly in recent times (Connell, Zurn, Stilwell, Awases, & Braichet, 2007). Throughout sub-Saharan Africa and other developing countries, migration has been at a considerable economic cost, including the depletion of workforces. Just like the inter-relationships between fertility and mortality that have been observed in prior scholarship, international migration also has profound implications for other components of population change such as health (Anglewicz, VanLandingham, Manda-Taylor, & Kohler, 2017; Kahn et al., 2007; Lagarde et al., 2003; Mulcahy & Kollamparambil, 2016; Weine & Kashuba, 2012) and fertility (Chattopadhyay, White, & Debpuur, 2006; Gyimah, 2006; White et al., 2008). A significant effect of migration on modern contraceptive use has also been documented in prior literature (Ochako, Askew, Okal, Oucho, & Temmerman, 2016).

Considering that almost all countries in the world are experiencing rapid rates of urban growth, further disaggregation of the demographic process by type of residence is imperative for a better appreciation of urbanization as a cause and consequence of demographic changes (Dyson, 2011). Such growth has been consistently associated with declines in urban fertility and mortality rates. Garenne and Joseph (2002) emphasized the key role of urban places in the onset of fertility transition in the region. Recent fertility levels are significantly higher in rural than urban areas in sub-Saharan Africa, where the rural populations of several countries have not yet experienced any decline (Corker, 2017; Shapiro & Tenikue, 2017). Available evidence from national surveys suggests that urban populations have started to experience a decline in fertility levels, while rural fertility has remained stable or increased. As migrants integrate within the destination society, they adapt to the lower fertility standards in urban areas. Similarly, some studies have also linked rural residence to higher mortality risk among children (Adewuyi & Zhao, 2017; O. K. Ezeh, Agho, Dibley, Hall, & Page, 2015), while others have reported contradictory findings (Morakinyo & Fagbamigbe, 2017).

Structure of the book

This Handbook comprehensively documents the methodological, theoretical, practical, and substantive issues in African demography. By providing an exhaustive review of demographic changes in the sub-Saharan African region, the Handbook will also be an essential collection for teachers, researchers, policymakers, and programmers in the field of population research covering the critical components of demography and population change such as fertility, ageing, mortality, and migration, as well as the causes and consequences of those changes. The handbook has 45 chapters encompassing various aspects of demographic changes in sub-Saharan Africa countries. These are arranged thematically to cover introductions, demographic training and research in Africa, marriage, fertility and reproductive health, and gender issues. Chapters addressing some demographic crises, particularly those emanating from and attributable to environment and health, are presented next, followed by those on migration. Other themes addressed are demographic dividend, ageing, mortality, and aspects of anthropological demography and the role of quality data in enriching the narratives in demographical studies.

Introductory chapters

While this first chapter provides a general outline of the handbook, Chapter 2 by Yemi Adewoyin and Clifford O. Odimegwu contextualizes the spatial and temporal patterns and development linkages of the population structure of Africa. The authors argue that the population structure of a society has implications for the development of that society. They provide data on the temporal trends and geographic variation in the continent's total population, annual growth rate, dependency ratio, infant mortality, life expectancy, net migration, and mean population age and data on the continent's Human Development Index (HDI) to buttress their position. The authors assert that Africa has made appreciable progress since 1950 despite its physical geographical characteristics, locational disadvantage in world systems, and errors of development.

The chapter concludes that to accelerate the pace of development and derive the dividends of its young and mobile demographics, governments in Africa should prioritize investments in education, health, and infrastructure, as these have been shown to impact fertility behaviour, mortality, life expectancy, and migration – factors the authors contend hold the key to Africa's development goals. The chapter prepares the ground for the understanding and interpretation of the various demographic outcomes unveiled in subsequent chapters. Essentially, it suggests that outcomes should not be seen in isolation but appreciated in the context of various extraneous conditions peculiar to the African continent.

Demographic training and research

Alfred Agwanda Otieno and Lawrence Ikamari provide an overview of the nature of transition in demographic training in African institutions in Chapter 3. Their chapter was motivated by the shift in the diversification of the discipline of demography as well as debates and criticisms on its didactic enterprise. The authors show that institutions providing demographic training are few, and courses in the discipline are mostly embedded in other broader departments. In Chapter 4, Michel Garenne describes the progress in knowledge of African populations and their dynamics from the 1960s. It takes as a starting point the landmark series of studies published in *The Demography of Tropical Africa*. The author notices major progress in data collection and data analysis, especially with the direct and indirect methods of demographic estimation.

The emergence of Demographic and Health Surveys (DHSs) is acknowledged in the chapter as a major boost and a driver for the paradigm shift in demographic research towards epidemiology and public health issues. The indirect method of estimation and statistical modelling in demographic research in Africa is the focus of Joshua O. Akinyemi and Sunday A. Adedini's Chapter 5. The chapter attempts a systematic appraisal of the procedures for indirect estimation and provides an overview of the use of statistical models in African demographic research, particularly the kinds of demographic outcomes that have been subjected to statistical modelling.

In spite of advances in data collection and availability on the continent, Lusophone Africa, comprising Angola, Cape Verde, Guinea-Bissau, Mozambique, and São Tome and Principe, has been under-researched, as shown by Carlos Arnaldo, Rogers Hansine, and Nelson C. Zavale in Chapter 6. Using systematic descriptive meta-summary and meta-narrative literature reviews, the authors attribute the status of demographic research in the Portuguese-speaking African countries to the level of tertiary education development at the time of independence and the fluctuation in political and military stability during the post-colonial period in the countries. Babatunde M. Gbadebo discusses old, contemporary, and emerging data sources for demographic research in Chapter 7. Expectedly, population censuses remain the principal source of demographic data, but their inadequate coverage is their greatest limitation. A combination of two or more data sources is suggested for addressing the inadequacies of population censuses. Issues of population censuses receive further attention in Chapter 8, where Françoise Gubry and Francis Gendreau discuss data collection and archiving in Francophone sub-Saharan Africa. The chapter acknowledges the progress made by national statistical offices in the subregion in making demographic data available and accessible.

Marriage, fertility, and sexual and reproductive health

Chapter 9 presents the basics of the demographic analysis of marriage and nuptiality in sub-Saharan Africa. Here, Michel Garenne documents country variations in age at marriage, proportion ever married, marriage types, age patterns, trends, and socio-economic differentials. The chapter also documents the data collection methods in nuptiality studies in Africa. Age at marriage and teen pregnancy constitute the fulcrum of Timalizge Zgambo's Chapter 10. Departing from what the author describes as the one-sided narrative that emphasizes the negative consequences of child marriage and teen pregnancy, the chapter provides a balanced review of the subject prevalence in the context of African cultural practices and predisposing factors. This, according to the author, becomes imperative to avoid importing foreign policies for addressing local issues. Age at marriage has been shown to impact fertility patterns. This much is also shown in Chapter 11, where David I. Ojakaa examines the sub-regional trends and patterns in the fertility transition in the continent. Two fertility patterns characterize the African fertility transition – an early childbearing peak and, to some extent, one slightly later, while the fertility transition is most advanced in Southern Africa.

David A. Sánchez-Páez and Bruno Schoumaker discuss fertility stalls in Africa in Chapter 12. They look at the fertility trend and decline since the 1950s and 1990s, respectively, and describe methods and findings on the dynamics of fertility stalls by focusing on factors such as changes in the proximate determinants of fertility; birth intervals; fertility desires; fertility preferences; and other socioeconomic variables like education, wealth, and effects of diseases. In Chapter 13, Boladé Hamed Banougnin and Obasanjo Afolabi Bolarinwa extend the discussions on fertility by looking at issues around contraception in Africa. Fertility and population growth rates are higher in Africa than in any other continent in the world. Over the past decade, increases in contraceptive use in Africa led to a slight decline in birth rates, which is still not enough to slow down the rapid population growth and ensure economic development. Evidence shows that progress towards contraceptive adoption is very slow in Western and Central African countries, with a risk of population size exceeding the United Nations population projections. The prospects for a future fertility decline are much more positive in Southern Africa, followed by Northern and Eastern Africa. Addressing contraceptive needs would be a starting point in furthering fertility decline in countries with low contraceptive prevalence and high fertility. Justin Dansou, Fidelia Dake, and Robert Y. Djogbenou, however, suggest in Chapter 14 that without paying appropriate attention to traditional contraceptive practice in sub-Saharan Africa, achieving contraceptive targets for family planning may remain elusive.

In Chapter 15, Sasha Frade reflects on the (un)changing ideas of reproductive health and family planning in Africa from the post-colonial period, through the Cairo Conference on Population and Development (ICPD), to the present. The author argues that the unquestioning use of and reliance on certain questions and data sets and the lack of new theory has led to a situation in which the identified challenges and issues around reproductive health, particularly the perception that high fertility and population growth are a problem and inimical to sound reproductive health outcomes, have remained unchanged and unchallenged. The author concludes that what is required now from African demographers is a re-thinking of agreed-upon terms, definitions, and concepts around reproductive health, fertility, and family planning. For Joshua O. Akinyemi, Nicole De Wet, and Clifford O. Odimegwu, at the nexus between reproductive health and population and development is the subject of sexuality, which has generated extensive discourse in the past two decades. In Chapter 16, they review African sexuality studies and show that previous studies covered the five components of sexuality: practices, partners, pleasure/pressure/pain, procreation, and power to different extents and that risky sexual behaviour was prevalent from adolescence to older ages. Literature on pleasure, pain, procreation, and power reflects the complex diversity driven by traditional norms, gender roles, and attitudes across the continent. They conclude by highlighting gaps and suggesting new agenda for sexuality research on the continent.

Gender in African demography

The importance of gender in African demographic research is brought to the fore in Chapter 17, where Lorretta Ntoimo and Clifford O. Odimegwu provide a wide-ranging review of the literature on fertility, mortality, migration, and sexual and reproductive health from 1994 to 2020. From their review, most of the studies were micro-level woman-focused studies. The use of a gender analysis framework was grossly deficient, and the dominant gender themes in the studies include participation in household decision-making, attitude to wife beating, male dominance, and level of education. The authors recommend context-specific interrogation of gender using multi-methods and participatory action research and gender analysis frameworks in future studies of gender and demographic processes in Africa.

Beatrice W. Maina, Chimaraoke Izugbara, Yandisa Sikweyiya, Ivy Nandongwa, and Caroline W. Kabiru shine a light on gender norms and sexual behaviour among young adolescents (10–14) on the premise that gender norms contribute to the inequalities that shape sexual and reproductive health (SRH). Their broad review, as detailed in Chapter 18, shows a growing but limited body of research on gender norms and SRH among the cohort. Patterns suggestive of changing gender norms and beliefs also emerge, evidenced by opposition to inequitable gender norms and practices. Research remains scant among very young boys, adolescents living with disabilities, sexual minorities, and adolescents in humanitarian settings. Other under-researched issues include how the dynamics of gender attitudes during adolescence interact with SRH outcomes; the impact of policy and legal frameworks related to harmful traditional practices such as early marriages, sexual violence, and female genital mutilation/cutting; and the scope of gender norm interventions to foster change at individual and other levels. In Chapter 19, Marifa Muchemwa examines gender-based violence in Africa through a systematic review of the literature, with particular attention to the policies, programmes, and issues which have been raised as remedies for gender-based violence. The chapter provides suggestions for future research to assist in improving policy directed at reducing or ending violence against women.

Environment, health, and demography

Environmental and socioeconomic factors matter for population health outcomes on several fronts. The nexus between disasters consequent on climate extremities and fertility behaviour in Africa is examined in Chapter 20 by Khandaker Jafor Ahmed and Yan Tan. The chapter attempts a synthesis of the literature on how different disasters influence fertility trends in SSA countries. The literature discussed engages mostly with war, famine, pandemic, and extreme climatic events in several African countries. Against the background of the rapidly growing urban population in Africa, and the premise that the urban population constitutes both an opportunity and a threat to its own health and wellbeing, Yemi Adewoyin reviews the urban health dimensions of demographic research in Africa in Chapter 21. The review covers the urban health content, the demographic cohort studied, and the temporal shifts in the urban health focus of the studies reviewed. The review shows the interrelationship among urban population growth; quality of the urban social and physical environment; urban health outcomes; the population's access to urban resources; and how these impact or are impacted by migration, fertility behaviour, life expectancy, and ageing. Issues of inequality in healthcare access are further amplified by Samuel Mwangi Wanjiku, Giuseppe T. Cirella, Alex Njeru, and Jacob Kazungu in Chapter 22.

HIV/AIDS and malnutrition remain major demographic crises in Africa. The levels, correlates, impacts, and policies and programmes for the control and eradication of HIV/AIDS are discussed in Chapter 23 by Pamela Chirwa-Banda. The chapter reviews studies on the subject from 2000 to 2020 and highlights preventative measures useful in the elimination of HIV infection and achieving the 90–90–90 strategy by 2030. Mpho Keetile, Kannan Navaneetham, and Gobopamang Letamo focus on the burden of malnutrition among adults in sub-Saharan Africa in the succeeding chapter. Their systematic review of evidence shows that the most consistent factors associated with the double burden of malnutrition among adults were mostly sociodemographic and economic. Arlette Simo Fotso and Larissa Nawo look at economic deprivation among children living with disability in the chapter that follows. They show that the International Classification of Functioning, Disability and Health for Children and Youth (ICF-CY) is today almost universally recognized as the framework to understand child disability and that the Washington Group/UNICEF child functioning screening instrument is now well endorsed to measure disability in children aged 2–17 years, even though this is yet to be routinely integrated into national surveys. Their review highlights the diversity of theoretical frameworks used in economics and social science studies, while empirical literature shows that children with disability are living a vicious circle of social and material deprivation.

Helena Yeboah and Sanni Yaya assess the effect of economic growth on maternal and child health outcomes in sub-Saharan Africa in Chapter 26. They contend that to achieve reduction in maternal and child mortality and to achieve the Sustainable Development Goals (SDGs), there is a need for higher investments in evidence-based health programs. Economic investments are also critical to poverty alleviation among the population. As shown by Manikandan AD and Vinod Joseph Kannankeril Joseph in Chapter 27, poverty among the population is accentuated by desertification, with resulting adverse health outcomes. The most severe consequence of desertification is further stress on the human health-poverty trap. Their chapter opens new perspectives for future research on environmental health, environmental poverty, human health-poverty, and disease ecology from multi-disciplinary and interdisciplinary perspectives. The chapter by Roberto Ariel Abeldaño Zuñiga, Gabriela Narcizo de Lima, and Daniel Esteban Quiroga on climate change and population displacement in Africa provides a bridge between the section on demographic crises of environment and health and that on migration. Their chapter on climate migration shows that between 2000 and 2019, around 1143 disaster events occurred in Africa, of which 90% were caused by floods, droughts, and storms, inflicting more than 46,000 deaths, affecting more than 337 million people, and forcing millions to migrate.

Migration

The three chapters on migration start with Vollan O. Ochieng, Razak M Gyasi, and Blessing U Mberu's exploration of the underpinning dynamics, destinations, and effects of internal migration in Ghana, Kenya, and Nigeria. UNDESA/UNESCO estimates that about 763 million people are involved in internal migration, nearly three times higher than international migrants. This presents notable implications for a country's development and policy agendas. The analysis in the chapter shows that internal migration in SSA has both positive and negative effects on urbanization, education, health, and familial systems. In Chapter 30, Alfred Agwanda, Mary Muyonga, Milton Adieri, and George Odipo revisit the changing perspectives of internal migration in East Africa. Beyond engaging in contemporary theoretical debates about internal migration, the chapter also notes intra-rural migration, return migration, invisible forms of movement, and gender sensitivity of the migration process and its consequences as under-researched themes on the subject.

In Chapter 31, Aderanti Adepoju reflects on international migration and development in Africa. The chapter looks at the root causes of emigration dynamics in sub-Saharan Africa, as well as the migration configuration within and outside the region, emigration of skilled professionals, and diaspora and remittances. The chapter further focuses on the consequences of these dynamics for the region and concludes with some suggestions on how migration's potential win-win-win can be attained. Among other suggestions, poverty eradication strategies aligned with domestic mechanisms for generating employment opportunities and fostering enterprise and self-sustaining livelihoods should be at the forefront of development assistance from developed countries benefiting from the brain drain in the region. The chapter also aligns with the International Labour Organization's position that compensation for the brain drain could take the form of supporting projects which involve professionals going back to their countries of origin for short periods to work in special programmes and education.

Demographic dividend

With a focus on human capital formation, Claudia Reiter, Anne Goujon, and Samir K.C. examine how rapid population growth is affecting the potential of many African countries to achieve their Sustainable Development Goals regarding access to quality primary and secondary education. This authors describe the changes in levels of educational attainment from 1950 to 2015 in 50 sub-Saharan African countries and explore the potential future of levels of education and their impact on population size and structure. The results suggest that in 2015, the majority of the working-age population still had a low education in a majority of the countries sampled. At the general level, and using the demographic dividend framework, Patricia Agupusi examines the pathways African countries are taking to transform their young demography for development. The author observes that demographic transition in Africa is attracting debate from both scholars and policymakers on the implications of Africa's growing young demography in the face of developmental challenges and concludes that whether the current demographic structure would bring disaster, as predicted by some, or dividends that would accelerate development, which is dependent on the type of health, education, and economic policies being formulated and implemented to improve Africa's human capital.

In Chapter 34, Morné Oosthuizen examines evidence from national transfer accounts (NTAs) to discuss demographic dividend in Africa. The national transfer accounts approach provides a useful way to analyse intergenerational resource flows. According to Oosthuizen, based on NTA estimates, Africa's first dividend began in 1993. This highlights the urgency of required policy actions. The chapter further reveals the degree of heterogeneity amongst African countries in terms of both the timing of the first demographic dividend and its expected magnitude. While the NTA approach provides a useful tool for analysing how policy-induced changes may impact the magnitude of the dividend, an important area for future research on the continent relates to the interactions between inequality and the demographic dividend. Latif Dramani, Crispin Mabika, Camille Guidimé, Jean Baptiste Oga, Cheikh Tidiane Ndiaye, Dalomi Bahan, Edem Akpo, Sam Agbahoungba, and Silvère Konan propose a normative model as well as tools and an index for understanding the level of demographic dividend at the national and sub-national level. The Demographic Dividend Monitoring Index (DDMI) created for this purpose is a tool for summarizing different dimensions of demographic dividend and covers five dimensions: economic dependency, quality of life, poverty transitions, extended human development, and networks and territories.

Ageing

Ayo S. Adebowale, Obiageli Onwusaka, Mobolaji M. Salawu, Segun Bello, and David A. Adewole provide an historical perspective on ageing in Africa in Chapter 36. There is an increase in life expectancy across countries in sub-Saharan Africa, implying that an ageing population is imminent in the years ahead, and there is a need to understand its history and consequences for policy formulation. Their chapter provides exhaustive material and a record of methodological, theoretical, practical, and substantive issues on ageing in SSA. To sustain the growing life expectancy, Mark Aviisah, Hinke H. Haisma, and Tobias C. Vogt review the literature on intergenerational family support provided to older adults in SSA and its effects on their health and well-being in Chapter 37. Their results suggest that receiving social and financial support from family as well as having frequent contact with family were positively related to better psychological well-being, self-rated health, and quality of life of older adults.

Mortality

The five chapters on mortality cover the full spectrum of mortality studies: maternal, infant and child, adult, and whole population. Specifically, N.N. Wekwete and K. Mangombe in Chapter 38 provide evidence on the causes of death and the double burden of disease in Africa. While communicable diseases continue to be the major causes of death, non-communicable diseases such as stroke, ischemic heart disease, and road injuries were among the top ten causes of death. The major risk factors of non-communicable diseases the authors found in their review were unhealthy diet, physical inactivity, alcohol and tobacco abuse, and road traffic accidents. Beneath the general population mortality outlook, adult mortality has gone down across countries in SSA between 1950 and 2020, but almost all the countries will still have adult mortality rates of above 100 per 1000 by the year 2050. Ayo S. Adebowale, Adeniyi F. Fagbamigbe, Tubosun Olowolafe, and Rotimi F. Afolabi describe the dynamics of adult mortality in Africa and ask if there are prospects for recording a decline in Chapter 39. They cite inadequate credible vital statistics as the basis for the use of an indirect demographic approach for estimation and projection of adult mortality in Africa, and, in spite of training provided by Africa's tertiary institutions on the methods of estimating adult mortality, their utilization is yet to be fully translated into research practice.

In Chapter 40, Dorothy N. Ononokpono, Bernard Baffour, Nsidibe Usoro, and Olukemi Adebola examine the levels, methods of measurement, and determinants of maternal mortality in sub-Saharan Africa, their aim being to identify new approaches in the measurement of maternal mortality and obtain accurate information on maternal mortality. Among other findings, their chapter shows that most common method of maternal mortality estimation was sisterhood and sibling history. Of all the data sources, reproductive-age mortality studies (RAMOSs) are considered the best approach in the absence of vital registration. Oluwatosin Ariyo and Henry Victor Doctor highlight measurement and surveillance strategies implemented to reduce maternal mortality in SSA in Chapter 41. While they show that vital registration and the indirect sisterhood method were the most prevalent methods used, they suggest the need for improvement in these methods to generate high-quality data and effectively prevent maternal mortality. Sunday A. Adedini and Joshua O. Akinyemi provide a synthesis on data sources for monitoring infant and child mortality in Chapter 42. They also review existing child mortality frameworks and childhood mortality estimation techniques and analyse data on the levels, trends, and patterns of infant and child mortality in SSA.

Concluding matters

The last three chapters of this handbook are purposely positioned to achieve two aims, as shown in the following. Daniel Jordan Smith's chapter on anthropological demography calls attention to the need to integrate the methods of anthropological investigations into our understanding of demographic events and processes. As Africans with rich cultural characteristics and strong familial and kinship ties, it is not surprising that many of the explanations in African demographic research on the subjects of fertility, migration and remittances, ageing, and health behaviour, among others, revolve around culture and kinship ties directly or indirectly.

To that extent, Smith, in Chapter 43, traces the evolution and contributions of anthropological demography in Africa. The author goes further to demonstrate how this emerging subfield of demography enriches the understanding of population health issues, particularly HIV/AIDS. The role of quality data in changing the HIV/AIDS trajectory and narratives in sub-Saharan Africa examined by Jacob A. Adetunji in Chapter 44 highlights how population-based sero-data has led to an improved understanding of HIV/AIDS. It also shows its socio-demographic correlates and how quality data is leading to the correction of some wrongly held beliefs and biased assumptions about HIV/AIDS and its risk behaviours in the region. The evidence in Adetunji's contribution on HIV prevalence and transmission among couples further amplifies Smith's position on familial and kinship ties in understanding health issues in Africa.

With the array of data and statistics provided in the chapters to describe the African demographic situation and its several consequences for demographic training and research, marriage, fertility and reproductive health, gender, environment, health and development, migration, ageing, and mortality in Africa, Chapter 45 concludes with an examination of the state of demographic transition in Africa. In this chapter, Lungile Motsa and Clifford O. Odimegwu describe the current state of transition in African countries and its consequences for Africa's development and the achievement of the Sustainable Development Goals. Apart from Mauritius, African states were marked by slow-paced, unpredictable, and difficult-to-compare demographic transitions. Many countries are stuck between stages 2 and 3, resulting in continued rapid population growth due to incessantly lower crude birth rate decline compared to crude death rate decline. Higher mortality reductions characterized Central, Eastern, and Western African countries, whereas Northern and Southern African countries were characterized by higher fertility reductions. The chapter confirms similarities and differences in the African demographic transitions, with less conformity to the classic demographic transition model, and concludes with suggestions to inform appropriate population programmes and policies in Africa.

References

Adewuyi, E. O., & Zhao, Y. (2017). Determinants of neonatal mortality in rural and urban Nigeria: Evidence from a population-based national survey. *Pediatrics International*, *59*(2), 190–200. https://doi.org/10.1111/ped.13086

Anglewicz, P., VanLandingham, M., Manda-Taylor, L., & Kohler, H.-P. (2017). Cohort profile: Internal migration in sub-Saharan Africa – The Migration and Health in Malawi (MHM) study. *BMJ Open*, 7(5), e014799. https://doi.org/10.1136/bmjopen-2016-014799

Bongaarts, J., & Casterline, J. (2013). Fertility transition: Is sub-Saharan Africa different? *Population and Development Review*, *38*, 153–168. https://doi.org/10.1111/j.1728-4457.2013.00557.x

Casterline, J. B., & El-Zeini, L. O. (2014). Unmet need and fertility decline: A comparative perspective on prospects in sub-Saharan Africa. *Studies in Family Planning*, *45*(2), 227–245. https://doi.org/10.1111/j.1728-4465.2014.00386.x

Chattopadhyay, A., White, M. J., & Debpuur, C. (2006). Migrant fertility in Ghana: Selection versus adaptation and disruption as causal mechanisms. *Population Studies*, *60*(2), 189–203. https://doi.org/10.1080/00324720600646287

Connell, J., Zurn, P., Stilwell, B., Awases, M., & Braichet, J.-M. (2007). Sub-Saharan Africa: Beyond the health worker migration crisis? *Social Science & Medicine*, *64*(9), 1876–1891. https://doi.org/10.1016/j.socscimed.2006.12.013

Corker, J. (2017). Fertility and child mortality in urban West Africa: Leveraging geo-referenced data to move beyond the urban/rural dichotomy. *Population, Space and Place*, *23*(3), e2009. https://doi.org/10.1002/psp.2009

Dyson, T. (2011). The role of the demographic transition in the process of urbanization. *Population and Development Review*, *37*, 34–54. https://doi.org/10.1111/j.1728-4457.2011.00377.x

Ezeh, A. C., Mberu, B. U., & Emina, J. O. (2009). Stall in fertility decline in Eastern African countries: Regional analysis of patterns, determinants and implications. *Philosophical Transactions of the Royal Society B: Biological Sciences*, *364*(1532), 2991–3007. https://doi.org/10.1098/rstb.2009.0166

Ezeh, O. K., Agho, K. E., Dibley, M. J., Hall, J. J., & Page, A. N. (2015). Risk factors for postneonatal, infant, child and under-5 mortality in Nigeria: A pooled cross-sectional analysis. *BMJ Open*, *5*(3), e006779. https://doi.org/10.1136/bmjopen-2014-006779

Garenne, M., & Joseph, V. (2002). The timing of the fertility transition in Sub-Saharan Africa. *World Development*, *30*(10), 1835–1843.

Gerland, P., Biddlecom, A., & Kantorová, V. (2017). Patterns of fertility decline and the impact of alternative scenarios of future fertility change in sub-Saharan Africa. *Population and Development Review*, *43*, 21–38. https://doi.org/10.1111/padr.12011

Gyimah, S. O. (2006). Migration and fertility behavior in sub-Saharan Africa : The case of Ghana. *Journal of Comparative Family Studies*, *37*(2), 235–252. https://doi.org/www.jstor.org/stable/41604071

Hertrich, V. (2017). Trends in age at marriage and the onset of fertility transition in sub-Saharan Africa. *Population and Development Review*, *43*, 112–137. https://doi.org/10.1111/padr.12043

Kahn, K., Tollman, S. M., Collinson, M. A., Clark, S. J., Twine, R., Clark, B. D., . . . Garenne, M. L. (2007). Research into health, population and social transitions in rural South Africa: Data and methods of the Agincourt Health and Demographic Surveillance System1. *Scandinavian Journal of Public Health*, *35*(Suppl. 69), 8–20. https://doi.org/10.1080/14034950701505031

Lagarde, E., Schim van der Loeff, M., Enel, C., Holmgren, B., Dray-Spira, R., Pison, G., . . . MECORA Group. (2003). Mobility and the spread of human immunodeficiency virus into rural areas of West Africa. *International Journal of Epidemiology*, *32*(5), 744–752. https://doi.org/10.1093/ije/dyg111

Lee, R. (2003). The demographic transition: Three centuries of fundamental change. *Journal of Economic Perspectives*, *17*(4), 167–190. https://doi.org/10.1257/089533003772034943

Lee, R., & Mason, A. (2010). Fertility, human capital, and economic growth over the demographic transition. *European Journal of Population/Revue Européenne de Démographie*, *26*(2), 159–182. https://doi.org/10.1007/s10680-009-9186-x

Mensch, B., Grant, M., & Blanc, A. (2006). The changing context of sexual initiation in sub-Saharan Africa. *Population and Development Review*, *32*(4), 699–727.

Morakinyo, O. M., & Fagbamigbe, A. F. (2017). Neonatal, infant and under-five mortalities in Nigeria: An examination of trends and drivers (2003–2013). *PLoS One*, *12*(8), e0182990. https://doi.org/10.1371/journal.pone.0182990

Mulcahy, K., & Kollamparambil, U. (2016). The impact of rural-urban migration on subjective well-being in South Africa. *The Journal of Development Studies*, *52*(9), 1357–1371. https://doi.org/10.1080/00220388.2016.1171844

Ndagurwa, P., & Odimegwu, C. (2019). The elasticity of marital fertility in three sub-Saharan African countries: A decomposition analysis. *Genus*, *75*(1), 17. https://doi.org/10.1186/s41118-019-0064-z

Ochako, R., Askew, I., Okal, J., Oucho, J., & Temmerman, M. (2016). Modern contraceptive use among migrant and non-migrant women in Kenya. *Reproductive Health*, *13*(1), 67. https://doi.org/10.1186/s12978-016-0183-3

Osili, U. O., & Long, B. T. (2008). Does female schooling reduce fertility? Evidence from Nigeria. *Journal of Development Economics*, *87*(1), 57–75. https://doi.org/10.1016/j.jdeveco.2007.10.003

Ratha, D., Mohapatra, S., Ozden, C., Plaza, S., Shaw, W., & Shimeles, A. (2011). *Leveraging migration for Africa*. https://doi.org/10.1596/978-0-8213-8257-8

Reher, D. S. (2004). The demographic transition revisited as a global process. *Population, Space and Place*, *10*(1), 19–41. https://doi.org/10.1002/psp.313

Shapiro, D. (2012). Women's education and fertility transition in sub-Saharan Africa. *Vienna Yearbook of Population Research*, *10*, 9–30. https://doi.org/www.jstor.org/stable/41940995

Shapiro, D., & Gebreselassie, T. (2013). Fertility transition in sub-Saharan Africa: Falling and stalling. *African Population Studies*, *23*(1). https://doi.org/10.11564/23-1-310

Shapiro, D., & Tenikue, M. (2017). Women's education, infant and child mortality, and fertility decline in rural and urban sub-Saharan Africa. *Demographic Research*, *37*, 669–708. https://doi.org/10.4054/DemRes.2017.37.21

Timaeus, I. M., & Moultrie, T. A. (2008). On postponement and birth intervals. *Population and Development Review*, *34*(3), 483–510. https://doi.org/10.1111/j.1728-4457.2008.00233.x

Weine, S. M., & Kashuba, A. B. (2012). Labor migration and HIV risk: A systematic review of the literature. *AIDS and Behavior*, *16*(6), 1605–1621. https://doi.org/10.1007/s10461-012-0183-4

White, M. J., Muhidin, S., Andrzejewski, C., Tagoe, E., Knight, R., & Reed, H. (2008). Urbanization and fertility: An event-history analysis of coastal Ghana. *Demography*, *45*(4), 803–816. https://doi.org/10.1353/dem.0.0035

You, D., Hug, L., Ejdemyr, S., Idele, P., Hogan, D., Mathers, C., . . . Alkema, L. (2015). Global, regional, and national levels and trends in under-5 mortality between 1990 and 2015, with scenario-based projections to 2030: A systematic analysis by the UN Inter-agency Group for Child Mortality Estimation. *The Lancet*, *386*(10010), 2275–2286. https://doi.org/10.1016/S0140-6736(15)00120-8

You, D., Jones, G., Hill, K., Wardlaw, T., & Chopra, M. (2010). Levels and trends in child mortality, 1990–2009. *The Lancet*, *376*(9745), 931–933. https://doi.org/10.1016/S0140-6736(10)61429-8

2

POPULATION STRUCTURE OF AFRICA – SPATIOTEMPORAL PATTERNS AND DEVELOPMENT LINKAGES

Yemi Adewoyin and Clifford O. Odimegwu

Introduction

In its simplest form, population structure describes the composition of a population group. This chapter attempts a description of the population structure of Africa, with a focus on its age-sex distribution, fertility and mortality patterns and migration dynamics. In describing these key demographic elements, variables employed include total population, population growth rate, median age, sex ratio, total fertility rate, mean childbearing age, infant mortality rate, life expectancy at birth and net migration. Data on the selected variables are presented for the years 1950, 1970, 1995 and 2020 to allow for a temporal comparison of progress made with each of the variables. The data are also presented at country and subregional levels to expound on their spatial dimensions. In discussing the data, relevant literature evidence is provided to explain the findings and patterns. As population is intrinsically linked to development, an analysis of the continent's progress on human development is equally presented in the chapter. The analysis is preceded by a discussion to contextualize the state of development in Africa as a consequence of geography, spatial organization within the world-systems framework, statehood age and the error of developmentalism.

General overview

Africa is estimated to have a total population of 1.34 billion people as of 2020. Seventy years earlier in 1950, the population was 224.7 million. In the 70-year period, the annual population growth rate in Africa oscillated around 2.42%, with a peak at 2.64% in 1970. As shown in Table 2.1, the continent's median population age has typically been less than 20, while for every 100 females, there have been 99 males. The proportion of dependent population on the continent has been declining since 1970 just as the total fertility rate has dropped significantly from 6.7 in 1970 to 4.4 in 2020. Equally declining visibly are infant mortality and under-five mortality rates on the continent. From 183 per 1,000 live births in 1950, infant mortality stood at 47 in 2020, while under-five mortality was 71 per 1,000 live births in 2020 as against 311 in 1950. The long-term effects of the decline in mortality were reflected in the increasing life expectancy from a dismal 37.5 years in 1950 to 62.3 years in 2020. Mean childbearing age remained 29, while net loss from migration was 0.4.

DOI: 10.4324/9780429287213-3

Table 2.1 Overview of African Population Structure, 1950–2020

Population Component	*1950*	*1970*	*1995*	*2020**
Total Population (millions)	224.7	363.4	717.3	1,340.6
Annual Pop Growth Rate (%)	2.08	2.64	2.46	2.51
Median Age	19.3	17.9	18.0	19.7
Sex Ratio (males/100 females)	98.8	99.3	99.4	99.9
Dependency Ratio (per 100 population aged 15–64)	80.5	90.1	88.6	78.1
Total Fertility (live births per woman)	6.6	6.7	5.7	4.4
Mean Childbearing Age	29.5	29.6	29.5	29.1
Infant Mortality (per 1,000 live births)	183	133	93	47
Under-Five Mortality (per 1,000 live births)	311	220	151	71
Life Expectancy at Birth	37.5	46.6	52.3	62.3
Net Migration (per 1,000 population)	–0.5	–1.0	–0.6	–0.4

Note: *2015–2020 Estimates
Source: United Nations, Department of Economic and Social Affairs, Population Division (2019)

Intra-continental variations

Population growth and fertility rates

At the subcontinental level, the seemingly static annual population growth rate has declined in both the Southern and Northern Africa subregions. In the former, the growth rate dropped from 2.16% in 1950 to 1.39% in 2020, while it dropped from 2.49% to 1.91% in the same period in Northern Africa. A notable decline was seen in Eswatini, Lesotho, South Africa, Morocco and Western Sahara. Countries from other subregions with significant declines in their growth rate were Reunion, Seychelles, Mauritius and South Sudan. While the growth rate has been rising marginally in Eastern and Western Africa, it has nearly doubled between 1950 and 2020 in the middle of Africa. The largest contributors to Africa's increasing annual population growth rate, as shown in Table 2.2, were Niger (3.82%), Equatorial Guinea (3.66%), Uganda (3.59%), Angola (3.29%), Burundi (3.15%) and Chad (3.04%).

Across Africa, total fertility rates were lowest in Southern and Northern Africa, at 2.50 and 3.25 live births per woman, respectively. The rates are a decline from 6.06 and 6.80 for both subregions in 1950. Countries in Middle and Western Africa had the highest fertility rates at 5.53 and 5.18, respectively. Despite the relatively high rates in both subregions, fertility rates have been declining generally in all the African countries, as shown in Table 2.2. The most improvements in the decline in fertility rates were recorded in the Maghreb countries, Egypt, Eswatini, South Africa, Cape Verde, Mauritius, Seychelles, Rwanda and Kenya. In contrast, Niger (6.95), Somalia (6.12), Democratic Republic of Congo (5.96), Mali (5.92) and Chad (5.80) recorded very marginal progress and were still having at least six live births per woman.

The variation in population distribution across the continent is consequent mainly on the differential fertility behaviour and adoption of contraceptive utilization in the countries. The country variation in contraceptive utilization ranges from 5.0% in Chad to 65.8% in Zimbabwe (United Nations, 2020). The literature is replete with studies on the underlying factors for the variations. The factors are broadly categorized as socioeconomic, demographic and ideational (Odimegwu & Adewoyin, 2020a) and include such issues as women's empowerment, education, religion, sex preference, intimate partner violence, community structures and internal migrations (Adebowale & Palamuleni, 2015; Blackstone, Nwaozuru, & Iwelunmor, 2017; Yaya,

Table 2.2 Subregional Population Growth and Fertility Rates, 1950–2020

Subregion/Country	*Annual Pop Growth Rate (%)*				*Total Fertility Rate*			
	1950–1955	*1970–1975*	*1995–2000*	*2015–2020*	*1950–1955*	*1970–1975*	*1995–2000*	*2015–2020*
Eastern Africa	2.24	2.85	2.78	2.67	6.99	7.14	6.09	4.43
Burundi	1.89	1.24	1.27	3.15	6.80	7.26	7.05	5.45
Comoros	1.96	2.24	2.64	2.24	6.00	7.05	5.60	4.24
Djibouti	2.31	6.79	2.59	1.56	6.31	6.85	4.81	2.76
Eritrea	1.80	2.77	0.79	1.18	6.97	6.62	5.60	4.10
Ethiopia	1.91	2.73	2.98	2.62	7.17	7.10	6.83	4.30
Kenya	2.79	3.67	2.82	2.32	7.48	7.99	5.35	3.52
Madagascar	2.14	2.78	3.14	2.67	7.30	7.20	5.80	4.11
Malawi	2.04	2.70	2.49	2.66	6.85	7.40	6.20	4.25
Mauritius	2.92	1.53	0.98	0.20	5.90	3.47	2.03	1.39
Mayotte	4.52	4.15	3.98	2.56	7.91	7.91	5.08	3.73
Mozambique	1.76	2.38	2.69	2.90	6.34	6.68	5.85	4.89
Réunion	3.23	0.96	1.79	0.73	6.93	3.88	2.33	2.27
Rwanda	2.90	3.00	6.14	2.61	8.00	8.28	5.90	4.10
Seychelles	1.40	2.58	1.11	0.70	5.00	5.38	2.18	2.46
Somalia	1.92	2.38	3.38	2.83	7.25	7.10	7.70	6.12
South Sudan	1.08	2.41	3.83	0.87	6.65	6.90	6.42	4.74
Uganda	2.65	2.65	2.94	3.59	6.90	7.10	6.95	5.01
United Republic of Tanzania	2.64	3.20	2.44	2.97	6.74	6.75	5.75	4.92
Zambia	2.70	3.36	2.71	2.93	6.70	7.40	6.10	4.66
Zimbabwe	3.14	3.48	0.81	1.46	6.80	7.40	3.89	3.63
Middle Africa	1.91	2.69	2.75	3.05	5.84	6.46	6.52	5.53
Angola	2.07	3.52	3.24	3.29	6.00	7.50	6.75	5.55
Cameroon	1.78	2.67	2.63	2.61	5.49	6.31	5.75	4.60
Central African Republic	1.10	1.56	2.44	1.45	5.52	5.95	5.55	4.75
Chad	1.78	2.30	3.51	3.04	6.10	6.67	7.41	5.80
Congo	1.93	2.94	2.88	2.56	5.68	6.30	4.90	4.45
Democratic Republic of the Congo	2.08	2.70	2.50	3.22	5.98	6.29	6.77	5.96
Equatorial Guinea	1.23	-3.45	3.98	3.66	5.67	5.80	5.94	4.55
Gabon	0.46	1.88	2.48	2.67	3.99	5.23	4.77	4.00
Sao Tome and Principe	-0.40	2.18	1.55	1.89	6.20	6.52	5.30	4.35
Southern Africa	2.16	2.67	1.66	1.39	6.06	5.60	3.00	2.50
Botswana	2.32	3.33	2.24	2.07	6.50	6.55	3.49	2.89
Eswatini	2.09	2.95	1.63	0.99	6.70	6.87	4.14	3.03
Lesotho	1.69	2.41	1.37	0.79	5.84	5.80	3.96	3.16
Namibia	1.98	2.96	1.95	1.86	6.00	6.60	4.26	3.42
South Africa	2.19	2.65	1.64	1.37	6.05	5.50	2.88	2.41
Western Africa	1.69	2.51	2.64	2.67	6.43	6.80	6.15	5.18
Benin	0.42	2.29	3.01	2.73	5.86	6.83	6.16	4.87
Burkina Faso	1.06	1.80	2.80	2.87	6.10	6.70	6.73	5.23
Cabo Verde	2.04	0.12	2.06	1.16	6.57	6.86	3.94	2.29
Côte d'Ivoire	2.66	4.57	2.95	2.55	7.45	7.93	6.05	4.68
Gambia	1.56	3.02	3.10	2.94	6.35	6.20	5.95	5.25
Ghana	2.58	2.68	2.50	2.19	6.44	6.90	5.02	3.89

(*Continued*)

Subregion/Country	*Annual Pop Growth Rate (%)*				*Total Fertility Rate*			
	1950–1955	*1970–1975*	*1995–2000*	*2015–2020*	*1950–1955*	*1970–1975*	*1995–2000*	*2015–2020*
Guinea	1.39	1.56	2.51	2.77	6.00	6.29	6.24	4.74
Guinea-Bissau	1.47	1.66	1.97	2.50	5.90	6.10	6.05	4.51
Liberia	1.68	2.67	6.63	2.46	6.27	6.80	6.05	4.35
Mali	1.10	1.72	2.66	2.99	6.95	7.15	6.95	5.92
Mauritania	2.50	2.97	2.57	2.78	6.34	6.75	5.52	4.59
Niger	2.88	2.79	3.55	3.82	7.30	7.60	7.70	6.95
Nigeria	1.64	2.48	2.49	2.59	6.35	6.61	6.17	5.42
Senegal	0.39	1.82	-0.63	0.71	6.80	7.25	5.70	4.65
Sierra Leone	2.43	2.93	2.40	2.77	6.03	6.57	6.48	4.32
Togo	1.19	2.02	1.26	2.13	6.33	7.20	5.54	4.35
Northern Africa	2.49	2.49	1.81	1.91	6.80	6.53	3.54	3.25
Algeria	1.94	2.76	1.53	1.98	7.28	7.57	2.89	3.05
Egypt	2.54	2.21	1.98	2.03	6.75	6.00	3.60	3.33
Libya	2.04	4.30	1.59	1.36	7.14	8.10	3.20	2.25
Morocco	3.12	2.12	1.29	1.26	6.61	6.40	2.97	2.42
Sudan	2.66	3.33	2.48	2.39	6.65	6.90	5.65	4.43
Tunisia	1.79	2.22	1.24	1.11	6.65	6.39	2.34	2.20
Western Sahara	8.59	-0.51	4.12	2.54	6.34	6.57	3.40	2.41

Source: United Nations, Department of Economic and Social Affairs, Population Division (2019)

Uthman, Ekholuenetale, & Bishwajit, 2018; Odimegwu & Adedini, 2017; Odimegwu, Akinyemi, Banjo, Olamijuwon, & Amoo, 2018; Ene, Adewoyin, & Chukwu, 2019; Odimegwu & Adewoyin, 2020b).

Population age and net migration rate

Africa is a very youthful continent, with a median population age less than 20. Middle Africa, with a median population age of 17.3, had the youngest population, followed by Western Africa (18.2) and Eastern Africa (18.7). In addition to the Northern and Southern African subregions, where the median age was close to 30, countries with a much older population relative to the continental average were Mauritius (37.5), Reunion (35.9), Seychelles (34.2) and Cape Verde (27.6). The youngest populations were in Niger (15.2), Mali (16.3), Chad (16.6), Somalia (16.7), Uganda (16.7) and Angola (16.7). While the median age has slightly increased since 1950 in Eastern, Southern and Northern Africa, it has witnessed a decline in Middle and Western Africa, as shown in Table 2.3.

There are two sides to Africa's youth bulge. First, having a population with an average age of 20 and a mean childbearing age of 29.1, as shown in Table 2.1, implies that in the next 10 years, there would be a population explosion in Africa. Going by United Nations estimates using constant fertility rates, in the 10 years, Africa's population would have increased by 400 million (United Nations, 2019). Without proper planning and an acceleration of the current pace of development, the increase may be a burden and put pressure on both the socioeconomic and physical environments in Africa (Fadayomi, 2011; Sippel, Kiziak, Woellert, & Klingholz, 2011; Agbor, Taiwo, & Smith, 2012; Omoju & Abraham, 2014). On the flip side however, the bulge may well catalyze the pace of development in Africa, because it implies a growing pool of human resources whose entry into the labour force is only a matter of years. According to Cummins (2019, p. 5), 'the obvious benefits of such labour force growth feeds into the narrative of a demographic dividend – a time-bound opportunity to catalyze economic growth and poverty reduction'. Investing in the youth population matters for achieving demographic dividend in Africa (Mumah, Brinton, Mukiira, Kabiru, & Izugbara, 2015; Canning, Raja, & Yazbeck, 2015; Bloom, Kuhn, & Prettner, 2017).

Apart from Southern Africa, with a positive net migration rate since 1970, and Middle Africa with a zero net migration rate in both 1950 and 2020, all other subregions on the African continent were net migration losers (Table 2.3). At the country level, for every 1,000

Table 2.3 Median Age and Net Migration in Africa, 1950–2020

Subregion/Country	*Median Age*				*Net Migration (per 1,000 population)*			
	1950	*1970*	*1995*	*2020*	*1950–1955*	*1970–1975*	*1995–2000*	*2015–2020*
Eastern Africa	18.4	17.2	16.9	18.7	−0.3	−1.1	−0.3	−0.6
Burundi	19.5	17.1	14.9	17.3	−5.8	−14.8	−14.7	0.2
Comoros	21.2	17.7	17.1	20.4	0	−4.5	−2.4	−2.4
Djibouti	16.5	17.5	18.1	26.6	3.0	36.5	3.0	0.9
Eritrea	17.3	18.1	15.6	19.2	0.2	1.4	−11.6	−11.6
Ethiopia	17.9	18.0	16.7	19.5	−0.2	−0.4	−0.5	0.3
Kenya	20.0	15.4	16.4	20.1	0	−0.3	−0.1	−0.2
Madagascar	20.9	17.2	17.2	19.6	0	−0.5	−0.1	−0.1
Malawi	17.1	17.9	17.4	18.1	0	−0.6	−1.1	−0.9
Mauritius	17.3	17.8	26.8	37.5	1.0	−4.8	−1.5	0
Mayotte	30.3	16.7	17.0	20.1	30.7	2.4	6.8	0
Mozambique	19.1	18.4	17.7	17.6	−0.8	−0.5	−0.6	−0.2
Réunion	20.3	17.1	26.1	35.9	1.9	−10.0	2.8	−1.4
Rwanda	18.0	16.0	18.3	20.0	0	−1.0	36.2	−0.7
Seychelles	26.1	18.0	24.5	34.2	−12.6	0.6	−0.6	−2.1
Somalia	19.5	18.3	17.3	16.7	0	0	0	−2.7
South Sudan	18.5	18.6	17.7	19.0	0	1.3	10.6	−15.9
Uganda	18.2	16.5	15.5	16.7	0	−5.5	−1.6	4.0
United Republic of Tanzania	16.9	17.0	17.2	18.0	0.2	1.6	−2.5	−0.7
Zambia	17.5	16.0	16.4	17.6	0	−0.9	0.4	−0.5
Zimbabwe	19.0	15.6	17.6	18.7	−0.3	−1.6	−9.0	−8.2
Middle Africa	19.5	18.4	16.9	17.3	−0.0	0.3	−1.4	0.0
Angola	19.8	17.6	16.1	16.7	0	6.2	2.6	0.2
Cameroon	20.4	19.1	16.8	18.7	0	−0.1	−0.7	−0.2
Central African Republic	22.5	20.1	18.2	17.6	0	−5.3	1.7	−8.6
Chad	21.5	18.6	15.8	16.6	0	−2.5	1.8	0.1
Congo	20.1	17.8	18.0	19.2	0	0	3.4	−0.8
Democratic Republic of the Congo	18.1	18.1	17.2	17.0	0	0.3	−4.3	0.3
Equatorial Guinea	23.8	20.9	18.9	22.3	0	−50.0	12.7	12.4
Gabon	28.1	25.4	19.0	22.5	1.3	1.0	1.7	1.6
Sao Tome and Principe	24.5	16.2	16.3	18.6	−30.8	−6.4	−13.9	−8.0
Southern Africa	20.9	18.9	20.8	27.0	−0.3	1.4	2.4	1.9
Botswana	19.2	16.1	18.3	24.0	−3.5	1.2	4.7	1.3

(*Continued*)

Subregion/Country	*Median Age*				*Net Migration (per 1,000 population)*			
	1950	*1970*	*1995*	*2020*	*1950–1955*	*1970–1975*	*1995–2000*	*2015–2020*
Eswatini	18.4	16.3	16.6	20.7	–3.9	–4.9	–5.4	–7.4
Lesotho	19.1	17.1	18.2	24.0	–5.4	–4.4	–3.8	–4.8
Namibia	20.9	18.4	18.0	21.8	0	–0.6	–2.5	–2.0
South Africa	21.1	19.1	21.3	27.6	0.1	1.9	3.0	2.5
Western Africa	19.2	18.4	17.4	18.2	–0.1	–0.3	–0.4	–0.5
Benin	24.2	19.1	17.2	18.8	–2.0	–1.6	–0.1	–0.2
Burkina Faso	19.5	18.3	16.3	17.6	–4.6	–5.8	–2.5	–1.3
Cabo Verde	23.0	15.7	17.1	27.6	–6.3	–25.9	–2.7	–2.5
Côte d'Ivoire	18.3	17.8	17.8	18.9	4.9	13.7	2.3	–0.3
Gambia	17.9	19.0	17.1	17.8	0	5.7	–0.7	–1.4
Ghana	17.1	16.8	18.1	21.5	2.2	–3.1	–1.4	–0.3
Guinea	21.9	19.2	17.0	18.0	0	–4.1	–4.7	–0.3
Guinea-Bissau	21.8	19.7	16.8	18.8	–3.6	–4.1	–7.2	–0.8
Liberia	19.1	18.3	18.0	19.4	–0.0	1.5	37.8	–1.0
Mali	20.9	18.8	16.5	16.3	–1.4	–3.1	–2.8	–2.1
Mauritania	17.9	17.0	17.6	20.1	–0.4	–1.0	–3.6	1.2
Niger	15.2	15.6	16.0	15.2	0.4	–0.6	–0.2	0.2
Nigeria	19.1	18.7	17.7	18.1	0.0	–0.1	–0.2	–0.3
Senegal	19.1	17.7	16.9	18.5	2.5	2.9	–4.9	–1.3
Sierra Leone	20.4	20.3	17.7	19.4	0	0	–6.8	–0.6
Togo	19.4	17.6	17.1	19.4	–6.5	–4.4	3.5	–0.3
Northern Africa	19.8	17.6	19.9	25.5	–1.6	–3.1	–1.9	–0.6
Algeria	19.4	16.4	19.4	28.5	–7.7	–3.3	–1.1	–0.2
Egypt	20.5	19.1	20.2	24.6	–0.5	–3.1	–0.6	–0.4
Libya	21.0	17.0	20.2	28.8	0	4.9	–2.2	–0.3
Morocco	19.5	16.2	21.1	29.5	0	–6.0	–3.8	–1.4
Sudan	18.1	16.8	17.7	19.7	0	0.4	–4.7	–1.2
Tunisia	20.3	17.0	23.1	32.8	–1.0	–3.6	–0.8	–0.3
Western Sahara	18.7	20.2	21.2	28.4	64.2	–29.5	21.4	9.9

Source: United Nations, Department of Economic and Social Affairs, Population Division (2019)

population in 2020, Equatorial Guinea (12.4), Western Sahara (9.9), Uganda (4.0), South Africa (2.5), Gabon (1.6), Botswana (1.3) and Mauritania (1.2) were the only countries in Africa with a positive net migration rate greater than one. The highest net migration losers in the same period were South Sudan (–15.9), Eritrea (–11.6), Central African Republic (–8.6), Zimbabwe (–8.2) and Sao Tome and Principe (–8.0). This is not unexpected considering the political and economic crises in the countries. The effects of politics and civil wars on net migration are best epitomized by Equatorial Guinea and Liberia. While Equatorial Guinea recorded a net migration rate of –50.0 between 1970 and 1975 at the height of the country's political crisis under President Francisco Macias Nguema, Liberia recorded a net migration rate of 37.5 between 1995 and 2000 when the country's civil war ended.

The negative net migration in Africa is attributable mainly to economic reasons. While the outflow from the African continent has been shown to positively impact the socioeconomic statuses of migrants' families left behind (Afaha, 2013; Kangmennaang, Bezner-Kerr, & Luginaah, 2018; Ajaero, Nzeadibe, Obisie-Nmehielle, & Ike, 2018; Chukwu, Ene, & Adewoyin, 2018), it equally has negative consequences on Africa's development. Thomas (2016), for instance, shows that the outflow of highly skilled Africans to the United States grew by more than 100% in 30 years between 1980 and 2010. The implication of such outflows, commonly referred to as brain-drain, is that the human resources and capacities required for economic and social capital production in various African countries have been depleted (Mutume, 2003; Adepoju, 2003; Dovlo, 2004; De Haas, 2008).

Infant mortality and life expectancy

Progress in reducing infant mortality across the continent has been tremendous. The greatest leap is noted in the Northern Africa subregion, where the infant mortality rate declined steeply from 201 per 1,000 live births in 1950 to 23 in 2020. Egypt, Libya and Tunisia recorded the largest improvements in the subregion, with infant mortality rates of less than 20 per 1,000 live births in 2000 from around 250 in the 1950s. The progress in Northern Africa was closely followed by that of Western Africa in absolute terms, with a reduction from 196 per 1,000 in 1950 to 57 in 2020. The change translates to a 71% reduction in infant mortality rates. Relatively, however, the Southern Africa subregion recorded a 78% reduction. On an individual country basis, and as shown in Table 2.4, Reunion (3), Mayotte (4), Mauritius (11), Seychelles (11) and Cape Verde (17) were the other countries that have reduced infant mortality to less than 20 per 1,000 population. Central African Republic (82), Sierra Leone (81) and Chad (75) had the highest prevalence rate of infant mortality on the continent.

Intensifying efforts at addressing the determinants of infant mortality on the continent would further accelerate the progress made in lowering and ultimately eradicating infant mortality in Africa. Factors underlying infant mortality on the continent include infant exposure to poor physical environmental conditions, including household habitat and hygiene conditions and the negative consequences of climate change (Muttunga, 2007; Akinyemi, Adedini, & Odimegwu, 2016; Onyekwelu et al., 2018; Adeboyejo, Adejumobi, Adewoyin, & Oyawoye, 2020). They also include socioeconomic, cultural and bio-demographical factors such as the mothers' age, their employment and empowerment status, their choices of delivery outlets and health-seeking behaviour, adoption of exclusive breastfeeding and intimate partner violence (Omariba, Beaujot, & Rajulton, 2007; Muttunga, 2007; Odimegwu, Chadoka, & De Wet, 2014; Chadoka-Mutanda & Odimegwu, 2016; Akinyemi, Adedini, & Odimegwu, 2017; Akinyemi, Solanke, & Odimegwu, 2018; Ene, Adewoyin, Olaitan, Nnama-Okechukwu, & Okafor, 2020). Government economic and health policies and their consequences for health seeking are also implicated (Osawe, 2014).

While life expectancy has almost doubled across the continent since 1950, expectedly and following from their achievements in reducing infant mortality, countries in the Northern subregion had the highest life expectancy (72 years). The Eastern African subregion followed, with 64 years. Life expectancy was still under 60 years in Middle and Western Africa in spite of their 57% and 71% improvements, respectively, as shown in Table 2.4. The positive impacts of longer life expectancy on regional economic development are well documented (Jie, Zhang, & Lee, 2001; Acemoglu & Johnson, 2005; Cervellati & Sunde, 2009). Prioritizing attention to the political, economic, sociodemographic and environmental determinants of health and longevity (Lin, Chen, & Chien, 2012; Adewoyin & Adeboyejo, 2016; Adeboyejo & Adewoyin, 2017; Adewoyin & Adeboyejo, 2017; Adewoyin, 2017a, 2017b; Chisumpa & Odimegwu, 2018; Ene, Adewoyin, & Uche, 2020) will further improve current life expectancy outcomes in Africa.

Table 2.4 Infant Mortality Rate and Life Expectancy in Africa, 1950–2020

Subregion/Country	*Infant Mortality (per 1,000 live births)*				*Life Expectancy at Birth*			
	1950–1955	*1970–1975*	*1995–2000*	*2015–2020*	*1950–1955*	*1970–1975*	*1995–2000*	*2015–2020*
Eastern Africa	171	129	95	42	37.42	46.34	49.24	64.15
Burundi	166	136	103	42	39.03	44.23	47.32	61.03
Comoros	192	139	74	53	38.72	46.85	59.29	63.98
Djibouti	154	104	72	33	41.04	50.90	57.02	66.54
Eritrea	199	140	71	35	34.08	44.12	53.97	65.74
Ethiopia	199	140	97	37	34.08	43.52	50.70	65.97
Kenya	142	97	71	36	42.57	53.96	51.77	66.18
Madagascar	183	134	78	29	36.32	45.97	56.68	66.49
Malawi	178	162	106	41	34.85	41.07	45.55	63.43
Mauritius	103	61	20	11	50.20	63.53	70.39	74.76
Mayotte	143	46	10	4	47.26	63.87	74.86	79.35
Mozambique	164	153	121	54	35.00	41.91	47.95	60.05
Réunion	142	46	10	3	47.86	64.59	75.28	80.03
Rwanda	150	135	122	29	40.15	44.95	45.09	68.44
Seychelles	81	47	12	11	61.90	67.35	70.80	73.29
Somalia	200	147	105	69	33.99	41.91	49.80	56.94
South Sudan	248	181	114	64	27.93	36.70	48.17	57.43
Uganda	150	117	94	46	40.13	49.56	44.32	62.76
United Republic of Tanzania	148	125	94	41	41.01	47.77	49.54	64.84
Zambia	138	107	109	46	43.24	51.19	43.36	63.26
Zimbabwe	114	76	69	39	49.68	57.45	46.97	60.83
Middle Africa	171	136	115	64	37.76	44.81	48.56	59.36
Angola	193	162	142	61	35.85	41.82	45.65	60.54
Cameroon	155	123	106	61	38.53	47.85	50.82	58.77
Central African Republic	170	137	110	82	32.74	44.26	45.04	52.67
Chad	186	146	114	75	36.06	42.56	47.65	53.80
Congo	134	86	74	35	40.43	51.69	51.91	64.16
Democratic Republic of the Congo	166	134	113	65	39.06	44.77	48.89	60.21
Equatorial Guinea	167	149	106	66	33.96	40.68	52.34	58.25
Gabon	160	118	62	35	36.82	49.20	59.40	66.06
Sao Tome and Principe	138	87	71	26	46.73	56.70	59.90	70.05
Southern Africa	134	89	50	29	44.61	53.84	58.21	63.28
Botswana	128	71	56	30	44.90	55.08	52.68	69.10
Eswatini	145	108	76	41	40.36	49.87	52.64	59.31
Lesotho	128	105	73	62	45.00	51.83	52.00	53.51
Namibia	144	88	51	33	40.70	53.88	55.04	63.02
South Africa	134	89	47	27	44.83	53.99	58.97	63.62
Western Africa	196	145	108	57	33.47	41.85	48.42	57.32
Benin	208	151	93	61	33.71	43.48	54.96	61.30
Burkina Faso	228	153	99	54	30.94	40.27	49.86	60.92
Cabo Verde	131	96	37	17	47.57	54.90	67.11	72.70
Côte d'Ivoire	189	129	99	60	30.17	46.26	50.44	57.25
Gambia	156	113	67	45	30.25	40.10	54.95	61.54
Ghana	147	106	67	36	42.17	50.03	57.00	63.65

(*Continued*)

Table 2.4 (Continued)

Subregion/Country	*Infant Mortality (per 1,000 live births)*				*Life Expectancy at Birth*			
	1950–1955	*1970–1975*	*1995–2000*	*2015–2020*	*1950–1955*	*1970–1975*	*1995–2000*	*2015–2020*
Guinea	207	185	112	52	33.08	37.43	51.63	61.04
Guinea-Bissau	163	146	115	57	35.59	41.42	49.45	57.82
Liberia	165	150	136	54	32.62	40.93	50.82	63.60
Mali	242	176	121	66	26.96	34.20	46.75	58.71
Mauritania	148	103	70	53	39.57	51.31	60.56	64.61
Niger	161	151	103	46	34.50	36.32	48.36	61.80
Nigeria	200	147	119	62	33.81	42.03	46.00	54.18
Senegal	128	108	68	33	35.47	40.91	57.24	67.47
Sierra Leone	237	190	157	81	28.79	37.32	37.61	54.07
Togo	186	113	80	50	35.30	48.07	53.71	60.53
Northern Africa	201	134	45	23	42.27	53.19	66.45	72.27
Algeria	163	122	38	21	42.89	51.49	69.52	76.59
Egypt	249	165	37	16	41.13	52.95	67.97	71.74
Libya	254	90	26	11	36.67	58.41	70.43	72.70
Morocco	151	113	44	20	45.67	53.53	67.65	76.33
Sudan	135	93	70	43	44.54	53.06	57.58	64.95
Tunisia	232	140	29	13	38.81	54.08	72.43	76.41
Western Sahara	217	160	64	29	35.52	43.26	61.28	69.86

Source: United Nations, Department of Economic and Social Affairs, Population Division (2019)

Childbearing age and sex ratio

On aggregate, mean age at childbirth declined slightly from 30 to 29 in Eastern Africa and 28 in Southern Africa, whereas it increased marginally in the other subregions (Table 2.5). This shows that despite pockets of teen pregnancies and their associated risk factors and health implications (Odimegwu & Mkwananzi, 2018; Yakubu & Salisu, 2018; Wado, Sully, & Mumah, 2019), Africa still has a preponderance of fully developed adult mothers. From the general outlook, the sex composition of Africa's population is largely balanced between both sexes. At the subregional level, however, the proportion of males to females was higher in Western and Northern Africa. While the trend has been ongoing since 1950 in Northern Africa, it began in Western Africa in 1995. Beneath the regional level, Equatorial Guinea (125.3), Djibouti (110.7), Western Sahara (109.5), Seychelles (105.3), Gabon (103.7), Ghana (102.8), Nigeria (102.8), Algeria (102.1), Egypt (102.1) and Libya (101.9) were the countries on the continent with a substantially higher proportion of males per 100 female population. Conversely, Mozambique (94.5), Reunion (93.8) and all the countries in the Southern Africa subregion had much fewer males per 100 female population, as shown in Table 2.5.

Sex ratio has implications for union formation. Where the numbers of females are a lot fewer than those of males, union formation, particularly with the ascendancy of monogamy in modern Africa, may become difficult. Such a scenario and its consequences for union formation may partly account for the prevalence of single motherhood on the continent. Behind Latin America, sub-Saharan Africa has the highest prevalence of single motherhood (10%), higher than in North America, Australia, Europe and Asia (United Nations Women, 2019). Studies

Table 2.5 Childbearing Age and Sex Composition of Africa's Population, 1950–2020

Subregion/Country	*Mean Childbearing Age*				*Sex Ratio (males/100 females)*			
	1950–1955	*1970–1975*	*1995–2000*	*2015–2020*	*1950*	*1970*	*1995*	*2020*
Eastern Africa	30.14	30.02	29.59	29.06	98.3	98.5	98.2	98.5
Burundi	30.92	30.95	30.98	31.06	91.9	94.5	95.5	98.5
Comoros	30.62	30.62	30.55	30.05	98.8	99.4	100.9	101.8
Djibouti	32.28	31.85	31.75	32.16	98.6	99.1	101.3	110.7
Eritrea	30.89	30.89	30.13	29.54	98.2	99.4	99.1	100.5
Ethiopia	30.75	30.75	30.07	29.73	98.6	99.0	99.4	100.1
Kenya	29.14	29.14	29.17	28.70	101.7	99.7	98.9	98.8
Madagascar	29.34	29.31	28.85	27.96	105.9	101.8	99.4	99.6
Malawi	29.71	29.71	29.10	28.04	92.3	97.7	98.4	97.3
Mauritius	28.06	28.41	27.17	28.14	99.2	100.1	99.4	97.4
Mayotte	28.68	28.68	29.84	29.84	119.7	110.5	103.2	96.8
Mozambique	30.38	29.80	28.82	28.60	95.6	96.0	91.1	94.5
Réunion	30.38	28.71	28.28	28.29	92.1	93.0	95.5	93.8
Rwanda	31.57	31.57	30.95	30.32	96.6	96.6	94.7	96.7
Seychelles	27.83	27.83	27.09	27.51	90.5	100.3	100.3	105.3
Somalia	32.16	32.16	31.37	29.68	98.6	97.8	100.6	99.4
South Sudan	29.25	29.27	30.12	29.57	104.1	99.5	99.0	100.2
Uganda	29.44	29.38	28.89	28.84	99.5	99.0	97.6	97.2
United Republic of Tanzania	29.67	29.52	29.45	28.76	95.2	97.8	99.0	99.9
Zambia	29.89	29.49	28.92	28.76	99.1	98.8	98.7	98.1
Zimbabwe	29.55	29.55	28.49	28.20	99.4	99.3	97.8	91.3
Middle Africa	28.76	28.82	29.35	29.10	92.3	96.8	98.4	99.6
Angola	28.21	28.21	28.47	28.79	94.2	106.6	99.7	97.9
Cameroon	28.61	28.61	28.34	28.91	96.1	97.6	99.1	100.1
Central African Republic	28.50	28.50	28.92	28.92	97.2	96.9	97.2	98.3
Chad	28.21	28.21	28.24	28.76	97.5	96.1	98.8	99.7
Congo	29.39	29.39	29.12	29.01	97.7	96.4	96.9	99.8
Democratic Republic of the Congo	29.22	29.23	30.17	29.36	88.1	94.0	98.0	99.7
Equatorial Guinea	28.83	28.71	29.03	28.06	96.7	98.8	102.6	125.3
Gabon	27.67	27.79	28.25	29.21	95.2	92.2	97.1	103.7
Sao Tome and Principe	28.23	28.23	28.37	28.81	124.9	100.5	98.0	100.2
Southern Africa	30.98	30.28	28.41	27.78	100.1	97.9	96.9	96.9
Botswana	29.72	29.93	28.72	28.06	93.8	92.8	92.6	93.9
Eswatini	30.54	29.12	28.45	27.70	94.6	93.4	91.3	96.7
Lesotho	31.07	30.06	29.13	27.91	80.8	80.0	94.5	97.4
Namibia	30.52	30.42	29.84	29.01	98.7	96.3	93.2	94.1
South Africa	31.04	30.33	28.32	27.72	101.6	99.1	97.5	97.1
Western Africa	29.16	29.58	29.68	29.54	99.5	99.8	100.3	101.4
Benin	30.63	30.79	29.58	28.86	87.2	92.6	96.1	99.8
Burkina Faso	27.60	29.38	30.01	29.23	110.3	99.1	96.0	99.9
Cabo Verde	30.46	30.46	28.60	27.38	89.3	91.0	92.4	100.8
Côte d'Ivoire	28.02	29.56	29.53	29.08	102.8	107.8	107.9	101.7
Gambia	27.83	27.99	29.21	30.40	96.1	101.9	100.0	98.4
Ghana	30.09	30.18	30.16	29.79	102.2	103.1	101.7	102.8
Guinea	27.56	29.31	29.07	29.10	100.0	97.3	92.0	93.7

(Continued)

Table 2.5 (Continued)

Subregion/Country	*Mean Childbearing Age*				*Sex Ratio (males/100 females)*			
	1950–1955	*1970–1975*	*1995–2000*	*2015–2020*	*1950*	*1970*	*1995*	*2020*
Guinea-Bissau	28.96	28.98	29.68	29.56	97.8	96.5	93.7	95.8
Liberia	28.25	28.89	29.74	28.45	108.5	99.5	98.9	101.1
Mali	29.05	29.41	29.13	29.01	104.8	100.2	97.8	100.4
Mauritania	29.39	30.36	30.72	30.49	96.7	98.5	98.2	100.9
Niger	28.90	29.10	29.12	29.06	82.3	93.8	97.0	101.1
Nigeria	29.50	29.55	29.70	29.81	99.5	100.0	101.4	102.8
Senegal	28.64	29.60	30.09	30.26	95.4	101.4	98.4	95.3
Sierra Leone	28.72	28.72	29.94	28.73	96.0	96.3	98.0	99.6
Togo	28.18	30.54	30.02	28.93	97.2	97.4	96.9	99.0
Northern Africa	29.12	29.31	29.54	29.30	101.8	101.3	101.4	101.0
Algeria	29.89	30.42	31.43	31.66	103.5	100.9	102.6	102.1
Egypt	28.42	28.42	27.99	27.60	103.1	103.2	101.4	102.1
Libya	29.35	29.35	32.65	32.82	107.2	106.5	110.0	101.9
Morocco	29.23	29.60	30.58	30.29	99.0	97.8	99.0	98.5
Sudan	29.28	29.28	29.88	30.02	99.8	100.1	100.6	99.8
Tunisia	30.75	30.88	30.58	31.04	98.7	100.5	102.0	98.4
Western Sahara	29.22	29.59	30.40	30.99	98.0	121.2	108.3	109.5

Source: United Nations, Department of Economic and Social Affairs, Population Division (2019)

have, however, shown that there is a spatial pattern to single motherhood (Ntoimo & Mutanda, 2020; Adewoyin, Awelewa, Uzoma, & Anazonwu, 2021). The Southern Africa subregion, where the sex distribution shows fewer males per 100 females, has been shown to have the highest prevalence of never-married mothers in Africa, at 50.5% (Ntoimo & Mutanda, 2020).

Contextualizing development and the African population structure

The population structure of a locale matters for both the social and economic development of the locale. The literature is replete with evidence to buttress this relationship at local, national and regional scales. In that context, the development profile of Africa is blamed on the size and composition of the continent's 1.3 billion inhabitants. International development agencies, development theorists and researchers cite a high fertility rate, high incidence of maternal and child mortality, poor and unequal access to social infrastructure by the population and lack of skills consequent on low literacy as some attributes of the population slowing down the pace of development on the continent. Their accounts, albeit true, did not, however, take cognizance of the peculiarities of the continent, how these peculiarities impede pace and how, despite them, the continent has still been able to make appreciable progress over the years. These impedances include landmass and geographical variation in terrain, spatial organization, statehood age and the error of developmentalism.

In the first instance, Africa has a landmass of 30.4 million square kilometres. This size is slightly bigger than the whole of Europe (10.2 million square kilometres), the United States (9.8 million square kilometres) and China (9.6 million square kilometres) combined. This implies a population density of 43 per square kilometre, against an average of 73 and 150 persons per square kilometre in Europe and China, respectively. With a more dispersed population, as is the case with Africa, providing services such as health, education, transportation and security becomes more expensive than when the population is clustered over a small area. The provision is made more difficult with a terrain that is as low as 155 meters below sea level at Assal, Djibouti, as high as 5.9 kilometres at Kilimanjaro, Tanzania, and interspersed with forests, mangroves, mountainous ranges and other physical geographical barriers, especially south of the Sahara Desert.

The world-systems theory (Wallerstein, 2004) describes the interrelationship among countries of the world with regard to international economics and the production of capital. The theory categorizes countries as core, semi-periphery and periphery based on their mode of economic production. While core countries (developed economies) are characterized by capital-intensive production, the periphery countries (Africa and other least-developed economies) are known by their labour-intensive production and extraction of raw material. This, Wallerstein (2004) argues, perpetuates underdevelopment in the periphery countries, whose only contributions to the international division of labour are rudimentary. D. M. Smith (1987), however, provides an alternative explanation for the perpetuation of underdevelopment in the periphery countries. In Smith's view, underdevelopment in the periphery countries is a factor of their spatial organization. This refers to the geographical location of the countries relative to other countries and how they are interconnected. In the regional context, this refers to the location of Africa relative to North America, Europe and China and how trade flows, and the diffusion of innovation and modernization are supposed to trickle down from the core regions to Africa. Not only is Africa locationally disadvantaged (with the few exceptions being African countries bordering the Mediterranean), the volume of trade and investment flows to Africa is paltry when compared with core-core flow.

Prior to the Berlin conference of 1855 that partitioned Africa and the subsequent colonization, the African population lived in empires, kingdoms and a variety of self-governed smaller states. Modern statehood on the continent didn't start until about a hundred years later. In Europe, in contrast, England has existed as a unified state since the 10th century, as has France. China has been a centre of civilization since around 1600 BC, and the United States became an independent state in 1776. Benchmarking Africa with these states is akin to wishing away the several generations of statehood experience and progressive growth that separate the regions. According to Rostow (1959), every society evolves through five stages of growth. These are the traditional society stage, where economic activities are only limited to a few production functions and more than 75% of the workforce are engaged in farming and food production. This is followed by the preconditions for the take-off stage, which is based on the adoption of technology for increased agricultural productivity, advancement in transportation systems and expansion of imports in exchange for natural resources. The third stage, the take-off, involves rapid and sustained expansion in major sectors of the economy where modern industrial technologies are required. The fourth and fifth stages are the drive to maturity and the age of high mass consumption. Using the characteristics of regions to rank them on Rostow's (1959) stages of growth would show Africa as evolving.

The stages of growth hypothesis by Rostow (1959) typify the basic tenets of developmentalism. Developmentalism as an economic theory argues that every society progresses linearly from one stage of development to the next higher stage by adopting a variety of internally centred market strategies, including import substitution (T. Smith, 1985). Essentially, developmentalism emphasizes societal development along a continuum by focusing more on a set of internal dynamics and less on what happens elsewhere. Expecting each society to develop at its own pace, using its own internal strategies, and yet comparing the rank of societies on the ladder of development is what Taylor (1989) describes as the error of developmentalism. Taylor (1989) contends that if social change is a matter of the internal dynamics of each country, then the position of other countries on the development ladder is irrelevant. This implies that progress in a society should only be compared with that society's pedigree and not with the progress in other climes. Avoiding the error of developmentalism would allow Africa to appreciate its own modest progress.

Progress in human development

Development is multidimensional, and defining it is complex. Its impacts on the population, however, remain one incontrovertible measure of its performance. The Human Development Index (HDI) provides one such measure. The HDI is a composite measure of development impacts on a population using three variables – health, education and standard of living. The value ranges from 0 (lowest) to 1 (highest). In 1990, only 12 of the 38 (31.6%) African countries ranked by the United Nations had an HDI value of 0.500 and above. These, as shown in Table 2.6, included Libya, South Africa, Mauritius and Gabon. By 2019, however, 36 of the 53 (67.9%) African countries ranked had an HDI value of at least 0.500. Mauritius, Seychelles, Algeria and Tunisia made it into the top half of the 189-country ranking in 2019.

A year-on year comparison of the HDI scores of countries ranked between 1990 and 2019 showed that no Africa country recorded a negative growth. With the exception of Libya, with a static growth rate, all the countries made some form of progress, ranging from 0.20% per annum in Lesotho to 2.74% per annum in Rwanda (Table 2.6). What this implies is that despite all the

Table 2.6 Human Development in Africa, 1990–2019

S/N	*Country*	*HDI Value 1990*	*HDI Value 2019*	*HDI Rank 2019 (n = 189)**	*Average Annual Growth 1990–2019 (%)***
1	Mauritius	0.624	0.804	66	0.88
2	Seychelles	–	0.796	67	..
3	Algeria	0.572	0.748	91	0.93
4	Tunisia	0.567	0.740	95	0.92
5	Botswana	0.573	0.735	100	0.86
6	Libya	0.724	0.724	105	0.00
7	South Africa	0.627	0.709	114	0.42
8	Egypt	0.548	0.707	116	0.88
9	Gabon	0.613	0.703	119	0.47
10	Morocco	0.457	0.686	121	1.41
11	Cabo Verde	–	0.665	126	..
12	Namibia	0.581	0.646	130	0.37
13	Sao Tome and Principe	0.452	0.625	135	1.12
14	Eswatini (Kingdom of)	0.541	0.611	138	0.42
15	Ghana	0.465	0.611	138	0.95
16	Kenya	0.482	0.601	143	0.76
17	Equatorial Guinea	–	0.592	145	..
18	Zambia	0.421	0.584	146	1.13
19	Angola	–	0.581	148	..
20	Congo	0.500	0.574	149	0.48

(*Continued*)

S/N	Country	HDI Value 1990	HDI Value 2019	HDI Rank 2019 (n = 189)*	Average Annual Growth 1990–2019 (%)**
21	Zimbabwe	0.478	0.571	150	0.61
22	Cameroon	0.448	0.563	153	0.79
23	Comoros	–	0.554	156	..
24	Mauritania	0.397	0.546	157	1.10
25	Benin	0.364	0.545	158	1.40
26	Uganda	0.320	0.544	159	1.85
27	Rwanda	0.248	0.543	160	2.74
28	Nigeria	–	0.539	161	..
29	Côte d'Ivoire	0.404	0.538	162	0.99
30	Tanzania (United Republic of)	0.368	0.529	163	1.26
31	Madagascar	–	0.528	164	..
32	Lesotho	0.498	0.527	165	0.20
33	Djibouti	–	0.524	166	..
34	Togo	0.406	0.515	167	0.82
35	Senegal	0.376	0.512	168	1.07
36	Sudan	0.331	0.510	170	1.50
37	Gambia	0.349	0.496	172	1.22
38	Ethiopia	–	0.485	173	..
39	Malawi	0.333	0.483	174	1.29
40	Congo (Democratic Republic of the)	0.369	0.480	175	0.91
41	Guinea-Bissau	–	0.480	175	..
42	Liberia	–	0.480	175	..
43	Guinea	0.282	0.477	178	1.83
44	Eritrea	–	0.459	180	..
45	Mozambique	0.227	0.456	181	2.43
46	Burkina Faso	–	0.452	182	..
47	Sierra Leone	0.287	0.452	182	1.58
48	Mali	0.234	0.434	184	2.15
49	Burundi	0.299	0.433	185	1.29
50	South Sudan	–	0.433	185	..
51	Chad	–	0.398	187	..
52	Central African Republic	0.334	0.397	188	0.60
53	Niger	0.220	0.394	189	2.03

Notes: *Number of countries ranked
**A smoothed annualized growth of the HDI calculated as the annual compound growth rate.
Source: United Nations (2020)

challenges African countries face, human development hasn't retrogressed but is, instead, getting better. The magnitude of the progress becomes more apparent when viewed along regional lines. As shown in Table 2.7, sub-Saharan Africa as a bloc had an HDI value of 0.404 in 1990. This increased to 0.547 in 2019. In both periods, the values were the lowest when compared with other regional blocs. In terms of average annual growth, however, its growth rate of 1.05% was higher than those of Europe and Central Asia, the Arab States, and Latin America and the Caribbean.

Table 2.7 Regional Average Annual HDI Growth, 1990–2019

Regions	*HDI Value 1990*	*HDI Value 2019*	*Average Annual Growth 1990–2019*
Arab States	0.556	0.705	0.82
East Asia and the Pacific	0.517	0.747	1.28
Europe and Central Asia	0.662	0.791	0.62
Latin America and the Caribbean	0.632	0.766	0.67
South Asia	0.437	0.641	1.33
Sub-Saharan Africa	0.404	0.547	1.05

Source: United Nations (2020)

Conclusion

An analysis of the population structure of Africa has shown that despite subcontinental spatial variations in levels of progress, the continent as a whole is making progress on all of its population components that matter for health and regional economic development. To accelerate the pace of development and derive the dividends of its young and mobile demographics, governments on the continent should prioritize investments in education, health and infrastructure. These have been shown to impact fertility behaviour, mortality and life expectancy and migration.

References

Acemoglu, D., & Johnson, S. (2005, July). *Disease and development: The effect of life expectancy on economic growth*. Cambridge, MA: Department of Economics, Massachusetts Institute of Technology.

Adebowale, A. S., & Palamuleni, M. E. (2015). Influence of gender preference and sex composition of surviving children on childbearing intention among high fertility married women in stable union in Malawi. *African Health Sciences*, *15*(1), 150–160.

Adeboyejo, A. T., Adejumobi, D. O., Adewoyin, Y., & Oyawoye, A. O. (2020). Spatial and demographic patterns of climate related diseases among hospitalized children in parts of Southwest Nigeria. *Human Geographies*, *14*(1), 59–71.

Adeboyejo, A. T., & Adewoyin, Y. (2017). Climate change and health of the aged in Lagos, Nigeria. *Australian Journal of Basic and Applied Sciences*, *11*(13), 8–16.

Adepoju, A. (2003). Migration in West Africa. *Development*, *46*(3), 37–41.

Adewoyin, Y. (2017a). Neoliberalism, public health, and malaria prevalence in Nigeria. *Asian Pacific Journal of Health Sciences*, *4*(4), 168–171.

Adewoyin, Y. (2017b). National treatment policy for whom? Analysis of malaria treatment choices in urban Nigeria. *Journal of Behavioral Health*, *6*(3), 120–123.

Adewoyin, Y., & Adeboyejo, A. T. (2016). People, places, and health variations: A case of malaria prevalence in Ibadan, Nigeria. *African Population Studies*, *30*(2), 3006–3015.

Adewoyin, Y., & Adeboyejo, A. T. (2017). Aspects of climatic and socioeconomic parameters and malaria prevalence: Evidence from Nigeria. *International Journal of Tropical Diseases and Health*, *28*(4), 1–9.

Adewoyin, Y., Awelewa, O. F., Uzoma, I. E., & Anazonwu, N. P. (2021). Prevalence pattern and sociodemographic correlates of single motherhood in Nigeria. *Sexuality Research and Social Policy*. https://doi.org/10.1007/s13178-020-00523-0

Afaha, J. S. (2013). Migration, remittance and development in origin countries: Evidence from Nigeria. *African Population Studies*, *27*(1). doi.org/10.11564/27-1-7

Agbor, J., Taiwo, O., & Smith, J. (2012). *Sub-Saharan Africa's youth bulge: A demographic dividend or disaster?* Africa Growth Initiative. Washington, DC: The Brookings Institutions.

Ajaero, C. K., Nzeadibe, C. T., Obisie-Nmehielle, N., & Ike, C. C. (2018). The linkages between international migration, remittances and household welfare in Nigeria. *Migration and Development*, 7(1). doi.org/10.1080/21632324.2017.1322171

Akinyemi, J. O., Adedini, S. A., & Odimegwu, C. O. (2016). Independent and combined effects of maternal smoking and solid fuel on infants and child mortality in sub-Saharan Africa. *Tropical Medicine & International Health Journal, 21*(12), 1572–1582.

Akinyemi, J. O., Adedini, S. A., & Odimegwu, C. O. (2017). Individual v. community-level measures of women's decision-making involvement and child-survival in Nigeria. *South African Journal of Child Health, 11*(1), 26–32.

Akinyemi, J. O., Solanke, B. L., & Odimegwu, C. O. (2018). Maternal employment and child survival during the era of Sustainable Development Goals: Insights from proportional hazards modelling of Nigeria birth history data. *Annals of Global Health, 84*(1).

Blackstone, S. R., Nwaozuru, U., & Iwelunmor, J. (2017). Factors influencing contraceptive use in sub-Saharan Africa: A systematic review. *International Quarterly of Community Health Education, 37*(2), 79–91.

Bloom, D., Kuhn, M., & Prettner, K. (2017). Africa's prospects for enjoying a demographic dividend. *Journal of Demographic Economics (JODE), 83*(1), 63–76.

Canning, D., Raja, S., & Yazbeck, A. (2015). *Africa's demographic transition: Dividend or disaster?* Washington, DC: World Bank.

Cervellati, M., & Sunde, U. (2009). *Life expectancy and economic growth: The role of the demographic transition.* IZA DP No. 4160, Berlin.

Chadoka-Mutanda, N., & Odimegwu, C. (2016). Maternal health-seeking behaviour and under-fives mortality in Zimbabwe. *Journal of Biosocial Science*, 1–14.

Chisumpa, V. H., & Odimegwu, C. O. (2018). Decomposition of age and cause specific adult mortality contributions to the gender gap in life expectancy from census and survey data in Zambia. *SSM – Population Health, 5*, 218–226.

Chukwu, N. A., Ene, J. C., & Adewoyin, Y. (2018). Impact of international migration of parents on academic performance of left-behind undergraduate students in the University of Nigeria, Nsukka: Implication for social work practice in Nigeria. *Journal of Social Works in Developing Societies, 1*(1), 408–416.

Cummins, M. (2019). *Population dynamics and the demographic dividend potential of Eastern and Southern Africa: A primer.* MPRA Paper No. 97735. Munich.

De Haas, H. (2008). The myth of invasion: The inconvenient realities of African migration to Europe. *Third World Quarterly, 29*(7), 1305–1322.

Dovlo, D. (2004). The brain drain in Africa: An emerging challenge to health professionals' education. *Journal of Higher Education in Africa, 2*(3), 1–18.

Ene, J. C., Adewoyin, Y., & Chukwu, N. A. (2019). Patterns and determinants of contraceptives utilization in a religiously homogeneous settlement: A Nigerian case study. *Research Journal of Health Sciences*, 7(3), 217–226.

Ene, J. C., Adewoyin, Y., Olaitan, M. T., Nnama-Okechukwu, C. U., & Okafor, A. (2020). Where do women choose to give birth in Enugu State, Nigeria? *Nigerian Journal of Social Sciences, 14*(1), 157–169.

Ene, J. C., Adewoyin, Y., & Uche, I. B. (2020). Coping with health and psychosocial well-being of older cohorts: Impact of medical social workers in Nigeria. *Journal of Medical Science and Clinical Research, 8*(4), 530–543.

Fadayomi, T. O. (2011). The demographic bonus: How prepared is Africa for the gains? *African Population Studies, 25*(2), 226–249.

Jie, Z., Zhang, J., & Lee, R. (2001). Mortality decline and long run economic growth. *Journal of Public Economics, 80*, 485–507.

Kangmennaang, J., Bezner-Kerr, R., & Luginaah, I. (2018). Impact of migration and remittances on household welfare among rural households in Northern and Central Malawi. *Migration and Development*, 7(1). doi.org/10.1080/21632324.2017.1325551

Lin, R. T., Chen, Y. M., Chien, L. C., & Chan, C. C. (2012). Political and social determinants of life expectancy in less developed countries: A longitudinal study. *BMC Public Health, 12*, 85. https://doi.org/10.1186/1471-2458-12-85

Mumah, J., Brinton, J., Mukiira, C., Kabiru, C. W., & Izugbara, C. O. (2015). *Invest in urban youth sexual and reproductive health to achieve a demographic dividend in Africa.* STEP UP Policy Brief. Nairobi: African Population and Health Research Center.

Muttunga, C. J. (2007). *Environmental determinants of child mortality in Kenya*. WIDER Research Paper, No. 2007/83, ISBN 978-92-9230-036-4, The United Nations University World Institute for Development Economics Research (UNU-WIDER), Helsinki.

Mutume, G. (2003). Reversing Africa's brain drain. *Africa Recovery, 17*(2), 1–9.

Ntoimo, L. F. C., & Mutanda, N. (2020). Demography of single parenthood in Africa: Patterns, determinants and consequences. In C. O. Odimegwu (Ed.), *Family demography and post-2015 development agenda in Africa*. Cham, Switzerland: Springer.

Odimegwu, C. O., & Adedini, S. (2017). The role of community structure in shaping African fertility patterns: Evidence from demographic and health surveys. *Journal of Biosocial Science, 49*(1), S46–S61.

Odimegwu, C. O., & Adewoyin, Y. (2020a). Latent and under-explored determinants of contraceptive use in Nigeria. *Sexuality Research and Social Policy*. doi.org/10.1007/s13178-020-00495-1

Odimegwu, C. O., & Adewoyin, Y. (2020b). Ethnic fertility behaviour and internal migration in Nigeria: Revisiting the migrant fertility hypotheses. *Genus, 76*(3), 1–17.

Odimegwu, C. O., Akinyemi, J., Banjo, O. O., Olamijuwon, E., & Amoo, E. (2018). Fertility, family size preference and contraceptive use in sub-Saharan Africa: 1990–2014. *African Journal of Reproductive Health, 22*(4), 44–53.

Odimegwu, C. O., Chadoka, N., & De Wet, N. (2014). Gender-based violence and child survival: Exploring the association between domestic violence and child health consequences in three African countries. *Gender and Behavior, 12*(4), 6071–6092.

Odimegwu, C. O., & Mkwananzi, S. (2018). Family structure and community connectedness: Their association with teenage pregnancy in South Africa. *Journal of Psychology in Africa, 28*(6), 479–484.

Omariba, D. W. R., Beaujot, R., & Rajulton, F. (2007). Determinants of infant and child mortality in Kenya: An analysis controlling for frailty effects. *Population Research and Policy Review, 26*(3), 299–321.

Omoju, O. E., & Abraham, T. W. (2014). Youth bulge and demographic dividend in Nigeria. *African Population Studies, 27*(2), 352–360.

Onyekwelu, C. A., Obienusi, E. A., Mozie, A. T., Ayadiuno, R. U., Nwosu, I. G., Adewoyin, Y., . . . Igboeli, E. E. (2018). Mapping incidents of infant mortality arising from gastroenteritis: A case study from South-East Nigeria. *African Population Studies, 32*(2), 4134–4154.

Osawe, O. W. (2014). Determinant of infant mortality rate: A panel data analysis of African countries. *Developing Country Studies, 4*(18), 111–115.

Rostow, W. W. (1959). The stages of economic growth. *The Economic History Review, 12*(1), 1–16.

Sippel, L., Kiziak, T., Woellert, F., & Klingholz, R. (2011). *Africa's demographic challenges: How a young population can make development possible*. Berlin: Berlin Institute for Population and Development.

Smith, D. M (1987). *Geography, inequality and society*. Oxford: Oxford University Press.

Smith, T. (1985). Requiem or new agenda for third world studies? *World Politics, 37*(4), 537.

Taylor, P. J. (1989). The error of developmentalism in human geography. In D. Gregory & R. Walford (Eds.), *Horizons in human geography*. London: Palgrave.

Thomas, K. J. A. (2016). Highly skilled migration from Africa to the US: Exit mechanisms, demographic determinants, and the role of socioeconomic trends. *Population Research and Policy Review, 35*, 825–849.

United Nations. (2019). *World population prospects 2019*. New York: United Nations Department of Economic and Social Affairs, Population Division, Online Edition. Rev. 1.

United Nations. (2020). *Human development report 2020: The next frontier – Human development and the Anthropocene*. Geneva: United Nations.

United Nations, Department of Economic and Social Affairs, Population Division. (2020). *World contraceptive use 2020* (POP/DB/CP/Rev2020). Geneva: United Nations.

United Nations Women. (2019). *Progress of the World's Women 2019–2020 – Families in a Changing World*. New York: United Nations.

Wado, Y. D., Sully, E. A., & Mumah, J. N. (2019). Pregnancy and early motherhood among adolescents in five East African countries: A multi-level analysis of risk and protective factors. *BMC Pregnancy Childbirth, 19*, 59.

Wallerstein, I. (2004). World-systems analysis. In G. Modelski (Ed.), *World system history*. Oxford: Eolss Publishers.

Yakubu, I., & Salisu, W. J. (2018). Determinants of adolescent pregnancy in sub-Saharan Africa: A systematic review. *Reproductive Health, 15*(1), 15.

Yaya, S., Uthman, O. A., Ekholuenetale, M., & Bishwajit, G. (2018). Women empowerment as an enabling factor of contraceptive use in sub-Saharan Africa: A multi-level analysis of cross-sectional surveys of 32 countries. *BMC Reproductive Health, 15*, 24.

PART 2

Demographic training and research

3

DEMOGRAPHIC TRAINING IN AFRICAN INSTITUTIONS

Past, present and future

Alfred Agwanda Otieno and Lawrence Ikamari

Introduction

At the turn of this century, there was a heightened discussion on demographic training globally. Most notable and relevant to training of demographers in Africa are the International Union for the Scientific Study of Population (IUSSP) through its working group on training and the Mellon Foundation-funded Population Council project to assess future needs for training and support of population scientists from developing countries. The results of the proceedings of these meeting have several implications for demographic training in Africa. First, demographic inquiry has shifted from the initial focus on describing and explaining population growth and fertility decline in developing countries. The discipline has expanded into areas that demand greater inter-disciplinary focus, such as persistent poverty and inequality, preservation of the environment and the HIV/AIDS pandemic, amongst others. Second, the growing demand for researchers with cross-disciplinary competencies entails that practitioners should be able to understand that there are alternative ways of generating knowledge and appreciate the theoretical basis of different research methods. Third, the changing job market in some countries in Africa demands that training in demography be refocused not only on government needs but also other sectors. The job market has undergone significant changes because government structures are being modified, universities are evolving, non-governmental organizations (NGOs) have increasingly acquired importance in the job market and there is potential for private-sector growth due to the expanding commercial sector and the associated needs. These shifts require demographic inquiry to contribute to clarifying both the population consequences of individual behaviour and the effect of macro-level population processes. Demographers need to have the skills necessary to employ methodologies that can provide explanations of behaviour at multiple levels incorporating individual, household and institutional factors and also changes over time. This implies the need to train demographers capable of fitting into the current and future job market. This chapter provides an overview of the past trends in training needs, focus areas and opportunities and challenges which calls for critical reflection. An important limitation is that it does not in any way prescribe a particular pathway for didactic practices on training in demography in African institutions of higher learning.

 DOI: 10.4324/9780429287213-5

Historical foundations and initiation of demographic training in Africa (1960–1990)

Demography as a discipline emerged in the 1920s and 1930s (Vance, 1952 cf. Greenhalgh, 1996; Tabutin, 2007) in the United States and later in France after the Second World War in 1945 (Tabutin, 2007). In Africa, the study of demography emerged in the early 1960s when colonialism ended for most countries and most African countries were beginning to build independent states (United Nations Economic Commission for Africa [UNECA], 1992; UN, 1995; Ntozi, 2011). At the first population conference held at Ibadan University with support from the Population Council in 1966, it was noted that by 1966, at least 15 countries had started teaching courses in demography (Caldwell & Okonjo, 1968), but the training involved introducing course units in established disciplines such as geography, sociology and economics, mostly at undergraduate level.

Post-graduate training in demography in Africa can be said to have been born in the Cairo Demographic Centre (CDC) in Egypt in the year 1963 with support from the United Nations (UN). Thereafter, the United Nations, in particular United Nations Population Fund (UNFPA), was instrumental in the initiation of the teaching of demography in African institutions. The initial institutions were the Regional Institute for Population Studies (RIPS) hosted at the University of Ghana in Accra in 1971 and the Institut de Formation et de Recherche Démographiques (IFORD) in Yaoundé, Cameroon, 1972 (UNECA, 1992). UNFPA was also instrumental in setting up other centres within national universities supporting curriculum development and reviews, staff capacity building and resources to support research (financial and teaching inputs such as computers and software). Apart from the UN system, the Population Council, Rockefeller Foundation and Ford Foundation leveraged their resources to help support infrastructure for population training, including capacity building and research (UNECA, 1992; Klancher, 2017). Bilateral agencies like United States Agency for International Development (USAID) and International Development Research Centre (IDRC) also supported the establishment of many centres (UNECA, 1992). Most of the centres were established in the 1980s (UNECA, 1992), with the most recent being in Southern Africa.

The notable features of post-graduate training programs in Africa are: 1) most of the training programs were established with some external funding, and 2) the departmental locations of the programs varied, implying the structural foundations were not similar. Most programs were initiated in the departments of sociology, economics, statistics or geography. In a few cases, programs were offered in a combined Department of Statistics and Demography, while others, such as the Population Studies and Research Institute of the University of Nairobi, were established as standalones similar to the programs at the RIPS in Ghana, CDC in Egypt and International Institute for Population Sciences (IIPS) in India. Worldwide, demography, as a discipline, is often attached to the faculties of economics, political or social sciences or statistics. Standalone institutions are found in Asia, Latin America and Africa.

Training needs and broad curriculum areas

Training needs

Two early writings describe the general foundations of demographic training needs in Africa. Okonjo (1966) was among the earliest writers on demographic training in Africa. In an article published in the *Journal of Modern African Studies*, the training needs were anchored on the fact that governments of Africa, in planning for economic and social development, became increasingly aware that they could no longer afford to treat population as an exogenous variable. At that time, the major population issues were the conduct, management and analysis of population census or demographic surveys. The focus was on getting accurate data on population size and structures and on basic demographic dynamics. Hence, studying the component variables of population change, and their interrelationships, became the core of curriculum, with special attention to the role of fertility and mortality. Igun (1976) later, in the earliest journal on population for African professionals, noted that at that time, training for African demographers should emphasize problems in data collection, data manipulation and innovation in solving methodological problems. The training was expected to focus on producing teachers of demography at institutions of higher learning; high-level professionals in governments, especially national statistical offices; middle-level professionals and low-level workers (Igun, 1976). Thus, during the first decade after the initiation of graduate programs, training emphasized the technical aspects of demography in order to meet the needs of the African governments to be able to collect and analyse census and demographic surveys to aid planning for national development.

However, the training needs expanded in the 1980s following the recommendations of the 1984 Second African Population Conference held in Arusha, Tanzania, and the World Population Plan of Action (United Nations [UN], 1979). At the Second African Population Conference, African countries adopted the Kilimanjaro Plan of Action, which called for the need to strike a balance between socio-economic development objectives and demographic objectives in order to improve quality of life for individuals and societal welfare (Van de Walle, Ohadike, & Sala-Diakanda, 1988). The plan of action following the Mexico City declaration on population and development and encouraged countries to establish long-term plans for the regular collection of various demographic and interrelated socio-economic variables, particularly for improvement of the level of living. The plan of action further recommended that training in various aspects of population activities should not be restricted to the higher level of specialization but should also extend to personnel at other levels. These recommendations led UNFPA to initiate long-term financial assistance to establish training and support research in a number of institutions in Africa. The UNFPA project initiation was preceded by a needs assessment prior to formulation and implementation. The needs assessment yielded two important factors that guided the establishment and support for training in several institutions. The first was the need to raise awareness among policy makers about the consideration of population factors. The second was to train personnel who could use population statistics and at the same time confidently talk about the interlinkages between population and other socio-economic factors (UN, 1995). The results of the needs assessment led to the revision of earlier programs and initiation of new programs. The main objective of the training programs was integrating population factors into national development planning. This initiative resulted in some countries initiating demographic programs at undergraduate levels and also at the post-graduate level. The purpose of undergraduate programs was to introduce courses on demography and population studies into professional training of administrators, economists, sociologists and geographers to create awareness and to use and integrate population factors in their future work. The second was to provide a basis for further training in demography for students who wished to specialize. A brief of the historical aspects of demographic training from the 1970s to 1990s was described by the UNECA in the Third African Population Conference held in Dakar, Senegal, 7–10 December 1992 and the UN Report 1995. Later in the mid-1990s, the UNFPA was also instrumental in directly setting up global training programs in three African countries to further create awareness and interest in population and development among policy makers.[1]

Broad curriculum areas

The initial graduate-level program started with postgraduate diplomas (lasting between 9 and 12 months) and master's degree courses (lasting on average 2 years). The curriculum in the early 1970s was largely broad and similar in all institutions. The course content included substantive demography; technical demography; family planning programs; auxiliary subjects including mathematics, statistics, sampling and research methods; and other complementary subjects such as economics, sociology, physiology of reproduction and genetics. This subject matter echoed the needs of African governments as well as citizens for basic demographic information. However, much of the training emphasized demographic data collection and analysis to support statistical agencies and planning departments. Thus, major issues revolved around how to manage population censuses and demographic surveys and to some extent vital statistics.

During this period, a range of techniques were also developed for estimating fertility and mortality for African populations because of the nature of data – incomplete and/or error prone. These methodological approaches formed the foundation of demographic analysis, especially in the use of census data. The seminal book published in 1968 by the Princeton Group, *The Demography of Tropical Africa*, represented a core reference work on fertility and mortality estimation from incomplete data (Brass & Coale, 1968). This period was also marked by the theory of modernization in the social sciences and measurement of the diffusion of western-style urban development and their associated demographic, social, economic and political transitions. The emergent theory highly influenced the nature of social science research and training. Examples of such works included Rostow's (1964) stages of economic growth, Soja's (1968) geography of modernization in Kenya, Mabogunje (1970) hypothesis about migration systems in Nigeria and Amin's (1974) research on modern forms of migration in West Africa. Kpedekpo's (1982) text *Essentials of Demographic Analysis for Africa* introduced students to methods of analysis using typical problems of data in Africa. In summary, the course content of formal demography in the 1970s and 1980s can largely be grouped into a mixture defined by the following categories (Bah (2001): a 'pure' demographic approach (British/North American variant or the French/German variant), statistical approach (including stochastic processes) and indirect approaches to estimation of demographic indicators (as exemplified by United Nations manuals). An example of a typical curriculum for early training programs as described by Bah (2001) is shown in Appendix Table 3.1.

Changing scope and diversity in demographic inquiry: 1990 to the present

In the 1990s, demographers' scope and areas of interest became more diversified (Keilman, 1992), driven by crises and their consequences such as HIV and AIDS, social and political demand (national or international) and funding requirements. Demography as a discipline not only began to venture out of its own territory but opened up to the major issues of society, moving into fields that had once belonged to other disciplines (Palloni, 2002). In Africa, the United Nations International Conference on Population and Development (ICPD), held at Cairo in 1994, and its subsequent plan of action shifted population policy focus by emphasizing human welfare rather than the population stabilization objectives of the previous decade. This shift in policy focus contributed to the diversification of demography to expand beyond its traditional core concerns.

These shifts brought in new themes in demography such as gender dimensions, reproductive health, population and environment and population and development, among others (Caselli,

2002; Tabutin, 2007). The emergence of new themes shifted the research agenda as well as the training needs amidst dwindling financial resources. Menken, Blanc, and Lloyd (2002) indicated that two of the largest donors in the population field (USAID and UNFPA) ceased funding long-term training in the second half of the 1990s. In addition, some centres suffered when support in the form of visiting instructors, teaching materials and training of their instructors was stopped. A review undertaken by Committee for International Cooperation in National Research in Demography (CICRED), covering centres in both English-speaking and French-speaking Africa with respect to their activities, resources, interests and modes of operation, noted a number of challenges (Goldstein, 1994). These challenges included limited funding, problems with structural autonomy within the government or institution, inadequate evaluation of research and too many poor and superficial research products. The inadequate staff often led to low levels of exploitation of data collected in field surveys or available in censuses and other government statistics, while lack of demographic expertise was due to lack of exposure to and use of newly emerging technology (UNECA, 1992; Goldstein, 1994; UN, 1995). In addition, as survey data, including prospects for longitudinal data, especially from demographic surveillance sites, became increasingly available, new insights in analysis techniques were introduced in training modules which were once not available to demographers in the 1970s and 1980s. These expanded the demographic knowledge base to include not only descriptions from estimates but also explanations of the results of the estimation.

The diversification raised debates on and criticisms of the didactic enterprise in demography in terms of course structure, textbook content and teaching style. Many institutions expanded the content and training curricula based on the extended diversity to accommodate new thinking (examples of master's degree curricula post-1994 are given in Appendix Table 3.2 for select institutions in West, East and Southern Africa; see also Wajnman, Rio Neto, & Eduardo, 2003 for Latin America). Some critics did not approve of these new directions (see Margolis, 1997), claiming that the demographic training was veering off the mark. This led to some diversity in the nature of training in several major demographic institutions (Bah, 2001). For example, RIPS revised the academic curriculum from mostly technical demography to a broader and more interdisciplinary program with a representation of quantitative and qualitative perspectives (Madise, 2015).

Worldwide, demography as a discipline has developed, both in terms of its themes and instruments of research and in its teaching, following different pathways and advancing at different speeds (Tabutin, 2007). In the last two and half decades, the science of demography has considerably changed – improving on its original expertise anchored on data collection and measurement to the development of new methodological approaches and diversifying its research topics (Tabutin, 2007). Demography as a science had been highly criticized to be good at measuring but poor or unreliable at explaining (Greenhalgh, 1996). This debate about explanatory or causal research in demography is not new but recurrent (Palloni, 2002; Tabutin, 2007; Burch, 2018). Some observers see demography as being restricted to the analytical, which was originally its strength but is now a serious handicap, while others argue that 'demography does not, in general, deserve to be qualified as theoretically weak' (Poirier & Piché, 1999, p. 42 cf. Tabutin, 2007). The attempts to widen the scope of the discipline have also led to the fragmentation of the discipline (Tabutin, 2007; Courgeau & Franck, 2007).

Doctoral training in demography

Between 1960 and 1990, doctoral training was mainly done outside the African countries, especially in the United States, France, Netherlands, Britain and Australia. A few students who enrolled in African institutions in doctoral programs sometimes took sandwich courses in developed countries because of limited research infrastructure such as computing and library facilities, amongst other needs. Doctoral training has been offered by thesis only.

Most doctoral-level programs in Africa (South Africa may be an exception) have been described as weak, and the weakest point is the long duration to complete the program (Obamba, 2017). The doctoral student's average desired duration of completion ranges from 36 to 48 months, but the actual period of time may extend by up to 18 months or more (Obamba, 2017). There are several factors behind the long durations to completion, but many are context dependent, such as structure of institutions, funding for training and research and nature of previous student training both at the undergraduate and master's levels (Obamba, 2017).

In general, problems of doctoral training in Africa are not confined to demography only. Africa has a low higher education participation rate (Obamba, 2017). Universities in Africa have a relatively smaller pool of students who can potentially proceed on to PhD programs compared to universities in other continents. The narrow pool syndrome is compounded by the pipeline effect, whereby master's enrolments are growing exponentially, whereas PhD enrolments remain significantly low and stagnant or decline altogether (Obamba, 2017). A study conducted in eight African universities reported that the total master's enrolments in the eight universities more than doubled from 9,625 in 2001 to 25,652 students in 2011 (cf. Obamba, 2017). During the same period, PhD enrolments grew from 1,165 in 2001 to only 2,584 students in 2011 (Bunting, Cloete, & Van Schalkwyk, 2014, cf. Obamba, 2017). The point to note is that there has been no comprehensive review of the discipline of demography covering many parts of the continent ever since the CICRED study in the early 1990s.

According to a recent scoping review (Obamba, 2017) of doctoral studies and research in Africa, there are reports that many institutions of higher learning are preoccupied with a singular focus on the quantity of people holding doctoral degrees. The extent to whether they are enough to replenish the dwindling stock of senior faculty and Africa's aging professoriate (British Academy, 2012; Tettey, 2010) has not been the focus of restructuring higher education training. A large proportion of studies on doctoral programs in Africa has been concerned primarily with quantitative measures, including enrolment numbers, completion rates, numbers of faculty with doctorate degrees, how long it takes to complete the doctorate and similar kinds of directly measurable parameters. This narrative is often framed within the broader structural challenge of producing and retaining the next generation of senior academic staff in most African universities (Obamba, 2017). For demography, this may be an enormous challenge in a number of countries; however, at present, the magnitude of the challenge is still anecdotal.

The present challenge for higher doctoral training and research in demography requires greater focus beyond 'bean-counting' sorts of indicators, although a substantial number of Southern African-focused studies have examined issues around doctoral enrolments, graduation patterns and policy of doctoral programs (Cloete, Mouton, & Sheppard, 2015). There are relatively fewer studies that have focused on doctoral studies at universities in other parts of Africa (Obamba, 2017). An International Association of Universities (IAU) study focused on doctoral enrolments and completions in Rwanda, Kenya, Nigeria, Benin, Cameroon and Senegal (Cross and Backhouse, 2014). Bunting et al. (2014) covered eight flagship universities across Kenya (Nairobi), Ghana (University of Ghana), Nigeria (Ilorin), Tanzania (Dar es Salaam), Mozambique (Eduardo Mondlane), Botswana (University of Botswana), Uganda (Makerere University), Mauritius (University of Mauritius) and South Africa (Cape Town). These studies examined general higher-level education but not demography. The future requires a critical examination of the structure of demography doctoral programs concerning such themes as the logical organization of demographic and related contents; learning resources and pedagogical activities; and sequencing, objectives and scope (Obamba, 2017).

Prospects for future training

In order to discern what the future holds for demographic training, it is important to reflect on what has happened in the past five decades, when the training programs were initiated and expanded. According to a database maintained by CICRED, the period between 1980 and 1990 was the time when demographic training programs expanded in Africa. The number of centres offering graduate training in demography expanded (see Appendix Table 3.3 for list), but the exact number may be unknown because currently no database exists on university-based demographic training centres. The training needs to be expanded from offering courses to enable graduates to plan, manage and analyse large-scale demographic data sets to those that integrate population factors in development planning. Ever since the ICPD 1994, these needs not only include the capacity to integrate population factors in development planning but also the ability to explain complex societal issues (see examples in Appendix Table 3.2). The centres that offer training in demography in Africa currently offer mainly master's-level training, of which three types can be distinguished. First, the 'traditional' type with a strong quantitative orientation and about two-thirds or more of the coursework consisting of courses in population/demography orientation. The second type seeks to train population scientists in conjunction with other disciplines, and about one-quarter of the coursework in these programs consists of population courses. The third type consists of degrees in other disciplines with one or two population courses such as in public health, sociology, economics, geography or statistics. The great majority of professionals who graduate with master's degrees work for government agencies, NGOs, private firms and even international projects.

Ntozi (2011) indicated that post-graduate diploma and master's programs have been successful despite challenges experienced by various institutions. However, some master's programs have an enormous dimension of courses and a rigid sequential scheme between master's and doctoral programs. PhD training programs have been described as weak (Ntozi, 2011; Ezeh et al., 2010; Menken et al., 2002), and as a result, some centres have introduced taught PhD programs in addition to thesis writing. PhD-level training in demography is still largely conducted in developed countries.

A critical factor in training is the labour market. In the recent decade, the academic job market appears to be stagnant in a number of countries in Africa. The NGO and private sectors are providing a growing number of opportunities for experts in population and related studies. This section highlights the opportunities and challenges to re-invigorate training programs to meet future needs in Africa and includes three major interrelated factors: the changing nature of the discipline; complex policy debates including their formulation, implementation and evaluation; and the labour market prospects.

1 The changing nature of the discipline and inputs for training

Demography has extended its field of investigation from the macro- to the micro-longitudinal and places greater emphasis on gaining new insight by devising or using more complex information systems and using a variety of statistical tools, often borrowed from outside[2] and adapted to its needs. There has been extensive growth in terms of new thematic areas in the discipline such as household and family dynamics, gender issues in development and program evaluation and increased interest in the use of qualitative methods. The individual, for example, is no longer seen as a simple trajectory made up of distinct demographic events, each analyzed separately, but as a complex life-course comprising various interconnected types of events (demographic, occupational, residential, etc.), a life of stages and periods with variable causalities (Billari, 2001). This has moved inquiry into a multi-factorial approach giving full place to the family; to the social circle and networks; and to social, economic and cultural factors (Tabutin, 2007). But the move into new frontiers is not without its faults. Tabutin (2007), citing earlier works by Poirier and Piché (1999), raised concerns on the various types of compartmentalization, such as between objects of research, levels of analysis, explanatory factors, critical theoretical thinking and demographic production centres (cf. Tabutin, 2007).

Demography is empirical, with demands on precise analysis, which has been revolutionized by the internet, growth in analysis software ranging from spreadsheets to general-purpose statistical software and simulation techniques. In the 1980s and much of the 1990s, these were hardly available to many teachers and students in Africa. The growth in the use of the internet has changed the scale of intellectual exchanges, while rapid change in the availability of data and computing technologies changed both demographic analysis and teaching. The power of desktop and local computing environments increased and created decentralized data processing environments, which are different from what was in Africa in the 1980s. Two factors have driven the change in approaches to quantitative analysis and teaching: the availability of high-quality large datasets such as censuses and labour-force surveys, Demographic and Health Surveys (DHSs) and multi-cluster indicator surveys (MCISs) and the growing power of computer analysis packages and increasing availability and affordability of computers and associated software. Although in many countries in Africa, censuses and other official data collections may be absent, irregular or unreliable (as in cases of countries in conflict), the collection of such data and establishment of open access platforms such as International Public Use Microdata Series have greatly improved access for many teachers and students to aid teaching and learning.

In addition to increased data availability, students and teachers of demography now have access to e-books and digital publication platforms making referencing easier and quicker, especially through use of citation managers such as Zotero. The internet has also increased chances for consultation and discussion, especially on difficult topics; techniques for analysis; and discussion fora. It has also led to quick remote supervisor–student interactions, especially through mail, chat platforms and virtual exchanges through webinars, among others. The internet is also changing learning platforms – from face to face to virtual systems.

The changing nature of the discipline itself is both an opportunity and a challenge. Tabutin (2007) summarized the status of demography in the 21st century as a long river, but a much broader, more tumultuous and many-branched one. The discipline is challenged from within and in competition with the outside world, which some demographers see as under threat, while some see progress. Demography has assets and achievements, but there are also weaknesses and constraints. The history, institutional status and place of demography vary enormously from one part of the world to another and from one country to another (Tabutin, 2007). However, there is a consensus that demography has certainly become a science,[3] with its body of research objects, methods and paradigms, but the general view is that demography is not, or is no longer, simply a technique for computing rates (Tabutin, 2007).

The rapidly changing nature of demography and its increasingly interdisciplinary nature have implications for the type and content of training. This requires adjustments in what is taught, taking into account new technologies in data collection and access and innovations in academic enquiry (Palloni, 2002; Burch, 2018). In the 21st century, students in post-graduate training in demography may be expected to cover enormous volumes of subject matter. But despite the increasingly wide subject, extending the course is not a suitable option but demands the choice of minimum core courses to be pragmatic. Reflection is needed to examine program structure and degree requirements due to the interdisciplinary character of demography and, for same countries, the absence of undergraduate degree programs in demography/population studies. The peculiar nature of the discipline demands reviews to identify and reflect on several dichotomies which currently exist. First, there is need for clear distinctions between programs in which demography is a field within another discipline and others in which it is the central axis of a program offered to students from different backgrounds. Second is reflecting between programs that emphasize teaching at least core content with light dissertation work and the others that place emphasis on the thesis research. Third is reflecting on the quantitative–qualitative distinction. The fourth dichotomy is about rigidity and flexibility. These dichotomies need reflections on whether students should specialize in areas such as fertility, mortality or migration without knowing about the others or whether there should be homogeneity. This is one of the greatest challenges in developing appropriate curricular as well as teaching approaches.

Three aspects of the discipline need to be strengthened: 1) its identity or specificity, 2) its social and political utility and 3) its public visibility (see also Tabutin, 2007). Graduates of this century may not find the labour market that requires only measurements or public policy; hence, the competencies must satisfy not only government and quasi-government needs but also those of NGOs and the private sector, for example, exploiting new frontiers, such as applications of demography (Swanson, Burch, & Tedrow, 1996) and expansion to spatial demography, may offer opportunities to meet private-sector needs.

2 The changing population policy environment

Policy frameworks since the ICPD at Cairo 1994 and subsequent reviews for many African countries have changed considerably, requiring complex investigations, debates on formulations and evaluations. More importantly, the success and sustainability of development strategies require that countries proactively address, rather than merely react to, population dynamics. This necessitates countries mapping population characteristics and needs and understanding how changes in structure and dynamics affect development. The availability of data and the analytical capacity to forecast population dynamics and assess demographic and development linkages are critical for the design of effective, evidence-based population policies and programs. This new perspective is also reflected in emerging 'demographic intelligence'.[4] How are the various institutions training demographers in Africa preparing for this opportunity? A response to this question requires that institutions reflect on the rationale for demographic intelligence operations. First, are the changing needs related to challenges of development, including the fact that population issues may be both a cause as well as a consequence of development challenges? Second, skill sets are changing to accommodate a data-driven world. It is increasingly valuable for professionals to be able to use data to make decisions and use visuals to tell stories of when data informs the who, what, when, where and how. There is rapid growth in demand for 'data scientists'[5] and expansion of data sources for demographic inquiry such as data from private-sector domains. A refocus on data generation processes, including the use of 'big data' from the private sector, expanded administrative/routine data and surveillance data, is imperative. For example, studies on migration (whether internal, international or transnational) impact have in recent times focused on the role played by remittances. But remittance transaction data is not only within the domain of government agencies such as national statistical offices or central banks but also with the private sector such as the telecommunication/mobile phone industry. Policy makers also need to understand data better in addition to current demand to determine who is being left behind. Thus, training is needed to produce demographers capable of developing careers in data science, which requires knowledge in appropriate data visualization, data mining and data analytics, including machine learning processes and reintegration of spatial data in analysis.

3 Labour market dynamics

Prior to the beginning of the 21st century, the largest number of demographers were employed in the government sector. Those with master's-level training or even undergraduate-level training in population or statistics were employed in technical positions such as national statistical agencies, planning ministries, finance and health. Many countries in Africa also established national population councils/secretariats that worked on population policies and occasionally conducted research. Government-sector job opportunities, particularly those with master's-level training, increased in Africa as governments decentralized, and population issues were increasingly recognized as key to development planning. Those with doctoral training were most likely to be found in senior-level positions in these agencies in the government, but the majority joined teaching (especially at universities), which has expanded in many countries.

After the ICPD held at Cairo, a large number of NGOs working in the areas of reproductive health and HIV/AIDS were established. The increase in the NGO sector can be attributed to the reluctance of governments to tackle controversial issues and, more recently, to the decline in government-sector employment opportunities. Population specialists were sought by NGOs to provide technical expertise in project monitoring and evaluation. As the requirements of some donors for 'results-based management' of projects has grown over the last several years, so has the demand for such expertise. Job opportunities in the NGO sector therefore require additional skills beyond training in demographic estimations.

Many African countries provide few employment opportunities for population specialists in the private sector, especially expanding actuary markets, market surveys and analysis, amongst others. The types of skills population experts can bring to private industry include analysis of the impact of demographic changes on the business environment and business decision-making using techniques of projection and forecasting. Healthcare organizations and market research organizations are also potential employers of population experts. These changes provide opportunities for employment of those with advanced demographic skills (examples include private industry in Mexico and India).

Related to the labour market is that students who were registered for the graduate level were often supported from scholarships by national governments, bilateral agencies, UN systems or philanthropic organizations. In a number of countries, this support for training has dwindled. With the severe reduction in funding, students have resorted to paying fees on their own. This has been one of the major challenges facing a number of institutions, and these institutions need to turn to resources generated within Africa and in particular the private sector; hence, training and research need to include meeting the needs of this sector.

Conclusion

The opportunities and challenges arising from the changing nature of the discipline, labour demands and government needs have training implications. The challenges in conducting an interdisciplinary course in demography should be considered in terms of the principal dimensions of a teaching program, namely teachers, students, level of teaching and institutional or organizational framework (such as course structure and content, resources that facilitate teaching-learning interactions and quality assurance schemes). Similarly, efforts should be made to establish and nurture close collaboration with the industry both in the public and private sectors for purposes of increasing and sustaining enrolment, research funding and utilization of demographic data and research information. Burch (2018), in reflections on the principles of teaching demography, mentions the major ones that can be used to shift from a rather 'abstract' demography to a more practical and probably more attractive demography. These include 1) integration of 'techniques' and 'explanatory factors' rather than teaching them in separate courses; 2) giving more weight to theories and conceptual frameworks; 3) paying greater attention to practical illustrations of the history of change in the world; and 4) developing computer tools needed for application exercises, simulation and error testing in data collection and methods. The expansion of internet technology and more recent experience with COVID-19 pandemic consequences also need review, especially mode of learning and associated infrastructure requirements.

Appendix Table 3.1 An Example of Training Curricula 1980–1984 at the Population Studies and Research Institute, University of Nairobi, Kenya

Year 1
Term 1
Introduction to Demographic Techniques
Basic Mathematics for Population Studies
Applied Probability and Stochastics Processes
Term 2
World Population Trends and Population Situation in Africa
Social Statistics for Population Analysis
Fertility and Development
Advanced Demographic Techniques
Population Mathematics
Term 3
Theories of Population and Socioeconomic Development
Urbanization and Human Settlements
Population Estimates and Projections
Stable Population Theory
Year 2
Thesis

Appendix Table 3.2 A Summary of Selected Demographic Training Centres in Africa Curricula

Name of the Centre/ Institution	*Details of the Centre/Institution*
Cairo Demographic Centre	The Cairo Demographic Centre was established in 1963 according to an agreement between the Egyptian government and the United Nations. In 1992, the CDC was declared an independent institution, marking the end of the three decades of UN support. Starting that year, the CDC operated under the auspices of the Egyptian government. The CDC provides training at various academic levels to persons working in the field of population in the countries of the Middle East, Africa and Asia. The CDC executes and conducts training programs and awards students with a general diploma in demography, special diploma in population and development, master of philosophy (MPhil) in demography and

(*Continued*)

Appendix Table 3.2 (Continued)

Name of the Centre/ Institution	*Details of the Centre/Institution*
	post-graduate diploma in population and sustainable development in collaboration with the United Nations Population Fund. The CDC organizes intensive programs, symposia and workshops on demography, statistics, computer research monographs, working papers, occasional papers and population and development series. UN translated series, and newsletters are regularly published by the CDC. The CDC cooperates and exchanges expertise with regional and international organizations, universities and institutes. The United Nations Population Fund in New York approved giving full accreditation to the CDC as an executing agency. The CDC has one of the richest demographic libraries in the Middle East. The library uses the POPLINE Program obtained from Johns Hopkins University.
Regional Institute of Population Studies, University of Ghana	The RIPS was established in 1972 by the United Nations in partnership with the government of Ghana as a regional centre of excellence for teaching and research on population and related disciplines, including health and environment and their implications for development. The RIPS is an important institution in Anglophone Africa for the training of population scientists and generation of high-quality research in population and related disciplines in order to provide solutions for solving development challenges in Ghana and beyond. The RIPS currently offers the following programs: MA, MPhil and PhD in population studies. **Master of arts (MA), population studies** Code Course title **First semester core courses** POPS 601 Sources, Evaluation, and Adjustment of Demographic Data POPS 603 Population and Development Theories and Policies POPS 605 Basic Population Analysis POPS 607 Introduction to Statistical and Computing Techniques POPS 609 Methods of Social Research POPS 610 Seminar POPS 600 Dissertation (both semesters) **Prescribed electives** POPS 611 Qualitative Research Methodology POPS 613 Population and Family Health POPS 615 Population, Ageing and Development POPS 617 Population, Human Resources and Development POPS 619 Population, Environment and Development POPS 621 Population, Health and Development POPS 623 Population Change, Agriculture and Food Security POPS 625 Population, Urbanization and Development **Second semester core courses** POPS 602 Population Variables and Development Planning POPS 604 Social Demography POPS 606 Advanced Population Analysis POPS 608 Advanced Quantitative Analysis POPS 612 Population Estimation and Projection

(Continued)

Appendix Table 3.2 (Continued)

Name of the Centre/ Institution	*Details of the Centre/Institution*
	Prescribed electives POPS 614 Gender and Reproductive Health POPS 616 Population, Housing, and Development POPS 616 Population, Housing, and Development POPS 618 Mathematical Demography POPS 622 Quantitative Research Methodology POPS 624 Population Change, Governance and Development POPS 626 Population, Education and Development POPS 628 Population, Culture and Development
Population Studies and Research Institute (PSRI), University of Nairobi	The Population Studies and Research Institute of the University of Nairobi was established in 1977 by the government of the Republic of Kenya with the support of the Population Council (New York) to train population scientists/demographers at the postgraduate levels. Since its inception, the programs have been revised several times. The course offered are: **MSc in population studies** **Year 1** **Semester one course units**: PMC 500: Population Theories PMC 501: Demographic Techniques 1 PMC 503: Population Dynamics 1 PMC 508: Theory and Methods of Research 1 PMA 506: Mathematics for Population Studies **Semester two course units:** PMC 502: Demographic Techniques 2 PMC 504: Population Dynamics 2 PMC 505: Computer Applications PMC 509: Theory and Methods of Research 2 PMA 516: Applied Statistics **Elective course units** PMA 510: Population Policies & Sustainable Development PMA 511: Population & Health PMA 512: Family and Household Demography PMC 513: Economic Demography PMA 514: Labour Force Dynamics PMC 515: Monitoring and Evaluation of Population and Health Programs PMC 516: Population Aging PMC 519: Urbanization and Population Change PMC 520: Biodemography PMA 523: Gender Issues in Population Studies PMC 524: Design and Management of Large Surveys and Censuses Year 2 PMC 526: Research Project **MA course units** **Year 1** **Semester one course units** PMC 500: Population Theories

(*Continued*)

Appendix Table 3.2 (Continued)

Name of the Centre/ Institution	*Details of the Centre/Institution*
	PMC 501: Demographic Techniques 1 PMC 503: Population Dynamics 1 PMC 508: Theory and Methods of Research 1 PMA 506: Mathematics for Population Studies **Semester two course units:** PMC 502: Demographic Techniques 2 PMC 504: Population Dynamics 2 PMC 505: Computer Applications PMC 509: Theory and Methods of Research 2 PMA 507: Statistics for Population Studies **Elective course units** PMA 510: Population Policies & Sustainable Development PMA 511: Population & Health PMA 512: Family and Household Demography PMC 513: Economic Demography PMA 514: Labour Force Dynamics PMC 515: Monitoring and Evaluation of Population and Health Programs PMC 516: Population Aging PMC 519: Urbanization and Population Change PMC 520: Biodemography PMA 523: Gender Issues in Population Studies PMC 524: Design and Management of Large Surveys and Censuses **Year 2** PMC526: Research Project **PhD program** **Semester one courses** PMC 700: Theories and Contemporary Issues in Population and Development PMC 701: Advanced Demographic and Statistical Analysis **Semester two courses** PMC702: Advanced Social Science Research Methods PMC 703: Independent Research Seminar **Elective courses** PMC 704: Fertility, Family Dynamics and Development PMC 705: Health, Mortality and Development PMC 706: Migration, Urbanization and Development **Two- and 3-year** PMC 800: Thesis
Demography and Population Studies Program at Wits University	Demography and Population Studies (DPS) Program at the University of the Witwatersrand started in 2003. The Wits Program in Demography and Population Studies offers interdisciplinary graduate teaching and research in demography and population studies. Demography as an academic discipline seeks to explore the dynamics of human populations in relation to the changes in their sizes, structures and distributions. Population changes have implications for the environment, employment, work, family relations, health, ageing and urbanization. The key features are of the programs are:

(*Continued*)

Appendix Table 3.2 (Continued)

Name of the Centre/ Institution	*Details of the Centre/Institution*
	• Interdisciplinary – involving the schools of Public Health and Social Sciences • A focus on public and reproductive health • Global partnerships with Northern and Southern Institutions **BA program course units** The BA honours program consists of five equally weighted units, three of which are compulsory. Honours students are required to complete two other units approved by the Head of School from those offered at the Honours level and which are related to demography and population studies SOSS 4012: Introduction to Population Studies SOSS 4047: Statistics for Demographic Survey and Analysis SOSS 4048: Health Demography SOSS 4015: Basic Demographic Methods SOSS 4016: Migration & Spatial Demography SOSS 4049: Demography of Fertility & Reproduction **MA program course units** Students are required to complete and pass three course units, which are related to demography and population studies, provided that the unit has not been completed at the undergraduate level. In addition, students must complete a research report on a topical demographic or population health issue. The courses offered are: SOSS 7012: Introduction to Population Studies SOSS 7070: Advanced Statistics for Demographic Survey and Analysis SOCL 7071: Health Demography SOSS 7003: Basic Demographic Methods SOSS 7023: Advanced Demographic Methods SOSS 7018: Migration & Spatial Demography SOSS 7072: Demography of Fertility and Reproduction **PhD program** This is done by thesis only.

Appendix Table 3.3 Population/Demography Centres

Algeria	Département de Démographie, Université d'Oran
Angola	Centre de Formation et Recherche sur la Population, Université Augustinho Neto
Benin	Centre de Formation et de Recherches en Matière de Population, Université Nationale du Bénin
	Centre de Recherche en Reproduction Humaine et en Démographie, Faculté des Sciences de la Santé, Clinique Universitaire de Gynécologie et d'Obstétrique
Botswana	Department of Demography, University of Botswana
Burkina Faso	Unité d'Enseignement et de Recherche en Démographie, Université de Ouagadougou
Cameroon	Institut de Formation et de Recherche Démographiques, Université de Yaoundé II
	Unité de Recherche en Population et Développement Durable, Faculté des Lettres et Sciences Humaines, Université de Dschang

(*Continued*)

Appendix Table 3.3 (Continued)

Democratic Republic of the Congo	Centre d'Etudes et de Recherches Scientifiques sur les Relations entre l'Education et la Population Département de Démographie, Faculté des Sciences Economiques, Université de Kinshasa
Ghana	Regional Institute for Population Studies, University of Ghana
Kenya	African Population and Health Research Center,
	Population Studies and Research Institute, University of Nairobi
Mali	Centre d'Etudes et Recherche sur la Population pour le Développement, Institut du Sahel, Comité permanent Inter-Etats de Lutte contre la Sécheresse dans le Sahel
Morocco	Centre d'Etudes et de Recherches Démographiques, Haut Agdal Département de Démographie, Institut
	National de Statistique et d'Economie Appliquée Program de Formation en Population et Développement Durable,
	Institut National de Statistique et d'Economie Appliquée
Nigeria	Department of Demography and Social Statistics, Faculty of Social Sciences, Obafemi Awolowo University
	Population Research Unit, Nigerian Institute of Social and Economic Research
	Population Research Unit, Nigerian Institute of Social and Economic Research
Senegal	Association pour la Promotion des Activités de Population-Sénégal, African Population Advisory Committee Département de la Statistique et de la Démographie, Ecole Nationale d'Economie Appliquée Laboratoire Population et Santé, Institut de Recherche pour le Développement Union for African Population Studies
Egypt	Cairo Demographic Center, Ministry of Population and Family Welfare Centre for Applied Demography and Human Resources Development,
	Institute of Statistical Studies and Research, Cairo University
	Department of Demographic Statistics and Biometries, Institute of Statistical Studies and Research, Cairo University
	Population Research Unit, League of Arab States Population Studies and Research Centre, Central Agency for Public Mobilisation and Statistics Social Research Center, American University in Cairo
Sierra Leone	Institute for Population Studies, Fourah Bay College, University of Sierra Leone
South Africa	Demography and Population Studies (DPS), University of the Witwatersrand
	Department of Statistics and Population Studies, University of Western Cape
	Population Studies and Demography, North-West University
	Development Studies & Population Studies, University of Kwa Zulu Natal
	Centre for Actuarial Research (CARe), Faculty of Commerce, University of Cape Town
	Centre for Regional and Urban Innovation and Statistical Exploration (CRUISE), Department of Geography and Environmental Studies, Stellenbosch University
	Centre for Population Studies, Department of Sociology, University of Pretoria
Sudan	Population Studies Centre, Faculty of Economics and Rural Development, University of Gezira
Ethiopia	Demographic Training and Research Centre, Institute of Development Research, Addis Ababa University
Swaziland	Statistics and Demography Department, Demographic Unit, University of Swaziland

(*Continued*)

Appendix Table 3.3 (Continued)

Togo	Unité d'Enseignement et de Recherche Population et Développement, Faculté des Sciences Economiques et Sciences de Gestion, Université du Bénin Unité de Recherche Démographique,
Tunisia	Office National de la Famille et de la Population, Tunis Research and Evaluation Division, Arab World Regional Office, International Planned Parenthood Federation
Uganda	Department of Population Studies, Institute of Statistics and Applied Economics, Makerere University
Zambia	Demography Training Unit, Department of Social Development Studies, School of Humanities and Social Sciences, University of Zambia
Zimbabwe	Centre for Population Studies, University of Zimbabwe

Source: Menken et al., 2002

Additional information has been added for more recent centres with websites.

Notes

1 According to Ntozi, 2011, regional centres in Dakar (Senegal), Rabat (Morocco) and Gaborone (Botswana) closed shop by the end of the 1990s.

2 Tools such as log-linear and multi-level models were used in sociology, psychology and economics before they were adopted by demographers.

3 Greenhalgh Susan (1996) notes that the 'major aim of this is to construct demography as a science, that is, to prove that demography possesses all the characteristics of a pure science'.

4 Demographic intelligence can be considered 'a set of methodologies, processes, architectures, and technologies that transform raw data into meaningful and useful information used to enable more effective strategic, tactical, and operational insights and decision-making'. Under this definition, Demographic intelligence encompasses information management (data integration, data quality, data warehousing, meta-data management, text- and content-analytics). Data preparation and data usage are two separate but closely linked segments of the intelligence architectural stack. This definition used here borrows heavily from business intelligence (BI), which refers to technologies, applications and practices for the collection, integration, analysis and presentation of business information.

5 Traditional education typically draws a distinct line between creative storytelling and technical analysis; the modern professional world also values those who can cross between the two. Data visualization sits right in the middle of analysis and visual storytelling, which may be important for the visibility that Tabutin, 2007, calls for.

References

Amin, S. (Ed.). (1974). *Modern migrations in Western Africa*. Oxford: Oxford University Press for the International African Institute.

Bah, S. (2001, May 15–18). *Tailoring demographic training in a transitional country: The case of South Africa*. Paper presented at the Seminar on Demographic Training in the Third Millennium organized by the IUSSP working group on Teaching and INSEA, Rabat, Morocco.

Billari, F. C. (2001). Sequence analysis in demographic research special issue on longitudinal methodology. *Canadian Studies in Population, 28*(2), 439–458.

Brass, W., & Coale, A. J. (1968). Methods of analysis and estimation. In W. Brass, A. J. Coale, P. Demeny, D. F. Heisel, F. Lorimer, A. Romaniuk, & E. van de Walle (Eds.), *The demography of tropical Africa* (pp. 88–142). Princeton, NJ: Princeton University Press.

British Academy. (2012). *Working with Africa: Human and social science research in action*. London: British Academy/Association of Commonwealth Universities.

Bunting, I., Cloete, N., & Van Schalkwyk, F. (2014). *An empirical overview of eight flagship universities in Africa: 2001–2011*. A report of the Higher Education Research and Advocacy Network in Africa (HERANA). Cape Town: Centre for Higher Education Transformation.

Burch, T. K. (2001). Teaching demography: Ten principles and two rationales. *Genus, 58*, 21–34.
Burch, T. K. (2018). Model-based demography, demographic research monographs. doi:10.1007/978-3-319-65433-1_7.
Caldwell, J. C., & Okonjo, C. (Eds.). (1968). *The population of tropical Africa*. New York: Longmans, Columbia University Press.
Caselli, G. (2002). Teaching demography: A number of priorities from the IUSSP Working Group. *Genus: Teaching Demography in the Early 21st Century, 58*(3–4), 11–17.
Cloete, N., Mouton, J., & Sheppard, C. (2015). *Doctoral education in South Africa: Policy, discourse and data*. Cape Town: African Minds.
Courgeau, D., & Franck, R. (2007). Is demography, a fully formed science or a science in the making? An outline program. *Population, 62*(1), 39–45.
Cross, M. & Backhouse, J. (2014). Evaluating doctoral programmes in Africa: context and practices. *Higher Education Policy, 27*(2), 155–174
Ezeh, A. C., Chimaraoke, O., Kabiru, C., Sharon, F., Kahn, K., Manderson, L., . . . Thorogood, M. (2010). Building capacity for public and population health research in Africa: The consortium for advanced research training in Africa (CARTA) model. *Global Health Action, 3*, 5693. doi:10.3402/gha.v3i0.5693
Goldstein, S. (1994, December 6–8). *Third regional conference of population research centers organized by CICRED held at Addis-Ababa, Ethiopia*. Report on Lessons from the Meeting.
Greenhalgh, S. (1996, January). The social construction of population science: An intellectual, institutional, and political history of twentieth-century demography. *Comparative Studies in Society and History, 38*(1), 26–66. Cambridge University Press Stable URL. Retrieved January 14, 2020, from www.jstor.org/stable/179337 11:19 UTC.
Igun, A. A. (1976, September). Demographic training and research in Africa. *Jimla Mutane, 1*(2), 281–293.
Keilman, N. (1992). *Emerging issues in demographic methodology*. Revised version of a paper written for the European Population Conference, Paris, 21–25 October 1991.
Klancher, E. (2017). A digital history of anglophone demography and global population control, 1915–1984. *Population and Development Review, 43*(1), 83–117. https://doi.org/10.1111/padr.12044
Kpedekpo, G. M. K. (1982). *Essentials of demographic analysis for Africa*. Exeter, NH: Heinemann Educational Books, Inc.
Mabogunje, A. L. (1970). Systems approach to a theory of rural-urban migration. *Geographical Analysis, 2*(1), 1–18.
Madise, N. J. (2015). *Towards financial sustainability: A case study of the Regional Institute for Population Studies at the University of Ghana*. Report Submitted to the William and Flora Hewlett Foundation.
Margolis, S. (1997). Population policy, research and the Cairo Plan of Action: New directions for the Sahel? *International Family Planning Perspectives, 23*(2), 86–89.
Menken, J., Blanc, A., &. Lloyd, C. (Eds.). (2002). *Training and support of developing-country population scientists: A panel report*. New York: Population Council.
Ntozi, J. (2011, December). Training of population specialists for Africa's needs: Past, current and future. *African Population Studies, 25*(2).
Obamba, M. (2017). *Constructing "innovative" doctorates: Scoping evidence on doctoral structure and practices from six African countries*. Scoping Report to the Partnership for African Social and Governance Research (PASGR) University of Central Lancashire, UK.
Okonjo, C. (1966, December). Demographic research and training in Africa. *The Journal of Modern African Studies, 4*(4), 540–548. Cambridge University Press. Retrieved from www.jstor.org/stable/159110
Palloni, A. (2002, July–December). Rethinking the teaching of demography: New challenges and opportunities. *Genus: Teaching Demography in the Early 21st Century, 58*(3–4), 35–70. Retrieved on July 7, 2020, from https://about.jstor.org/terms 07:39:57 UTC.
Poirier, J., & Piché, V. (1999). Trente ans de recherche explicative en démographie. Réflexions autour des dangers du cloisonnement. In D. Tabutin et al. (Eds.), *Théories, paradigmes et courants explicatifs en démographie* (pp. 41–64), Chaire Quetelet: Louvain la Neuve. Academia/L'Harmattan.
Rostow, W. W. (1964). *The stages of economic growth*. Cambridge: Cambridge University Press.
Soja, A. W. (1968). *The geography of modernization in Kenya: A spatial analysis of social, economic and political change*. Syracuse: Syracuse University Press.
Swanson, D. A., Burch, T. K., & Tedrow, L. M. (1996). What is applied demography? *Population Research and Policy Review, 15*, 403–418.

Tabutin, D. (1988). Training and research in demography: A survey of problems and prospects. In E. Van de Walle, P. O. Ohadike, & M. D. Sala-Diakanda (Eds.), *The state of African demography* (pp. 139–155). Liege: IUSSP.

Tabutin, D. (2007). Whither demography? Strengths and weaknesses of the discipline over fifty years of change. (Roger Depledge, Trans.). *I.N.E.D Population*, *1*(62), 15–31. ISSN 0032-4663 ISBN 2733230770

Tettey, W. (2010). *Challenges of developing and retaining the next generation of academics: Deficits in academic staff capacity at African universities*. New York: Partnership for Higher Education in Africa.

United Nations (UN). (1979). *Review and appraisal of the world population plan of action*. Population Studies No 71. ST/ESA/SER.A/71.Sales No E.71.XIII.7

United Nations (UN). (1995). *Developments in demographic training and research projects: Aspects of technical cooperation*. New York. Sales Number E.95.XIII.13, ST/ ESA/ SER.R/143.

United Nations. Economic Commission for Africa (UNECA). (1992). *Demographic training and research in Africa review and prospects. UN.* ECA African Population Conference (3rd: 1992, Dec. 7–10: Dakar, Senegal). Addis Ababa. Retrieved from http://hdl.handle.net/10855/14064

Vance, R. B. (1952). Is theory for demographers? *Social Forces*, *31*, 9–13.

Van de Walle, E., Ohadike, P., & Sala-Diakanda, M. (Eds). (1988). *The state of African demography*. Liege: IUSSP, pp. 139–155.

Wajnman, S., Rio Neto, G., & Eduardo, L. (2003). Is there a basic framework for training in demography? *Papeles de Población*, *9*(36), 21–46.

4
AFRICAN DEMOGRAPHIC RESEARCH
Progress and challenges

Michel Garenne

Introduction

Just 50 years ago, in 1961, two books were published summarizing what was known about the demography of tropical Africa (Galeotti, 1961; Lorimer, 1961). The first one is now largely ignored and rarely cited. Lorimer's book was very influential, as it started the adventure, leading seven years later to the publication of *The Demography of Tropical Africa*, a collection of articles that have been the origin of research on African demography (Brass et al., 1968). A first seminar on African demography was held in Paris in 1959 by Lorimer, followed in the 1960s and early 1970s by others in Ibadan, Nairobi and Accra (Caldwell & Okonjo, 1968; Ominde & Ejiogu, 1972; Cantrelle, 1974). These were followed by a long series of meetings, seminars and conferences on African demography, the last of which was the 6th UAPS conference in Ouagadougou, Burkina Faso, in December 2011. Another landmark was the creation of the Union for African Population Studies (UAPS/UEPA) in 1984.

This chapter provides a personal view on the development of African demography over this 50-year period. It conveniently divides this time frame into two periods of about 25 years each. These two periods are arbitrary and correspond to the creation of a journal (*African Population Studies*) in 1986, just two years after the development of Demographic and Health Surveys (DHSs), an event which has dramatically changed our level of knowledge and understanding of African populations and their dynamics. In this contribution to the 25th anniversary of African population studies, the author would like to share a few ideas and facts dealing with his own experience with African demography. Ironically, the author received his training in demography at the end of the first period (1977–1982) in France and the United States, with the main focus on the issues specific to this period, which are detailed in the following, and primarily data collection and demographic estimation techniques. But most of his research work has been conducted during the second period, with totally different paradigms and the need to conduct research on different topics with different tools and a multidisciplinary approach.

The colonial period (1880–1960)

During the colonial period, the focus was on getting cheap labour to provide the work force for development projects: basic infrastructure and communication (towns, roads, railways), mines

DOI: 10.4324/9780429287213-6

and quarries, and estates producing agricultural export goods (sugar cane, peanuts, cocoa, coffee, tea, palm oil, rubber, etc.). So the main concern for managing the colonial economy was with the number of people and their geographical distribution. The focus was therefore on administrative censuses, which were conducted on a routine basis (every year or every five years) in most areas under colonial control (Cordell & Gregory, 1980). In terms of issues, the main concern was with low population density and tropical diseases, which were seen as considerable limitations to economic development. Efforts were made to understand and reduce infertility, and large programs were developed to control infectious and parasitic diseases, such as malaria, sleeping sickness (trypanosomiasis), yellow fever, yaws, syphilis and schistosomiasis, as well as tuberculosis, leprosy and smallpox (Badoo, 2005; Retel-Laurentin, 1974). The first modern censuses were conducted at the end of the colonial period, and the first demographic sample surveys seem to be that conducted in 1948 in Southern Rhodesia, now Zimbabwe, among the Anglophone countries and that conducted in 1954 in Guinea among the Francophone countries (Shaul & Myburgh, 1949; Gendreau, 1993).

Part 1 – the first quarter-century in post-colonial times (1961–1985)

The crucial period of the early 1960s was the end of the colonial period in most African countries and the beginning of the new era of building modern independent states. The needs for demographic and health information systems became different, as they were required for building a modern administration. For demographers, the focus was on getting accurate data on population size and structures and on basic demographic dynamics (fertility, mortality, nuptiality, migration, urbanization, labour force). The concerns shifted towards rapid population growth, changing levels of mortality, rapid urbanization and major migration movements. For demographic research, the focus was on measurement tools and the development of appropriate data collection methods because vital registration was deficient. Later, a series of research studies focused on the impact of family planning programs which had started in the 1960s and 1970s.

The Niakhar surveys (1963–1982)

A good example of this concern for data collection was a demographic surveillance system (DSS) started in 1963 by Pierre Cantrelle in Senegal. In the original enterprise, two sites were originally set up: Niakhar and Paos-Koto (Niakhar, 2010), which had been elected because the first one was an area with high population density and net outmigration and the second an area of low population density and net in-migration. The focus of the research was on proper measurement of basic demographic rates of fertility, mortality, migration and nuptiality, all parameters which were simply not available at that time. The data collection technique was simple: a comprehensive census with some retrospective information on mortality and fertility and yearly rounds updating the population file by recording births, deaths, in- and out-migration and changes in marital status (marriages, divorces, separations) that had occurred since the previous round, realizing a full-scale population register on a small population. More information was collected, such as cause of death, reasons for migration, breastfeeding and weaning status, measles and measles vaccination.

The first series of rounds lasted five years, and the sample was later reduced to a smaller size and continued until 1982 on the same model. The outcome was very successful and showed that with simple means and appropriate interview techniques and questionnaires, reliable information could be gathered at low cost. Detailed research was conducted on the intermediate variables of natural fertility, as well as the age pattern of mortality (Cantrelle, 1969; Cantrelle & Leridon, 1971; Garenne & Cantrelle, 1991).

Years later, it became obvious that measurement was no longer an issue and that more data were needed than basic demographic events if one wanted to better understand the complex demographic processes underway. The Niakhar site is still running in 2011 and has hosted major studies of worldwide scope, such as a study on the relationship between nutritional status and mortality, vaccine trials, various studies on malaria and other diseases and numerous studies in all fields of social sciences (Garenne, Leroy, Beau, & Sene, 1991; Garenne & Fontaine, 1990, 2006; Garenne, Maire, & Fontaine, 2000; Lericollais et al., 1995; Niakhar, 2010).

French National Institute of Statistics surveys and other demographic surveys

As part of an effort to set up a new administration in independent states, the French National Institute of Statistics (INSEE) organized a series of demographic sample surveys in many Francophone countries, starting with Guinea in 1954–1955 (GDA, 1971; Gendreau, 1977, 1993; Lohlé-Tart, Clairin, François, & Gendreau, 1988; Tabutin & Schoumaker, 2004). Similar surveys were conducted in countries under Belgian colonial administration, in particular the famous 1955–1957 survey in Congo (Romaniuk, 1961). A similar survey was conducted in Sudan (1955–1956). Here, again, the focus was on measurement of basic demographic parameters. The INSEE surveys were based on fairly large samples (typical size was some 30,000 households). They were of good quality and produced reliable data on fertility rates, mortality rates, age structures and numerous other indicators. The first life tables were calculated, which were used later to produce model life tables (Clairin, Condé, Fleury-Brousse, Waltisperger, & Wunsch, 1980). Some of the original data still exist and might eventually be deposited at the Integrated Public Use Microdata Series (IPUMS) network of Minnesota University.

Another major advance in the 1970s was the development of the World Fertility Survey (WFS), the aims of which were to produce reliable data on fertility and family planning, and which also produced data on child mortality and various contextual variables. For sub-Saharan Africa, the WFSs had serious limitations: they covered only ten countries, had limited scope, and they were based on tiny samples, which hampered detailed statistical analysis

Censuses

Modern censuses, with detailed individual information (age, sex, marital status, education, occupation, housing, etc.) were already conducted at the end of the colonial period in the British colonies of East Africa (since 1948), in the Portuguese colonies (since 1940) and later in French and Belgian colonies. The quality of the data was mixed. Major problems were detected with inaccurate information, in particular age, and with missing values. These early censuses were often poorly analysed, as researchers had no access to original data. However, they produced estimates of fertility and child mortality for numerous countries and were used extensively for the first synthesis of mortality trends in Africa (Hill, 1991; Feachem & Jamison, 1991). Much has been learned since, and the quality of census data improved over time. However, some basic problems noted in the early censuses, such as large numbers of missing values for the number of children ever born among young women, which led to the development of a correction method by El Badry (1961), still existed in the 2001 census of South Africa. The censuses have been the main source of population reconstruction and projects by international and specialized agencies, such as the United Nations Population Division and the US Census Bureau.

The contribution of *The Demography of Tropical Africa*

The work synthesized in *The Demography of Tropical Africa* focused on data availability, data quality and adjustment of poor-quality data. The studies covered most of what is now called "sub-Saharan Africa", starting from the Sahelian band going from Mauritania to Sudan in the north to southern Rhodesia and Mozambique in the south, while ignoring the southern cone (South Africa, Namibia, Botswana) and Madagascar, as well as Ethiopia and Somalia in the East. Some countries were not covered because of a lack of data (Chad, Sierra Leone), as was the case for the African islands. Nevertheless, the study was fairly comprehensive and produced estimates of fertility, mortality and nuptiality for most countries considered. Data quality was seen as a major problem, and a full chapter is devoted to this issue, in particular to reporting births and deaths in censuses and retrospective surveys and to age misreporting. Special attention was also devoted to sex ratios at birth, sex ratios in the population and biases associated with age of respondent. Various techniques of adjustment were developed. The most striking example of data quality and adjustment is probably the correction of +40% for under-five mortality in Mozambique. This study was also the beginning of the adventure of indirect methods of demographic estimation, namely the P/F ratio method correcting for possible underestimation of fertility and the Brass methods converting the proportion of children dead to women of a given age group into life table estimates. These were followed by numerous other indirect methods (see the following).

Part 2 – the second quarter-century in post-colonial times (1986–2010)

A change in paradigm occurred around 1985, which can be symbolized by the development in 1984 of demographic and health surveys by the Institute for Resource Development (IRD)/Macro, later renamed the *DHS program*. These were the years of new integrated programs such as the "Child Survival program", large-scale programs aiming at reducing under-five mortality through various means. The focus was on a broader view of maternal and child health, with family planning being seen as only one element of population health, and above all on evaluation of interventions. Since a considerable amount of money was spent on family planning programs and health programs, government and international agencies wanted to have precise information about the effects of these programs and to know more about the context and other determinants of population change.

The contribution of DHSs

The IRD/Macro Institute, later renamed Inner City Fund (ICF/Macro), celebrated its 25th anniversary recently in 2009 (DHS Program, 2010). It conducted five rounds of surveys of five years each and started its sixth round, with a total of more than 100 surveys in sub-Saharan Africa. Over the years, the DHSs became more and more comprehensive, including not only demographic variables but also lots of contextual variables on perception; attitudes and behaviour; anthropometric measures for adults and children; and more recently biomarkers focusing on infectious diseases (HIV/AIDS, malaria, syphilis, Chlamydia), on nutritional status (Vitamin A, anaemia, iodine deficiency, zinc, lead poisoning) and on some chronic diseases (hypertension, diabetes, cholesterol). Beyond classic DHSs, special surveys were conducted on HIV (AIDS Interview surveys [AIS]); on malaria (Malaria Interview surveys [MIS]); on service provision (Service Provision Assessment surveys [SPA]); and on various topics, including education, maternal mortality and cause of death. They now systematically include GPS coordinates of household clusters, allowing detailed mapping.

Within a few years, DHSs became the leading source of knowledge on demographic parameters and their determinants as well as the main source of population-based information on HIV/AIDS prevalence, malaria and malnutrition. They are the basis of a huge amount of demographic and epidemiologic research. They allowed detailed mapping of HIV prevalence and of specific health problems such as malnutrition and anaemia. In-depth research on these data is possible through the open-access policy for individuals' data, which led to very innovative research and new findings. Of course, they do have limitations: they are missing the marriage histories which were available in WFSs, and they do not provide life tables and do not have information on causes of death, except in a few studies such as that of Ghana in 2007. Much of what has been learned on the erratic patterns of the demographics and health transition in Africa originates from DHSs. Extensive use of DHSs allows one to study changes in – and patterns of – mortality, fertility, nuptiality, adult and child anthropometry, HIV/AIDS, sexual behaviour and even sex ratios at birth (Garenne & Gakusi, 2005; Garenne & Zwang, 2006, 2008; Zwang & Garenne 2008; Garenne, 2003, 2004b, 2008a, 2008d, 2009, 2011a, 2011b, 2011d; Matthews, Leclerc & Garenne 2009). The DHSs could by themselves answer important questions, such as the demographic impact of male circumcision on HIV prevalence, found to be nil, or the impact of hormonal contraception on susceptibility to HIV (Garenne, 2006, 2008a; Leclerc, Matthews, & Garenne, 2009; Leclerc, Dubois-Colas, & Garenne, 2008). These results are important since they directly measure a population impact, and so the DHSs appear more cost effective than complex epidemiological studies such as clinical trials or case-control studies aiming at answering similar questions. DHSs also provide the key parameters for simulation exercises, such as those conducted on the HIV epidemics (Leclerc et al., 2009).

Other programs of sample surveys

Another program of a demographic health survey covering sub-Saharan Africa is the Multiple Indicator Cluster Surveys (MICSs) Program run by the United Nations Children's Fund (UNICEF). These surveys are much less detailed and of lower quality. They provide information on fertility, mortality and selected health indicators in countries lacking such information. Other countries had special series of national demographic surveys, such as the October household surveys in South Africa, and numerous surveys on migration (Bocquier & Traoré, 2000; Zachariah & Condé, 1980), as well as a number of population-based surveys on HIV seroprevalence. There are also many more small-scale surveys which have only a local scope and which often are not known because they are not disseminated.

Demographic surveillance systems

Another major development for demographic research over the past 25years has been the development of DSS in many African countries (Das Gupta, Garenne, & Pison, 1997; Garenne, 1998). They are now grouped into the In-Depth network, whose first meeting was in 2001. The network includes some 17 demographic surveillance systems, also called sentinel demographic sites, in sub-Saharan Africa. They have been very influential in promoting in-depth, high-quality research, as exemplified by a series of comparative studies on mortality, fertility, migration, causes of death and inequalities.

Censuses and the contribution of the IPUMS project

The idea of gathering and making systematic use of the information in population censuses for demographic research started with the African Census Analysis Project (ACAP, 2010). Unfortunately, this project did not go very far, and the fact that the leaders did not share the data provided by national agencies hampered any further research. Fortunately, much census data is now archived by the IPUMS international project, which provides open access to individual data, harmonized and unharmonized. This program offers a huge potential for research of population structures, household structures, migration, social composition, geographical patterns and urbanization. They also often include data on fertility, mortality and maternal mortality, which could make a huge contribution because of their large sample size. They seem particularly useful for studying maternal mortality, although they focus only on pregnancy-related deaths and lack information on obstetric deaths (Garenne, McCaa, & Nacro, 2008, 2011; Garenne, Leclerc, & Matthews, 2011).

The issue of vital registration

Vital registration remains poorly utilized in African demography, despite some positive experience (Garenne & Zanou, 1995). Among the negative experiences are many failed experiments throughout Africa. For instance, Lorimer (1968) noted that vital registration started in Uganda in 1904, which has worked ever since but remains very incomplete and still not usable a century later.

A similar experience could be found in Ouagadougou, where completeness went down from 1960 to 1990, making it now useless. There are, however, a few examples of vital registration systems that maintained good coverage in large cities such as Dakar in Senegal, Abidjan in Cote d'Ivoire for adults, Brazzaville in Congo and Libreville in Gabon, which were used for estimating the impact of HIV/AIDS (Garenne, Madison, Tarantola, Zanou et al., 1995; Garenne, Madison, Tarantola, Testa et al., 1995; Pictet, Le Coeur, M'Pelé, Brouard, & Lallemant, 1998). One of the oldest and most successful examples of vital registration is that of Antananarivo in Madagascar, which started even before the colonial period, and has been maintained at high coverage ever since, allowing detailed mortality calculations by age, sex and cause of death (Garenne, Waltisperger, Cantrelle, & Ralijaona, 1999). In the past 25 years, one of the success stories has been South Africa, where death registration was very weak before 1990 for the Black/African population but became almost complete for adults by the year 2005, allowing detailed demographic analysis. However, coverage for children still remains low in that country.

Past and present of indirect methods

Indirect methods were developed by William Brass, who was a statistician at the East-African Statistical Office at the end of the colonial period, when the first censuses were conducted. They were extended by himself and his students at Princeton University and at the Centre for Population Studies at the London School of Hygiene and Tropical Medicine over a period of some 25 years. The indirect methods aim at producing average estimates of past fertility and mortality using simple questions and calculations, which also allow occasionally for trend estimations. They are based on restrictive assumptions, which are increasingly violated due to the erratic patterns of population changes in Africa. They have become less useful over the years, and the DHSs hardly use them, preferring more precise direct calculations, with proper point estimates and confidence intervals. A few examples of the limitations of indirect methods are given in the following.

1 *The "P/F ratio method" in situations of changing fertility levels*
Cameroon underwent ups and downs in fertility trends with estimated values of TFR of 5.7 in 1963, 7.0 in 1983 and 5.3 in 2003, the age pattern of fertility remaining similar over the years. The impact of these changes on P/F ratios can be estimated, assuming perfect data, by recalculating cohort fertility assuming regular period changes with a constant age pattern. In 1983, after a period of rising fertility, the P/F would be 1.18 at age 25–29, 1.04 at 45–49 and below 1 before age 20. In 2003, after a period of declining fertility, the P/F ratio would be 1.01 at 25–29 but now 1.15 at 45–49, all these differences being only due to violation of the hypothesis of constant fertility and not to miscounting events. This was already noted by *The Demography of Tropical Africa*, which states on page 61: "Unfortunately, the P/F ratios are almost certainly affected by other factors than forgetting". It notes that more than half the African countries experienced fluctuations in fertility trends, and all are now undergoing fertility decline, at least in urban areas.

2 *The "Brass Method" in situation of changing mortality*
Mozambique underwent major changes in mortality due to the severe impact of the civil war which raged between 1975 and 1992. For the country as a whole, the under-five death rate declined from about 400 per 1000 in 1960 to 208 per 1000 in 1980, rose to 251 per 1000 in 1991 and declined to 134 per 1000 in 2003.
Mortality changes were even more dramatic in the central part of the country, the most affected by the civil war. In this type of situation, Brass estimates would simply smooth out all the changes and lead to very inaccurate results for the critical years (Garenne, Coninx, & Dupuy, 1996). This type of situation is not unique, since more than half of the African countries went through phases of decreasing and increasing mortality, the most recent example being countries highly affected by HIV/AIDS. Another shortcoming of the Brass method is the use of age of mother as a main criterion for stratification, since age of mother is in itself a risk factor of child mortality (Garenne 1982, 1994). In particular, the inclusion of the 15–19 age group is misleading for readers not aware of this bias. This is a recurrent problem in figures produced by MICSs, which show systemically increasing mortality for the most recent period corresponding to the 15–19 age group.

3 *Adult mortality*
Some of the indirect estimates allow one to compute the mortality of young adults from questions on survival of parents or brothers and sisters. Here again, severe violation of hypotheses, in particular the correlation between the survivorship of persons belonging to the same family, seriously biases the estimates. This has been recognized for a long time in the Agincourt study in South Africa (Tollman, Kahn, Garenne, & Gear, 1999).

4 *Completeness of death registration*
Brass and others have developed techniques for estimating completeness of death registration. These are based on numerous assumptions.
Here again, when violated, they may lead to inconsistent results. For instance, estimates made from the 2001 census in South Africa suggest an undercount of 45%, which would imply implausibly high level of mortality and would imply an increase in fertility to abnormally high levels to match the observed population growth (Hill, Queiros, Stanton, & AbouZahr, 2007).

5 *Sisterhood method*

Last, an indirect method allows one to compute estimates of maternal mortality from questions on the survival of sisters. The overall idea may look great, but the outcome may lead to nonsense results. First, counting as maternal death any death during the maternal risk period (pregnancy, delivery, post-partum), whatever the cause, produces non-specific results, since this mixes obstetric deaths with deaths that are unrelated to the pregnancy and with coincidental deaths. This is particularly the case in countries with high HIV prevalence. Second, as for the Brass method, the sisterhood method does not provide a proper confidence interval, which is far from trivial. This is, in fact, the worst scenario for estimating progress in safe methods. The opposite is needed: a specific case definition, precise point estimates and proper confidence intervals. (Garenne & Friedberg, 1997; Garenne, 2011c).

Discussion: current challenges

Measurement

The measurement issue, which was the core of demographic research more than 25 years ago, is no longer a serious problem for demographers. Most issues of data quality have been sorted out, and we have the tools to conduct precise interview surveys. In Africa, age missing values and inconsistent answers are still problematic but affect only a small proportion of questionnaires when surveys are well conducted (Pullum, 2006, 2008). These minor errors do not affect levels and trends in demographic indicators, nor do they affect the effects of explanatory variables in multivariate analysis. Furthermore, proper procedures of imputation for missing values may allow compensation for the inaccuracy. One of the recurrent problems using survey data is the calculation of confidence intervals for point estimates, which is not always done in demographic analysis, although statistical methods and software are widely available. Furthermore, the issue of estimating trends from retrospective sample survey data still remains, although many options are available (Garenne, 2011b). Of course, these issues do not apply to censuses, which have huge samples and small confidence intervals.

With a few exceptions, African countries still lack life tables at the national level and even more at the sub-national level, at least for urban and rural areas. This is primarily due to the fact that data on deaths in the past 12 months have not been systematically recorded in censuses, despite recommendations form the United Nations, and when it happened, it was often not carefully done. Of course, there is no reason that "deaths in the past 12 months" could not be recorded properly by age and sex if appropriate questions were asked in a census and if great care were taken for age estimation.

Demography and public health

In the field of public health and epidemiology, more work could be done to better understand the complex processes underway and their rapid changes.

Here demographers can make a big contribution by bringing in a population approach, which is very different from that of clinical epidemiology. This field typically requires multidisciplinary research. A good example of what has been achieved is the research on HIV/AIDS epidemiology and its demographic impact, where demographers had to develop new tools and new surveys and where they made a very significant contribution over the past 25 years (Newell, Brahmbhatt, & Ghys, 2004; Marston, Zaba, Salomon, Brahmbhatt, & Bagenda, 2005). This is a typical example of a new problem; emerging diseases, which, beyond demographic models, required understanding of the epidemiology of sexually transmitted diseases, of sexual behaviour, of mortality and of the cultural context of African societies and the numerous effects of economic development. Another issue, which remains under-researched, is the recent dynamics in the huge pockets of extreme poverty in the booming African cities. A good example is the research conducted by the African Population and Health Research Centre (APHRC, 2010) in Nairobi since 1997. More of those studies are needed to better document these new dynamics. Numerous health issues have emerged in recent years which have obliged demographers to develop new approaches. These include the resurgence of tuberculosis; the emergence of resistant malaria; the ups and downs of cholera epidemics throughout the continent; the emergence of obesity, diabetes and hypertension among the wealthier strata of African populations; and the severe stress associated with rapid social change. More research is also needed on adolescents, beyond contraception and sexually transmitted diseases, from nutrition to stress and adaptation to fast-changing social environments. All these issues deserve more research from demographers with a proper population approach.

Towards ecology and environmental studies

With rapid population growth since 1930 and its numerous consequences on the environment in a context of globalization of national economies and of global warming, the next series of issues to be addressed by demographers will deal with the environment and the population approach of ecological problems. For this, we will need new forms of training and an adaptation to new types of issues, as happened 25 years ago when the focus shifted to public health.

Open access to data and results

A key factor of the outstanding development of African demography over the last 25 years has been the new policy of open access to original individual data. In this respect, the DHS project and the IPUMS project are the best examples of what can be achieved and of the immense benefit of open access.

The few countries in Africa which refused to release their data have lost the richness of further analysis and do not appear in many detailed international comparisons. They did not have any gain from their restrictive policy.

Likewise, the publication of findings made immense progress over the past 25 years, as exemplified by the journal *African Population Studies*. The development of the internet simply changed the scale of intellectual exchanges. Finding a paper, even a working paper, is no longer the issue that it was 25 years ago. Here, again, open access to scientific journals is very important for optimal dissemination of findings, and some initiatives, such as Bioline International, have made an immense contribution for African researchers. Open access and rapid dissemination have also narrowed the gap between scientists and decision makers and made the results of the researcher more useful for the whole community.

This chapter covers a series of classic issues. Of course, there are many other issues which were not addressed, which will be dealt with in other parts of this collection. To list a few: the huge migration flows and changes in labour force participation that are occurring in Africa and their relationships with economic development and globalization, plus changing laws and rules of the game which have been so rapid in the past 25 years, with numerous dramatic consequences. Needless to say, there is a huge amount of work to be done for the coming generations.

References

Badoo, J. P. (2005). *Conquêtes médicales: histoire de la médecine moderne et des maladies en Afrique*. Paris: Karthala.

Bocquier, P., & Traoré, S. (2000). *Urbanisation et dynamique migratoire en Afrique de l'Ouest: La croissance urbaine en panne*. Paris: L'Harmattan.

Brass, W., Coale, A. J., Demeny, P., Heisel, D. F., Lorimer, F., Romaniuk, A., & van de Walle, E. (1968). *The demography of tropical Africa*. Princeton, NJ: Princeton University Press.

Caldwell, J. C., & Okonjo, C. (1968). *La population de l'Afrique tropicale*. New York: Population Council.

Cantrelle, P. (1969). *Etude démographique dans la région du Sine-Saloum (Sénégal): état civil et observation démographique 1963–1965*. Paris: ORSTOM.

Cantrelle, P. (Ed.). (1974). *Population in African development* (Vol. 1). Belgium: Ordina Editions.

Cantrelle, P., & Leridon, H. (1971). Breast feeding, mortality in childhood and fertility in a rural zone of Senegal. *Population Studies, 25*(3), 505–533.

Clairin, R., Condé, J., Fleury-Brousse, M., Waltisperger, D., & Wunsch, G. (1980). *La mortalité dans les pays en développement*. Tome III: Nouvelles tables types de mortalité à l'usage des pays en développement. Paris: Centre de Développement de l'OCDE.

Cordell, D.D., & Gregory, J.W. (1980). Historical demography and demographic history in Africa: Theoretical and methodological considerations. *Canadian Journal of African Studies/La Revue Canadienne Des Études Africaines, 14*(3), 389–416.

Das Gupta, M., Garenne, M., & Pison, G. (Eds.). (1997). *Prospective community studies in developing countries*. Oxford: Oxford University Press.

DHS Program (Demographic and Health Surveys). (2010). Retrieved from www.measuredhs.com

El-Badry, M. A. (1961). Failure of enumerators to make entries of zero: Errors in recording childless cases in population censuses. *Journal of the American Statistical Association, 56*(296), 909–924.

Feachem, R., & Jamison, D. (1991). *Disease and mortality in sub-Saharan Africa*. Oxford: Oxford University Press.

Galeotti, G. (1961). *Problemi demografici dei paesi sottosviluppati e solidarieta internazionale*. Bologna: Malipiero.

Garenne, M. (1982). Problems in applying the Brass method in tropical Africa: A case study in rural Senegal. *Genus, 38*(1–2), 119–134.

Garenne, M. (1994). Do women forget their births? A study of maternity histories in a rural area of Senegal (Niakhar). *Population Bulletin of the United Nations, 36*, 43–54.

Garenne, M. (1998). Potentiel et limites des observatoires démographiques. In R. Clignet (Ed.), *Observatoires du développement, observatoires pour le développement* (pp. 159–172). Paris: éditions de l'ORSTOM.

Garenne, M. (2003). Sex differences in health indicators among children in African DHS surveys. *Journal of Biosocial Science, 35*(4), 601–614.

Garenne, M. (2004a). Age at marriage and modernisation in sub-Saharan Africa. *Southern African Journal of Demography, 9*(2), 59–79.

Garenne, M. (2004b). Sex ratios at birth in populations of Eastern and Southern Africa. *Southern African Journal of Demography, 9*(1), 91–96.

Garenne, M. (2006). Male circumcision and HIV control in Africa. *PLoS Medicine, 3*(1), e78.

Garenne, M. (2008a). Long-term population effect of male circumcision in generalised HIV epidemics in sub-Saharan Africa. *African Journal of AIDS Research, 7*(1), 1–8.

Garenne, M. (2008b). *Fertility change in sub-Saharan Africa*. DHS Comparative Reports, No. 18. Calverton, MD: Macro International Inc.

Garenne, M. (2008c). Situations of fertility stall in sub-Saharan Africa. *African Population Studies, 23*(2), 173–188.

Garenne, M. (2008d). Poisson variations of the sex ratio at birth in African demographic surveys. *Human Biology, 80*(5), 473–482.

Garenne, M. (2009). Sex ratio at birth and family composition in sub-Saharan Africa: Inter-couple variations. *Journal of Biosocial Science, 41*(3), 399–407.

Garenne, M. (2011a). *Trends in nutritional status of adult women in sub-Saharan Africa DHS surveys*. DHS Comparative Reports, No. 27. Calverton, MD: Macro International Inc.

Garenne, M. (2011b). Testing for fertility stalls in demographic and health surveys. *Population Health Metrics, 9*(1), 1–8.

Garenne, M. (2011c). Estimating obstetric mortality from pregnancy-related deaths recorded in demographic censuses and surveys. *Studies in Family Planning, 42*(4), 237–246.

Garenne, M. (2011d). The impacts of HIV/AIDS on the health transition among under-five children in Africa. In G. Letamo (Ed.), *Social and psychological aspects of HIV/AIDS and their ramifications* (Chapter 13, pp. 237–248). Rijeka, Croatia: In-Tech Publishers.

Garenne, M., & Cantrelle, P. (1991). Three decades of research on population and health: The ORSTOM experience in rural Senegal: 1962–1991. In M. Das Gupta & M. Garenne (Eds.), *Prospective community studies in developing countries* (pp. 233–252). Oxford: Oxford University Press, 1997.

Garenne, M., Coninx, R., & Dupuy, C. (1996). Direct and indirect estimates of mortality changes: A case study in Mozambique. In *Demographic evaluation of health programs* (pp. 53–74). Paris: Committee for International Cooperation in National Research in Demography (CICRED).

Garenne, M., & Fontaine, O. (2006). Assessing probably causes of death using a standardized questionnaire: A study in rural Senegal. *Bulletin of the World Health Organization, 84*(3), 248–253.

Garenne, M., & Friedberg, F. (1997). Accuracy of indirect estimates of maternal mortality: A simulation model. *Studies in Family Planning, 28*(2), 132–142.

Garenne, M., & Gakusi, E. (2005). *Under-five mortality trends in Africa: Reconstruction from demographic sample surveys*. DHS Working Papers, No. 26. IRD-Macro.

Garenne, M., Leroy, O., Beau, J. P., & Sene, I. (1991). Child mortality after high-titre measles vaccines: Prospective study in Senegal. *The Lancet, 338*(8772), 903–907.

Garenne, M., Madison, M., Tarantola, D., Testa, J., Mboup, S., Wade, A., & Hane, A. (1995). *The demographic impact of HIV/AIDS in West Africa, Vol. II: Dakar and Ouagadougou (A report to USAID/REDSO)*. Harvard School of Public Health, François-Xavier Bagnoud Center for Health and Human Rights (No. 5). Working Paper Series.

Garenne, M., Madison, M., Tarantola, D., Zanou, B., Aka, J., & Dogoré, R. (1995). *The demographic impact of HIV/AIDS in West Africa, Vol. I: Abidjan (A report to USAID/REDSO)*. Harvard School of Public Health, François-Xavier Bagnoud Center for Health and Human Rights (No. 4). Working Paper Series.

Garenne, M., Maire, B., & Fontaine, O. (2000). *Risques de décès associés à différents états nutritionnels chez l'enfant d'âge préscolaire*. Paris: Centre français sur la population et le développement (CEPED).

Garenne, M., McCaa, R., & Nacro, K. (2008). Maternal mortality in South Africa in 2001: From demographic census to epidemiological investigation. *Population Health Metrics, 6*(1), 1–13.

Garenne, M., McCaa, R., & Nacro, K. (2011). Maternal mortality in South Africa: An update from the 2007 Community Survey. *Journal of Population Research, 28*(1), 89–101.

Garenne, M., Waltisperger, D., Cantrelle, P., & Ralijaona, O. (1999). Impact démographique d'une famine ignorée: Antananarivo: 1985–1987. *Economie de Madagascar, 4*, 247–264.

Garenne, M., & Zanou, B. (1995). L'état civil en Afrique: que peut-on en tirer? In *Clins d'oeil de démographes à l'Afrique et à Michel François* (No 2: 29–42). Paris: Documents et Manuels du CEPED.

Garenne, M., & Zwang, J. (2004). Social change and premarital fertility in Madagascar. *Southern African Journal of Demography, 9*(1), 27–48.

Garenne, M., & Zwang, J. (2006). *Premarital fertility and ethnicity in Africa*. DHS Comparative Reports, No. 13. Calverton, MD: Macro International Inc.

Garenne, M., & Zwang, J. (2008). Premarital fertility and HIV/AIDS in sub-Saharan Africa. *African Journal of Reproductive Health, 12*(2), 64–74.

Garenne, M. L. (2011). Testing for fertility stalls in demographic and health surveys. *Population Health Metrics, 9*(1), 1–8.

Garenne, M. L., Leclerc, P. M., & Matthews, A. P. (2011). Parameterisation of the transition to first marriage with the Picrate model. *Southern African Journal of Demography, 12*(1), 109–124.

Gendreau, F. (1977). La démographie des pays d'Afrique: Revue et synthèse. *Population (French Edition)*, 32(4–5), 899–943.

Gendreau, F. (1993). *La population de l'Afrique: manuel de démographie*. Paris: Karthala.

GDA: Groupe de Démographie Africaine. (1971). *Afrique Noire, Madagascar, Comores, Démographie Comparée*. Paris: DGRST.

Hill, A. (1991). Infant and child mortality: Levels, trends and data deficiencies. In R. G. Feachem & D. T. Jamison (Eds.), *Disease and mortality in sub-Saharan Africa*. New York: World Bank and Oxford University Press.

Hill, K., Queiros, B., Stanton, C., & AbouZahr, C. (2007). Measuring maternal mortality through the population census: Examples from Africa. In *UAPS Conference*, Arusha, Tanzania.

Leclerc, P. M., Dubois-Colas, N., & Garenne, M. (2008). Hormonal contraception and HIV prevalence in four African countries. *Contraception*, 77(5), 371–376.

Leclerc, P.M., Matthews, A.P., & Garenne, M.L. (2009). Fitting the HIV epidemic in Zambia: A two-sex micro-simulation model. *PLoS One*, *4*(5), e5439.
Lericollais, A. (Ed.). (1995). *Les paysans Sereer (Sénégal): permanences et changements*. Paris: ORSTOM.
Lohlé-Tart, L., Clairin, R., François, M. D., & Gendreau, F. (1988). *De l'homme au chiffre: Réflexions sur l'observation démographique en Afrique*. Paris: Etude du CEPED.
Lorimer, F. (1961). *Demographic information on Tropical Africa*. Boston, MA: Boston University Press.
Lorimer, F. (1968). Introduction. In W. Brass et al. (Eds.), *The demography of Tropical Africa*. Princeton, NJ: Princeton University Press.
Marston, M., Zaba, B., Salomon, J. A., Brahmbhatt, H., & Bagenda, D. (2005). Estimating the net effect of HIV on child mortality in African populations affected by generalized HIV epidemics. *JAIDS Journal of Acquired Immune Deficiency Syndromes*, *38*(2), 219–227.
Matthews, A. P., Leclerc, P. M., & Garenne, M. L. (2009). The Picrate model for fitting the age pattern of first marriage. *Mathématiques et sciences humaines: Mathematics and Social Sciences*, *47*(2), 17–28.
Newell, M. L., Brahmbhatt, H., & Ghys, P. D. (2004). Child mortality and HIV infection in Africa: A review. *Aids*, *18*, S27–S34.
Niakhar. (2010). Demographic surveillance systems in Senegal. Retrieved from www.ird.sn/activites/niakhar/
Ominde, S. H., & Ejiogu, C. N. (1972). *L'accroissement de la population et l'avenir économique de l'Afrique*. New York: Population Council.
Pictet, G., Le Coeur, S., M'Pelé, P., Brouard, N., & Lallemant, M. (1998). Contribution of AIDS to the general mortality in Central Africa: Evidence from a morgue-based study in Brazzaville, Congo. *Aids*, *12*(16), 2217–2223.
Pullum, T. W. (2006). *An assessment of age and date reporting in the demographic and health surveys, 1985–2003*. Calverton, MD: Demographic and Health Surveys Project, ORC Macro.
Pullum, T. W. (2008). *An assessment of the quality of data on health and nutrition in the DHS Surveys, 1993–2003*. DHS Methodological Reports, No. 6. Calverton, MD: Macro International Inc.
Retel-Laurentin, A. (1974). *Infécondité en Afrique noire: maladies et conséquences sociales*. Paris: Masson.
Romaniuk, A. (1961). *Tableau général de la démographie congolaise: Enquête démographique par sondage 1955–1957*. République du Congo: Ministère du plan et de la coordination économique, Service des statistiques, Kinshasa, p. 214.
Shaul, J. R. H., & Myburgh, C. A. L. (1949). Provisional results of the sample survey of the African population of Southern Rhodesia, 1948. *Population Studies*, *3*(3), 274–285.
Tabutin, D., & Schoumaker, B. (2004). La démographie de l'Afrique au sud du Sahara des années 1950 aux années 2000. *Population*, *59*(3), 521–622.
Tollman, S. M., Kahn, K., Garenne, M., & Gear, J.S. (1999). Reversal in mortality trends: Evidence from the Agincourt field site, South Africa, 1992–1995. *Aids*, *13*(9), 1091–1097.
Zachariah, K. C., & Condé, J. (1980). *Migration in West Africa – Demographics aspects*. Oxford: Oxford University Press (A joint World Bank-OECD Study).
Zwang, J., & Garenne, M. (2008). Social context of premarital fertility in rural South-Africa. *African Journal of Reproductive Health*, *12*(2), 98–110.

5

INDIRECT ESTIMATION TECHNIQUES AND STATISTICAL MODELING IN AFRICAN DEMOGRAPHIC RESEARCH

Joshua O. Akinyemi and Sunday A. Adedini

Introduction

Historically, demography has been popularly defined as "the statistical study of human populations". As a scientific subject, statistics deals with methods of data collection, summarization, analysis and interpretation and presentation. These definitions underscore the reason estimation of summary indices in forms of rates, ratios and percentages is at the core of demographic enterprise. "Statistical study" usually involves analysis which can range from simple analytical comparisons to fitting of complex statistical models to explain demographic processes.

In a treatise on the evolution of demography between 1950 and 2000, Poston et al. (2006) stated that there has been significant growth and change in disciplinary resources vis-à-vis demographic theories and models, methods, infrastructure of demography and demographic praxis (Poston & Micklin, 2006). A detailed elucidation on the growth and changes in these "demography resources" is outside the scope of this chapter. Methods comprise a body of procedures and techniques for collecting, evaluating, adjusting, estimating and analyzing demographic data (Poston & Micklin, 2006). With a focus on Africa, the interest of this chapter is methods for estimating and analysing demographic data. As a caveat, we do not intend to trace the development of "demographic methods" in Africa. Rather, this chapter is aimed at presenting a "bird's-eye" view of demographic estimation and statistical modelling in African demography.

Without prejudice to earlier seminal work, the publication of *Demography of Tropical Africa* (Brass et al., 1968) is an important landmark. It was a formal compendium on the characteristic features of data and the array of techniques deployed to derive plausible estimates by which some sense was made of Africa demography. At the time, it was a showpiece on fertility, mortality and nuptiality in what is today referred to as sub-Saharan Africa (SSA). In a nice commentary and illuminating perspective on "fifty years of research in African demography", Garenne (2011) referred to it as "the beginning of the adventure of indirect methods of demographic estimation". As a further reflection, this chapter begins with a systematic assessment of publications on or using indirect estimation[1] and then provides brief overview on the use of statistical

DOI: 10.4324/9780429287213-7

models. The concluding section presents some thoughts on the future of estimation and statistical modelling in African demographic research.

Appraisal of direct and indirect estimation (technical demography)

Hauser and Duncan (1959) defined demography as "the study of the size, territorial distribution, composition of population, changes therein, and the components of such changes". This definition clearly portrays the interdisciplinary nature of demography. For instance, population change could be economical, sociological, biological and so on – all of which rests in another discipline (Xie, 2000). It is unequivocal that measurement, estimation and analysis are the bedrock of demography. This aspect of the field is also known as technical demography – the branch of the discipline that deals with the methods, techniques and measures used in demographic estimation and analysis (Ramakumar & Gopal, 1986). Traditionally, it constitutes the core of demography as a discipline. This is underscored by historical developments in the field. From John Graunt's life tables to Alfred J. Lotka (who first proved the stable population theory) and several others, the discipline has thrived on the innovations, theories and models developed in technical demography.

The conventional sources of data for demographic estimation are vital registration systems (for continuous registration of births, deaths and marriages/divorces) and population censuses. Over the years, these data sources have been at different levels of advancement and completeness in different regions of the world. In the western countries, vital registration systems (VRSs) and censuses have existed for long enough and been sophisticated enough to provide reliable data for direct estimation of demographic parameters, but the situation in developing countries, especially sub-Saharan Africa, is different. In the latter, though censuses were sometimes conducted, VRSs were rare, especially during the colonial and early independence era. To overcome this challenge, demographers led by William Brass and others pioneered the development of techniques for "indirect estimation" of demographic parameters.

Indirect demographic estimation involves the use of methods and procedures to estimate demographic parameters from data that are defective, indirect or both (Brass & Coale, 1968; United Nations, 1983). Vital registration data could be defective as a result of low levels of completeness in recording births and deaths. Coverage and content errors such as age misstatement are common sources of defect in census data. Development of indirect techniques followed two pathways – the search for methods to analyse data from defective traditional sources (surveys, censuses and VRSs) and the use of indirect evidence on births and deaths. From the second path, a wide array of indirect techniques emerged from three ideas: (i) estimation of fertility from data on births in previous year and children ever born to women of childbearing age (ii) estimation of infant and childhood mortality from data on children ever born and surviving; and (iii) the use of model life tables and stable populations to estimate fertility, mortality and adjusted age distributions (Brass & Coale, 1968). These three innovations underwent refinements, extensions and different forms of adaptation and applications before culminating in the publication of the popular *Manual X* by the United Nations in 1983. Many of the techniques developed have also been applied in developed countries for assessment of the quality of census data and historical estimation of fertility and mortality rates. These efforts have enriched the subject of technical demography and the broader discipline as a whole.

In a commentary on the dying art of technical demography, Saxena (2011) alluded to the roles of the International Conference on Population and Development (ICPD) and further attributed the dwindling fortune to the replacement of technical demography courses by other topics on population and development issues. As a result, most demography and population studies graduates lack in-depth knowledge in technical demography and are therefore not adequately equipped to drive further development in the subject area. A paper presented at the Population Association of America annual meeting also decried the weak status of demographic training in South Africa amid the hope of improved data quality in censuses and VRSs in Africa as a whole (Pali, 2015). The situation is not much different in other African countries.

Though these problems are real, there has not been empirical evidence on the dearth of technical demographic research outputs in peer-review publications. Meanwhile, it is opined that journal publication is not just a means of communication among researchers; it also reflects developments in a discipline (Keyfitz, 1993). This implies that one way to assess how the field of technical demography has fared is by checking articles published in relevant journals and quantifying the proportion of technical demographic studies therein. Therefore, in the first section of this chapter, we report a systematic assessment of the proportion of technical demographic studies published in demographic journals since the ICPD of 1994 to 2015, which was the cut-off year for the belated Millennium Development Goals (MDGs).

Selection of journals

In order to ascertain the percentage of technical demographic studies published between 1994 and 2015, we reviewed all publications in nine leading demographic journals: *African Population Studies*, *Canadian Studies in Population*, *Demography*, *Demographic Research*, *GENUS*, *Journal of Population Research*, *Mathematical Population Studies*, *Population*, and *Population Studies*. *African Population Studies* was launched in 1984 by the Union for African Population Studies, while *Canadian Studies in Population* has been published by the Canadian Population Society since 1974. *Demography* has been published bi-monthly by the Population Association of America since 1964, while the *Journal of Demographic Research* was launched in 1999 by the Max Planck Institute for Demographic Research, Germany. *GENUS* is published by the University of Rome in Italy and was founded in 1934. The *Journal of Population Research*, known as the *Journal of the Australian Population Association* until 1999, was first published in 1984. *Mathematical Population Studies* was founded by a group of mathematical demographers in 1988. *Population Journal* has been published by *Institut National D'études Démographiques* (INED) since 1946, while *Population Studies* has been published at the London School of Economics since 1947. These journals were selected to reflect the various regions, Thus *African Population Studies* for Africa; *Demography*, *Mathematical Population Studies* and *Canadian Studies in Population* for North and South America; *Demographic Research*, *GENUS*, *Population and Population Studies* for Europe; and the *Journal of Population Research* for Australia and Asia. These journals have international focus and do not restrict publication to papers from any region of the world.

For *Population Journal*, only issues published from 2002 onward were available and reviewed. Those for 1994–2001 were not available in the online archive of the journal. In addition, a few prominent journals of statistics (such as *Journal of the American Statistical Association*, *Biometrics* and *Indian Statistical Journal*) occasionally publish articles on technical demography. Further review of a few issues of these journals revealed that they published predominantly statistics-related topics. If they were to be included, the proportion of technical demographic studies would be very small, as a result of which the overall percentage of technical demography papers would be drastically reduced. To avoid the effect of this potential selection bias, these statistical journals were not included in the review.

Sources and assessment of articles

Articles published in *Canadian Studies in Population*, *Demography*, *Journal of Population Research*, *Demographic Research*, *Mathematical Population Studies*, *Population* and *Population Studies* were obtained from the online archives of each journal. Articles published in *GENUS* were retrieved via JSTOR, while those of *African Population Studies* were sourced from Bioline International, a free open-access database.

All articles in every issue of the selected journals were screened to determine whether they could be classified as a technical demographic study. The screening process involve reviewing the abstract and method section of each article to ascertain whether it could be classified as a technical study. For this review, an article was deemed technical if it involved the use of any concept in technical demography (methods, measures and techniques of demographic analysis). As such, we included articles that involved demographic estimation (direct and indirect), life table techniques, population projections and assessment of quality of census or survey data. Articles on family demography and historical demography and those that merely used advanced statistical models were not classified as technical demographic studies.

For each issue of the journal, we recorded information on the year of publication, volume, issue, total number of articles and number of technical demographic studies. The technical demographic studies were further sub-classified under mortality, fertility, nuptiality, migration, data quality assessment, projection and others (e.g. stable population theory, decomposition of changes in life expectancies, etc.). We derived a yearly aggregate for total number of articles and number of technical demographic studies for 1994 to 2015 and subsequently computed the proportion of technical studies for each year. We illustrated the trends in the proportion of technical demographic studies in a graph and also estimated the annual rate of decline using least-square regression techniques.

Trends in publication of technical demography papers

A total of 4091 original studies were published in 465 issues of the selected journals between 1994 and 2015. The number of original articles in these journals grew at an exponential rate of 5.66% over the review period (Figure 5.1). Overall, 371 (7.0%) of the 4067 articles were based on technical demography. The proportion of technical demographic studies ranged from 12.0% in 1994 to 10.0% in 2015. Figure 5.2 shows that the proportion declined gradually at an annual rate of 0.42% (CI = 0.29–0.62) between 1994 and 2015.

The results further show that the technical demographic studies were devoted to mortality (44.2%), fertility (23.9%), data quality assessment and population projections (10.8%), migration (8.0%) and nuptiality (2.1%). Another wide range of topics, such as population momentum, stable population theory, relational life table and so on, constituted 11.0%.

Main themes covered in published technical demography paper

The mortality studies covered infancy and childhood, adulthood and older ages. Many of the childhood mortality studies utilized techniques such as the children ever born/children surviving method (Adetunji, 1996; Blacker, Ali, & Jones, 2007), preceding birth technique (Aguirre, 1994; Bairagi, Shuaib, & Hill, 1997) and hazard and frailty models (Bocquier, Madise, & Zulu, 2011; Sastry, 1997). For adult mortality, widowhood (Ahmed, 1995), sibling suvivorship (Gakidou & King, 2005; Masquelier, 2013), orphanhood methods (Grassly, Lewis, Mahy, Walker, & Timaeus, 2004; Udjo, 2014), the Lee-Carter model (Booth, Hyndman, Tickle, & de Jong,

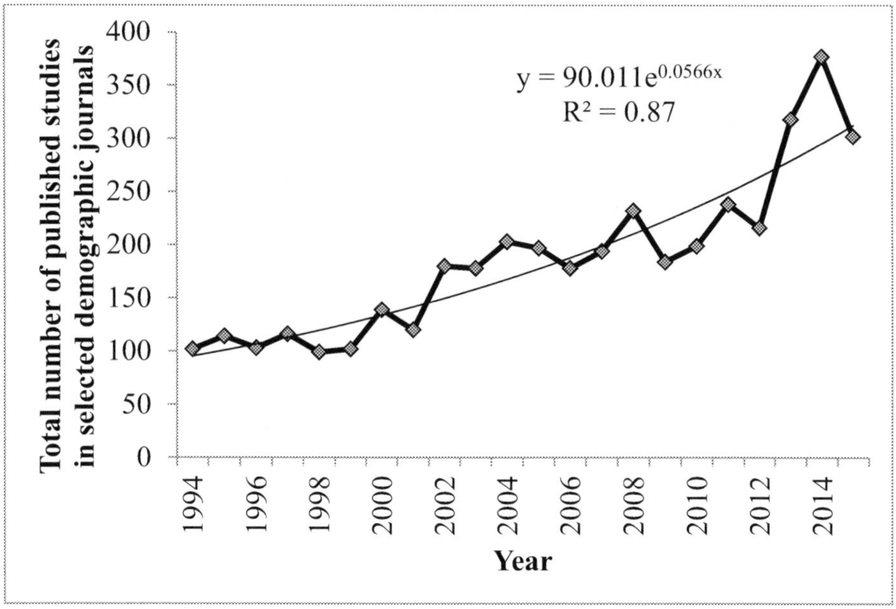

Figure 5.1 Total number of original articles published in selected demographic journals, 1994–2015
Source: Akinyemi and Adedini, 2018

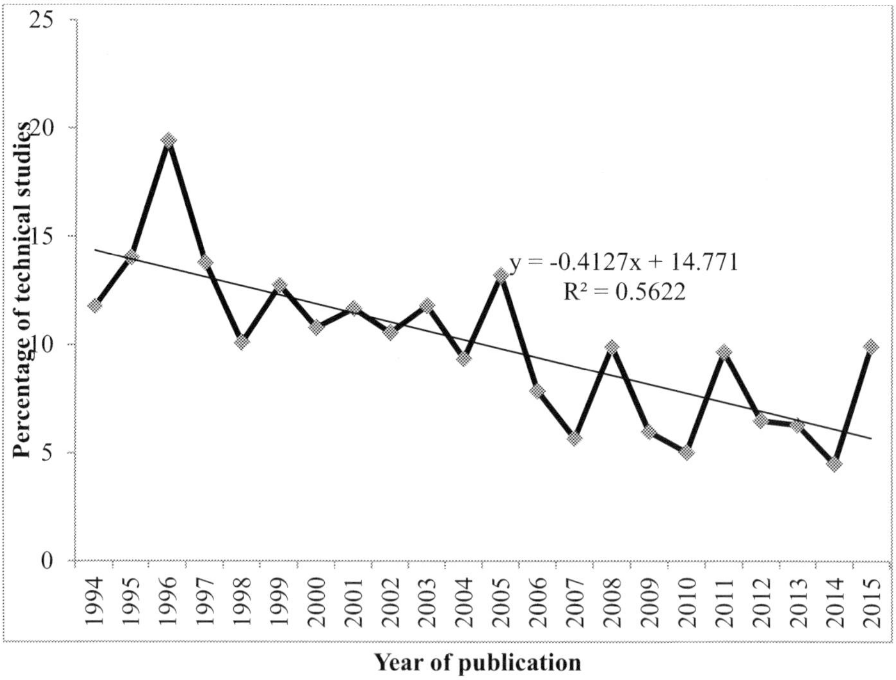

Figure 5.2 Trends in percentage of technical studies published in selected demographic journals, 1994–2015
Source: Akinyemi and Adedini, 2018

2006; Booth, Maindonald, & Smith, 2002; Miller & Lee, 2001), method of extinct generation (Bourbeau, 2000; Elo, 2001; Guillot, 2003; Hill, Choi, & Timaeus, 2005; Preston, Elo, & Stewart, 1999), survival ratio (Spoorenberg, 2008) and life tables (Kannisto, Nieminen, & Turpeinen, 1999; Kostaki & Panousis, 2001; Nath & Choudhury, 1995; Rowland, 1996; Zaba & Paes, 1995) were quite common. A few studies also explored new developments such as Bayesian extension to the Lee-Carter model (Booth et al., 2006; Wisniowski, Smith, Bijak, Raymer, & Forster, 2015; Zhao, 2012) and the multi-dimensional life table method (Eini-Zinab, 2013). However, most of the latest developments have only been used in developed countries and applied to census and VRS data.

Fertility studies cut across different regions of the world and were based on censuses, surveys and VRS data. Analytical approaches included use of the parity progression ratio (Kohler & Ortega, 2002; Moultrie, Sayi, & Timaeus, 2012; Sibanda, 1999), relational Gompertz model (Paget & Timaeus, 1994; Udjo, 1998, 2014), own-children method (Abbas-Shavazi, 1997; Avery, St Clair, Levin, & Hill, 2013; Dubuc, 2009), P/F ratio (Hinde & Mturi, 2000; Moultrie & Dorrinton, 2008; Moultrie & Timaeus, 2003; Udjo, 1998), variable-r method (Alkema et al., 2011; Cai, 2008) and the Bongaarts model (Bongaarts, 1999; Kohler & Ortega, 2002; Odimegwu & Zerai, 1996).

Studies on population projections were also fairly common based on methods such as cohort-component projection and Bayesian approaches (Alkema et al., 2011; Bocquier, 2005; Keilman, Pham, & Hetland, 2002; Thomas & Clark, 2011; Wisniowski et al., 2015). With the exception of South Africa (Udjo, 2013, 2014, 2015), population projections were scarce for sub-Saharan African countries.

This review of technical demography may have been limited due to the fact that we purposively selected only nine of the available demographic journals. No doubt, some technical studies in other journals may have been left out; however, we strongly believe that the journals selected gave a fair reflection of happenings in the field of demography over the period considered.

Reflections on indirect demographic estimation

The review shows that whereas the number of original articles in the selected journals has increased exponentially, there has been a significant decline in the percentage of technical demographic studies since 1994. It's also observed that some demographic topics, such as population projection and census data quality assessment, were rarely published for developing countries, especially in sub-Saharan Africa. Censuses and vital registration systems were supposed to be the prime sources of demographic data for population projection, estimation of demographic parameters and monitoring of population policies. Unfortunately, these traditional sources of demographic data are very poor and unreliable in many developing countries (Mathers, Fat, Inoue, Rao, & Lopez, 2005). VRSs in most places are passive, and level of completeness is low. Consequently, surveys have become popular alternatives, though with their own inherent data quality challenges. The popularity of surveys and collection of data on full birth histories permit direct estimation of fertility and mortality. This may have created a misconception that indirect techniques are obsolete (Moultrie et al., 2013).

Non-availability of requisite data may be partly responsible for the decline in use of indirect techniques. Censuses are rarely regular, and when conducted at all, they are fraught with political and technical controversies. Worse still, the census data are not made available to researchers. Efforts by Integrated Public Use Microdata Series (IPUMS) (Ruggles, King, Levison, McCaa, & Sobek, 2003) to overcome this challenge are commendable and need to be expanded.

To overcome the lacuna created by challenges associated with census and VRS data, nationally representative household surveys have become very common. Interestingly, the funders and agencies implementing these surveys make the data available for further analysis. Many demographers and population scientists have had to leverage these alternative data sources at least to keep the discipline alive. Aside, many of the indirect methods are known to depend on some restrictive assumptions that are difficult to meet due to changes in African demographic patterns compared to when the methods were developed (Garenne, 2011).

The interdisciplinary nature of demography may have also contributed to the declining trend. Consequently, demography journals have expanded in scope to include a wider range of topics. It may be that the field of demography has become considerably broader, thereby making technical demography a smaller proportion of the field (and the published papers). In addition, the interdisciplinary nature has caused demography to be seen as a step-child of many disciplines. Thus, in many developing countries, demographic training is based in schools of public health, statistics, sociology, geography and economics. Both teaching, research and practice of technical demography may have declined as a result of the interplay of these factors. Indeed, over the years, demography has expanded in scope. There has been more focus on understanding and explanation of causes and consequences of population change (Tabutin & Depledge, 2007). To do justice to these emerging interests, methodological change became necessary, with a shift towards the use of microdata from surveys and less technical demography.

The notable fall in the percentage of technical demography papers in the journals could also be traced to some developments in the population field. Since the late 1990s, teaching, training, research and further development have been observed to be diminishing. This observation has been made at two separate seminars organized six years apart by the International Union for Scientific Study of Populations (IUSSP). The first was the seminar on demographic training in the third world in 2001 (Tomassini, 2001), while the second one, in 2007, was focused on data needs for monitoring the Millennium Development Goals in developing countries (IUSSP, 2007). Some of the reasons adduced at the seminars include dwindling support for demographic training and ageing and subsequent retirement of skilled professionals, especially in developing countries (Moultrie, 2009). The few demographic training centres that could survive in the poor funding climates had to revise their curricula to accommodate more substantive topics in tandem with the new realities (Saxena, 2011).

Existing interventions to tame the declining fortunes of technical demography

In response to the decline in technical demography expertise, a special meeting was convened by the IUSSP on teaching and training in applied and technical demography in developing countries in 2009 (Moultrie, 2009). At the meeting, the genesis of the problem was traced to the outcome of the 1994 International Conference on Population and Development, after which funding for population and demography was channelled to other areas such as human rights and sexual and reproductive health. It is critical to sustain the expertise and arts of demographic estimation, especially in low-middle-income countries (LMICs) to salvage the weak and underdeveloped state of VRSs, as well as contentious features of population censuses (Moultrie et al., 2013). This is not to say that Africa and other LMICs have made no progress in their demographic data ecosystems; rather, there is still much to be done.

Two of the short-term interventions suggested at the 2009 IUSSP meeting have since been implemented. The first is a much-updated version of *Manual X*, titled *Tools for Demographic Estimation* (Moultrie et al., 2013). The web-based tools for demographic estimation comprised dynamic web pages on description of the methods, rationale and data requirements, as well as illustrative examples with downloadable Excel spreadsheets. They include new methods and advances and exposition on how well each method works under different conditions. Materials on measurement of migration from census data, which were not part of *Manual X*, have been included in the web-based tool. The second intervention is an online training course on "population analysis for policies and programmes" (IUSSP & UNFPA, 2013). This online course module provides users with basic knowledge on technical population analysis. It covers topics ranging from sources, collection and evaluation of demographic data to advanced methods of demographic analysis such as model life tables, population dynamics/projections and advanced fertility analysis.

Statistical modelling in African demography

A statistical model is a mathematical representation of a process that generates sample data based on certain assumptions. Models are never perfect, but researchers have ways of checking their appropriateness and fit. Amid other goals, a key interest in regression models is explanation and prediction of outcomes of interest. Demography as a subject is deeply statistical, with developments in population studies having heavier demand for application of advances in statistical modelling. The phrases "population composition" and "changes therein" refer to "population heterogeneity" and "dynamic processes", respectively (Xie, 2000). No doubt, these require extensive application of statistical models. This was aptly captured by Xie (2000), who stated: "Indeed, it is the integration of statistical methods into demographic research that has enabled demographers to study population heterogeneity and change with sample data". In Africa, this is very true because most demographic research in the past four decades has thrived mostly on data from "sample surveys". In fact, availability of data from nationally representative household data collection such as the World Fertility Survey (WFS), Demographic and Health Surveys (DHSs) and multiple indicator cluster surveys (MICSs) has expanded the subject matter of interest to demographers beyond the traditional focus on nuptiality, fertility, mortality and migration. This section of the chapter provides a brief overview on application of statistical models to demographic research in Africa. We summarize the type of dependent variables (outcomes) and kind of multivariable models employed. In doing this, we undertook a quick search of publications in leading demography and population studies journals between 2010 and 2020. Our targets were papers on African population and those in which the outcome of interest was related to demography, population health and development.

Outcome measures (dependent variables) and study population

Between 2010 and 2020, the majority of published papers in which statistical models were deployed fell into three broad areas: maternal and child health/nutrition, sexual and reproductive health (SRH) and mortality. Under maternal and child health/nutrition are outcome variables such as utilization of maternal health services (antenatal care, delivery and postnatal care), child health care services (immunization, treatment of childhood illnesses), childhood malnutrition and other related topics. SRH outcomes often include contraceptive use, sexual behaviour, gender-based violence and female genital cutting. Mortality was dominated by papers on childhood mortality (neonatal, infant and under-five), with very few papers on adult mortality. Very few papers reported on adolescent mortality in South Africa. The data sources for most of the studies were population-based or facility-based cross-sectional surveys. By implication, the statistical models often focused on exploration of association. Though a few studies used data from health and demographic surveillance sites, causal models were quite uncommon. One component of the demographic process that is grossly understudied is migration. This is understandable because population-based surveys rarely collect migration data. Another observation is that the age group usually covered 15–49 years. As a result, rarely is there sufficient information about elderly persons, especially those aged 60 years and above. There was also a preponderance of papers on women compared to those on men. Therefore, there is a significant knowledge gap on men and the elderly in SSA.

Statistical modelling frameworks

On a global scale, following widespread use of survey data, the use of statistical models by demographers has continued to evolve from techniques such as linear and log-linear models, structural equations, econometric models, path analysis and event history models (Xie, 2000). The case with demographic research is not different. The modelling frameworks in many published demographic papers on issues related to Africa can be classified as: generalized linear models (GLMs), hierarchical models and geo-additive models. This classification is by no means exhaustive, neither is it by type of outcome variable. Rather it follows the methodological evolution of the modelling frameworks. A detailed explanation of these model types is not the focus in this chapter. The most applied of these were GLMs, under which we have those for categorical outcomes (binary, ordinal and multinomial logistic models) and those for count outcomes (Poisson model and its variants [negative binomial, zero-inflated Poisson, etc.]).

Hierarchical or multilevel models were also used, with authors occasionally providing justifications for their use. Usually, such models are employed to analyze data from complex surveys where participants are likely to share certain characteristics in common at the cluster level. The levels commonly considered were individual, household and community. Though very few, papers that involve multi-country analyses add another level for the country. Community variables are often derived or aggregated from individual-level covariates. Multilevel models permit statistical investigation of population heterogeneity and also help to reduce bias in the estimation of standard errors and confidence intervals for explanatory variables. Further, random effects are often presented in form of intra-cluster correlation coefficient (ICC) and variance-partition coefficients. The meanings of these statistical parameters may not be easily understood by readers who are not familiar with the method.

A few studies went beyond GLMs and multilevel models to employ geo-additive models (GAMs) for the same kind of outcomes mentioned earlier. The distinguishing feature of GAMs is the inclusion of spatial effects and the ability to explore both linear and non-linear effects of explanatory variables (Kandala & Ghilagaber, 2014). With these, spatial and spatio-temporal models can be fitted to demographic outcomes. Inference is based on Bayesian techniques, especially Markov chain Monte Carlo (MCMC) simulations. The availability of GPS coordinates in DHS data permit the use of GAMs. This is a relatively new area of demographic research because very few people have expertise in Africa. It holds a lot of promise for precision public health.

Some studies also employed regression decomposition methods. These methods originated from econometrics but are becoming popular in other subject areas and have been employed in African demographic research. Though the original Oaxaca-Blinder decomposition was applied to investigate income differentials, the method has been further extended to binary and count and comes with software modules developed for platforms such as Stata and R. This has enhanced wider application of multivariate decomposition techniques to investigate changes over time or assess differentials between two population sub-groups. There have been instances where the original Oaxaca-Blinder techniques meant for a continuous outcome were applied to a dichotomous outcome. An important caution in the use of multivariate decomposition is that the choice of method must match the type of outcome.

Approaches to model building

Model building in African demographic research has commonly followed one of two pathways. Fist and most common is what can be referred to as the traditional approach to multivariable analysis. In this clime, explanatory variables found statistically significant in bivariate analyses are all entered into a regression model to identify the "predictors" or "determinants" of an outcome. This approach is not advisable because demographic or population processes rarely follow such a simplistic "mechanical" pathway. The second approach usually involves fitting of "sequential" models based on a carefully constructed or adapted conceptual framework. Relationships between dependent and explanatory variables are hypothesized, illustrated in diagrams (conceptual framework) and tested via empirical models. This is the preferred and a better approach to model social processes. This practice is in tandem with the notion that selection of variables for regression models should be theory based and motivated by the extant literature (Aneshensel, 2002). This approach applies beyond demography or population studies to other quantitative disciplines such as epidemiology and public health (Greenland, 1989).

Thoughts about the future

On the global scene, similar to other scientific disciples, demographic research has always been undergoing transition in response to technological, socio-cultural and economic development. For instance, there has been evolution from formal demography to population studies, with expanded attention to many of the underlying factors driving demographic processes (Xie, 2000). Methodological advances have continued unabated. For instance, as an offshoot of the data revolution, we have seen the emergence of new allied subjects such as "Bayesian demography", "digital and computational demography" (Bijak & Bryant, 2014, 2016; Bohon, 2018) among others.

What will the future be for technical and statistical demography in Africa? What does the future hold for direct/indirect estimation and statistical modelling in Africa demography? Or what should be the next steps in advancing this sub-area of the discipline? These are not questions that can be answered once and for all or in a section of a book chapter. There will continue to be methodological advances coupled with larger volume and newer types of data with increasing complexity. Also, computational tools will get more sophisticated. Similarly, research questions will become more complex, requiring multidisciplinary, interdisciplinary and transdisciplinary solutions. African demographers and population scientists need to brace for these realities.

Without losing disciplinary identity, independence and methodological rigour, Africa demographic practitioners will need to take advantage of the digital revolution, because it will impact African demographic research in different ways. A few of those related to the focus of this chapter are briefly highlighted. At present, notwithstanding the perpetual weaknesses of vital registration systems in many African countries, there has been an upsurge in availability of data from population-based surveys, demographic surveillance systems and routine health information systems. While direct estimation from VRSs may not be as popular, indirect estimation will still be relevant, albeit with modifications. There are opportunities for further refinement of the techniques to accommodate demographic changes in Africa in particular. There are increasing possibilities to combine data from multiple sources and use them for demographic estimation with objective estimates of uncertainty. This is one of the selling points in the bourgeoning field of Bayesian demography. African demographic researchers need to join the league of Bayesian population scientists and provide much-needed contextual perspectives so that Africa is not left behind. It will also become necessary to widen the use of small-area estimation techniques to provide estimates for sub-populations. Bayesian techniques are also applied in this area. All these will be necessary to deepen the quality of contributions to evidence-informed population policies and development.

Furthermore, the data revolution will have a huge impact on methodological approaches to statistical modelling in demography and many other social science disciplines. Analytical models are expected to be theory driven. However, a paradigm shift will be necessary in order to take full advantage of data-driven techniques such as machine learning and other emerging computational methodologies that characterize the data revolution. In short, digital and computational demography need to come alive in Africa.

With respect to modelling, though the existing framework may still be relevant, the range of outcomes will need to be expanded to migration, labour force, nuptiality and family. Also, the discipline will need to leap beyond the current dominance of GLMs. The use of causal inference and modelling procedures (Wunsch & Gourbin, 2020) should attract greater empirical interest. This may be necessary to fill the gap created by the non-feasibility of experimental studies to inform many population health and development initiatives. Undoubtedly, to set the stage for sustained development in this subject area, Africa needs to invest more to enrich the data ecosystems for longitudinal and life course analysis.

Note

1 This section of the chapter is an excerpt from our previous publication in *African Population Studies* (APS): Akinyemi, J. O., & Adedini, S. A. (2018). Is technical demography becoming less relevant? Two decade review of published articles in selected demography journals. *African Population Studies*, *32*(2), 4396–4404. Copyright permission to reference the earlier work has been obtained from the editorial office of APS.

References

Abbas-Shavazi, M. J. (1997). An assessment of the own-children method of estimating fertility by birthplace in Australia. *Journal of the Australian Population Association*, *14*(2), 167–185.

Adetunji, J. A. (1996). Infant mortality levels in Africa: Does method of estimation matter? *Genus*, *52*(3–4), 89–106.

Aguirre, A. (1994). Extension to the preceding birth technique. *Genus*, *50*(3–4), 151–169.

Ahmed, M. F. (1995). Recent estimates of adult mortality from widowhood in Bangladesh: A critical comparison. *Genus*, *51*(3–4), 97–116.

Akinyemi, J. O., & Adedini, S. A. (2018). Is technical demography becoming less relevant? Two decade review of published articles in selected demography journals. *African Population Studies*, *32*(2), 4396–4404.

Alkema, L., Raftery, A. E., Gerland, P., Clark, S. J., Pelletier, F., Buettner, T., & Heilig, G. K. (2011). Probabilistic projections of the total fertility rate for all countries. *Demography*, *48*(3), 815–839. doi:10.1007/s13524-011-0040-5

Aneshensel, C. S. (2002). *Theory-based data analysis for the social sciences*. Thousand Oaks, CA: Pine Forge Press.

Avery, C., St Clair, T., Levin, M., & Hill, K. (2013). The 'own children' fertility estimation procedure: A reappraisal. *Population Studies (Cambridge)*, *67*(2), 171–183. doi:10.1080/00324728.2013.769616

Bairagi, R., Shuaib, M., & Hill, A. (1997). Estimating childhood mortality trends from routine data: A simulation using the preceding birth technique in Bangladesh. *Demography*, *34*(3), 411–420.

Bijak, J., & Bryant, J. (2014). Bayesian demography. *Wiley StatsRef: Statistics Reference Online*, 1–6.

Bijak, J., & Bryant, J. (2016). Bayesian demography 250 years after Bayes. *Population Studies*, *70*(1), 1–19.

Blacker, J., Ali, M. M., & Jones, G. (2007). A response to criticism of our estimates of under-5 mortality in Iraq, 1980–98. *Population Studies (Cambridge)*, *61*(1), 7–13. doi:10.1080/00324720601122031

Bocquier, P. (2005). World urbanization prospects: An alternative to the UN model of projection compatible with the mobility transition theory. *Demographic Research*, *12*, 197–236. doi:10.4054/DemRes.2005.12.9

Bocquier, P., Madise, N. J., & Zulu, E. M. (2011). Is there an urban advantage in child survival in sub-Saharan Africa? Evidence from 18 countries in the 1990s. *Demography*, *48*(2), 531–558. doi:10.1007/s13524-011-0019-2

Bohon, S. A. (2018). Demography in the big data revolution: Changing the culture to forge new frontiers. *Population Research and Policy Review*, *37*(3), 323–341.

Bongaarts, J. (1999). The fertility impact of changes in the timing of childbearing in the developing world. *Population Studies (Cambridge)*, *53*(3), 277–289. doi:10.1080/00324720308088

Booth, H., Hyndman, R. J., Tickle, L., & de Jong, P. (2006). Lee-Carter mortality forecasting: A multi-country comparison of variants and extensions. *Demographic Research*, *15*, 289–310. doi:10.4054/DemRes.2006.15.9

Booth, H., Maindonald, J., & Smith, L. (2002). Applying Lee-Carter under conditions of variable mortality decline. *Population Studies (Cambridge)*, *56*(3), 325–336. doi:10.1080/00324720215935

Bourbeau, R. (2000). Mortality statistics for the oldest-old: An evaluation of Canadian data. *Demographic Research*, *2*. doi:10.4054/DemRes.2000.2.2

Brass, W., & Coale, A. J. (1968). Methods of analysis and estimation In W. Brass, A. J. Coale, P. Demeny, F. Hiesel, F. Lorimer, A. Romaniuk, & E. Van dan Walle (Eds.), *The demography of tropical Africa* (pp. 88–139). Princeton, NJ: Princeton University Press.

Brass, W., Coale, A. J., Demeny, P., Heisel, D. F., Lorimer, F., Romaniuk, A., & Van De Walle, E. (1968). *The demography of tropical Africa*. Princeton, NJ: Princeton University Press.

Cai, Y. (2008). An assessment of China's fertility level using the variable-r method. *Demography*, *45*(2), 271–281.

Dubuc, S. (2009). Application of the own-children method for estimating fertility by ethnic and religious groups in the UK. *Journal of Population Research*, *26*, 207–225. doi:10.1007/s12546-009-9020-7

Eini-Zinab, H. (2013). Multidimensional life-table analysis of the effect of child mortality on total fertility in India, 1992–93, 1998–99, 2005–06. *Population Studies (Cambridge)*, *67*(1), 7–23. doi:10.1080/00324728.2012.737473

Elo, I. T. (2001). New African-American life tables from 1935–11940 to 1985–1990. *Demography*, *38*(1), 97–114.

Gakidou, E., & King, G. (2005). Death by survey: Estimating adult mortality without selection bias from sibling survival data. *Demography*, *43*(3), 569–585.

Garenne, M. (2011). Fifty years of research in African demography: Progresses and challenges. *African Population Studies*, *25*(2), 151–167.

Grassly, N., Lewis, J., Mahy, M., Walker, N., & Timaeus, I. M. (2004). Comparison of household-survey estimates with projections of mortality and orphan numbers in sub-Saharan Africa in the era of HIV/AIDS. *Population Studies (Cambridge)*, *58*(2), 207–217. doi:10.1080/0032472042000224431

Greenland, S. (1989). Modeling and variable selection in epidemiologic analysis. *American Journal of Public Health*, *79*(3), 340–349.

Guillot, M. (2003). The cross-sectional average length of life (CAL): A cross-sectional mortality measure that reflects the experience of cohorts. *Population Studies (Cambridge)*, *57*(1), 41–54. doi:10.1080/0032472032000061712

Hauser, P. M., & Duncan, O. D. (1959). *The study of population: An inventory and appraisal*. Chicago: University of Chicago Press.

Hill, K., Choi, Y., & Timaeus, I. M. (2005). Unconventional approaches to mortality estimation. *Demographic Research*, *13*, 281–300. doi:10.4054/DemRes.2005.13.12

Hinde, A., & Mturi, A. J. (2000). Recent trends in Tanzanian fertility. *Population Studies (Cambridge)*, *54*(2), 177–191. doi:10.1080/713779080

IUSSP. (2007). *Report of meeting on taking stock of data needs and monitoring for the millennium development goals in developing countries*. Rabat, Morocco: IUSSP.

IUSSP & UNFPA. (2013). *Population analysis for policies & programmes*. Retrieved from https://papp.iussp.org/

Kandala, N.-B., & Ghilagaber, G. (2014). *Advanced techniques for modelling maternal and child health in Africa.* New York: Springer.

Kannisto, V., Nieminen, M., & Turpeinen, O. (1999). Finnish life tables since 1751. *Demographic Research, 1*. doi:10.4054/DemRes.1999.1.1

Keilman, N., Pham, D. Q., & Hetland, A. (2002). Why population forecasts should be probabilistic – illustrated by the case of Norway. *Demographic Research, 6*, 409–454. doi:10.4054/DemRes.2002.6.15

Keyfitz, N. (1993). Thirty years of demography and demography. *Demography, 30*(4), 530–548.

Kohler, H., & Ortega, J. A. (2002). Tempo-adjusted period parity progression measures, fertility postponement and completed cohort fertility. *Demographic Research, 6*, 91–144. doi:10.4054/DemRes.2002.6.6

Kostaki, A., & Panousis, V. (2001). Expanding an abridged table. *Demographic Research, 5*, 1–22. doi:10.4054/DemRes.2001.5.1

Masquelier, B. (2013). Adult mortality from sibling survival data: A reappraisal of selection biases. *Demography, 50*(1), 207–228. doi:10.1007/s13524-012-0149-1

Mathers, D. C., Fat, D. M., Inoue, M., Rao, C., & Lopez, A. D. (2005). Counting the dead and what they died from: An assessment of the global status of cause of death data. *Bulletin of the World Health Organization, 83*(3), 171–180.

Miller, T., & Lee, R. (2001). Evaluating the performance of the Lee-Carter method for forecasting mortality. *Demography, 38*(4), 537–549.

Moultrie, T. A. (2009). *IUSSP/UNFPA meeting on applied and technical demographic training in developing countries: Towards an agenda for revitalisation.* Aubervilliers: IUSSP.

Moultrie, T. A., & Dorrinton, R. (2008). Sources of error and bias in methods of fertility estimation contingent on the P/F ratio in a time of declining fertility and rising mortality. *Demographic Research, 19*, 1635–1662. doi:10.4054/DemRes.2008.19.46

Moultrie, T. A., Dorrington, R., Hill, A., Hill, K., Timaeus, I. M., & Zaba, B. (Eds.). (2013). *Tools for demographic estimation.* Paris: International Union for the Scientific Study of Population.

Moultrie, T. A., Sayi, T. S., & Timaeus, I. M. (2012). Birth intervals, postponement, and fertility decline in Africa: A new type of transition? *Population Studies (Cambridge), 66*(3), 241–258. doi:10.1080/00324728.2012.701660

Moultrie, T. A., & Timaeus, I. M. (2003). The South African fertility decline: Evidence from two censuses and a demographic and health survey. *Population Studies (Cambridge), 57*(3), 265–283. doi:10.1080/0032472032000137808

Nath, D. C., & Choudhury, L. (1995). Two regional (rural-urban) life tables for India. *Genus, 51*(1–2), 45–67.

Odimegwu, C. O., & Zerai, A. (1996). Understanding the proximate determinants of fertility of a Nigerian ethnic group. *Genus, 52*(3–4), 67–87.

Paget, W. J., & Timaeus, I. M. (1994). A relational Gompertz model of male fertility development and assessment. *Population Studies (Cambridge), 48*, 333–340. doi:10.1080/0032472031000147826

Pali, L. (2015). *Whither indirect demographic estimation methods: Africa's data revolution coming of age.* Paper presented at the Population Association of America Annual Meeting, San Diego.

Poston, D. L., & Micklin, M. (2006). The demographer's ken: 50 years of growth and change. In D. L. Poston & M. Micklin (Eds.), *Handbook of population.* New York: Springer.

Preston, S. H., Elo, I. T., & Stewart, Q. (1999). Effects of age misreporting on mortality estimates at older ages. *Population Studies (Cambridge), 53*, 165–177. doi:10.1080/00324720308075

Ramakumar, R., & Gopal, Y. S. (1986). *Technical demography.* New Delhi: Wiley Eastern Limited.

Rowland, D. T. (1996). Cohort survival in ageing populations: A model life table approach. *Genus, 52*(1–2), 71–82.

Ruggles, S., King, M. L., Levison, D., McCaa, R., & Sobek, M. (2003). IPUMS-International. *Historical Methods, 36*(2), 60–65.

Sastry, N. (1997). Family-level clustering of childhood mortality risk in Northeast Brazil. *Population Studies (Cambridge), 51*, 245–261. doi:10.1080/0032472031000150036

Saxena, P. C. (2011). Commentary – The dying art of technical demography. *Asian Population Studies*, 7(1). doi:10.1080/17441730.2011.558673

Sibanda, A. (1999). The Kenyan fertility transition: An age-specific analysis of fertility levels and trends. *Genus, 55*(3–4), 153–194.

Spoorenberg, T. (2008). What can we learn from indirect estimations on mortality in Mongolia, 1969–1989? *Demographic Research, 18*, 285–310. doi:10.4054/DemRes.2008.18.10

Tabutin, D., & Depledge, R. (2007). Whither demography? Strengths and weaknesses of the discipline over fifty years of change. *Population*, *62*(1), 15–31.

Thomas, J. R., & Clark, S. J. (2011). More on the cohort-component model of population projection in the context of HIV/AIDS: A Leslie matrix representation and new estimates. *Demographic Research*, *25*, 39–102. doi:10.4054/DemRes.2011.25.2

Tomassini, C. (2001). *Report of seminar on demographic training in the third millennium*. Aubervilliers: IUSSP.

Udjo, E. O. (1998). Trends in level and tempo of fertility in Botswana. *Genus*, *54*(3–4), 285–301.

Udjo, E. O. (2013). Estimating South Africa's black adult female social classes, demographic differentials and determinants. *Genus*, *69*(1), 1–23.

Udjo, E. O. (2014). Estimating demographic parameters from the 2011 South Africa population census. *African Population Studies*, *28*(1), 564–578.

Udjo, E. O. (2015). Projecting population, numbers of households and dwelling units in South Africa 2011–2021. *African Population Studies*, *29*(1), 1511–1526.

United Nations. (1983). *Manual X: Indirect techniques for demographic estimation* (Vol. ST/ESA/Series A/81). New York: Department of International Economic and Social Affairs.

Wisniowski, A., Smith, P. W., Bijak, J., Raymer, J., & Forster, J. J. (2015). Bayesian population forecasting: Extending the Lee-Carter method. *Demography*, *52*(3), 1035–1059. doi:10.1007/s13524-015-0389-y

Wunsch, G., & Gourbin, C. (2020). Causal assessment in demographic research. *Genus*, *76*(1), 1–20.

Xie, Y. (2000). Demography: Past, present, and future. *Journal of the American Statistical Association: Vignettes*, *95*(450), 670–673.

Zaba, B., & Paes, N. (1995). An alternative procedure for fitting relational model life tables. *Genus*, *51*(1–2), 19–43.

Zhao, B. B. (2012). A modified Lee-Carter model for analysing short-base-period data. *Population Studies (Cambridge)*, *66*(1), 39–52. doi:10.1080/00324728.2011.636839

6

THE DEMOGRAPHIC RESEARCH IN LUSOPHONE AFRICA

What is known and what needs to be done?

Carlos Arnaldo, Rogers Hansine and Nelson C. Zavale

Introduction

Background and objective

Demographic research in Africa is hampered by empirical constrains which affect theoretical formulations. Insufficient, unreliable, outdated, unsystematic and unsegregated demographic data often frustrate efforts to understand population dynamics in the continent (Bongaarts, 2017; Caldwell & Okonjo, 1968; Mbacke, 1994). Conceptual and theoretical frameworks developed to understand demographic phenomena elsewhere have not been able to provide a deeper and satisfying account of demographic dynamics in Africa (Adepoju, 1994), partly because of insufficient data and the tendency to take the African continent as homogenous (Bradshaw, Kaiser, & Ndegwa, 1995; Macamo, 2017; Adepoju, 1994). The pattern and trends of African demographic changes are unique, particularly concerning reproductive choices and their effects on population growth (Bongaarts, 2017; Bongaarts & Casterline, 2013). For instance, the demographic response to persistent poverty across the continent has been baffling. Whereas in some cases, urban poverty has been linked with fertility decline (Gurmu & Mace, 2008), in other cases, it has been associated with high fertility (Weeks, Hill, & Agyei-Mensah, 2008).

Although these problems are well documented across the continent, little is known about Portuguese-speaking African countries (Angola, Cape Verde, Guinea-Bissau, Mozambique and São Tomé and Príncipe). These countries share a similar historical trajectory: they are former Portuguese colonies and were among the last countries to become independent, between 1973 and 1975. Lusophone African countries were among the last countries to establish and develop research institutions, including those for demographic and populations analysis (Beverwijk, 2005). Furthermore, the few research institutions inherited from the Portuguese colonial administration were relatively weak and poorly equipped, and most qualified Portuguese staff, including researchers, were forced to leave after independence (Khan, 2016).

Noteworthily, most of the independent period of the Lusophone countries, in particular Angola, Guinea-Bissau and Mozambique, has been marked by political and military instability. This negatively impacts socioeconomic and political structures and inhibits the normal process

DOI: 10.4324/9780429287213-8

of collecting reliable demographic data. It was not until the mid-1990s that these countries began to experience extended periods of political stability and peace that made it possible to conduct comprehensive censuses and nationally representative surveys.

During the last three decades, demographic research on Lusophone Africa has remained scanty. Little is known about which demographic issues have deserved attention, let alone what the empirical and theoretical issues faced by African countries are. Without pointing at what is known with respect to demography in Lusophone Africa, it is virtually impossible to pinpoint what needs to be done. Our analysis in this chapter aims at documenting the demographic research done on Lusophone African countries during the post-colonial period and tracing directions for future research.

Overview of demographic research in Africa

The state of theoretical demographic debate in Africa is fairly recent (Kirk, 1996). The concern about demographic data gathering and analysis has been presented as urgent. Many African nations have been facing the task of accelerating their socioeconomic transformation, which may be difficult to attain without a systematic understanding of demographic patterns and trends and their relationship with socioeconomic development.

In the 1950s and 1960s, when the majority of African countries obtained their independence, African demography was characterized by early and universal marriage, high fertility and mortality, which led to rapid population growth (Tabutin & Schoumaker, 2004). The demographic transition had not begun, and Africa was viewed as demographically homogeneous. Today, the evidence that demographic transition is underway across the continent is overwhelming, and it is expected that the transition will continue throughout the 21st century despite regional disparities (Bongaarts, 2017; Bongaarts & Casterline, 2013). Theoretically, the onset of demographic transition has been linked with modernization (Davis, 1945) and socio-cultural shifts (Caldwell, 1976) but also with widespread urban poverty (Gurmu & Mace, 2008). In addition, the regional, national and urban versus rural differences in fertility rates have been theoretically linked with different degrees of economic development (Bongaarts, Frank, & Lesthaeghe, 1984), as well as sociocultural differences (Lesthaeghe, 1989).

Since the 1970s, the continent witnessed improvements in demographic data collection, particularly with the World Fertility Survey (WFS) and Demographic and Health Survey (DHS) programmes (Tabutin & Schoumaker, 2004). The analysis of these data showed that the pattern of fertility decline was, in certain nations, disturbed either by continued political and military instability and AIDS or even both. Demographic research in Africa and throughout the developing world has been carried out by research institutions in the global North not only to understand the demographic phenomena but essentially to shape population policies (Ross, 1998). In addition, nuptiality patterns and trends of HIV were and continue to be extensively examined to understand their links with reproductive behaviour.

Adult mortality and migration remain poorly examined. Migration patterns and trends that have been often examined are related to forced migration due to war and natural disasters. Over the years, demographic research on the population and development nexus has primarily been done through studying fertility. Recently, these debates have been taking place under the demographic dividend framework, particularly on whether Africa will harness the economic dividends of the ongoing and potential shifts in the demographic structure driven by the ongoing and expected fertility declines (Bloom, Canning, Fink, & Finlay, 2007; Cleland, 2012; Eastwood & Lipton, 2011).

Lusophone Africa

A brief history

Lusophone African countries[1] became independent between 1973 and 1975 mostly through armed struggle: Guinea-Bissau[2] in 1973 and in 1975 Mozambique, Cape Verde, São Tomé and Príncipe and Angola (Furtado, 2016; Seibert, 2016; Vidal, 2016). Although Cape Verde and São Tomé and Príncipe did not have armed struggles, the independence of these two archipelagos resulted from the liberation struggles in Angola, Guinea-Bissau and Mozambique and the Portuguese Revolution of April 25, 1974 (Seibert, 2016).

The recent history of three of the five Lusophone African countries has been marked by violent armed conflicts. In Angola, the conflict started right after independence and opposed UNITA (*União Nacional para a Independência Total de Angola*) to the government of the MPLA (*Movimento Popular de Libertação de Angola*). A cease-fire agreement was signed in May 1991, but the war resumed after the first multiparty elections held in 1992, when the UNITA opposition contested the victory of the MPLA party at the first round. A new peace protocol was signed in 1994, but all-out war resumed in December 1998 until April 2002, when the last cease-fire agreement was signed (Agadjanian & Prata, 2002). In Mozambique, the conflict started in 1976 and opposed RENAMO (*Resistência Nacional Moçambicana*) to the ruling FRELIMO (*Frente de Libertação de Moçambique*). The conflict ended in 1992 after a General Peace Agreement was signed between the government and RENAMO (Newitt, 1995). Guinea-Bissau did not have a civil war but has been living in continuous political instability marked by incessant cycles of military coups.

Demographic data sources and profile

The history of demographic data collection in the Lusophone countries dates back to the 1930s and 1940s when the series of modern censuses began and was generally repeated decennially up to 1970 (Heisel, 1968; INE, 1999). After independence, with the exception of Cape Verde, in the other countries, the sequence of the census was affected by political instability (Table 6.1).

Other important demographic data sources in Africa are surveys, particularly those conducted under the DHS Program. The only country that has not conducted a DHS is Guinea-Bissau. The Multiple Indicator Cluster Surveys (MICSs), Malaria Indicator Surveys (MISs) and AIDS Indicator Surveys (AISs) are also relevant demographic data sources in these countries (Table 6.1).

The Lusophone African countries belong to the categories of low- and middle-income countries. The gross domestic product (GDP) per capita in 2019 ranged from 491.8 US dollars in Mozambique to 3603.8 US dollars in Cape Verde (World Bank, 2019). The group is home to 66.9 million people, about 5% of Africa's total population (United Nations, 2019). Angola and Mozambique have large population sizes, above 30 million people each, and the remaining countries have relatively smaller population sizes, less than 2 million people. The population growth rate in Angola and Mozambique is above the averages for the continent and sub-Saharan region, about the average in Guinea-Bissau and below the average in Cape Verde and São Tomé and Príncipe. These rates of population growth are consistent with the prevailing high fertility rates and significant declines in mortality throughout Africa. With the exception of Cape Verde, with a total fertility rate (TFR) of 2.3 children per woman, in the remaining countries, the TFR is above 4 children per woman. With the exception of Guinea-Bissau, with a life expectancy at birth of 57.8 years, in the remaining countries, the life expectancy is above 60 years. The use of modern contraception by married women is below 15% in Angola and Guinea-Bissau, between 25 and 40% in Mozambique and São Tomé and Príncipe and above 50% in Cape Verde (Table 6.2).

Table 6.1 Sources of Demographic Data in Lusophone African Countries in the Post-Independence Period

	Numbers of Census or Surveys					
Country	*Censuses*	*DHS*	*MICS*	*MIS*	*AIS*	*Other*
Angola	1	1	4	2		7
Cape Verde	4	1	7			1
Guinea-Bissau	3	0	5			2
Mozambique	4	3	2	1	2	7
São Tomé and Príncipe	4	1	1	5		1

Note: DHS = Demographic and Health Survey; MICS = Multiple Indicator Cluster Survey; MIS = Malaria Indicator Survey; AIS = AIDS Indicator Survey.
Source: National Institutes of Statistics of the respective countries; DHS program website

Table 6.2 Socioeconomic and Demographic Characteristics of Lusophone Countries

Country	*GDP per Capita (2019) (USD)*	*Population in Thousands (2020)*	*Growth Rate (2015–2020) (%)*	*TFT (2015–2020) Children/ Woman)*	*e^0 (2015–2020) (Years)*	*Modern CPR (year) (%)*
Angola	2973.6	32,866	3.29	5.55	60.54	12.5 (2016)
Cape Verde	3603.8	556	1.16	2.29	72.7	57.1 (2005)
Guinea-Bissau	697.8	1968	2.5	4.51	57.82	14.4 (2014)
Mozambique	491.8	31,255	2.9	4.89	60.05	25.3 (2015)
São T. and Príncipe	1994.9	219	1.89	4.35	70.05	37.4 (2014)
Average Africa			2.51	4.44	62.66	
Average sub-Saharan Africa			2.65	4.72	60.52	

Source: United Nations, 2019; World Bank, 2019.

Methods

We have undertaken a systematic review of relevant demographic literature that has targeted the five countries. Our methodological approach applied descriptive meta-summary and meta-narrative typologies of systematic review based on Xiao and Watson (2017). Following the procedures for these typologies of review, we have reviewed the literature in two phases.

Phase 1. Search of relevant publications

We targeted peer-reviewed articles about demographic topics focusing on the five countries as an empirical field of research, authored by scholars affiliated with African and non-African institutions, published since 1975. The search was undertaken in three sub-phases.

First, a Boolean search was made in main scientific databases, namely Web of Science (WoS) and Scopus, combining the following keywords: "population dynamics", "fertility", "reproductive health", "mortality", "migration", "demographic dividend" and the individual names of the five Lusophone African countries. In order to ensure that all possible research is traced, we have additionally searched, in WoS and Scopus, publications appearing in each journal authored by African countries/institutions. Moreover, as some publications are not traced by WoS and

Scopus, a search in volumes and issues of each journal was made (for a complete list, see Appendix Table 6.1). If a journal was systematic in publishing relevant research, an individualized search, including in the journal's webpage, was made.

Second, articles published in African non-indexed journals were targeted. This was done because most of Africa's science is published in internationally non-indexed and less visible

Appendix Table 6.1 List of Journals

No.	*Name of Journal*
1	*African Journal of Reproductive Health*
2	*Aids*
3	*Aids Education and Prevention*
4	*American Journal of Tropical Medicine and Hygiene*
5	*BMC Public Health*
6	*BMC Women's Health*
7	*BMJ Global Health*
8	*Cadernos De Saúde Pública*
9	*Ciência & Saúde Coletiva*
10	*Demographic Research*
11	*Demography*
12	*Epidemiology and Infection*
13	*Family Medicine and Community Health*
14	*Geoforum*
15	*Global Public Health*
16	*Health & Place*
17	*International Journal of Epidemiology*
18	*International Journal of Health Geographics*
19	*International Migration*
20	*International Migration Review*
21	*Journal of Biosocial Science*
22	*Journal of Family Planning and Reproductive Health Care*
23	*Journal of Global Health*
24	*Journal of Health Population and Nutrition*
25	*Journal of International Migration and Integration*
26	*Journal of Marriage and Family*
27	*Journal of Population Research*
28	*Journal of Southern African Studies*
29	*Lancet Global Health*
30	*Open Access Journal of Contraception*
31	*PLoS One*
32	*Population Studies-A Journal of Demography*
33	*Public Health*
34	*Reproductive Health*
35	*Research in Economics*
36	*Social Biology*
37	*Social Forces*
38	*Social Science & Medicine*
39	*Studies in Family Planning*
40	*Tijdschrift Voor Economische En Sociale Geografie*

(*Continued*)

Appendix Table 6.1 (Continued)

No.	*Name of Journal*
41	*Transactions of The Royal Society of Tropical Medicine and Hygiene*
42	*Tropical Doctor*
43	*Tropical Medicine & International Health*

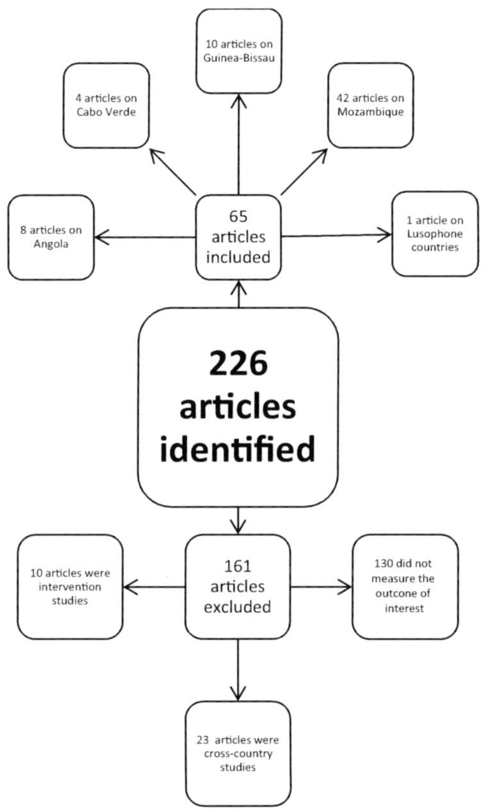

Figure 6.1 Inclusion and exclusion criteria

outlets (Tijssen, 2007). Nevertheless, given prevailing predatory publishing practices (Mouton & Valentine, 2017), the review strived to include journals with minimum quality standards. Two databases were used for this purpose: the African Journal Online[3] (AJO) and Scielo[4] databases.

During the search, we read the titles and abstracts and, whenever necessary, full texts to see if a publication fit our inclusion criterion. We targeted studies that had a demographic (fertility, mortality and migration) or proximate determinant of fertility (Bongaarts, 1978) as an outcome conducted on a Lusophone country from 1975 to 2020. The search identified a total of 226 articles, which are composed of 216 original articles and 10 intervention studies. Of the 226 articles, 161 articles were excluded because they did not measure the outcome of interest (130), were intervention studies (10) or were cross-country studies where the Lusophone countries appeared among a group of non-Lusophone countries (23). Therefore, 65 articles were included in the study, as shown in Figure 6.1.

Our methodology and sample size have the shortcoming of not including books, book chapters and edited books (hereafter referred to as books). Although we recognize books as relevant publication venues of demographic research, they are difficult to trace through conventional available online scientific database and indexes. Nevertheless, we believe that reviewing journal articles allows a reliable portrait of the state of literature, given that some books usually report, in a comprehensive and aggregate way, findings that first appeared in journal articles.

Demographic research in Lusophone Africa

We present the findings in three sections: 1) quantitative portrait of demographic research focusing on the five countries under analysis, 2) analysis of the main research findings and 3) directions for future research.

Quantitative overview

Countries' coverage

The review validated 65 studies conducted on five Lusophone African countries. More than half (42) focused on Mozambique, 10 on Guinea-Bissau, 8 on Angola and 4 on Cape Verde (Figure 6.1). There were no articles on São Tomé and Príncipe. The five countries have different levels of research capabilities or are not equally preferred as empirical sites of research. Mozambique is more targeted and seems to have stronger capabilities. Mozambique is home to the top-ranked university in Lusophone Africa, the Eduardo Mondlane University (see, e.g., Webometrics ranking), but its eventual stronger research capabilities may not be domestic but rather associated with stronger collaboration or connectivity of Mozambican scholars with foreign scholars. In fact, 60 out of 65 studies were either authored or co-authored by non-Lusophone-based researchers.

Temporal evolution

Figure 6.2 shows that most of the published research (60) we analysed is rather recent, published from 2000 onwards. This is consistent with the tragic post-colonial history of Lusophone Africa we described previously, which essentially affected most Lusophone countries from the 1970s to the early 1990s. Although the spectrum of armed and structural violence has not completely disappeared (particularly in Guinea-Bissau and Mozambique), it has dropped considerably, at least from the mid-1990s. A more peaceful environment may have contributed to the strengthening of research capacities and the rising trend in published demographic research.

Methodological approaches

Quantitative studies are overrepresented: of the 65 articles, 53 were quantitative research, 9 were qualitative and 3 used mixed methods. In addition, 8 used census data and 51 analysed survey data, of which 9 were nationally representative surveys and 42 were subnational or small-area surveys. While the dominance of quantitative data suggests that most studies are also methodologically underpinned by demography's dominant tradition of relying on a quantitative approach, qualitative and more in-depth studies are still needed to understand in full the demographic reality of Lusophone Africa.

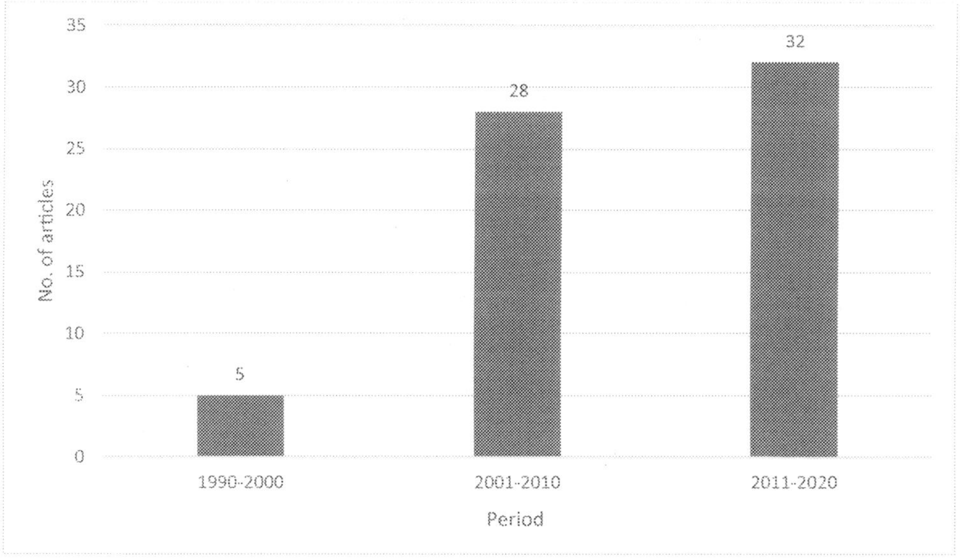

Figure 6.2 Evolution of reviewed articles

Thematic portrait

Table 6.3 shows that most articles cover three themes: fertility and reproductive health (25), mortality (22) and migration (14). Population dynamics and conflict are the least-researched topics, with only 4 studies all together targeting these topics. While the dominance of fertility and mortality is consistent with rather poor demographic profile of these countries and the significant presence of migration also consistent with the history of emigration in Cape Verde and Mozambique, the fact that *conflict* is among the under-researched topics is curious given the history of conflict in these countries. This suggests that topics like population dynamics and conflict should be targeted by future research, as well as the mortality, fertility and migration dynamics of less researched countries.

Fertility and reproductive health

Understanding fertility transition in Africa has been drawing the attention of demographers during the last three decades (Adegbola, 1988; Adewuyi, 1988; Caldwell & Caldwell, 1990; Caldwell, Orubuloye, & Caldwell, 1992; Cohen, 1998; Eastwood & Lipton, 2011; Ortega, 2008). In Lusophone countries, the dynamics of fertility transition are hardly known. Most studies are on Mozambique, some on Angola and Cape Verde and none on Guinea-Bissau and São Tomé and Príncipe (Table 6.4). The review paints a picture of countries that are generally at the initial stages of fertility transition, characterized by high fertility related to early start of childbearing and low contraceptive use (Agadjanian & Prata, 2001, 2002; Arnaldo, 2004; Cau, 2015). In Mozambique (Agadjanian, 1998; Arnaldo, 2004; Cau, 2015, 2016) and Angola (Agadjanian & Prata, 2001, 2002), urban residence and education are found to be the main drivers of both fertility decline and modern contraceptive use.

Table 6.3 Reviewed Articles by Country and Thematic Area

Countries	*Thematic Area*					*Total*
	Fertility and Reproductive Health	*Mortality*	*Migration*	*Population Dynamics*	*Conflict*	
Angola	4	0	2	0	2	8
Cape Verde	1	0	3	0	0	4
Guinea-Bissau	0	10	0	0	1	11
Mozambique	20	12	8	1	0	41
Group of Lusophone countries	0	0	1	0	0	1
Total	25	22	14	1	3	65

Agadjanian, Hayford and colleagues showed that in southern Mozambique, sociocultural factors at both individual and community levels, perception of HIV risk and possession or access to material goods and men's labour migration shape reproductive behaviour (Agadjanian, 2000, 2013; Agadjanian & Hayford, 2018; Agadjanian, Yabiku, & Cau, 2011; Hayford & Agadjanian, 2017, 2019; Hayford, Agadjanian, & Luz, 2012). Hayford and Agadjanian found evidence of the usefulness of demographic surveys to measure fertility desires. Data on the desire to stop childbearing in that context neither nearly followed nor completely diverged from classic demographic models of fertility preferences (Hayford & Agadjanian, 2017). There was strong evidence for a postponement mindset in the population, a coexistence of postponement with stopping and spacing goals and some consistency between the desire and the actual behaviour (Hayford & Agadjanian, 2019).

A number of the reviewed articles paid attention to reproductive health issues, particularly contraceptive use and reproductive health of adolescents and youth. Studies focusing on contraceptive use have highlighted the role of contextual factors such as community norms and cultural habits (Cau, 2015) and the influence of characteristics of host communities in urban areas (Cau, 2016) in shaping migrant women's contraceptive knowledge and usage.

Early sexual activity and childbearing are common characteristics of Lusophone countries (Frederico, Michielsen, Arnaldo, & Decat, 2018; Morris & Prata, 2018; Prata, Morris, Mazive, Vahidnia, & Stehr, 2006; Rosário, Gomes, Brito, & Costa, 2019; Speizer & White, 2008; Tavares, Schor, França Junior, & Diniz, 2009; Villela, Lima, & Brito, 2018). Early sexual initiation is rarely followed by condom use. This puts adolescents not only at risk of an early and unintended pregnancy that can result in unsafe and illegal abortion but also puts them at risk of contracting sexually transmitted infections (STIs), including HIV. However, in Cape Verde, there is a high prevalence of condom use, and adolescents are able to begin sexual activity relatively safe from STIs (Tavares et al., 2009). The reviews show that biological (Jaén-Sánchez et al., 2020) and sociocultural factors are associated with adolescent childbearing behaviour (Frederico et al., 2018; Rosário et al., 2019; Speizer & White, 2008). Speizer and White (2008), on Mozambique, show that youth fertility desires are important factors in adolescent early and unsafe sexual activity, since youth who intend to became pregnant soon are more likely to engage in unprotected sex with nonmarital partners.

Although fertility can be influenced by conflict (see Lindstrom & Berhanu, 1999), and three of the five Lusophone countries have been under some kind of conflict throughout most of their recent history, few studies on the effect of conflict on demographic behaviour, fertility in particular, were identified. Studies in Angola (Agadjanian & Prata, 2001, 2002; W. Avogo &

Table 6.4 Patterns and Determinants of Demographic Behaviour in Lusophone African Countries

No.	*Title*	*Year/Country*	*Thematic Area*	*Study Type*	*Pattern and Determinants of Demographic Behaviour*
1	Persistent and acute diarrhoea as the leading causes of child mortality in urban Guinea-Bissau	1992/Guinea-Bissau	Mortality	Survey/longitudinal	Persistent and acute diarrhoea were the most frequent causes of death, accounting for 43 and 31 deaths per 1000 children, respectively. Fever deaths (possibly malaria), neonatal deaths, acute respiratory infections and measles were other frequent causes (Mølbak et al., 1992).
2	Reason for termination of breastfeeding and the length of breastfeeding	1996/Guinea-Bissau	Mortality	Survey/longitudinal	The median weaning age was 22.6 months; illness of the child, new pregnancy of the mother and illness of the mother were associated with a significantly shorter lactation period compared with children weaned because they were "healthy" or "old enough" (M. S. Jakobsen et al., 1996).
3	Termination of breastfeeding after 12 months of age due to a new pregnancy and other causes is associated with increased mortality in Guinea-Bissau	2003/Guinea-Bissau	Mortality	Survey/longitudinal	Median length of breastfeeding was 22 months. Following termination of breastfeeding, 66 children died before 36 months of age. In all, 62% (879/1423) were weaned because they were 'healthy'. Compared with the "healthy" children; all other causes of weaning were associated with a higher mortality (mortality ratio [MR] = 2.97, 95% CI: 1.54–5.73) (M. S. Jakobsen et al., 2003).
4	Changes in prevalence and incidence of HIV-1, HIV-2 and dual infections in urban areas of Bissau, Guinea-Bissau: is HIV-2 disappearing?	2008/Guinea-Bissau	Mortality	Survey/cross-sectional	The incidence rate between 1996 and 2006 was 0.5 per 100 person-years for HIV-1 and 0.24 per 100 person-years for HIV-2. Compared with a previous period from 1987 to 1996, the incidence of HIV-2 is declining, whereas no significant increase in the incidence of HIV-1 was observed (da Silva et al., 2008).
5	Trends and determinants of mortality in women of reproductive age in rural Guinea-Bissau, West Africa – a cohort study	2013/Guinea-Bissau	Mortality	Survey/longitudinal	We followed 27,185 women of reproductive age (WRA) for 141,693 person-years-at-risk (PYO), among whom 9093 moved out and 1006 died. Overall standardized mortality rate was 759 per 100,000 PYO. WRA mortality did not decline (Mane et al., 2013).
6	Breastfeeding status as a predictor of mortality among refugee children in an emergency situation in Guinea-Bissau	2003/Guinea-Bissau	Mortality	Survey/cross-sectional	Controlling for age, weaned children experienced a six-fold higher mortality [mortality rate (MR) = 5.73 (95% CI 2.40–13.71)] during the first 3 months of the war compared with children still breastfeeding (M. Jakobsen et al., 2003).

(*Continued*)

Table 6.4 (Continued)

No.	*Title*	*Year/Country*	*Thematic Area*	*Study Type*	*Pattern and Determinants of Demographic Behaviour*
7	Knowledge and reported practices of men and women on maternal and child health in rural Guinea Bissau: a cross sectional survey	2010/Guinea-Bissau	Mortality	Survey/cross-sectional	There are low levels of appropriate knowledge on child health, some inappropriate practices and generally low vaccination coverage. Health knowledge scores improve significantly amongst those who have accessed higher education. Differences in health knowledge between women and men become insignificant once age and education are accounted for (King et al., 2010).
8	Cause of death among people with retroviral infection in rural Guinea-Bissau	2010/Guinea-Bissau	Mortality	Survey/cross-sectional	The results were reviewed by two doctors to conclude cause of death. A cause of death was agreed upon for 49/84 subjects. Nineteen of these 49 were infected with HIV-2 alone and 7 with both HIV-2 and HTLV-1. Among these, the main causes of death were pulmonary tuberculosis (n = 5), AIDS (n = 5), cerebrovascular accident (n = 5), sepsis (n = 3) and hepatocellular carcinoma (n = 2). Death associated with traditional HIV-related causes was implicated in 13/26 (50%) of those with HIV-2 (Cooper et al., 2010).
9	Temporal trends (1977–2007) and ethnic inequity in child mortality in rural villages of southern Guinea Bissau	2011/Guinea-Bissau	Mortality	Survey/cross-sectional	High levels of child mortality were found at all ages under five, with a significant reduction in child mortality over the time periods of birth except for 1997–2001. That period comprises the 1998/99 civil war interval, when child mortality was 1.5% higher than in the previous period (Fazzio et al., 2011).
10	Causes of death among women aged 17–49 years between 2007 and 2010 in Maputo, Mozambique	2017/Mozambique	Mortality	Mixed	A total of 9640 deaths (6510 for residents of Maputo City) were registered, and 77% had a specified cause of death reported. HIV deaths represented 36% of all deaths and 40% among 25–39-year-olds. The death rate did not increase linearly by age, as there was a peak among women aged 30–34 years (Parkkali et al., 2017).
11	Inequalities in child mortality in Mozambique: differentials by parental socio-economic position	2003/Mozambique	Mortality	Survey/cross-sectional	The results partly showed a parental socioeconomic gradient of infant and child mortality in Mozambique. Father's education seemed to reflect the family's social standing in the Mozambique context, showing a strong statistical association with post-neonatal and child mortality (Macassa, Ghilagaber, Bernhardt, Diderichsen et al., 2003).

12	Trends in infant and child mortality in Mozambique during and after a period of conflict	2003/ Mozambique	Mortality	Survey/cross-sectional	The levels of infant, child and under-5 mortality were considerably higher in rural than in urban areas. The difference in mortality between urban and rural areas increased over time until 1988–1992 and thereafter diminished (Macassa, Ghilagaber, Bernhardt, & Burstrom, 2003).
13	Impact of maternal human immunodeficiency virus infection on birth outcomes and infant survival in rural Mozambique	2009/ Mozambique	Mortality	Survey/ longitudinal	Women positive for HIV were more likely to have anaemia at delivery than women negative for HIV (51.3% versus 35.4%; $P < 0.001$). Infants born to HIV-positive mothers had a significantly higher post-neonatal mortality rate than infants born to HIV-negative mothers (7.8% versus 1.9%; $P < 0.001$). The rate of transmission of HIV by breastfeeding during the first year of life was 15.1% (95% confidence interval = CI 7.6–22.4) (Naniche et al., 2009).
14	A 10-year study of the cause of death in children under 15 years in Manhica, Mozambique	2009/ Mozambique	Mortality	Survey/ longitudinal	From January 1997 to December 2006, 568,499 person-year at risk (pyrs) and 10,037 deaths were recorded in the Manhica DSS. 3730 deaths with 246,658 pyrs were recorded for children under 15 years of age. Verbal autopsy interviews were conducted on 3002 (80.4%) of these deaths. 73.6% of deaths were attributed to communicable diseases; non-communicable diseases accounted for 9.5% of the defined causes of death and injuries for 3.9% of causes of deaths. Malaria was the single largest cause, accounting for 21.8% of cases. Pneumonia, with 9.8%, was the second leading cause of death, followed by HIV/AIDS (8.3%) and diarrhoeal diseases, with 8% (Sacarlal et al., 2009).
15	Spatio-temporal analysis of mortality among children under the age of five in Manhica (Mozambique) during the period 1997–2005	2011/ Mozambique	Mortality	Survey/ longitudinal	The results showed that childhood mortality in all the areas was modified from year to year, describing a convex time trend, but the spatial pattern described by the neighbourhood-specific underlying mortality rates did not change during the entire period from 1997 to 2005, where neighbourhoods with highest risks are situated in the peripheral side of the district (Escaramís et al., 2011).

(*Continued*)

Table 6.4 (Continued)

No.	*Title*	*Year/Country*	*Thematic Area*	*Study Type*	*Pattern and Determinants of Demographic Behaviour*
16	Labour migration and child mortality in Mozambique	2012/ Mozambique	Mortality	Survey/ longitudinal	We find no difference in mortality rates across migrant and nonemigrant men's children. When we separated successful from unsuccessful migration based on the wife's perception, however, stark contrasts emerge: children of successful migrants have the lowest mortality, followed by children of non-migrant men, followed by children of unsuccessful migrants (Yabiku et al., 2012).
17	Geographic differentials in mortality of children in Mozambique: their implications for achievement of Millennium Development Goal 4	2012/ Mozambique	Mortality	Survey/cross-sectional	Results of univariate and multivariate analyses showed a significant association between under-5 mortality and province (region) of mother's residence. Children of mothers living in the North provinces (Niassa, Cabo Delgado and Nampula) and the Central provinces (Zambezia, Sofala, Manica and Tete) had higher risks of mortality than children whose mothers lived in the South provinces, especially Maputo province and Maputo city (Macassa et al., 2012).
18	Religious affiliation and under-five mortality in Mozambique	2013/ Mozambique	Mortality	Survey/cross-sectional	Mother's affiliation with any religious organization, as compared with non-affiliation, has a significant positive effect on child survival, net of education and other socio-demographic factors (Cau et al., 2013).
19	Effects of health-system strengthening on under-5, infant, and neonatal mortality: 11-year provincial-level time-series analyses in Mozambique	2014/ Mozambique	Mortality	Survey/cross-sectional	Under-5 mortality rate was heterogeneous across provinces, with yearly decreases ranging from 11.1% (Nampula) to 1.9% (Maputo Province). Heterogeneity was greater for neonatal mortality rate, with only 7 of 11 provinces showing significant yearly decreases, ranging from 13.6% (Nampula) to 4.2% (Zambezia) (Fernandes et al., 2014).
20	Estimated coverage of death counts and adult mortality in Mozambique based on census data	2015/ Mozambique	Mortality	Survey/cross-sectional	The 2007 census enumerated between 65% and 90% of deaths in Mozambique, suggesting that mortality estimates using direct methods underestimate mortality in the country. The study showed that there has been progress in the quality of death counts in the census and that in the absence of high-quality vital statistics, population censuses can be a good source of mortality data in developing countries (Alberto & Queiroz, 2015).

21	Intervention heroes of Mozambique from 1997 to 2015: estimates of maternal and child lives saved using the lives saved tool	2018/ Mozambique	Mortality	Survey/cross-sectional	Our modelled estimates show that increases in intervention coverage from 1997 to 2011 saved an additional 422,282 child lives (0–59 months), 85,450 neonatal lives (0–1 month), and 6528 maternal lives beyond those already being saved at baseline coverage levels in 1997 (Macicame et al., 2018).
22	Improving sexual and reproductive health knowledge and practice in Mozambican families with media campaign and volunteer family health champions	2019/ Mozambique	Mortality	Survey/cross-sectional	A health education intervention, using a media campaign and local volunteers, is useful to promote mother and child health. There is an unmet need for family planning, and the use of modern contraception is below desired practice, needing further research about cultural barriers (Pires, Siemens, & Mupueleque, 2019).
23	Mortality patterns during a war in Guinea-Bissau 1998–99: changes in risk factors?	2006/Guinea-Bissau	Mortality	Survey/ longitudinal	In the first half-year, the mortality rate saw a 78% [mortality ratio (MR) = 1.78; 95% CI 1.61–1.97] increase, and mortality for children < 5 years of age doubled (MR = 2.07; 95% CI 1.79–2.38). In the last 6 months of the war, mortality was slightly increased for children and not at all for the total population (Nielsen, Jensen, Andersen, & Aaby, 2005).
24	Forced migration and child health and mortality in Angola	2010/Angola	Migration	Survey/cross-sectional	Authors observe a disadvantage of forced migrants, but this disadvantage is explained by other characteristics. When looking at the place of delivery, number of antenatal consultations and age-adequate immunization of children born in Luanda, we again detect a disadvantage of forced migrants relative to non-migrants, but now this disadvantage also extends to migrants who came to Luanda for reasons other than war. No differences across the three groups in child morbidity and related health care-seeking behaviour in the two weeks preceding the survey are found (W. A. Avogo & Agadjanian, 2010).

(*Continued*)

Table 6.4 (Continued)

No.	*Title*	*Year/Country*	*Thematic Area*	*Study Type*	*Pattern and Determinants of Demographic Behaviour*
25	Forced migration and HIV/AIDS risks in Angola	2008/Angola	Migration	Survey/cross-sectional	The analysis detects differences between forced migrants and the other groups in HIV/AIDS-related knowledge and attitudes, but these differences are explained away by the demographic characteristics and socioeconomic disadvantages of forced migrants. With respect to behaviour, we find that regardless of other characteristics, forced migrant men are more likely to engage in practices that may lead to increased HIV risks than long-time male city dwellers (Agadjanian & W. Avogo, 2008).
26	Luanda – Holanda: irregular migration from Angola to the Netherlands	2010/Angola	Migration	Mixed	The study shows that the migrants can be described as opportunity-seeking migrants rather than survival migrants. Most migrants made no use of typical human smugglers during their travel. They rather used assistance from their social network and the services of middlemen, called *esquemas*, on an ad-hoc basis (Van Wijk, 2010).
27	Toward a demography of immigrant communities and their transnational potential	2008/Cape Verde	Migration	Mixed	The article explores relationships between the demographic structure of immigrant populations and their transnational orientation. The analyses are demonstrated empirically through a case study of migration from Cape Verde to the Netherlands (Carling, 2008).
28	Mobility at the heart of a nation: patterns and meanings of Cape Verdean migration	2009/Cape Verde	Migration	Qualitative	The article traces the changing migration flows to, through and from the archipelago. These trends are related to developments in transportation technology and changes in the world economy, which have created fluctuations in the attractiveness of Cape Verde's location (Carling & Åkesson, 2009).
29	The queue outside the embassy: remittances, inequality and restrictive migration regimes	2013/Cape Verde	Migration	Qualitative	The article demonstrates that remittances in some cases benefit the poorest in Cape Verde and that this has to do with the long history of migration, which means that nearly everyone, irrespective of class, has a close relative abroad. It also shows that Cape Verdeans generally receive quite small amounts of money, which implies that they are seldom able to improve their economic situation in a more substantial way (Åkesson, 2013).

30	Information and refugee migration: The case of Mozambicans in Malawi	1996/ Mozambique	Migration	Qualitative	The decision-making of refugees can be critically compared with that of other migrants. Refugees also receive and evaluate information about prospective destinations in the decision-making process. This hypothesis was tested in the context of Mozambican refugees in Malawi in 1992 and 1993 (Koser, 1996).
31	From circular migrants in the mines to transnational polygynists in the townships: a century of transformation in central Mozambican male migration regimes (1900–1999)	2009/ Mozambique	Migration	Qualitative (historical analysis)	This article tracks the most significant transformations in the international migration regime between central Mozambique and South Africa throughout the twentieth century as the product of complex and continuous interactions between the broader political-economic environment and local forms of gendered and inter-generational social struggle (Lubkemann, 2009).
32	Husbands' labour migration and wives' autonomy, Mozambique 2000–2006	2010/ Mozambique	Migration	Survey/cross-sectional	Results show that both men's cumulative migration history and current migration status are positively associated with women's autonomy and that the effects on autonomy may persist even after the man's return. Three intervening factors, women's employment outside the home, lower fertility and residential independence from extended family members, did not fully mediate the effects of men's labour migration (Yabiku et al., 2010).
33	Social networks and undocumented Mozambican migration to South Africa	2010/ Mozambique	Migration	Mixed	Migrant social networks are not limited to a spatially bounded area; they transcend geography, location and territory; can be considered spatial conveyors of social capital; and operate transnationally at three different locations: in the sending communities, on borders and in the destination areas (Muanamoha et al., 2010).
34	Men's migration and women's fertility in rural Mozambique	2011/ Mozambique	Migration	Survey/ longitudinal	The model detects a lower birth rate among migrants' wives, which tends to be partially compensated for by an increased birth rate upon cessation of migration (Agadjanian et al., 2011).
35	Health costs of wealth gains: labor migration and perceptions of HIV/AIDS risks in Mozambique	2011/ Mozambique	Migration	Survey/ longitudinal	The analysis finds that the economic success of men's migration, rather than migration itself, significantly predicts women's worries about getting infected by their husbands or their own extramarital partners and their husbands' stance on condom use (Agadjanian et al., 2011).

(Continued)

Table 6.4 (Continued)

No.	*Title*	*Year/Country*	*Thematic Area*	*Study Type*	*Pattern and Determinants of Demographic Behaviour*
36	Father's migration and leaving the parental home in rural Mozambique	2016/ Mozambique	Migration	Survey/ longitudinal	The results showed that father's migration delays home-leaving for adolescent girls and that these effects are not mediated by school enrolment. The results for boys were inconclusive (Chae et al., 2016).
37	International migration and informal social protection in rural Mozambique	2017/ Mozambique	Migration	Qualitative	Results show that migration associated with remittances increases community group participation. In particular, while there is no significant relationship with group membership related to credit or self-help activities, remittance recipients are more likely to join groups that provide insurance (Mendola, 2017).
38	Looking (also) at the other side of the story. resilience processes in migrants	2016/CC_ PALOPs	Migration	Qualitative	The study identifies and explains the resources used by migrants to overcome adversity in the host countries. The thematic analysis revealed five main themes in the adversity dimension, with some of its topics further grouped in specific subtopics: socioeconomic changes, difficulties in relating to structures of social organization, insufficient proficiency of the language, rejection and devaluation and culture shock (Roberto & Moleiro, 2016).
39	Economic security, informational resources, and women's reproductive choices in urban Mozambique	1998/ Mozambique	Fertility and reproductive health	Survey/cross-sectional	The study found that women's perception of their material conditions and socioeconomic security were the main drivers of the intention to stop childbearing, while women's exposure to Western-origin information and technologies was the main driver of contraceptive use in Maputo (Agadjanian, 1998).
40	Religion, social milieu, and the contraceptive revolution	2001/ Mozambique	Fertility and reproductive health	Survey/cross-sectional	A socioculturally diverse religious social environment favours the exchange of reproductive experiences, which promotes the use of contraception (Agadjanian, 2001b).
41	Religious denomination, religious involvement, and modern contraceptive use in southern Mozambique.	2013/ Mozambique	Fertility and reproductive health	Survey/cross-sectional	The study shows that religious belonging and involvement are important predictors of contraceptive use in rural southern Mozambique. Women of Catholic and traditional Protestant relations had high contraceptive use compared to women of other religions and frequent religious attendance was positively associated with contraceptive use (Agadjanian, 2013).

42	Women's work and fertility in a sub-Saharan urban setting: a social environment approach	2000/ Mozambique	Fertility and reproductive health	Survey/cross-sectional	The findings show that women who work in more collectivized environments have fewer children and are more likely to use modern contraception than women who work in more individualized environments and those who do not work outside the home (Agadjanian, 2000).
43	Negotiating through reproductive change: gendered social interaction and fertility regulation in Mozambique	2001/ Mozambique	Fertility and reproductive health	Qualitative	The study finds that informal social interaction is important in shaping reproductive choices. Gender matters in the interactions, as men and women focus on different aspects of fertility and family planning and construe them in distinctly gendered ways (Agadjanian, 2001a).
44	HIV status, fertility intentions, and contraception in the area of expanded access to antiretroviral therapy: a case study of rural southern Mozambique	2018/ Mozambique	Fertility and reproductive health	Survey/cross-sectional	The findings for a study of HIV-positive and HIV-negative women who had given birth show that HIV status did not influence contraceptive use but had some moderating effect on fertility intentions in a context of a rapid widening of access to post-partum antiretroviral therapy in southern Mozambique (Agadjanian & Hayford, 2018).
45	War and reproduction: Angola's fertility in a comparative perspective	2001/Angola	Fertility and reproductive health	Survey/cross-sectional	The study suggests a depressive effect of war on fertility, with fertility dropping in periods of hostility peaks and rebounding in the periods of less hostility. These fluctuations were more pronounced in the most affected regions (Agadjanian & Prata, 2001).
46	War, peace and fertility in Angola	2002/Angola	Fertility and reproductive health	Survey/cross-sectional	The study shows evidence of a wartime drop and a post-war rebound in fertility and fertility intentions. These trends vary greatly, depending on the type and degree of exposure to war, urban rural residence and women's socioeconomic characteristics (Agadjanian & Prata, 2002).
47	Regional fertility trends in Mozambique	2004/ Mozambique	Fertility and reproductive health	Census/survey/ cross-sectional	The study documents the beginning of fertility decline in Mozambique but with regional differences in the magnitude of the decline. In the southern region, the fertility decline was well established, while in northern and central regions, the decline was still incipient (Arnaldo, 2004).

(*Continued*)

Table 6.4 (Continued)

No.	*Title*	*Year/Country*	*Thematic Area*	*Study Type*	*Pattern and Determinants of Demographic Behaviour*
48	Community influences on contraceptive use in Mozambique	2015/ Mozambique	Fertility and reproductive health	Survey/cross-sectional	In examining the mechanisms through which community context may influence the use of modern methods of contraception in Mozambique, the study found that community context influences modern contraceptive use by shaping the state of women's empowerment and accessibility and quality of family planning services in the community and by keeping strong fertility desires in the community (Cau, 2015).
49	Female migration, local context and contraception use in urban Mozambique	2016/ Mozambique	Fertility and reproductive health	Survey/cross-sectional	The study found that recent female rural-urban migrants are likely not to use modern contraceptives. the context of migrant-receiving areas in urban areas is important in shaping migrants' use of contraceptives. The characteristics of destination communities in urban areas are determinant in helping recent female migrants to adapt to urban lifestyle and use contraception (Cau, 2016).
50	Assessing women's satisfaction with family planning services in Mozambique	2017/ Mozambique	Fertility and reproductive health	Survey/cross-sectional	This study reported levels of overall satisfaction among women using family planning (FP) services in Mozambique. Provider/client interaction played an important role in determining the level of women's satisfaction. However, a waiting time of more than 4 hours, self-employment and wage employment were associated with women's dissatisfaction with the services (Chavane et al., 2017).
51	The National Reproductive Health Programme in Cape Verde: scope, limits and challenges	2018/Cape Verde	Fertility and reproductive health	Qualitative	This study reflected on the Cape Verde National Reproductive Health Program and found that it has been relevant for the reduction in maternal and infant mortality and the possibility of Cape Verdean women's control over decisions related to reproduction. However, the country's socio-cultural transitional process, the characteristics of the primary health services and the organization of health services and practices are still a challenge (Villela et al., 2018).

52	Factors influencing abortion decision-making processes among young women	2018/ Mozambique	Fertility and reproductive health	Qualitative	The study explores the individual, interpersonal and environmental factors behind the abortion decision-making process among young women experiencing unwanted pregnancy in two urban areas in Mozambique. It found that a low degree of autonomy for women (gender and power inequalities obstructed young women in making their decision with autonomy), the limited availability of health facilities providing abortion services and a lack of patient-centeredness of health services are the main barriers for young women to access abortion services (Frederico et al., 2018).
53	Now or never: perceived HIV status and fertility intentions in rural Mozambique	2012/ Mozambique	Fertility and reproductive health	Survey/cross-sectional	The study suggests that HIV infection might be incompatible with childbearing in the long run, as higher perceived risk of HIV infection was associated with the likelihood of wanting to speed up childbearing and wanting to stop having children. The decision to limit or accelerate childbearing is driven by uncertainty about the long-term outcomes (Hayford et al., 2012).
54	From desires to behaviour: Moderating factors in a fertility transition	2012/ Mozambique	Fertility and reproductive health	Survey/cross-sectional	The study found that fertility preferences have predictive power to explain fertility behaviour beyond the variance explained by sociodemographic characteristics. Also, individual and community characteristics moderate the correspondence between preferences and behaviour for women who want to stop childbearing (Hayford & Agadjanian, 2012).
55	Adolescent motherhood in Mozambique. consequences for pregnant women and new-borns	2020/ Mozambique	Fertility and reproductive health	Survey/cross-sectional	The study found a significant association between adolescent pregnancy and lower body mass index and follow-up during pregnancy (Jaén-Sánchez et al., 2020).
56	Abortion history and its association with current use of modern contraceptive methods in Luanda, Angola	2018/Angola	Fertility and reproductive health	Survey/cross-sectional	The history of induced abortion was associated with use of a modern contraceptive method in Luanda, Angola. The most common contraceptive used by women with a history of induced abortion was condoms, indicating that despite adoption of a modern method, many women are still at risk for an unintended pregnancy (Morris & Prata, 2018).

(Continued)

Table 6.4 (Continued)

No.	*Title*	*Year/Country*	*Thematic Area*	*Study Type*	*Pattern and Determinants of Demographic Behaviour*
57	Partner support for family planning and modern contraceptive use in Luanda, Angola.	2017/Angola	Fertility and reproductive health	Survey/cross-sectional	This study examined the role of husband/partner in contraceptive use in Luanda (Angola) and found that perceived husband/partner approval of family planning was strongly associated with current contraceptive use. These results suggest that intervention aimed at promoting male involvement in FP may significantly increase contraceptive use (Prata et al., 2017).
58	Determinants of maternal health care and birth outcome in the Dande Health and Demographic Surveillance System area, Angola	2019/Angola	Fertility and reproductive health	Survey/cross-sectional	The study identified factors that influence the utilization of health services by pregnant women and the associated risk factors for pregnancy outcome. Having at least one antenatal care (ANC) visit decreased the odds of stillbirth and abortion. Also, ANC attendance was associated with institutional delivery. The study suggested the existence of difficulties in the implementation of more demanding models of access to maternal health care. Rich-poor and rural-urban gaps persisted in women's access to maternal health care services. Essential improvements were needed in the country's capacity to address the determinants of maternal health and to adopt more appropriate interventions for local contexts (Rosário et al., 2019).
59	The unintended consequences of intended pregnancies: youth, condom use, and HIV transmission in Mozambique	2008/ Mozambique	Fertility and reproductive health	Survey/cross-sectional	This study demonstrates the importance of considering youth fertility desires in assessments of youth HIV risk and HIV prevention programs for youth. Youth who wanted to get pregnant soon were significantly less likely to use condoms with nonmarital partners than were youth who wanted to delay childbearing (Speizer & White, 2008).
60	Factors associated with sexual initiation and condom use among adolescents on Santiago Island, Cape Verde, West Africa	2009/Cape Verde	Fertility and reproductive health	Survey/cross-sectional	This study found that in Santiago Island (Cape Verde), there were a high prevalence of condom use during initial sexual activity. Adolescents were able to safely begin sexually active life if they had access to information, sex education and other STD prevention and contraceptive methods. Sexual initiation was found to be associated with age over 14 years, Catholic religion and alcohol consumption among boys and with 9 years of schooling and involvement in an affective-sexual relationship, among girls (Tavares et al., 2009).

61	Relationship between HIV risk perception and condom use: evidence from a population-based survey in Mozambique	2006/ Mozambique	Fertility and reproductive health	Survey/cross-sectional	The study found a tendency for young adults, especially young men, to underestimate their risk of contracting HIV. Even though men and women overall had accurate knowledge of HIV transmission modes, they did not know how to assess their risk. Having known someone with AIDS, having used voluntary counselling and testing services and correctly assessing one's own risk were also positively associated with condom use (Prata et al., 2006).
62	Men's migration and women's fertility in rural Mozambique.	2011/ Mozambique	Fertility and reproductive health	Survey/cross-sectional	The study found a relationship between man's labour migration and wives' reproductive behaviour. Wives of migrants had higher birth rates than the wives of non-migrants. Women married to more successful migrants had higher fertility intentions and were significantly more likely to be using modern contraceptives than either women married to less successful migrants or to non-migrants (Agadjanian et al., 2011).
63	Determined to stop? longitudinal analysis of the desire to have no more children in rural Mozambique	2017/ Mozambique	Fertility and reproductive health	Survey/ longitudinal	The study found evidence of the usefulness of a demographic measure of fertility desires in Southern Mozambique, in particular the desire to stop childbearing. Survey measures of the desire to stop childbearing in this context neither neatly followed nor completely diverged from classic demographic models of fertility preferences. Fertility desires both reflected stable underlying goals and evolved in response to individual and social circumstances (Hayford & Agadjanian, 2017).

(*Continued*)

Table 6.4 (Continued)

No.	Title	Year/Country	Thematic Area	Study Type	Pattern and Determinants of Demographic Behaviour
64	Spacing, stopping, or postponing? fertility desires in a sub-Saharan setting	2019/ Mozambique	Fertility and reproductive health	Survey/ longitudinal	Findings show strong evidence for a postponement mindset in this population, but postponement coexists with stopping and spacing goals. They find some consistency between the desire and the actual behaviour, as the study demonstrates that some women who want to delay a birth persist in this desire rather than transitioning to wanting a child soon as would be predicted by the classic definition of spacing. Patterns associated with a postponement orientation can be identified using standard demographic survey questions on fertility desires, although identification is easier when these questions are supplemented by additional questions about motivations or administered longitudinally (Hayford & Agadjanian, 2019).
65	Induced abortion: a cross-sectional study on knowledge of and attitudes toward the new abortion law in Maputo and Quelimane cities, Mozambique	2010/ Mozambique	Fertility and reproductive health	Survey/cross-sectional	A total of 1657 women (827 Maputo and 830 Quelimane) were interviewed between August 2016 and February 2017. 45.7% were married, and 75.5% had ever been pregnant. 9.2% of the women reported having had an induced abortion, of which 20.0% (17) had an unsafe abortion (Frederico et al., 2020).

Agadjanian, 2008) and Mozambique (Arnaldo, 2014) suggest that fertility might have been depressed by armed conflict.

Mortality

With respect to mortality, our review reveals that infant, child and maternal death rates have been the focus of demographic analysis in Lusophone African countries. The identified and reviewed articles are on Guinea-Bissau and Mozambique and show a pattern of high rates of child and maternal mortality (Cau, Sevoyan, & Agadjanian, 2013; Cooper et al., 2010; Escaramís et al., 2011; Fernandes et al., 2014; Mølbak et al., 1992; Nielsen, Jensen, Andersen, & Aaby, 2006; Parkkali et al., 2017; Sacarlal et al., 2009).

In Guinea-Bissau, the levels of child mortality were generally going down, but prolonged war was found to increase under-five mortality by up to 1.5% (Fazzio, Mann, & Boone, 2011; Nielsen et al., 2006). Diarrhoea, malaria, acute respiratory infections and measles were found to be the most frequent causes of child death (Mølbak et al., 1992). Maternal mortality has also been a concern, and one longitudinal study found that mortality among women did not decline (Mane, Fisker, Ravn, Aaby, & Rodrigues, 2013).

The duration of breastfeeding, which is heavily influenced by cultural practices, was found to be associated with infant mortality (M. Jakobsen et al., 2003; M. S. Jakobsen, Sodemann, Mølbak, & Aaby, 1996; M. S. Jakobsen et al., 2003). King, Mann and Boone (2010) found that there were low levels of appropriate knowledge on child health, some inappropriate practices and generally low vaccination coverage. In Guinea-Bissau, HIV was found to be an important determinant of mortality patterns, although its incidence showed signs of decline (Cooper et al., 2010; Silva, Oliveira, Andersen, Dias, & Rodrigues, 2008).

In Mozambique, along with studies about war-induced child mortality (Arnaldo, 2014; Macassa, Ghilagaber, Bernhardt, & Burstrom, 2003), considerable attention has been devoted to examining inequalities in child mortality (Fernandes et al., 2014; Macassa, Ghilagaber, Bernhardt, Diderichsen, & Burstrom, 2003; Macassa et al., 2012). Mother's religious affiliation (Cau et al., 2013), urban-rural residence and parental socioeconomic status (Macassa, Ghilagaber, Bernhardt, Diderichsen et al., 2003) were important post-neonatal and child mortality predictors.

In Manhiça (Mozambique), communicable diseases accounted for three-quarters of the causes of death in children under 15 years, with malaria (21.8%), pneumonia (9.8%), HIV/AIDS (8.3%) and diarrheal diseases (8%) the leading causes of deaths (Sacarlal et al., 2009). In the same site, Escaramís et al. (2011) conducted a spatio-temporal analysis of mortality patterns and found that there was a change in mortality from one year to another, but the spatial pattern remained unchanged.

The association between labour migration and child mortality in Mozambique has also been examined. The results show that while there was no difference between the children of migrant and non-migrant men, children of successful migrants had lower mortality compared to those of less successful migrants or of non-migrant men (Yabiku, Agadjanian, & Cau, 2012). HIV-positive mothers and their children were found most vulnerable to both childbirth-related diseases and deaths (Naniche et al., 2009; Parkkali et al., 2017).

Migration

Fifteen articles were identified on migration covering Angola, Cape Verde and Mozambique. In Angola, the articles have focused on both international (Van Wijk, 2010) and war-related internal migration (Avogo & Agadjanian, 2010; Agadjanian & Avogo, 2008). Van Wijk (2010) shows that the migrants can be described as opportunity-seeking migrants rather than survival migrants, who are typical in the case of forced migration due to war. Most of these opportunity seekers made no use of human smugglers during their travel. They rather used assistance from their social network and the services of middlemen, called *esquemas*, on an ad-hoc basis. Agadjanian and Avogo observed that forced migrants, mainly due to war and war-related instability in Angola, were disadvantaged relative to non-migrants in the host communities. Migrants were likely to experience difficulties in accessing place of delivery, had a limited number of antenatal consultations and had limited age-adequate immunization of children. These contributed to high child mortality. In addition, forced migrant men were more likely to engage in practices that could lead to increased HIV risks than long-time male city dwellers (Agadjanian & Avogo, 2008; Avogo & Agadjanian, 2010).

The articles on Cape Verde focused on transnational migration. This country is well known for its historical pattern of intense international migration (Carling, 2008). However, the intensity fluctuates, and Åkesson (2013) shows that the fluctuating trends are related to the developments in transportation technology and changes in the world economy. Carling and Åkesson (2009) demonstrate that remittances in some cases benefit the poorest in Cape Verde and that this has to do with the fact that there is a very long history of migration. In general, in Cape Verde, nearly everyone, irrespective of class, has a close relative abroad, but Cape Verdeans generally receive quite small amounts of money, which implies that they are seldom able to improve their economic situation in a more substantial way.

Nine articles on migration were found on Mozambique, focusing on forced migration (Koser, 1996) and labour migration (Muanamoha, Maharaj, & Preston-Whyte, 2010). Lubkemann (2009) shows that the most significant transformations in the international migration regime between central Mozambique and South Africa throughout the twentieth century were the product of complex and continuous interactions between the broader political-economic environment and local forms of gendered and inter-generational social struggle. Muanamoha et al. (2010) highlighted the importance of migrant social networks on Mozambican migration to South Africa. The networks transcend geography, location and territory and can be considered spatial conveyors of social capital. These networks operate transnationally at three different locations: in the sending communities, on borders and in the destination areas. A study about husbands' labour migration to South Africa and wives' autonomy shows that both men's cumulative migration history and current migration status are positively associated with women's autonomy and that the effects on autonomy may persist even after the man's return (Yabiku, Agadjanian, & Sevoyan, 2010).

Other studies are those about male migration and its effects on demographic and health-related factors. Victor Agadjanian et al. (2011) show that the economic success of men's migration, rather than migration itself, significantly predicts women's worries about getting infected by their husbands or their own extramarital partners and their husbands' stance on condom use. Agadjanian et al. (2011) show that these migratory patterns have important effects on demographic outputs. They have detected that there was a lower birth rate among migrants' wives, which tends to be partially compensated for by an increased birth rate upon cessation of migration. Additional analysis showed that father's migration to South Africa delays home-leaving for adolescent girls and that these effects are not mediated by school enrolment (Chae, Hayford, & Agadjanian, 2016).

Finally, Roberto and Moleiro (2016) show that migrants are able to adapt and adjust to their environments, resorting to various strategies of resilience. This study shows that some analysis on migration in Lusophone Africa has gone beyond the question of determinants, patterns and effects of migration.

Findings and overall gap in the demographic research of Lusophone Africa

This review shows that research in these countries was shaped by the same forces and institutions that shaped research across the continent, but with less research done compared with Anglophone and Francophone countries. The demographic issues that have deserved more attention have been similar to those that have been examined across the continent, but Lusophone Africa is relatively under-researched. Fertility and reproductive health dominated the research topics identified on Lusophone Africa. Out of the 65 papers, 25 were on fertility and reproductive health and 22 on mortality, in which the vast majority dealt with infant mortality. Concerning migration, 14 papers were shortlisted, in which the majority dealt with international migration. The analysis shows that the gaps in demographic research in Lusophone Africa are consistent with the gaps in the demographic research in Africa.

As late-comers with respect to independence, Lusophone African countries benefited from the advancement in data collection, particularly regarding the WFSs and DHSs that were initiated in 1970s and continue to this day. However, despite improvements in data availability and quality, robust practices of data analysis to strengthen or challenge existing theories remain weak. In fact, studies on fertility have been based on demographic transition theory, often without discussing the shortcomings of this framework in the African context. Little attention has been given to how sociocultural and political contexts shape the pattern and the dynamics of fertility transition in these countries. Yet is known that increasing data availability has prompted researchers to expose the shortcomings of the traditional demographic theories in Africa.

All together, this analysis provides evidence that demographic research across Lusophone African countries remains concentrated in describing trends and patterns of demographic change. Like elsewhere in Africa, there is potential for exploring alternative theoretical pathways to understanding African demography. As these countries continue to improve with respect to data availability, the existing gaps in the understanding of demographic patterns and behaviour may gradually be reduced. The availability of high-quality population data is important to improve our understanding of the demographic phenomena within the complexities of the political, historical, social, cultural and economic diversity of these countries and of African countries in general.

Summary and directions for future research

Summary

The aim of this chapter was to review the demographic research done on Lusophone African countries during the post-colonial period and trace directions for future research. Our analysis shows that a combination of factors shaped the demographic research in these countries. Among these factors are the level of tertiary education development at the time of independence and the fluctuation in political and military stability during the post-colonial period. Availability and quality of demographic data have been improving since the 1990s, but their use in demographic analysis to expand existing knowledge on population dynamics remains low. Over 90% of the reviewed articles were authored or co-authored by non-Lusophone scholars, which may suggest that language barriers may prevent local researchers from publishing in mainly English- and French-dominant literature. The limited presence of Lusophone-authored demographic research in Portuguese journals, mainly based in Brazil, indicates a low level of demographic research in Lusophone countries.

Despite a common historical past, demographic research in Lusophone countries has been developing at a different pace. The regional context of each Lusophone country and contemporary socioeconomic and political development have been more determinant in the development of demographic research capacity than common language and shared colonial experience. Thus, it was the contemporary context and political dynamics that considerably influenced the nature and quantity of demographic research.

In general, the Lusophone countries are demographically under-researched, and there are important disparities among the countries. This may reflect different levels of research capabilities in the field of demography and/or different preferences as empirical sites of research. Because of its stronger research capabilities and collaboration or connectivity of local scholars with foreign scholars, Mozambique is a dominant research site of the published studies on Lusophone countries, followed by Angola and Cape Verde. In contrast, very few studies on São Tomé and Príncipe and Guinea-Bissau were found.

Forty-two percent of published research was on fertility (mainly reproductive health), 35% on mortality and 23% on migration. Fertility and reproductive health were the dominant research topics in Mozambique, Angola and Cape Verde; mortality, basically under-five mortality, was the main research topic in Mozambique and Guinea-Bissau; and migration dominated the research on Mozambique, Angola and Cape Verde.

Directions for future research

Lusophone African countries still have a lot of ground to cover in relation to demographic research. Most of the demographic dynamics of these countries are still unknown. Although much attention has been given to fertility, much of it is on reproductive health and on how sociocultural factors influence the desire for childbearing and contraceptive use. The dynamics of fertility change, including sub-national patterns and how the proximate determinants shape that change, has not been researched and should be one of the focuses for future research, particularly in Angola and Mozambique, where a general fertility transition is uncertain or in the early stages.

The most-researched proximate determinant is contraceptive use and to some extent the beginning of sexual activity. Given that apart from low use of contraceptive methods, early marriage has been an important factor in shaping the fertility of Lusophone countries, understanding nuptiality patterns and marriages or family formation dynamics are relevant issues to explore, particularly in the multicultural contexts that characterize Lusophone countries.

Regarding mortality, the focus has been mostly on infant and child mortality. Very little has been done in order to understand the dynamics of adult mortality and how socioeconomic dynamics marked by prolonged conflict and the HIV and AIDS pandemic has contributed to adult mortality and survivorship in the study countries, including differences by sex and other demographically relevant categories.

In relation to migration, most studies have focused on international migration, including the networks that assist migration, adaptation strategy at the destination country and the relationship with family left behind. Little is known about internal migration and migration to other African countries. Except for Mozambique, where extensive analysis exists in relation to migration to South Africa, in the remaining countries, attention is required. Even in Mozambique, there are important migration dynamics with other neighbouring countries to be researched and understood. Comparative studies on migration among the Lusophone African countries have not received further attention. This is critical considering the linguistic and historical commonalities as well as the existence of political institutions, namely African countries with

Portuguese as official language (PALOP) and Community of Portuguese Language Countries (CPLP),[5] aiming at enhancing cooperation among Portuguese-speaking countries in Africa and beyond.

Finally, our study shows that attention must be paid to gender disparities and how gender dynamics interplay with demographic behaviour. Across the three demographic outcomes of interest, that is, fertility including reproductive health, mortality and migration, we observe that gender disparities remain to be thoroughly studied. Mortality rates are known to differ by gender, and this aspect has yet to be systematically addressed. A similar gap can be observed in relation to migration. Men's and women's migratory experiences are different and have been historically constructed in different historical, sociocultural and political frames. The effects of these temporal, sociological and gendered patterns in migration in Lusophone Africa remain to be examined.

Notes

1 Equatorial Guinea has limited historical and cultural commonalities with the other countries, and Portuguese is sparsely used throughout the country.
2 Guinea-Bissau unilaterally declared its independence in 1973 but was formally recognized in 1974.
3 www.ajol.info/index.php/ajol
4 https://scielo.org/
5 The CPLP includes also the likes of Portugal, Brazil and East Timor.

References

Adegbola, O. (1988). Religion and reproduction of sub-Saharan Africa. In *African Population Conference, Dakar* (Vol. 1). Liege: International Union for the Scientific Study of Population (IUSSP).

Adepoju, A. (1994). *Rethinking the approaches to the study of population dynamics in Africa*. Dakar: Union for African Population Studies (UAPS). Paper No. 1.

Adewuyi, A. A. (1988). Marital fertility in polygynous unions in Nigeria. *Journal of Biosocial Sciences, 20*, 393–400.

Agadjanian, V. (1998). Economic security, informational resources, and women's reproductive choices in urban Mozambique. *Social Biology, 45*(1–2), 60–79. https://doi.org/10.1080/19485565.1998.9988964

Agadjanian, V. (2000). Women's work and fertility in a sub-Saharan urban setting: A social environment approach. *Journal of Biosocial Science, 32*(1), 17–35.

Agadjanian, V. (2001a). Negotiating through reproductive change: Gendered social interaction and fertility regulation in Mozambique. *Journal of Southern African Studies, 27*(2), 291–309. www.jstor.org/stable/823330

Agadjanian, V. (2001b). Religion, social milieu, and the contraceptive revolution. *Population Studies, 55*(2), 135–148. https://doi.org/10.1080/00324720127691

Agadjanian, V. (2013). Religious denomination, religious involvement, and modern contraceptive use in southern Mozambique. *Studies in Family Planning, 44*(3), 259–274. Retrieved from www.jstor.org/stable/23654758

Agadjanian, V., Arnaldo, C., & Cau, B. (2011). Health costs of wealth gains: Labor migration and perceptions of HIV/AIDS risks in Mozambique. *Social Forces, 89*(4), 1097–1117. https://doi.org/10.1093/sf/89.4.1097

Agadjanian, V., & Avogo, W. (2008). Forced migration and HIV/AIDS risks in Angola. *International Migration, 46*(3), 189–216. https://doi.org/https://doi.org/10.1111/j.1468-2435.2008.00466.x

Agadjanian, V., & Hayford, S. R. (2018). HIV status, fertility intentions, and contraception in the era of expanded access to antiretroviral therapy: A case study of rural Mozambique. *Global Public Health, 13*(5), 582–596. https://doi.org/10.1080/17441692.2016.1268188

Agadjanian, V., & Prata, N. (2001). War and reproduction: Angola's fertility in comparative perspective. *Journal of Southern African Studies, 27*(2), 329–347. Retrieved from www.jstor.org/stable/823332

Agadjanian, V., & Prata, N. (2002). War, peace, and fertility in Angola. *Demography, 39*(2), 215–231.

Agadjanian, V., Yabiku, S. T., & Cau, B. (2011). Men's migration and women's fertility in rural Mozambique. *Demography, 48*(3), 1029–1048. https://doi.org/10.1007/s13524-011-0039-y

Åkesson, L. (2013). The queue outside the embassy: Remittances, inequality and restrictive migration regimes. *International Migration*, *51*(Suppl. 1), e1–e12. https://doi.org/https://doi.org/10.1111/imig.12045

Alberto, S. A., & Queiroz, B. L. (2015). Estimativas de cobertura de óbitos e da mortalidade adulta em Moçambique a partir de dados censitários. *Cadernos de Saude Publica*, *31*(10). https://doi.org/10.1590/0102-311X00158714

Arnaldo, C. (2004). Regional fertility trends in Mozambique. *Journal of Population Research*, *21*(2), 177–197.

Arnaldo, C. (2014). Armed conflict and demographic outcome in Mozambique and Rwanda: What can censuses tell us? In C. O. Odimegwu & J. Kekovote (Eds.), *Continuity and change in sub-Saharan African demography* (pp. 284–302). New York and London: Routledge.

Avogo, W., & Agadjanian, V. (2008). Childbearing in crisis: War, migration and fertility in Angola. *Journal of Biosocial Sciences*, *40*(5), 725–742.

Avogo, W. A., & Agadjanian, V. (2010). Forced migration and child health and mortality in Angola. *Social Science & Medicine*, *70*(1), 53–60.

Beverwijk, J. M. R. (2005). *The genesis of a system: A coalition formation in Mozambican higher education, 1993–2003* (PhD Thesis, Center for Higher Education Policy Studies (CHEPS)/University of Twente, Enschede, The Netherlands).

Bloom, D. E., Canning, D., Fink, G., & Finlay, J. (2007). *Realizing the demographic dividend: Is Africa any different?* Program on the Global Demography of Aging. Harvard University, Massachusetts. Retrieved from www.aercafrica.org/documents/reproductive_health_working_papers/Bloom_Canning_et_al_Demographic_Dividend_in_Africa.pdf

Bongaarts, J. (1978). A framework for analyzing the proximate determinants of fertility. *Population and Development Review*, *4*(1), 105–132.

Bongaarts, J. (2017). Africa's unique fertility transition. *Population and Development Review*, *43*(Suppl. 1), 39–58. https://doi.org/10.1111/j.1728-4457.2016.00164.x

Bongaarts, J., & Casterline, J. (2013). Fertility transition: Is sub-Saharan Africa different? *Population and Development Review*, *38*(Suppl. 1), 153–168.

Bongaarts, J., Frank, O., & Lesthaeghe, R. (1984). The proximate determinants of fertility in sub-Saharan Africa. *Population and Development Review*, *10*(3), 511–537.

Bradshaw, Y. W., Kaiser, P. J., & Ndegwa, S. N. (1995). Rethinking theoretical and methodological approaches to the study of African development. *African Studies Review*, *38*(2), 39–65. https://doi.org/10.2307/525317

Caldwell, J. C. (1976). Toward a restatement of demographic transition theory. *Population and Development Review*, *2*(3–4), 231–366. Retrieved from www.jstor.org/stable/1971615

Caldwell, J. C., & Caldwell, P. (1990). High fertility in sub-Saharan Africa. *Scientific American*, *262*(5), 82–89.

Caldwell, J. C., & Okonjo, C. (1968). The population of tropical Africa. *Studies in Family Planning*, *1*(29), 10–12. Retrieved from www.jstor.org/stable/1965301

Caldwell, J. C., Orubuloye, I. O., & Caldwell, P. (1992). Fertility decline in Africa: A new type of transition? *Population and Development Review*, *18*(2), 211–242.

Carling, J. (2008). Toward a demography of immigrant communities and their transnational potential. *International Migration Review*, *42*(2), 449–475. https://doi.org/10.1111/j.1747-7379.2008.00131.x

Carling, J., & Åkesson, L. (2009). Mobility at the heart of a nation: Patterns and meanings of Cape Verdean migration. *International Migration*, *47*(3), 123–155. https://doi.org/10.1111/j.1468-2435.2009.00526.x

Cau, B. M. (2015). Community influences on contraceptive use in Mozambique. *Health & Place*, *31*, 10–16.

Cau, B. M. (2016). Female migration, local context and contraception use in urban Mozambique. *African Journal of Reproductive Health/La Revue Africaine de la Santé Reproductive*, *20*(1), 52–61. Retrieved from www.jstor.org/stable/26357080

Cau, B. M., Sevoyan, A., & Agadjanian, V. (2013). Religious affiliation and under-five mortality in Mozambique. *Journal of Biosocial Science*, *45*(3), 415–429. https://doi.org/10.1017/s0021932012000454

Chae, S., Hayford, S. R., & Agadjanian, V. (2016). Father's migration and leaving the parental home in rural Mozambique. *Journal of Marriage and Family*, *78*(4), 1047–1062. https://doi.org/10.1111/jomf.12295

Chavane, L., Dgedge, M., Bailey, P., Loquiha, O., Aerts, M., & Temmerman, M. (2017). Assessing women's satisfaction with family planning services in Mozambique. *Journal of Family Planning and Reproductive Health Care*, *43*(3), 222–228. https://doi.org/10.1136/jfprhc-2015-101190

Cleland, J. (2012). *Will Africa benefit from a demographic dividend*. The Health & Education Advice & Resource Team (HEART). Retrieved from www.heart-resources.org

Cohen, B. (1998). The emerging fertility transition in sub-Saharan Africa. *World Development, 26*(8), 1431–1461.

Cooper, M., van der Loeff, M. S., McConkey, S., Cooper, S., Vincent, T., & Whittle, H. (2010). Cause of death among people with retroviral infection in rural Guinea-Bissau. *Tropical Doctor, 40*(3), 181–183. https://doi.org/10.1258/td.2010.090460

da Silva, Z. J., Oliveira, I., Andersen, A., Dias, F., Rodrigues, A., Holmgren, B., . . . Aaby, P. (2008). Changes in prevalence and incidence of HIV-1, HIV-2 and dual infections in urban areas of Bissau, Guinea-Bissau: Is HIV-2 disappearing? *Aids, 22*(10), 1195–1202. https://doi.org/10.1097/QAD.0b013e328300a33d

Davis, K. (1945, January). The world demographic transition. *Annals of the American Academy of Political and Social Sciences, 273*, 1–11.

Eastwood, R., & Lipton, M. (2011). Demographic transition in sub-Saharan Africa: How big will the economic dividend be? *Population Studies, 65*(1), 9–35.

Escaramís, G., Carrasco, J. L., Aponte, J. J., Nhalungo, D., Nhacolo, A., Alonso, P., & Ascaso, C. (2011). Spatio-temporal analysis of mortality among children under the age of five in Manhiça (Mozambique) during the period 1997–2005. *International Journal of Health Geographics, 10*(1), 14. https://doi.org/10.1186/1476-072X-10-14

Fazzio, I., Mann, V., & Boone, P. (2011). Temporal trends (1977–2007) and ethnic inequity in child mortality in rural villages of southern Guinea Bissau. *BMC Public Health, 11*(1), 683. https://doi.org/10.1186/1471-2458-11-683

Fernandes, Q. F., Wagenaar, B. H., Anselmi, L., Pfeiffer, J., Gloyd, S., & Sherr, K. (2014). Effects of health-system strengthening on under-5, infant, and neonatal mortality: 11-year provincial-level time-series analyses in Mozambique. *The Lancet Global Health, 2*(8), e468–e477. https://doi.org/10.1016/S2214-109X(14)70276-1

Frederico, M., Arnaldo, C., Decat, P., Juga, A., Kemigisha, E., Degomme, O., & Michielsen, K. (2020). Induced abortion: A cross-sectional study on knowledge of and attitudes toward the new abortion law in Maputo and Quelimane cities, Mozambique. *BMC Women's Health, 20*(1), 129. https://doi.org/10.1186/s12905-020-00988-6

Frederico, M., Michielsen, K., Arnaldo, C., & Decat, P. (2018). Factors influencing abortion decision-making processes among young women. *International Journal of Environmental Research and Public Health, 15*(2), 329. Retrieved from www.mdpi.com/1660-4601/15/2/329

Furtado, C. A. (2016). Cabo Verde e as quatro décadas de independência: dissonâncias, múltiplos discursos, reverberações e lutas por imposições de sentido à sua história recente. *Estudos Ibero-Americanos, 42*(3), 855–887. https://doi.org/10.15448/1980-864X.2016.3.22888

Gurmu, E., & Mace, R. (2008). Fertility decline driven by poverty: The case of Addis Ababa, Ethiopia. *Journal of Biosocial Science, 40*(3), 339–358. Retrieved from http://journals.cambridge.org/abstract_S002193200700260X

Hayford, S. R., & Agadjanian, V. (2012). From desires to behavior: Moderating factors in a fertility transition. *Demographic Research, 26*, 511–542. https://doi.org/10.4054/DemRes.2012.26.20

Hayford, S. R., & Agadjanian, V. (2017). Determined to stop? Longitudinal analysis of the desire to have no more children in rural Mozambique. *Population Studies (Cambridge), 71*(3), 329–344. https://doi.org/10.1080/00324728.2017.1334957

Hayford, S. R., & Agadjanian, V. (2019). Spacing, stopping, or postponing? Fertility desires in a sub-Saharan setting. *Demography, 56*(2), 573–594. https://doi.org/10.1007/s13524-018-0754-8

Hayford, S. R., Agadjanian, V., & Luz, L. (2012). Now or never: Perceived HIV status and fertility intentions in rural Mozambique. *Studies in Family Planning, 43*(3), 191–199. https://doi.org/10.1111/j.1728-4465.2012.00317.x

Heisel, D. F. (1968). The demography of the Portuguese territories: Angola, Mozambique, and Portuguese Guinea. In W. Brass, A. J. Coale, P. Demeny, D. F. Heisel, F. Lorimer, A. Romaniuk, & E. van de Walle (Eds.), *The demography of tropical Africa* (pp. 440–465). Princeton, NJ: Princeton University Press.

INE. (1999). *Recenseamentos Realizados no Período Colonial (1928 a 1970)*. Maputo: Instituto Nacional de Estatística, Direcçào de Censos e Inquéritos.

Jaén-Sánchez, N., González-Azpeitia, G., Saavedra-Santana, P., Saavedra-Sanjuán, E., Manguiza, A. A., Manwere, N., . . . Serra-Majem, L. (2020). Adolescent motherhood in Mozambique: Consequences for pregnant women and newborns. *PLoS One, 15*(6), e0233985. https://doi.org/10.1371/journal.pone.0233985

Jakobsen, M., Sodemann, M., Nylén, G., Balé, C., Nielsen, J., Lisse, I., & Aaby, P. (2003). Breastfeeding status as a predictor of mortality among refugee children in an emergency situation in Guinea-Bissau. *Tropical Medicine and International Health, 8*(11), 992–996. https://doi.org/10.1046/j.1360-2276.2003.01122.x

Jakobsen, M. S., Sodemann, M., Mølbak, K., & Aaby, P. (1996). Reason for termination of breastfeeding and the length of breastfeeding. *International Journal of Epidemiology, 25*(1), 115–121. https://doi.org/10.1093/ije/25.1.115

Jakobsen, M. S., Sodemann, M., Mølbak, K., Alvarenga, I., Nielsen, J., & Aaby, P. (2003). Termination of breastfeeding after 12 months of age due to a new pregnancy and other causes is associated with increased mortality in Guinea-Bissau. *International Journal of Epidemiology, 32*(1), 92–96. https://doi.org/10.1093/ije/dyg006

Khan, S. (2016). Moçambique 41 anos Depois: 'Crónica' de uma Imaturidade Política. *Estudos Ibero-Americanos, 42*(3), 944–960. https://doi.org/10.15448/1980-864X.2016.3.25257

King, R., Mann, V., & Boone, P. D. (2010). Knowledge and reported practices of men and women on maternal and child health in rural Guinea Bissau: A cross sectional survey. *BMC Public Health, 10*, 319. https://doi.org/10.1186/1471-2458-10-319

Kirk, D. (1996). Demographic transition theory. *Population Studies, 50*, 361–387.

Koser, K. (1996). Information and refugee migration: The case of Mozambicans in Malawi. *Tijdschrift voor Economische en Sociale Geografie, 87*(5), 407–418. https://doi.org/10.1111/j.1467-9663.1998.tb01573.x

Lesthaeghe, R. J. (1989). *Reproduction and social organization in sub-Saharan Africa*. Los Angeles, CA: University of California Press.

Lindstrom, D. P., & Berhanu, B. (1999). The impact of war, famine, and economic declined on marital fertility in Ethiopia. *Demography, 36*(2), 247–261.

Lubkemann, S. C. (2009). From circular migrants in the mines to transnational polygynists in the townships: A century of transformation in central Mozambican male migration regimes (1900–1999). *International Migration, 47*(3), 51–92. https://doi.org/10.1111/j.1468-2435.2009.00524.x

Macamo, E. (2017). *The taming of fate: Approaching risk from a social action perspective: Case studies from Southern Mozambique*. Dakar, Senegal: CODESRIA.

Macassa, G., Ghilagaber, G., Bernhardt, E., Diderichsen, F., & Burström, B. (2003). Inequalities in child mortality in Mozambique: Differentials by parental socio-economic position. *Social Science and Medicine, 57*(12), 2255–2264. https://doi.org/10.1016/s0277-9536(02)00545-2

Macassa, G., Ghilagaber, G., Charsmar, H., Walander, A., Sundin, Ö., & Soares, J. (2012). Geographic differentials in mortality of children in Mozambique: Their implications for achievement of Millennium Development Goal 4. *Journal of Health, Population and Nutrition, 30*(3), 331–345. https://doi.org/10.3329/jhpn.v30i3.12297

Macicame, I., Magaço, A., Cassocera, M., Amado, C., Feriano, A., Chicumbe, S., . . . Roberton, T. (2018). Intervention heroes of Mozambique from 1997 to 2015: Estimates of maternal and child lives saved using the Lives Saved Tool. *Journal of Global Health, 8*(2), 021202. https://doi.org/10.7189/jogh.08.021201

Mane, M., Fisker, A. B., Ravn, H., Aaby, P., & Rodrigues, A. (2013). Trends and determinants of mortality in women of reproductive age in rural Guinea-Bissau, West Africa – A cohort study. *BMC Women's Health, 13*(1), 48. https://doi.org/10.1186/1472-6874-13-48

Mbacke, C. (1994). Family planning programs and fertility transition in sub-Saharan Africa. *Population and Development Review, 20*(1), 188–193.

Mendola, M. (2017, June 1). International migration and informal social protection in rural Mozambique. *Research in Economics, 71*(2), 282–290. https://doi.org/10.1016/j.rie.2017.04.002

Mølbak, K., Aaby, P., Ingholt, L., Højlyng, N., Gottschau, A., Andersen, H., . . . Jose da Silva, A. P. (1992). Persistent and acute diarrhoea as the leading causes of child mortality in urban Guinea Bissau. *Transactions of the Royal Society of Tropical Medicine and Hygiene, 86*(2), 216–220. https://doi.org/10.1016/0035-9203(92)90580-6

Morris, N., & Prata, N. (2018). Abortion history and its association with current use of modern contraceptive methods in Luanda, Angola. *Open Access Journal of Contraception, 9*, 45–55. https://doi.org/10.2147/oajc.S164736

Mouton, J., & Valentine, A. (2017). The extent of South African authored articles in predatory journals. *South African Journal of Science, 113*(7–8), art. #2017–0010. https://doi.org/10.17159/sajs.2017/20170010

Muanamoha, R. C., Maharaj, B., & Preston-Whyte, E. (2010). Social networks and undocumented Mozambican migration to South Africa. *Geoforum, 41*(6), 885–896. https://doi.org/10.1016/j.geoforum.2010.06.001

Naniche, D., Bardají, A., Lahuerta, M., Berenguera, A., Mandomando, I., Sanz, S., . . . Menéndez, C. (2009). Impact of maternal human immunodeficiency virus infection on birth outcomes and infant survival in rural Mozambique. *American Journal of Tropical Medicine and Hygiene, 80*(5), 870–876.

Newitt, M. (1995). *A history of Mozambique*. Bloomington, IN: Indiana University Press.

Nielsen, J., Jensen, H., Andersen, P. K., & Aaby, P. (2005). Mortality patterns during a war in Guinea-Bissau 1998–99: Changes in risk factors? *International Journal of Epidemiology, 35*(2), 438–446. https://doi.org/10.1093/ije/dyi246

Nielsen, J., Jensen, H., Andersen, P. K., & Aaby, P. (2006). Mortality patterns during a war in Guinea-Bissau 1998–99: Changes in risk factors? *International Journal of Epidemiology, 35*(2), 438–446.

Ortega, J. A. (2008). *The fertility transition in sub-Saharan Africa: A comparative perspective*. Cape Coast, Ghana: USSP International Union for the Scientific Study of Population International Seminar on Human Fertility in Africa: Trends in the Last Decade and Prospects for Change, Cape Coast.

Parkkali, S., Nwaru, B. I., Augusto, O., Abacassamo, F., Cliff, J., & Hemminki, E. (2017). Causes of death among women aged 17–49 years between 2007 and 2010 in Maputo, Mozambique. *Journal of Global Health*, 7(2), 020411. https://doi.org/10.7189/jogh.07.020411

Pires, P. H., Siemens, R., & Mupueleque, M. (2019). Improving sexual and reproductive health knowledge and practice in Mozambican families with media campaign and volunteer family health champions. *Family Medicine and Community Health*, 7(7), e000089. https://doi.org/10.1136/fmch-2018-00008

Prata, N., Bell, S., Fraser, A., Carvalho, A., Neves, I., & Nieto-Andrade, B. (2017). Partner support for family planning and modern contraceptive use in Luanda, Angola. *African Journal of Reproductive Health, 21*(2), 35–48. https://doi.org/10.29063/ajrh2017/v21i2.5

Prata, N., Morris, L., Mazive, E., Vahidnia, F., & Stehr, M. (2006). Relationship between HIV risk perception and condom use: Evidence from a population-based survey in Mozambique. *International Family Planning Perspectives, 32*(4), 192–200. https://doi.org/10.1363/3219206

Roberto, S., & Moleiro, C. (2016). Looking (also) at the other side of the story: Resilience processes in migrants. *Journal of International Migration and Integration, 17*(3), 929–946. https://doi.org/10.1007/s12134-015-0439-8

Rosário, E. V. N., Gomes, M. C., Brito, M., & Costa, D. (2019). Determinants of maternal health care and birth outcome in the Dande Health and Demographic Surveillance System area, Angola. *PLoS One, 14*(8), e0221280. https://doi.org/10.1371/journal.pone.0221280

Ross, E. B. (1998). *The Malthus factor: Poverty, politics and population in capitalist development*. New York: Zed Books.

Sacarlal, J., Nhacolo, A. Q., Sigaúque, B., Nhalungo, D. A., Abacassamo, F., Sacoor, C. N., . . . Alonso, P. L. (2009). A 10 year study of the cause of death in children under 15 years in Manhiça, Mozambique. *BMC Public Health, 9*(1), 67. https://doi.org/10.1186/1471-2458-9-67

Seibert, G. (2016). São Tomé and Príncipe 1975–2015: Politics and economy in a former plantation colony. *Estudos Ibero-Americanos, 42*(3), 987–1012. https://doi.org/10.15448/1980-864X.2016.3.22842

Silva, Z. d., Oliveira, I., Andersen, A., Dias, F., & Rodrigues, A. (2008). Changes in prevalence and incidence of HIV-1, HIV-2 and dual infections in urban areas of Bissau, Guinea-Bissau: is HIV-2 disappearing? *AIDS, 22*(10), 1195–1202.

Speizer, I. S., & White, J. S. (2008). The unintended consequences of intended pregnancies: Youth, condom use, and HIV transmission in Mozambique. *AIDS Education and Prevention, 20*(6), 531–546. https://doi.org/10.1521/aeap.2008.20.6.531

Tabutin, D., & Schoumaker, B. (2004). La démographie de l'Afrique au sud du Sahara des années 1950 aux années 2000: Synthèse des changements et bilan statistique [The demography of sub-Saharan Africa from the 1950s to the 2000s]. *Population, 59*(3), 521–622. https://doi.org/10.3917/popu.403.0521

Tavares, C. M., Schor, N., França Junior, I., & Diniz, S. G. (2009). Factors associated with sexual initiation and condom use among adolescents on Santiago Island, Cape Verde, West Africa. *Cadernos de Saude Publica, 25*, 1969–1980. Retrieved from www.scielo.br/scielo.php?script=sci_arttext&pid=S0102-311X2009000900011&nrm=iso

Tijssen, R. J. W. (2007). Africa's contribution to the worldwide research literature: New analytical perspectives, trends, and performance indicators. *Scientometrics, 71*(2), 303–327.

United Nations. (2019). *World population prospects 2019*. Online Edition, Rev. 1. Retrieved from https://population.un.org/wpp/

Van Wijk, J. (2010). Luanda – Holanda: Irregular migration from Angola to the Netherlands. *International Migration*, *48*(2), 1–30. https://doi.org/10.1111/j.1468-2435.2008.00485.x

Vidal, N. d. F. (2016). O MPLA e a governação: entre internacionalismo progressista marxista e pragmatismo liberal-nacionalista. *Estudos Ibero-Americanos*, *42*(3), 815–854. https://doi.org/10.15448/1980-864X.2016.3.23461

Villela, W. V., Lima, R. W., & Brito, C. F. d. (2018). O Programa Nacional de Saúde Reprodutiva de Cabo Verde: alcances, limites e desafios. *Ciência & Saúde Coletiva*, *23*, 3631–3636. Retrieved from www.scielo.br/scielo.php?script=sci_arttext&pid=S1413-81232018001103631&nrm=iso

Weeks, J. R., Hill, A. G., & Agyei-Mensah, S. (2008). *Do slums promote high urban fertility? Neighborhood differences in Accra, Ghana*. Princeton University. Retrieved from https://paa2007.princeton.edu/papers/70904

Xiao, Y., & Watson, M. (2017). Guidance on conducting a systematic literature review. *Journal of Planning Education and Research*, 1–20. doi:10.1177/0739456X17723971

Yabiku, S. T., Agadjanian, V., & Cau, B. (2012). Labor migration and child mortality in Mozambique. *Social Science & Medicine*, *75*(12), 2530–2538. https://doi.org/https://doi.org/10.1016/j.socscimed.2012.10.001

Yabiku, S. T., Agadjanian, V., & Sevoyan, A. (2010). Husbands' labour migration and wives' autonomy, Mozambique 2000–2006. *Population Studies*, *64*(3), 293–306. https://doi.org/10.1080/00324728.2010.510200

7

OLD, CONTEMPORARY AND EMERGING SOURCES OF DEMOGRAPHIC DATA IN AFRICA

Babatunde M. Gbadebo

Introduction

Demographic statistics are results of data collected about population characteristics, such as age, sex, education, and income. They are usually used as an index for the measurement of development in any society. This is because any meaningful national development relies mostly on the availability of viable, reliable, and adequate demographic data. Up to the recent time, many African countries' developmental programmes have been jeopardised due to a lack of reliable demographic data. The lack of credible data has facilitated poor planning and implementation of programmes and policies that can address issues around population health and well-being. Accurate and reliable demographic data are not only essential for functional developmental programme planning and implementation but also useful in policy formulation, resource allocation, healthcare service delivery, monitoring, and evaluation of developmental programmes (Donatien, 2016). However, concerted efforts towards the collection of demographic data have propelled various countries in sourcing accurate and reliable demographic data through diverse methods such as population census, sample survey, population registers, and administrative records. These data sources have generated a lot of demographic data to countries, but some of the data generated were inaccurate and costly to obtain. This has led to the adoption of new and less costly technologies for obtaining reliable data. African countries, in particular, have been facing various challenges in their developmental programmes due to inaccurate data (Adedini et al., 2021). They, therefore, need to adopt innovative technologies for obtaining accurate and reliable socio-demographic data to achieve the Sustainable Development Goals.

In view of this background, this chapter provides answers to the following questions: What are the sources of demographic data in African countries? What are the various demographic data collection methods in Africa? What are the strengths and weaknesses of these sources of demographic data? What are the policy issues surrounding demographic data sources? This chapter provides answers to the aforementioned questions with the aim of aiding policy formulation and implementation in this contemporary time when many African countries face a dearth of reliable demographic data for meaningful development. Unveiling other complementary sources of demographic data will also improve the sustainability of quality demographic data collection in Africa.

 DOI: 10.4324/9780429287213-9

Methods

Demographic data in Africa are faced with inadequacies in spite of the importance of demographic data to social and economic development. In order to present detailed information on this subject matter, both offline and online literature reviews and book searches were carried out in line with the stated objectives between October 2019 and October 2020. About 150 articles were initially searched, but, using some inclusion and exclusion criteria, only 65 articles that met the criteria were systematically reviewed. An article is said to meet the inclusion criteria if it wholly or partially covers the specific objectives of the study and was published between 2000 and 2021 (except those on definition of terms). However, articles that were published by non-African scholars and those that covered countries beyond Africa were excluded. The electronic databases used in searching for relevant materials on the subject included Pubmed/ Medline (https://pubmed.ncbi.nlm.nih.gov/), AJOL (www.ajol.info/index.php/ajol), Google Scholar (http://scholar.google.com/), and Directory of Open Access Journals (www.doaj.org/). The findings were organised, formatted, and presented in a standard quality format.

Literature review

What are demographic data?

Demographic data are statistical data collected about population characteristics, such as age, sex, education, income, and marital status of the people. They are usually used as a proxy to national development; this is because any meaningful national development relies solely on the availability of viable and accurate demographic statistics.

Sources of demographic data

This chapter classifies sources of demographic data in Africa countries into traditional or old sources, contemporary or non-traditional sources, and emerging or new sources. The traditional sources are those data collection sources that are long standing in Africa; they were in existence and widely practised before 1960. They serve as principal and comprehensive sources of information for demographic, economic, and health planning and implementation. These sources include the population census, the sample survey, the vital statistics registration system, the administrative records, and the population registers. The contemporary sources of demographic data are those that are recent and relatively widespread. They include the World Fertility Survey, Demographic and Health Survey, Malaria Indicator Survey, and AIDS Indicator Survey. The emerging sources are those sources that are relatively new and not widespread. These sources include register-based census, Health and Demographic Surveillance System, Bank Verification Number, and National Identification Number.

The traditional sources of demographic data

The population census

This is the main source of demographic data on the size, structure, and spatial distribution of population practicable in virtually all African countries. It is an important instrument used in gathering reliable and detailed demographic, economic, and social data about the population of a country. It is the enumeration of the total population in a particular country or sub-division. It collects information on the characteristics of the population such as age, sex, education, marital status, household composition, family characteristics, household size, and economic activities of the population. It is the "total process of collecting, compiling and publishing demographic, economic and social data pertaining at a specified time to all persons in a country or delineated area" (United Nations, 2008). This implies that the population census not only collects information but also compiles and publishes the results for demographic, economic, and health planning. There is no doubt that census conducts in terms of contents, coverage, and methodology have changed greatly from what was obtainable in the past. Recent censuses (population and housing censuses) have included information on housing conditions, needs, and housing policies; this is because they are all crucial in evaluating citizens' well-being.

Census in African countries

Virtually all African countries have conducted censuses prior to, during, and after their independence using different approaches and methodologies so as to generate demographic data for programme planning and implementations. Globally, censuses were either conducted using the *de facto* or *de jure* method of enumeration. In the case of *de facto enumeration*, only people who are physically present at the census period are counted, while *de jure enumeration*, on the other hand, involves counting of people by proxy, that is, enumeration of persons who usually reside in a place; it is known as an enumeration by residence. These two methods of enumeration have also been employed at one time or the other in African countries. In Nigeria, all the censuses conducted during the pre-independence and early post-independence era employed the de jure method of enumeration (Okolo, 1999). Censuses at those periods were primarily aimed at determining the number of taxable adults so as to estimate the amount of revenue that could be obtained from the populace or the number who could be conscripted into military service or enlisted in forced work (United Nations, 1952). However, the censuses taken in 1991 and 2006 in Nigeria employed the de facto method of enumeration (NPC, 2006). Previous censuses in Liberia also employed de jure enumeration, but there was a shift to de facto enumeration in 2008 to improve census methodology (LISGIS, 2011; UNFPA et al., 2019). Censuses in Malawi used the de jure method of enumeration up to the 2018 census (NSO, 2019), while Ghana in 2000 started using de facto enumeration (GSS, 2000). The most recent 2014 population and housing census in Uganda used de facto enumeration (Dfid et al., 2014), and Sierra Leone adopted it in 2015 (GSO, 2015).

According to the modern and internationally accepted standard, all countries are expected to conduct a population census between 3 and 5 days at every 10-year interval in order to avoid vital data gaps. An irregular census taken has been the trend in most African countries, and this has been contributing to a retrogression in programme planning and implementation. The census in Nigeria between 1871 and 1911 was conducted every 10 years, after which it was not carried out decennially due to a paucity of funds and insecurity in some parts of the country. In Ghana, a decennial census was conducted from 1891 to 1931 before interruption by the Second World War and also between 1960 and 1970 (GSS, 2010). Over the past few decades, some countries, like Kenya and Namibia, have been conducting decennial censuses. For instance, the first census conducted in Kenya was in 1948, but the country has been conducting a census every 10 years from 1969 to 2019, and Namibia has done so from 1991 to 2011 (NPCN, 2012).

A population census requires that all parts of the country be universally enumerated. Censuses in Nigeria between 1871 and 1911 were restricted to the Lagos colony and its immediate environs in the southern part of the country. The 1881 census was mainly restricted to foreign nationals (Adegbola, 1980; United Nations, 1988), while universal enumeration commenced in the country from 1921 (Okolo, 1999; NPC, 2006). In South Africa, census enumerations in 1918, 1926, 1931, and 1941 were carried out only among the Europeans; all South Africans were counted for the first time in 1996 (Christopher, 2002).

A population census requires that every individual be separately enumerated. The 1952/53 population census in Nigeria was the first to adopt the principle of individual enumeration in that country (Adegbola, 1980). The 1931 census in Ghana was also the first one that embraced the principle of individual enumeration across the country (GSS, 2010). However, virtually all the recent population and housing censuses fulfil the modern principle of individual enumeration.

Early censuses conducted in African countries were restricted to assessing the socio-demographic and economic characteristics of the human population and do not include enumeration of buildings and living quarters; contemporary census administration in Africa covers both the population and housing characteristics (population and housing census). For instance, the 1991 and 2006 censuses in Nigeria were population and housing censuses: the characteristics of people's housing were captured during the census exercise. Ghana also started conducting a population and housing census in 2000 (GSS, 2010). Recent censuses in Sierra Leone, Liberia, Uganda, Malawi, South Africa, and most of the African countries included housing characteristics in their census questionnaires.

In most African countries, censuses are carried out following the conventional interview method of collecting data from the population by face-to-face interviews, most of which are paper based. Nigeria, Uganda, Malawi, Sierra Leone, and South Africa, just to mention a few African countries, in their last censuses collected their census data using face-to-face interviews through administration of questionnaire. The United Nations recommended conducting a census using contemporary emerging technologies to get accurate, detailed, and reliable population estimates. The 1996 census in South Africa employed the use of cellular phones as a means of data transfer, while the use of new scanning technology was adopted in 2001 (Juan, 2011). Nigeria started the use of GPS and satellite imagery during the 2006 population census to carve out geo-referenced enumeration area maps (Obasanjo, 2006). Also, Malawi employed scanning for the first time during the 2008 population and housing census and computer-assisted personal interviews (through which data were captured electronically with the use of a tablet and transmitted through the internet to the National Statistical Office) in 2018 (NSO, 2019). Ethiopia in 2007 and Liberia in 2008 for the first time also employed the use of GPS to demarcate their countries into enumeration areas and used satellite images to map urban areas (Liberty, 2010; CSA, 2012).

As part of internationally accepted practice, a post-enumeration survey is usually conducted to estimate and validate the extent of coverage error so as to produce robust and high-quality demographic data. The first post-enumeration survey in Africa was carried out in Ghana during the 1960 census (UGB, 2005) and South Africa in 1996. Following the conduct of the 2006 census in Nigeria, a post-enumeration survey was conducted shortly after the actual census to adjust the raw census figures (NPC, 2006). Uganda in 2014, Malawi in 2018, and other African countries have also carried out post-enumeration surveys to validate the quality of their census data.

Unlike in the past when the whole region, state, or district could be regarded as an enumeration area, contemporary censuses regard a small sample area as an enumeration area and household as a unit of enumeration (Van De Walle, 2006). This is done to facilitate easy enumeration, better monitoring, and wide coverage. The 2001 census in South Africa started using an enumeration area in the conduct of the census. Nigeria in 1991 adopted the use of enumeration areas; at that time, the country was divided into 210,000 enumeration areas. Similarly, Malawi demarcated the country into 18,772 enumeration areas in 2018 for easy census administration (NSO, 2019)

Issues in population census in African countries

A major setback confronting the decennial census in Africa is the paucity of funds. Virtually every country is expected to conduct a census once every 10 years (United Nations, 1998); this has not been the case in most African countries. It is unfortunate that about 13 African countries have not even conducted a census since 1990 (United Nations, 2007). Census enumeration requires a huge amount of money, and virtually all African countries find it difficult to fund this huge census bill alone. Most African countries depend on international bodies such as USAID, the United State Census Bureau, UNFPA, and the UN Statistics Division for financial and technical assistance. The 1996 South Africa census that was supposed to take place in March did not take place until October 1996 due to paucity of funds; the government of Ghana could not undertake decennial census in 1980 and 1984 and also postponed the census from March to September 2010, while Nigeria was supposed to have conducted another census since 2016 but did not due to paucity of funds. In addition, some census results have been cancelled due to inadequate coverage. The Nigeria 1962 census results were cancelled due to reports of gross under-counts in some parts of the country (Bamgbose, 2009). Another major reason the census has been irregular in some African countries is due to insecurity arising from insurgence, ethnopolitical crises, and militancy. Ethiopia has postponed censuses more than three times (Borkena News, 2020), while Nigeria and Somalia have also been facing some security challenges.

High-level professionals such as demographers, statisticians, sociologists, and cartographers are needed to effectively conduct a census. The lack of such adequately trained personnel in many Africa countries has been another issue in the conduct of verifiable population censuses. Some African governments also lack the political will to conduct a reliable census, and this has led to postponements of the census in such countries. In addition, only a few African countries have at one time or another been able to validate their census results through the conduct of a post-enumeration survey to adjust for undercounts made during the census.

Sample surveys

Most African countries embark on sample surveys as a source of securing basic demographic data because of census complexity and the cost implications. Sample surveys collect data from a representative sample that is randomly selected from the entire population in order to arrive at estimates of demographic characteristics of the population. The accuracy of any sample survey, therefore, depends on the size of the selected samples and the absence of bias. Sample surveys in Nigeria, Malawi, Liberia, Lesotho, and some North African countries have been organised in multi-round phases, while Kenya and Uganda have collected samples in single rounds, with questions modified to generate reliable and better results.

Vital registration statistics system

There is a need for reliable data on fertility and mortality. This will help us to understand the dynamics of population change, as well as with population projection, public administration, and developmental planning. Such information on births and deaths is provided by the vital registration statistics system (VRSS).

> Vital registration statistic system (or civil registration system) is the continuous, permanent, compulsory and universal recording of occurrence and characteristics of vital events pertaining to the population as provided through decree or regulation in accordance with the legal requirements of a country.
>
> (United Nations Department of Economic and Social Affairs Statistics Division, 2014)

Unlike population census, VRSS is designed to record vital demographic events such as births, deaths, marriages, and divorces that occur among individuals as the events occur. Unfortunately, most African countries lack an effective and comprehensive VRSS. Registration of births and deaths was extremely low despite several laws and attempts to improve vital registration (United Nations Department of Economics and Social Affairs, 2010; Makinde, Olapeju, Ogbuoji, & Babalola, 2016). Until recently, most African countries did not have legal provisions to ensure adequate records of vital events. Vital statistics in Africa are usually obtained from district civil registration offices, health facilities, courts, and district representatives. Most recently, the Ministry of Health, maternity centres and clinics, private and traditional health care providers, non-governmental organisations (NGOs), religious institutions, and the Ministry of Education serve as sources of vital data. One major problem confronting the collection of vital events in Africa is the completeness of events covered. Births and deaths are under-reported, as many of them are not reported to a government facility. Infant deaths suffer major under-reporting, as it is seen as a sad event and people may find it difficult to recall such sad experiences.

In Nigeria, for example, vital registration statistics are inadequate and incomplete despite the enactment of decrees and laws aimed towards making registration of vital events compulsory; the coverage was as low as less than 10% in 2019 (Centre of Excellence for CRVS Systems, 2019). One major contributing factor to this is that the technique used in collecting vital events is passive; laws about registration were made but not enforced. The completeness of vital registration statistics is also low in Ghana due to a passive method of data collection. Up to 2013, registration of vital events only covered 66% of births and 20% of deaths in Ghana despite efforts to improve collection of vital events (Ghana Statistical Office, 2015).

Administrative records

An important source of demographic data that has been in use in African countries is administrative records. Administrative records are records that contain adequate and proper documentation of the organization, functions, policies, decisions, procedures, and essential transactions of the agency and that are designed to furnish information to protect the rights of this state and of persons directly affected by the agency's activities. Statistics from this source are very valuable to the overall national statistical system, as many social statistics are produced from these administrative processes. Examples of administrative statistics include education statistics from schools, local school boards, and the Ministry of Education; health statistics from clinics, hospitals, and the Ministry of Health; and employment statistics from the Ministry of Labour. Unlike sample surveys, administrative statistics are collected on the entire population participating in the event and as such are more error-free. Administrative records are not well developed in Africa despite being a very cost effective and sustainable source of demographic data (Banda, 2003). Recently, only a few African countries have applied administrative data for demographic analysis or population projections (Lehohla, 2019).

Population register

One major traditional source of demographic data that has been in existence for a long time but is relatively new in some of the African countries is the population register. It is a registration system that maintains central databases of every individual in the country; the records are continuously updated as the characteristics of the individual change. A population register is

> an individualized data system, that is, a mechanism of continuous recording, and/or of coordinated linkage, of selected information pertaining to each member of the resident population of a country in such a way to provide the possibility of determining up-to-date information concerning the size and characteristics of that population at selected time intervals.
>
> (United Nations, 1969)

Population registers are longitudinal in nature, as the preparation of the registers entails following individuals through time and recording their histories. The register should contain detailed information on name, sex, date and place of birth, marital status, date of arrival/departure, citizenship(s), educational attainment, parity, occupation, ethnicity and language(s), and date and place of death. All the recorded information in the register can, therefore, be compiled and produced as a register-based census. Once the population register has been fully established, it is relatively inexpensive and rapid in producing reliable demographic statistics. Though some forms of population register have been found to exist in some parts of Africa, most African countries have yet to develop a comprehensive population register, except South Africa, which has developed a national population register (Statistics South Africa, 2014).

Contemporary sources of demographic data

World fertility survey

As part of international efforts to improve demographic data collection, especially in the less developed countries, the World Fertility Survey (WFS) was established in 1972, with funding received from UNFPA, USAID, and the UK Overseas Development Administration. The surveys are nationally representative and scientifically designed sample surveys on fertility and generally include both household and individual (female) components. They also cover economic status, marital status, religion and race, family composition, reproductive health, water sanitation, and mortality (GHDx, 2020). The first set of the surveys in Africa was conducted in Lesotho (1977) and Kenya (1977–78). Other African countries that have conducted WFS were: Bénin, Cameroon, Cote d'Ivoire, Egypt, Ghana, Mauritania, Morocco, Nigeria, Rwanda, Senegal, North Sudan, and Tunisia.

Demographic and health survey

One important source of sample surveys across Africa is the Demographic and Health Survey (DHS). It is a principal source of reliable as well as high-quality demographic data that is currently in practice in many African countries. The DHS programme was established in 1984 by the United States Agency for International Development (USAID). It is a large retrospective and nationally representative household-based sample survey designed to collect data on fertility, mortality, reproductive health, family planning, child health, nutrition, HIV/AIDS, malaria, and a of host of other topics. The survey, which is being implemented in a 5-year phase, is carried out using a stratified multi-stage cluster design. It makes use of GPS in collecting geographic information in all surveyed countries. DHSs have been carried out in many African countries using a similar methodology. For instance, six phases of the surveys were carried out in Nigeria between 1990 and 2018; most of the surveys adopted a stratified two-stage sampling procedure. Sample selection was carried out using a probability proportion to size (with enumeration areas serving as the primary sampling units), while household selection (secondary sampling units) was performed by equal probability systematic sampling with the use of computer programming (NPC [Nigeria] & ICF Int., 2019). Similar methodology was adopted for the 2019–20 Gambia Demographic and Health Survey (GBoS & ICF, 2021) and South Africa in 2016 (NDoH et al., 2019). Other surveys conducted by DHS include the Aids Indicator Survey, Malaria Indicator Survey, Service Provision Assessment, and Key Indicator Survey.

Malaria Indicator Survey

Another contemporary source of demographic data in African countries is the Malaria Indicator Survey. It is an evidence-based sample survey on malaria programme implementation and progress towards malaria control in a country. The survey covers questions on household characteristics, respondent background, reproduction, pregnancy, fever in children, intermittent preventive treatment, and knowledge of malaria. The survey is usually carried out in multi-stages using stratified sampling methods in the selection of eligible respondents. The one implemented in Nigeria both in 2010 and 2015 adopted two-stage sampling procedures in the selection of respondents (NMEP et al., 2016). One great advantage of this survey to African countries is that, if it is well implemented, it will help in achieving a malaria-free country.

The AIDS Indicator Survey

AIDS Indicator Survey (AIS) is another contemporary source of demographic data in Africa. It is a national sample survey that was developed to obtain indicators for effective monitoring and evaluation of national HIV/AIDS programmes at a reasonable cost. The survey design involves interviewing a group of respondents aged 15–49 years who are randomly selected. The survey includes questions on respondent's background, marriage, sexual behaviour, and number of children ever born, as well as awareness about HIV/AIDS and sexually transmitted diseases. A recent example of this kind of survey called the Nigeria HIV/AIDS Indicator and Impact Survey (NAIIS) was conducted in Nigeria in 2018. The survey assessed the prevalence of human immunodeficiency virus as well as other related health indicators. Data were collected from household members aged 0–64 years from July through December 2018 (NAIIS, 2019).

Emerging sources of demographic data

Register-based census

One of the demographic data sources practised in most developed countries which is closely related to the population register is a register-based census. This system, which could be adopted in Africa countries, is now emerging in South Africa. The government of South Africa, with a well-developed population register, is considering embracing the use of the population-based census (WHO, 2020). It is a kind of census based on an administrative data register. It involves combining demographic information on population (births and deaths), households, and dwellings from existing population-based registers with data from other administrative registers such as education, employment, housing, and migration. If well developed, it produces census information from the linked registers without the need for periodical census enumeration. A few high-income countries such as Denmark, Turkey, Finland, Norway, Singapore, Germany, Belgium, Netherlands, and Slovenia have adopted the register-based census (Boycroft, 2011; WHO, 2015). Some of these countries are henceforth not conducting decennial population and housing censuses but are moving from the traditional census to the register-based census (Boycroft, 2011). The register now serves as the basis for the population and housing census in these countries. The most recent census taken in the United Kingdom in 2011 made use of a national address register in conducting the census. Some of the advantages of census-based register include being relatively cheaper to maintain, reduction in the burden of respondents reporting the same information to different government departments, and enhanced use of administrative data. In addition, demographic statistics can be produced more frequently.

Health and Demographic Surveillance System

A Health and Demographic Surveillance System (HDSS) is another source of demographic data that is now gaining popularity across Africa, South Asia, and other parts of the world. This demographic source could be found to be highly useful in low-resource African countries with defective national civil registration and vital statistics systems. It is a platform through which longitudinal data on vital events such as births, deaths, migration, socio-economic information, and disease surveillance are collected within a geographical region of a country over time. In the country where an HDSS has been established, it is used to track population and demographic changes, as well as the evolution of health threats within their surveillance areas or research sites. An HDSS is used specifically to collect information on household members' education and marital status, mothers' pregnancy history, antenatal care, delivery, and children's immunisation history. Others include collection of information on household assets, malaria control measures, water and sanitation practices, building materials of dwellings, and number of rooms.

In conducting HDSSs, longitudinal population monitoring is carried out by enumerating all residents of a selected demographic surveillance site, and at least two routine visits per year will be paid to all homesteads to collect data on all births, other pregnancy outcomes, deaths, and migrations within the demographic surveillance area. Other relevant health information will also be collected, including the cause of death (which is carried out through verbal autopsies). The information collected is analysed with the use of computers (Doctor et al., 2012; Odhiambo et al., 2012; Alabi, Doctor, Afenyadu, & Findley, 2014; Adedini et al., 2021).

South Africa, Mozambique, Ethiopia, Kenya, Tanzania, Senegal, Guinea Bissau, Malawi, Uganda, Burkina Faso, Cote d'Ivoire, Mali, Nigeria, and Bangladesh have established HDSS sites in their countries, while Sierra Leone is presently in the early planning stage of implementing an HDSS. A major advantage of HDSS is that it provides accurate information for formulating, monitoring, and assessing the impacts of health policies. It can also be used to determine health service needs. In addition, an HDSS can be used to complement information collected through the vital statistic registration system.

Bank verification number

The Central Bank of Nigeria, in collaboration with Banker's Committee, on 14 February 2014 launched a centralised biometric identification system for the banking industry tagged bank verification number (BVN) (CBN, 2019). This was to complement the other means of identification for customers and to give a unique identity to customers which can be verified across the banking industry in the country. Moreover, the plan in the near future is to authenticate transactions with biometrics alone and without use of the card and also possibly to link to personal health insurance to facilitate easy and regular updates of central records. Record linkage through which the BVN could be linked to other registers relating to population characteristics could be adopted by African countries to produce demographic data.

National Identification System

Another emerging source of data collection is the use of the National Identification System (NIS). Many African countries are now trying to roll out a national identification system in which residents are to register for biometric national identity cards that assign a unique national identity number to every individual. In the future, a well-developed NIS may eventually replace the census and some other traditional sources of demographic data. The Nigerian government has commenced enforcement of the National Identification Number (NIN) on the new enhanced 10-year validity e-passport. This will be inserted as additional data in the new e-passports (NIMC, 2020). The government of South Africa is also making concerted efforts to replace the current national population register in the country with the NIS in the future (Maluleke, 2019).

Table 7.1 Strengths and Weaknesses of Some Sources of Demographic Data Used in African Countries

	Strengths	*Weaknesses*
Population Census	It covers the entire population and therefore serves as the most accurate source of demographic data. Serves as sample frame for a sample survey.	It is too costly. Data may not be timely. Data collection is not regular. Limited questions can be asked. It takes a longer period to process and release results. It is subject to under-enumeration and a low-response rate.
Survey	It is more cost effective than the census. Easy to generalise to a larger population. It is very reliable. It is versatile in nature. It serves as source of additional information to the census. May be used to check imbalance in the census results.	Not flexible. Lack of potential depth. It requires close supervision of field workers.
Vital Statistics Registration System	Provides data on a regular basis. Provides data for small areas or sub-divisions of a country.	Records are relatively incomplete. The completeness of the registration system needs to be evaluated before use of information from the system.

(*Continued*)

	Strengths	*Weaknesses*
Administrative Records	Provides data on a regular basis. Provides data for small areas or subdivisions of a country.	It may be difficult to access due to confidentiality and bureaucratic issues in securing official approval. Inaccuracy can render the data useless for statistical uses. It may not collect important variables needed for a particular research study.
Population Register	Uses fewer resources. It overcomes non-sampling errors.	Collection and compilation of data are very complex. It requires well-trained workers.

Quality of demographic data in African countries

Designing appropriate policies toward equitable national development involves suitable and reliable demographic data. Unfortunately, the quality of demographic data in most African countries is very poor. Many African censuses suffer poor gross coverage, while only a few countries in Africa have well-developed civil and vital registration systems. In addition, administrative records in African countries are not well documented to meet the contemporary demographic and economic needs, while the population register is virtually nonexistent in Africa. However, many African countries have made several attempts to improve the collection of accurate and more reliable demographic data. These include conducting several surveys such as World Fertility Surveys and Contraceptive Prevalence Surveys, as well as Demographic and Health Surveys. Though these surveys have provided useful demographic information that gives room for a more accurate assessment of demographic data, much still needs to be done. There is, therefore, a need to improve the collection of demographic data in Africa.

Improving birth and death records in Africa

Records on births and deaths in African countries are grossly inadequate, inaccurate, and under-enumerated, but there is a need to improve on the collection and documentation of vital events, especially birth and death statistics in Africa. This will not only increase their usability for good governance but will also help in achieving Africa's development agenda (Agenda 2063 – The Africa We Want) and monitor progress towards the Sustainable Development Goals. Most African countries use the passive method of civil registration: laws for registering vital events are made but not enforced. There is, therefore, a need for every African country to maintain a universal registration system that will cover all vital events and make their registration compulsory.

Like birth statistics, death records also suffer gross inadequacies in African countries (Makinde et al., 2020). Preliminary results of a Countrywide Mortality Surveillance for Action (COMSA) in Mozambique in 2018 indicated that only 40% of all births in the selected Mozambique provinces had been registered, and only a quarter of all deaths occurred in health facilities (Nkengasong et al., 2020). In Africa, birth registration has only progressed from 40% in 2012 to 57% in 2015, while registration of deaths remained stagnant (ECA, 2017). Similarly, global deaths resulting from COVID-19 in many countries were regarded as grossly under-reported; this is because most countries only reported COVID-19 deaths that occurred mainly in the hospitals. There is, therefore, a need to develop inclusive systems to capture deaths outside health facilities.

Another major problem facing the collection of vital statistics in African countries is the scantiness of funds allocated to data collection (Makinde et al., 2016). Adequate resources should therefore be allocated to the collection of vital events in the countries of Africa in order to further improve the collection of birth and death statistics. African governments should source funds both within and outside their respective countries. Registration of births and deaths should be at affordable or no cost, and registration platforms should be easily accessed.

Apart from funding, most African governments lack the political will for the registration of vital events. There is, therefore, a dire need to strengthen the required political will of African leaders regarding the wide coverage of vital events. In addition, African policymakers should be more enlightened on the importance of reliable vital events as a means of improving policy effectiveness.

Since most African countries face inadequate expertise to handle registration of vital events, more local technical and administrative staff should be trained and deployed for registration of vital events. Advanced technologies should also be deployed to facilitate easy and quick registration.

Emerging methods of data collection in Africa

Accurate population data are essential for proper planning in governance, resource allocation, implementation of programmes, and healthcare (disaster preparedness and response operations, estimating people at risk of infectious disease, etc.), especially in resource-poor countries (UNFPA, 2020). However, population data are only available every 10 years with the national census survey. This clearly does not meet the rapid growth and development of a population. In the face of census operation, many advanced countries have adopted new technologies for census capturing; these include the use of the internet, mobile devices, and geospatial information systems. The key drivers of technological innovation in census data collection are many. Some of these are to ensure data completeness, improve efficiency, reduce cost, minimise respondent burden, and enhance quality and reliability of census results (United Nations, 2019). As modernisation and civilisation abound in Africa, new methods of data collection are also emerging. Most of the data collection processes in old and contemporary Africa are now becoming archaic. For instance, a face-to-face interview was a data collection instrument used in collecting census data up to the present day in most African countries. Nowadays, the use of the internet, mobile devices, geospatial information systems, and mailed questionnaires, as well as digital censuses, are emerging. Other emerging sources include the National Identification System and bank verification number. These emerging methods, most importantly, give results in real time.

Online/web-based surveys

One of the primary methods of data collection in many developed countries over a decade is an online or web-based survey. The survey can be accessed on a variety of electronic devices such as laptops, smartphones, tablets, and so on. The device randomly selects people to be interviewed through software. Future surveys in African countries could adopt online surveys; this will not only fast-track data collection but enhance data quality, as interviewer bias is eliminated (Harvey, 2002).

Satellite data

These are information about Earth and other planets in space, gathered by man-made satellites in their orbits. The data are generated via remote sensing technologies, such as synthetic-aperture radar (SAR) technology, which provides reliable and timely data stream opportunities for a myriad of applications at land and sea. This method of data collection is based on population estimation approaches that use remotely sensed data. It is based on counts of individual dwelling units using high spatial resolution data such as aerial photographs, measurements of urbanised land areas, estimates derived from land-use classification, and automatic image analysis based on spectral features. This is a method of population estimation with a short cycle and reliability that changes the way the world works.

Mobile data

This is a method of collecting information (qualitative and quantitative information with the help of a mobile device [e.g., mobile phone, tablet, etc.]). This method has been verified to increase the speed and accuracy of data collection. Features of mobile data collection, such as decision support and checklists, improve the quality of the data collected while also ensuring adherence to data collection and care protocols, which is important in the population census. Its functionality requires an application on which the population information to be collected is built (UNFPA Malawi, 2018).

Digital census

Paper records deteriorate with time, while poor handling and storage also increase their chances of deterioration. Digital records have the advantages of being protected from deterioration and being less capital and labour intensive. Future modes of data collection in Africa should change from paper-based to digital data collection methods. As practised in developed countries such as the United States and Switzerland, modern technology in Africa is moving away from the pencil-and-paper-based method of collecting census data to the digital census, which involves the use of a tablet loaded with a questionnaire and GPS. In Africa, only a few countries have adopted a digital census, for instance, Malawi in 2019; Kenya and Ghana also planned to adopt the digital census in their 2020 decennial censuses, and Ghana has done that in its trial census (UNFPA, 2016; Christensen, 2019). Swaziland has succeeded in adopting a digital census, which was conducted in 2017, while Ghana for the first time planned to use a digital census in 2020 to survey the population (Duke-Williams & Rees, 1998). Nigeria and some other African countries are now planning to adopt this method.

Geographical information system

This is a computer-based system that allows geographically referenced information to be captured, stored, manipulated, analyzed, managed, and presented. It analyses spatial information that is referenced to locations on the earth (Laldaparsad, 2007). A geographical information system (GIS) provides substantial benefits to the census process in relation to reducing cost and time for pre-census activity. The growth of GIS through the 1990s led to a dramatic increase in the use of digital geographic data. In the past three decades, most developed countries and some developing countries have adopted the use of GIS applications in the census, such as the United States, United Kingdom, Japan, France, Australia, Canada, China, South Africa, Nigeria, Uganda, Malawi, Israel, India, Nepal, and many others. GIS technologies are still new in most African countries (Laldaparsad, 2007).

Policy implications

A deeper knowledge of various sources of demographic data will not only assist in policy formulation but also in policy implementation in these contemporary times when many African countries face a dearth of reliable demographic data for meaningful development. In addition, unveiling other complementary sources of demographic data through this study will also aid developmental planning and implementation in African societies through the usage of combinations of two or more sources of demographic data. African governments should as a matter of necessity and urgency develop a reliable and accurate source of demographic data that will be able to meet the contemporary challenges.

Discussion

This chapter provided an overview of old, contemporary, and emerging sources of demographic data in Africa and highlighted data collection methods used in sourcing data. The chapter revealed that census, sample surveys, and vital statistics registration systems constitute the old major sources of data collection; administrative records constitute the contemporary source; and population registers, register-based censuses, and the combination of registers and sample surveys are the emerging sources of data collection in African countries. Of all the sources, the chapter documented the population census to be the principal source of demographic data in Africa countries. This has also been documented by Mbondji et al. (2014). The chapter also revealed irregular conducts of population censuses in African countries despite their importance. This had been ascertained earlier (UNFPA, 2004).

The chapter further revealed that vital statistics registration systems as a source of data collection in African countries are beset with a lot of coverage errors (under-coverage). This was in line with the finding of the Centre of Excellence for CRVS Systems (2019) that most deaths, especially infant and child deaths, are under-reported, as they are seen as sad events. UN IGME (2017) also found that many births in African countries are not reported unless there is a need for a birth certificate.

It was also unveiled in this chapter that due to irregularity and unreliability of the old and contemporary sources of demographic data in most African countries, there is a need to adopt new source(s) of data collection, which may involve complementary use of data from one source with another. According to Sulaiman (2015), South Africa, for instance, is considering adopting a population-based register to replace the future population census so as to save cost and improve data quality.

It was further discussed that using one source of demographic data may not be sufficient to meet the contemporary and future needs of most African countries, hence the need to link data sources in generating credible data. In addition, new and advanced methods of data collection should be adopted in data collection and analyses in African countries so as to fast-track data collection, analysis, and dissemination of findings in order to enhance developmental programmes.

Conclusion

This chapter discussed old, contemporary, and emerging sources of demographic data in African countries. As discussed earlier, adequate and reliable demographic data are needed for meaningful national development; however, considering the potential uses of demographic data in improving the quality of life and the global changes in the demographic data regime, the traditional and current sources of data seem to be inadequate for the future needs of many African countries and may be inadequate to satisfy the urgent requirements to meet the Sustainable Development Goals. There is, therefore, a need to improve the way Africa countries source their data. The existing sources of data in Africa need to be strengthened and revitalised. Regular household surveys should also be strengthened in making inter-census estimates and used in checking the accuracy of census data. Also, African countries must as a matter of necessity look beyond the current traditional sources of data collection and seek information from a number of sources to obtain reliable demographic data. If possible, there should be an attempt to integrate traditional data sources into new ones to produce high-quality, reliable, and timely statistics for decision-making, especially during this period of the coronavirus epidemic, and to be able to meet future health challenges. In addition, administrative records could be incorporated into the decennial census to strengthen data quality as well as to lessen data collection costs. Population registers could also be combined with other records to produce a register based-census as it is practised in developed countries.

Future research agenda

The census has been identified as a major source of demographic data in African countries, while other sources have been used as complementary. However, due to the shortcomings of all the existing sources of demographic data, there is a need to improve the current sources of demographic data in Africa. This may involve combining two or more reliable sources of data to produce robust results. Future research should target the linkages between data sources in generating credible, reliable, and efficient data that are pertinent to policy formulation and implementation in African countries.

References

Adedini, S. A., Thaele, D., Sello, M., Mutevedzi, P., Hywinya., C, Ngwenya, N., . . . Madhi, S. A. (2021). Approaches, achievements, challenges, and lessons learned in setting up an urban-based Health and Demographic Surveillance System in South Africa. *Global Health Action, 14*(1), 1874138. doi:10.1080/16549716.2021.1874138

Adegbola, O. (1980). The nature of Nigerian census. In *Population data assessment in Nigeria: Proceedings No. 1*. Lagos: Population Association of Nigeria.

Alabi, O., Doctor, H. V., Afenyadu, G. Y., & Findley, S. E. (2014). Lessons learned from setting up the Nahuche Health and Demographic Surveillance System in the resource-constrained context of northern Nigeria. *Global Health Action*, 7(1), 23368. https://doi.org/10.3402/gha.v7.23368

Bamgbose, J. A. (2009). Falsification of population census data in a heterogeneous Nigerian state: The fourth republic example. *African Journal of Political Science and International Relations, 3*(8), 311–319. Retrieved from www.academicjournals.org/AJPSIR

Banda, J. P. (2003, December 3–5). Main sources of socio-demographic statistics. In *Expert Group Meeting to Review the Draft Handbook on Designing of Household Surveys*.

Borkena News. (2020, August 24, Monday). *Ethiopia postponed population census for the 3rd time*.

Boycroft, C. A. (2011). *Register-based census: What is the potential for New Zealand*. Wellington: Statistics New Zealand. Retrieved from www.stats.govt.nz/~/media/Statistics/surveys-and-methods/methods/research-papers/topss/a-register-based-census.pdf [cited January 29, 2015].

Central Bank of Nigeria. (2019). *Payment system: Bank verification number (BVN)*. Retrieved on August 21, 2020, from www.cbn.gov.ng/Paymentsystem/BVN.asp

Central Statistical Authority (CSA). (2012). *2007 Population and housing census of Ethiopia*. Administrative Report.

Centre of Excellence for CRVS Systems. (2019). *Snapshot of civil registration and vital statistics systems of Nigeria* [Internet]. Retrieved July 16, 2020, from https://crvssystems.ca/country-profile/nigeria#footnote4_en3l66p

Christensen, S. (2019, May 28). Africa: Ghana aims to capture vulnerable populations in first digital census. *Voice of America*. (Last updated June 22, 2020).
Christopher, A. J. (2002). To define the indefinable: Population classification and the census in South Africa. *Area, 34*(4), 401–408.
Department of International Development (DFiD), Uganda Bureau of Statistics, UNICEF, UNFPA. (2014). *Uganda population and housing census*. Global Health Data Exchange.
Doctor, H. V., Findley, S. E., Ager, A., Cometto, G., Afenyadu, G. A., Adamu, F., & Green, C. (2012). Using community-based research to shape the design and delivery of maternal health services in northern Nigeria. *Reproductive Health Matters, 20*, 10412.
Donatien, B. (2016, August 18). Poor data affects Africa's ability to make the right policy decisions. *The Conversation*.
Duke-Williams, O., & Rees, P. (1998). Can offices publish statistics for more than one small area geography? An analysis of the differencing problem in statistical disclosure. *International Journal of Geographical Information Science, 12*(6), 579–605.
Economic Commission for Africa. (2017). *Report on the status of civil registration and vital statistics in Africa*. Addis Ababa: ECA.
Gambia Bureau of Statistics (GBoS) and ICF. (2021). *The Gambia demographic and health survey 2019–20*. Banjul, The Gambia and Rockville, MD: GBoS & ICF.
Ghana Statistical Services. (2000). *Population and housing census 2000*. Accra: Government Press.
Ghana Statistical Services. (2010). *Population and housing census 2000*. Accra: Government Press.
Ghana Statistical Office. (2015). *Civil registration and vital statistics system in Ghana: Report on the Comprehensive Assessment*. Accra: Government Press.
Global Health Data Exchange (GHDx). (2020). *World Fertility Survey (WFS)*. Retrieved on October 28, 2020, from http://ghdx.healthdata.org/series/world-fertility-survey-wfs
Harvey, J. T. (2002). Population estimation models based on individual TM pixels. *Photogrammetric Engineering and Remote Sensing, 68*(11), 1181–1192.
Juan, A. X. F. (2011). Lessons from census taking in South Africa: Budgeting and accounting experiences. *The African Statistical Journal, 13*.
Laldaparsad, S. (2007, May 29–June 1). Census mapping and the use of geo-spatial technologies (A case of South Africa). In *United Nations Expert Group Meeting on Contemporary Practices in Census Mapping and Use of Geographical Information Systems*, New York.
Lehohla, P. (2019). *Data and methods needs: Regional perspective from Africa, IUSSP – EGM*.
Liberia Institute of Statistics and Geo-Information Services (LISGIS). (2011). *Republic of Liberia 2008 population and housing census: The administrative report*. Monrovia: Government Press.
Liberty, E. T. (2010, February 19–26). *Population census in post-conflict countries: The Liberian experience*. A Presentation at the 41st Session of the United Nations Statistical Commission, HDQ, New York.
Makinde, O. A., Odimegwu, C. O., Udoh, M. O., Adedini, S. A., Akinyemi, J. O., Atobatele, A., . . . Orobaton, N. (2020). Death registration in Nigeria: A systematic literature review of its performance and challenges. *Global Health Action, 13*(1).
Makinde, O. A., Olapeju, B., Ogbuoji, O., & Babalola, S. (2016). Trends in the completeness of birth registration in Nigeria: 2002–2010. *Demographic Research, 35*, 315–338.
Maluleke, R. (2019). *South Africa's progress in civil registration*. Presentation to the 5th Annual Meeting of the ID4Africa Movement Johannesburg, South Africa.
Mbondji, P. E., Kebede, D., Soumbey-Alley, E. W., Zienliski, C., Kouvividila, W., & Lusamba-Dikassa, P. (2014). Health information systems in Africa: Descriptive analysis of data sources, information products and health statistics. *Journal of the Royal Society of Medicine, 107*(15), 34–45.
National Department of Health and ICF. (2019). *South Africa demographic and health survey 2016*. Pretoria: National Department of Health – NDoH – ICF. Retrieved from http://dhsprogram.com/pubs/pdf/FR337/FR337.pdf
National Identity Management Commission (NIMC). (2020). *Nigerian Immigration Service (NIS) to commence enforcement of NIN on the new Enhanced e-Passports*. Retrieved on August 2020, from www.nimc.gov.ng/nimc-nis-to-commence-enforcement-of-nin-on-the-new-enhanced-e-passports/
National Malaria Elimination Programme (NMEP), National Population Commission (NPopC), National Bureau of Statistics (NBS), and ICF International. (2016). *Nigeria malaria indicator survey 2015*. Abuja, Nigeria; & Rockville, MD, USA: NMEP, NPopC, and ICF International.
National Planning Commission of Namibia (NPCN). (2012). *Census summary results*. Retrieved July 16, 2020, from https://cms.my.na/assets/documents/p19dmn58guram30ttun89rdrp1.pdf

National Population Commission, Nigeria. (2006, March). *Federal Republic of Nigeria 2006 population and housing census enumerator's manual*. Abuja, Nigeria: National Population Commission.

National Statistical Office. (2019). *2018 Malawi population and housing census main report*. Retrieved July 30, 2020, from http://arks.princeton.edu/ark:/88435/dsp0105741v60z

Nigeria HIV/AIDS Indicator and Impact Survey. (2019). *National summary sheet*. Retrieved July 15, 2020, from https://www.naiis.ng/resource/factsheet/NAIIS%20PA%20NATIONAL%20FACTSHEET%20FINAL.pdf

Nkengasong, J., Gudo, E., Macicame, I., Maunze, X., Amouzou, A., Banke, K., . . . Jani, I. (2020). Improving birth and death data for African decision making. *The Lancet Global Health*, *8*(1), e35–e36. https://doi.org/10.1016/S2214-109X(19)30397-3

Obasanjo, O. (2006, March 21). Census is indispensable to the nations quest of sustainable development. *The Guardian*, 9.

Odhiambo, F. O., Laserson, K. F., Sewe, M., Hamel, M. J., Feikin, D. R., Adazu, K., . . . Vulule, J. M. (2012). Profile: KEMRI/CDC health and demographic surveillance system-Western Kenya. *International Journal of Epidemiology*, *41*, 97787. doi:10.1093/ije/dys108

Okolo, A. (1999). The Nigerian census: Problems and prospects. *The American Statistician*, *53*(4), 321–325. doi:10.2307/2686050

Statistics South Africa. (2014). *Statistical release P0309.3: Mortality and causes of death in South Africa, 2013: Findings from death notification*. Pretoria. Retrieved from http://beta2.statssa.gov.za/publications/P03093/P030932013.pdf [cited January 29, 2015].

Sulaiman, B. (2015). Should the next South African census be register-based? *Bulletin of the World Health Organization*, *93*, 134. http://dx.doi.org/10.2471/BLT.14.148502

Uganda Bureau of Statistics. (2005). *Post enumeration survey: 2005 Uganda population and housing census*. Retrieved August 1, 2020, from https://unstats.un.org/unsd/censuskb20/KnowledgebaseArticle10682.aspx

UNFPA East and Southern Africa. (2016). *Swaziland goes digital for 2017 census*. Retrieved on August 20, 2020, from https://esaro.unfpa.org/en/news/swaziland-goes-digital-2017-census

UNFPA Malawi. (2018). *Malawi launches first ever digital census*. Retrieved on August 20, 2020 from https://malawi.unfpa.org/en/news/malawi-launches-first-ever-digital-census

United Nations. (1952). *Manual I: Methods for estimating total population for current dates*. United Nations Publications, Sales No. 52.XIII.5. New York: United Nations.

United Nations. (1969). Methodology and evaluation of population registers and similar systems. *Studies in Methods*, Series F, No. 5.

United Nations. (1988). *Case studies in population policy: Nigeria*. Population Policy Paper, No. 16. ST/ESA/SER/R.83.

United Nations. (1998). *Principles and recommendations for population and housing censuses, Revision 1*. New York: United Nations.

United Nations. (2007). *Population and vital statistics report: Department of Economic and Social Affairs, Statistics Division, 2010 World Population and Housing Census Programme: Census dates for all countries*. Retrieved from http://unstats.un.org

United Nations. (2008). *Principles and recommendations for population and housing censuses, Revision 2*. New York: United Nations.

United Nations. (2019). *Guidelines on the use of electronic data collection technologies in population and housing censuses*. Retrieved on August 19, 2020, from https://unstats.un.org/unsd/demographic/standmeth/handbooks/data-collection-census-201901.pdf

United Nations Department of Economics and Social Affairs. (2010). *Status of civil registration and vital statistics in the SADC region*. UN/DESA Technical Report. New York, NY: United Nations.

United Nations Department of Economic and Social Affairs Statistics Division. (2014). *Principles and recommendations for a vital statistics system*. New York: United Nations.

United Nations Inter-agency Group for Child Mortality Estimation (UN IGME). (2017). *Levels & trends in child mortality: Report 2017, estimates developed by the UN Inter-agency Group for Child Mortality Estimation*. New York: United Nations Children's Fund.

United Nations Population Fund. (2004). *African population database documentation*. New York: United Nations.

United Nations Population Fund. (2020). *Census: Overview*. Retrieved on August 19, 2020 from www.unfpa.org/census

United Nations Population Fund, Liberia Institute of Statistics and Geo-Information Services. (2019). *Liberia population and housing census 2008*. Ref. LBR_2008_PHC_v01_M.Dataset. New York: United Nations.

Van De Walle, E. (2006). African households: Censuses and surveys. *A General Demography of Africa*. https://doi.org/10.4324/9781315497532

WHO. (2015). Should the next South African census be register-based? *Bulletin of the World Health Organization*, *93*, 134. http://dx.doi.org/10.2471/BLT.14.148502

WHO. (2020). Should next South African census be register-based? *Bulletin of the World Health Organization*, *93*(2015), 134. http://dx.doi.org/10.2471/BLT.14.148502

8

DEMOGRAPHIC OPERATIONS IN DISTRESS? THE CASE OF FRENCH-SPEAKING AFRICAN COUNTRIES SOUTH OF THE SAHARA

Françoise Gubry and Francis Gendreau

Introduction

The foundations of African demography are to be found in the results of demographic data collection, censuses and surveys, the registration of vital events still being very incomplete in most African countries today. Since the 1950s, these data collection operations have grown considerably, gradually constituting a precious "demographic heritage", and have made it possible to progressively improve the knowledge that one can have about the dynamics of African populations.

In this general context, the situation of French-speaking African countries south of the Sahara has specific characteristics. In particular, their demographic heritage is relatively recent insofar as the colonial powers, French and Belgian, paid little attention to the collection of demographic data. It was therefore only after independence that the need for precise demographic data for development purposes became clear. Unfortunately, there was no concern to preserve this heritage until recently (early 21st century), and the oldest part of this heritage has often been forgotten over the years.

The result is that it is often difficult for a researcher to find even the publication of a census or a survey results dating back only about 40 years, a modest duration compared to the demographic temporality. Of course, many users are primarily interested in recent demographic data. But older demographic operations, that is, those dating back several decades, are of interest to other users, including statisticians-demographers and researchers working on demographic topics for which the study period may extend over several years or even several decades. It should be remembered that demographic trends are most often assessed over a long period of time.

The question of archiving demographic data has thus gradually become stronger, and this has been facilitated by the development of computers and the Internet. There has therefore been real progress, in particular for the demographic operations implemented by national statistical

 DOI: 10.4324/9780429287213-10

offices (NSOs), which have created archiving websites and which often preserve microdata. But it must be noted that there are still many operations which have not been saved or archived, in particular old operations, as well as those which are not carried out by NSOs.

This chapter develops these questions in three parts. The first presents the context of the study: its fields (thematic, geographic and temporal) and the sources on which the study is based. The second part gives a summary history of demographic operations in French-speaking African countries south of the Sahara and ends with an overview of the national operations that have been carried out (by decade, by type of operation and by country). Finally, the third part deals with the archiving of these operations: a brief history is drawn of the rise in power of data archiving before taking stock of the current situation not only for "classic" operations usually carried out by NSOs but also for demographic surveys carried out by research centres.

Context of the study

Fields of study

Thematic scope

The operations taken into account in this chapter are demographic data collection operations, either exhaustive (censuses) or by sampling (surveys).

For censuses, these are population censuses (and possibly housing or accommodation censuses), which play an important role due to their exhaustive nature and their interest in providing data at the finest geographical level. These are "statistical censuses", which we distinguish from "administrative censuses", implemented in many countries by the colonial administration before the first statistical censuses. These will be mentioned for the colonial period, but there are also some administrative censuses after independence, sometimes "improved", used in some countries before the first statistical census.

As for surveys, we consider demography in the traditional sense of demographic analysis (state and movement data). We therefore take into account household surveys with purely demographic objectives, but we also consider surveys with other objectives (employment, health, living conditions and poverty, budget/consumption, knowledge, attitudes and practices on contraception or AIDS, etc.) and also providing demographic data.

Geographic scope

This chapter focuses on French-speaking countries of Africa south of the Sahara, with the exception of non-independent territories (Mayotte, Reunion Island). The countries that we have chosen are those that emerged at their independence from the Belgian and French colonial empires. A total of 20 countries: Benin, Burkina Faso, Burundi, Cameroon, Central African Republic, Chad, Comoros, Congo, Congo (D.R.), Côte d'Ivoire, Djibouti, Gabon, Guinea, Madagascar, Mali, Mauritania, Niger, Rwanda, Senegal and Togo.[1]

In general, we have considered in these countries only national operations (those which cover the whole country). However, in certain cases, regions are excluded from the scope of the operation for various reasons (rainy season, floods, insecurity, etc.). In addition, we will evoke certain old local operations because of their historical importance as being among the first statistical operations carried out.

Temporal scope

In these 20 countries, there was no "scientific" demographic operation before the Second World War. The colonizers, Belgian and French, only carried out "administrative censuses", which we will briefly discuss in the following. The first scientific operations (surveys and censuses) date from the 1950s, during colonization. They developed after independence under the aegis of the national statistical offices, which continued the study of populations with new operations.

Therefore, the temporal scope covers the post-war period, that is, from January 1, 1950 (date of the first demographic data collections) to December 31, 2019 inclusive. In total, the study thus covers 70 years.

Sources: Inventaire des recensements et enquêtes démographiques en Afrique, archiving sites, documents

The inventory of operations between 1950 and 2019 that we use is the one we have developed for the Inventaire des recensements et enquêtes démographiques en Afrique (IREDA) site,[2] created in 2008 by the two authors of this chapter and whose purpose is to enhance the African demographic heritage of the 20th century, often more and more difficult to find. It is interested in the whole of Africa, in particular with a list of demographic operations in all countries that is regularly updated. But the description of the operations only concerns French-speaking African countries south of the Sahara (i.e., the 20 countries under review, plus Mauritius and the Seychelles) and Equatorial Guinea. In total, 440 demographic operations, 365 national and 75 local, are currently described for these 23 countries, and more than 4,700 resources are referenced, including 3,000 in full text.

The data on this site correspond to the time and thematic fields defined previously.

The main sources used to produce this inventory are:

- bibliographies on sources of demographic data in Africa, in particular: Population Research Center (1965), Pinfold (1985), Domschke and Goyer (1986), Mbaye (1986) and Lloyd and Marquette, 1992);
- a few books and articles, including lists of statistical operations (surveys and censuses) (de Graft-Johnson et al., 1988; Gendreau, 1996; Tabutin & Schoumaker, 2004);
- some international websites (or those with international content) having been created with the aim of promoting the safeguarding of demographic archives (or, more broadly, statistical archives) like those of the following organizations: World Bank, US Census Bureau (USCB), United Nations Statistics Division, International Household Survey Network (IHSN), Demographic and Health Surveys (DHSs), Multiple Indicator Cluster Surveys (MICSs), Integrated Public Use Microdata Series-International (IPUMS-International)[3];
- and, of course, the national data archive (NADA) sites of the national statistical offices.

For older operations, we mainly use two publications from the Groupe de Démographie Africaine (GDA): "Recensements africains, 1ère partie: Monographies méthodologiques" (GDA, 1980) and "Population Size in African Countries: An Evaluation" (GDA, 1986, 1988). Only Guinea is not covered by these publications.

Finally, we use old reference publications such as Brass et al. (1968), Caldwell and Okonjo (1968), Caldwell, Addo, Gaisie, Igun, and Olusanya (1975), Ominde and Ejiogu (1972), INSD (1975) and Fetter (1990).

History of demographic operations in French-speaking African countries south of the Sahara

Counting populations until independence

Administrative censuses

In most countries having experienced colonization, various "administrative" objectives, especially fiscal (levying of per capita tax), have led to what have been called "administrative censuses" (Sanogoh, 1972).

The methodology of these operations is often uncertain because the texts on which they are based are often imprecise: the first professional statistician was recruited at the Ministry of Colonies at the end of 1933 (Sanner, 1993). In addition, "the French Administration in Africa has hardly felt the need to base its action on a real demographic knowledge of the administered populations", the important thing for it being "to classify the individuals between taxable and non-taxable" (Sarton du Jonchay, 1958). Finally, the administrators in charge of carrying out these operations encountered many difficulties on the field (notably the reluctance of the populations) and "adapted" to this reality – see, for example, Gervais (1993) for the ex-Afrique Occidentale Française.

One of the main complaints against administrative censuses is that they underestimate the size of the population. This very general phenomenon is due to the distrust of a population anxious to escape conscription, recruitment for work or tax and the imperfection of census methods, not to mention the interest that local authorities sometimes had in not counting everyone (P. Gubry, 1984; Lohlé-Tart & François, 1999). This underestimation varies widely across countries, regions and time periods. It is estimated at more than 30% in Mauritania (1946) but seems almost zero in Congo (D.R.) (1940 and 1959) and Madagascar (1962).

These administrative censuses are found in most countries until independence. But whereas their methodology has been quickly clarified in countries under British, Portuguese or Spanish domination to become statistical censuses, it has remained much less elaborate for the Belgian and French colonizers (except in Algeria and Morocco), who carried them out until independence.

The beginnings of the statistical era

However, after the Second World War, the same colonizers set up in the 1950s the beginnings of the statistical era, in particular with the creation of statistical services in the various territories (Ficatier, 1981), and carried out the first scientifically conducted surveys, especially:

- Urban demographic censuses, first in Senegal: Diourbel and Ziguinchor (1951), Thiès (1953), Saint-Louis (1954), Dakar (1955); then in 1955 in Cameroon (Douala), Oubangui-Chari (Bangui), Congo (Brazzaville), Côte d'Ivoire (Abidjan) and so on;
- National retrospective surveys: Burundi and Rwanda (1952), Guinea (1955) and Zaire (1955–1958), before their implementation became widespread around the 1960s.

Finally, let us note two particular cases in this landscape, the realization of real national censuses in the Comoros (1958 and 1966) and in Togo (1958–1960).

There was also a (modest) initiation of demographic research with, for example, regional research operations, often qualified as socio-demographic or socio-economic, for example: the

Bangassou Region (Central African Republic 1954), the Niari Region (Congo 1954), the Bas-Mangoky (Madagascar 1955), the Bongouanou subdivision (Côte d'Ivoire 1955–1956), the Koukouya Plateau (Congo 1956), the Androy Region (Madagascar 1956), the Lobi Region (Burkina Faso 1956–1957) and, last but not least, the remarkable survey in the middle valley of Senegal (Mauritania-Senegal 1957).

Operations carried out by NSOs after independence

Governments and demographic data collection

The interest of demographic data for governments has evolved with changing needs. The 1960s were the highlight of "planning for development", and statistical offices are subject to the timetable for drawing up successive development plans to produce data in good time. Subsequently, this need fades with the gradual abandonment of planning and Keynesian economics. The liberal economy became dominant in the early 1980s with the "Washington consensus", and statistical data were considered less important. In addition, to face the economic crisis of the 1970s, the International Monetary Fund and the World Bank implemented "structural adjustment programmes" (SAPs). Such programmes began emerging in the French-speaking countries under review from the end of the 1970s. They considerably reduced the budgetary means of the governments, and the importance of the statistical offices decreased sharply. It would only resume in the 1990s with the importance given to the fight against poverty, the status of women, the environment, the Millennium Development Goals (MDGs) and then the Sustainable Development Goals (SDGs), all areas where the statistician-demographer has his or her place provided to adapt reference frameworks and data collection and analysis methods. Finally, demography "must respond more to the new problems of society" (Tabutin, 2006).

For the recent period, statistical offices could not escape the deterioration caused by the serious political and economic difficulties which have affected most of the African countries south of the Sahara, hence a lack of budgetary means, not always compensated for by international donors.

A gap should be pointed out here in this demographic observation system: in no country is there a framework integrating the different data sources (census, surveys, civil registration, administrative sources) into a coherent system and articulating them in a "programme" with priorities, timetable and budget (Dackam Ngatchou, 2005; Tabutin, 2006; Gendreau & Gubry, 2009).

The end of administrative censuses

After independence, and in the absence of a "statistical tradition", administrative censuses continued and sometimes continued to be processed (for example, each year in Madagascar until the early 1970s). In some French-speaking countries, what were commonly known as "improved censuses" were also organized, when, given the need for demographic statistics and the difficulty in organizing a real census, governments have chosen to use the existing system by improving it on various points: reduction of the duration of field operations, recruitment of enumerators, allocation of specific resources for its realization. Two examples can be cited here:

- Chad (1968): this census was thus able to provide alternative sources despite its incompleteness (70% of the population was actually counted) with results that are really useful for assessing the population figure of this country;

- Zaire, now Congo (D.R.) (1970): if the total population size obtained, clearly overestimated, is questioned in different regions, it seems to reflect reality fairly well for a series of cities and areas.

The explosion of surveys

But what most marked the beginnings of demographic data collection after independence was the implementation of numerous surveys. As the censuses were considered in the countries under review to be too difficult to carry out, and the civil registration system did not work, there was first of all the generalization of retrospective surveys until the end of the 1960s. They were then taken up by the surveys carried out within the international programme of the World Fertility Survey (WFS) from 1972 in six of the countries (Benin, Cameroon, Côte d'Ivoire, Mauritania, Rwanda, Senegal). Then there were numerous DHSs (from 1986) and MICSs (from 1995) in all countries. We can also cite here the migration surveys of the Réseau Migrations et Urbanisation en Afrique de l'Ouest (REMUAO), implemented under the coordination of the Centre d'études et de Recherche sur la Population et le Développement (CERPOD, closed today) and the Institut du Sahel and carried out in eight countries (Burkina Faso, Côte d'Ivoire, Guinea, Mali, Mauritania, Niger, Nigeria and Senegal).

Others, less known and often difficult to find, were carried out by NSOs but also by universities and research institutions, such as the Institut de Formation et de Recherche Démographiques (IFORD) (Cameroon).

Finally, especially since the early 1990s, many surveys should be noted carried out by NSOs on budget-consumption of households, on poverty or in the context of the MDGs and then the SDGs, with a demographic component, sometimes not negligible.

The first censuses

Except the specific cases of Comoros and Togo, which experienced their first censuses under colonization, the first censuses were spread from the beginning of the 60s (Central African Republic and Gabon) to the beginning of the 80s, with the exception of Chad, whose first census dates from 1993.

The implementation of these first censuses was made possible for many countries by the support of the Economic Commission for Africa (ECA) and the United Nations Population Fund (UNFPA), which set up in 1971 the African Census Programme to help countries which found it difficult to carry out a census (often the first). Funded by UNFPA, this programme made it possible to provide personnel and material assistance to the 20 countries which were covered by it from 1972 to 1979, including 12 countries under review (Benin, Burkina Faso, Burundi, Cameroon, Central African Republic, Congo, Côte d'Ivoire, Madagascar, Mali, Mauritania, Niger, Senegal) which, apart from the Central African Republic, had never carried out a census: this shows the importance that this programme had for these countries (Blanc, 1978).

From the decade 1980–1989, the implementation of censuses has been generalized, even if it encounters many difficulties, as shown in particular by P. Gubry (1995): "Besides the technical aspects, the political aspects completely determine the realization and the future of a census." But most countries fail to achieve them at a ten-year pace as recommended by the United Nations. It even seems that the countries are finding it increasingly difficult to carry out these operations, undoubtedly for two main reasons: the question of financing and political problems (ECA, 1996; Gendreau, 2019).

Overview of national operations carried out

The demographic data collection operations identified in the IREDA inventory for the 20 countries studied according to the criteria indicated previously are in total 334. This means an average of 47.7 operations per decade and 16.7 per country, or 2.4 operations per country and per decade. They will be presented according to three simple criteria: the decade, the type of operation and the country.

By decade and by type

Not surprisingly, the number of operations has grown from decade to decade (Table 8.1), with one exception, however, for the last decade, during which the number of operations declined after a maximum observed during the period 2000–2009 but which may also be due to too short a time to exhaustively present the operations of the last period. What appears, however, is that, over the period 1950–1989, the average number of operations by country and by decade was 1.2, whereas it rose to 4.0 for the period 1990–2019.

We combined the type of operation with the decade to highlight the variations over time of the different types of operation.

- The censuses (cen) are generalized in all countries, but their number seems to have peaked at around 15 per decade since 1970. Note also that one country, the Congo (D.R.), has only known one single census, carried out in 1984.
- Demographic and Health Surveys (DHS), to which we have added three "dhs-type" surveys (std) because they were developed in the same spirit but were not part of the DHS programme, have multiplied: from the period 1990–1999, more than one is done per country per decade.
- Multiple indicator cluster surveys (mic), a programme launched by UNICEF, are also becoming more widespread.
- The other demographic surveys (ods) are those that do not belong to an international program. We added to them national operations which we qualified as complex (cns) because the include several local components, censuses or surveys, carried out over a few years. These operations are mainly old surveys, prior to 1970.
- There are significantly fewer surveys on migration and possibly on labour force (mig) than the previous ones, the migratory phenomena having obviously presented less interest for decision makers, governments and NSOs.

Table 8.1 Number of Operations by Decade and Type

Type	*1950–1959*	*1960–1969*	*1970–1979*	*1980–1989*	*1990–1999*	*2000–2009*	*2010–2019*	*Total*
cen	2	4	14	15	12	15	12	**74**
dhs and std	0	0	0	4	23	22	25	**74**
mic	0	0	0	0	8	22	17	**47**
ods and cns	10	11	4	3	4	1	2	**35**
mig	0	0	3	1	8	4	0	**16**
oss	0	0	0	2	16	28	17	**63**
Others	2	5	10	6	2	0	0	**25**
Total	**14**	**20**	**31**	**31**	**73**	**92**	**73**	**334**

Source: IREDA

- The other statistical surveys containing demographic questions (oss) are, as already indicated, surveys not having the objective of demographic knowledge but nevertheless providing information in this field. They appear and develop especially from the 1990s.
- Under the heading "Others", we have gathered the operations which were not mentioned previously and which have been much less numerous: administrative censuses (adc); additional surveys to a census (ads), identified as going beyond a simple post-census survey; fertility surveys of the World Fertility Survey programme; and multi-round surveys (mrs). These operations seem to have disappeared around the 2000s.

By country

The number of operations varies widely depending on the country (Table 8.2): it ranges from 9 (Comoros, Congo and Gabon) to 25 (Senegal and Mali). Besides these last two countries, three other countries carried out at least three operations per decade during the considered period: Burkina Faso, Madagascar and Rwanda.

Table 8.2 Number of Operations by Country

Country	*Number of Operations*	*Country*	*Number of Operations*	*Country*	*Number of Operations*
Benin	15	**Congo**	9	**Mali**	25
Burkina Faso	24	**Congo (D.R.)**	10	**Mauritania**	18
Burundi	19	**Côte d'Ivoire**	19	**Niger**	19
Cameroon	19	**Djibouti**	11	**Rwanda**	23
Central African Rep.	12	**Gabon**	9	**Senegal**	25
Chad	13	**Guinea**	18	**Togo**	15
Comoros	9	**Madagascar**	22	**Total**	**334**

Source: IREDA

Archiving of these operations

The rise of data archiving

To know and manage populations, it was essential to count and describe them, but for the oldest demographic operations, the archiving of the collected data was not really developed. It is indeed astonishing to see that the first versions of the "Principles and Recommendations for Population and Housing Censuses" published in 1958 and then in 1969 by the United Nations simply stipulate that "it is most useful to assemble complete records on the methodology of each census, an evaluation of the techniques employed and the costs" (United Nations, 1969). Updates took into account, thanks to technological progress, new user requests such as the creation of databases, and they finally recommend the archiving of individual data in the latest version of 2017 (United Nations, 2017). On the other hand, archiving and dissemination of the surveys of the WFS (which took place from 1972 to 1984) and then of the DHS that followed were immediately put in place.

It was towards the end of the 20th century that considerable progress was made, obviously thanks to the development of information technology and the Internet, but also to a change in mentalities and uses of the collected statistical data. Until then, access to results was obtained through the tables of printed reports, often published late, more or less available in libraries (rare or scarce) of NSOs, universities or research centres. To be visible on the Internet, the NSOs first developed websites to display statistical and demographic indicators, then digital survey reports, and more recently microdata files. This visibility on the Internet to disseminate information, more gratifying than the archiving of data, for which there was also no particular incentive, required documenting and structuring the information for its dissemination, that is to say concretely to archive. Subsequent access to survey microdata also freed researchers from the constraint of using only data as they were published in the producer reports.

The archiving of statistical surveys has developed thanks to the creation of new technological tools based on recognized standards:

- Dublin Core Metadata Initiative (DCMI) came from the world of libraries and museums in 1995 to describe digital resources in a simple and standardized way.[4]
- Data Documentation Initiative (DDI), started in 1995, is an international standard for the description of data from the social, behavioural and economic sciences (or metadata).[5]

This has enabled the creation of various thematic or international archives (cited in our sources) which make it possible to identify statistical surveys carried out by or in partnership with NSOs.

Numerous surveys have been carried out following the adoption by the United Nations of the MDGs, then SDGs, which encouraged NSOs to provide many reliable indicators. The consortium The Partnership in Statistics for Development in the 21st Century (PARIS21)[6] was then created "to strengthen statistics and promote the use of robust statistical information by policy makers and citizens with a primary focus on low income countries". In 2004, the Marrakech Action Plan for Statistics was set up, followed by the creation of the International Household Survey Network in charge of improving the availability, accessibility and quality of survey data in developing countries and encouraging the analysis and use of these data (guidelines, training, dedicated software such as Nesstar Publisher or NADA, etc.) and managing its catalogue of statistical surveys.[7]

Data revolution

The 21st century has also seen the arrival of statistical data of a very different nature, called *big data* (mainly produced from private organizations), characterized by high volume, velocity and variety and requiring specific technologies and methods of analysis. The fifth "International Conference on Big Data for Official Statistics" organized by the United Nations took place in May 2019 in Kigali.

This explosion of data has given birth to a new term, *the data revolution*. In May 2013, at the request of the United Nations, the authors of the report entitled "A New Global Partnership: Eradicate Poverty and Transform Economies through Sustainable Development" launched an appeal: "We also call for a data revolution for sustainable development, with a new international initiative to improve the quality of statistics and information available to people and governments" (United Nations, 2013, p. 21). In 2016, "The Africa-Data-Revolution-Report: Highlighting Developments in African Data Ecosystems" (ECA, 2016) emphasized the importance of administrative data (including civil registration) and the central role that the national statistical system can play in national ecosystems. Regarding demography, we can also consult the reflections initiated by the Digital Demography Panel of the International Union for the Scientific Study of Population (IUSSP) on the web page devoted to this subject.[8]

A new demand also appears with the movement of *open data*. "Open means anyone can freely access, use, modify, and share for any purpose (subject, at most, to requirements that preserve provenance and openness)", as explained by the Open Knowledge Foundation.[9] The use of these public data, more and more numerous, can be the subject of different licenses for their use (such as anonymization of microdata) and is promoted in *The Africa Data Revolution Report 2018* (Van Belle, 2018).

These developments have made it possible to create archives of interoperable statistical surveys because they are built on the same standards. Finally, researchers can now find data on the African population in specialized international archives that can provide microdata such as that of DHS, MICS and IPUMS-International but also in general catalogues such as those of IHSN or the World Bank. They can also consult the national archiving sites of NSOs when they exist, the IREDA site for French-speaking African countries and the DEMOSTAF inventory (described in the following) for four countries (Burkina Faso, Madagascar, Mali, Senegal).

What visibility for ancient demographic surveys?

The IREDA project started, as mentioned, in 2008. Around this time, the first national archives of the NSOs (NADA) also started, as well as the international catalogue of surveys of the IHSN, the historical dimension of which seems rather limited.

Unlike the first part of our study, we are interested here in all demographic operations (in the traditional sense of state and movement data), whether national or not, which we were able to describe in IREDA thanks to the sources cited previously. Old local surveys and urban censuses were also taken into account for their historical interest since, as we have seen, in the 1950s, there were very few data on the population. All of these surveys are compared to those found in NADAs and the IHSN catalogue (Table 8.3).

Table 8.3 Comparison of the Demographic Operations of the Ten NADAs and IHSN with IREDA

Period	*IREDA (10 Countries)*	*NADAs (10 Countries)*		*IHSN (10 Countries)*	
	Number	*Number*	*%IREDA*	*Number*	*%IREDA*
Population censuses only					
Before 1980	10	5	*50*	7	*70*
1980–1999	13	10	*77*	10	*77*
After 2000	15	13	*87*	10	*67*
All censuses	38	28	*74*	27	*71*
All demographic operations					
1950–1959	23	9	*39*	1	*4*
1960–1969	33	3	*9*	0	*0*
1970–1979	24	8	*33*	7	*29*
1980–1989	23	13	*57*	13	*57*
1990–1999	43	23	*53*	33	*77*
2000–2009	57	41	*72*	51	*89*
2010–2019	52	37	*71*	42	*81*
Total demography	255	134	*53*	147	*58*
All operations (10 countries)	255	625	-	473	-

Source: IREDA, NADAs, IHSN

For the studied countries, only ten NADA archives could be taken into account by mid-2020.[10] Two other archives, which had not been maintained for a long time, have disappeared since a previous examination in 2017. Detailed research on these NADA archives has moreover shown that there are great disparities between them and that access to microdata files is often difficult (Gueye & Ihadjadene, 2017 and Gueye, 2019).

The comparison therefore relates only to these ten countries and only to their demographic surveys because these archives obviously contain many other national or local surveys on specific subjects.

The ten NADA archives are very heterogeneous, since four, among the least provided, have not been updated since 2016, whereas those of Senegal and Mali use the interoperability of the different archives to enrich the catalogue with old surveys. This partly explains the good result of NADAs compared to IHSN until 1980. The trend then reversed in favour of IHSN, but IREDA, which remains the most complete archive, also benefited from the contributions of the others. Figure 8.1 shows that the gap is narrowing now and that new surveys are being taken more and more into account.

National censuses are much better archived (more than 70%), even in ancient periods, probably because they are expensive and essential operations. Eight countries have signed an agreement with IPUMS-International to provide researchers with an anonymized file of 10% of the records (Table 8.4).

Their oldest African microdata are those of the 1958 Togo urban census, which were recreated in 2013 following the digitization of the questionnaires of this census, which had been found and entrusted to CEPED by Pierre Cantrelle (Cantrelle & Peltier-Charrier, 1975). The 1970 Togolese census file had previously also been recreated with the Unité de Recherche Démographique (URD, Lomé) by recoding a 1/20 sample of the questionnaires (Nomenyo & Assogba, 1994).

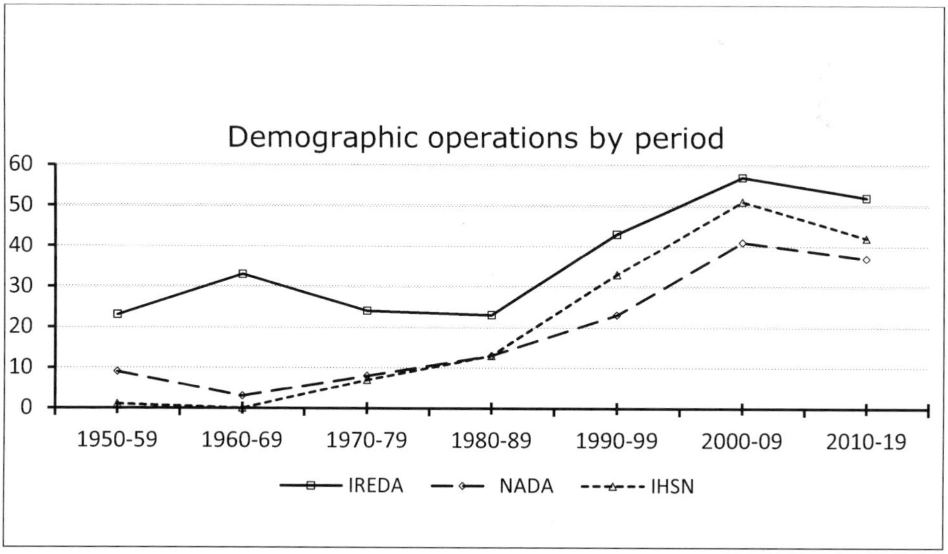

Figure 8.1 Number of demographic operations in IREDA, the ten NADAs and IHSN per decennial period

Table 8.4 African Censuses. Microdata Available in IPUMS-International

Period	*IPUMS Microdata*	*IREDA*	*% IREDA*
Before 1980	4	8	50
1980–1999	10	10	100
After 2000	9	12	75
All censuses	23	30	77

Benin, Burkina Faso, Cameroon, Guinea, Mali, Rwanda, Senegal, Togo

Source: IPUMS-I, IREDA

Other projects for digitizing census questionnaires have been carried out in partnership with the Observatoire Démographique et Statistique de l'Espace Francophone (Mali: 1976, 1987 and 1998; DRC: 1984) (Marcoux, Richard, & Kani Konate, 2014).

The dissemination of census results has long been a problem (Dackam, 2003), but the situation has considerably improved, and the first results are now fairly readily available on the NSOs' websites. The use of digital tablets and smartphones accelerates the processing of these data, but more needs to be done to access microdata.

What is the future for demographic surveys carried out by research centres?

Surveys outside NSOs are hardly archived

We have just seen that the old surveys rarely appear in these archives because they are difficult to find and that they are rarely archived in the NADAs.

But then what happens to the demographic surveys carried out by researchers belonging to research centres? In the 20 countries, there are many researchers who have carried out demographic surveys within their research centres or in partnership with other researchers: these are specific local surveys with funding for research projects or surveys for training of students. The results can be found inside publications in journals, but the microdata do not seem to have been systematically archived or even preserved.

Among the best-known demographic research centres in the French-speaking countries of the region, only IFORD has set up a NADA-type archive (IREDIF)[11] visible on its website, which partially describes 99 surveys between 1973 and 2008 without reporting the related resources or giving information about the existence of microdata; it is no longer updated. The ISSP has announced the creation of its survey archive, but nothing has emerged to date. The other demographic research centres in the region have no known or accessible data archive, and some of them do not exist any more. Among the ancient innovative surveys, the "Enquête sur la mortalité infantile et juvénile" (EMIJ) initiated by IFORD in Yaoundé in 1978 was then reproduced with the support of the other research centres in seven other countries of the region, and they led to more than 120 publications (F. Gubry, 1993). The files for all of these EMIJ surveys, or even their simple remembrance, seem to have been largely lost. Unfortunately, this situation can only deteriorate over the years if no partnership is created between NSOs and the research centres because developing and maintaining such archives requires training and retaining specialized staff.

Partnership does not necessarily improve the situation

The situation is also not very bright for African surveys in the 20 countries carried out in partnership with research centres of non-African countries. Their social science surveys archives are relatively new there, independent of those of the NSOs, and research organizations do not necessarily have them. The results of a quick round-up of African surveys in the region in various archives (Europe, United States, Canada, South Africa) are quite meagre, with a large dispersion of surveys across various sites. In France, the French Institute for Demographic Studies (INED) has had an archive for a long time, and there are around 15 African surveys carried out in partnership with its researchers;[12] however, the French National Research Institute for Sustainable Development (IRD) did not have any, and only publications have been widely cited and digitized in its Horizon bibliographic database.[13] For example, the implementation of biographical surveys has given rise to many methodological studies leading to the creation in 1998 of the international Groupe de Réflexion sur Approche Biographique (GRAB).[14] Between 1986 and 2001, 11 African biographical surveys were cited on this site with information on questionnaires and publications, but the only two microdata files from surveys carried out in partnership with INED researchers were archived.

An inventory of national and local statistical surveys belonging to the broad demographic field (such as surveys on employment or schooling) was implemented within the framework of the "Data documentation" component of the European project piloted by INED and Demography Statistics for Africa (DEMOSTAF)[15] and covers four countries (Burkina Faso, Madagascar, Mali, Senegal). Carried out in partnership with the relevant NSOs and IREDA and in accordance with the DDI and Dublin Core standards, this inventory identified numerous surveys, in particular local ones, implemented by research organizations or NGOs (F. Gubry, Diguet, Sohler, & Gueye, 2019). ANADS (Archivage National des Données du Sénégal),[16] institutional archive of the Senegalese Agence Nationale de la Statistique et de la Démographie (ANSD), faithful to its policy of visibility of all Senegalese surveys, immediately integrated the missing surveys, while that of Mali favoured surveys of ministerial bodies or United Nations agencies.

We should also welcome the initiative of the ANSD of Senegal, which initiated a project in 2018 to install data access centres in Senegalese universities in order to facilitate the accessibility and use of survey data for researchers and academic staff in a secure environment and in compliance with the provisions of the statistical law. The pilot project is located at Cheikh Anta Diop University (ANSD, 2018).

The situation is therefore still very fragile for these categories of surveys from the research world, unlike those now implemented by or with NSOs, which are increasingly better described and archived.

Conclusion

If, 70 years ago, Africa, especially French-speaking countries south of the Sahara, was in dire need of reliable demographic data, this is no longer the case today. Admittedly, all the problems are not resolved: civil registration still does not work well in most countries, few have defined a demographic observation strategy, certain themes are still little studied (for example, migration) and so on. But countries have carried out an average of 2.4 operations per decade (censuses, but above all surveys) for all the past 70 years, and most importantly, this figure has risen to almost 4.0 for the past three decades.

The risk today is that NSOs are faced with a plethora of data, especially with those collected for the implementation of the SDGs. Without increased resources, especially in qualified and long-term staff, they may not be able to cope with the processing and archiving of all this data. Already, the creation of NADAs and their updating were obviously not easy for many NSOs, access to these sites is sometimes uncertain and the situation should not be allowed to deteriorate.

We must hope that governments will continue to support the development of NSOs because the data revolution is underway, with numerous statistical data and abundant surveys whose open data will enable re-processing and to which will be added more and more big data whose methods and related techniques will develop rapidly. The horizon will then offer immense opportunities for researchers on the continent to study the African population and its long-term developments and therefore consolidate a booming African demography in light of the many publications that are produced.

Notes

1 In these countries, members of the Organisation Internationale de la Francophonie (OIF), French is the (or one) official language (except Mauritania, where the official language is Arabic, French however being widely spoken as use and work language). Seven countries that are members of the OIF are not among the countries selected: Equatorial Guinea (where the official languages are Spanish, French and Portuguese), Seychelles (where the official languages are English and French), and five countries where French is not an official language and whose last colonial power was not France: Cabo Verde, Guinea Bissau and Sao Tome y Principe (Portugal), and Egypt and Mauritius (United Kingdom).
2 https://ireda.ceped.org/inventaire/
The interested reader will find at this address all the information on the origins and the content of this project.
3 https://microdata.worldbank.org/index.php/home; www.census.gov/; https://unstats.un.org/; https://ihsn.org/; https://dhsprogram.com/; https://mics.unicef.org/; https://international.ipums.org/
4 www.dublincore.org
5 https://ddialliance.org
6 https://paris21.org
7 www.ihsn.org
8 https://iussp.org/en/panel/digital-demography
9 https://opendefinition.org
10 Benin, Burkina Faso, Burundi, Cameroon, Côte d'Ivoire, Mali, Niger, Rwanda, Senegal, Togo.
11 Inventaire des recensements et enquêtes démographiques de l'IFORD: www.iford-cm.org/iredif
12 http://nesstar.ined.fr/webview/
13 https://horizon.documentation.ird.fr
14 https://grab.site.ined.fr/fr
15 DEMOSTAF has 14 associated academic institutions, most located in Europe and Africa, and 4 African statistical institutes from 2016 to 2020. The project enters the framework of the UN SDGs with research using data produced by statistical institutes (censuses, surveys) at the national level and local data (population monitoring, local civil status): https://demostaf.site.ined.fr/
16 ANADS claims to be "A database of surveys for the promotion of research": www.ansd.sn/

References

ANSD. (2018). *Rapport d'activité 2018 de l'Agence nationale de la statistique et de la démographie (Sénégal)*. Dakar: ANSD.

Blanc, R. (1978). Le programme africain de recensements: une opération d'assistance internationale spécialement adaptée à l'Afrique. *Population, 33*(2), 460–463.

Brass, W., Coale, A. J., Demeny, P., Heisel, D. F., Lorimer, F., Romaniuk, A., & van de Walle, E. (1968). *The demography of tropical Africa*. Princeton, NJ: Princeton University Press.

Caldwell, J. C., Addo, N. O., Gaisie, S. K., Igun, A., & Olusanya, P. O. (1975). *Population growth and socio-economic change in West Africa*. New York: Population Council.

Caldwell, J. C., & Okonjo, C. (Eds.). (1968). *The population of tropical Africa*. New York: Columbia University Press.

Cantrelle, P., & Peltier Charrier, M. C. (1975). Pour un inventaire des archives des recensements et enquêtes démographiques réalisés en Afrique d'expression française. In *Actes du Colloque de Démographie Africaine* (Vol. 4, pp. 40–51). Ouagadougou: INSTAT (BF), CRDI, OCAM.

Dackam Ngatchou, R. (2003, November 10–12), *The strategies of dissemination of census products: Lessons learnt from some African countries*. Presentation paper, Population Census Data Dissemination and Use, Pretoria. UNFPA, PARIS21.

Dackam Ngatchou, R. (Ed.). (2005). *Besoins d'informations statistiques dans les documents de stratégie de réduction de la pauvreté, Atelier régional de formation sur les nouveaux outils d'analyse des données sociodémographiques issues d'opérations de collecte de grande envergure*. Dakar: UNFPA.

De Graft-Johnson, K. T. (1988). Demographic data collection in Africa. In E. Van de Walle, M. Sala-Diakanda, & P. Ohadike (Eds.), *The state of African demography* (pp. 13–28). Liège: IUSSP.

Domschke, E., & Goyer, D. S. (1986). *The handbook of national population censuses, Africa and Asia*. Westport: Greenwood Press.

ECA, UNDP & et al. (2016). *The Africa data revolution report: Highlighting developments in African data ecosystems*. Addis Ababa: UNDP.

ECA & United Nations Economic and Social Council. (1996). *Making population censuses cost-effective and pertinent for African development*. Addis Ababa: ECA.

Fetter, B. (1990). *Demography from scanty evidence: Central Africa in the colonial era*. Boulder, CO: Lynne Rienner Publishers.

Ficatier, A. (1981). *Un certain regard sur une des fonctions de l'INSEE: de la statistique coloniale à la coopération technique*. Paris: INSEE.

Gendreau, F. (1996, October 21–23). *L'avenir de l'observation démographique en Afrique*. Presentation paper, Chaire Quetelet, Entre l'utile et le futile, pistes pour une démographie du XIXe siècle, Louvain-la-Neuve. UCL

Gendreau, F. (2019, October 16–18). *Le recensement de population en Afrique, une opération encore problématique*. Paper presentation, Colloque international Enjeux démographiques en Afrique: l'apport des données de recensement et d'état civil, Paris. INED.

Gendreau, F., & Gubry, F. (2009). L'observation démographique en Afrique, Leçons du passé, perspectives d'avenir, préservation et valorisation des opérations. In R. Marcoux & J. Dion (Eds.), *Mémoires et démographie: regards croisés au Sud et au Nord* (pp. 61–97). Québec: AUF, Les Presses de l'Université Laval.

Gervais, R. (1993). Contribution à l'étude de l'évolution de la population de 1'Afrique Occidentale Française – 1904–1960. *Les Dossiers du CEPED, 23*.

Groupe de Démographie Africaine. (1980). *Recensements africains: 1ère partie: Monographies méthodologiques*. Paris: GDA.

Groupe de Démographie Africaine. (1986). *Population size in African countries: An evaluation* (Vol. 1 & Vol. 2). Paris: GDA.

Gubry, F. (1993, July 19–23). *EMIJY, EMIJO, EMIJUL, EMIS ou la déclinaison des enquêtes EMIJ sur la mortalité infantile et juvénile dans la littérature démographique*. Paper presentation, Séminaire sur la mortalité infantile et juvénile en Afrique: Bilan des recherches et politiques de santé, Yaoundé. IFORD.

Gubry, F., Diguet, D., Sohler, K., & Gueye, M. (2019, October 16–18). *Données d'enquêtes démographiques africaines: des accès plus performants*. Paper presentation, Colloque international Enjeux démographiques en Afrique: l'apport des données de recensement et d'état civil, Paris. INED.

Gubry, P. (1984). Évolution de la collecte et des recherches démographiques au Cameroun (1884–1984). *Démographie Africaine, 44*, 17–22.

Gubry, P. (1995). Recensement et Démocratie. In J. Vallin (Ed.), *Clins d'œil de démographes à l'Afrique et à Michel François* (pp. 43–56). Paris: CEPED.

Gueye, M. (2019). *Politiques d'accès aux données statistiques sur le Web à l'ère de l'open data: pratiques et perspectives: Cas des Instituts nationaux de statistique d'Afrique membres du réseau AFRISTAT* (Thèse de doctorat, Université Paris 8).

Gueye, M., & Ihadjadene, M. (2017). Accès aux données d'enquêtes statistiques en Afrique: Étude de cas des plateformes nationales d'archives de données (NADA) des Instituts nationaux de statistique (INS). In M. Hassoun, K. Zreik, O. Larouk, & G. Besacier (Eds.), *Le Document? Actes du 20e colloque international sur le document numérique (CiDE.20)* (pp. 175–188). Lyon: Europia.

Institut National de la Statistique et de la Démographie. (1975, January 20–24). *Actes du 4e colloque de démographie africaine: Migrations, État civil, Recensements administratifs*. Ouagadougou: CRDI, OCAM.

Lloyd, C., & Marquette, C. (1992). *Directory of surveys in developing countries, 1975/92*. New York: Population Council.

Lohlé-Tart, L., & François, M. (1999). *État civil et recensement en Afrique francophone: Pour une collecte administrative de données démographiques*. Paris: CEPED.

Marcoux, R., Richard, L., & Kani Konaté, M. (2014). Sauvegarde numérique des patrimoines démographiques: les recensements de la population et les expériences du Mali et de la République démocratique du Congo. In J. F. Simard & A. E. Ouedraogo (Eds.), *Une Francophonie en quête de sens: Retour sur le 1er Forum mondial de la langue française* (pp. 329–346). Québec: PUL.

Mbaye, S. (1986). *Sources de l'histoire démographique des pays du Sahel conservées dans les archives (1816–1960)*. Bamako: CILSS.

Nomenyo, M. A., & Assogba, M. L. (1994). Expérience togolaise de récupération du recensement de 1970. In *Actes du Colloque sur les sources de l'histoire démographique des pays du Sahel conservées dans les archives*, Dakar, 1987, March 9–12 (pp. 21–31). Bamako: CERPOD.

Ominde, S. H., & Ejiogu, C. N. (1972). *Population growth and economic development in Africa*. New York: Population Council.

Pinfold, J. R. (Ed.). (1985). African population census reports: A bibliography and checklist. In *The Standing Conference on Library Materials on Africa*. Munich: Zell.

Population Research Center. (1965). *International population census bibliography: Africa*. Austin: University of Texas.

Sanner, P. (1993). *Contribution à un mémorial du service colonial des statistiques 1923–1958*. Paris: INSEE.

Sanogoh, G. (1972). Une expérience d'amélioration des recensements administratifs. *Statéco*, *2*, 53–72.

Sarton du Jonchay, J. (1958). Recensement administratif et recensement démographique en zone rurale sous-développée: La réforme des méthodes de recensement administratif. *Supplément du Bulletin mensuel de la Statistique d'Outre-mer, Série Études*, 36.

Tabutin, D. (2006). Les systèmes d'information en démographie. In G. Caselli, J. Vallin, & G. Wunsch (Eds.), *Démographie. Analyse et synthèse VIII* (pp. 13–64). Paris: INED.

Tabutin, D., & Schoumaker, B. (2004). The demography of sub-Saharan Africa from the 1950s to the 2000s: A survey of changes and a statistical assessment. *Population*, *59*(3–4), 455–555. https://doi.org/10.3917/popu.403.0521

United Nations. (1969). *Principles and recommendations for population and housing censuses* (2nd ed.). New York: United Nations.

United Nations. (2013). *A new global partnership: Eradicate poverty and transform economies through sustainable development: The report of the high-level panel of eminent persons on the post-2015 development agenda*. New York: United Nations.

United Nations. (2017). *Principles and recommendations for population and housing censuses*. New York: United Nations.

Van Belle, J. P. (Ed.). (2018). *Africa data revolution report: Status and emerging impact of open data in Africa*. Addis Ababa: ECA, OD4D, UNDP, WWWF.

Appendix

A reminder of the typology of operations, already described inside the text:

- *adc:* *administrative census*
- *ads:* *additional survey, carried out after a census*
- *cen:* *census*
- *cns:* *complex national survey with some local components, census or surveys*
- *dhs:* *demographic and health survey*
- *mic:* *multiple indicators cluster survey*
- *mig:* *migration (and possibly manpower) survey*
- *mrs:* *multi-round survey*
- *ods:* *other demographic survey*

oss: *other statistic survey with demographic questions*
std: *survey type dhs*
wfs: *fertility survey of the World Fertility Survey (WFS)*

Operations that took place before independence are underlined and in italics. Those that took place during a period including the Independence Day are simply in italics.

Table 8.5 List of demographic operations in Africa (1950–2019)

Pays	*1950-1959*	*1960-1969*	*1970-1979*	*1980-1989*	*1990-1999*	*2000-2009*	*2010-2019*
Benin		61-ods	79-cen	81–83-mrs 82-wfs	92-cen 96-dhs	00-mig 01-dhs 02-cen 06-dhs 06–07-oss	11–12-dhs 13-cen 14-mic 17–18-dhs
Burkina Faso		60–62-cns 69-ods	72–73-mig 74–75-mig 75-cen 76-ads	85-cen	91-ods 92–93-dhs 93-mig 94–95-oss 96-mic 96-cen 98-oss 98–99-dhs	00–02-mig 03-dhs 03-oss 06-mic 06-cen 07-oss 09-mig	10–11-dhs 19 – cen
Burundi	*52-ods*	65-ods	70–71-mrs 74-ods 79-ads 79-cen	86-mig 87-dhs	90-cen 96-mic 98–99-oss	00-mic 02-ods 05-mic 06-oss 08-cen	10–11-dhs 13–14-oss 16–17-dhs
Cameroon	*58–65-cns*	66–69-rad	76-cen 78-wfs	83–84-oss 87-cen	91-dhs 96-oss 98-dhs	00-mic 01-oss 04-dhs 05-cen 06-mic 07-oss	11-dhs 14-oss 14-mic 18–19-dhs
Central African Republic	*55–60-cns*	61–63-cen 65-rad	75-cen	88-cen	92–93-oss 94–95-dhs	00-mic 03-cen 06-mic	10–11-mic 18–19-mic
Chad		62–64-cns 68-rad			93-cen 95–96-oss 96–97-dhs 98-mig	00-mic 04-dhs 09-cen	10-mic 11-oss 14–15-dhs 19-mic
Comoros	*58-cen*	*66-cen*		80-cen	91-cen 96-dhs	00-mic 03-cen	12-dhs 17-cen
Congo	*58–62-cns*		74-cen	84-cen	96-cen	05-oss 05-dhs 07-cen	11–12-dhs 14–15-mic
Congo (D.R.)	*55–58-ods*		70-rad 74–77-cns	84-cen	95-mic	01-mic 07-dhs	10-mic 13–14-dhs 17–18-mic

(*Continued*)

Table 8.5 (Continued)

Pays	*1950-1959*	*1960-1969*	*1970-1979*	*1980-1989*	*1990-1999*	*2000-2009*	*2010-2019*
Côte d'Ivoire	*50–55-rad* *55–58-cns*	60–65-rad 61–68-cns	75-cen 78–79-mrs	80–81-wfs 85–89-oss 88-cen	93-mig 94-dhs 98-cen 98–99-dhs	00-mic 05-dhs 06-mic	11–12-dhs 14-cen 16-mic
Djibouti				83-cen 89-ods	91-ods 96-ods	02-std 02-oss 06-mic 09-cen	12-oss 12-std 17–18-oss
Gabon		60–61-ods 60–61-cen 69–70-cen		80-cen	93-cen	00–01-dhs 03-cen	12-dhs 13-cen
Guinea	*55-ods*		72-rad	83-cen	90-rad 92-dhs 93-mig 94–95-oss 96-cen 99-dhs	02–03-oss 05-dhs 07-oss 07–08-mic	12-oss 12-dhs 14-cen 16-mic 18-dhs
Madagascar	*55–58-rad* *59–64-cns*	66-ods	75-cen	84-ods	92-dhs 93-cen 93–94-oss 95-mic 97-oss 97-dhs 99-oss	00-mic 01-oss 03-oss 03–04-dhs 04–05-oss 08–09-dhs	10-oss 12–13-oss 18-mic 18-cen
Mali		*60–61-ods*	76-cen	85-ods 87-dhs 87-cen	92–93-mig 94-oss 95–96-dhs 95–96-rad 96-mic 98-cen	01-dhs 01–02-oss 03–04-oss 04-oss 06-dhs 06–07-oss 07–08-oss 09-cen 09–10-mic	10-oss 11–19-oss 12–13-dhs 15-mic 18-dhs
Mauritania		61–66-cns	76–77-cen	81–82-wfs 88-cen	90–91-std 93-mig 95–96-oss 95–96-mic	00–01-dhs 00–01-cen 03–04-dhs 07-mic 08-oss	04-oss 11-mic 13-cen 14-oss 15-mic
Niger	*59–64-cns*		70–71-ods 77–78-cen	88-cen	92-dhs 93-mig 94-oss 95–96-oss 96-mic 98-dhs	00-mic 01-cen 05-oss 06-dhs 07–08-oss	12-dhs 12-cen 15-ods 17–18-dhs

(*Continued*)

Pays	*1950-1959*	*1960-1969*	*1970-1979*	*1980-1989*	*1990-1999*	*2000-2009*	*2010-2019*
Rwanda	*52-ods*		70-ods 78-cen	81-ads 83-wfs	91-cen 92-dhs 96-ods 99–01-oss	00-dhs 00-mic 02-cen 03-oss 05-oss 05-dhs 07–08-dhs	10–11-oss 10–11-dhs 11-ods 12-cen 13–14-oss 14–15-dhs 16–17-oss
Senegal		*60–61-ods*	70–71-mrs 76-cen 78-wfs 79–80-mig	86-dhs 88-cen	92–93-dhs 93-mig 94–95-oss 96-mic 97-dhs 99–00-dhs	00-mic 01–02-oss 02-cen 05-dhs 05–06-oss 06–07-oss 09-mig	10–11-dhs 10–12-oss 11-oss 12–17-dhs 13-cen
Togo	*58–60-cen*	61-ads	70-cen 71-ads	81-cen 88-dhs	98-dhs	00-mic 06-oss 06-mic	10-mic 10-cen 11-oss 13–14-dhs 17-mic

Source: IREDA

PART 3

Marriage, fertility and SRH

9

MARRIAGE IN SUB-SAHARAN AFRICA

Michel Garenne

Introduction

Marriage, the institutional alliance between a man and a woman, is a fundamental structure of both traditional and modern societies. Marriage is universal in societies, although not for individuals. Marriage is eminently social: it must be recognized and sanctioned by a special event: a traditional ceremony, an exchange of gifts, a religious ceremony, a civil ceremony, or a legal act. Marriage usually implies living together, although not always. Marriage usually implies sexual relationships, although not always. Marriage usually implies having children, although not always. Marriage implies sharing resources, although not always. In rare cases, it may be extended to single-sex unions, to unions of sterile persons, or to persons sharing only economic interests.

Marriage has many functions. The reproductive functions define the nuclear family (the reproductive unit) and imply child bearing and rearing, child care and education up to adulthood, and the reproduction of the population. The social functions define the basic social structure (the family); imply rights and duties for husband, wife, and children; and also social status and identity (name, race, ethnicity, descent), as well as lineages (patrilineal and matrilineal) and inheritance. In addition, religion is usually acquired within the family, especially when the mother and father belong to the same faith. Psychological functions structure the relationships between men and women and have many implications on psychological development and equilibrium, fulfillment of emotional needs, happiness, and solidarity between family members. The economic functions define the household (the economic unit) and have implications for income, assets, property, inheritance, and so on, as husband, wife, and children share many common resources. Living together (cohabitation) defines the housing unit, fundamental for demographic purposes and social research.

In Western and Northern Europe, the pattern of marriage changed in the 15th and 16th centuries after the Black Death. This change was made possible because in the 12th century, the Catholic Church imposed consensual unions (mutual agreement of bride and groom) over the family control in place formerly and also by neolocality (husband and wife build a new household elsewhere, away from their parents). This major innovation was closely related to

 DOI: 10.4324/9780429287213-12

the emergence of vital registration by the Church (birth, death, marriage), which gave a new social and legal status to individuals (Garenne & Cantrelle, 2019). The changing pattern of marriage in the 16th century is considered an institutional adaptation to expanding employment opportunities and higher wages following the depopulation resulting from the plague. It is associated with the changing balance of power between husband and wife and parents and children, resulting in women' greater autonomy made possible by wage labor and the development of market economy (De Moor & Van Zanden, 2009). The European marriage pattern of the 19th century was characterized by late marriage (around age 25 for women), high proportions (10% to 20%) of women who never married, and small age difference between spouses (1 to 2 years); it covered most of Europe west of a line linking Saint Petersburg and Trieste (Hajnal, 1953a, 1965). Ironically, this pattern appears unique in the world until the 20th century but remained the standard against which African and Asian patterns were contrasted by Western scholars. The marriage pattern changed again after 1950 in Europe, first with the marriage boom (Hajnal, 1953b) associated with the baby boom following recovery after World War II, then with a rapid decline in marriage rates, older age at marriage, and a larger proportion of women who never married. For instance, in France, the mean age at marriage of women increased from 25.4 to 33.9 years between 1950–59 and 2010–2017, and terminal celibacy increased from 9.3% (women born in 1910–1919) to 24.0% (women born in 1960–69) (source: National Institute for Statistics and Economic Studies [INSEE], 2018, vital registration and census).

With respect to Africa, marriage could be approached in several ways. From an anthropological or sociological perspective, marriage appears particularly complex in African societies when compared with European or Asian societies. Anthropologists working during the colonial period discovered many forms of marriages and living arrangements specific to sub-Saharan Africa. One of the striking features of African marriages is the widespread occurrence of polygyny (one husband, several wives), especially in West Africa (Radcliffe-Brown & Forde, 1950; Lyimo, 2000; Welch & Glick, 1981; Zeitzen, 2008). Polygyny may be associated with separate living arrangements of husband and wife, as it is the case for the "visiting husbands" in West Africa. Another peculiar and widespread feature is levirate, the inheritance of a widowed woman by a close relative of the deceased husband, often a younger brother, and its correlate: sororate, the inheritance of a widowed man by a close relative of the deceased wife, often a younger sister (Radcliffe-Brown & Forde, 1950). Other forms of marriage have also been described, such as rare cases of polyandry (one wife, several husbands), as among the Bashilele of Kasaï in Congo (Ngondo & Pitshandenge, 1996), although this case is different from polyandry described in Tibet and India and could be considered a form of organized prostitution. Cases of 'ghost marriage' (marriage with a deceased person) or same-sex symbolic marriage (also called woman-marriage to women) were also described, as among the Nuer of Southern Sudan (Evans-Pritchard, 1937; Schwartze, 2010), and among the Tswana and Zulu of Southern Africa (Radcliffe-Brown & Forde, 1950). Marriage rules in Africa are complex and specific to each ethnic group: they involve a variety of rules of endogamy/exogamy (marriage permitted or prohibited) related to lineages, clans, caste, orders, social status, and ethnicity, as well as preferential marriage, often with a cross-cousin or a parallel cousin (see details in Murdock, 1967; Radcliffe-Brown & Forde, 1950; Goody & Goody, 1967; Goody, 1976; Singer, 1973). Even in the same country, and among groups with similar socio-economic characteristics, endogamy/exogamy rules may differ radically (Cantrelle, 1960; Cantrelle & Dupire, 1964).

Box 9.1: Specific features of African marriages

- Universal marriage for men and women (declining in past 50 years and often replaced by consensual unions)
- Age at marriage early for women (increasing in past 50 years)
- Large age difference between husband and wife
- Preferential marriage with cross or parallel cousin (frequent in West Africa)
- Cohabitation not universal
- Polygyny: frequent, especially in West Africa
- Levirate/sororate: probably frequent (prevalence unknown)
- Ghost marriage: rare, few cases described
- Polyandry: very rare, one case described

From a demographic perspective, marriage in Africa became documented when censuses and demographic surveys were conducted after 1950. A pioneering work was conducted by Etienne van de Walle in the early 1960s at Princeton University, based on colonial censuses and surveys, which was published in the classic *The Demography of Tropical Africa* (van de Walle, 1968, 1993). Another pioneering work was conducted by French demographers of INSEE and Office for Scientific and Technical Research Overseas, now renamed as Institute for Research on Development, and based mainly on the INSEE demographic surveys conducted in Francophone Africa from 1954 to 1971 (Tabutin & Vallin, 1975; Gendreau, 1993). With the development of demographic surveys, in particular the World Fertility Surveys (WFSs) and the Demographic and Health Surveys (DHSs), as well as with regular censuses, many demographic data on marriage became available, allowing for a variety of new analyses (Lesthaeghe, 1989; Lesthaeghe, Kaufman, & Meekers, 1989; Pebley & Mbugua, 1989; Westoff, 2003; Shapiro & Gebreselassie, 2013; Koski, Clark, & Nandi, 2017; DHS, 2018; IPUMS, 2018).

This chapter covers some of the salient features of marriage in Africa from a demographic perspective. In this chapter, Africa refers to sub-Saharan Africa, as North Africa was excluded because marriage patterns are different. The chapter follows, therefore, a demographic approach that is population based and not based on individual or social relationships. It covers some of the links with fertility (reproduction), with mortality (widowhood), with nuptiality (divorce), and with migration. It presents the basics of demographic analysis: indicators, trends, age patterns, sex differences, socio-economic factors, and cultural factors and briefly addresses the issue of mathematical modeling of the nuptiality processes.

Basic concepts

Marriage is socially defined by a ceremony, a ritual, or a legal act. In demographic surveys, marriage is reported as such by interviewed persons, usually without checking whether there was a ceremony or a legal act, unless the survey focuses on type of marriage. For instance, in DHSs, the field worker conducting the interview asks the following question: "Are you married or living with someone?" Or "Are you currently married or living together with a man as if married? Possible answers are "Yes, Currently married/Yes, Living with a man/No, Not in union". Therefore the field worker relies on the respondent's declaration, and there is no checking whether a ceremony, a ritual, or a legal act was performed. In most cases, marriage is clearly defined, and reports from individuals coincide with those from family members or other persons. However, self-reporting might sometimes lead to inaccurate reporting or to differences between the individual viewpoint and that of the family or society. For instance, a young woman betrothed and pregnant might declare herself married, a young man who has not finished paying the bride-price might declare himself married, a person recently separated might declare a divorce, and so on. In some rare cases, potential spouses may give different answers, especially in the case of levirate marriage where the woman considers herself remarried, whereas the man does not. Conflicts could also arise between traditional and legal statuses: for instance, child marriage or polygynous marriage acceptable in traditional societies might be illegal in modern states; legal civil marriage could also be considered not acceptable religiously or socially if it occurred between persons who did not comply with social rules (prohibited marriage between mixed races, among different orders or castes, etc.). However, as will be seen in the following, minor inaccuracies in self-reporting usually have no impact on the proportion married in a population, which remains one of the most reliable demographic indicators.

Marital status is defined at one point in time (period) and in several categories, such as single (i.e., never-married), currently married or in a stable union, divorced or separated, or widowed. The polygamy status is usually added, with number of wives for men and rank in the union for women. In demographic surveys, one often adds whether partners live together and sometimes whether all the time or part time, as cohabitation plays a role in fertility as well on family structure and economic and social ties between family members.

The first marriage is crucial in demographic research, as it signals the beginning of the reproductive life. The age at first marriage has a wide distribution, usually ranging from age 12 (puberty) to 35 for women and from age 18 to 50 for men, although the first marriage might occur outside these age bands, for children as for older persons. The distribution of ages at first marriage is described by ways of classic statistics, such as median, mean, and standard deviation, or by mathematical modeling. Terminal celibacy is defined as the proportion in a cohort who never marry, usually taken as the proportion never-married by age 50 (or age 40–49) for women and by age 60 (or age 50–59) for men. The classic calculation of median age at first marriage takes into account the proportion ever-married, and therefore the median age is defined as the age at which half of a cohort is ever-married among those who will eventually marry (which could be labeled 'relative median'). Another calculation of median age is possible in censuses and surveys: the age at which half of a cohort is ever-married, whether or not they will eventually marry (which could be labeled 'total median'). This second definition is much easier to apply in cohort analysis since it does not depend on future behavior past the median age and summarizes at the same time information on age at marriage and on proportion ever-marrying. It allows for detailed trend analysis by cohort (year of birth) in censuses and surveys (for examples, see Garenne, 2014, and Garenne, 2016a).

Marital fertility is defined as fertility after the first marriage, and premarital fertility as fertility before the first marriage. Note that this definition, inherited from historical demography in Europe, is easy to apply in demographic surveys recording the date of birth of the first child and the date of first marriage of the mother, as in DHSs. The concept of marital/premarital fertility is different from the concept of legitimate/illegitimate fertility, which is defined by a legal status (married or not) at time of birth, as done in European populations. This definition of premarital fertility has a straightforward meaning in most cases in African surveys: it applies primarily to adolescent and very young women, as this situation is often stigmatized in societies (unwed mother, *fille-mère*). For instance, in DHSs, dates are defined by month and year and are recorded as a century month code (CMC), where 1 is January 1900, 1201 is January 2000, 1441 is January 2020, and so on. It is therefore easy and efficient to define premarital and marital fertility by comparing date of first birth with date of first marriage (for details, see: Garenne & Zwang, 2006; Zwang, 2004). It should be noted, however, that in some instances, the societal viewpoint might differ from the demographic viewpoint. For instance, among the Sereer of Senegal, it happens occasionally that a young betrothed woman delivers before marriage and gets formally married the day of the baptism of the child, usually seven days after delivery. Applying a strict definition will consider this birth premarital, whereas for the family, this birth is obviously marital.

Data collection

There are several ways of recording nuptiality events in demographic surveys. The method of choice is marriage history, where one records retrospectively all marriages or unions and their eventual breaking (separation, divorce, widowhood), with date and age for each event. Further information can be gathered on type of marriage (traditional, religious, legal) and on spouse characteristics (age, ethnicity, socio-economic status, etc.). This method was used in the World Fertility Surveys.

The Demographic and Health Surveys record less information, typically current marital status, first marriage, and number of unions, with current spouse characteristics. This allows for less analysis, in particular for marital duration and marriage breaking, but is still very informative for the analysis of the first marriage by age, cohort, and period. Censuses record even less information, usually only the current marital status at time of interview and cohabitation with spouse.

Full-scale prospective studies recording all changes in marital status over time are often conducted in population observatories with a demographic surveillance system (DSS). (See In-Depth network web site for a list of DSSs in Africa, 2018.) In sub-Saharan Africa, civil registration of marriages and divorces is very weak and incomplete and cannot be used for demographic analysis, as done routinely in European populations.

Age patterns, cohort, and period effects

Age patterns of first marriage

In Western societies, age patterns of marriage are usually calculated from civil registration data, because marriages and divorces are all registered by law. In Africa, civil registration of changes in marital status also exists, but its completeness is so low that it is not used for statistical purposes. However, age patterns of first marriages can be calculated from censuses and surveys. In censuses, the Hajnal method allows estimating the "singulate mean age at marriage" (SMAM) from the proportion ever-married (Hajnal, 1953a). Similarly, the Coale method allows fitting a model on the proportion ever-married on the same data (Coale, 1971; Coale & McNeil, 1972). This model is based on a translation from the age pattern of marriage found in Sweden. A new model, the Picrate model (for phased-in constant-rate), is a more general model, based on a Weibull distribution, which has only three parameters (a_0 the earliest age, C_{max} the proportion who eventually marry, and r_{max} the maximum rate of marriage) and is not based on any empirical pattern (see description of the model in Appendix 9.1). It directly provides the median, mean, and standard deviation of the distribution of the marriage function from the three parameters based on proportions ever-married by age (Matthews, Leclerc, & Garenne, 2009). This model can fit virtually any empirical distribution and has been applied to a variety of African countries for men and woman alike (Garenne, Leclerc, & Matthews, 2011). The model can be applied to period data (as in a census), as well as to cohort data (as in a DHS, where the age at first marriage is known). In this case, it requires first calculating the proportion ever-married by age in the cohort before applying the model.

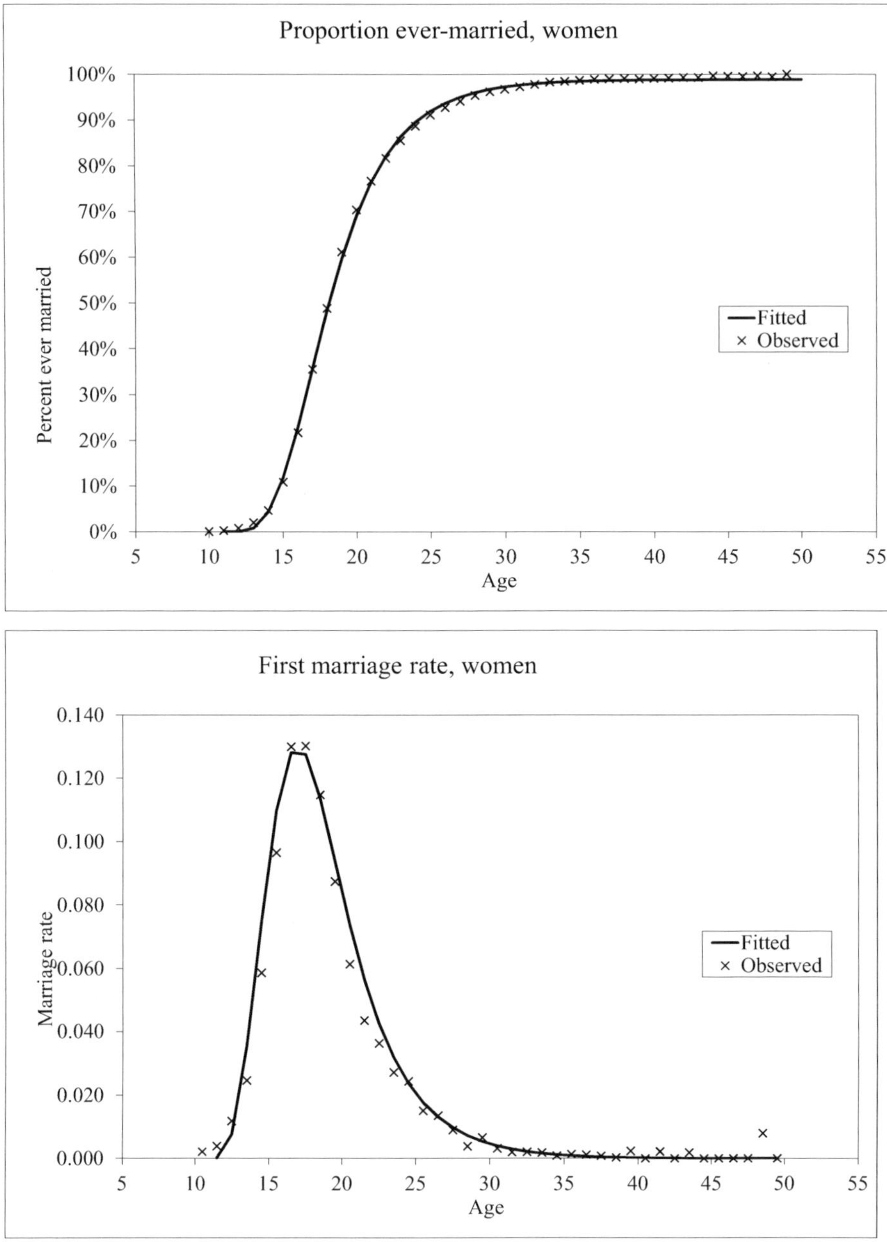

Figure 9.1 Example of fitting the proportion ever-married with the Picrate model and underlying age pattern of entry into first marriage, Zambia 2001

Source: Computed from DHSs

Figure 9.1 provides an example of the Picrate model applied to the Zambia 2001 DHS. Since the fitting is based on many points, the standard error on the estimates of mean, median, and standard deviation is very small. This is why the precision of estimates of median age at first marriage is very high and why minor changes in the median age could be identified with great reliability.

Cohort effects

There are several ways to approach cohort effects in marriage analysis. One method is to study the proportions ever-married by age over time, as in censuses or surveys conducted in the same country. This has been done repeatedly in Africa, a good example being that of Botswana (Mokomane, Baker, & van de Walle, 2006, p. 160).

The easiest and most efficient method to investigate cohort effects is probably to study trends in median age at first marriage, median being defined as the age at which half of a cohort is ever-married ('total median'). The main advantage of this method is that it can be computed for recent cohorts: for instance, if the median age is 20 years in 2020, it can be computed for women born in year 2000. Using DHSs recording age at first marriage, this method allows reconstructing trends in median age at first marriage (in year and month) for some 25 yearly cohorts (aged 25–49 at time of survey) and when several surveys are available in the same country for a longer period of 50 years or more. This was tried, for instance, for a variety of African countries, and it could done be by place of residence, ethnicity, socio-economic status, and so on (Garenne, 2014).

Figure 9.2 shows such reconstruction for a country (Ghana, urban) and for Africa as a whole. It shows that marriage is undergoing major changes in urban areas and some mild changes in rural areas. In urban Ghana, the median age at first marriage increased by about 4 years between cohorts born in 1950 and 1985. For the continent as a whole, it increased by about 5 years between 1940 and 1990 (from 17.5 years to 22.5 years) in urban Africa and by about 2 years in rural Africa.

Period effects

Marriage data in DHSs also permit investigation of the effect of a shock on marriage patterns. Here the method is simple: calculating marriage rates from DHS data with age at marriage (calculated as first marriages at year *t* divided by person-years as risk among never-married women). This was tried in Rwanda to estimate the effect of the shock produced by the 1994 civil war (genocide). Calculations show that the pre-war period saw fewer marriages and that the post-genocide period was largely compensated with higher marriage rates and younger ages at marriage. The genocide period was also followed by an increase in fertility a year later (Figure 9.3) (Garenne & Gakusi, 2014).

Ending marriage

Marriage can be ended by divorce or death of one of the spouses. The proper method to study marriage breaking is through longitudinal analysis, where one computes divorce and widowhood rates and considers them competitive risks. In this case, the construction of a multiple decrement life table is recommended. Formulae to calculate multiple decrement life tables can be found in textbooks (Manton & Stallard, 1984; Preston, Heuveline, & Guillot, 2001). Unfortunately, the data needed to construct such a table are usually not available in censuses or demographic surveys. Only DSS with prospective data, or full-scale marriage history with retrospective data, allow one to calculate multiple decrement nuptiality tables.

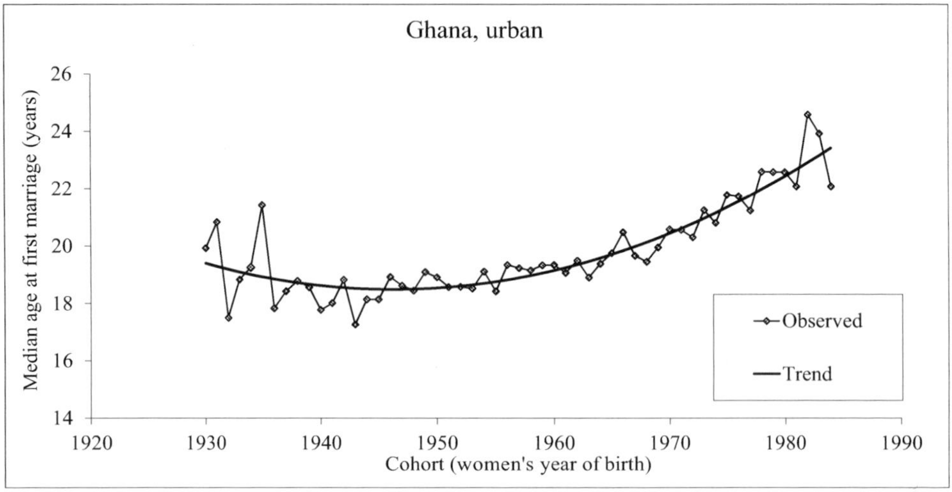

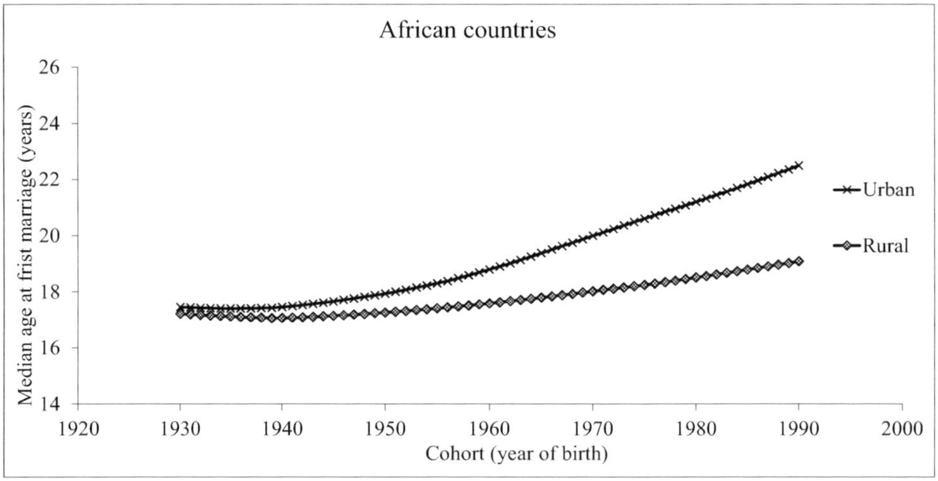

Figure 9.2 Examples of trends in median age at first marriage by cohort, women: (a) Ghana, urban areas; (b) average of African countries

Source: Computed from DHSs (Garenne, 2014)

Multi-state nuptiality tables

Classic multi-state nuptiality tables including marriage formation and dissolution can be computed when longitudinal data are available, as in DSS sites. However, in Africa, the matter is further complicated by polygamy. For instance, for men, one could distinguish five categories of marital status: single, married in monogamious union, married in polygamous union, divorced, widowed. This stratification gives seven possible transitions for changes in marital status, plus five transitions to mortality (see Figure 9.4). Furthermore, if one studies polygamy by number of wives (for instance, up to 4 or more), selecting ever-married men, then seven marital status

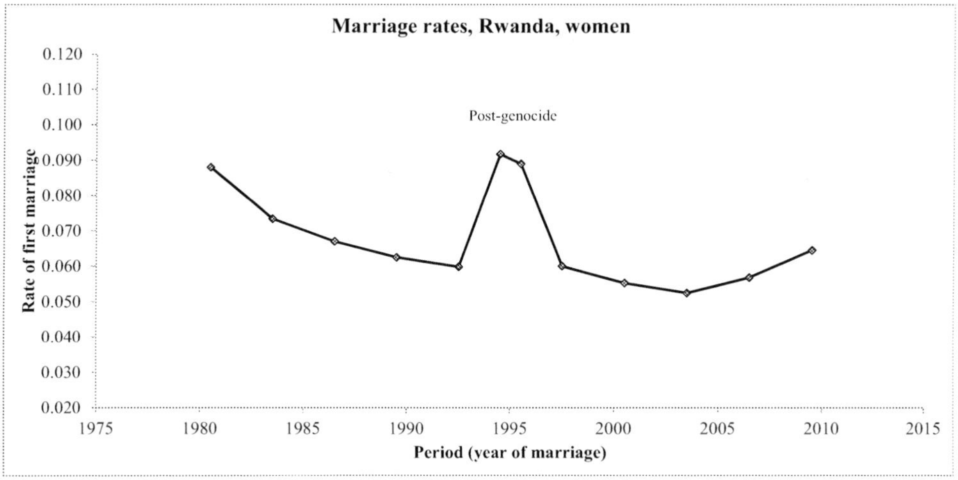

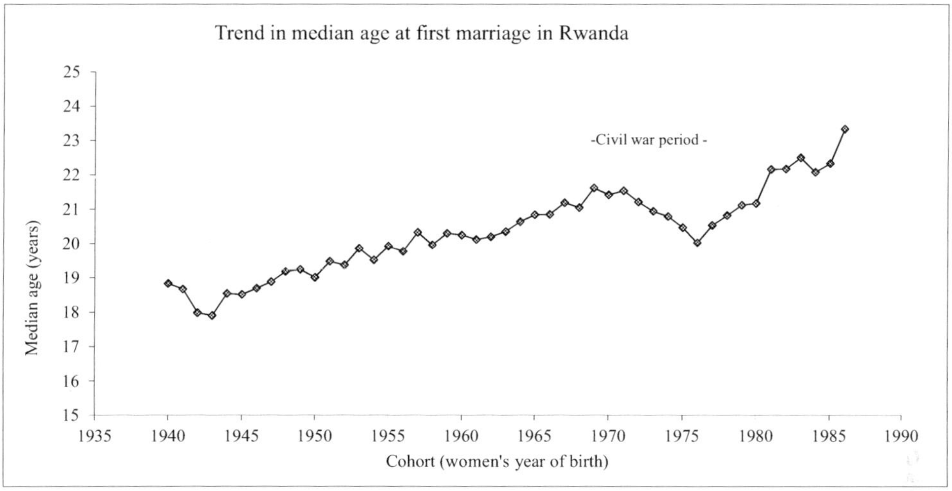

Figure 9.3 Effect of civil war on marriage incidence and age at marriage in Rwanda

Source: Computed from DHSs (Garenne & Gakusi, 2014)

need to be considered: never married, married in monogamous union, married 2 wives, married 3 wives, married 4+ wives, divorced, widowed. Including more wives further complicates the issue, but these are rare events. For women, the matter is even more complicated: a proper investigation should include the husband's marital status and calculate the rank of the wife in the polygamous union. Therefore, all changes in marital status for the two sexes need to be considered. This seems never to have been studied.

An example of a multi-state nuptiality table is given in Appendix 9.2. It is derived from the Niakhar DSS site for the 1983–1989 period for men age 15 and above. Appendix Table 9.1A provides the empirical data: (a) the distribution of population by marital status, including polygamy; (b) the transition rates for the changes in marital status; (c) the mortality rates by marital status. Marital status of men changes rapidly over time, with acquisition of a first wife, followed by that of other wives and various losses due to divorce and mortality. Appendix Table 9.1B

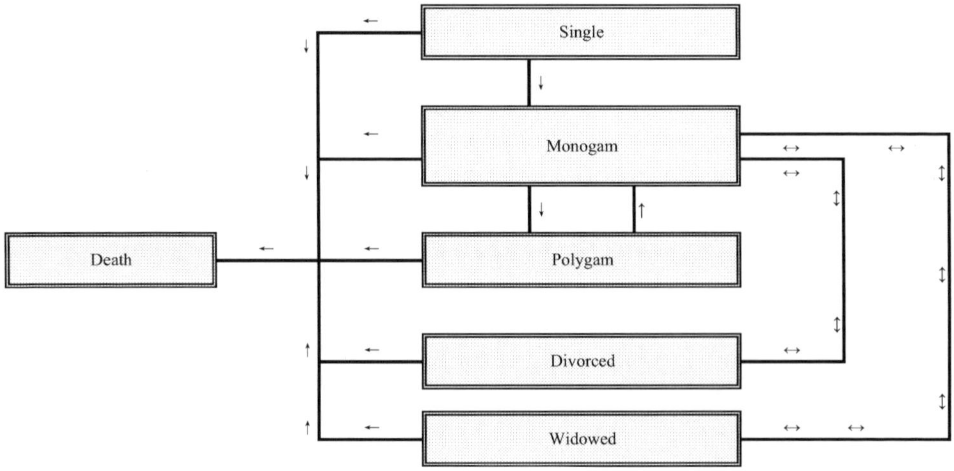

Figure 9.4 Example of transitions for building a multi-state nuptiality table with polygamy

displays the associated transitions in the multi-state nuptiality table and Appendix Table 9.1C the resulting marital status by age.

Current status and trends

In DHSs, as well as in censuses, data on current status (proportions divorced or widowed at one point in time) provide useful information on prevalence and trends in marriage breaking. When these proportions by age remain approximately constant, one can assume that rates of divorce and widowhood are constant. When they change, these proportions reveal changing processes. However, this could be due either to changes in the event (divorce or death of spouses), in competing events, or in remarriage. For instance, if remarriage is quicker after a divorce (for instance because of better economic conditions), the proportion of divorced persons in the population will decline. Conversely, if remarriage is less frequent after the death of the spouse (for instance because the spouse died of HIV/AIDS), the proportion widowed will increase in the population.

According to DHSs, it appears that divorce tended to remain steady in a majority of countries and either declined or increased in others. Figure 9.5 displays examples of two countries with changing proportions of divorced adults age 25–49: Ghana, where divorce seems to be declining from high values, and Mozambique, where divorce seems to be increasing from low values.

With the general mortality decline, mortality of spouses tends to decline and therefore the proportions widowed decline as well. However, in countries severely affected by HIV/AIDS, the proportion widowed tended to increase before the implementation of anti-retroviral therapy (ARV) and to decline thereafter when AIDS mortality was strongly reduced. Figure 9.6 displays such examples: Senegal, where the proportion of widowed men declined steadily from 1992 to 2017, and Zimbabwe, where the proportion of widowed women first increased from 1988 to 2005, then declined from 2005 to 2015, following the dynamics of AIDS mortality.

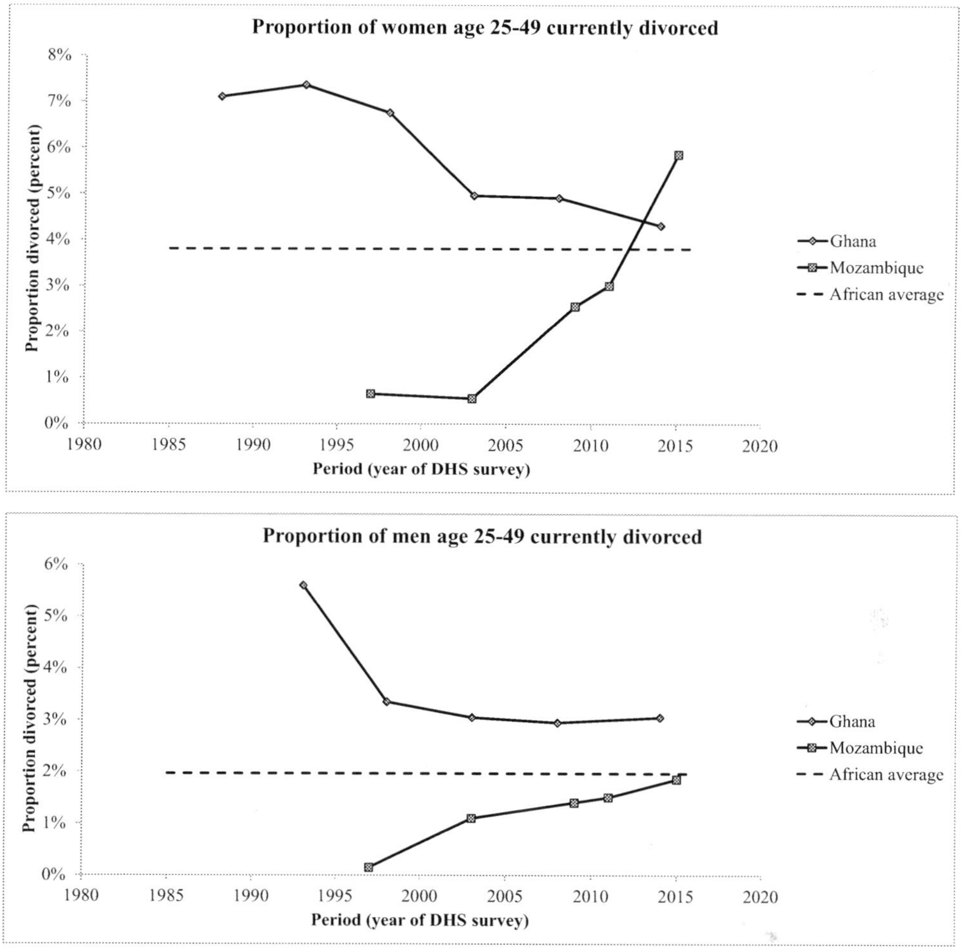

Figure 9.5 Examples of changing proportions of divorced women or men age 25–49
Source: DHS web site

Marriage breaking by duration in DHSs

Whereas WFS surveys provided information on marriage history, DHSs provide information only on survival of the first marriage by its status at time of survey (currently divorced, widowed, or remarried). Since date of first marriage and date of survey are also known, DHS data allow computing the probability that a marriage is still in course after a number of years. And for broken marriages, one could compute the proportions of women still divorced, still widowed, or remarried. An example from women in Senegal is displayed in Figure 9.7: 25.6% of first marriages were broken within 20 years, and among those women, 83.7% were remarried, 9.7% were still divorced, and 8.6% still widowed. Measuring the same proportions in other DHSs could provide indicators of trends in divorce, widowhood, and remarriage in the same country,

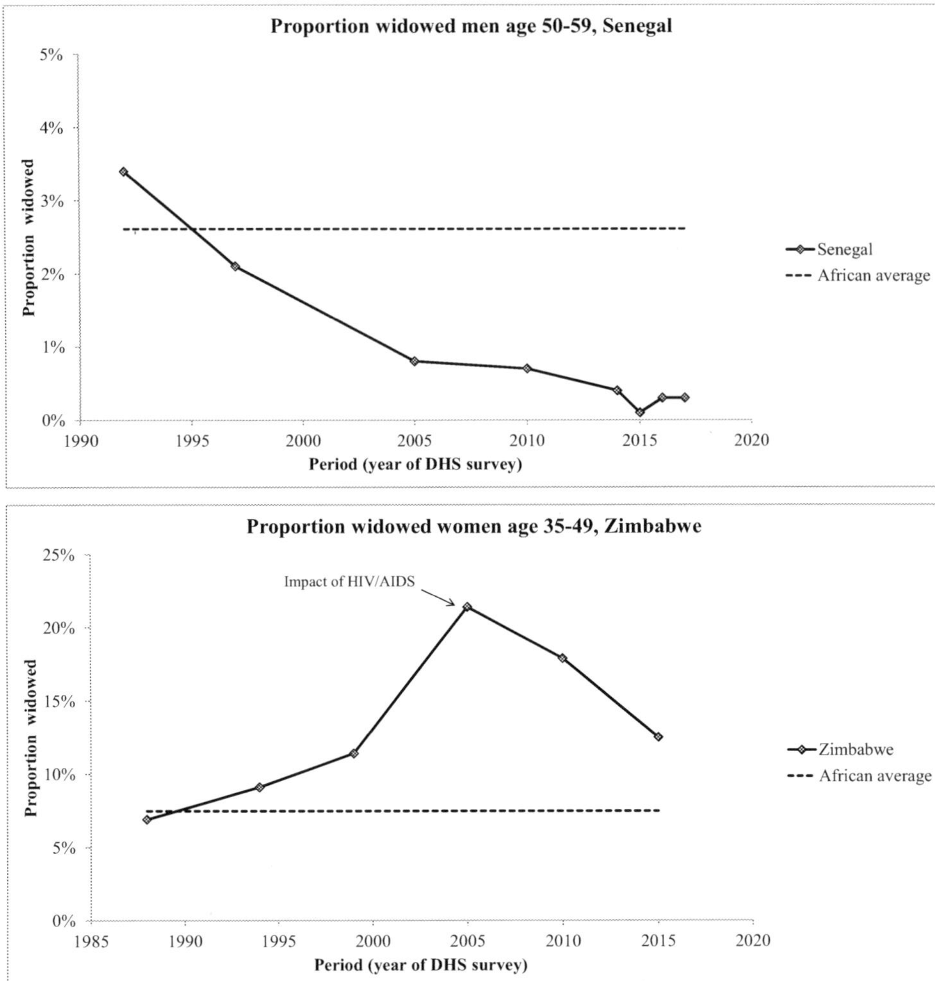

Figure 9.6 Changing proportions widowed over time: (a) effect of mortality decline on widowhood among men age 50–59 in Senegal; (b) effect of the AIDS epidemic on widowhood among women age 35–49 in Zimbabwe

Source: DHS web site

as well as differences across countries. For instance, in Senegal, the proportion of first marriages dissolved after 20 years declined somewhat from 1986 (32%) to 2017 (27%), but the proportion of women who remarried strongly declined over the same period of time, from 96% to 81%. As a consequence, the proportion of women still divorced after 20 years of marriage increased from 1.4% to 14.8%, that is, it was multiplied by 10 in about 30 years, a major change in remarriage, which seems correlated with the decline in polygamy.

For men, the matter is further complicated because of polygamy. Indeed, in DHSs for men, there is no way to find out the fate of the first marriage, since acquisition of a new wife is counted as being married more than once, as is the case for the breaking of the first marriage by divorce or widowhood.

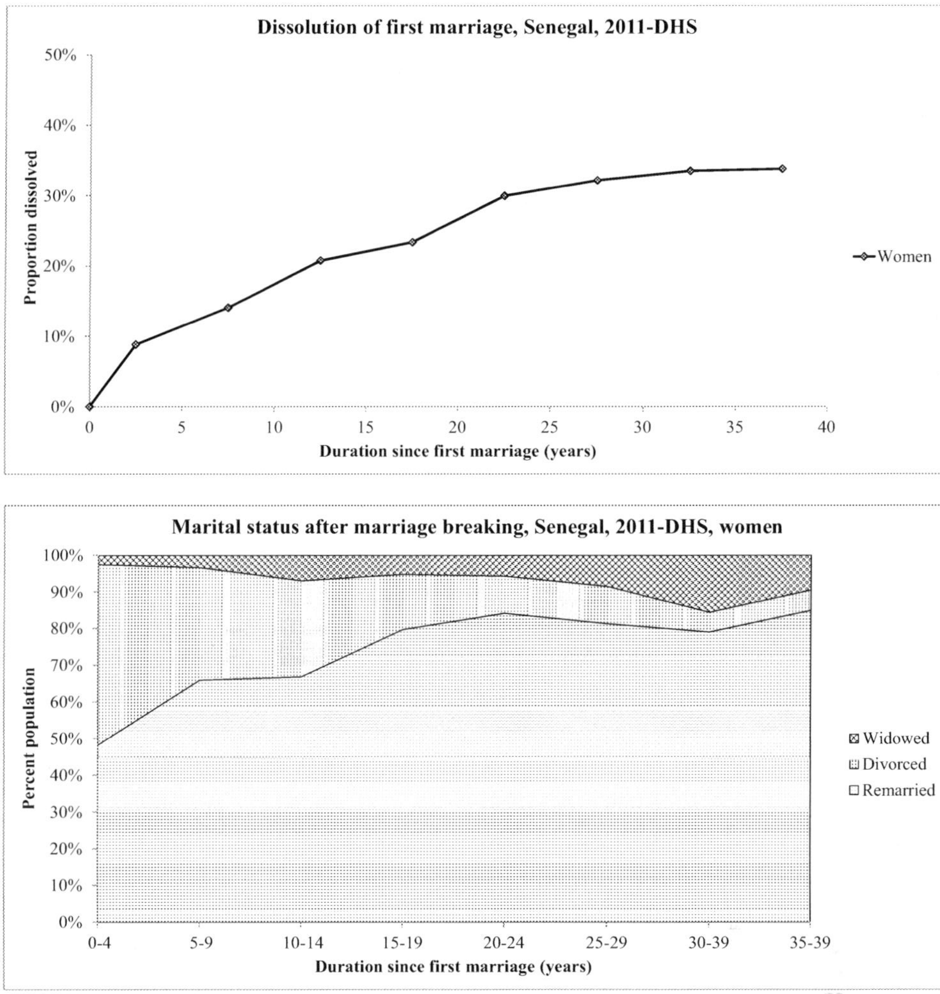

Figure 9.7 Example of indicators of marriage breaking by duration, Senegal, 2011 DHS, women age 15–49

Source: Computed from DHSs

Features of marriage patterns across sub-Saharan Africa

Universal and early marriage

In Africa, early censuses and surveys conducted in the 1950s and 1960s revealed virtually universal marriage for men and women, except for rare cases of mental disorders or physical handicaps. Universal and early marriage for women appears as a necessary condition for maximizing reproduction in situations of very high mortality, such as those prevailing in Africa before the 20th century. Universal and early marriage requires a specific social organization, with strong power relationships between elderly and young adults, huge pressure on young women and young men to marry, and strong ties of solidarity to ensure raising children in the best conditions. In early censuses and surveys, universal and early marriage for women was general in Africa, except in countries of Southern Africa already in transition, which were strongly affected by labor migration and apartheid (Timaeus & Graham, 1989).

Since these early studies, recent DHSs, conducted after 2000, revealed a great variety of situations in terminal celibacy for women, around an average of 4%. In West Africa, terminal celibacy is rare (<1%), whereas in Southern Africa, it is outstandingly frequent, the world record being held by South Africa (33% at the 2016 DHS). Figures are even higher for selected ethnic groups, such as the Zulus and the Swazis, among which more than 50% of women never marry (Garenne, 2016a). Figure 9.8 displays the variations in proportions never-married at age 40–49 for men and women and Figure 9.9 the geographical distribution of terminal celibacy for women. Three countries in Southern Africa (South Africa, Botswana, Namibia) appear outstanding by any world standard. For men, distributions were somewhat more homogeneous, also averaging 4% at age 40–49, and never exceeded 10%, with the exception of the same Southern African countries.

Polygyny

Rationales for polygyny

Polygyny is rare in Asia and the Middle East, frequent all over Africa, and the norm in many West African societies. Rationales for frequent polygyny have been discussed at

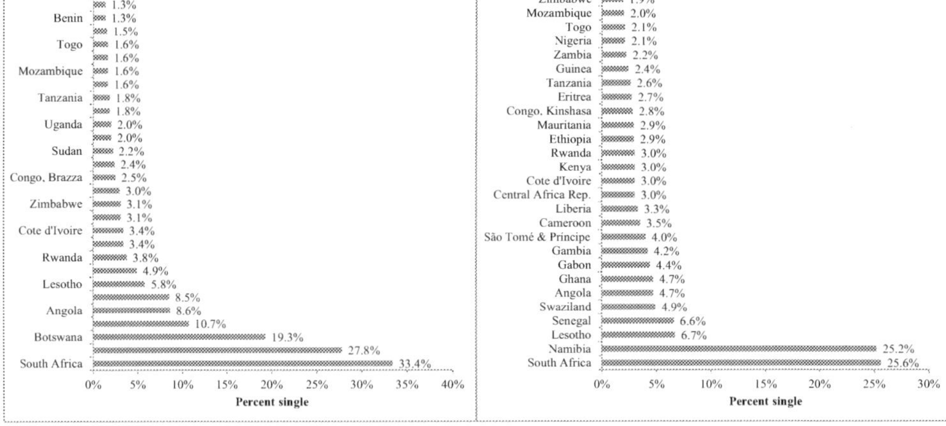

Figure 9.8 Distribution of African countries by the proportions of women and men in terminal celibacy (age 40–49)

Source: DHS web site, last DHS available

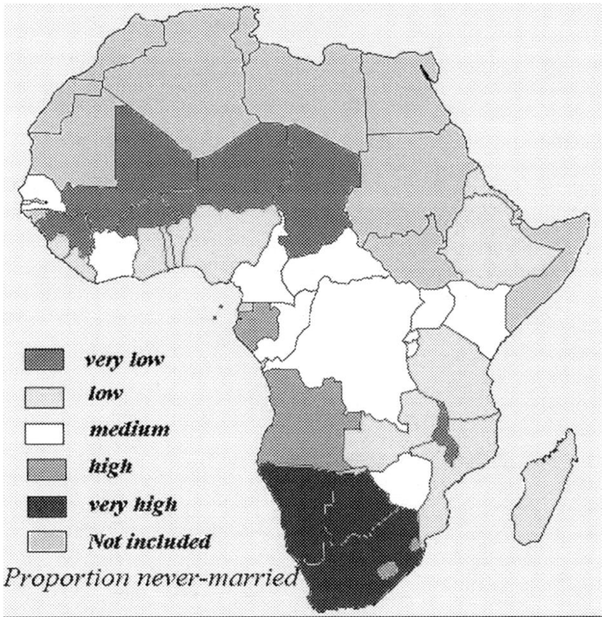

Figure 9.9 Map of terminal celibacy (last survey available)

Source: DHSs

length in the literature, and in fact there are several rationales: demographic, social, and economic. Polygyny is above all the result of power relationships, where men manage to acquire more than one wife. From a demographic perspective, polygyny ensures that all women are married, whatever the number of marriageable men. It therefore compensates for imbalance in the marriage market, in particular that due to differential mortality of men and women and for the age difference between spouses. As a result, it ensures maximizing the offspring of the women and the reproduction of the society. However, the system implies a large age gap between men and women and therefore limits somewhat the fertility effect, because older men have somewhat lower fertility (Garenne & van de Walle, 1989; Lardoux & van de Walle, 2003). From the men's viewpoint, the rationale is above all social, since polygyny is associated with prestige. Furthermore, polygyny offers many economic advantages to the men: more offspring, more manpower for agriculture, and therefore more production and more wealth. It also has limitations, since it implies more duties and equal treatment of the wives. From women's viewpoint, polygyny also offers some advantages: women in polygynous unions can get support from cowives, and they can share duties with respect to the husband, such as food preparation, fetching water, taking care or children, and other thankless domestic tasks. However, it has serious limitations, especially on the psychological and emotional aspects, as it may generate conflicts between cowives and may affect self-esteem. Monotheist religions interfere with traditional marriage systems in Africa: Islam permits and regulates polygamy, whereas Christian religions discourage the practice. Therefore, during the 20th century, polygamy tended to regress in Christian countries, whereas it tended to maintain itself in many Islamic countries, in particular in West Africa.

Polygyny indicators

Several indicators of polygyny have been presented in the demographic literature: (*p*) the proportion of married men who have more than one wife, (*f*) the proportion of married women who are in a polygynous union, (*m*) the ratio of married women to married men, and (*w*) the mean number of wives per polygynous man (Goldman & Pebley, 1989). These indicators are linked by simple relationships:

$$p = \frac{(m-1)}{(w-1)}$$

$$f = \frac{p \times w}{m} = \frac{w \times (m-1)}{m \times (w-1)}$$

The first equation states that the proportion of men in polygynous unions (*p*) decreases with the mean number of wives per polygynous man (*w*): when some men acquire more wives, there are fewer women available to others. Conversely, the proportion of married women who are in a polygynous union (*f*) increases with the mean number of wives per polygynous man (*w*): when men can acquire more wives, there are more opportunities for women. Note that these relationships apply only to adults of all ages, typically age 15+ (and not by age group), and only in a closed population, that is, without selective international migration. In practice, these theoretical relationships are not necessarily verified in censuses (Goldman & Pebley, 1989). For instance, in Senegal, the 1988 census, which includes information on polygyny, showed a difference of 3% between the two sides of the equations and the 2002 census a difference of 25%. Discrepancies could be due to a variety of factors: international migration (some married men living abroad with a wife at home are not resident and therefore not counted in the census); undercount in the census (married men living in hostels or in informal quarters, while wives stay in rural areas); errors in marital status at the census or in the imputation of missing values, and so on. In any case, (*p*) and (*f*) are usually more reliable and easier to record and furthermore can be computed by age, as done in DHSs.

Frequency of polygyny

DHSs provide several indicators of polygyny, in particular the proportion of married men (*p*) and women (*f*) in polygynous unions. Variations by country are impressive, ranging from a few percent to more than half the female population in a polygamous union. Highest values are found in West Africa, in particular in Senegal, Mali, Guinea, Gambia, Burkina-Faso, and Niger, and the lowest values in Southern Africa, in particular in South Africa, Namibia, and Madagascar. Among African DHSs, the highest value among men was in Senegal, 1992 (55% of men age 50–59 in a polygamous union), and the highest value among women was in Guinea, 1999 (67.6% of women age 35–49). Figure 9.10 displays the variations in prevalence of polygamy among adults age 35–49 by country, at last DHS: among women, it ranges from 6.4% in South Africa, 2016, to 62.6% in Guinea, 2012, with an average of 30%; among men, it ranges from 1.3% in Madagascar, 2008, to 35.1% in Guinea, 2012, with an average of 14%.

The geographical distribution of polygyny is displayed in Figure 9.11. Note that this map bears similarities to the map of terminal celibacy: in polygamous systems, women are not supposed to live alone, and therefore all women tend to marry and remarry, as there is no shortage

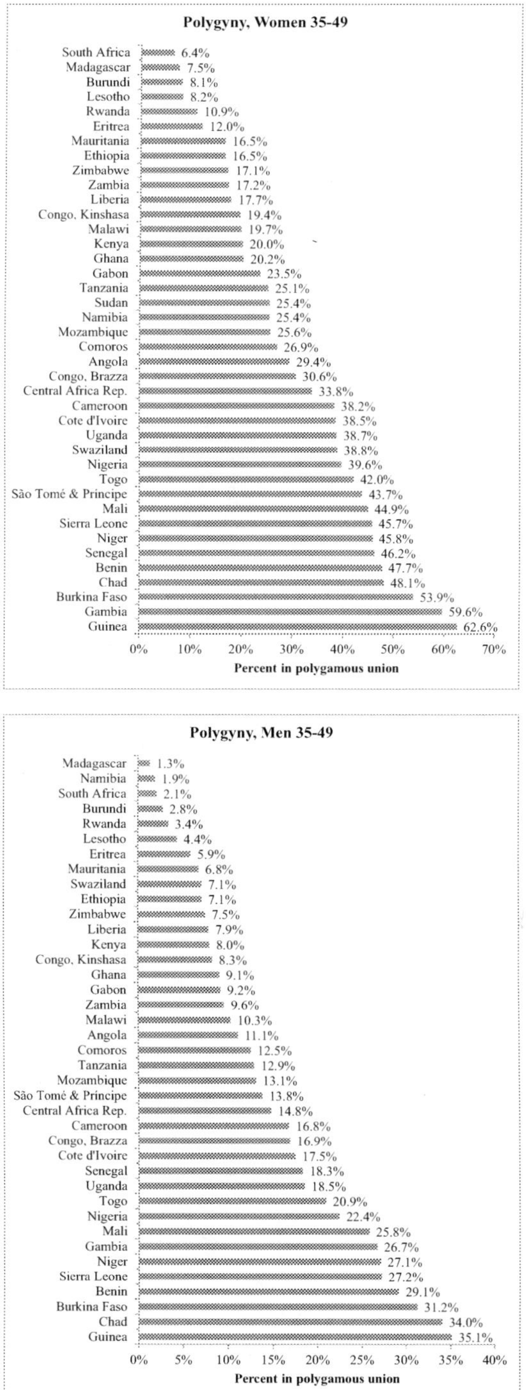

Figure 9.10 Frequency of polygyny in African countries, last DHS available.

Source: DHS web site

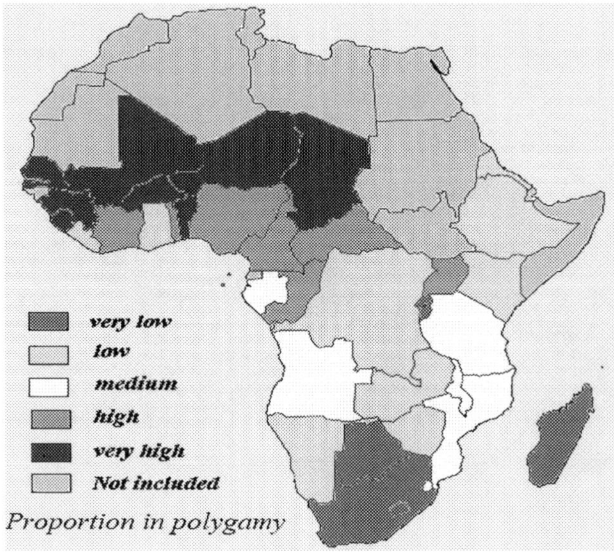

Figure 9.11 Map of the prevalence of polygyny, adults age 35–49

of husbands. Note also that this map bears similarities to the map of fertility levels, and Niger, the world record of high fertility, is also a country with a very high level of polygyny.

Trends in polygyny

In most countries with several DHSs, polygyny tended to decline over time, with only a few exceptions such as Uganda. For instance, in Senegal, the proportion of women age 35–49 in polygamous unions declined from 62% to 46% between 1978 and 2017, even more for younger women age 20–34 (from 46% to 25%), and likewise for men: from 31% to 18% from 1993 to 2017 at age 35–49 and from 12% to 4% for younger men age 20–34. These trends reveal cohort effects: women born after independence (1960), who married in the late 1970s or after, were less and less likely to be in a polygamous marriage compared with women born earlier (Figure 9.12).

Age pattern of polygamy

Polygamy is a process during which men acquire wives over time. As a result, the age pattern of polygamy is very marked (Figure 9.13). In Senegal, for men who marry early, polygamy was virtually non-existent, whereas for the older generations (born in 1924–1933), about 2/3 of men were in polygamous unions at age 60–69 in 1993. In contrast, women may enter in polygamy at their first marriage (30% in 1978), and their likelihood to be in a polygamous union also increases with age, as their husband may acquire new wives. It is therefore necessary to standardize by age when analyzing polygamy. Note that in Senegal, polygamy affected about 2/3 of men and women during the life cycle and that this proportion seems to be decreasing rapidly with time.

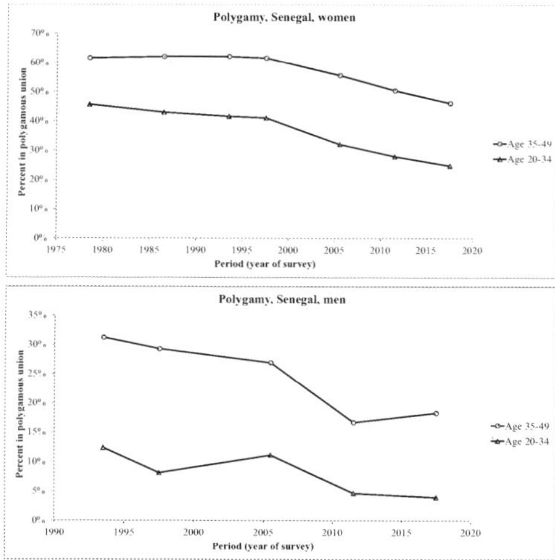

Figure 9.12 Trends in the prevalence of polygyny in Senegal

Source: Computed from WFS and DHSs

Levirate and sororate

Levirate (inheritance of a widowed woman by her former husband's brother or close relative) is reported in many parts of Africa and common in West and East Africa. The rationale for levirate seems to be primarily social: to provide a status to the widow and to guarantee the continuation of the patrilineage, and second, economical, as the new husband must support the inherited wife and provide some basic commodities (cloth, medicines, etc.), as well as food and shelter if needed. However, levirate does not necessarily imply cohabitation, and often widowed women stay in the extended family where they used to live with their former husband. There are no demographic data on levirate in censuses and demographic surveys, and it is not even mentioned in the Murdoch ethnographic atlas. However, DSS sites can provide some quantitative data. For instance, in the Niakhar DSS, for the 1983–1989 period, some 51% of widowed women remarry within 2 years, and in about half of the cases (53%) they marry a man in the same patrilineage at that of the former husband, in most cases a brother (Author's unpublished data). It seems that there is no published value on the prevalence of sororate in Africa.

Socio-economic differentials on marriage patterns

Socio-economic differentials in age at marriage, proportion ever-married, and polygamy are usually very marked in Africa. Most common differentials studied in DHSs deal with level of education, urbanization, household wealth, regional differences, and occasionally ethnicity. Typically, groups of more educated women, wealthier women, women living in cities, and women living in more developed areas have a higher median age at marriage and a larger proportion never-married and are less likely to be in polygamous unions. Table 9.1 provides such typical differentials for Kenya (DHS-2014). The largest differentials were for level of education (7 years difference in age at marriage between lowest and highest categories), then for wealth

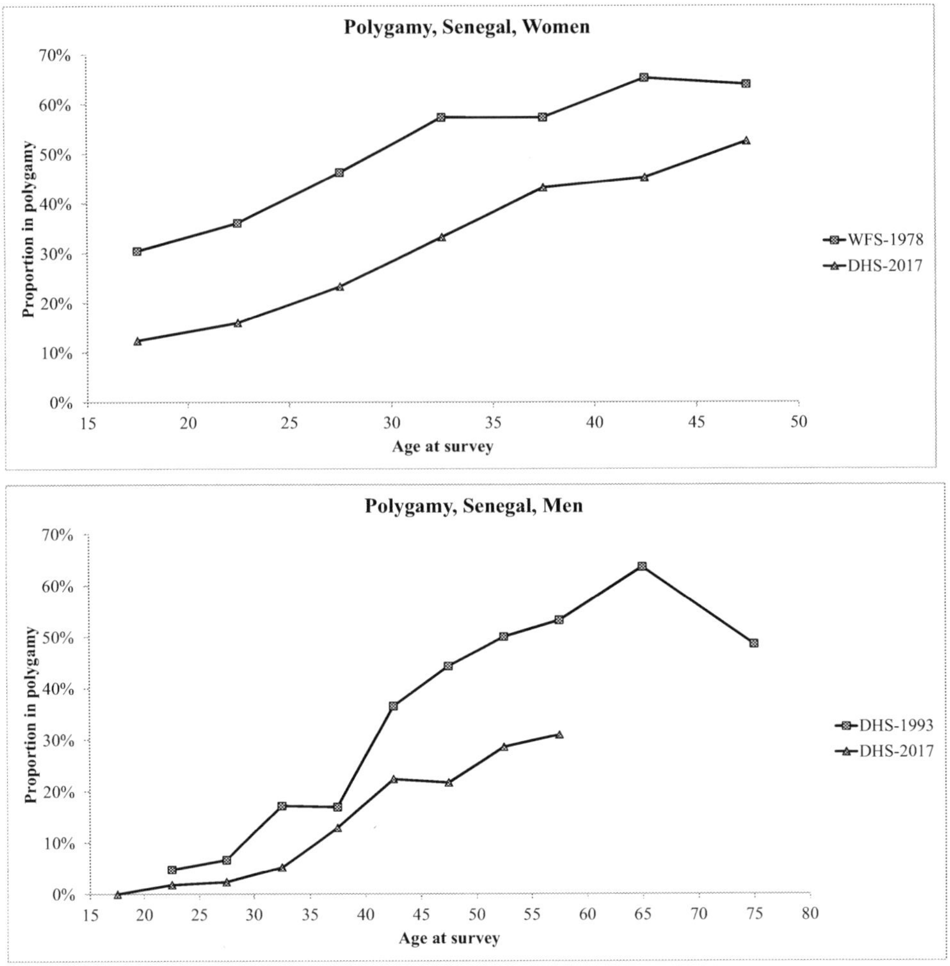

Figure 9.13 Age pattern of polygamy, Senegal

Source: Computed from WFS and DHSs

(4.3 years) and region or district of residence, and smaller for urban/rural residence. Note the large differentials in polygamy by district (county), because this category is closely linked with ethnicity and with the social practice of polygyny. This type of differential is almost universal in Africa; however, the magnitude of differences may vary considerably across countries and over time.

For age at first marriage, the lowest values were found in North-Eastern and Migori, while the highest values were found in Nairobi. For proportions never-married, the lowest values were found in Kwale and Tana River, while the highest values were found in Kirinyaga and Nyeri. For proportions in polygamous unions, the lowest values were found in Kirinyaga and Nyeri, while the highest values were found in Nyandarua and Narok.

Table 9.1 Examples of Socio-Economic Differentials in Nuptiality, Kenya, 2014 DHS

Socio-Economic Variables	*Age at First Marriage (Median)*	*Proportion Never Married (Age 40–49)*	*Proportion in Polygamous Unions (Age 40–49)*
Place of residence			
Urban	21.5	7.4%	13.4%
Rural	19.5	3.7%	21.0%
Level of education			
None	17.9	1.4%	40.1%
Primary	19.0	3.6%	19.9%
Secondary	21.5	7.2%	10.6%
Higher	24.9	11.6%	7.4%
Household wealth (quintile)			
Q1 (poorest)	18.3	2.4%	35.1%
Q2 (poorer)	19.1	4.2%	22.0%
Q3 (middle)	19.6	4.2%	16.5%
Q4 (richer)	20.6	5.2%	19.2%
Q5 (richest)	22.6	7.6%	7.1%
Region of residence			
Lowest value	18.6	1.1%	7.6%
Highest value	22.1	9.8%	40.0%
District of residence (county)			
Lowest value	17.1	0.0%	2.6%
Highest value	21.8	14.5%	62.1%

Source: Computed from 2014 DHS

Socio-economic differentials are suitable for numerous multivariate analyses, and invariably, level of education appears as the leading variable accounting for differentials, usually followed by household wealth. This can be interpreted as the effect of modernization, as modern education appears to be the main mechanism leading to adopting modern behavior. A study conducted in Malawi provides an example of such multivariate analysis (Palamuleni, 2011).

Changing marriage patterns and social change in Africa

Major changes in marriage patterns occurred in Africa in the 20th century, in particular after independence (since 1960). These changes are due to a variety of factors: social change (emerging new family models, often imitated from Western societies), modern education (especially for women), exposure to mass media, urbanization, economic development, and the spread of monotheist religions (Christianity and Islam). This section briefly explores some of these relationships from a longitudinal perspective in national populations.

Age at marriage and modernization

A study investigated the relationships between changes in female median age at first marriage with those in modernization (education, urbanization, economic development, polygyny, religion, acculturation, traumatic events, etc.). This study was based on 32 African countries and conducted at the population level from a longitudinal perspective, that is, over time (Garenne, 2004a). Results showed that increasing women's education and income per capita over time were the leading factors of rising age at marriage, whereas the spread of monotheist religions had a negative effect. Declining polygyny was associated with increasing age at marriage. The raw effect of urbanization was positive, because it was correlated with level of education and income, but its net effect (controlling for other factors) was negative, as if urban residence were favoring the marriage market (more opportunities for finding a partner). A typical evolution of an average country over a 50-year period induced an increase of 2.9 years in the median age at marriage, most of which was associated with increasing levels of education and income and declining polygyny, despite negative changes induced by other factors.

Other effects of modernization

Social change and modernization have an effect on terminal celibacy and polygyny. These relationships have not yet been investigated for the continent as a whole. They bear some relationships with fertility decline, although this remains a controversial issue because of the independent effect of modern contraception (see discussion in Garenne, 2014).

Premarital fertility and ethnicity

Sub-Saharan Africa hosts great diversity in ethnicity, with some 2100 ethno-linguistic groups being recorded in the Ethnologue database (Gordon, 2005; Ethnologue, 2018), of which some 500 groups recorded in censuses and DHSs. Each group has its own rule for marriage, polygyny, exogamy, and so on, with numerous demographic consequences. Research on the effect of ethnicity on marriage is limited in Africa, mainly because of the great complexity of the matter. Some of the DHSs publish nuptiality indicators by large ethnic groups, but this is not routine. A detailed analysis of some 500 ethnic groups related the median age at first marriage to the prevalence of premarital fertility (Garenne & Zwang, 2006). Results showed huge gradients, even in the same country. For instance, among 25 large ethnic groups in Cameroon, median age at marriage ranged from 14.7 to 20.8 years, and premarital fertility from 1.0% to 49.1%, the relationship being linear (later age at marriage implying more premarital fertility).

Outstanding marriage patterns in Southern Africa

South Africa: terminal celibacy and infertility

In South Africa, as well as in neighboring countries (Namibia, Botswana, Swaziland), female marriage occurs very late in life (median age is about 30 years), and terminal celibacy is extremely frequent. These outstanding patterns seem to be due to the huge trauma caused by the migrant labor system, which often obliged spouses to be separated, and by apartheid and its social consequences. As a result, premarital fertility is very frequent in this area (Garenne, Tollman, & Kahn, 2000; Garenne & Zwang, 2004, 2005, 2006; Zwang, 2004). In addition, some of the women who never marry also have no children (Garenne, 2016b). This increase in infertility is therefore no longer due to biological sterility (as in other places in Africa) but to voluntary infertility (as in some developed countries). Furthermore, South Africa is also one of the rare cases where higher social status is associated with lower prevalence of terminal celibacy (Garenne, 2016a). This seems to be due to the effect of social trauma on family stability: the poorer strata of the population were more affected and therefore less likely to end up in stable marital relationships.

Madagascar: reversal in nuptiality trends

Madagascar underwent a series of dramatic adverse events since independence (1960), in particular severe and repeated political crises and long-standing economic downturn: GDP per capita was cut by about half from 1975 to 1995 and never recovered afterwards (WDI, 2015). This crisis had several demographic and health consequences, in particular increasing child mortality, declining adult heights, and decreasing level of education (Garenne & Zwang, 2004; Garenne, 2017). As a result, the whole society was affected, as well as nuptiality. Madagascar is one of the rare documented cases of decreasing age at marriage and increasing polygamy, associated with decreasing levels of education, summarized in Table 9.2.

Marriage markets and the two-sex problem

Marriage markets are extremely difficult to study in Africa because of polygyny: a lack of marriageable men does not necessarily translate into fewer married women, as elsewhere. Furthermore, a deficit in marriageable women (as in China) has never been documented in African countries; this latter situation is made even less likely to happen in Africa because of the low sex ratio at birth, often in the 100–104 range, lower than in Europe or Asia, not counting the fact that sex-selective abortion does not exist so far in Africa (Garenne, 2002, 2004b).

Marriage markets

The dynamics of marriage markets have rarely been formally studied so far in Africa. Traditionally, women were reputed marriageable when reaching puberty. Since the age at puberty tends to decline, there are slightly more marriageable women than before. Furthermore, when fertility was increasing, and because of the large age difference between men and women, the number of never-married women tended to exceed that of never-married men simply because of the age structure. On the contrary, over time, the level of education increased, new job opportunities were created, women's autonomy improved, and new family models emerged: as a result, women are now less likely to marry, or they marry later, as shown in most African countries, especially in urban areas.

Traditionally, men were constrained by the control of the elderly and access to wealth, in particular the payment of bride-wealth and access to land and cattle. With urbanization, cash

Table 9.2 Example of Reversal in Nuptiality Trends, Madagascar

	Year of DHS Survey			
	1992	*1997*	*2003–04*	*2008–09*
Women, 15–49				
Median age at first marriage	18.2	18.5	19.1	18.9
Percent married before age 25	82.1%	82.9%	84.7%	91.4%
Percent in polygamy	6.6%	4.0%	3.4%	7.7%
Men, 15–59				
Median age at first marriage			23.3	22.8
Percent married before age 30			79.8%	90.4%
Percent in polygamy			0.4%	1.5%

Source: DHS web site

economy, increasing levels of education, new job opportunities, and higher income, men could be more likely to marry or to marry earlier. However, more freedom from the extended family, more sexual freedom in cities, and new family models could decrease their willingness to marry, the balance between these factors being unclear, and most likely context specific.

In addition, marriage markets could be affected by economic and political crises, here again either way, as shown by the examples of Rwanda and Madagascar mentioned previously. Marriage markets could also be affected by sex-selective migration. In places where men migrate for employment (to mines or industrial sites), there could be a deficit of men. However, this does not necessarily translate into less marriage, since cohabitation is not required for marriage, as shown by the case of Lesotho. Conversely, in big cities where educated women tend to migrate, there could be an excess of highly educated marriageable women. But here again, motivations for marriage are probably more important than the number of marriageable mates. Last, HIV/AIDS has probably affected marriage markets in several ways: young men and women avoiding premarital intercourse and waiting longer for first marriage, widowed men and women being less likely to remarry when their partners died of AIDS, and so on. This great variety of situation deserves in-depth and context-specific studies.

Example of a marriage-market simulation model

A recent simulation model was developed to fit the changes in the marriage market induced by a shock and changing numbers of marriageable men and women. This model was developed to simulate the dynamics of the HIV/AIDS epidemic in a two-sex population (Matthews & Garenne, 2013a, 2013b). This dynamic model simulates the marriage market over time in the following way: at each step, marriageable women offer a bid to marriageable men depending on their age, who offer a counter-bid also depending on their age, and equilibrium is searched for in a few simulation rounds so that the numbers of men and women who get married in the next step are equal. The model could be applied to a variety of situations, at least to investigate the potential effect of changing numbers of marriageable persons, and could potentially reveal indirectly changing behaviors due to other causes.

Discussion

In the earlier literature, marriage in Africa was often presented as traditional, universal, early, and stable over time. Demographic surveys published in the past 30 years revealed much more complex patterns. First, diversity in age at marriage, proportion marrying, polygyny, divorce rates, mortality rates (widowhood), and migration appear very marked across the continent by country, province, and socio-economic status, and even more when ethnicity is taken into account. Sub-Saharan Africa hosts at the same time countries with the highest and lowest ages at marriage, highest and lowest proportions ever-married, and lowest or highest levels of polygamy. Second, marriage has been changing rapidly in many places, as a consequence of modernization, social change, economic development, and in some cases acculturation or social trauma. These changes compare with corresponding changes in Western populations in speed and magnitude and are sometimes even more drastic, as in South Africa.

The future of marriage in Africa appears uncertain. In some cases, it has stayed stable so far, as in rural areas of West-Africa; in other cases, it has evolved like in Western countries (later and less marriage), such as among highly educated groups all over the countries; in other cases, marriage has tended to disappear rapidly, such as among selected ethnic groups in South

Africa; in Madagascar, it evolved in a direction opposite to expectations (earlier marriage, more polygamy). In most cases, later and less marriage is positively related to socio-economic status, whereas it is the opposite in other cases, as in South Africa. There are therefore ample opportunities to study these emerging processes from a demographic perspective and to relate these changes to social change and economic development as much as possible. Compared with the early days of African demographic research, there is now an abundant documentation and a huge amount of data waiting for in-depth analysis.

Acknowledgments

The author warmly thanks Dr. Pierre Cantrelle for providing useful comments and references.

References

Cantrelle, P. (1960). L'endogamie des populations du Fouta sénégalais. *Population, 15*, 665–676.

Cantrelle, P., & Dupire, M. (1964). L'endogamie des Peul du Fouta-Djallon. *Population, 19*, 529–558.

Coale, A. J. (1971). Age patterns of marriage. *Population Studies, 25*(12), 193–214.

Coale, A. J., & McNeil, D. R. (1972). The distribution by age of the frequency of first marriage in a female cohort. *Journal of the American Statistical Association, 67*(340).

De Moor, T., & Van Zanden, J. L. (2009). Girl power, the European marriage pattern and labour markets in the North Sea region in the late medieval and early modern period. *Economic History Review, 63*(1), 1–33.

Evans-Pritchard, E. E. (1937). *The Nuer*. Oxford: Clarendon Press. [French translation: *Les Nuers*, Paris, Gallimard, 1968].

Garenne, M. (2002). Sex ratios at birth in African populations: A review of survey data. *Human Biology, 74*(6), 889–900.

Garenne, M. (2004a). Age at marriage and modernization in sub-Saharan Africa. *Southern African Journal of Demography, 9*(2), 57–77.

Garenne, M. (2004b). Sex ratios at birth in populations of Eastern and Southern Africa. *Southern African Journal of Demography, 9*(1), 91–96.

Garenne, M. (2014). *Trends in marriage and contraception in sub-Saharan Africa: A longitudinal perspective on factors of fertility decline*. DHS Analytical Studies No. 42. Rockville, MD: ICF International.

Garenne, M. (2016a). A century of nuptiality decline in South Africa: A longitudinal analysis of census data. *African Population Studies, 30*(2), 2403–2414.

Garenne, M. (2016b). Dynamics of marriage and infertility in South Africa: An analysis of census data. *African Population Studies, 30*(2), 2550–2563.

Garenne, M. (2017). Crises and resilience in Madagascar: Relationships with demographic and social dynamics. In O. Wilson-Flores (Ed.), *Economic crises: Risk factors, management practices and social impacts* (Chapter 8, pp. 245–263). New York: Nova Publishers.

Garenne, M., & Cantrelle, P. (2019). *Forging a new identity: The development of civil registration & vital statistics, an African perspective*. Paper prepared for the United Nations Population Division, Special issue on Civil Registration and Vital Statistics.

Garenne, M., & Gakusi, E. (2014). Résilience du Rwanda aux chocs des années 1990: une perspective démographique. *Ethique et Economie, 11*(1), 16–28.

Garenne, M., Leclerc, P., & Matthews, A. (2011). Parametrisation of the transition to first marriage with the Picrate model: Application to African countries using DHS surveys. *Southern African Journal of Demography, 12*(1), 109–124.

Garenne, M., Tollman, S., & Kahn, K. (2000). Marital and premarital fertility in a rural area of South Africa: A challenge to existing population policy. *Studies in Family Planning, 31*(1), 47–54.

Garenne, M., & van de Walle, E. (1989). Polygyny and fertility among the Sereer of Senegal. *Population Studies, 43*(2), 267–283.

Garenne, M., & Zwang, J. (2004). Social change and premarital fertility in Madagascar. *Southern African Journal of Demography, 9*(1), 27–48.

Garenne, M., & Zwang, J. (2005). Premarital fertility in Namibia: Levels, trends and factors. *Journal of Biosocial Science, 37*(1), 1–23.

Garenne, M., & Zwang, J. (2006). *Premarital fertility and ethnicity in Africa*. DHS Comparative Reports No. 13. Calverton, MD: Macro International Inc., p. 87.

Gendreau, F. (1993). *La population de l'Afrique: manuel de démographie*. Paris: CEPED et Karthala (Chapter 12: La nuptialité, pp. 241–266).

Goldman, N., & Pebley, A. (1989). The demography of polygyny in sub-Saharan Africa. In R. K. Lesthaeghe (Ed.), *Reproduction and social organization in sub-Saharan Africa* (pp. 212–237). Berkeley, CA: University of California Press.

Goody, J. (1976). *Production and reproduction: A comparative study of the domestic domain*. Cambridge & New York: Cambridge University Press, p. 157.

Goody, J., & Goody, E. (1967). The circulation of women and children in Northern Ghana. *Man, New Series*, *2*(2), 226–248.

Gordon, R. G., Jr. (Ed.). (2005). *Ethnologue: Languages of the world* (15th ed.). Dallas, TX: SIL International.

Hajnal, J. (1953a). Age at marriage and proportions of marrying. *Population Studies*, 7(2), 111–136.

Hajnal, J. (1953b). The marriage boom. *Population Index*, *19*(2), 80–101.

Hajnal, J. (1965). European marriage patterns in perspective. In D. V. Glass & D. E. Eversley (Eds.), *Population in history: Essays in historical demography* (pp. 101–143). Chicago, IL: Aldine Publishing Company.

Koski, A., Clark, S., & Nandi, A. (2017). Has child marriage declined in sub-Saharan Africa? An analysis of trends in 31 countries. *Population and Development Review*, *43*(1), 7–29.

Lardoux, S., & van de Walle, E. (2003). Polygyny and fertility in rural Senegal. *Population*, *58*(6), 717–744.

Lesthaeghe, R. K. (Ed.). (1989). *Reproduction and social organization in sub-Saharan Africa*. Berkeley, CA: University of California Press.

Lesthaeghe, R. K., Kaufman, G., & Meekers, D. (1989). The nuptiality regimes in sub-Saharan Africa. In R. K. Lesthaeghe (Ed.), *Reproduction and social organization in sub-Saharan Africa* (pp. 238–337). Berkeley, CA: University of California Press.

Lyimo, P. B. (2000). *Polygamy in Africa* (Ph.D. dissertation, University of Ottawa, Canada). Retrieved from https://ruor.uottawa.ca › bitstream › Lyimo_Prosper_2011_thesis

Manton, K. G., & Stallard, E. (1984). *Recent trends in mortality analysis*. New York: Academic Press.

Matthews, A. P., & Garenne, M. L. (2013a). A dynamic model of the marriage market – Part 1: Matching algorithm based on age preference and availability. *Theoretical Population Biology*, *88*, 78–85.

Matthews, A. P., & Garenne, M. L. (2013b). A dynamic model of the marriage market – Part 2: Simulation of marital states and application to empirical data. *Theoretical Population Biology*, *88*, 86–93.

Matthews, A. P., Leclerc, P., & Garenne, M. (2009). The Picrate model for fitting the age pattern of first marriage. *Mathématiques et Sciences Humaines, No. 186*, *47*(2), 17–28.

Mokomane, Z., Baker, K. R., & van de Walle, E. (2006). Extramarital childbearing and the residence of children in Botswana. In E. van de Walle (Ed.), *African households, censuses and surveys* (pp. 159–177). London & New York: M.E. Sharpe.

Murdock, G. P. (1967). Ethnographic atlas: A summary. *Ethnology*, *1*, 109–236.

Ngondo, A., & Pitshandenge, S. (1996). *La polyandrie chez les Bashilele du Kasaï Occidental (Zaïre): Fonctionnement et rôles: Les Dossiers du CEPED*, N°42. Paris: CEPED.

Palamuleni, M. E. (2011). Socioeconomic determinants of age at marriage in Malawi. *International Journal of Sociology and Anthropology*, *3*(7), 224–235.

Pebley, A., & Mbugua, W. (1989). Polygyny and fertility in sub-Saharan Africa. In R. K. Lesthaeghe (Ed.), *Reproduction and social organization in sub-Saharan Africa* (pp. 338–364). Berkeley, CA: University of California Press.

Preston, S. H., Heuveline, P., & Guillot, M. (2001). *Demography: Measuring and modeling population processes*. Malden, MA: Blackwell Publishing.

Radcliffe-Brown, A. R., & Forde, D. (1950). *African systems of kinship and marriage*. London: Routledge and Kegan.

Schwartze, L. J. (2010). Grave vows: A cross-cultural examination of the varying forms of ghost marriage among five societies. *Nebraska Anthropologist*, *60*, 82–95.

Shapiro, D., & Gebreselassie, T. (2013). Marriage in sub-Saharan Africa: Trends, determinants, and consequences. *Population Research and Policy Review*, *33*(2), 229–255.

Singer, A. (1973). Marriage payments and the exchange of people. *Man, New Series*, *8*(1), 80–92.

Tabutin, D., & Vallin, J. (1975). La nuptialité. In *Sources et analyse des données démographiques* (Vol. III, pp. 3–56). Paris: Groupe de Démographie Africaine.

Timaeus, I., & Graham, W. (1989). Labor circulation, marriage and fertility in Southern Africa. In R. K. Lesthaeghe (Ed.), *Reproduction and social organization in sub-Saharan Africa* (pp. 365–400). Berkeley, CA: University of California Press.

Van de Walle, E. (1968). Marriage in African censuses and inquiries. In W. Brass et al. (Eds.), *The demography of tropical Africa* (pp. 183–238). Princeton, NJ: Princeton University Press.

Van de Walle, E. (1993). Recent trends in marriage ages. In K. A. Foote, K. H. Hill, & L. G. Martin (Eds.), *Demographic change in sub-Saharan Africa* (pp. 117–152). Washington, DC: National Academy Press.

Welch, C. E., & Glick, P. C. (1981). The incidence of polygamy in contemporary Africa: A research note. *Journal of Marriage and the Family*, *43*(2), 191–193.

Westoff, C. F. (2003). *Trends in marriage and early childbearing in developing countries*. DHS Comparative Reports No. 5. Calverton, MD: ORC Macro.

Zeitzen, M. K. (2008). *Polygamy: A cross-cultural analysis*. New York: Berg.

Zwang, J. (2004). Perceptions and attitudes towards late marriage and premarital fertility in rural South Africa. *Cahiers de l'IFAS*, *4*, 57. (Johannesburg, South Africa, IFAS).

Web sites

DHS. (2018). *Demographic and Health Surveys program*. Retrieved from https://dhsprogram.com/

Ethnologue. (2018). *Ethnologue database*, online version. Retrieved from www.ethnologue.com

In-Depth. (2018): *In-Depth network*. Retrieved from www.indepth-network.org/

INSEE. (2018) *Institut National de la Statistique et des Etudes Economiques*. Retrieved from www.insee.fr

IPUMS. (2018): *IPUMS International*. Retrieved from https://international.ipums.org/international/

WDI. (2015). *World Bank Development Indicators*. Retrieved from http://datatopics.worldbank.org/world-development-indicators/

Appendix 9.1

DESCRIPTION OF THE PICRATE MODEL FOR FITTING PROPORTIONS EVER-MARRIED

Picrate is an acronym for "phased-in-constant-rate". Full documentation on the model is available in Matthews et al. (2009). The Picrate model is designed to fit proportions ever-married and to derive the underlying marriage rates and related indicators (median, mean, standard deviation of age at first marriage).

Proportion ever married at age (*a*)

$$p(a) = p_{\max}\left\{1 - \exp\left[-r_{\max}(a - a_0) + I\left(r_{\max}(a - a_0)\right)\right]\right\}$$

where: $I(x) = \int_0^x \exp\left(-\frac{1}{2}u^2\right)du = \sqrt{2\pi}\left[N_C(x) - \frac{1}{2}\right]$

Marriage rate at age (*a*)

$$m(a) = \frac{dp}{da} = p_{\max} r_{\max}\left(1 - e^{-\frac{1}{2}r_{\max}^2(a-a_0)^2}\right)\exp\left\{-r_{\max}(a - a_0) + I\left(r_{\max}(a - a_0)\right)\right\}$$

Recruitment rate for entry into first marriage per susceptible, at age (*a*)

$$r(a) = r_{\max}\left\{1 - \exp\left[-\frac{1}{2}r_{\max}^2(a - a_0)^2\right]\right\}$$

And $r(a)/r_{\max}$ is a cumulative Weibull function.

Median age:

$$MED(a) = a_0 + 1.869 / r_{\max}$$

Mean age:

$$AVG(a) = a_0 + 2.090 / r_{\max}$$

Standard deviation:

$$STD(a) = 1.137 / r_{\max}$$

Appendix Table 9.1A Example of a Multi-State Nuptiality Table with Polygamy: Empirical data, Niakhar, 1983–1990, Men Age 15+

	Age Group			
	15–29	*30–44*	*45–59*	*60+*
Distribution of marital status in population				
Single	0.759	0.085	0.022	0.009
Monogam	0.226	0.702	0.525	0.424
Polygam	0.010	0.174	0.406	0.501
Divorced	0.004	0.032	0.034	0.032
Widowed	0.001	0.007	0.014	0.033
Total	1.000	1.000	1.000	1.000
Transitions of marital status (per 1000)				
First marriage, single	46.3	129.7	44.9	0.0
New wife, monogam	28.7	34.2	42.1	40.6
Divorce, monogam	8.8	8.0	8.0	5.5
Widowed, monogam	2.3	2.9	6.7	8.5
Loss of second wife, polygam	39.2	28.2	22.4	18.0
Remarriage, divorced	295.3	132.2	95.2	95.5
Remarriage, widowed	193.4	286.8	96.7	88.0
Mortality by marital status (per 1000)				
Single	3.3	13.9	19.3	38.3
Monogam	3.3	6.1	14.9	65.7
Polygam	5.6	4.5	11.7	53.1
Divorced	0.0	12.3	29.0	73.0
Widowed	0.0	14.3	87.1	148.5

Source: NB: All rates calculated per 1000 person-years lived in each marital status

Appendix Table 9.1B Example of a Multi-State Nuptiality Table with Polygamy: Transitions per 1,000,000 Men at Age 15 (Computed from Data in Appendix Table 9.1A)

	Events Occurring in Each Age Group, Cohort of 1,000,000 Men							
	Mariage, single	*New Wife, Monogam*	*Divorce, Monogam*	*Widowed, Monogam*	*Loss Of Wife, Polygam*	*Mariage, Divorced*	*Mariage, Widowed*	*Deaths*
15–19	44,119	0	0	0	0	0	0	14,404
20–24	174,839	6856	2510	376	0	0	329	19,380
25–29	440,073	33,145	10,953	2128	1228	1657	1747	24,457
30–34	135,376	97,743	29,156	7345	6284	7143	5673	26,499
35–39	54,402	100,957	27,177	8879	19,055	18,572	6694	33,940
40–44	24,582	93,496	22,711	9621	27,729	19,829	6910	43,257
45–49	12,017	83,370	18,270	10,035	32,127	17,245	6770	54,545
50–54	6150	72,447	14,322	10,196	33,209	13,747	6380	67,759
55–59	3197	61,159	10,905	10,059	31,850	10,376	5769	82,230
60–64	1639	49,660	7986	9540	28,721	7460	4953	96,344
65–69	801	38,195	5539	8563	24,362	5078	3976	107,349
70–74	360	27,245	3563	7123	19,278	3232	2921	111,624
75+	142	17,530	2067	5339	14,004	1885	1908	105,810

Appendix Table 9.1C Example of a Multi-State Nuptiality Table with Polygamy: Survivors in Each Marital Status, per 1,000,000 Men at Age 15 (Computed from Data in Appendix Table 9.1B)

Exact Age (a)	*Marital Status at Exact Age (a)*				
	Single	*Monogam*	*Polygam*	*Divorced*	*Widowed*
15	1,000,000	0	0	0	0
20	941,477	44,119	0	0	376
25	747,753	209,089	6856	2510	2136
30	286,826	604,501	38,685	11,627	7465
35	140,353	612,167	129,454	32,624	9541
40	78,440	555,875	208,143	37,743	10,740
45	48,075	486,030	266,737	35,707	11,549
50	31,202	414,154	305,251	31,082	12,025
55	20,767	342,862	324,391	25,711	12,087
60	13,729	273,027	324,380	20,326	11,607
65	8714	205,952	305,337	15,266	10,479
70	5109	144,092	268,304	10,751	8703
75	2640	90,937	216,557	6959	6458
80	1131	49,962	156,637	4030	642

10

THE CONSTRUCTION OF TEEN PREGNANCY AND CHILD MARRIAGE IN AFRICA

Timalizge Zgambo

Introduction

Teen pregnancy is considered a global phenomenon and child marriage a violation of human rights. The two issues combined are now at the epicentre of the adolescent sexual and reproductive health agenda in Africa. A teen mother is perceived as doomed to failure, all opportunities of attaining a good future lost post-motherhood or matrimonial union. This situation relates to the health risks of childbearing and the hardships associated with a lack of educational attainment, ultimately leading to poverty.

A child is defined as any person below 18 years, as prescribed by the Convention on the Rights of a Child (United Nations Human Rights, 1990). According to the international standard definition, child marriage is a legal or formal/customary union of two persons below 18 years and if one of the spouses is above 18 (United Nations population fund, 2012). However, many countries have varying legal frameworks guiding age at first marriage.

Teen pregnancy, which may also be called adolescent or early pregnancy, in this chapter refers to pregnancy between ages 10–19 years. Teen pregnancy has now become closely linked to child marriage, and the two issues are intertwined in that either one of them might be the cause of the other.

Three issues show how the two are linked: first, delaying or preventing child or early marriage can help reduce early/teen pregnancy and other related sexual risks (United Nations population fund, 2012). Second, early or teen pregnancy may be the gateway to early/child marriage, ultimately disrupting a teenager's life (Agege, Nwose, & Odjimogho, 2018). Third, teen pregnancy is seen both as a cause and a consequence of child marriage (Menon, Kusanthan, Mwaba, Juanola, & Kok, 2018). Since motherhood is a desirable thing in most African societies (Ahonsi et al., 2019; Kane et al., 2019; Mwape, Katowa-mukwato, Dixey, & Maimbolwa, 2014; Schaffnit, Urassa, & Lawson, 2019), once married, childbearing is expected to commence immediately, regardless of the age of the woman or girl. Therefore, this clearly marks a direct link between teen pregnancy and child marriage.

Teen pregnancy has been linked to health complications, low education attainment/school dropout, poverty, and intimate partner violence, among other things. Reports from the United Nations agencies involved in youth health and wellbeing highlight the harmful consequences and dangers of teen pregnancy and child marriage with a special focus on low- and

 DOI: 10.4324/9780429287213-13

middle-income countries (UNFPA, 2017; UNICEF, 2018, 2019; United Nations population fund, 2012; United Nations Zambia, UNFPA, & population Council, 2017). To this effect, the solution presented is to eliminate child marriages with the hope of preventing teen pregnancy. Girls Not Brides and the International Center for Research on Women (ICRW) have actively launched a global movement to particularly advocate ending child marriage, especially in Africa and Asia, where the practice is seen to be common.

There appears to be extensive research on teen pregnancy in general and (now) more studies on child marriage in the African context. However, most of the research conducted by both international organisations and African researchers highlights the negative consequences of teen pregnancy and child marriage (Macleod, 1999). Thus, the argument presented about teen pregnancy and child marriage in Africa is one sided, dominantly highlighting how problematic teen pregnancy is without particularly examining the context in which it occurs. Contrary to this view is what I refer to as the "open" view argument that teen pregnancy may not always lead to a disastrous life but (in some cases) yields positive outcomes. This side of the story is often undocumented and dominated by the more negative aspects.

This chapter focuses on exploring both the negative and the other (seemingly positive) side of the story that is not fully documented. The examination helps gain a deeper understanding of the context, circumstances, and setting in which teen pregnancy and child marriage occur in Africa. This also helps to gain a broader perspective of the 'harmfulness' of child marriage. To whom is it harmful? And this looks at the issue from the perspective of those who have experienced it, not only from those who write reports about it. Thus, these insights are gathered through a selection of studies that show both negative and some positive experiences of teen pregnancy and child marriage.

Some studies conducted in Africa have highlighted that (in some cases) teen mothers have experienced both positive and negative feelings about pregnancy and marriage. Others have displayed resilient coping strategies to continue managing their lives (Baba, Yendork, & Atindanbila, 2020; Chohan & Langa, 2011; Kane et al., 2019; Katowa, Maimbolwa, Mwape, & Muleya, 2017; Mwape et al., 2014; Schaffnit et al., 2019). These studies are discussed in detail later in the chapter. Most of this kind of literature remains limited and is not documented in most international reports or government official documents. Moreover, there appears to be scarce research that examines different constructs (both positive and negative views) of teen pregnancy and child marriage in Africa compared to the vast literature from high-income countries. Even though this chapter only examines teen pregnancy research in Africa, the previous point is worth noting.

This chapter seeks to question the dominant constructs and the unbalanced representation of teen pregnancy and child marriage research in Africa, as well as providing an agenda for future research on the subject. African researchers and demographers should respond to the problem of teen pregnancy and child marriage with an African lens in mind. It is important to note that the local, cultural, historical, and social circumstances within which teen pregnancy and child marriage occur are different and should not be treated or viewed similar to Asia or other continents. As such, I utilise a social construction perspective to question the universal problematisation of teen pregnancy, similar to what other African researchers have done before (Macleod, 2001; Mkhwanazi, 2006, 2015, 2016; Preston-Whyte, 1989; Preston-Whyte & Zondi, 1991).

I argue that there appears to be a copycat style of researching teen pregnancy that does not fit into the African context. In a nutshell, this chapter tacitly questions the temptation to see homogeneity where it does not exist. This resolve even fails to consider some fundamental African customary practices which opportunists have since hijacked by attempting to create a universal culture.

The call to eliminate teen pregnancy and child marriage in Africa

The problem of teen pregnancy and child marriage has led to campaigns focused on 'eliminating' child marriage and preventing teen pregnancy as much as possible in most parts of lower- and middle-income countries (LMICs). It is certain that teen pregnancy and child marriage are not new but have long existed before gaining the 'serious social problem' status. This status has been fuelled by comparative studies from the Demography and Health Survey (DHS), showing high indicators and the human rights fight against harmful traditions.

The UNFPA (2012) 'Marrying Too Young' report highlighted the global prevalence of child marriage using data from the DHS, indicating high child marriage practices in South Asia and West and Central Africa. The report showed child marriage rates above 30 per cent (considered most prevalent) in Burkina Faso, Cameroon, Chad, Ethiopia, Malawi, Mauritania, Mozambique, Nigeria, Niger, Sierra Leone, and Zambia. These statistics raised a call for action. Meanwhile, an international advocacy organisation, Girls not Brides, called child marriage a 'harmful traditional practice' and strongly condemned it.

The key message presented globally is that child marriage is a 'traditional' harmful practice and a violation of human rights. Other international reports show a similar view (Dethloff, 2018; Steinhaus, Gregowski, Fenn, & Petroni, 2016; UNICEF, 2019). Thus, the elimination of child marriage is now perceived as a matter of urgency for Africa. However, the description of child marriage as a traditional practice, first of all, needs to be distinguished, as it is misleading. Even though child marriage is most prevalent in Africa, this does not make it absent anywhere else. If it happened in the global north, would it still be classified as a harmful traditional practice? There should be substantive evidence to qualify the description of child marriage as a traditional practice. Otherwise, it suggests an agenda manufactured to give a bad representation of African culture.

The child marriage elimination agenda was flagged by the 1994 International Conference on Population and Development (ICPD) programme of action, which called for eliminating all forms of gender inequality against women and children to ensure that sexual reproductive rights are safeguarded (United Nations, 1995). The ICPD specifically stipulated that:

> countries should create a socio-economic environment conducive to the elimination of all child marriages and other unions as a matter of urgency and should discourage early marriage. The social responsibilities that marriage entails should be reinforced in countries' educational programmes. Governments should take action to eliminate discrimination against young pregnant women.
>
> (United Nations, 1995, p. 34)

To this effect, governments were instructed to enforce and stiffen marriage laws regarding the age deemed appropriate for marriage.

However, most African governments achieved little success after the ICPD (Hindin & Fatusi, 2009; Kalamar, Lee-Rife, & Hindin, 2016). There appears to be a tendency for African leaders to blindly commit and adhere to these agreements without a contextual view. Some struggles leading to this lack of success are attributed to deep-rooted societal values embedded in the African culture, customs, and identity as a continent. Even though not all African countries practice the same traditions, many traditions, customs, and values cut across geographical boundaries. Research has proved this, as highlighted in the studies presented in the next section. It is clear that policymakers, politicians, and some researchers seem to overlook the complexities of a 'one size fits all' solution to the problems of teen pregnancy and child marriage, as expounded later in the chapter.

To reinforce the ICPD-prescribed guidelines, the African Union (AU) set out an agenda to wipe out child marriage in Africa, 'Campaign to End Child Marriage in Africa: Call to Action' 2014–2017 (African Union, 2013). Then, AU chairperson Nkosazana Dlamini-Zuma, at an international conference on family planning, stated that 'We must do away with child marriage. Girls who end up as brides at a tender age are coerced into having children while they are children themselves' (African Union, 2013, p. 1).

In 2016, the United Nations Population Fund (UNFPA) and United Nations Children's Fund (UNICEF) launched the Global Programme to End Child Marriage in 12 countries, targeting a total elimination of all child marriages by 2030 (UNFPA & UNICEF, 2019). Burkina Faso, Ethiopia, Ghana, Mozambique, Sierra Leone, Uganda, and Zambia are among the African governments involved in the programme. National plans and policy documents on ending child marriage have since been launched and implemented in these countries. Thus, it is believed that child marriage is on the decline.

An analysis of child marriage trends in 31 sub-Saharan Africa countries showed a decline in teen pregnancy and child marriage rates (Koski, Clark, & Nandi, 2017), even though it is unclear if this decline is due to the recent massive campaigns. What seems to be clear is that most African governments are under external pressure to meet unrealistic targets without fully understanding the problem and the context in which it occurs. Koski et al. (2017) state that eliminating child marriage in Africa cannot happen without additional research. They state:

> in particular, we must learn more about what characterizes marriage among the youngest girls and the social forces that perpetuate it in the face of a rising trend in the average age at marriage throughout most of sub-Saharan Africa.
>
> (Koski et al., 2017, p. 26)

According to the Global Programme to End Child Marriage Phase 1 (2016–2019) evaluation report (UNFPA & UNICEF, 2019), many countries have managed to modify legal frameworks that predispose girls to child marriage and adopt policies that do not discriminate against married or pregnant adolescents. The report further states:

> most countries have reached or exceeded their targets, and there have been significant improvements in programme achievements over the four years of the Global Programme implementation.
>
> (UNFPA & UNICEF, 2019, p. 9)

However, the progress reported has not taken place without resistance from certain societal norms, including strong religious beliefs. In the 1990s, when many African governments embraced neo-liberalism, health reforms became more rights based and led to an influx of partnerships with European and US-based health research organisations. Consequently, adolescent sexual reproductive health policies have since been influenced by external culture and now amongst the popular topics not only in reproductive health but politically too.

The strong advocacy for sexual and reproductive rights as a human right has resulted in significant backlash in African culture (Tamale, 2011). Culture serves as a "double-edged sword that can be wielded creatively and resourcefully to enhance women's access to sexual justice" (Tamale, 2011, p. 20). The persistent negative description – "harmful traditional practices" – as a hindrance to what is perceived as a progressive society generally blocks deeper understandings of African sexual behaviour.

Method

The studies reviewed in this chapter were selected by searching relevant empirical, conceptual, and theoretical articles covering an open timeline. Databases searched include Taylor and Francis Publications, Sage, Google Scholar, Sabinet Reference, Academic Search Complete, and JSTOR. However, only a few of these searches yielded fruitful outcomes relevant to the subject. This highly suggests a gap in the literature.

The search covered both broad and specific terms: "Social construction", "Social construction and teen pregnancy", "teen pregnancy", "teen pregnancy in developing countries", "adolescent pregnancy". The purpose of this broad search was to scan the global literature to be able to compare it with the African literature. The search was then narrowed specifically to Africa using terms like "child marriage in Africa", "ending child marriage in Africa", "Adolescent pregnancy in Africa", "teen pregnancy in Africa". The focus was to retrieve articles on both positive and negative views on teen pregnancy and child marriage specific to Africa.

This review comprises studies selected from Ghana, Kenya, Nigeria, South Africa, South Sudan, Tanzania, and Zambia. Few of these studies were selected to present both sides of the argument. Although extensive reading was done in preparation for this chapter, not everything can be presented due to word count limitations. Thus, the articles were selected in line with the aim and objective of this chapter. I found that the search term "Social construction and teen pregnancy in Africa" produced a few materials. Evidently, this shows there is little research analysing the different constructs around teen pregnancy and child marriage in African countries compared to the international literature by American and British researchers across different disciplines in the social sciences (Arai, 2009; Furstenberg, 2007; Luker, 1996; Nathanson, 1991; Rhode, 1994; Weatherley, 1987) who have examined the subject thoroughly. Thus, few non-African researchers are cited with relevance to the arguments presented due to the limited African literature. This presents the need for more research on the problematisation of teen pregnancy and child marriage, focusing on context, circumstances, and setting. This helps to get a clear perspective of the problem and therefore seek suitable policy intervention.

Review of the literature: the problem of teen pregnancy

Teen pregnancy is a subject that has been well researched around the globe, and many different aspects of it have been explored in various professions and disciplines in the fields of psychology, sociology, anthropology, health and others. Each has provided their insights on the subject. This section reviews and discusses both positive and negative views about teen pregnancy and child marriage in the African context. Some studies highlight the devastating effects and problematic nature of teen pregnancy and child marriage as a combined issue. Other studies show that teen pregnancy and child marriage may be a rational choice, perceived positively. There are two parts to this section; the first describes teen pregnancy as a "public health" problem and a "social" problem. The second part presents the other side of the story that is often untold – the open view.

As presented in most local and international literature, the dominant view associates teen pregnancy and child marriage with bad and negative outcomes. The counter-argument I present here goes beyond simply looking at the 'problem' of teen pregnancy but paying close attention to how this theme is researched and presented. As pointed out earlier, a one-sided view has dominated the African literature on teen pregnancy and child marriage. Thus, the purpose of this review is to synthesise views from both sides while highlighting the implications of such dominant constructs.

Teen pregnancy as a public health problem

From a health perspective, pregnancy is said to endanger a pregnant teenager's health at birth and also affect the infant's health. Some studies (Envuladu, Umaru, & Iorapuu, 2016; Groot, Kuunyem, & Palermo, 2018; Moraes, Likwa, & Nzala, 2018; Omoro et al., 2017; Wadhawan, Narone, & Narone, 1982) associate teen pregnancy with health risks and complications such as sepsis, preeclampsia, anaemia, high blood pressure, and premature labour, among others. In theory, every pregnant woman, regardless of age, is susceptible to the mentioned diseases. However, the risk is said to be higher in younger females.

A study was conducted in Zambia (Luapula province) comparing two different age groups of females aged 10–15 and 20–24. High rates of eclampsia, haemorrhage, and prolonged labour were found in those below 16 (Moraes et al., 2018). This shows that there was a higher rate of eclampsia. But this does not indicate a direct link between maternal age and the other diseases. As the authors state:

> there was no significant association between maternal age and prolonged labour, anaemia, haemorrhage, sepsis, maternal death, preterm delivery, asphyxia and low Apgar scores.
>
> (Moraes et al., 2018, p. 5)

Moraes et al. (2018) further observed that adolescents did not frequently attend antenatal care visits as much as older women due to hindering factors: adolescents mostly hide their pregnancies for fear of scolding and stigma from parents, the community, and health workers. This limits close monitoring and early detection of threatening conditions. Additionally, the lack of attendance is linked to adolescents not having access to tailored 'adolescent-friendly' services that cater specifically to their needs. Moreover, a study conducted in Zambia showed that increased adolescent use of services has much to do with community-level influences of health-seeking behaviours (Mmari & Magnani, 2003). The more community acceptance and less stigma attached to teen sexual activity, the greater the accessibility of such services to young people. Thus, Moraes et al. (2018) recommend better antenatal, obstetric care and services targeted at adolescents as well as the overall strengthening of reproductive health services for women to reduce maternal morbidity and mortality.

Meanwhile, Omoro et al. (2017) state that teen pregnancy is unwanted and is a public health issue, which presents a high risk of acquiring HIV in Kenya. The authors conclude that:

> while HIV infection is a large public health issue in developing countries like Kenya, teenage pregnancy and the associated lack of education, as well as partner violence among teen girls are the more important public health issues.
>
> (Omoro et al., 2017, p. 8)

These authors suggest that teen pregnancy should be taken as a public health issue in the same way as contracting an HIV infection. In other words, teen pregnancy itself seems to be perceived as a medical condition, but other researchers disagree with the medicalisation of teen pregnancy. Lawlor and Shaw (2002, p. 553) state, "researchers and health practitioners should think more carefully about why something is labelled a public health problem together with the social and moral context in which it occurs and in which they practice". Lawlor and Shaw (2002) argue against the negative labelling of teen pregnancy as a sickness and a shameful thing.

It is assumed that there is insufficient convincing biological evidence that ties teen pregnancy to maternal deaths. In their article, they highlight that:

> medical consequences of teenage pregnancy concluded that Critical appraisal suggested that increased risks of these outcomes [anaemia, pregnancy-induced hypertension, low birth weight, prematurity, intrauterine growth retardation and neonatal mortality] were predominantly caused by the social, economic, and behavioural factors that predispose some young women to pregnancy.
>
> (Lawlor & Shaw, 2002, p. 552)

Thus, there are many other factors to consider before teen pregnancy can be labelled a public health problem or a clinical condition. For example, the physiological body capacity to carry a pregnancy regardless of age has been ignored. However, from the studies presented previously, it is clear that there are "some" possible complications or diseases that put pregnant adolescents and teenagers at risk. However, the pregnancy itself may not be the main determinant of exposure to high-pregnancy risk complications for younger females. The alternative to the problem here is to review care, access, and services for specific adolescent needs. With this in mind, teen pregnancy prevention may be an appropriate measure to avoid certain health complications but may not be the ultimate solution to curb these complications/diseases. Teen pregnancy cannot simply be controlled like an infectious pandemic, as it is interlinked to a combination of factors. Bearing in mind that all women, regardless of age, are susceptible to pregnancy-related complications depending on varying circumstances, it becomes more commendable to improve overall health care services. As Cherry and Dillon (2014, p. 3) state:

> the focus may be on some aspects of providing adequate medical and social services to reduce adolescent maternal and child risks. In these countries [developing countries], the major challenges being addressed are often the ability of the country's public health sector to provide adequate and effective contraception, prenatal and postnatal care, and well-baby programs.

Thus, governments need to direct more efforts towards improving the quality of reproductive health services, including youth/adolescent-friendly services, in addition to ensuring early monitoring of pregnancy and follow-ups.

Teen pregnancy as a 'social problem'

Teen pregnancy as a social problem is associated with an endless list of social and economic consequences in a young girl's life. Teen pregnancy is also said to be unplanned and unwanted. Therefore it leads to low or no educational attainment, leading to poverty, gender inequality, and intimate partner violence (IPV), a long inheritance of poverty from generation to generation (Edin et al., 2016; Efevbera, Bhabha, Farmer, & Fink, 2017).

Educational attainment is considered a key weapon in ensuring that a teenager succeeds in life. With pregnancy or marriage in the way, success cannot be achieved. Instead, the consequences are disastrous. Therefore, teenage girls 'must' be prevented from pregnancy and child marriage and be encouraged to be in school instead. Gyan (2013) conducted a qualitative study in Ghana to identify what factors lead to teen pregnancy and determine the effects of teen pregnancy on educational attainment. Gyan (2013, p. 58) states that "some of the respondents dropped out of school due to the pregnancy while others became pregnant because they dropped out of school". This shows that school dropout is both a cause and consequence of teen pregnancy. Nonetheless, the article does not show whether teenagers choose to get pregnant and drop out of school or if the pregnancy was unplanned, leading them to leave school. Gyan's study also points to poverty as a contributing factor to teen pregnancy due to material deprivation.

Poverty has frequently appeared in teen pregnancy literature as a leading factor or cause of teen pregnancy. Rural areas tend to have higher rates of teen pregnancy than urban areas. Odimegwu and Mkwananzi's study (2016) described an association between teen pregnancy and social disadvantage in most communities with high poverty levels. Another study found inconsistencies between wealth and sexual behaviour among young people, but wealthy females were not more vulnerable to contracting infections (Madise, Zulu, & Ciera, 2007). Yakubu and Salisu (2018) concluded that teen pregnancy occurs under multiple factors, including sociocultural, environmental, and economic factors.

However, there appears to be unsubstantiated evidence that poverty is one of the leading causes of child marriage because the term itself is defined narrowly and used loosely. For example, would the desire for material gain by young girls be classified as deprivation or poverty? Does this desire for material things imply poor living conditions? Or poverty? These are some of the questions that are rarely asked or answered when linking poverty to teen pregnancy. Thus, researchers need to be more critical in questioning the social and economic conditions rather than seeing poverty as a consequence of teen pregnancy.

Ahonsi et al. (2019) conducted a study in Ghana to establish the predators of child marriage and the norms that inform it. The study showed that 21 per cent of women got married before the age of 18, and the norm was that after a girl gets pregnant, the next thing that follows is marriage. Similarly, a study conducted in a Nigerian community concluded that "unexpected pregnancy is the highest cause of early marriage" (Agege et al., 2018, p. 1). It affirms the two issues cannot be easily separated. The circumstances leading to marriage (in most cases) emanate from the need to create a family unit consisting of father, mother, and child.

Ahonsi et al. (2019) further point out that there has been a decline in child marriage due to increased efforts in promoting girl child education. But the study also found that different factors lead to child marriage. These include cultural practices of child betrothal and exchange marriages in the family; low bride price; marriage for financial gain; societal, family, and peer influence; and pressure to wed, as marriage is a highly socially acceptable norm. Those who are not married face mockery and admire their peers who seem to be happily married (Ahonsi et al., 2019). Thus, fear of mockery and admiration might be circumstances that create room for young girls to find marriage or pregnancy/childbearing an attractive option.

Financial gain out of marriage is another factor tied to early/child marriage resulting from poverty. "Parents who could not take care of the needs of their young girls either encouraged or forced them into early marriage. In other cases, it was the desires and wants of young girls that led them into early marriage" (Ahonsi et al., 2019, p. 13). From this study, two things stand out. In some cases, young girls get married out of desire, and in other cases, circumstances may force or lead them to resort to marriage as a means of survival rather than continuing with education. Education is used as a weapon against child marriage. The assumption is that keeping girls in school may prevent them from the destruction of getting married early or that pregnancy leads to school dropouts.

However, Cobbett (2014) points out that education advocacy carries problematic constructions about schooling. Cobbett (2014, p. 313) argues that "the continuing hegemony in which schooling for girls is considered as 'a good thing' disrupts our ability to 'hear' girls and blurs understandings of empowerment". While many governments have made efforts to implement the education re-entry policy that allows girls to return to school after pregnancy, there is still room for other support avenues. Thus, as pointed out by Cobbett (2014), education is not synonymous with empowerment. Expanding the understanding of empowerment becomes crucial here, for example, exploring empowerment tools within the community that can be employed to develop the wellbeing and capacity of young mothers or married adolescents who forgo formal education.

Teen pregnancy unplanned/unwanted: the other side of the story

The general assumption that teen pregnancies are often unplanned and unwanted tends to overlook the case of desired, wanted, and planned pregnancy. Unwanted or unplanned teen pregnancy tends to imply a general rule that it is a mistake or an accident when a teenager gets pregnant. Unwanted pregnancy should not appear the most acceptable way of viewing the problem of teen pregnancy.

Preston-Whyte's (1991) study revealed that teenagers might decide to become mothers (by free choice) in order to uphold social norms, customs, or traditions to acquire a respectable status in that particular community. Thus, "becoming pregnant was a rational and conscious decision that a teenager made in light of her particular circumstances rather than merely something that happened to her" (extracted from Mkhwanazi, 2010, p. 348). In line with this view, an ethnographic study in a South African township concluded that "despite the negative perception of teenage pregnancy within the township, particular social and cultural circumstances provided fertile ground for its occurrence" (Mkhwanazi, 2010, p. 348).

Another qualitative study conducted in Zambia's six districts by Child frontiers showed that marriages occurring between teenage girls and boys of almost the same age were consensual. The study revealed that:

> the most common unions are those that take place between peers – girls (from age 12 or 13) and boys (from age 14), usually with an age difference of about two to three years. The majority of marriages involving children do not adhere to traditional processes. Children often decide on their own to marry.
>
> (Mann, Quigley, & Fischer, 2015, p. 39)

This study shows that child marriage is not associated with any cultural practices but occurs according to personal choice, contrary to the general assumption that it is a traditional practice or a matter of forced marriage.

Other studies show that pregnancy may be stressful, particularly for teenagers, and it is not experienced without difficulties. For example, a study conducted in Zambia revealed negative feelings experienced about getting pregnant and receiving negative reactions from their families (Katowa et al., 2017). This made them feel "distressed, [embarrassed], disappointed, frightened, and ashamed that they were pregnant" (Katowa et al., 2017, p. 66).

The point here is that the pregnancy itself was not stressful, but a combination of feelings, reactions, and expressions from the family/peers made it stressful. However, despite these circumstances, they were able to cope through different mechanisms.

> As a means to withstand the negative experiences and live within the circumstances of unmet teenage and motherhood needs, the pregnant and parenting teenagers used

> a number of adaptive coping strategies, including avoidance of negativity, embracing support from family and partner, repentance and dependence on God, and focusing on own and the child's future.
>
> (Katowa et al., 2017, p. 67)

This study is an example of the effects of dominant negative constructions about teen pregnancy that increase the burden rather than reducing it. Thus, it calls for more supportive intervention strategies to help pregnant teens and mothers cope and rebuild their lives.

Another study conducted in Ghana further reveals young girl's positive and negative experiences of marriage, pregnancy, and motherhood (Baba et al., 2020). It highlighted married girls' (12–19 years) negative experiences: financial difficulties, struggling with parenting (as new parents), pregnancy-related discomfort, and childbirth-related distresses/childcare challenges. Simultaneously, the positive aspects included high social status, the joy of motherhood, increased self-esteem, less stress, and successful delivery (Baba et al., 2020). Notably, the study also highlights successful delivery as a positive aspect but also 'pregnancy-related discomfort' but makes no mention of any distinct pregnancy-related medical health condition/diseases reported among these girls, in contrast with the dominant view that predominantly links pregnancy-related complications to early pregnancy.

The marriage and motherhood experience seem to suggest positive growth and responsibility, personal fulfilment, joy, and achievement in life. This presents the other side of the story.

> For some of these girls, childbirth transformed them positively and they tended to demonstrate that in the love they had for their children. Providing their children's basic needs such as food, clothing and motherly warmth demonstrates a mother's love for her child. . . . having a child was an essential ingredient in their marriage and without it there would be no joy.
>
> (Baba et al., 2020, pp. 201–202)

The authors further highlight mixed views about the timing of pregnancy.

> The majority of married girls perceived the timing of their marriages as early and negative, while a few others considered it as timely and positive. However, married girls reported more positive aspects in their marriage than they did negative aspects. These findings challenge reports of previous studies that have focused mainly on the negative experiences associated with child marriage.
>
> (Baba et al., 2020, p. 205)

These study findings challenge the bias and condemnation approach by policymakers and the research community. "The positive experiences serve as manifestations of positive outcomes that could further be explored by identifying personal strengths in resilience and coping in the context of child marriage" (Baba et al., 2020, p. 206).

Another study conducted in Zambia by Mwape et al. (2014) showed similar findings. A child was perceived as a future investment, strengthening the marital relationship and giving a sense of prestige and honour for the woman (Mwape et al., 2014). If a woman does not have a child, they are ridiculed, stigmatised, and excluded from society. Thus, "childlessness may contribute to [the] immense value attached to having children in low resource setting[s] such as Zambia" (Mwape et al., 2014, p. 105). Hence pregnancy, in this case, becomes a positive aspect of social life. Thus, the authors conclude that:

> it is essential that both positive and negative experiences of motherhood are acknowledged without concealing the complexity of their interaction. The co-existence of both negative and positive aspects would probably help to create a balanced view of motherhood and render it a worthwhile process for women to experience.
>
> (Mwape et al., 2014, p. 105)

Additionally, a study conducted in South Sudan found the same (Kane et al., 2019). The reasons for child marriage included motherhood seen as a fulfilling and meaningful experience, a home-making experience that implies stability and a passage to adulthood, and carrying one's name forward (Kane et al., 2019). As the authors state,

> having a child seems to somehow define one's worth and establish one's claim to adulthood. . . . [T]he girls who had children of their own, whether they were in school or not, seemed to take much pride in being mothers.
>
> (Kane et al., 2019, p. 7)

Here again, the assumption made is that the adolescent's decisions about childbearing reproduce the high value placed on motherhood. The authors argue that such decisions are also shaped by "harsh economic and social realities. . . [therefore] it is important to pay attention to whether adolescent pregnancy causes poorer life prospects or if poor life prospects motivate early pregnancy" (Kane et al., 2019, p. 7). This is an important matter for further exploration in teen pregnancy research.

Like Kane et al. (2019), Schaffnit et al.'s (2019) study found among the reasons given for marrying were: childbearing is God's law (implying that it is natural to reproduce), partnership, respect, and status. Schaffnit et al. (2019) point out that a high degree of autonomy in marital processes (by females themselves) and marrying to gain respect and status can hinder the progression of the ending child marriage agenda. The authors recommend that it is "essential to engage with the reality that marrying early is attractive to young people in some contexts, while in other contexts marriage may indeed infringe upon women's autonomy regardless of their age" (Schaffnit et al., 2019, p. 103).

Currently, the solution to teen pregnancy seems to be a 'one size fits all' approach prescribed by the UN. The universal minimum age set for marriage is 18 years; below this is considered child marriage. There appears to be a universally defined problem, accompanied by a single universal solution (to eliminate it). Thus, it does not consider the various faces of understandings of adulthood that are not numerical. Distinguishing notions about 'adulthood' become crucial in understanding the circumstances and context in which child marriage occurs.

"Adulthood and marriage are integrally linked to local concepts of adulthood but adulthood is only partially linked to age" (Schaffnit et al., 2019, p. 100). For example, in Schaffnit et al.'s (2019) study, the respondents used the word "adult" to measure when one can marry. This is a common feature of most African societies, where adulthood is often marked by puberty, not age. Moreover, it is permitted by customary law, which almost runs parallel with constitutional law. Thus, the diversity of what it means to be old enough or too young has been overtly ignored in most policy interventions targeting the elimination of child marriage. It is important to think critically about who determines the appropriate age for sexual activity and what criteria are used. Additionally, the high value placed on marriage and motherhood makes it difficult to set a standard age to be considered old enough to start sexual activities, marry, or have children. This creates the need for critical analysis, particularly capturing local ideas and interpretations about age and marriage for appropriate policy intervention.

Notably, most decisions on marriage in African societies are largely influenced by what the community or society dictates (social norms). In addition to localised concepts of adulthood, there are varying views expressed about marrying 'too late' for both males and females. If a woman delays getting married, she is considered worthless, not contributing to society, while in the case of a man, it is a sign of irresponsibility Schaffnit et al. (2019). Such social norms often appear to conflict with the legal frameworks that seek to regulate social behaviour. It then becomes crucial to question if and how governments can successfully attempt to 'control' or regulate sexual activities among young people.

For example, Marphatia et al. (2020) point out that in the case of child marriage, if the norm is to marry below the legally accepted age, does the government hold the whole community to account, and how do they achieve it, if at all it is attainable? To this effect, most African governments have launched campaigns working with traditional leaders to renounce what are being called 'harmful' practices embedded in their culture and identity. The questions raised here should provoke policymakers and researchers to rethink the chances of success in implementing the total elimination of child marriage in Africa, as this issue appears more complex and dynamic than one that can be solved with a narrow perspective.

Implications for African future research

Dominant constructs

Constructions about Africa have influenced the course of teen pregnancy research, adopting a path-dependent view of how the problem is perceived and solved. Constructions about Africa refer to how the African continent is viewed from a global perspective. The world's view of Africa is that of a troubled continent. As Ferguson (2006, p. 2) puts it,

> when we hear about "Africa" today [from the international community], it is usually in urgent and troubled tones. It is never just Africa but always the crisis in Africa, the problems of Africa, the failure of Africa.

The picture painted consistently about Africa, in the media and international reports or documentaries, is one which depicts the continent negatively, with many endless problems. Similarly, the perceived problem of teen pregnancy and child marriage reflects how Africa as a continent is positioned and labelled and how it has been construed historically. "The African human experience constantly appears in the discourse of our times as an experience that can only be understood through a negative interpretation" (Mbembe, 2001, p. 1). The social construction view illustrates how meanings can be attached to a place, issue, or problem based on conditions that turn out to be viewed as common sense. This is ideally achieved by using power to influence and continuously direct a belief into an unchangeable condition (Schneider & Ingram, 1993). As such, notions about Africa as a place of all manner of problems and failures continue to influence all Africa-related issues. Thus, Africa is historically and socially constructed as a failed and dysfunctional continent. This has been for a long time the kind of label that Africa has in the world and ultimately has implications on how Africa is researched.

According to Mbembe (2001), the general assumption is that African traditional societies are characterised by customs that appear "questionable". Thus, some cultural practices are described as human rights violations. With such a worldview, problems and solutions cannot be analysed objectively. This is a taken-for-granted view of the continent that leads to questioning some of the consistently highlighted issues as problematic. Ultimately, it can be argued that the "status" that Africa holds has consequences on the way it is researched.

Some general problems have been identified in African literature. First, most disciplines conduct research that focuses on symbolic representations rather than unveiling the materiality of power and the state in influencing discourses and representations (Mbembe, 2001). For example, the combination of power and the state can be described as the UN (powerful force) influencing the global policymaking and African states implementing these global policies just to fulfil international commitments and access financial resources. Therefore, some of the policy interventions become more symbolic than realistic.

Second, some Western theories, concepts, and frameworks that dominate African research on sexuality produce distorted and unreliable information/knowledge (Tamale, 2011). These borrowed concepts provide a different representation of the African experience and reality.

For example, Aniekwu (2006) distinguishes African feminists from Western ones in that they take pride in childbearing as a distinctive biological role. This means that even though feminists challenge the domination of men over women in the African context, this does not compromise their desire for motherhood. Thus, the author advises that all African feminist research should recognise this distinctive pro-natal factor. This also applies to other disciplines, including demography research on reproduction and motherhood in Africa.

Copying the Western style of researching (due to the different meanings attached) potentially leads to incompatible solutions to African problems. It is rather more useful to develop these frameworks and concepts according to our local setting. Macleod (2001) and Mkhwanazi (2006) state that South African research on teen pregnancy adopts US- and UK-based models and frameworks that do not fit into the local context. Understandably, this is due to Africa's colonial ties that cannot be easily broken off but at the same time should not be ignored. Therefore, the contextualisation of sexual activity and the concepts of adulthood, childbearing, and marriage remain crucial in understanding the dynamics of African research. Mkhwanazi (2006, p. 103) recommends contextualising "early childbearing with recourse to local people's everyday practices and to their subjective understandings of the social world".

Future African demographic research agenda

As African researchers, let us begin to question critically and examine thoroughly the taken-for-granted dominant constructs about Africa and how they skew the indigenous perspective to fit into the negative narrative. However, despite having a system deep-rooted in its colonial past, African researchers are not passive. They are aware of the need to reproduce African indigenous knowledge systems by having more narratives of their own stories to change the negative construct. There (Aniekwu, 2006; Basedau, 2020; Kaputa, 2015; Mbembe, 2001; Mkhwanazi, 2016; Tamale, 2011) are examples of this awareness. Going forward, I would like to propose three future research agendas on teen pregnancy and child marriage as part of demography studies.

First is the need for more critical African studies that present different sides to the story. As seen from the research search, few African researchers have sought to analyse teen pregnancy from this perspective by examining the context and unique African setting. The key argument presented is the wealth of information that is generated from contextualising a problem. Thus, there is a need to change the approach to research. Demographers and other social science disciplines need to be more conscious of Africa's unique status as a continent and the implications of this position in research. This calls for a move to the Africanisation research agenda, with Africans themselves conducting African research.

Second, even though African research may be deeply rooted in Western models, concepts, and methodologies, there is still room for Africanising research by creatively developing indigenous knowledge. The most effective way to achieve this is for more African researchers to conduct and document African lived experiences that reflect the African reality.

Last, teen pregnancy is an important subject in demography. While DHSs serve as a reliable and official source of information for policy intervention, it is critical that we do not rely only on indicators. In-depth qualitative studies can provide critical insights and understanding of teen pregnancy and child marriage complexities in Africa that can help solve associated problems.

Moreover, most of the statistical indicators on teen pregnancy and child marriage do not capture data widely in terms of the age range. For example, DHSs often exclude ages below 15 years due to methodological approaches (Koski et al., 2017). This presents limitations on the accuracy of the child marriage and teen pregnancy prevalence rates.

Therefore, including a wider age group and definitions of adulthood and marriage can help capture the actual prevalence of child marriage and teen pregnancy (which presents a clearer picture of the situation).

Conclusion

In summary, this chapter has discussed the problem of teen pregnancy presented as one of the biggest problems on the global health agenda and the call to eliminate child marriage in Africa. Teen pregnancy has been described as a social and health problem. The trend in describing teen pregnancy as a problem points to the grave consequences of a teenager falling pregnant, whether planned or unplanned, forced, or personal choice. The picture presented is that there is no chance of achieving a better life during or after teen pregnancy, which leads to poverty, violence, less/no educational attainment, and so on.

Meanwhile, some studies show that pregnant teenagers may indeed face hardships but at the same time still derive positive experiences and fulfilment from motherhood (depending on particular circumstances). In some cases, as the studies have shown, teen mothers and teen wives are resilient, endure certain hardships and are able to sustain a normal life. However, what has not been explored much in the literature is comparing non-pregnant teenagers with pregnant or married ones to capture and analyse the outcomes, especially in the context of poverty as a consequence of teen pregnancy. The same can be applied in terms of health care services and implications on maternal-related morbidity according to age.

Amidst all the negative notions of teen pregnancy and child marriage, one thing that remains critical, as some authors have pointed out, is the deep-rooted desire for motherhood and the high value placed on attaining a "married" rather than "single" status. The problematic definition of "child marriage" is that there are different local understandings of adulthood. It is difficult to attach an age, and therefore, it cannot or should not be standardised. All these factors make teen pregnancy and child marriage more complex, with interlinked issues that cannot be analysed from one dimension. The overall understanding and description of teen pregnancy are that it represents doom and failure in the eyes of policymakers and international organisations. Yet the other side of the story presents critical insights to aid wider policy intervention. A one-size-fits-all solution to eliminate child marriage in Africa may be less achievable due to the factors highlighted previously.

Finally, there is a need for alternative problem representations for teen pregnancy and child marriage research in Africa that does not focus only on the negative aspects in line with borrowed US and UK research models. While some problems may be genuine, others are not. African researchers need to be mindful and critical of how Africa is constructed, as this has implications on African research. The new way of researching teen sexual and reproductive health should include a critical analysis of such understandings in order to tailor policy interventions with a contextual outlook.

References

African Union. (2013). Campaign to end child marriage in Africa : Call to action. Addis Ababa.

Agege, E. A., Nwose, E. U., & Odjimogho, S. (2018). Parental perception of girl-child early marriage amongst the Urhobos in Nigeria. *International Journal of Community Medicine and Public Health*, *5*(8), 3185–3190.

Ahonsi, B., Fuseini, K., Nai, D., Goldson, E., Owusu, S., Ndifuna, I., . . . Tapsoba, P. L. (2019). Child marriage in Ghana : Evidence from a multi-method study. *BMC Women's Health*, *19*(126), 1–15.

Aniekwu, N. I. (2006). Converging constructions : A historical perspective on sexuality and feminism in. *African Sociological Review*, *10*(1), 143–160.

Arai, L. (2009). What a difference a decade makes : Rethinking teenage pregnancy as a problem. *Social Policy and Society*, *8*(2), 171–183.

Baba, H., Yendork, J. S., & Atindanbila, S. (2020). Exploring married girls' subjective experiences of well-being and challenges. *Journal of Adolescence*, *79*, 193–207. https://doi.org/10.1016/j.adolescence.2020.01.009

Basedau, M. (2020). Rethinking African studies : Four challenges and the case for comparative African studies. *Africa Spectrum*, *55*(2), 194–206.

Cherry, A. L., & Dillon, M. E. (2014). *International handbook of adolescent pregnancy*. New York: Springer.

Chohan, Z., & Langa, M. (2011). Teenage mothers talk about their experience of teenage motherhood. *Agenda*, *25*(3), 87–95. https://doi.org/10.1080/10130950.2011.610993

Cobbett, M. (2014). Beyond 'victims' and 'heroines': Constructing 'girlhood' in international development. *Progress in Development Studies*, *14*(4), 309–320. https://doi.org/10.1177/1464993414521523

Dethloff, N. (2018). Child brides on the move: Legal responses to culture clashes. *International Journal of Law, Policy and the Family*, *32*(3), 302–315. https://doi.org/10.1093/lawfam/eby008

Edin, K., Nilsson, B., Ivarsson, A., Kinsman, J., Norris, S. A., & Kahn, K. (2016). Perspectives on intimate relationships among young people in rural South Africa: The logic of risk. *Culture, Health & Sexuality*, *18*(9), 1010–1024. https://doi.org/10.1080/13691058.2016.1155749

Efevbera, Y., Bhabha, J., Farmer, P. E., & Fink, G. (2017). Girl child marriage as a risk factor for early childhood development and stunting. *Social Science & Medicine*, *185*, 91–101. https://doi.org/10.1016/j.socscimed.2017.05.027

Envuladu, E., Umaru, R., & Iorapuu, N. (2016). Determinants and effect of girl child marriage : A cross sectional study of school girls in Plateau State, Nigeria. *International Journal of Medicine and Biomedical Research*, *5*(3).

Ferguson, J. (2006). *Global shadows: Africa in the neoliberal world order*. Durham & London: Duke University Press. Retrieved from https://books.google.co.za/books?id=X1K4-wfXZeUC

Furstenberg, F. F. (2007). *Destinies of the disadvantaged: The politics of teen childbearing*. New York: Russell Sage Foundation. Retrieved from https://books.google.co.za/books?id=ROqFAwAAQBAJ

Groot, R. de, Kuunyem, M. Y., & Palermo, T. (2018). Child marriage and associated outcomes in northern Ghana : A cross-sectional study. *BMC Public Health*, 1–12.

Gyan, C. (2013). The effects of teenage pregnancy on the educational attainment of girls at Chorkor, a Suburb of Accra. *Journal of Educational and Social Research*, *3*(3), 53–60. https://doi.org/10.5901/jesr.2013.v4n3p53

Hindin, M., & Fatusi, A. (2009). Adolescent sexual and reproductive health in developing countries : An overview of trends and interventions. *International Perspectives on Sexual and Reproductive Health*, *35*(2), 58–62.

Kalamar, A. M., Lee-Rife, S., & Hindin, M. J. (2016). Interventions to prevent child marriage among young people in low- and middle-income countries: A systematic review of the published and gray literature. *Journal of Adolescent Health*, *59*(3), S16–S21. https://doi.org/10.1016/j.jadohealth.2016.06.015

Kane, S., Miedema, E., Dieleman, M., Broerse, J., Kane, S., Miedema, E., . . . Miedema, E. (2019). 'You have a child who will call you "mama"': Understanding adolescent pregnancy in South Sudan pregnancy. *Global Health Action*, *12*(1), 1–10. https://doi.org/10.1080/16549716.2018.1553282

Kaputa, A. J. (2015). *Wrongly framed*. Windhoek: Rhingo G.K Mutambo.

Katowa, P. M., Maimbolwa, M. C., Mwape, L., & Muleya, M. C. (2017). Experiences, needs and coping strategies of pregnant and parenting teenagers : A perspective from Lusaka and North Western Provinces of Zambia. *Journal of Research in Nursing and Midwifery*, *6*(4), 56–67.

Koski, A., Clark, S., & Nandi, A. (2017). Has child marriage declined in sub-Saharan Africa ? An analysis of trends in 31. *Population and Development Review*, *43*(1), 7–29.

Lawlor, D. A., & Shaw, M. (2002). Too much too young ? Teenage pregnancy is not a public health problem. *International Epidemiological Association*, *31*, 552–554. https://doi.org/10.1093/ije/31.3.554

Luker, K. (1996). *Dubious conceptions: The politics of teenage pregnancy*. Cambridge, MA: Harvard Press.

Macleod, C. (1999). Teenage pregnancy and its 'negative' consequences: Review of South African research – Part 1. *South African Journal of Psychology*, *29*(1), 1–7. https://doi.org/10.1177/008124639902900101

Macleod, C. (2001). Teenage motherhood and the regulation of mothering in the scientific literature : The South African example. *Feminism &Psychology*, *11*, 493–510. https://doi.org/10.1177/0959353501011004004

Madise, N., Zulu, E., & Ciera, J. (2007). Is poverty a driver for risky sexual behaviour ? Evidence from national surveys. *African Journal of Reproductive Health Introduction*, *11*(3), 83–98.

Mann, G., Quigley, P., & Fischer, R. (2015). *Qualitative study of child marriage in six districts of Zambia*. Lusaka, Zambia: UNICEF.

Marphatia, A. A., Saville, N.M., Amable, G.S., Manandhar, D.S., Cortina-Borja, M., Wells, J.C. & Reid, A.M. (2020, January). How much education is needed to delay women's age at marriage and first pregnancy? *Frontiers in Public Health*, 7, 1–17. doi:10.3389/fpubh.2019.00396

Mbembe, A. (2001). *On the postcolony*. Los Angeles, CA: University of California Press. Retrieved from https://books.google.co.za/books?id=S6FCpnfU8noC

Menon, J. A., Kusanthan, T., Mwaba, S. O. C., Juanola, L., & Kok, M. C. (2018). 'Ring' your future, without changing diaper – Can preventing teenage pregnancy address child marriage in Zambia ? *PLoS One*, *13*(10), 1–17.

Mkhwanazi, N. (2006). Partial truths: Representations of teenage pregnancy in research. *Anthropology Southern Africa*, *29*(3–4), 96–104. https://doi.org/10.1080/23323256.2006.11499935

Mkhwanazi, N. (2010). Understanding teenage pregnancy in a post-apartheid South African township. *Culture, Health & Sexuality*, *12*(4), 347–358. https://doi.org/10.1080/13691050903491779

Mkhwanazi, N. (2015, April). Twenty years of democracy and the politics of reproduction in South Africa. *African Identities*, 37–41. https://doi.org/10.1080/14725843.2015.1009618

Mkhwanazi, N. (2016). Medical anthropology in Africa : The trouble with a single story. *Medical Anthropology*, *35*(2), 193–202. https://doi.org/10.1080/01459740.2015.1100612

Mmari, K. N., & Magnani, R. J. (2003). Does making clinic-based reproductive health services more youth-friendly increase service use by adolescents? Evidence from Lusaka, Zambia. *Journal of Adolescent Health*, *33*(03), 259–270. https://doi.org/10.1016/S1054-139X(03)00062-4

Moraes, A. N., Likwa, R. N., & Nzala, S. H. (2018). A retrospective analysis of adverse obstetric and perinatal outcomes in adolescent pregnancy : The case of Luapula Province, Zambia. *Maternal Health, Neonatology, and Perinatology*, *4*(20), 1–11.

Mwape, L., Katowa-mukwato, P., Dixey, R., & Maimbolwa, M. (2014). A sweet and sour taste : Motherhood as an ambivalent experience in Zambia. *International Journal of Psychology and Counseling*, *6*(8), 99–106. https://doi.org/10.5897/IJPC2014.0263

Nathanson, C. A. (1991). *Dangerous passage: The social control of sexuality in women's adolescence*. Philadelphia, PA: Temple University Press. Retrieved from https://books.google.co.za/books?id=WKuUQgAACAAJ

Odimegwu, C., & Mkwananzi, S. (2016). Factors associated with teen pregnancy in sub-Saharan Africa : A multi-country cross-sectional study. *African Journal of Reproductive Health*, *20*(3), 94–107.

Omoro, T., Gray, S. C., Otieno, G., Mbeda, C., Penelope, A., Hayes, T., . . . Gust, D. A. (2017). Teen pregnancy in rural western Kenya : A public health issue. *International Journal of Adolescence and Youth*, *3843*, 1–10. https://doi.org/10.1080/02673843.2017.1402794

Preston-Whyte, E., & Zondi, M. (1989). To control their own reproduction: The agenda of black teenage mothers in Durban. *Agenda*, *4*, 47–68.

Preston-Whyte, E., & Zondi, M. (1991). Adolescent sexuality and its implications for teenage pregnancy and AIDS. *South African Journal of Continuing Medical Education*, *9*, 1389–1394.

Preston-Whyte, E. M. (1991) *Teenage pregnancy in selected coloured and black communities*. Pretoria: Human Sciences Research Council.

Rhode, D. L. (1994). Adolescent pregnancy and public policy. *Political Science Quarterly*, *108*(4), 635–669.

Schaffnit, S. B., Urassa, M., & Lawson, D. W. (2019). "Child marriage" in context : Exploring local attitudes towards early marriage in rural Tanzania. *Sexual and Reproductive Health Matters*, *27*(1). https://doi.org/10.1080/09688080.2019.1571304

Schneider, A., & Ingram, H. (1993). The social construction of target populations: Implications for politics and policy. *American Political Science Association*, *87*(2), 334–347. https://doi.org/10.2307/2939044

Steinhaus, M., Gregowski, A., Fenn, N. S., & Petroni, S. (2016). *She cannot just sit around waiting to turn twenty: Understanding why child marriage persists in Kenya and Zambia*. Washington, DC: International Center for Research on Women.

Tamale, S. (2011). *African sexualities: A reader*. Cape Town: Pambazuka Press. Retrieved from https://books.google.co.za/books?id=xSqIrrswbG0C

UNFPA. (2017). *The Safeguard Young People Programme three years on addressing the urgent needs of youth across Southern Africa*. Johannesburg: UNESCO.

UNFPA & UNICEF. (2019). *UNFPA–UNICEF Global Programme to end child marriage, Phase I (2016–2019) Report*. New York: UNFPA-UNICEF.

UNICEF. (2018). *Child Marriage latest trends and future prospects*. New York: UNICEF.

UNICEF. (2019). *Advancing the evidence base on child marriage and HIV white paper*. London & New York: UNICEF.

United Nations. (1995). *Report of the international conference on population and development, Cairo, 5–13 September 1994*. New York: United Nations.

United Nations Human Rights. (1990). *Convention on the rights of the child*. Retrieved September 15, 2020, from www.ohchr.org/EN/ProfessionalInterest/Pages/CRC.aspx

United Nations population fund. (2012). *Marrying too young*. Retrieved from www.unfpa.org/end-child-marriage

United Nations Zambia, UNFPA, & population Council. (2017). *Policy brief status of sexual and reproductive health and rights in Zambia*. Zambia: United Nations.

Wadhawan, S., Narone, R. K., & Narone, J. (1982). Obstetric problems in the adolescent Zambian mother studied at the University Teaching Hospital, Lusaka. *Medical Journal of Zambia*, *16*(3), 64–68.

Weatherley, R. A. (1987). Teenage pregnancy, professional agendas, and problem definitions. *Journal of Sociology and Social Welfare*, *14*(2).

Yakubu, I., & Salisu, W. J. (2018). Determinants of adolescent pregnancy in sub-Saharan Africa : A systematic review. *Reproductive Health*, *15*(15), 1–11. https://doi.org/10.1186/s12978-018-0460-4

11

TRENDS AND PATTERNS IN FERTILITY AND ITS PROXIMATE DETERMINANTS IN SUB-SAHARAN AFRICA

David I. Ojakaa

Introduction

The essence of fertility is that it combines with mortality and migration to constitute the factors in population change; the three are enjoined through what is often referred to as the demographic balancing equation (Brown, 1997). Thus formulated, it is an important input in population projections. For sub-Saharan Africa, systematic collection of information on fertility, mortality, and migration, and population in general, rather than reliance on crude sources for demographic data, although recent, has been spectacular (Brass, 2016). Indeed, with the entrenchment of decennial censuses in all countries in sub-Saharan Africa since the early 1960s and the entry of the World Fertility Surveys (WFSs) and later the Demographic and Health Surveys (DHSs), the availability of demographic data for sub-Saharan Africa has greatly improved. Nevertheless, this period of improved availability of data had been preceded by a phase of near total lack or gross incompleteness of data on African demography, prompting the ingenious development of indirect methods of demographic estimation. This chapter is about the trends in fertility and two of its proximate determinants (age at first marriage and contraceptive use) in sub-Saharan Africa. It was motivated, to a great extent, by my curiosity about the fertility transitions (and stalls) that were taking place in several countries in sub-Saharan Africa, Kenya in particular. The work is based on datasets collected so far by the Demographic and Health Surveys in sub-Saharan Africa, which are readily accessed in the STATCOMPILER menu of the DHS website.

The rest of this chapter is structured as follows. The next part of this introductory section presents a theoretical framework for considering fertility change in sub-Saharan Africa. In the second section, a selection of the repertoire of theories for examining the phenomenon of fertility transitions globally is presented. The third section provides a review of literature on the fertility transition in sub-Saharan Africa, while the fourth describes the methods used to analyse data for this chapter. In the fifth section, empirical findings on the trends and patterns of fertility and its proximate determinants in sub-Saharan Africa are provided. The paper concludes in the sixth section with a brief discussion of the findings and recommendations for further research as well as programme implementation.

The phenomenon of fertility change in sub-Saharan Africa can be explained through the framework of a family building pattern, as illustrated in Figure 11.1.

DOI: 10.4324/9780429287213-14

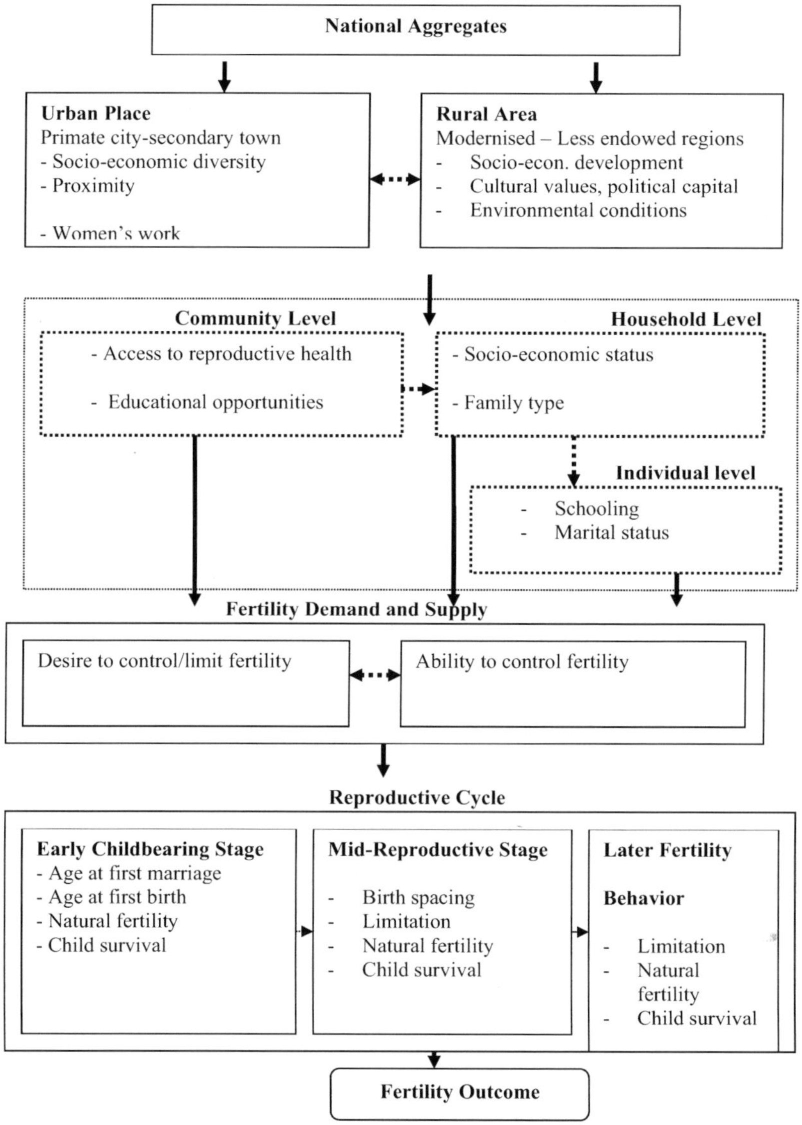

Figure 11.1 Family formation pattern at the sub-national levels in sub-Saharan Africa

Please note that while in this case we are concerned with fertility at the national levels, the explanation for these aggregates comes from sub-national considerations, hence the need to consider them. This conceptual framework is inspired by the framework on child mortality in the urban and rural Sahel (Lalou & LeGrand, 1997), on the micro-determinants (Entwisle & Mason, 1985), and the dynamic model of fertility (Newman, 1988). Four points summarise the conceptual framework. First, it is important to consider sub-national groupings, since they reveal residual variations in fertility which are often masked at the national level. The first and most obvious of the sub-national groupings is the urban-rural gradient. Urban areas can be sub-divided into the primate city and other smaller cities, towns, urban areas, and municipalities. Rural areas in turn can be grouped by levels of socio-economic development, other unique endowments, or political capital. Second, the patterns in fertility and its intermediate variables are manifested in the reproductive stage that individual women and couples find themselves in – whether early, middle, or later reproductive stages. Third, the fertility patterns and determinants act at a minimum of three levels – the community, the household, and the individual. An important aspect that affects change in fertility is the demand for fertility control on the one hand and access to services for fertility control on the other. Finally, all these factors operate to bring about the fertility outcome (a birth or no birth) at a particular point in time (Ojakaa, 2008, p. 13).

The range of perspectives for analysing change in fertility

A number of theories of fertility decline are fundamental to any study on the subject; it is therefore worth briefly outlining them. As other population writers have acknowledged (Cleland & Wilson, 1987; van de Kaa, 1996; Mason, 1997), what emerges from the literature is the multiplicity of theories that explain change in fertility; they should be viewed eclectically. These ideas, presented in the following subsections, include demographic transition, natural fertility, fertility demand and supply, proximate determinants of fertility, and the institutional approach.

Demographic transition

The theory of demographic transition was first applied to explain the high population growth in Europe and particularly Great Britain during the industrial revolution, the phrase referring to technical innovations that led to improvements in agriculture, transport, manufacturing, and sanitation as well as medicine. In this classic formulation, it was postulated that high population growth resulted from improvements in food supplies and personal living standards. According to the theory, fertility only declined following continued industrialisation and modernisation, which changed the economic and social structure of society, ultimately leading to a fertility decline. In this approach, it is the ready accessibility of family planning services through modernisation that leads not only to the satisfaction of unmet needs created by diminished fertility preferences but equally to further declines in fertility demand.

Under this concept, the role of the two other demographic variables, namely mortality and migration, clearly emerges. With a decrease in infant and child mortality, it is argued that parents no longer need many children, and fertility should equally decline. Similarly, rural-urban migration plays an important role in the transformation of the economy from one that is rural based and agricultural to one that is urban based and industrial. Due to lack of industrialisation and mortality decline in some regions of the developing world, and sub-Saharan Africa in particular, the application of this concept, however, waned. More recently, it has also been argued that the demographic transition theory focused on specific historical demographic events and is unsuitable for long-term explanations (Caldwell & Schindlmayr, 2003; Caldwell, 2004).

Natural fertility

The idea of natural fertility, first attributed to the French demographer Louis Henry, applies to couples living in long-term sexual unions (married) and is characterised by the absence of parity-specific birth control (Knodel, 1977). The definition of control is significant – it means behaviour affecting fertility which is changed as the number of children increases. When the number of children that the couple desires is attained, beyond which they do not want any more, control starts to take place. Behaviour such as breastfeeding, abstinence, and spousal separation which affects fertility levels (frequent in sub-Saharan Africa) but which is not dependent on parity is not considered to contradict the definition of natural fertility. The practice whereby parents deliberately space their births but do not have a targeted family size in mind, a situation prevailing in most of sub-Saharan Africa, is also considered part of natural fertility.

Proximate determinants

The framework of proximate fertility determinants (Bongaarts, 1978) is a modification of the idea of intermediate fertility variables (Davis & Blake, 1956). In the model of proximate determinants, the initial 11 intermediate fertility variables are reduced to eight. They are grouped under three categories: exposure aspects (the proportion of women married), deliberate marital fertility control (contraceptive use and abortion), and aspects related to natural marital fertility (lactational infecundability, frequency of intercourse, sterility, spontaneous intrauterine mortality, and the duration of the fertile period). To estimate the effect of each of the variables in reducing fertility from its natural level (estimated at 15.3, which represents the total natural marital fertility in the absence of contraception), an index for each determinant is calculated. The model of the proximate determinants has, however, been put to criticism (Reinis, 1992). Following the use of simulation methods, it is concluded that the method provides poor estimates of marriage delay, contraception, and induced abortion. In spite of this criticism, the model remains popular, being used to analyse effects of various proximate determinants such as abortion on fertility.

The institutional approach to fertility change

The purpose of the institutional approach in the analysis of fertility decline is to link macro and micro demographic levels (Simmons & Farooq, 1985). The approach focuses on the intervening structures and the different contexts within which these operate (Piché & Poirier, 1995). The emphasis is on institutions within which material production takes place and in which demographic reproduction occurs as well. Feedback is suggested between production and reproduction at the level of an individual family. Demographic explanations thus have to take into account the interaction between the different forms of production and modes of reproduction (Simmons & Farooq, 1985; Piché & Poirier, 1995; van de Kaa, 1996). In these relationships, there will be elements of choice (fertility preferences) and decision-making or fertility behaviour (Lesthaeghe, 1989).

The fertility supply-demand framework

The theory of fertility demand and supply takes as its departure point the micro-economic theory of fertility demand and adds to it a sociological variable, the supply of children (Easterlin & Crimmins, 1985; Mason, 1997). Change in fertility is then explained in terms of three factors – the supply of children, the demand, and the costs of fertility regulation. The supply of children is defined as the number of surviving children that couples would have in the absence of fertility control. The demand, on the other hand, refers to the number of surviving children parents would have if fertility regulation were costless. The costs for fertility regulation in turn cover both the couple's attitudes towards fertility control and the access to the means for fertility control. Several criticisms have been levelled at the supply-demand framework – one of which is that it is silent on the institutional determinants of the fertility transition (Mason, 1997; Robinson, 1997).

Diffusion of innovations

Another idea that has been applied to the study of fertility decline is that of diffusion of innovations. Started in the 1920s when the American Department of Agriculture embarked on efforts to assist small-scale farmers by encouraging them to adopt new products such as hybrid seeds, fertilisers, and pesticides, the concept of diffusion of innovations has been subsequently applied to the study of fertility change and adoption of family planning methods (Cleland, 2001). In the family planning program, medical programs (that had emphasised an epidemiological and preventive approach) gave way to diffusion programs that emphasised communications, incentives, and change agents or field workers. Note that diffusion has been traditionally defined as the process through which a new idea is communicated through a given set of channels over time and among members of a social system (Rogers, 1995).

Literature review

Fertility change in the southern shores of the Mediterranean

Contrasting fertility dynamics in five Arab states

Empirical studies conducted in sub-Saharan Africa on the subject of the fertility transition were examined. On a sub-regional basis, the following outline emerges: fertility dynamics for the countries in the southern shores of the Mediterranean, fertility in West Africa, and fertility change in Southern and Eastern Africa. The fertility changes in the countries bordering sub-Saharan Africa to the north, those in the so-called southern shores of the Mediterranean Sea, have received considerable attention in the demographic literature and serve as neighbourly comparisons for sub-Saharan Africa. Examination of the fertility dynamics in five Arab countries (Algeria, Egypt, Morocco, Yemen, and Sudan) reveals the different childbearing patterns in each country. In Yemen, where fertility is highest among the five, reaching over seven children per woman, childbearing starts early, and a large proportion of ever-married women reach high parities at a fast pace. Morocco and Egypt, which were characterised by lower fertility of about four births per woman at the beginning of the 21st century, exhibit a pattern of delay in the onset of childbearing, a slow pace of childbearing, and a smaller proportion of ever-married women that reach high parities. In Algeria and Sudan, on the other hand, where fertility was between four and five children per woman in the same time period, a delay in the beginning of childbearing plays a greater role in fertility change, while the timing and volume of childbearing play a smaller role (Eltigani, 2001).

Fertility dynamics in West Africa

Family planning and population policy concerns

The demographic literature on West Africa that bears on fertility change addresses many issues, and two of these are family planning and population policy. In the first theme, family planning and population policy, three salient issues that emerge are fertility intentions, the introduction of family planning interventions, and population policy. Demand for contraception in the West African countries of Mali and Burkina Faso, in comparison to Ghana, is heterogeneous, as it is dictated by men's attitudes, women's counting little (Andro & Hertrich, 2002). In contrast, contraceptive demand is found to be significant among women, less strong among men, and negligible among couples. The pattern is nevertheless changing among the younger generations, where women's and men's attitudes are converging.

Several studies treat the subject of family planning services in sub-Saharan Africa as a whole. One such theme is the future of family planning in Africa; more precisely the suggestion that Africa will be the family planning frontier of the twenty-first century echoes in a number of studies (Caldwell & Caldwell, 2002; Caldwell, Phillips, & Barkat-e-Khuda, 2002). This forecast is based on the observation that fertility levels and population growth rates persist at high levels and also in noting that appropriate family planning programs suitable for the region are still being developed. In this regard, the studies note that successful family planning programs will depend on political leadership, emphasis on hormonal contraceptives, and development of family planning programs that meet the needs of all segments of the population and not just married women. However, constraints include stagnation in economic growth, increasing child mortality, and the persistence of HIV/AIDS.

Research conducted in northern Ghana in the Navrongo integrated family planning program has demonstrated a number of findings. One of these (Bawah, 2002) is that communication between husband and wife does indeed lead to increased use of contraception. In addition, the introduction of health and family planning services through the deployment of nurse-midwives in a traditional African setting leads to reproductive change (Debpuur et al., 2002). Other studies conducted in the Republic of Gambia (Luck et al., 2000) show that the service delivery approach whereby village women provide basic health and family planning counselling and services to fellow women in their extended families has a high impact. Similarly, in Cameroon, family planning campaigns have an impact on the demand for and use of family planning services (Babalola, Vondrasek, Brown, & Traoré, 2001).

The fertility literature on Nigeria indicates that the country's population policy has had at most a moderate effect in reducing the country's high fertility (Obono, 2003). This is because of the policy's assumption of a single cultural system and disregard for male attitudes. Belief systems in the country are diverse but share a common interest in the fertility of crops, livestock, and people. Patterns of social organisation are similarly varied. For the population policy to succeed, there is a need to include, and not suppress, elements of the distinct cultures of the different ethnic groups. In addition, in the ongoing fertility transition in the country, Nigerians have to steer carefully through a political, economic, and cultural paradox: they have to balance between powerful forces that seek lower fertility and urge large families at the same time (Smith, 2004).

Fertility dynamics in Southern and Eastern Africa

A number of empirical research findings that have a bearing on fertility in Southern and Eastern Africa are presented here. They comprise social interaction and religion in Mozambique, civil strife in Angola, the fertility transition in South Africa, natural fertility in Malawi, the fertility transition and HIV/AIDS in Tanzania, and a comparison of fertility in Uganda and Kenya. Qualitative research on informal social interactions (verbal and non-verbal communication) among men and women in the capital city of Mozambique – Maputo – demonstrates the process through which people obtain family planning and related information in order to develop their attitudes and fertility intentions (Agadjanian, 2001, 2002). Not only are the interactions gendered, they hardly overlap, and rarely are similar issues discussed in the often-separate interactions.

Religion and fertility

The influence of religion on fertility can be considered as taking place through the idea of adoption of innovations and, within this idea, through the perspective of social interaction. It is often argued that diffusion of innovations is most effective when participants in the communication process are diverse with respect to the innovation but similar on other social characteristics (Rogers, 1995). These ideas are tested with qualitative and qualitative data collected from the city of Maputo in Mozambique (Agadjanian, 2001). In this metropolitan milieu, approval and use of modern contraception is more favourable in areas where social life and culture are more heterogeneous and two main religions – the Roman Catholic and other Christian denominations – prevail, but less so in parts of the city dominated by homogeneous small churches. In the rural areas, on the other hand, socio-cultural heterogeneity within and between religious groups being negligible, adherence to these religious faiths fosters learning behaviour about contraception.

The effect of war on fertility

The effects of war on a pre-transitional society's fertility are illustrated by a number of studies in Angola (Agadjanian & Prata, 2001; 2002), a nation that has known a drawn-out civil war for four decades. Demographically, the country is characterised by natural fertility – early initiation of reproduction, high ultimate family size, and low contraceptive prevalence. The studies show two fluctuations – a drop in fertility during times of war and a baby boom after the war, with the intensity of this cycle being more marked in areas that are more involved in combat and according to women's socio-economic status (more educated and less poor women being more responsive in their reproductive behaviour to the war). These immediate variations resulting from the war will most probably chart the future path of the demographic transition in the country.

The transition in South Africa

The characteristics and causes of the silent fertility revolution that has been taking place not just in South Africa but a number of its neighbours as well – Zimbabwe, Botswana, and Lesotho – are documented in the literature (Potts & Marks, 2001). The total fertility rate (TFR) in Southern Africa at the turn of the twenty-first century was three to four children and represents a decline of 40–50% from peak levels for Zimbabwe, Botswana, and South Africa. Although the fertility transition was taking place and the economic value of children was declining, the cultural values attached to reproduction remained high, and this new trend towards smaller family sizes has not undermined the fundamental position of fertility in the society. For many women, bearing children remains the most common avenue to achieving social status; for men, it is a means for social esteem. Children are viewed as an important part of marriage, but the literature points out that the value placed upon having children is so high that marriage often does not count in childbearing. Understanding the effects of the apartheid-era (1948–1994) conditions on the racial patterns of contraceptive use is a theme addressed in several studies on the fertility of South Africa (Burgard, 2004). Results of these studies show that despite strong state family planning programs that targeted black women, use of modern contraception among the latter remained lower than that for other racial groups in the country before and after the political transition in 1994.

Postpartum sexual abstinence in Malawi

Ethnic differences in postpartum sexual abstinence in Malawi are related to variations in perceptions about it in three communities inhabiting northern, central, and southern Malawi. Research results on the subject (Zulu, 2001) show that the duration and pattern of breastfeeding did not change much in the three communities between 1988 and 1998. The duration of post-partum abstinence, on the other hand, is much longer in the north, at a mean of 17 months, and shorter in the south and centre, at 10 and 6.6 months, respectively. In particular, it is the differences in the definition and timing of child-strengthening rituals that couples are required to perform before resuming sexual intercourse following the birth of a child that are important. The study underscores the utility of the micro-level approach in understanding fertility in sub-Saharan Africa.

The transition in Tanzania

The number of countries in sub-Saharan Africa joining the fertility transition is growing, Tanzania being one of the new entrants (Hinde & Mturi, 2000). Commencing in the late 1970s and early 1980s, the fertility transition in Tanzania shows patterns that are similar to those in Zimbabwe and Kenya. The fertility decline has been most marked in urban areas, and there has been a rapid uptake in contraceptive use from low levels before the 1990s to about 20% in the late 1990s. Falling marital fertility, which is associated with increased contraceptive use, rising age at first marriage, and the HIV/AIDS epidemic, have been the major causes of this decline. A conclusion of the study is that the three conditions for a fertility decline prescribed (Caldwell, Orubuloye, & Caldwell, 1992) – infant mortality rates of below 80 per 1,000 live births; high levels of primary-school education; and use of any contraceptive method of between 20 and 44%, as in Zimbabwe, Kenya, and Botswana – need to be applied selectively.

In addition to documenting the nature of the fertility transition in Tanzania, the impact of HIV/AIDS on fertility has also been examined in the country. Survey findings on this subject (Ainsworth, Filmer, & Semali, 1998) indicate that individual perceptions of mortality are likely to be influenced by mortality in the respective community, as well as by deaths in the household and extended family. The results also confirm the positive but weak relationship between community levels of child mortality and recent fertility. Community levels of adult mortality are negatively correlated with recent fertility. Deaths of female adults are associated with lower fertility among surviving women from the same household as the deceased. However, a male death is not correlated with fertility of surviving women. Thus, high adult mortality will lead to lower fertility, with the relation of the deceased adult to the surviving woman also mattering.

The transitions in Kenya and Uganda compared

Comparison of the fertility dynamics in neighbouring Uganda and Kenya (Blacker, Opiyo, Jasseh, Sloggett, & Ssekamatte-Ssebuliba, 2005) shows that between 1980 and 2000, the TFR in Kenya fell by 40% from some eight births per woman to around five. During the same period, fertility in Uganda declined by less than 10%. The higher drop in fertility registered in Kenya was mainly due to an increase in contraceptive use; in Uganda, there was also a decrease in pathological sterility. Women in Kenya wanted fewer children than in Uganda, but there was also greater unmet need in Uganda. This may be attributed to the divergent paths to economic development pursued in the two countries; and also, to the Kenyan government's active promotion of family planning services through the health system, an activity that did not start in earnest in Uganda until 1995.

Methods and measures

Exploratory analysis

An appropriate way in which to commence quantitative analysis of such a multifaceted yet rewarding subject as the fertility dynamics of sub-Saharan Africa is through descriptive and exploratory, rather than inferential and multivariate, analysis. In this regard, three particular methods are applied. These are the estimation of period fertility rates, medians for age at first marriage, and contraceptive prevalence. In estimating the age-specific fertility rate (ASFR), we use the period rather than the cohort or longitudinal approach. To arrive at the ASFR, we start by defining the TFR:

$$\text{TFR} = \text{summation of ASFRs} \times 5$$

Where:

The summation ranges from the beginning of childbearing (15 years) to the end (49 years). Please note that it is necessary to multiply by five in order to capture the five years within each of the seven five-year age groups. It is also conventional to divide by 1,000 in order to convert the ASFRs (which are expressed in terms of per 1,000 women) into births per woman.

The ASFR is next defined as:

$$\text{ASFR} = \text{Births in the } 1-36 \text{ months before the interview for the age group } \div$$
$$\text{Woman years of exposure in } 1-36 \text{ months before interview in age group}$$

In this case, the question of the reference period to which the births refer is important. Due to the possibility of birth displacement at five-year age-intervals, the reference period is taken as three years, or 36 months (Croft, Aileen, & Courtney, 2018) and, in terms of point estimation, to 1.5 years before the survey.

The median age at first marriage or union is defined as the median age in years when the woman first started living with the spouse or partner (Croft et al., 2018). The formula for calculating the medians, as in DHS statistics, is given as:

$$Median = Ai + (0.5 - Ci) \div (C_{i+1} - Ci) + 1$$

Where:

A_i is the age before reaching 50%; C_i is the cumulative percentage in the age before reaching 50% (i.e., at age A_i) and C_{i+1} is the cumulative percentage in the age immediately above 50%. The contraceptive prevalence rate (CPR) is the percentage of married women who are using a (modern) method of family planning.

A number of errors in the reporting of demographic data can in this particular case bias the intended fertility and nuptiality estimates. For fertility computations, these constitute errors in the mis-reporting of the age of the mother, omission of births, and mis-allocation of the date of birth of the child (Henin et al., 1982; United-Nations, 1983; Goldman, Rutstein, & Singh, 1985; Brass & Jolly, 1993). For nuptiality, data errors include mis-reporting of the date of first marriage as well as omission of the first marriage itself. In such situations, the solution involves a combination of data smoothing and imputation techniques which includes the use of parametric models. Since 1986, at least seven DHS-type surveys, including Malaria Indicator Surveys (MISs) and AIDS Indicator Surveys (AISs), have been conducted in the various countries in sub-Saharan Africa through the DHS program. Data used in this chapter are obtained from these surveys, available on the DHS website.

Empirical findings

Fertility

Patterns

The ASFRs for all countries in sub-Saharan Africa derived from DHSs undertaken between 1986 and 2018 by sub-region show at least one pattern – the peak age pattern of ASFRs. For all countries and all sub-regions, the peak age of childbearing is either within the early age group of 20–24 or the later age group of 25–29 years; both patterns can be found in each sub-region. For the early childbearing peak of 20–24 years, Kenya in Eastern Africa, Niger in West

Africa, and Malawi in Southern Africa exemplify this tendency. It is in the later peak childbearing group of ages 25–29 that most of the countries of Central Africa, such as the Democratic Republic of Congo (DRC), are found. Others in this grouping are Ghana in West Africa, Rwanda and Burundi in Eastern Africa, and South Africa in Southern Africa.

Levels

An examination of the TFR levels (not shown) for each country and sub-region over time in sub-Saharan Africa shows ubiquitous reductions in fertility over the period 1986–2018. An equally important observation is the variation in the level of fertility between sub-regions and countries. To view this result more clearly, we added estimated projections for the period 2015–2020 (UN, 2019) to the results from the most recent DHSs to produce the map shown in Figure 11.2.

The TFR estimates have been provided for all counties in Africa for comparative purses; analysis is limited to those in sub-Saharan Africa. The results show that West and Middle Africa have the most countries with a TFR of 5 and above, with Uganda and Burundi in Eastern Africa and Mozambique in Southern Africa included. Seven countries have a TFR of between 3.0 and 3.9 during the period 2015–2020. These are Namibia, Botswana, Zimbabwe, Lesotho, Swaziland, Kenya, and Ghana. Only one country in sub-Saharan Africa – South Africa – has a TFR of 2.4, which is approaching replacement level. This is in contrast to other developing

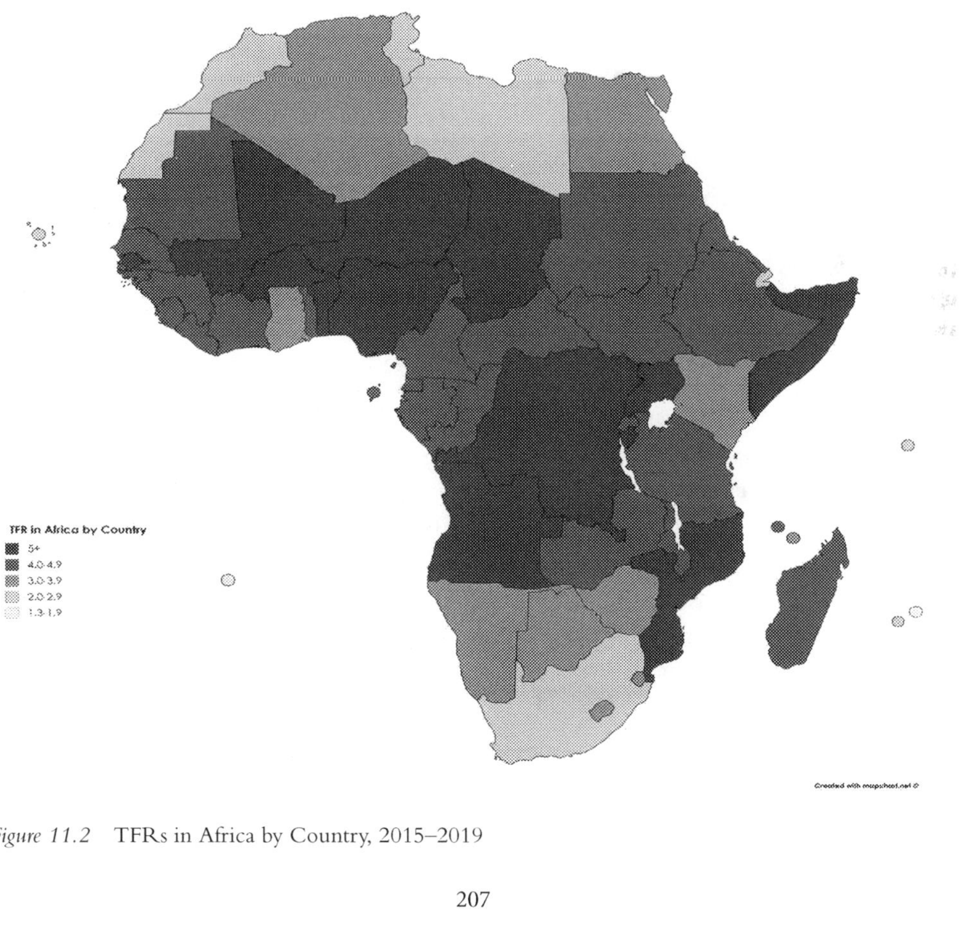

Figure 11.2 TFRs in Africa by Country, 2015–2019

world regions, where the mean TFR is 2.9, 2.4, 1.8, and 2.0, respectively, for Northern Africa and Western Asia, Central and Southern Asia, Eastern and South-eastern Asia, and Latin America and the Caribbean.

Age at first marriage

Trends

Trends in median age at first marriage for cohorts of women aged 25–29 years at the time of the respective survey were examined. For the West African sub-region, the median age at first marriage rose most in Ghana, from 18.5 years for the cohort aged 25–29 at the time of the 1988 DHS to 22.4 years for a similar age cohort at the time of the Ghana DHS 2014 survey. The trend was lowest for the West Africa sub-region in Niger, where it increased from 14.9 years for the cohort of women aged 25–29 years for the Niger 1992 DHS to 15.9 years for a similar age cohort reporting during the country's 2012 DHS. The data for Middle Africa are much more limited but show that that median age at first marriage for the 25–29 age cohorts increased most in Gabon (from 20.4 to 22.2 years, as reported in the country's 2000 and 2012, DHS respectively) and increased least in Chad, where it rose from 15.9 years, as reported in the 1996–1997 DHS, to 16.1 years, reported in 2014–15. For Eastern Africa, the median age at first marriage for the 25–29 age cohorts increased most remarkably in Rwanda (20.9 to 22.3) and Kenya (18.6 to 20.5 years). It was lowest in Uganda (17.5 to 18.6 years). It is in Southern Africa that the marriage pattern can be termed relatively late by standards of sub-Saharan Africa. According to the South Africa 2016 DHS report, early unions are rare in the country, with less than half of the women having started to live with a partner by age 25. For all five-year age cohorts, the median age at first union is more than 30 years (NDoH, Statistics South Africa (Stats SA), South African Medical Research Council (SAMRC), & ICF, 2019). Even in Botswana, where the last DHS results available are for 1988, the median age at first union for the 25–29 cohort then was relatively late, at 24.9 years.

Correlation

The correlation between median age at first union for cohorts aged 25–29 years at the time of the survey and the corresponding fertility for the three years before the survey for sub-Saharan countries is shown in Figure 11.3.

With a negative correlation coefficient of 0.592, the results show that countries with a lower median age at first marriage are associated with higher fertility and, conversely, those with a higher median age with lower fertility. In keeping with this result, the results for the 2012 DHS results for Niger are located at the topmost left part of the graph and those for Lesotho at the bottom right foreground section.

Contraceptive prevalence

Prevalence in the sub-regions

Contraceptive prevalence rates as well as their trends for individual countries are shown in Figures 11.4a–11.4d. For countries in the West Africa sub-region, the results from the 2018 round of DHS give an average CPR of 20.5%, with Guinea scoring the minimum of 10.4% and Senegal registering the maximum of 26.3%, closely followed by Ghana at 25% in the range. An

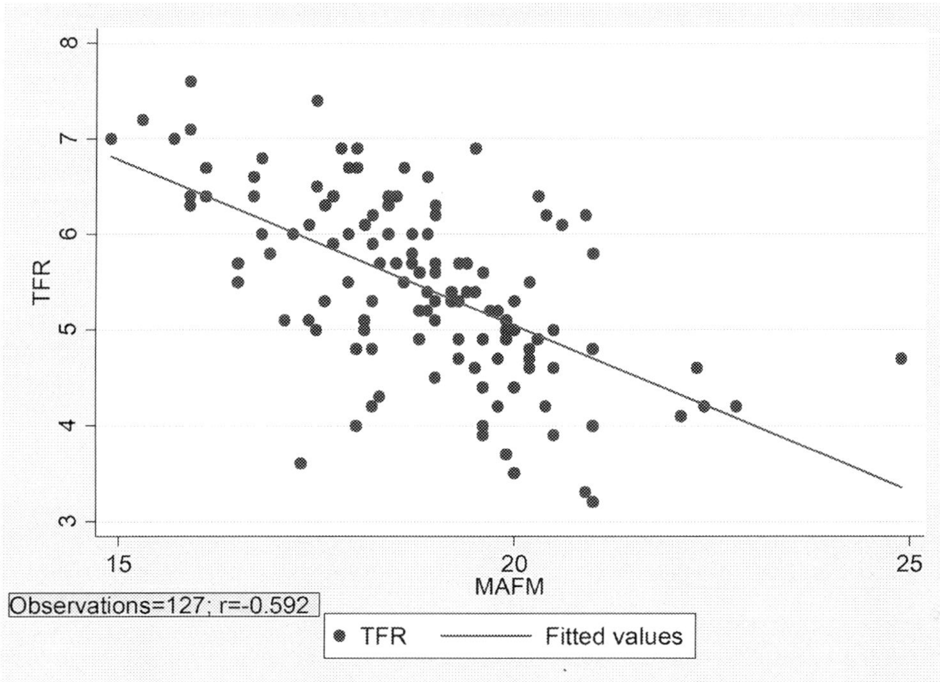

Figure 11.3 Correlation between age at first marriage and TFR

examination of the trend in modern contraceptive use among married women shows that there has been a substantial increase in the sub-region, from an average of 3.5% at the time of the 1988 DHS to the 20.5 registered at the time of 2018 DHSs. Fewer countries in Middle Africa document complete information in the demographic and health surveys conducted. Nevertheless, Cameroon has more complete information; for the 2011 DHS, the CPR is 14.4%, having risen from 4.3% in 1991.

Among all four sub-regions, it is in Southern Africa that contraceptive prevalence is highest. By the 2013 round of DHSs, the CPR in Zimbabwe was highest in sub-Saharan Africa at 65.8%, followed by that in Lesotho (59.8%), Namibia (55.3%), and South Africa (54%). Nevertheless, the DHS 2016 results for South Africa available in the country report indicate a CPR of 59% in 2016 and 61% in 1998. This variance may be related to the multi-racial classification of results. In contrast to other countries in the Southern Africa sub-region, CPR is lowest in Mozambique, where in the most recent survey (2015 AIS), it was 25.3%, compared to 10.4% in the 2013 DHS. Other countries in Southern Africa for which recent DHS results are available are Botswana, for which the CPR by 2018 was 67.4%; Malawi (58%); and Zambia (47.5%).

Most of the countries in the Eastern Africa sub-region, led by Kenya, have more consistent DHS datasets from which it is possible to more confidently infer trends in contraceptive prevalence. From the 2013 round of DHSs, the average CPR for the sub-region was 40.7%, up from 8.6% in 1988/89. The 2013 CPR is highest in Kenya (53%) and Rwanda (47.5%) and lowest in Tanzania (27.4%). Nevertheless, these sub-regional trends rapidly evolve with the publication of each new survey. For example, the CPR results for the 2018 DHS for Burundi and Tanzania have increased to 22.9% and 32%, respectively.

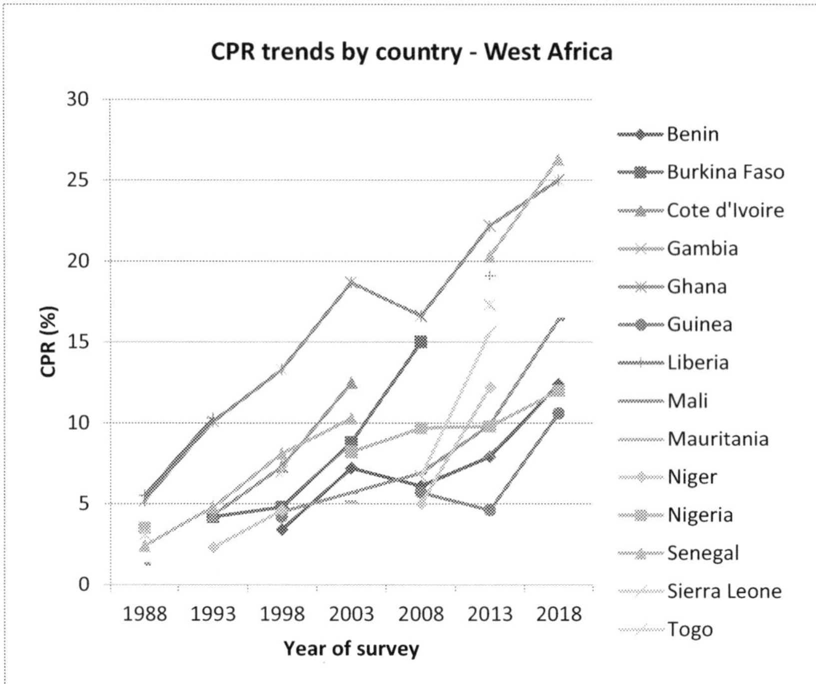

Figure 11.4a CPR trends by country – West Africa

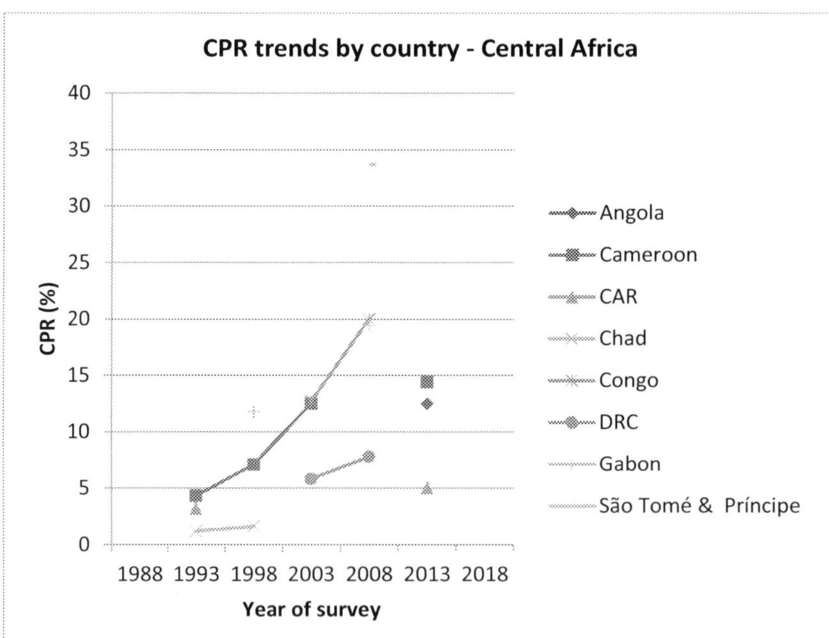

Figure 11.4b CPR trends by country – Central Africa

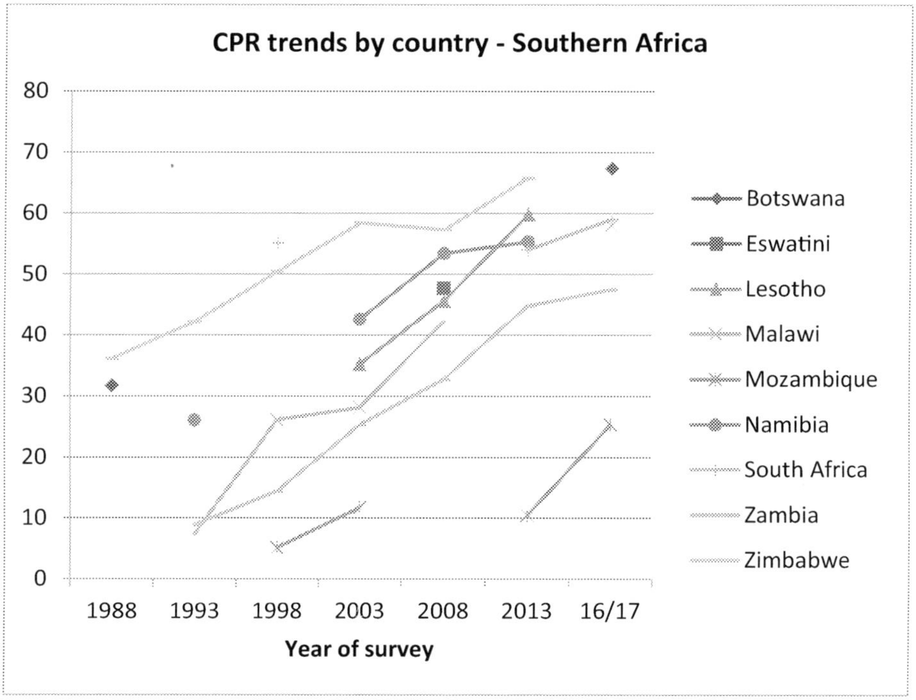

Figure 11.4c CPR trends by country – Southern Africa

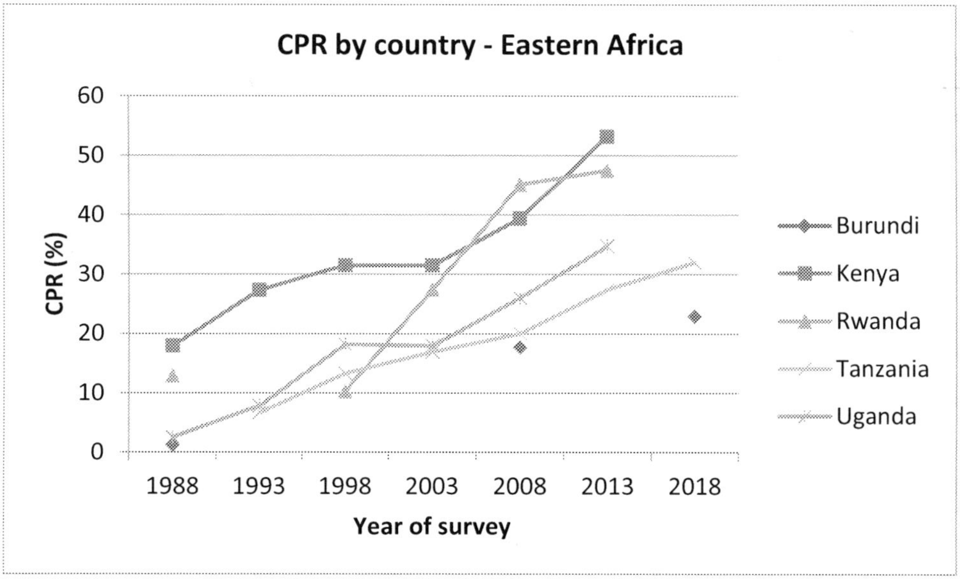

Figure 11.4d CPR trends by country – Eastern Africa

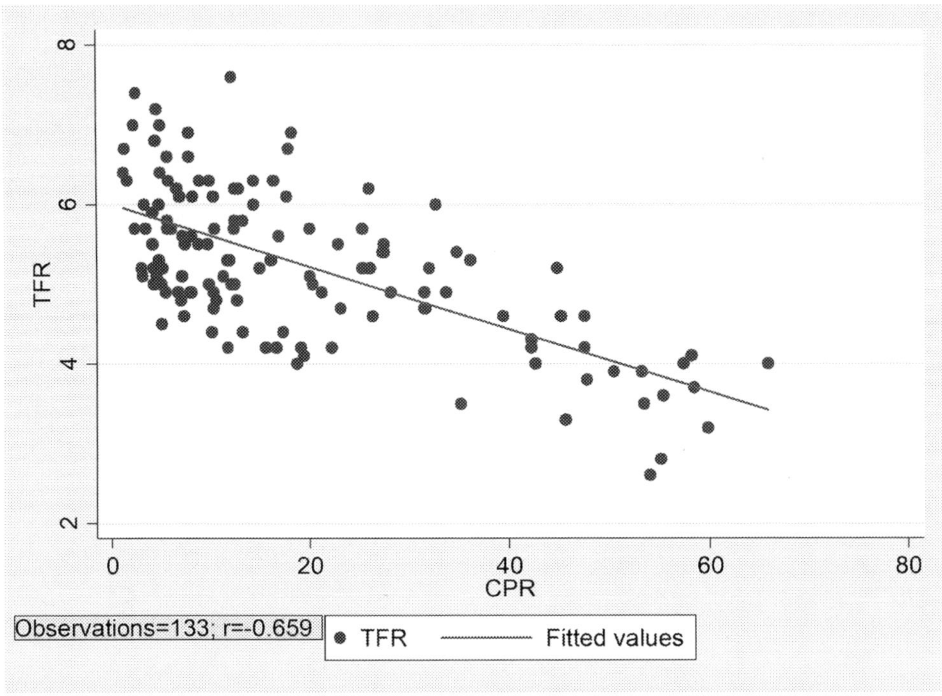

Figure 11.5 Correlation between contraceptive prevalence and TFR

Correlation between contraceptive prevalence and fertility

The association between the TFR and contraceptive prevalence is shown in Figure 11.5.

As with the association between age at first marriage and fertility, the graph shows that CPR and fertility are closely but negatively related, with a negative 0.659 correlation coefficient. Thus, countries with higher contraceptive prevalence such as Zimbabwe, Namibia, and South Africa are associated with lower fertility. In contrast, those with lower CPRs such as Niger and Mali will, at any particular time, tend to have higher fertility.

Discussion, conclusion, and research agenda

Discussion

Five areas from this study merit discussion. The fertility schedule is the first, and of the most visible patterns: peak fertility occurs during age groups 20–24 or 25–29 for individual countries. Even within some countries, nevertheless, it is observed that the shape of the fertility curve changes from one survey to another. While historically natural populations would be characterised by early childbearing climaxing at age 20 (Schmertmann, 2003), it is not immediately clear for each specific country now which among the factors of later marriage, education, and employment for women are behind the shifting of the fertility curve. Second, a number of African authors (Gayawan, Adebayo, Ipinyomi, & Oyejola, 2010; van Gijsen, 2009) call for a review of fertility models and standards currently applied to data from sub-Saharan Africa. This is in part due to the observation that the Booth correction factors that are often used to adjust for the Gompertz model may be inaccurate. A point to be noted nevertheless is that while period datasets are currently available in virtually every sub-Saharan country which has conducted a DHS, cohort fertility data that would reveal long-term fertility levels without timing effects are rare (Goldstein, 2010).

Third, another method for the estimation of transitions in reproductive events (such as first sex, marriage, and birth) has been suggested (Bongaarts et al., 2015, Bongaarts, Mensch, & Blanc, 2017). The merits of this methodology over the cohort approach include the ability to assess recent trends in the onset of childbearing. Fourth, indeed, this study has established a negative correlation between age at first marriage and fertility. Moreover, other studies find that increase in age at first marriage leads to a decrease of between 17% and 33% in fertility declines in several countries of Eastern and Southern Africa; a decline in the proportion of pre-marital fertility is also noted (Harwood-Lejeune, 2001). For both the observed increase in age at first marriage and decrease in pre-marital fertility, one explanatory factor could be increased contraceptive use. Others could include structural modernisation as well as the intervention of conjugal and gender relations (Hertrich, 2017). From a programme perspective, international, regional, national, and non-governmental communities have undertaken, for several decades now, intervention programmes aimed at addressing problems related with adolescence and teen-age reproductive health. Programmes supported and implemented by organisations such as the United Nations Population Fund (UNPF), the International Planned Parenthood Federation Africa Region (IPPFAR), National Ministries of Health, National Councils for Population and Development (NCPDs), and the African Medical and Research Foundation (Amref) belong in this group. Thus, family planning programme effort is an important factor in the equation for the proximate determinants of fertility.

Last, as expected, contraceptive prevalence is strongly associated with variations in fertility. Nevertheless, recent studies advise that the TFR-contraceptive use relationship should be analysed with appropriate econometric adjustments and methods in order to obtain less biased results (Bongaarts, 2017). Other emerging aspects which point to the direction of new research include rising contraceptive use among sexually active unmarried users, contraceptive discontinuation, expanding the range of long-acting contraceptive methods, contraception during the postpartum period, involvement of community health workers, strong government support, and sustained donor funding (Tsui, Brown, & Li, 2017; Askew Maggwa, & Obare, 2017). The conclusion of this chapter is therefore that age at first marriage and contraceptive prevalence are strongly but negatively associated with variations in fertility.

On the basis of these issues, it is recommended that the following areas be considered for further research and programme implementation:

Further research

- Conduct formal demographic studies to review period and cohort fertility models which predict African fertility and its transition more accurately;
- Apply other methods for computation of reproductive transition events such as age at first sex, marriage, and birth in the current monitoring of fertility transitions in sub-Saharan Africa;
- Studies on the new dynamics and pathways of the nuptiality-fertility relationship during the course of the transition;
- Within-country and inter-sub-regional studies on contraceptive use dynamics and organisation of family planning programmes in relation to the fertility transition.

Policy and programme interventions

- Strengthen country-specific adolescent and teenage reproductive programmes to address persistent issues of adolescent and teenage pregnancy, child marriage, and female genital mutilation (FGM).
- Enhance national public, non-governmental, and private, as well as community-level reproductive health services with a view to improving their accessibility and use.

Acknowledgements

The author acknowledges the DHS Program for the use of country DHS data, The United Nations Population Division for TFR estimates, and authors cited.

References

Agadjanian, V. (2001). Negotiating through reproductive change: Gendered social interaction and fertility regulation in Mozambique. *Journal of Southern African Studies*, *27*(2), 291–309.

Agadjanian, V. (2002). Men's talk about women's matters: Gender, communication, and contraception in urban Mozambique. *Gender and Society*, *16*(2), 194–215.

Agadjanian, V., & Prata, N. (2001). War and reproduction: Angola's fertility in comparative perspective. *Journal of Southern African Studies*, *27*(2), 329–347.

Agadjanian, V., & Prata, N. (2002). War, peace, and fertility in Angola. *Demography*, *39*(2), 215–231.

Ainsworth, M., Filmer, D., & Semali, I. (1998). The impact of AIDS mortality on individual fertility: Evidence from Tanzania. In *From death to birth: Mortality decline and reproductive change*. Washington, DC: The National Academy Press.

Andro, A., & Hertrich, V. (2002). Demand for contraception in Sahelian countries: Are men's and women's expectations converging? Burkina Faso and Mali, compared to Ghana. *Population (English Edition, 2002-)*, *57*(6), 929–957.

Askew, I., Maggwa, N., & Obare, F. (2017). Fertility transitions in Ghana and Kenya: Trends, determinants and implications for policy and programs. *Population and Development Review*, *43*(Suppl. 1), 289–307.

Babalola, S., Vondrasek, C., Brown, J., & Traoré, R. (2001). The impact of a regional family planning service promotion initiative in sub-Saharan Africa: Evidence from Cameroon. *International Family Planning Perspectives*, *27*(4), 186–216.

Bawah, A. A. (2002). Spousal communication and family planning behaviour in Navrongo: A longitudinal assessment. *Studies in Family Planning*, *33*(2), 185–194.

Blacker, J., Opiyo, C., Jasseh, M., Sloggett, A., & Ssekamatte-Ssebuliba, J. (2005). Fertility in Kenya and Uganda: A comparative study of trends and determinants. *Population Studies*, *59*(3), 355–373.

Bongaarts, J. (1978). A framework for analysing the proximate determinants of fertility. *Population and Development Review*, *4*(1), 105–132.

Bongaarts, J. (2017). The effects of contraception on fertility: Is sub-Saharan Africa different? *Demographic Research*, *37*, article 6, 129–146. doi:10.4054/DemRes.2017.37.6. Retrieved from http://www.demographic-research.org/Volumes/Vol37/6/

Bongaarts, J., & Blanc, A. K. (2015). Estimating the current age of mothers at the birth of their first child from household surveys. *Population Health Metrics*, *13*(25).

Bongaarts, J., Mensch, B. S., & Blanc, A. K. (2017). Trends in the age at reproductive transitions in the developing world: The role of education. *Population Studies*, *71*(2), 139–154.

Brass, W. (2016). *The demography of tropical Africa*. Copyright 1968. Collections: Princeton Legacy Library. Princeton, NJ: Princeton University Press. Retrieved from https://press.princeton.edu/books/hardcover/9780691649368/demography-of-tropical-africa

Brass, W., & Jolly, C. L. (1993). *Population dynamics of Kenya*. Washington DC: The National Academies Press. https://doi.org/10.17226/2210.

Brown, R. L. (1997). *Introduction to the mathematics of demography*. Winsted, CT: ACTEX Publications, Inc.

Burgard, S. (2004). Factors associated with contraceptive use in late- and post-apartheid South Africa. *Studies in Family Planning*, *35*(2), 91–104.

Caldwell, J. C. (2004). Demographic theory: A long view. *Population and Development Review, 30*(2), 297–316.

Caldwell, J. C., & Caldwell, P. (2002). Africa: The new family planning frontier. *Studies in Family Planning, 33*(1), 76–86.

Caldwell, J. C., Orubuloye, I. O., & Caldwell, P. (1992). Fertility decline in Africa: A new type of transition? *Population and Development Review, 18*(2), 211–242.

Caldwell, J. C., Phillips, J. F., & Barkat-e-Khuda. (2002). The future of family planning programs. *Studies in Family Planning, 33*(1), 1–10.

Caldwell, J. C., & Schindlmayr, T. (2003). Explanations of the fertility crisis in modern societies: A search for commonalities. *Population Studies, 57*(3), 241–263.

Capo-chichi, V., & Juarez, F. (2001). Is fertility declining in Benin? *Studies in Family Planning, 32*(1), 25–40.

Cleland, J. (2001). Potatoes and pills: An overview of innovation-diffusion contributions to explanations of fertility decline. In J. Casterline (Ed.), *Diffusion processes and fertility transition*. Washington, DC: National Academies Press.

Cleland, J., & Wilson, C. (1987). Demand theories of the fertility transition: An iconoclastic view. *Population Studies, 41*(1), 5–30.

Croft, T. N., Aileen, M. J. M., & Courtney, K. A. (2018). *Guide to DHS statistics*. Rockville, MD: ICF.

Davis, K., & Blake, J. (1956). Social structure and fertility: An analytic framework. *Economic Development and Cultural Change, 4*(3), 211–235.

Debpuur, C., Phillips, J. F., Jackson, E. F., Nazzar, A., Ngom, P., & Binka, F. N. (2002). The impact of the Navrongo Project on contraceptive knowledge and use, reproductive preferences, and fertility. *Studies in Family Planning, 33*(2), 141–164.

Easterlin, R. A., & Crimmins, E. M. (1985). *The fertility revolution: A supply-demand analysis*. Chicago: University of Chicago Press.

Eltigani, E. E. (2001). Childbearing in five Arab countries. *Studies in Family Planning, 32*(1), 17–24.

Entwisle, B., & Mason, W. M. (1985). Multilevel effects of socioeconomic development and family planning programs on children ever born. *The American Journal of Sociology, 91*(3), 616–649.

Gayawan, E., Adebayo, S. B., Ipinyomi, R. A., & Oyejola, B. A. (2010). Modelling fertility curves in Africa. *Demographic Research, 22*(10), 211–236.

Goldman, N., Rutstein, S. O., & Singh, S. (1985). *Assessment of the quality of data in 41 WFS Surveys: A comparative approach*. Voorburg, the Netherlands: International Statistical Institute.

Goldstein, J. R. (2010). *A behavioral Gompertz model for cohort fertility schedules in low and moderate fertility populations*. MPIDR Working Papers WP-2010-021. Rostock: Max Planck Institute for Demographic Research.

Harwood-Lejeune, A. (2001). Rising age at first marriage and fertility in Southern and Eastern Africa. *European Journal of Population, 17*, 261–280.

Henin, R. A., Korten, A., & Werner, L. H. (1982). *Evaluation of birth histories: A case study of Kenya. World Fertility Survey: Scientific Reports, 36*. Voorburg, the Netherlands: International Statistical Institute Permanent Office.

Hertrich, V. (2017). Trends in age at marriage and the onset of fertility transition in sub-Saharan Africa. *Population and Development Review: Fertility Transition in sub-Saharan Africa, 43*(Suppl. 1), 112–137.

Hinde, A., & Mturi, A. J. (2000). Recent trends in Tanzanian fertility. *Population Studies, 54*(2), 177–191.

Knodel, J. (1977). Family limitation and the fertility transition: Evidence from the age patterns of fertility in Europe and Asia. *Population Studies, 31*(2), 219–249.

Lalou, R., & LeGrand, T. K. (1997). Child mortality in the urban and rural Sahel. *Population, An English Selection, 9*, 147–168.

Lesthaeghe, R. J. (1989). *Reproduction and social organization in sub-Saharan Africa*. Berkeley, CA: University of California Press.

Luck, M., Jarju, E., Nell, M.D. & George, M.O. (2000). Mobilizing demand for contraception in rural Gambia. *Studies in Family Planning, 31*(4), 325–335.

Mason, K. O. (1997). Explaining fertility transitions. *Demography, 34*(4), 443–454.

National Department of Health (NDoH), Statistics South Africa (Stats SA), South African Medical Research Council (SAMRC), & ICF. (2019). *South African Demographic and Health Survey 2016*. Maryland: SAMRC & ICF

Newman, J. L. (1988). A stochastic dynamic model of fertility. *Research in Population Economics, 6*, 41–68.

Obono, O. (2003). Cultural diversity and population policy in Nigeria. *Population and Development Review, 29*(1), 103–111.

Ojakaa, D. (2008). *The fertility transition in Kenya: Patterns and determinants* (Ph.D. Thesis, Département de Démographie, Faculté des Arts et des Sciences, Université de Montréal), Québec, Canada.

Piché, V., & Poirier, J. (1995). Les Approches Institutionnelles de la Fécondité. In H. Gerard & V. Piché (Eds.), *La Sociologie des Populations*. AUPELF.UREF. Montreal: Les Presses de l'Université de Montréal.

Potts, D., & Marks, S. (2001). Fertility in Southern Africa: The quiet revolution. *Journal of Southern African Studies*, *27*(2), 189–205.

Reinis, K. I. (1992). The impact of the proximate determinants of fertility: Evaluating Bongaarts's and Hobcraft and Little's methods of estimation. *Population Studies*, *46*(2), 309–326.

Robinson, W. C. (1997). The economic theory of fertility over three decades. *Population Studies*, *51*(1), 63–74.

Rogers, E. M. (1995). *Diffusion of innovation*. New York: The Free Press.

Schmertmann, C. P. (2003). A system of model fertility schedules with graphically intuitive parameters. *Demographic Research*, *9*(5), 81–110.

Simmons, G. B., & Farooq, G. M. (1985). *Fertility in developing countries: An economic perspective on research and policy issues*. New York: St. Martin's Press.

Smith, D. J. (2004). Contradictions in Nigeria's fertility transition: The burdens and benefits of having people. *Population and Development Review*, *30*(2), 221–238.

Tsui, A. O., Brown, W., & Li, Q. (2017). Contraceptive practice in sub-Saharan Africa. *Population and Development Review*, *43*(1), 166–191.

United-Nations. (1983). *Manual X: Indirect techniques for demographic estimation*. New York: Department of International Economic and Social Affairs.

United Nations, Department of Economic and Social Affairs, Population Division. (2019). *World population prospects 2019: Data Booklet (ST/ESA/SER.A/424)*. Annex Table: Key Indicators. New York: United Nations.

Upton, R. L. (2001). 'Infertility makes you invisible': Gender, health and the negotiation of fertility in Northern Botswana. *Journal of Southern African Studies*, *27*(2), 349–362.

van de Kaa, D. J. (1996). Anchored narratives: The story and findings of half a century of research into the determinants of fertility. *Population Studies*, *50*(3), 389–432.

Van Gijsen, R. (2009). *Defining a sub-Saharan fertility pattern and a standard for use with the relational Gompertz model* (Thesis, Master of Philosophy (Demography), University of Cape Town). South Africa.

Zulu, E. M. (2001). Ethnic variations in observance and rationale for postpartum sexual abstinence in Malawi. *Demography*, *38*(4), 467–479.

12

FERTILITY TRANSITION IN AFRICA

What do we know and what have we learned about fertility stalls?

David A. Sánchez-Páez and Bruno Schoumaker

Introduction: the (particular) demographic transition

In the early 1990s, scholars on Africa announced the first evidence of the fertility transition in Africa, the last region in the world to initiate fertility decline (Caldwell, Orubuloye, & Caldwell, 1992; Caldwell, 1994; Robinson & Harbison, 1995; Walle & Foster, 1990). Comparative studies identified three groups of countries regarding their stage in demographic transition (Cleland, Onouha, & Timaeus, 1994; Cohen, 1998; Kirk & Pillet, 1998). Botswana, Ghana, Kenya, Namibia, South Africa, and Zimbabwe were leading the fertility decline, followed by Côte d'Ivoire, Cameroon, Madagascar, Nigeria, Rwanda, Senegal, Tanzania, Togo, and Zambia. The third group, the least advanced, included countries like Burkina Faso, Burundi, Liberia, Malawi, Mali, Niger, and Uganda.

Rapidly however, it was anticipated that the fertility transition in Africa, specifically in sub-Saharan Africa (SSA), was likely to differ from European and Asian transitions. Caldwell et al. (1992) argued that the onset of fertility decline would come from all ages and from both married and unmarried women demanding contraceptives to maintain or lengthen traditional birth intervals rather than from older women wishing to cease family building (Caldwell et al., 1992). The pace of fertility decline was also likely to be slow, it was noted, because of the "cultural, and socio-structural supports for high fertility" and the high demand for children among both men and women (Frank & McNicoll, 1987). It was also thought that the economic crises in African countries in the late 1980s and the rapid spread of HIV/AIDS across the continent could possibly lead to an 'African path' to low fertility (McNicoll, 1992). Interestingly, Lesthaeghe (1989) already speculated in the late 1980s that African countries could experience "a partial fertility transition . . . with ultimate fertility levels well above replacement".

SSA has indeed shown a somewhat different transition from that of other developing countries (Bongaarts, 2017; Shapiro & Hinde, 2017). While new data in the 1990s confirmed that the demographic transition was underway, the slow pace of fertility decline in Africa was a cause of concern (Caldwell et al., 1992; Casterline, 2001; Cleland et al., 1994; Cohen, 1998; Garenne & Joseph, 2002; Indongo & Pazvakawambwa, 2012; Kirk & Pillet, 1998; Mbamaonyeukwu, 2000; Mturi & Joshua, 2011; Onuoha & Timaeus, 1995; Shapiro & Hinde, 2017; Tabutin & Schoumaker, 2004). By the turn of the 21st century, fresh survey data showed

 DOI: 10.4324/9780429287213-15

unexpected findings. A reversal or interruption of fertility decline – stalled fertility – was found in Ghana, Kenya, and Nigeria at much higher rates than replacement level (Bongaarts, 2006; Shapiro & Tambashe, 2002; Westoff & Cross, 2006), and similar halts were also identified in the rural areas of Burkina Faso, Mali, Niger, Senegal, and Tanzania (Shapiro & Tambashe, 2002).

Since then, Africa's unique fertility transition has been discussed in several papers (Bongaarts, 2017; Bongaarts & Casterline, 2013; Casterline, 2017; Casterline & Agyei-Mensah, 2017; Eloundou-Enyegue, Giroux, & Tenikue, 2017; Gerland, Biddlecom, & Kantorova, 2017; Lesthaeghe, 2014; Moultrie, Sayi, & Timaeus, 2012). For instance, Bongaarts (2017) identified four characteristics that make Africa's transition different from the rest of the World. First, it started later than other less developed regions. Second, the level of fertility was higher at the time of onset of transition. Third, it started earlier compared to the level of development at the time of onset compared to other less developed countries. And fourth, the pace of decline and the improvement in development indicators are slower than elsewhere. Another unique feature of the African transition is related to long birth intervals. Moultrie et al. (2012) find that birth intervals have lengthened considerably in almost every African country. According to them, these long birth intervals reflect postponement of births rather than spacing of births and more broadly reflect uncertainties in family building behavior (Timaeus & Moultrie, 2008, 2013). Finally, fertility stalls have been found in a large number of countries and subnational areas (Al Zalak & Goujon, 2017; Bongaarts, 2006, 2008; Garenne, 2008; Howse, 2015; Ouadah-Bedidi, Vallin, & Bouchoucha, 2012; Schoumaker, 2019b; Schoumaker & Sánchez-Páez, 2020; Shapiro, Kreider, Varner, & Sinha, 2013; Shapiro & Gebreselassie, 2008) and are also part of the uniqueness of Africa's transitions.

In this chapter, we review the literature regarding fertility stalls in Africa since the 2000s. We first summarize fertility trends in Africa, comparing them with trends in other regions of the world. Next, we review existing studies on the identification of stalls, discussing some measurement issues and uncertainties regarding whether and where stalls have occurred. In the fourth section, we synthesize the literature on the demographic dynamics of fertility stalls, focusing mainly on knowledge about the proximate determinants in times of stalling fertility. In the fifth section, the literature on the causes of the stalls is explored. Finally, we discuss research perspectives and implications.

Fertility trends in Africa: a brief description

Figure 12.1 displays the fertility trends of Africa, SSA, Latin America and the Caribbean, Southern Asia, and Southeast Asia using data from the World Population Prospects (United Nations, 2020). Circles show the highest value of total fertility rate (TFR), while the Xs indicate the time of onset, measured as a decline by 10% from the maximum TFR. In Latin America and Southern and Southeast Asia, the time elapsed between the maximum TFR and onset of decline was, on average, 15 years. For these three regions, the decline started in the 1970s. Five years later, all of them were considered mid-transition regions; that is, the TFR was below 5 children per woman. The case of Africa, and particularly of SSA, is different. At the time the other regions were at the onset of their fertility transition, Africa was reaching its maximum TFR. Moreover, Africa needed around 25 years to begin the transition – from the 1970s to mid-1990s – and 15 more years to reach 5 children per woman. The onset in SSA occurred 5 years later than the average of Africa. Currently, the TFR in Africa and SSA is twice as high as in the other regions.

Africa took longer to reach mid-transition, reflecting the slow pace with which fertility has decreased (Shapiro & Hinde, 2017). Table 12.1 shows the variations of TFR between 5-year periods by region. The average fertility decrease in Africa and SSA from the maximum TFR to the time of onset was 0.196 and 0.222 children per woman per 5-year period, respectively. In the same period, the reductions in Latin America, Southern Asia, and Southeast Asia were 0.310, 0.254, and 0.210 children per woman per 5-year period, respectively. Moreover, the average decline in fertility from the time of onset to 2015–2020 in the three regions is 0.320, 0.364, and 0.363 children per woman per 5-year period, while in Africa and SSA, it is 0.257 and 0.290. The pace of decline in Africa after the time of onset is around 25% slower.

Results from Figure 12.1 and Table 12.1 show that fertility in Africa, at the regional level, has been declining since the 1970s. However, there are dissimilarities between subregions. Figure 12.2 displays fertility trends by subregion in Africa. As previously, circles and Xs stand for the maximum TFR and the time of onset, respectively.

Northern and Southern Africa were the first two regions to begin the demographic transition. For the former, the maximum TFR was reached in 1960–1965, while for the latter, it was in 1955–1960. In both cases, the time of onset was in 1975–1980 at levels of 6.2 and 5.2 children per woman, respectively. For the following 25 years, fertility declined consistently in both subregions until it stalled in the early 2000s. In Northern Africa, TFR slightly increased from 3.1 in the early 2000s to 3.3 in 2015–2020. In Southern Africa, TFR only marginally decreased from 2.7 to 2.5 since 2000.

Eastern, Middle, and Western Africa have taken longer to begin the demographic transition. Eastern Africa reached the highest TFR recorded among all African subregions: 7.1

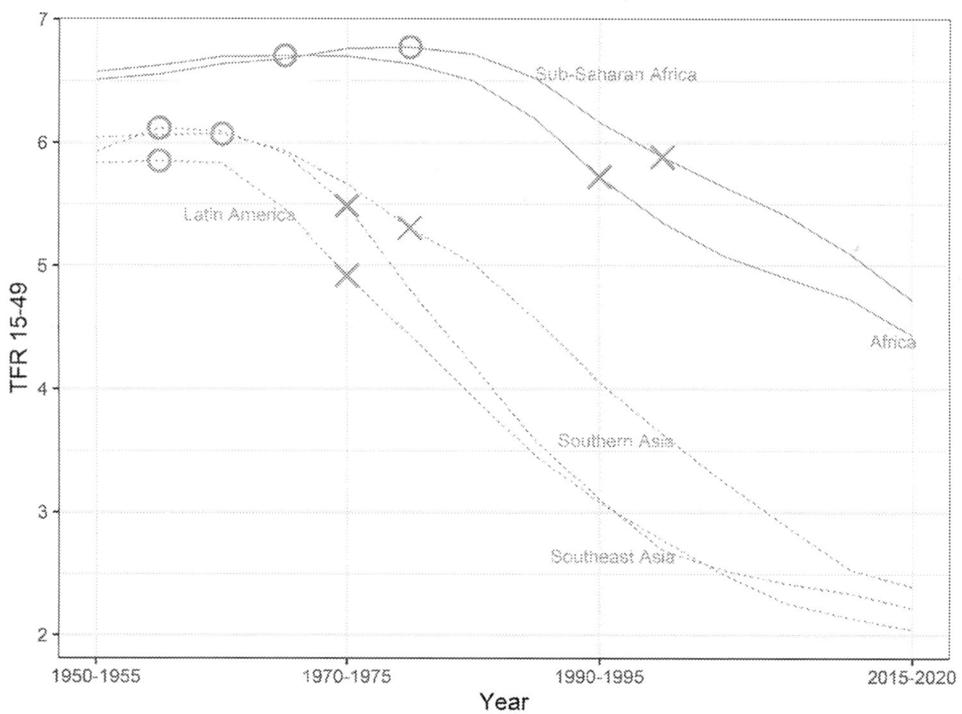

Figure 12.1 Fertility trends of less-developed regions

Source: World Population Prospects, United Nations, 2020

Note: Circles and Xs stand for the maximum TFR and the time of onset, respectively.

Table 12.1 Variations of TFR from the Previous 5-Year Period by Region

Year	Africa		Sub-Saharan Africa		Latin America		Southern Asia		Southeast Asia	
	Δ	Avg.	Δ	Avg.	Δ	Avg.	Δ	Avg.	Δ	Avg.
1955–1960	0.051		0.044		0.019		0.021		0.190	
1960–1965	0.075		0.083		–0.018	–0.310	0.006		–0.028	–0.210
1965–1970	0.007		0.046		–0.374		–0.133	–0.254	–0.174	
1970–1975	–0.003	–0.196	0.083		–0.539		–0.270		–0.429	
1975–1980	–0.063		0.011		–0.485	–0.320	–0.359		–0.678	–0.363
1980–1985	–0.139		–0.054	–0.222	–0.498		–0.284	–0.364	–0.611	
1985–1990	–0.314		–0.202		–0.485		–0.456		–0.623	
1990–1995	–0.463		–0.353		–0.376		–0.513		–0.469	
1995–2000	–0.373	–0.257	–0.281		–0.305		–0.422		–0.416	
2000–2005	–0.274		–0.245	–0.290	–0.284		–0.394		–0.163	
2005–2010	–0.177		–0.235		–0.228		–0.357		–0.107	
2010–2015	–0.170		–0.307		–0.122		–0.348		–0.078	
2015–2020	–0.292		–0.372		–0.094		–0.136		–0.118	

Source: World Population Prospects, United Nations, 2020. Estimates are calculated by the authors

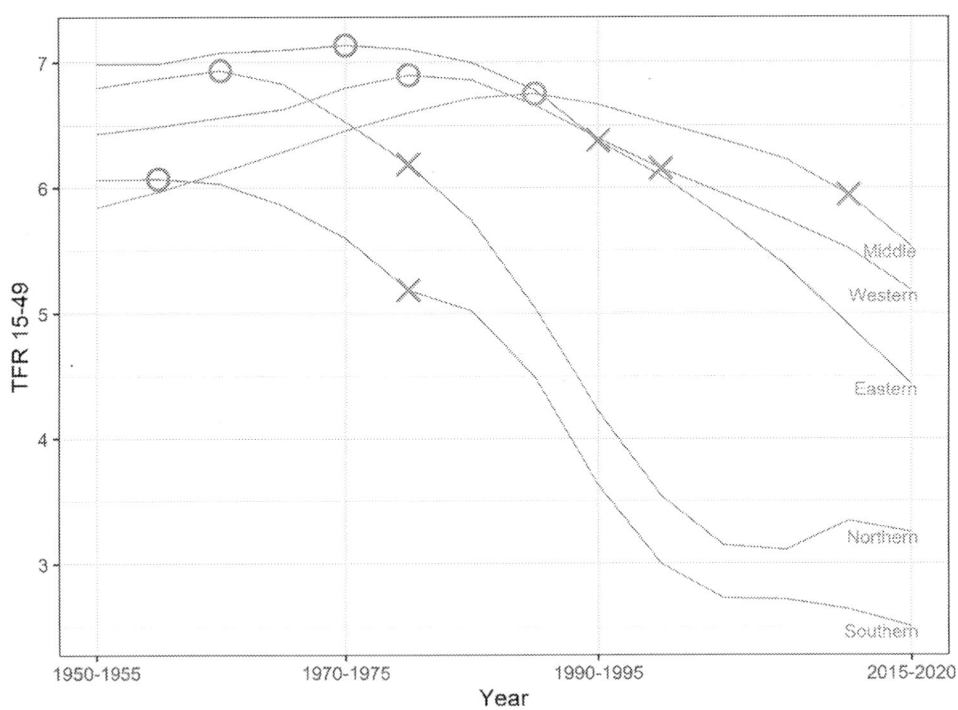

Figure 12.2 Fertility trends by subregion in Africa

Source: World Population Prospects, United Nations, 2020

Note: Circles and Xs stand for the maximum TFR and the time of onset, respectively.

children in 1970–1975. Fertility then declined at a pace of 0.190 children per woman per 5-year period, and the time of onset came 20 years later. Since then, TFR has decreased to reach 4.4 children in 2015–2020. In Western Africa, 20 years also elapsed between its peak TFR (6.9 children in 1975–1980) and the time of onset. Transition started after TFR declined at a pace of 0.186 children per woman per 5-year period. The decrease accelerated to 0.243 children per woman per 5-year period to reach 5.2 children in 2015–2020. Middle Africa was the last subregion to begin the fertility transition. The maximum TFR, 6.8, was reached in 1985–1990, and the time of onset arrived 25 years later, after fertility decreased by 0.162 children per woman per 5-year period. Afterwards, the pace of decline accelerated to 0.411. Both Middle and Western Africa, at the subregional level, are considered to be at an early stage of transition, while Eastern Africa is considered to have been in mid-transition since 2010–2015.

Country-level analysis shows heterogeneity within subregions. Figure 12.3 displays fertility trends by country and subregion in Africa. The subregional average from Figure 12.2 is included for reference (colored dashed lines). Country trends present patterns that make Africa unique. On the one hand, reversals and the slowdown in the pace of fertility decline are found among many countries. On the other, high levels of fertility are found at the onset of the transition and in recent years. Detailed TFRs by country from 1950 to 2020 can be found in Sánchez-Páez and Schoumaker (2020a).

Fertility transition in Northern Africa has been different from that in SSA. While in the former, fertility was dropping rapidly, in the latter, it was still high or even increasing. Also, Northern Africa is culturally different, as it has an Arab heritage. Moreover, Northern Africa is more developed than SSA from various perspectives such as education, health, and living standards. These differences have led researchers on the fertility transition to study SSA and Northern Africa separately. However, our case is different. We include both of them in our analysis, as they show evidence of fertility stalls, well above replacement level.

Table 12.2 Variations of TFR from the Previous 5-Year Period by Subregion in Africa

Year	Northern		Eastern		Middle		Western		Southern	
	Δ	Avg.	Δ	Avg.	Δ	Avg.	Δ	Avg.	Δ	Avg.
1955–1960	0.072		0.000		0.123		0.056		0.006	
1960–1965	0.064		0.090		0.156		0.071		–0.040	–0.221
1965–1970	–0.106	–0.249	0.021		0.167		0.067		–0.172	
1970–1975	–0.303		0.038		0.168		0.172		–0.259	
1975–1980	–0.337		–0.031	–0.190	0.143		0.101		–0.414	
1980–1985	–0.447	–0.367	–0.107		0.115		–0.040	–0.186	–0.167	–0.336
1985–1990	–0.696		–0.218		0.035		–0.199		–0.525	
1990–1995	–0.824		–0.404		–0.085	–0.162	–0.265		–0.863	
1995–2000	–0.679		–0.284	–0.389	–0.148		–0.242		–0.627	
2000–2005	–0.393		–0.337		–0.137		–0.204	–0.243	–0.280	
2005–2010	–0.039		–0.379		–0.153		–0.208		–0.010	
2010–2015	0.231		–0.473		–0.285		–0.227		–0.079	
2015–2020	–0.090		–0.470		–0.411	–0.411	–0.332		–0.135	

Source: World Population Prospects, United Nations, 2020. Estimates are calculated by the authors

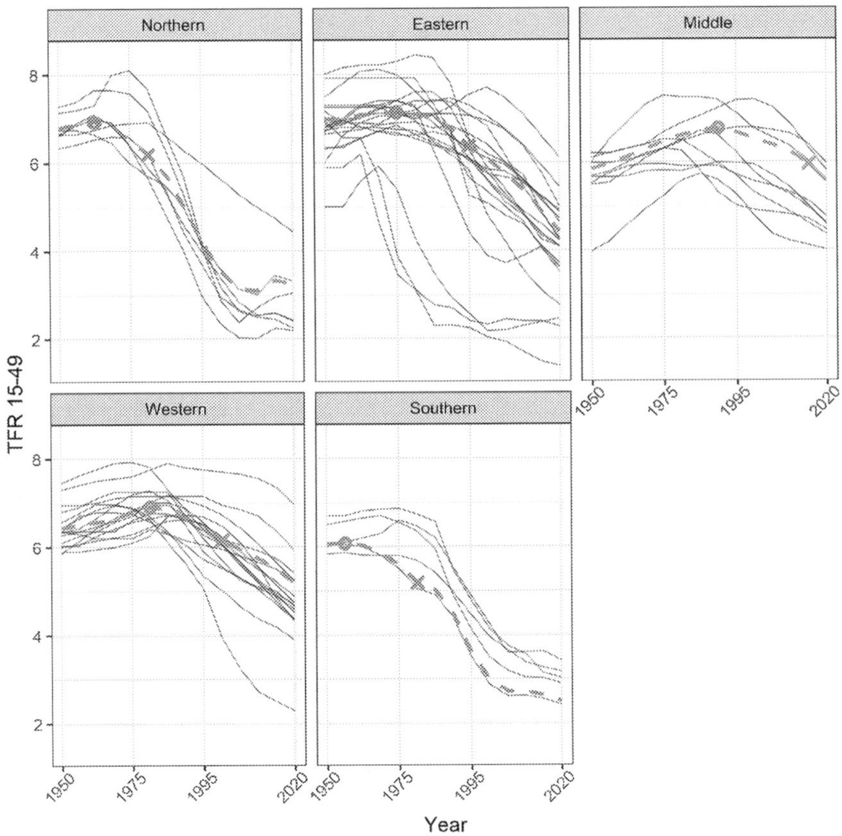

Figure 12.3 Fertility trends by country and subregion in Africa

Source: World Population Prospects, United Nations, 2020

Note: Circles and Xs stand for the maximum TFR and the time of onset, respectively.

Fertility stalls: how, when, and where to find them?

As just discussed, fertility transition in Africa has been different from other low- and middle-income regions. Stalls are one of the specificities of African transitions that have attracted the attention of many researchers over the last 20 years.

In general terms, a fertility stall is the interruption of an ongoing fertility transition by a period of no significant change in fertility before the country reaches the end of the transition (Bongaarts, 2008). Even though there is a consensus on what a fertility stall should mean, its operationalization varies across authors. This has led to some countries being classified differently (stalling or not), even with the same data over the same periods (Agyei-Mensah, 2006; Bongaarts, 2006; Garenne, 2011; Machiyama, 2010; Schoumaker, 2019b; Shapiro & Gebreselassie, 2008). Regarding the data sources, most of the reviewed literature uses the Demographic and Health Surveys (DHS), while some studies use the World Population Prospects, Multiple Indicator Cluster Surveys (MICS), and national data provided by national institutions (e.g., surveys or censuses).

The first mention of fertility stalls goes back to the 1980s, when Gendell (1985, 1989) identified stalls in Costa Rica, South Korea, and Sri Lanka. Although Gendell proposed a formal definition of stalled fertility,[1] a simpler approach was used in the early works on stalls in Africa. In these, stalls are identified as periods of non-decreasing fertility (TFR) between two dates (usually two surveys). As early as 2002, Shapiro and Tambashe (2002) pointed out some unusual trends in fertility with this method. Although Shapiro and Tambashe (2002) did not consider non-decreasing fertility a fertility stall (since it does take into account the stage in the transition process or previous pace of decline), several studies used this approach to determine whether fertility was declining or stalling (Askew, Maggwa, & Obare, 2017; Bongaarts & Casterline, 2013; Eltigani, 2003; Ibisomi et al., 2014; Kabagenyi et al., 2015; Ndagurwa & Odimegwu, 2019; Odwe, Agwanda, & Khasakhala, 2015; Ouadah-Bedidi et al., 2012; Palamuleni, 2017; Sayi, 2016; Shapiro et al., 2013; Shapiro & Gebreselassie, 2008; Westoff & Cross, 2006).

In parallel, Bongaarts adapted Gendell's criteria to the African context. For instance, Bongaarts (2006) proposes that a country has stalled fertility if its TFR fails to decline between two estimates while the country is in mid-transition. A decrease in TFR of less than about 0.25 births per woman in a 5-year period is considered a non-significant fertility decline (Bongaarts, 2008). In this regard, the generalization of mid-transition country replaces the first Gendell requirement. To be classified as a mid-transition country, the TFR should be below 5.0, and contraceptive prevalence among married women should be higher than 10% (Bongaarts, 2008). Also, Bongaarts does not include the relative slowdown proposed by Gendell, since the pace of fertility decline in Africa is already slow. Instead, he states that the decrease in the TFR should be less than 0.25 children per woman in a 5-year period. Of the 22 African countries surveyed in the early 2000s, only Ghana and Kenya were classified in the stalled fertility group (Bongaarts, 2006). A second study including four more countries and new datasets increased the number of cases of stalled fertility in Africa at any period since the 1990s to 14: Cameroon, Côte d'Ivoire, Egypt, Ethiopia, Ghana, Kenya, Morocco, Mozambique, Nigeria, Rwanda, Tanzania, Uganda, Zambia, and Zimbabwe (Bongaarts, 2008). Non-decreasing fertility was also found in Chad, Guinea, and Mali, but they were ruled out since they were considered pre-transitional. This method served as a basis for methodological refinements when defining the existence or not of a halt in the fertility decline (Agyei-Mensah, 2006; Ezeh, Mberu, & Emina, 2009; Howse, 2015; Machiyama, 2010; Moultrie et al., 2008; Muza, 2019; Nzimande & Mugwendere, 2018; Schoumaker, 2009, 2019b).

Some researchers proposed refining the methods due to concerns about the robustness of estimates. For instance, Bongaarts (2008) proposes the decrease in TFR of more than about 0.25 in a 5-year period as one of the requirements prior considering a period stalled. However, this threshold is to some extent ad hoc. On the other hand, using the non-decreasing TFR definition could drive one to debatable conclusions, since measurement and sampling errors exists in the estimates. In this regard, some researchers considered that all changes in the fertility trends, regardless of their magnitude, were relevant for fertility stalls as long as they were statistically significant. For instance, Garenne (2008) tests the statistical significance (p-value < 0.05) of the change of slope from negative (fertility decline) to nil or positive (fertility stall). Using data from 1985 to 2008, Garenne (2008) classified Ghana, Kenya, and Nigeria in the group of countries having experienced fertility stalls. Further research added Madagascar, Rwanda, Senegal, Tanzania, and Zambia to the list (Garenne, 2011). Testing the statistical significance of the change in fertility from one period to the next has been used by several studies (Ibisomi et al., 2014; Nzimande & Mugwendere, 2018; Palamuleni, 2017; Schoumaker & Sánchez-Páez, 2020; Sneeringer, 2009).

Some authors have used methods not related to the criteria proposed by Gendell or his subsequent refinements. For instance, Al Zalak and Goujon (2017) find a fertility stall in Egypt since the early 2000s after reconstructing TFR by year and smoothing it using the locally weighted scatterplot smoothing method. Moultrie et al. (2008) check for statistically significant differences in the rate of fertility decline over two time periods in South Africa (Rural KwaZulu-Natal) by testing whether two exponential curves fit the data better than a single exponential curve fitted to all the data. Ezeh et al. (2009) use probit models to test whether the change during a third period is equal to or greater than zero while changes in the previous two periods are negative in four countries of Eastern Africa. Goujon et al. (2015) compute fertility ratios by dividing the TFR of a 5-year period by the TFR of the previous 5-year period. Then, they define a fertility stall if the ratio is at or above 0.98.

Mixed evidence in classifying countries in the stalled fertility category (e.g., Ghana) led researchers to take into account concerns about data quality. For instance, Schoumaker (2009) proposed the reconstruction of fertility rates by pooling full birth histories from several surveys for assessing changes in fertility trends. This idea was based on the possible underestimation of fertility in recent years in surveys because of birth displacements, omitted births, or sampling issues; therefore, changes (or the absence of them) in TFR could be explained by measurement errors and their variations over time rather than declining or stalling fertility. Of the 24 African countries analyzed between 1986 and 2006, only Kenya and Rwanda were confirmed as cases of stalled fertility (Schoumaker, 2009). From there, the interest in re-examining the stall periods began. Besides checking the problems in the data suggested by Schoumaker (2009), Machiyama (2010) included an analysis using women's average parity and educational attainment. As a result, using Gendell's criteria on data from nine SSA countries, the stalls in Benin, Kenya, Rwanda, and Zambia were confirmed. Both studies used DHS for their analysis. In a further study, Schoumaker (2019b) compared different data sources in 32 SSA countries to identify stalls. Published fertility rates were compared with reconstructed trends from full birth histories, as well as with trends from censuses and other surveys (mainly MICS). A consistency index was computed, with a score varying from −1 – strong support of fertility decline – to 1 – strong support of fertility stall – (Schoumaker, 2019b). From this, unambiguous evidence of stalls was found in Namibia and Zimbabwe; very strong evidence in Congo, Kenya, and Zambia; and strong evidence in Cameroon.

Table 12.3 presents a summary of the number of studies on fertility transition in Africa by country, classified according to whether they have identified fertility stalls. We group them by subregion using the United Nations groups. In the case of comparative analyses, we include them for each country covered by the study. All the studies were published after the 2000s since previous evidence confirmed only declining fertility periods. Studies checking for fertility stalls have covered virtually all countries of Africa. Appendix Table 12.1 includes full details of the studies reviewed in Table 12.3. Overall, 33 of the 46 analyzed countries were classified under the stalled category at some point. At the subnational level, stalls in capital cities are apparently more common than elsewhere, while most rural areas are still pre-transitional.

However, the conclusions vary substantially across studies, depending mainly on the method used to define the stall. For instance, for the same period, countries such as Côte d'Ivoire, Senegal, or Uganda are in and out of the stalled category in parallel studies. Nine studies find stalls in Ghana, while 14 conclude there is no stall. Similar conclusions emerge in Cameroon, Nigeria, or Rwanda. For other countries, there is widespread agreement, as in Congo, Egypt, or Kenya. In some others, it is clear that most studies do not find evidence of fertility stalls, as in Botswana, Chad, Madagascar, Malawi, or South Africa. Finally, the time of the study also leads to different conclusions as new information becomes available and as new stalls emerge, as in Cameroon, Namibia, Zambia, or Zimbabwe.

Table 12.3 Number of Studies on Fertility Transition 2000–2020

Country	*Stall Period*	*Place of Stall*			*No Stall*
		National	*Urban*	*Rural*	
Northern Africa					
Algeria	2000–2010	1			1
Egypt	1993–1998, 2006–2014	5	2	1	2
Libya					2
Morocco	1992–2004	1			4
Sudan					3
Tunisia	2000–2010	1			1
Western Africa					
Benin	2001–2006, 2012–2017	5	2	1	14
Burkina Faso	1993–1999, 2003–2010	1		1	17
Côte d'Ivoire	1994–2011	3		2	14
Gambia	2004–2013	1	1		
Ghana	1993–2004, 2008–2014	9	3	1	14
Guinea	1999–2012	4	3	3	9
Guinea-Bissau					1
Liberia					9
Mali	1987–2012	2	1	1	13
Niger	1992–2006	5	2	2	12
Nigeria	2003–2013	8	2	1	12
Senegal	1997–2005, 2011–2016	3	2	2	14
Sierra Leone					2
Togo	1998–2013		1		12
Middle Africa					
Cameroon	1998–2011	11	4	4	8
Central African Republic					5
Chad	2004–2015			2	12
Congo	2005–2011	5	2	1	
D.R. Congo	2007–2013	3	2	1	2
Equatorial Guinea					1
Gabon	2000–2012	2	2	1	4
Eastern Africa					
Burundi	1980–2010		1		5
Comoros					6
Eritrea					6
Ethiopia	2000–2005, 2011–2016	1	1	1	12
Kenya	1998–2003	21	3	2	5
Madagascar	1992–1997	2	1		14
Malawi	2004–2010	1			19
Mozambique	1997–2011	8	1	2	9
Rwanda	2000–2005	10	2	2	9
Somalia					1
Tanzania	1996–2010	12	3	4	7
Uganda	1995–2006	2	2		18

(Continued)

Table 12.3 (Continued)

Country	*Stall Period*	*Place of Stall*			*No Stall*
		National	*Urban*	*Rural*	
Zambia	1996–2007	11	2	3	8
Zimbabwe	1999–2015	10	2	3	14
Southern Africa					
Botswana					3
Eswatini					3
Lesotho	2009–2014		2		6
Namibia	2007–2013	2	1	1	14
South Africa	1990–2013	2		2	10

Note: Full details of the studies included in this table are provided in Appendix Table 12.1.

Fertility dynamics in stall periods

In this section, we focus on the proximate determinants of fertility and their changes in periods of fertility stalls. This popular framework allows identifying the contribution of key behavioral and biological factors in the variations of fertility (Bongaarts, 1978, 2015). Many of the scholars researching fertility stalls in Africa have attempted to explain the reversals in fertility decline through the proximate determinants of fertility. We would expect to find a direct relation between fertility stalls and earlier age at union or increased sexual activity, lower contraceptive use, shorter periods of postpartum insusceptibility, or declines in abortion. However, results show mixed evidence.

An early age at first **union or marriage** increases the time that a women is exposed to childbearing. Factors associated with increasing age at marriage include education and income, while those associated with lower age include religion, polygyny, and urbanization (Garenne, 2004). On average, age at marriage has increased in Africa (Gebreselassie, 2012; Shapiro & Tenikue, 2017; Tabutin & Schoumaker, 2020; United Nations, 2002). It has contributed to lower fertility (Agyei-Mensah & Owoo, 2015; Burger, Burger, & Rossouw, 2012; Finlay, Mejía-Guevara, & Akachi, 2018; Guillaume, 2003; Johnson et al., 2011; Laelago, Habtu, & Yohannes, 2019), especially in urban areas (Garenne, 2004; Shapiro & Tenikue, 2017). As far as fertility stalls are concerned, some studies show that age at marriage decreased during periods of stalled fertility, while others do not. For instance, in Algeria and Tunisia, age at marriage decreased at the same time fertility stopped declining (Ouadah-Bedidi et al., 2012). Also, as expected, the increase in the proportion of married women was related to the increase in fertility in Zambia from 2002 to 2007 (Chola & Michelo, 2016). In contrast, TFR and age at marriage went up together in Benin, Cameroon, Guinea, Malawi, Mozambique, Nigeria, Uganda, and Zambia (Finlay et al., 2018); Egypt (Eltigani, 2003); Kenya (Bongaarts, 2006; Finlay et al., 2018; Garenne, 2008); Madagascar and Rwanda (Garenne, 2008), Namibia (Indongo & Pazvakawambwa, 2012); and Tanzania (Finlay et al., 2018; Garenne, 2008). While this may seem counterintuitive, it indicates that – although increasing age at marriage is expected to lead to lower fertility – this effect is counterbalanced by other proximate determinants.

Actually, in most countries, marriage does not account for fertility stalls since it has remained at the same level as before the stagnation in fertility, as in Eastern Africa (Ezeh et al., 2009), Ghana (Bongaarts, 2006; Garenne, 2008), or Zimbabwe (Nzimande & Mugwendere, 2018; Sayi, 2016). Unlike in other developing regions, the connection between marriage and fertility in SSA is also weak since premarital fertility is common (Garenne & Joseph, 2002; Johnson et al., 2011). In this regard, in countries such as Botswana, Kenya, Madagascar, Rwanda, and Tanzania, the trends of age at first marriage and age at first birth followed opposite directions, translating into increasing premarital fertility (Gaisie, 1998; Garenne, 2008; Ndahindwa et al., 2014). In the case of Zimbabwe, no significant changes in age at first birth were found at the time of stall (Sayi, 2016), although the marital fertility inhibition decreased over time (Muza, 2019).

Contraceptive use is the proximate determinant that has attracted the most attention from researchers exploring the stalls, for three main reasons. First, contraception is major factor to limit and to space births. Second, it helps to prevent sexually transmitted diseases. Third, contraceptive prevalence is also used as criterion for a country to be considered in demographic transition (Bongaarts, 2008; Nzimande & Mugwendere, 2018; Schoumaker, 2019b). However, we find mixed evidence on the association between contraception and fertility stalls.

As one might expect, increasing use of contraceptives has been connected to declining fertility periods in many countries (Finlay et al., 2018; Rossier & Corker, 2017; Shapiro et al., 2013), such as in Botswana (Gaisie, 1998), Eswatini (Chemhaka & Odimegwu, 2019), Ethiopia (Laelago et al., 2019), Malawi (Palamuleni, 2010), Namibia (Indongo & Pazvakawambwa, 2012; Shapiro & Gebreselassie, 2008; Shemeikka, Notkola, & Siiskonen, 2005), South Africa (Burger et al., 2012; Moultrie & Timaeus, 2003), Uganda (Kabagenyi et al., 2015), or Zimbabwe (Mturi & Joshua, 2011). As expected, in several countries, contraceptive use contributes to explaining stalls, as it leveled off or decreased: Cameroon (Jadhav & Short Fabic, 2019), D.R. Congo (Jadhav & Short Fabic, 2019; Romaniuk, 2011), Ghana (Agyei-Mensah, 2006; Bongaarts, 2006; Jadhav & Short Fabic, 2019), Kenya (Askew et al., 2017; Bongaarts, 2006; Ezeh et al., 2009; Garenne, 2008; Westoff & Cross, 2006), Mozambique (Jadhav & Short Fabic, 2019), Namibia (Jadhav & Short Fabic, 2019; Palamuleni, 2017), Niger (Jadhav & Short Fabic, 2019), Nigeria and Rwanda (Garenne, 2008), Tunisia (Ouadah-Bedidi et al., 2012), Uganda (Ezeh et al., 2009), and Zimbabwe (Nzimande & Mugwendere, 2018; Sayi, 2016). However, changes in fertility do not always correspond to changes in contraceptive use (Shapiro & Gebreselassie, 2008). Despite the increasing contraceptive prevalence, fertility stalled in some countries: Algeria (Ouadah-Bedidi et al., 2012); Benin (Johnson et al., 2011); Cameroon (Johnson et al., 2011; Shapiro & Gebreselassie, 2008); Guinea, Kenya, Mozambique, and Senegal (Shapiro & Gebreselassie, 2008); Egypt (Al Zalak & Goujon, 2017; Eltigani, 2003; United Nations, 2002), Ghana (Askew et al., 2017; Garenne, 2008; Shapiro & Gebreselassie, 2008); Madagascar (Garenne, 2008); Rwanda (Johnson et al., 2011; Shapiro & Gebreselassie, 2008; Westoff, 2013); South Africa (Moultrie et al., 2008); Tanzania (Ezeh et al., 2009; Garenne, 2008; Johnson et al., 2011); Zambia (Johnson et al., 2011); and Zimbabwe (Ezeh et al., 2009; Muza, 2019). In many of these countries, total demand for contraceptives has stalled – no additional women are willing to use contraceptives – while unmet need still remains at high levels – women cannot access or use contraceptives, even though they have intentions of doing so (Bongaarts & Casterline, 2013). These high levels translate into unwanted fertility. Evidence shows a link between stalled fertility and unwanted fertility in Ghana (Askew et al., 2017), Kenya (Askew et al., 2017; Ezeh et al., 2009), Tanzania and Uganda (Ezeh et al., 2009), and Zimbabwe (Sayi, 2016). Regarding the place of residence, increase in contraceptive use is more common in urban areas, and it is connected to fertility decline (Gebreselassie, 2012; Ross, Abel, & Abel, 2004; Shapiro, 2010;

Shapiro & Tambashe, 2002; Shapiro & Tenikue, 2017). However, periods where contraceptive use leveled off in urban areas are linked to stalled fertility, especially in SSA capital cities (Sánchez-Páez & Schoumaker, 2020b).

Average duration of **postpartum infecundability** summarizes both the length of amenorrhea (which depends on the length of breastfeeding) and postpartum abstinence. Historically, SSA has been characterized by longer periods of postpartum insusceptibility than other developing regions, resulting in longer birth intervals (Bongaarts & Casterline, 2013), with a strong inhibiting effect on fertility (Agyei-Mensah & Owoo, 2015; Capo-chichi & Juarez, 2001; Palamuleni, 2010). For instance, the fertility-inhibiting effect of postpartum infecundability has already contributed to the drop in fertility through longer periods of breastfeeding or abstinence in Benin (Capo-chichi & Juarez, 2001; Finlay et al., 2018), Burkina Faso, Ghana, Madagascar, Mali, Namibia, Niger, Rwanda, Senegal, Tanzania, and Zimbabwe (Finlay et al., 2018); Côte d'Ivoire (Finlay et al., 2018; Guillaume, 2003); Ethiopia (Finlay et al., 2018; Laelago et al., 2019); and Malawi (Palamuleni, 2010). In contrast, as far as fertility stalls are concerned, postpartum insusceptibility is the only proximate determinant with no mixed evidence. At the national level, reversals in fertility decline and shorter periods of insusceptibility were found in Cameroon, Guinea, Kenya, Malawi, Mozambique, Nigeria, Uganda, and Zambia (Finlay et al., 2018); D.R. Congo (Romaniuk, 2011); Ghana (Agyei-Mensah, 2006; Agyei-Mensah & Owoo, 2015); Egypt (Al Zalak & Goujon, 2017); Namibia (Palamuleni, 2017); and Zimbabwe (Muza, 2019). At the subnational level, Sánchez-Páez and Schoumaker (2020b) found that declining postpartum insusceptibility is the single most important factor of fertility stalls in SSA capitals. If not accompanied by a sufficient increase in contraceptive use effectiveness (Lesthaeghe, 2014; Tabutin & Schoumaker, 2004, 2020), shortened postpartum insusceptibility is expected to lead to more stalls.

The role of **abortion** in fertility stalls has been much less analyzed due to scarcity of information. Estimates of the abortion rate in Africa are around 34 per 1,000 women (Sánchez-Páez & Ortega, 2019; Singh, Remez, Sedgh, Kwok, & Onda, 2018). Evidence shows that abortion rates increase at the beginning of transition (Dickson, Adde, & Ahinkorah, 2018; Rossier & Corker, 2017) and possibly play a substantial role in fertility regulation in some settings, such as large cities (e.g., Accra, Cotonou, and Dakar. See Capo-chichi and Juarez, 2001; Garenne and Joseph, 2002; and Agyei-Mensah, 2006). Abortion could contribute to fertility stalls if it becomes less common. Using the Bongaarts model to identify the role of proximate determinants in capital cities in Africa, Sánchez-Páez and Schoumaker (2020b) find that a large share of stalls are not explained by the three previous proximate determinants, suggesting changes in abortion practices may be part of the explanation. Unfortunately, very little information is available, and special efforts should be made to improve estimates of abortions. On that basis, the effect of abortion on fertility, including on stalls, could be better addressed.

In addition to proximate determinants, research has also focused on **fertility preferences.** Africa has long been considered and defined as a pronatalist region (Bongaarts, 2017; Bongaarts & Casterline, 2013; Caldwell et al., 1992; Casterline, 2017; Ibisomi, 2008; Lesthaeghe, 1989), and African women still declare they want large families, partly reflecting cultural traditions. For instance, in Nigeria, ideal family size remains high, as society first honors fertile women and second considers children should take care of the elderly (Ibisomi, 2008). Also, for many African women, the number of children becomes the most important object of reproductive management (Johnson-Hanks, 2007). Overall, desired family size in SSA has stagnated at around four children in recent years (Casterline & Agyei-Mensah, 2017), and most births are reported as wanted. Since African women tend to translate their fertility preferences into birth outcomes (Cleland, Machiyama, & Casterline, 2019), high ideal family size will probably not allow fertility to decline rapidly. In this regard, stalled periods have been associated with stagnating or increasing wanted fertility in Algeria and Tunisia (Ouadah-Bedidi et al., 2012), Egypt (Al Zalak & Goujon, 2017; Eltigani, 2003; El-Zeini, 2008), Ghana (Agyei-Mensah, 2006; Askew et al., 2017; Bongaarts, 2006), Kenya (Askew et al., 2017; Bongaarts, 2006; Westoff & Cross, 2006), and Zimbabwe (Ndagurwa & Odimegwu, 2019; Nzimande & Mugwendere, 2018; Sayi, 2016). Also, the same association was found in most SSA capitals (Sánchez-Páez & Schoumaker, 2020b), where the demand for children also remains high (Casterline & Agyei-Mensah, 2017; Fuchs & Goujon, 2014; Gerland et al., 2017; Howse, 2015; Sánchez-Páez & Schoumaker, 2020b). Conversely, lower demand for children is linked to lower fertility in studies in Kenya (Blacker et al., 2005), Namibia (Indongo & Pazvakawambwa, 2012) and Uganda (Blacker, Opiyo, Jasseh, Sloggett, & Ssekamatte-Ssebuliba, 2005; Kabagenyi et al., 2015). In contrast, the decrease in desired family size and wanted fertility do not account for the fertility stall in Rwanda (Westoff, 2013). All in all, high and fairly stable ideal family sizes appear to be correlated with fertility stalls.

Finally, some research has also addressed the **age patterns of fertility** in times of stalling fertility. For instance, age-specific fertility rate shows decreasing fertility by age when fertility stalled in Egypt, except for those aged 15–24 (Al Zalak & Goujon, 2017; Eltigani, 2003). In the case of Kenya, there was a significant increase in fertility of women aged 25–29 at the time of the stall (Odwe et al., 2015). Nevertheless, and for all age groups, fertility is currently lower than it used to be (Shapiro & Gebreselassie, 2008). However, surprisingly little research has focused on age-specific factors in fertility stalls.

Potential causes of fertility stalls

Besides the fertility dynamics during periods of stagnated fertility, scholars have been interested in finding the underlying causes of the stalls. Among the most cited socioeconomic reasons are leveling off in education, high prevalence of HIV/AIDS, slow increases in national income or wealth, non-decreasing infant and child mortality, rising or persistent female unemployment, and weak family planning (FP) programs. As before, results show mixed evidence in some of them.

The effects of increasing the level of **education** or improving its quality have perhaps the most lasting impacts on a society. Literature shows the benefits of better education and its support to development and well-being. One of them is the potential contribution to the reduction of fertility, since more educated women have lower fertility (Askew et al., 2017; Gebreselassie, 2012; Hertrich, 2017; Shapiro, 2015; Shapiro & Tenikue, 2017; Westoff & Cross, 2006). It decreases unwanted fertility through increased contraceptive use and wanted fertility through reduction of desired family size (Bongaarts, 2017; Caldwell et al., 1992; Casterline, 2017; Fuchs & Goujon, 2014; Lesthaeghe, 1989; Uchudi, 2001). Also, education contributes to decreasing fertility by delaying sexual activity, marriage, and initiation of childbearing (Chemhaka & Odimegwu, 2019; United Nations, 2002). In this regard, comparative studies show that having more educated women is correlated to lower fertility (Kebede, Goujon, & Lutz, 2019; Shapiro, 2010; Shapiro et al., 2013; Shapiro & Gebreselassie, 2008). Also, increasing female education is correlated to decreasing fertility in several countries[2]: Benin (Capo-chichi & Juarez, 2001), Eswatini (Chemhaka & Odimegwu, 2019), Ghana (Agyei-Mensah & Owoo, 2015; Derose & Ezeh, 2005), Namibia (Indongo & Pazvakawambwa, 2012), Rwanda (Ndahindwa et al., 2014; Westoff, 2013), Uganda (Kabagenyi et al., 2015), South Africa (Moultrie & Timaeus, 2003), and Zambia (Chola & Michelo, 2016). As far as fertility stalls are concerned, it has been shown that they occurred after periods of non-increasing schooling in several countries, as in Côte d'Ivoire and Cameroon (Kebede et al., 2019); D.R. Congo (Kebede et al., 2019; Romaniuk, 2011); Congo, Niger, Nigeria, and Zambia (Goujon et al., 2015; Kebede et al., 2019); Gambia, Mali, and Mozambique (Goujon et al., 2015); Kenya (Askew et al., 2017; Bongaarts, 2006; Ezeh et al., 2009; Goujon et al., 2015; Kebede et al., 2019; Odwe et al., 2015); and Tanzania (Ezeh et al., 2009; Goujon et al., 2015; Kebede et al., 2019). For instance, Goujon et al. (2015) use reconstructed data on population by age and education to show that eight out of ten countries classified under the stall category had a stall in the progress of education during the 1980s. Conversely, fertility stalls are less common in countries with no evidence of an education stall (Goujon et al., 2015). In contrast, no supporting evidence has been found in Algeria, Egypt, and Tunisia, where fertility and schooling increased in parallel (Al Zalak & Goujon, 2017; Ouadah-Bedidi et al., 2012). In Egypt, high levels of unemployment among the most educated women translated into increased fertility. On the other hand, mixed evidence exists in Ghana (Agyei-Mensah, 2006; Askew et al., 2017; Bongaarts, 2006) and Zimbabwe (Ezeh et al., 2009; Goujon et al., 2015; Kebede et al., 2019; Ndagurwa & Odimegwu, 2019), since results show education accounts for stalls in some studies while it does not in others.

Female labor increases the opportunity cost of having a child. Around 16% of African women are currently working in contrast to 48% and 63% in South and Southeast Asia and Latin America, respectively (World Bank, 2020). However, this lower rate should be nuanced, as a significant share of female work in Africa is informal or in agriculture and not visible in the statistics (Romaniuk, 2011). In Africa, women are usually in charge of parenting, and their time should be shared between working and caring for the children. Hence, there is an inverse relation between fertility and female labor. The mechanism consists of lowering the desired number of children in exchange for greater involvement in work (Casterline, 2017; Dodoo & Frost, 2008; Uchudi, 2001). For instance, increased female participation in the labor market in Namibia contributed to the decline in fertility in the early 2000s (Indongo & Pazvakawambwa, 2012).

In this regard, long-term **female unemployment** can lead women to rethink their desired number of children. In Egypt, the persistent high rate of unemployment among women over age 25 contributed to the increase in fertility (Al Zalak & Goujon, 2017). Also, fewer women were working than before at the time of stalled fertility in Nigeria and Rwanda (Garenne, 2008). In contrast, increases in female labor were registered during the stalled periods in Ghana and Madagascar (Garenne, 2008), Kenya and Tanzania (Ezeh et al., 2009; Garenne, 2008), Uganda (Ezeh et al., 2009), and Zimbabwe (Ezeh et al., 2009; Muza, 2019; Ndagurwa & Odimegwu, 2019). Overall, there is mixed evidence between female unemployment and stalls.

Under-five mortality in Africa has decreased from 180 in 1990 to 75.8 children per thousand in 2019 (World Bank, 2020); however, it has increased in several countries (Tabutin & Schoumaker, 2004). Under-five mortality in Africa is 4.7 times higher than in Latin America and 1.9 times higher than in South and Southeast Asia.

According to the demographic transition theory, mortality decline – and especially child mortality decline – is a key factor in the fertility decline (Bongaarts, 2008; Caldwell et al., 1992; Casterline, 2017; Shapiro, 2010, 2015; Shapiro et al., 2013; Shapiro & Gebreselassie, 2008; Shapiro & Tambashe, 2002). In SSA, the reduction in under-five mortality explains 30% and 35% of the total decline in fertility in urban and rural areas in 31 countries (Shapiro & Tenikue, 2017). In Benin and Ghana, research shows substantial reductions in fertility after decreases in under-five mortality (Agyei-Mensah & Owoo, 2015; Capo-chichi & Juarez, 2001). Leveling off in under-five mortality was accompanied by fertility stalls in Ghana (Agyei-Mensah, 2006; Bongaarts, 2006; Garenne, 2008), Kenya (Bongaarts, 2006; Garenne, 2008; Gebreselassie, 2012; Westoff & Cross, 2006), and Zimbabwe (Gebreselassie, 2012). In contrast, stalled fertility occurred despite decreasing infant and child mortality in Cameroon, Chad, Congo, D.R. Congo, Côte d'Ivoire, Gabon, Lesotho, Niger, and Zambia (Shapiro & Tenikue, 2017); Rwanda (Garenne, 2008; Gebreselassie, 2012; Westoff, 2013); and Madagascar, Nigeria, and Tanzania (Garenne, 2008).

Since **HIV** was declared a pandemic in the late 1980s, African governments, especially in SSA, shifted priorities towards reducing the infected cases and containing the infection (Askew et al., 2017). HIV has several effects on fertility. It contributes to lower fertility by decreasing sexual activity to avoid getting infected and marital dissolution after infection, as in Ghana (Agyei-Mensah, 2006) and Kenya (Magadi & Agwanda, 2010), and by increasing the use of condoms during sexual intercourse to prevent contagion, as in Namibia (Shemeikka et al., 2005). The increase in intrauterine deaths, as in Kenya (Magadi & Agwanda, 2010) and South Africa (Moultrie & Timaeus, 2003), also contributes to lower fertility. On the other hand, HIV may also contribute positively to fertility through several mechanisms. The increase in under-five mortality, as in countries strongly affected by HIV/AIDS, may lead to birth replacement. For instance, in Kenya (Magadi & Agwanda, 2010; Westoff & Cross, 2006) and South Africa (Houle et al., 2016) women who have recently lost a child report wanting another one. Birth intervals are also decreased, including through reduced breastfeeding, as in Kenya (Magadi & Agwanda, 2010) and South Africa (Garenne, Tollman, Collinson, & Kahn, 2007). In addition, new and more effective treatments for the prevention of mother-to-child transmission could increase the possibility of bearing more children. Apparently, women infected with HIV are increasing their fertility in South Africa due to the lower risk of transmission (Moultrie et al., 2008). As a result, the fertility trend will depend on which of the two effects counterbalances the other and how they evolve over time. For instance, Lewis, Ronsmans, Ezeh, and Gregson (2004), using pooled data from Burkina Faso, Cameroon, Ghana, Kenya, Madagascar, Mali, Senegal, Tanzania, Togo, Uganda, Zambia, and Zimbabwe, show that an increase in HIV prevalence of one percentage point leads to a decline in total fertility of 0.37%. In contrast, Gori, Lupi, Manfredi, and Sodini (2020) conclude that HIV has triggered reversals of fertility in SSA, while Sánchez-Páez and Schoumaker (2021) find that the fertility of HIV-positive women may have contributed to fertility stalls. In this regard, HIV prevalence was found as one of the causes of stalled fertility, mainly due to replacement births, in Kenya (Magadi & Agwanda, 2010; Westoff & Cross, 2006) and South Africa (Garenne et al., 2007; Houle et al., 2016). HIV might also substantially delay the fertility transition in SSA by halting economic development (Gori et al., 2020).

As mentioned previously, African governments focused their efforts on the HIV pandemic. Budgetary constraints forced them to prioritize certain initiatives to the detriment of others, such as **family planning programs**. The idea behind FP programs is to increase the total demand for contraception, promote the supply of contraceptives, and reduce unmet need (Bongaarts, 2011). Thus, reducing fertility could be addressed by decreasing both, desired and unwanted fertility (Casterline & Agyei-Mensah, 2017). In general terms, the lack of organized FP programs in Africa has been identified as part of the problem leading to fertility stalls since they have generally been considered weak and a low priority for governments (Bongaarts, 2008, 2017; Fuchs & Goujon, 2014; Ross et al., 2004). However, in the specific case of Ghana, no link was found between FP programs and the stalls (Bongaarts, 2006), unlike Kenya, where there were shortages of contraceptive supplies while fertility was stalling (Westoff & Cross, 2006). It is worth noting that Ghana is one of the cases where the stalled period was recognized as possibly spurious. Although strong FP programs contribute to fertility decline, especially in pre-transitional countries (Bongaarts, 2017; Jadhav & Short Fabic, 2019; Lesthaeghe, 2014), evidence regarding the link between investments in family planning programs and fertility stalls in Africa is limited. For instance, we only have found evidence for D.R. Congo, where the lack of a national FP program reflects the increasing fertility (Romaniuk, 2011).

Wealth is usually inversely correlated with fertility, with the expectation of wealthier families having fewer children (Bongaarts, 2017). To rank families according to wealth, researchers have used indicators at the micro level – household income or wealth indexes computed from housing characteristics – and at the macro level – gross domestic product (GDP) per capita. In either case, they aim to measure the well-being of a family or the stage of development of a country from an economic perspective. Africa is the least developed region with the lowest income levels worldwide despite GDP per capita having increased steadily since the mid-1990s. Currently, per-capita GDP in Africa is almost six times lower than in Latin America and four times lower than in South and Southeast Asia (World Bank, 2020).

Literature finds in some countries an inverse relation between fertility and wealth (Bongaarts, 2017; Casterline, 2001; Chola & Michelo, 2016; Finlay et al., 2018; Fuchs & Goujon, 2014; Kabagenyi et al., 2015; Lesthaeghe, 1989), while in others, fertility decline is not explained by wealth indicators (Garenne & Joseph, 2002; Gurmu & Mace, 2008; Shapiro, 2010; Shapiro et al., 2013; Shapiro & Gebreselassie, 2008; Shapiro & Tambashe, 2002). From country-case research, the link between wealth and fertility stalls also presents mixed evidence. Some studies find that the decline in wealth accounts for fertility stalls, such as in Egypt (Eltigani, 2003); Kenya (Askew et al., 2017; Bongaarts, 2006; Garenne, 2008); and Madagascar, Nigeria, and Tanzania (Garenne, 2008), unlike in Ghana (Askew et al., 2017; Bongaarts, 2006; Garenne, 2008); Kenya, Tanzania, and Uganda (Ezeh et al., 2009), Rwanda (Garenne, 2008; Westoff, 2013); and Zimbabwe (Ezeh et al., 2009; Muza, 2019).

Conclusions

Fertility decline provides health and economic benefits and improves the lives of women and children (Bongaarts & Casterline, 2013). The current African population is around 1,340 million and, according to the ongoing fertility rates, is expected to triple by the end of the century (United Nations, 2020). The pace of decline in Africa, especially in sub-Saharan countries, will play a large role in the magnitude of future growth in world population (Gerland et al., 2017). Pace of decline is a positive function of social and economic change, economic aspirations and expectations, improvement in the provision of birth control services, and reduction in the psychological and social costs of birth control (Casterline, 2001). Uncertainty and failure to meet the objectives of these determinants have led to the transition taking longer than expected and to the process being exceptional. Studying stalls is important, as they represent somewhat extreme situations and highlight the slow and uncertain path in fertility transitions. A key factor in this uncertainty is the speed at which fertility will decline, including whether ongoing stalls will persist and/or new stalls will be found.

We summarize some of the main findings:

1 Fertility stalls in Africa have been identified in a large number of countries at some point. About three-quarters of African countries have been included in the stalled category at any point over the last 20 years. There is no general agreement on the number of stalls, when they occurred, and which countries did indeed experience fertility stalls. Differences in definitions of stalls and methods, as well as data quality issues, may lead to varying conclusions.
2 It is important to focus on trends within countries. Stalls are more common in capital cities than in other urban and rural areas, even in settings without fertility reversal at the national

level (Schoumaker & Sánchez-Páez, 2020). As far as urban areas are often pioneers in terms of demographic changes, the widespread stalls in urban areas may herald future stalls at the national level.

3 A key factor in stalls seems to be the fairly high and stable demand for children. Existing studies suggest that fertility stalls are – at least to some extent – stalls in wanted fertility and that failure of the ideal number of children to decline has contributed to stalls (Ndagurwa & Odimegwu, 2019; Nzimande & Mugwendere, 2018). Unless fertility preferences decrease substantially, it is probable that stalls will persist and other stalls will occur.

4 Fertility stalls occurred in some countries at a time when investments in family planning programs were slowed down. Even if demand for children decreases, securing fertility transition will clearly depend on strengthening FP programs. High desired family size, high unmet need for contraception, and ineffective ways to stop childbearing are responsible for high fertility (Bongaarts & Casterline, 2013; Casterline & Agyei-Mensah, 2017). The implementation or strengthening of FP programs can modify contraceptive demand (Bongaarts, 2011).

5 Child mortality, HIV/AIDS, changes in wealth, female employment, and female education have all – to varying extents – been analyzed in the search for causes of stalls. Overall, the evidence is mixed and varies across countries. Even if improvements in socioeconomic variables have a proven effect on fertility decline, the reversal of one of them does not necessarily translate into a fertility stall. Deteriorating economic conditions do not systematically lead to higher fertility. Overall, stagnation is more likely to occur as a result of the interaction of some variables than the individual effect of a single one, unless its impact is extremely strong. Mixed evidence may suggest that the analysis should be done on a case-by-case basis.

6 Moreover, analyses are fraught with difficulties. The impact of changes is probably lagged, such as the effect of mortality on fertility. Effects may be non-linear. Some factors – such as the spread of HIV/AIDS – may have several effects on fertility in opposite directions, which may unfold differently over time. Absence of strong evidence regarding the effects of these variables on stalls does not mean they are not important. Taking a long-term perspective, it is likely that a sustainable fertility decline will not occur with some improvements in health, education, and standard of living. Female education and labor contribute to reduce the desired number of children (Casterline, 2017). Improvements in both indicators will favor a better standard of living for African women.

7 As far as the proximate determinants of fertility are concerned, the role of postpartum insusceptibility in explaining stalls seems to have been somewhat neglected. Shortening of the insusceptibility period is one of the factors consistently associated with stalls. The contribution of the decrease in postpartum insusceptibility to increasing fertility is nothing new (Bongaarts, Frank, & Lesthaeghe, 1984). It seems it is also an important factor in stalls. Unless this decrease is offset by contraceptive use, stalls are likely to endure. While abortion may also influence fertility trends, we lack information on the levels and trends of abortion and on its role on fertility stalls.

8 Some other aspects also seem to have been somewhat neglected in existing research. For instance, few studies look at changes by age groups or take a cohort perspective. Parity progression ratios have also not been used but could be useful – for instance, to evaluate the role of gender composition of living children on the progression to higher parities. The role of men has also often been neglected in fertility analysis, even though they have a higher TFR than women (Schoumaker, 2019a). Africa is still patriarchal, which favors

fertility remaining at high levels (Dodoo & Frost, 2008), and men affect, among others, the decision to use contraceptives (Uchudi, 2001)

9 Predicting forthcoming stalls may be more difficult than it seems. There may be clues that warn that the fall in fertility will be halted or at least slowed down, as shown by trends in the proximate determinants of fertility and in ideal family size. But things could change rapidly and unexpectedly. It may prove as difficult as predicting when fertility decline will resume after a stall.

Research agenda

Further research is thus needed to continue the process of understanding the dynamics of fertility stalls. There are still gaps in the literature that need to be filled.

1 Some cases of stalls, such as Kenya or Ghana, have been widely studied and documented. However, recent findings show that there is strong evidence of fertility stagnation in countries such as Cameroon, Egypt, Namibia, Zambia, or Zimbabwe but they have been little explored.
2 More research should be conducted at the subnational level. Recent evidence shows that some stalls at the country level can be explained, at least partly, by composition effects. Research is needed to understand the differences of the fertility transition in urban and rural areas.
3 Research has focused primarily on contraceptive use, and to a lesser extent on sexual activity, to explain fertility patterns in Africa. However, evidence is lacking on the causes leading to reduced breastfeeding and postpartum abstinence and, therefore, their effects on fertility.
4 The literature should delve into the demographic transition driven by the lengthening of birth intervals and the extent to which they mean a decrease in demand for children or for the postponement of childbearing. Since period TFRs are sensitive to drastic changes in birth intervals, research linking birth intervals and stalls may be of interest, as may research comparing period TFR and cohort fertility and analysis of age-specific fertility rate patterns.
5 Little is known about the most sensitive determinants that contribute to high levels of demand for children and the reasons the improvement in socioeconomic conditions has not been accompanied by a fall in fertility, as has been seen in other less developed regions.
6 Research linking HIV to stalls is still lacking. It is important to know if there is a connection between them and, if so, what the transmission mechanisms are.
7 Although female labor, child mortality, or wealth appear as potential causes of fertility stalls, little research has focused on them. The mixed evidence found so far provides an opportunity to refine the analyses and explore in greater detail.
8 More and more research is analyzing fertility differences between men and women, as well as their roles in reproductive decisions. The direct influence of men on women's fertility outcomes and whether they are contributing to continued high fertility rates in Africa needs to be further explored.

Acknowledgments

We thank Dominique Tabutin for his comments on an earlier version of this chapter. This work was supported by the Fonds de la Recherche Scientifique – FNRS – under Grant No. T.0210.19 (STALLS).

Notes

1 Gendell (1985, 1989) proposes four requirements for a period to be considered stalled fertility. First, the TFR should have dropped from 5.0 by at least 20%. Second, TFR should have been decreasing by 0.2 per year for at least 5 years before stalling. Third, substantial deceleration as at least a halving of the rate of decline in one period compared with the rate that immediately preceded it, if the first two requirements have been met. Fourth, cases where the stall occurred at rates near the replacement level should be excluded.

2 However, earlier evidence from two comparative studies, both in the same 29 countries (Garenne & Joseph, 2002; Shapiro & Tambashe, 2002) and country-case studies in Egypt (Amin & Lloyd, 2002), Kenya (Shreffler & Dodoo, 2009), and Mozambique (Hayford & Agadjanian, 2012) show fertility decline during the 1990s is not fully accounted for by increased education.

References

Agyei-Mensah, S. (2006). Fertility transition in Ghana: Looking back and looking forward. *Population, Space and Place*, *12*(6), 461–477. https://doi.org/10.1002/psp.425

Agyei-Mensah, S., & Owoo, N. S. (2015). Explaining regional fertility variations in Ghana. *Journal of Population Research*, *32*(3), 157–172. https://doi.org/10.1007/s12546-015-9147-7

Al Zalak, Z., & Goujon, A. (2017). Exploring the fertility trend in Egypt. *Demographic Research*, *37*(32), 995–1030. https://doi.org/10.4054/DemRes.2017.37.32

Amin, S., & Lloyd, C. B. (2002). Women's lives and rapid fertility decline: Some lessons from Bangladesh and Egypt. *Population Research and Policy Review*, *21*(4), 275–317. https://doi.org/10.1023/A:1020030616075

Arnaldo, C. (2004). Regional fertility trends in Mozambique. *Journal of Population Research*, *21*(2), 177–197. https://doi.org/10.1007/BF03031897

Askew, I., Maggwa, N., & Obare, F. (2017). Fertility transitions in Ghana and Kenya: Trends, determinants, and implications for policy and programs. *Population and Development Review*, *43*(Suppl. 1), 289–307. https://doi.org/10.1111/padr.12010

Blacker, J., Opiyo, C., Jasseh, M., Sloggett, A., & Ssekamatte-Ssebuliba, J. (2005). Fertility in Kenya and Uganda: A comparative study of trends and determinants. *Population Studies*, *59*(3), 355–373. https://doi.org/10.1080/00324720500281672

Bongaarts, J. (1978). A framework for analyzing the proximate determinants of fertility. *Population and Development Review*, *4*(1), 105–132. https://doi.org/10.2307/1972149

Bongaarts, J. (2006). The causes of stalling fertility transitions. *Studies in Family Planning*, *37*(1), 1–16. https://doi.org/10.1111/j.1728-4465.2006.00079.x

Bongaarts, J. (2008). Fertility transitions in developing countries: Progress or stagnation? *Studies in Family Planning*, *39*(2), 105–110. https://doi.org/10.1111/j.1728-4465.2008.00157.x

Bongaarts, J. (2011). Can family planning programs reduce high desired family size in sub-Saharan Africa? *International Perspectives on Sexual and Reproductive Health*, *37*(4), 209–216. Retrieved from www.guttmacher.org/sites/default/files/article_files/3720911.pdf

Bongaarts, J. (2015). Modeling the fertility impact of the proximate determinants: Time for a tune-up. *Demographic Research*, *33*(19), 535–560. https://doi.org/10.4054/DemRes.2015.33.19

Bongaarts, J. (2017). Africa's unique fertility transition. *Population and Development Review*, *43*(Suppl. 1), 39–58. https://doi.org/10.1111/j.1728-4457.2016.00164.x

Bongaarts, J., & Casterline, J. B. (2013). Fertility transition: Is sub-Saharan Africa different? *Population and Development Review*, *38*(Suppl. 1), 153–168. https://doi.org/10.1111/j.1728-4457.2013.00557.x

Bongaarts, J., Frank, O., & Lesthaeghe, R. (1984). The proximate determinants of fertility in sub-Saharan Africa. *Population and Development Review*, *10*(3), 511–537. https://doi.org/10.2307/1973518

Burger, R. P., Burger, R., & Rossouw, L. (2012). The fertility transition in South Africa: A retrospective panel data analysis. *Development Southern Africa*, *29*(5), 738–755. https://doi.org/10.1080/0376835X.2012.731779

Caldwell, J. C. (1994). Fertility in sub-Saharan Africa: Status and prospects. *Population and Development Review*, *20*(1), 179–187. https://doi.org/10.2307/2137636

Caldwell, J. C., Orubuloye, I. O., & Caldwell, P. (1992). Fertility decline in Africa: A new type of transition? *Population and Development Review*, *18*(2), 211–242. https://doi.org/10.2307/1973678

Capo-chichi, V., & Juarez, F. (2001). Is fertility declining in Benin? *Studies in Family Planning, 32*(1), 25–40. https://doi.org/10.1111/j.1728-4465.2001.00025.x

Casterline, J. B. (2001). The pace of fertility transition: National patterns in the second half of the twentieth century. *Population and Development Review, 27*(Suppl. 1), 17–52. Retrieved from www.jstor.org/stable/3115248

Casterline, J. B. (2017). Prospects for fertility decline in Africa. *Population and Development Review, 43*(Suppl. 1), 3–18. https://doi.org/10.1111/padr.12055

Casterline, J. B., & Agyei-Mensah, S. (2017). Fertility desires and the course of fertility decline in sub-Saharan Africa. *Population and Development Review, 43*(Suppl. 1), 84–111. https://doi.org/10.1111/padr.12030

Chemhaka, G. B., & Odimegwu, C. (2019). The proximate determinants of fertility in Eswatini. *African Journal of Reproductive Health, 23*(2), 65–75. https://doi.org/10.29063/ajrh2019/v23i2.7

Chemhaka, G. B., Odimegwu, C., Zwane, E., Chadoka, N., & Gumbo, J. D. (2016). Estimation of Swaziland fertility: What do the methods tell us? *Southern African Journal of Demography, 17*(1), 7–66.

Chola, M., & Michelo, C. (2016). Examining the underlying determinants of fertility rates in Zambia: Evidence form the 2007 Zambia Demographic and Health Survey. *African Population Studies, 30*(2), 2318–2327. https://doi.org/10.11564/30-2-829

Cleland, J., Machiyama, K., & Casterline, J. B. (2019). Fertility preferences and subsequent childbearing in Africa and Asia: A synthesis of evidence from longitudinal studies in 28 populations. *Population Studies*, 1–21. https://doi.org/10.1080/00324728.2019.1672880

Cleland, J., Onouha, N., & Timaeus, I. (1994). *The onset of fertility transition in sub-Saharan Africa* (T. Locoh & V. Hertich, Eds.). Liege: Ordina Editions, pp. 1–20. Retrieved from https://pdfs.semanticscholar.org/0ff6/d57ab3056538a8048eff6e82edce46305265.pdf

Cohen, B. (1998). The emerging fertility transition in sub-Saharan Africa. *World Development, 26*(8), 1431–1461. https://doi.org/10.1016/S0305-750X(98)00058-8

Derose, L. F., & Ezeh, A. C. (2005). Men's influence on the onset and progress of fertility decline in Ghana, 1988–98. *Population Studies, 59*(2), 197–210. https://doi.org/10.1080/00324720500099496

Dickson, K. S., Adde, K. S., & Ahinkorah, B. (2018). Socio-economic determinants of abortion among women in Mozambique and Ghana: Evidence from Demographic and Health Survey. *Archives of Public Health, 76*, 36–46. https://doi.org/10.1186/s13690-018-0286-0

Dodoo, F. N.-A., & Frost, A. E. (2008). Gender in African population research: The fertility/reproductive health example. *Annual Review of Sociology, 34*, 431–452. https://doi.org/10.1146/annurev.soc.34.040507.134552

Eloundou-Enyegue, P., Giroux, S., & Tenikue, M. (2017). African transitions and fertility inequality: A demographic Kuznets hypothesis. *Population and Development Review, 43*(Suppl. 1), 59–83. https://doi.org/10.1111/padr.12034

Eltigani, E. E. (2003). Stalled fertility decline in Egypt, why? *Population and Environment, 25*(1), 41–59. https://doi.org/10.1023/A:1025547622370

El-Zeini, L. O. (2008). The path to replacement fertility in Egypt: Acceptance, preference, and achievement. *Studies in Family Planning, 39*(3), 161–176. https://doi.org/10.1111/j.1728-4465.2008.164.x

Ezeh, A. C., Mberu, B. U., & Emina, J. O. (2009). Stall in fertility decline in Eastern African countries: Regional analysis of patterns, determinants and implications. *Philosophical Transactions of the Royal Society B, 364*(1532), 2991–3007. https://doi.org/10.1098/rstb.2009.0166

Finlay, J. E., Mejía-Guevara, I., & Akachi, Y. (2018). Inequality in total fertility rates and the proximate determinants of fertility in 21 sub-Saharan African countries. *PLoS One, 13*(9), e0203344. https://doi.org/10.1371/journal.pone.0203344

Frank, O., & McNicoll, G. (1987). An interpretation of fertility and population policy in Kenya. *Population and Development Review, 13*(2), 209–243. https://doi.org/10.2307/1973192

Fuchs, R., & Goujon, A. (2014). *World population and human capital in the 21st century* (W. Lutz, W. P. Butz, & S. KC, Eds.). Oxford: Oxford University Press, pp. 147–225. https://doi.org/10.1093/acprof:oso/9780198703167.003.0004

Gaisie, S. K. (1998). Fertility transition in Botswana. *Journal of Contemporary African Studies, 16*(2), 277–296. https://doi.org/10.1080/02589009808729631

Garenne, M. (2008). Situations of fertility stall in sub-Saharan Africa. *African Population Studies, 23*(2), 173–188. https://doi.org/10.11564/23-2-319

Garenne, M., & Joseph, V. (2002). The timing of the fertility transition in sub-Saharan Africa. *World Development, 30*(10), 1835–1843. https://doi.org/10.1016/S0305-750X(02)00069-4

Garenne, M. L. (2004). Age at marriage and modernisation in sub-Saharan Africa. *Southern African Journal of Demography*, *9*(2), 59–79.

Garenne, M. L. (2011). Testing for fertility stalls in demographic and health surveys. *Population Health Metrics*, *9*, 59. https://doi.org/10.1186/1478-7954-9-59

Garenne, M. L., Tollman, S. M., Collinson, M. A., & Kahn, K. (2007). Fertility trends and net reproduction in Agincourt, rural South Africa, 1992–2004. *Scandinavian Journal of Public Health*, *35*(Suppl. 69), 68–76. https://doi.org/10.1080/14034950701355650

Gebreselassie, T. (2012). *The demographic transition and development in Africa: The unique case of Ethiopia* (C. Teller & A. Hailemariam, Eds.). Netherlands: Springer, pp. 19–44. https://doi.org/10.1007/978-90-481-8918-2_2

Gendell, M. (1985). *Stalls in the fertility decline in Costa Rica, Korea, and Sri Lanka*. World Bank Staff Working Papers No. 693 [Research report]. World Bank. Retrieved from http://documents.worldbank.org/curated/en/654971468770654787/Stalls-in-the-fertility-decline-in-Costa-Rica-Korea-and-Sri-Lanka

Gendell, M. (1989). Stalls in the fertility decline in Costa Rica and South Korea. *International Family Planning Perspectives*, *15*(1), 15–21. https://doi.org/10.2307/2133274

Gerland, P., Biddlecom, A., & Kantorova, V. (2017). Patterns of fertility decline and the impact of alternative scenarios of future fertility change in sub-Saharan Africa. *Population and Development Review*, *43*(Suppl. 1), 21–38. https://doi.org/10.1111/padr.12011

Gori, L., Lupi, E., Manfredi, P., & Sodini, M. (2020). A contribution to the theory of economic development and the demographic transition: Fertility reversal under the HIV epidemic. *Journal of Demographic Economics*, *86*(2), 125–155. https://doi.org/10.1017/dem.2019.21

Goujon, A., Lutz, W., & KC, S. (2015). Education stalls and subsequent stalls in African fertility: A descriptive overview. *Demographic Research*, *33*(47), 1281–1296. https://doi.org/10.4054/DemRes.2015.33.47

Guillaume, A. (2003). The role of abortion in the fertility transition in Abidjan (Côte d'Ivoire) during the 1990s. *Population*, *58*(6), 657–686. https://doi.org/10.3917/popu.306.0741

Gurmu, E., & Mace, R. (2008). Fertility decline driven by poverty: The case of Addis Ababa, Ethiopia. *Journal of Biosocial Science*, *40*(3), 339–358. https://doi.org/10.1017/S002193200700260X

Hayford, S. R., & Agadjanian, V. (2012). From desires to behavior: Moderating factors in a fertility transition. *Demographic Research*, *26*(20), 511–542. https://doi.org/10.4054/DemRes.2012.26.20

Hertrich, V. (2017). Trends in age at marriage and the onset of fertility transition in sub-Saharan Africa. *Population and Development Review*, *43*(Suppl. 1), 112–137. https://doi.org/10.1111/padr.12043

Houle, B., Pantazis, A., Kabudula, C., Tollman, S., & Clark, S. J. (2016). Social patterns and differentials in the fertility transition in the context of HIV/AIDS: Evidence from population surveillance, rural South Africa, 1993–2013. *Population Health Metrics*, *14*(1), 10–20. https://doi.org/10.1186/s12963-016-0079-z

Howse, K. (2015). What is fertility stalling and why does it matter? *Population Horizons*, *12*(1), 13–23. https://doi.org/10.1515/pophzn-2015-0003

Ibisomi, L. D. G. (2008). Fertility transition in Nigeria: Exploring the role of desired number of children. *African Population Studies*, *23*(2), 207–222. https://doi.org/10.11564/23-2-321

Ibisomi, L. D. G., Williams, J., Collinson, M. A., & Tollman, S. (2014). The stall in fertility decline in rural, northeast, South Africa: The contribution of a self-settled, Mozambican, refugee sub-population. *African Population Studies*, *28*(Suppl. 1), 590–600. https://doi.org/10.11564/28-0-517

Indongo, N., & Pazvakawambwa, L. (2012). Determinants of fertility in Namibia. *African Journal of Reproductive Health*, *16*(4), 50–57. www.ajrh.info/index.php/ajrh/article/view/1195

Jadhav, A., & Short Fabic, M. (2019). Dynamic stagnation: Reasons for contraceptive non-use in context of fertility stall. *Gates Open Research*, *3*, 1458. https://doi.org/10.12688/gatesopenres.12990.1

Johnson, K., Abderrahim, N., & Rutstein, S. O. (2011). *Changes in the direct and indirect determinants of fertility in sub-Saharan Africa*. DHS Analytical Studies No. 23. Rockville, MD: ICF Macro. Retrieved from https://dhsprogram.com/pubs/pdf/AS23/AS23.pdf

Johnson-Hanks, J. (2007). Natural intentions: Fertility decline in the African Demographic and Health Surveys. *American Journal of Sociology*, *112*(4), 1008–1043. https://doi.org/10.1086/508791

Kabagenyi, A., Reid, A., Rutaremwa, G., Atuyambe, L. M., & Ntozi, J. P. M. (2015). Has Uganda experienced any stalled fertility transitions? Reflecting on the last four decades (1973–2011). *Fertility Research and Practice*, *1*(1), 14–23. https://doi.org/10.1186/s40738-015-0006-1

Kebede, E., Goujon, A., & Lutz, W. (2019). Stalls in Africa's fertility decline partly result from disruptions in female education. *Proceedings of the National Academy of Sciences*, *116*(8), 2891–2896. https://doi.org/10.1073/pnas.1717288116

Kirk, D., & Pillet, B. (1998). Levels, trends, and differentials in sub-Saharan Africa in the 1980s and 1990s. *Studies in Family Planning*, *29*(1), 1–22. https://doi.org/10.2307/172178

Laelago, T., Habtu, Y., & Yohannes, S. (2019). Proximate determinants of fertility in Ethiopia. An application of revised Bongaarts model. *Reproductive Health*, *16*(13), 1–9. https://doi.org/10.1186/s12978-019-0677-x

Lesthaeghe, R. (1989). *Reproduction and social organization in sub-Saharan Africa* (R. J. Lesthaeghe, Ed.). Berkeley, CA: University of California Press, pp. 475–506. Retrieved from https://publishing.cdlib.org/ucpressebooks/view?docId=ft2m3nb1cw&chunk.id=d0e50582&toc.depth=1&toc.id=d0e50582&brand=ucpress

Lesthaeghe, R. (2014). *The fertility transition in sub-Saharan Africa into the 21st century* (Research Report 14–823). Ann Arbor, MI: Population Studies Center, University of Michigan.

Lewis, J. J. C., Ronsmans, C., Ezeh, A., & Gregson, S. (2004). The population impact of HIV on fertility in sub-Saharan Africa. *AIDS*, *18*(Suppl. 2), S35–S43. https://doi.org/10.1097/00002030-200406002-00005

Machiyama, K. (2010). *A re-examination of recent fertility declines in sub-Saharan Africa*. DHS Working Papers No. 68. Rockville, MD: ICF Macro. Retrieved from https://dhsprogram.com/pubs/pdf/WP68/WP68.pdf

Magadi, M. A., & Agwanda, A. O. (2010). Investigating the association between HIV/AIDS and recent fertility patterns in Kenya. *Social Science & Medicine*, *71*(2), 335–344. https://doi.org/10.1016/j.socscimed.2010.03.040

Mbamaonyeukwu, C. J. (2000). Signs of fertility transition in Nigeria. *African Population Studies*, *15*(1), 23–42.

McNicoll, G. (1992). Changing fertility patterns and policies in the Third World. *Annual Review of Sociology*, *18*, 85–108. https://doi.org/10.1146/annurev.so.18.080192.000505

Moultrie, T. A., Hosegood, V., McGrath, N., Hill, C., Herbst, K., & Newell, M.-L. (2008). Refining the criteria for stalled fertility declines: An application to rural KwaZulu-Natal, South Africa, 1990–2005. *Studies in Family Planning*, *39*(1), 39–48. https://doi.org/10.1111/j.1728-4465.2008.00149.x

Moultrie, T. A., Sayi, T. S., & Timaeus, I. M. (2012). Birth intervals, postponement, and fertility decline in Africa: A new type of transition? *Population Studies*, *66*(3), 241–258. https://doi.org/10.1080/00324728.2012.701660

Moultrie, T. A., & Timaeus, I. M. (2003). The South African fertility decline: Evidence from two censuses and a Demographic and Health Survey. *Population Studies*, *57*(3), 265–283. https://doi.org/10.1080/0032472032000137808

Mturi, A., & Joshua, K. (2011). Falling fertility and increase in use of contraception in Zimbabwe. *African Journal of Reproductive Health*, *15*(2), 31–44. https://doi.org/10.4314/ajrh.v15i2.69621

Muhwava, W. (2002). The onset of fertility transition in Zimbabwe: A re-analysis of census and survey data using robust demographic techniques. *African Population Studies*, *17*(1), 1–17.

Muza, C. (2019). The fertility revolution in Zimbabwe with special regards to proximate determinants of fertility. *AUC Geographica*, *54*(2), 182–193. https://doi.org/10.14712/23361980.2019.16

Ndagurwa, P., & Odimegwu, C. (2019). Decomposition of Zimbabwe's stalled fertility change: A two-sex approach to estimating education and employment effects. *Journal of Population Research*, *36*, 35–63. https://doi.org/10.1007/s12546-019-09219-8

Ndahindwa, V., Kamanzi, C., Semakula, M., Abalikumwe, F., Hedt-Gauthier, B., & Thomson, D. R. (2014). Determinants of fertility in Rwanda in the context of a fertility transition: A secondary analysis of the 2010 Demographic and Health Survey. *Reproductive Health*, *11*, 87–95. https://doi.org/10.1186/1742-4755-11-87

Nzimande, N., & Mugwendere, T. (2018). Stalls in Zimbabwe fertility: Exploring determinants of recent fertility transition. *Southern African Journal of Demography*, *18*(1), 59–110. Retrieved from www.jstor.org/stable/e90022345

Odwe, G., Agwanda, A., & Khasakhala, A. (2015). *Trends in socio-economic differentials in fertility in Kenya*. Paper presented at PAA 2015 Annual Meeting. Retrieved from https://paa2015.princeton.edu/papers/152428

Onuoha, N. C., & Timaeus, I. M. (1995). Has a fertility transition begun in West Africa? *Journal of International Development*, 7(1), 93–116. https://doi.org/10.1002/jid.3380070107

Ouadah-Bedidi, Z., Vallin, J., & Bouchoucha, I. (2012). Unexpected developments in Maghrebian fertility. *Population & Societies*, *486*, 1–4. Retrieved from www.ined.fr/en/publications/editions/population-and-societies/unexpected-developments-maghrebian-fertility/

Palamuleni, M. E. (2010). Fertility decline in Malawi: An analysis of the proximate determinants. *Journal of Social Development in Africa, 25*(1), 1–8. https://doi.org/10.4314/jsda.v25i1.54277

Palamuleni, M. E. (2013). Estimates of fertility for South Africa based on Rele method, 1996–2011. *Journal of Human Ecology, 43*(3), 257–265. https://doi.org/10.1080/09709274.2013.11906633

Palamuleni, M. E. (2017). Determinants of fertility decline in Namibia: An analysis of the proximate determinants. *Bangladesh E-Journal of Sociology, 14*(2), 41–63. Retrieved from www.bangladeshsociology.org/Determinants14.2.pdf

Robinson, W. C., & Harbison, S. F. (1995). The fertility decline in Kenya. *Journal of International Development, 7*(1), 81–92. https://doi.org/10.1002/jid.3380070106

Romaniuk, A. (2011). Persistence of high fertility in tropical Africa: The case of the Democratic Republic of the Congo. *Population and Development Review, 37*(1), 1–28. https://doi.org/10.1111/j.1728-4457.2011.00388.x

Ross, J., Abel, E., & Abel, K. (2004). Plateaus during the rise of contraceptive prevalence. *International Family Planning Perspectives, 30*(1), 39–44. Retrieved from www.guttmacher.org/journals/ipsrh/2004/03/plateaus-during-rise-contraceptive-prevalence

Rossier, C., & Corker, J. (2017). Contemporary use of traditional contraception in sub-Saharan Africa. *Population and Development Review, 43*(Suppl. 1), 192–215. https://doi.org/10.1111/padr.12008

Sánchez-Páez, D. A., & Ortega, J. A. (2019). Reported patterns of pregnancy termination from Demographic and Health Surveys. *PLoS One, 14*(8), e0221178. https://doi.org/10.1371/journal.pone.0221178

Sánchez-Páez, D. A., & Schoumaker, B. (2020a). *What do we know about fertility stalls in Africa? A literature review.* UCLouvain, Centre for Demographic Research. Working Paper No. 16. Retrieved from https://cdn.uclouvain.be/groups/cms-editors-demo/isa/DT162s1.pdf

Sánchez-Páez, D. A., & Schoumaker, B. (2020b). *The role of proximate determinants and ideal family size on fertility stalls in capital cities of sub-Saharan Africa.* Paper presented at PAA 2020 Annual Meeting.

Sánchez-Páez, D. A., & Schoumaker, B. (2021). *Fertility trends in sub-Saharan Africa: Has HIV contributed to fertility stalls?* Paper presented at PAA 2021 Annual Meeting.

Sayi, T. S. (2016). *Stall fertility decline in Zimbabwe.* Paper presented at PAA 2016 Annual Meeting. Retrieved from https://uaps2015.princeton.edu/papers/151666

Schoumaker, B. (2009). *Stalls in fertility transition in sub-Saharan Africa: Real or spurious?* UCLouvain, Centre for Demographic Research. Working Paper No. 30. Retrieved from https://cdn.uclouvain.be/public/Exports%20reddot/demo/documents/DT_SPED_30_corrige.pdf

Schoumaker, B. (2019a). Male fertility around the world and over time: How different is it from female fertility? *Population and Development Review, 45*(3), 459–487. https://doi.org/10.1111/padr.12273

Schoumaker, B. (2019b). Stalls in fertility transitions in sub-Saharan Africa: Revisiting the evidence. *Studies in Family Planning, 50*(3), 257–278. https://doi.org/10.1111/sifp.12098

Schoumaker, B., & Sánchez-Páez, D. A. (2020). *Identifying fertility stalls by place of residence in sub-Saharan Africa.* Paper presented at PAA 2020 Annual Meeting.

Shapiro, D. (2010). Women's education and fertility transition in sub-Saharan Africa. *Vienna Yearbook of Population Research, 10*(1), 9–30. https://doi.org/10.1553/populationyearbook2012s9

Shapiro, D. (2015). Accelerating fertility decline in sub-Saharan Africa. *Population Horizons, 12*(1), 3–12. https://doi.org/10.1515/pophzn-2015-0002

Shapiro, D., & Gebreselassie, T. (2008). Fertility transition in sub-Saharan Africa: Falling and stalling. *African Population Studies, 23*(1), 3–23. https://doi.org/10.11564/23-1-310

Shapiro, D., & Hinde, A. (2017). On the pace of fertility decline in sub-Saharan Africa. *Demographic Research, 37*(40), 1327–1338. https://doi.org/10.4054/DemRes.2017.37.40

Shapiro, D., Kreider, A., Varner, C., & Sinha, M. (2013). *Ralentissements, résistances et ruptures dans les transitions démographiques* (D. Tabutin & B. Masquelier, Eds.). Belgium: Chaire Quetelet 2010, Université Catholique de Louvain, pp. 47–64. Retrieved from https://pdfs.semanticscholar.org/2529/db4af2c4385d493f1a7bc93238c9402a93bc.pdf

Shapiro, D., & Tambashe, B. O. (2002). Fertility transition in urban and rural areas of sub-Saharan Africa: Preliminary evidence of a three-stage process. *Journal of Africa Policy Studies, 8*(2), 103–127.

Shapiro, D., & Tenikue, M. (2017). Women's education, infant and child mortality, and fertility decline in rural and urban sub-Saharan Africa. *Demographic Research, 37*(21), 669–708. https://doi.org/10.4054/DemRes.2017.37.21

Shemeikka, R., Notkola, V., & Siiskonen, H. (2005). Fertility decline in North-Central Namibia: An assessment of fertility in the period 1960–2000 based on parish registers. *Demographic Research*, *13*(4), 83–116. https://doi.org/10.4054/DemRes.2005.13.4

Shreffler, K. M., & Dodoo, N.-A. F. (2009). The role of intergenerational transfers, land, and education in fertility transition in rural Kenya: The case of Nyeri district. *Population and Environment*, *30*(3), 75–92. https://doi.org/10.1007/s11111-009-0077-1

Singh, S., Remez, L., Sedgh, G., Kwok, L., & Onda, T. (2018). *Abortion worldwide 2017: Uneven progress and unequal access*. New York: Guttmacher Institute. Retrieved from www.guttmacher.org/sites/default/files/report_pdf/abortion-worldwide-2017.pdf

Sneeringer, S. E. (2009). *Fertility transition in sub-Saharan Africa: A comparative analysis of cohort trends in 30 countries*. DHS Comparative Reports No. 23. Rockville, MD: ICF Macro. Retrieved from https://dhsprogram.com/pubs/pdf/CR23/CR23.pdf

Spoorenberg, T., & Issaka Maga, H. (2018). Fertility compression in Niger: A study of fertility change by parity (1977–2011). *Demographic Research*, *39*(24), 685–700. https://doi.org/10.4054/DemRes.2018.39.24

Tabutin, D., & Schoumaker, B. (2004). The demography of sub-Saharan Africa from the 1950s to the 2000s. A survey of changes and a statistical assessment. *Population*, *59*(3–4), 457–519. https://doi.org/10.2307/3654914

Tabutin, D., & Schoumaker, B. (2020). The demography of sub-Saharan Africa in the 21st century: Transformations since 2000, outlook to 2050. *Population*, *75*(2–3), 163–286. https://doi.org/10.3917/popu.2002.0167

Timaeus, I. M., & Moultrie, T. A. (2008). On postponement and birth intervals. *Population and Development Review*, *34*(3), 483–510. https://doi.org/10.1111/j.1728-4457.2008.00233.x

Timaeus, I. M., & Moultrie, T. A. (2013). Distinguishing the impact of postponement, spacing and stopping on birth intervals: Evidence from a model with heterogeneous fecundity. *Journal of Biosocial Science*, *45*(3), 311–330. https://doi.org/10.1017/S0021932012000648

Uchudi, J. M. (2001). Spouses' socioeconomic characteristics and fertility differences in sub-Saharan Africa: Does spouse's education matter? *Journal of Biosocial Sciences*, *33*(4), 481–502. https://doi.org/10.1017/s0021932001004813

United Nations. (2002). *Fertility levels and trends in countries with intermediate levels of fertility*. New York: United Nations.

United Nations. (2020). *World population prospects*. New York: United Nations, Department of Economic and Social Affairs. Retrieved from https://population.un.org/wpp/

Walle, E. van de, & Foster, A. D. (1990). *Fertility decline in Africa: Assessments and prospects*. Technical paper No. WTP 125. Washington, DC: World Bank.

Westoff, C. F. (2013). The recent fertility transition in Rwanda. *Population and Development Review*, *38*(Suppl. 1), 169–178. https://doi.org/10.1111/j.1728-4457.2013.00558.x

Westoff, C. F., & Cross, A. R. (2006). *The stall in the fertility transition in Kenya*. DHS Analytical Studies No. 9. Calverton, MD: ORC Macro. Retrieved from http://dhsprogram.com/pubs/pdf/AS9/AS9.pdf

World Bank. (2020). *World Bank Open Data*. Retrieved from https://data.worldbank.org/

Appendix Table 12.1 Literature Review of Studies on Fertility Transition 2000–2020

Country	*Stall Period*	*Place of Stall*			*No Stall*
		National	*Urban*	*Rural*	
Northern Africa					
Algeria	2000–2010	Ouadah-Bedidi, Vallin, and Bouchoucha (2012)			United Nations (2002)
Egypt	1993–1998, 2006–2014	United Nations (2002), Eltigani (2003), Bongaarts (2008), El-Zeini (2008), Al Zalak and Goujon (2017)	Shapiro et al. (2013), Al Zalak and Goujon (2017)	Al Zalak and Goujon (2017)	Amin and Lloyd (2002), Bongaarts (2006)
Libya					United Nations (2002), Ouadah-Bedidi, Vallin, and Bouchoucha (2012)
Morocco	1992–2004	Bongaarts (2008)			United Nations (2002), Bongaarts (2006), Ouadah-Bedidi, Vallin, and Bouchoucha (2012), Shapiro et al. (2013)
Sudan					Garenne and Joseph (2002), United Nations (2002), Garenne (2008)
Tunisia	2000–2010	Ouadah-Bedidi, Vallin, and Bouchoucha (2012)			United Nations (2002)
Western Africa					
Benin	2001–2006, 2012–2017				Capo-chichi and Juarez (2001), Garenne and Joseph (2002), Bongaarts (2006), Bongaarts (2008), Garenne (2008)
Burkina Faso	1993–1999, 2003–2010	Machiyama (2010), Johnson, Abderrahim, and Rutstein (2011), Gebreselassie (2012), Shapiro et al. (2013), Finlay, Mejía-Guevara, and Akachi (2018)	Shapiro et al. (2013), Schoumaker and Sánchez-Páez (2020)[1]	Gebreselassie (2012)	Shapiro and Gebreselassie (2008), Schoumaker (2009), Sneeringer (2009), Shapiro (2010), Goujon, Lutz, and KC (2015), Howse (2015), Shapiro and Tenikue (2017), Kebede, Goujon, and Lutz (2019), Schoumaker (2019a)

(*Continued*)

Appendix Table 12.1 (Continued)

Country	*Stall Period*	*Place of Stall*			*No Stall*
		National	*Urban*	*Rural*	
Côte d'Ivoire	1994–2011	Howse (2015)		Shapiro and Tambashe (2002)	Garenne and Joseph (2002), Bongaarts (2006), Bongaarts (2008), Garenne (2008), Shapiro and Gebreselassie (2008), Schoumaker (2009), Sneeringer (2009), Shapiro (2010), Johnson, Abderrahim, and Rutstein (2011), Gebreselassie (2012), Shapiro et al. (2013), Goujon, Lutz, and KC (2015), Shapiro and Tenikue (2017), Finlay, Mejía-Guevara, and Akachi (2018), Kebede, Goujon, and Lutz (2019), Schoumaker (2019a), Schoumaker and Sánchez-Páez (2020)
Gambia	2004–2013	Bongaarts (2008), Howse (2015), Kebede, Goujon, and Lutz (2019)		Shapiro et al. (2013), Shapiro and Tenikue (2017)	Garenne and Joseph (2002), Shapiro and Tambashe (2002), Guillaume (2003)[1], Bongaarts (2006), Garenne (2008), Shapiro and Gebreselassie (2008), Schoumaker (2009), Sneeringer (2009), Shapiro (2010), Gebreselassie (2012), Goujon, Lutz, and KC (2015), Finlay, Mejía-Guevara, and Akachi (2018), Schoumaker (2019a), Schoumaker and Sánchez-Páez (2020)
Ghana	1993–2004, 2008–2014	Goujon, Lutz, and KC (2015)	Schoumaker and Sánchez-Páez (2020)[1]		
Guinea	1999–2012	Agyei-Mensah (2006), Bongaarts (2006), Bongaarts (2008), Garenne (2008), Shapiro and Gebreselassie (2008), Sneeringer (2009), Shapiro (2010), Garenne (2011), Askew, Maggwa, and Obare (2017)	Shapiro and Gebreselassie (2008), Shapiro et al. (2013), Schoumaker and Sánchez-Páez (2020)[2]	Shapiro and Gebreselassie (2008)	Garenne and Joseph (2002), Shapiro and Tambashe (2002), United Nations (2002), Derose and Ezeh (2005), Schoumaker (2009), Machiyama (2010), Johnson, Abderrahim, and Rutstein (2011), Gebreselassie (2012), Goujon, Lutz, and KC (2015), Howse (2015), Shapiro and Tenikue (2017), Finlay, Mejía-Guevara, and Akachi (2018), Kebede, Goujon, and Lutz (2019), Schoumaker (2019a)

Guinea-Bissau		Shapiro and Gebreselassie (2008), Gebreselassie (2012), Shapiro et al. (2013), Finlay, Mejía-Guevara, and Akachi (2018)	Gebreselassie (2012), Shapiro et al. (2013), Schoumaker and Sánchez-Páez (2020)[1]	Shapiro and Gebreselassie (2008), Gebreselassie (2012), Shapiro et al. (2013)	Bongaarts (2008), Schoumaker (2009), Sneeringer (2009), Shapiro (2010), Goujon, Lutz, and KC (2015), Howse (2015), Shapiro and Tenikue (2017), Kebede, Goujon, and Lutz (2019), Schoumaker (2019a),
Liberia					Goujon, Lutz, and KC (2015)
Mali	1987–2012	Shapiro et al. (2013), Goujon, Lutz, and KC (2015)	Schoumaker and Sánchez-Páez (2020)[1]	Shapiro and Tambashe (2002)	Garenne and Joseph (2002), Bongaarts (2006), Bongaarts (2008), Garenne (2008), Shapiro and Gebreselassie (2008), Schoumaker (2009), Sneeringer (2009), Shapiro (2010), Gebreselassie (2012), Howse (2015), Shapiro and Tenikue (2017), Finlay, Mejía-Guevara, and Akachi (2018), Schoumaker (2019a),
Niger	1992–2006	Shapiro and Tambashe (2002), Shapiro et al. (2013), Goujon, Lutz, and KC (2015), Spoorenberg and Issaka Maga (2018), Kebede, Goujon, and Lutz (2019)	Shapiro et al. (2013), Schoumaker and Sánchez-Páez (2020)[1]	Shapiro and Tambashe (2002), Shapiro and Tenikue (2017)	Garenne and Joseph (2002), Bongaarts (2006), Bongaarts (2008), Garenne (2008), Shapiro and Gebreselassie (2008), Schoumaker (2009), Sneeringer (2009), Shapiro (2010), Gebreselassie (2012), Howse (2015), Finlay, Mejía-Guevara, and Akachi (2018), Schoumaker (2019a)
Nigeria	2003–2013	Bongaarts (2008), Garenne (2008), Garenne (2011), Gebreselassie (2012), Shapiro et al. (2013), Goujon, Lutz, and KC (2015), Howse (2015), Kebede, Goujon, and Lutz (2019)	Gebreselassie (2012), Schoumaker and Sánchez-Páez (2020)[1]	Shapiro et al. (2013)	Mbamaonyeukwu (2000), Garenne and Joseph (2002), Shapiro and Tambashe (2002), Bongaarts (2006), Shapiro and Gebreselassie (2008), Schoumaker (2009), Sneeringer (2009), Machiyama (2010), Shapiro (2010), Shapiro and Tenikue (2017), Finlay, Mejía-Guevara, and Akachi (2018), Schoumaker (2019a)

(Continued)

Appendix Table 12.1 (Continued)

Country	Stall Period	Place of Stall			No Stall
		National	Urban	Rural	
Senegal	1997–2005, 2011–2016	Shapiro and Gebreselassie (2008), Shapiro (2010), Garenne (2011)	Shapiro and Gebreselassie (2008), Schoumaker and Sánchez-Páez (2020)[2]	Shapiro and Tambashe (2002), Shapiro and Gebreselassie (2008)	Garenne and Joseph (2002), Bongaarts (2006), Bongaarts (2008), Garenne (2008), Schoumaker (2009), Sneeringer (2009), Johnson, Abderrahim, and Rutstein (2011), Gebreselassie (2012), Shapiro et al. (2013), Goujon, Lutz, and KC (2015), Howse (2015), Shapiro and Tenikue (2017), Finlay, Mejía-Guevara, and Akachi (2018), Schoumaker (2019a)
Sierra Leone					Goujon, Lutz, and KC (2015), Schoumaker (2019a)
Togo	1998–2013		Schoumaker and Sánchez-Páez (2020)[2]		Garenne and Joseph (2002), Shapiro and Tambashe (2002), Bongaarts (2006), Garenne (2008), Shapiro and Gebreselassie (2008), Schoumaker (2009), Sneeringer (2009), Shapiro (2010), Gebreselassie (2012), Shapiro et al. (2013), Shapiro and Tenikue (2017), Schoumaker (2019a)
Middle Africa					
Cameroon	1998–2011	Bongaarts (2008), Shapiro and Gebreselassie (2008), Shapiro (2010), Johnson, Abderrahim, and Rutstein (2011), Gebreselassie (2012), Shapiro et al. (2013), Howse (2015), Shapiro and Tenikue (2017), Finlay, Mejía-Guevara, and Akachi (2018), Kebede, Goujon, and Lutz (2019), Schoumaker (2019a)	Shapiro and Gebreselassie (2008), Gebreselassie (2012), Shapiro et al. (2013), Schoumaker and Sánchez-Páez (2020)[1]	Shapiro and Gebreselassie (2008), Gebreselassie (2012), Shapiro et al. (2013), Shapiro and Tenikue (2017),	Garenne and Joseph (2002), Shapiro and Tambashe (2002), Bongaarts (2006), Garenne (2008), Schoumaker (2009), Sneeringer (2009), Machiyama (2010), Goujon, Lutz, and KC (2015)

Central African Republic					Garenne and Joseph (2002), Garenne (2008), Sneeringer (2009), Goujon, Lutz, and KC (2015), Schoumaker and Sánchez-Páez (2020)
Chad	2004–2015			Shapiro et al. (2013), Shapiro and Tenikue (2017)	Garenne and Joseph (2002), Bongaarts (2008), Garenne (2008), Shapiro and Gebreselassie (2008), Schoumaker (2009), Sneeringer (2009), Shapiro (2010), Gebreselassie (2012), Goujon, Lutz, and KC (2015), Howse (2015), Schoumaker (2019a), Schoumaker and Sánchez-Páez (2020)
Congo	2005–2011	Sneeringer (2009), Goujon, Lutz, and KC (2015), Shapiro and Tenikue (2017), Kebede, Goujon, and Lutz (2019), Schoumaker (2019a)	Shapiro and Tenikue (2017), Schoumaker and Sánchez-Páez (2020)[2]	Shapiro and Tenikue (2017)	
D.R. Congo	2007–2013	Romaniuk (2011), Shapiro and Tenikue (2017), Kebede, Goujon, and Lutz (2019)	Shapiro and Tenikue (2017), Schoumaker and Sánchez-Páez (2020)[1]	Shapiro and Tenikue (2017)	Goujon, Lutz, and KC (2015), Schoumaker (2019a)
Equatorial Guinea					Goujon, Lutz, and KC (2015)
Gabon	2000–2012	Howse (2015), Shapiro and Tenikue (2017)	Shapiro and Tenikue (2017), Schoumaker and Sánchez-Páez (2020)[2]	Shapiro and Tenikue (2017)	Sneeringer (2009), Goujon, Lutz, and KC (2015), Kebede, Goujon, and Lutz (2019), Schoumaker (2019a)
Eastern Africa					
Burundi	1980–2010		Schoumaker & Sánchez-Páez (2020)[2]		Sneeringer (2009), Goujon, Lutz, and KC (2015), Howse (2015), Shapiro, and Tenikue (2017), Schoumaker (2019a)
Comoros					Garenne and Joseph (2002), Garenne (2008), Sneeringer (2009), Shapiro and Tenikue (2017), Schoumaker (2019a), Schoumaker and Sánchez-Páez (2020)

(*Continued*)

Appendix Table 12.1 (Continued)

Country	*Stall Period*	*Place of Stall*			*No Stall*
		National	*Urban*	*Rural*	
Eritrea					Shapiro and Gebreselassie (2008), Schoumaker (2009), Shapiro (2010), Gebreselassie (2012), Shapiro et al. (2013), Howse (2015)
Ethiopia	2000–2005, 2011–2016	Bongaarts (2008)	Schoumaker, and Sánchez-Páez (2020)[1]	Shapiro et al. (2013)	Gurmu and Mace (2008)[1], Shapiro and Gebreselassie (2008), Schoumaker (2009), Shapiro (2010), Gebreselassie (2012), Goujon, Lutz, and KC (2015), Howse (2015), Shapiro and Tenikue (2017), Finlay, Mejía-Guevara, and Akachi (2018), Kebede, Goujon, and Lutz (2019), Laelago, Habtu, and Yohannes (2019), Schoumaker (2019a)
Kenya	1998–2003	Bongaarts (2006), Westoff and Cross (2006), Bongaarts (2008), Garenne (2008), Shapiro, and Gebreselassie (2008), Ezeh, Mberu, and Emina (2009), Schoumaker (2009), Sneeringer (2009), Machiyama (2010), Shapiro (2010), Garenne (2011), Johnson, Abderrahim, and Rutstein (2011), Shapiro et al. (2013) Goujon, Lutz, and KC (2015), Howse (2015),	Shapiro and Gebreselassie (2008), Odwe, Agwanda, and Khasakhala (2015), Schoumaker and Sánchez-Páez (2020)[2]	Shapiro and Gebreselassie (2008), Odwe, Agwanda, and Khasakhala (2015)	Garenne and Joseph (2002), Shapiro and Tambashe (2002), United Nations (2002), Blacker et al. (2005), Gebreselassie (2012)

		Odwe, Agwanda, and Khasakhala (2015), Askew, Maggwa, and Obare (2017), Shapiro and Tenikue (2017), Finlay, Mejía-Guevara, and Akachi (2018), Kebede, Goujon, and Lutz (2019), Schoumaker (2019a)		
Madagascar	1992–1997	Sneeringer (2009), Garenne (2008), Garenne (2011)		Garenne and Joseph (2002), Bongaarts (2006), Bongaarts (2008), Shapiro and Gebreselassie (2008), Schoumaker (2009), Shapiro (2010), Johnson, Abderrahim, and Rutstein (2011), Gebreselassie (2012), Shapiro et al. (2013), Howse (2015), Shapiro, and Tenikue (2017), Finlay, Mejía-Guevara, and Akachi (2018), Schoumaker (2019a), Schoumaker and Sánchez-Páez (2020)
Malawi	2004–2010	Finlay, Mejía-Guevara, and Akachi (2018)		Garenne and Joseph (2002), Shapiro and Tambashe (2002), Bongaarts (2006), Bongaarts (2008), Garenne (2008), Shapiro and Gebreselassie (2008), Schoumaker (2009), Sneeringer (2009), Palamuleni (2010), Shapiro (2010), Johnson, Abderrahim, and Rutstein (2011), Gebreselassie (2012), Shapiro et al. (2013), Goujon, Lutz, and KC (2015), Howse (2015), Shapiro and Tenikue (2017), Kebede, Goujon, and Lutz (2019), Schoumaker (2019a), Schoumaker and Sánchez-Páez (2020)

(Continued)

Appendix Table 12.1 (Continued)

Country	*Stall Period*	*Place of Stall*			*No Stall*
		National	*Urban*	*Rural*	
Mozambique	1997–2011	Bongaarts (2008), Shapiro and Gebreselassie (2008), Shapiro (2010), Gebreselassie (2012), Shapiro et al. (2013), Goujon, Lutz, and KC (2015), Howse (2015), Finlay, Mejía-Guevara, and Akachi (2018)	Gebreselassie (2012)	Shapiro and Gebreselassie (2008), Shapiro et al. (2013)	Garenne and Joseph (2002), Arnaldo (2004), Bongaarts (2006), Garenne (2008), Schoumaker (2009), Sneeringer (2009), Shapiro and Tenikue (2017), Schoumaker (2019a), Schoumaker and Sánchez-Páez (2020)
Rwanda	2000–2005	Bongaarts (2008), Shapiro and Gebreselassie (2008), Schoumaker (2009), Sneeringer (2009), Machiyama (2010), Shapiro (2010), Garenne (2011), Johnson, Abderrahim, and Rutstein (2011), Gebreselassie (2012), Westoff (2013)	Gebreselassie (2012), Shapiro et al. (2013)	Garenne (2008), Shapiro and Gebreselassie (2008)	Garenne and Joseph (2002), Bongaarts (2006), Ndahindwa et al. (2014), Goujon, Lutz, and KC (2015), Howse (2015), Shapiro and Tenikue (2017), Finlay, Mejía-Guevara, and Akachi (2018), Schoumaker (2019a), Schoumaker and Sánchez-Páez (2020)
Somalia					Goujon, Lutz, and KC (2015)
Tanzania	1996–2010	Bongaarts (2008), Shapiro and Gebreselassie (2008), Ezeh, Mberu, and Emina (2009), Sneeringer (2009), Shapiro (2010), Garenne (2011), Johnson, Abderrahim, and Rutstein (2011),	Shapiro and Gebreselassie (2008), Shapiro et al. (2013), Schoumaker and Sánchez-Páez (2020)[1]	Shapiro and Tambashe (2002), Garenne (2008), Shapiro and Gebreselassie (2008), Shapiro et al. (2013)	Garenne and Joseph (2002), Bongaarts (2006), Schoumaker (2009), Machiyama (2010), Gebreselassie (2012), Shapiro and Tenikue (2017), Schoumaker (2019a)

		Shapiro et al. (2013), Goujon, Lutz, and KC (2015), Howse (2015), Finlay, Mejía-Guevara, and Akachi (2018), Kebede, Goujon, and Lutz (2019)			
Uganda	1995–2006	Bongaarts (2008), Finlay, Mejía-Guevara, and Akachi (2018)	Shapiro et al. (2013), Schoumaker and Sánchez-Páez (2020)[1]		Garenne and Joseph (2002), Shapiro and Tambashe (2002), Blacker et al. (2005), Bongaarts (2006), Garenne (2008), Shapiro and Gebreselassie (2008), Ezeh, Mberu, and Emina (2009), Schoumaker (2009), Sneeringer (2009), Machiyama (2010), Shapiro (2010), Gebreselassie (2012), Goujon, Lutz, and KC (2015), Howse (2015), Kabagenyi et al. (2015), Shapiro and Tenikue (2017), Kebede, Goujon, and Lutz (2019), Schoumaker (2019a)
Zambia	1996–2007	Bongaarts (2008), Machiyama (2010), Garenne (2011), Johnson, Abderrahim, and Rutstein (2011), Gebreselassie (2012), Shapiro et al. (2013), Goujon, Lutz, and KC (2015), Howse (2015), Finlay, Mejía-Guevara, and Akachi (2018), Kebede, Goujon, and Lutz (2019), Schoumaker (2019a)	Shapiro et al. (2013), Schoumaker and Sánchez-Páez (2020)[1]	Gebreselassie (2012), Shapiro et al. (2013), Shapiro and Tenikue (2017)	Garenne and Joseph (2002), Shapiro and Tambashe (2002), Bongaarts (2006), Garenne (2008), Shapiro and Gebreselassie (2008), Schoumaker (2009), Sneeringer (2009), Shapiro (2010),

(Continued)

Appendix Table 12.1 (Continued)

Country	*Stall Period*	*Place of Stall*			*No Stall*
		National	*Urban*	*Rural*	
Zimbabwe	1999–2015	Bongaarts (2008), Ezeh, Mberu, and Emina (2009), Goujon, Lutz, and KC (2015), Howse (2015), Sayi (2016), Nzimande and Mugwendere (2018), Kebede, Goujon, and Lutz (2019), Muza (2019), Ndagurwa and Odimegwu (2019), Schoumaker (2019a)	Nzimande and Mugwendere (2018), Schoumaker and Sánchez-Páez (2020)[2]	Shapiro et al. (2013), Nzimande and Mugwendere (2018), Schoumaker and Sánchez-Páez (2020)	Garenne and Joseph (2002), Muhwava (2002), Shapiro and Tambashe (2002), Bongaarts (2006), Garenne (2008), Shapiro and Gebreselassie (2008), Schoumaker (2009), Sneeringer (2009), Shapiro (2010), Johnson, Abderrahim, and Rutstein (2011), Mturi and Joshua (2011), Gebreselassie (2012), Shapiro and Tenikue (2017), Finlay, Mejía-Guevara, and Akachi (2018)
Southern Africa					
Botswana					Garenne and Joseph (2002), United Nations (2002), Garenne (2008)
Eswatini					Goujon, Lutz, and KC (2015), Chemhaka, Odimegwu, Zwane, Chadoka, and Gumbo (2016), Chemhaka and Odimegwu (2019)
Lesotho	2009–2014		Shapiro and Tenikue (2017), Schoumaker and Sánchez-Páez (2020)[2]		Garenne and Joseph (2002), United Nations (2002), Garenne (2008), Sneeringer (2009), Howse (2015), Schoumaker (2019a)
Namibia	2007–2013	Palamuleni (2017), Schoumaker (2019a)	Schoumaker and Sánchez-Páez (2020)[2]	Schoumaker and Sánchez-Páez (2020)	Garenne and Joseph (2002), Bongaarts (2008), Garenne (2008), Shapiro and Gebreselassie (2008), Schoumaker (2009), Sneeringer (2009), Shapiro (2010), Johnson, Abderrahim, and Rutstein (2011), Gebreselassie (2012), Indongo and Pazvakawambwa (2012), Shapiro et al. (2013), Howse (2015); Shapiro and Tenikue (2017); Finlay, Mejía-Guevara, and Akachi (2018)

South Africa	1990–2013	Palamuleni (2013), Houle et al. (2016)		Moultrie et al. (2008), Ibisomi et al. (2014)	Garenne and Joseph (2002), United Nations (2002), Moultrie and Timaeus (2003), Garenne et al. (2007), Garenne (2008), Sneeringer (2009), Burger, Burger, and Rossouw (2012), Shapiro et al. (2013), Schoumaker (2019a), Schoumaker and Sánchez-Páez (2020)

Note:
[1] Only the capital city.
[2] In both the capital city and other urban areas.

13
CONTRACEPTION

Boladé Hamed Banougnin and Obasanjo Afolabi Bolarinwa

Introduction

In the absence of any conscious effort of birth control, the average woman will bear about 15 children over her reproductive years (Bongaarts, 1982). In Africa, where the fertility rate has always been the highest, no population has ever come close to this hypothetical maximum. Several analysts point to the high fertility in Africa as a serious threat to its socio-economic progress (Bongaarts, 2017a; van Dalen & Henkens, 2020). The use of contraception aims to regulate fertility to ensure economic development and improve child and maternal health. Empirical evidence from the earliest surveys in Africa's more isolated countries shows widespread ignorance of any method of contraception (Cleland & Potter, 2019). Between 1955 and 1960, many populations in Africa were expanding at a pace that implied a doubling in size every 30 years (UN Population Division, 2019c). Yet it was only in 1967 that, for the first time, an African country (Kenya) adopted a population policy and initiated a family planning programme (Robinson & Ross, 2007). Likewise, in countries of the rest of the world, family planning programmes in African countries aimed at promoting contraceptive use among couples of reproductive age. Estimates from the UN Population Division (2019a) indicate that the contraceptive prevalence among married women aged 15–49 years has increased from 8.9% in 1970 to 34.3% in 2015. This is very low compared to increases from 34.8% to 65.7% in Asia and from 45.4% to 77.1% in South America over the same period (UN Population Division, 2019b). The increase in contraceptive use in Africa led to a decline in the total fertility rate and population growth rate: the fertility level fell from 6.7 to 4.1 children per woman, and the population growth declined from 2.64% to 2.58% over the period from 1970–1975 to 2010–2015 (UN Population Division, 2019c).

This chapter surveys contraceptive use and some of its closely related indicators, including the unmet need for contraception, discontinuation, and method switching in Africa.

Concept definitions and context

Contraceptive use refers to the use of devices or medications in the reduction of pregnancy likelihood. Contraceptives could be modern or traditional. Modern contraception is either permanent or temporary. It's temporary if it's long-acting reversible or short-acting reversible but permanent if it's male or female sterilization.

DOI: 10.4324/9780429287213-16

Temporary contraceptives include oral pills, injectables, condoms, implants, and intrauterine devices (IUDs), while permanent contraceptives are vasectomy for males and tubal litigation for females. Traditional contraceptives are coitus interruptus (withdrawal), lactational or postpartum amenorrhea, and periodic abstinence (Shah, 2010).

Contraceptive discontinuation is regarded as starting the use of contraceptives and then halting the use for any reason despite being at risk of unwanted pregnancy. Besides the desire to become pregnant, any other reasons for discontinuation of contraceptives contribute to unintended fertility and can lead to pregnancy termination through unsafe abortion. However, some women discontinue a particular contraceptive method because of its side effects or spousal opposition, but in most cases, these women often switch to an available method immediately (Perez & Tabije, 1996).

Contraceptive method switching is referred to when a woman reported having used different contraceptive methods in consecutive months. This can also be an event where a woman considered not using any form of contraceptive because she was not having sexual intercourse in the month she previously used a method (Grady, Billy, & Klepinger, 2002).

Unmet need for contraception is regarded as women considered sexually active who want to avoid becoming pregnant but are not using contraception (Sedgh, Hussain, Bankole, & Singh, 2007). Essentially, an unmet need is a conflict between what a woman wants and what she does about it. She may want less fertility but fail to take the necessary steps to prevent pregnancy. The ratio of married women with unmet needs and married women with met contraceptive needs is the total demand for contraception. In other words, it is the amount of contraceptive prevalence plus the unmet need for contraceptives (Aliyu, 2018).

The debate on unmet needs started in the 1960s. The first important definition of unmet need for family planning emerged from family planning knowledge, attitudes, and practice (KAP) surveys in sub-Saharan African countries in the 1988–1990s (Ashford, 2003; Cottingham, Germain, & Hunt, 2012; Dixon-Mueller & Germain, 1992; Nair & Devi, 2017; Rossier, Bradley, Ross, & Winfrey, 2015; Sedgh et al., 2007; Staveteig, 2017; Westoff, 1988b, 1988a).

Contraception use theoretical and conceptual issues in Africa

The marked family planning movement began in the 20th century to liberate women from the social and health consequences of unintended pregnancies. However, the beginning of family planning programmes in developing countries, including African countries, in the early 1950s was targeted towards alleviating the pressure of rapid population growth on economic development (Eko Jimmy, Kalu, & Osuchukwu Nelson, 2013). For instance, the health model belief (HMB), as developed by Becker (1974), was tested in Nigeria on contraceptive use. The model illustrated that unplanned pregnancy could be prevented when the individual perception of pregnancy's perceived seriousness and perceived benefits of contraception changed (Eko Jimmy et al., 2013).

Parents and partners have been identified as the major drivers of perceived benefits of contraception in high-income countries (HICs) through efficient communication. However, Africa's cultural belief system has left a gap between parental sexual and reproductive health (SRH) discussion and its benefits to young girls (Challa et al., 2020; Wamoyi, Fenwick, Urassa, Zaba, & Stones, 2010). Similarly, ineffective communication between women of reproductive age and their partners on the choice of contraception or opposition from sexual partners due to method choice has been identified as a perceived barrier in efficient contraceptive use (Eko Jimmy et al., 2013). Becker (1974)'s HBM can also be used to explain limited access to SRH services and providers as a perceived barrier to contraceptive uptake (Eko Jimmy et al., 2013).

It's important to understand that limited access to SRH services or providers is not limited to young girls and women alone; it has also been established that all women of any age are likely to have limited access to SRH service, which includes contraceptive uptake due to place or region of residence in Africa (Yao, Murray, & Agadjanian, 2013).

Another theory or model that can be used to explain the use of contraceptives in Africa is the theory of planned behaviour (TPB) developed by Ajzen (1985), later reviewed in Ajzen (1991), which explained how both internal and external factors could influence behavioural intention. The theory established how individual behaviour can be compelled by perceived social pressure or perceived behavioural control. That is, individual perception about contraceptives will determine the use, taking into consideration that the need for it will facilitate individual behaviour. Also, individual perception about contraceptive use is likely to facilitate or hinder interest in contraceptive use. In order words, an individual positive attitude towards using contraceptives is based on the importance of contraceptive consequences and the individual perceived social pressure to use a contraceptive and feel control over using it make an individual more likely to effectively use a contraceptive.

For instance, a study conducted in South Africa among a sexually active and not sexually active population using TPB on the use of condom as a form of contraceptive during sexual intercourse explained about 44% of the variance of intentions to use condom among the sexually active sample and more than 30% of the variance among the sample that was sexually inactive. The theory in the same study also predicted about 57% of actual condom use variance among the sexually active participants, and attitude was noted to have been the strongest predictor of condom use (Protogerou, Flisher, Wild, & Aarø, 2013). Consequently, individual attitude toward contraceptives will determine their use, as broadly argued using TBP, and this has been noted as one of the determinants of contraceptive use in Africa (DeMaria, Sundstrom, Faria, Saxon, & Ramos-Ortiz, 2019).

Methods and measures

Data source

This chapter utilizes published material and data from Demographic and Health Surveys (DHSs), StatCompiler, and United Nations Population Division.

Empirical findings

Level and trend of contraceptive use

Data are increasingly available for men in Demographic and Health Surveys and Multiple Indicators Cluster Surveys (MICSs) data. However, numerous studies pinpointed the major unresolved issue of husband-wife inconsistencies in contraceptive use responses (Gasca & Becker, 2018; Shakya et al., 2018; Uddin, Hossin, & Pulok, 2017). They argued that men typically report higher contraceptive use than women, especially for male contraception methods (Shakya et al., 2018; Uddin et al., 2017). Furthermore, the DHS and MICS questionnaires contain more detailed information on women's family planning than for men (ICF, 2020b; UNICEF, 2015). As a consequence, the focus of this chapter is mainly only women.

Figure 13.1 shows considerable variation in contraceptive prevalence across major African regions in 2019, based on UN Population Division estimates (United Nations, 2019b). In Africa, 28.7% of women used any contraceptive methods, which is a lower rate than the world

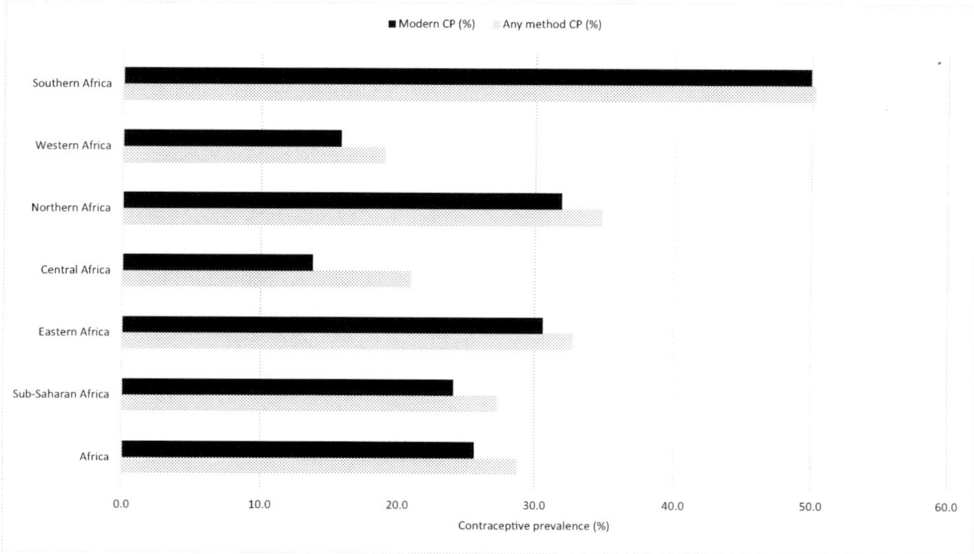

Figure 13.1 Percent distribution of modern and any contraceptive users, major African regions in 2019
Source: UN Population Division, 2019b

average (48.9%) and very low compared to Northern America and Europe (60.3%). The contraceptive prevalence rate in Asia (50.5%) was less than two-fold higher as compared to that in Africa. The disparities follow the same pattern for modern methods of contraception. Approximately one woman in four (25.6%) residing in Africa used modern contraceptives. The sub-Saharan part of Africa has the lowest prevalence rate (27.3% for any methods of contraception and 24.1% for modern methods of contraception). There are also disparities in contraceptive use across African countries. Contraceptive prevalence rates were higher in Southern, Northern, and Eastern Africa than in the other regions of Africa. About half the women living in Southern African countries used any methods of contraception (50.2%) and modern methods of contraception (49.9%). They are followed by women residing in Northern African countries (34.8% contraceptive prevalence rate and 31.9% modern contraceptive prevalence rate) and Eastern African countries (32.8% contraceptive prevalence rate and 30.6% modern contraceptive prevalence rate). Western Africa and Central Africa had the lowest contraceptive prevalence rates. Only 13.8% of women in Central Africa used modern contraceptives, against 19.0% for women in Western Africa.

Within the aforementioned major African regions, there are disparities between countries in terms of contraceptive use. Table 13.1 presents modern contraceptive prevalence rate by African region countries with countries with the lowest and highest rates. In Africa, Botswana (a Southern African country) had the highest modern contraceptive prevalence rate (55.2%), whereas Chad (a Central African country) had the lowest modern contraceptive prevalence rate (5.8%) in 2019. For each region, most of the women using modern contraceptives were living in Zimbabwe (in Eastern Africa: 48.5%), in Cameroon (in Central Africa: 46.3%), in Egypt (in Northern Africa: 42.0%), and in Burkina Faso (Western Africa: 27.1%). The lowest prevalence rate of modern contraception was in Eastern Africa (in Somalia) and Central Africa (Chad), and it was about 6%. In Western Africa, Guinea had the lowest modern contraceptive prevalence

Table 13.1 Distribution (%) of Modern Contraceptive Prevalence Rate by Major African Regions According to Countries with the Lowest and Highest Rates in 2019

Region	*Lowest*		*Highest*	
	Country	*CPR (%)*	*Country*	*CPR (%)*
Africa	Chad	5.8	Botswana	55.2
Eastern Africa	Somalia	5.9	Zimbabwe	48.5
Central Africa	Chad	5.8	Cameroon	46.3
Northern Africa	Libya	15.2	Egypt	42.0
Western Africa	Guinea	9.6	Burkina Faso	27.1
Southern Africa	South Africa	49.5	Botswana	55.2

Source: UN Population Division, 2019b

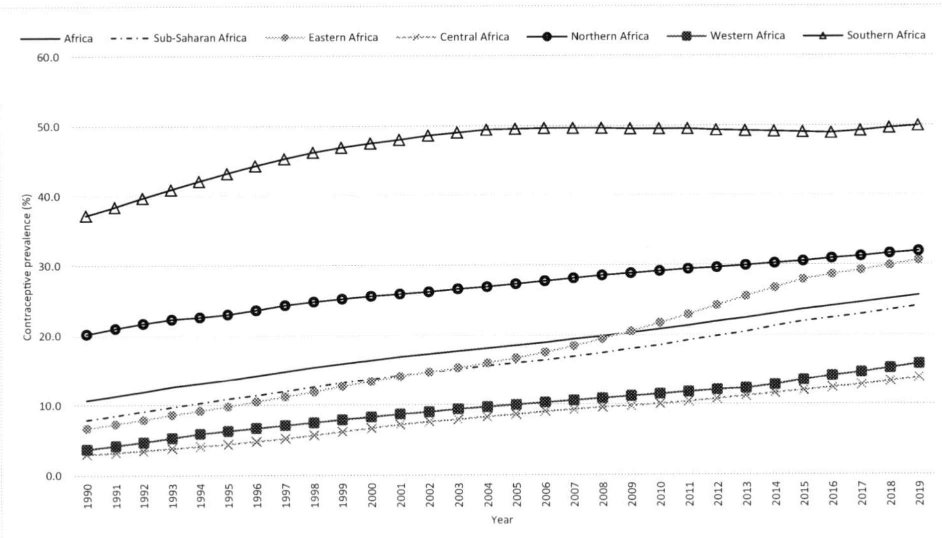

Figure 13.2 Trends in percent of women using a modern method of contraception, major regions of Africa 1990–2019

Source: UN Population Division, 2019b

rate (9.6%), and Libya had the lowest modern contraceptive prevalence rate (15.2%) in Northern Africa. South Africa has the lowest modern contraceptive prevalence rate in Southern Africa (49.5%). However, this prevalence rate is even higher than that of the highest of Africa's other regions all together.

Figure 13.2 shows trends since 1990 in the use of any modern method of contraception by major regions of Africa, as reported by the UN Population Division (2019b). Generally (in Africa), the prevalence of modern contraceptive use has risen from 10.7% in 1990 to 25.6% in 2019. In sub-Saharan Africa, the prevalence increased from 7.9% in 1990 to 24.1% in 2019. In 1990, modern contraceptive use was already relatively high in Southern Africa at 37.2%; it

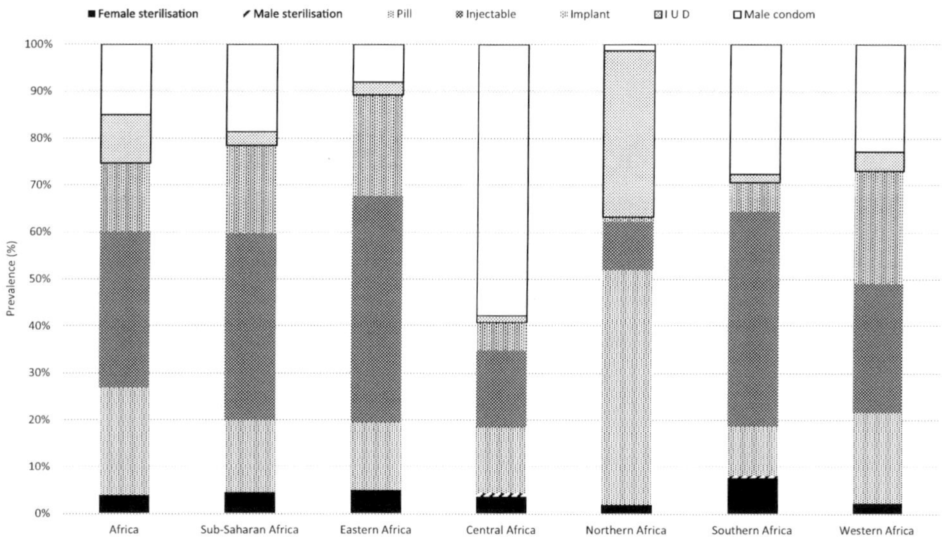

Figure 13.3 Percent distribution of contraceptive users by method, major African regions 2019

Source: UN Population Division, 2019a

was 20.2% in Northern Africa, 6.7% in Eastern Africa, and less than 4% in Central (3.0%) and Western Africa (3.7%). The graph pinpoints large increases in modern method use over the period 1990–2019.

In 1990, the proportion of women using traditional methods (not shown here) was higher than those using modern methods in Central African countries (9.8% vs. 3.0%) and in Western African countries (5.1% vs. 3.7%). The period 1990–2019 saw decreases in the use of traditional methods of contraception. In Africa, very few countries had traditional contraceptive prevalence rates above 10% in 2019. Those countries are Mauritius (15.3%), Congo (14.6%), and the Democratic Republic of Congo (10.8%). In countries such as Gabon, Libya, and Somalia, the traditional contraceptive prevalence was around 9%.

Use of specific modern methods

In 2019, injectables were by far the most commonly used modern contraceptive method, accounting for 33% of all users in Africa, followed by pills (23%), male condoms and implants (15%), and IUDs (10%). The same pattern applies for sub-Saharan African countries except for the fact that very few women used IUDs (3%). The popularity of pills and IUDs in Africa is somewhat more pronounced in Northern Africa. Half of the modern contraceptive users in Northern Africa used pills, and 35% used IUDs. In Southern Africa, injectables (46%) and male condoms (28%) are the most popular modern methods used. Just as women in Southern African countries did, most of the women users of modern methods of contraception in Eastern African countries used injectables (48%). The latter (Eastern African countries' women users of modern contraception) also used mostly implants (22%). In Central and Western African countries where the prevalence of modern contraceptive use is very low, the most common method used was male condoms and injectables. More than half (58%) of users of modern contraceptives in

Central African countries used male condoms. The proportions of them using injectables and pills were around 14%. Among users of modern contraceptives in Western African countries, 27% used injectables, approximately 23% used implants or male condoms, and 19% used pills.

Contraceptive use and fertility

Empirical evidence suggests an inverse relationship between levels of fertility and contraceptive use (Bongaarts, 2017a, 2017b). Figure 13.4 shows trends in contraceptive prevalence (CP) and total fertility rate (TFR) in major African regions between 1990 and 2020 (UN Population Division, 2019c, 2019b). As plotted in Figure 13.4, the contraceptive prevalence in all major regions is inversely related to the fertility rate. From 1990–1995 to 2015–2020, the contraceptive prevalence in Southern Africa increased from 41% to 50%, while the total fertility rate decreased from 3.6 to 2.5 children per woman. In Eastern Africa during the same period (from 1990–1995 to 2015–2020), the total fertility rate decreased from 6.4 to 4.4 children per woman, with the contraceptive prevalence rising from 12% to 32%.

In Central and Western African countries where contraceptive prevalence rates are still low with steady increases, fertility rates remain high. In 1990–1995, Central and Western African regions had a total fertility rate of 6.4. In 2015–2020, women living in Central African countries had higher number of children (5.5) than those living in Western African countries (5.2). The high fertility rate in the Western African region is driven by countries such as Niger (7.2 children per woman in 2012) and Mali (6.3 children per woman in 2018) (ICF, 2020a). Chad (6.4 children per woman in 2014–15), the Democratic Republic of Congo (6.6 children per woman in 2013–14), and Angola (6.2 children per woman in 2015–16) contribute most to the high fertility rate in the Central Africa region (ICF, 2020a).

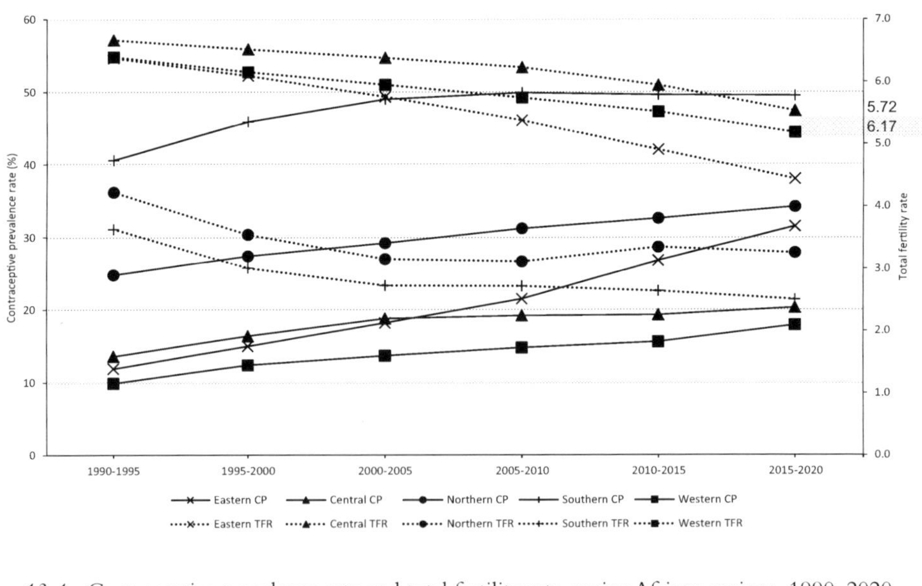

Figure 13.4 Contraceptive prevalence rate and total fertility rate, major African regions, 1990–2020

Source: ICF, 2020a

Contraceptive prevalence in Northern African countries has also risen during 1990–2020 (from 25% to 34%), but the total fertility rate was fairly stable during 2000–2020, with around 3 children per woman. The total fertility rate in this region was 4.2 in 1990–1995.

Contraceptive use: discontinuation and reasons for discontinuation

The emphasis in much of the contraceptive literature on current use and unmet need gives a misleadingly static impression of reproductive behaviour (Cleland & Potter, 2019). Except in societies such as Northern America and Europe, where sterilization dominates, considerable turbulence underlies contraceptive use episodes. This is due to the fact that couples move from use to non-use, and vice versa, or switch from one contraceptive method to another. The study of discontinuation of modern methods of contraception makes a large contribution to unmet need (Igras, Diakité, & Lundgren, 2017; Jain, Obare, RamaRao, & Askew, 2013; Jain & Winfrey, 2017; Senderowicz, 2020).

The DHS calendar – which collects a complete history of women's reproduction and contraceptive use for a period of between 5 and 7 years prior to the survey – provides key variables for the analysis of discontinuation of contraceptive use (ICF, 2018). This section uses the 28 most recent DHS datasets (1 from 2004 and 27 during the period 2010–2018) containing variables on first-year discontinuation in Africa. Results plotted in Figure 13.5 show that the Central African region had the highest rate of discontinuation (41%), followed by Eastern Africa (35%), Western Africa (34%), and Southern Africa (23%). The discontinuation rate is very low in Northern Africa (5%). Guinea (a Western African country) had the highest discontinuation rate (66% in 2018), whereas Egypt (a Northern African country) had the lowest discontinuation rate (4% in 2014).

African major regions differ from each other by reasons for discontinuation. The proportion of women who discontinued within 12 months of starting due to method failure is higher in

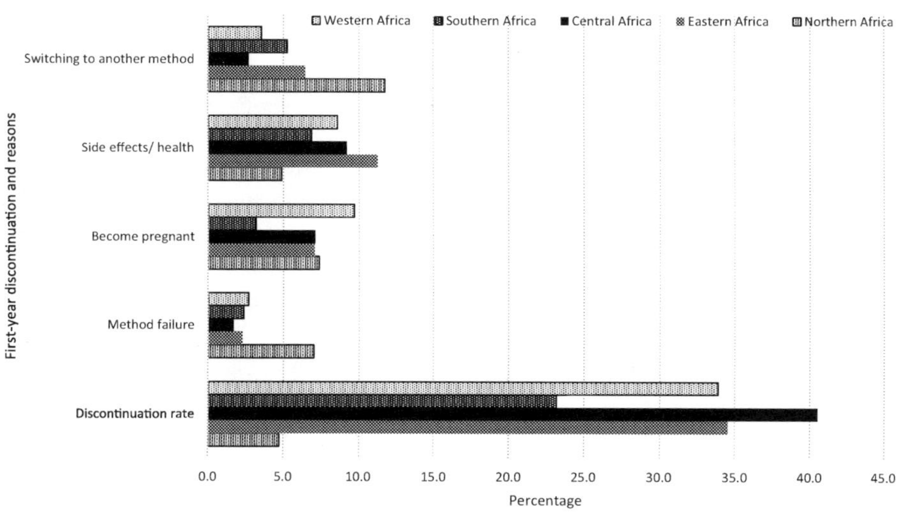

Figure 13.5 Discontinuation and reasons for discontinuation by Africa major regions for 28 countries

Source: ICF, 2020a

Northern Africa (7%) than in the other regions of Africa (2–3%). The rate of discontinuation due to switching to another method is (as expected) higher among Northern African women (12%, with a high of 17% in Morocco) than among women from the other regions (3–6%). The Western African region had the highest percentage of discontinuation due to the desire to become pregnant (10%, with a high of 16% in Guinea), followed by Northern Africa, Eastern Africa, Central Africa (7%), and Southern Africa (3%). Women who discontinued due to side effects or health matters were found more in Eastern Africa (11%) than in Central Africa and Western Africa (9%), as well as in the other regions of Africa. More the 25% of women residing in Guinea discontinued because of side effects.

Unmet need for contraception

Using data from KAP surveys, researchers found that some women who wanted no more children or who wanted to space their childbirths were not using any method of contraception. They identified those women as having an unmet need for contraception. The main concept of the unmet need was first developed by Westoff (1988b) through the World Fertility Survey (WFS) programmes. This concept depicts the gap between the demand for family planning and access to family planning services (Banougnin, Adekunle, Oladokun, & Sanni, 2018).

In regions with high fertility and low contraceptive prevalence, addressing the unmet need for family planning can be a better alternative to increasing contraceptive use (Ahinkorah, 2020; Cordero et al., 2019; Kulczycki, 2018; Lutalo et al., 2018). Identifying persons with an unmet need for contraception can help to implement efficient family planning programmes (Ahinkorah, 2020; Cordero et al., 2019; Kulczycki, 2018; Lutalo et al., 2018; Nair & Devi, 2017; Staveteig, 2017). Also, any strategy that addresses unmet needs for family planning reinforces reproductive health care services access (Ashford, 2003). Therefore, unmet need for family planning is a key indicator that should be considered by population policymakers. Capurchande, Coene, Roelens, and Meulemans (2017) found in a recent study conducted in Mozambique that family planning programmes aiming to meet women's need for contraception are more efficient. Indeed, these programmes focus more on how to fill the gap between women's fertility preferences and their behaviours towards contraception utilization.

Unmet need for family planning refers to the percentage of women who are not using any contraceptive method while wanting to stop or postpone childbearing (Bradley, Croft, Fishel, & Westoff, 2017). Unmet need for contraception can lead to unintended pregnancies, which pose risks for women, their families, and society (Bizuneh, Shiferaw, & Melkamu, 2008). A recent study conducted in 36 low- and middle-income countries found that one-quarter of pregnancies were unintended (Bellizzi, Mannava, Nagai, & Sobel, 2020). One particularly harmful consequence of unintended pregnancies is unsafe abortion. About one in five of 205 million pregnancies each year end in abortion, and of the equivalent number of abortions, approximately half are unsafe (Sedgh et al., 2016). In addition, unwanted births pose risks to children's health and wellbeing and contribute to rapid population growth in already resource-strapped countries (Bearak et al., 2020; Bishwajit, Tang, Yaya, & Feng, 2017).

In 1990, the estimated levels of unmet need for modern contraception in Africa were high: 31% in Central Africa, 27% in Eastern Africa, 25% in Western Africa, 18% in Northern Africa, and 16% in Southern Africa (ICF, 2020a). Unmet need in sub-Saharan Africa stems primarily from women wishing to delay pregnancy. Almost three decades later (in 2019), these figures remain high. Twenty percent of women living in Africa still had an unmet need for modern contraception; 28% in Central African countries, 21% in Western Africa, 18% in Eastern Africa, and 12–13% in Southern and Northern Africa (ICF, 2020a). Based on most recent DHS data, countries with the highest levels of unmet need for family planning in Africa were: Angola (38% in 2015–16), Benin (32% in 2017–18), Liberia (31% in 2013), and Mauritania (32%) (ICF, 2020a). According to the same data, Morocco (in 2003–4), Egypt (in 2014), and Zimbabwe (in 2015) had the lowest levels of unmet need in Africa (7–14%).

Research agenda

This chapter focused on contraceptive use in Africa using available data from secondary sources. The focus was specifically on the levels and trends of contraception, the specific method, the relationship between fertility rate and contraceptive use, discontinuation in contraceptive use and reason for discontinuation, and unmet contraceptive needs. Future research should consider how effectively family planning policies are implemented in scaling up the use of contraceptives in Africa.

Conclusion

There is a plethora of data on contraception globally, particularly in Africa (e.g., DHS, MICS, among others). However, macro-level standardized data are still lacking. The most used are data from the UN Population Division and StatCompiler. Evidence from these data shows that contraceptive use had increased, though slightly, and unmet need has remained fairly stable and high in Africa. Northern and Southern African countries had the highest levels of contraceptive use and lowest levels of unmet need for modern contraception. They are followed by Eastern Africa, whereas Central and Western African countries are still behind (with very low contraceptive prevalence rates and high unmet need for family planning). Most of the Western and Central African countries such as Chad, Niger, Mali, Guinea, and Somalia had critical contraceptive needs. A starting point could be the implementation of programmes aiming to address unmet need for family planning in these countries and many other countries, even from the other regions of Africa.

References

Ahinkorah, B. O. (2020). Predictors of unmet need for contraception among adolescent girls and young women in selected high fertility countries in sub-Saharan Africa: A multilevel mixed effects analysis. *PLoS One*, *15*(8), e0236352.

Ajzen, I. (1985). From intentions to actions: A theory of planned behavior. In *Action control* (pp. 11–39). Berlin, Heidelberg: Springer.

Ajzen, I. (1991). The theory of planned behavior. *Organizational Behavior and Human Decision Processes*, *50*(2), 179–211.

Aliyu, A. A. (2018). Family planning services in Africa: The successes and challenges. *Family Planning*, *69*.

Ashford, L. (2003). *Unmet need for family planning: Recent trends and their implications for programs*. Washington, DC: Population Reference Bureau.

Banougnin, B. H., Adekunle, A. O., Oladokun, A., & Sanni, M. A. (2018). Internal migration and unmet need for family planning in Cotonou, Benin Republic. *African Population Studies*, *32*(2).

Bearak, J., Popinchalk, A., Ganatra, B., Moller, A.-B., Tunçalp, Ö., Beavin, C., . . . Alkema, L. (2020). Unintended pregnancy and abortion by income, region, and the legal status of abortion: Estimates from a comprehensive model for 1990–2019. *The Lancet Global Health*, *8*(9), 52–61.

Becker, M. H. (1974). The health belief model and sick role behavior. *Health Education Monographs*, *2*(4), 409–419.

Bellizzi, S., Mannava, P., Nagai, M., & Sobel, H. (2020). Reasons for discontinuation of contraception among women with a current unintended pregnancy in 36 low and middle-income countries. *Contraception*, *101*(1), 26–33.

Bishwajit, G., Tang, S., Yaya, S., & Feng, Z. (2017). Unmet need for contraception and its association with unintended pregnancy in Bangladesh. *BMC Pregnancy and Childbirth*, *17*(1), 186.

Bizuneh, G., Shiferaw, S., & Melkamu, Y. (2008). *Unmet need and evaluation of programme options to meet unmet need for contraception in Ethiopia, 2000 and 2005: Further analysis of the 2000 and 2005 Ethiopia Demographic and Health Surveys*. Calverton, MD: Macro International.

Bongaarts, J. (1982). The fertility-inhibiting effects of the intermediate fertility variables. *Studies in Family Planning*, 179–189.

Bongaarts, J. (2017a). Africa's unique fertility transition. *Population and Development Review*, *43*, 39–58.

Bongaarts, J. (2017b). The effect of contraception on fertility: Is sub-Saharan Africa different? *Demographic Research*, *37*, 129–146.

Bradley, S., Croft, T., Fishel, J., & Westoff, C. (2017). *Revising unmet need for family planning*. DHS Analytical Studies No. 25. Calverton, MD: ICF International, 2012.

Capurchande, R., Coene, G., Roelens, K., & Meulemans, H. (2017). "If I have only two children and they die . . . who will take care of me?" – A qualitative study exploring knowledge, attitudes and practices about family planning among Mozambican female and male adults. *BMC Women's Health*, *17*(1), 66.

Challa, S., Shakya, H. B., Carter, N., Boyce, S. C., Brooks, M. I., Aliou, S., & Silverman, J. G. (2020). Associations of spousal communication with contraceptive method use among adolescent wives and their husbands in Niger. *PLoS One*, *15*(8), e0237512.

Cleland, J., & Potter, J. E. (2019). 30 Fertility regulation. In *Handbook of population* (pp. 793–817). Cham: Springer.

Cordero, J. P., Steyn, P. S., Gichangi, P., Kriel, Y., Milford, C., Munakampe, M., . . . Smit, J. (2019). Community and provider perspectives on addressing unmet need for contraception: Key findings from a formative phase research in Kenya, South Africa and Zambia (2015–2016). *African Journal of Reproductive Health*, *23*(3), 106–119.

Cottingham, J., Germain, A., & Hunt, P. (2012). Use of human rights to meet the unmet need for family planning. *The Lancet*, *380*(9837), 172–180.

DeMaria, A. L., Sundstrom, B., Faria, A. A., Saxon, G. M., & Ramos-Ortiz, J. (2019). Using the theory of planned behavior and self-identity to explore women's decision-making and intention to switch from combined oral contraceptive pill (COC) to long-acting reversible contraceptive (LARC). *BMC Women's Health*, *19*(1), 1–10.

Dixon-Mueller, R., & Germain, A. (1992). Stalking the elusive "unmet need" for family planning. *Studies in Family Planning*, *23*(5), 330–335.

Eko Jimmy, E., Kalu, O., & Osuchukwu Nelson, C. (2013). Prevalence of contraceptive use among women of reproductive age in Calabar metropolis, Southern Nigeria. *International Journal of Humanities and Social Science Invention (IJHSSI)*, *2*(6).

Gasca, N. C., & Becker, S. (2018). Using couples' discordant reports to estimate female covert use of modern contraception in sub-Saharan Africa. *Journal of Biosocial Science*, *50*(3), 326–346.

Grady, W. R., Billy, J. O., & Klepinger, D. H. (2002). Contraceptive method switching in the United States. *Perspectives on Sexual and Reproductive Health*, 135–145.

ICF. (2018). *DHS contraceptive calendar tutorial, The Demographic and Health Surveys Program*. Funded by USAID. Retrieved from www.DHSprogram.com

ICF. (2020a). *The DHS Program STATcompiler*. Funded by USAID. Retrieved from www.statcompiler.com

ICF. (2020b). *The DHS Program website*. Funded by USAID. Retrieved from www.dhsprogram.com

Igras, S., Diakité, M., & Lundgren, R. (2017). Moving from theory to practice: A participatory social network mapping approach to address unmet need for family planning in Benin. *Global Public Health*, *12*(7), 909–926.

Jain, A. K., Obare, F., RamaRao, S., & Askew, I. (2013). Reducing unmet need by supporting women with met need. *International Perspectives on Sexual and Reproductive Health*, 133–141.

Jain, A. K., & Winfrey, W. (2017). Contribution of contraceptive discontinuation to unintended births in 36 developing countries. *Studies in Family Planning*, *48*(3), 269–278.

Kulczycki, A. (2018). Overcoming family planning challenges in Africa: Toward meeting unmet need and scaling up service delivery. *African Journal of Reproductive Health*, *22*(1), 9–19.

Lutalo, T., Gray, R., Santelli, J., Guwatudde, D., Brahmbhatt, H., Mathur, S., . . . Makumbi, F. (2018). Unfulfilled need for contraception among women with unmet need but with the intention to use contraception in Rakai, Uganda: A longitudinal study. *BMC Women's Health*, *18*(1), 1–7.

Nair, A., & Devi, S. (2017). Knowledge and attitude of puerperal women towards family planning practices in a tertiary care hospital. *Journal of Evidence Based Medicine and Healthcare*, *4*(5), 212–216.

Perez, A. E., & Tabije, T. L. (1996). *Contraceptive discontinuation, failure, and switching behavior in the Philippines*. DHS Working Papers No. 18. Calverton, MD: Macro International. Retrieved from http://dhsprogram.com/pubs/pdf/WP18/WP18.pdf

Protogerou, C., Flisher, A. J., Wild, L. G., & Aarø, L. E. (2013). Predictors of condom use in South African university students: A prospective application of the theory of planned behavior. *Journal of Applied Social Psychology, 43*, E23–E36.

Robinson, W. C., & Ross, J. A. (2007). *The global family planning revolution: Three decades of population policies and programs*. Washington, DC: The World Bank.

Rossier, C., Bradley, S. E., Ross, J., & Winfrey, W. (2015). Reassessing unmet need for family planning in the postpartum period. *Studies in Family Planning, 46*(4), 355–367.

Sedgh, G., Bearak, J., Singh, S., Bankole, A., Popinchalk, A., Ganatra, B., . . . Johnson Jr, B. R. (2016). Abortion incidence between 1990 and 2014: Global, regional, and subregional levels and trends. *The Lancet, 388*(10041), 258–267.

Sedgh, G., Hussain, R., Bankole, A., & Singh, S. (2007). Women with an unmet need for contraception in developing countries and their reasons for not using a method. *Occasional Report, 37*, 5–40.

Senderowicz, L. (2020). Contraceptive autonomy: Conceptions and measurement of a novel family planning indicator. *Studies in Family Planning, 51*(2), 161–176.

Shah, I. H. (2010). Family planning and reproductive health. *Demography, 1*, 162–184.

Shakya, H. B., Dasgupta, A., Ghule, M., Battala, M., Saggurti, N., Donta, B., . . . Raj, A. (2018). Spousal discordance on reports of contraceptive communication, contraceptive use, and ideal family size in rural India: A cross-sectional study. *BMC Women's Health, 18*(1), 147.

Staveteig, S. (2017). Fear, opposition, ambivalence, and omission: Results from a follow-up study on unmet need for family planning in Ghana. *PLoS One, 12*(7), e0182076.

Uddin, J., Hossin, M. Z., & Pulok, M. H. (2017). Couple's concordance and discordance in household decision-making and married women's use of modern contraceptives in Bangladesh. *BMC Women's Health, 17*(1), 107.

UNICEF. (2015). *Monitoring the situation of children and women for 20 years: The multiple indicator cluster surveys (MICS) 1995–2015*. New York: UNICEF.

UN Population Division. (2019a). *Contraceptive use by method 2019: Data booklet* (ST/ESA/SER.A/435). New York: United Nations, Department of Economic and Social Affairs. Retrieved from https://digitallibrary.un.org/record/3849735?ln=en

UN Population Division. (2019b). *Estimates and projections of family planning indicators 2019*. New York: United Nations, Department of Economic and Social Affairs. Retrieved from www.un.org/en/development/desa/population/theme/family-planning/cp_model.asp

UN Population Division. (2019c). *World population prospects 2019, Online Edition*. United Nations, Department of Economic and Social Affairs. Retrieved from https://population.un.org/wpp/Download/Standard/Population/van

Dalen, H. P., & Henkens, K. (2020). *When is fertility too low or too high*? Population policy preferences of demographers around the world. *Population Studies*, 1–15.

Wamoyi, J., Fenwick, A., Urassa, M., Zaba, B., & Stones, W. (2010). Parent-child communication about sexual and reproductive health in rural Tanzania: Implications for young people's sexual health interventions. *Reproductive Health*, 7(1), 1–18.

Westoff, C. F. (1988a). Is the KAP-gap real? *Population and Development Review*, 225–232.

Westoff, C. F. (1988b). The potential demand for family planning: A new measure of unmet need and estimates for five Latin American countries. *International Family Planning Perspectives*, 45–53.

Yao, J., Murray, A. T., & Agadjanian, V. (2013). A geographical perspective on access to sexual and reproductive health care for women in rural Africa. *Social Science & Medicine, 96*, 60–68.

14

BEFORE PILLS AND INJECTABLES

Systematic review of drivers of traditional contraceptive practice in sub-saharan africa

Justin Dansou, Fidelia A. A. Dake and Robert Y. Djogbenou

Background

In 1960, few women in the developing world used contraceptives (Robinson & John, 2007). Family planning programs that started at the time across sub-Saharan Africa (SSA) made steady progress, but contraceptive prevalence rates are still very low, and unmet need for contraception in SSA is still unacceptably high (Aliyu, 2018). In 2019, it was estimated that more than 214 million women in the developing world wanted to avoid pregnancy but had an unmet need for contraceptives (Guttmacher Institute, 2017). Again, of the estimated 206 million pregnancies that occurred in 2017 in developing regions, 43% were unintended (Guttmacher Institute, 2017). Recent analysis of data from 24 SSA countries show that more than 50% of married women (15–49 years) with a need for family planning were not using modern methods (Population Reference Bureau (PRB), 2020).

Contraception is a means of enabling individuals and couples to control their reproductive life (Cleland et al., 2006) and contraception allows women to be more economically active (Global Health Council, 2019). Furthermore, contraception has numerous benefits for the mother, the child and the community at large (Aliyu, 2018; Dansou, 2017). Generally, planned pregnancies are safer for the mother and produce healthier children than unplanned pregnancies. Additionally, the cost of averting unwanted births is quite insignificant compared to the cost of unwanted births (Cleland et al., 2006). Expanding access to and use of contraception and reduction of unmet need for family planning are key components of improving reproductive health (Leontine, Kantorova, Menozzi, & Biddlecom, 2013) and are also vital to avoiding maternal deaths by preventing unwanted pregnancies (World Health Organization, 2019a).

Methods of contraception are broadly classified into modern and traditional methods. Modern methods are defined as using one or more of the following methods: male and female condoms, oral contraceptive pills, injectables, intra-uterine devices (IUDs), sub-dermal implants, male and female sterilization, or emergency contraceptive pills. It is worth mentioning that the inclusion of lactational amenorrhea and/or the standard days method in modern methods varies across countries (PRB, 2020). Additionally, it should be noted that the use of modern methods of contraception requires the involvement of at least some basic health system such as a clinic with health personnel and supply systems for providing contraceptives such as the pill,

DOI: 10.4324/9780429287213-17

injectable, implant, IUD, condom, and sterilization. Traditional methods of contraception, on the other hand, are regarded as those methods which do not involve the use of orthodox medicine (Aliyu, 2018). Traditional contraception is defined as using one or more of the following methods: lactational amenorrhea method (LAM), standard days method (SDM), rhythm/calendar method, withdrawal, or abstinence (Hubacher & Trussell, 2015). Throughout human history, traditional family planning practices for fertility regulation have been rich and varied (Centre for Disease Control and Prevention, 2000), and some of these methods have existed since prehistoric times (Aliyu, 2018).

In general, modern and traditional methods of contraception are distinguished from one another based on effectiveness (Gebreselassie, Kristin, Sarah, & Thomas, 2017). Traditional methods of contraception have been thought of as being less effective compared to modern methods, yet 59 million women of reproductive age in developing regions rely on traditional methods for fertility regulation (Guttmacher Institute, 2017). Furthermore, despite global commitment and mounting investment aimed at improving access to and use of modern methods of contraception, traditional contraceptive practice persists in SSA, even if the decline has already begun.

In addition to the decline in traditional contraceptive prevalence in SSA, inequities in contraceptive practice, including traditional contraceptives, exist both within and between the various sub-regions and countries. Among the various sub-regions, the highest level of contraceptive prevalence has been recorded in Southern Africa (55% and 1% for modern and traditional methods, respectively), while Western Africa with (16% and 3%) and Middle Africa (15% and 7%) for modern and traditional methods, respectively, stand out with the lowest contraceptive practice in the region. Northern Africa and Eastern Africa have 46% and 5% and 39% and 5% contraceptive prevalence for modern and traditional methods, respectively.

Notwithstanding the low prevalence of traditional versus modern methods of contraception as earlier mentioned, traditional methods have been the foundation for fertility regulation in many societies, including the developed world, before the development of modern methods. And although modern methods of contraception are gaining ground in SSA, traditional contraceptive practice still persists. However, while the factors associated with the use of modern methods, have been well documented and synthesized over time, there is little synthesis of such evidence on traditional methods at the global SSA level. This chapter thus systematically reviews literature on the drivers of traditional contraception in SSA.

Data and methods

Review approach

The Preferred Reporting Items for Systematic Reviews and Meta-Analyses (PRISMA) (Shamseer et al., 2015) checklist was applied in screening papers/articles/studies for eligibility and inclusion in the review.

Search strategy and data extraction

Peer-reviewed articles on traditional contraception, published in English between 1990 and 2019, were retrieved from PubMed and Web of Science. Data from PubMed were retrieved using the RISmed (Kovalchik, 2017) package in R, while data for Web of Science were retrieved manually based on the same search terms used for the PubMed search. Additional studies were retrieved from an advanced search in Google Scholar and JSTOR, again based on the same search terms.

Search query and study selection

A number of tools from the R software were employed to automate the study eligibility check and selection process. RISmed (Kovalchik, 2017) was used for reference extraction from bibliographic data in PubMed. The extraction of references in both PubMed and Web of Science was aided by using the following search terms *'(driver OR determinant OR factor OR barrier OR facilitator) AND (use OR practice OR behavior OR preference) AND (contraception OR traditional contraceptive OR family planning) AND (sub-Saharan Africa OR resource limited OR low income OR middle income OR Africa OR SSA OR Angola OR Benin OR Botswana OR Burkina Faso OR Burundi OR Cameroon OR Cape Verde OR Central African Republic OR Chad OR Comoros OR Congo OR Congo Democratic Republic OR Ivory Coast OR Djibouti OR Equatorial Guinea OR Eritrea OR Ethiopia OR Gabon OR Gambia OR Ghana OR Guinea OR Guinea-Bissau OR Kenya OR Lesotho OR Liberia OR Madagascar OR Malawi OR Mali OR Mauritania OR Mauritius OR Mozambique OR Namibia OR Niger OR Nigeria OR Reunion OR Rwanda OR Sao Tome OR Senegal OR Seychelles OR Sierra Leone OR Somalia OR South Africa OR Sudan OR Swaziland OR Tanzania OR Togo OR Uganda OR Western Sahara OR Zambia OR Zimbabwe)'*. Following the initial search, the inclusion and exclusion criteria for selecting studies to be included in the study were applied.

Inclusion and exclusion criteria

One of the features that distinguishes a systematic review from a narrative review is that in conducting a systematic review, the authors need to pre-specify the criteria for including and excluding studies in the review (McKenzie et al., 2019). Accordingly, the inclusion criteria for this review were: (1) peer-reviewed studies that addressed traditional contraception use – enablers, barriers, and interventions in sub-Saharan Africa; (2) conducted between 1990 and 2019; (3) published in English; (4) measured barriers and/or enablers related to traditional contraceptive uptake and/or use; and (5) employed quantitative, qualitative, or mixed methods approaches. The exclusion criteria were: (1) studies that did not examine traditional contraceptive through quantitative, qualitative, or mixed-methods approaches; (2) studies that focused solely on modern contraception or condom use only; (3) studies with insufficient information on study design, time frame, and measures used; and (4) studies that were not published in English and cross-country studies that included regions outside SSA. The PRISMA plot in Figure 14.1 shows how the search strategy was applied in arriving at the studies/articles included in the review.

Following the automated extraction process, the titles and abstracts of papers that met the inclusion and exclusion criteria were manually reviewed to select eligible studies. The title and abstract screening was performed by all three authors (JD, FD, and RD). In carrying out the screening, abstracts of references in the data retrieved from PubMed and Web of Science were evenly distributed into three efforts for screening using the Metagear package (Lajeunesse, 2016). The titles and abstracts of studies that clearly mentioned the outcomes of the review (factors associated/determinants/predictors/drivers of family planning service utilization with a focus on traditional methods) were considered for further evaluation and inclusion in the systematic review. The full text of the studies/papers that were selected from the title and abstract screening stage were further evaluated based on the objectives, methods, participants/population, and key findings. A total of 18 full papers that met all the evaluation criteria were included in the final review.

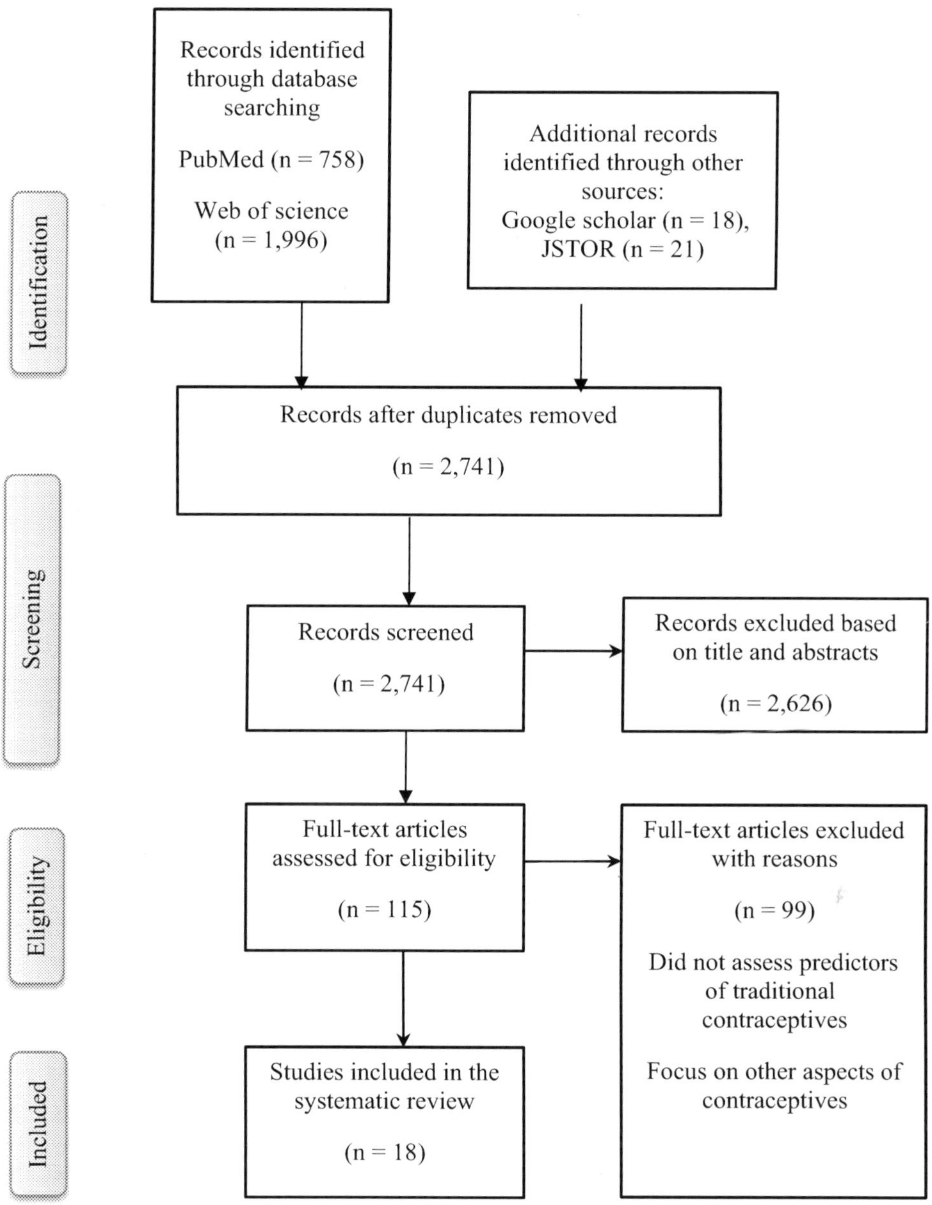

Figure 14.1 Application of inclusion and exclusion criteria for selecting articles for the review

Quality appraisal

The quality assessment tool for observational cohort and cross-sectional studies which consists of 14 criteria used in assessing different aspects of a study was employed in this review. Previous studies (Njagi, Arsenijevic, & Groot, 2018; Okedo-Alex, Ifeyinwa, Obumneme, & Chigozie,

2019; Wardle & Steel, 2015) have applied this quality assessment tool in conducting systematic reviews.

Synthesis methods

The reviewers discussed the full text of the 18 studies/papers that met all the evaluation criteria, and selected studies were accessed to analyze similarities and discrepancies in the key findings especially in the key drivers identified by each paper/study. The results were then summarized by sub-region and presented by category of factors associated with traditional contraceptive practice.

Results

Studies included in review

The search query in PubMed yielded 758 articles, while the same search query yielded 1,996 articles in Web of Science. The manual search in Google Scholar and JSTOR yielded another 39 articles. A total of 2,741 primary articles on the determinants of traditional contraception in SSA were realized from the search of all the various databases after excluding duplicates. After reviewing the title and abstract of the 2,741 retrieved articles, 2,626 were excluded as inappropriate for the current systematic review and meta-analysis. A total of 115 full-text articles were assessed for eligibility, and 99 of these were excluded because they either did not address determinants of traditional contraception or focused on other aspects of contraception. The review is thus based on 18 full-text articles appropriately selected as being eligible according to the inclusion and exclusion criteria.

The reviewed studies used different study designs, most of which were cross-sectional studies and secondary analyses of data at the national or sub-national level. Table 14.1 shows a summary

Table 14.1 Summary of Studies Included in the Review by Sub-Region

Sub-Region/Country	*References*	*Study Design and Subject of Focus*
Eastern Africa		
Malawi	(Kalipeni & Zulu, 1993)	– Secondary data analysis – Men (aged 20–59) and women (aged 15–54)
Uganda	(Ntozi & Kabera, 1991)	– Secondary data analysis – Women aged 15–49 years
Zimbabwe	(Guilkey & Jayne, 1997)	– Secondary data analysis – Women aged 15–35
Kenya	(Magadi & Siân, 2003; Ochako, Gichuhi, & Open, 2016)	– Cross-sectional quantitative study and secondary data analysis – Women aged 15–49 years
Middle Africa		
Cameroon	(Ekani-Bessala, Carre, Thierry, & Patrick, 1998; Johnson-Hanks, 2002)	– Secondary data analysis – Women aged 15–49 years
West Africa		
Benin	(Dansou et al., 2017)	– Secondary data analysis – Women aged 15–49 years

(*Continued*)

Sub-Region/Country	References	Study Design and Subject of Focus
Ghana	(Addai, 1999; Oheneba-Sakyi, 1990, 1992)	– Secondary data analysis – Women aged 15–49 years
Nigeria	(Adanikin, Nuala, & Sabu, 2017; Jinadu & Ajuwon, 1997; Ujuju et al., 2011)	– Secondary data analysis – Women aged 15–49 years – Cross-sectional study – Women aged 19–40 years
The Gambia	(Bledsoe et al., 1994)	– Cross-sectional study (qualitative) – Women aged 15–54 years
Multi-country	(Rossier & Jamaica, 2017; Staveteig, Lindsay, & Rebecca, 2015; Sullivan, Jane, Janet, & James, 2006)	– Secondary data analysis – Women aged 15–49 years

of the studies included in the systematic review by country and sub-region. The review includes studies that were conducted in Benin (Dansou, Adekunle, & Arowojolu, 2017), Cameroon (Ekani-Bessala, Carre, Thierry, & Patrick, 1998; Johnson-Hanks, 2002), Ghana (Addai, 1999; Oheneba-Sakyi, 1990, 1992), Kenya (Magadi & Siân, 2003; Ochako, Gichuhi, & Open, 2016), Malawi (Kalipeni & Zulu, 1993), Nigeria (Adanikin, Nuala, & Sabu, 2017; Ujuju et al., 2011), Uganda (Ntozi & Kabera, 1991), The Gambia (Bledsoe, Hill, D'alessandro, & Langerock, 1994), and Zimbabwe (Guilkey & Jayne, 1997). The review also includes two multi-country studies (Rossier & Jamaica, 2017; Staveteig, Lindsay, & Rebecca, 2015) involving Niger, Nigeria, Senegal, Sierra Leone, Liberia, Rwanda Burundi, Zambia, and Zimbabwe conducted by Staveteig and colleagues (2015) and another study involving 29 countries conducted by Rossier and Jamaica (2017).

The traditional methods of contraception mentioned in the studies included in the review include periodic abstinence, the withdrawal method, and natural method or fertility awareness, among others. Table 14.2 shows a description of the traditional methods of contraception mentioned in the studies included in the systematic review.

Factors associated with traditional contraceptive methods practice

Sociodemographic characteristics and traditional contraceptive practice

The results of the review show that the characteristics of individual women, their partners, and the household the women belong to are associated with traditional contraceptive practice among sub-Saharan African women (Table 14.3). Key among these individual characteristics are demographic and socio-economic factors such as age and wealth. Considering age, older women were found to be more likely to use a traditional method, and the age effect was found to exist in all sub-regions except West Africa (Rossier & Jamaica, 2017). Similar results have also been found in specific countries. For example, in rural Gambia, young women relied more on traditional methods (herbs, charms, and abstinence) compared to the older women, and in the North Bank area of Gambia, charms were often prepared for very young married women who were deemed physically immature to carry a child to term and deliver safely (Bledsoe et al., 1994). Similarly, 15–35-year-old women in Zimbabwe were found to be less likely to use traditional methods of contraception relative to modern methods (Guilkey & Jayne, 1997). In the Cameroonian context, Johnson-Hanks (2002) found that periodic abstinence is the most

Table 14.2 Description of Traditional Contraceptive Methods Explored by Studies Included in the Review

Traditional Contraceptive Method	*Description*	*References*
Abstinence	It is the most widely known and practiced method of birth spacing in sub-Saharan Africa. Although also used for stopping childbearing, periodic abstinence is particularly important for birth spacing and for postponing the first birth.	(Adanikin et al., 2017; Addai, 1999; Bledsoe et al., 1994; Dansou et al., 2017; Guilkey & Jayne, 1997; Johnson-Hanks, 2002; Kalipeni & Zulu, 1993; Magadi & Siân, 2003; Ntozi & Kabera, 1991; Oheneba-Sakyi, 1990, 1992; Rossier & Jamaica, 2017; Staveteig et al., 2015; Sullivan et al., 2006)
Herbal juices and concoctions (drink herbs, belt herbs, and herbs cut in body)	Herbally treated strings with wooden beads are among the most widely known traditional methods of birth spacing in SSA, particularly in Malawi. Herbally treated strings and beads are tied around the woman's waist throughout the time when a pregnancy is not desired. Herbal juices can also be taken orally as a contraceptive, much like the modern pill. Sometimes juices or concoctions are inserted in the vagina to act as spermicides during copulation.	(Addai, 1999; Kalipeni & Zulu, 1993; Ntozi & Kabera, 1991; Staveteig et al., 2015)
Traditional abortifacients	In rare circumstances, herbal medicines or abortifacients are administered to effect induced abortion, even though abortion is condemned in most SSA countries.	(Kalipeni & Zulu, 1993)
Natural method or fertility awareness: Safe period/ rhythm	It is a method of contraception where women monitor and record fertility signals during their menstrual cycle to work out when they are likely to get pregnant. Safe period is also called the rhythm method. It refers to the period during the menstrual cycle when conception is considered least likely to occur. It is usually a number of days prior and subsequent to the onset of menstruation.	(Addai, 1999; Ekani-Bessala et al., 1998; Guilkey & Jayne, 1997; Kalipeni & Zulu, 1993; Magadi & Siân, 2003; Ochako et al., 2016; Ujuju et al., 2011)

Coitus interruptus (withdrawal)	It is a method of preventing pregnancy in which the man removes his penis from the woman's vagina before sperm is released. It is also called the pulling-out method, aiming to prevent sperm from entering the vagina. There are two types of withdrawal. Coitus interruptus is the Latin name for withdrawal with ejaculation taking place afterwards. Coitus reservatus is the Latin name for withdrawal without ejaculation. Both have been used since ancient times for contraception and for other reasons.	(Adanikin et al., 2017; Addai, 1999; Bledsoe et al., 1994; Dansou et al., 2017; Ekani-Bessala et al., 1998; Guilkey & Jayne, 1997; Kalipeni & Zulu, 1993; Magadi & Siân, 2003; Ntozi & Kabera, 1991; Ochako et al., 2016; Oheneba-Sakyi, 1990, 1992; Rossier & Jamaica, 2017; Staveteig et al., 2015; Sullivan et al., 2006)
Wearing amulets/rings	The amulets (engisha) are sewn into a garment worn close to the body. It is a practice which consists of wearing amulets such as a ring or the testicles of a weasel on their thighs or hanging its amputated foot from around their necks or wearing wreaths of herbs or desiccated cat livers.	(Ntozi & Kabera, 1991)
Burying carrier	When a child dies, it is buried with the cloth that was used to carry it, and thereby, it is believed the mother cannot conceive again.	(Ntozi & Kabera, 1991)
Douche/douching	It is a method of washing out the vagina, usually with water or a spermicidal agent after sex. It affects only sperm that remain in the vaginal canal.	(Oheneba-Sakyi, 1990)
Soup, incision, waistband, ring	Explored among the Yoruba of Southwestern Nigeria. No specific description is available.	(Jinadu & Ajuwon, 1997)
First child ritual	The first-born carries the last-born in the first-born's baby carrier and places him/her on the eaves of the house. It includes 'putting a child on eaves of the house', 'hot food', and 'first born behind the house'.	(Ntozi & Kabera, 1991)
Baby's foot	Immediately after delivery, the baby's foot is inserted back in the opening of the womb, and the person inserting it says: 'Let the productivity stop here'.	(Ntozi & Kabera, 1991)

(*Continued*)

Table 14.2 (Continued)

Traditional Contraceptive Method	*Description*	*References*
Umbilical cord	The umbilical cord of the last-born is worn by the mother around the waist. When she wants to conceive again, she may remove the umbilical cord.	(Ntozi & Kabera, 1991)
Placenta on ant hill	After delivery, the first-born takes the placenta of the last-born to an ant hill. The placenta is then inverted, and a big stone is placed on it.	(Ntozi & Kabera, 1991)
Son-in-law	A woman puts on her son-in-law's clothes when she is having her monthly periods, and this is said to stop her menstrual cycle	(Ntozi & Kabera, 1991)
Leaves inserted	The leaves of some plants, like esitaimwe or shagama nungi, are softened by either half drying or boiling them. They are then inserted before sexual intercourse to prevent the semen from reaching the womb.	(Ntozi & Kabera, 1991)
Prolonged breastfeeding	Breastfeeding for more than 19 months.	(Ntozi & Kabera, 1991)
Postpartum	Period of voluntary sexual abstinence after delivery; when combined with postpartum amenorrhea, this is the period of insusceptibility to pregnancy.	(Guilkey & Jayne, 1997; Kalipeni & Zulu, 1993)

Table 14.3 Summary of Studies Included in the Review by Key Drivers

Factor/Driver	*References*
Male partners' contraceptive perceptions and involvement	(Adanikin et al., 2017; Ekani-Bessala et al., 1998; Sullivan et al., 2006; Ujuju et al., 2011)
Decision-making power	(Adanikin et al., 2017)
Reproductive health behaviors	(Dansou et al., 2017)
Household wealth index	(Adanikin et al., 2017; Dansou et al., 2017; Ochako et al., 2016; Rossier & Jamaica, 2017)
Age	(Bledsoe et al., 1994; Guilkey & Jayne, 1997; Johnson-Hanks, 2002; Magadi & Siân, 2003; Oheneba-Sakyi, 1990; Rossier & Jamaica, 2017)
Female education	(Adanikin et al., 2017; Guilkey & Jayne, 1997; Johnson-Hanks, 2002; Magadi & Siân, 2003; Ntozi & Kabera, 1991; Ochako et al., 2016; Oheneba-Sakyi, 1990; Rossier & Jamaica, 2017)
Occupation	(Ntozi & Kabera, 1991; Ochako et al., 2016; Oheneba-Sakyi, 1990)
Place of residence	(Adanikin et al., 2017; Guilkey & Jayne, 1997; Ochako et al., 2016)
Region of residence	(Adanikin et al., 2017; Addai, 1999; Dansou et al., 2017; Guilkey & Jayne, 1997; Magadi & Siân, 2003; Ochako et al., 2016; Oheneba-Sakyi, 1990)
Household size	(Ochako et al., 2016)
Fertility desire	(Dansou et al., 2017; Guilkey & Jayne, 1997; Oheneba-Sakyi, 1990)
Desire for pregnancy	(Ochako et al., 2016)
Knowledge of traditional methods	(Kalipeni & Zulu, 1993; Rossier & Jamaica, 2017)
Number of living children	(Addai, 1999, 1999; Bledsoe et al., 1994; Ekani-Bessala et al., 1998; Jinadu & Ajuwon, 1997; Magadi & Siân, 2003; Ochako et al., 2016)
Marital status	(Johnson-Hanks, 2002; Magadi & Siân, 2003; Rossier & Jamaica, 2017)
Discussion about FP and consent seeking	(Bledsoe et al., 1994; Dansou et al., 2017; Ekani-Bessala et al., 1998; Kalipeni & Zulu, 1993; Oheneba-Sakyi, 1992)
Cultural and religious membership	(Adanikin et al., 2017; Dansou et al., 2017; Guilkey & Jayne, 1997; Magadi & Siân, 2003; Ntozi & Kabera, 1991; Ochako et al., 2016; Oheneba-Sakyi, 1990; Rossier & Jamaica, 2017; Ujuju et al., 2011)
Perceived effectiveness and purpose of the method	(Jinadu & Ajuwon, 1997; Ntozi & Kabera, 1991)

prevalent method of contraception among young women aged 20–24 years (Johnson-Hanks, 2002). He further argues that the category of women who turn to periodic abstinence are highly motivated to avoid a mistimed birth and are amply informed about available methods. Their choice of a traditional method is grounded precisely in the modern conjuncture that they face: postponing childbearing while finishing school and seeking formal-sector employment (Johnson-Hanks, 2002). Magadi and Siân (2003) also found that younger women in Kenya tend to be more likely to use traditional methods compared to their older counterparts.

The findings with regard to women's level of education and traditional contraceptive practice show a mixed pattern. While women with some level of schooling in Ghana were less likely to use traditional contraceptive methods (TCMs) (Oheneba-Sakyi, 1990), Kenyan women with secondary and higher education were more likely to use TCMs (Ochako et al., 2016). Similarly, highly educated women in Uganda were more likely to have ever used TCMs compared to less educated women or women with no formal education (Ntozi & Kabera, 1991). And in Zimbabwe, women with 4–6 years of schooling were more likely to use TCMs (Guilkey & Jayne, 1997). Similarly, in Nigeria, women with higher level of education were more likely to use TCMs (Adanikin et al., 2017). Another study found that educated women are more likely to use TCMs rather than no method when in need, but when the sample is limited to women who use any method of contraception, traditional or modern, the association between education and TCM use is significant only in East Africa (Rossier & Jamaica, 2017). In Cameroon, the use of TCMs was found to be most prevalent among educated women (Johnson-Hanks, 2002). But in Kenya, it was found that variations in the choice of different types of methods by level of educational attainment seems minimal, although highly educated women are more likely to use long-term methods, whereas those with no formal education are more likely to use TCMs (Magadi & Siân, 2003). The results also reveal a mixed pattern when considering women's employment status and traditional contraceptive practice (Ntozi & Kabera, 1991; Ochako et al., 2016; Oheneba-Sakyi, 1990). While currently employed women in Uganda were more likely to have ever used TCMs (Ntozi & Kabera,1991), in Kenya, the reverse was true: unemployed women were more likely to use a TCM rather than no method compared to those who were self-employed (Ochako et al., 2016). And in Ghana, women who were working in the agriculture sector were found to be more likely to use TCMs (Oheneba-Sakyi, 1990).

Aside from the individual characteristics of women themselves, the characteristics of the household women belong to were found to influence traditional contraceptive practice (Adanikin et al., 2017; Ochako et al., 2016). One of the household factors that was found to influence traditional contraceptive practice is household size. In Kenya, household size was found to be an important determinant of choice of contraceptive method. Specifically, women in households with four or more members were more likely to use a traditional method (Ochako et al., 2016). Another household factor found to be associated with traditional contraceptive practice is household wealth status. The findings from the review, however, show some indications that are contrary to expectation. For example, in Nigeria, women living in households belonging to the richer/richest wealth quintile were more likely to use TCMs compared to women belonging to poor households (Adanikin et al., 2017), and in Kenya, women from rich households were more likely to use a TCM rather than no method compared to women from poor households (Ochako et al., 2016).

Residence characteristics were also found to influence traditional contraceptive practice among women in SSA. Rural residence was associated with a lower likelihood of traditional contraception among Nigerian women (Adanikin et al., 2017), but in Zimbabwe, urban rather than rural residence was found to be associated with traditional contraception. In Benin, women from the Alibori, Mono, and Oueme regions were less likely to use TCM compared to their counterparts living in Littoral (Dansou et al., 2017), while in Zimbabwe, women residing in urban areas were found to be less likely to use TCM rather than modern or no method of contraception (Guilkey & Jayne, 1997). Again, in the context of Kenya, it was found that women living in non-slum settlements were more likely to use traditional methods of contraception compared to their counterparts living in slum settlements (Ochako et al., 2016). An earlier study conducted in Kenya also found that the probability of using TCMs was higher in rural than in urban areas among married women (15–49 years) (Magadi & Siân, 2003). In some specific countries, there were further geographic variations in the chances of traditional contraceptive practice. For example, women living in the northern part of Nigeria were less likely to use TCMs (Adanikin et al., 2017), and women from the Volta region in Ghana were more likely to use TCM, while those from the Eastern/Ashanti/Brong Ahafo regions were less likely to use TCMs relative to those from the Northern, Upper East, and Upper West regions (Addai,

1999). Earlier studies in the same setting found that women from the Northern region were less likely to use TCM (Oheneba-Sakyi, 1990, 1992).

Cultural beliefs, religious membership, and traditional contraceptive practice

In SSA, fertility and reproductive behaviors such as contraception are influenced by cultural beliefs and religious practices (Adanikin et al., 2017; Guilkey & Jayne, 1997; Ntozi & Kabera, 1991; Ochako et al., 2016; Oheneba-Sakyi, 1990; Ujuju et al., 2011). Contraception in particular is influenced by the religious belief of individuals and couples and also prevailing cultural practices as defined by ethnic or some other form of cultural grouping. Sometimes religious and cultural factors act synergistically to influence contraceptive practice. One religious group that has been documented to have unique stances on contraception is the Catholic faith. Women of the Catholic faith in Nigeria have been found to be less likely to use TCMs compared to women of the Protestant and Islamic faith (Adanikin et al., 2017). Another qualitative study in Enugu and Katsina states in Nigeria found that both users and providers perceive the standard days method as religiously and culturally acceptable. The standard days method was also found to be particularly useful among women who could not use hormonal methods for medical reasons. Additionally, it was realized that involving religious and community leaders contributed significantly to acceptance of the method (Ujuju et al., 2011). Similarly, in Uganda, Anglican women were found to be more apt to have ever used traditional methods compared to women of other religious faiths (Ntozi & Kabera, 1991). In Ghana, non-Christian women were more likely to use TCMs (Oheneba-Sakyi, 1990), but in Zimbabwe, Christian women were less likely to use TCM relative to modern methods of contraception (Guilkey & Jayne, 1997). Considering ethnic variations, Luo women in Kenya were more likely to use a traditional method compared to their Kikuyu counterparts (Ochako et al., 2016).

Reproductive behaviors, spousal characteristics, and TCMs

Certain reproductive behaviors are associated with contraception and fertility in general, and this review found that these reproductive behaviors are related to traditional contraceptive practice among women in SSA (Guilkey & Jayne, 1997; Oheneba-Sakyi, 1990). Considering marital status and traditional contraceptive practice, Johnson-Hanks (2002) found that in the Cameroonian context, periodic abstinence is the most common method used by women of most social categories; however, its use is most prevalent among unmarried women. In Kenya, single women were found to be more likely to use TCMs compared to their married counterparts (Magadi & Siân, 2003). Considering age at first marriage, evidence from Ghana suggests that women who go into marriage at or after age 20 were less likely to use TCMs (Oheneba-Sakyi, 1990), and women who desire a large number of children were more likely to use TCM relative to modern methods (Oheneba-Sakyi, 1990). But in Zimbabwe, women who want a child soon were less likely to use TCMs, and they were also more likely to use TCMs instead of modern methods compared to women who did not want any more children (Guilkey & Jayne, 1997). The odds of using contraception were also found to vary depending on whether contraception was being used for the purpose of limiting or spacing births. Some studies suggest that, in general, women in SSA tend to use TCMs for limiting births, but there is also indication that limiters have almost 40% greater odds of using a modern method compared to spacers (Rossier & Jamaica, 2017). Additionally, studies on pregnancy wantedness in Kenya show that compared to women who have never been pregnant, women who reported that their pregnancy was intended were less likely to use a traditional method (Ochako et al., 2016). In Cameroon, it has been found that having had an illegal abortion increases the odds of TCM use among women (Ekani-Bessala et al., 1998).

In terms of having children and using traditional contraception, the results are mixed. While Kenyan women with at least one child were less likely to report using TCM (Ochako et al., 2016), Magadi and Siân (2003) found that the probability of using TCM was highest for women who have no living children. In Ghana, women without children were more likely to use TCMs, while those with three or four children were less likely to use TCMs (Addai, 1999). But in Cameroon, women with three or more children were more likely to use TCMs (Ekani-Bessala et al., 1998). In The Gambia, women whose last child was still alive were more likely to use TCM compared to those whose last child had died (Bledsoe et al., 1994). There is limited evidence on the sex of living children and traditional contraceptive practice, but among the Yoruba in Southwestern Nigeria, users of TCM were found to have more sons than non-users, and non-users were found to have more daughters than users (Jinadu & Ajuwon, 1997).

Male partners' contraceptive perceptions and involvement, discussion about family planning, and consent

The decision to use contraception or not and which methods of contraception to use is also driven by discussions among partners and sometimes other family members. Partners' knowledge about method types also influences which type of method(s) the couple use. Magadi and Siân (2003) report that partner's approval of family planning is important in method choice and that women whose partners disapprove of family planning are most likely to use TCMs. Similarly, in Malawi, more men compared to women report knowledge and practice of traditional methods, and a greater proportion of men indicated that the majority of the decisions to use herbal juices were initiated by them (men), while decisions to use strings were generally made by women (Kalipeni & Zulu, 1993). However, the women's reports show that women themselves were the main decision-makers for both methods (Kalipeni & Zulu, 1993). There were also appreciable differences between males and females in their reasons for favoring or disliking the use of contraception. Men tended to emphasize economic factors in their approval of contraception, while women emphasized factors related to health. In some countries, the decision to use traditional contraception is required to be a joint decision by the couple. For example, in rural Gambia, most ritual specialists refused to prepare charms (one of the most common TCMs in the region) for women without the husband's consent (Bledsoe et al., 1994), while in Benin, women who reported having discussed family planning topics with their partners within the last four weeks were more likely to use TCM (Dansou et al., 2017). The decision to use TCM is also influenced by the opinion of partners. For example, in Ghana, women were more likely to use TCMs if they approved family planning alone compared to if the husband also approved family planning (Oheneba-Sakyi, 1992), and in Cameroun, women who had the approval of the partner (if present) were more likely to use TCMs (Ekani-Bessala et al., 1998), while in other settings, women whose husbands were absent were less likely to use any contraception (Guilkey & Jayne, 1997).

Drivers of traditional contraceptive practice in SSA and knowledge of traditional methods

The level of knowledge about TCMs as well as the actual use of TCMs in SSA varies from country to country. But lack of knowledge about TCMs seems to contribute to lower rates of use in SSA, particularly among the uneducated, the very poor, and Muslim women. Rossier and Jamaica (2017) found that although knowledge of periodic abstinence or withdrawal is lower than knowledge of modern methods, traditional contraceptive practice appears to be fairly widespread in SSA, especially in Central Africa, where knowledge of traditional methods is greater than knowledge of modern methods. The results of the present review indicate that higher modern contraceptive prevalence at the country level is significantly associated with decreased odds of using TCMs. However, it was also realized that lack of knowledge of traditional methods most likely contributes to lower levels of use among the poorest and less/uneducated women. Additionally, the fact that periodic abstinence and promotion of the standard days method are often associated with Catholic/Christian outreach programs probably explains why Muslim women are less likely to know about or use traditional methods of contraception (Rossier & Jamaica, 2017). However, the propensity to use TCMs appears to be lower in countries with a higher prevalence of modern method use, which seems to suggest that women's ease of access to modern methods also influences method choice (Rossier & Jamaica, 2017). Country-specific studies also show different results. For example, a survey conducted in Malawi found that most people are knowledgeable about both traditional and modern methods of contraception (Kalipeni & Zulu, 1993). However, in spite of the general positive associations between knowledge and use of TCMs, in some instances, lack of knowledge about TCMs resulted in method discontinuation. Additionally, analysis of data from four sub-Saharan Africa countries indicates that women relied on postpartum amenorrhea as a traditional method without knowing its limitations (Gebreselassie et al., 2017).

Perceived effectiveness, purpose, and motivation for using different methods of contraception

Traditional methods of contraception are preferred by some women over modern methods because of the perceived benefits and effectiveness of TCMs. For example, in rural Uganda, although women pointed out a long list of TCMs, they did not use methods they did not believe were effective. The so-called effective TCMs that were widely used were prolonged breastfeeding, withdrawal, and abstinence. Again, it appeared the main purpose of practicing traditional contraception for these women in rural Uganda was the benefit of increasing birth intervals for the health of the child rather than for family planning reasons. In Nigeria, Jinadu and Ajuwon (1997) found that users of traditional contraceptives had great confidence in their effectiveness and the absence of side effects. In addition, users of TCMs trusted the traditional healers whom they consulted regularly for other health issues and who prescribed contraceptive methods. In contrast, none of the women in this study encouraged their husbands to practice coitus interruptus or use condoms, fearing their husbands would not like either method (Jinadu & Ajuwon, 1997). Cameroonian women have also been found to prefer periodic abstinence for two reasons. First, it is not associated with any negative effects – whether reproductive, sexual, or social – in contrast to nearly all other methods. Second, periodic abstinence is perceived as uniquely modern and morally acceptable, as it conforms almost perfectly to local notions of self-discipline, temporal management, and measured self-restraint (Johnson-Hanks, 2002). Furthermore, many Cameroonian women were concerned that in addition to causing physical harm, medical contraceptive techniques will inhibit a natural and healthy sexual life, making the woman unattractive or destroying her desire for sex. As such, while some older women whose identity as honorable mothers has already been established might be willing to give up their future fecundity for the ease and convenience of sterilization, for young women, periodic abstinence is more appealing. Furthermore, there are indications that most Cameroonian women and most users of periodic abstinence are highly motivated to protect their sexual and reproductive health, ensuring their physical desirability and their future marriage (Johnson-Hanks, 2002). In southern Cameroon, a healthy sexual life is considered essential to physical well-being, both for men and women, and disturbances to pleasurable sex are considered problematic (Laburthe-Tolra, 1977; Ombolo, 1990). Modern methods of contraception are thus not only considered inconvenient or undesirable but actually physically dangerous and disruptive to normal sexual function (Johnson-Hanks, 2002). Thus, when contraceptive methods are perceived to inhibit good sex, they are largely rejected. This rejection applies not only to condoms but also to pills, which are said to make a woman unattractive and decrease her physical desire for her partner. In a qualitative study, one woman explained that "Taking the pill, I find that ugly, bad, whatever. That will come to change your body, the way your body works. So it is not useful to take the pill". Similarly, many women consider the IUD harmful to sexual welfare, because a partner could get pierced or harmed during sex, making intercourse physically uncomfortable and emotionally tense. Additionally, long-term hormonal contraceptives are thought to make a woman lifeless and physically undesirable and inhibit fertility much longer after the clinical effects (Johnson-Hanks, 2002).

Discussion

The current study systematically reviewed and synthesized evidence on the drivers of traditional contraceptive practice in SSA, focusing on studies published on traditional family planning in SSA between 1990 and 2019. The drivers of TCMs identified in the review include socio-demographic characteristics of women (including their age, marital status, level of education, and type of occupation), household characteristics (including household wealth status, household size, decision-making power), residence characteristics (place of residence, region of residence), and reproductive behaviors (fertility desire, pregnancy history and desire for pregnancy, number of living children, and sex preference of children). Other factors include male partners' perception of and involvement in the use of contraception, discussion about family planning, and consent seeking. Knowledge about traditional methods of contraception, cultural and religious membership, perceived effectiveness and purpose of methods, social motivation, and community effect, among others, were also found to be associated with traditional contraceptive practice in SSA.

Considering marital status as one of the demographic factors identified to be associated with traditional contraceptive practice, all the studies that were reviewed were unanimous: single/never-married women were more likely to use TCMs compared to their married counterparts (Johnson-Hanks, 2002; Magadi & Siân, 2003; Rossier & Jamaica, 2017). This could be explained by the fear of side effects often associated with modern methods which tend to be reported by single women who fear the possibility of primary sterility before marriage from using modern methods of contraception, as reported in Nigeria (Jinadu & Ajuwon, 1997). Similar explanations were provided among young, educated Cameroonian women, who overwhelmingly preferred periodic abstinence (Johnson-Hanks, 2002). Thus the fear of side effects and the social acceptability of TCMs makes traditional contraception a much preferred option among women SSA, particularly young women.

Another key driver of traditional contraceptive practice reported by the studies included in this review was educational attainment. Educated women showed higher odds of TCM practice from the studies highlighting these relationships in Ghana (Oheneba-Sakyi, 1990), Uganda (Ntozi & Kabera, 1991), Zimbabwe (Guilkey & Jayne, 1997), Nigeria (Adanikin et al., 2017), Cameroon (Johnson-Hanks, 2002), and Kenya (Ochako et al., 2016). These findings are, however, contrary to previous reports that show that lack of knowledge of traditional methods seems to contribute to lower rates of use among uneducated women in SSA (Rossier & Jamaica, 2017). The higher likelihood of traditional contraceptive practice among educated women could be because educated women would be more likely to have better understanding of how traditional contraceptives work, which may seem less complex compared to modern methods. For instance, withdrawal, which does not require supplies or visits to the clinic or pharmacy and only requires male involvement and couple communication at the act of sex (World Health Organization Department of Reproductive Health and Research [WHO/RHR] and Johns Hopkins Bloomberg School of Public Health/Center for Communication Programs [CCP], Knowledge for Health Project, 2018), may be viewed as a less complex option with no side effects. Educated women may thus see traditional methods as safe and prefer such methods over modern methods. Additionally, educated women, particularly those who are highly educated, may want to have children after delaying childbearing due to schooling. Such women would thus prefer to use traditional methods rather than long-acting modern methods of contraception. Despite these findings, the available evidence is not consistent. For example a study conducted in Kenya found that females with no formal education were most likely to use traditional methods (Magadi & Siân, 2003). Again, this could be because of the lack of understanding of how modern methods work on the part of these women who are not formally educated.

The findings regarding wealth status are also somewhat similar to those of educational attainment. The findings of two studies included in the current review reported significant association between TCM practice and household wealth index (Adanikin et al., 2017; Ochako et al., 2016), such that living in a high wealth status household was associated with increased odds of using traditional methods. This finding suggests that the preferred use of TCMs over modern methods is not necessarily due to financial constraints. It is plausible that rich women may be more informed about the side effects of modern methods, and thus their fear of the side effects of modern methods drives the use of TCMs.

Spousal/partners' characteristics, including their perception and involvement in contraceptive decision-making, were also found to be predisposing factors for traditional contraceptive practice in Nigeria (Adanikin et al., 2017; Ujuju et al., 2011), Ghana (Oheneba-Sakyi, 1992), and Cameroon (Ekani-Bessala et al., 1998). In Nigeria, men's fear that women who use family planning may become promiscuous was associated with increased odds of using traditional methods; however, this method was seen as a less effective family planning method with short-term actions. The reason for this finding could be because men with such beliefs do not trust their partners. Therefore women use TCMs, which can be discontinued immediately if their partners do not agree to using contraception. Again, some of the TCMs, for example, withdrawal, are within the control of male partners and thus can be employed as and when needed. This plausibly explains why men's involvement in communication about contraception among couples was associated with a choice of TCM, as reported in the Katsina and Enugu states in Nigeria (Ujuju et al., 2011). Such beliefs are also in line with the findings of a study conducted in Cameroon which found that women who did not have a partner regularly present at home were more likely to use TCMs (Ekani-Bessala et al., 1998). Furthermore, in highly traditional societies, extramarital sexual relationships are not acceptable and sometimes come with great consequences for women. In such a context, when the decision-making power is given to women, they will prefer to use traditional rather than modern methods, as reported in Nigeria (Adanikin et al., 2017), to avoid any form of suspicion. This could be because of the fact that women, even with good decision-making power, fear being accused of being promiscuous when adopting modern contraceptive methods, especially long-acting methods. Furthermore, in some contexts, apart from the partners in a union, the decision to use family planning sometimes involves people other than the couple. For example, the role of mothers-in-law in family planning has been reported in Malawi (Kalipeni & Zulu, 1993). In rural Gambia, most ritual specialists refuse to prepare charms – one of the most common TCMs in the region – for women without the husband's consent (Bledsoe et al., 1994). These perceptions are also influenced by cultural and religious differences in traditional contraceptive practice, as has been reported in the studies included in the present review (Adanikin et al., 2017; Guilkey & Jayne, 1997; Ochako et al., 2016; Oheneba-Sakyi, 1990; Ujuju et al., 2011). These influences are further compounded by ethnic and religious differences. These cultural, religious, and ethnic influences of traditional contraception are probably driven by, for example, some Christian religious doctrines that disapprove of traditional methods such as withdrawal, as it is believed this method goes against the mandate of procreation instructed by God.

Fertility desire was also widely documented among the key drivers of TCMs in the current review. The desire for many children was positively associated with traditional contraceptive use in Ghana (Oheneba-Sakyi, 1990) and Zimbabwe (Guilkey & Jayne, 1997). For women who desire to have a child/more children, the fear of the effects of long-acting modern methods may drive them towards the use of TCMs instead. This was found to be true in Zimbabwe, where women who want a child soon were more likely to use traditional methods instead of modern methods (Guilkey & Jayne, 1997; Kalipeni & Zulu, 1993). Similar findings pertaining to number of living children have also been reported in Ghana (Addai, 1999), Cameroon (Ekani-Bessala et al., 1998), Kenya (Magadi & Siân, 2003; Ochako et al., 2016), and The Gambia (Bledsoe et al., 1994). The influence of high parity on traditional contraceptive use may be because women with high fertility use TCM for birth spacing. In rural Uganda, it appears that the main purpose of practicing traditional contraception was to increase the birth intervals for the health of the child rather than for family planning reasons (Ntozi & Kabera, 1991). These findings therefore suggest that traditional contraception may be preferred for child spacing and not necessarily for limiting. There is a need for more research to unpack the nuances in the use of traditional contraception for spacing versus limiting births.

The current review also revealed geographic variations in the odds of TCMs use; the findings are, however, not consistent. While women dwelling in rural areas in Nigeria were less likely to use TCMs (Adanikin et al., 2017), urban women in Zimbabwe were less likely to use TCMs (Guilkey & Jayne, 1997), and women living in non-slum settlements in Kenya were more likely to use TCMs (Ochako et al., 2016). In addition to urban versus rural variations, variations across sub-regions and within countries were also reported (Adanikin et al., 2017; Addai, 1999; Dansou et al., 2017; Oheneba-Sakyi, 1990). Additionally, significant community effects were discovered in a multilevel model analysis in Kenya, suggesting that unobservable community factors influence the choice of contraceptive methods. The results also imply a high degree of homogeneity in the use of traditional methods within communities (Magadi & Siân, 2003). These geographic variations may be suggestive of external community influences which could be driven by cultural and socio-economic factors independent of individual characteristics.

Study strengths and limitations

This study provides evidence on the drivers of traditional contraceptive practice in SSA. The studies included in the review were evaluated for methodological quality using standardized tools. However, contextual differences in study settings may affect the interpretation and meaning of the results in different contexts. This notwithstanding, some drivers showed similarities, while others showed differences within and between countries. A number of limitations are worth mentioning. First, this review used only studies published in English. Findings from publications reported in languages other than English and in local languages are likely to have been missed. Second, this review does not include studies from the Southern Africa region. The review therefore does not include perspectives from Southern Africa. There is therefore a need for future reviews to explore studies from the Southern Africa region to provide a holistic view of traditional contraception in Africa.

Conclusion

Despite campaigns and several interventions over the past decades aimed at improving access to and use of modern contraceptive methods while discouraging access to and use of traditional methods, the expected results have not been realized, especially in SSA. Traditional contraceptive practice still persists in SSA, and in some settings, TCMs are still the main method of family planning. The studies included in the current review show a number of drivers of traditional contraceptive practice, though the evidence is not always consistent. These drivers include the persistence of country-specific cultural, religious, and traditional practices of birth regulation. In addition, being educated, living in high wealth status households, and desiring large family size, and to a lesser extent being single/never-married, are among the key drivers influencing the use of traditional methods of contraception. Lack of information and knowledge were among the key explanations for underutilization of traditional methods of contraception among less-educated women and women living in poor/low wealth status households. The finding that most educated and rich women were more likely to use TCM show that access, particularly economic access, may not be the only reason women use TCMs. Additionally, the persistence of traditional and cultural practices and other means for birth regulation suggests a need for more investigation into the patterns of traditional contraceptive use and how they may complement the use of modern methods. Such investigation could inform policies and interventions that will help harness the benefits of traditional methods of contraception as a complement to modern methods of contraception, particularly in contexts where traditional contraceptive practice is still prevalent and preferred.

References

Adanikin, I. A., Nuala, M., & Sabu, S. P. (2017). Impact of men's perception on family planning demand and uptake in Nigeria. *Elsevier – Sexual & Reproductive Healthcare, 14*, 55–63. https://doi.org/10.1016/j.srhc.2017.10.002

Addai, I. (1999). Ethnicity and contraceptive use in sub-Saharan Africa: The case of Ghana. *Journal of Biosocial Science, 31*, 105–120. https://doi.org/10.1017/S0021932099001054

Aliyu, A. A. (2018). Chapter 5: Family planning services in Africa: The successes and challenges. In *Family planning* (pp. 69–93). IntechOpen. https://doi.org/10.5772/intechopen.72224

Bledsoe, H. C., Hill, A. G., D'alessandro, U., & Langerock, P. (1994). Constructing natural fertility: The use of western contraceptive technologies in rural Gambia. *Population and Development Review, 20*(1), 81–113. Retrieved from www.jstor.com/stable/2137631

Centre for Disease Control and Prevention [CDC]. (2000). *Family planning methods and practice: Africa*. Atlanta, Georgia: CDC.

Cleland, J., Bernstein, S., Ezeh, A., Faundes, A., Glasier, A., & Innis, J. (2006). Family planning: The unfinished agenda. *Lancet, 368*, 1810–1827.

Dansou, J. (2017). The benefits of family planning (FP) use in Benin: An application of the demographic dividend model (DemDiv). *Gates Open Research, 3*(1110), 9. https://doi.org/10.12688/gatesopenres.12906.1

Dansou, J., Adekunle, A. O., & Arowojolu, A. O. (2017). Factors behind the preference in contraceptives use among non-pregnant and sexually active women in Benin Republic. *Central African Journal of Public Health, 3*(5), 80–89. https://doi.org/10.11648/j.cajph.20170305.15

Ekani-Bessala, M., Carre, N., Thierry, C., & Patrick, T. (1998). Prevalence and determinants of current contraceptive method use in a palm oil company in Cameroon. *Elsevier Contraception, 58*, 29–34.

Gebreselassie, T., Kristin, B., Sarah, S., & Thomas, P. (2017). *Trends, determinants, and dynamics of traditional contraceptive method use*. DHS Analytical Studies No. 63. Rockville, MD: ICF Macro.

Global Health Council. (2019). *Let's end preventable child and maternal deaths once and for all*. Retrieved on July 10, 2020, from https://globalhealth.org/lets-end-preventable-child-and-maternal-deaths-once-and-for-all/; www.globalhealth.org/lets-end-preventable-child-and-maternal-deaths-once-and-for-all/

Guilkey, D. K., & Jayne, S. (1997). Fertility transition in Zimbabwe: Determinants of contraceptive use and method choice. *Population Studies, 51*(2), 173–189. https://doi.org/10.1080/0032472031000149896

Guttmacher Institute. (2017). *Adding it up: Investing in contraception and maternal and newborn health, 2017*. Retrieved on July 10, 2020, from https://globalhealth.org/lets-end-preventable-child-and-maternal-deaths-once-and-for-all/; www.guttmacher.org/fact-sheet/adding-it-up-contraception-mnh-2017

Hubacher, D., & Trussell, J. (2015). A definition of modern contraceptive methods. *Elsevier, Commentary/Contraception, 92*, 420–421. https://doi.org/10.1016/j.contraception.2015.08.008

Jinadu, M. K., & Ajuwon, B. (1997). Traditional fertility regulation methods among the Yoruba of southwestern Nigeria: II. A prospective study of use-effectiveness. *African Journal of Reproductive Health, 1*(1), 65–73. Retrieved from www.jstor.com/stable/3583276

Johnson-Hanks, J. (2002). On the modernity of traditional contraception: Time and the social context of fertility. *Population and Development Review, 28*(2), 229–249. Retrieved from www.jstor.com/stable/3092811

Kalipeni, E., & Zulu, E. M. (1993). Gender differences in knowledge and attitudes toward modern and traditional methods of child spacing in Malawi. *Population Research and Policy Review, 12*, 103–121.

Kovalchik, S. (2017). *RISmed: Download content from NCBI databases*. Retrieved from https://CRAN.R-project.org/package=RISmed

Laburthe-Tolra, P. (1977). *Minlaaba: histoire et société traditionnelle chez les Béti du Sud Cameroun*. Paris: Honore Champion. Atelier Reproduction des thèses, Université de Lille III; diffusion H. Champion.

Lajeunesse, M. J. (2016). Facilitating systematic reviews, data extraction, and meta-analysis with the Metagear package for R. *Methods in Ecology and Evolution, 7*, 323–330.

Leontine, A., Kantorova, V., Menozzi, C., & Biddlecom, A. (2013). National, regional, and global rates and trends in contraceptive prevalence and unmet need for family planning between 1990 and 2015: A systematic and comprehensive analysis. *United Nations, eISBN: 978-92-1-004369-4, 381*, 1642–1652. https://doi.org/10.1016/S0140-6736(12)62204-1

Magadi, M. A., & Siân, C. L. (2003). Trends and determinants of contraceptive method choice in Kenya. *Studies in Family Planning, 34*(3), 149–159. Retrieved from www.jstor.com/stable/3181102.

McKenzie, J., Brennan, S., Ryan, R., Thomson, H., Johnston, R., & Thomas, J. (2019). Chapter 3: Defining the criteria for including studies and how they will be grouped for the synthesis. In J. Higgins, J. Thomas, J. Chandler, M. Cumpston, T. Li, M. J. Page, & V. A. Welch (Eds.), *Cochrane handbook for systematic reviews of interventions* (2nd ed., pp. 33–66). Chichester, UK: John Wiley & Sons.

Njagi, P., Arsenijevic, J., & Groot, W. (2018). Understanding variations in catastrophic health expenditure, its underlying determinants and impoverishment in sub-Saharan African countries: A scoping review. *Systematic Reviews*, 7(136). https://doi.org/10.1186/s13643-018-0799-1

Ntozi, J. P., & Kabera, J. B. (1991). Family planning in rural Uganda: Knowledge and use of modern and traditional methods in Ankole. *Studies in Family Planning, 22*(2), 116–123. Retrieved from www.jstor.com/stable/1966781

Ochako, R., Gichuhi, W., & Open, A. (2016). Pregnancy wantedness, frequency and timing of antenatal care visit among women of childbearing age in Kenya. *Reproductive Health, 13*(51), 8. https://doi.org/10.1186/s12978-016-0168-2

Oheneba-Sakyi, Y. (1990). Socio-economic and cultural differentials in contraceptive usage among Ghanaian women. *International Journal of Sociology of the Family, 20*(2), 139–161. Retrieved from www.jstor.com/stable/23028503

Oheneba-Sakyi, Y. (1992). Determinants of current contraceptive use among Ghanaian women at the highest risk of pregnancy. *Journal of Biosocial Science, 24*, 463–475.

Okedo-Alex, I. N., Ifeyinwa, C. A., Obumneme, B. E., & Chigozie, J. U. (2019). Determinants of antenatal care utilisation in sub-Saharan Africa: A systematic review. *BMJ Open*. https://doi.org/10.1136/bmjopen-2019-031890

Ombolo, J.-P. (1990). *Sexe et société en Afrique noire: L'anthropologie sexuelle beti: essai analytique, critique et comparatif*. Paris: L'Harmattan.

PRB. (2020). *2020 World population data*. Washington, DC: Population Reference Bureau.

Robinson, W. C., & John, A. R. (2007). 24 Family planning: The quiet revolution. In W. C. Robinson & A. R. John (Eds.), *The global family planning revolution: Three decades of population policies and programs* (pp. 85–102). USA: Library of Congress Cataloging-in-Publication Data. https://doi.org/10.1596/978-0-8213-6951-7

Rossier, C., & Jamaica, C. (2017). Contemporary use of traditional contraception in sub-Saharan Africa. *Population and Development Review, 43*, 192–215. https://doi.org/10.1016/S0140-6736(12)62204-1

Shamseer, L., David, M., Mike, C., Davina, G., Alessandro, L., Mark, P., . . . the PRISMA-P Group. (2015). Preferred reporting items for systematic review and meta-analysis protocols (PRISMA-P) 2015: Elaboration and explanation. *BMJ Research Methods & Reporting, 349*, 25. https://doi.org/10.1136/bmj.g7647

Staveteig, S., Lindsay, M., & Rebecca, W. (2015). *Uptake and discontinuation of long-acting reversible contraceptives (LARCS) in low-income countries*. DHS Analytical Studies No. 54. Rockville, MD: ICF International.

Sullivan, T. M., Jane, T. B., Janet, R., & James, S. D. (2006). Skewed contraceptive method mix: Why it happens, why it matters. *Journal of Biosocial Science, 38*, 501–521. https://doi.org/10.1017/S0021932005026647

Ujuju, C., Anyanti, J., Adebayo, B. S., Muhammad, F., Oluigbo, O., & Gofwan, A. (2011). Religion, culture and male involvement in the use of the standard days method: Evidence from Enugu and Katina states of Nigeria. *International Nursing Review, 58*, 484–490.

Wardle, J., & Steel, A. (2015). Systematic reviews in integrative medicine: A clinician's guide to publication. *Advances in Integrative Medicine, 2*, 103–109.

World Health Organization. (2019a). *Maternal mortality*. Retrieved on July 10, 2020, from www.who.int/news-room/fact-sheets/detail/maternal-mortality; www.who.int/news-room/fact-sheets/detail/maternal-mortality

15

FROM POST-COLONIALISM TO CAIRO TO NOW

The (un)changing ideas of reproductive health and family planning in africa

Sasha Frade

The unfolding of conceptual definitions and concepts in reproductive health: a conceptual shift?

Despite the work done and plethora of research conducted over the past five decades, in many African countries, reproductive health remains a key challenge. Reproductive health, according to the WHO, is

> a state of complete physical, mental and social well-being and not merely the absence of disease or infirmity, in all matters relating to the reproductive system and to its functions and processes. Reproductive health implies that people are able to have a satisfying and safe sex life and that they have the capability to reproduce and the freedom to decide if, when and how often to do so.

Until the ICPD[1] in 1994, the popularized opinion and public discourse around reproductive health for Africa centred around family planning and fertility in relation to population growth and extremely high fertility levels (Birdsall, 1976; Adepoju, 1975; Pearce, 1994). In terms of fertility regulation and reproductive health generally, family planning programmes and contraceptives were the policies of choice (Pearce, 1994). Control of population was the way in which development would be reached in Africa (Adepoju, 1975), or rather, population growth was the reason for Africa's underdevelopment (Abate, 1978; Pearce, 1994). This sentiment was spearheaded by the United States and was incorporated into the ideals of the United Nations and particular governments – especially in the Global North (Pearce, 1994). However, most African countries believed that family planning should be centred more around reproductive health rather than fertility decrease and only the promotion of contraception (Birdsall, 1976). Reproductive health was far broader and included the idea of population and development being inextricably linked rather than one preceding the other (Birdsall, 1976; Adepoju, 1975).

The ICPD marked a significant turning point in how reproductive health and rights, and by extension family planning programmes, were understood and conceptualized. The international consensus was brought about by a lengthy process of negotiation and discussions leading to the actual conference (McIntosh & Finkle, 1995). This was necessitated by the fact that

DOI: 10.4324/9780429287213-18

there existed two opposing views on the "problem" of population. At the ICPD, there was a mutual global understanding that population matters (generally), but reproductive health and fertility more specifically needed to be understood, researched, and promoted within the realm of sustainable development, gender equality and women's empowerment. However, as Richey (1999) has noted

> Although an international consensus on questions of population and family planning may have been reached at the 1994 International Conference on Population and Development in Cairo, when we look at actual cases of policy formulation and implementation, the discourse reflects ambiguity and conflict rather than consensus.

Although some agreement was reached in terms of the questions and discourse around population, reproductive health and rights, and family planning, the population policies, and therefore the research, that have been developed post-ICPD still reflect a very neo-Malthusian rationale. By the early 1990s, most African countries had at least a population policy or family planning programme in draft form. However, the focus remained on fertility regulation and population control rather than a holistic view of population, health, and development (Pearce, 1994; Starrs et al., 2018). According to the ICPD Plan of Action, one of the key factors that needed to be promoted was the access to reproductive and sexual health services including family planning.[2] However, most of the focus in Africa specifically has been on family planning, to the detriment of other reproductive health matters (Lince-Deroche et al., 2016).

Specifically, among population scientists, there was an increased understanding that family planning was needed together with economic and social development (Adepoju, 1975; Birdsall, 1976). Without commensurate economic and social development, families and women would still desire a higher number of children (Birdsall, 1976). The idea of modernization and development in demography and population studies came mainly from the theories of demographic and fertility transition (Adepoju, 1975; Segal, 1993; Wado, Gurmu, Tilahun, & Bangha, 2019). In brief, the theories depict that a process of development and modernization per the European and American experiences would eventually lead to fertility decline in Africa (Pearce, 1994; Potts & Marks, 2001; Wado et al., 2019). However, despite this new awareness that arose in the 1980s and 1990s, many of the factors researched and assessed during the pre-ICPD years are the same as those researched post-1994 as partial determinants of high fertility and reproductive health outcomes.

This beginning section is critical in contexualizing the idea of reproductive health in Africa over the last 50 years. The (un)evolving discourse around reproductive health and family planning has framed and guided the research, and policies and programmes, on the continent over the period. As such, this chapter assesses the research conducted over the past 50 years in this field – which must be understood by first problematizing the theoretical and substantive ideas that have led to the research questions posed by demographers and population scientists about Africa. The trajectory of research, and the way in which reproductive health has been understood and defined, has largely been due to the popular discourse of the day.

Theories and conceptual models in reproductive health

For the most part, there is a paucity of theory and conceptual models in the field of reproductive health per se. Most theories and conceptual models used for reproductive health research in demography and population science have been fertility theories and conceptual models, all with the aim to explain what factors can explain a move from high to low fertility rates. These too have remained rather stagnant over the past several decades. Malthusian and neo-Malthusian ideas, together with the popularization of the demographic and fertility transition theories (DTT and FTT), have spearheaded the rather simplistic and unilateral view of the pathways from a high fertility to low fertility transition. Reproductive health has been a by-product or seen as a proximate factor leading to this goal. These theories and conceptual models, however, have also provided a wealth of information and direction – having guided a lot of what we do know today regarding reproductive health and fertility among women of reproductive age.

Thomas Malthus spearheaded the idea of the population problem and the social and economic ills that would ensue if population growth and fertility continued unabated in his book *An Essay on the Principle of Population* (1872). However, this idea of the population problem was once again popularized in the book *Population Bomb* by Paul Ehrlich (1968), not at first, but over the years, the ideas of the book and the neo-Malthusian warnings and predictions gained sway in international discourse and debate, much of which continues today.

Furthermore, DTT – and by extension FTT – was created in the 1940s and 1950s by Frank Notestein, based on the results of a historical demographic review of several countries in the Global North (Kirk, 1996). This theory states that all countries will pass through a transition from high death and fertility rates to a phase of low death and high fertility rates (in which population growth occurs); eventually fertility rates match the lowered death rates, and population growth ceases. For most of the world, this has happened, but particularly in Africa, most countries are transitioning slowly or have regressed somewhat in their transition (Shapiro & Gebreselassie, 2008; Bongaarts & Casterline, 2013). Most research today still attempts to understand why African countries have not followed the same path as their counterparts in the Global North and now in Asia and Latin America as well.

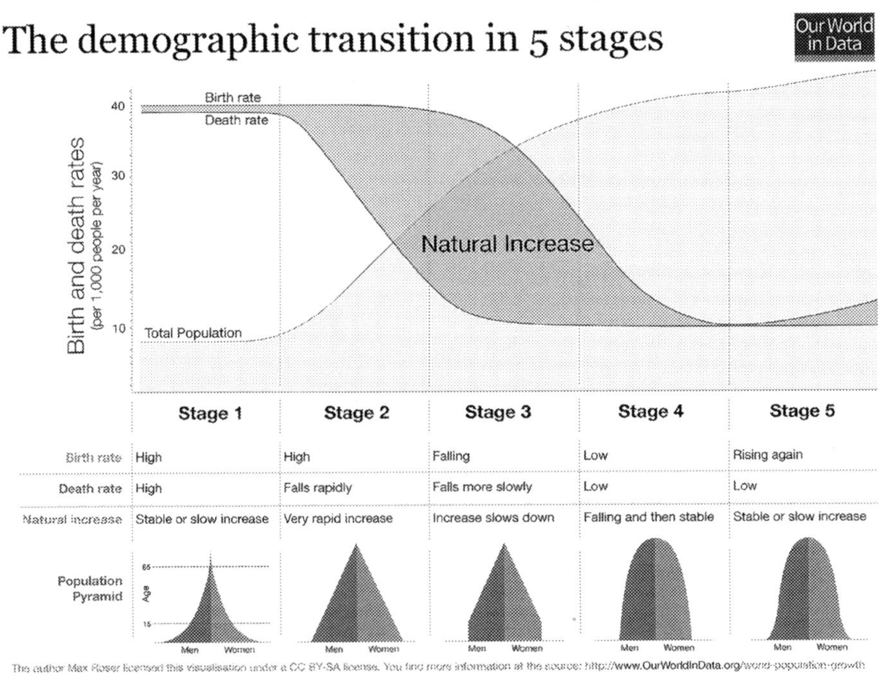

Figure 15.1 The demographic and fertility transition theories

Source: http://ourworldindata.org/data/population-growth-vital-statistics/world-population-growth

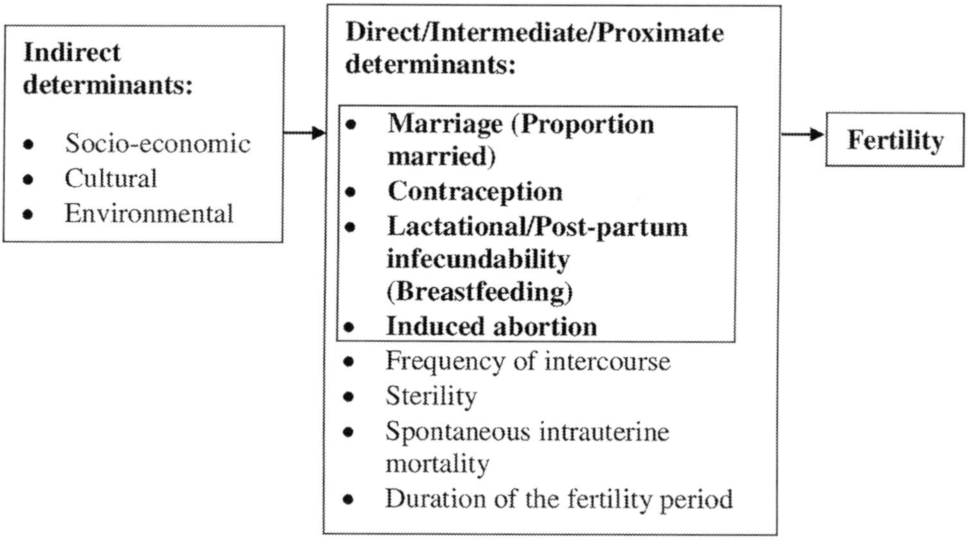

Figure 15.2 Bongaarts' proximate determinants framework

Source: Lai, S. L. (2016). Recent fertility and its proximate determinants in 3 ASEAN countries/Lai Siow Li (Doctoral dissertation, University of Malaya)

Arguably the most popular and widely used theory and conceptual model is Bongaarts' proximate determinants model (Bongaarts, Frank, & Lesthaeghe, 1984). Refined and revised from the Davis and Blake model, Bongaarts' model remains popular due to several reasons.

1 It can be quantified and is not simply a theory – its theoretical and empirical applicability has been widely used and verified (Letamo & Letamo, 2001);
2 It links the social, demographic, and economic spheres to the biomedical (or reproductive) determinants that either lead to high or low fertility. The refined logic of this socio-medical model has subsequently been refined and re-used to explain other demographic and health processes;
3 It is simple to understand and conceptualize; and
4 There are data that can be used to prove or disprove the theory in any given context – thanks mainly to the DHS.

However, although these have been applied to Africa, none were derived specifically to explain fertility and reproductive health in Africa. To date, there is no African theory of reproductive health in demography and population studies, and all other theories available still concentrate on fertility and its attempt to have countries transition from the first to final stages of the demographic, or fertility, transitions and not necessarily on reproductive health.

Methodological approaches and implications

Much of the population-based information collected prior to the colonial period was due to anthropologists, sociologists, historians, and philosophers and was mainly qualitative in nature (Pearce, 1994). During the colonial period, and even prior, quantitative data collection in the form of censuses and surveys were limited, and, where conducted, they were not collected in a systematic way or even periodically (Abate, 1978; Pearce, 1994). The data that were available remained of poor quality, either being incomplete, inconsistent, or both from the end of the colonial period right until the 1980s and 1990s (Segal, 1993). In some countries, this remains the case. Further, population studies and demography as skills and as a profession had not been taught in Africa. However, as of the 1970s and 1980s, the collection and analysis of comprehensive demographic data from African countries began to increase. By the late 1980s/ early 1990s, there was a general increase of available data that allowed for more reliable, comparative, and generalizable research (Segal, 1993). Furthermore, around the 1980s, training and opportunities for demographers and population scientists on the continent also increased due to funding (Segal, 1993; Potts & Marks, 2001) from (mainly) the United Nations Population Fund (UNFPA) (Segal, 1993). Although training and skills development on the continent gained momentum during this time, a shortfall of demographers and population scientists remained until well into the 1990s, and therefore a large proportion of research and studies on reproductive health and fertility, as with other demographic and population-based research, was conducted by non-African demographers and population scientists trained and/or living elsewhere (Segal, 1993).

Specifically, with reference to fertility and reproductive health, the World Fertility Survey (WFS) was launched in the 1970s. The WFS was the most comprehensive, international demographic data collection exercise at the time – and between 1973 and 1984, surveys regarding human fertility were conducted in 66 (mainly developing) countries. The WFS was supported by the UNFPA but remained under the headship of the Office of Population at the US Agency for International Development. Specifically, several African countries were included in the initial 66 – Bénin, Cameroon, Cote d'Ivoire, Egypt, Ghana, Kenya, Lesotho, Mauritania, Morocco, Nigeria, Rwanda, Senegal, Sudan (North), and Tunisia.

The main reason or rationale for the creation of the WFS was specifically to resolve conflicting views and assessments about family planning programmes all over the world. The WFS aimed to ensure the availability of complete and internationally comparable quantitative data, and therefore developed standardized tools for data collection that were used in all participating countries. The tools were split into three questionnaires – the first was a household schedule, the second was a detailed questionnaire administered to ever-married women (single women were only included in some of the countries) who were of reproductive age, and the final questionnaire was administered to their husbands. The last questionnaire, however, was only administered in three countries. It was, however, the women's questionnaire that included the fertility and reproductive health questions – namely around complete marriage and pregnancy histories and sections on socioeconomic background, contraception, breastfeeding, and fertility preferences. Further, the WFS allowed for additional questions, known as modules, that countries could opt for to allow for more in-depth analysis – the initial surveys allowed for modules on family planning and the biological determinants of childbearing.

The datasets produced from the cross-sectional exercise allowed for comparisons across time and space for the first time. Furthermore, they now allowed for certain statistical techniques to be applied to the areas of fertility and reproductive health, including family planning questions, such as linear regression models to individual-level measures of fertility, as well as the application of hazard models to event histories. However, the WFS did not provide much insight into fertility determinants or policy-related questions with regard to family planning (Cleland & Verma, 1989; Cleland & Scott, 1987; Kendall, 1979; Population Information Programme, 1985).

In 1984, the decision was made to expand the WFS to ensure inclusivity of other key and important demographic, population, and health-related factors. The expanded version of the

WFS, the Demographic and Health Survey (DHS), was launched that year. The DHS has since been expanded to over 90 countries, and 43 are in sub-Saharan Africa. Many of the countries have undergone multiple DHSs over the last 30 years, and therefore the DHS remains arguably the most-used and cited international survey in demographic and population-based quantitative research (Potts & Marks, 2001). This is mainly due to its comprehensiveness and comparability over time and space and the fact that despite several revisions and updates over the years, the data have remained consistent and of generally high quality. Therefore, many methods and measures used since the 1980s in reproductive health research in demography and quantitative population sciences have been due to the DHS

At the core of many of the questions posed and the way in which data have been collected, specifically in relation to fertility and reproductive health but generally on population-based issues in DHS and DHS-type surveys, is the idea that the data will be allowed to resolve or assist African countries in modernizing the same way as the Western world has over the last 200 years. As such, small families and low fertility rates and population growth have been the associative outcome of a modernized context (Pearce, 1994) vis-à-vis fertility. As Pearce (1994) mentions

> the major concern is with the presentation and interpretation of much of the data. The "deficit" image of Africa comes as much from the manner of presentation as from the statistics themselves.

More recently, from around the late 1990s/early 2000s, however, there has been an increase in the number, types, and variation of data being collected – albeit in some African countries more than others. There is now far more variation in in-country data that is being utilized to assess fertility and reproductive health outcomes. Vital registration systems and centralized health data remain rather poor and incomplete throughout the continent. As such, demographers and population scientists have continued to rely on the DHS and, where available, health and demographic surveillance sites, panel data sets, national surveys, and smaller site-based local research and data. Further, there has been a renewed appreciation and need for qualitative studies on issues relating to fertility and reproductive health – to reassess many of the established ideas and concepts but also to provide in-depth understanding of some of the quantitative and statistical results over the last several decades. Despite the availability of different types of data and the application of various techniques today, many of the key challenges and issues in reproductive health and family planning reported in journals and research studies have remained consistent – even since the 1970s.

Key issues and challenges in reproductive health in Africa

In the 1970s, many African countries had recently gained independence, whilst others would only gain independence over the next few decades. As such, some research had begun to recognize that the policies and programmes in place, as well as many of the social and institutional structures, had been disrupted and informed by colonial interests rather than for the betterment and benefit of local populations (Valentine & Revson, 1979; Caldwell & Caldwell, 2002). Furthermore, the research showed that as a repercussion of colonial policies and unequal distribution of resources between local populations and colonial expatriates, most clinics and health care services were concentrated in urban areas, to the detriment of the predominantly rural local populations. As such, reproductive health measures showed skewed differentiation between those living in rural and urban areas (Adepoju, 1975; Birdsall, 1976).

Also, much of the research in reproductive health during this time looked at social and cultural differentials that attempted to explain why Africa was undergoing a different fertility experience to other countries – both developed and developing. Subsistence farming, the lack of technological advancement, certain cultural practices and customs (Caldwell, 1997), an inherent pro-natalist social structure which encouraged family formation and childbearing (Shah, 1998), and certain customary marital practices (such as polygyny and early marriage) (Valentine & Revson, 1979; Adepoju, 1975; Pearce, 1994), as well as the non-use of contraceptives, were found as reasons for the high fertility at this time (Adepoju, 1975). Furthermore, reasons for the high fertility in Africa were linked to the communal nature of African culture, which was closely linked to kinship and subsistence farming – and with family members each having their own role and responsibility, and as such, children themselves were seen to hold certain roles within the family's organization and the division of work or labour. Due to these practices and customs, researchers and theorists in demography and population studies often referred to the value of children in terms of family prestige, wealth, and prosperity, providing a safety net for parents in their old age, but also the immediate benefit of increasing agricultural output (Valentine & Revson, 1979; Caldwell, 2005). One of the other reasons noted for the high fertility rates in Africa was also due to the high infant and child mortality rates on the continent – the replacement effect (Grieser et al., 2001). As such, parents produced more children given the uncertainty of how many of those children would survive (Birdsall, 1976; Snyder, 1974).

Many of the aspects of reproductive health research conducted in and by African demographers and population scientists have been guided by either/or one rationale. The first is the fixation on the transition to lower fertility rates and the proximate determinants that could explain the non or slow transition. The second is that much research in this area has been guided by the availability of questions around reproductive health, many of which were guided by popular discourse around population growth and what was required to regulate fertility but more specifically by the questions in the DHS and WFS. Subsequent datasets have used similar questions to assess reproductive health in Africa. There is much that is now known but far more that needs to be researched – specifically with regard to non-fertility related reproductive health from a demographic and health perspective. According to the research and data available, in general, Africa fares poorly on all reproductive health indicators and factors – albeit with some improvements in the region over the past 50 years (Wado et al., 2019).

Socio-demographic and economic factors associated with reproductive health issues have been widely researched in Africa. In fact, most of the research that looks at these factors in relation to reproductive health, irrespective of the variable or indicator used, shows that the heightened reproductive health issues in Africa are due to poor socio-economic conditions and country-level economic development (Okonofua, 1997; Bongaarts et al., 1984; Garenne, 2008) but also due to individual behaviour and social norms (Shah, 1998; Valentine & Revson, 1979; Potts & Marks, 2001). It is now widely acknowledged that there are several socio-demographic and economic factors that have been found to either have a positive or negative effect on reproductive health: place of residence (Caldwell & Caldwell, 2002; Bongaarts et al., 1984; Garenne, 2008), educational level of the woman (Okonofua, 1997; Caldwell, 1997; Shah, 1998; Caldwell & Caldwell, 2002; Bongaarts et al., 1984; Garenne, 2008), employment status, household wealth (Shah, 1998), and even religion (Letamo & Letamo, 2001; Garenne, 2008), as well as the women's relationship status (Letamo & Letamo, 2001) and the type of marriage (Garenne, 2008).

Use of contraceptives and the idea of unmet need

The use of modern contraceptives in Africa has increased over time, albeit differentially between different sub-groups (Garenne, 2018; Shah, 1998; Letamo & Letamo, 2001), but levels remain low (Shah, 1998; Wado et al., 2019). The uptake in modern contraceptives, however, has been shown to be the leading cause of (albeit slow) fertility decline on the continent (Letamo & Letamo, 2001). Further, there are marked differences between women who live in urban and rural areas (Garenne, 2018), those of different educational status, those of different age groups, parity, and even between countries and sub-regions on the continent (Wado et al., 2019).

However, although an increase in the use of modern contraceptives has been seen over the past 50 years, largely due to the family planning programme rolled out in most African countries over this time, there is still a large proportion of women who do not access contraception (Shah, 1998; Starrs et al., 2018). The concept of unmet need, otherwise known as the knowledge, attitudes, and practice (KAP)-gap, is based on a huge body of demographic research that shows that there is a large proportion of women in Africa whose actual fertility does not match with their desired fertility (Dodoo & Landewijk, 1996; Westoff, 1988; Bongaarts, 1991; Starrs et al., 2018). However, these same women often do not use the family planning programme or, more specifically, are not on any form of contraception (Dodoo & Landewijk, 1996; Starrs et al., 2018; Shah, 1998). One of the other key factors regarding unmet need and contraceptive use is the fact that this measure does not differentiate between those who would want to stop or simply space births – which invariably has much to do with the women's age and parity, as much as with other key socio-demographic factors (Dodoo & Landewijk, 1996).

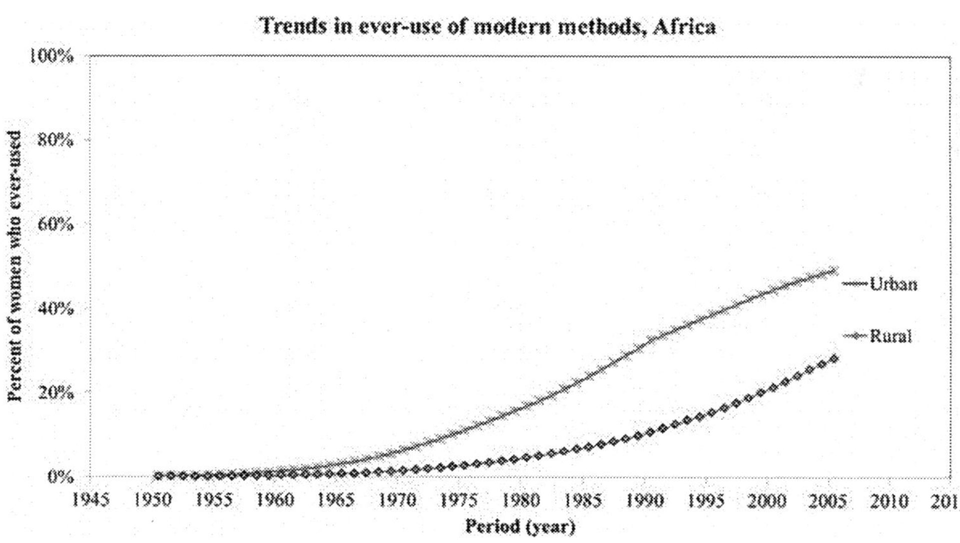

Figure 15.3 Trends in ever-use of modern methods by place of residence in Africa from 1950–2005 (from DHS data for 35 African countries)

Source: Garenne, 2018

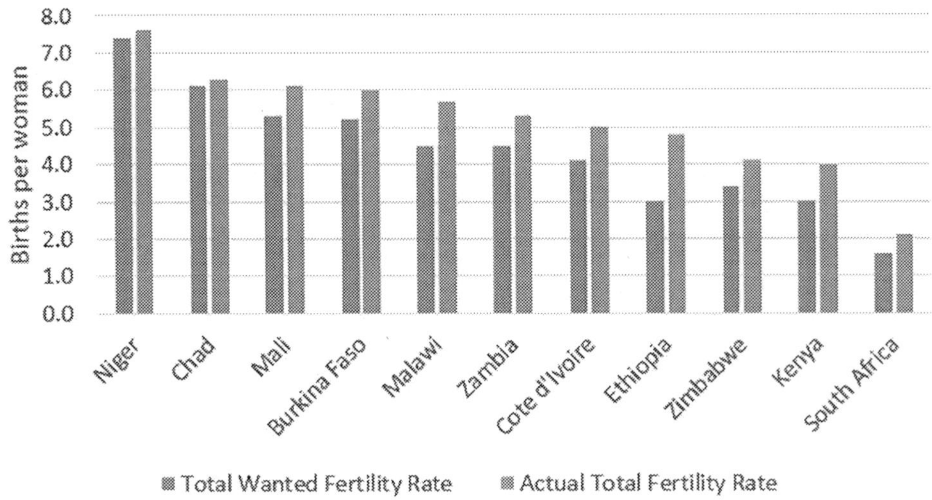

Figure 15.4 Differences between wanted and actual fertility in selected African countries (from DHS data)

Source: Canning, D., Raja, S., & Yazbeck, A. S. (Eds.). (2015). *Africa's Demographic Transition: Dividend or Disaster?* Washington, DC: The World Bank

Wanted and actual fertility

Dodoo and Landewijk (1996) estimated that in the 1990s, around 30% of married women in Africa, although wanting to decrease their fertility levels, were not using any form of family planning. As such, in many African countries, there is a stark difference between the wanted and actual fertility levels among women, albeit with large variations within and between different countries (Canning, Raja, & Yazbeck, 2015).

One argument, however, is that the family planning programmes in Africa remain solely focused on women and exclude men. This has been underpinned as one of the reasons that the family planning programme model in Africa may not have met with the same level of success as seen in other countries (Dodoo & Landewijk, 1996). Specifically, the exclusion of men is said to not consider the cultural practices and context of fertility in Africa, given that men have a significant role in the decision-making regarding children and fertility (Dodoo & Landewijk, 1996; Potts & Marks, 2001). Dodoo and Landewijk (1996) believe that excluding men from this measure, whilst it may be correctly calculating women's desire for contraception (or not), incorrectly assesses whether contraception will be taken up by excluding the role the male partner has in fertility-related decisions.

The importance of age

Fertility transitions are often studied by looking at the age structure and to follow the changes in the age-specific fertility rates. The countries where fertility rates have decreased globally have seen a commensurate increase in the age at first birth – which is often closely related to the age at first union (Garenne, 2004). However, in most African countries, both the age at first union and the age at first birth are far lower than the global averages – which research has found to be one of the contributing factors to the persistently higher-than-global-average fertility levels on the continent. This is even though, over the last 50 years, there has been some increase in the age at first birth and first union (Garenne, 2004; Melesse et al., 2020) and even though there are also increasing rates of pre-union or pre-marital pregnancies on the continent (Garenne, 2004). However, again, these also vary according to several sub-populations and by key socio-demographic factors. Those living in urban areas and those with higher levels of education, for instance, have shown consistently higher ages at both first union (Garenne, 2004, 2008) and first birth (Garenne, 2004).

Teenage pregnancies and adolescent reproductive health

Teenage pregnancies have remained of great concern throughout Africa over time (Mturi & Moerane, 2001; Valentine & Revson, 1979; Okonofua, 2000) and remain a high contributor to overall fertility levels in many African countries (Defo, 2011). Teenage pregnancies have for the most part remained relatively high and stable (Mkwananzi & Odimegwu, 2015; Okonofua, 2012) – in comparison to other world regions. Due to these high levels, much of the research regarding adolescents in the field of reproductive health has therefore centred around

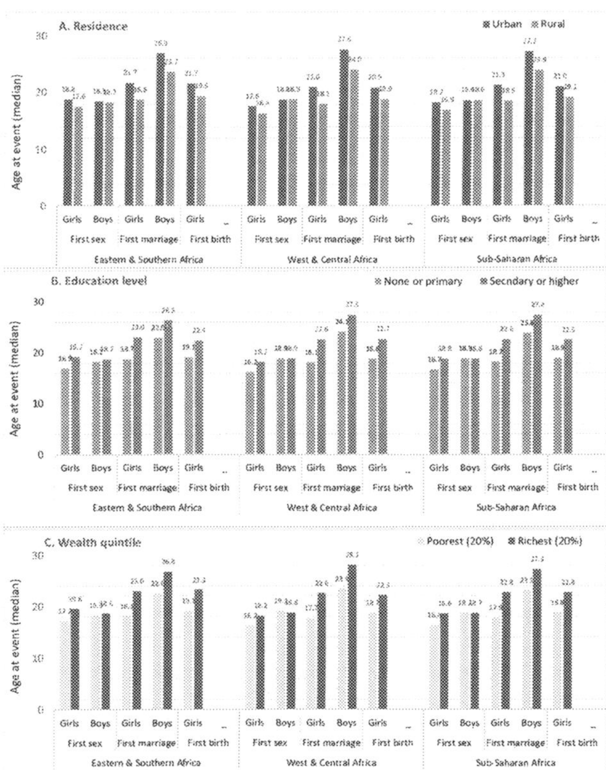

Figure 15.5 Median age at first sex, age at first marriage, and age at first birth for girls and boys by level of education, urban–rural residence, and household wealth in sub-Saharan Africa (from DHS data)

Source: Melesse, D. Y., Mutua, M. K., Choudhury, A., Wado, Y. D., Faye, C. M., Neal, S., & Boerma, T. (2020). Adolescent sexual and reproductive health in sub-Saharan Africa: Who is left behind? *BMJ Global Health*, *5*, e002231

risky sexual behaviours and, therefore, teenage pregnancies. Most African cultures discourage premarital sex and childbearing, and therefore associated stigma and shame increase the risk of these women undergoing unsafe and (in many African countries) illegal abortions – increasing their risk of long-term reproductive, mental, and other health issues and which account for around 13% of all maternal deaths in Africa (Shah, 1998). Furthermore, risky sexual behaviours and unprotected sex also increase the risk of HIV and other STIs (Mturi & Moerane, 2001; Okonofua, 2012). Despite the risks, and the discouragement of the practice, there are several African countries that have seen an increase, rather than a decrease in teenage pregnancies and risky sexual behaviours (Mturi & Moerane, 2001; Mkwananzi & Odimegwu, 2015; Okonofua, 2000).

Available indicators do show that adolescents have the highest percentage of unmet need for all reproductive health services, including access to contraception and barrier methods – such as condoms (Shah, 1998; Okonofua, 2012). Furthermore, adolescents continuously report high levels of multiple concurrent partners (Okonofua, 2000), inconsistent and non-condom use, low contraceptive prevalence rates, and early debut of sexual activities. Furthermore, due to these risky sexual behaviours, this age group also have a high risk of transmission, and high prevalence, of HIV/AIDS and other STIs (Mturi & Moerane, 2001). However, given the taboos associated with premarital sex, adolescents often are not able to access the services they need – often due to stigma and fear of being victimized by other adolescents, health care providers, and community members.

Sexually transmitted infections

Africa has the highest HIV/AIDS and STI infection rates in the world. Unfortunately, these pandemics have only served to increase the impact of other negative reproductive health outcomes on the continent (Caldwell, 1997; Shah, 1998). Furthermore, with specific reference to HIV/AIDS, given the sheer magnitude and severity of the epidemic over the last few decades in many countries, the HIV/AIDS programmes were separate to the reproductive health

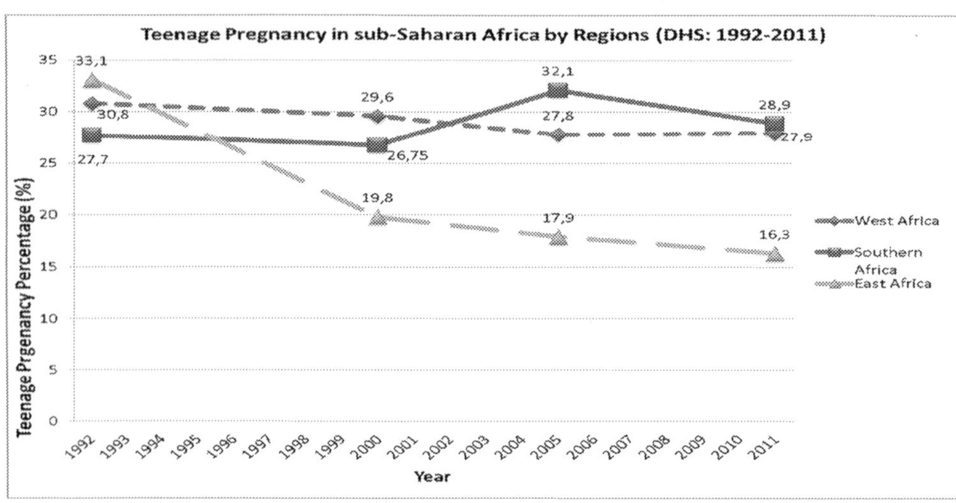

Figure 15.6 Trends in teenage pregnancies in sub-Saharan Africa from 1992 to 2011 (from DHS data)
Source: Mkwananzi and Odimegwu, 2015

programme (Richey, 2003). The convergence between the two only came in the form of the prevention of mother to child transmission programme much later. However, research has widely shown the impact that these infections have had on both women and their children (Potts & Marks, 2001; Grieser et al., 2001; Letamo & Letamo, 2001).

Women's roles, autonomy, and decision-making power

Research on reproductive health and family planning in Africa often reflects on the role of women's autonomy and their decision-making role in the household or union, vis-à-vis high fertility and (non-)contraceptive use but also whether women access clinics on their own (Dodoo & Landewijk, 1996; Dodoo, 1993; Ezeh, 1997; Okonofua, 1997; Potts & Marks, 2001; Odimegwu & Adedini, 2014). It is largely understood that women with higher levels of autonomy and decision-making power are more likely to negotiate for condom use and contraceptives and for their ideal number of children but will also be able to go the clinic on their own if the need arises (Corroon et al., 2014). It is also understood that it would contribute to lowering unmet need (Sougou, Bassoum, Faye, & Leye, 2020; Dodoo & Landewijk, 1996; Odimegwu & Adedini, 2014). Factors found to have a positive effect on women's autonomy and decision-making power are place of residence, their age, their own and partner's level of education, and their occupation (Darteh, Dickson, & Doku, 2019; Woldemicael, 2009), as well as the household's economic situation (Woldemicael, 2009).

However, the measure of autonomy and decision-making has been inconsistent – and therefore, there are studies that have also found no interlinkage between indicators of autonomy and decision-making with reproductive health outcomes and contraceptive use (Loll et al., 2019). This has made the interlinkages and pathways between women's empowerment, autonomy, and decision-making in the reproductive area altogether unclear – despite the widely held belief that the two are highly related.

Concluding remarks: research agenda and way forward

There is now a dire need to rethink the idea, and programme of, family planning. Although we have seen a shift in the discourse around reproductive health over the last 50 years – policies and programmes, and research, have not changed. It may in fact be that we need to enquire whether the term family planning is the correct term at all – the term lacks inclusivity of adolescents, those outside of the reproductive ages, and those belonging to vulnerable and minority groups such as sex workers and those in the LGBTQI+ community. Further, family planning programmes have for the most part excluded men as well – the other half of the decision-making process in terms of fertility and family formation. Finally, the term family planning does not encompass the full spectrum of what constitutes reproductive health; the focus of most family planning programmes has been around contraceptive use (Dodoo & Landewijk, 1996; Caldwell & Caldwell, 2002).

The unquestioning use and reliance on certain questions and data sets, and the lack of new theory in the field of fertility and reproductive health, has led to a situation in which the identified challenges and issues around reproductive health have remained unchanged and unchallenged. Albeit with slight improvements and shifts in rates and percentages, the plethora of research done on the topic in Africa has not led to massive improvements in the reproductive health of women. The research, and subsequent polices, have also not led to a decrease to (at least close to) replacement level fertility or successes in the "modernization" process as envisioned by the demographic and fertility transition theories.

One then needs to begin to question whether the "lack of" or slow progress in these areas is due to some deficit in Africa or whether in fact we are asking the right questions in the right context. Issues of desire for children, contraceptive use, fertility intentions, and other key variables included in fertility and reproductive health questionnaires are, first, not all encompassing of the broader reproductive health definition, contain a majority focus on fertility as opposed to actual reproductive health, and are women centred as opposed to couple or even family centred. Furthermore, these questions and variables assume that given the choice, women in Africa will opt for the answer that validates the experience and definition of modernization and decreased fertility seen in America and Europe at first, and then in Asia and elsewhere. As such, there needs to be a distinct move away from the idea of fertility being the focus of reproductive health and by extension family planning programmes. A concerted effort is required to interrogate the types of questions and variables that have been in use to explain reproductive health in quantitative terms and interrogate whether we are measuring what we have intended to. It also needs to be interrogated whether these questions are contextually relevant and align with the needs and desires of women in Africa – both across time and space.

The use of qualitative methods can, at least in part, begin the process of interrogation and ensure that the questions, and the way in which they are asked, are in fact relevant and understood to those who are answering them. This needs to be followed by the formation and piloting of various types of questions and the ways in which we ask them to women (and men). This process of how we ask and interpret the results of analyses and research would need to work in tandem with expanding our theoretical and conceptual understanding of fertility and reproductive health in Africa. There is a need to move beyond 1970s post-colonial theories and concepts popularized and diffused by a select number of nations, institutions, and groups.

There are some key questions that we can ask as the initial phase. What do we mean when we say reproductive health in Africa today, and what should this include? What does reproductive health mean to an Africa woman, couple, and family, and do these ideas differ? What are the reproductive health needs and gaps, and therefore questions, that are needed for those below menarche and beyond menopause? What are the reproductive health needs and gaps for those that are in minority, vulnerable and/or disenfranchised groups – such as sex workers, those in the LGBTQI+ community, and those who are voluntarily or involuntarily remaining childless? What are the reproductive health needs of men? And, finally, is simply assessing adolescent use or non-use of contraception based on whether they want to fall pregnant enough, or could there be other reasons – such as fear of gaining weight – that we have not yet taken into account and therefore included in our communication and programmes to adolescents?

More concretely, this means that far more research is required into the differential needs of different groups and the factors that determine optimal or sub-optimal reproductive health – in terms of age, life course, and sex or rather sexual orientation. This is over and above education, employment status, place of residence, and any other key socio-demographic factors that are normally included in demographic and population-based research. Second, the definition and concept of reproductive health need to be re-defined and re-framed in quantitative questionnaires. This requires, as a start, a qualitative assessment on these issues, followed by the piloting and testing of various questions to ensure we are asking the questions that will lead to the outcomes desired by women, couples, and families in Africa over and above the aims and goals of governments. Third, such research initiatives must contribute to two further aims – one is to seek more in-depth theories and concepts that are applicable to contemporary Africa and lead to a regional and global discussion on whether policies and programmes need to be re-thought in line with this. Expanding demography and population-based research to fulfil its inter- and multi-disciplinary mandate, such theories and conceptual models should look beyond simply the link between socio-demographic factors and reproductive health outcomes and beyond the socio-biomedical model. There is scope to investigate and introduce aspects of the psychosocial and psychological, anthropological, economic, and sociological, amongst others, given that we continue to research the same thing expecting different results. Given the holistic nature of reproductive health, one further linked question to pose is whether the clinic-based model of the family planning programme is the most effective for Africa.

Furthermore, there are other topics around reproductive health that have been researched to a far lesser extent and require more information to reach proper conclusions on the way forward. Such topics include infertility (Okonofua, 1997), domestic and other forms of gender-based violence (Frade & Odimegwu, 2018; Loll et al., 2019; Somefun & Ibisomi, 2015), and more recently the impact that the COVID-19 pandemic will have on the supply chain and service delivery of the reproductive health programme in countries with already strained resources but also how, and if, it will alter some of the achievements in reproductive health on the continent (Riley, Sully, Ahmed, & Biddlecom, 2020). Finally, research has seen a continual changing of family dynamics and a nuptiality transition – including single parenthood, divorce and remarriage, and the addition of step and half siblings. The impact this could have on the reproductive preferences and choices that women and men make has not been extensively researched and requires much further investigation.

Much has been done over the last 50 years, but there are now many new questions that need to be posed and much new research that is required. As demographers and population scientists in the 21st century, new ways of understanding reproductive health and family planning will be critical if we are to see any major improvement in this area on the continent. The research should further drive the policy and programmatic agenda, and not the other way around. This is, essentially, the best way forward.

Notes

1 International Conference on Population and Development.

2 These services were broadly defined to include family planning counselling, pre-natal care, safe delivery and post-natal care, prevention and appropriate treatment of infertility, prevention of abortion and the management of the consequences of abortion, treatment of reproductive tract infections, sexually transmitted diseases and other reproductive health conditions, education, counselling as appropriate on human sexuality, reproductive health, and responsible parenthood. Services regarding HIV/AIDS, breast cancer, infertility, delivery, hormone therapy, sex reassignment therapy, and abortion should be made available, and there should be active discouragement of female genital mutilation (FGM) (UNFPA, 1995).

References

Abate, Y. (1978). African population growth and politics. *Issue: A Journal of Opinion*, *8*(4), 14–19.

Adepoju, A. (1975). Population policies in Africa: Problems and prospects. *African Affairs*, *74*(297), 461–479.

Birdsall, N. (1976). Health planning and population policy in Africa. *African Studies Review*, *19*(2), 19–33. doi:10.2307/523561

Bongaarts, J. (1991). The KAP-gap and the unmet need for contraception. *Population and Development Review*, 293–313.

Bongaarts, J., & Casterline, J. (2013). Fertility transition: Is sub-Saharan Africa different? *Population and Development Review*, *38*(Suppl. 1), 153.

Bongaarts, J., Frank, O., & Lesthaeghe, R. (1984). The proximate determinants of fertility in sub-Saharan Africa. *Population and Development Review*, 511–537.

Caldwell, J. C. (1997). The global fertility transition: The need for a unifying theory. *Population and Development Review*, 803–812.

Caldwell, J. C., & Caldwell, P. (2002, October). The fertility transition in sub-Saharan Africa. In *Conference on Fertility and the Current South African Issues of Poverty, HIV/AIDS and Youth*, Pretoria, South Africa.

Caldwell, J. C. (2005). On net intergenerational wealth flows: An update. *Population and Development Review, 31*(4), 721–740.

Cleland, J., & Verma, V. (1989). The World Fertility Survey: An appraisal of methodology. *Journal of the American Statistical Association, 84*(407), 756–767.

Cleland, J., & Scott, C. (1987). *The World Fertility Survey: An assessment*. Oxford: Oxford University Press.

Canning, D., Raja, S., & Yazbeck, A. S. (Eds.). (2015). *Africa's demographic transition: Dividend or disaster?* Washington, DC: The World Bank.

Corroon, M., Speizer, I. S., Fotso, J. C., Akiode, A., Saad, A., Calhoun, L., & Irani, L. (2014). The role of gender empowerment on reproductive health outcomes in urban Nigeria. *Maternal and Child Health Journal, 18*(1), 307–315.

Darteh, E. K. M., Dickson, K. S., & Doku, D. T. (2019). Women's reproductive health decision-making: A multi-country analysis of demographic and health surveys in sub-Saharan Africa. *PLoS One, 14*(1), e0209985.

Defo, B. (2011). The importance for the MDG4 and MDG5 of addressing reproductive health issues during the second decade of life: Review and analysis from times series data of 51 African countries. *African Journal of Reproductive Health/La Revue Africaine De La Santé Reproductive, 15*(2), 9–30.

Dodoo, F., & Van Landewijk, P. (1996). Men, women, and the fertility question in sub-Saharan Africa: An example from Ghana. *African Studies Review, 39*(3), 29–41. doi:10.2307/524942

Dodoo, F. N. A. (1993). Education and changing reproductive behavior in Ghana. *Sociological Perspectives, 36*(3), 241–256.

Ehrlich, P. R. (1968). *The population bomb* (pp. 72–80). New York: The Guilford Press.

Ezeh, A. C. (1997). Polygyny and reproductive behavior in sub-Saharan Africa: A contextual analysis. *Demography, 34*(3), 355–368.

Frade, S., & Odimegwu, C. (2018). What is the association between IPV and fertility in Uganda? *Population Horizons, 15*(2), 41–54.

Garenne, M. (2008). *Fertility changes in sub-Saharan Africa*. DHS Comparative Reports No. 18. Calverton, MD: Macro International Inc.

Garenne, M. (2018). *Family planning and fertility decline in Africa: From 1950 to 2010, in Family Planning*. London: IntechOpen.

Garenne, M. (2004). Age at marriage and modernisation in sub-Saharan Africa. *Southern African Journal of Demography*, 59–79.

Grieser, M., Gittelsohn, J., Shankar, A., Koppenhaver, T., Legrand, T., Marindo, R., . . . Hill, K. (2001). Reproductive decision making and the HIV/AIDS epidemic in Zimbabwe. *Journal of Southern African Studies, 27*(2), 225–243.

Kendall, M. (1979). *The world fertility survey: Current status and findings*. Johns Hopkins University Population Reports, Series M(3).

Kirk, D. (1996). Demographic transition theory. *Population Studies, 50*(3), 361–387.

Letamo, G., & Letamo, H. N. (2001). The role of proximate determinants in fertility transition: A comparative study of Botswana, Zambia and Zimbabwe. *Southern African Journal of Demography*, 29–35.

Lince-Deroche, N., Pleaner, M., Morroni, C., Mullick, S., Firnhaber, C., Harries, J., . . . Holele, P. (2016). Achieving universal access to sexual and reproductive health services: The potential and pitfalls for contraceptive services in South Africa. *South African Health Review, 2016*(1), 95–108.

Loll, D., Fleming, P., Manu, A., Morhe, E., Stephenson, R., King, E., & Hall, K. (2019). Reproductive autonomy and modern contraceptive use at last sex among young women in Ghana. *International Perspectives on Sexual and Reproductive Health, 45*, 1–12. doi:10.1363/45e7419

McIntosh, C. A., & Finkle, J. L. (1995). The Cairo conference on population and development: A new paradigm? *Population and Development Review*, 223–260.

Melesse, D. Y., Mutua, M. K., Choudhury, A., Wado, Y. D., Faye, C. M., Neal, S., & Boerma, T. (2020). Adolescent sexual and reproductive health in sub-Saharan Africa: Who is left behind? *BMJ Global Health, 5*, e002231

Mkwananzi, S., & Odimegwu, C. (2015, April 30–May 2). Teen pregnancy in sub-Saharan Africa: The application of social disorganisation Theory. In *2015 Annual Meeting*, San Diego, CA.

Mturi, A., & Moerane, W. (2001). Premarital childbearing among adolescents in Lesotho. *Journal of Southern African Studies, 27*(2), 259–275.

Odimegwu, C., & Adedini, S. A. (2014). Gender equity and fertility intention in selected sub-Saharan African countries. *Gender & Behaviour*, *12*(2), 5858–5881.

Okonofua, F. (1997). Economic development and reproductive health in Africa/Développement économique et santé reproductive en Afrique. *African Journal of Reproductive Health/La Revue Africaine De La Santé Reproductive*, *1*(2), 6–9. doi:10.2307/3583371

Okonofua, F. (2000). Adolescent reproductive health in Africa: Future challenges/Santé reproductive de l'adolescent en Afrique: Défis de l'avenir. *African Journal of Reproductive Health/La Revue Africaine De La Santé Reproductive*, *4*(1), 7–12. doi:10.2307/3583238

Okonofua, F. (2012). Promoting youth sexual and reproductive health in Africa: The need for a paradigm shift/Promotion de la santé sexuelle et de reproduction chez la jeunesse en Afrique: Nécessité d'un changement d'attitude et de politique. *African Journal of Reproductive Health/La Revue Africaine De La Santé Reproductive*, *16*(2), 9–15.

Pearce, T. (1994). Population policies and the 'creation' of Africa. *Africa Development/Afrique Et Développement*, *19*(3), 61–76.

Population Information Program. (1985). *Fertility and family planning surveys: An update*. Johns Hopkins University Population Reports, Series M(8).

Potts, D., & Marks, S. (2001). Fertility in Southern Africa: The quiet revolution. *Journal of Southern African Studies*, *27*(2), 189–205.

Richey, L. (1999). Family planning and the politics of population in Tanzania: International to local discourse. *Journal of Modern African Studies*, 457–487.

Richey, L. (2003). HIV/AIDS in the shadows of reproductive health interventions. *Reproductive Health Matters*, *11*(22), 30–35.

Riley, T., Sully, E., Ahmed, Z., & Biddlecom, A. (2020). Estimates of the potential impact of the COVID-19 pandemic on sexual and reproductive health in low- and middle-income countries. *International Perspectives on Sexual and Reproductive Health*, *46*, 73–76. doi:10.1363/46e9020

Segal, A. (1993). Africa's population and family planning dynamics. *Africa Today*, *40*(3), 25–37.

Shah, I. (1998). Sexual and reproductive health in sub-Saharan Africa: An overview. *African Journal of Reproductive Health/La Revue Africaine De La Santé Reproductive*, *2*(2), 98–107.

Shapiro, D., & Gebreselassie, T. (2008). Fertility transition in sub-Saharan Africa: Falling and stalling. *African Population Studies*, *23*(1).

Starrs, A. M., Ezeh, A. C., Barker, G., Basu, A., Bertrand, J. T., Blum, R., . . . Sathar, Z. A. (2018). Accelerate progress – sexual and reproductive health and rights for all: Report of the Guttmacher–Lancet Commission. *The Lancet*, *391*(10140), 2642–2692.

Snyder, D. W. (1974). Economic determinants of family size in West Africa. *Demography*, *11*(4), 613–627.

Somefun, D. O., & Ibisomi, L. (2015). Intimate partner violence and contraceptive behaviour: Evidence from Malawi and Zambia. *Southern African Journal of Demography*, *16*(1), 123–150.

Sougou, N. M., Bassoum, O., Faye, A., & Leye, M. M. M. (2020). Women's autonomy in health decision-making and its effect on access to family planning services in Senegal in 2017: A propensity score analysis. *BMC Public Health*, *20*, 1–9.

Wado, Y. D., Gurmu, E., Tilahun, T., & Bangha, M. (2019). Contextual influences on the choice of long-acting reversible and permanent contraception in Ethiopia: A multilevel analysis. *PLoS One*, *14*(1), e0209602.

UN Population Fund (UNFPA). (1995). *Report of the International Conference on Population and Development*, Cairo, 5–13 September 1994, A/CONF.171/13/Rev.1. Retrieved from www.refworld.org/docid/4a54bc080.html

Valentine, C. H., & Revson, J. E. (1979). Cultural traditions, social change, and fertility in sub-Saharan Africa. *The Journal of Modern African Studies*, *17*(3), 453–472.

Westoff, C. F. (1988). Is the KAP-gap real? *Population and Development Review*, 225–232.

Woldemicael, G. (2009). Women's autonomy and reproductive preferences in Eritrea. *Journal of Biosocial Science*, *41*(2), 161.

16

DEMOGRAPHY OF SEXUALITY STUDIES IN AFRICA

Joshua O. Akinyemi, Nicole De Wet and Clifford O. Odimegwu

Reproduced (with additions) following copyright permission by African Journal of Reproductive Health

Akinyemi, J. O., De Wet, N., & Odimegwu, C. O. (2016). Review of sexuality studies in Africa: setting a new post-2015 research agenda. *African Journal of Reproductive Health, 20*, 21–28.

Introduction

Since the introduction of the Millennium Development Goals (MDGs) and its successor, Sustainable Development Goals (SDGs), challenges facing sexual and reproductive health have been at the forefront. SDGs 3 and 5, which encompass five of the MDGs, were related in some ways to sexual and reproductive health. These include eradication of poverty and hunger; promotion of gender equality and women's empowerment; reduction of child mortality; improvement of maternal health; and combating HIV/AIDS, malaria and other diseases (UN Millennium Project, 2006; WHO, 2015). An important key to addressing the challenges and goals related to sexual and reproductive health is a better understanding of sexuality. Research has addressed aspects of sexuality including its definition, components and associated factors in African contexts (Dixon-Mueller, 1993; Oomman, 1998; Standing & Kisekka, 1989). While research has assisted in the partial achievement of the MDGs, many African countries were unable to meet the goals. This failure is indicative of the additional work that research, policy and practice need to do to further development on the continent. As the international community pursues the post-2015 agenda, it is necessary to appraise the knowledge gained from research in the past two decades and make suggestions for sustaining or improving the progress made so far.

Apart from a book on a review of sexual behaviour in sub-Sahara Africa published in the late 1980s (Standing & Kisekka, 1989), previous reviews of sexuality studies in sub-Saharan Africa focused on sexual behaviour of in-school adolescents and youths (Kaaya et al., 2002), school-based sexual health interventions to prevent STI/HIV (Paul-Ebhohimhen, Poobalan, & van Teijlingen, 2008) and parent-child communication about sexuality and HIV/AIDS (Bastien, Kajula, & Muhwezi, 2011). While these past reviews have contributed in no small measure to shaping the search for possible solutions to sexuality challenges, an inclusive examination of literature related to aspects of sexuality such as sexual practices, partners and pleasure, pressure

DOI: 10.4324/9780429287213-19

and pain is necessary. This review covers this broader context and therefore aims to synthesize existing research on sexuality in sub-Saharan Africa over the past two decades, identify knowledge gaps and subsequently suggest some research agenda for post-2015.

Methods

Literature search strategy

PubMed, Medline, African Journals Online (AJOL), Bioline International and POPLINE databases were searched for original articles published in English between 1994 and 2015. Different combinations of the following search terms were used: sexuality, sexual behaviour, sex practices, sexual pleasure, sexual satisfaction, sexual enjoyment, sexual assault, sexual coercion, forced intercourse, unwanted sex, gender roles, gender norms and sub-Saharan Africa. Tables of contents of major journals publishing articles in the subject area were also searched. These include: *African Population Studies*, *African Journal of Reproductive Health* and *Reproductive Health Matters*, among others.

Results

Findings from the review are described in a systematic manner under sub-headings that capture the five components of sexuality as articulated by Gupta (2000). These are: practices, partners, pleasure/pressure/pain, procreation and power. First, definitions of the term "sexuality" are briefly reviewed.

Sexuality definition(s)

Aside from the literary meaning of sexuality as the sexual functions and orientations of an individual, very few formal definitions abound. According to Gupta (2000), sexuality is a complex, dynamic, multidimensional phenomenon influenced directly and indirectly by society, culture, age, gender, socio-economic status and other factors. Its complexity perhaps explain why formal definition of the term is rare in the literature. Researchers at the International Centre for Research on Women have described five components of sexuality as practices, partners, pleasure/pressure/pain, procreation and power (Gupta, 2000). The first two components (sexual practices and partnerships) capture sexual behaviour, which arguably is the most-researched aspect of sexuality in sub-Saharan Africa. Sexuality is a word with interconnection with several other terms; notable among them are: gender, HIV/AIDS and reproductive health.

In the 1980s and early 1990s, sexuality was commonly studied within three contexts: (1) sexual behaviour and contraceptive use; (2) adolescent sexuality; and (3) high-risk sexual behaviour and sexually transmitted diseases, including HIV/AIDS (Dixon-Mueller, 1993). Taking cues from sociological and anthropological literature, Dixon-Mueller (1993) expanded an earlier framework for sexual behaviour (Standing & Kisekka, 1989) by proposing four dimensions of sexuality with a gender perspective and illustrated how these are linked to sexual and reproductive health. These four dimensions were: sexual partnerships, sexual acts, sexual meanings and sexual drives/enjoyment.

Meanwhile, the World Health Organization (WHO) defined sexual health as a:

> state of physical, mental and social well-being in relation to *sexuality*. It requires a positive and respectful approach to sexuality and sexual relationships, as well as the

> possibility of having pleasurable and safe sexual experiences, free of coercion, discrimination and violence.

This definition further shed light on different dimensions to sexuality. Apart from sexual relationships and sexual violence, components such as pleasurable and safe sexual experiences are rarely studied except among people who have health conditions that may affect their sexual functioning – for example, stroke survivors.

Sexual practices

At least one of three indices were commonly used to describe sexual behaviour. These indices were: condom use at last sex, multiple sexual partnership and sex with casual or commercial partner. Age at sexual debut/initiation was also reported in some studies. In this regard, the topical issues can be grouped under the following sub themes: adolescents and youth sexual behaviour, adult male and female sexual behaviour and sexual behaviour in special groups (such as older adults and persons living with HIV).

Sexual behaviour among adolescents and youths

Though there were variations in the age range for most of the studies on adolescents, many of them were among respondents aged 10–24 years. Male-female differences in condom use, age of sexual debut and multiple partnership were commonly reported. There were a few multi-country studies on adolescent sexual behaviour based on nationally representative data such as the Demographic and Health Surveys (DHSs) and AIDS indicator surveys (Curtis & Sutherland, 2004; Ferry et al., 2001). About a quarter had initiated sex before age 15 years, though the proportion declined over time. Female sex and low level of education were associated with early sex debut. Multiple sexual partnerships though decreased over time and were more common among males and urban residents.

Madise et al. contributed evidence on the link between poverty and risky sexual behaviour among adolescents using nationally representative data from Burkina Faso, Ghana, Malawi and Uganda (Madise, Zulu, & Ciera, 2007). Girls in the wealthiest wealth quintile in Burkina Faso, Ghana and Malawi had later sex debuts compared to those in the poorest quintile. Among boys, wealth was not significant, except in Malawi, where those in the middle quintile had earlier sexual debuts. There was no association between wealth status and multiple sex partnership.

The surge in the interest of researchers in adolescent sexual behaviour is related to the HIV/AIDS and STIs prevention programmes. As a follow-up to this, studies were conducted to assess the extent to which correct knowledge of HIV/AIDS has resulted in behaviour change. Unfortunately, evidence from Nigeria (Omoyeni, Akinyemi, & Fatusi, 2014), Botswana (Letamo, 2011) and Uganda (Rutaremwa, Ntozi, & Diana, 2011) showed that being knowledgeable about HIV/AIDS does not necessarily translate into safe sex practices by adolescents.

Though migration is the least-researched component of population change in sub-Saharan Africa, evidence emerging from an urban health and demographic surveillance system in a slum area of Nairobi suggests that there was no significant difference in risky sexual behaviour between migrant and non-migrant youths (Munindia, Mudege, Beguy, & Mberu, 2014). Further studies would be required to ascertain the generalizability of this observation.

Many of the studies among youths focused on young persons in-school or out-of-school or a combination of both. Most of the studies on in-school youths were conducted among undergraduates in tertiary institutions and therefore share a lot of similarities in their findings. In a study on sexual behaviour and contraceptive choice among Nigerian undergraduates, Arowojolu, Ilesanmi, Roberts and Okunola (2002) reported that 87% were sexually active and 66% had more than one sex partner. While 87.5% knew about contraceptives, only 34.2% were current users. Another study carried out more than a decade later found that alcohol use was associated with sexual activity, with 26.9% of alcohol users and 8.9% of non-users reportedly having engaged in sexual intercourse in the four weeks before the survey (Oye-Adeniran, Aina, Gbadegesin, & Ekanem, 2014). A similar study among female undergraduates in Tanzania showed that about 70% of the students were sexually active, with less than half of them (41.5%) currently using contraceptives (Somba, Mbonile, Obure, & Mahande, 2014). Mturi and Gaearwe (2014) added to this evidence base by reporting gender differences in age of sexual initiation and multiple sex partnership in a group of university undergraduates in Mahikeng, South Africa.

Out-of-school youths constitute a special group whose sexual behaviour has also been studied. Food deprivation was a significant predictor of early sex debut and multiple partnerships among youths in a slum area of Lagos State, Nigeria (Kunnuji, 2014). Other factors that predispose out-of-school youths to risky sexual behavior include alcohol consumption and influence of peer pressure (Khasakhala & Mturi, 2008).

Uchudi, Magadi, and Mostazir (2012) conducted a multilevel analysis of the determinants of multiple sexual partnerships in 20 SSA countries using DHS data collected in 2003–2008. The results showed that individual factors (early sexual initiation, young age, education, media exposure and working for cash away from home) and cultural context (permissive sexual norms) are the main determinants of multiple sexual partnerships. These patterns of results point to the need for life course perspectives on the determinants of sexual behavior.

The advent of new information and communication technology platforms seems to have increased the complexity of the dynamics of sexual behaviour among youths. These technological tools have resulted in a new phenomenon known as cybersex – involvement in online sexual activities. A study among youths and adolescents in Lagos, Nigeria, revealed that about 50% were involved in online sexual activities such as visiting pornographic sites, sex chats, cybering and satisfaction of sexual urges via the internet (Kunnuji, 2013). Intensity and time of internet use were the strongest predictors, among other factors.

While sexual behaviour among adult females has received greater attention from researchers, the experiences of males have more or less been neglected, aside from a few studies in which gender differences are reported. A qualitative study among sexually active men and women in Mozambique revealed that traditional norms and beliefs about masculinity played strong roles in forming male sexual behaviour (Macia, Maharaj, & Gresh, 2011). These community norms and beliefs about male sexual behaviour are not limited to Southern Africa alone. A community-based mixed method study in Nigeria found that most of the men and women believed that though sexual activity is permitted only in a marriage, men are by nature sexually polygynous (Orubuloye, Caldwell, & Caldwell, 1997). This was later corroborated by another study which showed that about 1 out of 10 sexually active Nigerian men were involved in extra-marital affairs (Mitsunga, Powell, Heard, & Larsen, 2005).

Sexual behaviour among other groups

Due to its connection to reproductive health, studies on sexual behaviour were most often conducted among men aged 15–59 years and women aged 15–49 years. Evidence shows that sexual activity is common among older persons. This was demonstrated in results from Malawi which indicated that 26.7% of women and 73.8% of men aged 65 years and above were sexually active (Freeman & Anglewicz, 2012). Findings from a qualitative study among older adults (age

50–75 years) in southwestern Nigeria also showed that sexual activity is viewed as important in old age and there were gender differences in sexual desire/pleasure (Agunbiade & Ayotunde, 2012). How older adults go about satisfying their sexual desire is therefore an important research question deserving further investigation, especially in high HIV prevalence settings.

Among sex workers, unsafe sex practices were associated with alcohol consumption, as revealed by a recent study in Uganda (Mbonye, Rutakumwa, Weiss, & Seeley, 2014). Also, there are speculations that initiation of antiretroviral treatment promotes risky sexual behaviour in HIV positive persons (De Coninck, 2014). The evidence is not consistent, given the different findings from diverse contexts (Diabate et al., 2013; Osinde, Kaye, & Kakaire, 2011).

Sexual partnership

Studies on different forms of sexual partnership seem to be scarce in sub-Saharan Africa. This may not be unconnected with the perceived stigma and unfavourable environment for these types of sexual relationships. For instance, South Africa is the only country in the sub-region that has decriminalized same-sex relationships. Rabie et al. investigated the construction of sexuality among young gay men in semi-rural South Africa and found that the respondents constructed their sexuality as "being like a woman" (Rabie & Lesch, 2009). Another South African study explored condom use experiences and reported on factors that inhibit and facilitate usage (Siegler et al., 2014). Factors found to aid condom use include alternative sexual strategies while reduced sexual pleasure was reported as discouraging condom use. Even though global evidence suggests that this group has higher risks of HIV, it is a bit challenging to conduct studies among them (Muraguri, Temmerman, & Geibel, 2012; Scheibe, Kanyemba, Syvertsen, Adebajo, & Baral, 2014).

Pleasure, pressure and pain

The quest for sexual pleasure and enjoyment/satisfaction is a major factor determining how men and women engaged in sexual acts. The literature on this aspect of sexuality appeared to be skewed towards certain issues. This review showed that sexual satisfaction/pleasure has most often been investigated in regard to contraceptive use (Cox, Hindin, Otupiri, & Larsen-Reindorf, 2013), male/female circumcision (Kigozi et al., 2008) and sexual functioning among survivors of non-communicable diseases such as diabetes (Olarinoye & Olarinoye, 2008) and stroke (Akinpelu, Osose, Odole, & Odunaiya, 2013). In addition, sexual pleasure was found to be studied while investigating different sex practices, especially among women. For example, Bagnol et al. reported on two sex practices among Mozambican women – elongation of the labia minora and insertion of natural or synthetic products into the vagina (dry sex) (Bagnol & Mariano, 2008). These practices were usually undertaken for female identity and enhancement of sexual pleasure. Another study among women in Uganda and Tanzania revealed that intravaginal practices were driven by cultural norms and social expectation on hygiene, sexual pleasure and relationship security, among others (Lees et al., 2014). Though these practices varied from culture to culture, the motivations were very similar, with sexual pleasure featuring repeatedly (Martin Hilber et al., 2010; Scorgie et al., 2009).

The promotion of male circumcision as a strategy for HIV prevention has also attracted the interest of researchers to investigate the effect of male circumcision on male sexual functioning and satisfaction (Kigozi et al., 2008). Evidence is, however, mixed. Results from Kenya suggest that male circumcision does not have any negative effect on sexual satisfaction or functioning (Krieger et al., 2008). A study in Malawi found that female partners of circumcised men had greater sexual satisfaction (Shacham, Godlonton, & Thornton, 2014), while another study in KwaZulu-Natal, South Africa, found that voluntary medical male circumcision was associated with better perception of masculinity, male identity, sexual performance and pleasure (Humphries, van Rooyen, Knight, Barnabas, & Celum, 2015). Concerning female circumcision, it is widely condemned in reproductive health circles. Though the evidence on its effect on sexual functioning is inconclusive, a study in Lagos, Nigeria, showed that female genital cutting adversely affects their sexual functioning (Oyefara, 2015).

The search for interventions to control or eradicate pressure/pain in sexuality must have contributed to the quantity of research in this area. Terms used to connote pains and pressures include sexual coercion, unwanted sex, non-consensual sex, forced intercourse, sexual assault, sexual abuse, sexual harassment and sexual violence. While prevalence varied widely depending on the context and definition of the term used, the summary is that these negative experiences are quite common in sub-Saharan Africa. While evidence on causes is sparse, there are overwhelming facts to show that male intimate partners are the greatest perpetrators and female partners are the victims (Bingenheimer & Reed, 2014; Stern, Cooper, & Greenbaum, 2015). There was evidence to show that females also inflict pains/pressures on their male counterparts (Haile, Kebeta, & Kassie, 2013; Sikweyiya & Jewkes, 2009). Findings also suggest that the main driving forces behind these attitude are traditional norms and cultural beliefs that portray men as being superior to women who therefore can use every means to get whatever they want, including sexual intercourse (Conroy, 2014; Dunkle et al., 2004; Erulkar, 2004). A common denominator for most of the pain/pressure experiences is alcohol use by either partner. In addition, males with multiple partners were very likely to inflict pain/pressure in form of coercion, forced sex, unwanted sex and so on (Agardh, Odberg-Pettersson, & Ostergren, 2011; van der Straten, King, Grinstead, Serufilira, & Allen, 1995). Sexually transmitted infections, HIV/AIDS, depression, low self-esteem and post-traumatic stress disorder are common consequences of these acts (Conroy & Chilungo, 2014; Dunkle et al., 2004; Hoffman, O'Sullivan, Harrison, Dolezal, & Monroe-Wise, 2006). In light of these, programmes on protection of women's reproductive health and rights need to be sustained. Research efforts on innovative and effective interventions have also become imperative.

Power and procreation

Power is the most important component of sexuality because it influences how all the other components are expressed and experienced (Gupta, 2000). For instance, power determines whose interest takes precedence in procreation (number of children), contraceptive use (sex practices) and sexual pleasure/pain. Power as a sexuality component has been operationalized in terms of gender imbalance in decision-making in sexual relationships. Specifically, power is viewed as ability to make choices (Kabeer, 2005). The distribution of this ability between men and women makes the concept of power and gender intertwined. This complex relationship underscores the relevance of the Sustainable Development Goal focused on gender and women's empowerment. The extant evidence is that unequal power balance in favour of men is driven largely by hegemonic masculinity and the predominant patriarchal beliefs and structure in sub-Saharan Africa (Jegede & Odumosu, 2003; Orubuloye et al., 1997; Rassjo & Kiwanuka, 2010). Caldwell et al. argued based on evidence from several countries that while constructs/definition of adolescence was driven by international, economic and social forces, in sub-Saharan Africa, contemporary adolescence has been shaped by the traditional culture, with implications for sexuality and reproduction (1998). This notion is supported by several empirical studies, especially those that investigated gender-based violence, condom use and HIV. Even though females are on the receiving end of male domination, they also believe it is right because that is what the traditional norms dictate (Orubuloye, Caldwell, & Caldwell, 1993; Rassjo & Kiwanuka, 2010). Evidence from post-apartheid South Africa showed that change is possible but challenging. A qualitative study among undergraduates showed that though there have been dramatic changes in gender norms and recognition of women's rights, women were still restrained by traditional construction of gender roles (Mantell et al., 2009). Gender power imbalance is one area that needs urgent intervention in sexual and reproductive health, especially in sub-Saharan Africa.

Sexuality data collection methodologies

Due to the complex and sensitive nature of data on sexuality, it has been suggested that creative approaches are needed to gather information on its various dimensions (Dixon-Mueller, 1993). Few methodological studies were found to have explored different techniques of collecting sensitive data apart from the conventional questionnaire interviews. A comparison of face-to-face interview with an audio-computer assisted survey instrument (ACASI) among adolescent girls in Kenya revealed that the latter is a better technique for eliciting data on sensitive issues such as types of sex partner and coerced sexual activity (Hewett, Mensch, & Erulkar, 2004). Langhaug et al. (2011) compared the validity and reliability of four modes of questionnaire administration among youths in rural Zimbabwe. The four methods were: self-administered questionnaire (SAQ), SAQ with an audio soundtrack (Audio-SAQ), informal confidential voting interview (ICVI) and audio-computer assisted survey instrument. Indices for comparison were item non-response and reporting of sensitive sexual behaviour. The results showed that item non-response was higher in SAQ and audio-SAQ than in ICVI and ACASI. Though the authors claimed that ACASI was acceptable in resource-poor settings, its feasibility has not been ascertained under field conditions. With further advancement in the digital revolution, data collection will go purely electronic because it conveys better efficiency for fieldwork activities.

A glimpse at post-2015 sexuality literature

To provide a glimpse into sexuality literature post-2015, a quick search in PubMed revealed that many of the findings earlier summarized still resonated quite well. Also, papers on sexual orientation are becoming very common, unlike in the past. Several new studies have focused on lesbian, gay, bisexual and transgender (LGBT) individuals – commonly referred to as key populations or "African sexual minorities" (Zaidi, Ocholla, Otieno, & Sandfort, 2016). The papers in this group were often about HIV treatment/prevention (Gamariel et al., 2020) and reproductive themes such as condom use (Bakai et al., 2016; Ochako, Temmerman, Mbondo, & Askew, 2017; Shangani, Naanyu, Operario, & Genberg, 2018), transactional sex (Kounta et al., 2019; Wamoyi, Ranganathan, Kyegombe, & Stoebenau, 2019) and access to healthcare services (Logie et al., 2019; Sekoni et al., 2016; Sithole, 2017). While very few countries, like South Africa, have legislation to protect different sexual identities, a few nations, such as Nigeria, had laws to criminalize these practices. The legality or otherwise in many other countries is not clearly known. Apart from the legal concerns, the socio-cultural norms and beliefs in much of SSA are not so friendly to these sexual minorities. Therefore, stigmatization is a source of concern. Attempts to look into different aspects of health and livelihood in this "key population" have been the driving force of many studies, and this is evident in the emerging literature. Availability of journals specifically dedicated to these groups must have also provided the impetus for increasing publications.

Knowledge gap and research agenda

Before proposing research agenda, we summarize the evidence as synthesized in this review. Sexuality cuts across different age strata in society, from adolescents to older persons. The majority of sexual relationships are heterosexual, and multiple sex partnership is common, especially among men, and seems unaffected by knowledge about HIV/AIDS and other STIs. Family setting, home environment and parent-child relationship/communication are associated with sexual behaviour among young persons. The Internet and information technology are adding to the complexity of sexual behaviour among adolescents and youths. Urbanization and poverty are among the factors associated with risky sexual behaviour among adolescents. Traditional norms and beliefs about gender roles are a driving force for gender power imbalance in sexuality-related matters. Concerning data collection, the face-to-face interview is not versatile enough to collect data needed to understand the complex nature of human sexuality.

In view of the available evidence, some knowledge gaps which could form the fulcrum of a new research agenda are highlighted. The majority of the existing studies do not provide useful information on the characteristics of sex partners apart from the type (regular, casual or commercial). It is necessary to collect richer data on the identity of sex partners and circumstances leading to formation and dissolution or concurrency of sexual relationships. Since sexuality is partly driven by cultural norms and beliefs, qualitative studies exploring the roles/influence of contextual characteristics are needed. Such studies would need to go beyond the conventional cross-sectional designs. This should be with a view to exploring how sexual identity, orientation, practices and other behaviour evolve, especially in adolescence and younger ages.

Further evidence is needed on determinants of specific sexual behaviour. This becomes important given the point that knowledge of HIV/AIDS does not result in safe sexual practices. A relevant question is why men/women adopt certain practices/behaviour. Have traditional/cultural norms about sex and sexuality changed over time, and how do such changes affect sexual and reproductive health? Since family setting also affects adolescent sexual behaviour and family changes is one of the consequences of population dynamics, the consequences of family change for adolescent sexuality need to be better described. With the onset of phenomenon such as cybersex, design of prevention programmes would benefit from an in-depth knowledge of the aspects of sexuality most affected by technological advancement. For instance, does involvement in cybersex have any implication for safe sex practices?

More work needs to be done in the area of data collection methodologies. Many of the existing studies are based on the conventional cross-sectional design, which is obviously deficient for causal inference. Mixed-methods designs that use qualitative techniques can be deployed to provide deeper understanding about sexual behaviour. Besides, health and demographic surveillance systems represent a rich source of longitudinal data with which cause-effect relationships can be appropriately studied.

Since gender imbalance in power is related to all other components of sexuality, and power is deeply entrenched in socio-cultural norms, that seems to be difficult to change. Thus, in pursuit of the WHO's definition of sexual health, there is a need for innovative approaches to achieve changes in socio-cultural norms and gender role attitudes. Programmes on gender equality and women's empowerment therefore need to look beyond the current approaches which are centred around education.

The global COVID-19 pandemic and previous epidemics in sub-Saharan Africa such as Ebola and Lassa fever also have diverse implications for sexual and reproductive health (SRH) service delivery and research. Disruption of service provision and uptake is one major immediate effect of travel restrictions and other measures introduced to curtail COVID-19 (Church,

Gassner, & Elliott, 2020). There were also reports of similar challenges during the Ebola outbreak in parts of West Africa. (Barden-O'Fallon, Barry, Brodish, & Hazerjian, 2015; Camara et al., 2017; Quaglio et al., 2019). The long-term consequences of these disruptions could be enormous. These emerging public health crises raise many questions, especially for Africa, which has always been confronted with health and developmental challenges. New research frontiers are needed to track these issues and respond adequately with innovative, feasible and acceptable strategies to ensure that the SRH gains of the recent past are not eroded by the COVID-19 crisis.

References

Agardh, A., Odberg-Pettersson, K., & Ostergren, P. O. (2011). Experience of sexual coercion and risky sexual behavior among Ugandan university students. *BMC Public Health, 11*, 527. doi:10.1186/1471-2458-11-527

Agunbiade, O. M., & Ayotunde, T. (2012). Ageing, sexuality and enhancement among Yoruba people in south western Nigeria. *Cult Health Sex, 14*(6), 705–717. doi:10.1080/13691058.2012.677861

Akinpelu, A. O., Osose, A. A., Odole, A. C., & Odunaiya, N. A. (2013). Sexual dysfunction in Nigerian stroke survivors. *African Health Sciences, 13*(3), 639–645. doi:10.4314/ahs.v13i3.17

Arowojolu, A. O., Ilesanmi, A. O., Roberts, O. A., & Okunola, M. A. (2002). Sexuality, contraceptive choice and AIDS awareness among Nigerian undergraduates. *African Journal of Reproductive Health, 6*(2), 60–70.

Bagnol, B., & Mariano, E. (2008). Vaginal practices: Eroticism and implications for women's health and condom use in Mozambique. *Cult Health Sex, 10*(6), 573–585. doi:10.1080/13691050801999071

Bakai, T. A., Ekouevi, D. K., Tchounga, B. K., Balestre, E., Afanvi, K. A., Goilibe, K. B., . . . Pitche, V. P. (2016). Condom use and associated factors among men who have sex with men in Togo, West Africa. *Pan African Medical Journal, 23*, 118. doi:10.11604/pamj.2016.23.118.7492

Barden-O'Fallon, J., Barry, M. A., Brodish, P., & Hazerjian, J. (2015). Rapid assessment of Ebola-related implications for reproductive, maternal, newborn and child health service delivery and utilization in Guinea. *PLoS Currents*, 7. doi:10.1371/currents.outbreaks.0b0ba06009dd091bc39ddb3c6d7b0826

Bastien, S., Kajula, L. J., & Muhwezi, W. W. (2011). A review of studies of parent-child communication about sexuality and HIV/AIDS in sub-Saharan Africa. *Reproductive Health, 8*(25), 1–17.

Bingenheimer, J. B., & Reed, E. (2014). Risk for coerced sex among female youth in Ghana: Roles of family context, school enrollment and relationship experience. *International Perspectives on Sexual and Reproductive Health, 40*(4), 184–195. doi:10.1363/4018414

Caldwell, J. C., Caldwell, P., Caldwell, B. K., & Pieris, I. (1998). The construction of adolescence in a changing world: Implications for sexuality, reproduction, and marriage. *Studies in Family Planning, 29*(2), 137–153.

Camara, B. S., Delamou, A., Diro, E., Béavogui, A. H., El Ayadi, A. M., Sidibé, S., . . . Zachariah, R. (2017). Effect of the 2014/2015 Ebola outbreak on reproductive health services in a rural district of Guinea: An ecological study. *Transactions of the Royal Society of Tropical Medicine and Hygiene, 111*(1), 22–29. doi:10.1093/trstmh/trx009

Church, K., Gassner, J., & Elliott, M. (2020). Reproductive health under COVID-19 – Challenges of responding in a global crisis. *Sexual and Reproductive Health Matters, 28*(1), 1773163. doi:10.1080/26410397.2020.1773163

Conroy, A. A. (2014). Gender, power, and intimate partner violence: A study on couples from rural Malawi. *Journal of Interpersonal Violence, 29*(5), 866–888. doi:10.1177/0886260513505907

Conroy, A. A., & Chilungo, A. (2014). Male victims of sexual violence in rural Malawi: The overlooked association with HIV infection. *AIDS Care, 26*(12), 1576–1580. doi:10.1080/09540121.2014.931562

Cox, C. M., Hindin, M. J., Otupiri, E., & Larsen-Reindorf, R. (2013). Understanding couples' relationship quality and contraceptive use in Kumasi, Ghana. *International Perspectives on Sexual and Reproductive Health, 39*(4), 185–194. doi:10.1363/3918513

Curtis, S. L., & Sutherland, E. G. (2004). Measuring sexual behaviour in the era of HIV/AIDS: The experience of Demographic and Health Surveys and similar enquiries. *Sexually Transmitted Infections, 80*(Suppl. 2), II22–27. doi:10.1136/sti.2004.011650

De Coninck, Z. (2014). Does access to antiretroviral drugs lead to an increase in high-risk sexual behaviour? *African Journal of Reproductive Health, 18*(3), 15–16.

Diabate, S., Chamberland, A., Zannou, D. M., Geraldo, N., Azon-Kouanou, A., Massinga-Loembe, M., . . . Alary, M. (2013). Sexual behaviour after antiretroviral therapy initiation in female sex workers and HIV-positive patients from the general population, Cotonou, Benin. *AIDS Care, 25*(11), 1426–1432. doi:10.1080/09540121.2013.772279

Dixon-Mueller, R. (1993). The sexuality connection in reproductive health. *Studies in Family Planning, 24*(5), 269–282.

Dunkle, K. L., Jewkes, R. K., Brown, H. C., Gray, G. E., McIntryre, J. A., & Harlow, S. D. (2004). Gender-based violence, relationship power, and risk of HIV infection in women attending antenatal clinics in South Africa. *Lancet, 363*(9419), 1415–1421. doi:10.1016/s0140-6736(04)16098-4

Erulkar, A. S. (2004). The experience of sexual coercion among young people in Kenya. *International Family Planning Perspectives, 30*(4), 182–189. doi:10.1363/ifpp.30.182.04

Ferry, B., Carael, M., Buve, A., Auvert, B., Laourou, M., Kanhonou, L., . . . Kaona, F. (2001). Comparison of key parameters of sexual behaviour in four African urban populations with different levels of HIV infection. *AIDS, 15*(Suppl. 4), S41–50.

Freeman, E., & Anglewicz, P. (2012). HIV prevalence and sexual behaviour at older ages in rural Malawi. *International Journal of STD and AIDS, 23*(7), 490–496. doi:10.1258/ijsa.2011.011340

Gamariel, F., Isaakidis, P., Tarquino, I. A. P., Beirão, J. C., O'Connell, L., Mulieca, N., . . . Venables, E. (2020). Access to health services for men who have sex with men and transgender women in Beira, Mozambique: A qualitative study. *PLoS One, 15*(1), e0228307. doi:10.1371/journal.pone.0228307

Gupta, G. R. (2000). *Gender, sexuality, and HIV/AIDS: The what, the why, and the how.* Paper presented at the XIIIth International AIDS Conference, Durban, South Africa.

Haile, R. T., Kebeta, N. D., & Kassie, G. M. (2013). Prevalence of sexual abuse of male high school students in Addis Ababa, Ethiopia. *BMC International Health and Human Rights, 13*, 24. doi:10.1186/1472-698x-13-24

Hewett, P. C., Mensch, B. S., & Erulkar, A. S. (2004). Consistency in the reporting of sexual behaviour by adolescent girls in Kenya: A comparison of interviewing methods. *Sexually Transmitted Infections, 80*(Suppl 2), II43–48. doi:10.1136/sti.2004.013250

Hoffman, S., O'Sullivan, L. F., Harrison, A., Dolezal, C., & Monroe-Wise, A. (2006). HIV risk behaviors and the context of sexual coercion in young adults' sexual interactions: Results from a diary study in rural South Africa. *Sexually Transmitted Diseases, 33*(1), 52–58.

Humphries, H., van Rooyen, H., Knight, L., Barnabas, R., & Celum, C. (2015). 'If you are circumcised, you are the best': Understandings and perceptions of voluntary medical male circumcision among men from KwaZulu-Natal, South Africa. *Cult Health Sex, 17*(7), 920–931. doi:10.1080/13691058.2014.992045

Jegede, A. S., & Odumosu, O. (2003). Gender and health analysis of sexual behaviour in south-western Nigeria. *African Journal of Reproductive Health*, 7(1), 63–70.

Kaaya, S. F., Flisher, A. J., Mbwambo, J. K., Schaalma, H., Aaro, L. E., & Klepp, K. I. (2002). A review of studies of sexual behaviour of school students in sub-Saharan Africa. *Scandinavian Journal of Public Health, 30*(2), 148–160. doi:10.1080/14034940210133807

Kabeer, N. (2005). Gender equality and women's empowerment: A critical analysis of the third millennium development goal. *Gender and Development, 13*(1), 13–24.

Khasakhala, A. A., & Mturi, A. J. (2008). Factors associated with risky sexual behaviour among out-of-school youth in Kenya. *Journal of Biosocial Science, 40*(5), 641–653. doi:10.1017/s0021932007002647

Kigozi, G., Watya, S., Polis, C. B., Buwembo, D., Kiggundu, V., Wawer, M. J., . . . Gray, R. H. (2008). The effect of male circumcision on sexual satisfaction and function, results from a randomized trial of male circumcision for human immunodeficiency virus prevention, Rakai, Uganda. *BJU International, 101*(1), 65–70. doi:10.1111/j.1464-410X.2007.07369.x

Kounta, C. H., Sagaon-Teyssier, L., Coulaud, P. J., Mora, M., Maradan, G., Bourrelly, M., . . . Spire, B. (2019). Transactional sex among men who have sex with men participating in the CohMSM prospective cohort study in West Africa. *PLoS One, 14*(11), e0217115. doi:10.1371/journal.pone.0217115

Krieger, J. N., Mehta, S. D., Bailey, R. C., Agot, K., Ndinya-Achola, J. O., Parker, C., & Moses, S. (2008). Adult male circumcision: Effects on sexual function and sexual satisfaction in Kisumu, Kenya. *Journal of Sexual Medicine, 5*(11), 2610–2622. doi:10.1111/j.1743-6109.2008.00979.x

Kunnuji, M. (2013). Prevalence and predictors of unsolicited exposure to and involvement in online sexual activities among young Internet users in Lagos metropolis. *African Population Studies, 27*(1), 1–13.

Kunnuji, M. (2014). Basic deprivation and involvement in risky sexual behaviour among out-of-school young people in a Lagos slum. *Cult Health Sex*, *16*(7), 727–740. doi:10.1080/13691058.2014.894206

Langhaug, L. F., Cheung, Y. B., Pascoe, S. J., Chirawu, P., Woelk, G., Hayes, R. J., & Cowan, F. M. (2011). How you ask really matters: Randomised comparison of four sexual behaviour questionnaire delivery modes in Zimbabwean youth. *Sexually Transmitted Infections*, *87*(2), 165–173. doi:10.1136/sti.2009.037374

Lees, S., Zalwango, F., Andrew, B., Vandepitte, J., Seeley, J., Hayes, R. J., & Francis, S. C. (2014). Understanding motives for intravaginal practices amongst Tanzanian and Ugandan women at high risk of HIV infection: The embodiment of social and cultural norms and well-being. *Social Science and Medicine*, *102*, 165–173. doi:10.1016/j.socscimed.2013.12.005

Letamo, G. (2011). Does correct knowledge about HIV and AIDS lead to safer sexual behaviour? The case of young people in Botswana. *African Population Studies*, *25*(1), 46–62.

Logie, C. H., Alschech, J., Guta, A., Ghabrial, M. A., Mothopeng, T., Ranotsi, A., & Baral, S. D. (2019). Experiences and perceptions of social constraints and social change among lesbian, gay, bisexual and transgender persons in Lesotho. *Cult Health Sex*, *21*(5), 559–574. doi:10.1080/13691058.2018.1498539

Macia, M., Maharaj, P., & Gresh, A. (2011). Masculinity and male sexual behaviour in Mozambique. *Cult Health Sex*, *13*(10), 1181–1192. doi:10.1080/13691058.2011.611537

Madise, N., Zulu, E., & Ciera, J. (2007). Is poverty a driver for risky sexual behaviour? Evidence from national surveys of adolescents in four African countries. *African Journal of Reproductive Health*, *11*(3), 83–98.

Mantell, J. E., Needham, S. L., Smit, J. A., Hoffman, S., Cebekhulu, Q., Adams-Skinner, J., . . . Milford, C. (2009). Gender norms in South Africa: Implications for HIV and pregnancy prevention among African and Indian women students at a South African tertiary institution. *Cult Health Sex*, *11*(2), 139–157. doi:10.1080/13691050802521155

Martin Hilber, A., Hull, T. H., Preston-Whyte, E., Bagnol, B., Smit, J., Wacharasin, C., & Widyantoro, N. (2010). A cross cultural study of vaginal practices and sexuality: Implications for sexual health. *Social Science and Medicine*, *70*(3), 392–400. doi:10.1016/j.socscimed.2009.10.023

Mbonye, M., Rutakumwa, R., Weiss, H., & Seeley, J. (2014). Alcohol consumption and high risk sexual behaviour among female sex workers in Uganda. *African Journal of AIDS Research*, *13*(2), 145–151. doi:10.2989/16085906.2014.927779

Mitsunga, T. M., Powell, A. M., Heard, N. J., & Larsen, U. M. (2005). Extramarital sex among Nigerian men: Polygyny and other risk factors. *Journal of Acquired Immune Deficiency Syndromes*, *39*, 478–488.

Mturi, A. J., & Gaearwe, L. (2014). Gender differences in sexual behaviour amongst university students in Mahikeng, South Africa. *African Population Studies*, *28*(1), 526–537.

Munindia, K., Mudege, N., Beguy, D., & Mberu, B. U. (2014). Migration and sexual behaviour among youth in Nairobi's slum areas. *African Population Studies*, *28*(3), 1297–1309.

Muraguri, N., Temmerman, M., & Geibel, S. (2012). A decade of research involving men who have sex with men in sub-Saharan Africa: Current knowledge and future directions. *SAHARA-J: Journal of Social Aspects of HIV/AIDS*, *9*(3), 137–147. doi:10.1080/17290376.2012.744176

Ochako, R., Temmerman, M., Mbondo, M., & Askew, I. (2017). Determinants of modern contraceptive use among sexually active men in Kenya. *Reproductive Health*, *14*(1), 56. doi:10.1186/s12978-017-0316-3

Olarinoye, J., & Olarinoye, A. (2008). Determinants of sexual function among women with type 2 diabetes in a Nigerian population. *Journal of Sexual Medicine*, *5*(4), 878–886. doi:10.1111/j.1743-6109.2007.00649.x

Omoyeni, S., Akinyemi, A. I., & Fatusi, A. (2014). Adolescents and HIV-related behaviour in Nigeria: Does knowledge of HIV/AIDS promote protective sexual behaviour among sexually active adolescents? *African Population Studies*, *27*(2), 331–342.

Oomman, N. (1998). Sexuality: Not just a reproductive health matter. *Reproductive Health Matters*, *6*(12), 10–12. doi:10.1016/S0968-8080(98)90001-5

Orubuloye, I. O., Caldwell, J. C., & Caldwell, P. (1993). African women's control over their sexuality in an era of AIDS: A study of the Yoruba of Nigeria. *Social Science and Medicine*, *37*(7), 859–872.

Orubuloye, I. O., Caldwell, J. C., & Caldwell, P. (1997). Perceived male sexual needs and male sexual behaviour in southwest Nigeria. *Social Science and Medicine*, *44*(8), 1195–1207.

Osinde, M. O., Kaye, D. K., & Kakaire, O. (2011). Sexual behaviour and HIV sero-discordance among HIV patients receiving HAART in rural Uganda. *Journal of Obstetrics and Gynaecology*, *31*(5), 436–440. doi:10.3109/01443615.2011.578228

Oye-Adeniran, B. A., Aina, O. F., Gbadegesin, A., & Ekanem, E. E. (2014). Substance use and sexual behaviour among female students in Nigerian universities. *International Quarterly of Community Health Education, 35*(1), 73–83. doi:10.2190/IQ.35.1.f

Oyefara, J. L. (2015). Female genital mutilation (FGM) and sexual functioning of married women in Oworonshoki Community, Lagos State, Nigeria. *African Population Studies, 29*(1), 1526–1540.

Paul-Ebhohimhen, V. A., Poobalan, A., & van Teijlingen, E. R. (2008). A systematic review of school-based sexual health interventions to prevent STI/HIV in sub-Saharan Africa. *BMC Public Health, 8*, 4. doi:10.1186/1471-2458-8-4

Quaglio, G., Tognon, F., Finos, L., Bome, D., Sesay, S., Kebbie, A., . . . Putoto, G. (2019). Impact of Ebola outbreak on reproductive health services in a rural district of Sierra Leone: A prospective observational study. *BMJ Open, 9*(9), e029093. doi:10.1136/bmjopen-2019-029093

Rabie, F., & Lesch, E. (2009). 'I am like a woman': Constructions of sexuality among gay men in a low-income South African community. *Cult Health Sex, 11*(7), 717–729. doi:10.1080/13691050902890344

Rassjo, E. B., & Kiwanuka, R. (2010). Views on social and cultural influence on sexuality and sexual health in groups of Ugandan adolescents. *Sexual and Reproductive Healthcare, 1*(4), 157–162. doi:10.1016/j.srhc.2010.08.003

Rutaremwa, G., Ntozi, J. P., & Diana, N. (2011). Has high knowledge of HIV/AIDS among the youth translated into positive sexual behavior in Northern Uganda? *African Population Studies, 25*(1), 95–114.

Scheibe, A., Kanyemba, B., Syvertsen, J., Adebajo, S., & Baral, S. (2014). Money, power and HIV: Economic influences and HIV among men who have sex with men in sub-Saharan Africa. *African Journal of Reproductive Health, 18*(3), 84–92.

Scorgie, F., Kunene, B., Smit, J. A., Manzini, N., Chersich, M. F., & Preston-Whyte, E. M. (2009). In search of sexual pleasure and fidelity: vaginal practices in KwaZulu-Natal, South Africa. *Cult Health Sex, 11*(3), 267–283. doi:10.1080/13691050802395915

Sekoni, A. O., Jolly, K., Gale, N. K., Ifaniyi, O. A., Somefun, E. O., Agaba, E. I., & Fakayode, V. A. (2016). Provision of healthcare services to men who have sex with men in Nigeria: Students' attitudes following the passage of the Same-Sex Marriage Prohibition Law. *LGBT Health, 3*(4), 300–307. doi:10.1089/lgbt.2015.0061

Shacham, E., Godlonton, S., & Thornton, R. L. (2014). Perceptions of male circumcision among married couples in rural Malawi. *Journal of International Association of Providers of AIDS Care, 13*(5), 443–449. doi:10.1177/2325957413508319

Shangani, S., Naanyu, V., Operario, D., & Genberg, B. (2018). Stigma and healthcare-seeking practices of men who have sex with men in Western Kenya: A mixed-methods approach for scale validation. *AIDS Patient Care and STDS, 32*(11), 477–486. doi:10.1089/apc.2018.0101

Siegler, A. J., Voux, A., Phaswana-Mafuya, N., Bekker, L. G., Sullivan, P. S., Baral, S. D., . . . Stephenson, R. (2014). Elements of condom-use decision making among South African men who have sex with men. *Journal of International Association of Providers of AIDS Care, 13*(5), 414–423. doi:10.1177/2325957414535979

Sikweyiya, Y., & Jewkes, R. (2009). Force and temptation: Contrasting South African men's accounts of coercion into sex by men and women. *Cult Health Sex, 11*(5), 529–541. doi:10.1080/1369105090 2912783

Sithole, B. (2017). HIV prevention needs for men who have sex with men in Swaziland. *African Journal of AIDS Research, 16*(4), 315–320. doi:10.2989/16085906.2017.1379420

Somba, M. J., Mbonile, M., Obure, J., & Mahande, M. J. (2014). Sexual behaviour, contraceptive knowledge and use among female undergraduates' students of Muhimbili and Dar es Salaam Universities, Tanzania: A cross-sectional study. *BMC Womens Health, 14*, 94. doi:10.1186/1472-6874-14-94

Standing, H., & Kisekka, M. N. (1989). *Sexual behaviour in sub-Saharan Africa: A review and annotated bibliography*. London: Overseas Development Administration.

Stern, E., Cooper, D., & Greenbaum, B. (2015). The relationship between hegemonic norms of masculinity and men's conceptualization of sexually coercive acts by women in South Africa. *Journal of Interpersonal Violence, 30*(5), 796–817. doi:10.1177/0886260514536275

Uchudi, J., Magadi, M., & Mostazir, M. (2012). A multilevel analysis of the determinants of high-risk sexual behaviour in sub-Saharan Africa. *Journal of Biosocial Science, 44*(3), 289–311. doi:10.1017/s0021932011000654

UN Millennium Project. (2006). *Public choices, private decisions: Sexual and reproductive health and the millennium development goals*. New York: United Nations Development Programme.

van der Straten, A., King, R., Grinstead, O., Serufilira, A., & Allen, S. (1995). Couple communication, sexual coercion and HIV risk reduction in Kigali, Rwanda. *AIDS*, *9*(8), 935–944.

Wamoyi, J., Ranganathan, M., Kyegombe, N., & Stoebenau, K. (2019). Improving the measurement of transactional sex in sub-Saharan Africa: A critical review. *Journal of Acquired Immune Deficiency Syndromes*, *80*(4), 367–374. doi:10.1097/qai.0000000000001928

WHO. (2015). *Health in 2015: From MDG to SDG*. Geneva: World Health Organization.

Zaidi, S. S., Ocholla, A. M., Otieno, R. A., & Sandfort, T. G. (2016). Women who have sex with women in Kenya and their sexual and reproductive health. *LGBT Health*, *3*(2), 139–145. doi:10.1089/lgbt.2014.0121

PART 4

Gender in African demography

17

GENDER IN AFRICAN DEMOGRAPHIC RESEARCH

A scoping review

Lorretta Favour Chizomam Ntoimo and Clifford O. Odimegwu

Introduction

"Gender refers to the roles, behaviours, activities, attributes and opportunities that any society considers appropriate for girls and boys, and women and men. Gender interacts with, but is different from the binary categories of biological sex" (World Health Organization, 2020). It is a socially constructed difference between femininity and masculinity. Gender is a central organizing principle of societies and often governs the processes of production and reproduction, consumption and distribution (March, Smyth, & Mukhopadhyay, 1999; UNDP, 2020). Through gendered structures and processes, advantages and disadvantages, exploitation and control, and identity are patterned in terms of a distinction between male and female. Gender attributes are, however, culturally specific, and can change over time.

The importance of gender in human development came to the fore from the early days of the feminist movement, particularly during the second-wave feminist movement in the 1970s. During the 1994 revolutionary International Conference on Population and Development (ICPD) in Cairo and the 1995 Fourth World Conference on Women in Beijing, the importance of gender was not only given priority attention in the global population and development discourse but made a mandatory policy and program focus for nations (UN Women, 2014). The ultimate milestones in prioritizing gender are equity and equality. Gender equity refers to the equivalence in life outcomes for men and women. It entails the provision of fairness and justice in the distribution of benefits and responsibilities between women and men and girls and boys (UNDP, 2020). The concept recognizes that women and men have different needs, interests, and power and that these differences should be identified and addressed to produce equitable outcomes, whereas gender equality refers to a situation where women and men have equal opportunities for realizing their full human rights and potential; can contribute equally to national, political, economic, social, and cultural development; and benefit equally from the results (Permanyer, 2010; UNDP, 2020). Gender equality entails that the underlying causes of discrimination based on sex, gender, and other social conditions be systematically identified and removed to give men and women equal opportunities. The concept of gender equality recognizes women's existing subordinate positions within social relations and aims at the structuring of society to eradicate male domination. Gender equality is not merely simple equality with men; it includes both formal equality and substantive equality (Kabeer, 2005; UNDP, 2020).

 DOI: 10.4324/9780429287213-21

Many countries have made great strides towards gender equity and equality, but no country has achieved equality between women and men in socially constructed roles, responsibilities, privileges, relations, and expectations (UNDP, 2020). A wide disparity still exists between women and men in both the public and private sphere, particularly in Africa (Omoluabi, Aina, & Attanasso, 2014; UNDP, 2016). Many girls still marry and commence childbearing in adolescence; maternal mortality is still highest in the region; and a wide gap persists in favour of males in the share of seats in parliament, in population with at least some secondary education, and labour force participation (UNDP, 2016, 2018, 2019; World Health Organization, 2019). In the most recent gender inequality index (GII) ranking (UNDP, 2019, 2020), no African country is among the first 40. Among the African countries categorized in the high human development category, the best in GII ranking are Libya (41), Tunisia (63), and South Africa (97); others fall in the ranks of 100 and above.

Gender intersects with other forms of inequality to affect personal and national development, and many studies have shown the negative impact of gender inequality on economic growth and other development indicators (Abu-Ghaida & Klasen, 2004; Aina & Olayode, 2012; Baliamoune-Lutz & McGillivray, 2007; Blackden & Wodon, 2006; Branisa, Klasen, & Ziegler, 2009; Cuberes & Teignier, 2011; Klasen, 2000, 2002; UNDP, 2020). Due to the pivotal link between gender equality and human development, gender equality and women's empowerment was one of the United Nations Millennium Development Goals (2000–2015). Despite the efforts made within the 15-year MDG era, gender disparities have remained in virtually all countries in the world. Thus, the United Nations continued the MDG unfinished agenda on gender equality by setting a more ambitious Sustainable Development Goal 5 to achieve gender equality and empower women and girls with six targets and three sub-targets. However, with the current global GII index value of 0.439, the chances of achieving SDG 5 are very grim (UNDP, 2019, 2020).

Gender analysis in research

The need to identify and address the different needs and interests of women and men and the causes of discrimination based on sex, gender, and other social conditions entails a systematic analytical approach. Gender analysis addresses this. Gender analysis enables researchers to ask questions that transcend mere male and female differences to uncover hidden processes that support and perpetuate gender-related disparities and to design and implement studies aimed at correcting or mitigating the effects of gender inequality (European Institute for Gender Equality (EIGE), 2019; March et al., 1999). Gender analysis enables the researcher to understand gender structures and process and how the research process itself can be permeated with power relations and biases. For instance, a researcher should consider how gender as a power relation influences the data collection and analysis process by considering questions such as 1) who participates as respondents, 2) when data is collected and where, 3) who is present, 4) who collects data, and 5) who analyses data (Morgan et al., 2016). Also, using a gender analysis framework, the components of gender can be incorporated into research as predictors of the expected outcome. Different gender analysis frameworks have been developed over time to effectively identify gendered processes and outcomes. Some of the frameworks are briefly described below.

1 The Harvard Analytical Framework is useful for collecting information from the community and households. It has four main components: activity profile, which describes who does what (reproductive and productive activities); access and control over resources, which describes who has what and benefits from each activity; influencing factors, referring to

the factors that influence gender roles; and project cycle analysis (European Institute for Gender Equality (EIGE), 2019; March et al., 1999).

2 The Moser Framework, also known as the triple role framework, identifies women's triple role at the micro level as productive, reproductive, and community activities. The Moser conceptual framework for gender analysis and planning emphasizes gender roles and gender needs. It describes and distinguishes two types of gender needs: 1) practical gender needs, which refers to needs that are related to women's daily lives but maintain existing gender relations, and 2) strategic gender needs, referring to needs that potentially transform existing gender subordination. This framework includes identification of gender role in production, reproduction, and community management; gender needs assessment; disaggregating control of resources and decision-making in the household; planning for balancing the triple role; distinguishing between different aims in policy interventions; and involving women and gender-aware organizations in planning.

3 Gender Analysis Matrix. This is a community-based technique to analyse gender differences at the household and community level and considers the impact on labour, time, resources, and social-cultural factors.

4 Capacities and Vulnerabilities Analysis (CVA) Framework. Used by external agencies in emergency relief interventions to meet immediate needs and to build on people's strengths to support long-term social and economic development.

5 Women's Empowerment Framework. This framework might be used to assess how a development intervention or programme might support greater women's empowerment. Focus on gender relations rather than only women's role.

6 Social Relation Approach. The approach uses institutional analysis to identify how institutions (community, market, state, and family) create and reproduce inequalities.

7 The People-Oriented Planning Framework. This framework is an adaptation of the Harvard Analytical Framework. The framework aims to ensure that there is efficient and equitable distribution of resources.

In general, gender analysis aims to identify gendered processes and outcomes in specific contexts by asking the following questions: 1) who has what (access to resources – education, information, skills, income, employment, services, benefits, time, space, social capital, etc.), 2) who does what (the division of labour and everyday practices – a division of labour within and beyond the household and everyday practices), 3) how values are defined (social norms, ideologies, beliefs, and perceptions), and 4) who decides (rules and decision-making – both formal and informal) (European Institute for Gender Equality (EIGE), 2019; March et al., 1999; Morgan et al., 2016).

Demographic research and gender

The prominence of demography, the scientific study of human population size, composition, distribution, and the processes of change, as a core behavioural discipline that is closely linked to human development goals, has continued to increase over time from the Malthusian treatise in 1798. Although demographic theories and discourse have influenced developmental milestone over the years, there is a paucity of gender perspectives in classical and contemporary demographic theories. For instance, Dodoo and Frost (2008) reviewed the classical and diffusion demographic theories of fertility decline and their application to Africa. They noted the exclusion of gender perspectives in the theories and submitted that it accounts for the limited applicability of the theories in explaining fertility behaviour in the highly gendered African context.

Despite the limited representation of gender in demographic theories, the central role of gender in explaining many developmental outcomes entails that demographic research in Africa should pay priority attention to gender for a more positive impact on development in Africa. Several reports and studies document the link between gender and different demographic outcomes. For instance, changes in attitude to gender roles and gender equality are associated with fertility (Arpino, Esping-Andersen, & Pessin, 2015; Myrskylä, Kohler, & Billari, 2011), and gender inequality is associated with high maternal mortality (Chirowa, Atwood, & Van der Putten, 2013) and higher rates of male mortality (Stanistreet, Bambra, & Scott-Samuel, 2005). This chapter presents a scoping review of the presentation of gender in demographic research in Africa. The objective is to document the presentation of gender in demographic research in Africa, identify gaps, and make recommendations for future demographic research in the region.

Methodology

Study design

This chapter is a scoping review of the literature. The review follows the methodological framework developed by (Arksey & O'Malley, 2005) which comprises five steps: 1) identifying of the question; 2) identifying relevant studies; 3) study selection; 4) charting the data – recording key themes emerging from the literature; and 5) collating, summarizing, and reporting the results.

Inclusion criteria

Quantitative and qualitative studies conducted in four major demographic subjects (fertility, mortality, migration, and sexual and reproductive health) in any African country from 1994 to 2020 and published in English were included. The time frame is informed by the need to assess how gender has been incorporated into demographic research in Africa from the 1994 ICPD to date. Nearly three decades of demographic research is considered sufficient to determine the trajectory of gender in African demographic research.

Search strategy

The search strategy was designed to access only published articles. The following databases were searched: Google Scholar, African Journal Online (AJOL), Directory of Open Access Journals (DAOJ), and PubMed. The reference lists of some articles were also searched. The search terms for gender included gender, gendered patterns, gender norms, gender lens, gender roles, gender relations, gender discrimination, gender equity, gender equality, gender gap, gender issues, gender indicator, gender perspective, gender bias, gender stereotyping, gender division of labour, gender empowerment, women's empowerment, women autonomy.

Demographic terms were migration, immigration, emigration, internal migration, in-migration, outmigration urban-rural migration, rural-urban migration, fertility, reproduction, birth, fertility intention, fertility preference, mortality, death, sexual and reproductive health, domestic violence, gender-based violence, contraceptive use. The gender terms were interacted with demographic terms in the search using the Boolean operators: "AND" "OR" and "NOT". Example: Gender AND fertility OR reproduction OR birth AND Africa.

Results

Articles in the four demographic thematic areas were retrieved by relevance from the databases. We reviewed the abstracts of the first 200 relevant articles for fertility, 200 for sexual and reproductive health, 200 for migration, and 260 for mortality. The full text of the articles that met the inclusion criteria was retrieved for the review. A total of 42 articles were included in the review, 16 for fertility, 16 for SRH, 4 for migration, and 6 for mortality. (See the flow chart in Figure 17.1.) The review is presented narratively by each demographic theme, and the summary of the gender themes in the reviewed articles is presented in Table 17.1. The measures of gender include participation in household decisions, attitude to wife beating, and approval of male dominance, among others.

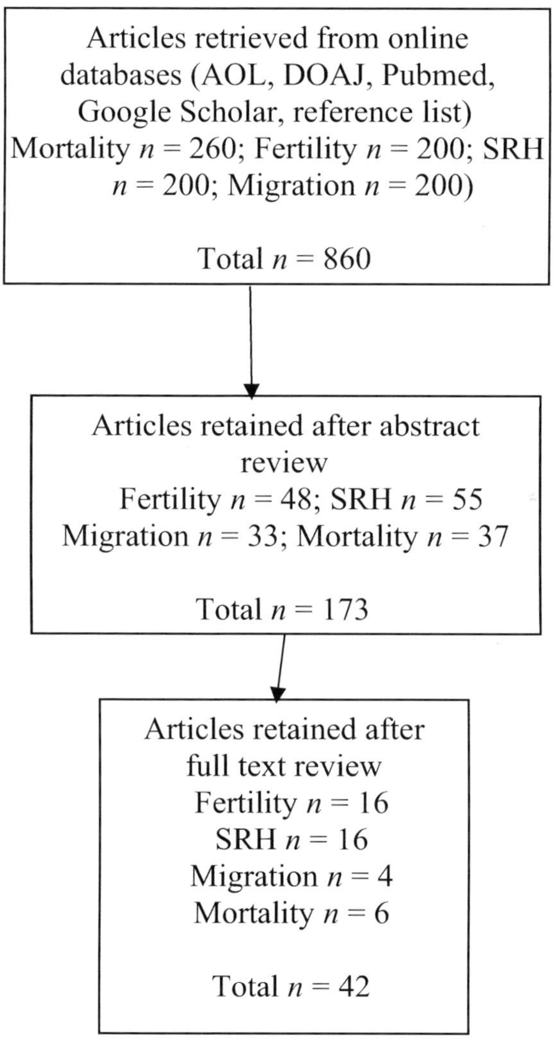

Figure 17.1 Flow chart of search results and included articles

Fertility

Studying fertility intentions, Odimegwu and Adedini (2014) measured gender relations as participation in household decisions about contraceptive use, what to do with money husband earns, how to spend own money, own health care, daily purchases, large household purchases, and visits to family or relatives. Ushie et al. (2010) also explained fertility preference from the perspective of gender indicated by participation in household decisions by males and females. This is the dominant application of gender in most of the articles. Other authors who have engaged the decision domain of gender to study fertility preferences and other aspects of fertility include Woldemicael (2009) in Eritrea, Larsen and Hollos (2003) in Tanzania, and Hindin (2000) in Zimbabwe. Others specifically focused on the gender concept of women's autonomy or empowerment and related it to family size and other aspects of fertility (Hindin, 2000; Hogan, Berhanu, & Hailemariam, 1999; Larsen & Hollos, 2003; Upadhyay & Karasek, 2012). The measures of women's empowerment in these studies included household decision-making, attitude toward wife beating, and refusing sex with one's husband. Snow, Winter, and Harlow (2013) studied young men's attitudes toward gender equality and their ideal family size in five countries in Eastern Africa.

A few other authors extended the measure of gender by including other domains. Wusu and Adedokun (2017) explained age at first marriage and children ever born to women age 35–49 by what they called gender revolution measured with engagement in paid employment and highest education. Dodoo and Tempenis (2002) explained reproductive decisions in rural areas in Kenya from the dimension of male dominance. In gender, lineage, and fertility-related outcomes in Ghana, Takyi and Dodoo (2005) analysed gender in terms of differentials in reproductive preference between husband and wife or both.

The use of a qualitative method was common in the interrogation of gender in fertility research in the continent. DeRose, Dodoo, and Patil (2002) demonstrate that gender norms indicated by attitude to men's dominance in fertility decisions influence fertility decision-making whether or not there are differences in reproductive goals of male and female in a union. Jensen (2015) explored the interaction of poverty, changing gender roles (sustained male privileges), and fertility in two rural communities in the Western province of Kenya. Izugbara, Ochako, and Izugbara (2011) engaged the lived experience of 80 women in Kenya to posit the centrality of gender in the definition of unwanted pregnancy by women. Adams, Salazar, and Lundgren (2013) investigated the influence of gender norms indicated by ideal woman definition, male control, and fertility as a symbol of masculinity and femininity on fertility desires of adolescents (male and female) in North-Central Uganda, and (Upton, 2001) explored the role of gender in negotiating infertility in Northern Botswana.

Conflating sex as gender was common in many analyses of gender and fertility in Africa. Ratcliffe, Hill, and Walraven (2000) documented the reproductive experiences of men and women in 40 villages in the Gambia. Their study revealed variation by sex in total fertility rate (TFR), marriage pattern, and fertility intentions. They attempted to explain the variations from a perspective of gender relations, but the analysis was essentially sex disaggregation. Gaisie's (2000) study on family structure, gender, and fertility in Botswana was also an analysis disaggregated by sex, as well as polygyny, gender relations, and reproduction in Ghana by Agadjanian and Ezeh (2000) and Bankole and Audam's (2011) analysis of fertility intentions as a predictor of contraceptive use.

Sexual and Reproductive Health

Women's empowerment or women's autonomy measured as participation in household decision-making is the dominant application of gender in sexual and reproductive health studies in Africa.. This measure was used to study contraceptive use (Alabi, Odimegwu, De-Wet, & Akinyemi, 2019; Bamiwuye, De Wet, & Adedini, 2013; Hindin, 2000), and use of maternal health services (Adjiwanou & LeGrand, 2014; Ntoimo & Odusina, 2019).

Other authors employed a broader measure of gender to explain aspects of reproductive health in the continent. Banda, Odimegwu, Ntoimo, and Muchiri (2016) measured gender inequality as women's attitude to domestic violence and participation in household decisions and linked it to maternal health indicators in Zambia. Corroon et al. (2014) defined gender inequality in terms of attitude to wife beating, prohibition from certain activities by husband/partner, participation in household decision-making, and access to own money. Using a qualitative approach, Izugbara, Ibisomi, Ezeh, and Mandara (2010) explained poor spousal contraceptive communication in Northern Nigeria from a gender perspective; Aransiola, Akinyemi, and Fatusi (2014), Bawah, Akweongo, Simmons, and Phillips (1999), and Harrington et al. (2016) explored the perspectives of men and women to understand the gendered power dynamics in negotiation for contraceptive use among couples. Male approval and male desire predicted the use of contraceptives in couples in Kenya (Kimuna & Adamchak, 2001). Yaya, Okonofua, Ntoimo, Udenige, and Bishwajit (2019) used a gender analysis framework as presented in Morgan et al. (2016) to explore barriers to the utilization of primary health care for maternal health in rural Nigeria. Elfstrom and Stephenson (2012) generated community gender norms and inequality by aggregating individual-level responses to questions in the Demographic and Health Survey on attitude to wife beating, participation in household decision-making, the proportion of women and men with at least a primary education, and the ratio of men to women who are employed. Gender norms and inequality as measured by them predicted modern contraceptive use in many African countries.

The role of men in contraceptive use was explored by some authors, albeit without in-depth explication of gender and a clear gender-related question (Mesfin, 2002; Tuloro, Deressa, Ali, & Davey, 2009), but gender relations as participation in decision-making was engaged in Adewuyi and Ogunjuyigbe (2003).

Many studies of domestic violence by demographers in the region did not adopt a gender approach. Even when the study is titled gender-based violence (GBV), gender is excluded from the research question and analysis. These studies are mainly explanations of experience of GBV, attitude to GBV, and the associated factors (e.g. Odimegwu, Bamiwuye, & Adedini, 2015; Okemgbo, Omideyi, & Odimegwu, 2002; Oluremi, 2015; Ononokpono & Azfredrick, 2014; Oyediran & Isiugo-Abanihe, 2005). However, McCloskey, Williams, and Larsen (2005) explained gender-based violence from a gender perspective. Studying intimate partner violence in Tanzania, they extended the measure of gender inequality to include educational attainment, type of union, participation in the decision to marry, partner's contribution to the household, children's health care, children's school fees, and her healthcare.

Migration and spatial distribution

Out of the 200 articles accessed and reviewed, only 4 engaged gender either as a key explanatory or moderating variable. Many of the studies were sex-disaggregated analyses of migration (e.g. Amoako & Apusigah, 2013; Camlin et al., 2010; Ranga, 2015; Toma & Vause, 2014). Raimundo (2008) examined how masculinity has been affected by the trend towards feminization of migration and to what extent the new trend of migration has affected the rural and urban household structure in Maputo, Mozambique. Analysing migration from a gendered perspective, other authors show that husband's labour migration enhanced wife's economic autonomy in rural Mozambique (Yabiku, Agadjanian, & Sevoyan, 2010) and Tanzania (Archambault, 2010).

Francis (2002) studied the implication of labour migration and the role of gender relations for rural livelihoods in Kenya, Lesotho, and South Africa. Contrary to studies in fertility, sexual and reproductive health (SRH) and mortality where gender domains were usually explanatory variables; in some of the migration studies, improved gender relations was an outcome.

Mortality

In an analysis of health systems in Africa using the example of Tanzania, Tibandebage and Mackintosh (2010) demonstrate how the gendered nature of health systems in Tanzania acts as a barrier to reducing avoidable maternal deaths. A macro-level analysis that relates gender inequality to high maternal mortality was conducted by Chirowa et al. (2013) in seven countries in Eastern and Southern Africa (Angola, Botswana, Malawi, Mozambique, South Africa, Zambia, and Zimbabwe). The authors constructed a Gender Inequality Index with reproductive health, women's empowerment, and labour force participation between women and men and related it to health expenditure and maternal mortality.

Neumayer and Plümper (2007) noted that natural disasters directly or indirectly lower women's life expectancy and kill more women than men where gender norms promote low socioeconomic status for women. Ratele (2008) relates the lower number of males compared to females as recorded in 1996 and 2001 censuses in South Africa to gender practices of masculinity that encourage risky behaviour. In a study of neonatal mortality in East and West Africa, Grady et al. (2017) included empowerment of women as an explanatory variable which was measured as the percentage of mothers who did not want or plan to have their last child, the percentage of mothers whose husbands decided on their contraceptive practices, and the percentage of mothers whose husbands justified wife-beating. Flatø and Kotsadam (2014) found a larger infant mortality effect of drought for girls compared to boys in sub-Saharan Africa, and they strongly associated the pattern to gender norms that encourage son preference and limited family size.

Other studies that included gender were simply disaggregation by sex. For instance, in the study of adult mortality in Zambia by Chisumpa, Odimegwu, and De Wet (2017), place of death differed by sex, a pattern that may have been explained by gender. Other examples are the study of factors associated with mortality among hospitalized infants in Asmara, Eritrea, by Shah, Zemichael, and Meng (2012); mortality among HIV-infected people in South Africa (Otwombe, Petzold, Modisenyane, Martinson, & Chirwa, 2014; Sartorius & Sartorius, 2013); analysis of poverty and mortality among persons aged 15–59 years in Zambia and Kenya (Chapoto, Kirimi, & Kadiyala, 2012); mortality experience of persons aged 50 years and over in South Africa (Gómez-Olivé et al., 2014); and risk factors for child mortality in rural South Africa (Sartorius, Kahn, Collinson, Vounatsou, & Tollman, 2011).

Discussion

This chapter examined gender in African demographic research from 1994 to 2020. Published literature on fertility, mortality, migration, and sexual and reproductive health was reviewed. The relationship between demographic processes and gender as a key determinant, moderator, or outcome and the impact on development is established in the literature. Migration as a gendered phenomenon and its significance to improving individual and national development is well documented in various reports and studies (Fleury, 2016; Jolly, Reeves, & Piper, 2005; Oishi, 2002; Piper, 2005; Sinke, 2006). Changes in attitude to gender roles and gender equality are associated with fertility (Arpino et al., 2015; Myrskylä et al., 2011). Ahonsi (1995) strongly posited that lower fertility and higher status for women is the most realistic road to sustainable

Table 17.1 Key Gender Themes in the Reviewed Articles

Fertility	*SRH*	*Migration*	*Mortality*
Participation in household decision-making	Women's empowerment and autonomy measured as participation in household decision-making	Wife's economic autonomy	Empowerment as husband decides on contraceptive use, husband justifies wife beating, last birth unwanted
Women's autonomy and empowerment – participation in household decision-making, attitude to wife beating, and refusing sex	Attitude to wife beating	Renegotiation of rights, power, and responsibilities by wives and husbands	Gender norms that encourage son preference, promote low social status for women
Engagement in paid employment and highest education	Attitude to domestic violence	Participation in migration decisions	Gendered health systems – health system structures that disadvantage women
Attitude supporting male dominance in decision-making	Prohibition from certain activities by husband/partner, participation in household decision-making, access to own money	Women's autonomy constructed with freedom – mobility, spending money, getting a job, or engaging in business. Women's employment outside the home.	Gender Inequality Index constructed with reproductive health, women's empowerment, and labour force participation between women and men
		Lower fertility.	
		Residential independence from extended family members	
Differential in reproductive preference between husband and wife	Male approval, male desires		Gender norms that promote masculinity as risky behaviour
Male privileges	The proportion of women and men with at least a primary education and the ratio of men to women who are employed		
Socially sanctioned notions of motherhood and 'proper' procreation			
Gender norms – ideal woman obeys husband, male control of women and resources, fertility as a core element of masculinity and femininity, and children as status and recognition to a young couple			

development in Africa. Gender inequality is associated with high maternal mortality (Chirowa et al., 2013) and higher rates of male mortality (Stanistreet et al., 2005). Sexual and reproductive health indicators such as maternal mortality, abortion, contraceptive use, and gender-based violence, among others, are driven by social determinants that are shaped by gender (MacPherson, Richards, Namakhoma, & Theobald, 2014). Despite the proven strong link, most of the reviewed studies were narrow analysis of only the decision domain of gender. There was an obvious deficiency in the use of gender analysis framework in the analysis of demographic processes of fertility, migration, mortality, and sexual and reproductive health in the included articles.

Contributory to the narrow analysis of gender in the reviewed studies is the heavy dependence on data from the Demographic and Health Survey (DHS) and other secondary sources. The DHS, for instance, captures a limited dimension of gender (participation in household decision-making) and attitude to wife beating. Even when this is used, many authors used this domain as a mere explanatory variable without engaging the gender issues. Also, the heavy reliance on DHS data limits analytical methodology. Incorporating gender into research entails considering who is empowered or disempowered by the results and the extent to which the research progressively transforms gender power relations in both the public and private spheres or at least does not make it worse (European Institute for Gender Equality (EIGE), 2019; Morgan et al., 2016). One way to focus on transformation is through the use of participatory action research (PAR). This research approach is not used in any of the reviewed articles.

In addition to the limited analysis of gender, most of the studies were micro-level analysis focused on women. Going further from the studies on the male role in different aspects of fertility in Africa (DeRose & Ezeh, 2005; Isiugo-Abanihe, 2003), only a few authors paid attention to gender and fertility from men's perspective. A robust and productive engagement of gender in demographic research in the region would require engaging both male and female perspectives.

Gender in most cases was interchangeably used with sex. Sex disaggregation is not gender analysis. It shows sex differentials in a demographic outcome but provides no insight into socially constructed roles and responsibilities that shape the observed differences by sex, thus making no direct input into gender transformation.

Except for one article that used a gender analysis (Yaya et al., 2019), others engaged gender in a limited measure of participation in decision-making, while a few extended the measure to include attitude to wife beating, educational attainment, and participation in the labour force. Participation in decision-making is only one aspect of gender analysis. The results of studies that engage only one aspect of gender analysis will find limited application in policy and programmes that can challenge and alter gender inequality (Ahonsi, 1995; Aina & Olayode, 2012; Baliamoune-Lutz & McGillivray, 2007). These studies were also disproportionally focused on women, obviously because of the patriarchal culture in many African societies that is reinforced by conservative Islam and Christianity, which emphasize male dominance in decision-making (Izugbara, 2004; Stanistreet et al., 2005; Ntoimo & Isiugo-Abanihe, 2014).

Incorporating gender into African demographic research would not provide answers to all the developmental problems of the regions. For instance, although gender equality is a positive predictor of reproductive and maternal health, findings from Lan and Tavrow (2017) suggest that improving gender equality alone will not achieve a desirable improvement in maternal health in Africa if corruption is not addressed. However, the established link between gender equality and equity and human development indicators suggests that a more holistic and robust analysis of gender in demographic research in Africa will advance the achievement of Sustainable Development Goals in the continent.

Limitations of the study

This study is a scoping review; thus, it provides an overview of the existing literature and lacks the methodological rigour of a systematic review. All the possible databases and grey literature were not searched. Also, limiting the review to publications in English and after 1994 may have excluded some relevant studies of gender in demographic research in Africa. Therefore, this study does not represent all that exists in African demographic research concerning gender. However, to the best of our knowledge, after Dodoo and Frost's (2008) review of gender in the application of classical and diffusion demographic theories of fertility in Africa, this is the first time a review of gender in African demographic research has been conducted. The review of gender equity in sexual and reproductive health by MacPherson et al. (2014) was limited to Eastern and Southern Africa and one subject area, like Dodoo and Frost's study. Therefore, the results of this review, though limited, provide useful insight into gender in demographic research in Africa, as well as highlighting the gaps for future demographic discourse and projects on gender in the continent.

Conclusion

Although gender and transition in gender norms are key determinants of many demographic outcomes, most of the reviewed demographic studies were either gender blind or limited in their analysis of gender. Sex-disaggregated data are important, but the incorporation of gender in research using a well-defined framework equips researchers to ask relevant questions that transcend mere male and female differences to why and how gender power relations create inequalities between males and females in ways that undermine sustainable development. We recommend context-specific interrogation of gender beyond women's autonomy or empowerment indicated by participation in household decision-making. Also, we recommend the use of multi-methods, and PAR and gender analysis frameworks in future studies of gender and demographic processes in Africa.

References

Abu-Ghaida, D., & Klasen, S. (2004). The costs of missing the Millennium Development Goal on gender equity. *World Development*, *32*(7), 1075–1107.

Adams, M. K., Salazar, E., & Lundgren, R. (2013). Tell them you are planning for the future: Gender norms and family planning among adolescents in northern Uganda. *International Journal of Gynecology & Obstetrics*, *123*, e7–e10.

Adewuyi, A., & Ogunjuyigbe, P. (2003). The role of men in family planning: An examination of men's knowledge and attitude to contraceptive use among the Yorubas. *African Population Studies*, *18*(1), 35–49.

Adjiwanou, V., & LeGrand, T. (2014). Gender inequality and the use of maternal healthcare services in rural sub-Saharan Africa. *Health & Place*, *29*, 67–78.

Agadjanian, V., & Ezeh, A. C. (2000). Polygyny, gender relations, and reproduction in Ghana. *Journal of Comparative Family Studies*, *31*(4), 427–441.

Ahonsi, B. A. (1995). Gender relations, demographic change and the prospects for sustainable development in Africa. *Africa Development/Afrique et Développement*, 85–114.

Aina, O. I., & Olayode, K. (2012). Gender equality, governance and women empowerment agenda in a democratizing society: Issues, prospects, and challenges. *The Nigerian Journal of Sociology and Anthropology*, *9*, 22.

Alabi, O., Odimegwu, C. O., De-Wet, N., & Akinyemi, J. O. (2019). Does female autonomy affect contraceptive use among women in northern Nigeria? *African Journal of Reproductive Health*, *23*(2), 92–100.

Amoako, E. E., & Apusigah, A. A. (2013). Gender, migration and remittances in Ghana: An overview. *Ghana Journal of Development Studies, 10*(1–2), 15–43.
Aransiola, J. O., Akinyemi, A. I., & Fatusi, A. O. (2014). Women's perceptions and reflections of male partners and couple dynamics in family planning adoption in selected urban slums in Nigeria: A qualitative exploration. *BMC Public Health, 14*(1), 869.
Archambault, C. S. (2010). Women left behind? Migration, spousal separation, and the autonomy of rural women in Ugweno, Tanzania. *Signs: Journal of Women in Culture and Society, 35*(4), 919–942.
Arksey, H., & O'Malley, L. (2005). Scoping studies: Towards a methodological framework. *International Journal of Social Research Methodology, 8*(1), 19–32.
Arpino, B., Esping-Andersen, G., & Pessin, L. (2015). How do changes in gender role attitudes towards female employment influence fertility? A macro-level analysis. *European Sociological Review, 31*(3), 370–382.
Baliamoune-Lutz, M., & McGillivray, M. (2007). Gender inequality and growth in sub-Saharan Africa and Arab countries. *International Centre for Economic Research Working Papers, 25*, 1–27.
Bamiwuye, S. O., De Wet, N., & Adedini, S. A. (2013). Linkages between autonomy, poverty and contraceptive use in two sub-Saharan African countries. *African Population Studies, 27*(2), 164–173.
Banda, P. C., Odimegwu, C. O., Ntoimo, L. F. C., & Muchiri, E. (2016). Women at risk: Gender inequality and maternal health. *Women & Health, 57*(4), 405–429. https://doi.org/10.1080/03630242.2016.1170092
Bankole, A., & Audam, S. (2011). Fertility preferences and contraceptive use among couples in sub-Saharan Africa. *African Population Studies, 25*(2), 556–586.
Bawah, A. A., Akweongo, P., Simmons, R., & Phillips, J. F. (1999). Women's fears and men's anxieties: The impact of family planning on gender relations in northern Ghana. *Studies in Family Planning, 30*(1), 54–66.
Blackden, M., & Wodon, Q. (2006). *Gender, time use, and poverty: Introduction*. World Bank Working Paper No. 11080. Washington, DC: World Bank.
Branisa, B., Klasen, S., & Ziegler, M. (2009). *Why we should all care about social institutions related to gender inequality*. Poverty, Equity and Growth-Discussion Papers, Courant Research Centre.
Camlin, C. S., Hosegood, V., Newell, M.-L., McGrath, N., Bärnighausen, T., & Snow, R. C. (2010). Gender, migration and HIV in rural KwaZulu-Natal, South Africa. *PLoS One, 5*(7), e11539.
Chapoto, A., Kirimi, L., & Kadiyala, S. (2012). Poverty and prime-age mortality in Eastern and Southern Africa: Evidence from Zambia and Kenya. *World Development, 40*(9), 1839–1853.
Chirowa, F., Atwood, S., & Van der Putten, M. (2013). Gender inequality, health expenditure and maternal mortality in sub-Saharan Africa: A secondary data analysis. *African Journal of Primary Health Care & Family Medicine, 5*(1).
Chisumpa, V. H., Odimegwu, C. O., & De Wet, N. (2017). Adult mortality in sub-Saharan Africa, Zambia: Where do adults die? *SSM-Population Health, 3*, 227–235.
Corroon, M., Speizer, I. S., Fotso, J.-C., Akiode, A., Saad, A., Calhoun, L., & Irani, L. (2014). The role of gender empowerment on reproductive health outcomes in urban Nigeria. *Maternal and Child Health Journal, 18*(1), 307–315.
Cuberes, D., & Teignier, M. (2011). *Gender inequality and economic growth*. Background paper for the World Development Report 2012 – Gender equality and development.
DeRose, L. F., Dodoo, F. N.-A., & Patil, V. (2002). Fertility desires and perceptions of power in reproductive conflict in Ghana. *Gender & Society, 16*(1), 53–73.
DeRose, L. F., & Ezeh, A. C. (2005). Men's influence on the onset and progress of fertility decline in Ghana, 1988–98. *Population Studies, 59*(2), 197–210.
Dodoo, F. N.-A., & Frost, A. E. (2008). Gender in African population research: The fertility/reproductive health example. *Annual Review of Sociology, 34*, 431–452.
Dodoo, F. N.-A., & Tempenis, M. (2002). Gender, power, and reproduction: Rural-urban differences in the relationship between fertility goals and contraceptive use in Kenya. *Rural Sociology, 67*(1), 46–70.
Elfstrom, K. M., & Stephenson, R. (2012). The role of place in shaping contraceptive use among women in Africa. *PLoS One, 7*(7), e40670.
European Institute for Gender Equality (EIGE). (2019). *Gender analysis*. Publications Office of the European Union. Luxembourg: European Union.
Flatø, M., & Kotsadam, A. (2014). *Droughts and gender bias in infant mortality in sub-Saharan Africa* (Memorandum No. 02/2014). University of Oslo, Department of Economics.

Fleury, A. (2016). *Understanding women and migration: A literature review*. Washington, DC: Global Knowledge Partnership on Migration and Development (KNOMAD).
Francis, E. (2002). Gender, migration and multiple livelihoods: Cases from Eastern and Southern Africa. *Journal of Development Studies, 38*(5), 167–190.
Gaisie, S. K. (2000). Family structure, gender and fertility in Botswana. *Pula: Botswana Journal of African Studies, 14*(2), 130–147.
Gómez-Olivé, F. X., Thorogood, M., Bocquier, P., Mee, P., Kahn, K., Berkman, L., & Tollman, S. (2014). Social conditions and disability related to the mortality of older people in rural South Africa. *International Journal of Epidemiology, 43*(5), 1531–1541.
Grady, S. C., Frake, A. N., Zhang, Q., Bene, M., Jordan, D. R., Vertalka, J., . . . Pierre, L.-M. (2017). Neonatal mortality in East Africa and West Africa: A geographic analysis of district-level demographic and health survey data. *Geospatial Health, 12*(1), 137–150.
Harrington, E. K., Dworkin, S., Withers, M., Onono, M., Kwena, Z., & Newmann, S. J. (2016). Gendered power dynamics and women's negotiation of family planning in a high HIV prevalence setting: A qualitative study of couples in western Kenya. *Culture, Health & Sexuality, 18*(4), 453–469.
Hindin, M. J. (2000). Women's autonomy, women's status and fertility-related behavior in Zimbabwe. *Population Research and Policy Review, 19*(3), 255–282.
Hogan, D. P., Berhanu, B., & Hailemariam, A. (1999). Household organization, women's autonomy, and contraceptive behavior in southern Ethiopia. *Studies in Family Planning, 30*(4), 302–314.
Isiugo-Abanihe, U. C. (2003). *Male role and responsibility in fertility and reproductive health in Nigeria*. Ibadan, Nigeria: The Centre for Population Activities and Education for Development (CEPAED).
Izugbara, C., Ibisomi, L., Ezeh, A. C., & Mandara, M. (2010). Gendered interests and poor spousal contraceptive communication in Islamic northern Nigeria. *BMJ Sexual & Reproductive Health, 36*(4), 219–224.
Izugbara, C. O. (2004). Patriarchal ideology and discourses of sexuality in Nigeria. *Understanding Human Sexuality Seminar Series, Department of Sociology and Anthropology, University of Uyo, Nigeria, 2*(21), 1–35.
Izugbara, C. O., Ochako, R., & Izugbara, C. (2011). Gender scripts and unwanted pregnancy among urban Kenyan women. *Culture, Health & Sexuality, 13*(9), 1031–1045.
Jensen, A.-M. (2015). Poverty, gender and fertility in rural Kenya. *African Population Studies, 42*(2), 311–332.
Jolly, S., Reeves, H., & Piper, N. (2005). *Gender and migration: Overview report*. London: Institute of Development Studies.
Kabeer, N. (2005). Gender equality and women's empowerment: A critical analysis of the third millennium development goal 1. *Gender & Development, 13*(1), 13–24.
Kimuna, S. R., & Adamchak, D. J. (2001). Gender relations: Husband-wife fertility and family planning decisions in Kenya. *Journal of Biosocial Science, 33*(1), 13.
Klasen, S. (2000). *Does gender inequality reduce growth and development? Evidence from cross-country regressions*. Sonderforschungsbereich 386: Analyse Diskreter Strukturen Discussion Paper No. 212.
Klasen, S. (2002). Low schooling for girls, slower growth for all? Cross-country evidence on the effect of gender inequality in education on economic development. *The World Bank Economic Review, 16*(3), 345–373.
Lan, C.-W., & Tavrow, P. (2017). Composite measures of women's empowerment and their association with maternal mortality in low-income countries. *BMC Pregnancy and Childbirth, 17*(2), 337.
Larsen, U., & Hollos, M. (2003). Women's empowerment and fertility decline among the Pare of Kilimanjaro region, Northern Tanzania. *Social Science & Medicine, 57*(6), 1099–1115.
MacPherson, E. E., Richards, E., Namakhoma, I., & Theobald, S. (2014). Gender equity and sexual and reproductive health in Eastern and Southern Africa: A critical overview of the literature. *Global Health Action*, 7(1), 23717.
March, C., Smyth, I. A., & Mukhopadhyay, M. (1999). *A guide to gender-analysis frameworks*. Great Britain: Oxfam.
McCloskey, L. A., Williams, C., & Larsen, U. (2005). Gender inequality and intimate partner violence among women in Moshi, Tanzania. *International Family Planning Perspectives*, 124–130.
Mesfin, G. (2002). The role of men in fertility and family planning program in Tigray Region. *Ethiopian Journal of Health Development, 16*(3), 247–255.
Morgan, R., George, A., Ssali, S., Hawkins, K., Molyneux, S., & Theobald, S. (2016). How to do (or not to do) . . . gender analysis in health systems research. *Health Policy and Planning, 31*, 1069–1078. https://doi.org/10.1093/heapol/czw037

Myrskylä, M., Kohler, H.-P., & Billari, F. C. (2011). *High development and fertility: Fertility at older reproductive ages and gender equality explain the positive link*. Rostock, Germany: Max Planck Institute for Demographic Research.

Neumayer, E., & Plümper, T. (2007). The gendered nature of natural disasters: The impact of catastrophic events on the gender gap in life expectancy, 1981–2002. *Annals of the Association of American Geographers*, *97*(3), 551–566.

Ntoimo, L. F. C., & Isiugo-Abanihe, U. (2014). Patriarchy and singlehood among women in Lagos, Nigeria. *Journal of Family Issues*, *35*(14), 1980–2008. https://doi.org/10.1177%2F0192513X13511249

Ntoimo, L. F. C., & Odusina, E. K. (2019). Family structure, women autonomy and utilization of maternal healthcare services in Nigeria. In Ezebunwa Nwokocha & Olufunke Fayehun (Eds.), *Concise Demography of Nigeria: A Festchrift for Prof Uche Isiugo-Abanihe* (pp. 124–143). BumbleBee Publishing.

Odimegwu, C., & Adedini, S. A. (2014). Gender equity and fertility intention in selected sub-Saharan African countries. *Gender & Behaviour*, *12*(2), 5858–5881.

Odimegwu, C., Bamiwuye, O. S., & Adedini, S. A. (2015). Gender-based violence as a new proximate determinant of fertility in sub-Saharan Africa. *Southern African Journal of Demography*, *16*(1).

Oishi, N. (2002). *Gender and migration: An integrative approach*. Working Paper No. 49. San Diego, CA: Center for Comparative Immigration Studies, University of California.

Okemgbo, C. N., Omideyi, A. K., & Odimegwu, C. O. (2002). Prevalence, patterns and correlates of domestic violence in selected Igbo communities of Imo State, Nigeria. *African Journal of Reproductive Health*, 101–114.

Oluremi, F. D. (2015). Domestic "violence against women in Nigeria." *European Journal of Psychological Research*, *2*(1), 24–33.

Omoluabi, E., Aina, O. I., & Attanasso, M. O. (2014). Gender in Nigeria's development discourse: Relevance of gender statistics. *African Population Studies*, *27*(2), 372–385.

Ononokpono, D. N., & Azfredrick, E. C. (2014). Intimate partner violence and the utilization of maternal health care services in Nigeria. *Health Care for Women International*, *35*(7–9), 973–989.

Otwombe, K. N., Petzold, M., Modisenyane, T., Martinson, N. A., & Chirwa, T. (2014). Factors associated with mortality in HIV-infected people in rural and urban South Africa. *Global Health Action*, 7(1), 25488.

Oyediran, K., & Isiugo-Abanihe, U. (2005). Perceptions of Nigerian women on domestic violence: Evidence from 2003 Nigeria Demographic and Health Survey. *African Journal of Reproductive Health*, *9*(2), 38–53.

Permanyer, I. (2010). The measurement of multidimensional gender inequality: Continuing the debate. *Social Indicators Research*, *95*(2), 181–198.

Piper, N. (2005). *Gender and migration*. Policy Analysis and Research Programme of the Global Commission on International Migration.

Raimundo, I. (2008). The interaction of gender and migration household relations in rural and urban Mozambique. *Masculinities in Contemporary Africa*, 7.

Ranga, D. (2015). Gender differences in the migration of Zimbabwean teachers to South Africa. *Eastern Africa Social Science Research Review*, *31*(1), 43–62.

Ratcliffe, A. A., Hill, A. G., & Walraven, G. (2000). Separate lives, different interests: Male and female reproduction in the Gambia. *Bulletin of the World Health Organization*, *78*(5), 570–579.

Ratele, K. (2008). Masculinity and male mortality in South Africa. *African Safety Promotion*, *6*(2), 19–41.

Sartorius, B., Kahn, K., Collinson, M. A., Vounatsou, P., & Tollman, S. M. (2011). Survived infancy but still vulnerable: Spatial-temporal trends and risk factors for child mortality in rural South Africa (Agincourt), 1992–2007. *Geospatial Health*, *5*(2), 285.

Sartorius, B., & Sartorius, K. (2013). Identifying and targeting mortality disparities: A framework for sub-Saharan Africa using adult mortality data from South Africa. *PLoS One*, *8*(8), e71437.

Shah, S., Zemichael, O., & Meng, H. D. (2012). Factors associated with mortality and length of stay in hospitalised neonates in Eritrea, Africa: A cross-sectional study. *BMJ Open*, *2*(5).

Sinke, S. M. (2006). Gender and migration: Historical perspectives. *International Migration Review*, *40*(1), 82–103.

Snow, R. C., Winter, R. A., & Harlow, S. D. (2013). Gender attitudes and fertility aspirations among young men in five high fertility East African countries. *Studies in Family Planning*, *44*(1), 1–24.

Stanistreet, D., Bambra, C., & Scott-Samuel, A. (2005). Is patriarchy the source of men's higher mortality? *Journal of Epidemiology & Community Health*, *59*(10), 873–876.

Takyi, B. K., & Nii-Amoo Dodoo, F. (2005). Gender, lineage, and fertility-related outcomes in Ghana. *Journal of Marriage and Family*, *67*(1), 251–257.

Tibandebage, P., & Mackintosh, M. (2010). Maternal mortality in Africa: A gendered lens on health system failure. *Socialist Register, 46.*

Toma, S., & Vause, S. (2014). Gender differences in the role of migrant networks: Comparing Congolese and Senegalese migration flows. *International Migration Review*, *48*(4), 972–997.

Tuloro, T., Deressa, W., Ali, A., & Davey, G. (2009). The role of men in contraceptive use and fertility preference in Hossana Town, Southern Ethiopia. *Ethiopian Journal of Health Development*, *20*(3).

UNDP. (2016). *Africa Human Development Report 2016 accelerating gender equality and women's empowerment in Africa*. New York: United Nations Development Programme Regional Bureau for Africa.

UNDP. (2018). *Human Development Indices and Indicators 2018 statistical update*. New York: United Nations Development Programme.

UNDP. (2019). *Human Development Report 2019 beyond income, beyond averages, beyond today: Inequalities in human development in the 21st century*. New York: United Nations Development Programme.

UNDP. (2020). *2020 Human development perspectives tackling social norms: A game changer for gender inequalities*. New York: United Nations Development Programme.

UN Women. (2014). *Beijing Declaration and platform for action*. New York: UN Women.

Upadhyay, U. D., & Karasek, D. (2012). Women's empowerment and ideal family size: An examination of DHS empowerment measures in Sub-Saharan Africa. *International Perspectives on Sexual and Reproductive Health*, 78–89.

Upton, R. L. (2001). "Infertility makes you invisible": Gender, health and the negotiation of fertility in Northern Botswana. *Journal of Southern African Studies*, *27*(2), 349–362.

Ushie, M., Abia, R., Osonwa, K., Ugal, D., Ushie, B., Mgbekem, M., . . . Eneji, J. (2010). Reproductive decisions between gender and fertility preferences among urban dwellers: The Case of Bette, Nigeria. *Annals of Humanities and Development Studies*, *1*(1), 329–334.

Woldemicael, G. (2009). Women's autonomy and reproductive preferences in Eritrea. *Journal of Biosocial Science*, *41*(2), 161–181.

World Health Organization. (2019). *Trends in maternal mortality 2000 to 2017: Estimates by WHO, UNICEF, UNFPA, World Bank Group and the United Nations Population Division*. Geneva, Switzerland: World Health Organization.

World Health Organization. (2020). *Gender*. Retrieved from www.who.int/health-topics/gender

Wusu, O., & Adedokun, O. A. (2017). Gender revolution prospects in Nigeria: Implications for marriage timing and fertility. *African Sociological Review/Revue Africaine de Sociologie*, *21*(2), 58–80.

Yabiku, S. T., Agadjanian, V., & Sevoyan, A. (2010). Husbands' labour migration and wives' autonomy, Mozambique 2000–2006. *Population Studies*, *64*(3), 293–306.

Yaya, S., Okonofua, F., Ntoimo, L., Udenige, O., & Bishwajit, G. (2019). Gender inequity as a barrier to women's access to skilled pregnancy care in rural Nigeria: A qualitative study. *International Health*, *11*(6), 551–560. https://doi.org/10.1093/inthealth/ihz019

18

GENDER NORMS AND SEXUAL BEHAVIOR AMONG VERY YOUNG ADOLESCENTS IN SUB-SAHARAN AFRICA

A scoping review

Beatrice W. Maina, Chimaraoke Izugbara, Yandisa Sikweyiya, Ivy Nandongwa and Caroline W. Kabiru

Introduction

Gender norms – socially constructed roles, behaviors and attributes considered appropriate for men and women (Brickell, 2006) – are major drivers of health and wellbeing (Fiaveh, Izugbara, Okyerefo, Reysoo, & Fayorsey, 2015; Kemigisha et al., 2018). Power differentials inherent in inequitable gender norms often position women as subordinate to men (Smith, Parrott, Swartout, & Tharp, 2015), shaping relational health behaviors and outcomes with potentially strong implications for sexual and reproductive behaviors (Ampofo, 2001; Fiaveh et al., 2015). For instance, existing evidence associates certain forms of masculinities with women's restricted autonomy (Smith et al., 2015), male sexual risk-taking (C. O. Izugbara & Undie, 2008) and women's passivity in sexual matters (MacPherson, Richards, Namakhoma, & Theobald, 2014), predisposing men and women to a wide range of sexual and reproductive health (SRH) risks.

Adolescence lays a foundation for lifelong health trajectories (Patton et al., 2016). Galambos, Berenbaum, and McHale (2009) argue that gender inequalities between boys and girls in sexual relationships begin to manifest at an early stage of development, as young people adopt their society's belief system, particularly with respect to gender and sexuality. While several factors contribute to SRH behaviors and outcomes among adolescents in sub-Saharan Africa (SSA) (Hervish & Clifton, 2012), gender and, more specifically, gendered beliefs and norms have far-reaching implications. Pubertal maturation in early adolescence heightens expectations related to gender (Galambos et al., 2009). Increased social interactions during this period are important in adopting a belief system critical for informing behavior (Brickell, 2006; Moreau et al., 2019), shaping adolescents' vulnerability to poor SRH outcomes (Fiaveh et al., 2015), with implications that extend beyond adolescence.

Globally, there is growing awareness that promoting equitable gender norms in early adolescence is key to securing young people's safe transition to adulthood (A. Kågesten et al., 2016; Lane, Brundage, & Kreinin, 2017). This growing awareness is exemplified in Sustainable Development Goal (SDG) 5, which recognizes gender equality as a fundamental human right and a

DOI: 10.4324/9780429287213-22

necessary foundation for a peaceful, prosperous and sustainable world (United Nations, 2015). With romantic and sexual relationships taking shape and gender roles playing out in early adolescence, promoting gender equality during this critical period of human development requires robust understanding of the intersections of gender norms and adolescent SRH behaviors and well-being.

In SSA, adolescents make up the greatest proportion of the population, with about 12 percent of the region's population aged 10–14 years (United Nations Population Division, 2019). While studies show that most very young adolescents in the region have not initiated sex, they engage in intimate relationships and non-coital sexual activities, including kissing, hugging and fondling and other behaviors that are only the beginning of patterns of gendered practices with potentially far-reaching implications for individuals, communities and society at large (Kabiru, Beguy, Undie, Zulu, & Ezeh, 2010; A. E. Kagesten, Kabiru, & Maina, 2018).

This chapter provides insights on the state of knowledge on the implications of gender norms for very young adolescents' SRH behaviors in SSA, highlights lessons emerging from the literature for policy and programmatic actions and identifies gaps for further research. The review was guided by the following research questions:

1. What are the key gender norms that circumscribe the socialization of very young adolescents (ages 10–14 years) in SSA region?
2. How do gender norms influence sexual and reproductive behaviors and outcomes of very young adolescents in SSA?
3. What are the barriers to addressing gender norms that influence SRH outcomes among very young adolescents in SSA?
4. What interventions have been implemented to improve gender-equitable norms and SRH outcomes among very young adolescents in SSA?

Methods

We conducted a scoping review of available literature to map and synthesize existing evidence on gender norms and SRH among very young adolescents aged 10–14 years in SSA.

Search strategy

We searched the following databases: PubMed, JSTOR, EbscoHost (PsychINFO, CINAHL, Psychology and Behavioral Sciences Collection, Global Health), Scopus, ScienceDirect, HINARI and the Web of Science. Geographically, search results were limited to countries in SSA and to peer-reviewed papers published between January 2000 and May 2020. Papers were included if they addressed 1) gender norms that circumscribe the socialization of very young adolescents and their influence on sexual and reproductive behaviors and outcomes of very young adolescents in SSA, 2) barriers to addressing gender norms that influence SRH outcomes among very young adolescents and 3) interventions to improve gender-equitable norms among very young adolescents in SSA.

Searches were conducted between April 30, 2020, and May 18, 2020, and while the exact search terms varied by database (available upon request), the four primary search components included were 1) very young/early adolescents/adolescents, 2) gender norms, 3) SRH/SRH behaviors and 4) sub-Saharan Africa. Studies were excluded if they focused exclusively on children younger than 10 years or adolescents older than 14 years. Also excluded were studies that included early adolescents but where data were not disaggregated by age.

Article selection

After removing duplicate search results, two authors, BM and IN, independently screened all titles and abstracts of potential articles identified in the search to determine which studies met the inclusion criteria. In the second stage, full texts of all studies that met the inclusion criteria in the title and abstract screening stage were reviewed independently by two primary reviewers to ascertain eligibility. In both screening stages, any discrepancies were jointly reviewed by all authors.

Data extraction and quality assessment

Data from included articles were extracted using a standardized form. Two reviewers independently assessed the internal validity of each included study using the appropriate Critical Appraisal Rating Programme (CASP) appraisal checklist and assigned each paper an overall quality ranking of "low," "medium" or "high." Any discrepancies in these rankings were resolved through discussion. While the majority of the studies ranked medium or high in quality, no studies were excluded because of this quality assessment. Results of the quality assessment are available on request.

Results

Figure 18.1 shows a flowchart of the study selection process. Table 18.1 describes the 23 articles that met the inclusion criteria. Results by the year of publication were indicative of increasing attention being paid to gender and SRH issues among very young adolescents in SSA. Studies varied by geographical regions: 14 studies were conducted in four countries in Eastern Africa,

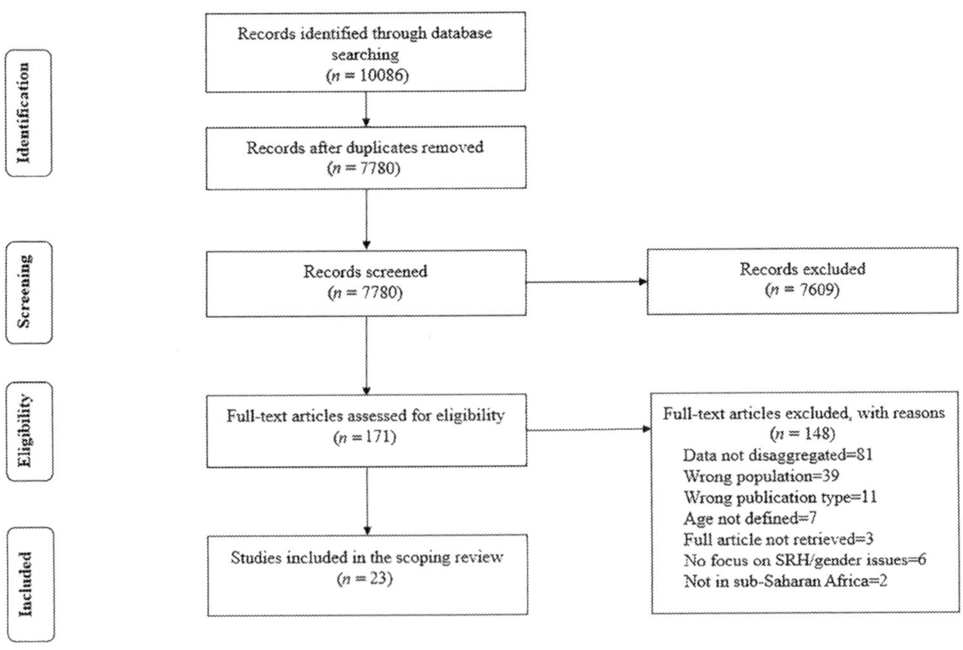

Figure 18.1 Literature search flow

6 studies in two countries in Southern Africa (mainly South Africa), 7 studies in five Western African countries and 3 studies in the Democratic Republic of the Congo (Central Africa). Four studies were multi-country, three of which included countries outside SSA.

The studies used different designs and data collection methods. Sixteen studies were based on cross-sectional data, four studies on randomized controlled trials data, one study used an ethnographic design, one a comparative multimethod design and one a convergent parallel mixed methods design. Ten studies applied qualitative and quantitative methods of data collection, while three studies applied mixed methods. Only nine studies clearly stated that their work was guided by a theoretical framework, with each study using a different framework, as shown in Table 18.1.

While we focused on findings from adolescents aged 10–14 years, study participants' ages varied. In ten studies, all participants were very young adolescents aged between 10 and 14 years, while three studies included very young adolescents and adults. In six studies, participants were aged between 10 and 24 years; two studies included participants aged 10–19 years and adults, one study had participants aged 12–27 years and one study conducted in South Africa recruited participants in 8th grade (8th graders in South Africa are aged around 13 and 14 years). By sex, 6 studies included females only, 17 studies included both male and females and 1 study focused on boys only.

Gender norms and gender socialization

The findings showed that not only were gendered behaviors prevalent among boys and girls, but such behaviors were similar in different settings. Ordinarily, girls assumed domestic roles presumed to be less physically demanding, while boys, perceived to be stronger than girls, were socialized to take up roles that were deemed hard or challenging for girls (Ampofo, 2001; Coast et al., 2019; De Meyer et al., 2017; Lundgren et al., 2019; Mmari et al., 2018; Ninsiima et al., 2018; Ortiz-Echevarria et al., 2017; Ragnarsson, Onya, Thorson, Ekström, & Aarø, 2008). Girls were socialized to be submissive, while boys were prepared for positions that gave them dominance, including in sexual and romantic relationships. While boys were considered strong enough to protect themselves, girls were viewed as weak and vulnerable (Lundgren et al., 2019; Mmari et al., 2018; Ninsiima et al., 2018; Ortiz-Echevarria et al., 2017) and hence in need of protection. Thus, girls' movements were restricted, while boys gained more independence.

Gendered norms operated in sexual relationships, with boys expressing more sexual freedom than girls (Ampofo, 2001; Coast et al., 2019; De Meyer et al., 2017; Ninsiima et al., 2018; Ragnarsson et al., 2008). For instance, in Ethiopia and Rwanda, boys were found to be free to experiment with sex, while girls' sexuality was highly policed (Coast et al., 2019). In all studies included in this review, adolescents perceived heterosexual relationships as the norm.

Our findings suggest that very young adolescents endorsed or challenged inequitable gender norms about sexual behaviors in almost equal measure. For instance, in a study focusing on young males' gendered sexuality in Limpopo Province, South Africa, girls approved of males having multiple sexual relationships (Ragnarsson et al., 2008). Boys were expected to take a leading and dominant role in sexual relationships (Ampofo, 2001), with their sexual desires being perceived as intrinsic (Vu et al., 2017).

The mixed findings on how gender norms were challenged and negotiated (De Meyer et al., 2017; DeLong et al., 2020; Kemigisha et al., 2018; Lundgren et al., 2019; Maina, Orindi, Sikweyiya, & Kabiru, 2020; Moreau et al., 2019; Ninsiima et al., 2018; Ortiz-Echevarria et al., 2017; Russell et al., 2014) are suggestive of changing gender norms and beliefs in different contexts. A study in South Africa found that young people supported domains of inequitable

Table 18.1 Description of the Included Articles

Author, Year	*Study Design*	*Study Aims*	*Country, Study Location*	*Theoretical Framework*	*Target Population (Age Range and Sex)*
Ampofo (2001)	Cross-sectional study, qualitative	Exploring gendered attitudes to social relations and reproductive and sexual behaviors among young people	Ghana, eastern region	Not stated	11–13 years, male and female
Ragnarsson et al. (2008)	Cross-sectional study, qualitative	Describing how young people, both boys and girls, depict and interpret male gender and sexuality in their community	South Africa, Mankweng	Not stated	12–14 years, male and female
Cho et al. (2011)	Randomized controlled trial, quantitative	Testing whether comprehensive support to keep adolescent orphans in school can reduce HIV risk factors	Kenya, Western province	Social development model	12–14 years, female
Ojo (2014)	Cross-sectional study, quantitative	Examining age and gender differences in the premarital sexual attitudes exhibited by adolescents and young adults	Nigeria, Lagos, Ogun & Osun in south west Nigeria	Sexual strategies theory	12–27 years, male and female
Russell et al. (2014)	Cross-sectional study, quantitative	Describing the potentially preventable factors in intimate partner violence (IPV) perpetration and victimization among South African 8th-grade students	South Africa, Cape Town	Jewkes' theoretical model of IPV causation	8th grade, male and female
De Meyer et al. (2017)	Cross-sectional study, qualitative	Exploring how gender norms emerge in romantic relationships among early adolescents living in five poor urban areas	USA, Ecuador, Scotland, Belgium, Kenya, urban poor settlements	Not stated	11–13 years, male and female
Falb et al. (2017)	Cross-sectional study, quantitative	Examining the association of gendered and parental attitudes of caregivers in South Kivu, Democratic Republic of Congo (DRC), with their early adolescent girls' (aged 10–14 years) experiences of violence and girls' attitudes towards IPV	Democratic Republic of the Congo, South Kivu	Not stated	10–14 years, female Also included adults

Ortiz-Echevarria et al. (2017)	Cross-sectional study, qualitative	Understanding the lived realities of very young adolescents in Kobe refugee camp and their related health and development needs, expectations and goals	Ethiopia, Kobe refugee camp	Blum et al.'s conceptual framework for early adolescence	10–16 years, male and female; also included adults
Stark et al. (2017)	Cross-sectional study, quantitative	Assessing whether attitudes toward traditional gender norms modify the effects of the relationship between violence exposure and future orientation in displaced girls	Democratic Republic of the Congo, South Kivu	Role congruity theory	10–14 years, female adolescents; also included adults
Vu et al. (2017)	Cross-sectional study, quantitative	Describing and comparing gender norms among 10- to 14-year-olds versus 15- to 24-year-olds and conducting a rigorous evaluation of the GEM scale's performance among these two age groups	Uganda, Wakiso and Kampala districts	Not stated	10–24 years, male and female
Kemigisha et al. (2018)	Cross-sectional study, quantitative	Assessing the factors associated with sexual wellbeing (defined as body image, self-esteem and gender-equitable norms) in young adolescents in Uganda	Uganda	Not stated	10–14 years, male and female
Merrill et al. (2018)	Convergent parallel mixed methods design, mixed methods	Exploring the preliminary outcomes of the SKILLZ Street program and the processes through which such outcomes were or were not achieved	South Africa, Gauteng province	Not stated	11–16 years, female
Mmari et al. (2018)	Cross-sectional study, qualitative	Comparing the perceived risks associated with entering adolescence among parents and adolescents and explore how these risks differ by gender and by cultural setting across six sites	Egypt, USA, Belgium, Nigeria, Nairobi and Shanghai, urban poor settlements	Not stated	11–13 years, male and female; also included adults
Ninsiima et al. (2018)	Cross-sectional study, qualitative	Exploring the gender-related sexuality norms among young adolescents in Uganda	Uganda, Mbarara, Western Uganda, rural and urban areas	Social learning theory	12–14 years, male and female; also included adults

(*Continued*)

Author, Year	*Study Design*	*Study Aims*	*Country, Study Location*	*Theoretical Framework*	*Target Population (Age Range and Sex)*
Coast et al. (2019)	Comparative multimethod qualitative design, qualitative	Assessing how gender and age affect adolescent boys' and girls' experiences of SRH in two East African countries: Ethiopia and Rwanda	Ethiopia and Rwanda	GAGE (Gender & Adolescence: Global Evidence) "3 Cs" conceptual framework	10–19 years, male and female; also included peers and adults
Kemigisha et al. (2019)	Randomized controlled trial, mixed methods	To evaluate the effectiveness of a comprehensive sexuality education (CSE) intervention for very young adolescents in Uganda	Uganda	Theory of planned behavior and the social ecological Model	11–15 years, male and female
Lundgren et al. (2019)	Ethnographic cohort study, qualitative	Understanding how gendered norms and practices develop during the transition from child to young adult in post-conflict northern Uganda	Uganda	Feminist theory, social constructivist theory, ecological systems theory	10–19 years, male and female
Moreau et al. (2019)	Cross-sectional study, mixed methods	To construct and test a cross-cultural scale assessing the perceptions of gender norms regulating romantic relationships between boys and girls in early adolescence	Egypt, USA, Malawi, South Africa, Bolivia, Ecuador, Scotland, Belgium, Vietnam, Nigeria, DRC, Kenya, India, Burkina Faso, China, urban poor settlements	Not stated	10–14 years, male and female
Austrian et al. (2020)	Randomized controlled trial, quantitative	Assessing the impact of a girls' empowerment program on social, economic, education and fertility outcomes	South Africa, rural and urban areas	Not stated	10–19 years, female

DeLong et al. (2020),	Randomized controlled trial, quantitative	To compare and contrast reproductive health, gender equity attitudes and intimate partner violence among married very young adolescent girls with married older adolescent girls and young women in rural Niger	Niger, rural areas	Not stated	13–19 years, female
Maina et al. (2020)	Cross-sectional study, quantitative	Exploring the association between gender norms about romantic relationships and sexual experiences of very young male adolescents	Kenya, urban slum in Nairobi	Not stated	10–14 years, male
Ninsiima et al. (2020),	Cross-sectional study, qualitative	Exploring how the intersection between poverty, unequal gender relations and restricted access to the law impacts on the sexual and reproductive choices of young women	Uganda	Not stated	12–14 years, female
Özler et al. (2020)	Randomized controlled trial, quantitative	Examining the potential of adding a cash transfer component to a gender-transformative mentoring intervention that aimed to reduce sexual abuse among females in early adolescence; equip adolescent girls with the skills to make healthy, strategic life choices; and to stay safe from sexual abuse using a cluster-randomized controlled trial with three arms: control, Girl Empower (GE) and GEþ.	Liberia, Nimba County	Not stated	13–14 years, female

gender norms that promoted male superiority and violence while disagreeing with those that promoted dating abuse (Merrill et al., 2018).

Three studies showed that very young adolescents were more likely to endorse inequitable gender norms than older adolescents (Kemigisha et al., 2018; Ojo, 2014; Vu et al., 2017), while one study did not find any differences in gender attitudes by age (DeLong et al., 2020). In a study conducted in South West Nigeria, Ojo (2014) found that boys were more likely than girls to hold permissive views about premarital sexual activity. Adolescents who reported sexual or physical violence and early sexual debut were more likely to support inequitable gender norms (Vu et al., 2017). A Ugandan study (Ninsiima et al., 2018) found that differentiated gender roles were more common in rural areas than in urban areas, while in Ghana, adolescents in matriarchal societies were more likely to endorse equitable norms than those in patriarchal societies (Ampofo, 2001). These results reflect commonalities in gender beliefs and perceptions across cultures, age groups and sexes.

Key actors in the gender socialization of boys and girls included parents, caregivers, schools, teachers, communities, peers, religious institutions and leaders (Ampofo, 2001; Coast et al., 2019; De Meyer et al., 2017; Lundgren et al., 2019; Mmari et al., 2018; Moreau et al., 2019; Ninsiima et al., 2018; Ortiz-Echevarria et al., 2017).

Gender norms and sexual and reproductive behaviors and outcomes

The pathways through which gender norms influenced SRH behaviors and outcomes among young adolescents was a common theme. The socialization of boys and girls often involved their early introduction to notions of proper gender behaviors and norms (Ampofo, 2001; Coast et al., 2019; De Meyer et al., 2017; DeLong et al., 2020; Kemigisha et al., 2018; Lundgren et al., 2019; Maina et al., 2020; Mmari et al., 2018; Moreau et al., 2019; Ninsiima et al., 2018; Ojo, 2014; Ortiz-Echevarria et al., 2017; Ragnarsson et al., 2008; Russell et al., 2014; Stark et al., 2017; Vu et al., 2017). These gender norms were often inherently inequitable, with strong potential to foster power differentials among boys and girls and promote sexual double standards that diminish girls' power, voice and agency and promote dominance, aggression, risk-taking, sexual activity and experimentation among boys (De Meyer et al., 2017; Mmari et al., 2018; Moreau et al., 2019; Ninsiima et al., 2018).

Inequitable gender norms put girls under pressure to demonstrate their femininity through sexual acquiescence, deference to men and boys and expectations of material and financial support from males, often with adverse SRH outcomes (Ragnarsson et al., 2008). Research conducted in Ethiopia among refugee populations showed that many of these inequitable gender norms found expression in cultural practices such as female genital mutilation/cutting (FGM/C), seclusion and early marriage (Coast et al., 2019; Ortiz-Echevarria et al., 2017). These cultural practices set the stage for early childbearing; girls' limited access to education, SRH information, and knowledge about their bodies, including menstruation; and several other adverse negative outcomes (Ortiz-Echevarria et al., 2017). The normative expectation for girls to be discreet about sexual matters and their own sexuality constrained very young adolescent girls in Uganda, South Africa, Malawi, Nigeria, DRC, Kenya and Burkina Faso from opening up about their own sexual relations; reporting their sexual victimization; safely negotiating relationship with boys and men; and seeking life-saving SRH services, support, and information (Coast et al., 2019; Ninsiima et al., 2018; Ninsiima et al., 2020; Ortiz-Echevarria et al., 2017; Ragnarsson et al., 2008; Russell et al., 2014). In rural Ethiopia, the belief that the onset of menarche and menstruation indicated girls' marriageability and sexual readiness was not only a dynamic in girl-child marriage, it also forced girls to conceal their menarche and menstruation in order to continue schooling or avoid being married off (Coast et al., 2019; Ortiz-Echevarria et al., 2017). In doing so, however, these girls may be exposed to unhygienic menstrual management practices and infections.

In the same vein, masculine ideals drove adolescent boys to experiment early with sex; initiate romantic relationships early; engage in multiple sexual partnerships; pursue reputation and peer respect through sexual activity, violence and risk-taking; and use bodily and material capital to gain authority over girls' bodies or win them over for sexual activity, all of which exposed them and their partners to harm and poor SRH outcomes (Ampofo, 2001; Coast et al., 2019; Kemigisha et al., 2018; Mmari et al., 2018; Ninsiima et al., 2018; Ortiz-Echevarria et al., 2017; Russell et al., 2014).

Some rites of passage in SSA, including male circumcision, provide a critical pathway for behaviors that compromise the SRH of very young adolescents. Writing specifically about very young boys in South Africa, Ragnarsson and colleagues reported that the cultural belief that circumcision qualifies boys for manhood and readies them for sexual activity encouraged early sexual debut among boys, who often lacked adequate information and knowledge to protect themselves and their partners from negative SRH outcomes (Ragnarsson et al., 2008).

Barriers to addressing gender norms that influence SRH outcomes among very young adolescents

Our findings suggest that very young people's capacity to negotiate and challenge patriarchal gender norms while exploring alternative gender norms is influenced by three factors: personal factors (knowledge, agency and aspirations), social factors (socialization processes, capital, costs and consequences) and structural factors (health/educational systems, religious institutions, government policies).

Personal factors: Limited agency for girls and women to negotiate safe sex practices was shown to have a negative effect on their SRH outcomes (Lundgren et al., 2019; Ninsiima et al., 2018; Ninsiima et al., 2020; Ortiz-Echevarria et al., 2017; Ragnarsson et al., 2008). For example, in a study conducted in Northern Uganda, Lundgren et al. found that girls' limited knowledge and myths about contraceptives restricted their autonomy in decision-making over their reproductive behaviors (Lundgren et al., 2019).

Socio-cultural factors: For adolescent girls and women, there were critical costs and consequences of challenging patriarchy, which included stigma, sanctions and violence (Ampofo, 2001; Coast et al., 2019; Lundgren et al., 2019; Ninsiima et al., 2018; Ninsiima et al., 2020; Ortiz-Echevarria et al., 2017; Ragnarsson et al., 2008). Furthermore, fear of embarrassment and loss of status were shown to motivate adolescent girls' and women's compliance with patriarchal norms (Ampofo, 2001; Coast et al., 2019; Lundgren et al., 2019). In the Ugandan study conducted by Lundgren et al., girls observed that women's lack of access to capital constrained their capacity to challenge patriarchal norms and that some women were forbidden from engaging in income-generating activities or making their own money, ensuring dependence on their husbands (Lundgren et al., 2019). Moreover, men were reported to use violence against women and girls as a tool or tactic to maintain their dominance (DeLong et al., 2020; Lundgren et al., 2019; Merrill et al., 2018; Russell et al., 2014; Stark et al., 2017). While these portray socio-cultural beliefs of male dominance over female, young adolescents' support for these inequitable norms across cultures may create barriers to addressing the inequitable gender norms.

Customary practices that promote early marriages (Ortiz-Echevarria et al., 2017; Özler et al., 2020) have been shown to be critical barriers to addressing gender norms. For instance, the acceptability of cultural practices such as FGM/C and early marriages, as shown in two studies conducted in Ethiopia and Rwanda (Coast et al., 2019; Ortiz-Echevarria et al., 2017), is a barrier to addressing gender inequitable norms. A study among adolescents and adults in a refugee camp in Ethiopia demonstrated that male dominance, early marriages and harmful traditional practices such as FGM/C were a reality for adolescent girls in the study setting (Ortiz-Echevarria et al., 2017), yet young people rarely discussed or questioned practices such as FGM/C in public (Ortiz-Echevarria et al., 2017), perhaps due to fear of consequences for challenging patriarchal norms.

Structural factors: Education, religious institutions, health systems, poverty, policies and legal and justice systems were critical structural barriers to addressing gender norms in relation to SRH by reinforcing patriarchal norms in these settings (Coast et al., 2019; Lundgren et al., 2019; Ninsiima et al., 2020; Özler et al., 2020; Stark et al., 2017). Despite legal provisions criminalizing rape, sexual violence and sexual harassment in Rwanda and Ethiopia, Coast et al. (2019) attributed low rates of reporting such occurrences to victim blaming, especially for rape, with girls often blamed for provoking a sexual assault. Lundgren et al. (2019) argued that girls' access to family planning services would give them power to make informed choices about their reproductive behaviors, thus challenging male dominance over reproductive decisions. In Western Uganda, Ninsiima et al. reported that structural weaknesses in the justice system, including ill-equipped police and health care services, coupled with poverty and unequal gender relations, restricted girls' ability to exercise their sexual and reproductive rights, leaving victims powerless and vulnerable (Ninsiima et al., 2020).

Interventions aimed at improving gender-equitable norms among very young adolescents in SSA

Five studies (Austrian et al., 2020; Cho et al., 2011; Kemigisha et al., 2019; Merrill et al., 2018; Özler et al., 2020) reported on the evaluation of interventions that have been implemented to, among other outcomes, improve gender-equitable norms among very young adolescents. Except for Özler et al. (2020), who found that the Girl Empowered program had significant positive effects on gender attitudes, overall, the other interventions had no or modest effects on increasing gender-equitable norms among adolescents. The Girl Empowered program, which was described as a gender-transformative mentoring intervention, was implemented among girls aged 13–14 years in rural Nimba County in Liberia (Özler et al., 2020) and had significant positive effects on gender attitudes as assessed by the gender attitudes index of the Gender Equity Index and Attitudes Towards IPV Index.

Similar to the Adolescent Girls Empowerment Program (AGEP) (Austrian et al., 2020) and the SKILLZ Street Program (Merrill et al., 2018) that both targeted very young adolescent girls, the Girl Empowered program offered girls life skills sessions facilitated by local female mentors. The Girl Empowered curriculum, for example, covered the following topics: sense of self, feelings and emotions, social networks, protection and safety, financial literacy, reproductive health, leadership and empowerment and setting life goals. Unlike the other interventions, however, the Girl Empowered curriculum also included caregiver training sessions, which aimed to familiarize caregivers with the content of the girls' curriculum and content, to enable them reinforce the skills that the girls learned and to encourage them to support and protect girls in their communities. The SKILLZ Street Program – a soccer-based life skills program – on the other hand, included a supplementary SMS platform through which participants could access additional information on key intervention topics and information on local health services (Merrill et al., 2018).

Both the Girls Empowered program (Özler et al., 2020) and AGEP (Austrian et al., 2020) offered girls training in financial literacy and supported the girls to set up individual savings. The Girl Empowered program also gave caregivers a cash incentive for girls' participation in the program in one of the study arms (Özler et al., 2020), while the AGEP program provided girls with a voucher that they could redeem to access free wellness and SRH services.

Cho et al. (2011) hypothesized that supporting both girls and boys to stay in school would increase equitable gender attitudes. In their randomized controlled trial conducted among adolescent orphans aged 12–14 years in western Kenya, they found that a lower proportion of adolescents who received a comprehensive community-based intervention aimed at keeping adolescents in school endorsed IPV. All participating households received mosquito nets, blankets and food supplies. Adolescents in intervention households also received uniforms and school fees and could receive additional support to address challenges, such as lack of sanitary towels, that increased school absenteeism. The intervention, however, had no significant effect on gender equity scores.

Kemigisha et al. reported on a comprehensive sexuality education intervention implemented in 33 primary schools in South Western Uganda (Kemigisha et al., 2019). The theory-based intervention, which aimed to enhance knowledge, attitudes and practices related to sexual health, comprised 11 lessons delivered by trained volunteer undergraduate university students. Topics covered were puberty, relationships and emotions, decision making, self-esteem skills, reporting of physical and sexual violence, knowing one's rights, sexually transmitted infections, HIV/AIDS and stigma, prevention of pregnancy, sexuality and gender and sexuality and media influence. At the end of the intervention, there was no significant difference between adolescents in the intervention and control group in endorsement of gender-equitable norms (Kemigisha et al., 2019).

Discussion

This scoping review aimed to explore and describe recent literature on gender norms and SRH behaviors among very young adolescents in sub-Saharan Africa. While the review demonstrates limited but increasing focus on gender norms and SRH among very young adolescents, the available evidence highlights commonalities on how inequitable gender norms are propagated across regions (Ampofo, 2001; Kemigisha et al., 2018; Maina et al., 2020; Ninsiima et al., 2018; Ojo, 2014; Vu et al., 2017). The study findings also underscore the harmful effects of inequitable gender norms on adolescent SRH and well-being (Coast et al., 2019; Ninsiima et al., 2020; Ortiz-Echevarria et al., 2017; Ragnarsson et al., 2008; Russell et al., 2014). We discuss the study findings, identifying the key gaps likely to inform future research and programmatic action.

Focus on boys

The review demonstrates a limited focus on boys and SRH outcomes for boys. While girls are often perceived to be at a disproportionate risk of poor SRH outcomes (DeLong et al., 2020; Fiaveh et al., 2015; Mmari et al., 2018), inadvertent failure to focus on boys may limit their engagement in gender equality debates, programs and policies and may derail or delay achievements of intended results in gender transformative programming (Ruane-McAteer et al., 2019). While these findings majorly reflect girls' heightened risk for poor SRH outcomes, they also highlight the marginalization of boys and men in gender and SRH research. As gender norms are conceptualized in relation to men and women, these results underscore the need for greater focus on boys, especially at the young age when behaviors likely to influence future health trajectories are being formed.

Marginalized and sexual minority groups

Scarcity of evidence limits the critical review of how gender norms impact SRH behaviors of very young adolescents in humanitarian settings and those living with disabilities, as well as sexual minorities. Only one study focused on adolescents in humanitarian settings – Kobe refugee camp in Ethiopia – and found that FGM/C and child marriages were prevalent in the setting (Ortiz-Echevarria et al., 2017). This finding reflects those of a scoping review on barriers and facilitators for sexual and reproductive health and rights of young people in refugee contexts globally, whereby Tirado, Chu, Hanson, Ekström, and Kågesten (2020) found 14 studies conducted in sub-Saharan Africa that included very young adolescents. Only three of the studies were published in peer-reviewed journals (Tirado et al., 2020).

None of the studies we reviewed focused on adolescents living with disabilities. In a study conducted in southwestern Nigeria, Afolayan (2015) reported that sexual abuse and violence were prevalent among people living with disability, disproportionately affecting women and girls. Disability stereotypes such as negative presentation of women and girls living with disabilities as helpless, incompetent, asexual and intellectually challenged diminishes women's sexual and reproductive agency and reinforces male dominance in intimate relationships (Afolayan, 2015).

The review findings also depict normalization of heterosexual relationships, despite extant evidence on same-sex relationships in SSA, albeit among older adolescents and young people (Mucherah, Owino, & McCoy, 2016). Similar to findings by Woog and Kågesten (2017) none of the reviewed studies focused on sexual minorities. While the evidence gap on sexual minorities could also be attributed to criminalization of same-sex relationships in a majority of countries in SSA (C. Izugbara et al., 2020), there is increasing regional effort targeting SRH needs of the sexual minorities (African Commission on Human and Peoples' Rights, 2014). All together, these marginalized and minority groups of young people are often adversely affected by poor SRH outcomes, as their stigmatization and social exclusion expose them to sexual risk-taking, sexual violence, gender-based violence and early marriages (Afolayan, 2015; Hanass-Hancock, 2009; Tirado et al., 2020), outcomes that are often associated with inequitable gender norms.

Policy and policy implementation gaps in elimination of traditional harmful practices

This scoping review also shows a grim picture on the nexus between inequitable gender norms and poor SRH outcomes among very young adolescents and highlights major policy and policy implementation gaps that may impede the realization of Sustainable Development Goal 5 on achieving gender equality and empowering all women and girls (UNFPA, n.d.). Early marriages, sexual violence, FGM/C and other harmful traditional practices are prevalent in SSA contexts and adversely affect girls (Hervish & Clifton, 2012; UNFPA, 2019). For instance, while most countries in SSA criminalize child marriages (The African Committee of Experts on the Rights and Welfare of the Child, 2015), Mashikwa and colleagues indicate that some countries have a provision for child marriages with parental consent (Maswikwa, Richter, Kaufman, & Nandi, 2015). Similarly, while most countries have laws that prohibit FGM/C, the practice remains pervasive in many practicing communities (Shell-Duncan, Naik, & Feldman-Jacobs, 2016). The seemingly limited effect of policy and legal frameworks calls for an urgent need to harmonize policies and laws on child protection across the region and strengthen legal and law enforcement frameworks to ensure that policies and laws are implemented accordingly. Moreover, these findings highlight an urgent need for countries to ensure multilateral collaborations in policy implementation to ensure that social, cultural and structural provisions that encourage harmful traditional practices are completely abandoned.

SRH programming focused on very young adolescents

Despite inequitable gender norms being associated with poor SRH outcomes among very young adolescents, this age-group is also highly neglected in terms of gender and SRH programming in SSA. Our review found only five peer-reviewed articles describing intervention studies that focused on very young adolescents (Austrian et al., 2020; Cho et al., 2011; Kemigisha et al., 2019; Merrill et al., 2018; Özler et al., 2020). Two of these interventions focused on boys and girls and three on girls alone, again highlighting the exclusion of boys in programming (Blum, Boyden, Erulkar, Kabiru, & Wilopo, 2019). However, we do recognize that there are recently completed but unpublished interventions targeting very young adolescents. For example, the DREAMS (Determined, Resilient, Empowered, AIDS-free, Mentored and Safe) initiative aims to reduce HIV incidence rates among adolescent girls and young women (AGYW) in 10 countries in SSA. The DREAMS core package of interventions includes individual-level (empowering AGYW and reducing their risk of HIV and violence) and contextual-level interventions (strengthening families through economic and parenting support, mobilizing community to address social norms and reducing HIV risk in male sex partners) (Gourlay et al., 2019). In some contexts, such as in Nairobi, Kenya, the DREAMS target population included very young adolescents aged 10–14 years (Birdthistle et al., 2018). The Adolescent Girl Initiative–Kenya (Austrian et al., 2016) was a randomized controlled trial conducted in two marginalized settings in Kenya – Kibera informal settlement, Nairobi County, and Wajir County – with a long-term goal to delay childbearing for adolescent girls by improving their wellbeing. The study followed adolescents aged 11–14 years for a period of two years and implemented four sector-specific interventions – violence prevention, education, health and wealth creation. At the end of the two-year intervention, there was no effect on gender attitudes (Austrian et al., 2020). The HERStory intervention (South African Medical Research Council, 2020), implemented in South Africa among AGYW aged 10–24 years, included a comprehensive package of health, education and support services for AGYW in and out of school. Overall, the intervention provided access to comprehensive HIV, TB and SRH services and commodities; rights-based SRH education; support to keep girls in school; therapeutic services for abused children; financial literacy and career development; vocational programs to promote economic empowerment; and interventions to maximize social support. AGYW who participated in the program made safer decisions and felt more empowered and less vulnerable to influence from peers and boyfriends. Also, the intervention enhanced AGYW's agency to negotiate contraceptive use with partners (South African Medical Research Council, 2020).

Programmatic scope

Reviewed interventions approached gender norms in regard to young people's SRH from a multilayered perspective, including comprehensive sexuality education, life skills, financial literacy and support, SRH services, food supplies, school support, protection and safety, leadership and empowerment (Austrian et al., 2020; Cho et al., 2011; Kemigisha et al., 2019; Özler et al., 2020). Further, most interventions targeted individual adolescents. However, gender is a social construct (Brickell, 2006), and thus, interactions that an individual has with their proximal and distal environments are likely to influence their gender attitudes and behaviors. In the current review, the only intervention – Girl Empowered program – that showed significant positive changes in gender attitudes also included caregiver training sessions, which aimed to enable caregivers to reinforce the skills that girls learned and to encourage them to support and protect girls in their communities (Özler et al., 2020). Interventions need therefore to consider and take into account other facets of social interactions. For instance, socio-ecological theorists argue that individual behavior is influenced by different layers of the eco-system, including individual characteristics, their immediate environment (e.g. family and peers) and distal environments (e.g. institutional and community level factors) as well as the macro-level factors (e.g. the policy environments) (Golden & Earp, 2012). The insignificant or marginally significant effects of these interventions on gender norms warrant further review of what works to address inequitable gender norms among young adolescents in SSA.

Reviewed interventions mainly focused on improving girls' sexual and reproductive agency (Austrian et al., 2020; Merrill et al., 2018; Özler et al., 2020) by empowering them to reject traditional harmful practices and inequitable gender norms and to make informed decisions about their sexual and reproductive behavior. This approach implies a personal responsibility to reject inequitable gender norms. However, existing evidence suggests that gendered norms and beliefs inherent in contexts where young people live may limit their agency in sexual relationships (Ninsiima et al., 2018; Tolman, Anderson, & Belmonte, 2015). The emphasis on agency among young people notwithstanding, there is little precision and consistency regarding what sexual and reproductive agency means for young girls (Tolman et al., 2015), a limitation that may pose challenges in designing and assessing the impact of gender-transformative interventions.

Strengths and limitations of the review

This is the first review to focus on gender norms and sexual behaviors among very young adolescents in SSA. While we did not assess the strength of the literature reviewed given the nature of scoping reviews, the findings are important in highlighting the emerging evidence and gaps in adolescent SRH. The review focused only on peer-reviewed articles covering SSA and published in English. While this demonstrated rigor in the evidence generated, considering only peer-reviewed articles and only those in English may have excluded important findings reported in study reports, gray literature materials and other languages.

Conclusions

This review is timely in that it demonstrates the limited but increasing evidence on gender norms and very young adolescents' SRH and accentuates several research, program and policy gaps that need to be addressed to improve adolescents' SRH. The review underscores the importance of focusing on very young adolescents, who, because of their developmental stage, are susceptible to pressure to conform to socio-cultural expectations. The review highlights the need for gender-transformative programs targeting not only adolescent girls but also boys and demonstrates the early adolescence age as a window of opportunity for gender-transformative programming when behaviors are being formed. While a majority of the reviewed interventions focused on individual-level factors, interventions should address contextual factors that are likely to influence negotiation and reproduction of gender norms. This review shows that lack of or failure to implement national laws and policies aimed at addressing inequitable gender norms and harmful traditional practices impacts women's and girls' health and well-being, as evidenced by their disproportionate share of poor SRH outcomes. Thus, there is a need to devise mechanisms and frameworks that will ensure development and/or effective implementation of policies and laws across the SSA region. Findings also demonstrate significant gaps in our current understanding of gender norms and adolescent SRH and highlight the need for more research, including longitudinal studies to understand how gender attitudes change over time and how these changes influence SRH behaviors as adolescents transition to adulthood.

Acknowledgments

Writing time for BM, IN and CK was partially supported by a grant from the African Regional Office of the Swedish International Development Cooperation Agency, Sida Contribution No. 12103 for APHRC's Challenging the Politics of Social Exclusion project. Writing time for BM was also partially supported by the International Development Research Centre grant number 108676–002 for the APHRC's Gendered Socialization of Very Young Adolescents and Sexual and Reproductive Health project

References

Afolayan, G. E. (2015). Contemporary representations of disability and interpersonal relationships of disabled women in south-western Nigeria. *Agenda, 29*(2), 54–65. doi:10.1080/10130950.2015.1061780

The African Committee of Experts on the Rights and Welfare of the Child. (2015). *Africa's agenda for children 2040: Fostering an Africa fit for children*. Retrieved from https://www.acerwc.africa/agenda-2040/

Ampofo, A. A. (2001). "When men speak women listen": Gender socialisation and young adolescents' attitudes to sexual and reproductive issues. *African Journal of Reproductive Health, 5*(3), 196–212. doi:10.2307/3583335

Austrian, K., Muthengi, E., Mumah, J., Soler-Hampejsek, E., Kabiru, C. W., Abuya, B., & Maluccio, J. A. (2016). The Adolescent Girls Initiative–Kenya (AGI-K): Study protocol. *BMC Public Health, 16*(1), 210. doi:10.1186/s12889-016-2888-1

Austrian, K., Soler-Hampejsek, E., Behrman, J. R., Digitale, J., Jackson Hachonda, N., Bweupe, M., & Hewett, P. C. (2020). The impact of the Adolescent Girls Empowerment Program (AGEP) on short and long term social, economic, education and fertility outcomes: A cluster randomized controlled trial in Zambia. *BMC Public Health, 20*(1).

Austrian, K., Soler-Hampejsek, E., Kangwana, B., Maddox, N., Shah, V., Wado, Y. D., . . . Maluccio, J. (2020). *Adolescent Girls Initiative–Kenya: Endline evaluation report*. Nairobi, Kenya: Population Council.

Birdthistle, I., Schaffnit, S. B., Kwaro, D., Shahmanesh, M., Ziraba, A., Kabiru, C. W., . . . Floyd, S. (2018). Evaluating the impact of the DREAMS partnership to reduce HIV incidence among adolescent girls and young women in four settings: A study protocol. *BMC Public Health, 18*(1), 912. doi:10.1186/s12889-018-5789-7

Blum, R. W., Boyden, J., Erulkar, A., Kabiru, C., & Wilopo, S. (2019). Achieving gender equality requires placing adolescents at the center. *Journal of Adolescent Health, 64*(6), 691–693. doi:10.1016/j.jadohealth.2019.02.002

Brickell, C. (2006). The sociological construction of gender and sexuality. *The Sociological Review, 54*(1), 87–113. doi:10.1111/j.1467-954X.2006.00603.x

Cho, H., Hallfors, D. D., Mbai, I. I., Itindi, J., Milimo, B. W., Halpern, C. T., & Iritani, B. J. (2011). Keeping adolescent orphans in school to prevent human immunodeficiency virus infection: Evidence from a randomized controlled trial in Kenya. *Journal of Adolescent Health, 48*(5), 523–526.

Coast, E., Jones, N., Francoise, U. M., Yadete, W., Isimbi, R., Gezahegne, K., & Lunin, L. (2019). Adolescent sexual and reproductive health in Ethiopia and Rwanda: A qualitative exploration of the role of social norms. *SAGE Open, 9*(1).

DeLong, S. M., Brooks, M. I., Aliou, S., Lundgren, R., Corneliess, C., Johns, N. E., . . . Silverman, J. G. (2020). Married very young adolescent girls in Niger at greatest risk of lifetime male partner reproductive coercion and sexual violence. *PLoS One, 15*(4).

De Meyer, S., Kågesten, A., Mmari, K., McEachran, J., Chilet-Rosell, E., Kabiru, C. W., . . . Michielsen, K. (2017). "Boys should have the courage to ask a girl out": Gender norms in early adolescent romantic relationships. *Journal of Adolescent Health, 61*(4).

Falb, K.L., Asghar, K., Laird, B., Tanner, S., Graybill, E., Mallinga, P. & Stark, L. (2017). Caregiver parenting and gender attitudes: Associations with violence against adolescent girls in South Kivu, Democratic Republic of Congo. *Child Abuse and Neglect, 69*, 278-284

Fiaveh, D. Y., Izugbara, C. O., Okyerefo, M. P., Reysoo, F., & Fayorsey, C. K. (2015). Constructions of masculinity and femininity and sexual risk negotiation practices among women in urban Ghana. *Culture, Health & Sexuality, 17*(5), 650–662. doi:10.1080/13691058.2014.989264

Galambos, N. L., Berenbaum, S. A., & McHale, S. M. (2009). Gender development in adolescence. *Handbook of Adolescent Psychology, 1*, 305–357.

Golden, S. D., & Earp, J. A. L. (2012). Social ecological approaches to individuals and their contexts: Twenty years of health education & behavior health promotion interventions. *Health Education & Behavior, 39*(3), 364–372.

Gourlay, A., Birdthistle, I., Mthiyane, N. T., Orindi, B. O., Muuo, S., Kwaro, D., . . . Floyd, S. (2019). Awareness and uptake of layered HIV prevention programming for young women: Analysis of population-based surveys in three DREAMS settings in Kenya and South Africa. *BMC Public Health, 19*(1), 1417. doi:10.1186/s12889-019-7766-1

Hanass-Hancock, J. (2009). Interweaving conceptualizations of gender and disability in the context of vulnerability to HIV/AIDS in KwaZulu-Natal, South Africa. *Sexuality and Disability, 27*(1), 35–47.

Hervish, A., & Clifton, D. (2012). Status report on adolescents and young people in sub-Saharan Africa: Opportunities and challenges. New York: UNFPA and Population Reference Bureau.

Izugbara, C., Bakare, S., Sebany, M., Ushie, B., Wekesah, F., & Njagi, J. (2020). Regional legal and policy instruments for addressing LGBT exclusion in Africa. *Sexual and Reproductive Health Matters, 28*(1), 1698905. doi:10.1080/26410397.2019.1698905

Izugbara, C. O., & Undie, C.-C. (2008). Masculinity scripts and the sexual vulnerability of male youth in Malawi. *International Journal of Sexual Health, 20*(4), 281–294. doi:10.1080/19317610802412043

Kabiru, C. W., Beguy, D., Undie, C. C., Zulu, E. M., & Ezeh, A. C. (2010). Transition into first sex among adolescents in slum and non-slum communities in Nairobi, Kenya. *Journal of Youth Studies, 13*(4), 453–471.

Kågesten, A., Gibbs, S., Blum, R. W., Moreau, C., Chandra-Mouli, V., Herbert, A., & Amin, A. (2016). Understanding factors that shape gender attitudes in early adolescence globally: A mixed-methods systematic review. *PLoS One, 11*(6), e0157805. doi:10.1371/journal.pone.0157805

Kagesten, A. E., Kabiru, C. W., & Maina, B. (2018). 'Inexperienced'? Patterns in romantic and sexual experiences among urban poor early adolescents in Nairobi, Kenya. *Culture, Health & Sexuality, 20*(12), 1299–1316. doi:10.1080/13691058.2018.1432765

Kemigisha, E., Bruce, K., Ivanova, O., Leye, E., Coene, G., Ruzaaza, G. N., . . . Michielsen, K. (2019). Evaluation of a school based comprehensive sexuality education program among very young adolescents in rural Uganda. *BMC Public Health, 19*(1), 1393–1393.

Kemigisha, E., Nyakato, V. N., Bruce, K., Ruzaaza, G. N., Mlahagwa, W., Ninsiima, A. B., . . . Michielsen, K. (2018). Adolescents' sexual wellbeing in Southwestern Uganda: A cross-sectional assessment of body image, self-esteem and gender equitable norms. *International Journal of Environmental Research and Public Health, 15*(2).

Lane, C., Brundage, C. L., & Kreinin, T. (2017). Why we must invest in early adolescence: Early intervention, lasting impact. *Journal of Adolescent Health, 61*(4), S10–S11. doi:10.1016/j.jadohealth.2017.07.011

Lundgren, R., Burgess, S., Chantelois, H., Oregede, S., Kerner, B., & Kågesten, A. E. (2019). Processing gender: Lived experiences of reproducing and transforming gender norms over the life course of young people in Northern Uganda. *Culture, Health & Sexuality, 21*(4), 387–403.

MacPherson, E. E., Richards, E., Namakhoma, I., & Theobald, S. (2014). Gender equity and sexual and reproductive health in Eastern and Southern Africa: A critical overview of the literature. *Global Health Action*, 7. doi:10.3402/gha.v7.23717

Maina, B. W., Orindi, B. O., Sikweyiya, Y., & Kabiru, C. W. (2020). Gender norms about romantic relationships and sexual experiences among very young male adolescents in Korogocho slum in Kenya. *International Journal of Public Health, 65*(4), 497–506.

Maswikwa, B., Richter, L., Kaufman, J., & Nandi, A. (2015). Minimum marriage age laws and the prevalence of child marriage and adolescent birth: Evidence from sub-Saharan Africa. *International Perspectives on Sexual and Reproductive Health, 41*(2), 58–68.

Merrill, K. G., Merrill, J. C., Hershow, R. B., Barkley, C., Rakosa, B., DeCelles, J., & Harrison, A. (2018). Linking at-risk South African girls to sexual violence and reproductive health services: A mixed-methods assessment of a soccer-based HIV prevention program and pilot SMS campaign. *Evaluation and Program Planning, 70*, 12–24.

Mmari, K., Moreau, C., Gibbs, S. E., De Meyer, S., Michielsen, K., Kabiru, C. W., . . . El-Gibaly, O. (2018). 'Yeah, I've grown; I can't go out anymore': Differences in perceived risks between girls and boys entering adolescence. *Culture, Health & Sexuality, 20*(7), 787–798.

Moreau, C., Li, M., De Meyer, S., Vu Manh, L., Guiella, G., Acharya, R., . . . Mmari, K. (2019). Measuring gender norms about relationships in early adolescence: Results from the global early adolescent study. *SSM – Population Health*, 7, 100314. https://doi.org/10.1016/j.ssmph.2018.10.014

Mucherah, W., Owino, E., & McCoy, K. (2016). Grappling with the issue of homosexuality: Perceptions, attitudes, and beliefs among high school students in Kenya. *Psychology Research and Behavior Management, 9*, 253–262. doi:10.2147/PRBM.S112421

Ninsiima, A. B., Leye, E., Michielsen, K., Kemigisha, E., Nyakato, V. N., & Coene, G. (2018). "Girls have more challenges; they need to be locked up": A qualitative study of gender norms and the sexuality of young adolescents in Uganda. *International Journal of Environmental Research and Public Health, 15*(2).

Ninsiima, A. B., Michielsen, K., Kemigisha, E., Nyakato, V. N., Leye, E., & Coene, G. (2020). Poverty, gender and reproductive justice: A qualitative study among adolescent girls in Western Uganda. *Culture, Health & Sexuality, 22*(Suppl. 1), 65–79.

Ojo, A. A. (2014). Age and gender differences in premarital sexual attitudes of young people in South West Nigeria. *Gender & Behaviour, 12*(2), 6301–6311.

Ortiz-Echevarria, L., Greeley, M., Bawoke, T., Zimmerman, L., Robinson, C., & Schlecht, J. (2017). Understanding the unique experiences, perspectives and sexual and reproductive health needs of very young adolescents: Somali refugees in Ethiopia. *Conflict and Health, 11.*

Özler, B., Hallman, K., Guimond, M.-F., Kelvin, E. A., Rogers, M., & Karnley, E. (2020). Girl Empower – A gender transformative mentoring and cash transfer intervention to promote adolescent wellbeing: Impact findings from a cluster-randomized controlled trial in Liberia. *SSM – Population Health, 10*, 100527–100527.

Patton, G. C., Sawyer, S. M., Santelli, J. S., Ross, D. A., Afifi, R., Allen, N. B., . . . Viner, R. M. (2016). Our future: A Lancet commission on adolescent health and wellbeing. *The Lancet, 387*(10036), 2423–2478. doi:10.1016/S0140-6736(16)00579-1

Ragnarsson, A., Onya, H. E., Thorson, A., Ekström, A. M., & Aarø, L. E. (2008). *Young males' gendered sexuality in the era of HIV and AIDS in Limpopo province, South Africa* (Vol. 18). Los Angeles, CA: Sage Publications.

Resolution 275: Resolution on protection against violence and other human rights violations against persons on the basis of their real or imputed sexual orientation or gender identity, ACHPR/Res.275(LV)2014 Stat. (2014).

Ruane-McAteer, E., Amin, A., Hanratty, J., Lynn, F., Corbijn van Willenswaard, K., Reid, E., . . . Lohan, M. (2019). Interventions addressing men, masculinities and gender equality in sexual and reproductive health and rights: An evidence and gap map and systematic review of reviews. *BMJ Global Health, 4*(5), e001634. doi:10.1136/bmjgh-2019-001634

Russell, M., Cupp, P. K., Jewkes, R. K., Gevers, A., Mathews, C., LeFleur-Bellerose, C., & Small, J. (2014). Intimate partner violence among adolescents in Cape Town, South Africa. *Prevention Science, 15*(3), 283–295.

Shell-Duncan, B., Naik, R., & Feldman-Jacobs, C. (2016). *A state-of-art-synthesis of female genital mutilation/cutting: What do we know now? Evidence to end FGM/C Research to help women thrive.* New York: Population Council.

Smith, R. M., Parrott, D. J., Swartout, K. M., & Tharp, A. T. (2015). Deconstructing hegemonic masculinity: The roles of antifemininity, subordination to women, and sexual dominance in men's perpetration of sexual aggression. *Psychology of Men & Masculinity, 16*(2), 160–169. doi:10.1037/a0035956

South African Medical Research Council. (2020). *HERStory: An evaluation of a South African combination HIV prevention intervention for adolescent girls and young women.* South Africa: South African Medical Research Council.

Stark, L., Asghar, K., Meyer, S., Yu, G., Bakemore, T., Poulton, C., & Falb, K. (2017). The effect of gender norms on the association between violence and hope among girls in the Democratic Republic of the Congo. *Global Mental Health, 4.*

Tirado, V., Chu, J., Hanson, C., Ekström, A. M., & Kågesten, A. (2020). Barriers and facilitators for the sexual and reproductive health and rights of young people in refugee contexts globally: A scoping review. *PLoS One, 15*(7), e0236316. doi:10.1371/journal.pone.0236316

Tolman, D. L., Anderson, S. M., & Belmonte, K. (2015). Mobilizing metaphor: Considering complexities, contradictions, and contexts in adolescent girls' and young women's sexual agency. *Sex Roles, 73*(7), 298–310. doi:10.1007/s11199-015-0510-0

UNFPA. (2019). *Beyond the crossing: Female genital mutilation across boarders, Ethiopia, Kenya, Somalia, Tanzania and Uganda.* New York: UNFPA.

UNFPA. (n.d.). *How changing social norms is crucial in achieving gender equality.* New York: UNFPA.

United Nations. (2015). *Sustainable development goals.* Retrieved on October 29, 2019, from https://sustainabledevelopment.un.org/?menu=1300

United Nations Population Division. (2019). *World population prospects 2019.* Retrieved from https://population.un.org/wpp/DataQuery/

Vu, L., Pulerwitz, J., Burnett-Zieman, B., Banura, C., Okal, J., & Yam, E. (2017). Inequitable gender norms from early adolescence to young adulthood in Uganda: Tool validation and differences across age groups. *Journal of Adolescent Health, 60*(2), S15–S21.

Woog, V., & Kågesten, A. (2017). *The sexual and reproductive health needs of very young adolescents aged 10–14 in developing countries: What does the evidence show* (G. Institute, Ed.). New York: Guttmacher Institute.

19

GENDER-BASED VIOLENCE IN AFRICA

Marifa Muchemwa

Introduction

Globally, studies have shown that in most instances, women are victims of gender-based violence. Several international conferences have addressed violence against women, including the 1979 Convection on Elimination of All Forms of Discrimination against Women, The UN General Assembly of 1993, Fourth World Conference on Women and others. In Africa, governments have enacted various legislation in efforts to address gender-based violence. Despite the existence of policies, laws and acts against gender-based violence, women in the region continue to experience violence.

Several studies have been conducted on gender-based violence in different parts of the world. The studies have focused on the different forms of gender-based violence experienced by victims, who in many cases are women (Scorgie et al., 2017). Some have focused on factors contributing to gender-based violence, characteristics of women who experience violence and the perpetrators of gender-based violence (Kalichman et al., 2007). Others have looked at the role of female empowerment in addressing gender-based violence (Green, Blattman, Jamison, & Annan, 2015; Wekwete, Sanhokwe, Murenjekwa, Takavarasha, & Madzingira, 2014).

Few studies in Africa have systematically reviewed the literature on gender-based violence intervention programmes (Gibbs, Jacobson, & Kerr Wilson, 2017; McCloskey, Boonzaier, Steinbrenner, & Hunter, 2016). Yet there are many studies on HIV intervention (Dworkin, Hatcher, Colvin, & Peacock, 2013; Kyegombe et al., 2014), with some of the studies combining gender-based violence and HIV interventions (Abramsky et al., 2012; Wagman et al., 2015). The studies on HIV intervention highlight that gender-based violence increases women's exposure to HIV (Abramsky et al., 2012; Wagman et al., 2015). By addressing gender-based violence, women's exposure to HIV is reduced, since there is an interplay in factors associated with gender-based violence and HIV. Studies which evaluate intervention programmes and policies on gender-based violence are essential in revealing the extent to which African countries are addressing violence against women. Gender-based violence is a public health concern; it has negative consequences on females and impacts the attainment of SDG 5 on gender equality. To the best of our knowledge, this chapter is the first work to systematically review the literature

 DOI: 10.4324/9780429287213-23

on intervention programmes together with policies that are in place in addressing gender-based violence in Africa.

This systematic review of gender-based violence intervention and policy-related studies draws attention to five themes. The first looks at gender equality; this involves economically empowering women through microfinance programmes. The second one is on the importance of including men in intervention programmes on violence against women. This involves targeting boys at a young age in schools and men. The third illustrates the micro- and macro-continuum interventions in addressing violence against women. The fourth is on the policies that have been put in place to address gender-based violence, including enforcement of existing laws. The review ends by discussing the potential gaps in knowledge regarding intervention programmes and policies developed to address gender-based violence in Africa. The review of the literature on gender-based violence intervention has led to the conclusion that in the presence of the five themes, there is a lot that still needs to be done in Africa to address the increasing cases of gender-based violence.

Defining gender-based violence

Gender-based violence encompasses all the harmful acts perpetrated against a person's will based on socially ascribed gender differences between males and females (Inter-Agency Standing Committee, 2015). It refers to any act of violence that results in physical, sexual or psychological harm to women. It includes deprivation of liberty and coercion (United Nations, 1993). Men and boys can be victims of gender-based violence; however, it impacts women and girls greatly compared to men and boys (Inter-Agency Standing Committee, 2015). Gender-based violence is interpreted in various ways, hence it uses different terminology such as sexual and gender-based violence or violence against women (UNICEF, 2010). The term violence against women, in the United Nations Declaration on the Elimination of Violence against Women, is used to refer to any acts of abuse. The terms 'gender-based violence' and 'violence against women' are often used interchangeably due to gender-based violence increasingly affecting women and girls (Sida, 2015).

The forms of gender-based violence differ across cultures but the most common forms include intimate partner violence, domestic violence, sexual violence, trafficking, forced or early marriage and harmful traditional practices such as female genital mutilation (Sida, 2015). Intimate partner violence is the most common form of gender-based violence. It refers to violence against an intimate partner, with perpetrators being men in most instances. It involves physical, sexual and psychological or emotional violence that could happen throughout the lifetime, posing both direct and indirect health consequences (Sida, 2015). Domestic violence refers to violence that occurs in a marital or live-in relationship. This means that the perpetrator lives within the victim's domestic environment (Flury & Nyberg, 2010). However, it does not always have to be live-in but also involves the closeness of the relationship between victims and perpetrators. This type of violence often goes beyond physical acts by involving economic and social forms of abuse (Barad & Slattery, 2007). Physical violence refers to acts such as slapping, something thrown at one, being pushed or hit with a fist, choked, burnt or threatened with a weapon (WHO, 2002). Sexual violence refers to being forced to have sexual intercourse, sexual assault, sexual harassment, rape and gang rape or being forced to do something which is sexual (Sida, 2015). Emotional violence refers to the humiliation and intimidation towards an individual (WHO, 2002).

Predictors of gender-based violence

Gender inequalities

The power inequalities between men and women are key to understanding gender-based violence. Men are portrayed as dominant and having power over women, and this allows them to control women. The economic inequalities between men and women result in women being financially dependent on men (Umubyeyi, Persson, Mogren, & Krantz, 2016). When women experience gender-based violence, they are left with no choice but to be tolerant. This is because they can be financially dependent on the perpetrator such that reporting them to the police will mean a loss of income for the family (Shamu, Abrahams, Temmerman, & Zarowsky, 2013). This results in some women normalizing or considering the beating part of the relationship (Strebel et al., 2006). Getting their partners arrested is not seen as an option, as it will leave the family without a breadwinner to provide for the children (Mukanangana, Moyo, Zvoushe, & Rusinga, 2014). The beating is often regarded by the women as a sign of love by the man towards their partner (Strebel et al., 2006).

Despite the existence of legislation meant to protect women from gender-based violence, some women fail to seek care or help due to gender inequalities. The inequalities that exist between men and women are portrayed as normal in most sub-Saharan countries due to traditional gender norms. When women seek help in matters regarding gender-based violence, they are viewed as acting contrary to what is expected by society, that is, being submissive. A study in Rwanda indicated that traditional gender norms such as men's superiority over women are supported by the church (Umubyeyi et al., 2016). Similarly, in Zimbabwe, the church is among the institutions which perpetuate inequalities between men and women (Magezi & Manzanga, 2019). Such inequalities result in policies and legislation which protect women against violence being viewed as opposing the cultural norms of men as responsible for dominating within the family.

Patriarchy and cultural practices

The patriarchy embedded in African culture makes men believe that they are entitled to control and beat women (Fidan & Bui, 2016). The cultural norms, value and beliefs within patriarchal societies promote gender-based violence (Magezi & Manzanga, 2019). A study in Nigeria highlighted that gender-based violence is rooted in the patriarchal, cultural, traditional and religious norms which allow men to dominate women (UN Women, 2020). The traditional culture in these sub-Saharan countries makes some women not report abusive partners and stay in abusive relationships. Reporting a husband is seen as improper, with the victim (the wife) who attempts to do so becoming a social outcast (Mukanangana et al., 2014). Forms of gender-based violence such as spousal rape are not taken as a form of violence by men, since they would have paid a bride price (Umubyeyi et al., 2016). The payment of a bride price gives men conjugal rights to sexual intercourse. This sees men controlling the reproductive health of women (Mukanangana et al., 2014). The bride price is often used as an excuse for gender-based violence, since women are viewed as the property of men (Dery, 2015).

Families and communities play a role in the endurance of abuse of women by exerting pressure to make the marriage work (Shamu et al., 2013) and by shunning women who attempt to report their partners (Mukanangana et al., 2014). This makes women persevere to avoid the social stigma associated with a failed marriage. Such circumstances make women develop a culture of silence (Umubyeyi et al., 2016). This is because of existing cultural practices which view the physical abuse of women as normal. Women end up believing that it is normal for them to be beaten by their partners, since it is something they grew up being told would happen and that when it happens, they should take it as a sign of love (Mukanangana et al., 2014). When women report violence to their families, they are told that this is how men behave (Mukanangana et al., 2014). Being exposed to such advice has seen some women accepting violence as part of the package of marriage (Rani, Bonu, & Diop-Sidibe, 2004).

Intervention programmes and policies for addressing gender-based violence

Gender equality

The World Health Organization called for gender equality as critical in the prevention of violence against women (WHO, 2009). Gender inequalities increase the violent practices of men towards women, making the victims fail to seek help (WHO, 2009). Studies in different countries in Africa have identified gender equality as important in addressing violence against women (Jewkes et al., 2014; Mukanangana et al., 2014). This can be done by government interventions that promote gender equality through laws and policies as well as the economic empowerment of women (Mukanangana et al., 2014), hence the need for gender-based violence prevention programs to target areas in which women are dominated economically by men (Tsai et al., 2011).

Intervention programmes in most parts of Africa have shown positive results in addressing gender-based violence, especially interventions which include economic empowerment of both females and males. In South Africa, economic interventions such as Stepping Stones and Creating Futures empowered both women and men, resulting in improved gender relations as well as reduced gender-based violence (Jewkes et al., 2014). Similarly, a microfinance programme, Intervention for AIDS and Gender Equity (IMAGE[1]) in the country involved training on HIV prevention, gender norms and domestic violence to reduce gender-based violence (Pronyk et al., 2006) and risky sexual behaviours (Pronyk et al., 2008). Microfinance[2] intervention and training in gender norms, HIV and domestic violence empower women economically, leading to a reduction in gender-based violence (Kim et al., 2007). Microfinance improves an individual's potential in income generation and secure livelihood (Kennedy, Fonner, O'Reilly, & Sweat, 2014). Economic empowerment of women through microfinance intervention is essential in building self-esteem and improving household decision-making power (Kim et al., 2007). However, it is argued that the strategies used to empower women disregard gender concerns (Phorano, Nthomang, & Ntseane, 2005) since gender equality is emphasized without paying attention to the concerns of men. This could be a reason women continue to experience gender-based violence in light of empowerment programmes.

Despite such calls for gender equality by studies as a remedy for gender-based violence, not many studies in Africa are being done to assess the impact of measures being suggested such as addressing gender inequalities through the economic empowerment of women if it is indeed a panacea to gender-based violence. A lot of literature in Africa offers remedies for gender-based violence (Mukanangana et al., 2014; Shamu et al., 2013;), with a few indicating that economic interventions are helpful to reduce violence against women (Kim et al., 2007; Knight et al., 2020).

School as sources to prevent violence against women

The World Health Organization points out that schools can be used as centres to prevent violence against women through school programmes that teach about gender norms and attitudes before they are instilled in childhood and youth (WHO, 2009). In such programmes, children are taught about gender-based violence attitudes and behaviour while they are young. Such types of school interventions have yielded positive results in the United States and in Canada's youth relationship project (WHO, 2009). In sub-Saharan Africa, a few studies have looked at schools as potential sources of learning about violence against women (Beninger, 2013; Haffejee, 2006; Prinsloo, 2006). Such interventions have the potential to prevent gender-based violence by restructuring stereotypes that allow men to dominate women (WHO, 2009). The programmes go a long way in promoting gender equality, which is essential in the prevention of gender-based violence (WHO, 2009).

In most sub-Saharan countries, gender-based violence exists in schools. These practices of violence are rooted in a society which instils gender inequalities between boys and girls (Modiba, 2018). Boys are taught to be superior, while girls are taught to be submissive. This type of socialization promotes dominant behaviours among boys over girls (Modiba, 2018). The way schoolchildren behave reflect their families and the communities they are from, hence the need for schools, communities and families to work together to reject behaviours that promote violence against women. A study in Kenya indicated that adolescent boys are a stage at which teaching on the attitudes and behaviours which lead to sexual violence can be done (Keller et al., 2017). This shows the importance of teaching boys in school about violence against women.

Community interventions

Communities are vital places for carrying out interventions on gender-based violence since it is in these spaces where violence against women takes place. Hence, awareness campaigns on violence against women should be carried out at the community level (Phorano et al., 2005). Intervention programmes should take note of the prevailing social context in communities such as levels of poverty, unemployment of men and substance abuse since these influence gender-based violence (Strebel et al., 2006). Community interventions should look at gender norms and attitudes as tools in the prevention of gender-based violence (WHO, 2009). Interventions should include microfinance programmes to empower women, with men being part of the measures taken to prevent gender-based violence (WHO, 2009).

In sub-Saharan Africa, microfinance interventions have been used as a strategy to empower women to reduce gender-based violence. In South Africa, IMAGE and Stepping Stones programmes have been initiated as strategies to address gender-based violence (WHO, 2009). A study in Limpopo province in South Africa indicated that IMAGE intervention reduced past-year physical and sexual intimate partner violence by 55% (Pronyk et al., 2006). The MAISHA intervention in Mwanza city in Tanzania focused on integrating a ten-session social empowerment intervention with a microfinance programme to assess its effect on the past-year experiences of physical and sexual violence among women (Kapiga et al., 2019). The women who participated in the MAISHA intervention had reduced reports of physical and sexual intimate partner violence. Similarly, the Start Awareness Support Action (SASA) intervention study in Uganda found a greater reduction in physical intimate partner violence than sexual intimate partner violence (Abramsky et al., 2014). The economic empowerment of women through microfinance programmes reduces intimate partner violence and improves self-esteem and self-confidence, including the power to make decisions within the household, increasing their social networks (Bourey et al., 2015). However, the MAISHA and SHARE intervention studies found no effect on emotional abuse (Kapiga et al., 2019; Wagman et al., 2015).

However, microfinance has been identified as possibly going against the established gender norms and male authority (Bourey, Williams, Bernstein, & Stephenson, 2015). This results in microfinance being associated with increased reports of intimate partner violence (Abramsky et al., 2011). A study in Uganda indicated that the economic success of women does not equate to protection from intimate partner violence (Green et al., 2015). The study further indicated that engaging men does not imply that there will be increased economic success for women or reduced reports of intimate partner violence (physical or emotional violence), but what improves is the quality of the relationship of the couples (Green et al., 2015).

Community interventions are essential in addressing gender-based violence by transforming expected gender norms and attitudes of individuals in communities (WHO, 2009). Some intervention programmes in Africa have trained communities on gender roles, cultural beliefs, relationships, intimate partner violence and HIV (Andersson, Cockcroft, & Shea, 2008). In the Gambia, the Stepping Stones programme promoted dialogue within marriage, resulting in reduced conflict and domestic violence (Paine et al., 2002). These forms of interventions improve women's self-esteem by making them leave abusive relationships. The intervention programmes act as a form of social support to women (Paine et al., 2002). Social capital and economic empowerment in women can reduce intimate partner violence.

Media interventions

The media can be used as a source of public awareness for gender-based violence. Through media interventions, gender norms can be challenged which promote violent behaviours against women, and women's rights can be promoted (WHO, 2009). The public can be made aware of violence against women through different media platforms such as television, radio and newspapers (WHO, 2009). In most instances, women are not aware of the services offered to those who are abused. A study in Zimbabwe indicated that a lower proportion of sexual violence survivors accessed post-rape services in clinics. This was due to lack of awareness of the program and its services (Sithole et al., 2018).

Different forms of gender-based violence such as wife-beating, rape, human trafficking and sexual harassment have been broadcast in the media through television dramas, music videos and soap operas. The broadcasting of gender-based violence on media can be positive or negative (Oladimeji & Osunkunle, 2020). The positive forms include discouraging any acts which promote gender-based violence, while the negative form involves portraying women as sex objects who can be violated, with the perpetrators getting away with the offence (Oladimeji & Osunkunle, 2020). The various media platforms are widely seen by most women, which makes them a vital tool in the intervention programmes which seek to protect women from gender-based violence.

Programmes must engage males and females

To improve the status of women in society, the 1995 Fourth World Conference on Women in Beijing pointed out the value of involving men. Studies on gender-based violence suggest the inclusion of men and boys in programmes that seek to address violence against women (Casey, Carlson, Two Bulls, & Yager, 2018). This allows teaching boys about attitudes and social norms which contribute to sexual violence towards women (Keller et al., 2017). This involves exposing boys to knowledge which puts them in a position where they can discern when consent for sex has been given or not (Keller et al., 2017). In South Africa, organisations such as Agisanang Domestic Abuse Prevention and Training (ADAPT) have seen men visiting informal places like bars and liquor stores to teach men about gender-based violence (Peacock, Khumalo, & McNab, 2006).

Governments in some African countries are working with men in programs and campaigns on the prevention of violence against women. In South Africa, civil society organizations such as Fathers Speak Out, the Men as Partners (MAP) Network and the South African Men's Forum are working with men to support gender equality (Peacock et al., 2006). Men's perceptions of women and masculinities changed after attending gender equality workshops (Peacock & Levack, 2004). In circumstances where men were not involved in the microfinance schemes which aimed at empowering women, there was conflict and tension between the partners, particularly in communities with rigid gender roles (WHO, 2009). This makes it vital for men to be involved in awareness programs aimed at the prevention of gender-based violence; this might contribute to changing their attitudes towards violence (Meskele, Khuzwayo, & Taylor, 2019).

Policies to address gender-based violence

Many countries in sub-Saharan Africa are signatory to international and regional frameworks aimed at protecting and promoting women's rights. These include the 1979 Universal Declaration on Human Rights Convention on the Elimination of All Forms of Discrimination Against Women (CEDAW), Protocol to the African Charter on Human and Peoples Rights on the Rights of Women in Africa and the SADC Declaration and Gender Protocol. The countries which are signatory are obliged to implement laws that protect women to ensure compliance with international rights. South Africa is among the signatories. It obliges by domesticating and implementing legislative and policy frameworks which are aligned with the international conventions (Mpani & Nsibande, 2015). Zimbabwe is also a signatory of CEDAW, and it has national policies formulated to prevent gender-based violence, such as the Domestic Violence Act 2006 (Magezi & Manzanga, 2019). The introduction of such policies shows the commitment that the governments in Africa have towards dealing with violence against women.

Nigeria is also a signatory. It has policy frameworks in place which address issues on gender equality and social inclusion (Mercy & Nanji, 2014). Nigeria's National Gender Policy (2006) was adopted by all states to promote gender equality as part of national development (Mercy & Nanji, 2014). However, the law does not clearly state the sanctions against any misconduct and infringement on women's rights surrounding gender-based violence. The laws in place to protect women against violence are outdated and need to be revised. There have been calls for laws that provide rehabilitation services, such as the provision of shelter and programs which offer skills to victims of gender-based violence (Mercy & Nanji, 2014). Despite such efforts by Nigeria, gender-based violence persists, and the COVID-19 pandemic has further increased its prevalence (UN Women, 2020).

Follow up on enacted policies

Studies have called for governments and their agencies to follow up on the enforcement of policies, including enacted laws on gender-based violence, to ensure compliance to curb violence against both women and men (Mukanangana et al., 2014). The enforcement of current laws on gender-based violence is vital in changing cultural norms and values that tolerate violence (Kalichman et al., 2007). Cases of gender-based violence are hardly reported, especially among married partners. Among the few cases which are reported, only a few cases go to court, with only a minority of the perpetrators being convicted (Andersson et al., 2008).

Policies and legislation are often conflicting, with some men not accepting what is regarded as law. The new policies on gender equality are viewed as threatening men's power within families (Umubyeyi et al., 2016). The gender equality policies are not in line with traditional cultural norms; this explains why women continue to experience violence in the presence of laws that condemn violence (Umubyeyi et al., 2016). Such notions among men show a need for interventions that educate men on the laws which protect women from gender-based violence. The new policies allow women to have access to freedom and improved rights, while on the other hand, this can trigger violence from their partners who feel undermined. Violent behaviours by men are meant to keep them as dominant figures who control women. Some studies have shown that the government has not taken strong action against the perpetrators of violence. The majority of the perpetrators of violence against women go unpunished. The resources to address gender-based violence provided by the state are insufficient. Insufficient resources make the implementation of laws on gender-based violence difficult, resulting in a lack of follow-up measures.

Research agenda

Research needs to move from describing factors that contribute to gender-based violence, since these are well known. What is needed is research that seeks to examine what is being done to fulfil the requirements of international policies. International policies such as the 1993 Declaration on the Elimination of Violence against Women and the 1995 Fourth World Conference on Women in Beijing released policy statements on gender-based violence (Michau, Naker, & Sauve, 2003). However, there is limited research aimed at investigating what countries in Africa are doing in efforts to meet the call by the international policies apart from the enactment of laws that prohibit violence. Yes, there exist laws in the countries to address gender-based violence, but to what extent are these laws enforced to ensure a reduction in violence against women?

We need research that examines areas or communities in which the United Nations Development Fund for Women (UNIFEM), women's groups and governments are operating to address gender-based violence to see if its goal to eliminate all forms of violence is being met. Research on gender-based violence needs to shift focus and be more eager to understand if women's groups, governments and NGOs are achieving their goals. Such research will form a basis for understanding if interventions on gender-based violence are indeed worthy to combat violent practices towards women. This will show the extent to which governments are working with women to empower them and to address gender equality.

In sub-Saharan African countries, some constitutions call for women's equality, with some nations developing laws and policies aimed at protecting women's rights. The problem in this region is ensuring that the policies and laws are put into practice (Michau et al., 2003). Governments need to ensure that there exists a conducive environment that allows gender-based violence programmes and policies to be implemented and put into practice. For instance, South Africa has laws that forbid gender-based violence and child abuse (Dworkin et al., 2013). But there is a higher prevalence of gender-based violence. So this raises a lot of question about the legal system. This creates a need for research studies that focus on investigating the legal system for what could be possibly influencing acts of violence against women. Such a move in research will move away from focusing on the victims of gender-based violence, but the focus should be centred on the legal system (police, judges, courts) and gender activists. The inclusion of gender activists in research is vital to understand what could be making the legal system fail the people it should protect. There is a need in the sub-Saharan region for studies that investigate how feminists and the legal system can work together in creating an environment that ensures gender equality and reduces violence against women.

Conclusion

The focus of this chapter was on intervention programmes and policies put in place to address gender-based violence in Africa. From the chapter, it is clear that gender-based violence is rife in Africa despite the existing policies that have been put in place to address violence against women. Gender equality has been identified as one of the steps in the prevention of violence against women. This involves economically empowering women to improve their economic position. Hence intervention studies on gender-based violence have used microfinance programmes as a strategy to empower women to reduce violence. There was reduced violence among women who participated in the microfinance programmes. This, in a way, highlighted that when women are economically empowered through income-generating projects, it reduces reports of gender-based violence. However, some of the studies indicated that the participation of women in microfinance programmes does not automatically end the occurrence of violence but improves the quality of the relationship with their partners.

The chapter indicates that sub-Saharan countries are signatories to the 1979 Universal Declaration on Human Rights Convention on the Elimination of All Forms of Discrimination against Women (CEDAW). This implies that countries have a mandate to protect and prevent women from experiencing gender-based violence. These countries have national policies aimed at preventing women from gender-based violence. However, studies have suggested a need to enforce or revise the existing national policies considering the increased cases of gender-based violence in different African countries.

The inclusion of men in intervention programmes aimed at addressing gender-based violence is identified as vital. In the programmes, men are taught to accept the changing gender roles of women, which includes active participation in income-generating projects, and to respect women by avoiding any form of violence directed towards women. Schools are identified in Africa as places that can assist in the restructuring of norms and values which promote violence against women.

The chapter ends by critically discussing what needs to be included in the research as a way of assisting in finding remedies against gender-based violence. This involves a strong transformation in gender-based violence research which moves away from taking victims as the centre of attention. The predictors of gender-based violence and what triggers its occurrence are known. The focus should be on institutions that have been put in place to deal with violence against women. Questions should be asked about whether such institutions are able to meet their mandate of protecting women if they are failing what could be the barriers. Identifying the barriers would be vital in improving existing policies directed at addressing violence against women. By so doing, the chapter provides interesting pointers on gaps in gender-based violence research which require attention.

Notes

1 IMAGE involves a combination of microfinance initiatives implemented by Small Enterprise Foundation (SEF), a training session on gender and HIV known as Sisters for Life (SfL) (Knight et al., 2020).

2 Microfinance is a development strategy targeting rural women to provide services such as credit for income-generating projects (Kim et al., 2007)

References

Abramsky, T., Devries, K., Kiss, L., Francisco, L., Nakuti, J., Musuya, T., . . . Michau, L. (2012). A community mobilisation intervention to prevent violence against women and reduce HIV/AIDS risk in Kampala, Uganda (the SASA! Study): Study protocol for a cluster randomised controlled trial. *Trials, 13*(1), 96.

Abramsky, T., Devries, K., Kiss, L., Nakuti, J., Kyegombe, N., Starmann, E., . . . Musuya, T. (2014). Findings from the SASA! Study: A cluster randomized controlled trial to assess the impact of a community mobilization intervention to prevent violence against women and reduce HIV risk in Kampala, Uganda. *BMC Medicine, 12*(1), 122.

Abramsky, T., Watts, C. H., Garcia-Moreno, C., Devries, K., Kiss, L., Ellsberg, M., . . . Heise, L. (2011). What factors are associated with recent intimate partner violence? Findings from the WHO multi-country study on women's health and domestic violence. *BMC Public Health, 11*(1), 109.

Andersson, N., Cockcroft, A., & Shea, B. (2008). Gender-based violence and HIV: Relevance for HIV prevention in hyperendemic countries of Southern Africa. *AIDS, 22*, S73–S86.

Barad, E., & Slattery, E. (2007). *Gender-based violence laws in sub-Saharan Africa*. Report prepared for the Committee on African Affairs of the New York City Bar.

Beninger, C. (2013). Combating sexual violence in schools in sub-Saharan Africa: Legal strategies under regional and international human rights law. *African Human Rights Law Journal, 13*(2), 281–301.

Bourey, C., Williams, W., Bernstein, E. E., & Stephenson, R. (2015). Systematic review of structural interventions for intimate partner violence in low-and middle-income countries: Organizing evidence for prevention. *BMC Public Health, 15*(1), 1165.

Casey, E., Carlson, J., Two Bulls, S., & Yager, A. (2018). Gender transformative approaches to engaging men in gender-based violence prevention: A review and conceptual model. *Trauma, Violence, & Abuse, 19*(2), 231–246.

Dery, I. (2015). Bride-price and domestic violence: Empirical perspectives from Nandom district in the north western region of Ghana. *International Journal of Development Sustainability, 4*(3), 258–271.

Dworkin, S. L., Hatcher, A. M., Colvin, C., & Peacock, D. (2013). Impact of a gender-transformative HIV and anti-violence program on gender ideologies and masculinities in two rural, South African communities. *Men and Masculinities, 16*(2), 181–202.

Fidan, A., & Bui, H. N. (2016). Intimate partner violence against women in Zimbabwe. *Violence Against Women, 22*(9), 1075–1096.

Flury, M., & Nyberg, E. (2010). Domestic violence against women: Definitions, epidemiology, risk factors and consequences. *Swiss Medical Weekly, 140*(3536).

Gibbs, A., Jacobson, J., & Kerr Wilson, A. (2017). A global comprehensive review of economic interventions to prevent intimate partner violence and HIV risk behaviours. *Global Health Action, 10*(Suppl. 2), 1290427.

Green, E. P., Blattman, C., Jamison, J., & Annan, J. (2015). Women's entrepreneurship and intimate partner violence: A cluster randomized trial of microenterprise assistance and partner participation in post-conflict Uganda (SSM-D-14–01580R1). *Social Science & Medicine, 133*, 177–188.

wHaffejee, S. (2006). *Waiting opportunities: Adolescent girls experiences of gender-based violence at schools*. Johannesburg: Centre for the Study of Violence and Reconciliation.

Inter-Agency Standing Committee. (2015). *Guidelines for integrating gender-based violence interventions in humanitarian action: Reducing risk, promoting resilience and aiding recovery*, pp. 1–340. Retrieved from https://gbvguidelines.org/wp/wp-content/uploads/2015/09/2015-IASC-Gender-based-Violence-Guidelines_lo-res.pdf

Jewkes, R., Gibbs, A., Jama-Shai, N., Willan, S., Misselhorn, A., Mushinga, M., . . . Skiweyiya, Y. (2014). Stepping Stones and Creating Futures intervention: Shortened interrupted time series evaluation of a behavioural and structural health promotion and violence prevention intervention for young people in informal settlements in Durban, South Africa. *BMC Public Health, 14*(1), 1325.

Kalichman, S. C., Simbayi, L. C., Cain, D., Cherry, C., Henda, N., & Cloete, A. (2007). Sexual assault, sexual risks and gender attitudes in a community sample of South African men. *AIDS Care, 19*(1), 20–27.

Kapiga, S., Harvey, S., Mshana, G., Hansen, C. H., Mtolela, G. J., Madaha, F., . . . Abramsky, T. (2019). A social empowerment intervention to prevent intimate partner violence against women in a microfinance scheme in Tanzania: Findings from the MAISHA cluster randomised controlled trial. *The Lancet Global Health*, 7(10), e1423–e1434.

Keller, J., Mboya, B. O., Sinclair, J., Githua, O. W., Mulinge, M., Bergholz, L., . . . Kapphahn, C. (2017). A 6-week school curriculum improves boys' attitudes and behaviors related to gender-based violence in Kenya. *Journal of Interpersonal Violence, 32*(4), 535–557.

Kennedy, C. E., Fonner, V. A., O'Reilly, K. R., & Sweat, M. D. (2014). A systematic review of income generation interventions, including microfinance and vocational skills training, for HIV prevention. *AIDS Care, 26*(6), 659–673.

Kim, J. C., Watts, C. H., Hargreaves, J. R., Ndhlovu, L. X., Phetla, G., Morison, L. A., . . . Pronyk, P. (2007). Understanding the impact of a microfinance-based intervention on women's empowerment and the reduction of intimate partner violence in South Africa. *American Journal of Public Health, 97*(10), 1794–1802.

Knight, L., Ranganathan, M., Abramsky, T., Polzer-Ngwato, T., Muvhango, L., Molebatsi, M., . . . Watts, C. (2020). Intervention with Microfinance for AIDS and Gender Equity (IMAGE): Women's engagement with the scaled-up IMAGE programme and experience of intimate partner violence in rural South Africa. *Prevention Science, 21*(2), 268–281.

Kyegombe, N., Abramsky, T., Devries, K. M., Starmann, E., Michau, L., Nakuti, J., . . . Watts, C. (2014). The impact of SASA! A community mobilization intervention, on reported HIV-related risk behaviours and relationship dynamics in Kampala, Uganda. *Journal of the International AIDS Society, 17*(1), 19232.

Magezi, V., & Manzanga, P. (2019). Gender-based violence and efforts to address the phenomenon: Towards a church public pastoral care intervention proposition for community development in Zimbabwe. *HTS Theological Studies, 75*(4), 1–9.

McCloskey, L. A., Boonzaier, F., Steinbrenner, S. Y., & Hunter, T. (2016). Determinants of intimate partner violence in sub-Saharan Africa: A review of prevention and intervention programs. *Partner Abuse*, 7(3), 277–315.

Mercy, O. A., & Nanji, U. C. (2014). National gender policy and sex-based violence against women in Nigeria. *Journal of Social Sciences and Public Affairs, 4*(1), 11–30.

Meskele, M., Khuzwayo, N., & Taylor, M. (2019). Intimate partner violence against women living with and without HIV, and the associated factors in Wolaita Zone, Southern Ethiopia: A comparative cross-sectional study. *PLoS One, 14*(8), e0220919.

Michau, L., Naker, D., & Sauve, S. (2003). *Mobilising communities to prevent domestic violence: A resource guide for organisations in East and Southern Africa*. Kampala: Raising Voices.

Modiba, N. S. (2018). Managing gender-based violence and harassment in African schools to enable performance of all genders. *Journal of Gender, Information and Development in Africa (JGIDA)*, 7(2), 185–203.

Mpani, P., & Nsibande, N. (2015). *Understanding gender policy and gender-based violence in South Africa: A literature review*. Johannesburg: Institute for Health and Development Communication.

Mukanangana, F., Moyo, S., Zvoushe, A., & Rusinga, O. (2014). Gender based violence and its effects on women's reproductive Health: The case of Hatcliffe, Harare, Zimbabwe. *African Journal of Reproductive Health, 18*(1), 110–122.

Oladimeji, O. K., & Osunkunle, O. (2020). Media channels and their potency in portraying gender based violence against women among Uitenhage Residents in the Eastern Cape Province of South Africa. *AFFRIKA Journal of Politics, Economics and Society, 10*(1), 143–164.

Paine, K., Hart, G., Jawo, M., Ceesay, S., Jallow, M., Morison, L., . . . Shaw, M. (2002). 'Before we were sleeping, now we are awake': Preliminary evaluation of the Stepping Stones sexual health programme in The Gambia. *African Journal of AIDS Research, 1*(1), 39–50.

Peacock, D., Khumalo, B., & McNab, E. (2006). Men and gender activism in South Africa: Observations, critique and recommendations for the future. *Agenda, 20*(69), 71–81.

Peacock, D., & Levack, A. (2004). The men as partners program in South Africa: Reaching men to end gender-based violence and promote sexual and reproductive health. *International Journal of Men's Health, 3*(3), 173–188.

Phorano, O., Nthomang, K., & Ntseane, D. (2005). Alcohol abuse, gender-based violence and HIV/AIDS in Botswana: Establishing the link based on empirical evidence. *SAHARA-J: Journal of Social Aspects of HIV/AIDS, 2*(1), 188–202.

Prinsloo, S. (2006). Sexual harassment and violence in South African schools. *South African Journal of Education, 26*(2), 305–318.

Pronyk, P. M., Hargreaves, J. R., Kim, J. C., Morison, L. A., Phetla, G., Watts, C., . . . Porter, J. D. (2006). Effect of a structural intervention for the prevention of intimate-partner violence and HIV in rural South Africa: A cluster randomised trial. *The Lancet, 368*(9551), 1973–1983.

Pronyk, P. M., Kim, J. C., Abramsky, T., Phetla, G., Hargreaves, J. R., Morison, L. A., . . . Porter, J. D. (2008). A combined microfinance and training intervention can reduce HIV risk behaviour in young female participants. *AIDS, 22*(13), 1659–1665.

Rani, M., Bonu, S., & Diop-Sidibe, N. (2004). An empirical investigation of attitudes towards wife-beating among men and women in seven sub-Saharan African countries. *African Journal of Reproductive Health*, 116–136.

Scorgie, F., Baron, D., Stadler, J., Venables, E., Brahmbhatt, H., Mmari, K., & Delany-Moretlwe, S. (2017). From fear to resilience: Adolescents' experiences of violence in inner-city Johannesburg, South Africa. *BMC Public Health, 17*(3), 51–64.

Shamu, S., Abrahams, N., Temmerman, M., & Zarowsky, C. (2013). Opportunities and obstacles to screening pregnant women for intimate partner violence during antenatal care in Zimbabwe. *Culture, Health & Sexuality, 15*(5), 511–524.

Sida. (2015). *Preventing and responding to gender-based violence: Expressions and strategies*, pp. 1–24. Retrieved from www.sida.se/contentassets/3a820dbd152f4fca98bacde8a8101e15/preventing-and-responding-to-gender-based-violence.pdf

Sithole, Z., Gombe, N. T., Juru, T., Chonzi, P., Shambira, G., Nsubuga, P., & Tshimanga, M. (2018). Evaluation of sexual and gender-based violence program in Harare City, Zimbabwe, 2016: A descriptive cross-sectional study. *The Pan African Medical Journal, 31*.

Strebel, A., Crawford, M., Shefer, T., Cloete, A., Henda, N., Kaufman, M., . . . Kalichman, S. (2006). Social constructions of gender roles, gender-based violence and HIV/AIDS in two communities of the Western Cape, South Africa. *SAHARA-J: Journal of Social Aspects of HIV/AIDS, 3*(3), 516–528.

Tsai, A. C., Leiter, K., Heisler, M., Iacopino, V., Wolfe, W., Shannon, K., . . . Weiser, S. D. (2011). Prevalence and correlates of forced sex perpetration and victimization in Botswana and Swaziland. *American Journal of Public Health, 101*(6), 1068–1074.

Umubyeyi, A., Persson, M., Mogren, I., & Krantz, G. (2016). Gender inequality prevents abused women from seeking care despite protection given in gender-based violence legislation: A qualitative study from Rwanda. *PLoS One, 11*(5), e0154540.

UNICEF. (2010). *Handbook for coordinating gender-based violence interventions in humanitarian settings*, pp. 1–348. Retrieved from www.unicef.org/protection/files/GBV_Handbook_Long_Version.pdf

United Nations. (1993). *The United Nations Declaration on the elimination violence against women*, pp. 1–7. Retrieved from www.refworld.org/docid/3b00f25d2c.html

UN Women. (2020). *Gender-based violence in Nigeria during the COVID-19 crisis: The shadow pandemic*, pp. 1–17. Retrieved from https://nigeria.un.org/sites/default/files/2020-05/Gender%20Based%20Violence%20in%20Nigeria%20During%20COVID%2019%20Crisis_The%20Shadow%20Pandemic.pdf

Wagman, J. A., Gray, R. H., Campbell, J. C., Thoma, M., Ndyanabo, A., Ssekasanvu, J., . . . Serwadda, D. (2015). Effectiveness of an integrated intimate partner violence and HIV prevention intervention in Rakai, Uganda: Analysis of an intervention in an existing cluster randomised cohort. *The Lancet Global Health, 3*(1), e23–e33.

Wekwete, N. N., Sanhokwe, H., Murenjekwa, W., Takavarasha, F., & Madzingira, N. (2014). The association between spousal gender based violence and women's empowerment among currently married women aged 15–49 in Zimbabwe: Evidence from the 2010–11 Zimbabwe Demographic and Health Survey. *African Population Studies, 28*(3), 1413–1431.

WHO. (2002). *World report on violence and health*. Retrieved from www.who.int/violence_injury_prevention/violence/world_report/en/summary_en.pdf

WHO. (2009). *Promoting gender equality to prevent violence against women*. Retrieved from www.who.int/violence_injury_prevention/violence/gender.pdf

PART 5

Environment, health and demography

20

THE DISASTER–FERTILITY NEXUS IN SUB-SAHARAN AFRICAN COUNTRIES

Khandaker Jafor Ahmed and Yan Tan

Introduction

Natural disasters are devastating events triggered by natural hazards, whose origins may be internal (below the Earth's surface), external (topographic), weather related (meteorological, hydrological), or biological. Typically beyond human control, such disasters include earthquakes, tidal waves and tsunamis, volcanic eruptions, landslides, avalanches, windstorms (cyclones, typhoons, hurricanes, tornadoes), floods, and droughts. Human-made or anthropogenic disasters are catastrophic events that result from human action or inaction. Like natural disasters, these can be sudden and acute or slow and prolonged in their effects. Some examples are explosions or bombings, pollution events, wars, and some wildfires. The economic, agricultural, and healthcare sectors are seriously disrupted by natural and human-made disasters alike. Both can have lasting consequences that perpetuate underdevelopment (Shaluf, 2007).

From 1999 to 2018, as we see from the Global Climate Risk Index (CRI) for 2020, the world experienced more than 12,000 extreme weather events, resulting in the death of over 495,000 people and economic losses totalling USD 3.54 trillion (Eckstein, Künzel, Schäfer, & Winges, 2020). Natural disasters have increased dramatically over the last 30 years (Figure 20.1), with a concentration in Asia. Floods and storms are the top categories. The total of 335 natural disasters recorded in 2017 included 126 floods and 127 storms (CRED, 2018), bringing significant changes in population dynamics (mortality, migration, and fertility) (Jiang & Hardee, 2011).

The world's nations are at different stages of demographic transition. Fertility is one of the most important mechanisms by which the transition takes place. Total fertility rate (TFR) is the average number of children that would be born alive to a woman (or group of women) during her lifetime if she were to pass through her childbearing years, conforming to the age-specific fertility rates of a given year. As the standardised fertility measure most commonly used, TFR is ideal for comparative purposes. It is a comprehensive summary measure that is readily understood, at least in general intuitive terms. The decline in fertility started in the late 19th century in Europe and South America, then spread to North America in the early 20th century. Asia underwent a similar transition in the 1950s and 1960s, but the change began slowly and fitfully in Africa, as late as the 1970s and 1980s (Reher, 2004). Since 1950, the global TFR has exhibited a remarkable decline due to demographic transitions in many

 DOI: 10.4324/9780429287213-25

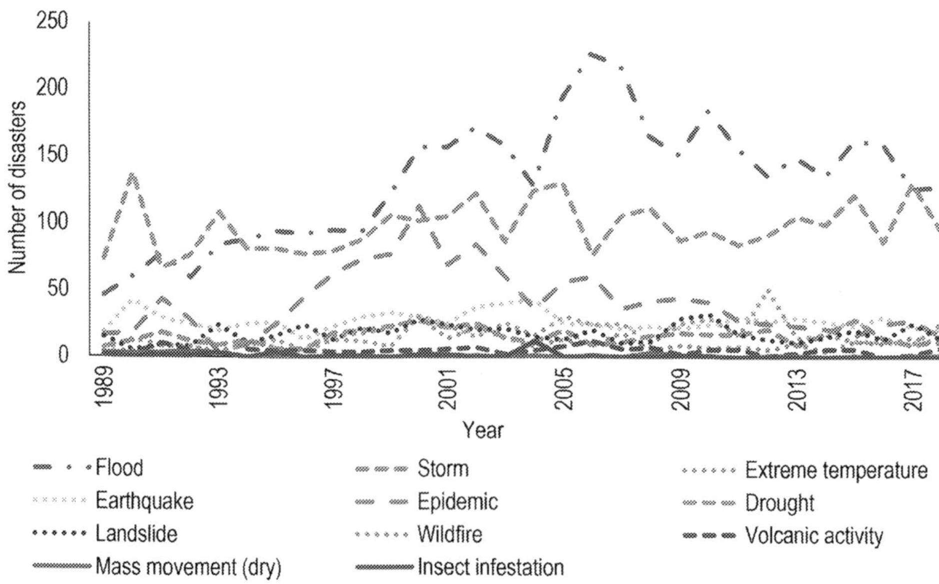

Figure 20.1 Global trends in disasters by type, 1989–2018

developed and some developing countries. The rate has roughly halved, from 5.5 in 1950 to 2.49 in 2015 (Roser, 2021). Figure 20.2 maps the distribution of TFRs by country in 2015. It shows that 80% of the world's population is distributed in countries with TFRs less than three children per woman. Strikingly, many countries, mainly concentrated in the sub-Saharan Africa (SSA) region, still have TFRs over five. These include Niger (7.29), Democratic Republic of Congo (6.2), Mali (6.15), Chad (6.05), Angola (5.77), Nigeria (5.59), and Zambia (5.04) (Roser, 2021). The pace of fertility decline in SSA countries is much slower than anywhere else (Shapiro & Hinde, 2017).

Increasingly frequent and intense natural disasters have had significant impacts on human settlements and population dynamics over the last seven decades. Some studies find negative associations between fertility and natural disasters (Hamamatsu, Inoue, Watanabe, & Umezaki, 2014; Lin, 2010), while other studies find an increase in fertility (Davis, 2017; Nobles, Frankenberg, & Thomas, 2015). Delineating the intricate relationship between natural disasters and human fertility is a necessary phase in the under-researched field of environment–population relations (Xiao & Hong, 2010). To understand human vulnerability to disasters at the household level, and to design effective climate adaptation and mitigation strategies, it is essential to take into account fertility rates in areas susceptible to climate extremes and variations (Jiang & Hardee, 2011).

In recent years, Africa has endured an increasing share of global disasters, reflected in the number of people affected and the number of fatalities. This is expected to continue because of the continent's growing share of the world's population: from 13% in 2000 to a projected 20% in 2050. High population growth increases the likelihood of urban growth in regions prone to environmental disasters and resource scarcity. As a result of climate change, SSA has undergone frequent and intense extreme temperatures. Regions across the African continent are expected to endure more extreme temperatures, droughts, and heavy rainfall. The demographic transition in SSA countries, expected on the basis of experience in other regions, is remarkably protracted.

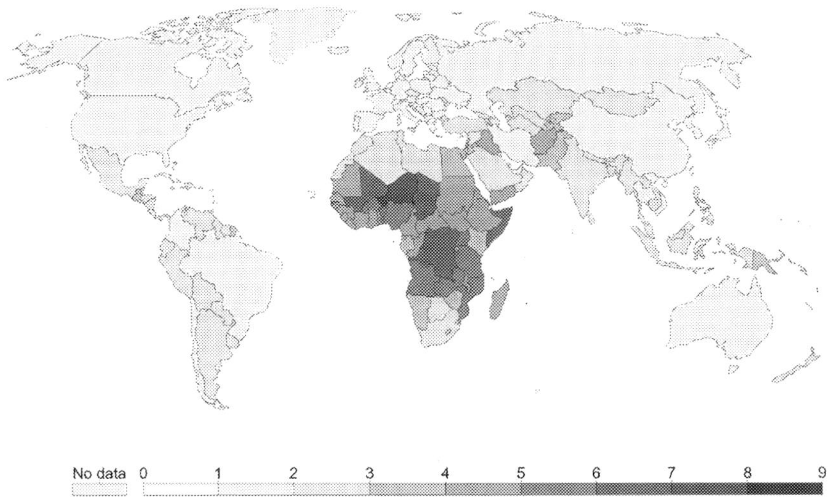

Figure 20.2 Total fertility rates (TFRs; children per woman) by country, 2015

Our aim here is to understand how different disasters influence fertility trends in these distressed polities. We review literature sourced from relevant databases including Web of Science, Scopus, CINAHL, and PubMed. Only peer-reviewed journal articles written in English were included in this analysis, and searches included *fertility terms* (fertility, fertility rate, birth, birth rate), *climate change terms* (climate, temperature, precipitation), and *disaster terms* (earthquake, hurricane, storm, tsunami, famine, flood, drought, war, bombing, pandemic, epidemic, disease). We use *total fertility rate* data curated by the World Bank (2020), and the *disaster records* for SSA countries are sourced from the Centre for Research on Epidemiology of Disasters (CRED) (2020).

Disasters in sub-Saharan Africa

Frequent droughts affect the regions of Southern Africa, the Horn of Africa, and the Sahel (a broad geographical transition between the Sahara to the north and savannah country to the south, stretching from the Red Sea to the Atlantic). By contrast, a vast area of Central and Western Africa experiences flooding, while countries in the southeast face cyclones and storms every year (CRED, 2019). The events of different disasters have increased substantially across 48 SSA countries over the last six decades (Figure 20.3). Disasters did not increase substantially in SSA before 1995 but have risen dramatically since then.

The International Disaster Database (EM-DAT) uses five broad categories: meteorological, climatological, hydrological, geophysical, and biological disasters. EM-DAT data (publicly available) shows that floods and epidemic events are the top two disaster types across SSA, followed by droughts and storms (Table 20.1). SSA countries experienced 243 storms, 280 droughts, 28 wildfires, 53 landslides, and 40 earthquakes over the period 1950–2019.

Fertility levels and trends in SSA countries

Although there had been significant fertility declines in developing areas such as Northern Africa, Asia, and Latin America before the 1980s, fertility decline in SSA began much later

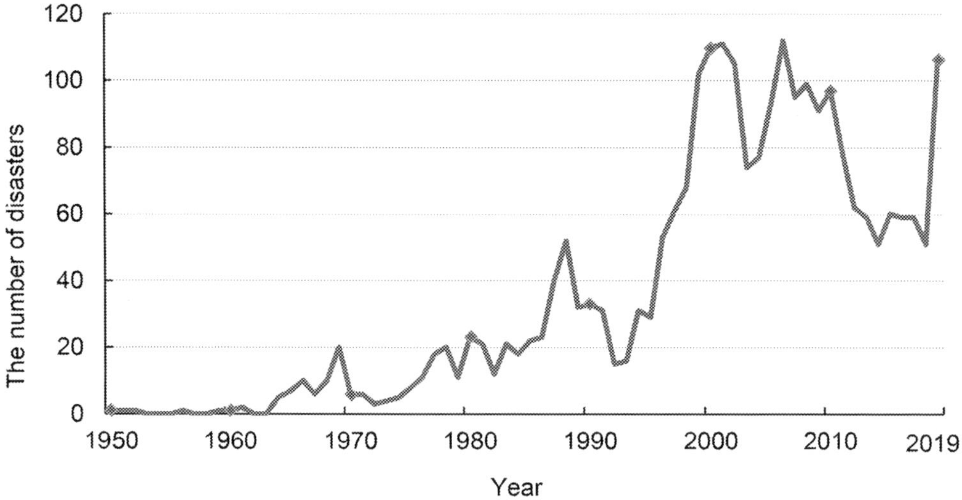

Figure 20.3 The trend of disasters in 48 sub-Saharan African countries, 1950–2019

Table 20.1 Natural Disasters in 48 Sub-Saharan African Countries, 1950–2019

Disaster Category	*Disaster Type*	*Frequency*
Meteorological	*Storm*	*243*
	Extreme temperature	*7*
Climatological	*Drought*	*280*
	Wildfire	*28*
Hydrological	*Flood*	*941*
	Landslide	*53*
Geophysical	*Earthquake*	*40*
	Mass movement	*2*
	Volcanic activity	*16*
Biological	*Animal accident*	*1*
	Epidemic	*852*
	Insect infestation	*65*

Source: Data source: CRED (2020)

and at a much slower pace (Bongaarts, 2017). Figure 20.4 shows TFR trends from 1960 to 2017 across four aggregations: SSA, East Asia and the Pacific, Europe and Central Asia, and Latin America and the Caribbean. In the early 1960s, birth levels in these four regions were persistently high. The average TFR in Africa (around 6.5) was substantially higher than in other regions (less than 3 in East Asia and the Pacific). Fertility declines began in the mid-1960s across all regions except SSA. The fertility trends in all areas, again except SSA, have since continued along similar pathways.

Fertility transition in SSA began at the end of the 1980s with an average TFR of 5.1, reducing to about half that in 2005–2010. Figure 20.4 indicates that recent declines in SSA fertility levels are slower than the 1970s rates for East Asia, Latin America, and Europe. Asia and Latin

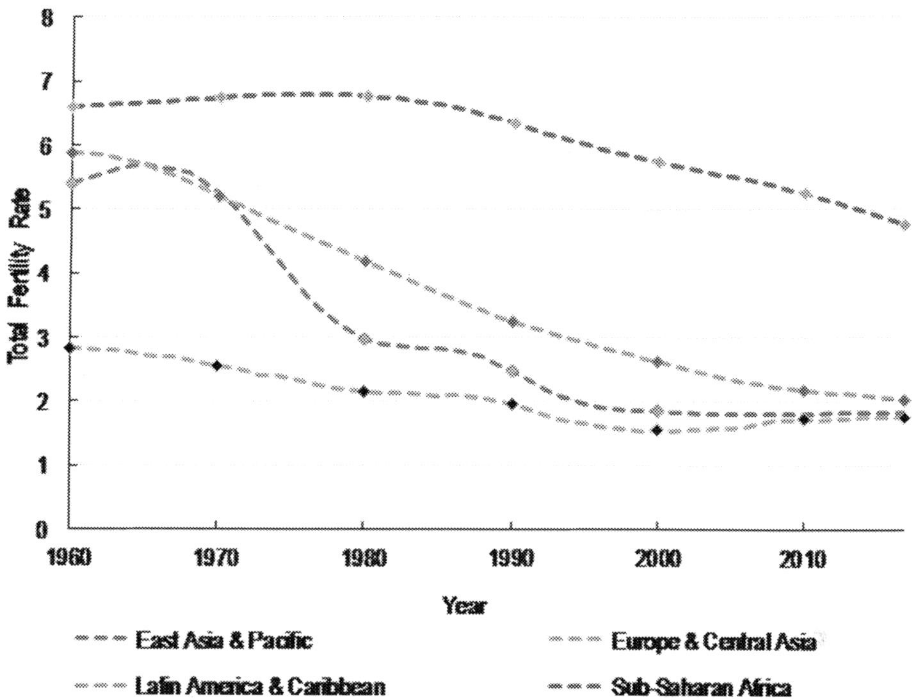

Figure 20.4 Regional trends in TFRs, 1960–2017

America had the same rates in their 1970s, early-to-middle stages of their transition. Bongaarts and Casterline (2013) analysed fertility levels and trends in Africa, Asia, and Latin America, finding that the present overall fertility rate in Africa is higher than in other regions and that SSA fertility changes differ in trajectory also. In sum, future trends in sub-Saharan fertility are proving hard to predict from present and past data (Mbacké, 2017).

While the expected fertility transition is now underway in most SSA countries, several countries still have high fertility rates. Figure 20.5 shows different trends of change in fertility rates in 48 selected SSA countries from 1960 to 2018. For example, in 2017 only two (Botswana and Cape Verde) of these selected countries had TFRs less than 3, with a similar trend of decline between 1960 and 2018, and only Mauritius, in SSA, had a TFR below the effective replacement level, at 2.1 (Figure 20.5a). There are also seven countries with TFR between 3.00 and 3.99 in 2017. TFRs of these countries, except Seychelles, halved between 1960 and 2018. In 1960, the TFRs of these countries were between 6 and 8 and declined to below 4 in 2018. As an exception, the Seychelles TFR increased from 2.1 in 1997 (there were missing records of TFR before 1997) to 3.44 in 2018 (Figure 20.5b). Figure 20.5c reveals exceptional fertility trends in 11 SSA countries: there were persistent stalls in TFR decline, and rates started a belated decline after the 2000s. Of these, three countries (the Democratic Republic of Congo, Niger, and Somalia) had TFRs over 6, and eight countries (e.g., Angola, Burundi, Burkina Faso, Gambia, Mali, Nigeria, Chad, and Uganda) had TFRs ranging between 5 and 6 (Figure 20.5c). Over half of SSA countries had TFRs of 4 to 5 (Figure 20.5d).

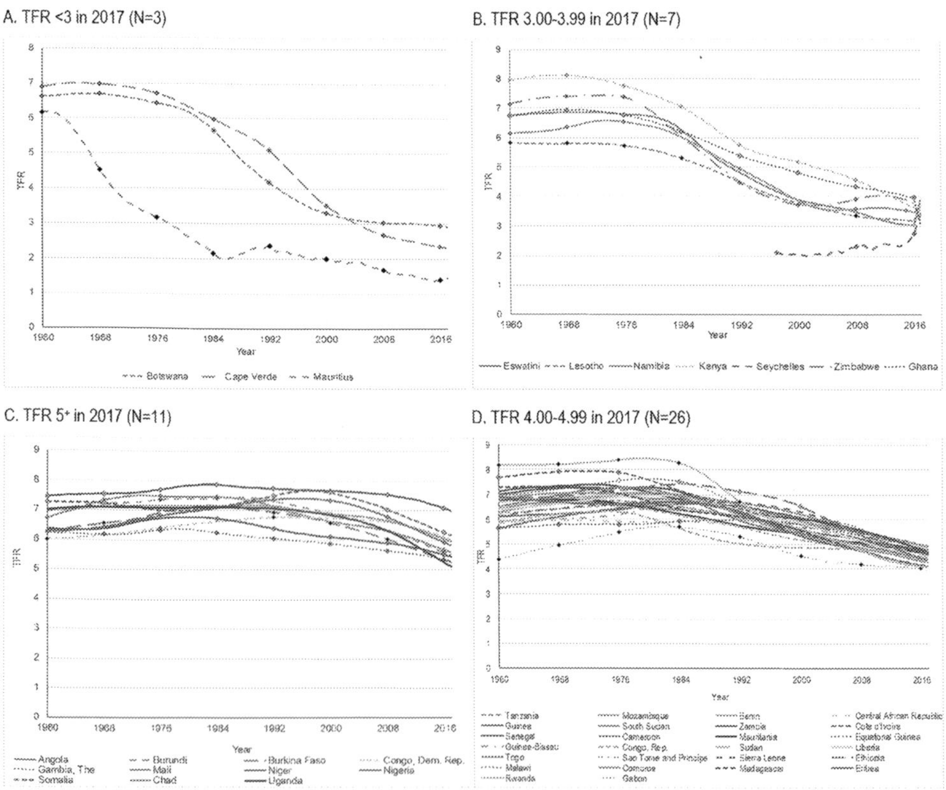

Figure 20.5 TFR trends for sub-Saharan African countries, 1960–2018

Research into disasters and fertility in the context of sub-Saharan Africa

Here we synthesise the literature on how different disasters influence fertility trends in SSA countries. The literature discussed here engages mostly with war, famine, pandemic, and extreme climatic events in Ethiopia, Angola, Eritrea, Malawi, Mali, Nigeria, Zimbabwe, Madagascar, Senegal, Kenya, Uganda, Lesotho, Burkina Faso, Guinea, Rwanda, Zambia, Sierra Leone, and Liberia. Most of the discussion of disasters and fertility is centred on epidemics or pandemics.

Despite generally higher TFRs in Angola and Ethiopia, studies show a decline in TFR during or after the war in Angola and the drought and famine in Ethiopia. For example, in 2017, the TFR was 5.6 for Angola and 4.35 for Ethiopia. Interestingly, disasters affected TFR in unaffected areas also. The study in Angola (Agadjanian & Prata, 2002) observed fertility decline during the 1992–1994 civil war and a subsequent rebounding after its conclusion. Their findings reveal variations in fertility between areas heavily affected and less affected by the war. Regarding fertility preference, women living in heavily affected areas were significantly less likely to want a pregnancy in the 12 months following the war than their counterparts in the less-affected areas. Socioeconomic factors shaped fertility responses to war regardless of the degree to which an area was affected. Women who were more educated and more affluent (typically less exposed to poverty) were more able to regulate their fertility. Worse experience of the war, more intrusively negative memories, and heightened anticipation of future wars were important reasons for interrupted reproduction in Angola (Agadjanian & Prata, 2002). In Ethiopia, fertility also responded to drought, famine, and transitions in economic and political conditions. For example, a decrease in conception probability was evident in the drought and famine of the 1970s. Coincidently, couples residing beyond the conflict- or drought-hit areas were also impacted by such developments (Lindstrom & Berhanu, 1999).

As a consequence of the 1998–2001 border conflicts with Ethiopia, both labour migration and displacement illustrated the decline in Eritrea's fertility from 1995 (TFR at 6.1) to 2002 (TFR at 4.8). While the decline aligned with a period of delayed marriages, it was significantly affected by the capacity of women and their husbands to stay together. There was no significant change in the rate of contraceptive use between 1995 and 2002. Data from the Demographic and Health Survey (DHS) in 1995 and 2002 showed that around 60% of married women lived with their husband in 1995, but this figure dropped to around 30% in 2002. Due to border conflicts in 1998–2001, substantial mobilisation took place; 55% of women surveyed in 2002 reported their husband's occupation as a military servant, up from 9% in 1995 (Blanc, 2004).

SSA countries are vulnerable to climate extremes. Recent research on SSA demonstrates an adverse impact on TFR in some countries. An investigation across 18 SSA countries provided insights into the short- and long-term effects of climate change on fertility. Eissler, Thiede, and Strube (2019) observed that varying temperatures, regardless of the time range, have detrimental effects on fertility, as do fluctuations in annual precipitation. By way of example, for every one-unit increase in temperature (a unit corresponding to one standard deviation) over 12 months or 60 months, the reported ideal family size would reduce by 0.042 children and 0.101 children, respectively. Similarly, for every one-unit increase in precipitation over a short period, women's preference for an ideal family size would decrease by 0.052 children, while over a long period, the decrease would be 0.059 children. The same study also identified spatial differences in fertility responses to climate impact. In West Africa, women's fertility goals are highly related to precipitation patterns, while in East and Southern Africa, fertility goals are affected mainly by rising temperature. The researchers called for future study to address potential moderating functions of the agro-ecological and socio-cultural contexts when analysing fertility responses to climate variability.

Another recent study by Davenport et al. (2020) in 15 SSA nations suggested that an increase in the number of days above 40 degrees Celsius, in some cases above 35 degrees Celsius, would increase spontaneous abortions and also the risk of unsafe births. They estimated that if the percentage of days between 35 and 37 degrees Celsius increases by 10%, the birth weight would reduce substantially: by 1.9%. The probability of a healthy birth weight would drop by 2.5% for every 10% increase in the number of days between 37 and 40 degrees Celsius. The probability of a healthy birth weight would decline by 4.4% for every 10% increase in the number of days hotter than 40 degrees Celsius.

Philibert, Tourigny, Coulibaly, and Fournier (2013) examined how birth seasonality responds to a changing climate in Mali's rural areas. Their findings showed that the childbirth rate in a health facility attended by a skilled birth attendant was high at the end of the dry season, April–June. Nevertheless, the rate fell rapidly in the first half of the rainy season in July, rose again during the later part of the rainy season in August–October, and fell to its lowest level after the rainy season. The birth rate pattern in Mali exhibited two peaks. The major spike happens in September–October (the second half of the rainy season), corresponding to a high conception rate nine months before in December–January. The secondary spike in the delivery rate in May–June (dry season) corresponds to a high conception rate nine months before, in August–September.

In the major spike, the excess in deliveries ranged from 5.5% to 6.5%, and in the secondary peak from 1.5% to 3.5%. Between these peaks, there was an abrupt trough in July.

However, the bulk of the disaster–fertility research in SSA countries has concerned epidemics or pandemics – and primarily HIV/AIDS. Heuveline (1997) shows that fertility decline is associated with the AIDS pandemic in SSA. The author distinguished that pandemic's impact on fertility among infected women and the general population. With an average infection rate of 30% for women of reproductive age, a 10% decrease in the infected women's fertility rates leads to a 3% decrease in fertility overall. Heuveline (1997) articulated the pandemic's indirect effects on fertility decline, surveying some more proximate determinants. First, the length of exposure to the risk of becoming pregnant could be affected by the salience of the AIDS pandemic. The couple may decrease sexual intercourse voluntarily if either partner is infected, or the death of one of them may mean that the partnership is in fact dissolved. Second, fertility may increase as a result of a child's death: then breast-feeding stops, and pregnancy becomes possible once again. However, the decreased fecundity may be a consequence of HIV infection itself. Third, in a crisis situation, the couple may turn away from their customs and traditional religious values and prefer longer birth intervals. Fourth and last, the decline in fertility may result from increased use of birth control measures, some of which overlap with measures against infection with HIV.

Hunter et al. (2003) examined the association between HIV and fertility of women in a rural area of Tanzania. They observed a substantial reduction in the fertility of infected compared to uninfected women. Data from two different surveys show that for women infected (or of unknown status) in the first round but infected in the second round the *age-specific fertility rate* (ASFR) was half in the second round compared to the ASFR for those who were uninfected in both rounds. However, among women of 15–19 years, the ASFR was higher for those who were HIV positive than for those who were HIV negative. The effect of duration of HIV infection on fertility was noteworthy, decreasing modestly over time. Though modern contraceptive use was higher among HIV positive women, there was a reduction in fertility regardless of contraceptive use. The authors attributed this reduction to behavioural and biological causes: behavioural causes, because HIV-positive women may have infrequent sexual intercourse or none at all or are more likely to use methods to avoid the risk of infection and therefore of conception also, and biological causes, because fecundity may be diminished as a consequence of HIV infection itself.

Daniel (2000) also found a decline in fertility in response to the HIV/AIDS epidemic and infers that associated behavioural and biological changes have a far-reaching impact on fertility trends in SSA. Of the behavioural changes, lower coital frequency and greater use of condoms are likely to reduce fertility. Of the biological changes, increased mortality of people in their reproductive ages and increased morbidity lower both opportunities for conception and fertility levels.

Terceira, Gregson, Zaba, and Mason (2003) examined the role of HIV/AIDS in fertility decline for a rural area of Zimbabwe. They compared fertility rates between HIV-positive and uninfected women and observed lower fertility among HIV-positive women. Moreover, the age-specific fertility rates and total fertility rate for sexually experienced women were consistently lower among HIV-infected women. The observed lower fertility and the reduced chance of pregnancy among HIV-infected women are characterised by older age, living in more developed areas, widowhood, non-use of contraceptives, reported lower coital frequency, more sexual partners, and no history of STD infection (as genital discharge). The researchers identified mechanisms of the lower fertility of HIV-infected women of different stages in Zimbabwe. They hypothesised that widowhood, divorce, reduced coital frequency and contraceptive use, amenorrhoea, miscarriage, and pelvic inflammatory disease could lower the fertility and pregnancy rates of HIV-positive women. Increased amenorrhoea has a greater effect on the reduction of fertility in advanced stages of infection. Miscarriage among both HIV-positive and non-infected women was not substantial. Pelvic inflammatory disorder has an adverse effect on women infected with symptomatic HIV. Modern contraceptives were less likely to be used by infected women because they decrease their coital frequency or experience increased amenorrhoea.

Castro, Behrman, Kohler, and Warren (2015) examined how HIV risk perception influences women's fertility intention. They found a negative association between women's perceived risk of HIV and their intention to have a child in the next two years. Their findings revealed a 25% reduction in the likelihood of giving birth in the two years when the HIV risk perception shifts from 'low' to 'high'. However, a study by Karlsson and Pichler (2015) in SSA did not find any association between HIV pandemic and fertility. They examined the effects of the HIV epidemic on life expectancy, mortality, and fertility in three sub-Saharan African countries – Mozambique, South Africa, and Zimbabwe. They demonstrated a shred of consistent and robust evidence for Zimbabwe and South Africa: the pandemic led to a substantial adverse effect on life expectancy and correspondingly positive impact on mortality rates. However, they found no evidence of change in fertility patterns caused by the pandemic.

Such studies reveal a decline in fertility in SSA countries. However, they are contradicted by a recent study by Chin and Wilson (2018). These researchers examined how and whether fertility responds to the HIV/AIDS pandemic in 14 SSA countries: Burkina Faso, Cameroon, Ethiopia, Ghana, Guinea, Kenya, Lesotho, Malawi, Mali, Senegal, Sierra Leone, Swaziland, Zambia, and Zimbabwe. They concluded that a doubling of HIV prevalence increased TFR by 1.37 and increased the number of surviving children by 0.38 children. Moreover, the effects were heterogeneous across ages: fertility responded more in these ways among women of older reproductive age than among younger women.

The associated effects of antiretroviral therapy (hereafter ART) for reducing morbidity and mortality can reverse some downward trends in the fertility of HIV-infected women in SSA. As ART is becoming increasingly accessible in SSA, improvements in health, quality of life, and survival are likely to influence both the biological and behavioural fertility determinants of infected women. Consequently, both fertility intentions and sexual activity may increase after ART initiation. Examining 49 DHS data of 27 SSA countries, Marston, Zaba, and Eaton (2017) revealed that the fertility differences between HIV-positive and HIV-negative women slightly reduced with increased ART coverage. For example, in urban Southern Africa, for women aged 30–34, the fertility ratio increased from 0.70 with <20% national ART coverage to 0.76 with 50% ART coverage. Another study in Tanzania reported a difference among women who initiated ART compared to those who did not. For example, the fertility rate among Tanzanian women living with HIV on ART was higher (by 50%) than women living with HIV without ART (Mbita, Renju, Lija, Conserve, & Todd, 2019). Myer et al. (2010) observed an increase in women's pregnancy rate across seven SSA countries who were married or cohabited and those who had a male partner enrolled in the program, and most male partners were receiving ART.

Discussion

Fewer studies of fertility responses to natural and human-made disasters have been conducted in SSA than elsewhere. Studies have primarily been undertaken by scholars from the United States, where most of the funding agencies are located. Recent research linking climate variability with fertility changes in SSA calls for further investigations. Population research has mostly concentrated on the consequences of impeding population growth, identifying social, cultural, and political obstacles to fertility decline (Issaka & Guengant, 2017; May, 2017). The principal emphasis has been on the total fertility rate and its proximate determinants, such as early marriage; the infrequency of contraceptive use; and women's general low status in terms of schooling, employment, and other indicators (Hertrich, 2017). The fertility trajectory in SSA is of great concern because it has influenced the demographics and impeded economic growth in the region for decades (Bongaarts & O'Neill, 2018). Moreover, decreases in fertility in this region have stalled over recent years (Schoumaker, 2019). Persistent population growth is assumed to be correlated with poverty and climate-related vulnerability (Schmidhuber & Tubiello, 2007). We now turn to considering how different types of disasters affect fertility changes in SSA, including examples of other countries for a comparison and a better understanding.

HIV/AIDS is one of the most deadly infectious diseases in the world – especially in SSA, where the disease has had a significant effect on health outcomes and life expectancy in recent decades. There is an exceptionally high death rate in some SSA countries. In 2017, HIV/AIDS caused more than one in four (28%) of deaths in South Africa and Botswana. Mozambique's share (24%) was also very high, as were the rates in Namibia (23%), Zambia (18%), Kenya (17%), and the Congo (15%) (Roser & Ritchie, 2018). HIV/AIDS pandemic and fertility-related studies conducted in SSA and published at the beginning of the 21st century reveal that fertility declined in response to the pandemic (Hunter et al., 2003; Daniel, 2000; Terceira et al., 2003). However, as we have seen, one recent investigation in 14 SSA countries found that TFR and the number of surviving children both grew despite increasing HIV prevalence (Chin & Wilson, 2018).

The slowing pace of fertility decline and the recent demographic transition in SSA could be attributable mostly to the impact of several pandemics (as well as other natural disasters). The incidence and the severity of different diseases and pandemics are still high in SSA. With poor health systems, people in SSA predictably suffer more than people elsewhere. From the pandemic–fertility literature, we can draw implications for SSA countries concerning the effects of COVID-19 on fertility. At the time of writing, the world community already feels momentous impacts from this pandemic on demographic dynamics: mortality, migration, and fertility. Increased fertility rates have been reported in the short and long term (Anser et al., 2020), but we might reasonably expect effects on both fertility and healthy birth rates to be heterogeneous and mutually antagonistic. Spikes in morbidity and mortality due to the pandemic may reduce birth rates in the short term, but on the other hand, rates of sexual activity (and fertility) may for various reasons increase or decrease at various stages. Birth rates may increase following the pandemic, as happened with other disasters such as war, flood, drought, and earthquake. Moreover, economic and social change triggered by a pandemic is likely to influence both fertility intentions and fertility rates. Aassve, Cavalli, Mencarini, Plach, and Bacci (2020, p. 370) sum it up well: "The unfolding effect of the COVID-19 pandemic on fertility will depend on the ways in which societies have developed and at what stage they are in the demographic transition, from regimes characterised by high birth rates and lack of contraception, to controlled and low fertility."

Though the countries of Africa were not well prepared, given that they lack available resources and public health infrastructure to fight against the COVID-19 pandemic, their response to the pandemic has been marked by resilience and innovation (Ihekweazu & Agogo, 2020). Effects of the COVID-19 pandemic on fertility changes in SSA ultimately call for more definitive investigation in the future, when more complete and more concrete evidence is reliably available. Acknowledging the effects of other pandemics and disasters, we need to pay particular attention to the COVID-19 impacts on fertility changes in SSA, both in the short and long run. Future research can be designed for further understanding the nexus between pandemics, disaster, and fertility in SSA.

Human-made disasters such as war or terrorist bombings are found to affect the fertility rate in SSA and other regions. War-related studies in SSA (such as in Angola and Eritrea) revealed falling fertility rates after the conflicts (Agadjanian & Prata, 2002; Blanc, 2004). This finding is consistent with a similar study conducted in a sub-district (Matlab Bazar thana) of Bangladesh stressing the effect of the 1971 civil war on fertility. The researchers (Curlin, Chen, & Hussain, 1976) attributed the disruption of marriage during the war to a decline in fertility, but findings in other contexts are different from those in SSA. For example, birth rates increased after the Oklahoma City bombing in the United States in 1995. Following the bombing of 1995, births in all counties of the Oklahoma metropolitan area increased by 3.9, 15.1, 22.4, and 22.8 in 1996, 1997, 1998, and 1999 respectively (Rodgers, John, & Coleman, 2005). Similarly, there was a positive reproductive response to a civil war from 1975 to 1978 in the time of Cambodia's Khmer Rouge or "KR" regime. In that time, the TFR declined to 3.7, which was 29% lower than that before the war. But after the war, in 1979–1980, there was a dramatic spike in TFR to over 7. The higher TFR after the fall of the KR regime was attributed to behavioural change, especially a marriage boom and high marital fertility (Heuveline & Poch, 2007).

War-induced changes in socio-demographic factors and migration patterns influenced the fertility behaviour of reproductive women in SSA countries' studied areas. In Angola, the effect of war on fertility was more pronounced in areas heavily impacted than in areas less impacted, and women who were more educated and more affluent were more able to regulate their fertility (Agadjanian & Prata, 2002). In Eritrea, couples' separation – through a temporary migration of husbands working as military – explained fertility decline (Blanc, 2004). Similarly, outside SSA, in Tajikistan, spousal separation during the war of 1992–1997 was reckoned as a pivotal contributor to declining fertility (Clifford, Falkingham, & Hinde, 2010).

Frequent droughts impact the Southern African, Horn of Africa and the Sahel regions. The severe drought in Somalia in 2010 caused the death of around 20,000 people, accounting for the majority of such deaths in the region. This drought, along with the Somali Civil War, led to a famine declaration due to high mortality and malnutrition (CRED, 2019). Fertility in SSA responds to drought and famine. In the months of severe food shortages in Ethiopia in the 1970s, a decline in pregnancy rates was apparent. Such events have also affected couples living outside war- or drought-hit regions. The separation of couples was a primary factor of fertility decline (Lindstrom & Berhanu, 1999). Similar findings of research conducted in Bangladesh, Finland, and Tajikistan confirm inferences that relate fertility to drought and famine in Ethiopia. In Bangladesh, Razzaque (1988) examined the effect of the 1975–1976 famine on fertility and discovered that the fertility effect varied by socioeconomic status. The separation of couples can primarily explain the pronounced effect on these lower socioeconomic groups. During the famine, males would migrate in large numbers to other regions of the country to seek sources of income, affecting the frequency of sexual activity (Razzaque, 1988). In Tajikistan, the decline in fertility following the drought of 2000–2001 was due to the promptness of men's migration (Clifford et al., 2010). In Finland, Fellman and Eriksson (2001) found a decline in births in the year following the 1967–1968 famine. Births were reduced by 30% in that subsequent year, compared to the 10-year average before the famine. Fewer conceptions were reported during the months from January to May when an extreme food shortage resulted from the famine. The researchers (Fellman & Eriksson, 2001) found a change in socioeconomic conditions resulting from the famine to be a critical contributor to the decline of births in Finland.

Flood is the topmost natural disaster in the SSA region; notably, much of Central Africa and Western Africa have been affected. From 2000 to 2019, floods were responsible for 64% of disaster events (CRED, 2019). Unfortunately, we find no research into the effects of the flood on fertility changes in SSA. However, we can assume fertility changes based on studies conducted in other different settings such as the United States and Bangladesh. Following the 1997 Red River flood in North Dakota, a study by Tong, Zotti, and Hsia (2011) identified a change in birth rates between pre-disaster years (1994–1996) and post-disaster years (1997–2000). Birth rates in the six counties of North Dakota that were most affected by flood (Cass, Grand Forks, Pembina, Richland, Trail, and Walsh) were also compared with the entire state, comprising 53 counties. The overall birth rate across all counties declined significantly after the disaster to 12.2 births per 1,000 population, from 13.1 births before. Compared to the rest of the state, post-flood birth rates in these six counties were higher than any of the other counties had been before and after the flood. Their study also found that the cohort of women with high birth rates following the flood was older, less likely to be married, more educated, and non-white (Tong et al., 2011). Similarly, in Bangladesh, higher fertility preference is evident among women of reproductive ages in flood- and cyclone-affected villages compared to regions not vulnerable to any extreme weather events (Haq & Ahmed, 2019). With changes in household socioeconomic conditions as adverse effects of extreme weather events (i.e., loss of land and crops and being forced to sell land) and a scarcity of natural resources, having more children could be thought beneficial (Sasson & Weinreb, 2017).

Countries in southEastern Africa confront an annual cyclone season each year, leaving them most affected by storms. These were the top ten deadliest storms in SSA between 1990 and 2019, causing deaths of around 2672 people in five countries: Mozambique, Madagascar, Zimbabwe, Senegal, and Somalia (CRED, 2019). In this review, we have not found any research examining the effects of the storms or cyclones on fertility changes in the SSA region. However, research conducted in Central and North America could help us to understand the mechanism of fertility changes in response to storms (including cyclones, hurricanes, and typhoons). Studies in Nicaragua and South Carolina showed an increase in fertility, but a decrease was found in Louisiana. Investigating the effect of Hurricane Mitch in Nicaragua on women's reproductive health, fertility increased following the storm in the two-year short term and normalised in six years (Davis, 2017). Hurricane Hugo hit South Carolina in 1989, and 24 counties of the 46 counties were declared disaster areas. A study by Cohan and Cole (2002) reported a significant increase in birth rates in the 24 affected areas during the year following Hurricane Hugo. Post-disaster fertility increases may have been due to more time spent bonding by couples. In contrast, another study (Antipova & Curtis, 2015) conducted on Hurricane Andrew of 1992 affecting Louisiana revealed different outcomes. Their research found fewer births in nearly all months following the hurricane. They also reported higher preterm births for the post-hurricane years.

Research linking climate with human fertility and reproductive health, and investigating proximate determinants at the individual and community level, has attracted significant attention in recent years. An interesting paper examined the effects of climate variables on fertility changes in SSA (Eissler et al., 2019). They found that an increase in temperature is associated with a decrease in perceptions of ideal family size. Further, an increase in precipitation leads to a decrease in fertility in the short term but an increase in the long term. This finding is consistent with studies conducted in Indonesia and South Korea which showed that increased temperature reduces birth rates (Sellers & Gray, 2019; Cho, 2020; Barreca, Deschenes, & Guldi, 2018). In contrast, a study in Mexico showed that fertility increased in the years following years of above-average precipitation. Absence of migration could be a pivotal contributor to the increased fertility in dry seasons in rural communities in Mexico (Simon, 2017). The decline in fertility following high temperature may well be associated with behavioural and biological drivers (Cho, 2020). Behaviourally, heat-related fatigue may reduce coital frequency. A biological perspective indicates that the likelihood of conception may decrease due to a worsening of female health at conception. Reduced sperm concentration as a consequence of elevated temperatures is another possible factor; but the place of male physiology and male fertility in this complex causal network is so far under-researched and barely touched on in what we have been able to survey for SSA.

Two studies conducted in Mali and Tanzania examined the seasonal variations of births, with higher birth rates in the rainy season (Philibert et al., 2013; Mulder, 1992). These two studies are unique, since they provide better explanations of mechanisms involving socio-cultural factors of fertility changes in SSA. The results of the study by Philibert et al. (2013) support a causal process linked to climate change that has direct and indirect implications for the seasonality of birth. Climate change affects conception and birth, with fetal loss due to annual precipitation variations that lead to the changed incidence of malaria. Climate change influences women's fertility due to changes in the crop production cycle, leading to food production adjustments, agricultural workload, and social-cultural behaviours that influence energy balance and sexual activity. Mulder (1992) also attributed the differences in seasonal birth to precipitation patterns. He demonstrated that seasonal variations in births from the effects of rainfall are mediated in a number of ways: nutritional and energetic factors, weaning practices, and spousal separations. Nutritional and energetic factors have an effect in two ways on women's reproductive health and birth rates. First, good provision of pasture land for animals provides an adequate supply of nutritious foods (e.g., milk production) to help women conceive. Second, rainfall allows women to shorten the time taken in exertions to get water, allowing women to save time and energy for sexual activity. Weaning practices are crucial for the studied population, and they too relate to precipitation patterns. In the Datoga community, women prefer to wean their offspring at the end of the rains. This practice unlocks late July as an opportunity for a peak in conceptions. As for spousal separation, the impact of precipitation on coital frequency is critical to evaluate the seasonal variations in Datoga's birth rate. The wet season starts in December and January when men are more likely to return home from the dry-season pastures. Also, in December and January, festival activities are widespread. The higher sexual frequency at the start of the rainy season may explain a surge of births in October.

Current studies in other parts of the world have investigated how fertility behaviour (measured as fertility rates) responds to climatic shocks and climate variability in different settings (Barreca et al., 2018; Fukuda et al., 2014; Helle, Helama, & Jokela, 2008; Sellers & Gray, 2019; Simon, 2017). Some studies revealed that fertility rates increase (Cohan & Cole, 2002; Davis, 2017), while others found decreased fertility rates (Antipova & Curtis, 2015), after hurricanes or severe stormy weather. Fertility rates also declined following droughts and associated famine in Bangladesh, China, Ethiopia, Finland, and Tajikistan (Ashton, Hill, Piazza, & Zeitz, 1984; Clifford et al., 2010; Coale, 1981; Fellman & Eriksson, 2001; Lindstrom & Berhanu, 1999; Razzaque, 1988). The effects of earthquakes on fertility in different contexts from Haiti, Italy, and Japan varied significantly (Behrman & Weitzman, 2016; Hamamatsu et al., 2014; Lin, 2010; Zhu et al., 2013). Clearly, disasters have diverse effects on fertility changes in different countries.

Clearly, fertility varies significantly following disasters. Nevertheless, the effects are not uniform; fertility increases in some areas, while it decreases in other regions, depending on the national and regional contexts. Considering our review of various research findings in various contexts, some important mechanisms for fertility responses to disasters can be summarised as follows:

- crisis-induced psychological stress, leading to a decrease in fecundity (Fellman & Eriksson, 2001);
- frequency of intercourse brought on by physical closeness (Carta et al., 2012) or separation of couples such as temporary migration of the husband or wife (Blanc, 2004; Clifford et al., 2010; Lindstrom & Berhanu, 1999; Razzaque, 1988; Simon, 2017);
- voluntary birth control due to bad experience or perceptions of the probability of a disaster (Agadjanian & Prata, 2002);
- increase (Cetorelli, 2014) or decrease of marriage (Clifford et al., 2010; Heuveline & Poch, 2007);
- insurance against child mortality (Nobles et al., 2015; Zhu et al., 2013);
- worse reproductive health at conception (Barreca et al., 2018);
- more bonding and time spent between couples during a disaster (Carta et al., 2012; Cohan & Cole, 2002);
- a decrease in contraceptive access (Behrman & Weitzman, 2016; Clifford et al., 2010);
- socioeconomic conditions of households (Agadjanian & Prata, 2002; Fellman & Eriksson, 2001).

Conclusion

Certain findings in this chapter deserve special emphasis. First, there appear to be more significant impacts on fertility from disasters in SSA than elsewhere. Flood, epidemics or pandemics, drought, and storms are the four major disaster types in SSA. Our survey reveals mixed and heterogeneous effects on fertility. Second, the impact of disasters on fertility could be a better explanation behind the slower pace of fertility decline and the late demographic transition in SSA compared to other regions of the world. Third, SSA has had several pandemics, such as HIV and Ebola, in recent decades. Surprisingly, the effect of an epidemic is unique in SSA compared to other regions. Other climate-related disasters, including flood, drought, and storms, have adverse effects on agriculture, inducing water scarcity, food security, and acute poverty. Environmental degradation, food insecurity, and poverty are associated with fertility changes (increase or decrease), sometimes understood as a household's coping mechanism. Fourth and last, many of the world's and Africa's low-income countries are focused on SSA, and they have inadequate health facilities and resources. SSA countries are still in the earlier stage of demographic transition, experiencing high mortality and high fertility.

Given the increasing frequency and intensity of natural disasters and a slow pace of decline in fertility in SSA, there is a need for special attention to understanding the complex relationship between disasters and fertility. Greater frequency and intensity of natural disasters might slow down the decline in the region's fertility rate. Since the fertility rate in SSA differs from other parts of the world, more empirical research will be needed to unravel the dynamics of fertility changes due to climate change (encompassing both variability and extremes) and natural disasters. Findings in this chapter suggest that the SSA countries are of central importance in any more general attempt to come to terms with the disaster–fertility nexus and the deep mechanisms of fertility changes. Engagement with local institutions and researchers from SSA countries could contribute to the investigation if the aim is to appreciate more of the socio-cultural wellsprings of fertility-related practices in sub-Saharan Africa.

Acknowledgements

This study was funded by the Beacon of Enlightenment Doctor of Philosophy Scholarship at The University of Adelaide, Australia.

References

Aassve, A., Cavalli, N., Mencarini, L., Plach, S., & Bacci, M. L. (2020). The COVID-19 pandemic and human fertility. *Science, 369*(6502), 370–371.

Agadjanian, V., & Prata, N. (2002). War, peace, and fertility in Angola. *Demography, 39*(2), 215–231.

Anser, M. K., Yousaf, Z., Khan, M. A., Voo, X. H., Nassani, A. A., Alotaibi, S. M., . . . Zaman, K. (2020). The impacts of COVID-19 measures on global environment and fertility rate: Double coincidence. *Air Quality, Atmosphere and Health, 13*, 1083–1092.

Antipova, A., & Curtis, A. (2015). The post-disaster negative health legacy: Pregnancy outcomes in Louisiana after Hurricane Andrew. *Disasters, 39*(4), 665–686.

Ashton, B., Hill, K., Piazza, A., & Zeitz, R. (1984). Famine in China, 1958–61. *Population and Development Review, 10*(4), 613.

Barreca, A., Deschenes, O., & Guldi, M. (2018). Maybe next month? Temperature shocks and dynamic adjustments in birth rates. *Demography, 55*(4), 1269–1293.

Behrman, J. A., & Weitzman, A. (2016). Effects of the 2010 Haiti Earthquake on women's reproductive health. *Studies in Family Planning, 47*(1), 3–17.

Blanc, A. K. (2004). The role of conflict in the rapid fertility decline in Eritrea and prospects for the future. *Studies in Family Planning, 35*(4), 236–245.

Bongaarts, J. (2017). Africa's unique fertility transition. *Population and Development Review, 43*(S1), 39–58.

Bongaarts, J., & Casterline, J. (2013). Fertility transition: Is sub-Saharan Africa different? *Population and Development Review, 38*(S1), 153–168.

Bongaarts, J., & O'Neill, B. C. (2018). Global warming policy: Is population left out in the cold? *Science, 361*(6403), 650–652.

Carta, G., Dalfonso, A., Colagrande, I., Catana, P., Casacchia, M., & Patacchiola, F. (2012). Post-earthquake birth-rate evaluation using the brief cope. *Journal of Maternal-Fetal and Neonatal Medicine, 25*(11), 2411–2414.

Castro, R., Behrman, J. R., Kohler, H. P., & Warren, F. J. (2015). Perception of HIV risk and the quantity and quality of children: The case of rural Malawi. *Journal of Population Economics, 28*(1), 113–132.

Cetorelli, V. (2014). The effect on fertility of the 2003–2011 War in Iraq. *Population and Development Review, 40*(4), 581–604.

Chin, Y. M., & Wilson, N. (2018). Disease risk and fertility: Evidence from the HIV/AIDS pandemic. *Journal of Population Economics, 31*(2), 429–451.

Cho, H. (2020). Ambient temperature, birth rate, and birth outcomes: Evidence from South Korea. *Population and Environment, 41*(3), 330–346.

Clifford, D., Falkingham, J., & Hinde, A. (2010). Through civil war, food crisis and drought: Trends in fertility and nuptiality in post-Soviet Tajikistan. *European Journal of Population, 26*(3), 325–350.

Coale, A. J. (1981). Population trends, population policy, and population studies in China. *Population and Development Review*, 7(1), 85–97.

Cohan, C. L., & Cole, S. W. (2002). Life course transitions and natural disaster: Marriage, birth, and divorce following Hurricane Hugo. *Journal of Family Psychology, 16*(1), 14–25.

CRED. (2018). *Natural disasters 2017*. Brussels, Belgium. Retrieved from https://cred.be/sites/default/files/adsr_2017.pdf

CRED. (2019). Disasters in Africa: 20 Year review (2000–2019*). *CRED Crunch, 56*. Retrieved from https://cred.be/sites/default/files/CredCrunch56.pdf.

CRED. (2020). *The CRED/OFDA International disaster database*. Belgium: Université catholique de Louvain-CRED. Retrieved from www.emdat.be

Curlin, G. T., Chen, L. C., & Hussain, S. B. (1976). Demographic crisis: The impact of the Bangladesh civil war (1971) on births and deaths in a rural area of Bangladesh. *Population Studies, 30*(1), 87–105.

Daniel, M. L. (2000). The demographic impact of HIV/AIDS in sub-Saharan Africa. *Geography, 85*(1), 46–55.

Davenport, F., Dorélien, A., & Grace, K. (2020). Investigating the linkages between pregnancy outcomes and climate in sub-Saharan Africa. *Population and Environment, 41*, 397–421.

Davis, J. (2017). Fertility after natural disaster: Hurricane Mitch in Nicaragua. *Population and Environment*, *38*(4), 448–464.

Eckstein, D., Künzel, V., Schäfer, L., & Winges, M. (2020). *Global climate risk index 2020*. Berlin: Germanwatch. Retrieved from http://germanwatch.org/sites/germanwatch.org/files/publication/1066.pdf

Eissler, S., Thiede, B. C., & Strube, J. (2019). Climatic variability and changing reproductive goals in sub-Saharan Africa. *Global Environmental Change*, *57*, 101912.

Fellman, J., & Eriksson, A. W. (2001). Regional, temporal, and seasonal variations in births and deaths: The effects of famines. *Social Biology*, *48*(1–2), 86–104.

Fukuda, M., Fukuda, K., Shimizu, T., Nobunaga, M., Mamsen, L. S., & Andersen, C. Y. (2014). Climate change is associated with male:female ratios of fetal deaths and newborn infants in Japan. *Fertility and Sterility*, *102*(5), 1364–1370.

Hamamatsu, Y., Inoue, Y., Watanabe, C., & Umezaki, M. (2014). Impact of the 2011 earthquake on marriages, births and the secondary sex ratio in Japan. *Journal of Biosocial Science*, *46*(6), 830–841.

Haq, S. M. A., & Ahmed, K. J. (2019). Is fertility preference related to perception of the risk of child mortality, changes in landholding, and type of family? A comparative study on populations vulnerable and not vulnerable to extreme weather events in Bangladesh. *Population Review*, *58*(2), 61–99.

Helle, S., Helama, S., & Jokela, J. (2008). Temperature-related birth sex ratio bias in historical Sami: Warm years bring more sons. *Biology Letters*, *4*(1), 60–62.

Hertrich, V. (2017). Trends in age at marriage and the onset of fertility transition in sub-Saharan Africa. *Population and Development Review*, *43*(S1), 112–137.

Heuveline, P. (1997). AIDS and population growth in sub-Saharan Africa: Assessing the sensitivity of projections. *Population Research and Policy Review*, *16*(6), 531–560.

Heuveline, P., & Poch, B. (2007). The phoenix population: Demographic crisis and rebound in Cambodia. *Demography*, *44*(2), 405–426.

Hunter, S. C., Isingo, R., Boerma, J. T., Urassa, M., Mwaluko, G. M., & Zaba, B. (2003). The association between HIV and fertility in a cohort study in rural Tanzania. *Journal of Biosocial Science*, *35*(2), 189–199.

Ihekweazu, C., & Agogo, E. (2020). Africa's response to COVID-19. *BMC Medicine*, *18*(151).

Issaka, H. M., & Guengant, J.-P. (2017). Countries with very slow or incipient fertility transitions. In H. Groth & J. F. May (Eds.), *Africa's population: In search of a demographic dividend* (pp. 147–164). Cham: Springer.

Jiang, L., & Hardee, K. (2011). How do recent population trends matter to climate change? *Population Research and Policy Review*, *30*(2), 287–312.

Karlsson, M., & Pichler, S. (2015). Demographic consequences of HIV. *Journal of Population Economics*, *28*(4), 1097–1135.

Lin, C. Y. (2010). Instability, investment, disasters, and demography: Natural disasters and fertility in Italy (1820–1962) and Japan (1671–1965). *Population and Environment*, *31*(4), 255–281.

Lindstrom, D., & Berhanu, B. (1999). The impact of war, famine, and economic decline on marital fertility in Ethiopia. *Demography*, *36*(2), 247–261.

Marston, M., Zaba, B., & Eaton, J. W. (2017). The relationship between HIV and fertility in the era of antiretroviral therapy in sub-Saharan Africa: Evidence from 49 Demographic and Health Surveys. *Tropical Medicine and International Health*, *22*(12), 1542–1550.

May, J. F. (2017). The politics of family planning policies and programs in sub-Saharan Africa. *Population and Development Review*, *43*(S1), 308–329.

Mbacké, C. (2017). The persistence of high fertility in sub-Saharan Africa: A comment. *Population and Development Review*, *43*(S1), 330–337.

Mbita, G., Renju, J., Lija, G., Conserve, D. F., & Todd, J. (2019). Effect of antiretroviral therapy on fertility rate among women living with HIV in Tabora, Tanzania: An historical cohort study. *PLoS One*, *14*(9), e0222173.

Mulder, M. B. (1992). Demography of pastoralists – Preliminary data on the datoga of Tanzania. *Human Ecology*, *20*(4), 383–405.

Myer, L., Carter, R. J., Katyal, M., Toro, P., El-Sadr, W. M., & Abrams, E. J. (2010). Impact of antiretroviral therapy on incidence of pregnancy among HIV-infected women in sub-Saharan Africa: A cohort study. *PLoS Medicine*, 7(2), e1000229.

Nobles, J., Frankenberg, E., & Thomas, D. (2015). The effects of mortality on fertility: Population dynamics after a natural disaster. *Demography*, *52*(1), 15–38.

Philibert, A., Tourigny, C., Coulibaly, A., & Fournier, P. (2013). Birth seasonality as a response to a changing rural environment (Kayes region, Mali). *Journal of Biosocial Science*, *45*(4), 547–565.

Razzaque, A. (1988). Effect of famine on fertility in a rural area of Bangladesh. *Journal of Biosocial Science*, *20*(3), 287–294.

Reher, D. S. (2004). The demographic transition revisited as a global process. *Population, Space and Place*, *10*(1), 19–41.

Rodgers, J. L., John, C. A. S., & Coleman, R. (2005). Did fertility go up after the Oklahoma City bombing? An analysis of births in metropolitan counties in Oklahoma, 1990–1999. *Demography*, *42*(4), 675–692.

Roser, M. (2021). *Fertility rate*. Published online at OurWorldInData.org. Retrieved from https://ourworldindata.org/fertility-rate

Roser, M., & Ritchie, H. (2018). *HIV/AIDS*. Published online at OurWorldInData.org. Retrieved from https://ourworldindata.org/hiv-aids

Sasson, I., & Weinreb, A. (2017). Land cover change and fertility in West-Central Africa: Rural livelihoods and the vicious circle model. *A Journal of Interdisciplinary Studies*, *38*(4), 345–368.

Schmidhuber, J., & Tubiello, F. N. (2007). Global food security under climate change. *Proceedings of the National Academy of Sciences of the United States of America*, *104*(50), 19703–19708.

Schoumaker, B. (2019). Stalls in fertility transitions in sub-Saharan Africa: Revisiting the evidence. *Studies in Family Planning*, *50*(3), 257–278.

Sellers, S., & Gray, C. (2019). Climate shocks constrain human fertility in Indonesia. *World Development*, *117*, 357–369.

Shaluf, I. M. (2007). An overview on disasters. *Disaster Prevention and Management*, *16*(5), 687–703.

Shapiro, D., & Hinde, A. (2017). On the pace of fertility decline in sub-Saharan Africa. *Demographic Research*, *37*(1), 1327–1338.

Simon, D. H. (2017). Exploring the influence of precipitation on fertility timing in rural Mexico. *Population and Environment*, *38*(4), 407–423.

Terceira, N., Gregson, S., Zaba, B., & Mason, P. (2003). The contribution of HIV to fertility decline in rural Zimbabwe, 1985–2000. *Population Studies*, *57*(2), 149–164.

Tong, V., Zotti, M., & Hsia, J. (2011). Impact of the Red River catastrophic flood on women giving birth in North Dakota, 1994–2000. *Maternal and Child Health Journal*, *15*(3), 281–288.

World Bank. (2020). *Fertility rate: Sub-Saharan Africa*. Retrieved from https://data.worldbank.org/country/ZG

Xiao, C., & Hong, D. (2010). Gender differences in environmental behaviors in China. *Population and Environment*, *32*(1), 88–104.

Zhu, H., Lei, H., Huang, W., Fu, J., Wang, Q., Shen, L., . . . Hu, L. (2013). Fertility in older women following removal of long-term intrauterine devices in the wake of a natural disaster. *Contraception*, *87*(4), 416–420.

21

URBAN HEALTH DIMENSIONS OF DEMOGRAPHIC RESEARCH IN AFRICA – A SYSTEMATIC REVIEW

Yemi Adewoyin

Introduction

The percentage of urban dwellers has been on a steady rise since 1950. From being 30% of the world's population in 1950, the proportion of urban dwellers rose to 55% in 2018 and is projected to further rise to 68% by the year 2050 (United Nations, Department of Economic and Social Affairs, Population Division, 2019). The projected growth is expected to be higher in low and lower-middle income countries of the global South. In Africa particularly, the annual growth rate is projected to be 3.0%, more than double the estimated 1.2% and 1.4% growth rates across most lower-middle and low-income countries, respectively. The United Nations' figures and estimates are based on urban centres with a minimum population of 300,000 people. If country-specific definitions of urbanity are considered, these figures are a gross underestimation of global urban population. For instance, in Nigeria, a settlement of 20,000 people qualifies as urban, while a settlement with a population density of 4,000 inhabitants per square kilometre in Japan, or with a local administrative authority in South Africa, irrespective of the population, is classified as urban. While there is no global consensus on the population threshold for defining an urban settlement, an incontrovertible issue, around which all urban stakeholders share a common position however, is the health effects of living in an urban settlement.

In spite of offering greater prospects for socioeconomic development and an enhanced quality of life for individuals and households with their better infrastructure, job opportunities, and array of goods and services, urban centres present many health challenges that are attributable to their particular social and physical environments and the population's level of access to resources and infrastructure in the urban space (Adewoyin & Adeboyejo, 2016; Adewoyin, 2018a). To illustrate, in-migration and natural increase fuel urban population growth, put pressure on housing and other social infrastructure, result in overcrowding and growth of slums and squatter settlements, exacerbate water and sanitation problems, constrain access to employment opportunities, and in turn create a class structure that impacts access to social services like healthcare, education, and security based on income and place of residence within the city. Infrastructural development, including building and road construction to accommodate the needs of the growing urban population, reduces the urban green canopy, aggravates the effects of climate change on urban residents, fuels ambient air and water pollution, and depletes available open spaces for physical exercise and recreation.

DOI: 10.4324/9780429287213-26

Increase in number of fossil energy-driven vehicles, stemming from population increase and advancement in transportation systems, not only contributes to polluting urban air but also increases the risks of road traffic accidents and injuries. Within the unequal social space created by differing access to income opportunities, nutrition and feeding patterns, lifestyle choices, and health seeking assume varying dimensions reflecting the social, spatial, and income inequalities within the city. The lifestyle choices include drugs; tobacco; alcohol and substance abuse; gangsterism; sedentary living; indulgence in food with high content of salt and sugar, especially from fast food outlets; risky sexual behaviour; and other behaviours that promote stress, depression, and/or anxiety. The health consequences of the interrelationships among the foregoing are implied by and define the scope of urban health (Vlahov & Galea, 2005; Mberu, Wamukoya, Oti, & Kyobutungi, 2015; Adewoyin & Adeboyejo, 2016; Oni et al., 2016; World Health Organization, 2016; Ezeh et al., 2017; Adewoyin, Chukwu, & Sanni, 2018). Simply put, urban health is any aspect of population health issues consequent on the interrelationships among the physical and social environments and the biodemographic composition of the population resident in an urban settlement.

According to the World Health Organization (WHO)'s 2016 global report on urban health, more than 880 million people live in slums around the world, including three out of five urban residents in sub-Saharan Africa (SSA); 2.4 billion people, including 40% of the urban population in SSA, lack access to improved sanitation facilities and are exposed to a wide range of infectious diseases like dysentery, cholera, typhoid, schistosomiasis, and trachoma, while children in the poorest quintile of urban households are twice as likely to die before their fifth birthday compared to children in the richest quintile (WHO, 2016). The report further shows that while undernutrition and food insecurity account for 45% of all deaths in children under five years, overweight and obesity, major risk factors for noncommunicable diseases like cardiovascular diseases, cancer, and diabetes, underlined about 63% of all deaths worldwide. The WHO estimates that more than 1.2 million lives are lost to road traffic accidents annually; 60% of all urban residents have been victims of crime, especially in overcrowded urban areas characterized by a spatial concentration of poverty, illicit drug use, and widespread substance abuse; and 3.7 million deaths in 2012 were attributed to outdoor air pollution, associated with ischaemic heart disease, stroke, chronic obstructive pulmonary disease, lung cancer, and lower respiratory infections in children (WHO, 2016). According to Mehta (2004), breathing Mumbai's air is the equivalent of smoking two-and-one-half packs of cigarettes per day.

Urban health is intrinsically and cyclically linked to the four pillars of demography in several ways. On the one hand, fertility, ageing, mortality, and migration patterns influence urban population growth rate and, in turn, define the quality of the urban social and physical environment and the population's access to urban resources. Access and quality of the urban environment, on the other hand, impact fertility behaviour; underlie sickness, diseases, violence, and injury with their consequences for mortality; impact life expectancy and the ageing process; and determine whether people migrate into or out of the urban centre. Given the higher rate of urbanization in Africa, the poor urban health outcomes in the continent that are likely to worsen with increased urban population, the linkage between urban health and demography, and the capacity of demographic research outputs to inform policies for improving the health outcomes, this chapter reviews the urban health dimensions of demographic research in Africa. The chapter particularly examines the urban health content, the demographic cohort studied, and the temporal shifts in the urban health focus of the studies.

Methods

Scope

The search focused only on publications from Nigeria, Kenya, and South Africa. The three countries were selected from the 25 English-speaking African countries for their geographical location, population, and number of universities. While Nigeria is the most populous from West Africa and has the subregion's highest number of universities, South Africa met the criteria from the Southern Africa subregion. Although it has a lower population than Ethiopia and Tanzania, Kenya has more universities and research institutions than the other East African countries. The number of universities, and by extension, researchers, is expected to be reflected in the number of publications from the selected countries and be sufficient to extract a pattern of study that represents the outputs from other African countries.

Search strategy

The Preferred Reporting Items for Systematic Reviews and Meta-Analyses (PRISMA) checklist (Moher, Liberati, Tetzlaff, & Altman, 2009) was employed for this review, and two databases were used: Scopus and Google Scholar. The African Journals Online (AJOL) database, which could possibly contain more scholarly works from Africa by Africans, which was intended to be used as the second database, was offline during the search period in June 2020. The use of Google Scholar, a repository of open-access publications ranked as the largest academic bibliographic database (Gusenbauer, 2018), in AJOL's stead, is believed to be sufficient for the purpose of this review. Specific search terms used were 'urban OR urbanization OR 'urban AND health' AND children OR youth OR aged OR elderly OR women OR men OR youth OR young OR adolescent OR teenage OR adult AND nigeria OR kenya OR south AND africa' and limited to article title and abstract in Scopus, and 'children OR teenage OR adult OR youth OR young OR adolescent OR women OR men OR aged OR older OR elder "urban" -rural' in the article title search in Google Scholar. While the search focused on Kenya, Nigeria, and South Africa, a few other multi-country studies that mentioned the three countries during the search were also included. The search covered 1970 to June 2020.

Inclusion and exclusion criteria

Only studies in the social sciences, environmental sciences, and public health disciplines and multidisciplinary journals were included in the review. All studies that were conducted in rural areas or compared rural-urban outcomes were excluded from the review. Studies that did not focus on the general population or at least a demographic cohort within the population were also excluded. Subjects excluded were contraceptive use and family planning, intimate partner violence, and coronavirus. While the first two subjects were excluded for being broad themed and not driven mainly by urban residency but largely by other sociodemographic determinants, coronavirus was excluded for its recency as a global pandemic and insufficient empirical studies on its urban aetiology.

Results

Study selection

Following the PRISMA checklist, the study selection process and the associated numbers are illustrated in Figure 21.1. From a total of 2,130 articles, 229 were included in the review.

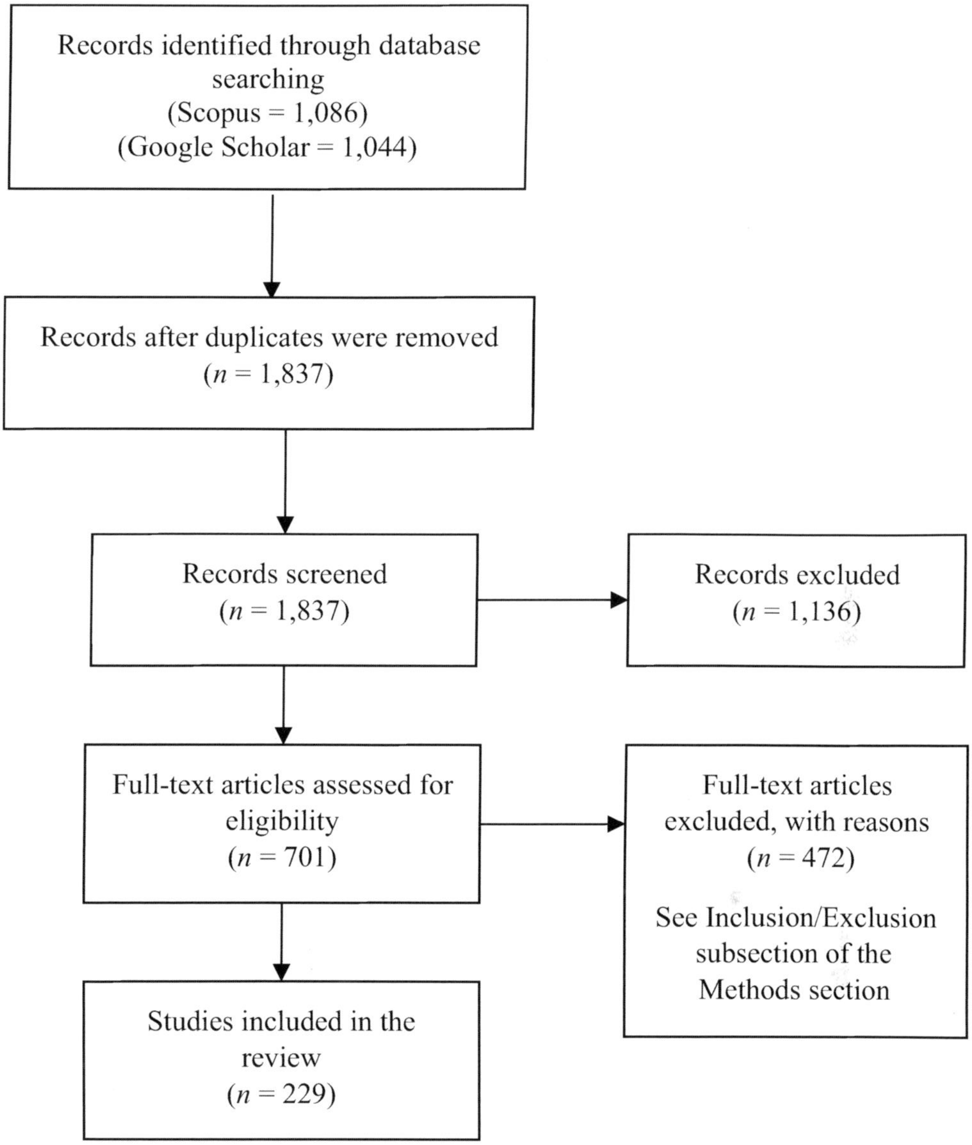

Figure 21.1 PRISMA flowchart of literature selection and inclusion criteria

Spatiotemporal distribution of studies

Eighty-six (37.6%) of the studies were conducted in Nigeria, 31.4% were from South Africa, 18.3% were from Kenya, and 12.7% of the reviewed works were multi-country. Only four (1.7%) of the studies were carried out before 1990, 3.5% were from the 1990s, and 11.8% were from 2000 to 2009, while 83% of the studies were conducted between 2010 and June 2020. The year 2019, with 14.4% of the total publications, emerged as the year with the highest number of publications. At half year, the year 2020, with 11.4% of the publications, and 2017, with 10.9%, followed in that order.

Urban health subject

From the studies reviewed, a number of urban health issues were observed. These included access to healthcare and health-seeking behaviour and how these are affected by location within the urban environment. Anxiety and depression; environmental issues including pollution and climate change; water availability and sanitation; diets and physical exercise; indulgence in tobacco, drugs, alcohol, and substance abuse; risky sexual behaviour; violence; and road-related health outcomes were also studied. Other issues addressed in the studies were socioeconomic status and inequality, malnutrition, and poor housing conditions. As illustrated in Table 21.1,

Table 21.1 Distribution of Urban Health Subjects in Demographic Publications, 1970–2020

Subject	*Proportion* (%)*	*Authors*
Access	2.7	Fotso and Mukiira (2012), Macharia, Ouma, Gogo, Snow, and Noor (2017), Idowu, Olowookere, Abiola, Akinwumi, and Adegbenro (2017), Adewoyin Chukwu, and Sanni (2018), Olusese, Petros, and Abuya (2018), Lawal and Anyiam (2019), Made et al. (2020)
Anxiety and depression	3.5	Frank-Briggs and Alikor (2010), Dewing, Tomlinson, le Roux, Chopra, and Tsai (2013), Tucker et al. (2014), Idowu, Amoo, Chiazor, and Adekeye (2015), Skeen, Macedo, Tomlinson, Hensels, and Sherr (2016), Marsay, Manderson, and Subramaney (2017), van Heyningen et al. (2017), Culbreth, Swahn, Ndetei, Ametewee, and Kasirye (2018), Ngocho et al. (2019), Kootbodien, Naicker, Wilson, Ramesar, and London (2020), Owusu-Ansah, Addae, Peasah, Oppong, and Osafo (2020), Baratin et al. (2020), Maina, Orindi, Osindo, and Ziraba (2020)
Environment, including pollution and climate change	17.9	Ogundipe (1975), Von Schirnding, Yach, Blignault, and Mathews (1991), Iyun (1992), Ebomoyi (1994), Penner et al. (2003), Zhou, Minakawa, Githeko, and Yan (2004), Nriagu et al. (2008), Maluleke and Worku (2009), Ojiezeh, Ibeh, Opedun, and Udoh (2010), Oluwatayo (2011), Ige, Falade, and Arinola (2012), Thompson, Matamale, and Kharidza (2012), Ajibade, McBean, and Bezner-Kerr (2013), Babatunde, Asaolu, and Sowemimo (2013), Bi and Okposio (2013), Boru et al. (2013), Ochodo, Ndetei, Moturi, and Otieno (2014), Suchdev et al. (2014), Shirinde, Wichmann, and Voyi (2014), Muriithi (2014), Nkosi, Wichmann, and Voyi (2015), Garl et al. (2015), Breiman et al. (2015), Baloye and Palamuleni (2015), Ayoade, Sikiru, and Okanlawon (2015), Smit et al. (2016), Nriagu, Udofia, Ekong, and Ebuk (2016), Orji (2017), Vanker et al. (2017), Owili, Lien, Muga, and Lin (2017), Thiam et al. (2017), Adeboyejo and Adewoyin (2017a), Adewoyin (2018a), Onyekwelu et al. (2018), Suter et al. (2018), Nyathi, Olowoyo, and Oludare (2018), Shezi and Wright (2018), Njoku, Edokpayi, and Odiyo (2019), Popoola, Popoola, and Purchase (2019), Schenck, Blaauw, Viljoen, and Swart (2019), Gyang et al. (2019), Apata et al. (2019), Winter, Obara, and Barchi (2019), Fakunle et al. (2020), Aigbokhaode, Isara, and London (2020), Rother (2020), Rollin, Channa, Olutola, Nogueira, and Odland. (2020), Adeboyejo, Adejumobi, Adewoyin, and Oyasiji (2020), Iyaloo et al. (2020), Tomita, Cuadros, Burns, Tanser, and Slotow (2020)

(*Continued*)

Subject	Proportion (%)*	Authors
Health seeking	5.2	Seeley (1984), Ludwar-Ene (1991), Fotso, Ezeh, and Oronje (2008), Maree and Wright (2010), Bocquier et al. (2011), Falkingham, Chepngeno-Langat, Kyobutungi, Ezeh, and Evandrou (2011), Fotso and Mukiira (2012), Griffiths, Johnson, Noël, and Norris (2013), Ananias and Strydom (2014), Aboyade, Beauclair, Mbamalu, Puoane, and Hughes (2016), Chadoka-Mutanda and Odimegwu (2017), Alfaro-Velcamp (2017), Makanda and Vearey (2017), Freeman (2017), Olubodun, Odukoya, and Balogun (2019), Okunade (2020), Ezedike, Ohazurike, Emetumah, and Ajaegbu (2020)
Healthy living (diet and exercise)	14.0	Haddock (1979), Monyeki, Pienaar, Mamabolo, and Temane (2009), Iloh, Amadi, and Nwankwo (2010), Ene-Obong, Ibeanu, Onuoha, and Ejekwu (2012), Durowade et al. (2012), Kalula (2016), Busayo, Jacob, and Abimbola (2014), Morar, Coopoo, Shaw, and Shaw (2014), Peltzer et al. (2014), Olack et al. (2015), Nnoka, Akinola, and Mosimabale (2016), Olagunju, Ayamolowo, and Sunmonu. (2016), Adam and Isah (2017), Okpokowuruk, Akpan, and Ikpeme (2017), Obuah, Moore, Altraide, and Asuquo. (2017), Adedokun, Goon, Owolabi, Adeniyi, and Ajayi (2017), Kambondo and Sartorius (2018), Toriola et al. (2018), Winter et al. (2019), Danquah et al. (2019), De Jong (2019), Adetunji et al. (2019), Muller et al. (2019), Kassier, Senekal, and Villiers (2019), Oyekale (2019), Onagbiye, Tshwaro, Barry, and Marie (2019), Sogunle, Masukume, and Nelson (2019), Baratin et al. (2020), Nkosi, Rathogwa-Takalani, and Voyi (2020), Kidokoro et al. (2020), Peer, Lombard, Steyn, and Levitt (2020), Darikwa and Manda (2020)
Housing	0.9	Ibem and Azuh (2016), Naicker, Teare, Balakrishna, Wright, and Mathee (2017)
Location	4.3	Breiman et al. (2015), Baloye and Palamuleni (2015), Tomita et al. (2017), Adeboyejo et al. (2020), Iyaloo et al. (2020), Tomita et al. (2020), Manda, Lombard, and Mosala (2012), Bigala and Ayiga (2014), Gibbs, Jewkes, Willan, and Washington (2018), Habyarimana et al. (2018), Makhubele et al. (2019), Darikwa and Manda (2020)
Road	1.3	Osuntogun and Koku (2007), Pepple and Adio (2014), Ntaji (2015), Adedokun et al. (2017)
Risky sexual behaviour	11.3	Adedimeji, Omololu, and Odutolu (2007), Mberu (2008), Adedimeji, Heard, Odutolu, and Omololu (2008), Marteleto, Lam, and Ranchhod (2008), Burrell, Mark, Grant, Wood, and Bekker (2010), Okonofua, Omo-Aghoja, Bello, Osughe, and Agholor (2010), Xu, Luke, and Msiyaphazi (2010), Mberu and White (2011), Olawuyi (2011), Marston, Beguy, Kabiru, and Cleland (2013), Kohli, Konya, Obura, Stones, and Revathi (2013), Speizer, Fotso, Davis, Saad, and Otai. (2013), Tucker et al. (2014), Muindi, Mudege, Beguy, and Mberu (2014), Beguy, Mumah, and Gottschalk (2014), Bajoga, Atagame, and Okigbo (2015), Okigbo et al. (2015), Arulogun, Ogbu, and Dipeolu (2016), Kamandaya (2016), Ajaero, Odimegwu, Mkwananzi, and Banjo (2018), K. C. Okafor, Adam, and Azuike (2018), Moodley (2019), Francis et al. (2019), Maina et al. (2020), Ajaero, Onuh, Amoo, and Adewoyin (2020), Mayo-Wilson et al. (2020)

(*Continued*)

Table 21.1 (Continued)

Subject	*Proportion (%)**	*Authors*
Sanitation and water	2.6	Von Schirnding et al. (1991), Ekejindu and Ochuba (2004), Fatiregun and Oluwatoba (2008), Ajibade et al. (2013), Babatunde et al. (2013), Bi and Okposio (2013), Boru et al. (2013), Muriithi (2014), Ayoade et al. (2015), Thiam et al. (2017), Adewoyin (2017a), Gbadegesin and Olayide (2019), Gyang et al. (2019), Apata et al. (2019), Medgyesi et al. (2019), Ezedike et al. (2020)
Socioeconomic status, inequality, and malnutrition	19.7	Osuhor and Etta (1980), Iyun (1992), Orindi et al. (2020), Elamass (1997), Porteus et al. (2000), Allu (2001), Abidoye and Ihebuzor (2001), Adeboyejo and Onyeonoru (2003), De Villiers and Senekal (2002), Cunnan (2002), Adeyeba and Tijani (2002), Kaufman and Stavrou (2004), Ezeh et al. (2006), Adedimeji et al. (2007), Fotso et al. (2008), Bocquier et al. (2011), Falkingham et al. (2011), Olack et al. (2011), Kimani-Murage et al. (2011), I. P. Okafor and Odeyemi (2012), Webb-Girard et al. (2012), Amoo, Adetoro, and Oluwole-Isaac (2013), Samuel et al. (2014), Kimani-Murage et al. (2014), Idowu et al. (2015), Kieni (2015), Kipyegon, Nyarombe, Achimba, and Kamar (2015), Soura et al. (2015), Mberu et al. (2015), Mutisya, Kandala, Ngware, and Kabiru (2015), Ombati and Ombati (2016), Adewoyin and Adeboyejo (2016), Tsai, Tomlinson, Comulada, and Rotheram-Borus (2016), Ojagbemi, Bello, Luo, and Gureje (2017), Ezeh et al. (2017), Lilford et al. (2017), Olusese et al. (2018), De Wet, Frade, and Akinyemi (2018), Amadi, Ezenwosu, and Odetunde (2018), Chikoko, Ruparanganda, Muzvidziwa, and Chimhowa (2019), Alawode, Chima, and Awoleye (2019), Olodu, Adeyemi, Olowookere, and Esimai (2019), Senekal et al. (2019), Makhubele et al. (2019), Medgyesi et al. (2019), Khulu and Ramroop (2020), Ikuteyijo (2020)
Substance abuse	7.4	Steyn, Yach, Stander, and Fourie (1997), Sitas et al. (2004), Obot (2005), Pengpid, Peltzer, & van der Heever (2011), Faronbi, Oginni, Olowookere, and Moronkeji (2012), Dewing et al. (2013), Ahaneku, Ahaneku, Osuji, Oguejiofor, and Opara (2014), Wijnberg and Green (2014), Akinyemi et al. (2016), Gibbs et al. (2018), Francis et al. (2019), Jacobs and Slabbert (2019), Ikoh, Smah, Okwanya, Clement, and Aposhi (2019), Korio and Nyavanga (2019), Oduaran and Akanni (2019), Itanyi et al. (2020), Ajayi and Somefun (2020), Harker, Londani, Morojele, Williams, and Parry (2020)
Violence and injury	9.2	Williams (1994), Orindi et al. (2020), Dissel (1997), Mamman (2004), Oruwari (2006), Burrows, Swart, and Laflamme (2009), Burrows, Niekerk, and Laflamme (2010), Smith and Sandra (2010), Igwe (2011), Ziraba, Kyobutungi, and Zulu (2011), Olasunkanmi (2012), Wijnberg and Green (2014), Meth (2014), Kyamana (2015), Skeen et al. (2016), Akwaji, Uyang, and Abonor (2017), Amali, Moshood, and Iliyasu (2017), Adeyemi and Oyetunde (2017), Kingsley, Emmanuel, and Vincent (2018), Kabiru, Mumah, Maina, and Abuya (2018), Edelstein (2018), Baiocchi et al. (2019), Mguzulwa and Gxubane (2019), Agunbiade (2019)
Total	**100.0**	**229**

*Double counts for studies in more than one category were excluded in computing the percentages.

about 20% of the works focused on the interrelatedness of socioeconomic status, inequality, and malnutrition. Studies on the physical environment, including pollution and climate change and their consequences for the health of urban dwellers ranked second (17.9%) in terms of subject investigated, while the third most investigated subject was the health consequences of unhealthy eating habits and physical exercise (14.0%). Housing (0.9%), roads (1.3%), sanitation (2.6%) and access (2.7%) were the least investigated urban health issues in the studies.

Demographic cohorts studied

Studies focusing on children (25.7%) and women (20.6%) dominated the reviewed works. Studies on youths (17.6%) and the whole population (13.5%) ranked next in the proportional distribution of demographic groups studied in the works. Aside from the study on orphans that was singled out from the general children cohort because of the extra vulnerability of orphans, men were the least-studied demographic group (2.6%). As shown in Table 21.2, other less-investigated groups were adults (4.4%), migrants (4.8%), adolescents (5.2%), and the aged (5.2%).

Table 21.2 Distribution of the Demographic Cohorts Studied in Reviewed Works

Demographic Group	*Proportion* (%)*	*Authors*
Adolescent	5.2	Adeboyejo and Onyeonoru (2003), Mberu (2008), Burrows et al. (2009), Ene-Obong et al. (2012), Amoo et al. (2013), Marston et al. (2013), Griffiths et al. (2013), Busayo et al. (2014), Idowu et al. (2015), Okpokowuruk et al. (2017), Kabiru et al. (2018), Francis et al. (2019), Jacobs and Slabbert (2019), Baiocchi et al. (2019), Nkosi et al. (2020), Maina et al. (2020), Itanyi et al. (2020)
Adults	4.4	Ilo et al. (2010), Ige et al. (2012), Ochodo et al. (2014), Pepple and Adio (2014), Ahaneku et al. (2014), Olack et al. (2015), Mberu et al. (2015), Danquah et al. (2019), De Jong (2019), Darikwa and Manda (2020)
Children	25.7	Ogundipe (1975), Osuhor and Etta (1980), Von Schirnding et al. (1991), Ebomoyi (1994), Elamass (1997), Porteus et al. (2000), Abidoye and Ihebuzor (2001), De Villiers and Senekal (2002), Adeyeba and Tijani (2002), Ekejindu and Ochuba (2004), Nriagu et al. (2008), Fatiregun and Oluwatoba (2008), Maluleke and Worku (2009), Monyeki et al. (2009), Frank-Briggs and Alikor (2010), Burrows et al. (2010), Olack et al. (2011), Kimani-Murage et al. (2011), Bocquier et al. (2011), Thompson et al. (2012), Ene-Obong et al. (2012), I. P. Okafor and Odeyemi (2012), Babatunde et al. (2013), Boru et al. (2013), Griffiths et al. (2013), Bi and Okposio (2013), Suchdev et al. (2014), Muriithi (2014), Morar et al. (2014), Samuel et al. (2014), Ayoade et al. (2015), Breiman et al. (2015), Kieni (2015), Kipyegon et al. (2015), Soura et al. (2015), Mutisya et al. (2015), Skeen et al. (2016), Ombati and Ombati (2016), Nnoka et al. (2016), Akinyemi, Adedini, Wandera, and Odimegwu (2016), Orji (2017), Vanker et al. (2017), Thiam et al. (2017), Chadoka-Mutanda and Odimegwu (2017), Adam and Isah (2017), Adeyemi and Oyetunde (2017), Okpokowuruk et al. (2017), Owili et al. (2017), Onyekwelu et al. (2018), Olusese et al. (2018), Suter et al. (2018), Kambondo and Sartorius (2018), Toriola et al. (2018), Amadi et al. (2018), Gyang et al. (2019), Adetunji et al. (2019), Muller et al. (2019), Olodu et al. (2019), Senekal et al. (2019), Medgyesi et al. (2019), Gbadegesin and Olayide (2019), Aigbokhaode et al. (2020), Fakunle et al. (2020), Kidokoro et al. (2020), Adeboyejo et al. (2020), Khulu and Ramroop (2020)

(*Continued*)

Table 21.2 (Continued)

Demographic Group	*Proportion (%)**	*Authors*
Men	2.6	Burrell et al. (2010), Tucker et al. (2014), Wijnberg and Green (2014), Meth (2014), Adedokun et al. (2017), Ajaero et al. (2020)
Migrants	4.8	Alfaro-Velcamp (2017), Mberu (2008), Amoo et al. (2013), Bocquier et al. (2011), Boru et al. (2013), Olusese et al. (2018), Ajaero et al. (2020), Ludwar-Ene (1991), Makandwa and Vearey (2017), Mberu and White (2011), Muindi et al. (2014), Ikuteyijo (2020)
Older adults	5.2	Haddock (1979), Ezeh, Chepngeno, Kasiira, and Woubalem (2006), Smith and Sandra (2010), Falkingham et al. (2011), Kalula (2016), Ananias and Strydom (2014), Bigala and Ayiga (2014), Nkosi et al. (2015), Freeman (2017), Adeboyejo and Adewoyin (2017), Ojagbemi et al. (2017), Agunbiade (2019), Okunade (2020)
Orphan	0.4	Kimani-Murage et al. (2011)
Whole population	13.5	Zhou et al. (2004), Sitas et al. (2004), Osuntogun and Koku (2007), Pengpid et al. (2011), Ziraba et al. (2011), Shirinde et al. (2014), Kimani-Murage et al. (2014), Garl et al. (2015), Baloye and Palamuleni (2015), Smit et al. (2016), Nriagu et al. (2016), Adewoyin and Adeboyejo (2016), Macharia et al. (2017), Naicker et al. (2017), Tomita et al. (2017), Ezeh et al. (2017), Lilford et al. (2017), Adewoyin et al. (2018), Adewoyin (2018a), Nyathi et al. (2018), Shezi and Wright (2018), Lawal and Anyiam (2019), Njoku et al. (2019), Apata et al. (2019), Alawode et al. (2019), Kootbodien et al. (2020), Rother (2020), Baratin et al. (2020), Peer et al. (2020), Iyaloo et al. (2020), Tomita et al. (2020)
Women	20.6	Seeley (1984), Ludwar-Ene (1991), Iyun (1992), Williams (1994), Steyn et al. (1997), Orindi et al. (2020), Cunnan (2002), Penner et al. (2003), Fotso et al. (2008), Ojiezeh et al. (2010), Maree and Wright (2010), Okonofua et al. (2010), Olawuyi (2011), Oluwatayo (2011), Fotso and Mukiira (2012), Durowade et al. (2012), Manda et al. (2012), Webb-Girard et al. (2012), Olasunkanmi (2012), Ajibade et al. (2013), Kohli et al. (2013), Dewing et al. (2013), Beguy et al. (2014), Bajoga et al. (2015), Okigbo et al. (2015) Aboyade et al. (2016), Olagunju et al. (2016), Ibem and Azuh (2016), Tsai et al. (2016), Idowu et al. (2017), Makandwa and Vearey (2017), Marsay et al. (2017), van Heyningen et al. (2017), Adewoyin (2017a), Owili et al. (2017), Habyarimana et al. (2018), De Wet et al. (2018), Ngocho et al. (2019), Olubodun et al. (2019), Winter et al. (2019), Kassier et al. (2019), Oyekale (2019), Gbadegesin and Olayide (2019), Moodley and Ebrahim (2019), Chikoko et al. (2019) Aigbokhaode et al. (2020), Rollin et al. (2020), Ezedike et al. (2020)
Youth	17.6	Dissel (1997), Kaufman and Stavrou (2004), Mamman (2004), Obot (2005), Oruwari (2006), Adedimeji et al. (2007), Adedimeji et al. (2008), Marteleto et al. (2008), Xu et al. (2010), Mberu and White (2011), Igwe (2011), Faronbi et al. (2012), Speizer et al. (2013), Peltzer et al. (2014), Muindi et al. (2014), Kyamana (2015), Ntaji (2015), Arulogun et al. (2016), Ombati and Ombati (2016), Kamandaya (2016), Obuah et al. (2017), Akwaji et al. (2017), Amali et al. (2017), Edelstein (2018), Culbreth et al. (2018), Ajaero et al. (2018), K. C. Okafor et al. (2018), Gibbs et al. (2018), Kingsley et al. (2018), Popoola et al. (2019), Schenck et al. (2019), Onagbiye et al. (2019), Mguzulwa and Gxubane (2019), Sogunle et al. (2019), Makhubele et al. (2019), Ikoh et al. (2019), Korio and Nyavanga (2019), Oduaran and Akanni (2019), Made et al. (2020), Owusu-Ansah et al. (2020), Mayo-Wilson et al. (2020), Ajayi and Somefun (2020), Harker et al. (2020), Ikuteyijo (2020)
Total	**100.0**	**229**

*Double counts for studies in more than one category were excluded in computing the percentages.

Temporal pattern of study focus

Between 1970 and 1989, four urban health issues dominated demographic research. These were environment, health seeking, healthy living, and health outcomes consequent on the socio-economic status of urban dwellers. Between 1990 and 1999, sanitation, substance abuse, and violence and injury surfaced in demographic studies with a focus on urban health. In the decade that followed, road-related issues and studies on risky sexual behaviour joined the list. Access, anxiety and depression, housing, and locational issues were urban health issues that emerged in the 2010–2019 period of demographic research in Africa. The temporal analysis of the subjects, as shown in Table 21.3, indicates that only studies on environment recorded a consistent upward trajectory from 1990. When the 2020 half year was taken into consideration, and subject to maintaining the current trend, studies on access, anxiety and depression, healthy living, location, and substance abuse are likely to join studies on environment in recording an upward trend on urban health subjects in demographic research in the coming years.

Discussion and gaps

The fact that socioeconomic status was the most-investigated urban health subject (19.7%) in the reviewed demographic studies underscores its importance as major determinant of health. Socioeconomic status of the urban population reflects income inequality within the urban space and affects where the population live, how they live, their feeding patterns, and the quality of their meals. These impacts affect the population's susceptibility and exposure to diseases (Adewoyin & Adeboyejo, 2016; Amadi et al., 2018; Adeboyejo et al., 2020). Uncontrolled and unplanned urbanization further exacerbates the health consequences of the susceptibility and exposure (Adeboyejo & Onyeonoru, 2003; Adewoyin, 2018a; Adewoyin et al., 2018). The socioeconomic status of urban residents also determines where they live within the city and

Table 21.3 Temporal Pattern of Urban Health Issues in Demographic Research, 1970–2020

Urban Health Issues	*Before 1990* (%)	*1990–1999* (%)	*2000–2009* (%)	*2010–2019* (%)	*2020* (%)
Access	—	—	—	3.0	3.8
Anxiety and depression	—	—	—	3.7	7.7
Environment, including pollution and climate change	25.0	12.5	14.8	18.9	15.4
Health seeking	25.0	12.5	—	5.5	3.8
Healthy living (diet and exercise)	25.0	—	3.7	15.2	19.2
Housing	—	—	—	1.2	—
Location	—	—	—	4.2	11.5
Road	—	—	3.7	1.2	—
Risky sexual behaviour	—	—	14.8	11.6	11.5
Sanitation and water	—	12.5	7.4	1.2	3.8
Socioeconomic status, inequality, and malnutrition	25.0	25.0	37.0	17.7	11.5
Substance abuse	—	12.5	7.4	6.7	11.5
Violence and injury	—	25.0	11.1	9.8	—

affects the population's access to social infrastructure and urban services that could enhance their well-being. Accessibility was, however, one of the least-investigated subjects (2.7%) in the studies. Amidst a spatial concentration of poverty and a class structure that constrains access to social services due to unequal income and socioeconomic status, emphasizing the role of access in demographic research possesses the capacity to influence policies to take care of the healthcare needs of the poor and vulnerable population. This becomes more imperative as studies have shown that government policies and the political economy of public goods provision matter for health outcomes (Adewoyin, 2017b, 2017c, 2017d, 2018b).

Housing, roads, and water and sanitation are other subjects less investigated. Their shares of representation in the sample were 0.9%, 1.3%, and 2.6%, respectively. Conditions within and around the house have consequences for health and diseases (Iyun, 1987; Egunjobi, 1995; Adewoyin, 2018a). These conditions include overcrowding – the number of rooms relative to the number of occupants, the location of the kitchen, whether there are mosquito nets, adequacy of ventilation, the types of materials the floor and roof are made of, proximity to noise and other pollutants, and adequacy of sanitation facilities. These conditions predispose the population to respiratory diseases; rapid spread of viral and bacterial infections including skin diseases, malaria, and other insect-borne diseases; high blood pressure; and anxiety, among others. The sanitation issues within the house and in the urban area in general indirectly account for a large proportion of infant and under-five mortality across the world through such diseases as dysentery, cholera, typhoid, schistosomiasis, and trachoma (WHO, 2016). Road traffic accidents, the pollution from road construction, and exposure from using both private and public transportation systems and their consequences for health are virtually non-existent in demographic studies with a focus on urban health. Transportation restrictions, including social distancing within the buses and taxis, as a mean of curtailing the spread of COVID-19 buttress the need to focus on roads and the transport system as an important component of urban health for demographic investigation.

Environmental pollution and climate change impacts are felt more in urban areas. According to a World Bank report, cities consume as much as 80% of energy production worldwide and also account for an almost equal share of global greenhouse gas emissions (World Bank, 2010). The health impacts of environmental pollution and climate change are well documented and are adequately represented in the number of demographic studies that addressed urban health issues in this review (17.9%). Beyond these external social and physical environmental factors (socioeconomic status, road housing, sanitation, pollution, and climate change), over which the population may not have total control, studies on the lifestyle choices of urban population ranked next in prevalence. These choices include unhealthy food consumption and lack of exercise (14.0%), risky sexual behaviour (11.3%), violence and injury (9.2%), and substance abuse (7.4%). This suggests that the urban environment predisposes the population to lifestyles and behaviours that further put them at risks of poor health (Ahaneku et al., 2014; K. C. Okafor et al., 2018; Kabiru et al., 2018; Ajaero et al., 2020; Itanyi et al., 2020). The preponderance of fast food outlets, conversion of exercise and recreational playgrounds into residential and commercial buildings to accommodate increase in urban population and their needs, peer influence, and inadequate security play a big role in creating the predisposing conditions. The temporal trends of studies on these subjects, as shown in Table 21.3, suggest that they will continue receiving adequate attention in the coming years.

Improved maternal and child health outcomes and gender equality are critical to achieving several of the targets of the global Sustainable Development Goals (SDGs). It is therefore not surprising that studies on children (25.7%) and women (20.6%) dominated demographic studies. While the pattern underscores the importance of women and children, studies on men, the third leg of the family tripod, are sparse (2.6%). This is in spite of the fact that men are more at risk of anxiety and depression if they are unable to provide for their families and indulge more in risky sexual behaviour, substance abuse, and violence (Burrell et al., 2010; Tucker et al., 2014; Wijnberg & Green, 2014; Gibbs et al., 2018; Ajaero et al., 2020). The health consequences of these conditions among men have implications for the family and national economies owing to loss of man-hours and production capacities. More attention should therefore be given to men's health in demographic research, especially urban-dwelling men. Equally deserving of more attention is the plight of orphan children in the urban space. Only one study focused on orphans (Kimani-Murage et al., 2011). The study's interest was on nutrition and food security among this vulnerable group in an urban slum. Their multiple levels of vulnerability will make further studies on urban orphans topical and relevant. More works are also expected on older adults and their urban health situation. Only 5.2% of the studies focused on older adults in a continent where life expectancy is still the lowest globally, a rise from 49.4 years in 1990 to 61.1 years in 2019 notwithstanding (United Nations, 2019). Such studies may illuminate how the additional 12 years were gained in order to sustain the increase.

Conclusion and research agenda

This chapter reviewed the urban health content in demographic research in Africa between 1970 and 2020. While all aspects of urban health were captured in the studies, the health consequences of constrained physical accessibility to urban infrastructure and social services based on the spatial distribution of the population within the city, housing conditions, and road and transportation systems, as well as water and sanitation, received very little attention in the studies. These aspects matter for contraction and transmission of infectious diseases, exposure and susceptibility to disease-promoting livelihoods, psychological well-being, and health seeking. As the bulk of the study focused on women, children and youths, a shift in focus to address the health conditions of urban men and older adults is suggested. This follows from the importance of men as the third leg of the family tripod, they being more prone to depression, risky sexual behaviour, substance abuse, and violence, and due to their roles in economic production. The shift with respect to older adults is also relevant for improving life expectancy in Africa.

References

Abidoye, R. O., & Ihebuzor, N. N. (2001). Assessment of nutritional status using anthropometric methods on 1–4 year old children in an urban ghetto in Lagos, Nigeria. *Nutrition and Health, 15*(1), 29–39.

Aboyade, O. M., Beauclair, R., Mbamalu, O. N., Puoane, T. R., & Hughes, G. D. (2016). Health-seeking behaviours of older black women living with non-communicable diseases in an urban township in South Africa. *BMC Complementary and Alternative Medicine, 16*(1), 410.

Adam, V. Y., & Isah, J. A. (2017). Prevalence and comorbidities of childhood overweight and obesity among school aged children in an urban settlement in Benin City, Nigeria. *Nigerian Journal of Paediatrics, 44*(1).

Adeboyejo, A. T., Adejumobi, D. O., Adewoyin, Y., & Oyasiji, A. O. (2020). Spatial and demographic patterns of climate related diseases among hospitalized children in parts of southwest Nigeria. *Human Geographies, 14*(1), 59–71.

Adeboyejo, A. T., & Adewoyin, Y. (2017). Climate change and health of the aged in Lagos, Nigeria. *Australian Journal of Basic & Applied Sciences, 11*(13), 8–16.

Adeboyejo, A. T., & Onyeonoru, I. P. (2003). Residential density and adolescent reproductive health problems in Ibadan, Nigeria. *African Population Studies, 18*(1), 81–95.

Adedimeji, A. A., Heard, N. J., Odutolu, O., & Omololu, F. O. (2008). Social factors, social support and condom use behavior among young urban slum inhabitants in southwest Nigeria. *East African Journal of Public Health, 5*(3), 215–222.

Adedimeji, A. A., Omololu, F. O., & Odutolu, O. (2007). HIV risk perception and constraints to protective behaviour among young slum dwellers in Ibadan, Nigeria. *Journal of Health Population and Nutrition, 25*(2), 146–157.

Adedokun, A. O., Goon, D. T., Owolabi, E. O., Adeniyi, O. V., & Ajayi, A. I. (2017). Driving to better health: Screening for hypertension and associated factors among commercial taxi drivers in Buffalo city metropolitan municipality, South Africa. *Open Public Health Journal, 10*, 303–312.

Adetunji, A. E., Adeniran, K. A., Olomu, S. C., Odike, A. I., Ewah-Odiase, R. O., Omoike, I. U., & Akpede, G. O. (2019). Socio-demographic factors associated with overweight and obesity among primary school children in semi-urban areas of mid-western Nigeria. *PLoS One, 14*(4), e0214570.

Adewoyin, Y. (2017a). Gender mainstreaming, solid waste management and urban health in Nigeria. In Adeboyejo et al. (Eds.), *Sustainable environmental planning and management in Nigeria* (pp. 209–220). Ogbomoso: Faculty of Environmental Sciences.

Adewoyin, Y. (2017b). National treatment policy for whom? Analysis of malaria treatment choices in urban Nigeria. *Journal of Behavioral Health, 6*(3), 120–123.

Adewoyin, Y. (2017c). Health, spatial justice and regional planning in Nigeria. In G. C. Emenike & T. C. Nzeadibe (Eds.), *Readings in human geography* (Chapter 10, pp. 159–172). Nigeria: Port-Harcourt, Uniport Press.

Adewoyin, Y. (2017d). Neoliberalism, public health, and malaria prevalence in Nigeria. *Asian Pacific Journal of Health Sciences, 4*(4), 168–171.

Adewoyin, Y. (2018a). A residential habitat quality model for population health vulnerability assessment in Urban Nigeria. *International Journal of Scientific Reports, 4*(3), 59–67.

Adewoyin, Y. (2018b). Political ecology of malaria prevalence in urban Nigeria. *Tanzania Journal of Development Studies, 16*(2), 74–86.

Adewoyin, Y., & Adeboyejo, A. T. (2016). People, places, and health variations: A case of malaria incidence in Ibadan, Nigeria. *African Population Studies, 30*(2), 3006–3015.

Adewoyin, Y., Chukwu, N. A., & Sanni, L. M. (2018). Urbanization, spatial distribution of healthcare facilities and inverse care in Ibadan, Nigeria. *Ghana Journal of Geography, 10*(2), 96–111.

Adeyeba, O. A., & Tijani, B. D. (2002). Intestinal helminthiasis among malnourished school age children in peri-urban area of Ibadan, Nigeria. *African Journal of Clinical and Experimental Microbiology, 3*(1), 24–28.

Adeyemi, O., & Oyetunde, O. (2017). Pattern of accidental femur fractures in children and the predictors of child abuse in an urban community in Nigeria. *Journal of Critical Care, 100*(38), 369–370.

Agunbiade, O. M. (2019). Explanations around physical abuse, neglect and preventive strategies among older Yoruba people (60+) in urban Ibadan Southwest Nigeria: A qualitative study. *Heliyon, 5*(11), e02888.

Ahaneku, G. I., Ahaneku, J. E., Osuji, C. U., Oguejiofor, C. O., & Opara, P. C. (2014). Lipid patterns, alcohol intake and BMI of adult Nigerians in a sub-urban slum in Enugu, Nigeria. *The Pan African Medical Journal, 18*, 37.

Aigbokhaode, A. Q., Isara, A. R., & London, S. (2020). Household air pollution and respiratory symptoms of women and children in a sub urban community in Nigeria. *American Journal of Respiratory and Critical Care Medicine, 201*, A1797.

Ajaero, C. K., Odimegwu, C. O., Mkwananzi, S., & Banjo, O. (2018). Inter-provincial migration effect on youth risk behaviors in South Africa: A multilevel analysis of contextual- and individual-level factors. *Cogent Social Sciences, 4*(1), 1.

Ajaero, C. K., Onuh, J. C., Amoo, E. O., & Adewoyin, Y. (2020). Contextual correlates of risky sexual behavior among migrant and non-migrant men in Nigeria. *SAGE Open, 10*(2), 1–10.

Ajayi, A. I., & Somefun, O. D. (2020). Recreational drug use among Nigerian university students: Prevalence, correlates and frequency of use, *PLoS One, 15*(5), e0232964.

Ajibade, I., McBean, G., & Bezner-Kerr, R. (2013). Urban flooding in Lagos, Nigeria: Patterns of vulnerability and resilience among women. *Global Environmental Change, 23*(6), 1714–1725.

Akinyemi, J. O., Adedini, S. A., Wandera, S. O., & Odimegwu, C. O. (2016). Independent and combined effects of maternal smoking and solid fuel on infant and child mortality in sub-Saharan Africa. *Tropical Medicine & International Health, 21*(12), 1572–1582.

Akwaji, F. N., Uyang, F. A., & Abonor, L. B. (2017). Urban slums and youth criminality in Calabar Municipality of Cross River State, Nigeria. *Annals of Humanities and Development Studies, 8*(1).

Alawode, O. A., Chima, V., & Awoleye, A. F. (2019). Household characteristics as determinants of ownership of mosquito nets in urban households in Nigeria. *Scientific African, 6*, e00156.

Alfaro-Velcamp, T. (2017). Don't send your sick here to be treated, our own people need it more: Immigrants' access to healthcare in South Africa. *International Journal of Migration, Health and Social Care, 13*(1), 53–68.

Allu, S. O. (2001). *Access to primary health care for low-income women in urban Kenya* (Unpublished master's thesis, University of Calgary, Calgary, AB). doi:10.11575/PRISM/22202

Amadi, O. F., Ezenwosu, O. U., & Odetunde, O. I. (2018). A cross-sectional study on nutritional status of preschool aged children in Enugu urban, Nigeria. *Journal of Experimental Research, 6*(2), 19.

Amali, S. E., Moshood, I., & Iliyasu, M. B. (2017). Impact and implications of youth involvement in urban gangs: A case study from Nasarawa, Kano State, Nigeria. *Acta Criminologica: African Journal of Criminology & Victimology, 30*(5), 150–169.

Amoo, E. O., Adetoro, W., & Oluwole-Isaac, A. (2013). Internal migration of young persons and street trading activities in urban areas of Nigeria. *IFE Psychologia: An International Journal, 21*(2), 113–122.

Ananias, J., & Strydom, H. (2014). Factors contributing to elder abuse and neglect in the informal caregiving setting. *Social Work (South Africa), 50*(2), 266–284.

Apata, T. G., Ogunjimi, S. I., Okanlawon, M. M., Bamigboye, O., Adara, C., & Egbunonu, C. (2019). Growing-city pollution and sanitation: Causality and evidence from major cities of southwestern Nigeria. *Urbe, 11*, e20180189.

Arulogun, O. S., Ogbu, I. A., & Dipeolu, I. O. (2016). Influence of internet exposure on sexual behaviour of young persons in an urban district of Southwest Nigeria. *The Pan African Medical Journal, 25*, 61.

Ayoade, A. A., Sikiru, S., & Okanlawon, P. O. (2015). Assessment of water provision and associated risks among children in Abeokuta peri-urban, Ogun state, Southwestern Nigeria: The gender implications. *wH2O: The Journal of Gender and Water, 4*(1), 9.

Babatunde, T. A., Asaolu, S. O., & Sowemimo, O. A. (2013). Urinary schistosomiasis among pre-school and school aged children in two peri-urban communities in Southwest Nigeria. *Journal of Parasitology and Vector Biology, 5*(7), 96–101.

Baiocchi, M., Friedberg, R., Rosenman, E., Amuyunzu-Nyamongo, M., Oguda, G., Otieno D., & Sarnquist, C. (2019). Prevalence and risk factors for sexual assault among class 6 female students in unplanned settlements of Nairobi, Kenya: Baseline analysis from the IMPower & Sources of Strength cluster randomized controlled trial. *PLoS One, 14*(6), e0213359.

Bajoga, U. A., Atagame, K. L., & Okigbo, C. C. (2015). Media influence on sexual activity and contraceptive use: A cross sectional survey among young women in urban Nigeria. *African Journal of Reproductive Health, 19*(3), 100–110.

Baloye, D. O., & Palamuleni, L. G. (2015). A comparative land use-based analysis of noise pollution levels in selected urban centers of Nigeria. *International Journal of Environmental Research and Public Health, 12*(10), 12225–12246.

Baratin, C., Beune, E., van Schalkwijk, D., Meeks, K., Smeeth, L., Addo, J., . . . Agyemang, C. (2020). Differential associations between psychosocial stress and obesity among Ghanaians in Europe and in Ghana: Findings from the RODAM study. *Social Psychiatry and Psychiatric Epidemiology, 55*(1), 45–56.

Beguy, D., Mumah, J., & Gottschalk, L. (2014). Unintended pregnancies among young women living in urban slums: Evidence from a prospective study in Nairobi city, Kenya. *PLoS One, 9*(7), e101034.

Bi, A., & Okposio, M. M. (2013). Risk factors for death in under-five children presenting with acute diarrhoea in an urban teaching hospital in Nigeria. *Pacific Journal of Medical Sciences, 12*(1), 45–54.

Bigala, P., & Ayiga, N. (2014). Prevalence and predictors of elder abuse in Mafikeng local municipality in South Africa. *Etude de la Population Africaine, 28*(1), 463–474.

Bocquier, P., Beguy, D., Zulu, E. M., Muindi, K., Konseiga, A., & Yé, Y. (2011). Do migrant children face greater health hazards in slum settlements? Evidence from Nairobi, Kenya. *Journal of Urban Health, 88*(2), S266–S281.

Boru, W. G., Kikuvi, G., Omollo, J., Abade, A., Amwayi, S., Ampofo, W., . . . Oundo, J. (2013). Aetiology and factors associated with bacterial diarrhoeal diseases amongst urban refugee children in Eastleigh, Kenya: A case control study. *African Journal of Laboratory Medicine, 2*(1).

Breiman, R. F., Cosmas, L., Njenga, M. K., Williamson, J., Mott, J. A., Katz, M. A., . . . Neatherlin, J. C. (2015). Severe acute respiratory infection in children in a densely populated urban slum in Kenya, 2007–2011. *BMC Infectious Diseases, 15*(1), 95.

Burrell, E., Mark, D., Grant, R., Wood, R., & Bekker, L. (2010). Sexual risk behaviours and HIV-1 prevalence among urban men who have sex with men in Cape Town, South Africa. *Sexual Health*, 7(2), 149–153.

Burrows, S., Niekerk, A., & Laflamme, L. (2010). Fatal injuries among urban children in South Africa: Risk distribution and potential for reduction. *Bulletin of the World Health Organization, 88*, 267–272.

Burrows, S., Swart, L., & Laflamme, L. (2009). Adolescent injuries in urban South Africa: A multi-city investigation of intentional and unintentional injuries. *International Journal of Child and Adolescent Health, 2*(1), 117–129.

Busayo, A. O., Jacob, M. L., & Abimbola, T. (2014). Lifestyle and genetic factors in the prevalence of adolescent underweight and obesity in an urban area in Nigeria. *Journal of Obesity and Metabolic Research, 1*(3), 164.

Chadoka-Mutanda, N., & Odimegwu, C. O. (2017). Maternal health-seeking behaviour and under-five mortality in Zimbabwe. *Journal of Biosocial Science, 49*(3), 408–421.

Chikoko, W., Ruparanganda, W., Muzvidziwa, V. N., & Chimhowa, E. C. (2019). Reasons for the street girl's entry into commercial sex work: A case study of the Harare central business district, Zimbabwe (RSGECSWH). *Journal of Sociology and Social Anthropology, 10*(1).

Culbreth, R., Swahn, M. H., Ndetei, D., Ametewee, L., & Kasirye, R. (2018). Suicidal ideation among youth living in the slums of Kampala, Uganda. *International Journal of Environmental Research and Public Health, 15*(2), 298.

Cunnan, P. (2002). *The health of urban poor, black women street traders in Durban, South Africa* (Unpublished Ph.D. thesis). London, Queen Mary, University of London.

Danquah, I., Addo, J., Boateng, D., Klipstein-Grobusch, K., Meeks, K., Galbete, C., . . . Smeeth L. (2019). Early-life factors are associated with waist circumference and type 2 diabetes among Ghanaian adults: The RODAM Study. *Scientific Reports, 9*(1), 10848.

Darikwa, T. B., & Manda, S. O. (2020). Spatial co-clustering of cardiovascular diseases and select risk factors among adults in South Africa. *International Journal of Environmental Research and Public Health, 17*(10), 3583.

De Jong, M. (2019). *From 'cleanliness is next to Godliness' to 'without perfect health, there is nothing': Discourses of healthy lifestyle in the construction of young adult identities in urban South Africa* (Ph.D. Thesis, Rhodes University, South Africa).

De Villiers, A., & Senekal, M. (2002). Determinants of growth failure in 12–24-month-old children in a high-density urban slum community in East London, South Africa. *European Journal of Clinical Nutrition, 56*(12), 1231–1241.

De Wet, N., Frade, S., & Akinyemi, J. (2018). Extra mouths to feed: The odds of young mothers engaging in transactional sexual relationships in South Africa. *Cogent Social Sciences, 4*(1), 1482986.

Dewing, S., Tomlinson, M., le Roux, I. M., Chopra, M., & Tsai, A. C. (2013). Food insecurity and its association with co-occurring postnatal depression, hazardous drinking, and suicidality among women in peri-urban South Africa. *Journal of Affective Disorders, 150*(2), 460–465.

Dissel, A. (1997). Youth, street gangs and violence in South Africa. In G. Herault & P. Adesanmi (Eds.), *Youth, street culture and urban violence in Africa* (pp. 405–411). Ibadan: French Institute for Research in Africa, Nigeria.

Durowade, K. A., Osagbemi, G. K., Salaudeen, A. G., Musa, O. I., Akande, T. M., Babatunde, O. A., . . . Ibrahim, O. O. K. (2012). Prevalence and risk factors of cervical cancer among women in an urban community of Kwara State, north central Nigeria. *Journal of Preventive Medicine and Hygiene, 53*(4), 213–219.

Ebomoyi, E. W. (1994). Pediculosis capitis among urban school children in Ilorin, Nigeria. *Journal of the National Medical Association, 86*(11), 861.

Edelstein, I. (2018). Pathways to violence propensity: Results from a two-wave study of young males in urban South Africa. *Journal of Psychology in Africa, 28*(1), 33–40.

Egunjobi, L. (1995). Urban environmental health and physical planning. In B. F. Iyun, Y. Verhasselt, & H. Anthony (Eds.), *The health of nations: Medicine, disease and development in the third world*. Aldershot: Avebury.

Ekejindu, I. M., & Ochuba, G. C. (2004). Cryptosporidium infection among young children in Onitsha Urban Area in South-Eastern Nigeria. *Tropical Journal of Medical Research, 8*(1), 17–20.

Elamass, I. A. (1997). *The prevalence of malnutrition and some associated factors among pre-school children in an urban slum, Kibera, Nairobi, Kenya* (Thesis, University of Nairobi, Kenya).

Ene-Obong, H., Ibeanu, V., Onuoha, N., & Ejekwu, A. (2012). Prevalence of overweight, obesity, and thinness among urban school-aged children and adolescents in southern Nigeria. *Food and Nutrition Bulletin, 33*(4), 242–250.

Ezedike, C., Ohazurike, E., Emetumah, F. C., & Ajaegbu, O. O. (2020). Health-seeking behavior and waste management practices among women in major urban markets in Owerri, Nigeria. *AIMS Public Health, 7*(1), 169.

Ezeh, A., Chepngeno, G., Kasiira, A., & Woubalem, Z. (2006). The situation of older people in poor urban settings: The case of Nairobi, Kenya. In B. Cohen & J. Menken (Eds.), *Aging in sub-Saharan Africa: Recommendations for furthering research* (pp. 189–213). Washington, DC: National Research Council (US) Committee on Population.

Ezeh, A., Oyebode, O., Satterthwaite, D., Chen, Y., Ndugwa, R., Sartori, J., . . . Watson, S. I. (2017). The history, geography, and sociology of slums and the health problems of people who live in slums. *The Lancet, 389*(10068), 547–558.

Fakunle, A. G., Olusola, B., Jafta, N., Faneye, A., Heederik, D., Smit, L. A. M., & Naidoo, R. N. (2020). Home assessment of indoor microbiome (Haim) in relation to lower respiratory tract infections among under-five children in Ibadan, Nigeria: The study protocol. *International Journal of Environmental Research and Public Health, 17*(6), 1857.

Falkingham, J. C., Chepngeno-Langat, G., Kyobutungi, C., Ezeh, A., & Evandrou, M. (2011). Does socioeconomic inequality in health persist among older people living in resource-poor urban slums? *Journal of Urban Health, 88*(2), S381–S400.

Faronbi, J. O., Oginni, M. O., Olowookere, A. E., & Moronkeji, D. (2012). Impact of drug abuse on the lives of youth in a semi-urban community setting in Nigeria. *Journal of Community and Health Sciences*, 7(1).

Fatiregun, A. A., & Oluwatoba, O. A. (2008). Pattern of intestinal helminth infections among school children in an urban community in Ibadan, Nigeria. *Asian Pacific Journal of Tropical Medicine, 1*(3), 42–47.

Fotso, J. C., Ezeh, A., & Oronje, R. (2008). Provision and use of maternal health services among urban poor women in Kenya: What do we know and what can we do? *Journal of Urban Health, 85*(3), 428–442.

Fotso, J. C., & Mukiira, C. (2012). Perceived quality of and access to care among poor urban women in Kenya and their utilization of delivery care: Harnessing the potential of private clinics? *Health Policy and Planning, 27*(6), 505–515.

Francis, J. M., Myers, B., Nkosi, S., Williams, P. P., Carney, T., Lombard, C., . . . Morojele, N. (2019). The prevalence of religiosity and association between religiosity and alcohol use, other drug use, and risky sexual behaviours among grade 8–10 learners in Western Cape, South Africa. *PLoS One, 14*(2), e0211322.

Frank-Briggs, A. I., & Alikor, E. A. D. (2010). Anxiety disorder amongst secondary school children in an urban city in Nigeria. *International Journal of Biomedical Science, 6*(3), 246.

Freeman, E. (2017, May 24). *Rethinking care for older Africans: Changing expectations and practices of long term care in urban South Africa.* LSE ALPHA/KCL Global Ageing and Health Seminar Series, Kings College, London.

Garl, R. M., Matooane, M., Engelbrecht, F. A., Bopape, M. J. M., Landman, W. A., Naidoo, M., . . . Wright, C. Y. (2015). Regional projections of extreme apparent temperature days in Africa and the related potential risk to human health. *International Journal of Environmental Research and Public Health, 12*(10), 12577–12604.

Gbadegesin, T. K., & Olayide, O. E. (2019). Assessment of women and children vulnerability to water use in low-income urban area of Agbowo community, Ibadan, Nigeria. *International Journal of Sustainability Management and Information Technologies, 5*(2), 29.

Gibbs, A., Jewkes, R., Willan, S., & Washington, L. (2018). Associations between poverty, mental health and substance use, gender power, and intimate partner violence amongst young (18–30) women and men in urban informal settlements in South Africa: A cross-sectional study and structural equation model. *PLoS One, 13*(10), e0204956.

Griffiths, P. L., Johnson, W. C., Noël, P. J. M., & Norris, S. A. (2013). In urban South Africa, 16 year old adolescents experience greater health equality than children. *Economics & Human Biology, 11*(4), 502–514.

Gusenbauer, M. (2018). Google Scholar to overshadow them all? Comparing the sizes of 12 academic search engines and bibliographic databases. *Scientometrics, 18*, 177–214.

Gyang, V. P., Chuang, T., Liao, C., Lee, Y., Akinwale, O. P., Orok, A., . . . Chou, C. (2019). Intestinal parasitic infections: Current status and associated risk factors among school aged children in an archetypal African urban slum in Nigeria. *Journal of Microbiology, Immunology and Infection, 52*(1), 106–113.

Habyarimana, F., Zewotir, T., & Ramroop, S. (2018). Spatial distribution and analysis of risk factors associated with anemia among women of reproductive age: Case of 2014 Rwanda demographic and health survey data. *Open Public Health Journal, 11*(1), 425–437.

Haddock, D. R. W. (1979). An analysis of adult admissions and deaths in a medical unit in a new teaching hospital in southern Nigeria, 1973–76: Possible changing patterns of serious morbidity and mortality in urban adult Nigerians. *Annals of Tropical Medicine & Parasitology*, *73*(1), 1–10.

Harker, N., Londani, M., Morojele, N., Williams, P. P., & Parry, C. D. H. (2020). Characteristics and predictors of heavy episodic drinking (HED) among young people aged 16–25: The international alcohol control study (IAC), Tshwane, South Africa. *International Journal of Environmental Research and Public Health*, *17*(10), 3537.

Ibem, E. O., & Azuh, D. E. (2016). Satisfaction with public housing among urban women in Ogun State, Nigeria. *Covenant Journal of Research in the Built Environment*, *1*(2).

Idowu, A., Olowookere, S. A., Abiola, O. O., Akinwumi, A. F., & Adegbenro, C. (2017). Determinants of skilled care utilization among pregnant women residents in an urban community in Kwara State, Northcentral Nigeria. *Ethiopian Journal of Health Sciences*, *27*(3), 291–298.

Idowu, A. E., Amoo, E. O., Chiazor, I. I., & Adekeye, O. (2015). Psychosocial health of adolescent living in urban slum Nigeria. *Review of Economics and Development Studies*, *1*(1), 1–10.

Ige, O. M., Falade, A. G., & Arinola, O. G. (2012). Atopy is a risk factor for adult asthma in urban community of Southwestern Nigeria. *Lung India: Official Organ of Indian Chest Society*, *29*(2), 114.

Igwe, D. O. (2011). Demographic delusion and urban violence: A challenge to youth development in Nigeria. *International Journal of Global Environmental Issues*, *11*, 218–230.

Ikoh, M. U., Smah, S. O., Okwanya, I., Clement, U. A., & Aposhi, Z. A. (2019). Factors affecting entry into drug abuse among youths in Lafia Metropolis: Implications on security. *SAGE Open*, *9*(1).

Ikuteyijo, L. O. (2020). Irregular migration as survival strategy: Narratives from youth in urban Nigeria. *West African Youth Challenges and Opportunity Pathways*, 53–77.

Iloh, G., Amadi, A., & Nwankwo, B. (2010). Obesity in adult Nigerians: A study of its prevalence and common primary co-morbidities in a semi-urban Mission General Hospital in South-Eastern Nigeria. *Nigerian Journal of Medicine*, *19*(4), 459–466.

Itanyi, I. U., Onwasigwe, C. N., Ossip, D., Uzochukwu, B. S. C., McIntosh, S., Aguwa, E. N., . . . Ezeanolue, E. E. (2020). Predictors of current tobacco smoking by adolescents in Nigeria: Interaction between school location and socioeconomic status. *Tobacco Induced Diseases*, *18*, 117959.

Iyaloo, S., Kootbodien, T., Naicker, N., Kgalamono, S., Wilson, K. S., & Rees, D. (2020). Respiratory health in a community living in close proximity to gold mine waste dumps, Johannesburg, South Africa. *International Journal of Environmental Research and Public Health*, *17*(7), 2240.

Iyun, B. F. (1987). Ecology and disease in Nigeria. *Geographia Medica*, *17*, 85–127.

Iyun, B. F. (1992). Women's status and childhood mortality in two contrasting areas in southwestern Nigeria: A preliminary analysis. *GeoJournal*, *26*(1), 43–52.

Jacobs, T., & Slabbert, I. (2019). Factors that could contribute to substance misuse and criminal activity amongst adolescents: An ecological perspective. *Social Work (South Africa)*, *55*(2), 223–235.

Kabiru, C. W., Mumah, J. N., Maina, B. W., & Abuya, B. A. (2018). Violence victimisation and aspirations – expectations disjunction among adolescent girls in urban Kenya. *International Journal of Adolescence and Youth*, *23*(3), 281–290.

Kalula, S. Z. (2016). Prevalence of and risk factors for falls in older people in an urban community in South Africa. *BMC Geriatrics*, *16*, 51.

Kamandaya, M. (2016). *Sex and young people in urban slums: Exploring the material deprivation and sexual risk nexus in Malawi and South Africa* (Ph.D. Thesis, University of the Witwatersrand, South Africa).

Kambondo, G., & Sartorius, B. (2018). Risk factors for obesity and overfat among primary school children in Mashonaland west province, Zimbabwe. *International Journal of Environmental Research and Public Health*, *15*(2), 249.

Kassier, S., Senekal, M., & Villiers, A. (2019). Baseline descriptors of urban overweight/obese Zulu women enrolled in a weight loss intervention, South Africa (P21–034–19). *Current Developments in Nutrition*, *3*(1), 21–34.

Kaufman, C. E., & Stavrou, S. E. (2004). 'Bus fare please': The economics of sex and gifts among young people in urban South Africa. *Culture, Health & Sexuality*, *6*(5), 377–391.

Khulu, C., & Ramroop, S. (2020). Determinants of malnutrition in under-five children in Angola, Malawi and Senegal. *Open Public Health Journal*, *13*(1), 55–61.

Kidokoro, T., Fuku, N., Yanagiya, T., Takeshita, T., Takaragawa, M., Annear, M., . . . Mwangi, F. M. (2020). Physical activity and sedentary behaviour patterns among Kenyan and Japanese children: A comprehensive cross-country comparison. *International Journal of Environmental Research and Public Health*, *17*(12), 4254.

Kieni, S. K. (2015). *Factors influencing influx of street children in urban areas: A case of street children projects in Meru town-Kenya*. Kenya: University of Nairobi.

Kimani-Murage, E. W., Holding, P. A., Fotso, J. C., Ezeh, A. C., Madise, N. J., Kahurani, E. N., & Zulu, E. M. (2011). Food security and nutritional outcomes among urban poor orphans in Nairobi, Kenya. *Journal of Urban Health, 88*(2), S282–S297.

Kimani-Murage, E. W., Schofield, L., Wekesah, F., Mohamed, S., Mberu, B., Ettarh, R., . . . Ezeh, A. (2014). Vulnerability to food insecurity in urban slums: experiences from Nairobi, Kenya. *Journal of Urban Health, 91*(6), 1098–1113.

Kingsley, C. O., Emmanuel, C. A., & Vincent, Y. A. (2018). Sexual identity, preference and prevalence of forced sexual intercourse among young people in an urban community in Ovia North East local government area, Edo State, Nigeria. *Advances in Sexual Medicine, 8*(3), 25.

Kipyegon, K., Nyarombe, N. F., Achimba, O. C., & Kamar, K. I. (2015). Factors influencing rising number of street children in urban centers in Kenya: A survey of Eldoret Municipality, Kenya. *European Open Urban Studies & Development Journal, 1*(1), 1–14.

Kohli, R., Konya, W. P., Obura, T., Stones, W., & Revathi, G. (2013). Prevalence of genital chlamydia infection in urban women of reproductive age, Nairobi, Kenya. *BMC Research Notes, 6*(1), 44.

Kootbodien, T., Naicker, N., Wilson, K. S., Ramesar, R., & London, L. (2020). Trends in suicide mortality in South Africa, 1997 to 2016. *International Journal of Environmental Research and Public Health, 17*(6), 1850.

Korio, A. A., & Nyavanga, E. J. (2019). Alcoholic beverage use among Somali youth living in Eastleigh, an urban suburb in Nairobi, Kenya. *European Journal of Preventive Medicine*, 7(1), 23–28.

Kyamana, S. (2015). Factors contributing to crime among male urban youth: A case of Pumwani-Majengo ward, Nairobi Kenya. Kenya: University of Nairobi.

Lawal, O., & Anyiam, F. E. (2019). Modelling geographic accessibility to Primary Health Care facilities: Combining open data and geospatial analysis. *Geo-Spatial Information Science, 22*(3), 174–184.

Lilford, R. J., Oyebode, O., Satterthwaite, D., Melendez-Torres, G. J., Chen, Y., Mberu, B., . . . Caiaffa, W. (2017). Improving the health and welfare of people who live in slums. *The Lancet, 389*(10068), 559–570.

Ludwar-Ene, G. (1991). Spiritual church participation as a survival strategy among urban migrant women in Southern Nigeria. In G. Ludwar-Ene (Ed.), *New religious movements and society in Nigeria* (pp. 53–67). Bayreuth: Eckhard Breitinger.

Macharia, P. M., Ouma, P. O., Gogo, E. G., Snow, R. W., & Noor, A. M. (2017). Spatial accessibility to basic public health services in South Sudan. *Geospatial Health, 12*(1), 510.

Made, F., Ntlebi, V., Kootbodien, T., Wilson, K., Tlotleng, N., Mathee, A., . . . Naicker, N. (2020). Illness, self-rated health and access to medical care among waste pickers in landfill sites in Johannesburg, South Africa. *International Journal of Environmental Research and Public Health, 17*(7), 2252.

Maina, B. W., Orindi, B. O., Osindo, J., & Ziraba, A. K. (2020). Depressive symptoms as predictors of sexual experiences among very young adolescent girls in slum communities in Nairobi, Kenya. *International Journal of Adolescence and Youth, 25*(1), 836–848.

Makandwa, T., & Vearey, J. (2017). Giving birth in a foreign land: Exploring the maternal healthcare experiences of Zimbabwean migrant women living in Johannesburg, South Africa. *Urban Forum, 28*(1), 75–90.

Makhubele, M., Ravhuhali, K., Kuonza, L., Mathee, A., Kgalamono, S., Made, F., . . . Naicker, N. (2019). Common mental health disorders among informal waste pickers in Johannesburg, South Africa 2018 – A cross-sectional stud. *International Journal of Environmental Research and Public Health, 16*(14), 2618.

Maluleke, K. R., & Worku, Z. (2009). Environmental determinants of asthma among school children aged 13–14 in and around Polokwane, Limpopo Province, South Africa. *International Journal of Environmental Research and Public Health, 6*(9), 2354–2374.

Mamman, M. (2004). Urban youth violence as a threat to urban security and governance in Nigeria. *Savanna: A Journal of the Environmental and Social Sciences, 19*(1), 87–101.

Manda, S. O. M., Lombard, C. J., & Mosala, T. (2012). Divergent spatial patterns in the prevalence of the human immunodeficiency virus (HIV) and syphilis in South African pregnant women. *Geospatial Health, 6*(2), 221–231.

Maree, J. E., & Wright, S. C. D. (2010). How would early detection be possible? An enquiry into cancer related knowledge, understanding and health seeking behaviour of urban black women in Tshwane, South Africa. *European Journal of Oncology Nursing, 14*(3), 190–196.

Marsay, C., Manderson, L., & Subramaney, U. (2017). Validation of the Whooley questions for antenatal depression and anxiety among low-income women in urban South Africa. *South African Journal of Psychiatry, 23*, 1013.

Marston, M., Beguy, D., Kabiru, C., & Cleland, J. (2013). Predictors of sexual debut among young adolescents in Nairobi's informal settlements. *International Perspectives on Sexual and Reproductive Health, 39*(1), 22–31.

Marteleto, L., Lam, D., & Ranchhod, V. (2008). Sexual behavior, pregnancy, and schooling among young people in urban South Africa. *Studies in Family Planning, 39*(4), 351–368.

Mayo-Wilson, L. J., Mathai, M., Yi, G., Mak'anyengo, M. O., Davoust, M., Massaquoi, M. L., . . . NAHEDO Study Group. (2020). Lessons learned from using respondent-driven sampling (RDS) to assess sexual risk behaviors among Kenyan young adults living in urban slum settlements: A process evaluation. *PLoS One, 15*(4), e0231248.

Mberu, B., Wamukoya, M., Oti, S., & Kyobutungi, C. (2015). Trends in causes of adult deaths among the urban poor: Evidence from Nairobi urban health and demographic surveillance system, 2003–2012. *Journal of Urban Health, 92*(3), 422–445.

Mberu, B. U. (2008). Internal migration and premarital reproductive behavior among adolescents in Nigeria. *Social Science & Medicine, 72*(8), 1284–1293.

Mberu, B. U., & White, M. J. (2011). Internal migration and health: Premarital sexual initiation in Nigeria. *Social Science & Medicine, 72*(8), 1284–1293.

Medgyesi, D., Sewell, D., Senesac, R., Cumming, O., Mumma, J., & Baker, K. K. (2019). The landscape of enteric pathogen exposure of young children in public domains of low-income, urban Kenya: The influence of exposure pathway and spatial range of play on multi-pathogen exposure risks. *PLoS Neglected Tropical Diseases, 13*(3), e0007292.

Mehta, S. (2004). *Maximum city; Bombay lost and found*. New York: Vintage.

Meth, P. (2014). *Violence and men in urban South Africa: The significance of home: Masculinities and place*. Farnham: Ashgate, pp. 159–172.

Mguzulwa, S., & Gxubane, T. (2019). The impact of youth gang violence on the educational attainment of male high school learners in Khayelitsha. *Social Work (South Africa), 55*(3), 266–283.

Moher, D., Liberati, A., Tetzlaff, J., & Altman, D. G. (2009). Preferred reporting items for systematic reviews and meta-analyses: The PRISMA statement. *PLoS Med, 6*(7), e1000097.

Monyeki, M. A., Pienaar, A. E., Mamabolo, R. L., & Temane, M. (2009). Effect of obesity on physical self-concept of urban school children living in Potchefstroom, South Africa. *African Journal for Physical Health Education, Recreation and Dance, 15*(1), 1–4.

Moodley, P., & Ebrahim, S. (2019). #Blesser: A critical evaluation of conceptual antecedents and the allure of a transactional relationship. *Acta Academica, 51*(2).

Morar, D., Coopoo, Y., Shaw, I., & Shaw, B. S. (2014). Health and fitness attitudes and lifestyle habits of urban children in South Africa. *African Journal for Physical Health Education, Recreation and Dance, 20*(2), 102–112.

Muindi, K., Mudege, N., Beguy, D., & Mberu, B. U. (2014). Migration and sexual behaviour among youth in Nairobi's slum areas. *African Population Studies, 28*(3), 1297–1308.

Müller, I., Schindler, C., Adams, L., Endes, K., Gall, S., Gerber, M., . . . Pühse, U. (2019). Effect of a multidimensional physical activity intervention on body mass index, skinfolds and fitness in South African children: Results from a cluster-randomised controlled trial. *International Journal of Environmental Research and Public Health, 16*(2), 232.

Muriithi, D. I. (2014). *Risk factors influencing diarrhoea occurrence among children under five years old in informal urban settlements: A case study of Korogocho, in Nairobi county, Kenya*. Kenya: University of Nairobi.

Mutisya, M., Kandala, N., Ngware, M. W., & Kabiru, C. W. (2015). Household food (in) security and nutritional status of urban poor children aged 6 to 23 months in Kenya. *BMC Public Health, 15*(1), 1052.

Naicker, N., Teare, J., Balakrishna, Y., Wright, C. Y., & Mathee, A. (2017). Indoor temperatures in low cost housing in Johannesburg, South Africa. *International Journal of Environmental Research and Public Health, 14*(11), 1410.

Ngocho, J. S., Watt, M. H., Minja, L., Knettel, B. A., Mmbaga, B. T., Williams, P., & Sorsdahl, K. (2019). Depression and anxiety among pregnant women living with HIV in Kilimanjaro region, Tanzania. *PLoS One, 14*(10), e0224515.

Njoku, P. O., Edokpayi, J. N., & Odiyo, J. O. (2019). Health and environmental risks of residents living close to a landfill: A case study of Thohoyandou landfill, Limpopo province, South Africa. *International Journal of Environmental Research and Public Health, 16*(12), 2125.

Nkosi, V., Rathogwa-Takalani, F., & Voyi, K. (2020). The frequency of fast food consumption in relation to wheeze and asthma among adolescents in Gauteng and North West Provinces, South Africa. *International Journal of Environmental Research and Public Health, 17*(6), 1994.

Nkosi, V., Wichmann, J., & Voyi, K. (2015). Chronic respiratory disease among the elderly in South Africa: Any association with proximity to mine dumps? *Environmental Health: A Global Access Science Source, 14*(1), 33.

Nnoka, K. O., Akinola, O. O., & Mosimabale, M. M. (2016). Prevalence of overweight and obesity among school age children (6–9years) in six selected rural and urban schools of Osun State, Nigeria. *Nigerian Journal of Nutritional Sciences, 37*(1), 171–176.

Nriagu, J., Afeiche, M., Linder, A., Arowolo, T., Ana, G., Sridhar, M. K. C., . . . Orisakwe, O. E. (2008). Lead poisoning associated with malaria in children of urban areas of Nigeria. *International Journal of Hygiene and Environmental Health, 211*, 591–605.

Nriagu, J., Udofia, E. A., Ekong, I., & Ebuk, G. (2016). Health risks associated with oil pollution in the Niger Delta, Nigeria. *International Journal of Environmental Research and Public Health, 13*(3), 346.

Ntaji, M. (2015). Epidemiological features of road traffic accidents among young adults in a semi urban community of Southern Nigeria. *The Nigerian Postgraduate Medical Journal, 22*(1).

Nyathi, S., Olowoyo, J. O., & Oludare, A. (2018). Perception of scavengers and occupational health hazards associated with scavenging from a waste dumpsite in Pretoria, South Africa. *Journal of Environmental and Public Health, 2018*, 9458156.

Obot, I. S. (2005). *Substance use among students and out-of-school youth in an urban area of Nigeria*. Geneva: WHO.

Obuah, P. U., Moore, B., Altraide, D. D., & Asuquo, E. O. (2017). Pondering over the lifestyle and hypertension status of young adults in Alakahia: A semi-urban community in Rivers State, Nigeria. *International Journal of Public Health Research, 5*(4), 49.

Ochodo, C., Ndetei, D. M., Moturi, W. N., & Otieno, J. O. (2014). External built residential environment characteristics that affect mental health of adults. *Journal of Urban Health, 91*(5), 908–927.

Oduaran, C. A., & Akanni, A. A. (2019). Perceived stress effect and socio-demographic factors in substance use: A study of undergraduate students in a South African university. *Studies on Ethno-Medicine, 13*(2).

Ogundipe, O. (1975). Poisoning in children in an urban area of Nigeria. *Nigerian Medical Journal, 5*, 431–434.

Ojagbemi, A., Bello, T., Luo, Z., & Gureje, O. (2017) 0. Living conditions, low socioeconomic position, and mortality in the Ibadan Study of Aging. *Journals of Gerontology – Series B Psychological Sciences and Social Sciences, 72*(4), 646–655.

Ojiezeh, T. I., Ibeh, N. I., Opedun, D. O., & Udoh, S. J. (2010). Malaria endemicity among pregnant women in urban and semi-urban areas in Southwest, Nigeria. *American-Eurasian Journal of Scientific Research, 5*, 207–211.

Okafor, I. P., & Odeyemi, K. A. (2012). Use of insecticide-treated mosquito nets for children under five years in an urban area of Lagos State, Nigeria. *Nigerian Journal of Clinical Practice, 15*(2), 220–223.

Okafor, K. C., Adam, V. Y., & Azuike, E. C. (2018). Risky sexual behavior of young people in an urban community, South – South, Nigeria. *Global Journal of Medicine and Public Health*, 7(4).

Okigbo, C. C., & Speizer, I. S. (2015). Determinants of sexual activity and pregnancy among unmarried young women in urban Kenya: A cross-sectional study. *PLoS One, 10*(6), e0129286.

Okonofua, F., Omo-Aghoja, L., Bello, Z., Osughe, M., & Agholor, K. (2010). Self-reporting of induced abortion by women attending prenatal clinics in urban Nigeria. *International Journal of Gynecology & Obstetrics, 111*(2), 122–125.

Okpokowuruk, F. S., Akpan, M. U., & Ikpeme, E. E. (2017). Prevalence of hypertension and prehypertension among children and adolescents in a semi-urban area of Uyo Metropolis, Nigeria. *Pan African Medical Journal, 28*, 303.

Okunade, O. O. (2020). Adults and social supports for older parents in peri-urban Ibadan, Nigeria. *Journal of Caring Sciences, 9*(2), 65–72.

Olack, B., Burke, H., Cosmas, L., Bamrah, S., Dooling, K., Feikin, D. R., . . . Breiman, R. F. (2011). Nutritional status of under-five children living in an informal urban settlement in Nairobi, Kenya. *Journal of Health, Population, and Nutrition, 29*(4), 357.

Olack, B., Wabwire-Mangen, F., Smeeth, L., Montgomery, J. M., Kiwanuka, N., & Breiman, R. F. (2015). Risk factors of hypertension among adults aged 35–64 years living in an urban slum Nairobi, Kenya. *BMC Public Health, 15*(1), 1251.

Olagunju, O. E., Ayamolowo, S. J., & Sunmonu, W. O. (2016). Health promoting lifestyles and frequency of hospitalization market women in an urban settlement in South West Nigeria. *International Journal of Basic, Applied and Innovative Research*, *5*(4), 120–129.

Olasunkanmi, A. (2012). Women and urban violence in Nigeria: A study of Ibadan metropolis. *Studies on Home and Community Science*, *6*(2), 87–93.

Olawuyi, O. (2011). The prevalence of bacterial vaginosis among young women in urban areas in Nigeria and its major risk factors. *Sexually Transmitted Infections*, *87*(l), A299–A300.

Olodu, M. D., Adeyemi, A. G., Olowookere, S. A., & Esimai, O. A. (2019). Nutritional status of under-five children born to teenage mothers in an urban setting, south-western Nigeria. *BMC Research Notes*, *12*(1), 116.

Olubodun, T., Odukoya, O. O., & Balogun, M. R. (2019). Knowledge, attitude and practice of cervical cancer prevention, among women residing in an urban slum in Lagos, South West, Nigeria. *The Pan African Medical Journal*, *32*, 130.

Olusese, A., Petros, S., & Abuya, E. O. (2018). Under siege: Alternative care for urban unaccompanied and separated refugee children in Kenya. In *Protecting Migrant Children*. Cheltenham: Edward Elgar Publishing.

Oluwatayo, I. B. (2011). Climate change and adaptive capacity of women to water stress in urban centers of Nigeria: Emerging concerns and reactions. *Resilient Cities*, 69–78.

Ombati, M., & Ombati, V. F. O. (2016). Resilience of children and youth negotiating urban vulnerabilities and livelihoods in the Langas slums of Eldoret, Kenya. *Urbana*, *17*, 1–13.

Onagbiye, S. O., Tshwaro, R. M. T., Barry, A., & Marie, Y. (2019). Physical activity and non-communicable disease risk factors: Knowledge and perceptions of youth in a low resourced community in the western cape. *Open Public Health Journal*, *12*(1), 558–566.

Oni, T., Smit, W., Matzopoulos, R., Adams, J. H., Pentecost, M., Rother, H. A, . . . RICHE Members. (2016). Urban health research in Africa: Themes and priority research questions. *Journal of Urban Health*, *93*(4), 722–730.

Onyekwelu, C. A., Obienusi, E. A., Mozie, A. T., Nwosu, I. G., Adewoyin, Y., Ndichie, C. C., . . . Ayadiuno, R. U. (2018). Mapping incidents of infant mortality arising from gastroenteritis: A case study from South-East Nigeria. *African Population Studies*, *32*(2), 4134–4154.

Orindi, B. O., Maina, B. W., Muuo, S. W., Birdthistle, I., Carter, D. J., Floyd, S., & Ziraba, A. (2020). Experiences of violence among adolescent girls and young women in Nairobi's informal settlements prior to scale-up of the DREAMS Partnership: Prevalence, severity and predictors. *PLoS One*, *15*(4), e0231737.

Orji, C. A. (2017). *Modelling the relation between urban malaria and environmental inequality a case study of children, in Abia, Nigeria*. Netherlands: Utretch University.

Oruwari, Y. (2006). *Youth in urban violence in Nigeria – A case study of urban gangs from Port Harcourt*. Nigeria Delta Economies of Violence Project Working Paper 14.

Osuhor, P. C., & Etta, K. M. (1980). Morbidity patterns amongst children in a semi-urban community in Northern Nigeria. *Journal of Tropical Pediatrics*, *26*(3), 99–103.

Osuntogun, B. A., & Koku, C. A. (2007). Environmental-impacts of urban road transportation in south-western states of Nigeria. *Journal of Applied Sciences*, 7(16), 2356–2360.

Owili, P. O., Lien, W. H., Muga, M. A., & Lin, T. H. (2017). The associations between types of ambient PM2.5 and under-five and maternal mortality in Africa. *International Journal of Environmental Research and Public Health*, *14*(4), 359.

Owusu-Ansah, F. E., Addae, A. A., Peasah, B. O., Oppong, A. K., & Osafo, J. (2020). Suicide among university students: Prevalence, risks and protective factors. *Health Psychology and Behavioral Medicine*, *8*(1), 220–233.

Oyekale, A. S. (2019). Effect of obesity and other risk factors on hypertension among women of reproductive age in Ghana: An instrumental variable probit model. *International Journal of Environmental Research and Public Health*, *16*(23), 4699.

Peer, N., Lombard, C., Steyn, K., & Levitt, N. (2020). Elevated resting heart rate is associated with several cardiovascular disease risk factors in urban-dwelling black South Africans. *Scientific Reports*, *10*(1), 4605.

Peltzer, K., Pengpid, S., Alafia Samuels, T., Özcan, N. K., Mantilla, C., Rahamefy, O. H., . . . Gasparishvili, A. (2014). Prevalence of overweight/obesity and its associated factors among university students from 22 countries. *International Journal of Environmental Research and Public Health*, *11*(7), 7425–7441.

Pengpid, S., Peltzer, K., & van der Heever, H. (2011). Prevalence of alcohol use and associated factors in urban hospital outpatients in South Africa. *International Journal of Environmental Research and Public Health, 8*(7), 2629–2639.

Penner, J., Meier, A. S., Mwachari, C. A., Francis, M. B., Odhiambo, J. C., & Craig, R. (2003). Risk factors for pneumonia in urban-dwelling HIV-infected women: A case – control study in Nairobi, Kenya. *JAIDS Journal of Acquired Immune Deficiency Syndromes, 32*(2), 223–228.

Pepple, G., & Adio, A. (2014). Visual function of drivers and its relationship to road traffic accidents in Urban Africa. *Springer Plus, 3*(1), 47.

Popoola, O. E., Popoola, A. O., & Purchase, D. (2019). Levels of awareness and concentrations of heavy metals in the blood of electronic waste scavengers in Nigeria. *Journal of Health and Pollution, 9*(21).

Porteus, K., Clacherty, G., Mdiya, L., Pelo, J., Matsai, K., Qwabe, S., & Donald, D. (2000). 'Out of school' children in South Africa: An analysis of causes in a group of marginalised, urban 7 to 15 year olds. *Support for Learning, 15*(1).

Röllin, H. B., Channa, K., Olutola, B., Nogueira, C., & Odland, J. Ø. (2020). In utero exposure to aluminium and other neurotoxic elements in urban coastal South African women at delivery: An emerging concern. *International Journal of Environmental Research and Public Health, 17*(5), 1724.

Rother, H. A. (2020). Controlling and preventing climate-sensitive noncommunicable diseases in urban sub-Saharan Africa. *Science of the Total Environment, 722*, 137772.

Samuel, G. W., Amoo, E. O., Ekanem, I. B., Ajayi, M. P., Olawole-Isaac, A., & Akanbi, M. A. (2014). Vulnerability of children of street trading nursing mothers to diseases in urban Nigeria: Strategies for mitigation. *International Journal of Humanities and Social Sciences*. Retrieved from http://eprints.covenantuniversity.edu.ng/4272/#.YW121tpBzIU on 06/10/2020

Schenck, C. J., Blaauw, P. F., Viljoen, J. M. M., & Swart, E. C. (2019). Exploring the potential health risks faced by waste pickers on landfills in South Africa: A socio-ecological perspective. *International Journal of Environmental Research and Public Health, 16*(11), 2059.

Seeley, J. (1984). 'We have the healing power. . .' independent churches and women in urban Kenya. *Cambridge Anthropology*, 58–70.

Senekal, M., Nel, J. H., Malczyk, S., Drummond, L., Harbron, J., & Steyn, N. P. (2019). Provincial dietary intake study (PDIS): Prevalence and sociodemographic determinants of the double burden of malnutrition in a representative sample of 1 to under 10-year-old children from two urbanized and economically active provinces in South Africa. *International Journal of Environmental Research and Public Health, 16*(18), 3334.

Shezi, B., & Wright, C. Y. (20180. Household air pollution exposure and respiratory health outcomes: A narrative review update of the South African epidemiological evidence. *Clean Air Journal, 28*(1), 43–56.

Shirinde, J., Wichmann, J., & Voyi, K. (2014). Association between wheeze and selected air pollution sources in an air pollution priority area in South Africa: A cross-sectional study. *Environmental Health: A Global Access Science Source, 13*(1), 32.

Sitas, F., Urban, M., Bradshaw, D., Kielkowski, D., Bah, S., & Peto, R. (2004). Tobacco attributable deaths in South Africa. *Tobacco Control, 13*(4), 396–399.

Skeen, S., Macedo, A., Tomlinson, M., Hensels, I. S., & Sherr, L. (2016). Exposure to violence and psychological well-being over time in children affected by HIV/AIDS in South Africa and Malawi. *AIDS Care – Psychological and Socio-Medical Aspects of AIDS/HIV, 28*(16), 25.

Smit, W., de Lannoy, A., Dover, R. V. H., Lambert, E. V., Levitt, N., & Watson, V. (2016). Making unhealthy places: The built environment and non-communicable diseases in Khayelitsha, Cape Town. *Health and Place, 39*, 196–203.

Smith, M., & Marais, S. (2010). A Profile of fatal injury risk for older adults in urban South Africa. *Injury Prevention, 16*(l), A208–A209.

Sogunle, E., Masukume, G., & Nelson, G. (2019). The association between caesarean section delivery and later life obesity in 21–24 year olds in an Urban South African birth cohort. *PLoS One, 14*(11), e0221379.

Soura, A. B., Mberu, B., Elungata, P., Lankoande, B., Millogo, R., Beguy, D., & Compaore, Y. (2015). Understanding inequities in child vaccination rates among the urban poor: Evidence from Nairobi and Ouagadougou health and demographic surveillance systems. *Journal of Urban Health, 92*(1), 39–54.

Speizer, I. S., Fotso, J. C., Davis, J. T., Saad, A., & Otai, J. (2013). Timing and circumstances of first sex among female and male youth from select urban areas of Nigeria, Kenya, and Senegal. *Journal of Adolescent Health, 53*(5), 609–616.

Steyn, K., Yach, D., Stander, I., & Fourie, J. M. (1997). Smoking in urban pregnant women in South Africa. *South African Medical Journal, 87*(4), 460–463.

Suchdev, P. S., Davis, S. M., Bartoces, M., Ruth, L. J., Worrell, C. M., Kanyi, H., . . . Montgomery, J. M. (2014). Soil-transmitted helminth infection and nutritional status among urban slum children in Kenya. *The American Journal of Tropical Medicine and Hygiene, 90*(2), 299–305.

Suter, M. K., Karr, C. J., John-Stewart, G. C., Gómez, L. A., Moraa, H., Nyatika, D., . . . Benki-Nugent, S. (2018). Implications of combined exposure to household air pollution and HIV on neurocognition in children. *International Journal of Environmental Research and Public Health, 15*(1), 163.

Thiam, S., Fuhrimann, S., Niang-Diène, A., Sy, I., Faye, O., Utzinger, J., & Cissé, G. (2017). Urbanisation and its effect on risk factors associated with childhood diarrhoea in Mbour, Senegal: A visualisation. *Geospatial Health, 12*(2), 632, 381–384.

Thompson, A. A., Matamale, L., & Kharidza, S. D. (2012). Impact of climate change on children's health in Limpopo province, South Africa. *International Journal of Environmental Research and Public Health, 9*(3), 831–854.

Tomita, A., Cuadros, D. F., Burns, J. K., Tanser, F., & Slotow, R. (2020). Exposure to waste sites and their impact on health: A panel and geospatial analysis of nationally representative data from South Africa, 2008–2015. *The Lancet Planetary Health, 4*(6), e223–e234.

Tomita, A., Vandormael, A. M., Cuadros, D., Di Minin, E., Heikinheimo, V., Tanser, F., . . . Burns, J. K. (2017). Green environment and incident depression in South Africa: a geospatial analysis and mental health implications in a resource-limited setting, *The Lancet Planetary Health, 1*(4), e152–e162.

Toriola, A., Ajayi-Vincent, O., Oyeniyi, P., Akindutire, I., Adeagbo, D., Konwea, P., . . . Monyeki, M. (2018). Comparison of the prevalence of overweight and obesity in 9–13 year-old children from two countries using CDC and IOTF reference charts. *Asian Journal of Scientific Research, 11*(4), 466–471.

Tsai, A. C., Tomlinson, M., Comulada, W. S., & Rotheram-Borus, M. J. (2016). Food insufficiency, depression, and the modifying role of social support: Evidence from a population-based, prospective cohort of pregnant women in peri-urban South Africa. *Social Science & Medicine, 151*, 69–77.

Tucker, A., Liht, J., de Swardt, G., Jobson, G., Rebe, K., McIntyre, J., & Struthers, H. (2014). Homophobic stigma, depression, self-efficacy and unprotected anal intercourse for peri-urban township men who have sex with men in Cape Town, South Africa: A cross-sectional association model. *AIDS Care, 26*(7), 882–889.

United Nations. (2019). *World population prospects: 2019 Highlights*. Geneva: United Nations, Department of Economic and Social Affairs, Population Division.

United Nations, Department of Economic and Social Affairs, Population Division. (2019). *World urbanization prospects: The 2018 revision* (ST/ESA/SER.A/420). New York: United Nations.

van Heyningen, T., Honikman, S., Myer, L., Onah, M. N., Field, S., & Tomlinson, M. (2017). Prevalence and predictors of anxiety disorders amongst low-income pregnant women in urban South Africa: A cross-sectional study. *Archives of Women's Mental Health, 20*(6), 765–775.

Vanker, A., Barnett, W., Workman, L., Nduru, P. M., Sly, P. D., Gie, R. P., & Zar, H. J. (2017). Early-life exposure to indoor air pollution or tobacco smoke and lower respiratory tract illness and wheezing in African infants: A longitudinal birth cohort study. *The Lancet Planetary Health, 1*(8), e328–e336.

Vlahov, D., & Galea, S. (2005). Urban health: Evidence, challenges and direction. *Annual Review of Public Health, 26*, 341–365.

Von Schirnding, Y. E. R., Yach, D., Blignault, R., & Mathews, C. (1991). Environmental determinants of acute respiratory symptoms and diarrhoea in young coloured children living in urban and peri-urban areas of South Africa. *South African Medical Journal, 79*(4), 457–461.

Webb-Girard, A., Cherobon, A., Mbugua, S., Kamau-Mbuthia, E., Amin, A., & Sellen, D. W. (2012). Food insecurity is associated with attitudes towards exclusive breastfeeding among women in urban Kenya. *Maternal & Child Nutrition, 8*(2), 199–214.

Wijnberg, M., & Green, S. (2014). Male gang members' perspectives on gang membership and the role of drugs. *Social Work (South Africa), 50*(2), 284–302.

Williams, P. (1994). *Women and urban violence: A reflection of the structural adjustment programme on urban violence in Nigeria*. Ibadan: IFRA.

Winter, S. C., Obara, L. M., & Barchi, F. (2019). Environmental correlates of health-related quality of life among women living in informal settlements in Kenya. *International Journal of Environmental Research and Public Health, 16*(20), 3948.

World Bank. (2010). *Cities and climate change: An urgent agenda*. Urban Development Series Knowledge Paper, 10. Washington, DC: World Bank.

World Health Organization. (2016). *Global report on urban health: Equitable, healthier cities for sustainable development*. Geneva: WHO.

Xu, H., Luke, N., & Msiyaphazi, Z. E. (2010). Concurrent sexual partnerships among youth in urban Kenya: Prevalence and partnership effects. *Population Studies*, *64*(3), 247–261.

Zhou, G., Minakawa, N., Githeko, A. K., & Yan, G. (2004). Association between climate variability and malaria epidemics in the East Africian highlands. *Proceedings of the National Academy of Sciences of the United States of America*, *101*(8), 2375–2380.

Ziraba, A. K., Kyobutungi, C., & Zulu, E. M. (2011). Fatal injuries in the slums of Nairobi and their risk factors: Results from a matched case-control study. *Journal of Urban Health*, *88*(2), S256–S265.

22

DEMOGRAPHY OF INEQUALITY IN HEALTHCARE ACCESS IN AFRICA

Samuel Mwangi Wanjiku, Giuseppe T. Cirella, Alex Njeru and Jacob Kazungu

Introduction

Eradicating extreme poverty in developing countries is linked to understanding and addressing socioeconomic, political, and structural inequalities in healthcare access. In the study of inequality in healthcare access, researchers have conducted narrow literature reviews that directly focus on and are relevant to their empirical cases. This has resulted in reviews that are limited in scope and scattered among different domains. To address this challenge, this chapter aims to review the literature and bring together perspectives of knowledge on inequality in healthcare access. This scholarship focuses on different levels, that is, regional, national, sub-national, and households. It also involves various dimensions of inequality in healthcare access, including different data sets, theories, analytical frameworks, and policy analysis. By so doing, we learn what researchers have found to date about inequality in healthcare access in Africa and the means through which those findings were reached.

The origin of healthcare inequality in Africa is unclear even though studies suggest it started during the colonial era and early days of independence, for example, the case of South Africa (van Rensburg, 2014). Overall, due to governance frameworks, inequality in healthcare access became systematic and, therefore, with time, has either decreased or increased to diverse degrees in different African countries.

There are multiple perspectives on health access that this chapter highlights. Health inequality is different from inequality in healthcare access. The former is a broader concept that involves disparity in health status. Health inequality can be caused by beyond factors of healthcare access, such as the difference in availability of nutrition or the high prevalence of diseases in a particular geographical location. For example, a study of inequality in healthcare among children and adolescents in Madagascar showed that infectious diseases and nutrition were among the highest causes of deaths among those 10–14 years old (Ratovoson et al., 2020). Inequality in healthcare access is a component and key determinant of health inequality.

Healthcare access has been defined differently and changes meaning relative to the context of the analysis. Deaton (1999, p. 4) defines inequality in healthcare access as the difference in the utilization of healthcare across different socioeconomic groups. One of the challenges in the definition is that the term can mean both 'the potential for healthcare use' and 'the utilization of healthcare'. As argued by Guagliardo (2004, p. 2), "this leads to confusion between the ability

DOI: 10.4324/9780429287213-27

to get care, the act of seeking care, the actual delivery of care, and indicators thereof". Perhaps, guided by Sen's capability approach theory, healthcare access can be classified as 'potential for utilization' and 'realized utilization'. Potential utilization of healthcare access occurs when a population in need of health services coexists with a functional healthcare delivery system.

On the other hand, realized healthcare refers to achieved healthcare services. A more comprehensive definition of healthcare access has been put forward by Khan and Bhardwaj (1994) as the ability to reach, obtain, or afford health services. The two perspectives have recently been brought together by Rispel, de Sousa, and Molomo (2009, p. 493), who define health inequalities as "the systematic and unfair differences in health experience or outcomes between different socioeconomic groups within or between societies or countries." In common parlance, inequality in healthcare access refers to the differential ability of a population or a segment of the population to obtain the available health services. Love-Koh et al. (2020, p. 2) expand the definition to "the differences in healthcare access or utilization, quality of care or health outcomes that are considered avoidable and unfair, such as those associated with socioeconomic status, ethnicity, or geographical region".

The World Health Organization (WHO) defines health inequalities as "differences in health status or the distribution of health determinants between different population groups" (Quigley et al., 2006). As WHO examines health determinants, other researchers focus on health outcomes. Tang, Petrie, and Rao (2009, p. 56) define "health inequality as differences in health status or distribution of health outcome across individuals in a population". Even though there is not a specific way of quantifying fairness in ensuring equity in healthcare access, avoidable disparities within the population are termed unfair. In this chapter, we do not attempt to differentiate the two concepts (i.e., potential and realized health access) but rather bring out dimensions of inequality in healthcare access in Africa.

Studies in healthcare access inequality are always comparativeand examine di erent characteristics of the healthcare system, availability and distribution ofresources and population at risk in a region. Inequality in healthcare access has broadly been categorized as horizontal and vertical inequality (Ngozi & Ngianga-Bakwin, 2011). Most of the literature on healthcare access in Africa has cited inequality in the form of poverty, including the inability of people to meet the cost of healthcare and lack of access marked by lack of facilities (Kabia et al., 2019; Baraza, Maina, & Ravishankar, 2017; Peters et al., 2008). Although a general lack of health facilities was predominant, some scholars focused on poverty and unequal healthcare access. Other scholars went beyond the problem of distance in accessing healthcare to examine gender and economic issues (Timyan, Brechin, Measham, & Ogunleye, 1993; Vlassoff, 1994). At the same time, others examined the impact of healthcare reforms in African countries on equal access to healthcare. However, there is a mixed reaction to how healthcare reforms in different countries have impacted inequality in healthcare access. For example, using a household survey method, Hjortsberg and Mwikisa (2002) concluded that the impact of Zambia's health sector reform did not reduce the costs of healthcare access for some rural dwellers. This was due to traveling long distances, which increased the cost of healthcare. In contrast, van Rensburg (2014) provides evidence that since 1994, the healthcare reform in South Africa, for example, the free provision of primary healthcare, contributed to reducing inequality in healthcare access.

Theoretical frameworks of inequality in healthcare access

Most researchers of inequality in healthcare access prefer empirical studies without any specific theoretical underpinning. The availability of new forms of data and empirical analysis of disparity in healthcare access has challenged some of the demographic transition theories. New empirical evidence has shown a varied rate of change and correlations related to inequality in healthcare access. For instance, studies have found changing fertility or death rate declines in different periods. This indicates a more complex correlation that defies a simple prediction by any single theory. A key challenge is the lack of a common theoretical understanding of the shifting inequality in healthcare access that can be used across diverse historical paths.

One significant theoretical framework applied in the study of inequality in healthcare access is the capability approach. The theory was developed by Amartya Sen and Martha Nussbaum in the 1980s (Sen, 1980, 1984, 1993) but has gained prominence in recent years in terms of inequality in human welfare (Haisma, Yousefzadeh, & Boele Van Hensbroek, 2018). According to the capability approach, inequality in healthcare access occurs when people have different capabilities to achieve it (Unterhalter, 2003). In 2014, the *Journal of African Population Studies*, Volume 28, Number 2 dedicated the entire issue to applying the capability approach in population studies in Africa. Some studies used this theory to study inequality in healthcare access (e.g., Douptcheva & Hill, 2014; Sauvain-Dugerdil, 2014).

Quantifying various forms of inequality in healthcare access is important, since it shows 'unjust' or 'unfair' concerns related to the social determinants of those disparities. However, there is no unanimous approach to measuring fairness in the evaluation of inequality in healthcare access. Some theoretical frameworks focus on health sector governance, where policy interventions are informed by the concepts of egalitarianism, libertarianism, and utilitarianism (Faden & Powers, 2008; Ridde, 2008). The logic of egalitarianism aims to achieve equality in the distribution of resources and equality of people in terms of worth and value. Utilitarianism is concerned with the maximum benefit to the majority. In this case, the number of people and maximization of the usefulness (utility) of resources can justify inequality. According to utilitarianism, it is justifiable to allocate health facilities in urban areas where population density is high, since, in these areas, there is a higher need for healthcare services as opposed to sparsely populated rural ones. Health sector reforms and policy interventions based on one of these two perspectives of equality in healthcare access are founded on the governance theory of social justice (Rispel, 2016; Frimpong, 2013; Amu, Dickson, Kumi-Kyereme, & Darteh, 2018). The social justice theory emphasizes optimizing economic, social, and political processes within society to address the marginalization of the disadvantaged in healthcare access.

There is still a lack of any hegemonic theoretical framework that guides empirical research in the study of healthcare access and demographic transition in Africa. One study can combine various aspects of inequality, including spatial analysis, rural-urban inequality, maternal education, ethnicity, and wealth inequality (see Gage, 2007; Haisma, 2018; McLaren, Ardington, & Leibbrandt, 2013; Rutaremwa, Wandera, Jhamba, Akiror, & Kiconco, 2015).

Data and methodologies used

Researchers use different analytical approaches depending on the objective of their studies. Most of the studies of inequality in healthcare access in Africa use Demographic and Health Survey (DHS) data and, at times, complement this with census and survey data (Brockerhoff & Hewett, 2000; Adedini, Odimegwu, Imasiku, & Ononokpono, 2015; Hanson et al., 2017; Andriano & Morden, 2019). Some of the methodologies applied include logistic regression (Adedini et al., 2015; Ruktanonchai et al., 2018). In the case of a multidimensional analysis of inequality in healthcare access, researchers use multivariate regression (McLaren et al., 2013) or multilevel structural equation modeling (MSEM) (Adjiwanou & LeGrand, 2014; Van Malderen, Van Oyen, & Speybroeck, 2013). MSEM has been used to measure gender norms, especially those related to violence against women, as well as their direct or indirect impact on women's decision-making behavior regarding healthcare access (Adjiwanou & LeGrand, 2014; Ng et al., 2010). Antai (2009) used multi-level regression analysis in studying inequality by examining the relationship between women's socioeconomic status and the pattern of immunization. A Bayesian framework in the spatial extrapolation of disparity in healthcare access has been applied as a predictive model (Ruktanonchai et al., 2018). This is because modeling using Bayesian estimation is ideal for quantifying uncertainties through posterior distributions (Fritzen, 2007; Ruktanonchai et al., 2018). Some of the methodologies applied to analyze the effect of maternal education on under-five mortality include logistic regression and Bois's decomposition (see Bado & Susuman, 2016; and Van Malderen et al., 2013). Gridded data are increasingly being used by researchers in the examination of healthcare access. However, gridded data are not a substitute for census data. Instead, all gridded data sets are based on census data.

Spatial analysis has commonly been applied to study inequality in healthcare access (Linard, Gilbert, Snow, Noor, & Tatem, 2012). Before 2000, few studies on inequality in healthcare access deployed geographic information systems (GISs). The use of GISs in examining the distribution of populations and location of healthcare facilities is on the rise (Gjesfjeld & Jung, 2011; Gething et al., 2012; Sudhof et al., 2013; Ouma et al., 2018). The travel distance and the time taken to reach a health facility by road are the two variable measurements where researchers use GIS. Although GIS is useful in mapping physical distance, researchers highlight challenges in modeling time to reach a health facility (Makanga, Schuurman, von Dadelszen, & Firoz, 2016). In most rural areas in Africa, roads and pathways that link communities and health facilities have not yet been mapped, leading to inaccurate estimation. Besides, different means of transportation to a health facility make measuring time taken to access a health facility a challenge. However, with spatially disaggregated data becoming more available in better resolutions and the recent development of more sophisticated GIS analytical tools (Neutens, 2015), such challenges are increasingly resolved.

Another approach to measuring healthcare access inequality in Africa is using the concentration index (CI) (Kakwani, Wagstaff, & Van Doorslaer, 1997; Erreygers, 2009; Van Malderen et al., 2013). The concept of CI explains how equally (or unequally) certain health status is distributed across a population. This is best demonstrated using a concentration curve whereby "the cumulative proportion of the population, ranked by socioeconomic status, is plotted against the cumulative amount of health" (Booysen, 2003, p. 661). The CI has been classified into standard concentration and general concentration. In other words, the CI examines healthcare service delivery and where it is most utilized. The generalized concentration involves the cumulative distribution of health share in a population ranked by socioeconomic status irrespective of variance in the mean health status. The standardized concentration, on the other hand, takes into consideration the population's mean health status. According to Kakwani et al. (1997), in a concentration graph, negative indices (i.e., down to −1) show that a majority of people who seek healthcare services are the poorest within a population. A zero value means equal health service utilization throughout socioeconomic status, and a positive value (i.e., up to +1) means that health is more concentrated in the population of higher socioeconomic status. The introduction of the CI contributed to the scholarship of healthcare access by bringing in population concentration and measures of poverty level such as socioeconomic status (Goli, Nawal, Rammohan, Sekher, & Singh, 2017; Love-Koh et al., 2020).

Researchers have used the Gini index, also referred to as the Gini coefficient or Lorenz curve, to measure the correlation between the variation in socioeconomic wellbeing and inequality in healthcare access. The Gini index is a measure of statistical dispersion that aims to represent the distribution of wealth or income inequality of a country's population. A Gini coefficient of 1 shows a 100% inequality. For example, if only one person has an income in a large population, the Gini coefficient will be almost 1. Healthcare inequality is typically treated separately from the overall average health status of a population. Studies using Gini coefficient measures show a positive relationship between income inequality and health inequality (Petrie & Tang, 2008; Tang et al., 2009; J. E. Ataguba, Akazili, & McIntyre, 2011; Van Malderen et al., 2013; Omer et al., 2014; Love-Koh et al., 2020). However, for any given income estimates, there are huge variations of healthcare inequality. This indicates that the Gini measure of inequality only captures a part of healthcare inequality. Tang et al. (2009) used Gini coefficients to measure the distribution of healthcare inequality in Tanzania. They used Lorenz and concentration curves to measure the distribution of the whole healthcare workforce. Munga and Mæstad (2009) used a similar methodological approach and found evidence of inequality in the distribution of the health workforce per capita. Gini index measures are useful statistical tools that examine the dispersion of income inequality within a country or any particular group of people.

Additionally, researchers have used some absolute measures of health inequality, such as the slope index of inequality (SII) (Regidor, 2004). An SII is a weighted measure of inequality generated from a regression model where the whole population is ranked from the most disadvantaged (at rank zero) to the most advantaged (at rank 1). Arsenault et al. (2018) used the SII to assess the inequalities in antenatal care coverage and quality. In a few cases, a systematic review has been used to study scholarship in health care access. The World Health Organization, for instance, used a systematic review to examine the impact of health insurance in Africa and Asia (Spaan et al., 2012).

Manifestations of inequality in healthcare access

In the study of (in)equality in healthcare access in Africa, the cost of access has been examined in two ways. First is the physical distance to reach a health facility (time), and second is the financial cost of reaching health facilities. The link between these two perspectives brings together other socioeconomic factors such as infrastructure, individual poverty level, population density, and rurality or urbanity of areas. All these are factors determining whether people will seek healthcare and the extent of healthcare access.

Physical distance to health services

Generally, the burden of accessing healthcare is highest among the poorest located farthest from the health facilities. The poorest in rural and hard-to-reach areas tend to experience minimal access compared to relatively wealthy individuals in urban areas. In most African countries, the population concentration is highest in urban areas rather than in rural areas, and so are the health facilities. This form of inequitable resource distribution results in skewed utilization patterns across geographic regions. The access also varies across geographical locations whereby rural dwellers are highly likely to incur a higher cost and time to access primary health than urban dwellers. Also, it might create diverse demographic and health-seeking behaviors as well as different prevalence and incidence of health issues in a country.

Sub-Saharan Africa has had the highest maternal mortality ratio (MMR) in the world. This ratio is, however, not even across the continent and within African countries. Access to healthcare facilities is one of the contributing factors to uneven maternal healthcare. There has been a concerted effort to examine the emergence and development of spatial inequality in healthcare access (Ruktanonchai et al., 2016, 2018). Ruktanonchai et al. (2018) conducted a study on the changing disparity in maternal and child health access in Kenya,

Uganda, Tanzania, and Rwanda. They found that inequality in healthcare access was diverse in all of the countries. Tanzania and Rwanda, for example, indicated a significant increase in healthcare coverage and therefore illustrated reduced inequality. However, in all the East African countries, there was a general decrease in the inequality gap. Although this meant that governments had made a significant effort to reduce spatial inequality (i.e., horizontal inequality) in healthcare access, it remains unclear whether such progress leads to a correlative reduction in inequality in healthcare access across the socioeconomic arena (ibid). Herman (2014) used a case study of Tanzania to explain changing disparities in maternal health access using changing political-economic contexts of healthcare access. He concluded that there was a significant relationship between the change in human welfare, healthcare access, and regional development. In other words, the overall development in an area resulted in a reduction in inequality in healthcare access. The spatial distribution of populations across a country and their proximity to urban areas is a key factor in determining economic development and healthcare access.

Inequality in healthcare access has been measured against different demographic variables in different African countries, indicating a significant correlation between the distance traveled to reach a health facility and infant and child mortality. Distance from a health facility affected the utilization of preventive care, including prenatal care, delivery assistance, and child immunization. It also changed the consumption of curative services (see Katende, 1992, 1994). In detail, the study involved various categories of health facilities available in the region, that is, categorizing them into three: hospitals, health centers, and private clinics. In the twenty-first century, however, new forms of classification of health services and facilities have emerged, and the classification in past studies might not be congruent with the recent grouping.

Ngozi and Ngianga-Bakwin (2011) conducted a study on the spatial distribution of health facilities in Nigeria by combining various data sources, including government surveys and census data, and analyzed the extent of healthcare access geospatially via GIS. They found a correlation between inequality in healthcare access and population size region-wide. They examined healthcare access from both the supply and demand sides. From the demand side, they used vertical disparities, that is, the wealth status of people and their ability to access health care, while from the supply side, they focused on health service delivery at the facilities. The supply side, also known as provider-to-population ratios, involved measuring the distribution of health facilities and health professionals. The study, however, experienced fundamental shortcomings. First, it did not link the demand perspective of healthcare access with the supply perspective. Second, the nature of a relationship between the distribution of health facilities and the number of physicians available in these health facilities in a region was not explicit. This is with the acknowledgment that the distribution of health facilities is based on the population density in an area, while service delivery is based on an average number of patients (McNamee, Ternent, & Hussein, 2009).

Inequality in spatial accessibility (distribution of health facilities)

One perspective of measuring healthcare access is examining the distribution of health facilities in a country. Studies have shown a high inequality in the distribution of maternal healthcare professionals and health facilities in many sub-Saharan African countries (Gerein, Green, & Pearson, 2006; Hanson et al., 2017). Ruktanonchai et al. (2018) conducted a comparative study on spatial heterogeneity and sub-national inequalities in maternal and newborn health in East African countries. The study concluded that reduced access to health facilities reduces the utilization of all forms of maternal healthcare services (ibid). Spatial disaggregation of data healthcare access has enabled a better understanding of the impact of the geographical factors that generate disparities (Østby, Nordås, & Rød, 2009; Macharia, Odera, Snow, & Noor, 2017).

Using the case of Tanzania, Hanson et al. (2017) conducted a study to examine whether improved geographic accessibility had raised maternity care uptake. The study used census data and extensive household surveys to examine the change in healthcare access that occurred between 2007–2013. They concluded that women living far from the hospital reported a greater increase in the utilization of maternity care in primary facilities than those living near the facilities.

The use of physical distance or the cost of traveling to a health facility to measure health access examines the people's potential to access health. One of the challenges of this measure of healthcare access experience is its application in determining realized access. For instance, researchers use the health facility's attendance list to identify the patient's location of residence and the distance traveled. Hanson et al.'s (2017) study failed to consider people who would have sought health services but did not manage due to distance or travel costs. Second, there was the assumption that ill health, for example, caused by a disease, was equally distributed across the study area, and therefore proximity to a health provider was the sole factor.

Rural-urban dynamics of inequality in healthcare access

The rural-urban gradient in healthcare access is highly noticeable in sub-Saharan Africa. The rural and urban communities experience different public health issues, including fertility rates, access to modern family planning, infectious diseases, mortality rates, and maternal health (Booysen, 2003; Kong, Van de Linde, Aldous, Handley, & Clarke, 2013; Yaya, Uthman, Okonofua, & Bishwajit, 2019). This difference in health status is based on differential urbanicity, which goes in tandem with population concentration. Although healthcare access is generally poor in rural areas, in some cases, the disparity in healthcare access could be much worse in urban areas (Booysen, 2003). Booysen presented evidence that there existed a rural-urban inequality in healthcare access. However, a higher disparity of healthcare access in rural areas than in urban areas would be expected. Contrastingly, using the case of South Africa, Booysen found the reverse – that disparity in healthcare access was even worse in urban areas than in rural ones; however, this cannot be generalized. In addition, whether in rural or urban areas, inequality in healthcare access was viewed to work against the less well off, that is, low-income individuals (Ataguba & Alaba, 2012). Besides, more rural dwellers seek healthcare services from public facilities than from private facilities compared to urban dwellers.

In other cases, spatial inequalities in healthcare access exist in urban areas. Spatial inequality in most urban areas in developing countries is a natural consequence of household income inequalities (Kilroy, 2007). Cities are explained by spatial patterning of economic activities and levels of economic welfare. The level of income usually clusters the residence. High-income residential areas have better access to healthcare than slum areas occupied by the extremely poor (Magadi, Zulu, & Brockerhoff, 2003). In most cases, there is a huge difference in the means of transport and health facilities (Ruktanonchai, 2016). According to Booysen (2003), when healthcare access in urban areas is zoomed out, another level of inequality is experienced. He found a higher inequality in small urban settlements than in big urban places, that is, a higher rate of intra-urban inequality in healthcare access within smaller urban settlements than in larger towns (Booysen, 2003). This observation presented yet unexplored research area related to the geography of inequality in healthcare access: first, the nature of inequality within peri-urban regions and, second, its comparability with that of rural and urban areas.

Need to go beyond the rural-urban dichotomy

The literature on the rural-urban divide in healthcare access, however, experiences one major problem. There is an assumption that any region has to be categorized as either rural or urban (i.e., the distinct border between the two regions). In reality, this does not exist. Recent scholarship on the rural-urban divide has yet to go beyond the traditional rural-urban categorization of geographic areas to include the in-between region commonly referred to as peri-urban. The inclusion of the third dimension creates a challenge in comparing healthcare access between the rural and urban divide. This, in retrospect, raises the potential problem of the definitions and categorization of spaces.

Unequal distribution of healthcare personnel

Another form of inequality in healthcare access is the availability of healthcare personnel inequality in healthcare access, in this regard, is quantified in terms of imbalance in the health workforce (Zurn, Dal Poz, Stilwell, & Adams, 2004; Dussault & Franceschini, 2006). The logic is that some health facilities might have inadequate medical personnel, thereby resulting in disproportionate availability of services or underperformance of crucial functions in certain areas. Unlike health facilities, workforce issues are strategic. They not only affect the entire system performance but also are a key factor in establishing sustainable health reforms. Imbalance in the health workforce emerges from geographic factors, such as hardship places, the geographical distribution of health facilities and local institutional environment (Fritzen, 2007), and complexities related to the centralization or decentralization of health sector governance (Jeppsson, 2002; Bossert & Beauvais, 2003). One or a combination of these factors contributes to the uneven distribution of the health workforce and unequal health access. Most health workers prefer an urban setting as compared to remote rural environments (Dussault & Franceschini, 2006). This 'urban bias' results in disparity in healthcare access, leaving rural areas poorer with disproportionately fewer medical personnel

The distribution of healthcare professionals is measured as the ratio of health personnel to the population in an area. From an economic viewpoint, the distribution of the health workforce is a function of the labor market. Inequality, therefore, arises when the demand for health professionals exceeds supply in a region compared to another. Moreover, a difference in wages of health professionals may result in migration and variance in the distribution of the workforce, that is, from one country to another. The second argument is that of health sector governance. Using the case of South Africa, Mayosi and Benatar (2014) argue that an imbalance in human resource for health (HRH) and the consequent inequality in healthcare access are caused by inappropriate policies that reproduce the historical maldistribution of health professionals. Imbalance in the health workforce traverses public-private disparities of HRH, rural-urban disparities, and geographic locations.

Healthcare inequality based on ethnicity

Studies show inequality in healthcare access in Africa along ethnic lines (Bachmann, London, & Barron, 1996; Fazzio, Mann, & Boone, 2011; Macassa Ghilagaber, Bernhardt, & Burstrom, 2006; Adedini et al., 2015; Victora et al., 2020). Both race and culture are constructs of ethnicity (Zierler & Krieger, 1997). Ethnicity is an element of differentiating cultures of different populations (DeAngelis, 2008). In Africa, healthcare access varies from one ethnic group to another. Some scholars used birth histories and under-five mortality rates to measure how much different ethnic groups accessed healthcare (Brockerhoff & Hewett, 2000; Fazzio, 2011). Using a multivariable analysis of child mortality by ethnicity and adjusted by maternal education, family economic conditions, and rural-urban locality, Victora et al. (2020) found inequality in child survival in most countries.

Brockerhoff and Hewett (2000) studied a 20-year trend of child mortality based on ethnic groups in 11 African countries. The study found that there were significant differentials in child mortality between ethnic groups in all of the countries. The study further revealed that over time, the change in child mortality rate varied between ethnic groups. For example, in Kenya, the Kikuyu community underwent a higher decline in mortality rate between the 1970s and 1980s compared to the rest of the ethnic groups, whereas in Senegal, between 1972 and 1992, the Serer community experienced a higher decline in child mortality than the rest of the ethnic communities. As such, the rate of ethnic-based healthcare inequality in Africa is dynamic. Some communities with an improving healthcare tread can later slow down and be overtaken by others. A good example was Senegal – in 1968–1972, the Serer community had a relatively higher child mortality rate than the rest of the ethnic groups. However, in 1988–1992, the Serer community had a lower average child mortality rate than other communities. A study of the relationship between ethnic affiliation and under-five mortality in Mozambique showed that the mortality rate among children from Emakua and Cisena communities was higher than that of other communities. Adedini et al. (2015) conducted a similar study of ethnic differentials in healthcare in Nigeria and found significant differences in under-five mortality rates between ethnic groups. Some communities, like Igbo and Yoruba, experienced lower under-five mortality compared to other minority tribes.

The changing inequality in healthcare access based on ethnicity is associated with the changing differences in socioeconomic conditions, geographic setting, and demographic behaviors (Brockerhoff & Hewett, 2000; Macassa et al., 2006). Social-cultural behavior can exacerbate or mitigate health risks. Moreover, resource-based barriers like lack of money for treatment contribute to shaping inequality along ethnic lines; that is, high poverty level links to low healthcare access. Another factor includes physical barriers to accessing healthcare within the region occupied by an ethnic community, for example, distance to health facilities (Adedini et al., 2014). The community's cultural norms are a crucial determinant of societal levels of education and community behavior in healthcare access. When these features characterize ethnic communities differently, inequality in healthcare access takes shape.

Maternal schooling and healthcare inequality

A difference in maternal schooling generates inequality in children's healthcare. An increase in maternal health is associated with a reduction of under-five mortality rates (Gakidou, Cowling, Lozano, & Murray, 2010; Bado & Susuman, 2016). Using DHS data from Malawi and Uganda, Andriano and Monden (2019) showed that in each country, each year of additional maternal schooling leads to a reduction of under-five mortality by 10% and 17%, respectively. There was a lower mortality rate for children of women with primary education than for those without. As Andriano and Monden (2019) explained, the quantity of education (i.e., the number of years spent in schooling) is not quality. They also only looked at the mother's number of years of accessing universal primary education. One strength of the study was the use of universal primary education as the standard measure of schooling between the two countries. Still, it was not clear whether the reduction in under-five mortality was attributed to the quality of education.

There is a rising complexity of the relationship between women's education and fertility – there are direct and indirect effects of education and family planning and reproductive behavior. Education is associated with improved nutrition and maternal health and therefore increased fertility. Women's schooling has also been linked to family planning and modern family planning methods. Also, access to family planning in rural areas is low compared to urban areas (Feyisetan & Ainsworth, 1996; Martin, 1995). As shown by Goli et al. (2017), maternal education can also serve as a proxy factor for inequality in healthcare since it promotes other socioeconomic welfare such as employment and income.

Socioeconomic inequality to healthcare access

The term 'socioeconomic' refers to both social and economic factors that influence the behavior of individuals and populations within societal structures. Socioeconomic factors also include social stratification and social class, occupation, and so on. In Africa, the population can be categorized according to socioeconomic characteristics, and, therefore, it is possible to measure the disparity in healthcare access. The difference in household socioeconomic status contributes to understanding inequality in healthcare access (Zierler & Krieger, 1997; Van Malderen et al., 2013; Olorunsaiye & Degge, 2016; Ratovoson et al., 2020). Economic factors such as income level or wealth determine who can access health services and how easy it is. Until the 2000s, most African countries did not have free healthcare. The affordability of healthcare was a key factor. But still, many people living in extreme poverty cannot afford the cost of basic healthcare even though they are exposed to the highest health risks. This has shifted the point of analysis to the effect of wealth inequality on healthcare access within a population (Omer et al., 2014). The level of income and wealth status are constituents and directly impact many healthcare access variables, such as level of education. One approach to measuring the impact of economic status on healthcare access is examining ill health and premature death across people of different income and wealth statuses. The extremely poor are commonly disadvantaged since they bear a disproportionate share of poor health.

A high rate of preventable deaths is a variable of the effect of low income on healthcare access. Socioeconomic determinants also affect access to childcare programs such as immunization. Goli et al. (2017) used the impact of income on maternal mortality to measure inequality in healthcare access. Van Malderen et al. (2013) examined the relationship between wealth-related inequality and under-five mortality in 13 African countries. Overall, these studies found a correlation between household wealth inequality, including father's occupation and mother's education, and variation in healthcare access. Ruktanonchai et al. (2018) found a disparity in access to maternal and newborn healthcare across the level of education, wealth, and rurality in all the countries studied.

Inequality in financial risk protection has contributed to the disparity in healthcare access resulting from out-of-pocket (OOP) payments for healthcare (Carrin, Buse, Heggenhougen, & Quash, 2010). In this regard, studies have looked into the inequalities in health insurance coverage and the catastrophic and impoverishing effect of OOP healthcare expenditure. For instance, Kazungu and Barasa (2017) found that the distribution of health insurance coverage in Kenya was significantly pro-rich. On the other hand, studies have also examined the incidence of catastrophic expenditure and the impoverishing impact of OOP healthcare payments (Chuma & Maina, 2012). Barasa, Okiro, Munge, and Njeru (2020) found that the high financial burden of healthcare access resulted in both catastrophic health expenditure and impoverishment of the population. Although the direct cost of healthcare access pushed people into poverty, when the transport cost was added (i.e., indirect cost of healthcare access), this number significantly rose.

Most importantly, the effect of catastrophic health expenditure was not equal across the country. The unemployed, the poorest, the elderly, and those in marginalized places were more disadvantaged. These categories of people are, therefore, less likely to access health services. A study conducted in Nigeria by Aregbeshola and Khan (2018) found that high reliance on out-of-pocket payment for healthcare pushed many people into poverty and led to less healthcare access. Indeed, catastrophic health expenditure is more likely to hurt the poorest cohorts than the well off. Lack of healthcare insurance leads to out-of-pocket payments and reduced healthcare access.

Another way of measuring inequality in healthcare access is the assessment of the financial-related unmet need for healthcare. Although there are many forms of unmet health needs, financial barriers (i.e., the cost of health) are major determinants of who gains healthcare and who does not. Using the case of Kenya, Njagi, Arsenijevic, and Groot (2020) studied the extent of unmet need for healthcare and regional inequalities. The study found that the cost-related unmet need was higher among the poor, uneducated, and uninsured households.

The barriers to healthcare access are interlinked in a complex way and form a multidimensional cause-effect relationship. For instance, Barasa et al. (2020) suggested that even when free health programs are available, some people fail to access services due to a lack of proper information, fearing they would be charged a high price. Generally, the correlation between the economic status of different populations and health inequality expresses the analytical gap. There is a lack of solid analytical approaches to differentiate poverty as a cause of poor health among the extremely poor and hence a high need to seek healthcare and extreme poverty as a barrier to accessing healthcare among the extremely poor. This further pulls attention to the need to differentiate health inequality from inequality in healthcare access.

Gender and inequality in healthcare access

Women's access to healthcare is not only determined by their own decision-making on sexual and reproductive behaviors but also dependent on the normative limitations imposed by the society they live in. The idea is that gender construction within society either promotes or hinders women's access to healthcare. As such, gender relations have been found to affect healthcare access (DeRose & Ezeh, 2005; Dodoo & Frost, 2008). In this context, gender issues comprise women's household decision-making, gender norms, and their impact on the utilization of health services, particularly maternal health (Horne, Dodoo, & Dodoo, 2013). Adjiwanou and LeGrand (2014) used the case of Kenya, Uganda, Tanzania, and Ghana to measure the effect of gender norms on healthcare access. The study found that gender norms that tolerate violence against women have a detrimental impact on maternal healthcare access. In such settings, women are less likely to access timely antenatal care. As women's education and wealth have the highest impact on healthcare access, there is a weak relationship between the autonomy of a woman's decision-making and health-service use. Another study by Izugbara and Ezeh (2010) on women and the high fertility rate in Northern Islamic Nigeria found that women would deliberately bear more children to avoid divorce or engage in plural marriage.

Understanding the gender roles in a society helps explain access to healthcare and various dynamics of maternal healthcare, such as reproductive attitudes and behavior. Studies have shown that the high fertility in northern Nigeria was contributed to by the religion where women's role has been reduced to childbearer (Mazrui, 1994; Izugbara & Ezeh, 2010). The socioeconomic status of women has been found to be a critical factor for healthcare access.

Challenges in the scholarship of inequality in healthcare access

One of the challenges facing the scholarship of inequality in healthcare access in Africa is how to bring together the causes, manifestations, and implications of this inequality itself. For instance, if there exists inequality in healthcare access based on ethnicity in a country, then what effects do such disparities have on the socioeconomic livelihoods of the 'disadvantaged' population cohorts? At the core of the empirical analyses are the fundamental difficulties in operationalizing definitions related to inequality in healthcare access. Inequality in healthcare access is multidimensional, and, therefore, the valuation of the state of health using simple ratios will always experience a weakness. Most studies identified previously use one or several health measures as unidimensional proxies in examining inter-individual differences.

Studies on inequality in healthcare access in Africa highlight the challenge of data. The challenge is commonly highlighted by studies that require longitudinal data sets and those with spatially explicit population data across African countries. The lack of accurate and spatially detailed population data presents the unreliability of data on healthcare access. However, the availability of data varies from country to country and between sub-national regions.

The recent development in GIS and spatial analysis indicates promising research and open data on inequality in healthcare access. Researchers have opted for standardized global datasets such as the Gridded Population of the World and Global Rural-Urban Mapping Project to address the challenge of differing spatial modeling techniques. But still, due to the remoteness of some regions in Africa, gridded data sets lack or do not capture some critical details of population distribution and the resultant disparity in healthcare access. Some studies indicate a need for more spatial and temporal disaggregation of data to accommodate all dimensions of inequality in healthcare access analyzed across various subgroups. Other studies recommend exploring a new way of visualizing the evolution of spatial variation over time using a standard scale (Ruktanonchai et al., 2018).

Achievements in addressing inequality in healthcare access

Much of the efforts in addressing inequality in healthcare are concerned with reducing underdevelopment. They include reducing extreme poverty, which occurs in one or many forms of social exclusion, such as poor conditions of means of transport especially in rural areas, high cost of healthcare, lack of health insurance coverage among the poorest population, shortage of health professionals, and low or lack of education, especially among women (van Rensburg, 2014; Kabia et al., 2019). Just like inequality in healthcare access takes varied perspectives, policies that address social exclusion are dynamic and take multi-dimensional processes. These policies interact differently across economic, social, cultural, and political dimensions (Dussault & Franceschini, 2006). They also involve different levels and actors ranging from individuals and households, communities, and countries (Olorunsaiye & Degge, 2016). Some areas include poverty alleviation and increasing economic opportunities, especially to the most vulnerable population. Other policies revolve around the reduction of social barriers to social services (Willie, 2011).

Conclusion

A general overview of the scholarship in inequality in healthcare access since 1994 does not show significant changes in the study approach. All the perspectives of inequalities in healthcare access, which are interlinked and have a multidimensional cause-effect relationship, indicate different forms of vulnerabilities of various populations. For instance, socioeconomic inequality is a cause and an outcome of inequality in maternal education. In African countries, the geographical distribution of ethnic communities correlates with levels of healthcare access and the level of regional development in the respective regions occupied by these communities.

Inequality in healthcare access takes a multidimensional perspective, and it becomes complicated for researchers to put all these variables in a single study. Thus, researchers preferred to focus on one or a few elements of inequality in healthcare access in one or several African countries. Although the DHS data and census data are the predominant sources of evidence and have been useful in analyzing comparative cases across countries, they experience challenges. First, both data sets are collected at different times, and therefore the points of reference of demographic change are varied in different countries. In other cases, some countries have not been consistent in conducting national censuses, which leaves substantial missing data and analytical gaps in the study of inequality in healthcare access. However, gridded data are emerging not as a replacement but as a complement to DHS and census data.

Although this chapter brought out different ways of studying inequality in healthcare access and different dimensions of inequality, the literature does not explicitly show which dimension of inequality is more prevalent within the health access scholarship. A further systematic review would be necessary to examine which perspective of inequality in healthcare access scholarship in African is most dominant and why.

References

Adedini, S. A., Odimegwu, C., Bamiwuye, O., Fadeyibi, O., & Wet, N. D. (2014). Barriers to accessing health care in Nigeria: Implications for child survival. *Global Health Action*, 7(1), 23499.

Adedini, S. A., Odimegwu, C., Imasiku, E. N., & Ononokpono, D. N. (2015). Ethnic differentials in under-five mortality in Nigeria. *Ethnicity and Health*, *20*(2), 145–162.

Adjiwanou, V., & LeGrand, T. (2014). Gender inequality and the use of maternal healthcare services in rural sub-Saharan Africa. *Health and Place*, *29*, 67–78.

Amu, H., Dickson, K. S., Kumi-Kyereme, A., & Darteh, E. K. M. (2018). Understanding variations in health insurance coverage in Ghana, Kenya, Nigeria, and Tanzania: Evidence from demographic and health surveys. *PLoS One*, *13*(8), e0201833.

Andriano, L., & Monden, C. W. (2019). The causal effect of maternal education on child mortality: Evidence from a quasi-experiment in Malawi and Uganda. *Demography*, *56*(5), 1765–1790.

Antai, D. (2009). Inequitable childhood immunization uptake in Nigeria: A multilevel analysis of individual and contextual determinants. *BMC Infectious Diseases*, *9*(1), 181.

Aregbeshola, B. S., & Khan, S. M. (2018). Out-of-pocket payments, catastrophic health expenditure and poverty among households in Nigeria 2010. *International Journal of Health Policy and Management*, 7(9), 798–806.

Arsenault, C., Jordan, K., Lee, D., Dinsa, G., Manzi, F., Marchant, T., & Kruk, M. E. (2018). Equity in antenatal care quality: An analysis of 91 national household surveys. *The Lancet Global Health*, *6*(11), e1186–e1195.

Ataguba, J. E., Akazili, J., & McIntyre, D. (2011). Socioeconomic-related health inequality in South Africa: Evidence from General Household Surveys. *International Journal for Equity in Health*, *10*(1), 1–10.

Ataguba, J. E. O., & Alaba, O. (2012). Explaining health inequalities in South Africa: A political economy perspective. *Development Southern Africa*, *29*(5), 756–764.

Bachmann, M., London, L., & Barron, P. (1996). Infant mortality rate inequalities in the Western Cape Province of South Africa. *International Journal of Epidemiology*, *25*(5), 966–972.

Bado, A. R., & Susuman, A. S. (2016). Women's education and health inequalities in under-five mortality in selected sub-Saharan African countries, 1990–2015. *PLoS One*, *11*(7).

Barasa, E., Okiro, E., Munge, K., & Njeru, A. (2020). *What is equity in health, and are Kenyans accessing equitable healthcare?* Nairobi: KEMRI Wellcome Trust.

Baraza, E. W., Maina, T., & Ravishankar, N. (2017). Assessing the impoverishing effects, and factors associated with the incidence of catastrophic health care payments in Kenya. *International Journal for Equity in Health, 16*(1), 1–14.

Booysen, le R. F. (2003). Urban–rural inequalities in health care delivery in South Africa. *Development Southern Africa, 20*(5), 659–673.

Bossert, T. J., & Beauvais, J. C. (2003). Decentralization of health systems in Ghana, Zambia, Uganda and the Philippines: A comparative analysis of decision space. *Health Policy and Planning, 17*(1), 14–31.

Brockerhoff, M., & Hewett, P. (2000). Inequality of child mortality among ethnic groups in sub-Saharan Africa. *Bulletin of the World Health Organization, 78*, 30–41.

Carrin, G., Buse, K., Heggenhougen, K., & Quah, S. R. (Eds.). (2010). *Health systems policy, finance, and organization*. Academic Press.

Chuma, J., & Maina, T. (2012). Catastrophic health care spending and impoverishment in Kenya. *BMC Health Services Research, 12*(1), 1–9.

DeAngelis, T. (2008). A fresh look at race and ethnicity. *Monitor on Psychology, 39*, 30.

Deaton, A. (1999). *Inequalities in income and inequalities in health*. Research Program in Development Studies. Princeton, NJ: Princeton University Press.

DeRose, L. F., & Ezeh, A. C. (2005). Men's influence on the onset and progress of fertility decline in Ghana. *Population Studies, 59*(2), 197–210.

Dodoo, F. N. A., & Frost, A. E. (2008). Gender in African population research: The fertility/reproductive health example. *Annual Review of Sociology, 34*, 431–452.

Douptcheva, N., & Hill, A. G. (2014). Functionings and capabilities as tools for explaining differences in self-assessed health: The case of women's health in Accra, Ghana. *African Population Studies, 28*(2), 744–757.

Dussault, G., & Franceschini, M. C. (2006). Not enough there, too many here: Understanding geographical imbalances in the distribution of the health workforce. *Human Resources for Health, 4*(1), 1–16.

Erreygers, G. (2009). Correcting the concentration index. *Journal of Health Economics, 28*(2), 504–515.

Faden, R. R., & Powers, M. (2008). Health inequities and social justice. *Bundesgesundheitsblatt-Gesundheitsforschung-Gesundheitsschutz, 51*(2), 151–157.

Fazzio, I., Mann, V., & Boone, P. (2011). Temporal trends (1977–2007) and ethnic inequity in child mortality in rural villages of southern Guinea Bissau. *BMC Public Health, 11*(1), 1–8.

Feyisetan, B. J., & Ainsworth, M. (1996). Contraceptive use and the quality, price, and availability of family planning in Nigeria. *The World Bank Economic Review, 10*(1), 159–187.

Frimpong, P. B. (2013). The quest for equity in the provision of health care in Ghana. *African Review of Economics and Finance, 4*(2), 254–272.

Fritzen, S. A. (2007). Strategic management of the health workforce in developing countries: What have we learned? *Human Resources for Health, 5*(1), 1–9.

Gage, A. J. (2007). Barriers to the utilization of maternal health care in rural Mali. *Social Science and Medicine, 65*, 1666–1682.

Gakidou, E., Cowling, K., Lozano, R., & Murray, C. J. (2010). Increased educational attainment and its effect on child mortality in 175 countries between 1970 and 2009: A systematic analysis. *The Lancet, 376*(9745), 959–974.

Gerein, N., Green, A., & Pearson, S. (2006). The implications of shortages of health professionals for maternal health in sub-Saharan Africa. *Reproductive Health Matters, 14*(27), 40–50.

Gething, P. W., Johnson, F. A., Frempong-Ainguah, F., Nyarko, P., Baschieri, A., Aboagye, P., . . . Atkinson, P. M. (2012). Geographical access to care at birth in Ghana: A barrier to safe motherhood. *BMC Public Health, 12*(1), 1–13.

Gjesfjeld, C. D., & Jung, J. K. (2011). How far? Using geographical information systems (GIS) to examine maternity care access for expectant mothers in a rural state. *Social Work in Health Care, 50*(9), 682–693.

Goli, S., Nawal, D., Rammohan, A., Sekher, T. V., & Singh, D. (2017). Decomposing the socioeconomic inequality in utilization of maternal health care services in selected countries of South Asia and sub-Saharan Africa. *Journal of Biosocial Science, 50*(6), 749–769.

Guagliardo, M. F. (2004). Spatial accessibility of primary care: Concepts, methods and challenges. *International Journal of Health Geographics, 3*(1), 1–13.

Haisma, H., Yousefzadeh, S., & Boele Van Hensbroek, P. (2018). Towards a capability approach to child growth: A theoretical framework. *Maternal and Child Nutrition, 14*(2), e12534.

Hanson, C., Gabrysch, S., Mbaruku, G., Cox, J., Mkumbo, E., Manzi, F., . . . Ronsmans, C. (2017). Access to maternal health services: Geographical inequalities, United Republic of Tanzania. *Bulletin of the World Health Organization, 95*(12), 810.

Herman, M. O. (2014). Political-economic transitions and the changing context of maternal health access in Tanzania: Evidence from DHS data. *African Population Studies, 28*, 1072–1087.

Hjortsberg, C. A., & Mwikisa, C. N. (2002). Cost of access to health services in Zambia. *Health Policy and Planning, 17*(1), 71–77.

Horne, C., Dodoo, F. N. A., & Dodoo, N. D. (2013). The shadow of indebtedness: Bridewealth and norms constraining female reproductive autonomy. *American Sociological Review, 78*(3), 503–520.

Izugbara, C. O., & Ezeh, A. C. (2010). Women and high fertility in Islamic northern Nigeria. *Studies in Family Planning, 41*(3), 193–204.

Jeppsson, A. (2002). SWAp dynamics in a decentralized context experiences from Uganda. *Social Science and Medicine, 55*(11), 2053–2060.

Kabia, E., Mbau, R., Oyando, R., Oduor, C., Bigogo, G., Khagayi, S., & Barasa, E. (2019). "We are called the et cetera": Experiences of the poor with health financing reforms that target them in Kenya. *International Journal for Equity in Health, 18*(1), 1–14.

Kakwani, N., Wagstaff, A., & Van Doorslaer, E. (1997). Socioeconomic inequalities in health: Measurement, computation and statistical inference. *Journal of Econometrics*, 77(1), 87–103.

Katende, C. (1992). *The effect of accessibility to clinics on infant and child mortality: The cases of Liberia and Zimbabwe.* Commissioned paper for the working group on the Effects of Child survival and General Health Programs on Mortality, Panel on the Population Dynamics of Sub-Saharan Africa, Committee on Population, National Research Council, Washington, DC.

Katende, C. (1994). The impact of access to health services on infant and child mortality in rural Uganda. *African Population Studies, 9*(1).

Kazungu, J. S., & Barasa, E. W. (2017). Examining levels, distribution and correlates of health insurance coverage in Kenya. *Tropical Medicine and International Health, 22*(9), 1175–1185.

Khan, A. A., & Bhardwaj, S. M. (1994). Access to health care: A conceptual framework and its relevance to health care planning. *Evaluation and the Health Professions, 17*(1), 60–76.

Kilroy, A. (2007). *Intra-urban spatial inequality: Cities as "urban regions": Reshaping economic geography.* World Development Report. Washington: World Bank

Kong, V. Y., Van de Linde, S., Aldous, C., Handley, J. J., & Clarke, D. L. (2013). Quantifying the disparity in outcome between urban and rural patients with acute appendicitis in South Africa. *South African Medical Journal, 103*(10), 742–745.

Linard, C., Gilbert, M., Snow, R. W., Noor, A. M., & Tatem, A. J. (2012). Population distribution, settlement patterns and accessibility across Africa in 2010. *PLoS One*, 7(2), e31743.

Love-Koh, J., Griffin, S., Kataika, E., Revill, P., Sibandze, S., & Walker, S. (2020). Methods to promote equity in health resource allocation in low-and middle-income countries: An overview. *Globalization and Health, 16*(1), 6.

Macassa, G., Ghilagaber, G., Bernhardt, E., & Burstrom, B. (2006). Inequalities in under-five mortality in Mozambique: Differentials by region of residence and ethnic affiliation of the mother. *East African Medical Journal, 83*(5), 259.

Macharia, P. M., Odera, P. A., Snow, R. W., & Noor, A. M. (2017). Spatial models for the rational allocation of routinely distributed bed nets to public health facilities in Western Kenya. *Malaria Journal, 16*(1), 367.

Magadi, M. A., Zulu, E. M., & Brockerhoff, M. (2003). The inequality of maternal health care in urban sub-Saharan Africa in the 1990s. *Population Studies, 57*(3), 347–366.

Makanga, P. T., Schuurman, N., von Dadelszen, P., & Firoz, T. (2016). A scoping review of geographic information systems in maternal health. *International Journal of Gynecology and Obstetrics, 134*(1), 13–17.

Martin, T. C. (1995). Women's education and fertility: Results from 26 Demographic and Health Surveys. *Studies in Family Planning*, 187–202.

Mayosi, B. M., & Benatar, S. R. (2014). Health and health care in South Africa – 20 years after Mandela. *New England Journal of Medicine, 371*(14), 1344–1353.

Mazrui, A. A. (1994). Islamic doctrine and the politics of induced fertility change: An African perspective. *Population and Development Review, 20*, 121–134.

McLaren, Z., Ardington, C., & Leibbrandt, M. (2013). *Distance as a barrier to health care access in South Africa.* A Southern Africa Labour and Development Research Unit Working Paper No. 97. Cape Town: SALDRU, University of Cape Town.

McNamee, P., Ternent, L., & Hussein, J. (2009). Barriers in accessing maternal healthcare: Evidence from low-and middle-income countries. *Expert Review of Pharmacoeconomics and Outcomes Research*, *9*(1), 41–48.

Munga, M. A., & Mæstad, O. (2009). Measuring inequalities in the distribution of health workers: the case of Tanzania. *Human Resources for Health*, 7(1), 1–12.

Neutens, T. (2015). Accessibility, equity and health care: Review and research directions for transport geographers. *Journal of Transport Geography*, *43*, 14–27.

Ng, N., Kowal, P., Kahn, K., Naidoo, N., Abdullah, S., Bawah, A., . . . Xavier Gómez-Olivé, F. (2010). Health inequalities among older men and women in Africa and Asia: Evidence from eight Health and Demographic Surveillance System sites in the INDEPTH WHO-SAGE Study. *Global Health Action*, *3*(1), 5420.

Ngozi, M. N., & Ngianga-Bakwin, K. (2011). The spatial distribution of health establishments in Nigeria. *African Population Studies*, *25*(2), 680–696.

Njagi, P., Arsenijevic, J., & Groot, W. (2020). Cost-related unmet need for healthcare services in Kenya. *BMC Health Services Reviews*, *20*, 322.

Olorunsaiye, C. Z., & Degge, H. (2016). Variations in the uptake of routine immunization in Nigeria: Examining determinants of inequitable access. *Global Health Communication*, *2*(1), 19–29.

Omer, A. S., Bezruchka, S., Longhi, D., Kelly, Z., Brown, M., & Hagopian, A. (2014). The effects of household assets inequality and conflict on population health in Sudan. *African Population Studies*, *28*(3), 1216–1232.

Østby, G., Nordås, R., & Rød, J. K. (2009). Regional inequalities and civil conflict in Sub-Saharan Africa. *International Studies Quarterly*, *53*(2), 301–324.

Ouma, P. O., Maina, J., Thuranira, P. N., Macharia, P. M., Alegana, V. A., English, M., . . . Snow, R. W. (2018). Access to emergency hospital care provided by the public sector in sub-Saharan Africa in 2015: A geocoded inventory and spatial analysis. *The Lancet Global Health*, *6*(3), e342–e350.

Peters, D. H., Garg, A., Bloom, G., Walker, D. G., Brieger, W. R., & Hafizur Rahman, M. (2008). Poverty and access to health care in developing countries. *Annals of the New York Academy of Sciences*, *1136*, 161–171.

Petrie, D., & Tang, K. K. (2008). *A rethink on measuring health inequalities using the Gini coefficient*. Discussion Paper Series, 381. University of Queensland, Australia.

Quigley, R., den Broeder, L., Furu, P., Bond, A., Cave, B., & Bos, R. (2006). *Health impact assessment international best practice principles*. Special Publication Series No. 5. Fargo, North Dakota: International Association for Impact Assessment.

Ratovoson, R., Masquelier, B., Andriatahina, T., Mangahasimbola, R., Andrianirina, Z., Pison, G., & Baril, L. (2020). Inequalities in cause-specific mortality in children and adolescents in the Moramanga health survey, Madagascar. *International Journal of Public Health*, 1–10.

Regidor, E. (2004). Measures of health inequalities: Part 2. *Journal of Epidemiology and Community Health*, *58*(11), 900.

Ridde, V. (2008). Equity and health policy in Africa: Using concept mapping in Moore (Burkina Faso). *BMC Health Services Research*, *8*(1), 1–12.

Rispel, L. (2016). Analysing the progress and fault lines of health sector transformation in South Africa. *South African Health Review*, *2016*(1), 17–23.

Rispel, L. C., de Sousa, C. A. P., & Molomo, B. G. (2009). Can social inclusion policies reduce health inequalities in sub-Saharan Africa? A rapid policy appraisal. *Journal of Health, Population, and Nutrition*, *27*(4), 492.

Ruktanonchai, C. W., Nilsen, K., Alegana, V. A., Bosco, C., Ayiko, R., Kajeguka, A. C. S., . . . Tatem, A. J. (2018). Temporal trends in spatial inequalities of maternal and newborn health services among four east African countries, 1999–2015. *BMC Public Health*, *18*(1), 1339.

Ruktanonchai, C. W., Ruktanonchai, N. W., Nove, A., Lopes, S., Pezzulo, C., Bosco, C., . . . Lambert, N. (2016). Equality in maternal and newborn health: Modelling geographic disparities in utilization of care in five East African countries. *PLoS One*, *11*(8).

Rutaremwa, G., Wandera, S. O., Jhamba, T., Akiror, E., & Kiconco, A. (2015). Determinants of maternal health services utilization in Uganda. *BMC Health Services Research*, *15*(1), 271.

Sauvain-Dugerdil, C. (2014). Targeting inequalities: A contribution of the capability approach to population studies. *African Population Studies*, *28*(2), 721–731.

Sen, A. (1980). Equality of what? In S. McMurrin (Ed.), *The Tanner Lectures on human values*. Salt Lake City, UT: University of Utah Press.

Sen, A. (1984). The living standard. *Oxford Economic Papers*, *36*, 74–90.

Sen, A. (1993). Capability and well-being. In M. Nussbaum & A. Sen (Eds.), *The quality of life*. Oxford: Clarendon Press.

Spaan, E., Mathijssen, J., Tromp, N., McBain, F., Have, A. T., & Baltussen, R. (2012). The impact of health insurance in Africa and Asia: A systematic review. *Bulletin of the World Health Organization, 90*, 685–692.

Sudhof, L., Amoroso, C., Barebwanuwe, P., Munyaneza, F., Karamaga, A., Zambotti, G., . . . Hirschhorn, L. R. (2013). Local use of geographic information systems to improve data utilisation and health services: Mapping caesarean section coverage in rural Rwanda. *Tropical Medicine and International Health, 18*(1), 18–26.

Tang, K. K., Petrie, D., & Rao, D. P. (2009). Measuring health inequality with realization of potential life years (RePLY). *Health Economics, 18*(S1), S55–S75.

Timyan, J., Brechin, S. J. G., Measham, D. M., & Ogunleye, B. (1993). Access to care: More than a problem of distance. *The Health of Women: A Global Perspective*, 217–234.

Unterhalter, E. (2003). The capabilities approach and gendered education: An examination of South African complexities. *Theory and Research in Education, 1*(1), 7–22.

Van Malderen, C., Van Oyen, H., & Speybroeck, N. (2013). Contributing determinants of overall and wealth-related inequality in under-5 mortality in 13 African countries. *Journal of Epidemiology and Community Health, 67*(8), 667–676.

Van Rensburg, H. C. (2014). South Africa's protracted struggle for equal distribution and equitable access – Still not there. *Human Resources for Health, 12*(1), 26.

Victora, C. G., Barros, A. J., Blumenberg, C., Costa, J. C., Vidaletti, L. P., Wehrmeister, F. C., . . . You, D. (2020). Association between ethnicity and under-5 mortality: Analysis of data from demographic surveys from 36 low-income and middle-income countries. *The Lancet Global Health, 8*(3), e352–e361.

Vlassoff, C. (1994). Gender inequalities in health in the third world: Uncharted ground. *Social Science and Medicine, 39*(9), 1249–1259.

Willie, M. M. (2011). Access to public health facilities: Taking stock of South Africa's Rural Eastern Cape Province. *World Medical Journal, 57*(5), 6–12.

Yaya, S., Uthman, O. A., Okonofua, F., & Bishwajit, G. (2019). Decomposing the rural-urban gap in the factors of under-five mortality in sub-Saharan Africa? Evidence from 35 countries. *BMC Public Health, 19*(1), 616.

Zierler, S., & Krieger, N. (1997). Reframing women's risk: Social inequalities and HIV infection. *Annual Review of Public Health, 18*(1), 401–436.

Zurn, P., Dal Poz, M. R., Stilwell, B., & Adams, O. (2004). Imbalance in the health workforce. *Human Resources for Health, 2*(1), 1–12.

23

HIV/AIDS IN THE POPULATION: ITS LEVELS, CORRELATES, IMPACT, POLICIES AND PROGRAMS

Pamela Chirwa-Banda

Introduction

HIV continues to be a major global public health issue, with an estimated 38 million people living with HIV by the end of 2019 and almost 33 million lives lost so far (WHO, 2020a). The vast majority of people living with HIV are located in low-and middle-income countries, with an estimated 68% living in sub-Saharan Africa (SSA). Among this group 20.7 million are living in East and Southern Africa which saw 700,000 new HIV infections in 2019 (UNAIDS, 2019a). However, with proper adherence to HIV treatment, people living with HIV are able to manage the condition and continue living a healthy life. Heightened prevalence rates of HIV are mostly among key populations such as sex workers, prisoners, men who have sex with men, vulnerable individuals like adolescent girls and young women (WHO, 2018). Many policies and programs have been aligned to mitigate the spread of HIV (Kenworthy, 2018). This review focuses on the levels, correlates, impact, policies and programs of HIV in African countries.

Literature review

People living with HIV (levels)

In 2020, out of the 38 million people across the globe living with HIV/AIDS, 36.2 million were adults and 1.8 million were children, with an estimated 68% living in sub Saharan Africa, among this group, 20.7 million (54%) in Eastern and Southern Africa, 4.9 million (13%) in Western and Central Africa and 0.24 million in Middle East and North Africa (UNAIDS, 2020b).

East and Southern Africa are the regions hardest hit by HIV. These regions are home to around 6.2% of the world's population with close to three quarters (73%) of the total number of people living with HIV in the world (20.7 million people). At least 85% of people living with HIV were aware of their status by end of 2018 (UNAIDS, 2020b) (see Figure 23.1).

Men who have sex with men (MSM)

While data on men who have sex with men (referred to as MSM) in East and Southern Africa is limited, reported HIV prevalence ranges from 2% in Angola to 31% in Zimbabwe (UNAIDS,

 DOI: 10.4324/9780429287213-28

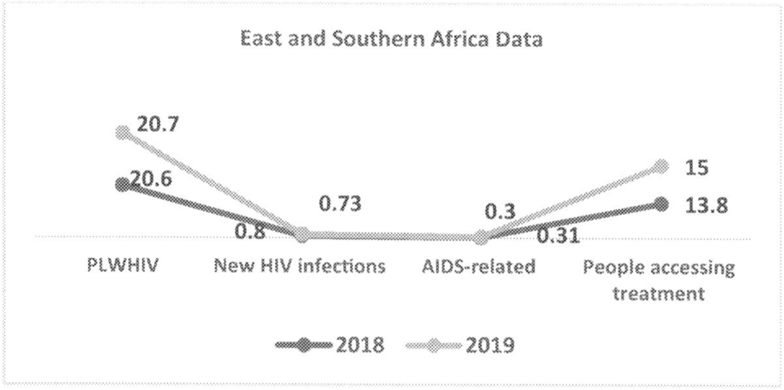

Figure 23.1 East and Southern Africa Data.

2020b). Overall, around one in five (20%) men who have sex with men in the region are estimated to be living with HIV. In Kenya, an annual incidence of greater than 20% was reported in Mombasa. Other countries in Africa reported high prevalence; for example, in South Africa, the Soweto men study confirmed high risk for HIV infection among MSM (Lane et al., 2011).

People in prison

In SSA, HIV prevalence among prisoners varied from 2.3% to 34.9% among different regions (Telisinghe et al., 2016). HIV prevalence among prisoners in Western Africa ranged from 2.3% to 10.8% and in Eastern Africa varied from 4.2% to 23% (Telisinghe et al., 2016). This is reflective of high HIV prevalence in the general population; and the fact that prisons are high risk environments for HIV transmission, fuelled by overcrowding, limited access to health care, drug use, unsafe injecting practices, sexual violence, unprotected sex and lack of access to HIV prevention commodities such as condoms and lubricants, means that transmission risk is very high (Jürgens, Nowak, & Day, 2011).

People who inject drugs

Regional HIV prevalence rates are high in people who inject drugs in all parts of the world (up to 15.5% in East and Southern Africa) (World Health Organization Statistics, 2020). Evidence from some African countries suggests many people who inject drugs acquire HIV before the age of 25 (UNAIDS, 2016). In Kenya, HIV prevalence among people who inject drugs was 18% in 2011, compared to 5.6% among the general population, whilst in Tanzania it was estimated that 15.5% of people who injected drugs were living with HIV, with the prevalence among women who inject drugs thought to be higher than among their male counterparts (UNAIDS, 2019a). In 2018, an estimated 21.8% of people who inject drugs in South Africa were living with HIV mainly because people who inject drugs usually shared syringes and other injecting instruments and also reused needles as found in a South African study (UNAIDS, 2019b).

Sex workers

Globally, the average HIV prevalence among sex workers is estimated to be approximately 12%. Although sex workers are disproportionately affected by HIV in every country, HIV prevalence among this population varies greatly between countries, ranging from 5.5% in Madagascar to more than 70% in Lesotho and Uganda (UNAIDS, 2020a). In Botswana, Malawi, Rwanda and Zimbabwe more than 40% of female sex workers were found to be living with HIV (UNAIDS, 2019b). In another study, HIV prevalence among sex workers in Nigeria was estimated at 24.5% (compared with 3.7% among the general population age 15–49 years), and in Rwanda at 50.8% (compared with 2.9% in the general population). Sex workers are at an increased risk due to exposure to multiple sexual partners and, sometimes, inconsistent condom use, often due to clients' unwillingness or coercion. Legal issues, stigma, discrimination and violence pose barriers to HIV services for sex workers (WHO, 2016).

New infections

An estimated 1.7 million individuals worldwide acquired HIV in 2019 compared to 2.8 million people in 1998, a reduction of new HIV infections of 40% since the peak in 1998 and declined by 23% since 2010, from 2.1 million to 1.7 million in 2019. Among children, new HIV infections have declined by 52% since 2000, from 310,000 in 2010 to 150,000 in 2019. However, progress on the prevention of HIV transmission remains far too slow, with the estimated total number of new infections in 2019 more than three times higher than UNAIDS's 2020 target (UNAIDS, 2020c). From the 1.7 million people newly infected in 2019, 20,000 new infections were recorded in Middle East and North Africa, whilst Western and Central Africa recorded 240,000, and East and Southern Africa had the highest number of new infections of 700,000. Children (age 0–14 years) accounted for 9% of new infections in 2019, with 84% of child infections occurring in SSA.

Adolescents and young people represent a growing share of people living with HIV worldwide. In 2019 alone, 460,000 young people between the ages of 10 and 24 were newly infected with HIV, of whom 170,000 were adolescents between the ages of 10 and 19. To compound this, most recent data indicate that only 27% of adolescent girls and 16% of adolescent boys aged 15–19 in Eastern and Southern Africa, the region most affected, have been tested for HIV in the past 12 months and received the result of the last test (UNICEF, 2020). Worse still, there is a challenge that if the current trend continues, there will still be some 183,000 annual new HIV infections among adolescents in 2030. Despite the continuing severity of the epidemic, huge strides have been made towards meeting the UNAIDS 90–90–90 targets with great annual declines observed in Comoros, Rwanda, South Africa and Uganda. However, progress on the prevention of HIV transmission remains far too slow, with the estimated total number of new infections in 2019 more than three times higher than UNAIDS's 2020 target of reducing new infections by less than 500,000 by end of 2020 (UNAIDS, 2020c).

AIDS-related deaths

Since the start of the epidemic, an estimated 74.9 million people have become infected with HIV and 32 million people have died of AIDS-related illnesses; however, AIDS-related deaths have been reduced by 60% since the peak in 2004 (UNAIDS, 2020a). About 690,000 people died from AIDS-related illnesses worldwide in 2019; of these, East and Southern Africa contributed 300,000, whilst Western and Central Africa had 140,000 deaths and 8,000 from Middle East and North Africa (UNAIDS, 2019a).

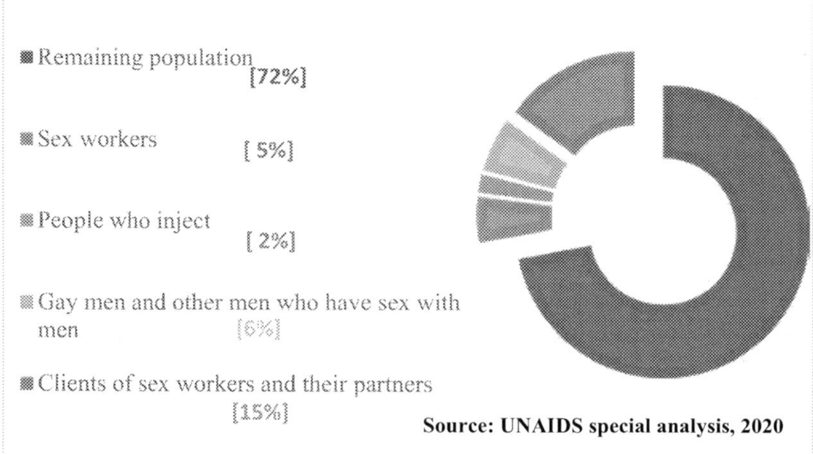

Figure 23.2 Distribution of new HIV infections by population (Age 15–49 years), Eastern and Southern Africa, 2019.

On treatment

HIV treatment access is key to the global effort to end AIDS as a public health threat. At least 15 million are receiving anti-retroviral therapy (ART) in East and Southern Africa, whilst 2.9 million are receiving ART in Western and Central Africa; and in the Middle East and North Africa, only 92,000 are receiving treatment. HIV treatment access is key to the global effort to end AIDS as a public health threat. UNAIDS reports that in 2019, of all people with HIV worldwide, 81% knew their HIV status; 82% of all people who knew their status were receiving ART; 88% of all pregnant women on ART, were virally suppressed mother-to-child transmission (PEPFAR, 2020).

Correlates

Late commencement of ART was found to be associated with diverse risk factors. In a study by Ndawin and colleagues conducted on 55 HIV-positive people in Cameroon, late ART initiation was associated with diverse risk factors operating at the individual, facility and regional levels (Ndawin et al., 2012). In another systematic review and meta-analysis of published studies until January 5, 2020 in SSA, the association between age-disparate relationships and risk of HIV infection among adolescent girls and young women (AGYW) aged 15–24 years was associated with increased risk of unprotected sexual intercourse and HIV infection in SSA (Bajunirwe, Semakula, & Izudi, 2020). In another population-based survey in Lesotho on correlates of HIV infection in adolescent girls and young women, results revealed that correlates of prevalent infection included reporting a history of anal sex, having a partner suspected or known to be HIV-positive and having two or more lifetime sexual partners (Low et al., 2019). Another study done in the Democratic Republic of Congo revealed having two or more multiple concurrent sexual partners and/or not using condoms were variables similarly and highly

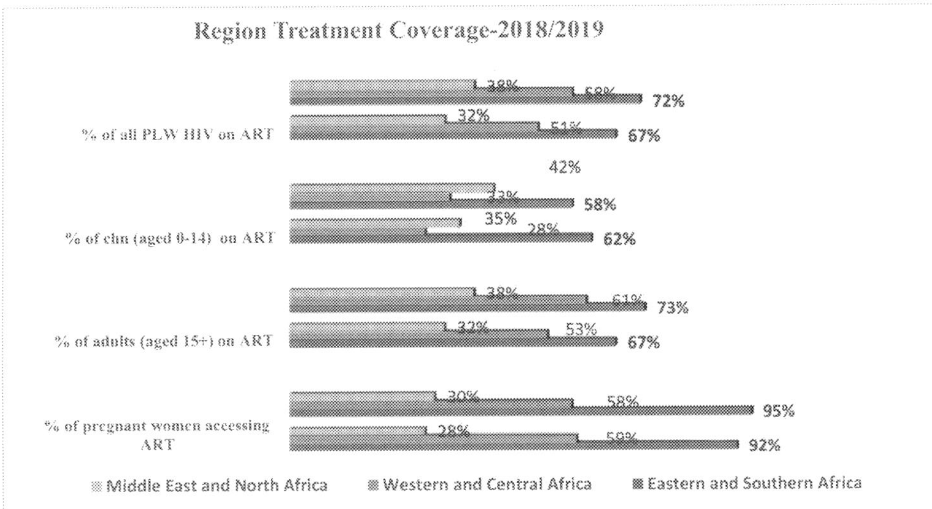

Figure 23.3 Regional HIV/AIDS treatment coverage.

associated with HIV risk. Local programs would benefit from comprehensive interventions targeting all behavioral and sociocultural determinants (Carlos et al., 2017).

In a study on risk factors for HIV infection among female sex workers in Bangui, Central African Republic, Age at first sexual intercourse, self-assessment of HIV risk, knowledge of HIV status, anal sex practice with last clients, irregular condom use in last week, consumption of alcohol, other psycho-active substances and past history of STIs showed statistically significant association with risk for HIV infection (Longo et al., 2017).

Various correlates of being HIV-positive from voluntary counselling and HIV testing centres have been identified: HIV risk behavior including multiple sex partners, lack of (consistent) condom use, anal sex, substance use (alcohol drinking), use of alcohol before sex, testing positive for HIV in the past, intention to reduce their HIV risk behaviour, health status-HIV symptomatic, and history of sexually transmitted infections (STI). Furthermore, previous studies found differences in HIV prevalence of persons at HIV counselling and testing clinics, with HIV mostly higher in women. One study found HIV higher in men than in women. Reviews on studies conducted in the general population in SSA have shown that alcohol use was associated with HIV risk behavior and HIV infection (Peltzer, 2012; Luseno & Wechsberg, 2009).

In another sub-Saharan study conducted by Kharsany and Karim, men who have sex with men, people who inject drugs (PWID) or sex workers were highly correlated with diverse HIV risk factors (Kharsany & Karim, 2016).

Regional impacts

The vast majority of people with HIV are in low- and middle-income countries. In 2019, there were 20.7 million people with HIV (54%) in Eastern and Southern Africa, 4.9 million (13%) in Western and Central Africa, 5.8 million (15%) in Asia and the Pacific, and 2.2 million (6%) in Western and Central Europe and North America (UNAIDS, 2020a).

Global information on the HIV/AIDS epidemic indicates the existence of an ever-increasing number of orphans and vulnerable children. Compared to other children, orphans are observed to be more depressed and anxious, less optimistic and to display angry feelings and disruptive behaviors (Doku, Akohene, Ananga, & Debrah, 2019).

Advanced HIV has been associated with the rise in orphanhood. A study on primary caregivers of HIV-infected children aged 5–18 years in rural South Africa confirmed that all forms of orphan-hood, i.e. loss of both parents or loss of father or mother had increased with high burden of perinatal HIV infection and compromised health among maternal orphans (Mokgatle & Madiba, 2015). The elderly have not been left out as proved by the study done by Ogunmefun and colleagues which showed that the AIDS pandemic has had direct and indirect effects which have manifested in a set of interrelated social, economic and psychological dimensions that could ultimately impact the health and well-being of the elderly persons affected by HIV and AIDS, with the main burden of their care resting almost entirely on family members, who in most cases are elderly females (Lekalakala-Mokgele, 2011). However, although there has been some progress in the containment of the epidemic worldwide, orphan-hood resulting from HIV/AIDS mortality remains a pressing problem, especially in SSA (Zagheni, 2011).

The impact of HIV/AIDS on children in sub-Saharan Africa

The HIV/AIDS epidemic has a negative effect on multiple aspects of children's lives. The vulnerabilities that children who are infected or affected by HIV/AIDS experience are multi-faceted, spanning physical and emotional health and schooling, encompassing poverty, transmission of opportunistic infections, care for unwell adults, adult distress, AIDS stigma, lack of social support, maternal breastfeeding issues, and vertical HIV transmission. Some evidence is provided that infants, adolescents, children with infected or ill mothers and children living with severely ill adults are particularly vulnerable (Goldberg & Short, 2016).

Household-level impacts

HIV/AIDS infects and kills young and middle-aged adults preferentially, the age group that comprises household heads, mothers and fathers of young children and adolescents, caregivers for the old and sick, transmitters of agricultural and livelihood knowledge and skills, and custodians of social safety nets. Some research reports greater negative impact from the loss of labor of an adult male household head, while others suggest that impacts on household food security are more severe if adult females are infected (Gill, 2010).

Impact on education

Although there are substantial variations across countries, several studies provide evidence that school enrolment rates for orphans are significantly lower than those of non-orphans. For instance, a study in eastern Zimbabwe showed that being a young caregiver was associated with lower attendance in secondary school and all forms of orphan-hood also significantly decreased the odds of primary school completion in youths surveyed from 1998 to 2011. The study however, found no evidence that HIV status affects education but did find further evidence that orphans do experience worse education outcomes than other children (Pufall et al., 2014). In contrast, earlier studies have found that HIV status does have an effect on educational outcomes of HIV-infected children, AIDS orphans and children with HIV infected parents differently. According to Zinyemba and colleagues, HIV-infected children mainly missed school due to illness and medical appointments, and orphans mainly faced financial problems and lacked motivation in their education, while children with HIV-infected parents faced financial problems and possibility of caring for their sick parents. They recommended that distinguishing these groups of children could help to formulate policies that adequately improved schooling outcomes of these vulnerable children (Zinyemba, Pavlova, & Groot, 2019). These results are in tandem with UNICEF findings that when a parent becomes sick, his or her children's education is often disrupted because they will have to perform domestic work or income-generating activities rather than attend school (UNICEF, 2006).

Impact on economic development

HIV/AIDS has affected the global human development of African countries through its devastating impact on health and demographic indicators such as life expectancy at birth, healthcare assistance, age and sex distribution; economic indicators like income, work force, and economic growth, education and knowledge acquisition; and other indicators like governance, gender inequality and human rights (Boutayeb, 2009). Another study on HIV/AIDS concerning economic growth in SSA using data from 46 SSA countries, spanning the period 2000–2015, revealed that a 1% increase in the HIV/AIDS prevalence rate in SSA decreased the growth in per capita income by 0.47%. The impact of HIV/AIDS on economic growth was felt most in East Africa followed by West Africa, although the prevalence rate was highest in Southern Africa. In particular, a 1% increase in the prevalence rate of HIV/AIDS in East Africa and West Africa retarded growth in per capita income by 0.64% and 0.47%, respectively, over the study period (Nketiah-Amponsah, Abubakari, & Baffour, 2019).

Studies show that HIV and AIDS attack mostly the reproductive and economically active section of the population, changing family composition by decimating the young adult population and creating elderly-female-headed and child-headed families (AVERT, 2019). Using data from Demographic and Health Surveys for fifteen countries in SSA, in estimating the relationship between regional HIV prevalence and the change in individual human capital investment over time, areas with higher levels of HIV experienced relatively larger declines in schooling (Fortson, 2011).

Impact on COVID-19

Members of key populations (KPs), including sex workers, men who have sex with men (MSM), people who inject drugs and transgender people are particularly vulnerable to COVID-19. KP individuals living with HIV who are not on antiretroviral therapy (ART) and not virally suppressed may have a compromised immune system, which may place them at higher risk of coronavirus acquisition and COVID-19 morbidity and mortality. Furthermore, emerging evidence shows that groups already experiencing a greater concentration of underlying health conditions are more affected by severe COVID-19 complications (Meeting Targets and Maintaining Epidemic Control (Epic), 2020).

Policies and programs

HIV is a socially, culturally induced crisis and, as such, a variety of measures are needed simultaneously to appeal to different people, groups and circumstances (Poku, 2016). Ending AIDS is a life-saving investment that pays for itself many times over. Success has been achieved where policies and programs focus on people, not diseases; policies and programs that are designed with communities and that respond to the ways that people live their lives (UNAIDS, 2019b; WHO, 2016).

The Fast Track strategy acknowledges that, without rapid scale-up, the HIV epidemic will continue to outrun the response; therefore, it outlines the need to reduce new HIV infections and AIDS-related deaths by 90% by 2030 (UNAIDS, 2014a). To achieve this, the Fast Track strategy sets out targets for prevention and treatment, known as the 90-90-90 targets (UNAIDS '90-90-90'). This includes reducing new annual HIV infections to fewer than 500,000 by 2020 and to fewer than 200,000 by 2030, ending AIDS as a public health threat (UNAIDS, 2014b). The 90-90-90 targets refer to the pathway by which a person is tested, linked and retained in HIV care, and initiates and adheres to antiretroviral drugs (ARVs), also known as the treatment cascade, to achieve viral suppression.

Most reductions in new infections have occurred in Eastern and Southern Africa but new HIV infections in other regions have declined more modestly. In 2017, UNAIDS released its Prevention 2020 Road Map, which outlined ten ways that intensified prevention efforts (UNAIDS, 2017a).

Effective HIV prevention programs require a combination of biomedical, structural and behavioral interventions. Combination prevention programs consider factors specific to each setting, such as levels of infrastructure, local culture and traditions as well as populations most affected by HIV. They can be implemented at the individual, community and population levels (UNAIDS, 2010).

Behavioral interventions

Behavioral interventions seek to reduce the risk of HIV transmission by addressing risky behaviors and addressing the cultural contexts within which risk behaviors occur, and aim to stimulate uptake of HIV prevention services such as knowledge, risk perception, norms, skills, sexual behaviors and HIV service demand (AVAC, 2018). Programs that offer support for testing people in social networks have also been an effective and acceptable approach for some populations. For instance, in a study by Somefun and colleagues found that mass media exposure and HIV testing among youth in SSA witnessed some growth in the percentage of youth who were tested, and an increasing trend was evident. The findings highlighted an increase in the number of youth testing for HIV who were exposed to mass media messages, thereby suggesting a continuous and proactive media movement that may lead to diffusion of ideas among youth and might ultimately promote HIV testing (Somefun, Wandera, & Odimegwu, 2019). The correct and consistent use of condoms with condom-compatible lubricants is recommended for all key populations to prevent sexual transmission of HIV and STIs (WHO/UNFPA/UNAIDS, 2012).

Biomedical interventions

Biomedical interventions use a mix of clinical and medical approaches to reduce HIV transmission. One example of a biomedical intervention, male circumcision, is a simple medical procedure that has been shown to reduce the risk of HIV transmission by up to 60% during unprotected heterosexual sex (UNAIDS, 2017b). In order to be effective, biomedical interventions are rarely implemented independently and are often used in conjunction with behavioral interventions. For example, during circumcision, voluntary medical male circumcision (VMMC) is treated as part of a comprehensive HIV prevention strategy, providing age appropriate sexual and reproductive health services alongside VMMC such as condom promotion, HIV testing and counselling, risk reduction counselling, testing for sexually transmitted infections (STIs), pre-exposure prophylaxis and interventions that address harmful gender norms (WHO/UNAIDS, 2016).

Pre-exposure prophylaxis

The WHO recommended PrEP and developed consolidated HIV guidelines for key populations for use among sero-discordant couples, men who have sex with men and transgender people on the basis that demonstration projects were needed to ascertain optimal delivery approaches (WHO, 2012, 2014). WHO HIV guidelines allows the offer of PrEP to be based on individual assessment, rather than risk group, and is intended to foster implementation that is informed by local epidemiological evidence regarding risk factors for acquiring HIV (WHO, 2012).

Post-exposure prophylaxis (PEP)

Post-exposure prophylaxis (PEP) is widely considered an integral part of the overall prevention strategy given to reduce the likelihood of acquiring HIV infection after possible exposure. HIV post-exposure prophylaxis is currently being considered for people presenting within 72 hours of a sexual assault. An HIV risk assessment and counselling specific to HIV and PEP should be part of the PEP intervention (WHO, 2014).

Voluntary medical male circumcision for HIV prevention

VMMC has been recommended as an additional, important strategy for the prevention of heterosexually acquired HIV infection in men, particularly in settings with hyperendemic and generalized HIV epidemics and low prevalence of male circumcision. Since 2007, more than 23 million VMMC procedures have been performed in the fifteen priority countries of East and Southern Africa, were in 2019 about half of all new HIV infections occurred (WHO, 2020b). In Uganda, the USAID-funded STAR-EC project worked from 2009–2016 to increase access to VMMC and other HIV prevention and treatment services in east central Uganda.

Countries with hyperendemic and generalized HIV epidemics and low prevalence of male circumcision should increase access to male circumcision services as a priority for adolescents and young men (Macintyre et al., 2014). Ambitious global targets for HIV testing and treatment have been set, aiming to have 90% of people living with HIV knowing their status, 90% of people who know their status receiving sustained antiretroviral therapy and 90% of people on antiretroviral therapy having viral suppression (UNAIDS, 2017b).

VMMC is being implemented in different countries as a priority component of HIV prevention programs, particularly in those countries with an increased burden of HIV, such as Malawi (UNAIDS, 2016). Currently, there is an ambitious global target of 20 million circumcisions (80% coverage) by end of 2020.

Antiretroviral treatment

Antiretroviral treatment (ART) programs have been scaled up dramatically in East and Southern Africa over the past decade. The 2013 WHO ART guidelines recommended initiating ART for all adults with HIV and a CD4 count at or below 500 cells/mm^3, regardless of WHO clinical stage, giving priority to those with severe or advanced HIV disease (WHO clinical stage 3 or 4) or a CD4 cell count at or below 350 cells/mm^3 (WHO, 2013). All countries in the region are at least implementing the 2013 WHO treatment guideline. Kenya, Malawi, Namibia, Uganda, Lesotho, Botswana, South Africa, Zambia, South Sudan, Eswatini and Ethiopia have adopted the guidelines to immediately offer treatment to people diagnosed with HIV, known as 'test and treat' or 'treat all' (AVERT, 2020). At least 15 million are accessing Art from East and Southern Africa, whilst 2.9 million are on ART from Western and Central Africa, and in the Middle East and North Africa only 92,000 are on treatment. A study assessing the change in the proportion of people staring treatment within 30 days of enrolment in HIV care after six countries adopted test and treat policies found the rate of ART initiation had sharply accelerated in Malawi, Uganda and Zambia, slowed in Kenya and had not changed in Rwanda and Burundi. (Tymejczyk et al., 2019).

HIV testing and counselling

Voluntary counselling and testing (VCT) for HIV has been promoted as a strategy to prevent HIV pandemics by changing sexual behavior. Community-based HIV testing and counselling for key populations, with linkage to prevention, care and treatment services, is recommended, in addition to provider-initiated testing and counselling. Provider-initiated testing remains the region's main approach, but community-based testing is growing since it has been shown to be effective in reaching large numbers of first-time testers, diagnosing people living with HIV at earlier stages of infection, and linking those who test positive to care. Workplace and door-to-door testing, using rapid diagnostic tests, is also increasing (UNAIDS, 2017a). HIV-related stigma remains a huge barrier to testing, something that self-testing kits may help to side-step. In 2015, self-testing began in Malawi, Zambia and Zimbabwe through the four-year Unitaid STAR (Self-Testing Africa Research) Initiative, the largest ever evaluation of self-testing. STAR's second phase expanded self-testing access to Eswatini, Lesotho and South Africa. By November 2018 the initiative had distributed 2.3 million HIV self-test kits in these countries and significantly increased HIV testing coverage, particularly among men, young people and first-time testers (UNITAID/WHO, 2018).

Prevention of mother-to-child transmission

Since the WHO issued revised guidelines in 2006, important new evidence has emerged on the use of antiretroviral (ARV) prophylaxis for the prevention mother-to-child transmission of HIV (PMTCT), and on safe feeding practices for HIV-exposed infants. The provision of antiretroviral medicines to prevent mother-to-child transmission scaled up from 44% globally in 2010 to 82% in 2018. Leading the charge are high-performing programs in much of Eastern and Southern Africa, where 92% of all pregnant women living with HIV received antiretroviral therapy in 2018, up from 49% in 2010. Integrating antenatal care and services for eliminating mother-to-child transmission of HIV with maternal, newborn and child platforms and nutrition services has proved important for retaining mothers in care after they have given birth. Community engagement is critical to ensuring that elimination goals are achieved. For instance, in South Africa, the Start Free Stay Free AIDS Free initiative promoting a range of policy and programmatic interventions aimed at reaching the elimination target, as well as other targets set by the United Nations General Assembly for women, young people and children. The most effective way to prevent children from acquiring HIV is to ensure women are empowered to protect themselves from acquiring the virus. Primary prevention therefore is paramount, but it is a major shortfall in the global AIDS response.

Structural interventions

Structural interventions seek to address underlying factors that make individuals or groups vulnerable to HIV infection. These can be social, economic, political or environmental. By successfully addressing these structural barriers, individuals are empowered and able to access HIV prevention services (Rao, Parkhurst, Ogden, Aggleton, & Mahal, 2008). Yet structural interventions are much more difficult to implement because they attempt to deal with deep-rooted socio-economic issues such as poverty, gender inequality and social marginalization.

Programs for young women

In 2013, ministers of health and education from countries across the region committed to bringing in a raft of programs to address the barriers that prevent girls and young women from accessing services. Focuses include empowering women and girls and people from groups most affected by HIV with the agency to claim their rights through programs like keeping girls in school, comprehensive sexuality education, girl-friendly sexual and reproductive health (SRH) services, eliminating gender-based violence and female genital mutilation, and economic and political empowerment (UNAIDS, 2016). Another program, Determined, Resilient, Empowered, AIDS-free, Mentored and Safe (DREAMS), aimed to reduce HIV infections among adolescent girls and young women by 40% in Kenya, Lesotho, Malawi, Mozambique, South Africa, Eswatini, Tanzania, Uganda, Zambia and Zimbabwe between 2015–2017/18. The program focused on social isolation, economic disadvantage, discriminatory cultural norms, orphan-hood, gender-based violence and education (USAID 'DREAMS: Partnership to Reduce HIV/AIDS in Adolescent Girls and Young Women).

In 2016, the South African government created She Conquers, a national campaign to implement the DREAMS program beyond the districts already being supported. Also in 2016, Eswatini partnered with the Global Fund and the National Emergency Response Council on HIV/AIDS, resulting in close to national coverage on HIV prevention for adolescent girls and young women (UNAIDS/UNICEF, 2016). Data on DREAMS's impact from one of the program's main donors, the US President's Emergency Plan for AIDS Relief (PEPFAR), suggests that communities or districts involved in DREAMS which had the highest HIV burdens when the program began had seen new HIV diagnoses among young women decline by between 25% to 40% as of 2017 (USAID, 2020). Another HIV prevention intervention grounded in the 'ABC' approach which encourages **a**bstinence, adhering to one sexual partner (**be** faithful) and the use of **c**ondoms has demonstrated some positive governance of behavior among young people; however, the latest studies have also found that in many countries that continue to invest in programs that promote abstinence and faithfulness, these interventions fail to deliver significant reductions in numbers of sexual partners, age at sexual debut, multiple sexual partnerships and teenage pregnancy (UNAIDS, 2016).

Other interventions have been implemented using multi-channel programs achieving high coverage and measurable effects on attitudes, condom use and uptake of HIV testing services, like Love Life multi-media campaign in South Africa that in 2017 reached more than 300,000 young people (Love Life Annual Reports); and Zimbabwe's national behaviour change program, which includes the Sista2Sista initiative that addresses the barriers young women face in accessing sexual reproductive health services (Ministry of Health/National AIDS Council Zimbabwe, 2018) and the multi-country One Love campaign which ran in nine Southern African cities between 2009 and 2011 to reduce multiple concurrent partnerships, one of the key drivers of HIV in the region (UNAIDS, 2016). Other studies have shown that school-based sex education is an effective strategy for reducing HIV-related risk. Students who receive school-based sex education interventions, particularly rights-based, sex-positive approaches, have been found to have significantly greater HIV knowledge and are more likely to use condoms, have fewer sexual partners and delay the age at which they start having sex (often referred to as 'sexual debut') (IPPF, 2016).

Conclusion

This chapter reviewed HIV levels, correlates, impact, policies and programs in African countries from 2000 to 2020. Studies on the prevalence of HIV have provided reliable insight into the magnitude of the problem in Africa. It is also shown that East and Southern Africa are the most affected by HIV in the world and are home to the largest number of people living with HIV. The number of people living with HIV in African countries continues to increase, although access of antiviral treatment is increasing well. The review also affirms that the African continent has achieved substantial success in slowing the epidemic, and continues to be a major public health concern.

Preventing new HIV infections is central to ending the AIDS epidemic. Despite the availability of a widening array of effective HIV-prevention tools and methods and a massive scale-up of HIV treatment in recent years, we have not made sufficient progress in reducing new infections in adults and adolescents globally. The target of the 2016 United Nations Political Declaration on Ending AIDS is to reduce new HIV infections among adults to fewer than 500,000 by 2020, from more than 1.8 million in 2010, and to scale up HIV primary prevention and treatment programs to achieve this (UNAIDS, 2018).

For close to two decades, the world has made tremendous progress in the AIDS response. HIV treatment scale-up has been particularly impressive, resulting in a 34% reduction in AIDS-related deaths between 2010 and 2017. While considerable progress has been made, there is a risk that momentum might be lost. If the world is to be on track to end AIDS by 2030, there must be adequate and predictable financing for development. However, since 2000, the resources available for the AIDS response globally have declined. Ending AIDS is a life-saving investment that pays for itself many times over. Efforts to engage and empower adolescent girls and young women, young men and key populations have been neglected, as has work to ensure a conducive policy environment in which barriers to service access are eliminated. As a result, the current pace of decline in new HIV infections is not enough to reach global HIV prevention targets (UNAIDS, 2019b).

References

AVAC. (2018). *No prevention, no end: Annual Report*. Retrieved from www.avac.org/sites/default/files/resource-files/AVACreport2018.pdf

AVERT. (2019). *HIV around the world: Sub Saharan Africa overview*. UNAIDS. Retrieved from www.avert.org/professionals/hiv-around-world/sub-saharan-africa/overview

AVERT. (2020). *HIV and AIDS in East and Southern Africa regional overview*. Retrieved from www.avert.org/professionals/hiv-around-world/sub-saharan-africa/overview

Bajunirwe, F., Semakula, D., & Izudi, J. (2020). Risk of HIV Infection among adolescent and young women in age disparate relationships in Subsaharan Africa. *AIDS*, *34*(10), 1539–1548.

Boutayeb, A. (2009). The impact of HIV/AIDS on human development in African countries. *BMC Public Health*, *9*(1). Retrieved from www.biomedcentral.com/1471-2458/9/S1/S

Carlos, S., López-del, B., Burgueño, E., Martínez-González, M., Osorio, A., Ndarabu, A., . . . Jokin, de I. (2017). Male condom use, multiple sexual partners and HIV: A prospective case-control study in Kinshasha (DRC). *AIDS Care*, *29*(6), 772–781. doi:10.1080/09540121

Doku, P., Akohene, K., Ananga, M., & Debrah, T. (2019). A systematic review of the mental health of orphans and vulnerable children within the context of HIV/AIDS in Africa. *International Journal of Psychiatry*, *4*(2), 1–20.

Fortson, J. (2011). Mortality risk and human capital investment: The impact of HIV/AIDS in sub-Saharan Africa. *The Review of Economics and Statistics*, *93*(1), 1–15.

Gill, T. (2010). Modelling the impact of HIV/AIDS upon food security of diverse rural households in Western Kenya. *Agricultural Systems*, *103*(5), 265–281.

Goldberg, R., & Short, S. (2016). What do we know about children living with HIV infected or AIDS ills adults in Sub saharan Africa? A systematic review of the literature. *AIDS CARE*, *28*(S2), 130–141.

IPPF. (2016). *Putting sexuality back into comprehensive sexuality education*. Retrieved from www.ippf.org/sites/default/files/2016

Jürgens, R., Nowak, M., & Day, M. (2011). HIV and Incarceration: Prisons and detention. *Journal of the International AIDS Society*, *14*(1), 1–17.

Kenworthy, N. (2018). From a global crisis to the 'end of AIDS': New epidemics of signification. *Global Public Health*, *13*(8), 960–971.

Kharsany, A., & Karim, Q. (2016). HIV infection and AIDS in sub-Saharan Africa: Current status, challenges and opportunities. *The Open AIDS Journal*, *10*, 34–48. doi:10.2174/1874613601610010034

Lane, T., Raymond, H. F., Dladla, S., Rasethe, J., Struthers, H., McFarland, W., & McIntyre, J. (2011). High HIV prevalence among men who have sex with men in Soweto, South Africa: Results from the Soweto men's study. *AIDS and Behaviour*, *15*(3), 626–634.

Lekalakala-Mokgele, E. (2011). A literature review of the impact of HIV and AIDS on the role of the elderly in the sub-Saharan African community. *Health SA Gesondheid*, *16*(1), 59–65.

Longo, J., Simaleko, M., Diemer, H., Grésenguet, G., Brücker, G., & & Belec, L. (2017). Risk Factors for HIV Infection among female sex workers in Bangui, Central African Republic. *PLos One*, *12*(11).

Low, A., Thin, K., Davia, S., Mantell, J., Koto, M., McCracken, S., . . . Frederix, K. (2019). Correlates of HIV infection in adolescent girls and young women in Lesotho: Results from a population based Survey. *Lancet HIV*, e613–e622. http://dx.doi.org/10.1016/S2352-3018(19)30183-3

Luseno, W. K., & Wechsberg, W. M. (2009). Correlates of HIV testing among South African women with high sexual and substance-use risk behaviours. *AIDS Care*, *21*(2), 178–184.

Macintyre, K., Andrinopoulos, K., Natome, M., Bornstein, M., Ochieng, A., Peacock, E., & Bertrand, J. (2014). Attitudes, perceptions and potential uptake of male circumcision among older men in Turkana country, Kenya using qualitative methods. *PLoS One*, 9(5); e83998.

Meeting Targets and Maintaining Epidemic Control (Epic). (2020). *Strategic consideration for mitigating the impact of COVID 19 on Key Population focused HIV Programs*. Durban: FHI 360.

Ministry of Health/National AIDS Council Zimbabwe. (2018). *Global AIDS Monitoring Zimbabwe Country Report*. Retrieved from www.unaids.org/sites/default/files/country/documents/ZWE_2018_countryreport.pdf

Mokgatle, M., & Madiba, S. (2015). The burden of disease on HIV-infected orphaned and non-orphaned children accessing primary health facilities in a rural district with poor resources in South Africa: A cross-sectional survey of primary caregivers of HIV-infected children aged 5–18 years. *Infectious Disease of Poverty*, *4*(1), 18.

Ndawin, J., Chaix, B., Koulla-Shiro, S., Delaporter, E., Okouda, B., Abanda, A., . . . Superviel, V. (2012). Facvtors associated with late antiretroviral theraphy initiation in Cameroon: A representative multilevel analysis. *Journal of Antimicrobial Chemotheraphy*. doi:10.1093/jac/dkt011

Nketiah-Amponsah, E., Abubakari, M., & Baffour, P. (2019). Effect of HIV/AIDS on economic growth in sub-Saharan Africa: Recent evidence. *International Advances in Economic Research*, *25*(4), 469–480.

Peltzer, K. (2012). Correlates of HIV infection among people visiting public HIV counseling and testing clinics in Mpumalanga, South Africa. *African Health Sciences*, *12*, 8–16.

PEPFAR. (2020). *Global HIV/AIDS overview*. Hiv.Org. Retrieved from www.hiv.gov/federal-response/pepfar-global-aids/global-hiv-aids-overview

Poku, N. (2016). HIV prevention: The key to ending AIDS by 2030. *The Open AIDS Journal*, *19*, 65–77. Retrieved from https://doi.org/10.2174/1874613601610010065

Pufall, E., Nyamukapa, C., Easton, J., Campbell, C., Skovdal, M., Munyati, S., . . . Gregson, S. (2014). The impact of HIV on children's education in Eastern Zimbabwe. *AIDS Care*, *26*(9), 1136–1143. Retrieved from https://doi.org/10.1080/09540121.2014.892564

Rao, G., Parkhurst, J., Ogden, J., Aggleton, P., & Mahal, A. (2008). Structural approaches to HIV prevention. *The Lancet, 372*(9640), 764–775. Retrieved from www.avert.org/professionals/hiv-programming/prevention/overview

Simooya, O. S. (2001). 'Behind Walls': A study of HIV risk behaviours and seroprevalence in Prisons in Zambia. *AIDS, 15*(13), 1741–1744.

Somefun, O., Wandera, S., & Odimegwu, C. (2019). Media exposure and HIV testing among youth in sub Saharan Africa: Evidence from Demographic and Health Surveys. *SAGE Open, 9*(2).

Telisinghe, L., Charalambous, S., Topppp, S., Herce, M., Hoffmann, C., Barron, P., . . . Amon, J. (2016). HIV and Tuberculosis in prisons in sub-Saharan Africa. *Lancet, 388*(10050), 1215–1227.

Tymejczyk, O., Brazier, E., Yiannoutsos, C., Vinikoor, M., van-Lettow, M., Nalugoda, F., . . . leDEA Consortium. (2019). Changes in rapid HIV treatment initiation after national "treat all" policy adoption in 6 sub-Saharan African countries: Regression discontinuity analysis. *PLoS Medicine, 16*(6), e1002822.

UNAIDS. (2010). *Combination HIV prevention: Tailoring and coordinating biomedical, behavioural and structural strategies to reduce new HIV infections*. Retrieved from http://files.unaids.org/en/media/unaids/contentassets/documents/unaidspublication/2011/20111110_JC2007_Combination_Prevention_paper_en.pdf

UNAIDS. (2014a). *Fast track ending the AIDS epidemic by 2030*. Retrieved from www.unaids.org/sites/default/files/media_asset/JC2686_WAD2014report_en.pdf

UNAIDS. (2014b). *Understanding Fast Track: Accelerating action to end the AIDS Pandemic 2030*.

UNAIDS. (2016). *Prevention gap report*. Retrieved from www.unaids.org/sites/default/files/media_asset/2016-prevention-gap-report_en.pdf

UNAIDS. (2017a). *HIV prevention 2020 road map: Accelerating HIV prevention to reduce new infections*. Retrieved from www.unaids.org/sites/default/files/media_asset/hiv-prevention-2020-road-map_en.pdf

UNAIDS. (2017b). Ending AIDS: Progress towards 90–90–90 targets. *Geneva: Joint United Nations Programme On, 3*(5). Retrieved from www.unaids.org/sites/default/files/media_asset/Global_AIDS_update_2017_en.pdf

UNAIDS. (2018). *Implementation of the HIV Prevention 2020 Road Map*.

UNAIDS. (2019a). *AIDSinfo*. Retrieved from http://aidsinfo.unaids.org/

UNAIDS. (2019b). *Global HIV prevention coalition second progress report: Implementation of the HIV prevention 2020 road map*. Geneva: United Nations.

UNAIDS. (2020a). *Global HIV & AIDS statistics: 2020 fact sheet*. Retrieved from www.unaids.org/en/resources/fact-sheet

UNAIDS. (2020b). *HIV and AIDS in East and Southern Africa regional overview (2019)*. Retrieved from www.avert.org/professionals/hiv-around-world/sub-saharan-africa/overview

UNAIDS. (2020c). *Seizing the moment global AIDS update | 2020 Tackling entrenched inequalities to end epidemics*. UNAIDS Joint United Nations Programme on HIV/AIDS. Retrieved from www.unaids.org/sites/default/files/media_asset/2020_global-aids-report_en.pdf

UNAIDS/UNICEF. (2016). *All in to end adolescent AIDS: A progress report*. Retrieved from www.unaids.org/sites/default/files/media_asset/ALLIN2016ProgressReport_en.pdf

UNICEF. (2006). *Africa's orphaned and vulnerable generations: Children affected by AIDS*. Retrieved from www.unicef.org/publications/index_35645.html

UNICEF. (2020). Retrieved from unicef.org website: https://data.unicef.org/topic/hivaids/adolescents-young-people/

UNITAID/WHO. (2018). *'Knowing your status-then and now': Realizing the potential of HIV self testing*. Retrieved from https://unitaid.org/assets/STAR-Initiative-Report-Knowing-your-status%E2%80%93then-and-now.pdf

USAID. (2020). *DREAMS: Partenrship to reduce HIV/AIDS in adolescent girls and young women*. Retrieved from www.usaid.gov/global-health/health-areas/hiv-and-aids/technical-areas/dreams

WHO. (2012). *Guidance on oral pre-exposure prophylaxis (PrEP) for serodiscordant couples, men and transgender women who have sex with men at high risk of HIV: Recommendations for use in the context of demonstration projects*. Geneva. Retrieved from www.who.int/hiv/pub/guidance_prep/en

WHO. (2013). *Consolidated guidelines on the use of antiretroviral drugs for treating and preventing HIV infection: Recommendations for a public health approach*. Retrieved from www.who.int/hiv/pub/guidelines/arv2013/en/

WHO. (2014). *Guidelines on Post Exposure Prophylaxis for HIV and the use of co-trimoxazole prophylaxis for HIV-related infections among adults, adolescents and children: Recommendations for a public health approach*. Retrieved from http://www/who.int/hiv/pub/guidelines/arv2013/arvs2013upplement_dec2014/en/

WHO. (2016). *Consolidated guidelines on HIV prevention, diagnosis, treatment and care for key populations*. Geneva: WHO. Retrieved from www.ncbi.nlm.nih.gov/books/NBK379696/
WHO. (2018). *Report on key populations in African HIV/AIDS: National strategic plans*. Brazzaville: WHO regional Office for Africa.
WHO. (2020a). *HIV/AIDS fact sheet*. Retrieved from www.who.int/fact-sheets/hiv-aids
WHO. (2020b). *Preventing HIV through safe voluntary medical male circumcision for adolescent boys and men in generalized HIV epidemics: Recommendations and key considerations*. Policy Brief.
WHO/UNAIDS. (2016). *A framework for voluntary medical male circumcision: Effective HIV prevention and a gateway to improved adolescent boys' & men's health in Eastern and Southern Africa by 2021*. Retrieved from http://apps.who.int/iris/bitstream/handle/10665/246234/WHO-HIV-2016.17-eng.pdf?
World Health Organization Statistics. (2020). *People who inject drugs*. Retrieved from www.who.int/hiv/topics/idu/en/
Zagheni. (2011). The impact of the HIV/AIDS epidemic on kinship resources for orphans in Zimbababwe. *Population and Development Review*, *37*(4), 761–783.
Zinyemba, T. P., Pavlova, M., & Groot, W. (2019). Effects of HIV/AIDS on Children's education attainment: A systematic literature review. *Journal of Economic Surveys*, *34*(1), 35–84. Retrieved from https://doi.org/10.1111/joes.12345

24

THE DOUBLE BURDEN OF MALNUTRITION AMONG ADULTS IN SUB-SAHARAN AFRICA

A systematic review of the literature

Mpho Keetile, Kannan Navaneetham and Gobopamang Letamo

Introduction

The sub-Saharan Africa (SSA) region is faced with the double burden (DB) of malnutrition (DBM) explained as simultaneous presence of undernutrition and overnutrition. We note that if current trends continue, the global goal of ending hunger and all forms of malnutrition by 2030 will not be achieved. Globally, 800 million people are still suffering from undernutrition and among them over 237 million live in SSA (Food and Agriculture Organization, 2019). At the same time, rates of overnutrition depicted as overweight and obesity are increasing rapidly in many African countries (Vorster, Kruger, & Margetts, 2011; Onyango et al., 2019). This has created a situation in which undernutrition and overnutrition (overweight/obesity) coexist in African countries leading to the double burden of malnutrition (DBM). DBM is characteristic of the nutrition transition, a phenomenon wherein increasing overweight/obesity emerges in predominantly undernourished populations, as is evident in the SSA region. The increase in malnutrition is attributed to several factors such as poverty, illiteracy, ignorance, big family size, climate change, poor nutrition policies and corruption (Amuna & Zotor, 2008; Bain et al., 2013).

Despite the Millennium Development Goals (MDGs) target of reducing hunger by half by 2015, major failures were recorded in Africa at the end of the MDGs (United Nations [UN], 2015). During the MDGs period SSA saw little or no change in the prevalence of malnutrition over the period 1990–2011 (Stevens et al., 2012). More recently, the Sustainable Development Goals (SDGs) recognize the need for better nutrition. For instance, SDG 2 aims to 'end hunger, achieve food security and improved nutrition, and promote sustainable agriculture" (United Nations, 2019). The SDGs aim to end all forms of hunger and malnutrition by 2030, making sure all people – including adults – have sufficient and nutritious food all the time (FAO/IFAD/UNICEF/WFP/WHO, 2018). This involves promoting sustainable agriculture, supporting small-scale farmers and equal access to land, technology and markets.

Even though there are numerous national initiatives aimed at ending all forms of malnutrition in Africa, the rates of hunger, under- and over-nutrition are poised to increase in the

DOI: 10.4324/9780429287213-29

future (Onyango et al., 2019). This is mainly because SSA is currently undergoing a nutritional transition. While other countries are lagging behind with high rates of under nutrition, other nations are experiencing an increasing incidence of overweight/obesity and diet-related non-communicable diseases (NCDs) in the adult population (Holmes et al., 2018). According to the Food Agricultural Organization (2017), a vast majority of the undernourished population is mostly found in countries affected by conflict. This is because people in conflict-affected countries do not have sustainable means of subsistence and rely most often on food aids. As a result the prevalence of undernourishment is about twice as high in conflict-affected countries with a protracted crisis than in countries not affected by conflict (Uchendu, 2018), and nutrition outcomes are also generally worse in those countries (Jones, Acharya, & Galway, 2016). Although the frequency of wars has decreased in most SSA countries, there has recently been an increase in the number of violent conflicts and conflict-related deaths in 13 SSA countries (Jones et al., 2016).

Undernutrition is still a major challenge in Africa. However, the nutritional transition has brought about overnutrition related conditions. Over the past two decades, the share of the overweight and obese population has increased rapidly in Africa (Hruby & Hu, 2015). Thus the share of overweight adults has nearly doubled, from 17% in 1980 to over 30% in 2015 (Agyemang, Boatemaa, Frempong, & Aikins, 2015). Notable regional differences in overweight and obesity levels have also been observed, with Southern Africa recording higher levels than other SSA regions (Ajayi et al., 2016). Southern Africa tops the scales across the continent, reporting adult obesity rates of 31% (Haggblade et al., 2016).

Available literature indicates that across all Africa regions, adult women are the most vulnerable to weight gain during the nutrition transition, given biological differences in how women and men metabolize fat (Barker, 1995, 2012; Neupane & Doku, 2015). The increasing numbers of overweight and obese populations coupled with the emerging NCDs, on top of already high levels of undernutrition, have begun to place a DB on the already stretched public health systems of Africa (Voster et al., 2011; World Health Organization, 2013b; Gomez et al., 2013; Tzioumis & Adair, 2014). This DB has emerged most prominently in the Southern African countries of South Africa, Swaziland and Lesotho, where rates of undernutrition and overnutrition both exceed 30% (Haggblade et al., 2016). This DB manifests itself in simultaneously high rates of underweight and overweight among adult women in many countries. Already, a majority of African countries have reached the point at which the share of overweight women exceeds underweight (WHO, 2018).

Efforts to encourage healthy diets and reduce undernutrition, obesity and diet-related NCDs in Africa are generally limited to diet or nutrition counselling, media campaigns, nutrient labelling or dietary guidelines. However, such actions have little public health impact unless many individuals in the population make sustained changes in their food consumption behaviours (Popkin, Adair, & Ng, 2012; WHO, 2018). At a time when warnings about health consequences of excess weight abound, much less attention seems to be paid to the implications of being underweight during adulthood (Bitew & Telake, 2010). This may partly be explained by the fact that due to westernization and modernization; thinness is commonly regarded as an ultimate goal to the extent that it is hard to think of thinness as a health concern. As such there is limited research on the health and well-being of adults in the SSA context (Letamo, 2011).

In African countries, most studies on malnutrition are often directed towards infants, young children and pregnant and lactating women. The lack of attention to the adult malnutrition in policies and programs is reflected by the paucity of information from research studies on their condition. The scant information that is available suggests that the nutrition problems of the adults are sizable which is contrary to the experiences of the adult population in the continent.

Given that Africa is poised to experience an marked increase in the number of adults in the next two decades, researchers and policymakers would do well to focus more attention on the nutrition and health of this group. The aim of this chapter is to synthesize available empirical evidence about the DBM of adults in Africa. In particular, we reviewed two broad areas of research: 1) the nutritional status of adult Africans, in terms of both under- and overnutrition, and 2) the social, cultural and economic determinants of malnutrition among the adult population in Africa. The study is relevant in that it would help policy makers to make policy interventions to reduce the consequences of undernutrition and overnutrition as high risk factors for NCDs. The main reason we select these areas is that they form the core of a problem statement on the DB of adult malnutrition. They are a key starting point for designing nutrition policies and programs for this group. As will be seen throughout this chapter, there are substantial gaps in the literature. A final section outlines some suggested future research and policy priorities.

Theoretical and conceptual issues

Conceptually, malnutrition generally involves undernutrition (underweight) and overnutrition (or overweight and obesity). A simplified definition of malnutrition is that it literally means 'bad nutrition' or 'dysnutrition' and theoretically includes both over- and under-nutrition (World Health Organization, 2018). According to the World Food Programme (WFP) malnutrition is defined as 'a state in which the physical function of a person is impaired to the point where he or she can no longer maintain adequate bodily performance processes such as growth, pregnancy, lactation, physical work and resisting and recovering from disease' (Bain et al., 2013). From a conceptual point of view, the dichotomy of undernutrition and overnutrition is no longer relevant. This is mainly because, while undernutrition is still prevalent in majority of African countries, overnutrition mirrored by a rapid rise in nutrition-related NCDs and risk factors such as overweight and obesity, diabetes and cardiovascular disease (CVD) is also increasing in some African countries. This DBM is defined by the World Health Organization (WHO) as the coexistence of undernutrition along with overweight/obesity or other nutrition-related NCDs (World Health Organization, 2018). 'Undernutrition' covers stunting, wasting or thinness, as well as specific micronutrient deficiencies. 'Overnutrition' refers primarily to overweight or obesity. Over nutrition-related conditions or cardio-metabolic risk factors other than obesity include high blood pressure, hyperglycaemia and diabetes and at-risk blood lipid profile (Alshehri, 2010).

For the most part, the conceptual understanding of malnutrition and its causes has been commonly guided by the UNICEF conceptual framework for the causes of malnutrition (Vogt, Rukooko, Iversen, & Eide, 2016). Similarly, most of the studies on malnutrition in SSA have been guided by the UNICEF framework. The UNICEF conceptual framework is an analytic tool that has been developed to portray causal determinants of malnutrition. The conceptual framework, originally designed in 1990, has been refined to be broad enough to encompass multiple sectors that impact the causes of malnutrition at each level (Levitt, Pelletier, & Pell, 2009; Black et al., 2013). It has been modified for various geographical contexts or with a focus on interventions. Its modification to suit various geographical contexts makes the conceptual framework applicable even in the African context.

The main premise of this framework is that adequate food intake and freedom from disease are the immediate conditions for good nutrition. It presumes that the underlying conditions are clustered under food security, adequate care and a proper healthy environment, which also constitutes the necessary components of nutrition security. According to the WHO (2013a) a good nutrition environment is the one in which food security is combined with a clean environment,

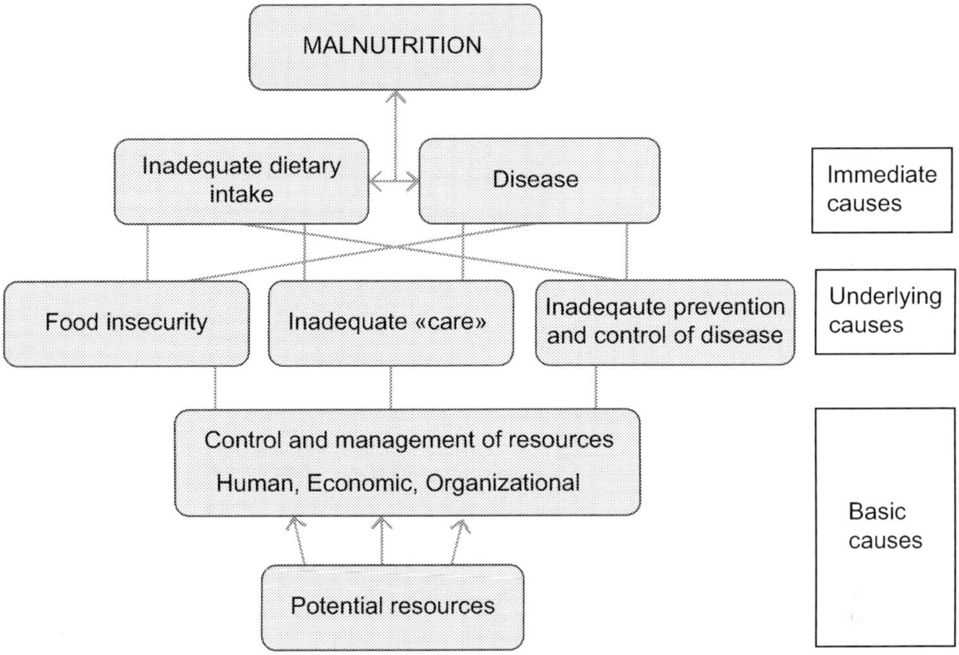

Figure 24.1 UNICEF's conceptual framework for the causes of malnutrition.

Source: Vogt et al., 2016

adequate health services and appropriate care and feeding practices to ensure a healthy life for all household members. The tenets of this framework have been succinctly used to understand determinants of malnutrition in both the developed and developing countries. It is therefore considered as a normative framework that can help conceptualize what measures are necessary to ensure conditions for good nutrition.

This framework provides a crossing point between the broader systemic-level issues and the community, household and individual levels. In most SSA countries, the quality of nutrition is still relatively very poor. Economic growth is slack and household purchasing power is very low. Meanwhile, malnutrition prevalence from 2000 to 2020 across SSA countries showed an overall decline in undernutrition as economic indicators improved (Stevens et al., 2012). As a result, there is a need to improve socioeconomic indicators in order to improve nutrition outcomes for the adult population in Africa. The increases in wealth at a country level need to be equitable and investments in health and nutrition are desired in order to impact the nutrition status of most adults.

There are several environmental and economic shocks that have caused disruptions in resources and livelihoods, leading to static or worsening prevalence of malnutrition, especially undernutrition in Africa (Frieden, 2010; Reinhardt & Fanzo, 2014). These shocks, especially droughts associated with civil conflicts, have led to an increased undernutrition in low-income settings of Africa. In Rwanda, for example, a study about the consequences of conflict and crop failure found that the impact of war has led to adult malnutrition, even post-conflict impact over the life course (Food and Agriculture Organization, 2013, 2017). Climate events and changes to the natural system can affect the prevalence of undernutrition through both increases in human morbidity and degradation of the local food system and resources. Exposure to these types of events can be associated with malnutrition through the impact on the quality and quantity of food or can indirectly be associated through the impact on the economy, political systems, public infrastructure and water systems.

Methodology

Malnutrition indicators

This review focuses on the DB of adult malnutrition in SSA, by considering both undernutrition and overnutrition.

Search strategy

We employed a systematic literature review using the Preferred Reporting Items for Systematic Reviews and Meta-Analyses (PRISMA) guidelines (Moher et al., 2015). A list of relevant words and sub-headings of keywords on 'adult malnutrition in SSA' was generated and used to comprehensively search peer-reviewed articles from four computerized bibliographic databases: Scopus, PubMed, CINAHL and Embase. We also used Google scholar to access some articles using the following key words: 'adult malnutrition', 'adult undernutrition (underweight)', 'adult overnutrition (overweight or obesity)' and 'in sub-Saharan Africa'. The search covered research conducted in 46 sub-Saharan African countries and published between January 2000 and January 2020. The year 2000 was used as a baseline for this review in order to capture articles published during the MDGs. The articles retrieved from each database were imported into an Excel template then later transferred to an EndNote library. For additional relevant publications that might have been missed, we searched the bibliographical references of all retrieved articles that met the inclusion criteria, complemented by citation tracking using Google Scholar. We also searched for articles using the country name and region as keywords. The following combination of keywords was used in the search:

- (malnutrition★ OR malnourished★ OR undernutrition★ OR undernourished★ OR underweight★ OR overnutrition★ OR overweight/obese★)
- (Adult★ or 15 years and over★ or elderly★ or old★ or men★ or women★)
- (Factor★ OR determinant★ OR correlate★ OR cause★ OR Patterns/Trends)

Exclusion and inclusion criteria

The studies were included in this review based on the following exclusion and inclusion criteria; they were included if they

1 focussed on adults (≥15 years);
2 were conducted in SSA;
3 analyzed factors associated with adult undernutrition (underweight) and overnutrition (overweight/obesity);
4 were published between 2000 and 2020;
5 were cross-sectional or longitudinal studies (qualitative studies, case studies, books, policy briefs or theses were excluded);

6 were published in a peer-reviewed journal (non-peer-reviewed research, reviews or commentaries were excluded);
7 were written in English or French by African scholars (either as principal or co-authors); and
8 were relevant United Nations documents and reports.

Data extraction

After collecting all the articles through the search, they were exported into an Excel data entry template which was later exported to EndNote library. All publications were screened by reading titles and abstracts and the complete text of the remaining articles that met the inclusion/exclusion criteria were retained studies. All data extraction and appraisals of retrieved studies were reviewed and the summary of the selected studies was recorded. The summaries included author, year of publication, country of publication, number of adults, factors associated with undernutrition indicators (underweight) and factors associated with overnutrition (overweight/obesity). These studies were also grouped by country into SSA sub-regions (East Africa, Southern Africa, West Africa and Central Africa) based on the United Nations (UN) geoscheme classification. The Strengthening the Reporting of Observational Studies in Epidemiology (STROBE) checklist was used to ascertain the quality of reviewed studies (Cuschieri, 2019). The STROBE checklist was also used to assess internal validity (based on potential measurement biases and confounding) of cross-sectional studies and external validity (based on potential selection bias). The assessment considered the following quality-appraisal criteria: sample size, sampling methodology, responses rate, outcome measures, methods of statistical analyses, limitation of the study, ethical consideration and control for confounding.

Data analysis

For this review, we retrieved a total of 1,753 articles from the four databases (PubMed, PsycINFO, Scopus and Embase) and Google scholar. After the removal of duplicates, 1003 articles were retained. A screening of the titles resulted in the exclusion of 702 articles. The abstracts of the resulting 301 articles were read and screened which led to the exclusion of another 107 articles. The full text of the remaining 94 articles was reviewed and 51 articles were further excluded. A further 13 studies were removed after reading references from retrieved articles. As a result the overall total of articles which met the inclusion criteria for the review was 30 as shown in the flowchart in Figure 24.2.

Results

Quality assessment for included studies

In order to assess the quality of studies which were used for this review, the Strengthening the Reporting of Observational Studies in Epidemiology (STROBE) checklist (Akombi et al., 2017) was used as a guide (Table 24.1). The STROBE checklist consists of 22 items which are used to evaluate the internal validity (based on potential measurement bias and cofounding) and external validity (which looks on the potential selection bias) of cross-sectional studies. At the first step we listed 22 STROBE items, which we later collapsed into 8 quality-appraisal criteria of response rate, outcome measures, sample size, sampling methodology, statistical analyses, study limitation, ethical consideration and control for confounding variables. Each reviewed

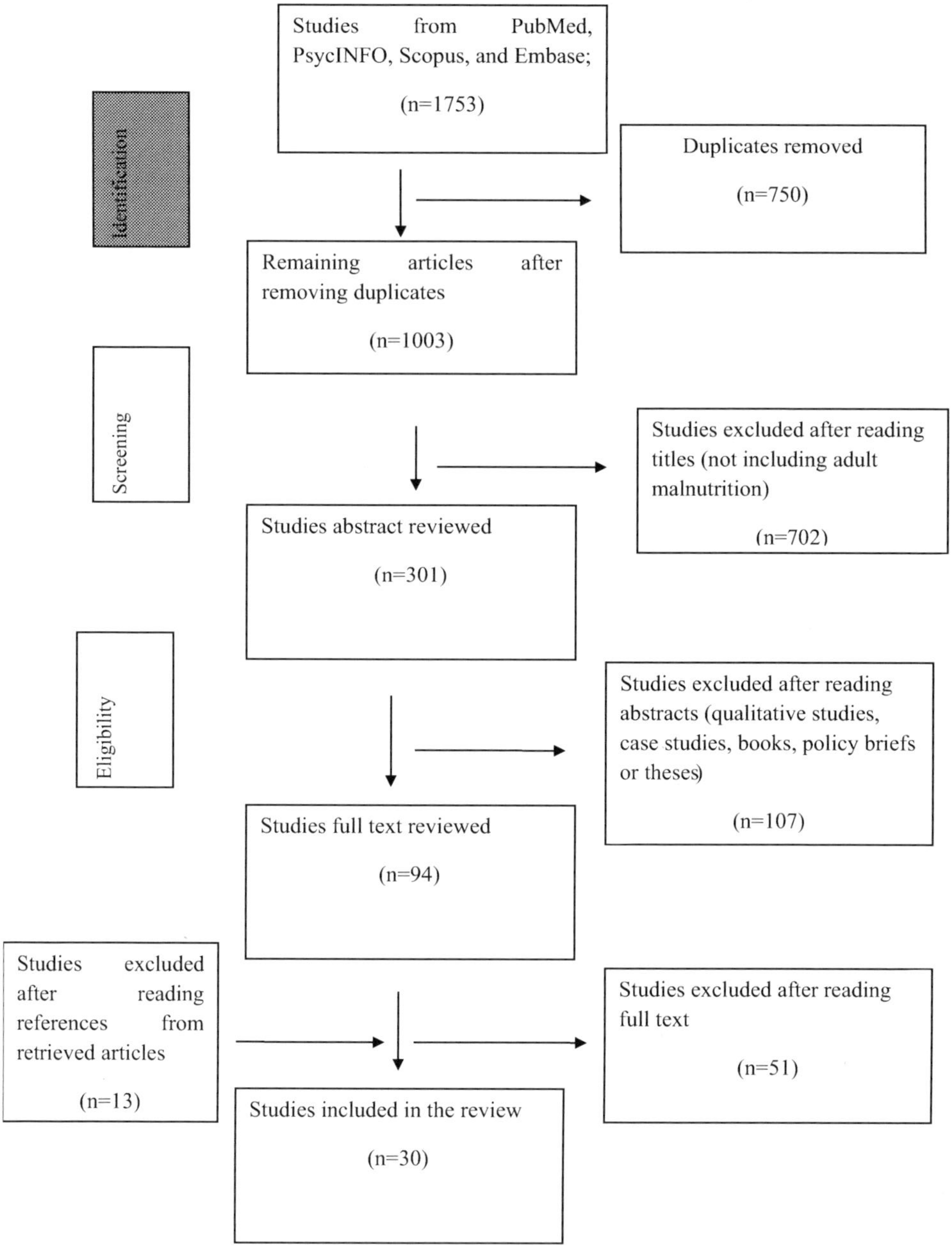

Figure 24.2 Flow chart for studies selected based on PRISMA 2015 guidelines

study was assigned scores ranging from 0 to 8 points (thus 0 if none of the criteria were met and 8 points if the study met all criteria). The overall quality of the study was then the sum of points awarded to that particular study. Studies scored as follows: ≤3 = poor quality; 4–6 = medium quality; and ≥7 = high quality.

Results

Characteristics of included studies

Table 24.1 shows a summary of the studies included in this review grouped by sub-region. Of the studies conducted, 8 were in Southern Africa, 13 in West Africa, 8 in East Africa and 1 in Central Africa. Sample sizes ranged from 95 to 48,966 participants. Fifteen studies reported on prevalence and determinants of overweight or obesity, 4 studies were on adult undernutrition, 9 studies on prevalence of and factors associated with adult malnutrition and 2 studies on HIV and adult malnutrition.

Twenty studies reported the factors associated with undernutrition (underweight), while 10 studies reported on overnutrition (overweight or obesity). When using the eight criteria used to evaluate the quality of included studies it was found that 17 studies (57%) were of high quality, while 12 studies (40%) were of medium quality and 1 study (3%) was of low quality. The details of domain-specific scores are provided in Table 24.3. During the search, 9 community-based cross sectional studies, 4 studies using DHS data, 1 meta-analysis, retrospective study and prospective cohort study and 14 population-based cross-sectional studies were found. All these studies were included in the review of the DBM in SSA.

Evidence from reviewed studies

Evidence from reviewed studies indicates that studies assessing the DBM are generally lacking in SSA. Consequently the search produced most of the studies which focused on either underweight or overweight or obesity, separately. Table 24.2 presents the summary of the selected studies. According to results in Table 24.2, the most consistent factors associated with underweight among adults were being male, young adults, low wealth status, low education, traditional dietary pattern, low income, sedentariness, ill health, low consumption of sugar and rural area residence. Factors identified to be associated with undernutrition were unemployment, HIV-positive status, hospitalization, poor environment and smoking. Results indicate that prevalence of various forms of malnutrition varied across study settings and overtime. While overweight/obesity were most common in the Southern Africa region, underweight was more common in the Central and East African regions. Since majority of the studies were cross-sectional in nature, causality could not be ascertained.

Most studies showed that being male was a factor associated with undernutrition, but a study conducted in Burkina Faso and the Democratic Republic of the Congo identified that undernourishment was more common among older women (Zeba, Delisle, & Renier, 2014). On the other hand, only one study in Burkina Faso found that undernutrition was associated with traditional dietary pattern and female sex. In Cameroon a study among adults admitted at the hospitals indicated that undernutrition was more common among patients with malignancy. Other studies conducted in Ethiopia, Ghana and Kenya identified factors such as gastrointestinal symptoms, previous opportunistic infections, low CD4 count and having tuberculosis to be significantly associated with malnutrition (Dagne, Mesfin, & Gebremedhin, 2019; Blaauw et al., 2019; Fongar, Gödecke, Aseta, & Qaim, 2019).

Factors such as being female; wealth; high education; residing in urban areas; television ownership; high income; low physical activity; frequent consumption of sweets, meat and eggs; alcohol consumption; being married and increasing age were found to be consistently associated with adult overweight or obesity. Other factors linked to overweight or obesity in the reviewed studies include hypertension, diabetes, high cholesterol level, greater maternal age and

Table 24.1 Assessment Tools Used for the Quality Appraisal of the Included Studies, Based on STROBE Checklist

Sample size	*Sampling methodology (representativeness)*	*Response rate*	*Outcome measure*	*Statistical analysis*	*Confounding*	*Study limitations*	*Ethical considerations*
1 point Study reported sample size calculation	1 point Random selection from representative list of the target population	1 point High response rate (>70%)	1 point Valid acceptable definition of adult malnutrition (undernutrition or overnutrition) based on WHO guidelines and objectively measured	1 point Statistical techniques and reasons for choosing techniques are fully explained	1 point Well adjusted (individual, household and community-level factors). Adjusted and unadjusted Odd ratio (OR) or Relative ratio (RR), confidence interval and p-values were well presented	1 point Stated study limitations	1 point Studies with ethical consideration
0 point No sample size calculation	0 point Non-random selection but from sampling frame that represent the community	0 point Moderate/Low response rate (<70%)	0 point No valid definition of malnutrition	0 point Statistical techniques are not explained	0 point Minimally adjusted for some or none of the confounders	0 point No stated study limitations	0 point Studies with no ethical consideration

Table 24.2 Summary of Selected Studies

Country	*Title*	*Author [Ref]Year, Country*	*Number of Adults (N), Age*	*Factors associated with underweight*	*Factors associated with overnutrition/ overweight/obesity*
Angola	Gender and sociodemographic distribution of Body Mass Index: the nutrition transition in an adult Angolan community	Pedro et al., 2018, Angola	N=2,357, 15–64 years	Men, underweight prevalent in 15–24 years	Women, increased with age, among people who lived with companions, decreased with education among women, higher in rural areas, higher family incomes, DBM among women
Benin	Prevalence and risk factors of overweight and obesity: findings from a cross-sectional community-based survey in Benin	Gbary et al., 2014, Benin	N=6,773, 25–64 years		Females, primary and tertiary education, occupation, dwelling and department
Botswana	Prevalence and Determinants of Adult Under-Nutrition in Botswana	Letamo & Navaneetham, 2014, Botswana;	N=9,052,20–49 years	Being male, low wealth status, low education	
	The prevalence of, and factors associated with, overweight and obesity in Botswana	Letamo, 2011, Botswana	N=9,023,20–49 years		Women, old age, urban residence, being married and high education
	Socioeconomic and behavioural determinants of overweight/ obesity among adults in Botswana	Keetile et al., 2019, Botswana	N=1,178, ≥15 years		Women, older ages, high education, smokers, poor physical activity
	The prevalence of, and factors associated with, overweight and obesity among University of Botswana students	Tapera et al., 2017, Botswana	N=202, 18–30 years		Overweight/obesity prevalence was 36.8%, associated with age, poor physical activity, year of study and an individual's opinion about him/her being overweight/obese
Burkina Faso	Prevalence and factors associated with overweight and obesity among rural and urban women in Burkina Faso	Diandere et al., 2019, Burkina Faso	N=2,191, 25–64 years		Urban, high cholesterol level, having high BP

(*Continued*)

Table 24.2 (Continued)

Country	*Title*	*Author [Ref]Year, Country*	*Number of Adults (N), Age*	*Factors associated with underweight*	*Factors associated with overnutrition/ overweight/obesity*
	Dietary patterns and physical inactivity, two contributing factors to the DBM among adults in Burkina Faso	Zeba et al., 2014, Burkina Faso	N=110, 25–60 years	Traditional dietary pattern, low income, female sex and sedentary time were significant contributing factors to the DBM	
	Wealth and under-nourishment among married women in two impoverished nations: evidence from Burkina Faso and Congo Democratic Republic	Adebowale, Palamuleni, & Odimegwu, 2015, Burkina Faso	N=4,233, 15–49 Years	Undernourishment among older women, poor, middle-class women	Obesity and overweight among rich women, rural areas, with no formal education, anaemic and unemployed
	Obesity and metabolic syndrome in a Burkina Faso Urban Area; Prevalence, Associated Factors and comorbidities	Sagna et al., 2014, Burkina Faso	N=632, 20–75 years		Obesity associated with hypertension, diabetes; older females were obese
Cameroon	Malnutrition in patients admitted to the medical wards of the Doula General Hospital: a cross sectional study	Luma et al., 2017, Cameroon	N=251, 18 years and above	Malnutrition was 19.34%, common among patients with malignancy	
	Prevalence and predictors of overweight and obesity among Cameroonian women in a national survey and relationships with waist circumference and inflammation in Yaoundé and Doula	Engle-Stone et al., 2018	N=704, 15–49 years		Residents in urban areas, greater maternal age and television ownership had overweight/ obesity
Cape Verde	No information				
Central African Republic	Under nutrition and obesity among elderly people living in two cities of developing countries; Prevalence and associated factors in EDAC study	Jésus et al., 2017, Central African Republic	N=990, <50 years	Undernutrition was 19.2%, Obesity was 8.8%; increasing age, occupation, smoking, low consumption of sugar associated with undernutrition, being female associated with obesity	Central African Republic the hungriest country

Ethiopia	Undernutrition and associated factors among adults living with Human Immune Deficiency Virus in Dembia District, northwest Ethiopia: an institution-based cross-sectional study	Mitiku et al., 2016, Ethiopia	N=2,803, ≥18 years	Young adults (18–29 years), widows, anaemic	
	Prevalence and factors associated with overweight and obesity among adults in Hawassa City, southern Ethiopia: a community based cross-sectional study	Darebo, Mesfin, & Gebremedhin, 2019, Ethiopia	N=531, 18–64 Years		Women, high income, low physical activity, daily alcohol intake, frequent consumption of sweets, meat and eggs were associated with overweight/obesity
	Factors associated with overweight and obesity among adults in northeast Ethiopia: A cross sectional study	Dagne et al., 2019, Ethiopia	N=751, 18–64 years		High among adults who have snack intake habit, drink alcohol, high wealth status, married
	Malnutrition: Prevalence and its associated factors in people living with HIV/AIDS, in Dilla University Referral Hospital	Hailemariam, Bune, & Ayele, 2013, Ethiopia	N=520, 18 years and above	Prevalence of malnutrition was 12.3%, after adjusting for covariates; unemployment, gastrointestinal symptoms, previous opportunistic infections were significantly associated with malnutrition	
	Prevalence of malnutrition and associated factors among adult patients on antiretroviral therapy follow-up in Jimma Medical Center, southwest Ethiopia	Daka & Ergiba, 2020	N=971, >15 years	Malnutrition was more likely among widowed patients, low CD4 count, bedridden	

(Continued)

Table 24.2 (Continued)

Country	*Title*	*Author [Ref]Year, Country*	*Number of Adults (N), Age*	*Factors associated with underweight*	*Factors associated with overnutrition/overweight/obesity*
Ghana	The Problem of Hospital Malnutrition in the African Continent	Blaauw et al., 2019, Ghana	N=2,126, 43.11 years	Nearly two thirds of patients were at risk of malnutrition on admission. This was associated with greater hospital mortality. The nutritional status of patients deteriorated during hospitalization	Prospective cohort study
	Overweight and obesity epidemic in Ghana: a systematic review and meta-analysis. BMC public health, 16(1), 1239. https://doi.org/10.1186/s12889-016-3901-4	Ofori-Asenso et al. (2016), Ghana	N=48,966, age not stated	The national prevalence of overweight and obesity were estimated as 25.4% and 17.1% respectively. Higher prevalence of overweight (27.2% vs 16.7%) and obesity (20.6% vs 8.0%) were estimated for urban than for rural dwellers. Prevalence of overweight (27.8% vs 21.8%) and obesity (21.9% vs 6.0%) were also significantly higher in women than men. About 45.6% of adult diabetes patients in Ghana are either overweight or obese.	Systematic review
Kenya	Various forms of DBM problems exist in rural Kenya	Fongar et al., 2019, Kenya	N=874, >15 years	DBM was 19% in adults, DB low at household level	
Malawi	Moderate to severe malnutrition in patients with tuberculosis is a risk factor associated with early death	Zachariah, Spielmann, Harries, & Salaniponi, 2002, Malawi	N=1,181, Age not stated	22% mild malnutrition, 14% moderate malnutrition and 21% severe malnutrition, malnutrition led to mortality	
Nigeria	Prevalence and pattern of overweight and obesity in three rural	Adebayo et al., 2014, Nigeria	N=777, 20–90 years		Increased with age, highest in 51–60-year age group,

	Some socioeconomic factors of malnutrition in Benin City, Nigeria	Osuhor & Ogbeide, 1982	N=570 families, age not stated	poor education, poor income and poor environment	
Senegal	HIV and the dual burden of malnutrition in Senegal, 1994–2012	Benzekri et al., 2018, Senegal	N=2,448, >18	Among HIV-negative individuals, the prevalence of undernutrition decreased from 23% in 1994–1999 to 5% in 2006–2012, while prevalence of overnutrition increased from 19 to 55%. Women had greater odds of obesity. Age >35 was associated with increased odds for obesity.	Retrospective study
Seychelles	The dimensions of food insecurity and malnutrition among people living with HIV in Senegal, West Africa	Benzekri et al., 2017, Senegal	N=95, 19–67 years	Economic access was the strongest predictor of severe food insecurity, and poorly controlled HIV was the strongest predictor of malnutrition	Cross-sectional
Somalia	Short-term prognosis in severe adult and adolescent malnutrition during famine: use of a simple prognostic model based on counting clinical signs	Collins & Myatt, 2000, Somalia.	N=383, 15 years and older		Cross-sectional
South Africa	Determinants of obesity and associated population attributability, South Africa: empirical evidence from the National Panel Survey	Sartorius, Veerman, Manyema, Chola, & Hofman, 2015, South Africa	N=22,218, ≥15 years		Females, living in formal urban areas, white ethnicity, being married, not exercising and high SES were associated with male obesity. Females in urban areas, African/white ethnicity, married, not exercising, high SES

(*Continued*)

Table 24.2 (Continued)

Country	*Title*	*Author [Ref]Year, Country*	*Number of Adults (N), Age*	*Factors associated with underweight*	*Factors associated with overnutrition/overweight/obesity*
	Differing patterns of overweight and obesity among black men and women in Cape Town: the CRIBSA study	Peer et al., 2014, South Africa	N=1,099, 25–74 years		Increasing age, wealth, hypertension and diabetes
Tanzania	Malnutrition and associated factors among adults starting on antiretroviral therapy at PASADA hospital in Temeke District, Tanzania	Kabalimu, Sungwa, & Lwabukuna, 2018, Tanzania	N=125, 20 years and older	Malnutrition prevalence was 19.4%, associated with irregular income, inability to at least get 2 meals	Cross-sectional
Uganda	Gender and age disparities in adult undernutrition in Northern Uganda: high-risk groups not targeted by food aid programmes	Schramm, Kaducu, Smedemark, Ovuga, & Sodemann et al., 2016	N=4,986, ≥15 years	For men, young age and older age, being divorced and smoking; for women, older age	
Zimbabwe	Trends in prevalence and related risk factors of overweight and obesity among women of reproductive age in Zimbabwe, 2005–2015	Mukora-Mutseyekwa, Zeeb, Nengomasha, & Kofi Adjei 2019, Zimbabwe	2005 ZDHS*, N=8,185 2010 ZDHS, N=8,448; ZDHS, N=9,066, 15–49 years		Being married, high SES, being employed, urban residence

*ZDHS-Zimbabwe Demographic Health Survey

Table 24.3 Quality Assessment of Included Studies

Author, Year, Country	*Sample size*	*Sampling methodology (Representativeness)*	*Response rate*	*Outcome measure*	*Statistical analysis*	*Confounding*	*Study limitations*	*Ethical considerations*	*Quality assessment core*
Southern Africa									
Letamo & Navaneetham, 2014, Botswana	1	1	1	1	1	1	1	1	8
Letamo, 2011, Botswana	1	1	0	1	1	1	1	1	7
Keetile et al., 2019, Botswana	1	1	1	1	1	1	1	1	8
Tapera et al., 2017, Botswana	1	1	1	1	1	0	0	1	6
Pedro et al., 2018, Angola	1	1	1	1	1	0	0	1	0
Sartorius et al., 2015, South Africa	1	1	1	1	1	1	1	0	7
Peer et al., 2014, South Africa	1	1	1	1	1	1	1	1	8
Mukora-Mutseyekwa et al., 2019, Zimbabwe	1	1	1	1	1	1	1	1	8
West Africa									
Adebayo et al., 2014, Nigeria	1	1	0	1	1	0	0	1	5
	1	1	0	0	1	1	1	1	6
Osuhor & Ogbeide, 1982, Nigeria	1	1	1	1	1	1	1	1	8
Gbary et al., 2014, Benin	1	1	1	1	1	1	1	1	8
Zeba et al., 2014, Burkina Faso	1	1	0	1	1	1	1	0	7
Adebowale et al., 2015, Burkina Faso	1	1	1	1	1	1	0	1	7
Sagna et al., 2014, Burkina Faso	1	1	0	1	1	0	0	0	4
Luma et al., 2017, Cameroon	1	1	0	1	1	0	1	1	6
Engle-Stone et al., 2018, Cameroon	1	1	1	1	1	1	1	1	8
Blaauw et al., 2019, Ghana	1	1	0	0	1	0	0	1	4
Ofori-Asenso et al., 2016, Ghana	1	0	0	1	1	1	1	1	6
Benzekri et al., 2018, Senegal	1	1	1	1	1	1	1	1	8
East Africa									
Darebo et al., 2019, Ethiopia	1	1	0	0	1	0	0	0	3
Dagne et al., 2019, Ethiopia	1	1	0	1	1	1	0	1	6
Hailemariam et al., 2013, Ethiopia	1	1	1	1	1	0	0	0	5

(*Continued*)

Table 24.3 (Continued)

Author, Year, Country	*Sample size*	*Sampling methodology (Representativeness)*	*Response rate*	*Outcome measure*	*Statistical analysis*	*Confounding*	*Study limitations*	*Ethical considerations*	*Quality assessment core*
Daka & Ergiba, 2019, Ethiopia	1	1	0	1	1	1	1	1	7
Fongar et al., 2019, Kenya	1	1	1	1	1	1	1	1	8
Zachariah et al., 2002, Malawi	1	1	0	1	1	1	0	0	5
Schramm et al., 2016, Uganda	1	1	0	1	1	1	0	1	6
Collins & Myatt, 2000, Somalia	1	1	0	1	1	1	1	1	7
Central Africa									
Jésus et al., 2017, Central African Republic	1	1	1	1	1	1	1	1	8

habitual snack intake. Contrary to findings in most of the studies, studies conducted in Angola and Burkina Faso found that overweight or obesity was significantly high in rural areas (Pedro et al., 2018). It was also found that overweight and obesity were more common among anaemic individuals in Burkina Faso and the Democratic Republic of the Congo (Akombi et al., 2017). Adult diabetic patients were also found to be overweight and obese in Ghana (Ofori-Asenso, Agyeman, Laar, & Boateng, 2016).

Discussion

The findings of the reviewed studies indicate the existence of the DBM in Africa. This is because dietary behaviours are increasingly changing in Africa (Blaauw et al., 2019; Bain et al., 2013). While some African countries are still struggling with adult undernutrition, others are far ahead and are faced with overnutrition. We found that undernutrition was consistently common among men while overnutrition (overweight/obesity) was disproportionately higher among women than men in all countries. This evidence is quite indicative, and it shows that generally men have low appetite. Overweight/obesity among women is an established finding and has several connotations in the African context. Observed gender differences in overweight/obesity have been explained by a myriad of sociocultural dynamics and complex sociocultural pathways that encourage weight gain among women than men (Kamadjeu et al., 2006). For example, cultural values favour larger body size among women as a sign of fertility, healthfulness or prosperity (Letamo, 2011). More recently, women have lower levels of physical activity due to modernization and sedentariness which may also contribute to higher prevalence of overweight/obesity among them.

Moreover, biological differences in women leave them particularly vulnerable to weight gains as diets shift to include greater proportions of oils and refined cereal and sugar-rich products. Over the past two decades, nationally representative data from demographic and health surveys in nineteen African countries identified an increasing proportion of overweight women, in both rural and urban areas. Underweight shares, though generally declining over the same period, show episodic increases in a few countries (Senegal, Rwanda and Madagascar), possibly as a result of intermittent poor harvests or food price spikes associated with the world food crisis (Jaacks et al., 2015).

In our review, low education and low wealth status were reported as one of the consistent factors associated with undernutrition in SSA. On the other hand, high education and high wealth status were consistently associated with overnutrition. A high education level translates into greater health care utilization, adoption of modern medical practices and nutritional knowledge, which in turn influence health-related decisions that improve nutritional outcomes of adults. Similarly, the availability and access to numerous food groups by the non-poor predisposes them to diet-related problems such as overweight/obesity due to overconsumption. Households with uneducated adults tend to have low income, and thus spend less on proper nutrition and are more susceptible to growth failure due to lack of access to sufficient food of adequate quality, poor living conditions, lack of access to basic health care services and greater exposure to diseases. This is quite comprehensive in SSA where the overall education level is low and poverty level is high.

In some African countries the double effect of inadequate dietary intake and an unhealthy environment increases susceptibility to water-borne conditions such as fever, diarrhoea, and infections, which may in turn depress appetite, inhibit the absorption of nutrients in food, and increase the need for caloric availability. This is often seen in war-torn African countries where the population does not have access to good sanitation. Consequently, in order to sustain an adequate dietary intake, it is crucial that adults obtain their daily energy from a varied, healthy and balanced diet. This can only be achieved through improving the quality of health environments through increase in access to safe water supply, proper housing, health services and sanitary facilities for disposing of human waste. This is important for maintaining a sanitary environment and preventing the spread of illness.

The finding from this review that factors such as traditional dietary pattern, ill health and low consumption of sugar or energy-giving food are the correlates of undernutrition is consistent with some studies in Asia (Akhtar, 2016). The prevalence of undernutrition in SSA, higher than any other continent globally, is worsened by the vicious cycle of poverty in the regions. However, one systematic review conducted on the determinants of malnutrition in low- and middle-income countries (LMICs) using the International Network for the Demographic Evaluation of Populations and Their Health (INDEPTH) surveillance systems stated that biological causes such as presence of infections and social causes such as wealth, education and urbanization are the key factors associated with adult malnutrition. Although undernutrition is common across the African continent, some of the countries in the Southern Africa region such as Botswana, South Africa, Namibia and Swaziland have already experienced nutritional transition typified by increased rates of overweight/obesity (Letamo, 2011; Cois & Day, 2015; Neupane et al., 2015).

This review showed that comparatively, Western, Central and Eastern Africa reported the highest number of studies on undernutrition while Southern Africa had the highest number of studies on adult overnutrition. The former could be a result of the need to address the high level of undernutrition observed within these sub-regions which are often susceptible to high levels of poverty. Furthermore, as observed by the Food Agricultural Organization (2017) a vast majority of the undernourished population is mostly found in countries affected by conflict. This is because people in conflict-affected countries do not have sustainable means of subsistence and rely most often on food aids. As a result the prevalence of undernourishment is about twice as high in conflict-affected countries with a protracted crisis as in countries not affected by conflict.

Meanwhile, the rapidly changing dietary patterns unfolding in some African countries provide an important window of opportunity to study the impact of these changes in health outcomes. Of particular importance is the fact that conducting research in these dynamic environments can help fill the gaps in our knowledge as to which of these factors can explain the increases in the DBM and how to come up with best policy initiatives. Strengthening the evidence base will support the development of more effective policies and programmes to prevent and ameliorate the growing burden of undernutrition and overnutrition and their consequent impacts. This can be achieved through the adoption of a food-systems approach to the DBM which will provide the opportunity to explore how a coherent approach to the way food is grown, processed and sold can address both the quality and the quantity of the food supply. Thus, a coherent approach that focusses on food systems and food security can ensure that those who are currently not getting enough of the right food can improve the quality of their diet, without healthy foods being displaced by the cheap, unhealthy, ultra-processed foods high in fat, salt and sugar that are driving the rise in rates of obesity and diet-related NCDs.

There is also a need to develop nutrition policies that are specific to the African context. To date, most of the evidence that supports global nutrition policy comes from high-income countries, with limited data from surveillance surveys and cross-sectional studies available from Africa. The lack of data from Africa is a function of limited support for infrastructure and human capacity to undertake and lead the research and data collection from within countries.

Without consideration of how to build and support this capacity, the opportunities that arise to learn from the rapid dietary changes that are occurring will be lost. It will also be difficult to provide reliable surveillance data for key indicators to assess progress on global targets for nutrition. Global funders need to consider how to support this capacity within Africa.

Strengths and limitations

This review provided a general view on the studies conducted in SSA given that most countries in the continent are undergoing nutritional transition and are facing the challenge of the DBM. As a result, this systematic review was a comprehensive search of the existing literature on the DBM in SSA, specifically focussing on undernutrition and overnutrition. The main strength of this study is that most of the studies included in the review were of medium to high quality and used large sample population data. However, there are several limitations to this study. First, this study mainly focused on quantitative cross-sectional studies and did not include qualitative studies. As a result it lacks the qualitative element, which could be used to triangulate the findings and offer explanations for the observed patterns.

Second, the search was not able to identify experimental trial/intervention studies which would provide evidence on attempts to curb the risks associated with the DBM among the adults in SSA. The third limitation is that this review does not report the pooled estimate for the effect of each factor on adult malnutrition across all sub-regions. The factors were measured differently in each study, and as a result reporting an estimate for the pool effect would misrepresent the impact of the factors on adult malnutrition. Lastly, the reviewed studies indicated the individual causes and some of the underlying causes of adult malnutrition, but did not address the basic or societal causes of malnutrition.

Future research and policy priorities

The insufficiency of data on the DBM highlighted by this chapter indicates an imperative need for research in a wide range of areas to inform nutrition-related policy development for adults in SSA countries. Data from some surveys which could be used to describe the nutritional status of adults in the continent are mostly small and slanted toward individuals expected to be at highest risk, such as children, pregnant women, refugees and displaced persons. Given that almost all the reviewed studies used cross-sectional data, there is need for longitudinal data. Longitudinal data relating the process of growth to lifestyle factors, including dietary intake patterns, are not available. Consequently there is need for more life course research, which will take cognizance of the dynamics of malnutrition not only at the childhood stage but at all the stages of life. The notable lack of systematic studies on nutrition and food intakes in this group limits the development of appropriate community-based strategies to improve nutritional status of the African adult population. Until recently, the adult population has not been considered a priority for targeting of nutrition interventions; as a result, it is not surprising that the effectiveness of different types of nutrition interventions has not been fully described in this population. Out of the 47 SSA countries considered during the review, only studies from 19 countries were included the review. This indicates the need for more research on adult malnutrition, particularly undernutrition in countries such as Chad, Comoros, Cote d'Ivoire, Djibouti, Equatorial Guinea, Eritrea, Gabon, the Gambia, Ghana, Guinea, Guinea-Bissau, Kenya, Liberia, Madagascar, Mali, Mauritania, Mauritius, Mozambique, Namibia, Niger, Rwanda, Sao Tome and Principe, Senegal, the Seychelles, Sierra Leone, Somalia, South Sudan, Sudan, Swaziland, Togo and Zambia. On a positive note, most SSA countries have adopted WHO nutritional guidelines.

Conclusion

This systematic review of literature has yielded insurmountable evidence indicating the need for further research on the DBM in SSA. Key determinants of malnutrition are common across countries. Consistently, the reviewed studies have indicated that factors associated with undernutrition among adults were being male, young adults, low wealth status, low education, traditional dietary pattern, low income, sedentariness, ill health, low consumption of sugar and rural area residence. Other factors identified to be associated with undernutrition were unemployment, HIV-positive status, hospitalization, poor environment and smoking. On the other hand, factors consistently associated with overnutrition resulting in overweight or obesity were being female; wealth; high education; residing in urban areas; television ownership; high income; low physical activity; frequent consumption of sweets, meat and eggs; alcohol consumption; being married and increasing age. Given that Africa is now faced with the DBM, there is a need for more nutrition-related research and policies in Africa. This is because most studies on malnutrition in Africa are often directed towards infants, young children and pregnant and lactating women. The lack of attention to the adult malnutrition in policies and programs is reflected by the paucity of information from research studies on their condition. The scant information that is available suggests that the nutrition problems of the adults are sizable, which is contrary to the experiences in most countries as shown by this review.

References

Adebayo, R. A., Balogun, M. O., Adedoyin, R. A., Obashoro-John, O. A., Bisiriyu, L. A., & Abiodun, O. O. (2014). Prevalence and pattern of overweight and obesity in three rural communities in southwest Nigeria. *Diabetes, Metabolic Syndrome and Obesity: Targets and Therapy*, 7, 153–158. https://doi.org/10.2147/DMSO.S55221

Adebowale, A. S., Palamuleni, M. E., & Odimegwu, C. O. (2015). Wealth and under-nourishment among married women in two impoverished nations: Evidence from Burkina Faso and Congo Democratic Republic. *BMC Research Notes, 8*, 34. https://doi.org/10.1186/s13104-015-1001-7

Agyemang, C., Boatemaa, S., Frempong, G. A., & Aikins, A. de-G. (2015). *Obesity in sub-Saharan Africa*. Switzerland: Metabolic Syndrome Springer International Publishing, pp. 1–13.

Ajayi, I. O., Adebamowo, C., Adami, H., Dalal, S., Diamond, M. B., Bajunirwe, F., . . . Holmes, M. D. (2016). Urban – rural and geographic differences in overweight and obesity in four sub-Saharan African adult populations: A multi-country cross-sectional study. *BMC Public Health, 16*, 1126. https://doi.org/10.1186/s12889-016-3789-z

Akhtar, S. (2016). Malnutrition in South Asia – A critical reappraisal. *Critical Reviews in Food Science and Nutrition, 56*(14), 2320–2330. doi:10.1080/10408398.2013.832143

Akombi, B. J., Agho, K. E., Hall, J. J., Wali, N., Renzaho, A., & Merom, D. (2017). Stunting, wasting and underweight in sub-Saharan Africa: A systematic review. *International Journal of Environmental Research and Public Health, 14*(8), 863. https://doi.org/10.3390/ijerph14080863

Alshehri, A. M. (2010). Metabolic syndrome and cardiovascular risk. *Journal of Family & Community Medicine, 17*(2), 73–78. https://doi.org/10.4103/1319-1683.71987

Amuna, P., & Zotor, F. B. (2008). Epidemiological and nutrition transition in developing countries: Impact on human health and development. *Proceedings of the Nutrition Society, 67*(1), 82–90.

Bain, L. E., Awah, P. K., Geraldine, N., Kindong, N. P., Sigal, Y., Bernard, N., & Tanjeko, A. T. (2013). Malnutrition in sub-Saharan Africa: Burden, causes and prospects. *Pan African Medical Journal, 15*(120). doi:10/11604/pamj.2013.15.120.2535

Barker, D. J. P. (1995). Fetal origins of coronary heart disease. *British Medical Journal, 311*(6998), 171–174.

Barker, D. J. P. (2012). Sir Richard Doll lecture: Developmental origins of chronic disease. *Public Health, 126*(3), 185–189.

Benzekri, N. A., Sambou, J. F., Diaw, B., Sall, E.H.I., Sall, F., Niang, A., Ba, S., Gueye, N.F.N., Diallo, M.B., Hawes, S.S., Seydi, M. & Gottlieb, G.S. (2017). The dimensions of food insecurity and malnutrition among people living with HIV in Senegal, West Africa. *AIDS Care, 29*(12), 1510–1516. doi: 10.1080/09540121.2017.1338652

Benzekri, N. A., Seydi, M., NDoye, I., Toure, M., Kiviat, N.B., Sow, P.S., Hawes, S.E. & Gottlieb, G.S. (2018). HIV and the dual burden of malnutrition in Senegal, 1994–2012. *International Journal of STD & AIDS, 29*(12), 1165–1173. doi: 10.1177/0956462418777364

Bitew, F. H., & Telake, D. S. (2010). *Under-nutrition among women in Ethiopia: Rural urban disparity.* DHS Working Papers No. 77. Calverton, MD: ICF Macro.

Blaauw, R., Osland, E., Sriram, K., Ali, A., Allard, J. P., Ball, P., . . . Berger, M. M. (2019). Parenteral provision of micronutrients to adult patients: An expert consensus paper. *Journal of Parenteral and Enteral Nutrition, 43*(S1), S5–S23.

Black, R. E., Victora, C. G., Walker, S. P., Bhutta, Z. A., Christian, P., de Onis, M., . . . Maternal and Child Nutrition Study Group. (2013). Maternal and child undernutrition and overweight in low-income and middle-income countries. *Lancet, 382*(9890), 427–451. doi:10.1016/ S0140-6736(13)60937-X

Cois, A., & Day, C. (2015). Obesity trends and risk factors in the South African adult population. *BMC Obesity, 2*(42). https://doi.org/10.1186/s40608-015-0072-2

Collins, S., & Myatt, M. (2000). Short-term prognosis in severe adult and adolescent malnutrition during famine: Use of a simple prognostic model based on counting clinical signs. *JAMA: The Journal of the American Medical Association, 284*, 621–626. doi:10.1001/jama.284.5.621

Cuschieri, S. (2019). The STROBE guidelines. *Saudi Journal of Anaesthesia, 13*(Suppl. 1), S31–S34. https://doi.org/10.4103/sja.SJA_543_18

Dagne, H., Raju, R. P., Andualem, Z., Hagos, T., & Addis, K. (2019). Food safety practice and its associated factors among mothers in Debarq Town, Northwest Ethiopia: Community-based cross-sectional study. *BioMed Research International*, Article ID 1549131. https://doi.org/10.1155/2019/1549131

Daka, D. W., & Ergiba, M. S. (2020). Prevalence of malnutrition and associated factors among adult patients on antiretroviral therapy follow-up care in Jimma Medical Center, Southwest Ethiopia. *PloS one, 15*(3), e0229883. https://doi.org/10.1371/journal.pone.0229883

Darebo, T., Mesfin, A., & Gebremedhin, S. (2019). Prevalence and factors associated with overweight and obesity among adults in Hawassa city, southern Ethiopia: A community based cross-sectional study. *BMC Obesity, 6*, 8 https://doi.org/10.1186/s40608-019-0227-7.

Engle-Stone, R., Nankap, M., Ndjebayi, A. O., Friedman, A., Tarini, A., Brown, K. H., & Kaiser, L. L. (2018). Prevalence and predictors of overweight and obesity among Cameroonian women in a national survey and relationships with waist circumference and inflammation in Yaoundé and Douala. *Maternal & Child Nutrition, 14*(4), e12648.

FAO/IFAD/UNICEF/WFP/WHO. (2018). *The State of Food Security and Nutrition in the World 2018: Building climate resilience for food security and nutrition.* Rome: Food and Agriculture Organization.

Fongar, A., Gödecke, T., Aseta, A., & Qaim, M. (2019). How well do different dietary and nutrition assessment tools match? Insights from rural Kenya. *Public Health Nutrition, 22*(3), 391–403. doi:10.1017/S1368980018002756

Food and Agriculture Organization. (2013). *The state of food and agriculture: Food systems for better nutrition.* Rome, Italy: Food and Agriculture Organization.

Food Agriculture Organization. (2017). *Africa Regional Overview of food security and nutrition report.* Rome: Food Agriculture Organization.

Food Agriculture Organization. (2019). *The state of food security and nutrition in the world-Safeguarding against economic slowdowns and downturns.* Rome: Food and Agriculture Organization of the United Nations.

Frieden, T. R. (2010). A framework for public health action: The health impact pyramid. *American Journal of Public Health, 100*(4), 590–595.

Gbary, A., Kpozehouen, A., Houehanou, Y., Djrolo, F., Amoussou, M., Tchabi, Y., . . . Houinato, D. (2014). Prevalence and risk factors of overweight and obesity: Findings from a cross-sectional community-based survey in Benin. *Global Epidemic Obesity, 2*, 3. doi:10.7243/2052-5966-2-3.

Gomez, M. I., Barrett, C. B., Raney, T., Pinstrup-Andersen, P., Meerman, J., Croppenstedt, A., Lowder, S., . . . Thompson, B. (2013). Post green revolution food systems and the triple burden of malnutrition. *Food Policy, 42*(1), 129–138.

Haggblade, S., Duodu, K. G., Kabasa, J. D., Minnaar, A., Ojijo, N. K. O., & Taylor, J. R. N. (2016). Emerging early actions to bend the curve in sub-Saharan Africa's Nutrition Transition. *Food and Nutrition Bulletin, 37*(2), 219–241. https://doi.org/10.1177/0379572116637723

Hailemariam, S., Bune, G. T., & Ayele, H. T. (2013). Malnutrition: Prevalence and its associated factors in People living with HIV/AIDS, in Dilla University Referral Hospital. *Archives of Public Health = Archives belges de sante publique*, *71*(1), 13. https://doi.org/10.1186/0778-7367-71-13

Holmes, M. D., Dalal, S., Sewram, V., Diamond, M. B., Adebamowo, S. N., Ajayi, I. O., . . . Fung, T. T. (2018). Consumption of processed food dietary patterns in four African populations. *Public Health Nutrition*, *21*(8), 1529–1537.

Hruby, A., & Hu, F. B. (2015). The epidemiology of obesity: A big picture. *Pharmaco Economics*, *33*(7), 673–689. https://doi.org/10.1007/s40273-014-0243-x

Jaacks, L. M., Sllining, M. M., & Popkin, B. M. (2015). Recent underweight and overweight trends by rural-urban residence among women in low- and middle-income countries. *Journal of Nutrition*, *145*(2), 352–357.

Jésus, P., Guerchet, M., Pilleron, S., Fayemendy, P., Mouanga, A., Mbelesso, P., . . . Desport, J. (2017). Undernutrition and obesity among elderly people living in two cities of developing countries: Prevalence and associated factors in the EDAC study. *Clinical Nutrition ESPEN*, *21*. doi:10.1016/j.clnesp

Jones, A. D., Acharya, Y., & Galway, L. P. (2016). Urbanicity gradients are associated with the household and individual level double burden of malnutrition in sub-Saharan Africa. *Journal of Nutrition*, *146*(6), 1257–1267.

Kabalimu, T. K., Sungwa, E., & Lwabukuna, W. C. (2018). Malnutrition and associated factors among adults starting on antiretroviral therapy at PASADA Hospital in Temeke District, Tanzania. *Tanzania Journal of Health Research*, *20*(2). https://doi.org/10.4314/thrb.v20i2.5

Kamadjeu, R. M., Edwards, R., Atanga, J. S., Kiawi, E. C., Unwin, N., & Mbanya, J.-C. (2006). Anthropometry measures and prevalence of obesity in the urban adult population of Cameroon: An update from the Cameroon burden of diabetes baseline survey. *BMC Public Health*, *6*, 228. doi:10.1186/1471-2458-6-228

Keetile, M., Navaneetham, K., Letamo, G., Bainame, K., Rakgoasi, S., Gabaitiri, L., . . . Molebatsi, M. R. (2019). Socioeconomic and behavioral determinants of overweight/obesity among adults in Botswana: A cross-sectional study. *BMJ Open* 9, e029570. doi:10.1136/ bmjopen-2019-029570

Letamo, G. (2011). The prevalence of and factors associated with overweight and obesity in Botswana. *Journal of Biosocial Sciences*, *43*, 75–84.

Letamo, G., & Navaneetham, K. (2014). Prevalence and determinants of adult under-nutrition in Botswana. *PLoS One* *9*(7), e102675. https://doi.org/10.1371/journal.pone.0102675

Levitt, E. J., Pelletier, D. L., & Pell, A. N. (2009). Revisiting the UNICEF malnutrition framework to foster agriculture and health sector collaboration to reduce malnutrition: A comparison of stakeholder priorities for action in Afghanistan. *Food Policy*, *34*, 156–165. doi:10.1016/j.foodpol.2008.07.004

Luma, H. N., Eloumou, S. A. F. B., Mboligong, F. N., Temfack, E., Donfack O. T., & Doualla M. S. (2017). Malnutrition in patients admitted to the medical wards of the Douala General Hospital: A cross-sectional study. *BMC Research Notes*, *10*, 238. https://doi.org/10.1186/s13104-017-2592-y

Mitiku, A., Ayele, T. A., Assefa, M., & Tariku, A. (2016). Undernutrition and associated factors among adults living with Human Immune Deficiency Virus in Dembia district, northwest Ethiopia: An institution based cross-sectional study. *Archives of Public Health*, *74*, 33. https://doi.org/10.1186/s13690-016-0143

Moher, D., Shamseer, L., Clarke, M., Ghersi, D., Liberati, A., Petticrew, M., . . . Stewart, L. A. (2015). Preferred reporting items for systematic review and meta-analysis protocols (PRISMA-P) 2015 statement. *Systematic Reviews*, *4*(1).

Mukora-Mutseyekwa, F., Zeeb, H., Nengomasha, L., & Kofi Adjei, N. (2019). Trends in prevalence and related risk factors of overweight and obesity among women of reproductive age in Zimbabwe, 2005–2015. *International Journal of Environmental Research and Public Health*, *16*(15), 2758. https://doi.org/10.3390/ijerph16152758

Neupane, S., & Doku, D. T. (2015). Overweight and obesity among women: Analysis of demographic and health survey data from 32 sub-Saharan African countries. *BMC Public Health*, *16*, 30. https://doi.org/10.1186/s12889-016-2698-5

Ofori-Asenso, R., Agyeman, A. A., Laar, A., & Boateng, D. (2016). Overweight and obesity epidemic in Ghana: A systematic review and meta-analysis. *BMC Public Health*, *9*(16(1)), 1239. doi:10.1186/s12889-016-3901-4. PMID: 27938360; PMCID: PMC5148846.

Onyango, A. W., Jean-Baptiste, J., Samburu, B., & Mahlangu, T. (2019). Regional overview on the double burden of malnutrition and examples of program and policy responses: African region. *Annals of Nutrition and Metabolism*, *75*, 127–130. doi:10.1159/000503671

Osuhor, P. C., & Ogbeide, O. (1982). Some socioeconomic factors of malnutrition in Benin city, Nigeria. *Public Health*, *96*(5), 288–291. doi: 10.1016/s0033-3506(82)80051-6.

Pedro, J. B., Jochum, M., Buizert, C., Hec, F., Barkerd, S. S., & Rasmussena, O. (2018). Beyond the bipolar seesaw: Toward a process understanding of interhemispheric coupling. *Quaternary Science Reviews*, *192*(1), 27–46.

Peer, N., Lombard, C., Steyn, K., Gwebushe, N., & Levitt, N. (2014). Differing patterns of overweight and obesity among black men and women in Cape Town: The CRIBSA study. *PLoS One*, *9*(9), e107471. doi:10.1371/journal.pone.0107471

Popkin, B. M., Adair, L. S., & Ng, S. W. (2012). Global nutrition transition and the pandemic of obesity in developing countries. *Nutritional Reviews*, *70*(1), 3–21.

Reinhardt, K., & Fanzo, J. (2014). Addressing chronic malnutrition through multi-sectoral, sustainable approaches: A review of the causes and consequences. *Frontiers in Nutrition*, *1*, 13. https://doi.org/10.3389/fnut.2014.00013

Schramm, S., Kaducu, F., Smedemark, S., Ovuga, E., & Sodemann, M. (2016). Gender and age disparities in adult undernutrition in northern Uganda: High-risk groups not targeted by food aid programmes. *Tropical Medicine & International Health*, *21*(6), 807–817. doi:10.1111/tmi.12708

Sagna, Y., Yanogo, D., Guira, O., Bagbila, A. P., Bognounou, R., Zoungrana, L., . . . Drabo, Y. J. (2014). Obesity and metabolic syndrome in a Burkina Faso urban area: Prevalence, associated factors and comorbidities. *Journal of Nutritional Disorders and Therapy*. doi:10.4172/2161-0509-4.100014.

Sartorius, B., Veerman, L. J., Manyema, M., Chola, L., & Hofman, K. (2015). Determinants of obesity and associated population attributability, South Africa: Empirical evidence from a National Panel Survey, 2008–2012. *PLoS One*, *10*(6), e0130218. https://doi.org/10.1371/journal.pone.0130218

Stevens, G. A., Finucane, M. M., Paciorek, C. J., Flaxman, S. R., White, R. A., Donner, A. J., . . . Ezzati, M. (2012). Trends in mild, moderate, and severe stunting and underweight, and progress towards MDG 1 in 141 developing countries: A systematic analysis of population representative data. *The Lancet*, *380*(9844), 824–834. doi:10.1016/S0140-6736(12)60647-3

Tapera, R., Marogwe, T. M., Tumoyagae, T., Maswabi, T. M., Erick, P., Letsholo, B., & Mbongwe, B. (2017). The prevalence and factors associated with overweight and obesity among University of Botswana students. *Cogent Medicine*, *4*, 1. doi: 10.1080/2331205X.2017.1357249

Tzioumis, E., & Adair, L. S. (2014). Childhood dual burden of under- and overnutrition in low- and middle-income countries: A critical review. *Food and Nutrition Bulletin*, *35*(2), 230–243.

Uchendu, F. N. (2018). Hunger influenced life expectancy in war-torn sub-Saharan African countries. *Journal of Health, Population and Nutrition*, *37*(1), 11. doi:10.1186/s41043-018-0143-3

United Nations (UN). (2015). *The millennium development goals report 2015*. Working Papers id: 7222. eSocialSciences.

United Nations. (2019). *United Nations Sustainable Development Goal 2: End hunger, achieve food security and improved nutrition and promote sustainable agriculture*. Retrieved on April 16, 2020, from www.un.org/sustainabledevelopment/hunger

Vogt, L. E., Rukooko, B., Iversen, P. O., & Eide, W. B. (2016). Human rights dimensions of food, health and care in children's homes in Kampala, Uganda – A qualitative stud. *BMC International Health and Human Rights*, *16*, 10. doi:10.1186/s12914–016–0086-y

Vorster, H. H., Kruger, A., & Margetts, B. M. (2011). The nutrition transition in Africa: Can it be steered into a more positive direction? *Nutrients*, *3*(4), 429–441. https://doi.org/10.3390/nu3040429

World Health Organization. (2013a). *Global nutrition policy review: What does it take to scale-up nutrition action?* Geneva: World Health Organization.

World Health Organization. (2013b). *World Health Statistics, 2013*. WHO Press, Geneva. World Health Organization.

WHO. (2018). *Global nutrition policy review 2016–2017: Country progress in creating enabling policy environments for promoting healthy diets and nutrition*. Geneva: World Health Organization.

World Health Organization. (2013a). *Global database on Body Mass Index*. Retrieved on April 4, 2020, from http://apps.who.int/bmi/index.jsp

World Health Organization. (2013b). *Fact sheet*. Retrieved from www.who.int/health-topics/malnutrition#tab=tab_13

World Health Organization. (2018). *Atlas of African Health Statistics 2018: Universal health coverage and the Sustainable Development Goals in the WHO African Region*. Brazzaville: WHO Regional Office for Africa.

Zachariah, R., Spielmann, M. P., Harries, A. D., & Salaniponi, F. M. L. (2002). Moderate to severe malnutrition in patients with tuberculosis is a risk factor associated with early death, *Transactions of the Royal Society of Tropical Medicine and Hygiene*, *96*(3), 291–294. https://doi.org/10.1016/S0035-9203(02)90103-3

Zeba, N. A., Delisle, H. F., & Renier, G. (2014). Dietary patterns and physical inactivity, two contributing factors to the double burden of malnutrition among adults in Burkina Faso, West Africa. *Journal of Nutritional Science*, *3*, e50.

25

CHILD DISABILITY AND DEPRIVATION

A Conceptual, theoretical and empirical review of the sub-Saharan African literature

Arlette Simo Fotso and Larissa Nawo

Introduction

The WHO and UNICEF estimate that about one billion people live with a form of disability across the world (WHO & UNICEF, 2012). In 2004, it was estimated that 5% of people aged 0–14 years old have a moderate or severe disability – even if figures for children are thought to be less reliable, representing about 93 million children. The largest proportion of these children live in developing countries with the highest percentage reported in sub-Saharan Africa (WHO & World Bank, 2011). Yet the scientific literature about disability remains relatively rare in the region compared to the Western world or other low- and middle-income countries (Banks, Kuper, & Polack, 2017; E. van der Mark, Conradie, Dedding, & Broerse, 2017), particularly the one focussing on children.

Several papers have reviewed the literature on the link between disability and poverty – or some aspect of it, overall (Anderson, Dumont, Jacobs, & Azzaria, 2007; Elwan, 1999; Groce, Kett, Lang, & Trani, 2011; Palmer, 2011; Pinilla-Roncancio, 2015). Others have focussed on developing countries, with the majority of studies carried on in China, India or Brazil (Banks et al., 2017; Groce, Kembhavi, et al., 2011). Few researchers have looked at child disability (Hunt & Watermeyer, 2017; Stabile & Allin, 2012; E. van der Mark et al., 2017), but none of these has focussed on Africa. To the best of our knowledge, this is the first paper to review the literature on the concept and measurements of child disability and how it relates to different types of deprivations in sub-Saharan Africa.

The aim of this paper is to provide a comprehensive review of economics and population-studies literature on the link between child disability and deprivation. We argue that it is important to understand the link between these two concepts, firstly because tackling deprivation experienced by children is necessary to achieve Sustainable Development Goals numbers 1, 2, 3, 4, 5, 6, 7, 8 and 10; and secondly, because deprivation in childhood is likely to have a long-term impact on the lives of the people and can have future economic consequences for the countries.

This document does not provide an exhaustive, but rather a comprehensive literature review, first of the child disability concept, definition and measurement challenges as experienced in

 DOI: 10.4324/9780429287213-30

African studies. Secondly, it enumerates the main theoretical framework used in African literature to understand and study the link between child disability and deprivation. Thirdly, it provides a summary of the main empirical results found in this area, and finally, it proposes new areas for research to advance the knowledge and understanding of the child disability-deprivation nexus in Africa.

Child disability concept and measures in African studies

Child disability: conceptual framework and definition

Disability can be defined as a process involving body functions and structure, activity limitations and participation restrictions, personal characteristics, aspects of environmental barriers and facilitators (Loeb, Cappa, Crialesi, & de Palma, 2017). If the definition seems simple, the concept is actually complex and necessitates a closer look especially when used for children – understood as persons below the age of 18, as per the definition of the United Nation Convention on the Rights of the Child.

The International Classification of Functioning is a widely admitted framework to understand disability. It was published by the World Health Organisation (WHO) in 1980, then modified and named International Classification of Functioning, Disability and Health (ICF) in 2001 (WHO, 2001). This framework makes a synthesis between the medical and social models of disability by using a biopsychosocial model in which disability has three dimensions: impairment, limitation and participation. It has inspired the definition of disability in many national policies and laws.

However, most of these laws do not provide a definition of disability specific to children. As early as 2007, the WHO developed the International Classification of Functioning, Disability and Health for Children and Youth (ICF-CY), which underlined the necessity of ICF to be adapted to children (WHO, 2007).

ICF-CY has been developed to cover an age range from birth to 18 years. As do the previous classifications, ICF-CY has four main components which can be classified with more or less details. Firstly, the body function and structure: body functions refer to the physiological and psychological functions of body systems such as seeing, hearing, understanding, while body structures refers to parts of the body, such as organs, limbs and their components. Impairments describe problems in body function and/or structure. The second component is activities and participation. Activities is the execution of a task (standing or walking) and participation implies taking part in a life situation (doing tasks as children of his or her age). Activity limitations and participation restrictions pinpoint difficulties in these domains. The third component is environmental factors – which can be the physical, social and attitudinal environment in which individuals live and conduct their life. It provides information on how attitudes and physical external environments can be a barrier or facilitator for a child with a specific health issue. Finally, we have personal factors, which capture internal influences on functioning. With environmental factors, these latter are part of contextual factors (WHO, 2007). Data collection on the child's disability should, therefore, try as much as possible to include these different elements (Simo Fotso, 2016).

If the ICF-CY is today almost universally recognised as the framework to understand child disability, multiple instruments have been used throughout the years to measure disability in children.

Measurement of child disability in African surveys and studies

The screening instruments used to measure disability usually depend on the model and aspect of disability considered (medical vs social or impairment vs participation). The purpose of data collection is also crucial (Institut national de la statistique, 2012). In fact, if the aim of the data collection is to identify the population with disabilities who are eligible to receive benefits, it is likely that individuals with moderate disabilities will not be included in the survey and therefore the population with disabilities, both adults and children, will be underestimated. In such a case, the effect of disability (severe in this case) on socioeconomic variables is likely to be overestimated (Simo Fotso, 2016).

One of the widely used disability screening instrument is the one using the direct word 'disability'. For example, one formulation of such an instrument can be, 'Does the X have any disability(-ies)?' It has been used in multiples countries (see Table 25.1). This instrument was in most cases used to measure disability among people 15 years of age and older, allowing some estimates for 15–17-year-old children. It focusses mainly on impairments and does not account for the social and environmental aspects of disability. This measurement has been criticised by many African studies (Schneider, 2009; Swartz, 2014), because the use of the word 'disability' is prone to stigma and can produce an under-declaration of disability. Moreover, Simo Fotso, Duthé and Odimegwu (2019) have shown that slight changes in the formulation such as using the word 'have' instead of 'being victim of' disability can give different results.

To provide global and African estimates on the prevalence of disability in 0–14-year-olds, the WHO and the World Bank have used the Global Burden of Disease. It was first developed in 1990 then subsequently improved and produced disability estimates in 46 African countries in 2004 (see the list in Table 25.1), in 2010 and 2017. This instrument uses the years lived with disability (YLD) – used to calculate disability-adjusted years (DALYs) – to quantify the functional status of an individual. If the instrument is adequate in ensuring internal consistency and cross-country comparability, it does not account for environmental factors and provides a description of disability limited to a health condition and impairment alone.

The Ten Questions screening (TQ) that was included in the MICS (Multiple Indicator Cluster Surveys) between 2000 and 2010 is the most widely used instrument to assess child disability in low- and middle-income countries. It attempts to include organ functions, anatomical structures, activity and participation as recommended by ICF-CY. It also takes into account context as children are compared to their peers. The measure was used in numerous African countries as shown in Table 25.1. However, evaluation studies of this measure have shown that it includes a high percentage of false positives and mild disabilities (Durkin et al., 1994).

Another disability screening instrument has been used in nationally representative surveys in Africa: the questions set used in the optional disability module included in Demographic and Health Surveys (DHS) of Cameroun and Chad in 2011 and 2014 respectively. The head of the household was asked to report body structure and function defects, as well as some activity limitation for all family members using seven questions reported in Table 25.1. (S)He assessed limitation in five areas, namely: sight, hearing, mobility, cognitive functions and communication. The response options were no, partial or total limitation. To the best of our knowledge, this instrument has not received scientific validation testing (Simo Fotso et al., 2019).

The Washington Group (WG) disability screening tools are now increasingly used to measure disability. It was built by the WG, a United Nations (UN)-sponsored group established in 2001 to improve the quality and international comparability of disability measures. It covers six functional domains and basic actions such as seeing, hearing, walking, cognition, communication

Table 25.1 Child Disability Screening Instruments in African Studies

Disability screening instrument	*Questions used* [a]	*Scale*	*Age groups targeted*	*Examples of data collected* [b]
Direct question using the word 'disability'	– Does the respondent have any disability(-ies)? functional impairment (deaf, mute, blind, lack of limb, mental disease) + leprosis + albinos. – Is (name) the victim of a handicap? If yes, functional impairment (visual, speaking, hearing, mental and motor disability, deaf-mute) – Does the person have a serious sight, hearing, physical or mental disability? If yes, circle all applicable disabilities for the person.	yes/no	All	Cameroon census (2005); Cameroun household survey (2007, 2014); South Africa census (1996, 2001); Burkina Faso census (2006); Namibia census (2011); Zambia Living Conditions Monitoring Survey VI (2010)
Ten Questions screening for disability	– Compared with other children, did (name) have any serious delay in sitting, standing or walking? – Compared with other children, does (name) have difficulty seeing, either in the daytime or at night? – Does (name) appear to have difficulty hearing? – When you tell (name) to do something, does he/she seem to understand what you are saying? – Does (name) have difficulty in walking or moving his/her arms or does he/she have weakness and/or stiffness in the arms or legs? – Does (name) sometimes have fits, become rigid or lose consciousness? – Does (name) learn to do things like other children his/her age? – Does (name) speak at all (can he/she make himself/herself understood in words; can he/she say any recognizable words)? – a. Ages 3–9: Is (name)'s speech in any way different from normal? – b. Age 2: Can he/she name at least one object (animal, toy, cup, spoon)? – Compared with other children of his/her age, does (name) appear in any way mentally backward, dull or slow?	yes/no	2–9 years	Cameroon MICS2&3; Central African Republic MICS3; Ghana MICS3; Mauritania MICS3; Sao Tome and Principe MICS2&3; Sierra Leone MICS3

Other DHS screening instrument	– 'Is there a person in your household who is missing a body part, for example, a hand, arm, foot or leg?' – 'Is there a person in your household who is missing an extremity, such as a fingertip, toe, nose or ear?' – 'Is there a person in your household who has a deformed upper or lower limb and cannot, or only with difficulty, walk and/or use his/her arms or hands?' – 'Is there a person in your household who can hardly see or is blind?' – 'Is there a person in your household who can hardly hear or is deaf?' – 'Is there a person in your household who finds it very hard to speak or is dumb?' – 'Is there a person in your household who has behavioural disorders?'	[illegible] yes: partial/ total	[illegible]	[illegible] (2011)
WG short screening for disability assessment	– Do you have difficulty seeing, even if wearing glasses? – Do you have difficulty hearing, even if using a hearing aid? – Do you have difficulty walking or climbing steps? – Do you have difficulty remembering or concentrating? – Do you have difficulty (with self-care such as) washing all over or dressing? – Using your usual (customary) language, do you have difficulty communicating (for example understanding or being understood by others)?	No difficulties, Some difficulties, A lot of difficulties, Cannot do it at all	5 years and older	Yaounde (city in Cameroon) HandiVIH survey (2015); Zambia Survey of Living Conditions among People with Disabilities in Zambia (2006); Uganda DHS 2016; Uganda census 2014; Senegal Census 2013; Mali DHS 2018; South Africa census 2011.
Global Burden of Disease	None, modelled using years lived with disability (YLD) estimates	No, moderate or severe disability	0–14 years and 15 years plus	Global Burden of Disease (1990, 2004, 2010). Regional figures.
Unicef/WG Module on Child Functioning	Questionnaire is accessible here: https://data.unicef.org/resources/module-child-functioning/	No difficulties, Some difficulties, A lot of difficulties, Cannot do it at all	2–4 years and 5–17 years	Northwest province of Cameroon (2013); Xhariep District of the Free State Province in central South Africa (2014); Turkana County, Kenya, between July and August 2013.

Source: Note: [a] Some surveys have used some slightly different wording for their questions.

and self-care. It also allows graduation of difficulties from using four possible answers: no, some or a lot of difficulties and cannot do it at all. The short set has been used at the national level in many African countries (see Table 25.1). It has also been tested in some small-scale surveys in provinces or cities.

However, this measure was not developed for children specifically. From 2011, UNICEF has decided to collaborate with the WG on Disability Statistics to revise the TQ included in MICS and construct a measure specific to children. The ICF-CY conceptual framework was used to select the domains relevant for this measurement. The WG/UNICEF child functioning screening instrument was finalised in 2016. It targets children 2–17 years of age and assesses functional difficulties domains such as seeing, hearing, mobility, communication/comprehension, learning, relationships, playing, emotions, behaviour, focussing attention/concentrating and coping with change (Loeb et al., 2017; WG & UNICEF, 2017). Some of the main sources of data on child disability have been indicated in Table 25.1.

Theoretical framework linking child disability and deprivation in African studies

Numerous theoretical frameworks have been harnessed to study the relationship between child disability and deprivation. This is somehow expected given the different forms deprivation can take (Kanamori & Pullum, 2013).

Economics theories for child disability and deprivation

Life cycle theory

One theory used to understand the link between child disability and education deprivation in African studies is the life cycle theory (Simo Fotso, Solaz, Diene, & Nanfosso, 2018). According to this theory, disability seen as a body function or structure limitation (health issue) will negatively affect a person's long-term health by affecting his/her education.

Human capital theory

Using Becker's human capital theory (Becker, 1962) some authors have also argued that disability can negatively affect the investment made in disabled children's education (Simo Fotso et al., 2018). In fact, in Becker's theory, the amount of investment made is a positive function of the expected return of the investment. In the case of disabled children, since they are less likely to find a job because of discrimination of morbidity, some parents may find it less advantageous to invest in their education. This will ultimately lead to a lower educational level for disabled children.

Theoretical models with health as a consumption commodity or investment

Grossman's model (Grossman, 1972) on health has been used to understand how disability can generate health deprivation for other children in the household. In fact, this model considers health as a consumption good that enters in the preference functions of parents. As such, these latter will use the household financial resources to provide for health care needs that can be generated by a disability, and improve the health condition of their disabled offspring. In a context of limited resources, as is the case in many African countries, it might create health deprivation for the other children (Simo Fotso, 2017b). However, if the health care cost for children with disability is higher, as is likely to be the case, parents will invest more in the well-endowed non-disabled child, depriving the disabled children of health care.

Domestic production model

The domestic production theory has also been used by some African authors to explain how child disability can affect time allocation of parents and family members with serious consequences for the time available for child care and resources (Simo Fotso, 2017a; Simo Fotso, Somefun & Odimegwu, 2020). In this theory, the household is considered a production unit using limited time either for unpaid work – for child care for example – or paid work (Becker, 1965). With a disabled child in the household, parents can spend extra time caring for this child and reduce their paid work. The consequence of this is less financial resources available in the household. This could cause deprivation for the family members who might be unable to afford basic needs such as health, education, housing, recreation etc. Simo Fotso et al. (2020) have used this model to explore the consequences of child disability on extended family employment in an African context.

The capability model

According to this model, disability can be seen as capability deprivation. An impairment (body function and structure limitations) deprives individuals of their capabilities, since it can cause constant pain. By adding an extra burden to household resources, impairment and its costs can also restrict individuals' functioning (like being well nourished, educated, healthy). Most of the previous models demonstrate that disability can be the cause of multiple deprivations; the capability model builds on that and demonstrates that poverty or resource limitations can cause disability (Graham, Moodley, & Selipsky, 2013; Mitra, 2006).

Other theories linking child disability to deprivation

Theory of quality of life

Some authors such as Zuurmond et al. (2019) have used developments of the theory of quality of life to understand how caring for a disabled child can affect the well-being of the caregiver. These theories go beyond individual achievement and stress the importance of social relationships to understand human well-being. Understanding how caring for a disabled child affects the caregiver is important for the caregiver's health but also the disabled child's and siblings' health. This is because the health (physical or psychological) of the caregiver can be a key factor in the health and well-being of all the children (s)he cares for (Geere et al., 2013).

Stress-coping model

On the same topic in Uganda, Hartley, Ojwang, Baguwemu, Ddamulira and Chavuta (2005) used the stress-coping model. According to the model, individuals' appraisal of events affects their ability to cope. This appraisal may be influenced by a number of elements including disability, demographic characteristics or demands or threats to individual goals and values. The coping strategy resulting from the appraisal of parents of disabled offspring is likely to have negative psychological, social and/or physical consequences. In such a case, social networks can help to mitigate these effects or, on the contrary, create additional stress.

Agency and adaptive preferences model

In a qualitative study on the adaptive strategy of the mother of disabled children, E. J. van der Mark, Conradie, Dedding and Broerse (2019) used the agency model that they combined with the adaptive preferences model to account for self-depriving expressions of agency. The model explains how already deprived people like mothers of disabled children can perpetuate their deprivation while being active, autonomous and reflective agents.

Alavi et al. (2012)'s conceptual model

Alavi et al. (2012) developed their own model to conceptualise the impact of musculoskeletal impairments (MSI) on the lives of children in an African context. Four main themes were underlined: the indignity; the exclusion from social life (like at school and in the household core); pain experienced when trying to participate; food deprivation outside their home (in part due to exclusion from core daily activities).

Social-ecological theory

Njelesani (2019) used the social-ecological theory to capture the responses to violence against disabled children in West Africa. According to this theory, the violence results from the confluence of multiple forces in which the child, family, community and culture interact. Those determine the child's experience and outcomes.

The evil circle of poverty model

This model was used by Ingstad, Munthali, Braathen and Grut (2012) to understand the link between disability and malaria. The evil circle occurs when poverty causes disability and disability keeps people in poverty. This model uses social violence to understand poverty. They describe social violence as a situation in which people are maintained in poverty because they are not allowed to meet basic needs, to fulfil their potential or to access fundamental social institutions.

Empirical findings: the key concerns, methods and results in the study of the theme in Africa

Though we are presenting a comprehensive rather than a systematic review of the empirical literature, we used the following approach to select the papers to be included. We focussed on the literature published from 2000 to 2020 which examines the nexus between disabilities and poverty and deprivation. Only studies conducted in Africa, with a focus on disabled children aged 0–17 years, have been included. Poverty was defined using mainly economic measures (e.g. assets, income), while disability included both broad assessments (e.g. self-reported functional or activity limitations) and specific impairments/disorders. Deprivation was measured both by a physical and social limited access to life facilities and well-being (e.g. access to formal education, health care and/or public transport, social stigmatization etc). We retrieved 204 articles using web search engines such as Google Scholar and PubMed. After removing duplicates, we screened 165 of them based on the study inclusion criteria mentioned earlier. After iterative reading and screening of these articles, we included a final count of 31 articles in this empirical review.

Disability and social and institutional challenges

In a selected sample of 15 articles focussing on sub-Saharan African countries, Adugna, Nabbouh, Shehata and Ghahari (2020) found that children with disabilities are exposed to many barriers which include stigma and negative behaviours, poverty and shortage of resources, inadequate policy implementations, physical inaccessibility, lack of transportation, lack of privacy, and inadequately trained health care professionals to deal with disability.

Mkabile and Swartz (2020) conducted 20 semi-structured interviews with primary caregivers and parents of children with intellectual disability living in a poor setting in Cape Town, South Africa. Their results suggest that there were a lot of difficulties in accessing services and support and struggling to cope in the context of extreme poorness and deprivation.

Based on a qualitative method, Njelesani (2019) explored the violence against children with disabilities. Responses to disability-related violence are driven at the mesosystem[1] and exosystem[2] levels. The prevailing views suggested that policies and legislation at the national level are not always taken into account as part of the solution. Communities are leading responses to violence, and children with disabilities are hidden at home or in institutions for both their own and their family's safety.

Disability and malnutrition

Alavi et al. (2012) developed a conceptual model representing the impact of musculoskeletal impairments (MSIs) in the day-to-day lives of children in Malawi. Based on a sample of 169 children with MSIs (CMSIs), family and other community members participated in 57 interviews, focus groups and observations. Using the inductive approach to analyse data, the authors found two key results: the major stigmatizations that emerged were indignity and exclusion, and pain and hunger.

In Turkana-Kenya, Kuper et al. (2015) found that children with disabilities were particularly vulnerable to malnutrition, particularly in the area of food insecurity and widespread malnutrition. Children with disabilities are vulnerable to malnutrition, as a result of exclusion and feeding difficulties.

Kerac et al. (2014) reviewed the link between malnutrition and neuro-disability in Africa. According to the authors, malnutrition occurs throughout life and starts with maternal malnutrition affecting fetal neurodevelopment with both immediate (e.g. folate deficiency causing neural tube defects) and lifelong implications (e.g. impaired cognitive function). In fact, macronutrient malnutrition can both generate and be caused by neuro-disability. Transmission channels include decreased food intake, increased nutrient losses and increased nutrient requirement. Specific micronutrient deficiencies can also lead to neuro-disability, such as blindness (vitamin A), intractable epilepsy (vitamin B6) and cognitive impairment (iodine and iron).

Disability and access to health care and reproduction health

Kalibala, Schenk, Weiss and Elson (2012) are the first scholars to quantify the vulnerability of children in Uganda and assess their resource needs. These authors quantified factors of vulnerabilities among children living with disabilities in Uganda. Their findings suggest that among the most important features were maternal mortality, disability, child labour and pregnancy before the age of 17. Their survey data suggest that the most vulnerable children are underrepresented in different types of support services.

In KwaZulu-Natal, South Africa, using the Ten Questions (TQ) screen in the isiZulu language, Jelsma, Davids and Ferguson (2011) studied high sensitivity for serious developmental disabilities in children. According to their results, children living with disabilities and HIV-positive status are significantly delayed regarding development compared to their HIV-negative counterparts. Moreover, children in foster care, and particularly those with HIV, were found to perform worse in the area of fine motor skills.

Recognizing that sexuality is shaped during childhood, McKenzie and Swartz (2011) found that there are high levels of stigma and negative attitudes (like psychological or/and physical abuse) toward children with disabilities in their community that limit the development of healthy sexuality.

In Malawi, Devendra, Makawa, Kazembe, Calles and Kuper (2013) conducted a case-controlled study of 296 HIV-infected children aged 2–9 years attending an Antiretroviral Therapy (ART) centre in Lilongwe (cases) and their uninfected siblings (controls). Disability was assessed using the WHO Ten Questions (TQ) screen. Authors found that 67% of cases with a disability had never attended any rehabilitative service and 29% of the caregivers reported facing stigma and discrimination because of the child's disability. This study reveals the magnitude of disability among HIV-infected children and the large unmet need for rehabilitation services.

In Cameroon, analysing on the Demographic Health and Multiple Indicator Cluster Survey (DHS-MICS) survey of 17,864 children under age 18 and using multivariate analyses (two-part model with logistic then GLM regression), Simo Fotso (2017b) found that an impairment considerably increases the monthly health care costs for the disabled child by XAF 204.[3] For two children sharing the same biological mother, having a disabled sibling reduces the health care expenditures allocated to that child by XAF 102.

In a township of Johannesburg, South Africa, Andrade et Baloyi (2011) found that deaf adolescents appear to be at risk for insufficient information about HIV/AIDS due to barriers such as literacy difficulties, language barriers and limited access to information.

Disability and school attendance

Using 14 household surveys from 13 developing countries Filmer (2008) found that 1–2% of the population have disabilities. In all countries children between 6–17 years old living with disabilities are significantly less likely to start school or to be enrolled at the time of the survey.

Using logistic regression model on a sample of 3,706 children and young adolescents aged 11–14 years randomly sampled from 42 primary schools in Uganda, Devries et al. (2014) found that (1) disabled girls are at particular risk of violence, notably sexual violence; and (2) disabled girls report slightly more physical (99.1% vs 94.6%, $p = 0.010$) and considerably more sexual violence (23.6% vs 12.3%, $p = 0.002$) than non-disabled girls; for disabled and non-disabled boys, levels are not statistically different.

In South Africa, Fleisch, Shindler and Perry's (2012) analysis revealed that certain sub-populations have higher non-attendance ratios, especially children with disabilities.

In a sample of disabled children in Cameroon, Simo et al. (2018) controlled for unobserved heterogeneity within the households by using a 'true' sibling fixed-effect model and the severity of the disability. Authors found that moderate and severe disabilities decrease the probability that a child pursues formal education, and reduce school advancement.

Child disability and direct and indirect costs to families

Direct costs

Guthrie (2002) demonstrates that South Africa's current system of social assistance makes a major contribution to the welfare of vulnerable children and their families. Overall, estimation of direct costs varies considerably, not only according to the level of the disability status but also within the level of poverty of families with disabled children; studies consistently indicate a significant increase in direct costs. However, households without access to at least two strands of the social protection net were impoverished by the increase direct and indirect costs of long-term child disabilities (Goudge et al., 2009).

A distorted distribution of costs, in particular medical costs, exists among families with children with special health needs (Simo Fotso, 2017c). However, direct monetary costs may be the smallest component of the costs borne by families, given a number of indirect costs associated with children's disabilities.

Indirect costs

Employment of mothers and other family members

Some studies have gone beyond mothers and assessed the effect of child disability on fathers' and other non-parent family members' employment. Simo Fotso's (2016) study shows that child disability has no effect on fathers' employment in Cameroon. In another study in South Africa, Simo Fotso et al. (2020) found that a child's serious illness or disability significantly increases the employment odds of fathers while reducing those of mothers. These effects were found to be even stronger among married parents.

Psychological impact

A study conducted in Uganda has shown feeling guilty, overwhelmed, sadness, anxiety or great stress (Hartley et al., 2005). Stigma and the resulting feelings of isolation have likewise been noted as a source of feelings of distress in Uganda (Hartley et al., 2005) and in Zimbabwe (E. van der Mark et al., 2017). Moreover, poor living conditions and lack of access to services cause further fear and concern in South Africa (Saloojee, Phohole, Saloojee & IJsselmuiden, 2007). 'The "daily grind" of living in poverty is often a source of chronic and pervasive tension' (McNally & Mannan, 2013, p. 325).

Socio-structural impact

Concerning the socio-structural impact, many issues are studied such as the effects of caring on finances, social relationships or family functioning. In impoverished households, findings suggest that the main burden is not only the time needed to cope with childhood disability. Rather, the shortfalling financial resources, a serious lack of existing services, limited knowledge of the services available and transport constraints in accessing them are experienced as the greatest struggles. The affordability, accessibility and availability of services are therefore important in a resource-poor context like South Africa (Jones, Weinberg, Ehrlich & Roberts, 2000). The

Triple-A puzzle also exacerbates the difficulty of obtaining information from services (Hartley et al., 2005; Philpott & McLaren, 2011), further reducing health literacy.

In Zambia, mothers of children with cerebral palsy (CP) feel socially isolated, owing to a shortage of support from family, community members and health care providers. This social segregation was aggravated by the behaviours of others towards the mothers; people felt that mothers were responsible for their children's disabilities. Mothers also had marital problems as a result of having a child with CP (Singogo, Mweshi & Rhoda, 2015).

Physical impact

In Kenya, Geere et al. (2013) found that the physical burden is more severe due to poverty; for example, there is a limited supply of wheelchairs, specialised means of transportation and personal lifts in the context of poor housing. Physical effort is thus an additional burden for parents. In some instances, constrained supply of assistive equipment and technologies in resource-poor areas are recognized as a source of poverty (Eide & Øderud, 2009).

New research agenda

We found potential gaps in knowledge of the relationship between children with disabilities and deprivation in sub-Saharan Africa.

At the institutional level: access to careers assistance, access to school, access to a rehabilitation centre, access to public transport etc.

Firstly, the areas of intervention, service utilization and legislation need more research. Even epidemiologic research is of inadequate quality, and research is scarce for conditions other than hearing and intellectual disabilities. Future works should not only solve these gaps in current knowledge but also find ways to transpose their results into public health policy advancements that would influence the lives of children with disabilities in low- and middle-income countries.

Secondly, measuring access to health services in developing contexts remains imprecise and relies mostly on asking patients about the time and distance they travelled. Future works should make use of a geographic information system (GIS) (a system designed to capture, store, manipulate, analyse, manage and present spatial and geographical data) because it will be more reliable and valid.

There is a lack of understanding of transport needs. Future works should explore in depth the complexities and nuances of disability in terms of access to health care. Issues of access for persons living with disabilities stretches far beyond questions about the health care system and have been deeply understood. The questions of transport, poverty, beliefs and attitudinal barriers require more attention in research.

At the household level

Despite slowly emerging evidence between the impact of poverty and deprivation on disabled children and their families, there is a significant knowledge gap on how political, cultural and socioeconomic exclusion stifles parents with disabled children, to improve their families' well-being and possibly reap the benefits of development policies.

It remains unclear what the consequences are of child disability, poverty or other contextual factors such as HIV/AIDS. What is the dynamic between public policy, poverty and the care for a child with a disability? Is social support for caregivers of children with disabilities limited by poverty or is it more related to urban migration?

Moreover, since the relationship between disability, poverty and care is linked to several academic disciplines, there is no universal conceptual framework for studying the impact of disability. In fact, parents of disabled children living in poverty are worried about fulfilling the needs of their offspring, stressed about the fact that their children will not fulfil their educational potential and are more vulnerable to serious illness. They also recognise the value and the drawbacks of public benefits (for instance, financial support by state is insufficient and stigmatising). They express concern about being unable to provide both basic needs and culturally enriching activities for their disabled children, and they say the stresses caused by poverty affect their parenting abilities. But the evidence remains fragmented and difficult to assess because of the multiple concepts used.

Next, given the various gaps in knowledge, we argue that future research should also focus in particular on parents of children with disabilities living in poverty and their experiences, practices and needs. The research should pay more attention to the conditions of poverty, analyse demographic and contextual differences in a resource-constrained environment, preferably be multidisciplinary, and involve parents in the research to ensure its practical relevance, and aim to develop a conceptual framework for the analysis.

Finally, further research needs to be conducted on exploration and critiques of responses to violence against children with disabilities. Future studies must also investigate the ways government and nongovernment actors can work with children with disabilities and their communities to decrease vulnerability and exposure to violence and to build prevention programs inclusive of children with disabilities.

Conclusion

The aim of this chapter was to provide a comprehensive survey on links between child disability and deprivation in Africa. To this end, it first attempts to clarify the notion of child disability, definition and measurement challenges as experienced in African studies. Secondly, it enumerates the core theoretical framework used in African literature to understand and study the linkage between child disability and deprivation. Thirdly, it provides a summary of the main empirical results found in this area; and finally, it proposes a new area for research to advance the knowledge and understanding of the child disability-deprivation relationship in Africa.

The nexus between disability, deprivation and poverty is of increasing interest to policy makers since children with disabilities are being mainstreamed into national and international poverty reduction programs. This literature is vast and has a long history. However, previous literature reviews on disability and poverty have not systematically addressed the concepts of poverty and deprivation especially for children living with disabilities in Africa. This review concentrates on children with disabilities for the empirical contributions in economics, public health, population studies and health policy.

From the conceptual discussion, the paper shows that the ICF-CY is today almost universally recognised as the framework to understand child disability. For measurement, the WG/UNICEF child functioning screening instrument, finalised in 2016, is now well endorsed to measure disability in children aged 2–17 years; however, the measurement is not yet routinely integrated into nationally representative surveys in sub-Saharan Africa.

The theoretical review shows that the life cycle theory, human capital theory, health as commodity and investment model, domestic production model, capability approach, the theory of quality of life, stress-coping model, the social-ecological theory and the evil circle of poverty model are some of the conceptual frameworks used in African studies to model the link between child disability and poverty.

The empirical review focussed on children with disabilities from neuro-development, to adolescence through birth and childhood and the associated direct and indirect costs of these disabilities on both the immediate family and the child. It showed that children with disabilities from poor urban and rural areas are living a vicious cycle of deprivation (stigma, social exclusion, discrimination, low self-esteem etc.) and extreme poverty (low access to health care special assistance, violence, low access to transport facilities, low access to sanitation and clean water).

By drawing attention to the limitations of existing findings, this chapter identifies literature gaps for future research, remaining empirical challenges and their implications for policy.

Notes

1 Mesosystems consist of interrelationships among the microsystems in which an individual participates.
2 The exosystem contains environmental elements that have a profound influence on a child's development, even though that child is not directly involved with them. The exosystem is a part of Urie Bronfenbrenner's ecological systems theory (Paquette & Ryan, 2001).
3 XAF is the monetary unit of the Central African Financial Community of Africa.

References

Adugna, M. B., Nabbouh, F., Shehata, S., & Ghahari, S. (2020). Barriers and facilitators to healthcare access for children with disabilities in low and middle income sub-Saharan African countries: A scoping review. *BMC Health Services Research*, *20*(1), 1–11. https://doi.org/10.1186/s12913-019-4822-6

Alavi, Y., Jumbe, V., Hartley, S., Smith, S., Lamping, D., Muhit, M., . . . Lavy, C. (2012). Indignity, exclusion, pain and hunger: The impact of musculoskeletal impairments in the lives of children in Malawi. *Disability and Rehabilitation*, *34*(20), 1736–1746. https://doi.org/10.3109/09638288.2012.662260

Anderson, D., Dumont, S., Jacobs, P., & Azzaria, L. (2007). The personal costs of caring for a child with a disability: A review of the literature. *Public Health Reports (Washington, D.C.: 1974)*, *122*(1), 3–16.

Banks, L. M., Kuper, H., & Polack, S. (2017). Poverty and disability in low- and middle-income countries: A systematic review. *PloS One*, *12*(12), e0189996. https://doi.org/10.1371/journal.pone.0189996

Becker, G. S. (1962). Investment in human capital: A theoretical analysis. *Journal of Political Economy*, *70*(5), 9–49.

Becker, G. S. (1965). A theory of the allocation of time. *Economic Journal*, *75*(4), 493–517.

De Andrade, V., & Baloyi, B. (2011). "Some of the things I understand but not all of it": A group of deaf adolescents' sources of knowledge and concerns regarding the adequacy of their level of knowledge about human immunodeficiency virus/acquired immune deficiency syndrome. *Vulnerable Children and Youth Studies*, *6*, 255–262. https://doi.org/10.1080/17450128.2011.597795

Devendra, A., Makawa, A., Kazembe, P. N., Calles, N. R., & Kuper, H. (2013). HIV and childhood disability: A case-controlled study at a paediatric antiretroviral therapy centre in Lilongwe, Malawi. *PloS One*, *8*(12), e84024. https://doi.org/10.1371/journal.pone.0084024

Devries, K. M., Kyegombe, N., Zuurmond, M., Parkes, J., Child, J. C., Walakira, E. J., & Naker, D. (2014). Violence against primary school children with disabilities in Uganda: A cross-sectional study. *BMC Public Health*, *14*(1), 1–9. https://doi.org/10.1186/1471-2458-14-1017

Durkin, M. S., Davidson, L. L., Desai, P., Hasan, Z. M., Khan, N., Shrout, P. E., . . . Zaman, S. S. (1994). Validity of the ten questions screen for childhood disability: Results from population-based studies in Bangladesh, Jamaica, and Pakistan. *Epidemiology*, *5*(3), 283–289.

Eide, A. H., & Øderud, T. (2009). Assistive technology in low-income countries. In *Disability and international development: Towards inclusive global health* (pp. 149–161). https://doi.org/10.1007/978-0-387-93840-0

Elwan, A. (1999). *Poverty and disability: A survey of the literature* (No. 21315; p. 1). The World Bank. http://documents.worldbank.org/curated/en/488521468764667300/Poverty-and-disability-a-survey-of-the-literature

Filmer, D. (2008). Disability, poverty, and schooling in developing countries: Results from 14 household surveys. *The World Bank Economic Review*, *22*(1), 141–163. https://doi.org/10.1093/wber/lhm021

Fleisch, B., Shindler, J., & Perry, H. (2012). Who is out of school? Evidence from the Statistics South Africa Community Survey. *International Journal of Educational Development, 32*(4), 529–536. https://doi.org/10.1016/j.ijedudev.2010.05.002

Geere, J. L., Gona, J., Omondi, F. O., Kifalu, M. K., Newton, C. R., & Hartley, S. (2013). Caring for children with physical disability in Kenya: Potential links between caregiving and carers' physical health. *Child, 39*(3), 381–392. https://doi.org/10.1111/j.1365-2214.2012.01398.x

Goudge, J., Russell, S., Gilson, L., Gumede, T., Tollman, S., & Mills, A. (2009). Illness-related impoverishment in rural South Africa: Why does social protection work for some households but not others? *Journal of International Development, 21*(2), 231–251. https://doi.org/10.1002/jid.1550

Graham, L., Moodley, J., & Selipsky, L. (2013). The disability – poverty nexus and the case for a capabilities approach: Evidence from Johannesburg, South Africa. *Disability & Society, 28*(3), 324–337. https://doi.org/10.1080/09687599.2012.710011

Groce, N., Kembhavi, G., Wirz, S., Lang, R., Trani, J.-F., & Kett, M. (2011). *Poverty and disability – A critical review of the literature in low and middle-income countries* (SSRN Scholarly Paper ID 3398431). Social Science Research Network. https://doi.org/10.2139/ssrn.3398431

Groce, N., Kett, M., Lang, R., & Trani, J.-F. (2011). Disability and poverty: The need for a more nuanced understanding of implications for development policy and practice. *Third World Quarterly, 32*(8), 1493–1513. https://doi.org/10.1080/01436597.2011.604520

Grossman, M. (1972). On the concept of health capital and the demand for health. *Journal of Political Economy, 80*(2), 223–255.

Guthrie, T. (2002). Family social security benefits in South Africa. *Social Dynamics, 28*(2), 122–145. https://doi.org/10.1080/02533950208458735

Hartley, S., Ojwang, P., Baguwemu, A., Ddamulira, M., & Chavuta, A. (2005). How do carers of disabled children cope? The Ugandan perspective. *Child: Care, Health and Development, 31*(2), 167–180. https://doi.org/10.1111/j.1365-2214.2004.00464.x

Hunt, X., & Watermeyer, B. (2017). A web of gaps: A discussion of research strands concerning Global South families with a disabled child. *Global Health Action, 10*(1), 1337355. https://doi.org/10.1080/16549716.2017.1337355

Ingstad, B., Munthali, A. C., Braathen, S. H., & Grut, L. (2012). The evil circle of poverty: A qualitative study of malaria and disability. *Malaria Journal, 11*(1), 1–6. https://doi.org/10.1186/1475-2875-11-15

Institut national de la statistique, I. I. (2012). *République du Cameroun: Enquête démographique et de santé et à indicateurs multiples (EDS-MICS) : 2011*. Calverton, MD: ICF International.

Jelsma, J., Davids, N., & Ferguson, G. (2011). The motor development of orphaned children with and without HIV: Pilot exploration of foster care and residential placement. *BMC Pediatrics, 11*(1), 1–7. https://doi.org/10.1186/1471-2431-11-11

Jones, S. L., Weinberg, M., Ehrlich, R. I., & Roberts, K. (2000). Knowledge, attitudes, and practices of parents of asthmatic children in Cape Town. *The Journal of Asthma: Official Journal of the Association for the Care of Asthma, 37*(6), 519–528. https://doi.org/10.3109/02770900009055479

Kalibala, S., Schenk, K. D., Weiss, D. C., & Elson, L. (2012). Examining dimensions of vulnerability among children in Uganda. *Psychology, Health & Medicine, 17*(3), 295–310. https://doi.org/10.1080/13548506.2011.597771

Kanamori, M. J., & Pullum, T. (2013). *Indicators of child deprivation in sub-Saharan Africa: Levels and trends from the Demographic and Health Surveys*. DHS Comparative Reports No. 32; DHS Comparative Reports, p. 164. Calverton, MD: ICF International. http://dhsprogram.com/pubs/pdf/CR32/CR32.pdf

Kerac, M., Postels, D. G., Mallewa, M., Alusine Jalloh, A., Voskuijl, W. P., Groce, N., . . . Molyneux, E. (2014). The interaction of malnutrition and neurologic disability in Africa. *Seminars in Pediatric Neurology, 21*(1), 42–49. https://doi.org/10.1016/j.spen.2014.01.003

Kuper, H., Nyapera, V., Evans, J., Munyendo, D., Zuurmond, M., Frison, S., . . . Kisia, J. (2015). Malnutrition and childhood disability in Turkana, Kenya: Results from a case-control study. *PLoS One, 10*(12), e0144926. https://doi.org/10.1371/journal.pone.0144926

Loeb, M., Cappa, C., Crialesi, R., & de Palma, E. (2017). Measuring child functioning: The Unicef/Washington Group Module. *Salud Publica De Mexico, 59*(4), 485–487. https://doi.org/10.21149/8962

Mckenzie, J., & Swartz, L. (2011). The shaping of sexuality in children with disabilities: A Q methodological study. *Sexuality and Disability – SEX DISABILITY, 29*. https://doi.org/10.1007/s11195-011-9221-9

McNally, A., & Mannan, H. (2013). Perceptions of caring for children with disabilities: Experiences from Moshi, Tanzania. *African Journal of Disability, 2*(1). https://doi.org/10.4102/ajod.v2i1.21

Mitra, S. (2006). The capability approach and disability. *Journal of Disability Policy Studies*. https://doi.org/10.1177/10442073060160040501

Mkabile, S., & Swartz, L. (2020). Caregivers' and parents' explanatory models of intellectual disability in Khayelitsha, Cape Town, South Africa. *Journal of Applied Research in Intellectual Disabilities: JARID*. https://doi.org/10.1111/jar.12725

Njelesani, J. (2019). 'A child who is hidden has no rights': Responses to violence against children with disabilities. *Child Abuse & Neglect*, *89*, 58–69. https://doi.org/10.1016/j.chiabu.2018.12.024

Palmer, M. (2011). Disability and poverty: A conceptual review. *Journal of Disability Policy Studies*, *21*(4), 210–218. https://doi.org/10.1177/1044207310389333

Paquette, D., & Ryan, J. (2001). *Bronfenbrenner's ecological systems theory*. Retrieved October 19, 2021, from https://www.dropoutprevention.org/wp-content/uploads/2015/07/paquetteryanwebquest_20091110.pdf

Philpott, S., & McLaren, P. (2011). *Hearing the voices of children and caregivers: Children with disabilities in South Africa* (No. 2001–2011; A Situation Analysis, p. 44). Department of Social Development/UNICEF. Retrieved from www.unicef.org/southafrica/reports/hearing-voices-children-and-caregivers

Pinilla-Roncancio, M. (2015). Disability and poverty: Two related conditions: A review of the literature. *Revista de La Facultad de Medicina*, *63*, 113–123. https://doi.org/10.15446/revfacmed.v63n3sup.50132

Saloojee, G., Phohole, M., Saloojee, H., & IJsselmuiden, C. (2007). Unmet health, welfare and educational needs of disabled children in an impoverished South African peri-urban township. *Child: Care, Health and Development*, *33*(3), 230–235. https://doi.org/10.1111/j.1365-2214.2006.00645.x

Schneider, M. (2009). The difference a word makes: Responding to questions on 'disability' and 'difficulty' in South Africa. *Disability and Rehabilitation*, *31*(1), 42–50. https://doi.org/10.1080/09638280802280338

Simo Fotso, A. (2016). *Coûts du handicap de l'enfant pour les ménages au Cameroun* (Thèse UCAD, Thèse de doctorat, Université Cheik Anta Diop & INED). Thèse UCAD. https://bibnum.ucad.sn/viewer.php?c=thd&d=thd%5f2016%5f0051

Simo Fotso, A. (2017a). Child disability and mothers' labour market participation in Cameroon. *Journal of African Development*, *19*(1), 27–60.

Simo Fotso, A. (2017b). Child disability and siblings' healthcare expenditures in a context of child fostering. *Social Science & Medicine*, *182*, 89–96. https://doi.org/10.1016/j.socscimed.2017.04.016

Simo Fotso, A. (2017c). Child disability and siblings' healthcare expenditures in a context of child fostering. *Social Science & Medicine*, *182*, 89–96. https://doi.org/10.1016/j.socscimed.2017.04.016

Simo Fotso, A., Duthé, G., & Odimegwu, C. (2019). A comparative analysis of disability measures in Cameroonian surveys. *Population Health Metrics*, *17*(1), 16. https://doi.org/10.1186/s12963-019-0198-4

Simo Fotso, A., Solaz, A., Diene, M., & Nanfosso, R. T. (2018). Human capital accumulation of children in Cameroon: Does disability really matter? *Education Economics*, *26*(3), 305–320. https://doi.org/10.1080/09645292.2017.1421619

Simo Fotso, A., Somefun, O. D., & Odimegwu, C. (2020). Child health and relatives' employment in South Africa: The gendered effect beyond parents. In M. Konte & N. Tirivayi (Eds.), *Women and sustainable human development: Empowering women in Africa* (pp. 205–223). Springer International Publishing. https://doi.org/10.1007/978-3-030-14935-2_12

Singogo, C., Mweshi, M., & Rhoda, A. (2015). Challenges experienced by mothers caring for children with cerebral palsy in Zambia. *The South African Journal of Physiotherapy*, *71*(1). https://doi.org/10.4102/sajp.v71i1.274

Stabile, M., & Allin, S. (2012). The economic costs of childhood disability. *The Future of Children*, *22*(1), 65–96.

Swartz, L. (2014). Five challenges for disability-related research in sub-Saharan Africa. *African Journal of Disability*, *3*(2). https://doi.org/10.4102/ajod.v3i2.149

van der Mark, E., Conradie, I., Dedding, C., & Broerse, J. (2017). How poverty shapes caring for a disabled child: A narrative literature review. *Journal of International Development*, *29*. https://doi.org/10.1002/jid.3308

van der Mark, E. J., Conradie, I., Dedding, C. W. M., & Broerse, J. E. W. (2019). Exploring adaptation and agency of mothers caring for disabled children in an urban settlement in South Africa: A qualitative study. *Women's Studies International Forum*, *76*, 102271. https://doi.org/10.1016/j.wsif.2019.102271

WG, & UNICEF. (2017). *Module on child functioning: Concept note*, p. 9 [Concept note]. UNICEF/Washington Group on Disability Statistics. https://data.unicef.org/resources/module-child-functioning-concept-note/

WHO. (2001). *International classification of functioning, disability and health: ICF*. Geneva: World Health Organization.

WHO. (2007). *International classification of functioning, disability, and health: Children & Youth Version : ICF-CY*. Geneva: World Health Organization.

WHO, & UNICEF, U. N. C. (2012). *Early childhood development and disability: A discussion paper*. Geneva: World Health Organization.

WHO, & World Bank. (2011). *World report on disability: Main report* (No. 62783; pp. 1–349). The World Bank & World Health Organisation. Retrieved from http://documents.worldbank.org/curated/en/665131468331271288/Main-report

Zuurmond, M., Nyante, G., Baltussen, M., Seeley, J., Abanga, J., Shakespeare, T., . . . Bernays, S. (2019). A support programme for caregivers of children with disabilities in Ghana: Understanding the impact on the wellbeing of caregivers. *Child: Care, Health and Development*, *45*(1), 45–53. https://doi.org/10.1111/cch.12618

26

EFFECT OF ECONOMIC GROWTH ON MATERNAL AND CHILD HEALTH OUTCOMES IN SUB-SAHARAN AFRICA

A review of the empirical evidence

Helena Yeboah and Sanni Yaya

Introduction

More than 300,000 women died from pregnancy-related deaths in 2015 with two thirds of this total occurring in sub-Saharan Africa (SSA) (Roser & Ritchie, 2020). The lifetime risk of women dying due to pregnancy-related causes as of 2017 was about 1 in 38 in SSA compared to 1 in 240 in South Asia and 1 in 4,300 in Europe and Central Asia (WDI Data, 2020). Similarly, out of the global estimate of 5.42 million children who died before their fifth birthday in 2017, sub-Saharan Africa recorded 2.8 million, representing over 51% (Roser, Ritchie, & Dadonaite, 2013). This makes the SSA region the riskiest region of maternal and under-five child death occurrences than in all other regions in the world and this has become a key health challenge in the region. To this end, the global community recognizes the importance of ending preventable maternal and child deaths, making it an essential part of global health initiatives such as the Sustainable Development Goals (SDGs) which was adopted by all United Nations Member States in 2015 and has its third goal of seeking to ensure healthy lives and to promote well-being for all at all ages (WHO, 2020). Particularly regarding maternal and child health, some of the targets for SDG 3 are to address and reduce the global maternal mortality rates to less than 70 per 100,000 live births, reduce neonatal deaths to 12 per 1,000 live births and under-five deaths to at least 25 per 1,000 live births by 2030, and these are important targets for sub-Saharan African countries where maternal and child deaths are notably high (United Nations, n.d.).

There have been concerted efforts by several governments of sub-Saharan African countries and international institutions including the World Health Organization (WHO), African Union (AU), the United Nations Population Fund (UNFPA) and the International Development Research Centre (IDRC) to promote health and curb these high levels of child and maternal mortality in the region. This notwithstanding, many countries in the region continue to record some of the highest mortality rates compared to other world regions (IDRC, 2019; UNFPA, 2013b). Although good health is a goal in itself, reduction in maternal and child health is among the key indicators of maternal and child health, child nutrition, overall well-being of a country's population as well as the economic growth and development of nations (Frimpong &

DOI: 10.4324/9780429287213-31

Adu, 2014; Reidpath & Allotey, 2003). Investment in population health in effect increases human capital, which is a key contributing factor to economic performance (Sharma, 2018). The health-growth relationship is, however, not unidirectional. While a healthy population increases productivity and national wealth, a growing economy also has the potential of increasing the health of the population (Ensor et al., 2010). For developing countries like those in SSA to achieve better health statuses, there is the need to invest in evidenced-based and sustainable health programs.

One of the key factors that are recognized as a necessary, sufficient or often-times the only policy instrument for the improvement in population health outcomes particularly in developing countries is macroeconomic growth (M. A. Subramanyam, Kawachi, Berkman, & S. V. Subramanian, 2011). This suggests that countries with high annual growth rates should record positive and high maternal and child health outcomes. Empirically, this is not the case for all countries. The impact of economic growth on maternal and child health has resulted in mixed or inconclusive empirical evidence across and within countries.

On the positive side of the growth-health relationship Ensor et al. (2010) found a negative association between changes in GDP per capita and maternal and infant mortality, particularly for countries which are at their early stages of development. Economic growth has also been found as a strong predictor of good nutritional performance in developing countries (Ariizumi & Schirle, 2012). Similarly, Harttgen, Klasen and Vollmer (2013) found that increase in GDP per capita reduces stunting, wasting and underweight, which are some of the indicators of childhood undernutrition. The authors however added that while economic growth reduces child undernutrition, the magnitude in SSA remains insufficient to eliminate childhood undernutrition in the near future. On the other hand, while Vollmer et al. (2014) found zero to little association between increase in per-capita GDP and reduction in early childhood undernutrition, M. A. Subramanyam, Kawachi, Berkman & S. V. Subramanian (2010) point to no consistent evidence that economic growth results in a decline in childhood undernutrition in India. In Canada, Headey (2013) found that a percentage point increase in unemployment rate decreases the mortality rate. According to Corsi and S. V. Subramanian (2014), although maternal, neonatal and child health (MNCH) interventions contribute to the reduction in under-five mortality rates, the effects of economic growth in sub-Saharan Africa remain weak and inconsistent.

These mixed results and inconsistent findings may be attributed to the differences in the levels and focus areas of investments and interventions in public health in the various countries as well as healthcare behaviour which influences individuals' willingness to access improved healthcare interventions, particularly the influences of traditions and culture on healthcare decision-making especially by women. The SSA region constitutes several countries with disparities in economic growth rates, investment abilities and culture, and thereby different maternal and child health outcomes. In employing extensive literature review; databases of the World Bank, UNICEF and the World Health Organization; and relevant secondary data, we seek to analyze the impact and relationship between economic growth and maternal and child health outcomes in sub-Saharan African countries.

Maternal and child health trend in sub-Saharan Africa

The African region recorded about 41% decline in maternal deaths between 1990 and 2010, but poor maternal health outcomes continue to be a key health concern in the sub-Saharan African region (UNFPA, 2013b). Maternal deaths often occur while a woman is pregnant, while giving birth or within 42 days of termination of pregnancy, caused by birth complications (UNFPA, 2013b; WHO, 2011). Such peculiar health challenges and conditions that increase women's morbidity and mortality include direct obstetric causes such as haemorrhage, pregnancy hypertensive disorders, obstructed labour, sepsis and major infectious diseases. Preterm birth complications and birth asphyxia and trauma for instance are ranked fifth and sixth respectively as causes of morbidity and are among the top ten causes of mortality in the African region. It has been recorded that for every death, about 20 to 30 women suffer from short- or long-term disabilities and illnesses like obstetric fistula, chronic pain, damage to reproductive organs or anaemia (UNFPA, 2013b). These deaths and illnesses are preventable and treatable, but the lack of basic healthcare and education for many women in the developing countries often leads to such life-threatening health issues which affect them and their children, families and community.

It is evidently known that access to healthcare in the form of skilled delivery, antenatal care and obstetric care can significantly reduce high maternal and child mortalities across countries. However, in most developing countries, specifically those in SSA, there are several factors that act as impediments to the access to healthcare services. These factors can be categorized into availability, geographic accessibility, affordability and acceptability (Peters et al., 2008). Geographic accessibility refers to the physical distance or travel time between the service location and household location. In rural areas where roads are poor, many of the people are not able to utilize healthcare facilities that are mostly found in the urban centres and it also results in unequal distribution of health supplies and delay during emergency situations. Availability has to do with the opportunity to access healthcare when needed, in the form of health workers, drugs and equipment, education, healthcare information, wages and quality of staff. Informal fees, direct costs and price of services, household resources and opportunity cost make up the affordability dimension and this is considered one of the most important determinants of access to healthcare. In rural areas where patriarchal control is prominent, women tend to rely financially on their husbands and in most cases are not able to financially afford certain healthcare services that could improve their health status. Acceptability refers to how healthcare service providers are responsive to the cultural and social expectations of the individual and the community, and these include the staff efficiency, household expectation, cultural and community norms, attitudes and preferences and all the other characteristics of the health services (Ensor & Cooper, 2004; Peters et al., 2008).

These factors are further classified under demand- and supply-side factors (Ensor & Cooper, 2004). The demand-side factors are those that influence demand and relate to the ability to use maternal health services at individual, household or community levels, including indirect transportation costs, information on healthcare services/providers, education, income, household expectations, community, and religious and cultural preferences. Particularly with education, high levels of mother's education positively influence health investment behaviours such as increased nutrition intake of children which significantly increases child health outcomes (Prickett & Augustine, 2016). Supply-side factors are those that influence the slope and position of the supply curve. These may include the price and quality of drugs, technology, efficiency of staff and other negative factors which may include absenteeism, scarcity of supplies, unfriendly attitude of service providers and poor management training that hinder service uptake by individuals, households and communities. There is also the interaction of the demand- and supply-side factors which include quantity rationing, long waits for service, high cost of service and unofficial payments of staff. In order to improve the overall well-being of women and children, there is the need to build the capacity of healthcare systems and providers, while reducing the barriers individuals face in their attempt to access healthcare.

Figure 26.1 shows the number of maternal deaths by world regions. At a glance, the numbers for the sub-Saharan African region are disconcerting and it clearly shows the regional disparities women face in their chances of survival. Since 1990, the numbers have remained high

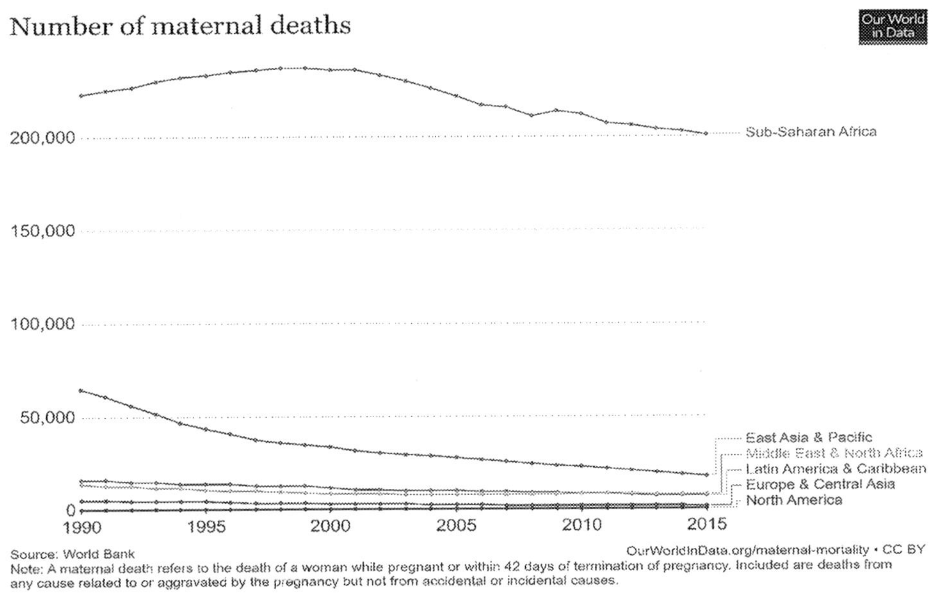

Figure 26.1 Number of maternal deaths by world regions.

Source: World Bank (2015)

compared to any of the other regions. In 1990, the number of maternal deaths was 223,000, increasing to 237,000 in 1999. A decline was experienced afterwards until 2008 at a value of 211,000. There was a slight increase in 2009 but a decline thereafter to a value of 201,000 in 2015. On the other hand, East Asia and the Pacific in the early 1990s had around 65,000 deaths but declined continuously along the years to 18,000 in 2015. Latin America and the Caribbean, and Europe and Central Asia have also made similar significant progress, with the 2015 values representing a decline of 50% and over. The Middle East and North Africa experienced falling numbers from 14,000 in 1990 to 8,200 in 2006 after which it obtained constant values until 2009. The numbers increased to 8,400 but declined to its 2015 value of 8,000. In comparison, while the other regions have maintained low figures and/or recorded greater percentage declines in their numbers, the sub-Saharan African region has only seen less than 10% decline in the number of maternal deaths.

Sub-Saharan African countries are however diverse and therefore bear different burdens of maternal deaths. Figure 26.2 shows the maternal mortality ratio (MMR), which is the number of maternal deaths in a given time period per 100,000 live births during the same time period. Central African Republic in 1992 recorded the MMR of 1,320 per 100,000 live births, but this declined to 882 in 2015. The decline notwithstanding, it has been the country with the highest MMR since 1992 among selected countries. Ethiopia records a steep decline in the MMR: in 1990, 1,250 per 100,000 live births was recorded which decreased to 353 per 100,000 live births in 2015. Remarkably, South Africa has obtained the lowest MMR values since 1990. The Central African Republic holds the highest MMR, but the actual number of maternal deaths has been the lowest and this is due to the low population of the country (World Bank, 2019). Ethiopia has also recorded a continuous decline in the number of maternal deaths, but the numbers are still high with 11,000 maternal deaths in 2015. While it has an upward trend

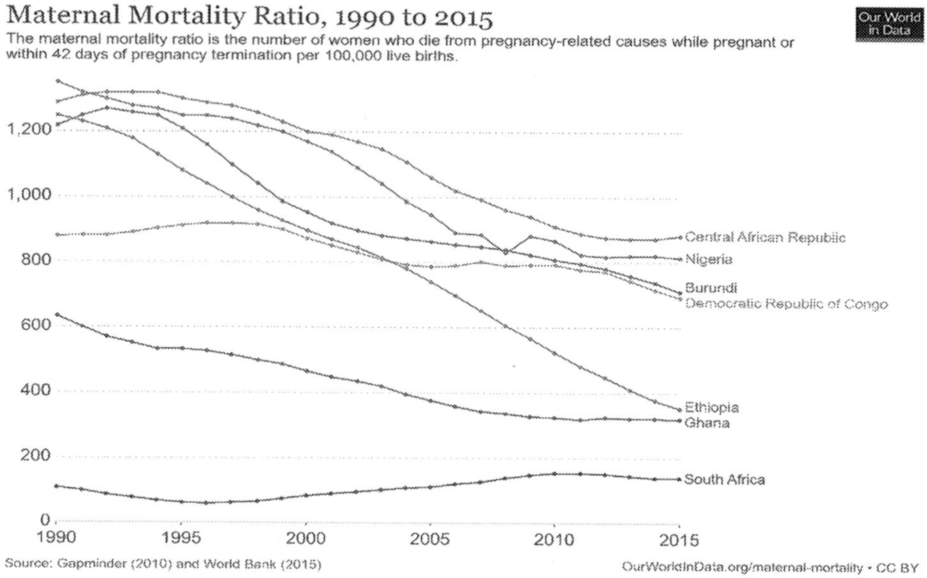

Figure 26.2 Maternal mortality ratio, 1990 to 2015.

Source: Gapminder (2010) and World Bank (2015)

of maternal deaths, Nigeria's trend is more volatile. Like DRC where the number of maternal deaths increased from 15,000 in 1990 to 20,000 in 2000 and up to 22,000 in 2015, Nigeria's 2015 value of 58,000 was higher than that of 1990. This means that for these two countries, that is, Nigeria and DRC, no significant improvements have been made in reducing the number of deaths (Roser & Ritchie, 2020). Nigeria, Ethiopia and DRC were among the five countries with the highest number of maternal deaths in the world as of 2015 (Roser & Ritchie, 2020).

This makes the burden of maternal mortality in sub-Saharan Africa very high in relation to the prevalence and incidence in other world regions. The impact of maternal deaths on the family and particularly on the children is huge. In addition to the psychological and emotional impacts and the loss of household incomes, newborns are more likely to die, and for surviving children, school participation and enrolment decrease substantially; older children are more likely to face higher rates of undernutrition, lower levels of education and therefore lower future incomes and health (Moucheraud et al., 2015; Roser & Ritchie, 2020). Banerjee and Duflo (2011) point out that when unborn babies and children receive better nourishment in the first two years of life, they tend to gain a lifetime income of US$3,269 PPP. This makes the optimal health of women an essential factor in child survival and improves overall health and well-being.

Just as maternal health outcomes in SSA are disturbing, child health outcomes in the region are alarming (UNFPA, 2013a). Africa reduced under-five child deaths by 33% between the period of 1990 and 2010, but SSA continues to record the highest under-five mortality rates compared to other world regions (as shown in Figure 26.3). The region had an average of 2.8 million child deaths in 2017 compared to 28,861 child deaths in North America, representing an average ratio of 1 in 99 in favour of North American countries. Undernutrition is one of the key indicators of child health which leaves long-term consequences on the well-being and survival of children and according to the WHO (2014), it should be a priority for policy-makers

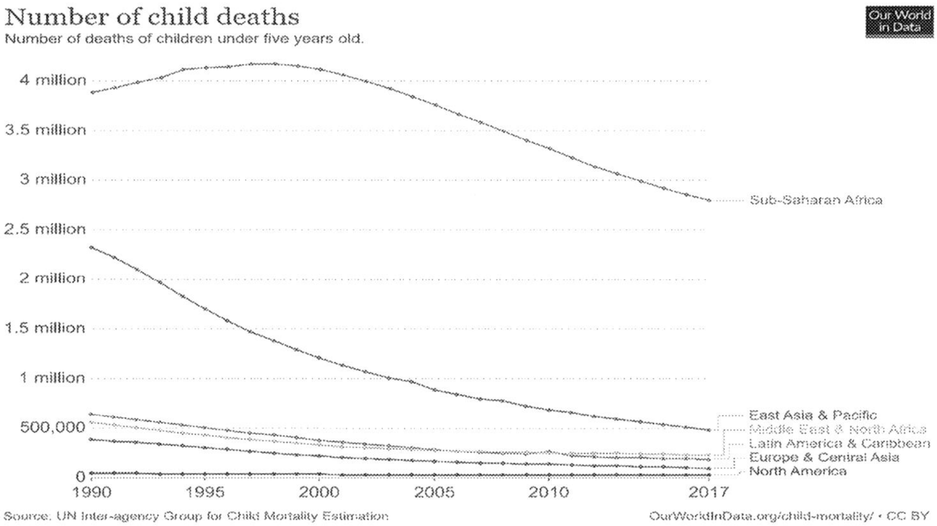

Figure 26.3 Number of under-five child deaths by world regions.

Source: UN Inter-agency Group for Child Mortality Estimation (2019)

and development concern for governments. Undernutrition is measured by three anthropometric dimensions of childhood nutrition: weight-for-age (underweight), height-for-age (stunting), and weight-for-height (wasting); however, unlike wasting and underweight, stunting is the most prevalent form of severe childhood malnutrition (Biadgilign, Shumetie, & Yesigat, 2016) Stunting is defined as the percentage of children between 0 and 59 months whose height for age is below minus two standard deviation from the median of the WHO Child Growth Standards (de Onis & Branca, 2016).

Stunting is associated with increased risk of death from infectious diseases including pneumonia, diarrhoea and measles, and for those who may survive, there is a long-term impact on their physical and cognitive development which is considered irreversible beyond the first 1,000 days of the child's life (de Onis & Branca, 2016; Roser & Ritchie, 2013). Such irreparable impact also results in reduced mental abilities and poor school performance, and this means lower education, incomes and health in their adult life. As shown in Figure 26.4, all the selected SSA countries recorded more than 30% of stunted growth before 1995 but show declining trends afterwards. Ghana recorded a continuous decline from 43.8% in 1993 to 18.8% in 2014. Similarly, Malawi recorded declining rates in stunting from 55.8% in 1992 to 37.1% in 2015. These represent a decline of about 57% and 33.5% respectively in the share of children under five who are stunted. Although this shows promising improvements, the rates are comparatively high. Nigeria on the other hand saw a sharp rise in stunting, recording a rate of 43.6% in 2016 and this value is only 6.9% less of its 1990 stunting rate.

Economic growth and maternal and child health in sub-Saharan Africa

Economic growth has been found to substantially reduce undernutrition in Ethiopia through the increase in health investment, public infrastructure and improved households' per-capita

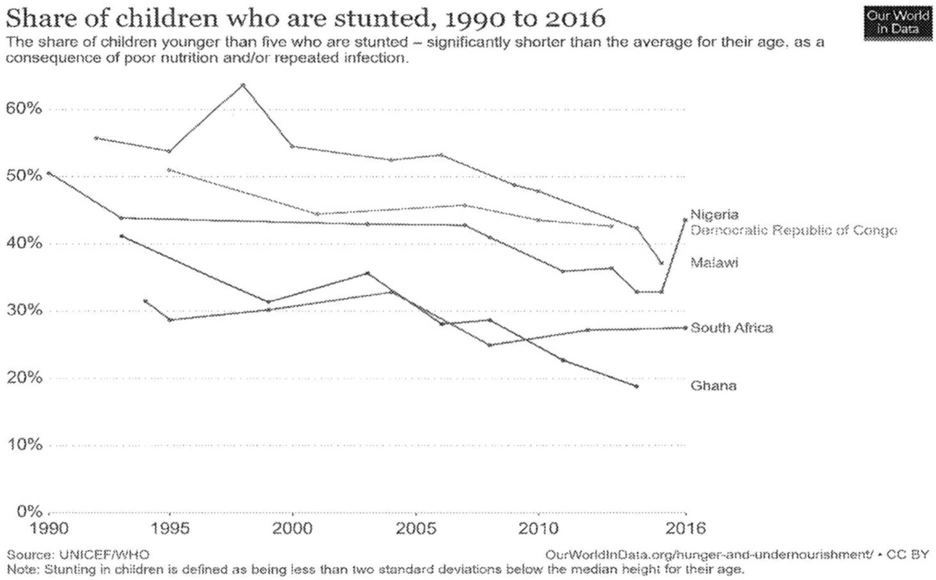

Figure 26.4 Share of children under five who are stunted, 1990 to 2016.

Source: UNICEF/WHO/The World Bank (2018)

income (Biadgilign et al., 2016). Ensor et al. (2010) also investigated the impact of previous economic recessions and booms on maternal and infant health outcomes for 14 high- and middle-income countries between 1936 and 2005. The authors separately used maternal mortality and infant mortality as the dependent variables, with GDP per capita as the main explanatory variable. They found that for both maternal and infant mortality, there exists a negative relationship between income and outcomes. Ensor et al. (2010), however, argued that the reasons for the differences in health outcomes when these countries were analyzed individually are not clear, and that for countries in the early stages of development, health gains are vulnerable to fluctuating GDP. This notwithstanding, they concluded that the relationship between economic growth and health outcomes is important for countries in the early stages of development.

Lange and Vollmer (2017) did an empirical review on the effect of economic development on population health by analyzing published economic journals between 1990 and 2015 on Google Scholar and PubMed. A total of 18 studies that considered mortality, life expectancy and malnutrition as the dependent variable and GDP, GDP per capita, growth in GDP, growth in GDP per capita or unemployment rate as the main independent variable were selected. The authors concluded that there exists a strong and positive relationship between incomes and population health status within and across countries. This relationship is, however, not unidirectional: a healthy population increases productivity which positively impacts national wealth, while a growing economy on the other hand can affect the health of the population, and although differences in health outcomes in many countries have been partly attributed to differences in economic growth, the relationship is also not consistent (Ensor et al., 2010). For countries with high records of annual growth rates, it is expected that maternal and child health outcomes remain positive and high. However, this is sometimes not the case, particularly in sub-Saharan African countries.

With the exception of Nigeria and South Africa, the sub-Saharan African region obtained an average growth rate of 2.4 percent in 2018, and for countries like Rwanda, Guinea, Ghana and Ethiopia, economic growth rate has averaged over 5% since 2016. For instance, in 2017, Ethiopia was named the fastest-growing economy in sub-Saharan Africa with an accelerated growth rate of 9.5%, followed by Ghana with a rate 8.5% (WDI Data, 2020). Despite these achievements in economic growth and several declines in the maternal and child death rates since the 1990s, the SSA region still could not advance the achievement of the MDGs 4 and 5, which targeted 75% reduction in Maternal Mortality Rates (MMR) and 67% reduction in under-five mortality rates by the end of 2015 (United Nations, 2015). Moreover, the maternal and child death rates are still high. Overall, SSA accounted for 66% of global maternal deaths in 2015, and by 2017, the region's record showed that 1 in 13 children died before their fifth birthday, representing 50% of global under-five deaths (UNFPA, 2013b; UNICEF, 2018). While many countries have already met the Sustainable Development Goal (SDG) target on under-five mortality, which aims to reduce under-five deaths to 25 or fewer deaths per 1,000 live births by 2030, about 53 countries including over 30 SSA countries are yet to make any progress (UNICEF, 2019). For these countries to meet the target, it has been recommended that they accelerate the decline in child deaths and for some of these countries, more than double of their current declines will be needed.

Figure 26.5 shows the relationship between maternal mortality ratio and GDP per capita. GDP per capita divides the total economic output of a country by its population. Equatorial Guinea, a country in the central part of Africa, recorded the highest GDP per capita of $27,554

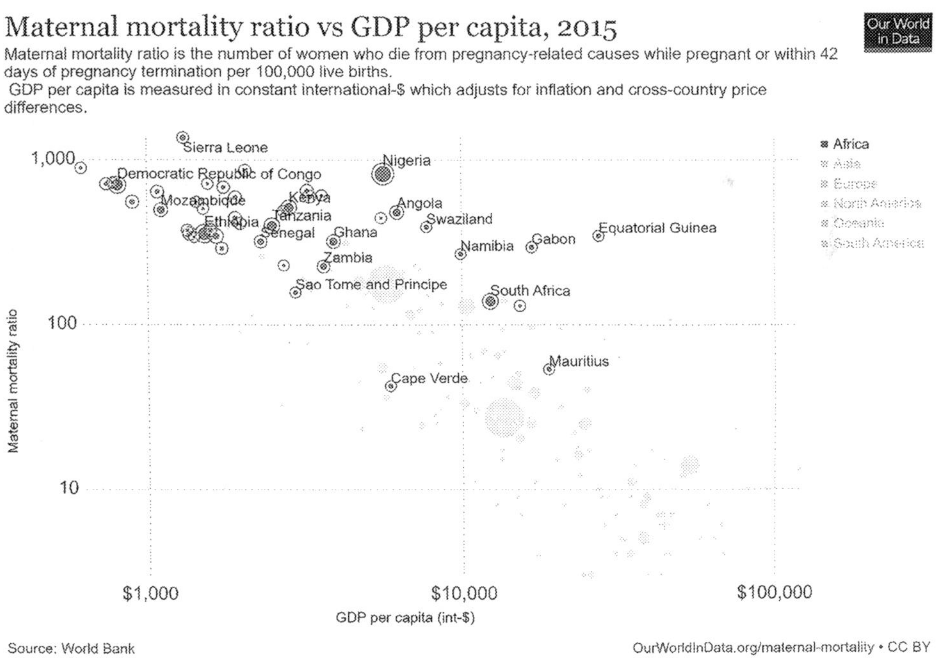

Figure 26.5 Maternal mortality ratio vs GDP per capita, 2015.
Source: World Bank (2015)

in 2015 and MMR of 342 deaths per 100,000; Cape Verde had $5,915 GDP per capita but recorded a lower MMR of 42 deaths per 100,000. The difference between the MMRs of Tanzania and Swaziland was 9 deaths per 100,000; however, Swaziland recorded $5,267 more GDP per capita than Tanzania. This uncertain relationship raises questions on the impact of economic growth on maternal and child health outcomes in sub-Saharan African countries.

These differences and variability in health outcomes point to the fact that although economic growth is important, it is not enough. It should be combined with the distribution of income and other prevailing factors such as information on healthcare services/providers, education, income, household expectations, community, religious and cultural preferences, because these factors impact maternal and child health outcomes (Ensor & Cooper, 2004). It is important to understand the overall relationship and direction between economic growth and maternal and child health outcomes in SSA, but more so, it is vital to understand the reasons for the differences in maternal and child health outcomes in these countries. This will enable more comprehensive and effective policy interventions and community-acceptable programmes which will aid in the reduction and prevention of maternal and child deaths and undernutrition in these countries and the region at large.

Economic growth and maternal and child health: a conceptual framework

The increase in economic growth is expected to increase incomes of household through employment opportunities, move individuals out of poverty, transform societies and improve the overall wellbeing of a country's population (DFID, n.d.). While it is recognized that the increase in economic growth improves household health outcomes, there have been mixed results. This is because the link between economic growth and household health outcomes operates through two channels: the macro (national) level, which deals with the impact of state-level economic growth on health outcomes; and the individual (micro) level which considers how the increase in household income affects household outcomes (Ensor et al., 2010). There are also several pathways that link economic growth and health at each level, and as a result, the pathway chosen by governments and households will determine the health outcome.

In Figure 26.6, we examine the pathways at the individual and macro levels to understand how the changes in income impact maternal and child health outcomes in the sub-Saharan African region.

At the individual level, the changes in income may have either positive or negative impact on maternal and child health outcomes. When household income increases, household nutrition also increases. Foods that contain more micronutrients and calories will be consumed, and this will put consumers in a better position to fight against infectious diseases as well as provide greater chance of recovering from illnesses. The household will be able to cover out-of-pocket health costs and invest in preventive and curative health goods, water and sanitation, which tackles the demand-side factors that impede healthcare utilization, thereby improving maternal and child health outcomes (Ensor et al., 2010; Lange & Vollmer, 2017). However, the increase in household income can also heighten maternal and child health problems, since certain illnesses and deaths commonly associated with prosperity, also called 'diseases of the affluent', come with poor lifestyles including tobacco use and poor diets which tend to increase in some households as income increases (Lange & Vollmer, 2017).

On the macro level, the link between economic growth and maternal and child health outcomes takes several pathways through the state's investment and interventions in different sectors of the country. Economic growth increases the state's ability to invest in many aspects of

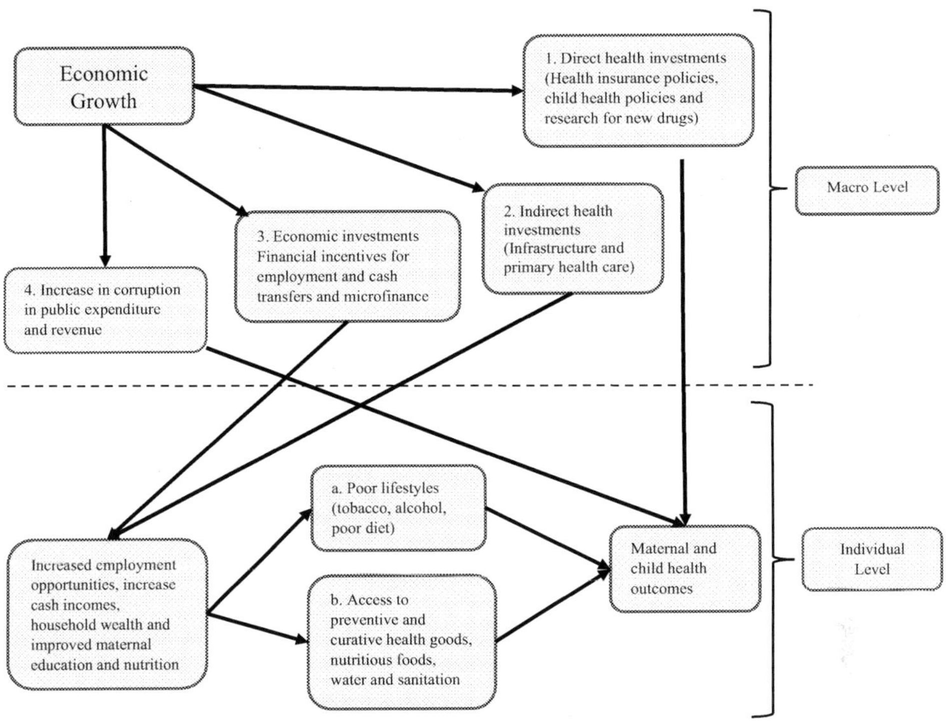

Figure 26.6 Conceptual framework.

the economy such as the following. (1) The state can increase direct health investment which includes investments in policies on health insurance, child health, immunization and nutrition, and policies on research for new drugs and diseases, which have a direct positive impact on maternal and child health outcomes. (2) The state can increase investment in infrastructure development: clinics, hospitals and roads, and primary healthcare. This constitutes the indirect health investment and tackles the supply-side issues of healthcare utilization. (3) The state can increase economic investments in the form of financial incentives for employment, cash transfers and microfinance targeted at women. It is a well-established fact that an increase in the income of women in the household directly impacts the health and overall well-being of the household (Morrison, Raju, & Sinha, 2007). (4) The increase in corruption in public expenditure and public income directly impacts the outcome of maternal and child health, because resources are channelled from investing in health policies and projects into the pockets of government officials and individuals. Both the indirect health investments and the economic investments lead to increased employment opportunities, cash incomes and household wealth. At this level, the impact follows the individual level as discussed previously (Ensor et al., 2010; Lange & Vollmer, 2017; M. A. Subramanyam et al., 2010).

Looking at the conceptual framework, it is important to note that the increase in economic growth increases government spending abilities, which further influences the health and well-being of individuals in a country, indicating that the positive impact of economic growth on the overall health of the population depends on how the state distributes resources as well as the behaviour and choices of the household and individuals within the country. Government health spending, investment in the economy and corruption are important factors that impact health outcomes and therefore need to be considered in order to understand the mechanisms between economic growth and health outcomes. Based on this framework and the pathways, we will examine the mechanisms through which economic growth impacts maternal and child health outcomes in SSA countries.

Exploring pathways and mechanisms

As shown in the first and second pathways, an increase in economic growth results in both direct and indirect health investments which will eventually increase maternal and child health outcomes. Evidently this has not been the case. According to the WHO Regional Office for Africa (2018), many health systems in SSA underperform when it comes to availability of essential services, coverage of essential interventions, financial risk protection from catastrophic health expenditures, service satisfaction and health security. Such an underperformance has resulted in a health deficit in SSA. To achieve universal health coverage among citizens, good population health outcomes and efficient health system performance, countries need to invest in both tangible and intangible inputs such as workforce, infrastructure, research and technologies, insurance and health information to provide the essential health services needed by the population (WHO Regional Office for Africa, 2018). It has however been recognized that poor economies tend to record significantly lower health expenditures, whereas those with larger per-capita GDP are more probable to spend greater portions of their income on healthcare (Ortiz-Ospina & Roser, 2016). The World Bank has classified its member states into four income groups, namely, low-income countries (LIC), lower middle-income countries (LMIC), upper middle-income countries (UMIC) and high-income countries (HIC) (The World Bank, 2020). For the 2020 fiscal year, countries with gross national income (GNI) per capita of $1,025 or less are low-income countries; lower middle-income countries have GNI per capita between $1,026 and $3,995; upper middle-income countries are those with GNI per capita between $3,996 and $12,375; countries with GNI per capita of $12,376 or above are classified as high-income countries. SSA has 27 LICs, 13 LMICs, 7 UMICs and only one HIC which is the Seychelles, a country in the eastern part of the region.

Table 26.1 shows the GNI per capita and current health expenditure per capita (CHE pc) of selected countries in the SSA region and their income classifications. The Seychelles as a high-income country spends more of its income on each individual in the country compared to South Africa, Nigeria and Guinea.

One debatable phenomenon is the relationship between health expenditure and health outcomes. This is because Rwanda as a low-income country in 2018 recorded a life expectancy of 68, which is higher than that of LMICs like the Democratic Republic of the Congo, Ghana and Kenya as well as UMICs including Botswana and Namibia (WDI Data, 2020). Similarly, the MMR of Guinea as of 2017 was 576 compared to Nigeria's rate of 917 in the same year. This may be the consequence of the inefficiencies in the way these countries apportion their resources in the health system. This may include poor governance which results in bribery and corruption, poor targeting, misallocation of resources and poor management (Makuta & O'Hare, 2015). According to Transparency International (2020), the sub-Saharan African region has an average corruption perception index of 32, with some countries like Somalia recording as low as 9. This means there are high corruption and bribery actions, in which public officials tend to embezzle monies meant for the healthcare system, including funds for the acquisition of medicines, improving healthcare facilities and hiring qualified health workers, which would have improved the health of the population, particularly the poorest who cannot

Table 26.1 GNI per Capita and Current Health Expenditure for Selected SSA Countries

Country	*Guinea (LIC)*		*Nigeria (LMIC)*		*South Africa (HMIC)*		*The Seychelles (HIC)*	
Year	*GNI pc*	*CHE pc*	*GNI pc*	*CHE pc*	*GNI pc*	*CHE pc*	*GNI pc*	*CHE pc*
2000	400	52.71524	470	75.90919	3070	562.2164	7290	674.0007
2001	360	57.01679	530	80.91418	2860	583.2636	7310	774.8258
2002	350	67.91682	630	71.96352	2670	559.5637	6850	659.8343
2003	340	61.0823	710	155.2128	2920	582.5018	7490	729.5383
2004	370	58.19341	870	151.6796	3720	608.8408	9280	693.5063
2005	360	63.43512	1030	157.7279	4990	643.6844	11140	736.8481
2006	400	40.31287	1350	156.9027	5630	680.6531	12580	772.9899
2007	470	44.82782	1610	154.8648	5910	711.2873	12270	760.8051
2008	620	44.01995	1960	159.8381	5980	753.7684	11130	737.3047
2009	670	44.05439	2040	170.6391	5850	803.8869	10220	712.4122
2010	690	46.58384	2140	166.7103	6190	863.4855	10190	945.83
2011	680	61.6019	2190	174.6496	6990	908.5803	11060	984.8821
2012	700	58.16825	2460	181.7129	7570	965.1554	11540	1264.078
2013	700	61.43481	2720	194.8448	7350	988.0589	12650	1067.165
2014	740	87.7672	2990	201.1753	6760	1038.216	13290	1187.87
2015	760	109.0881	2880	217.4599	6050	1083.678	14020	1213.827
2016	780	109.2372	2470	214.562	5470	1076.11	13830	1439.928
2017	820	89.17005	2100	221.095	5410	1097.819	14220	1485.474
2018	850	-	1960	-	5750	-	15600	-

Source: WDI Data (2020)

afford high out-of-pocket costs (Hsiao, Vogt, & Quentin, 2019). Witvliet, Kunst, Arah and Stronks (2013) analyzed 20 African countries, including 18 sub-Saharan African countries, and found that perceived higher national corruption contributes to the increase in poor health outcomes among the population. For countries with higher-quality governance, increase in public health spending lowers under-five mortality and increases life expectancy; as such, governments can pursue and implement quality policies and efficiently target and use resources in healthcare delivery. However, for countries with bad governance, an increase in public health spending has no or low impact on the rate of under-five mortality (Makuta & O'Hare, 2015).

Many SSA countries have borne and continue to face health shocks due to outbreaks and deaths which increase household risks and vulnerability, and lead to significant reduction in health service outcomes since this reduces the health system capacity and resilience (WHO Regional Office for Africa, 2018). Atake (2018) reveals that health shocks in the form of unpredictable diseases deteriorate the health of individuals, especially the poor and uninsured. For instance, in countries like South Africa where HIV is highly prevalent, households with HIV infections earn 35% to 50% lower incomes and tend to incur higher out-of-pocket costs compared to unaffected households (Alam & Mahal, 2014). While labour participation declines due to sickness and deaths of infected individuals, labour supply among adolescents and women in the household increase to offset the income losses. Similarly, the 2014 Ebola outbreak in West Africa presented significant health shocks to the health system due to deaths of many health workers and the closure of several health facilities (Brolin Ribacke, Saulnier, Eriksson, & von Schreeb, 2016). The total fiscal cost for the three most infected countries of Guinea, Liberia and Sierra Leone in 2014 was almost 5% of their combined GDP, representing more than

$500 million (Thomas et al., 2015). The current COVID-19 crisis has not only taken a toll on human life, but it has been predicted that SSA will experience between 2.1% and 5.1% decline in 2020 economic growth, costing between $37 billion and $79 billion (World Bank, 2020). Similar declines worldwide are expected to cause global economic downturn and recession which will be larger than any other previous pandemic. Households take their fair share at the end of the spectrum because they are faced with job losses and infections leading to loss in household welfare. According to the WHO Regional Office for Africa (2018), countries can have high resilience to fight disease outbreaks when they have higher income levels and high levels of health expenditure, but for many SSA countries with high fragility, low income, low health investments, weak health systems, large informal workforce and limited access to water and sanitation facilities, the overall health and well-being of the most vulnerable, including women and children, will significantly decline.

While economic growth enables the government and private businesses to invest in the economy through the provision of financial incentives including cash transfers, employment opportunities and microfinance for the population, particularly women, economic shocks and recessions on the other hand contract economies and this means that governments' ability to finance such investments will be impacted (Ensor et al., 2010). Resources will be channelled to areas that may need immediate attention. In the case of global recession, foreign investments and assistance from donors which in most cases constitute a substantial portion of developing countries' health sector finance may either diminish or cease (Ensor et al., 2010). The authors show that as countries grow, the impact of economic shocks becomes weak, and so suggest that for many developing countries in SSA, economic shocks will have severe consequences on the economy. Remittances may decline significantly, and together with declined public spending and social safety nets, households will experience substantial economic challenges (Arieff, Weiss, & Jones, 2010).

In the case in which governments are able to invest in direct and indirect sectors of the health system and in the economy in general, there is an increase in employment opportunities, cash incomes and household wealth. However, the increase in household income does not mean an automatic increase in child nutrition or maternal health outcomes. A positive association between household income and nutritional status of children will depend on how resources are apportioned to food and non-food items, level of quality of food purchased and how such foods are distributed among the individuals within the household (Vollmer et al., 2014). Also, behavioural changes that may occur due to the increase in income will have two distinct outcomes. As mentioned earlier, it will either increase or decrease maternal and child health outcomes. On the positive side, increased household resources will enable households to provide food with more calories and nutrients for the children, greater access to water and sanitation, health-relevant goods, social protection and access to quality healthcare services (Harttgen et al., 2013; Lange & Vollmer, 2017). In Tanzania, Fichera and Savage (2015) found that an income increase of 10% generally reduces the number of illnesses by 0.02 and increases vaccination of children under six by 0.1. On the other hand, households may increase risky health behaviours such as smoking, drinking and bad eating habits that have a high likelihood of increasing illnesses such as diabetes, hypertension and obesity (Lange & Vollmer, 2017).

Conclusion

Maternal and child mortality rates are not only among the key indicators of maternal and child health, child nutrition and overall well-being, but they remain a vital part of the development of countries. The reduction in maternal and child deaths is significant for human capital development and economic growth of countries, making the advancement of the health of women and children across all socio-economic statuses and geographical locations vital. For many countries in sub-Saharan Africa, maternal death, child death and child undernutrition rates are higher compared to other world regions. With such high rates, most of these countries in the region remain incapable of achieving the SDG 3 in a timely manner. Economic growth is considered a key instrument in the reduction of maternal and child deaths, but this relationship is not always positive. Countries with high growth rates may record debilitating population health outcomes. For instance, Ethiopia, which was named the fastest-growing economy with an accelerated growth rate of 9.5% in 2017, also recorded a maternal mortality ratio of 401 per 100,000 live births in the same year.

Moreover, many authors have found mixed results, and such inconsistencies have been attributed to the level of investments, focus of investments and interventions in the health system and, importantly, healthcare behaviour of the population. Poor countries with low income will have significantly low levels of health investments, which limits the essential services the population will need for positive health outcomes. Again, when economic growth boosts investments in the healthcare system, it may not increase health outcomes unless there are higher-quality governance and low corruption practices. In many SSA countries, health shocks such as HIV/AIDS, Ebola and COVID-19 have threatened and reduced the health system capacity and resilience, and coupled with economic shocks that come with such unpredictable illnesses, households have become more susceptible to risks and vulnerabilities. An increase in economic investment by the government can result in positive or negative individual and household health outcomes based on their healthcare behaviours. Households can either use such increased income to purchase foods and health items that can increase their health status or resort to the consumption of unhealthy foods and items like tobacco and alcohol which can lead to illnesses like hypertension and obesity.

All these factors influence the mechanism between economic growth and maternal and child health outcomes. These factors go a long way to show that although economic growth is important, it is not enough. Understanding the overall relationship and direction between economic growth and maternal and child health outcomes in SSA countries will enable more comprehensive and sound policies, and community-acceptable programs that will strengthen the capacity of the already fragile healthcare system and improve household health behaviours, which will aid in improving maternal and child health outcomes within countries in the region.

Abbreviations

AU	African Union
CHE	Current Health Expenditure
COVID-19	Corona Virus Disease of 2019
DFID	Department for International Development
IDRC	International Development Research Centre
GDP	Gross Domestic Product
GNI	Gross National Income
HIC	High-Income Country
HIV/AIDS	Human Immunodeficiency Virus/Acquired Immunodeficiency Syndrome
LIC	Low-Income Country
LMIC	Lower Middle-Income Country
MMR	Maternal Mortality Rate

(Continued)

AU	African Union
MNCH	Maternal, Neonatal and Child Health
PC	Per Capita
PPP	Purchasing Power Parity
SDG	Sustainable Development Goals
SSA	Sub-Saharan Africa
UMIC	Upper Middle-Income Country
UN	United Nations
UNICEF	United Nations International Children's Emergency Fund
UNFPA	United Nations Population Fund for Population Activities
WDI	World Development Index
WHO	World Health Organization

References

Alam, K., & Mahal, A. (2014). Economic impacts of health shocks on households in low and middle income countries: A review of the literature. *Globalization and Health, 10*(1), 1–18.

Arieff, A., Weiss, M. A., & Jones, V. C. (2010). *The global economic crisis: Impact on sub-Saharan Africa and global policy responses*. Retrieved from https://fas.org/sgp/crs/row/R40778.pdf

Ariizumi, H., & Schirle, T. (2012). Are recessions really good for your health? Evidence from Canada. *Social Science & Medicine, 74*(8), 1224–1231.

Atake, E.-H. (2018). Health shocks in Sub-Saharan Africa: Are the poor and uninsured households more vulnerable? *Health Economics Review, 8*(1), 26. https://doi.org/10.1186/s13561-018-0210-x

Banerjee, A. V., & Duflo, E. (2011). *A radical rethinking of the way to fight global poverty*. Retrieved from https://warwick.ac.uk/about/london/study/warwick-summer-school/courses/macroeconomics/poor_economics.pdf

Biadgilign, S., Shumetie, A., & Yesigat, H. (2016). Does economic growth reduce childhood undernutrition in Ethiopia? *PLoS One, 11*(8), e0160050. https://doi.org/10.1371/journal.pone.0160050

Brolin Ribacke, K. J., Saulnier, D. D., Eriksson, A., & von Schreeb, J. (2016). Effects of the West Africa Ebola virus disease on health-care utilization – A systematic review. *Frontiers in Public Health, 4*. https://doi.org/10.3389/fpubh.2016.00222

Corsi, D. J., & Subramanian, S. V. (2014). Association between coverage of maternal and child health interventions, and under-5 mortality: A repeated cross-sectional analysis of 35 sub-Saharan African countries. *Global Health Action, 7*. https://doi.org/10.3402/gha.v7.24765

de Onis, M., & Branca, F. (2016). Childhood stunting: A global perspective. *Maternal & Child Nutrition, 12*(Suppl. 1), 12–26. https://doi.org/10.1111/mcn.12231

DFID. (n.d.). Economic growth: The impact on poverty reduction, inequality, human development and jobs. *Growth Building Jobs and Prosperity in Developing Countries*. Retrieved May 19, 2020, from www.oecd.org/derec/?hf=5&b=15&q=Economic+growth%2C+income+inequality+and+poverty+reduction&s=score

Ensor, T., & Cooper, S. (2004). Overcoming barriers to health service access: Influencing the demand side. *Health Policy and Planning, 19*(2), 69–79. https://doi.org/10.1093/heapol/czh009

Ensor, T., Cooper, S., Davidson, L., Fitzmaurice, A., & Graham, W. J. (2010). The impact of economic recession on maternal and infant mortality: Lessons from history. *BMC Public Health, 10*, 727. https://doi.org/10.1186/1471-2458-10-727

Fichera, E., & Savage, D. (2015). Income and health in Tanzania. An instrumental variable approach. *World Development, 66*, 500–515. https://doi.org/10.1016/j.worlddev.2014.09.016

Frimpong, P. B., & Adu, G. (2014). Population health and economic growth in sub-Saharan Africa: A panel cointegration analysis. *Journal of African Business, 15*(1), 36–48. https://doi.org/10.1080/15228916.2014.881227

Gapminder. (2010). *Gapminder tools*. Retrieved from Gapminder.org.

Harttgen, K., Klasen, S., & Vollmer, S. (2013). Economic growth and child undernutrition in sub-Saharan Africa. *Population and Development Review, 39*(3), 397–412. https://doi.org/10.1111/j.1728-4457.2013.00609.x

Headey, D. D. (2013). Developmental drivers of nutritional change: A cross-country analysis. *World Development, 42*, 76–88.

Hsiao, A., Vogt, V., & Quentin, W. (2019). Effect of corruption on perceived difficulties in healthcare access in sub-Saharan Africa. *PLoS One, 14*(8), e0220583. https://doi.org/10.1371/journal.pone.0220583

IDRC. (2019). *Innovating for maternal and child health in Africa*. IDRC – International Development Research Centre. Retrieved from www.idrc.ca/en/initiative/innovating-maternal-and-child-health-africa

Lange, S., & Vollmer, S. (2017). The effect of economic development on population health: A review of the empirical evidence. *British Medical Bulletin, 121*(1), 47–60. https://doi.org/10.1093/bmb/ldw052

Makuta, I., & O'Hare, B. (2015). Quality of governance, public spending on health and health status in sub Saharan Africa: A panel data regression analysis. *BMC Public Health, 15*(1), 932. https://doi.org/10.1186/s12889-015-2287-z

Morrison, A., Raju, D., & Sinha, N. (2007). *Gender equality, poverty and economic growth*. Policy Research Working Paper Series No. 4349. The World Bank. Retrieved from https://ideas.repec.org/p/wbk/wbrwps/4349.html

Moucheraud, C., Worku, A., Molla, M., Finlay, J. E., Leaning, J., & Yamin, A. E. (2015). *Consequences of maternal mortality on infant and child survival: A 25-year longitudinal analysis in Butajira Ethiopia (1987–2011)*. ResearchGate. Retrieved from www.researchgate.net/publication/277079941_Consequences_of_maternal_mortality_on_infant_and_child_survival_A_25-year_longitudinal_analysis_in_Butajira_Ethiopia_1987-2011

Ortiz-Ospina, E., & Roser, M. (2016). Global health. *Our World in Data*. Retrieved from https://ourworldindata.org/health-meta

Peters, D. H., Garg, A., Bloom, G., Walker, D. G., Brieger, W. R., & Rahman, M. H. (2008). Poverty and access to health care in developing countries. *Annals of the New York Academy of Sciences, 1136*, 161–171. https://doi.org/10.1196/annals.1425.011

Prickett, K. C., & Augustine, J. M. (2016). Maternal education and investments in children's health. *Journal of Marriage and the Family, 78*(1), 7–25. https://doi.org/10.1111/jomf.12253

Reidpath, D. D., & Allotey, P. (2003). Infant mortality rate as an indicator of population health. *Journal of Epidemiology & Community Health, 57*(5), 344–346. https://doi.org/10.1136/jech.57.5.344

Roser, M., & Ritchie, H. (2013). Hunger and undernourishment. *Our World in Data*. Retrieved from https://ourworldindata.org/hunger-and-undernourishment

Roser, M., & Ritchie, H. (2020). Maternal mortality. *Our World in Data*. Retrieved from https://ourworldindata.org/maternal-mortality

Roser, M., Ritchie, H., & Dadonaite, B. (2013). Child and infant mortality. *Our World in Data*. Retrieved from https://ourworldindata.org/child-mortality

Sharma, R. (2018). Health and economic growth: Evidence from dynamic panel data of 143 years. *PLoS One, 13*(10). https://doi.org/10.1371/journal.pone.0204940

Subramanyam, M. A., Kawachi, I., Berkman, L. F., & Subramanian, S. V. (2010). Socioeconomic inequalities in childhood undernutrition in India: Analyzing trends between 1992 and 2005. *PLoS One, 5*(6), e11392. https://doi.org/10.1371/journal.pone.0011392

Subramanyam, M. A., Kawachi, I., Berkman, L. F., & Subramanian, S. V. (2011). Is economic growth associated with reduction in child undernutrition in India? *PLoS Medicine, 8*(3). https://doi.org/10.1371/journal.pmed.1000424

Thomas, R. M., Smith, G., Ferreira, F. H. G., Evans, D., Maliszewska, M., Cruz, M., . . . Over, M. (2015). *The economic impact of Ebola on sub-Saharan Africa: Updated estimates for 2015 (English) | The World Bank*. Retrieved from http://documents.worldbank.org/curated/en/541991468001792719/The-economic-impact-of-Ebola-on-sub-Saharan-Africa-updated-estimates-for-2015

Transparency International. (2020). *CPI 2019: Sub-Saharan Africa*. Retrieved from website: www.Transparency.Org; www.transparency.org/news/feature/cpi_2019_sub_saharan_africa

UN Inter-agency Group for Child Mortality Estimation. (2019). *CME info – Child Mortality Estimates*. Retrieved from https://childmortality.org/files_v22/download/UN%20IGME%20Child%20Mortality%20Report%202018.pdf

UNFPA. (2013a). *Investing in women's health – The key to Africa's economic development*. Retrieved from /press/investing-womens-health-key-africas-economic-development

UNFPA. (2013b). *Maternal health in Africa*. Retrieved from /resources/maternal-health-africa

UNICEF. (2018). *Maternal health*. UNICEF DATA. Retrieved from https://data.unicef.org/topic/gender/maternal-health-gender/

UNICEF. (2019, September 19). *Levels and trends in child mortality*. UNICEF DATA. Retrieved from https://data.unicef.org/resources/levels-and-trends-in-child-mortality/

UNICEF/WHO/The World Bank. (2018, May 14). *Joint child malnutrition estimates (JME)- 2018 edition*. UNICEF DATA. Retrieved from https://data.unicef.org/resources/levels-and-trends-in-child-malnutrition-2018/

United Nations. (n.d.). *Sustainable development goals: Sustainable development knowledge platform*. Retrieved May 10, 2020, from https://sustainabledevelopment.un.org/?menu=1300

United Nations. (2015). *United Nations millennium development goals*. United Nations. Retrieved from www.un.org/millenniumgoals/news.shtml

Vollmer, S., Harttgen, K., Subramanyam, M. A., Finlay, J., Klasen, S., & Subramanian, S. V. (2014). Association between economic growth and early childhood undernutrition: Evidence from 121 Demographic and Health Surveys from 36 low-income and middle-income countries. *The Lancet Global Health*, *2*(4), e225–e234. https://doi.org/10.1016/S2214-109X(14)70025-7

WDI Data. (2020). *World Development Indicators | DataBank*. Retrieved from https://databank.worldbank.org/source/world-development-indicators

WHO. (2011). *WHO | Investing in health for Africa: The case for strengthening systems for better health outcomes*. WHO; World Health Organization. Retrieved from www.who.int/pmnch/topics/economics/20110414_investinginhealth_africa/en/

WHO. (2014). *Global nutrition targets 2025: Policy brief* (No. WHO/NMH/NHD/14.3). World Health Organization. Retrieved from https://apps.who.int/iris/bitstream/handle/10665/149019/WHO_N?sequence=1

WHO. (2020). *WHO | SDG 3: Ensure healthy lives and promote wellbeing for all at all ages*. WHO; World Health Organization. Retrieved from www.who.int/sdg/targets/en/

WHO Regional Office for Africa. (2018). *State of health in the WHO African Region: An analysis of the status of health, health services and health systems in the context of the Sustainable Development Goals – World*. ReliefWeb. Retrieved from https://reliefweb.int/report/world/state-health-who-african-region-analysis-status-health-health-services-and-health

Witvliet, M. I., Kunst, A. E., Arah, O. A., & Stronks, K. (2013). Sick regimes and sick people: A multilevel investigation of the population health consequences of perceived national corruption. *Tropical Medicine & International Health*, *18*(10), 1240–1247. https://doi.org/10.1111/tmi.12177

World Bank. (2015). *Trends in maternal mortality: 1990 to 2015*. Estimates by WHO, UNICEF, UNFPA, World Bank Group and the United Nations Population Division. Retrieved from /publications/trends-maternal-mortality-1990–2015

World Bank. (2019). *Maternal mortality ratio (modeled estimate, per 100,000 live births) | Data*. Retrieved from https://data.worldbank.org/indicator/sh.sta.mmrt

World Bank. (2020, April 9). *COVID-19 (Coronavirus) drives sub-Saharan Africa toward first recession in 25 years* [Text/HTML]. World Bank. Retrieved from www.worldbank.org/en/news/press-release/2020/04/09/covid-19-coronavirus-drives-sub-saharan-africa-toward-first-recession-in-25-years

The World Bank. (2020). *World Bank country and lending groups – World Bank data help desk*. Retrieved from https://datahelpdesk.worldbank.org/knowledgebase/articles/906519-world-bank-country-and-lending-groups

27

HUMAN HEALTH EFFECTS OF DESERTIFICATION IN SUB-SAHARAN AFRICA

A systematic review

Manikandan AD and Vinod Joseph Kannankeril Joseph

Introduction

The term desertification was originated in connection with the Sahel region in Africa. The coinage goes back to the 1920s (Bovill, 1921; WIT, 2009) when the West African Sahara's extension into the Sahel zone was first noticed (Kertesz, 2009). Indeed, the term desertification was first used by Lavauden in 1927 to portrait severely overgrazed lands in Tunisia (Dregne, 2000) and was later popularized by Aubréville (Aubréville, 1949), a French botanist, to describe the transformation of productive agricultural land in Northern Africa into desert-like, uncultivable fallow land (Pannell & Duncan, 2020). Desertification, which is best conceived as land degradation[1] in drylands[2] (Darkoh, 2003), causes potential health problems such as malnutrition and meningococcal meningitis (Agier et al., 2013; Dukić et al., 2012; Molesworth, Cuevas, Connor, Morse, & Thomson, 2003; Prăvălie, 2016; UNICEF, 2020b) and found to be a persisting problem in Africa. The phrase 'desertification and public health' was first used by the World Ecology Report (WIT, 2009) which pointed out that 'the process of desertification presents a serious impact on the well-being and health of the populations living in the areas affected by drought and land degradation on an unprecedented global scale'. Many attempts have been made and are still venturing to explicate the link between desertification and health problems such as malnutrition, water- and food-borne diseases, other infectious diseases, respiratory diseases, and burning injuries at the global level (Menne & Bertollini, 2000; WHO, 2015, 2020; WIT, 2009).

Desertification has created a vicious circle of degradation of nature, mainly damaging the ecosystem's goods and services, decreasing the water level, soil fertility, and yields, and causing large scale poverty. It increases hidden hunger and health problems, which decreases investment in the conservation of soil and water, resulting in further desertification. Furthermore, the extent of desertification escalates when the population pressure and greed for surplus from agriculture land increase to the extent that it forces the farmers to exploit their land for survival and improve the standard of living. It degrades the ground further, and the vicious circle continues. Desertification also adds fuel to the ill health and poverty among people who depend more on drylands. The worst situation of such a case can be found in Africa (WIT, 2009). However, there is not much empirical evidence to either validate or invalidate this literature's hypothesized link. We do a systematic review of publicly available studies from the Sahel region of Africa

DOI: 10.4324/9780429287213-32

to demonstrate the human health impacts of desertification and the impacts of desertification on populations' health. The systematic review's main objective is to explore the bi-directional link between desertification and public health in the Sahel region. The systematic review will help the policymakers, academicians, and experts find gaps in the theoretical and empirical understandings of inextricable association or connection between desertification and public health. Moreover, the review will be helpful in initiating a program that addresses at least two sustainable development goals (SDGs), including one which is the eradication of hidden hunger and land degradation in drylands in the developing world and the Least-Developed Countries (LDCs), which include some Asian, Latin American, and the sub-Saharan countries.

Africa has become more vulnerable to drought, land degradation, and desertification over the past decades due to natural and human factors such as wind erosion, climate change, deforestation, overgrazing, and unsustainable cultivation. Darkoh (Darkoh, 2003) noted that 39 countries are susceptible to desertification in the African continent. However, a recent study of Prăvălie (Prăvălie, 2016) estimated that 46 out of 54 countries are vulnerable to desertification in Africa, with some already affected. The World Health Organization (WHO, 2015) noted that out of the 80 countries substantially affected by land degradation, 36 are situated in Africa. Some African countries are located in the semiarid region: Burkina Faso, Chad, Eretria, Mali, Mauritania, Niger, Nigeria, Sudan, and Senegal (Suleiman, 2017) are commonly called the Sahel region (Figure 27.1). Biophysically, the Sahel is a semiarid transition zone between the Sahara Desert and tropical Africa (O'Connor & Ford, 2014). This region stretching across Northern Africa from Senegal in the west to Sudan in the east (Hein & DE Ridder, 2006) is undergoing severe desertification (Ozer, Courel, & Goudie, 2006), which remains a significant threat to well-being (Ipbes & Willemen, 2018; Millennium Ecosystem Assessment, 2005) and public health (Olagunju, 2015). Besides, the growing desertification, which is a significant concern (IPCC, 2020), malnutrition (UNICEF, 2019, 2020a; UNSCN, 2010; Wuehler, Hess, & Brown, 2011) and infectious diseases (Darkoh, 1996, 2003; OCHA, 2014; UNICEF, 2019, 2020a; UNSCN, 2010; Wuehler et al., 2011) also appear to be burning health issues in the Sahel. The prime reason for this could be a hypothetical link between the desertification and health of populations. This hypothesized link works though complex pathways, e.g. desertification causes: i) higher threats of malnutrition from reduced food and water supplies; ii) more water- and food-borne diseases that result from poor hygiene and a lack of clean water; iii) respiratory diseases caused by atmospheric dust from wind erosion and other air pollutants; and iv) the spread of infectious diseases as populations migrate (WHO, 2020). As Sacande rightly said, 'For people living in those drylands largely in the developing world, the effects of desertification are hunger, malnutrition and poverty' (Martin, 2020). That is, the loss of resource productivity affects the health of populations under desertification (Roboff, 1977). All these points indicate that the crisis in soil health is one of the major root causes of malnutrition and subsequent social problems in Africa (Karlen & Rice, 2015; Sanchez & Swaminathan, 2005).

Many studies are available on the topics such as 'desertification' and 'public health' regarding the Sahel belt (Cairns et al., 2012; Gonzalez, 2001; Gorse et al., 1987; Hein & DE Ridder, 2006; L. Hein et al., 2011; Houndekon, De Groote, & Lomer, 2006; Prince, Wessels, Tucker, & Nicholson, 2007; Thomson, Jeanne, & Djingarey, 2009). However, the profound analysis of desertification and public health in the Sahel has not been receiving the deserved attention among the policymakers, experts, and academicians. There is little but growing literature in this field (Abu Ahmed, 1990; Olagunju, 2015). Therefore, a systematic review of publicly available data, evidence, and studies on the human health impacts of desertification and the desertification impacts of the health of populations from the Sahel assumes significance. The development of some necessary research fields, especially the desertification-related effects on human health,

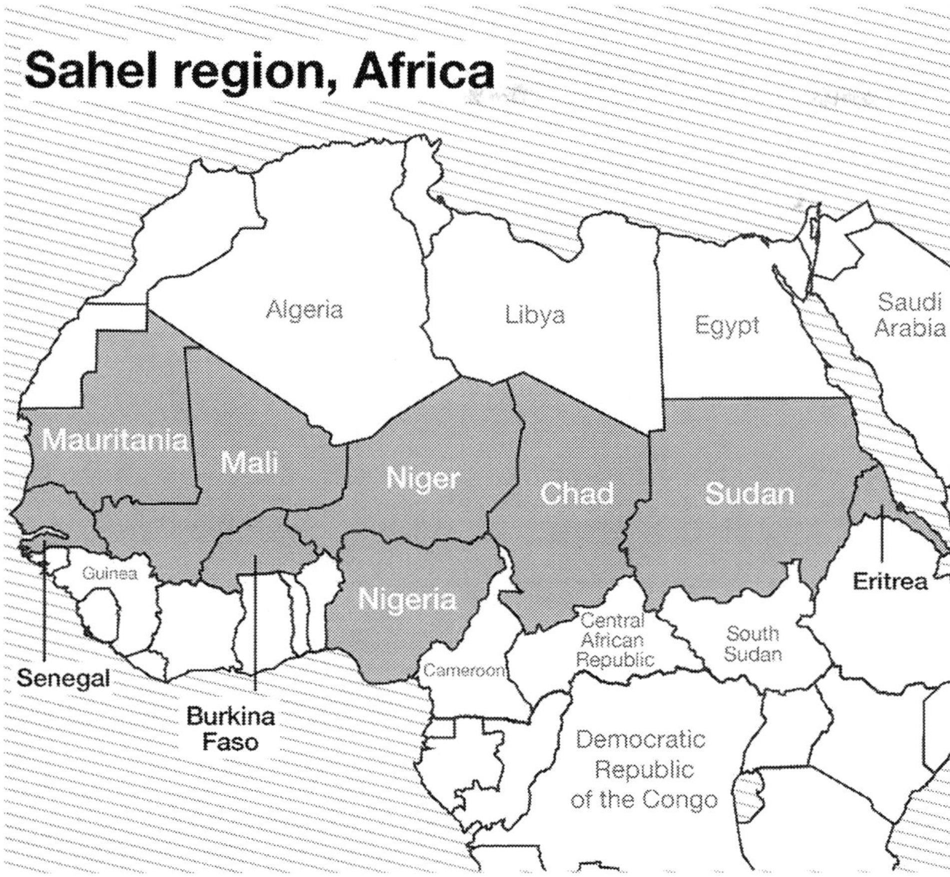

Figure 27.1 Sahel region in Africa,

Source: (Suleiman, 2017)

is the need of the hour (Ozer et al., 2006). The study will help facilitate a broader understanding of the bi-directional (hypothesized) link between these two important subjects. Therefore, the review will be helpful in eradicating some of the gravest developmental challenges of our time, such as hidden hunger, poverty, water- and food-borne diseases, other infectious diseases, and ecosystem degradation in drylands (Arid, Semiarid, and Dry sub-humid areas) in the sub-Saharan countries and other LDCs.

Conceptual framework

The review of publicly available studies on the desertification and health of populations from the Sahel showed that the association of desertification, ill health, and poverty is explicit. Poverty as a common denominator between desertification and ill health explains a chain of relationship. The increasing poverty among people who inhabit severely desertified areas leads to significant health issues. Agriculture is the backbone of livelihood in the Sahel belt. When a poor farmer becomes diseased, the entire household can become trapped in the downward spiral of lost income and high healthcare costs (OECD & WHO, 2003). Desertification-driven infectious diseases are severe problems in the Sahel. Thus, the most dangerous consequence of desertification is a further stress on health-poverty. It seems that people who live in severely desertified areas suffer from an environmental health-poverty trap. Accordingly, the conceptual framework presented here gives food for thought. It opens perspectives for future research. The social scientists and health experts would undertake using a methodology that considers environmental health, environmental poverty, the human health-poverty trap, and disease ecology in a multi-disciplinary and interdisciplinary perspective.

Figure 27.2 portrays that desertification increases the risks of poverty and ill health. Poverty in response also increases the chances of desertification and ill health further. And ill health increases the likelihood of poverty, which decreases investment in soil and water conservation, resulting in further desertification. The relation between these credentials is correlative, and each effects changes on the other. We will produce a simple example for validating our logic of this conceptual framework. For instance, the dust intensification, caused by human-induced desertification, affects populations' health in the Sahel (Moulin & Chiapello, 2006). Poor health[3] increases the likelihood of becoming poor. Poverty, in effect, causes further desertification because, as the livelihood pressure increases, poor farmers will be forced to rely more on their low-quality land[4] to survive. It degrades the land further and – the 'vicious circle continues' (Darkoh, 1996). This assumption suggests that both the health and poverty statuses cannot be uplifted by a single-handed policy intervention either in the healthcare system or through poverty alleviation strategies; rather it is advisable that at first, we should take strict actions for the improvement of the land resource which we call 'desertification control' measures (Berthe, 1997). The Great Green Wall initiative in the Sahel belt is a significant move in this direction (Gadzama, 2017).

Poor people of the Sahel belt are suffering from this vicious circle of action in which desertification causes diseases. The diseases intensify poverty[5] which further leads to more desertification and diseases. We should address all these issues simultaneously by introducing a program that addresses desertification, infectious disease, and poverty on a single platform. Figure 27.2 displays three types of circles: 1) desertification, ill health, and poverty; 2) ill health, poverty, and desertification 3) poverty, desertification, and ill health. The paper's complete analysis stands on this inextricable 'vicious circle' of desertification, ill health, and poverty. The impacts of the 'vicious circle' on people who inhabit desertified areas depend on many factors such as the degree of dependence on land-based livelihood, the extent and severity of desertification, topography, gender, age, education, income, and access to public services including healthcare, social security programme, etc. and climate conditions. The impacts of desertification on public health have been found to be disproportionate for any reason. For example, the poorest of poor, women, children, aged persons, and other vulnerable groups who are least accounted for in usual statistics are the first to suffer from the inextricable link between the desertification, diseases, and poverty.

Methods

An initial scoping literature search was done to identify the subject headings and relevant keywords, following which a final search strategy was developed. A systematic literature search in the PubMed, Medline, Cochrane Library, Mendeley, JSTOR, United Nations Convention to Combat Desertification (UNCCD), United Nations Office for the Coordination of Humanitarian Affairs (OCHA), United Nations Children's Fund (UNICEF), and United Nations Environment Program (UNEP) databases was conducted using relevant keywords. A manual search for additional studies was also performed using Google Scholar and the World Health

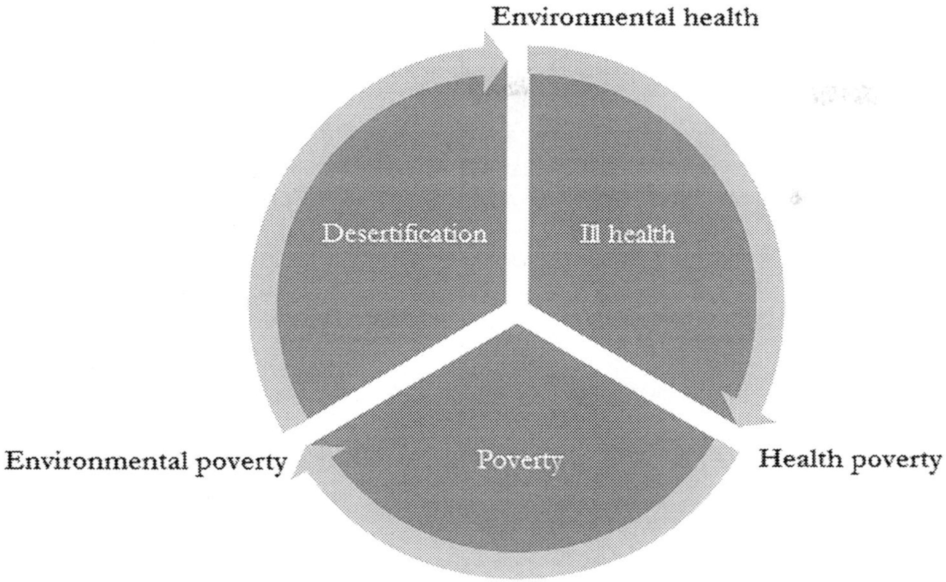

Figure 27.2 A vicious circle of desertification, poor health, and poverty.

Organization (WHO) websites. To strengthen the selected studies' quality, both the reviewers were independently screened using the inclusion and exclusion criteria. Any disagreements over article inclusion and exclusion were resolved through a presentation and thorough, in-depth discussion by both the reviewers.

Identification of studies which discuss desertification and public health in the Sahel was a major challenge because the association between desertification and public health is too elusive to find enough empirical support in the literature, based both on quantitative studies and qualitative case studies. But we decided to go ahead with the selection of publicly available studies from the Sahel. We used 'Desertification and Public Health in the Sahel' as our primary keyword in the paper. Surprisingly, we received only a few articles. To sidestep such difficulty in obtaining more studies, we re-phrased the keywords in the following manner: 'Desertification in the Sahel', 'Environmental health in Sahel', 'Public Health in the Sahel', 'Climate change and health in Sahel', and 'Health in the Sahel'. And we found many studies on these subjects. However, the number of desertification-related studies that discussed the effect of desertification on health in the Sahel was minimal. Likewise, public health studies which addressed the impact of health problems on desertification in the Sahel region were also very few to be found. This happened to be a significant challenge not only for the paper but also for the literature. However, despite all these challenges, we received nine papers that discussed the relationship between the desertification and health of the population in the Sahel. The keywords used were 'Desertification Other infectious diseases Sahel', 'Desertification Water- and food-borne diseases Sahel', 'Desertification Respiratory diseases Sahel', 'Desertification Health Sahel', 'Desertification Psychological or Mental problems Sahel', and 'Desertification Malnutrition Sahel'.

All the studies conducted on or before 30/06/2020 were considered for systematic literature search. Additional searches in Google Scholar, the WHO website, and other potential sources were also conducted for more literature or additional data for studies already selected. All those literatures obtained with the first keyword that met search criteria were directly selected for the study. All those literatures collected with the second keyword were filtered with two additional questions: i) whether they focused on the health impacts of desertification or not, and ii) whether they focussed on the desertification impacts of the health of populations or not. The literature which responded positively were included, and other studies were excluded. All the literature obtained using the third and fourth keywords were further filtered: those which dealt with desertification were included, and the rest were excluded. The reference lists of these identified articles were also critically reviewed in an attempt to identify more literature. Reference lists of initially selected studies were further hand-searched. Titles and abstracts were screened, and potentially relevant articles acquired.

Studies on non-human subjects and those that were replies, case reports, opinions, or editorials were excluded from the review. Articles only in the English language and published in peer-reviewed journals were selected. The literature search fetched a total of 2,155 studies. The studies were identified from the following databases: PubMed (658), Mendeley (789), JSTOR (630), Cochrane Library (13), United Nations UNCCD (15), OCHA (9), UNICEF (24), and UNEP (17). Additionally, 316 studies were identified from Google Scholar, the WHO, and manual Google searches. A total of 148 records remained after reviewing titles and removing duplicates. Therefore, the application of the selection criteria excluded 139 studies. A total of 9 studies were finally retained for the review (Figure 27.3).

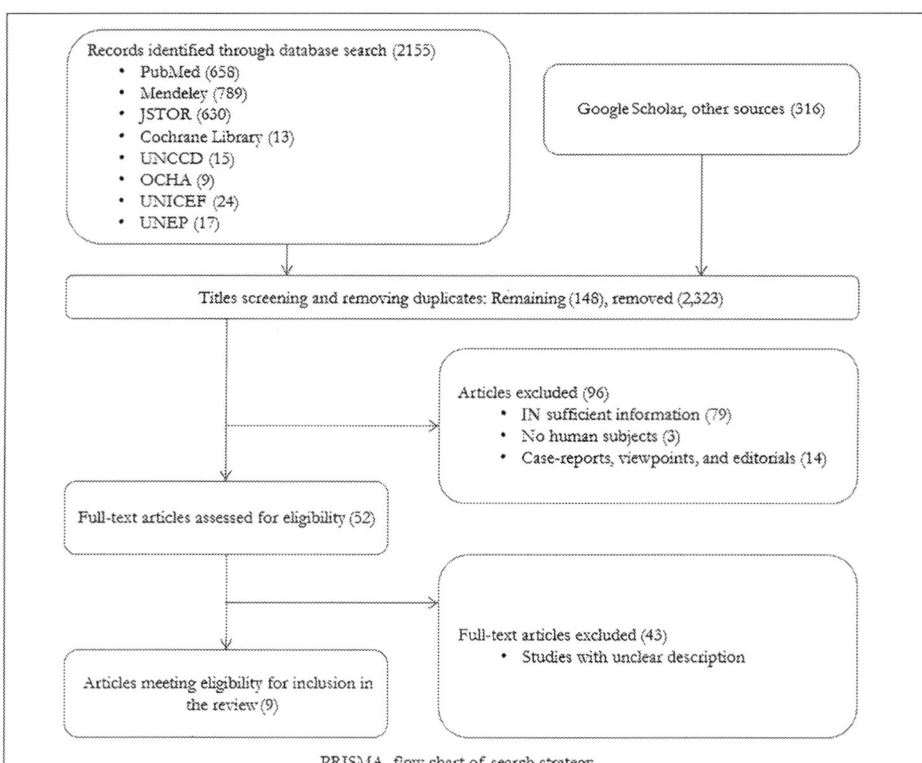

Figure 27.3 Strategy for a systematic review of desertification and public health in the Sahel region.

The specific objectives of the systematic review are as follows: 1) to list out publicly available studies on the desertification and public health in the Sahel region; 2) to review the methodologies of available studies on the desertification and public health in the Sahel region; 3) to analyze the results and findings of available studies on the desertification and public health in the Sahel region; and 4) to find the gaps and scope for future research.

Results

Desertification has not only social, economic, demographic, technical, and political dimensions (De Troyer, 1986), but also has a health implication. The results of various studies (Table 27.1) from the Sahel have shown that desertification, poverty, food insecurity, malnutrition, infectious diseases including water-borne diseases, and psychological problems are inextricably linked with each other through complex pathways. Therefore, it is challenging to segregate the effects of desertification from one another. A profound analysis of cause-and-effect mechanisms of desertification and public health is not available.

Desertification and malnutrition

Among other causes, desertification is one of the most important reasons for malnutrition in the Sahel. It is stated that the loss of resource productivity affects the health of populations under

Table 27.1 Desertification and Public Health in the Sahel Region

Studies	*Country/Region*	*Main focus of the study*	*Method of the study*
Farron Vogel Roboff, 1977	Sahel, Africa	Health impacts of desertification on nomadic peoples	Field-based descriptive study
Miriam K. Were, 1989	Ethiopia, Sahel[6]	Health impacts of ecological upheavals, including desertification	Descriptive
S.L. Laki, 1994	Sudan, Sahel	Desertification and its causes, effects, and policy options in Sudan	Descriptive
Hans Bruyninckx, 2004	Burkina Faso, Sahel	The Convention to Combat Desertification and the Role of Innovative Policy-Making Discourses	Case study
Cyril Moulin and Isabelle Chiapello, 2006	Sahel, Africa	Dust intensification caused by human-made desertification	Empirical study using long-term African dust data sets
Pierre Ozer, Marie-Francoise Courel, and Andrew S. Goudie, 2006	Sahel, Africa	Significance of international years of deserts, desertification, and dust.	Descriptive

(*Continued*)

Table 27.1 (Continued)

Studies	*Country/Region*	*Main focus of the study*	*Method of the study*
Temidayo Ebenezer Olagunju, 2015	Nigeria, Sahel	Drought and desertification in Nigeria. Its implications on health and solutions	Landscape metrics approach
Laura Swift and Jessica Saulle, 2015	Sahel, Africa	Food crises in the Sahel	Descriptive using the household economy approach (HEA)
Mahamane Mansour, Volker Hochschild, Alfred Schultz, and Jude NkuoKuma, 2016	Sahel, Africa	Investigate and monitor desertification process	Descriptive
Salisu Nura, F.M. Mairami and H.E. Negbenebor, 2018	Nigeria, Sahel	Food shortage and malnutrition and its solution using mutation breeding	Extensive review of mutation breeding
Mady Cissoko, Issaka Sagara, Moussa H. Sankaré, Sokhna Dieng, Abdoulaye Guindo, Zoumana Doumbia, Balam Allasseini, Diahara Traore, Seydou Fomba, Marc Karim Bendiane, Jordi Landier, Nadine Dessay and Jean Gaudart, 2020	Mali, Sahel	Geo Epidemiology of Malaria	Meteorological and environmental variables were synthesized using principal component analysis and multiple correspondence analysis; the relationship between malaria incidence and synthetic indicators was determined using a multivariate general additive model; hotspots were detected by SaTScan.

desertification (Roboff, 1977). Agriculture is the economic backbone of people in sub-Saharan Africa (Darkoh, 1996). Therefore, the deterioration of soil fertility and topsoil removal by wind caused by desertification has devastating impacts on people's health and nutritional status in those areas. According to M.S. Swaminathan "Micronutrient deficiency in the soil results in micronutrient malnutrition in people, and the crops grown in such soils tend to be deficient in the nutrients needed to fight hidden hunger" (FAO, 2015a). Were (Were, 1989) observed that desertification or land degradation causes micronutrient-deficiency-related health problems, including anaemia. Those people living in degraded lands may have no access to fresh vegetables, fruits, or legumes and often fall victim to micronutrient-related health issues. Abahussain (Abahussain, Abdu, Al-Zubari, El-Deen, & Abdul-Raheem, 2002) noted that reducing biodiversity affects the food and health of local people who rely on a large number of different animal and vegetable species. Desertification can have disastrous implications on women and children's health and well-being in the Niger Delta region of Nigeria (Etuonovbe, 2009). For example, women and children responsible for fetching water and collecting firewood for households are near the worst effects of drought and desertification (UNECA, 2007).

Moreover, women in rural areas derive micronutrients like iron and vitamins like B12 from non-haem sources such as grains, cereals, vegetables, pulses, beans, and lentils. Lack of vegetables in diets will cause protein-energy malnutrition (PEM). The high prevalence of malnutrition among women and children under five years of age in the Sahel, therefore, substantiates that (OCHA, 2014; USAID, 2017) desertification has an iconic impact on people's health status. Swift and Saulle (Swift & Saulle, 2015) clearly said that desertification, food crises, and malnutrition are commonly associated with the Sahel.

In Nigeria, the effect of desertification is devastating, with severe implications on food production (Thelma, 2015), which affects food affordability and food utilization adversely. Food insecurity and malnutrition are the most visible outcomes. Mansour (Mahamane, Hochschild, Alfred, & Jude, 2016) said that desertification aggravates poverty; decreases land productivity; increases the aridity of the climate; increases food insecurity; and further induces diseases and malnutrition in Niger. Thus, to avoid problems associated with desertification, such as decreased soil fertility, an increased risk of malnutrition and starvation in Nigeria, mutation breeding has been recommended by Salisu (Salisu, Mukhtar Mairami, & Negbenebor, 2018). Bruyninckx (Bruyninckx, 2004) noticed that the 'vicious circle' of desertification and impoverishment increased the stress on overall food security, resulting in malnutrition and poor health in Burkina Faso.

Desertification, infections, and other diseases

Desertification, infectious diseases and other diseases are found to be interconnected in studies conducted in the Sahel region. It is assumed that those living in drylands are more affected by water-borne diseases since land degradation leads to water scarcity, which causes poor-hygiene-related diseases such as trachoma and other eye infections (Were, 1989). Furthermore, desertification leads to loss of biological diversity, contributing to diseases (Olagunju, 2015). The loss of vegetation cover is a major phenomenon in the desertified areas that stimulates diseases like yellow fever, scrub typhus, malaria, and other mosquito- or fly-borne infections and diseases (Barrow, 1991). Cissoko (Cissoko et al., 2020) noticed that increasing desertification, accompanied by lower rainfall, higher temperature, and lighter vegetation, may partly explain malaria's lower risks in Mali.

Furthermore, human-induced desertification increasing the dust emission in the Sahel has profound health implications (Moulin & Chiapello, 2006). The primary source of atmospheric mineral dust is the Sahara and its desertified land, which produce about half of the yearly global mineral dust production, affecting people's health in Africa, Europe, and America (Ozer et al., 2006). The frequency of dust storms increased by desertification reduces air quality and causes respiratory and lung diseases in the Sahel.

Desertification and psychological problems

Desertification is regarded as a part of ecological degradation. The relationship between psychological conditions or mental health and ecological degradation is described in the literature. Loss of ecology by degradation processes and natural and human-made factors causes loss of a 'sense of place' or identity, leading to depression and emotional stress among people (Myers et al., 2013; Speldewinde, Cook, Davies, & Weinstein, 2009). Similarly, desertification causes psychological problems in the Sahel (Laki, 1994). Our findings also have substantial implications on the behavioural aspects of people living in desertified lands.

A review of publicly available studies conducted so far has revealed complex and multiple ways of linking desertification and populations' health in the Sahel. Desertification affects soils, water, air, vegetation cover, biodiversity, climate, food quality, habitation, mental health, animal health, and income. Thus, desertification increases soil-borne diseases, water-borne diseases, yellow fever and scrub typhus through diminished vegetation cover, respiratory and lung diseases, vector-transmitted human disease, malaria and other infectious diseases, food-borne diseases, infections through migration, mental stress, tension and headache, and nutrient deficiency problems including anaemia among the Sahelian people (Mandal, 2011; Menne & Bertollini, 2000; ole-MoiYoi, 2013; Osterwalder, 2011). Health problems of the Sahelian people, especially desertification-related health problems of women and children under five years of age, must be seen from a broader perspective. Many studies have to be undertaken for exploring the complex and multi-dimensional relationship between the desertification and health of populations (see Figure 27.4).

Conclusion

Among the natural material resources, the greatest, unquestionably, is the land (Schumacher, 1973). The land, as one of the most commonly accessed resources, mainly faces three challenges: aridity, recurrent drought, and desertification (Tolba, Saab, & Environment, 2008). Ever since land-human relation became worse, the problem of desertification and its catastrophic consequences on agronomic productivity, sustainability, and well-being began. Studies suggest that the Sahel region's land is highly prone to desertification, which poses a severe threat to the lands' productivity. Therefore, 'the health of the land', which is defined as the 'capacity of the land for self-renewal' (Leopold, 1949), is inherently connected with both the public health and sustainability of the ecosystem, and thus is to be maintained. Especially, healthy soil is crucial for both food security and nutrition (FAO, 2015b). The purpose of the paper is not to exaggerate the fact that desertification has severe implications on human health, but to highlight what literature says on health impacts of desertification in the Sahel, a region in which this topic is most relevant but least explored.

We presented a new way of assembling and analyzing the available information on the desertification and health of populations in the Sahel to reveal an inextricable bi-directional link

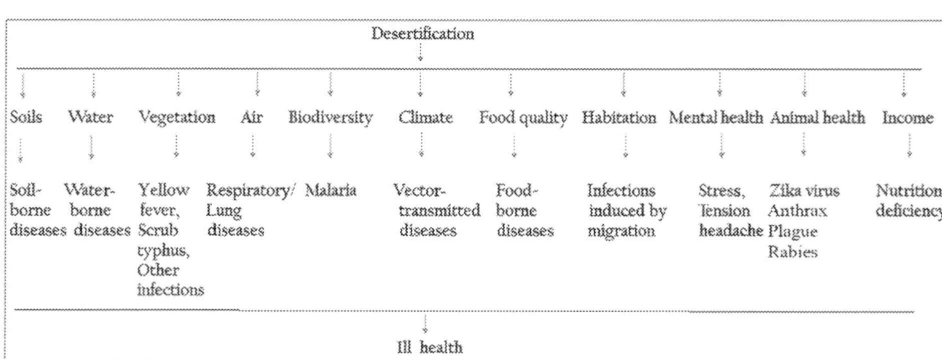

Figure 27.4 Desertification raises the risks of public health in complex and multiple ways.

between these two topics. We found that there is an association between the desertification and health of populations in the Sahel. However, more empirical studies have to be undertaken to validate this because there are considerable literature gaps. No severe systematic attempt has been made to validate or invalidate the relationship between the desertification and health of populations. Studies which link the ill health impacts on desertification are not available. Thus, more empirical and theoretical studies exploring the vicious circle of desertification and ill health are most welcome, although it is very challenging. It was understood that the association of desertification and impoverishment keeps well-being and sustainability at risk. Women, children, and other vulnerable groups are the first to suffer from this devastating association in the Sahel. We hope this paper will be the inspiration to develop some new research fields, especially desertification as related to health poverty, mental well-being, and behavioural aspects in people living in drylands using quantitative studies or qualitative case studies based on an interdisciplinary approach. Our results are certainly not conclusive: more studies have to be done to prove or disprove a hypothetical bi-directional link between desertification and public health. The discovery of such a relationship and its policy-based solutions will play a vital role in ensuring the Sahel region's well-being and sustainability.

Desertification, climate change, dust intensification, ill health, and poverty are inextricably associated with each other and within the Sahel region, each triggering and reinforcing the other. Socially weaker sections are the first to suffer from this. We cannot resolve these problems with one-directional intervention like a single medical treatment. Therefore, a confluence of multi-pronged strategy is needed: afforestation, re-distribution of fertile or productive lands, improving access to healthcare, provision of improved sanitation and drinking water facilities, discouraging the use of unclean energy (firewood, kerosene, and dung) by improving access to solar energy, and promotion of soil and water conservation through both modern and indigenous techniques.

Notes

1 There is no universally accepted definition of the term land degradation (Hoeschele, 1998). There are numerous terms and definitions for the land degradation that are a source of misunderstanding, misinterpretation, and confusion (Eswaran, Lai, & Reich, 2001). We used the Food and Agriculture Organization's (FAO) definition in our study (Ponce-Hernandez, 2004). It has defined land degradation as 'the set of processes that lowers the current and potential capability of the land to produce (quantitatively or qualitatively) goods and services'. In the study, desertification means that land degradation in arid, semiarid, and dry sub-humid areas results from various factors, including natural and human factors.
2 The arid, semiarid, and dry sub-humid areas are commonly known as drylands.
3 The terms poor health and ill health are used interchangeably in the paper.
4 Case study in the Darfur region of Sudan (Fuller, 1987) and in Ghana (Owusu, Cervone, & Luzzadder-Beach, 2013) are substantiated this argument.
5 For more details, see (Bonds, Keenan, Rohani, & Sachs, 2010).
6 The extreme north of Ethiopia is regarded as a part of the Sahel region.

References

Abahussain, A. A., Abdu, A. S., Al-Zubari, W. K., El-Deen, N. A., & Abdul-Raheem, M. (2002). Desertification in the Arab Region: Analysis of current status and trends. *Journal of Arid Environments*, *51*(4), 521–545. https://doi.org/https://doi.org/10.1006/jare.2002.0975

Abu Ahmed, H. (1990). Effects of drought and desertification on health and social life in the Sudan. *World Health Forum*, *11*(4), 424.

Agier, L., Deroubaix, A., Martiny, N., Yaka, P., Djibo, A., & Broutin, H. (2013). Seasonality of meningitis in Africa and climate forcing: Aerosols stand out. *Journal of the Royal Society Interface*, *10*(79), 20120814. https://doi.org/10.1098/rsif.2012.0814

Aubréville, A. (1949). *Climats: forêts et désertification de l'Afrique tropicale.* Société d'éditions géographiques, maritimes et coloniales. Retrieved from https://books.google.co.in/books?id=4Yg-PQAACAAJ

Barrow, C. J. (1991). *Land degradation: Development and breakdown of terrestrial environments.* Cambridge: Cambridge University Press.

Berthe, Y. (1997). *The role of forestry in combating desertification.* Antalya, Turkey: World Forestry Congress.

Bonds, M. H., Keenan, D. C., Rohani, P., & Sachs, J. D. (2010). Poverty trap formed by the ecology of infectious diseases. *Proceedings of the Royal Society B: Biological Sciences, 277*(1685), 1185–1192. doi:10.1098/rspb.2009.1778

Bovill, E. W. (1921). The encroachment of the Sahara on the Sudan (concluded). *Journal of the Royal African Society, 20*(80), 259–269. Retrieved from www.jstor.org/stable/715561

Bruyninckx, H. (2004). The convention to combat desertification and the role of innovative policy-making discourses: The case of Burkina Faso. *Global Environmental Politics, 4*, 107–127. https://doi.org/10.1162/1526380041748010

Cairns, M., Roca-Feltrer, A., Garske, T., Wilson, A. L., Diallo, D., Milligan, P. J., . . . Greenwood, B. M. (2012). Estimating the potential public health impact of seasonal malaria chemoprevention in African children. *Nature Communications, 3*, 881. https://doi.org/10.1038/ncomms1879

Cissoko, M., Sagara, I., Sankaré, M. H., Dieng, S., Guindo, A., Doumbia, Z., . . . Gaudart, J. (2020). Geo-epidemiology of malaria at the health area level, Dire Health District, Mali, 2013–2017. *International Journal of Environmental Research and Public Health, 17*(11), 3982. https://doi.org/10.3390/ijerph17113982

Darkoh, M. (1996). The human dimension of desertification in the drylands of Africa. *Journal of Social Development in Africa, 11*, 89–106.

Darkoh, M. (2003). Desertification in the drylands: A review of the African situation. *Annals of Arid Zone, 42*(3–4), 289–307.

De Troyer, C. (1986). Desertification control in the Sudanian and Sahelian zones of West Africa– Better management of the renewable resource base. *Forest Ecology and Management, 16*(1), 233–241. https://doi.org/https://doi.org/10.1016/0378-1127(86)90023-X

Dregne, H. E. (2000). Desertification: Problems and challenges. *Annals of Arid Zone, 39*, 363–371.

Dukić, V., Hayden, M., Forgor, A. A., Hopson, T., Akweongo, P., Hodgson, A., . . . Pandya, R. (2012). The role of weather in Meningitis outbreaks in Navrongo, Ghana: A generalized additive modeling approach. *Journal of Agricultural, Biological, and Environmental Statistics, 17*(3), 442–460. https://doi.org/10.1007/s13253-012-0095-9

Eswaran, H., Lai, R., & Reich, P. (2001). Land degradation: An overview: Responses to land degradation. *Proceedings of the 2nd International Conference on Land Degradation and Desertification*, Khon Kaen, Thailand (pp. 20–35).

Etuonovbe, A. K. (2009). *The devastating effects of environmental degradation – A case study of the Niger Delta Region of Nigeria.* Retrieved from https://www.fig.net/resources/proceedings/fig_proceedings/fig2009/papers/ts01d/ts01d_etuonovbe_3386.pdf

FAO. (2015a). *FAO urged to address land degradation, malnutrition, needs of family farms.* Retrieved on July 28, 2020, from www.fao.org/europe/news/detail-news/en/c/330659/

FAO. (2015b). *Healthy soils are the basis for healthy food production.* Retrieved on May 25, 2020, from www.fao.org/soils-2015/news/news-detail/en/c/277682/

Fuller, T. D. (1987). Resettlement as a desertification control measure: A case study in Darfur Region, Sudan – Part II: Recommendations. *Agricultural Administration and Extension, 26*(1), 39–55. https://doi.org/https://doi.org/10.1016/0269-7475(87)90026-2

Gadzama, N. (2017). Attenuation of the effects of desertification through sustainable development of Great Green Wall in the Sahel of Africa. *World Journal of Science, Technology and Sustainable Development, 14.* https://doi.org/10.1108/WJSTSD-02-2016-0021

Gonzalez, P. (2001). Desertification and a shift of forest species in the West African Sahel. *Climate Research, 17*(2), 217–228. https://doi.org/10.3354/cr017217

Gorse, E. J., & Steeds, R. D. (1987). *Desertification in the Sahelian and Sudanian zones in West Africa.* World Bank Technical Paper No. WTP 61. World Bank Group. Retrieved from http://documents.worldbank.org/curated/en/334511468768330211/Desertification-in-the-Sahelian-and-Sudanian-zones-in-West-Africa

Hein, L., & DE Ridder, N. (2006). Desertification in the Sahel: A reinterpretation. *Global Change Biology, 12*, 751–758. https://doi.org/10.1111/j.1365-2486.2006.01135.x

Hein, L., Ridder, N. d., Hiernaux, P., Leemans, R., Wit, A. d., & Schaepman, M. (2011). Desertification in the Sahel: Towards better accounting for ecosystem dynamics in the interpretation of remote sensing images. *Journal of Arid Environments*, *75*(11), 1164–1172. https://doi.org/10.1016/j.jaridenv.2011.05.002

Hoeschele, W. (1998). *Land degradation, state power, and peasant livelihood in Attappadi (Kerala), India*. State College, PA: Pennsylvania State University.

Houndekon, V. A., De Groote, H., & Lomer, C. (2006). Health costs and externalities of pesticide use in the Sahel. *Outlook on Agriculture*, *35*, 25–31. https://doi.org/10.5367/000000006776207627

Ipbes, & Willemen, L. (2018). *Summary for policymakers of the assessment report on land degradation and restoration of the Intergovernmental Science-Policy Platform on Biodiversity and Ecosystem Services*. Bonn, Germany: University of Twenty, Intergovernmental Science-Policy Platform on Biodiversity and Ecosystem Services.

IPCC. (2020). *Climate change and land: An IPCC special report on climate change, desertification, land degradation, sustainable land management, food security, and greenhouse gas fluxes in terrestrial ecosystems*. Intergovernmental Panel on Climate Change (IPCC). Retrieved from https://www.ipcc.ch/srccl/download/

Karlen, D., & Rice, C. (2015). Soil degradation: Will humankind ever learn? *Sustainability*, 7, 12490–12501. https://doi.org/10.3390/su70912490

Kertesz, A. (2009). The global problem of land degradation and desertification. *Hungarian Geographical Bullet*, *58*, 19–31.

Laki, S. L. (1994). Desertification in the Sudan: Causes, effects and policy options. *International Journal of Sustainable Development & World Ecology*, *1*(3), 198–205. https://doi.org/10.1080/13504509409469874

Leopold, A. (1949). *A Sand County almanac, and Sketches here and there*. New York: Oxford University Press. Retrieved from https://search.library.wisc.edu/catalog/9910065222502121

Mahamane, M., Hochschild, V., Alfred, S., & Jude, N. (2016). Fragmentation rate and landscape structure of the Tillabry landscape (Sahel region) with reference to desertification. *Journal of Geography and Regional Planning*, *9*, 77–86. https://doi.org/10.5897/JGRP2015.0538

Mandal, F. (2011). The changing ecology of infectious diseases in human. *World Environment*, *1*, 14–19. https://doi.org/10.5923/j.env.20110101.03

Martin, H. B. (2020). *How do we stop global desertification?* Retrieved from www.upm.com/articles/responsibility/20/how-do-we-stop-global-desertification/

Menne, B., & Bertollini, R. (2000). The health impacts of desertification and drought. *Down to Earth*. Retrieved from www.uncclearn.org/sites/default/files/inventory/who38.pdf

Millennium Ecosystem Assessment. (2005). *Ecosystems and human well-being: Desertification synthesis*. World Resources Institute. Retrieved from www.millenniumassessment.org/documents/document.355.aspx.pdf

Molesworth, A. M., Cuevas, L. E., Connor, S. J., Morse, A. P., & Thomson, M. C. (2003). Environmental risk and meningitis epidemics in Africa. *Emerging Infectious Diseases*, *9*(10), 1287–1293. https://doi.org/10.3201/eid0910.030182

Moulin, C., & Chiapello, I. (2006). Impact of human-induced desertification on the intensification of Sahel dust emission and export over the last decades. *Geophysical Research Letters, American Geophysical Union*, *33*(18). https://doi.org/10.1029/2006gl025923

Myers, S., Gaffikin, L., Golden, C., Ostfeld, R., Redford, K., Ricketts, T., . . . Osofsky, S. (2013). Human health impacts of ecosystem alteration. *Proceedings of the National Academy of Sciences of the United States of America*, *110*. https://doi.org/10.1073/pnas.1218656110

OCHA. (2014). *Humanitarian needs overview Sahel region*. United Nations Office for the Coordination of Humanitarian Affairs. Retrieved from https://reliefweb.int/sites/reliefweb.int/files/resources/2021%20Sahel%20Crisis%20HNRO%20EN.pdf

O'Connor, D., & Ford, J. (2014). Increasing the effectiveness of the "Great Green Wall" as an adaptation to the effects of climate change and desertification in the Sahel. *Sustainability*, *6*, 7142. https://doi.org/10.3390/su6107142

OECD, & WHO. (2003). *Poverty and health*. Organisation for Economic Cooperation and Development and World Health Organization. https://doi.org/10.1787/9789264100206-en

Olagunju, T. (2015). Drought, desertification and the Nigerian environment: A review. *Journal of Ecology and the Natural Environment*, 7, 196–209. https://doi.org/10.5897/JENE2015.0523

ole-MoiYoi, O. K. (2013). *Short- and long-term effects of drought on human health*. United Nations Office for Disaster Risk Reduction. Retrieved from www.preventionweb.net/english/hyogo/gar/2013/en/bgdocs/ole-MoiYoi,%202012.pdf

Osterwalder, K. (2011). *Migration and desertification*. United Nations Convention to Combat Desertification. Retrieved from http://catalogue.unccd.int/22_loose_leaf_Desertification_migration.pdf

Owusu, A., Cervone, G., & Luzzadder-Beach, S. (2013). Analysis of desertification in the Upper East Region (UER) of Ghana using remote sensing, field study, and local knowledge. *Cartographica: The International Journal for Geographic Information and Geovisualization, 48*, 22–37. https://doi.org/10.1353/car.2013.0009

Ozer, P., Courel, M.-F., & Goudie, A. S. (2006). International year of deserts, desertification and dust [Letter to the editor]. *Africa Health, 28*(4), 3. https://orbi.uliege.be/handle/2268/15856

Pannell, M., & Duncan, L. (2020). Desertification. Retrieved from *Encyclopedia.com*.

Ponce-Hernandez, R. (2004). *Land degradation assessment (Assessing carbon stocks and modelling win – win scenarios of carbon sequestration through land-use changes)*. Rome: Food and Agriculture Organisation.

Prăvălie, R. (2016). Drylands extent and environmental issues. A global approach. *Earth-Science Reviews, 161*. https://doi.org/10.1016/j.earscirev.2016.08.003

Prince, S., Wessels, K., Tucker, C., & Nicholson, S. (2007). Desertification in the Sahel: A reinterpretation of a reinterpretation. *Global Change Biology, 13*, 1308–1313. https://doi.org/10.1111/j.1365-2486.2007.01356.x

Roboff, F. V. (1977). The moving target: Health status of nomadic peoples. *Economic Geography, 53*(4), 421–428. https://doi.org/10.2307/142985

Salisu, N., Mukhtar Mairami, F., & Negbenebor, H. (2018). Mutation breeding as panacea for food shortage and malnutrition in Nigeria's Sahel (a review). *Bayero Journal of Pure and Applied Sciences, 10*, 133. https://doi.org/10.4314/bajopas.v10i1.27S

Sanchez, P., & Swaminathan, M. (2005). Cutting world hunger in half. *Science (New York, N.Y.), 307*, 357–359. https://doi.org/10.1126/science.1109057

Schumacher, E. F. (1973). *Small is beautiful; economics as if people mattered*. New York: Harper Collins.

Speldewinde, P. C., Cook, A., Davies, P., & Weinstein, P. (2009). A relationship between environmental degradation and mental health in rural Western Australia. *Health & Place, 15*(3), 880–887. https://doi.org/https://doi.org/10.1016/j.healthplace.2009.02.011

Suleiman, M. D. (2017). *Sahel region, Africa*. Retrieved from https://theconversation.com/sahel-region-africa-72569

Swift, L., & Saulle, J. (2015). Dealing with food crises in the Sahel. In M. Lakitsch, S. Wolter, & J. Pokoo (Eds.), *Humanitarian assistance in West Africa and beyond*. Austrian Study Centre for Peace and Conflict Resolution. Austria: Stadtschlaining.

Thelma, M. N. (2015). Desertification in northern Nigeria: Causes and implications for national food security. *Journal of Social Sciences and Humanities, 3*(2), 22–31.

Thomson, M., Jeanne, I., & Djingarey, M. (2009). Dust and epidemic meningitis in the Sahel: A public health and operational research perspective. *IOP Conference Series: Earth and Environmental Science*, 7, 012017. https://doi.org/10.1088/1755-1307/7/1/012017

Tolba, M. K., Saab, N. W., & Environment, A. F. f. (2008). *Arab environment: Future challenges*. Retrieved from https://wedocs.unep.org/handle/20.500.11822/9639

UNECA. (2007). *Africa review report on drought and desertification*. United Nations Economic and Social Council. United Nations Economic Commission for Africa. Retrieved from https://sustainabledevelopment.un.org/content/documents/eca_bg3.pdf

UNICEF. (2019). *Eastern and Southern Africa: Eritrea*. Retrieved from www.unicef.org/appeals/eritrea.html

UNICEF. (2020a). *Health & nutrition: Challenges*. Retrieved from www.unicef.org/sudan/health-nutrition

UNICEF. (2020b). *Malnutrition: A major cause of death in children, West and Central Africa*. United Nations Children's Fund. Retrieved July 30, 2020, from www.unicef.org/wca/malnutrition

UNSCN. (2010). *Food and nutrition security in West-Africa: Opportunities and challenges* (Vol. 38). United Nations Standing Committee on Nutrition. Retrieved from http://www.unscn.org/files/Publications/SCN_News/Supplement_ECOWAS_scnnews38_final.pdf

USAID. (2017). *Regional fact sheet, climate change risk profile, West Africa Sahel*. United States Agency for International Development. Retrieved from https://www.climatelinks.org/resources/climate-risk-profile-west-africa-sahel

Were, M. K. (1989). Ecological upheavals with special reference to desertification and predicting health impact. *Social Science & Medicine, 29*(3), 357–367. https://doi.org/https://doi.org/10.1016/0277-9536(89)90284-0

WHO. (2015). *Major risks resulting from human activities*. World Health Organization. Retrieved from https://apps.who.int/iris/bitstream/handle/10665/177155/Synt_R_5.pdf?sequence=5&isAllowed=y#:~:text=to%20climate%20change.-,Of%20the%2080%20countries%20substantially%20affected%20by%20land%20degradation%2C%2036,and%20residues%20from%20chemicals%2Fpesticides

WHO. (2020). *Land degradation and desertification*. World Health Organization. Retrieved from www.who.int/globalchange/ecosystems/desert/en/

WIT. (2009). Desertification: Its effects on people and land. *World Ecology Report*, *XXI*(1). World Information Transfer, Inc.

Wuehler, S. E., Hess, S. Y., & Brown, K. H. (2011). Accelerating improvements in nutritional and health status of young children in the Sahel region of Sub-Saharan Africa: Review of international guidelines on infant and young child feeding and nutrition. *Maternal and Child Nutrition*, 7(Suppl. 1), 6–34. https://doi.org/10.1111/j.1740-8709.2010.00306.x

28

CLIMATE CHANGE AND POPULATION DISPLACEMENT IN AFRICA

Roberto Ariel Abeldaño Zuñiga, Gabriela Narcizo de Lima and Daniel Esteban Quiroga

Introduction

There is sufficient evidence to argue that climate change causes an increasing frequency of disasters, with loss of human lives and structural assets that hit the least developed countries hardest. This situation is particularly relevant for countries on the African continent, where, despite having lower greenhouse gas emission indicators than countries with higher levels of development (such as the European countries), the effects of disasters related to climate change have shown greater impact in recent decades (Adenle, Manning, & Arbiol, 2017; Collier, Conway, & Venables, 2008; Conway & Schipper, 2011; Downing, Ringius, Hulme, & Waughray, 1997; Henderson, Storeygard, & Deichmann, 2017; Matondo, Alemaw, & Sandwidi, 2020).

Among the consequences of disasters to the population, damage to households should be pointed out, in addition to deaths and economic losses. In countries with lower levels of development, these damages sometimes turn dwellings into uninhabitable buildings (Abeldaño Zúñiga & González Villoria, 2018). Hence, one of the most significant impacts of disasters on the population is forced displacement due to disaster situations (Kolmannskog & Trebbi, 2010).

Owing to the various dimensions of social vulnerability faced by the countries of the African continent, population displacement is one of the main obstacles affecting post-disaster recovery. Some authors point out that individuals and families who are forced to leave their homes often lose their jobs and their primary source of income, but are also more likely to experience health problems during and after the period they remain displaced (Hori & Schafer, 2010).

Worldwide, the phenomenon of forced displacement by disasters is showing an increasing trend, partly due to the increase in the occurrence of disasters related to climate change. In this sense, Kälin points out that in 2008, 36 million people were displaced within their own countries due to a sudden onset disaster. Of that number, at least 20 million displacements were due to disasters related to climate change (Kälin, 2010).

Africa is no stranger to this trend since disaster situations have been evident in several countries on this continent in recent decades (Li, Chai, Yang, & Li, 2016; Manyena, 2016; Parkes, Cronin, Dessens, & Sultan, 2019). Additionally, Uganda and Ethiopia are among the countries in the world that most frequently receive and host displaced persons due to conflicts and disasters caused by climate change. In the year 2016 alone, these countries received, respectively, a total of 940,800 and 791,600 people, between refugees and displaced persons (Tafere, 2018).

DOI: 10.4324/9780429287213-33

Other African countries, such as Kenya, Sudan, Rwanda, and Tanzania, also host a large number of displaced persons (Fangama Abdalla, 2015; Kakonge, 2000; Solomon et al., 2018; Whitaker, 2002), even being among the least-developed countries in the world and presenting serious environmental problems, which can be aggravated by the large influx of people in their territories (Fangama Abdalla, 2015; Kakonge, 2000).

Considering that the incidence of disasters related to climate change will increase in the coming decades and that limited natural resources, such as clean water, are likely to become even more scarce in many parts of the African continent, threatening livelihoods, and exacerbating food insecurity (Manyena, 2016; Osima et al., 2018), this chapter aims to analyze the phenomenon of internal displacements due to disaster situations, trends in climate change, and incidence of disasters in the African countries, with the purpose of contributing to the understanding of the new patterns of displacement and competition for depleted natural resources, which can cause conflicts between communities or aggravate pre-existing vulnerabilities.

Climate change

Africa is the continent most vulnerable to climate change impacts in all climate scenarios above 1.5°C (Intergovernmental Panel on Climate Change, 2018). This vulnerability in the region derives from various pressures associated with low adaptive capacity. Firstly, the geographic location of many African countries is characterized by warmer climates and marginal areas that are more exposed to climatic risks such as variability in rainfall, poor soils, and flood plains. Secondly, the economies of most African countries still rely heavily on climate-sensitive sectors such as agriculture, fisheries, natural resources, and tourism, and thirdly, the continent does not have adequate capacity to respond to the direct and indirect effects of climate change due to the spread of poverty, poor economic and social infrastructure, conflicts, and limited human, institutional, and financial capacities (African Development Bank Group, 2019; The Centre for International Governance Innovation, 2009; United Nations Economic Commission for Africa, 2008).

The impacts of climate change on economies and societies in most of the continent are numerous and evident through the increase in natural disasters, including extreme droughts and floods, resulting in food insecurity, increased climate-related internal migration, extreme temperatures, and low labour productivity, mainly due to thermal stress during the warmer seasons in some parts of the continent (Intergovernmental Panel on Climate Change, 2018; The Centre for International Governance Innovation, 2009; United Nations Economic Commission for Africa, 2008).

According to the Intergovernmental Panel on Climate Change (IPCC) (2014), Africa will experience a temperature increase that will be one and a half times greater than the average experienced worldwide. Evidence suggests that a persistent 1°C rise on the continent will cause the loss of 65% of current maize growth capacity in producing countries, and an estimated 20% drop in world food production (Intergovernmental Panel on Climate Change, 2014; Research Program on Climate Change Agriculture and Food Security, 2011). Furthermore, it is estimated that the price of wheat will increase by 120%, corn by 177%, and processed rice by 107% before 2030 (Research Program on Climate Change Agriculture and Food Security, 2011). This would put the most basic foods out of reach for many Africans and undermine their fundamental right to food.

An average rise in temperature of 1.5°C in Africa is expected to lead to a 10% decrease in precipitation by 2050, causing water stress for approximately 480 million people on the continent. West Africa, the Horn of Africa, and the Sahel would be highly affected by desertification and droughts linked to climate change, despite the overall greening of the Sahel observed since the drought of the 1980s (Intergovernmental Science-Policy Platform on Biodiversity and Ecosystem Services, 2018). Africa also has large coastal areas at or near sea level, and warming by 2°C would produce a significant rise in sea levels, affecting many communities and destroying much of their coastal infrastructure (Intergovernmental Panel on Climate Change, 2018).

Following a path of sustainable development can reduce vulnerability to climate change by improving adaptive capacity and increasing resilience to its potential impacts, because degradation of natural resource-dependent livelihoods is likely to remain the main driver of long-term migration in Africa over the next two to three decades (The Centre for International Governance Innovation, 2009).

Impact of climate-related disasters

It is widely accepted that the impacts of disasters are related to socio-economic factors, frequency and intensity of events, local management capacities, and countries' political and financial instruments for disaster risk management (Banholzer, Kossin, & Donner, 2014). It is also accepted that in the most vulnerable populations, the effects of disasters are more lethal. The idea that disasters affect the development of nations in two ways has been developed by some authors, arguing that a disaster can reproduce conditions of poverty on the one hand, while on the other hand, poverty generates conditions of vulnerability that do not allow the risks to be adequately addressed (Daoud, Halleröd, & Guha-Sapir, 2016; Lopez-Calva y Ortiz-Juarez, 2009). This has important implications for its empirical approach since this complexity of two-way relationships creates a framework that is difficult to capture empirically. This is particularly important for Africa, since the geographical characteristics of this continent make it very prone to the occurrence of frequently occurring disasters of high intensity, mainly events of hydrometeorological and climatic origin.

According to data from the Centre for Research on the Epidemiology of Disasters (CRED), in the 2010s decade, there were about 1,143 disaster events throughout the African continent, which caused more than 46,000 deaths and affected more than 337,000,000 people. Of these disasters, 90% were caused by floods, droughts, and storms (Centre for Research on the Epidemiology of Disasters, 2019).

Although dozens of disasters occur every year, in every country on the African continent some, such as Kenya, Mozambique, and South Africa, are more affected than others (Centre for Research on the Epidemiology of Disasters, 2018, 2019; Guha-Sapir, Hoyois, & Below, 2015). It is assumed that with a growing population, added to climate change trends in the continent, climate-related disasters could increase in frequency and intensity, as well as increasing their effects on vulnerable populations in these countries.

The statistical data of the CRED show that Africa is in second place after Asia in experiencing disasters of hydrological origin, and in first place in experiencing disasters of climatological origin, compared to the rest of the continents. Due to the vulnerable conditions in which many African communities live, after Asia, this continent has the second-highest number of deaths from disasters.

Forced displacement due to disasters

The Migration Glossary of the International Organization of Migration (IOM) (2019) defined internally displaced persons as 'people or groups of people who have been forced or obliged to flee or leave their homes or their habitual residence, particularly as a result of, or to avoid, the effects of armed conflict, a situation of generalized violence, violation of human rights, or natural or human disasters and have not crossed a border of an internationally recognized State'.

Firstly, the situation of population displacement caused by disasters (regardless of whether they are related to climate change or not) must be distinguished from displacement caused by political or armed conflict situations. While displacements forced by political or armed conflicts practically do not allow people to return to their homes, disaster displacement, at least in theory, allows people to return home once the natural threat has subsided, although not all threats are treated in the same way, as will be detailed later (Shultz et al., 2014).

There are some discussions on the conceptualization of this phenomenon since some authors and International Organizations talk about 'environmental displacements'. In contrast, other authors discuss 'environmental migration' and others discuss 'environmental refugees' (El Hinnawi, 1985). IOM (2019) stated, 'Migrants for environmental reasons are people or groups of people who, mainly due to sudden and gradual changes in the environment, which have a negative impact on their lives or their living conditions, are forced, or decide, to abandon their habitual dwellings, either temporarily or permanently. They move to other parts of their own country or outside of it". This is not a minor issue because the moving people's status triggers other issues related to the protection of their rights in the displacement.

Another issue that should be pointed out is related to the right to property. In disaster displacement, the right to property is not taken away, as it is in some conflict situations in which people are stripped of their property and belongings by armed groups.

Walter Kalïn (2010) has proposed at least five possible scenarios to analyze the temporality of internal displacements forced by disaster situations.

Scenario 1: This is characterized by sudden-onset disasters. In the case of the African continent, within this category are floods, storms, hurricanes, typhoons, landslides, or avalanches that can cause sudden large forced displacement of people. However, it would be expected that this type of displacement is not long-term, and, depending on the management of the disaster situation by local and national official agencies, in most cases, people could return to their homes.

Scenario 2: This is a scenario of slow environmental degradation caused by the long-term effects of rising sea levels, droughts and soil desertification, and the mechanisms of degradation of drinking water sources. Since the availability of irrigation and drinking water is threatened in some regions, regional economies face an economic impact, as is the case of several countries on the African continent. In some cases, this long-term scenario can lead to a "voluntary" migration in search of adaptations to the changing environment. However, in cases in which the areas cannot be re-habitable, depending on the level of desertification, one would be talking about a permanent forced displacement.

Scenario 3: This scenario corresponds to that of the African states on the Atlantic coast, which present a particular case of slow-onset disasters. Due to rising sea levels and low elevations, these areas may become uninhabitable without desertification. Here the problem of displacement is pressing since, when dealing with small states (for example, the Gambia, Guinea-Bissau, and Sierra Leone, among others), the population would need to move to other countries. In this scenario, we should be thinking of a 'climate refugee'[1] situation, as El Hinnawi (1985) put it more than three decades ago.

Scenario 4: This is the case in which there is an active intervention by local authorities to evict households located in areas considered to be at risk (riverbanks, hillsides, and mountains). In these cases, unlike what was mentioned in Scenario 1, there are no possibilities of return, and due to permanent displacement, this can trigger legal problems.

Scenario 5: This is a more complex scenario. It relates to forced displacement in situations of violence caused by conflicts related to the availability of natural resources, the most important of which are driven by the availability of drinking and irrigation water. In these cases of displacement, the return would depend on the resolution of the conflict and the availability of natural resources (Kälin, 2010).

Political framework of internal displacements

Although the term 'environmental refugees' (El Hinnawi, 1985) first appeared in the mid-1980s to refer to people experiencing forced displacement due to environmental disasters, it was not until the publication of the Guiding Principles on Internal Displacement by the United Nations Office for the Coordination of Humanitarian Assistance in 1998 when the problem of internal displacement, particularly the gaps in the legal and humanitarian protection of displaced persons, began to be attended to (United Nations Office for the Coordination of Humanitarian Assistance, 1998).

By adopting the Sendai Framework for Disaster Risk Reduction in 2015, the Member States of the United Nations agreed to 'build resilience and reduce the risk of disasters', including the risk of displacement (UN Office for Disaster Risk Reduction, 2015). In December 2015, the adoption of the Paris Agreement by the United Nations Framework Convention on Climate Change convened a working group to develop recommendations and integrated approaches to avoid, minimize, and address displacement related to adverse impacts of climate change (United Nations Framework Convention on Climate Change, 2015).

This process was complemented by the World Humanitarian Summit in 2016 and marked a set of commitments and parallel actions in support of communities facing displacement in the face of a disaster situation. However, there is not yet enough evidence to argue whether the different processes will actually result in an integrated set of mutually reinforcing efforts, actions, and implementation (Guadagno, 2016).

In the specific case of the African continent countries, mention should be made of the treaty signed by the countries of the African Union in Kampala, Uganda, in 2009, which entered into force in 2012.

This treaty was the product of the African Union Convention for the Protection and Assistance of Internally Displaced Persons in Africa (African Union, 2009). It arose because Africa has been at the forefront in the development of binding legal instruments on internal displacement. This was born when the Organization of African Unity took the initiative to broaden the definition of refugee in 1969. The instrument adopted in Kampala constitutes the most important framework in the region to protect and assist internally displaced persons. Although initially few countries had ratified the Kampala Convention, by 2019, it had been ratified by 55 countries in the region.

The Kampala Convention affirms the importance of protecting and assisting internally displaced persons at all stages of displacement, from preventing displacement to protecting and assisting during displacement. This convention also incorporates the UN Guiding Principles on Internal Displacement declared in 1998, since it recognizes that they are 'an important international framework for the internal protection of displaced persons' that protect the inherent rights of internally displaced persons. The Kampala Convention includes a wide range of internal displacement causes due to environmental and conflict reasons and establishes obligations, responsibilities, and roles of the states parties concerning protection against displacement.

Table 28.1 International Agreements and Treaties on Internal Displacements Due to Disasters

Year	*Place*	*Agreement/Treaty*
1984	Cartagena	Cartagena Declaration on Refugees in the Organization of American States
1992	New York	United Nations Framework Convention on Climate Change
1998	Kyoto	Kyoto Protocol (Framework Convention on Climate Change)
1998	New York	Guiding Principles on Internal Displacement
1999	New York	Inter-Agency Standing Committee (IASC), 'Protection of Internally Displaced Persons', Committee Policy Documents No. 2
2005	Hyogo	Hyogo Framework for Action 2005–2015: Building the resilience of nations and communities to disasters
2006	Great Lakes	Protocol on the Protection and Assistance to Internally Displaced Persons
2008	Geneva	Intergovernmental Panel on Climate Change (IPCC). Fourth Assessment Report of the Intergovernmental Panel on Climate Change
2009	Kampala	Kampala Convention. African Union Convention for the Protection and Assistance of Internally Displaced Persons in Africa

Source: Elaborated by the authors.

Listed here are some of the agreements and political instruments reached by international organizations related to forced internal displacement due to disaster situations (Table 28.1).

Methods

Data from the National Oceanic and Atmospheric Administration (NOAA, 2020), the Royal Netherlands Meteorological Institute (2020), the World Bank Group (2020), and the Food and Agriculture Organization of the United Nations (FAO, 2019) were used to analyze climate change trends for the countries of the African continent.

NOAA's annual thermal anomaly data (2020) come from the Global Historical Climatology Network-Monthly and the International Comprehensive Ocean-Atmosphere Data Set. These two data sets are combined into a single product to produce the combined global anomalies of land and ocean temperatures.

The historical data series for mean temperature and precipitation by country comes from the Climate Change Knowledge Portal (World Bank Group, 2020). The series of temperature and precipitation data presented monthly values, and the annual averages of average temperature and total precipitation by country were calculated from them.

The percentages of forest and agricultural land by country and data on net CO_2 equivalent emissions (CO_2-eq) by year come from the FAOSTAT platform (FAO, 2019), which provides free access to data on food and agriculture for more than 245 countries and 35 regions, in the period from 1961 to 2017, in addition to future projections of GHG emissions for 2030 and 2050.

For the projections of future climate change, the resources of the KNMI Climate Explorer climate data web application of the Royal Netherlands Meteorological Institute (2020) were used to generate maps based on the data set used in the IPCC WG1 AR5 Annex I 'Atlas' (Intergovernmental Panel on Climate Change, 2013).

For its part, the analysis of disaster trends in the countries of the African continent was based on data from the International Disaster Database (EM-DAT), which is maintained by the Centre de Recherche sur l'Épidémiologie des Désastres de L'École de Santé Publique de l'Université Catholique de Louvain, Belgium (Centre for Research on the Epidemiology of Disasters, 2020). The information for this database begins in 1900, and around 300 events are added each year. For a disaster to be entered into the analyzed database, at least one of the following criteria must be met:

1 Ten (10) or more people reported as deceased
2 One hundred (100) or more people reported as affected
3 State of emergency declaration
4 Summon international assistance

In order to disaggregate related and non-related climate disasters, events were classified according to their threat of origin, as observed in the operationalization detailed in Table 28.2 (Centre for Research on the Epidemiology of Disasters, 2020).

The occurrence of disasters was characterized by decades for the period 1900–2019. Among the effects of disasters, the numbers of deaths and of injured and affected people were analyzed and operationalized according to the following definitions (Centre for Research on the Epidemiology of Disasters, 2020):

Deaths: number of people who lost their lives due to a disaster event.
Homeless: number of people whose homes were destroyed or heavily damaged, requiring shelter after a disaster.
Total affected: the sum of the injured people, plus those affected, plus the people who lost their homes.

The *economic cost pattern* is determined by the variable that estimates the total damage for each event, in US dollars at the time of the disaster. This places a value on all direct and indirect economic losses related to the disaster, including the following sectors: social infrastructure,

Table 28.2 Hazards Classification Based on Their Origin

Hazard groups		*Hazard subgroups*
Climate-related	Meteorological	Storms
		Cyclones and hurricanes
		Extreme temperatures
	Hydrological	Flood
		Landslide
		Wave action
	Climatological	Drought
		Wildfire
	Biological	Infectious diseases (Epidemics)
Non-climate-related	Geophysical	Earthquakes
		Volcanic activity
		Mass movement
	Technological incidents	Industrial
		Transport
		Miscellaneous

Source: Centre for Research on the Epidemiology of Disasters – CRED, School of Public Health, Université Catholique de Louvain.

production, environment, and others (Centre for Research on the Epidemiology of Disasters, 2020).

Data from the Internal Displacement Monitoring Centre (IDMC) based in Geneva, Switzerland, were used for assessing internal displacement by disasters. Together with the Norwegian Refugee Council, this body monitors the situation of internal displacement due to circumstances of violence and disaster (Internal Displacement Monitoring Centre, 2020).

In addition to the databases and platforms consulted for carrying out the analysis of trends in climate change, disasters, and internal displacement mentioned earlier, an extensive bibliographic review was also carried out. The literature search included abstracts, titles, and keywords of original research papers in peer-reviewed English-language academic journals using Scopus, Web of Science, and Scientific Electronic Library Online (SciELO) academic databases.

Articles published by African institutions or academics were of special interest for this work, however, to address the topic of climate change and climate-related population displacements in the African countries; it was also necessary to consult the information provided by the international literature and by organizations such as the IPCC (1996, 2013, 2014, 2018), FAO (2011), Intergovernmental Science-Policy Platform on Biodiversity and Ecosystem Services (2018), Research Program on Climate Change, and Agriculture and Food Security (2011), among others.

Results

Climate change trends

Africa is extremely vulnerable to the impacts of climate change, and temperatures in all countries of the continent are expected to rise more quickly than the global average. The NOAA (2020) data for temperature anomalies in Africa from 1910 to 2019 (Figure 28.1) shows that positive anomalies became frequent from the end of the 1970s, increasing gradually until 2019. At the end of the 1990s, positive anomalies exceeded 0.5°C in relation to the twentieth-century average, until the mid-2000s when anomalies above 1°C began to be recorded. These anomalies can cause significant losses in agricultural production and favour the increased occurrence of extreme climatic events. In 2014, thermal anomalies in Africa reached 1.5°C, with 2016 being the hottest year with a positive anomaly of 1.52°C.

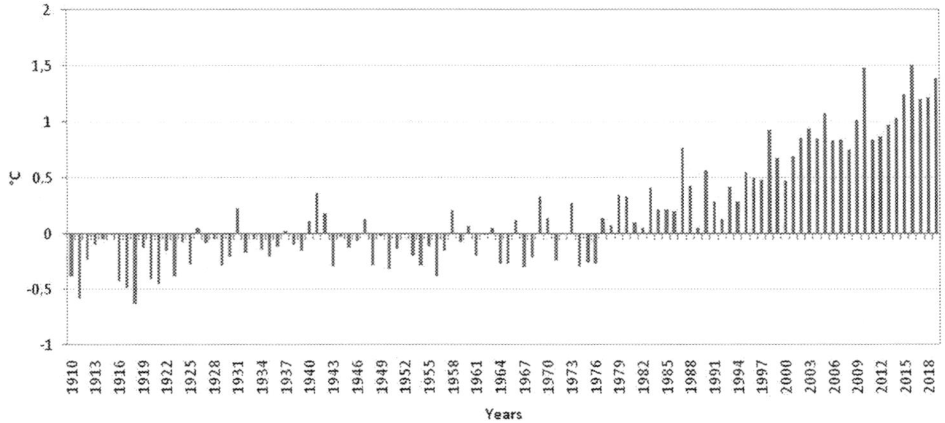

Figure 28.1 Surface temperature anomalies for the African continent between 1910 and 2019.

These temperature anomalies refer to the deviation of the annual mean temperatures from the twentieth-century average for the entire African continent. However, it is already possible to individually identify some impacts in the different regions of Africa resulting from the significant increase in temperatures.

According to data from the Climate Change Knowledge Portal (World Bank Group, 2020) (Figure 28.2), an increasing warming trend has been observed since the beginning of the twentieth century, mainly in the African regions where warm climates predominate. For the other areas, the increase in temperatures was not constant until the late 1970s, thus coinciding with NOAA's annual data on thermal anomalies for the African continent (2020) (Figure 28.1).

Analyzing the data by country from the years 1902 to 2016, it is possible to observe a considerable variation in warming rates, with values above 2°C in Lesotho, South Africa, Namibia, Eswatini, Tunisia, and Egypt, to values below 0.5°C in Guinea, Sierra Leone, Liberia, Comoros, and Mauritius; but, generally, warming rates in most countries exceeded 1°C for this data period.

Concerning rainfall, a decreasing trend is observed in the annual totals for 25 countries of the continent in the period from 1902 to 2016 (Figure 28.2), mainly generated by the increase in intense and prolonged droughts in some regions of Africa, especially in the last three decades.

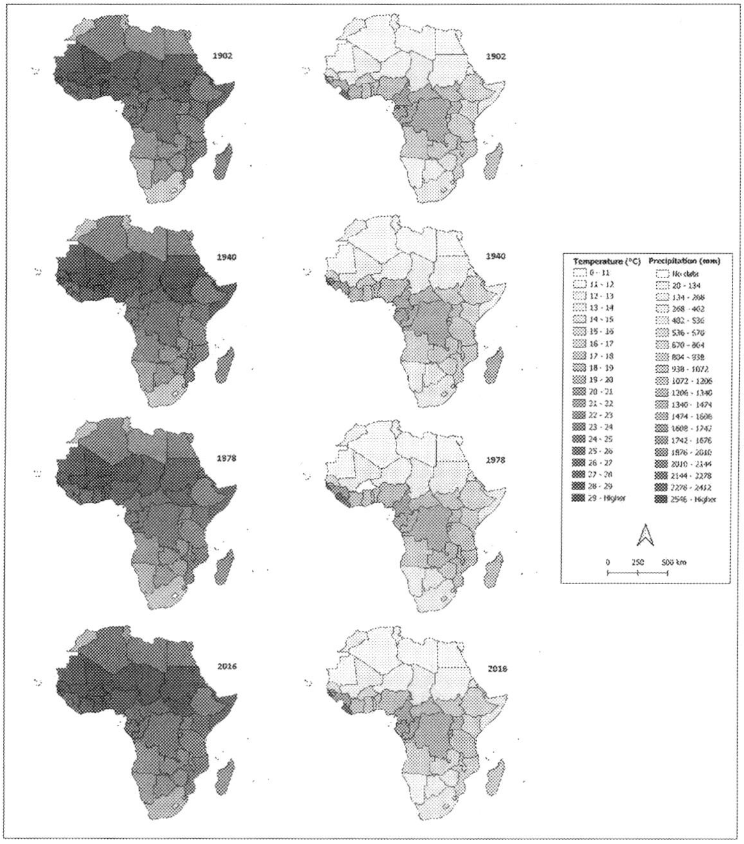

Figure 28.2 Average annual temperatures and annual total rainfall variations in Africa – Temperature values and annual rainfall per country from 1902 to 2016.

Libya, Algeria, Egypt, and Zimbabwe stand out as the countries that presented the most significant reductions in their annual rainfall totals, with values exceeding 30% for the entire period. For other countries, the average reduction in precipitation is around 14%.

On the other hand, in the last decades there has also been higher precipitation due to the intensification of the summer monsoons in West Africa; an increase in short rains in East Africa, due to the warming pattern of the Indian Ocean; and an increase in extreme precipitation caused by cyclones landing on the east coast of the continent (World Bank Group, 2020). Burundi, Eritrea, Eswatini, Rwanda, and Ethiopia stand out among the countries that showed a significant increase in rainfall in the period analyzed, with totals of over 34%. The average increase in annual precipitation totals for the other countries analyzed between 1902 and 2016 was approximately 21%.

It is important to clarify that these trends of increases or decreases in annual totals of precipitation and average temperatures for the different regions of Africa refer to more than 100 years of data. The values may vary significantly if shorter series are analyzed.

The increase in the concentration of greenhouse gasses (GHG) in the Earth's atmosphere is directly related to the rapid increase in average global temperature. Emissions occur in practically all human activities and sectors of the economy. In the African continent, the major responsibility for the growth of GHG emissions in recent decades is the expansion of agricultural and livestock activities, which accelerate deforestation and the loss of important forest areas (Intergovernmental Science-Policy Platform on Biodiversity and Ecosystem Services, 2018).

Agriculture is the backbone of most African economies, accounting for up to 40% of total export earnings and employing around 75% of the total workforce in sub-Saharan Africa. More than 50% of household food needs and an equivalent part of income come from agriculture (Research Program on Climate Change Agriculture and Food Security, 2011).

On the one hand, agriculture is one of the factors responsible for the increase in temperatures, since emissions from this sector, added to deforestation to convert the land for cultivation, represent a significant percentage of all GHG emissions generated by human activities in African countries (Intergovernmental Panel on Climate Change, 2018; MacCarthy et al., 2018). On the other hand, this activity can also become a victim of the problem it is helping to create, since most agricultural systems in Africa are directly dependent on climate. Climate change may affect the length of growing seasons and yield potential, particularly along the margins of semi-arid and arid areas, thus intensifying food insecurity as productivity decreases and food prices rise (Intergovernmental Panel on Climate Change, 2018; Research Program on Climate Change Agriculture and Food Security, 2011).

Among the African countries that most expanded their agricultural lands between 1961 and 2017 (Figure 28.3) are Uganda, Malawi, Benin, and Rwanda, with 26.7%, 25.9%, 22.2%, and 20.1% of the total of their respective territories, and this expansion accelerated mainly from the end of the 1980s. If these values are compared to the loss of forest areas between 1989 and 2017 (Figure 28.3), it is possible to observe that in Rwanda, Benin, and Uganda there were also significant reductions in the percentage of land allocated to forests, with 11.1%, 12.9%, and 13.4% respectively. Zimbabwe was the country that presented the highest loss rates of forest areas in the period analyzed, with 21% of its territory between 1989 and 2017.

Africa lost the highest percentage of its tropical forests compared to other continents during the 1980s, 1990s, and early 2000s. According to FAO (2011), the real loss was 3.4 million hectares per year between 2005 and 2010. Some of the main causes have been classified as commercial agriculture, the expansion of palm oil cultivation, and illegal industrial and artisanal logging (Intergovernmental Science-Policy Platform on Biodiversity and Ecosystem Services, 2018).

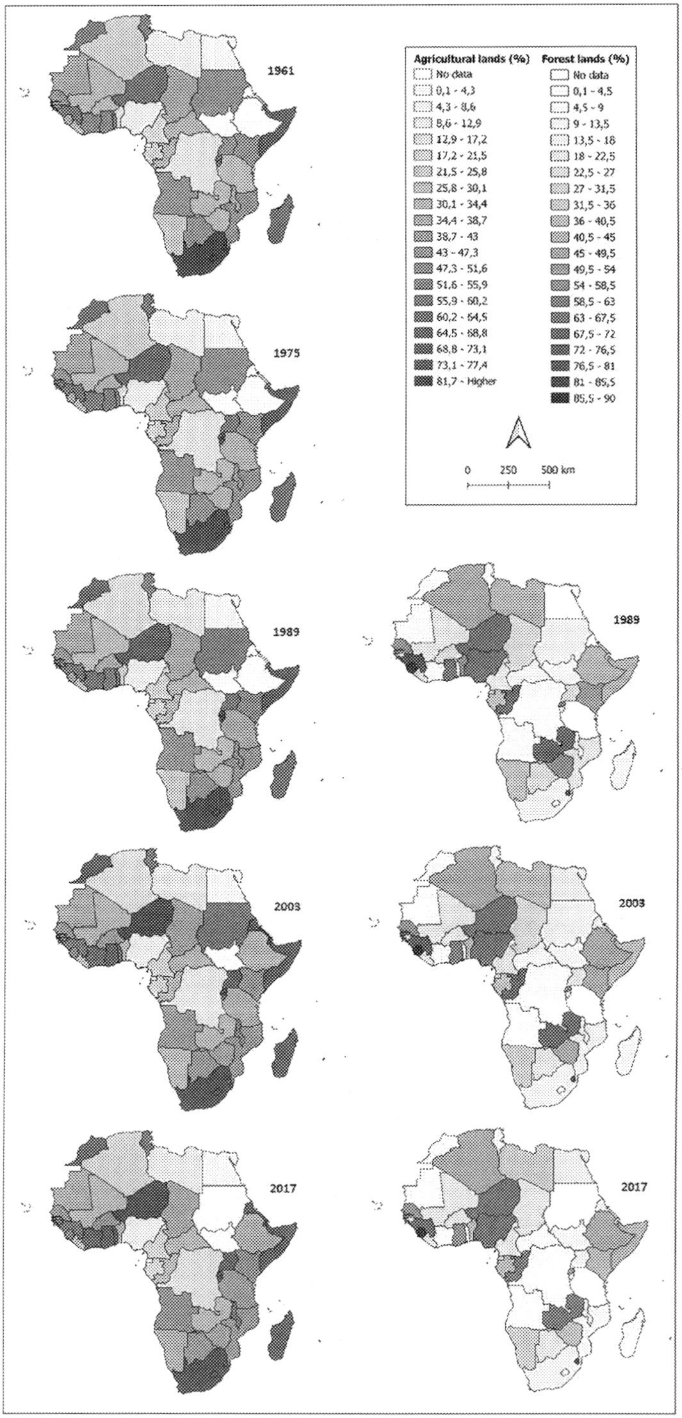

Figure 28.3 Agricultural and forest lands in Africa – Percentage of agricultural lands (1961–2017) and forest lands (1989–2017) per country.

During severe droughts such as the El Niño years, African rain forests can also become more susceptible to fire. The most destructive fires occur in forests that have been previously burned (Intergovernmental Science-Policy Platform on Biodiversity and Ecosystem Services, 2018; Kipalu, Koné, Bouchra, Vig, & Loyombo, 2016). Deforestation, in addition to contributing to the rapid increase in GHG emissions, also impacts the livelihoods of local peoples through the loss of natural resources and the loss of habitats on which they depend for food, medicine, and the maintenance of social stability (Kipalu et al., 2016).

The main problem related to the expansion of agriculture to the detriment of forests lies in GHG emissions promoted by land use and the conversion of forests to agricultural land. Burning or rotting vegetation releases carbon stored in logs, leaves, roots, and soil into the air. When these emissions are credited to the agriculture account, this sector's share of emissions globally and by country grows rapidly.

Data on net CO_2-eq emissions by country estimated by the FAO (2019) provide a complete picture of CH_4, N_2O, and CO_2 emissions from agriculture (expressed in Gigagrams of CO_2-eq per year) associated with the production of crops, livestock, and incorporated management activities (Ferranti, Berry, & Anderson, 2018). CO_2-eq is a measure used to compare the emissions of various GHGs based on their global warming potential, and is calculated using the parameters presented in the second IPCC assessment report on global warming potentials (GWP-SAR) (Intergovernmental Panel on Climate Change, 1996). Emission estimates are available for the period 1961–2017 and include the projection years 2030 and 2050.

Between 1961 and 2017, there was a rapid growth in agricultural GHG emissions in several African countries (Figure 28.4), with Angola, Benin, Burkina Faso, Central African Republic, Comoros, Congo, Eswatini, Gabon, the Gambia, Libya, Mauritius, Namibia, Niger, Nigeria, and Togo presenting an increase of more than 80% in emissions in the analyzed period. The most alarming growth was recorded from the late 1980s. An increase of approximately 46% in emissions from the continent has been observed in the last three decades. Even in relation to this period, it is important to mention that in South Africa, the Ivory Coast, and Mali reductions were registered in GHG emissions from agriculture.

Compared to 2017, an increase of 4.6% in the continent's emissions is estimated for 2030. For 2050, the projections for Africa show an increase of approximately 20% in relation to this same year, but it is expected that countries like Eritrea, the Gambia, and Somalia will reduce emissions from agriculture. This reduction, even if it seems positive, may be related to the fact that climate change will more intensely affect regions with a hot climate, and especially in arid and semi-arid zones, directly impacting the agricultural production of countries that already suffer from food and water shortages.

The future climate depends on how much the composition of the atmosphere and the properties of the earth change. Possible futures can be described through scenarios that are constructed so that the consequences of, and the options to limit, climate change can be researched. The Representative Concentration Pathways (RCPs) are the GHG concentration trajectories adopted by the IPCC in its fifth evaluation report (AR5) (Intergovernmental Panel on Climate Change, 2014), which describes different climatic scenarios, all of which are considered possible depending on the volume of GHG emitted in the coming years.

RCP4.5 and RCP6.0 are stabilization scenarios that assume, in the first case, a peak in emissions in 2040 and a sharp decrease until 2080, and in the second, a rapid increase in emissions until 2060 and then their decrease in future years. If these scenarios are compared with the actual values of temperature and precipitation for the period from 1986 to 2019 for the African continent, even with a high degree of uncertainty, it is possible to identify the areas that will be most impacted by climate change in the decades to come.

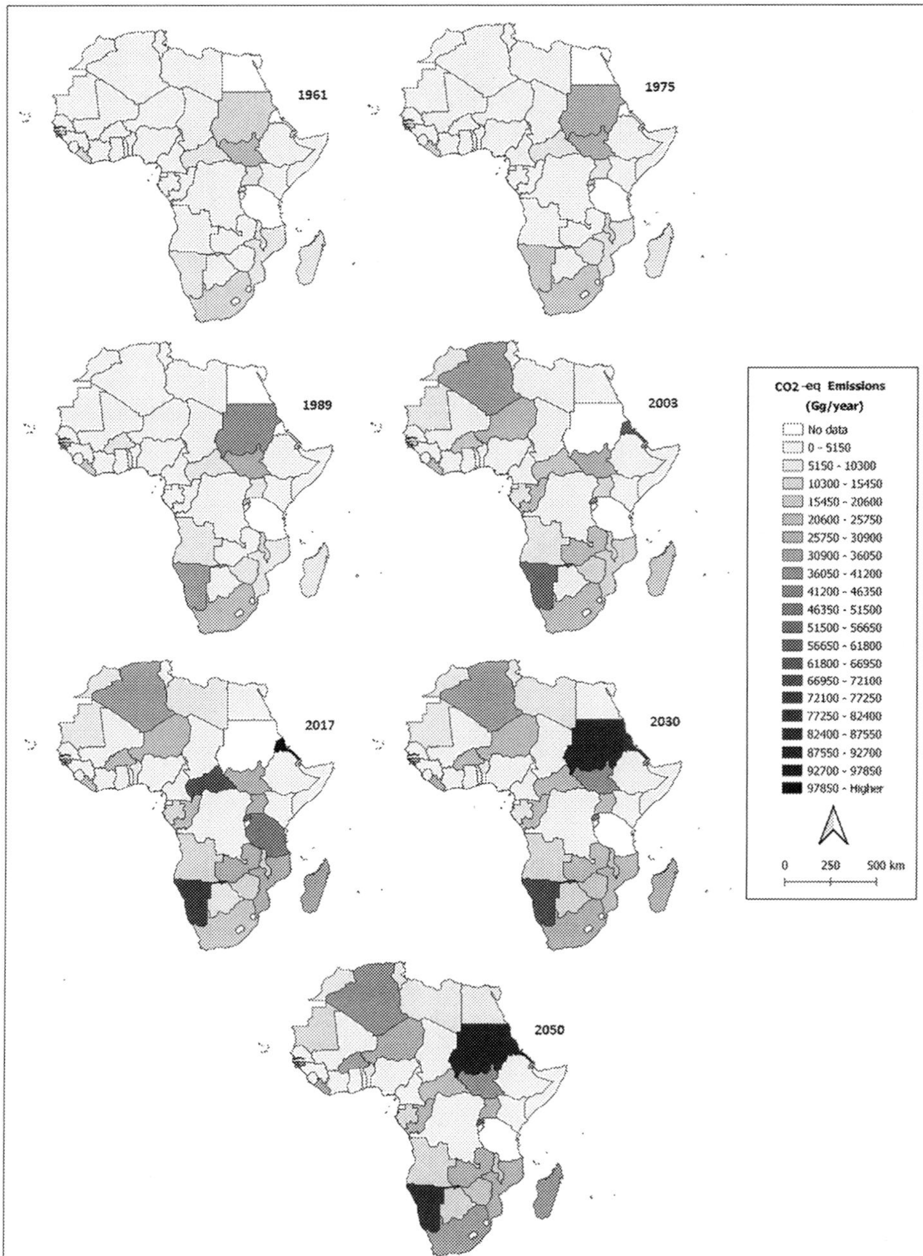

Figure 28.4 CO_2 equivalent emissions in Africa – Totals per country from 1961 to 2050 (Gg CO2-eq/year)

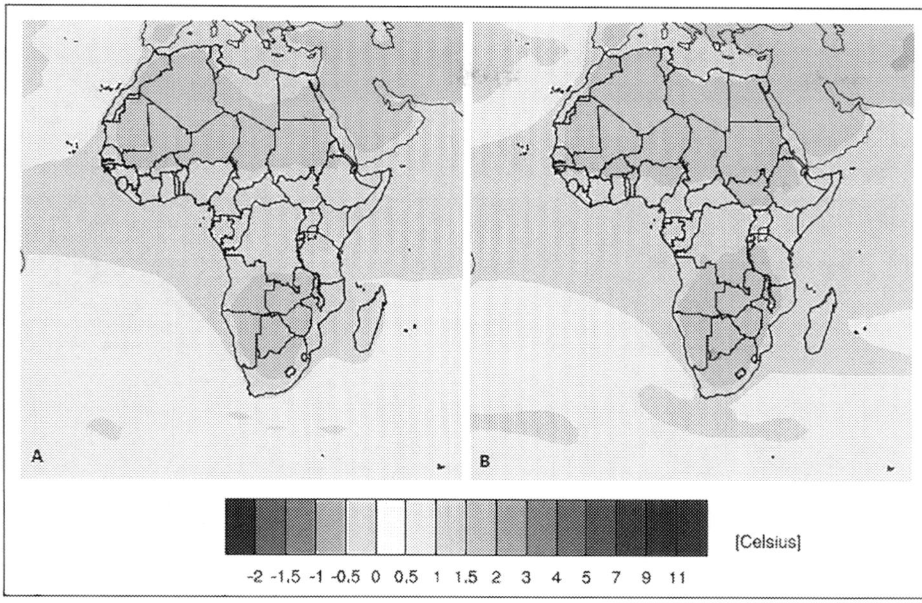

Figure 28.5 Mean RCP4.5 (A) and RCP6.0 (B) temperature 2020–2100 minus 1986–2019 (January – December/AR5 CMIP5 subset) – Africa.

According to the RCP4.5 scenario (Figure 28.5), a general warming is expected in the African continent by 2100, which will reach values of up to 2°C, especially in the arid and semi-arid zones of North and South Africa. The most affected countries will be Mauritania, Mali, Algeria, Niger, Chad, Libya, Egypt, Eritrea, Sudan, Zambia, Angola, Zimbabwe, Botswana, South Africa, and Namibia.

In the RCP6.0 scenario (Figure 28.5), the same pattern is repeated. However, the areas where temperatures are expected to rise the most will be more extensive, reaching countries like Ethiopia, Tanzania, the Democratic Republic of the Congo, and Nigeria, located in the regions of transition to the humid climates of the continent.

Future rainfall projections present a higher degree of uncertainty since they also depend on factors related to natural climate variability. Rainfall variability is projected to increase in most African regions. There is a high probability of a greater frequency of high-intensity rainfall events, especially on the Atlantic coasts of the countries of Central and Western Africa and in parts of Eastern Africa. Climate change could lead to significant losses of endemic plant species and more than 50% of some species of birds and mammals, and 20–30% decreased productivity of African lakes by 2100 (Intergovernmental Science-Policy Platform on Biodiversity and Ecosystem Services, 2018).

According to the RCP4.5 scenario (Figure 28.6), almost all countries in tropical climate zones will be impacted by an increase in rainfall by 2100 (compared to the period of 1986–2019). An increase of up to 0.5mm per day is expected in Nigeria, Cameroon, Equatorial Guinea, and Gabon. On the other hand, for dry climate zones, rainfall is expected to decrease even more, especially in Madagascar, Mozambique, and Malawi, which will decrease between 0.2mm and 0.5mm rainfall per day by 2100.

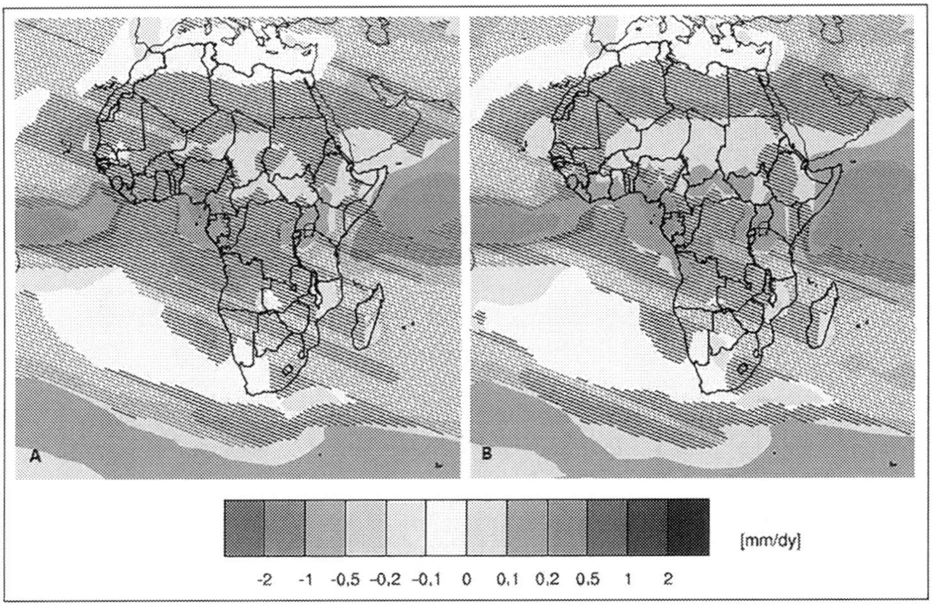

Figure 28.6 Mean RCP4.5 (A) and RCP6.0 (B) precipitation 2020–2100 minus 1986–2019 (January – December/AR5 CMIP5 subset) – Africa.

For the RCP6.0 scenario, it is expected that the areas that will register increases in precipitation will extend a little further to North Africa, reaching countries such as Mauritania, Algeria, Libya, and Egypt, in regions where an arid climate predominates. The most significant increase will be observed in parts of Nigeria, Cameroon, Equatorial Guinea, Gabon, Uganda, and Rwanda, reaching values of up to 0.5mm per day by 2100, compared to the period of 1986–2019. Towards Southern Africa, the projections continue to show that there is a trend towards less precipitation of up to 0.5mm per day in some areas.

Disasters

In the EMDAT database, a total of 5,014 disaster events that occurred in all the countries of the African continent between 1900 and 2019 were analyzed. Of these events, 54.2% were caused by climate-related threats.

The countries most affected by these climate-related events were Nigeria (129 events), the Democratic Republic of the Congo (123 events), Kenya (115 events), Mozambique (111 events), Ethiopia (110 events), and South Africa and the United Republic of Tanzania (101 events each) (Figure 28.7).

The 5,014 events registered show a total of 1,513,036 deaths, with Ethiopia, Uganda, Niger, Sudan, and Mozambique having the highest number of deaths. Among these five countries, 1 million deaths were accumulated in the period analyzed (Figure 28.7), and a total of 573,972,200 people were affected by disasters. The countries with the most affected people were Ethiopia, Kenya, Sudan, Mozambique, and Malawi, among which there were more than 250 million affected people throughout the period. The variable that accounts for people who lost their homes due to a disaster shows that a total of 9,666,244 lost their homes in this period.

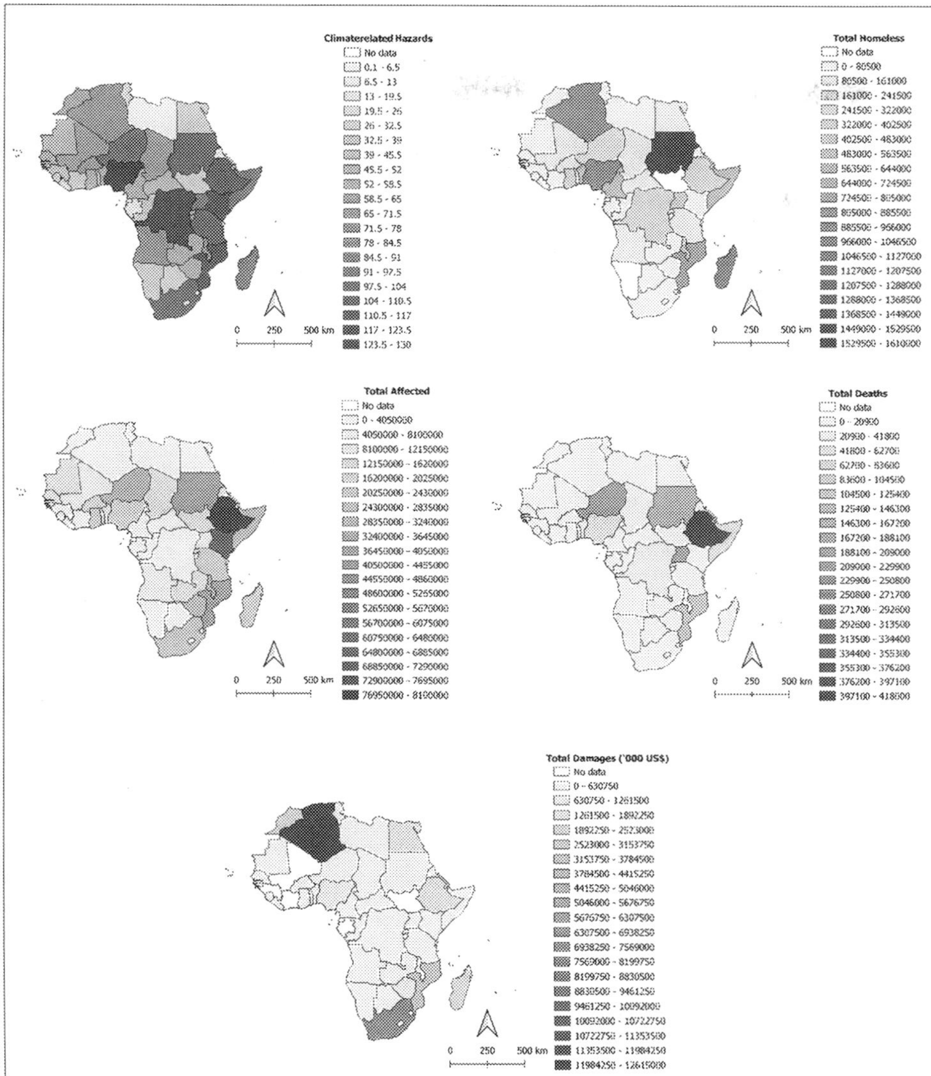

Figure 28.7 Climate-related hazards, homeless, affected, deaths, and total damages in Africa between 1900–2019.

The most affected countries were Sudan, Madagascar, Algeria, Nigeria, and Mozambique (55% of the total) (Figure 28.7).

The countries that suffered the most significant economic losses from disasters were Algeria, South Africa, and Mozambique, which account for 60% of the total damages calculated for the entire continent (a total of US$38,234,443,000).

Analysis by decades shows that the 2000s have been the most catastrophic for the continent, where 1,019 climate-related events have been recorded, equivalent to 27.5% of all climate-related disasters recorded throughout the studied period. Although for the first decades of the period (1900 to 1970) there are few records in the EMDAT database, this does not mean that

Table 28.3 Impacts of Climate-Related and Non-Climate-Related Disasters in Africa by Decade – Years 1900 to 2019

Decades	*Disasters*		*Total Deaths*		*Number of Homeless*		*Total Affected*		*Total Damages ('000 US$)*	
	Non-climate-related	*Climate-related*	*Non-climate-related*	*Climate-related*	*Non-climate-related*	*Climate-related*	*Non-climate-related*	*Climate-related*	*Non-climate-related*	*Climate-related*
	Total events	*Total events*	*Sum*	*Sum*	*Sum*	*Sum*	*Sum*	*Sum*	*Sum*	*Sum*
1900	2	4	117	211,000						
1910	1	10	12	85,000				32,000		
1920	1	3	12	127,000						
1930	4	2	57	2,000	7,500		7,630			
1940	8	14	398	61,941			1	15,000		
1950	7	9	1,411	879	129,250		136,282	72,162	6,000	
1960	23	70	13,510	7,062	19,405	42,636	100,173	10,739,509	153,570	627,420
1970	21	107	1,236	125,439	65,000	247,482	173,149	28,634,910	4,000	1,457,070
1980	134	291	11,356	582,426	493,200	1,891,943	1,059,985	92,316,091	5,317,400	2,377,276
1990	367	468	19,006	74,357	112,330	2,953,373	321,316	117,696,240	1,418,029	3,851,686
2000	1,104	1,019	36,215	58,327	496,610	2,151,456	1,128,338	152,624,836	6,478,200	4,224,141
2010	625	720	22,210	72,065	27,105	1,028,954	239,538	168,675,040	458,000	11,861,651
Total	2,297	2,717	105,540	1,407,496	1,350,400	8,315,844	3,166,412	570,805,788	13,835,199	24,399,244

Source: EMDAT, 2020

there were no disaster events, but instead that there was no permanent record system. However, the 1980s was the decade with the highest number of deaths (582,426), which is equivalent to 41.3% of all deaths recorded in the period. The countries most affected by deaths in the 1980s were Ethiopia, Sudan, and Mozambique, which suffered a drought between 1983 and 1985 that cost 300,000, 150,000, and 100,000 lives, respectively. These deaths during the drought are attributed to famine in these countries. While some sources report several hundred thousand more deaths, the EMDAT database is shown in Table 28.3.

The highest number of people who lost their homes was recorded in the 1990s. Mozambique (Cyclone Nadya in 1994), where 500,000 people lost their homes, and Nigeria, Somalia, Ghana, and Malawi, where more than 1 million people lost their homes due to floods stand out (Table 28.3).

Regarding the volume of people affected by climate-related disasters, this increases every decade, at the rate that disasters on the African continent increase. The same trend is observed in the analysis of climate change variables in the continent.

Internal displacements

According to the World Disaster Report (United Nations Office for the Coordination of Humanitarian Affairs, 2015), disasters have affected over 193 million people annually between 2005 and 2014 around the globe. Besides disasters, conflicts that may be related to internal disputes over scarce natural resources also force millions of people to flee their homes and settle as internally displaced persons in temporary camps.

Studies by Kakonge (2000), Fangama Abdalla (2015), Solomon et al. (2018), and Tafere (2018) agree that mass forced displacements and conflicts instigate significant environmental changes, including deforestation, soil degradation, depletion of water resources, and environmental waste, which, in turn, increase the vulnerability of these displaced groups to the effects of related and non-related climate disasters, and reinforce the possibility of new conflicts over resources.

IDMC data shows that the five countries in Africa where the most events that generated internal displacement between 2008 and 2019, were the Democratic Republic of the Congo, Burundi, Nigeria, Ethiopia, and Ghana (Figure 28.8).

Regarding the volume of people internally displaced by disasters, there were a total of 23,235,411 people displaced between 2008 and 2019. This volume is equivalent to the entire population of Madagascar or Cameroon, to cite some graphic examples of the situation. Of those displacements, 99% were caused by a climate-related disaster event. This confirms the vulnerability of the population to the effects of climate change, which forced them to abandon their homes.

The countries with the largest numbers of displaced persons were Nigeria (5,791,255), Somalia (2,195,266), Ethiopia (1,895,419), Niger (1,465,978), Sudan (1,298,278), Mozambique (1,294,066), Kenya (1,044,867) and Madagascar (1,024,182). All of these countries had more than one million displaced people in the period analyzed. Among these eight countries, there were 16,009,311 internally displaced persons, equivalent to 69% of the persons displaced by climate-related disasters in the period (Figure 28.8).

Although trends cannot be analyzed, due to the limited period in which the IDMC has kept records, it can be seen that there have been particularly severe years for the African population. One of those years was 2012, when 5,940,315 internal displacements were registered. This was mainly due to the floods that affected Nigeria, Niger, and Chad in 2012 that motivated the displacement of more than 5 million people (Table 28.4).

Regarding the threats that have caused internal displacement in African countries, 768 floods were identified (66.6%), 276 storms (23.9%), 55 movements of land (landslides) (4.8%), 40 wildfire events (3.5%), and 13 drought events (1.1%). Thus, taking up the scenarios proposed by Kälin, threats related to Scenario 1 of sudden-onset events, and events in Scenario 2 characterized by slow onset, were mainly identified. No event records were found within Scenario 3, which corresponds to movements due to the rise of sea levels on the Atlantic coast.

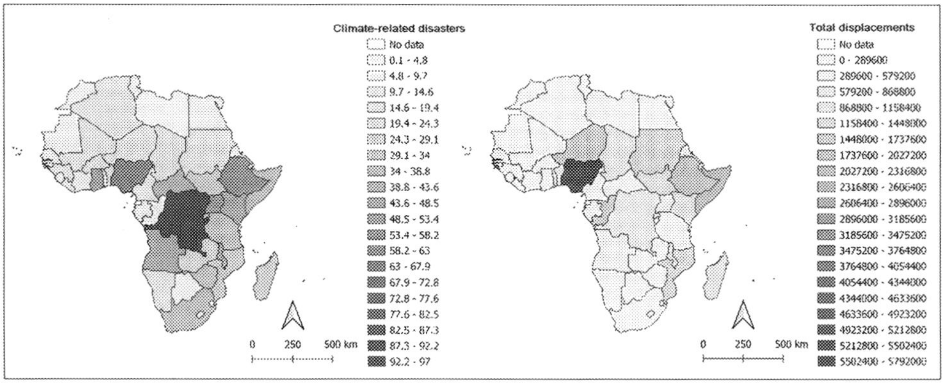

Figure 28.8 Internal displacements in Africa. 2008–2019.

Table 28.4 Internal Displacements in Africa, Due to Climate-Related and Non-Climate-Related Disasters – 2008–2019

Year	*Non-climate-related*	*Climate-related*	*Total*
	Sum	Sum	
2008	24,575	771,998	796,573
2009	20,550	1,098,843	1,119,393
2010	ND	1,707,549	1,707,549
2011	ND	603,321	603,321
2012	581	5,940,315	5,940,896
2013	6	1,599,154	1,599,160
2014	10,022	648,718	658,740
2015	3,900	1,126,051	1,129,951
2016	21,331	1,057,484	1,078,815
2017	74	2,561,591	2,561,665
2018	640	2,622,822	2,623,462
2019	128	3,415,758	3,415,886
Total	81,807	23,153,604	23,235,411

Source: IDMC, 2020

In light of what was exposed in this study, three important results stand out, which are essential to understand the intrinsic relationship between climate change, disasters, and displacements for environmental reasons:

1 Between 2000 and 2019, around 1,143 disaster events occurred in Africa.
2 Approximately 90% of disasters were caused by floods, droughts, and storms.
3 More than 46,000 deaths and more than 337 million affected people were caused by climate-related disasters.

Conclusions

Climate change in Africa is expected to severely compromise agricultural production, generate a rise of sea levels, cause the loss of natural resources, and have a substantial impact on social stability due to the lack of food, water scarcity, and impoverishment of cultivated soils caused by desertification.

Under a scenario of rapid global warming, large areas of Africa would experience changes in precipitation that would significantly exceed natural variability, with significant consequences for agricultural systems. The results of the IPCC climate change models (2018) indicate that warming above 1.5°C would result in a drastic reduction in the cultivation period and a consequent decrease in agricultural production on the continent.

A substantial impact on wildlife is also expected, mainly due to the continent's tropical forests' loss. The most extended droughts that are already occurring in some areas of Africa, which intensify in the El Niño years, are leading to an increase in forest fires. These cause a decrease in endemic species due to habitat loss and affect the livelihoods of millions of people who depend on biodiversity resources and forest products.

The rise in sea level due to climate change will displace the coastal limits, forcing the inhabitants of these areas to move to other regions of the continent. The west coast of Africa is one of the most vulnerable areas. The IPCC report (2018) projects that by the end of the twenty-first century, rising sea levels will affect low-lying coastal areas, further degrading mangroves and coral reefs, and threatening fishing activity, biodiversity, and tourism.

Disasters related to extreme climatic events, such as floods, prolonged droughts, and heatwaves, which have become more frequent in recent decades and threaten human security, are likely to force increasing numbers of people to move, generating competition between communities and nations for water and necessary essential resources, with possible negative consequences for political stability and conflict resolution.

Returning to the five scenarios proposed by Kalïn (2010), 99% of the internal displacement of people within the countries of Africa is included in Scenario 1, which involves sudden-onset disasters. The remaining 1% is included within the slow-onset disasters that Kalïn described in Scenario 2.

Although the volume of internal displacement due to slow-onset phenomena (droughts and consequent famines) represented a very low percentage of displaced people, these events significantly impacted mortality.

We expected to find internal displacements motivated by the increase in sea level (Scenario 3), widely described in the literature. However, it was not possible to identify this typology. There may be two reasons for this. The first could be due to the fact that there are no records of these events in the African Atlantic coast countries. Events happen, and also displacements, but they are not recorded. The second reason may have to do with the nomenclature of the events since these events could possibly be registered as 'floods' in the coastal areas, which were initially due to the rise in sea level. In this sense, an in-depth review of the nomenclatures and registration processes in international databases should be carried out to achieve greater precision in the analysis of possible causes and possible consequences to issue more accurate recommendations.

The consequences of the processes of climate change in Africa are visible. The increase in the frequency and intensity of climate-related disasters also has direct consequences for the population. We have seen the volume of displaced people, the mortality, the numbers of people affected, and the economic damage that disasters cause in the countries of the African continent.

While there are strategic governance frameworks for protecting the rights and guarantees of displaced persons that have been signed and ratified by all African Union countries, this is not enough. Work must be done on risk reduction strategies to reduce the number of displaced people in highly vulnerable countries such as Nigeria, Somalia, Ethiopia, Niger, Sudan, Mozambique, Kenya, and Madagascar, in which more than 16 million people have been displaced in just 13 years, while the volume of displacements in other countries continues to be important.

Regarding possible future lines of research, it is essential to focus the analysis on the political processes that followed the signing of protection agreements, such as the Kampala Convention, not only for the protection of the rights of displaced persons but for the prevention of displacement situations due to climate-related disasters. It is also necessary to continue with the research on displacements due to environmental change, in order to advance in a conceptual definition based on the particularities observed in Africa and to advance in the empirical experience through analysis of data specific to the continent.

Note

1 It should be noted that this concept of 'environmental refugees, or climate refugees' has been strongly criticized by academics, because the terms 'refugees', 'migrants', and 'displaced' carry different causes and different legal statuses. Academics recommend reserving the term 'refugee' for when there is active persecution (Kolmannskog & Trebbi, 2010).

References

Abeldaño Zúñiga, R. A., & González Villoria, A. M. (2018). Desastres en México de 1900 a 2016: patrones de ocurrencia, población afectada y daños económicos. *Revista Panamericana de Salud Pública, 42*(e55), 1–8. https://doi.org/10.26633/RPSP.2018.55

Adenle, A. A., Manning, D. T., & Arbiol, J. (2017). Mitigating climate change in Africa: Barriers to financing low-carbon development. *World Development, 100*, 123–132. https://doi.org/10.1016/j.worlddev.2017.07.033

African Development Bank Group. (2019). *Climate change in Africa*. Retrieved from www.afdb.org/en/cop25/climate-change-africa

African Union. (2009). *Kampala Convention: African Union for the protection and assistance of internally displaced persons in Africa*. Retrieved from https://au.int/sites/default/files/treaties/36846-treaty-kampala_convention.pdf

Banholzer, S., Kossin, J., & Donner, S. (2014). The impact of climate change on natural disasters. In Z. Zommers & A. Singh (Eds.), *Reducing disaster: Early warning systems for climate change* (Vol. 9789401785, pp. 21–49). Springer Netherlands. https://doi.org/10.1007/978-94-017-8598-3_2

The Centre for International Governance Innovation (CIGI). (2009). *Climate change in Africa: Adaptation, mitigation and governance challenges*. Retrieved from www.unicef.org/esaro/Climate_Change_in_Africa.pdf

Centre for Research on the Epidemiology of Disasters. (2020). *The International Disaster Database (EM-DAT)*. Belgique: Université Catholique de Louvain. Retrieved from www.emdat.be

Centre for Research on the Epidemiology of Disasters. (2018). *Natural Disasters 2017*. Belgium: Université Catholique de Louvain.

Centre for Research on the Epidemiology of Disasters. (2019). Disasters in Africa: 20 Year review (2000–2019). In *CRED Crunch*. Liege: Université Catholique de Louvain.

Collier, P., Conway, G., & Venables, T. (2008). Climate change and Africa. *Oxford Review of Economic Policy, 24*(2), 337–353. https://doi.org/10.1093/oxrep/grn019

Conway, D., & Schipper, E. L. F. (2011). Adaptation to climate change in Africa: Challenges and opportunities identified from Ethiopia. *Global Environmental Change, 21*(1), 227–237. https://doi.org/10.1016/j.gloenvcha.2010.07.013

Daoud, A., Halleröd, B., & Guha-Sapir, D. (2016). What is the association between absolute child poverty, poor governance, and natural disasters? A global comparison of some of the realities of climate change. *PLoS One, 11*(4), 1–20. https://doi.org/10.1371/journal.pone.0153296

Downing, T. E., Ringius, L., Hulme, M., & Waughray, D. (1997). Adapting to climate change in Africa. *Mitigation and Adaptation Strategies for Global Change, 2*(1), 19–44. https://doi.org/10.1023/B:MITI.0000004663.31074.64

El Hinnawi, E. (1985). *Environmental refugees*. United Nations Environment Programme. Retrieved from https://wedocs.unep.org/handle/20.500.11822/2651

Fangama Abdalla, I. M. (2015). Refugees consumption of Forest Products prior to Repatriation Kuna Zeberma Camp, Kassab Locality, Gedaref State. *International Journal of Current Microbiology and Applied Sciences, 4*(2), 843–846.

Ferranti, P., Berry, E., & Anderson, J. (2018). *Encyclopedia of food security and sustainability*. Amsterdam, the Netherlands: Elsevier.

Food and Agriculture Organization of the United Nations (FAO). (2011). *State of the world's forests 2011*. Retrieved from http://www.fao.org/3/i2000e/i2000e00.htm

Food and Agriculture Organization of the United Nations (FAO). (2019). *FAOSTAT [Dataset]*. Retrieved from www.fao.org/faostat/es/#data

Guadagno, L. (2016). Human mobility in the Sendai Framework for disaster risk reduction. *International Journal of Disaster Risk Science*, 7(1), 30–40. https://doi.org/10.1007/s13753-016-0077-6

Guha-Sapir, D., Hoyois, P., & Below, R. (2015). *Annual Disaster Statistical Review 2014: The numbers and trends*. Retrieved from www.cred.be/sites/default/files/ADSR_2010.pdf

Henderson, J. V., Storeygard, A., & Deichmann, U. (2017). Has climate change driven urbanization in Africa? *Journal of Development Economics, 124*, 60–82. https://doi.org/10.1016/j.jdeveco.2016.09.001

Hori, M., & Schafer, M. (2010). Social costs of displacement in Louisiana after Hurricanes Katrina and Rita. *Population and Environment, 31*(1–3), 64–86. https://doi.org/10.1007/s11111-009-0094-0

International Organization of Migration. (2019). Glossary on Migration No. 34. In *International Migration Law*. Retrieved from http://medcontent.metapress.com/index/A65RM03P4874243N.pdf%5Cn http://www.epim.info/wp-content/uploads/2011/01/iom.pdf

Intergovernmental Panel on Climate Change (IPCC). (1996). *IPCC Second Assessment Report (SAR) – Climate Change 1995*. Retrieved from www.ipcc.ch/site/assets/uploads/2018/06/2nd-assessment-en.pdf

Intergovernmental Panel on Climate Change (IPCC). (2013). *Climate Change 2013: The physical science basis*. Retrieved from www.climatechange2013.org/report/

Intergovernmental Panel on Climate Change (IPCC). (2014). *AR5 Climate Change 2014: Impacts, adaptation, and vulnerability: Part B Regional aspects*. Retrieved from www.ipcc.ch/report/ar5/wg2/

Intergovernmental Panel on Climate Change (IPCC). (2018). *Global Warming of 1.5°C: An IPCC Special Report on the impacts of global warming of 1.5°C above pre-industrial levels and related global greenhouse gas emission pathways, in the context of strengthening the global response to the threat of climate change*. Retrieved from www.ipcc.ch/site/assets/uploads/sites/2/2019/06/SR15_Full_Report_High_Res.pdf

Intergovernmental Science-Policy Platform on Biodiversity and Ecosystem Services (IPBES). (2018). *The IPBES regional assessment report on biodiversity and ecosystem services for Africa*. Retrieved from https://ipbes.net/policy-support/assessments/regional-subregional-assessment-report-biodiversity-ecosystem-services

Internal Displacement Monitoring Centre (IDMC) (2020). *Global Internal Displacement Database*. Retrieved from www.internal-displacement.org/database/

Kakonge, J. O. (2000). A review of refugee environmental-oriented projects in Africa: A case for environmental impact assessment. *Impact Assessment and Project Appraisal, 18*(1), 23–32. https://doi.org/10.3152/147154600781767565

Kälin, W. (2010). Conceptualizing climate-induced displacement. In J. McAdam (Ed.), *Climate change and displacement: Multidisciplinary perspectives* (1st ed., pp. 81–104). Oxford: Hart Publishing.

Kipalu, P., Koné, L., Bouchra, S., Vig, S., & Loyombo, W. (2016). *Securing forest peoples' rights and tackling deforestation in the Democratic Republic of Congo*. Forest Peoples Programme (FPP). Retrieved from www.forestpeoples.org/sites/fpp/files/publication/2016/05/fppdrcreportinternet-2.pdf

Kolmannskog, V., & Trebbi, L. (2010). Climate change, natural disasters and displacement: A multi-track approach to filling the protection gaps. *International Review of the Red Cross, 92*(879), 713–730. https://doi.org/10.1017/S1816383110000500

Li, C. J., Chai, Y. Q., Yang, L. S., & Li, H. R. (2016). Spatio-temporal distribution of flood disasters and analysis of influencing factors in Africa. *Natural Hazards, 82*(1), 721–731. https://doi.org/10.1007/s11069-016-2181-8

Lopez-Calva, L. F., & Ortiz-Juarez, E. (2009). *Evidence and policy lessons on the links between disaster risk and poverty in Latin America: Methodology and Summary of Country Studies* (MDG-01–2009; Research for Public Policy, MDGs and Poverty, Issue Research for Public Policy, MDGs and Poverty, MDG-01–2009, RBLAC-UNDP). Retrieved from https://mpra.ub.uni-muenchen.de/18342/1/01_RPPLAC_POV.pdf

MacCarthy, D. S., Zougmoré, R. B., Akponikpè, P. B. I., Koomson, E., Savadogo, P., & Adiku, S. G. K. (2018). Assessment of greenhouse gas emissions from different land-use systems: A case study of CO 2 in the Southern Zone of Ghana. *Applied and Environmental Soil Science, 2018*, 1–12. https://doi.org/10.1155/2018/1057242

Manyena, B. (2016). After Sendai: Is Africa bouncing back or bouncing forward from disasters? *International Journal of Disaster Risk Science*, 7(1), 41–53. https://doi.org/10.1007/s13753-016-0084-7

Matondo, J., Alemaw, B., & Sandwidi, W. (2020). *Climate variability and change in Africa* (J. I. Matondo, B. F. Alemaw, & W. J. P. Sandwidi, Eds.). Cham: Springer Nature Switzerland AG 2020. https://doi.org/10.1007/978-3-030-31543-6

National Oceanic and Atmospheric Administration (NOAA). (2020). *Climate at a glance | National Centers for Environmental Information (NCEI) [Dataset]*. Retrieved from www.ncdc.noaa.gov/cag/

Organización Internacional para las Migraciones (OIM). (2006). Glosario sobre Migración. *Derecho Internacional sobre Migración: Glosario sobre migración*, 7. https://doi.org/ISSSN: 1816–1014

Osima, S., Indasi, V. S., Zaroug, M., Endris, H. S., Gudoshava, M., Misiani, H. O., . . . Dosio, A. (2018). Projected climate over the Greater Horn of Africa under 1.5 °C and 2 °C global warming. *Environmental Research Letters, 13*(6). https://doi.org/10.1088/1748-9326/aaba1b

Parkes, B., Cronin, J., Dessens, O., & Sultan, B. (2019). Climate change in Africa: Costs of mitigating heat stress. *Climatic Change, 154*(3–4), 461–476. https://doi.org/10.1007/s10584-019-02405-w

Research Program on Climate Change Agriculture and Food Security (CCAFS). (2011). *Annual Report 2011: Groundwork for success*. https://cgspace.cgiar.org/bitstream/handle/10568/25195/http://CCAFS_AnnRpt2011.pdf

Royal Netherlands Meteorological Institute. (2020). *KNMI Climate Explorer [Dataset]*. https://climexp.knmi.nl/start.cgi

Shultz, J., Gómez Ceballos, Á. M., Espinel, Z., Rios Oliveros, S., Fonseca, M. F., & Hernandez Florez, L. J. (2014). Internal displacement in Colombia. *Disaster Health, 2*(1), 13–24. https://doi.org/10.4161/dish.27885

Solomon, N., Birhane, E., Gordon, C., Haile, M., Taheri, F., Azadi, H., & Scheffran, J. (2018). Environmental impacts and causes of conflict in the Horn of Africa: A review. *Earth-Science Reviews, 177*, 284–290. https://doi.org/10.1016/j.earscirev.2017.11.016

Tafere, M. (2018). Forced displacements and the environment: Its place in national and international climate agenda. *Journal of Environmental Management, 224*, 191–201. https://doi.org/10.1016/j.jenvman.2018.07.063

United Nations Economic Commission for Africa (UNECA). (2008). *Climate Change: African perspectives for a post-2012 Agreement*. Retrieved from www.uneca.org/sites/default/files/uploaded-documents/CoM/cfm2008/com2008_climatechange_en.pdf

United Nations Framework Convention on Climate Change. (2015). Paris Agreement of the United Nations Framework Convention on Climate Change. In *Cop21*. United Nations Framework Convention on Climate Change. Retrieved from http://unfccc.int/resource/docs/2015/cop21/spa/l09s.pdf%5Cnhttps://unfccc.int/files/meetings/paris_nov_2015/application/pdf/paris_agreement_spanish_.pdf

United Nations Office for the Coordination of Humanitarian Affairs. (2015). *World Disasters Report 2015: Focus on local actors, the key to humanitarian effectiveness*. Retrieved from https://reliefweb.int/report/world/world-disasters-report-2015

United Nations Office for the Coordination of Humanitarian Assistance. (1998). Guiding principles on internal displacement. In *Report of the Representative of the Secretary-General, Mr. Francis M. Deng, submitted pursuant to Commission resolution 1997/39*. Retrieved from https://digitallibrary.un.org/record/251017?ln=es

UN Office for Disaster Risk Reduction. (2015). Sendai Framework for disaster risk reduction 2015–2030. In UNISDR (Ed.), *Resolution approved by the General Assembly on June 3, 2015* (1st ed.). Oficina de las Naciones Unidas para la Reducción del Riesgo de Desastres. Retrieved from http://www2.ohchr.org/spanish/bodies/hrcouncil/docs/gaA.RES.60.1_Sp.pdf

Whitaker, B. E. (2002). Refugees in Western Tanzania: The distribution of burdens and benefits among local hosts. *Journal of Refugee Studies, 15*(4), 339–358. https://doi.org/10.1093/jrs/15.4.339

World Bank Group. (2020). *Climate change knowledge portal [Dataset]*. Retrieved from https://climateknowledgeportal.worldbank.org/

PART 6

Migration

29

INTERNAL MIGRATION IN SUB-SAHARAN AFRICA

Dynamics, destinations, and implications

Vollan O. Ochieng, Razak M Gyasi, and Blessing U Mberu

Introduction

Internal migration, particularly rural-urban migration, is considered the most common type of population movement in sub-Saharan Africa (SSA) with implications for long-term spatial population distribution, overwhelming emergence of agglomerates, and stimulating concentration of population in the region (Mberu, 2015; World Bank, 1999). Internal migration can either be voluntary or involuntary. The former includes those pertaining to a migrant's own pursuit to relocate to another area/region due to perceived or real, better prospects at the preferred destination. Involuntary migration, on the other hand, is induced by factors other than the migrant movement. It includes but is not limited to unwanted job transfers, conflicts, insecurities, and violent displacements at source or home (Oucho, Oucho, & Ochieng, 2014). In addition, internal migration takes the form of rural-urban migration, urban-rural migration, and urban-urban migration (Oucho & Oucho, 2015). Migration – internal and international – occurs as a result of individual's pursuit for better opportunities to counter challenges pertaining to access to better social welfare, health, poverty alleviating economic activities, and environmental quality (International Organization for Migration, 2018a; Mberu, Beguy, & Ezeh, 2017) with implications for migrants' socio-economic welfare. Migration also presents an implication for improved socio-economic status. Being a coping strategy, migration is largely driven by economic, environmental, political, and demographic factors both at origin and destination (Obuor et al., 2017). It has hence resulted in complex social and demographic policy challenges both at source and destination regions (International Labor Organization, 2018a). Existing evidence indicates that internal migration is more widespread than international migration, perhaps due to low-cost implications involved in relocation within a country rather than externally.

The evidence indicates that globally, internal migration is more widely practiced than international migration, thus warranting investigations into the effects of such population relocations on resources both at source and destination. Most African migrants resort to intra-country or inter-country movements within the continent (African Development

 DOI: 10.4324/9780429287213-35

Bank, 2019; 2018) compared to movement out of the continent due to the associated higher cost implications (UN CTAD, 2018; Fafchamps & Shilpi, 2013). Moreover, the pull factors at destinations require low or semi-developed skills sets that meet qualifications of most migrants. For instance, globally, internal migrants range between 740–763 million (UNESCO, 2019; International Organization for Migration, 2018a), while the number of international migrants nears 272 million people (UN DESA, 2019a). This explains why most educated youth in LMICs often migrate in search of employment opportunities within the confines of their countries (Fafchamps & Shilpi, 2013; Dudwick, 2011). Even for intra-country movements, distances covered by migrants are determined by migrants' financial capabilities. For instance, a Ghanaian study revealed that in Ghana's Upper West Region, rich migrants often migrated to distant urban towns in the south, including Accra, while poor migrants only managed shorter distances, mostly to the Brong Ahafo Region (Van der Geest, 2011).

More attention has been cast on the negative effects of rural-urban migration for both urban and rural political stability and economic development (Mberu, 2015; Chen, Valente, & Zlotnik, 1998). For instance, the effect of remittance reliance and population loss has been associated with limiting community's growth and encouraging underdevelopment (Oucho, 2019; Oucho, 2015). Evidence in SSA and much of the third world largely focus on four key migration spheres: migration in response to urbanization; migration for social networking; migration as a cushioning and/or safeguarding tool against risks, especially the economic risks; and migration due to emergence of tribal and peasant societies occasioned by capitalism (Mberu, 2015; Chapman & Prothero, 1984).

The evidence largely focuses on rural-urban migration and even in doing so, few focus in-depth on specific in-country migration destinations, effects (positive or negative using the economic and social lenses), and pull and push factors for internal migrants in three or more countries. By looking at evidence in more countries, it is possible to devise policy actions that speak to the effects and pull and push factors for or against internal migration in SSA especially if such effects and factors are cross-cutting and/or similar. Such will allow SSA to develop uniform policy actions that address common migration challenges. In light of this background, the potential impacts of migration may be determined by the kind of investments and opportunities accrued to migrants with diverse levels of skills from SSA. This chapter, therefore, seeks to explore the dynamics and effects of internal migration in Ghana, Kenya, and Nigeria, considering that they are countries with large economies in East and West Africa respectively as well as high migrant population (International Organization for Migration, 2018b, 2018c, 2019; UN DESA, 2019a, 2019b; Awumbila, 2017).

An extensive literature review and a content analysis were conducted. In the review, searches were primarily made from online sources including but not limited to UN databases (UNDP, UN DESA, ILO, UN CTAD, UNESCO, IOM, etc.), the World Bank, Google, Google Scholar, and grey literature. In the databases, the following were the search terms used: 'internal migration in SSA'; 'rural-urban migration in Ghana, Kenya, Nigeria'; 'rural-rural migration in Ghana, Kenya and Nigeria'; 'internal migration and rural development in Ghana/Kenya/Nigeria'; 'internal migration in Kenya'; 'internal migration in Ghana'; 'internal migration and rural development in Ghana, Kenya, and Nigeria'; 'internal migration and family systems/networks'; 'internal migration in Nigeria'; 'migration and rural challenges in SSA'; 'effects of internal migration'; 'migration destinations in Kenya, Ghana and Nigeria', and 'pull and push factors for internal migration in Ghana, Kenya and Nigeria'.

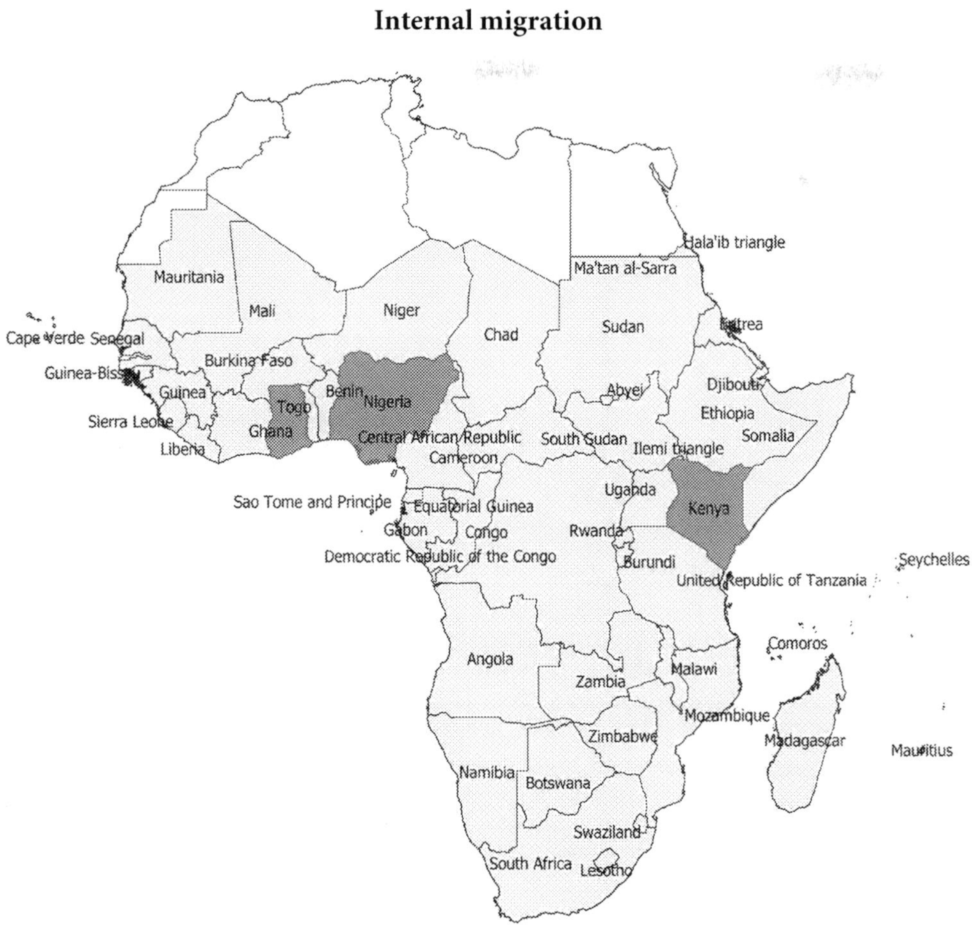

Figure 29.1 Sub-Saharan Africa, with countries of study (Ghana, Kenya, and Nigeria).

Internal migrants' destinations: Ghana, Kenya, and Nigeria

a) Ghana

The country has an estimated population of 29.8 million (UNDP, 2019), with high numbers concentrated in the southern half of the country especially near and along the Atlantic coast (CIA, 2017). Ghana enjoys a stable and strong economy which places it as one of the most advanced and largest West African markets, heavily relying on oil, cocoa, gold, diamonds, bauxite, and manganese (BBC Monitoring, 2017). The country is ranked 142 out of 188 countries, with a Human Development Index (HDI) value of 0.596. Despite the remarkable economic growth, Ghana has not been able to absorb the quickly growing labour force in its labour market leading to high youth unemployment and internal and international migration (UN DESA, 2019a). Ghana is recorded to be one of the fastest-growing economies in the world, with a growth of 8.9% for 2018 (UN DESA, 2019a). Much of the country's economy is capital-intensive with industries like services, oil, and mining dominating in the labour

Table 29.1 Key Demographic and Development Indicators: Ghana, Kenya, and Nigeria

Ghana		*Kenya*		*Nigeria*	
Indicator(s)		*Indicator(s)*		*Indicator(s)*	
Total area, *in sq km*[a]	238,533	Total area, *in sq km*[a]	580,367	Total area, *in sq km*[a]	923,768
Population (2019), *in million*[b]	**29.8**	Population (2019)[b]	**47,564,296**	Population (2019), *in million*[a]	205,430,839
Urban Population (2019), *% of total*[b]	56.1	Urban Population (2019), *% of total*[b]	27.3	Urban Population (2019), *% of total*[b]	51.2
Population Growth Rate, average annual growth (2015–2019) %[b]	2.3	Population Growth Rate, average annual growth (2015–2019) %[b]	2.3	Population Growth Rate, average annual growth (2015–2019) %[c]	2.6
Ethnic Groups[a]	Akan 47.5%, Ewe 13.9%, Mole 16.6%, Ga-Dangme 7.4%, Gurma 5.7%, Guan 3.7%, Mande 1.1%, Other 1.4%.	Ethnic Groups[b]	Kikuyu 17.2%, Luhya 13.8%, Kalejin 12.9%, Luo 10.5%, Kamba 10.1%, Somali 6.2%, Kisii 5.7%, Mijikenda 5.1%, Meru 4.3%, Turkana 2.6%, Masai 2.2%, Other 9.4%	Ethnic Groups[c]	Hausa – 25% Yoruba – 21% Igbo – 15% Ijaw – 10% Fulani – 4% Kanuri – 4% Ibibo – 3.5% Tiv – 3.5% Others – 12%
Human Development Index (HDI) (2019)[b]	0.596	Human Development Index (HDI) (2019)[d]	0.579	Human Development Index (HDI) (2019)[d]	0.534
***Country Rank out of 188*[b]**	142	*Country Rank out of 188*[c]	147	*Country Rank out of 188*[d]	158
GDP based on PPP per Capita, *current international dollars per capita* (2019)[c]	2,202.312	GDP based on PPP per Capita, *current international dollars per capita (2019)*[c]	3,467.60	GDP based on PPP per Capita, *current international dollars per capita (2020)*[d]	2,028.20

Life Expectancy at Birth (2019), *years*[b/c]	63.9	Life Expectancy at Birth (2019), *years*[c]	66	Life Expectancy at Birth (2019), *years*[d]	54
Unemployment (2019), ***% of labour force***[b]	6.78%	Unemployment (2019), *% of labour force*[c/e]	9.31	Unemployment (2019), *% of labour force*[c]	23.1
Youth Unemployment (2019), % ***ages 15–24***[b]	13.69%	Youth Unemployment (2019), *% ages 15–24*[e]	18.3	Youth Unemployment (2019), *% ages 15–24*[f]	19.6
Multidimensional Poverty Headcount (2018)[d], %	30.1	Multidimensional Poverty Headcount (2018)[c], %	38.7	Multidimensional Poverty Headcount (2018)[d], %	51.4
Foreign Direct Investment (net inflows, 2019), ***current USD millions***[e]	2.9	Foreign Direct Investment (net inflows, 2019), *current USD millions*[c]	1,625.9	Foreign Direct Investment (net inflows, 2019), *current USD millions*[d]	1,997.4
Net Official Development Assistance Received (2018), ***current USD millions***[c]	1,256.7	Net Official Development Assistance Received (2019), *current USD millions*[c]	2.5	Net Official Development Assistance Received (2019), *current USD millions*[d]	3.3
Personal Remittances Received (2019), ***current USD millions***[c]	5.37	Personal Remittances Received (2019), *current USD millions*[c]	2.7	Personal Remittances Received (2019), *current USD millions*[d]	24.3
Sources: [a](CIA, 2017); [b](UN DESA, 2019); [c](World Bank, 2019); [d](UNDP, 2019); [e](UN CTAD's World Investment Report 2019)		**Sources:** [a](CIA, 2017); [b](KNBS, 2019); [c](World Bank, 2019); [d](UNDP, 2019); [e](ILO, 2019)		**Sources:** [a](World Population Review, 2020); [b](Knoema 2019); [c](Findlay, 2019); [d](World Bank, 2019); [e](Nigeria National Bureau of Statistcs, 2019); [f](ILO, 2019)	

market. These industries are foreign direct investments (FDI) driven and, thus, are attracting expert labour force, with low capacities for absorption of the domestic labour – largely the youthful population (Honorati & De-Silva, 2016). Ironically, the country's 'actual economic engine', supported by agriculture, has witnessed steady declines occasioned by lack of innovation and modernization in all stages of production. The youth aged between 15 and 34 years have been unduly unable to access decent jobs, further worsening the unemployment status in the country attributed to the youth bulge (Maastricht Graduate School of Governance (MGSoG, 2017). In light of this fact, youth as well as persons within the productive age in Ghana have been left with no option but to migrate in search of better prospects elsewhere. Migration in Ghana is largely internal with predominantly north-south directional situation/occurrence (Quartey, 2006; Anarfi, Kwankye, Ababio, & Tiemoko, 2003), like many other West African nations since pre-colonial periods (International Organization for Migration, 2009a).

For instance, in 2010 more than 80% of Ghanaian migrants stayed in Ghana of which 70% were in cities and towns (Ackah & Medvedev, 2010; Black, King, & Tiemoko, 2003). The situation has remained unchanged over time, meaning more than 60% of households indicate having at least one migrant member residing in urban areas and sending remittances to family members in rural areas (Teye, 2018; Awumbila, Teye, & Yaro, 2016).

Evidence (Duplantier, Ksoll, Lehrer, & Seitz, 2017) indicates that Ghanaian youth post senior high school (SHS) prefer certain destinations over others. For instance, post-SHS youth prefer and migrate to the Ashanti, Greater Accra, Brong Ahafo, and northern regions. These areas not only attract youth from other regions but also retain youth who are originally from these areas. This implies that the areas are well endowed with better migrant pull factors like employment and educational opportunities among others. Regions like Eastern, Volta, Upper West, Western, and Upper East have very few migrants who received their schooling elsewhere. Equally, the regions have low retention rates for youth originally from these regions. Table 29.2 provides a detailed highlight.

Table 29.2 Migration Locations (Destinations) after Senior High School (SHS)

SHS Region										
	Ashanti	*Brong Ahafo*	*Central*	*Eastern*	*Greater Accra*	*Northern*	*Upper East*	*Upper West*	*Volta*	*Western*
Ashanti	80.94	15.04	8.15	3.51	2.17	2.99	17.65	9.76	2.13	5.08
Brong Ahafo	4.21	72.56	0.43	0.64	0	4.79	2.35	12.2	0	0.56
Central	3.22	0.75	55.79	3.19	2.17	0	2.35	0	2.39	3.39
Eastern	0.5	0	0.86	42.17	0.54	0	2.35	1.22	0.53	1.13
Greater Accra	7.92	6.02	27.47	47.6	92.39	6.59	21.18	4.88	29.79	13.56
Northern	0.25	1.88	0	0.96	0.54	80.84	10.59	6.1	0.80	0
Upper East	0	0	0	0.32	0.54	1.8	41.18	3.66	0.53	0.56
Upper West	0.25	0	0.86	0.32	0	2.4	1.18	56.1	0.53	0.56
Volta	0.25	0.75	0.43	0.32	1.09	0.6	0	1.22	62.5	0
Western	2.48	3.01	6.01	0.96	0.54	0	1.18	4.88	0.80	75.14
Total (%)	100	100	100	100	100	100	100	100	100	100

Source: Duplantier et al., 2017

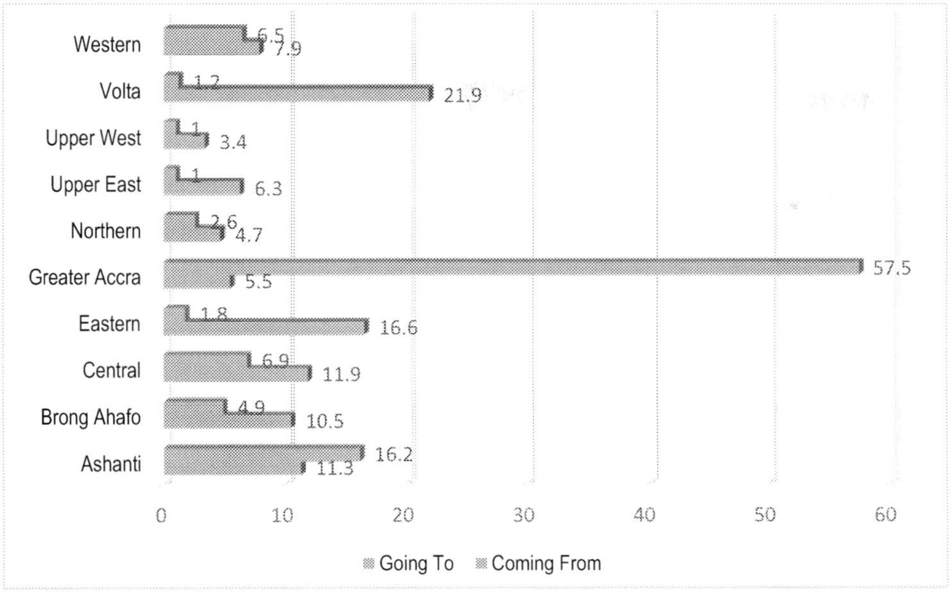

Figure 29.2 reveals that generally, majority of internal migrants migrate to Greater Accra region followed by Ashanti, Central and Western respectively while fewer migrants migrate to Eastern, Upper West, Volta, and Upper East respectively.

b) Kenya

Socially, Kenya is a multi-religious, multicultural, and multi-ethnic country that hosts one of the largest and world's oldest refugee populations in Africa (International Organization for Migration, 2018c). This makes the country more liable to internal migration – native or refugee status notwithstanding. The migration management is being informed by ongoing policy developments in Kenya as well as its strategic location in the East African region, which continue to affect the flow and structure of migration and its system in the country (Horwood, 2015; Methmann & Oels, 2015). More importantly, the country's internal migration is largely informed by its natural population increase as well as from in-migration refugee camps and other neighbouring countries prompting relocation to other areas in search of better livelihoods. It is such population increases that have pushed the country's population to approximately 48 million from about 39 million people, an increase of about 9 million people from the 2009 figures (Kenya National Bureau of Statistics, 2019; National Coordination Mechanism on Migration, 2018a, 2018b). The natural population increase further stems from the fact that the country's number of births by far exceeds total number of deaths. The country's sex ratio was 1.000 (1,000 males per 1,000 females) which is unlike the global sex ratio of 1,016 males to 1,000 females in 2017 (IOM, 2018c). This implies that internal migration for both males and females could take more or less the same proportion of the population.

Rural-urban migration is predominantly practiced in Kenya with major urban centres (Nairobi, Mombasa, and Kisumu) being major recipients of migrants (Oucho et al., 2014). Nairobi receives a majority of its in-migrants from central, eastern and Nyanza (western) regions of the country. In coastal and central regions, most rural-urban migration practice was to urban areas situated within the region, especially workers to huge sisal plantations in the coastal regions:

coffee plantations in Kiambu, Nyeri, and Kirinyaga as well as tea plantations in Kiambu (International Organization for Migration, 2018c). Likewise, a number of agricultural towns, mostly in the Rift Valley Region, have emerged as key destination areas due to the expansive plantation forms in these towns. For instance, Kericho and Naivasha are key migrant destinations due to tea and flower plantations respectively in those towns (Oucho, 2010, 2009, n.d.). Overall, migration to urban areas is predominantly male-led, compared to female migrants, a situation that is consistent with the migration pattern observed during the colonial era (pre-1963) (International Organization for Migration, 2018c). Table 29.3 highlights the demographics and patterns of migration in Kenya.

c) Nigeria

Nigeria, like most SSA countries is bedevilled by internal migration practices, fuelled by the country's prevailing economic, political, and labour market environment/dynamics, which have resulted in challenges in access to jobs, poverty, education, and challenges related to healthcare access (IOM & ICMPD, 2015; Oyeneyi, 2013; Taiwo, 2013). Evidence reveals that more than 10% of Nigerians live in states other than their birth states. Put in perspective, Nigerians with the highest internal migrants were those from Ogun, Kwara, Osun, and Imo, recording more than 20% of migrants living in other states (International Organization for Migration, 2016). Equally, high internal migration practices are evident in Abia, Akwa Ibom, Anambra, Delta, Edo, Kogi, Oyo, and Ondo, most of which are in the south part of the country except Kogi and Kware which are in the north-central part of the country. Migration data from the National Population Commission further reveal that 23% of the Nigerian population sampled were migrants who had relocated within ten years, while 2% were return migrants (National Population Commission (NPopC), 2012), indicating that the highest proportion of migrants were internal migrants.

Table 29.3 Number of Male Migrants per 100 Female Migrants by Destination and Age

Region	*Age Group*					
	Place of Destination	*0–14*	*15–24*	*25–59*	*60+*	*Total*
Central	Rural	98	86	120	85	105
	Urban	103	72	131	69	96
Coast	Rural	94	111	146	75	108
	Urban	103	79	125	57	95
Eastern	Rural	93	142	169	100	102
	Urban	95	76	142	62	97
Northeastern	Rural	95	144	120	111	99
	Urban	88	94	183	92	104
Nyanza	Rural	105	62	119	83	101
	Urban	103	70	139	63	99
Rift Valley	Rural	96	100	134	75	103
	Urban	98	83	131	69	96
Western	Rural	106	62	103	83	100
	Urban	102	72	133	71	100

Source: Data, IOM (2018c); Table by Author.

In terms of migration status, household population distribution shows that migrants compose at least two fifths of the total population in seven states including Abia, Imo, Anambra, Delta, Bayelsa, Ekiti, and Lagos, out of 36 states in the country. Additionally, more than 20 states including the Abuja Federal Capital Territory record higher percentages than the national average of 23%. Few migrant households (2%) report return migration, associated with retirement with only five states recording over 5% return migrants, including Ekiti (7.4%), Edo (6.2%), Anambra (6%), Delta (5.5%), and Imo (5.1%) (NNBS, 2014). The fact that these states are adjoining could imply that there exists a unifying or crosscutting sociocultural norm or attachment associated with home return at old age/retirement that is not area or ethnic specific.

In terms of gendered migration, a new trend is observable in which more females (51.5%) migrate than males (48.5%). This trend was evident in 21 of the 36 states with Sokoto, Plateau, Adamawa, Jigawa, and Katsina recording the highest proportion of female migrants (International Organization for Migration, 2016; Oyeniyi, 2013). The states together with seven states [total of 12 states] are all in the northern part of the country which could imply an emerging sociocultural female behaviour including but not limited to marriages, more household leadership roles and the need to migrate in search of employment to support families back home, and restrictive female practices from which women are running. States leading in male internal migration include Delta, Oyo, Ogun, Akwa Ibom, Enugu, and Taraba. In comparison, there are more male return migrants (61.3%) over females (38.7%) (Okoronkwo, 2014), implying that female migrants may have migrated to urban or other areas and gotten married in their destinations.

Urban areas attract the largest (60%) share of internal migrants compared to rural areas (40%). States attracting rural migrants are those with extensive plantations like Taraba, Nasarawa, Kebbi, Jigawa, Benue, Bauchi, and Akwa Ibom while urban areas with the highest concentration of migrants are Anambra, Ebonyi, Lagos, Ogun, Enugu, Oyo, and Delta (NNBS, 2014, 2013).

In terms of migrants' flow, Nigeria's north-central area attracts more internal migrants than other areas. It is followed by south-south, south-west, and south-east intra-country internal migration flows. This indicates that north-central and south-south zones are the epicentres of internal migration flows in Nigeria chiefly attributable to the south-south's wealth in natural resources (e.g. petroleum), and the north-central's administrative attraction rising from elevation of Abuja as the country's capital city (De-Haas, 2008). Other migration push factors in Nigeria are involuntary including civil strife, climate change, and insecurities (Oyeniyi, 2013).

In general, internal migration tilts the net lifetime migration towards Anambra (98%), the west-central areas that the Federal Capital Territory of Abuja occupies (85.1%), as well as the Lagos Metropolitan area (97%), while the south-east geo-political zones are key out migration centers (source/origin areas for migrants) (International Organization for Migration, 2009b; Oyeniyi, 2013).

Pull and push factors

The pull and push factors for Ghana, Kenya, and Nigeria are largely similar. For instance, youth in Ghana are attracted to urban areas due to perceived and/or actual existing employment opportunities at destinations (cities), modern and well-equipped schools, adequate and well-maintained road or rail network, decent housing, and other infrastructure like electricity, internet, and water sewerage (Edwin, 2016). The Ghanaian pull factors are consistent with the Kenyan factors in addition to existing security, self-independence for youth migrants, access to foreign investors, social security, food security, and healthcare at destinations of choice in Kenya (Oucho, 2019; Ratha et al., 2011). For Nigeria, other than the captured pull factors for Ghana

Table 29.4 Distribution of Migrants and Their Destination: Urban-Rural Dynamics

States	*Urban (in %)*	*Rural (in %)*
Abuja (FCT)	85.1	14.9
Abia	48.4	51.6
Adamawa	58.3	41.7
Anambra	98.0	2.0
Bayelsa	62.4	37.6
Cross River	41.5	58.5
Gombe	58.5	41.5
Kaduna	68.4	31.6
Kano	55.1	44.9
Kwara	69.7	30.3
Lagos	97.0	3.0
Oyo	84.0	16.0

Source: Oyeniyi (2013).

and Kenya, perceived availability or ease of access to reliable and stable marriage or marital partners, civil service (in-service) jobs, National Youth Service (NYSC), and freedom from parents are cited as key drivers or pull factors for Nigerian migrants (Oyeniyi, 2013).

Push factors include insecurities (e.g. post-election violence), developmental marginalization, poor or inadequately resourced educational institutions and lack of (farming) land for youth at points of origin (rural homes) (Edwin, 2016), food insecurity, climate change, development-based displacement, poor and lacking basic healthcare needs (Oucho, 2019), increased youth unemployment, parental neglect, and the consistent breakdown of social support networks in rural areas, which forces migrants to relocate to other areas, mostly cities in pursuit of employment (International Organization for Migration, 2016; Oyeniyi, 2013; NPopC, 2012). It is important to point out that the pull and push factors captured in this section are cross-cutting among countries and none of them are unique to only one country.

Effects of internal migration

There exists an inextricable link between internal migration, health, education, and urbanization that studies and research in SSA seldom focus on, and this is not strange in the three countries' contexts (Nyaoro, Schade, & Schmidt, 2016).

i) Urbanization

The urban environment is a dynamic and complex setting with a serious impact on individuals' well-being, health, and related health practices. Putting dynamism and complexity in perspective, three features of contemporary urbanization differentiate it from previous processes: a) proliferation of informal settlements and their effects and impacts on the urban environment and the same environment's impact on the informal settlements; b) the high rate of urban growth and its effects on local governments; and c) the explosion of poverty and its effects on the urban economy (Duplantier et al., 2017; Awumbila, Manuh, Quartey, Tagoe, & Bosiakoh, 2008). Together, the three characteristics have yielded 'new urban settings' synonymized by deep-seated change processes with both negative and positive effects, an expanded metropolitan

Figure 29.3 A view of slums in Accra and Nairobi.

area, infiltration and proliferation of informal settlements, widespread environmental impacts, and increased inequities and inequalities (WHO, 2005).

Ghana like any other country, is witnessing rapid urbanization levels attributable to internal migration (International Organization for Migration, 2018b). As previously captured, the majority of the migrants are either unskilled, semi-skilled, and/or illiterate or semi-illiterate, which works against them in terms of access to and retention of decent jobs as well as in creation of employment for themselves or others (African Development Bank, 2018; Mberu et al., 2017). As a result, the youth and the migrant community at large in Ghana often contend with challenges associated with low or lack of income attributed to poor pay from informal employments. This, however, does not mean that internal migrants perform dismally in terms of socio-economic attainments but rather that the vast majority are not as privileged and endowed as would be expected of a migrant. For instance, with low or lack of employment, migrants have no alternative but to contend with poor accommodation in informal settlements that they can afford (Awumbila, 2017; Ochieng & Onyatta, 2016).

With rural-urban migration as well as urban-urban migration still on the rise, Ghana's urban informal settlements continue to spread to accommodate the ever-increasing migrant populations, most of which have no or limited educational qualification (UN-Habitat, 2018). Such expansion has widened existing urban informal settlements in Ghana that even the neighbouring communities have been merged with the urban centre forming a metropolis (Ghana Statistical Service, 2016). For instance, Accra and Kumasi are examples that suffice (Teye, 2018; Owusu, 2018). Equally, issues to do with inadequate essential infrastructure like health, road networks, educational facilities, and decent and affordable accommodation as well as waste disposal systems and infrastructures have compounded rapid urbanization in Ghana's major urban centres (Awumbila, 2017), leading to what is termed as the 'urbanization of poverty' (Oucho et al., 2014).

In Kenya, rapid population growth triggered by both internal and natural population growth is playing a leading role in the country's urbanization process. With internal migration, spurred by natural population increase, there is an observable reclassification of previously rural areas, subjecting the already delicate urban milieu in precarious states of development (Oucho & Oucho, 2010). Rural-urban migration has particularly been a key contributor to the urbanization trends witnessed in Kenya's old and emerging towns. As a result, 31.1% (14.83 million) of the total population (47,564,296 people), with major urban centres accommodating the highest proportion – Nairobi city ranking highest with 4.397 million, Mombasa 1.208 million, Nakuru 570,674, Kisumu 440,891, and Eldoret 475,716 (Kenya National Bureau of Statistics, 2019). More importantly, internal migration has significantly contributed to Kenya's urban sprawl in major and emerging urban centres. The key observable effect of internal migration is rapid urbanization, engulfing former rural communities at the periphery of major urban centres – known as peri-urban (J. O. Oucho et al., 2014).

Due to limited space available for further expansion, compounded by lack of jobs or existence of poor-paying jobs for migrants, informal settlements took precedence in Kenya's major urban centres – Nairobi, Mombasa, Kisumu, Nakuru, and Eldoret just to name a few (Kenya National Bureau of Statistics, 2019; International Organization for Migration, 2018c). This has led to increased resources channelled to these areas to offer health, education, and infrastructural needs beyond the capacities of both the national and local governments. Consequently, it is not surprising to find informal settlements characterized by poor sanitation (water sanitation and hygiene), poor housing conditions, high joblessness and related insecurities, poor environmental conditions, and limited or lacking infrastructural systems (Desgroppes & Taupin, 2011). However, urbanization is still perceived in Kenya as a sure way to gain easy access to better services like education, health, and employment, thus still attracting immigrants (Regional Mixed Migration Secretariat, 2018). In fact, Kenyan internal migrants contend that there is an intricate relationship between rural-urban migration and reduction of rural poverty (Oucho & Oucho, 2010). Against this backdrop, challenges and benefits adduced from migration at individual levels and from the country's economic perspective will still be an issue of contention.

Nigerian urbanization, occasioned by natural population increase at destination as well as by internal migration and immigration, has resulted in high urban population growth that has remained above 2% per annum in the past several years (UN DESA, 2019b; Aliyu &

Amadu, 2017). Consequently, Nigerian cities have witnessed rapid growth of uncontrolled and unplanned urban settlements in major cities and towns (The Cities Alliance, 2007). Existing supportive evidence shows that inefficient and ineffective urban land-use planning in Nigeria plays a central role in worsening experienced urban challenges like poverty, congestion, unemployment, air pollution, and environmental degradation, among others (Avis, 2019; Onibokun & Faniran, 2015; The Cities Alliance, 2007).

Internal migration, specifically rural-urban and urban-urban migration, to major urban areas in Nigeria has resulted in immense pressure on the urban environment, resulting in challenges synonymous with most urban settlements – poverty, un/under-employment, crime and insecurities, a sprawl of informal settlements, and environmental pollution among others (Avis, 2019). With every population increase in Nigeria's urban centres, the urban edge undergoes constant metamorphosis (OECD, 2016; Bloch, Fox, Monroy, & Ojo, 2015). In Nigeria, an area is considered urban if it has 20,000 or more inhabitants, which is higher than the proportion used to constitute an urban area in most countries (Ofem, 2012). While the current urbanization trends in most Nigerian urban centres are high, projections are that the country's urban population will continue to grow in the foreseeable future with projections that the country's population will double within the next 30 years (UN DESA, 2019b).

Populations in pursuit of better economic prospects in Nigeria continue to influx major cities in Nigeria – Abuja, Lagos, and Ibadan as well as other major urban settlements. The urban influx in these cities has been so severe that the country's capacity to adequately provide basic services like decent housing, employment, and related infrastructure has been compromised (Aliyu & Amadu, 2017; Angel, 2011), leading to the urbanization of poverty in these cities (Oucho & Oucho, 2010). Internal migration has significantly reduced the rural population in Nigeria with over 50% of the country's total population residing in urban areas (UN DESA, 2019a, 2019b).

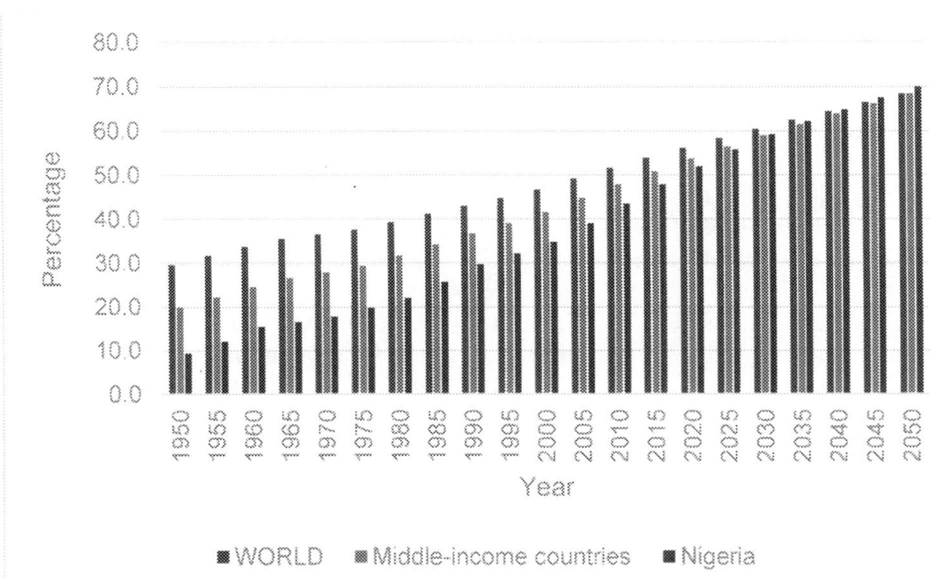

Figure 29.4 Nigeria's urban population, 1950–2050.

As a result, there is an insurgence of urban poor settlements – slums or informal settlements – in major cities and urban centres in Nigeria, where populations daily contend with hazardous environmental conditions, poor water and sanitation access, crimes and insecurities due to un/under-employment, poor and/or inadequate infrastructure, and poor access to health and educational service (Avis, 2019; Farrell, 2018a, 2018b).

ii) Education

Internal migration has noteworthy effects on education and educational outcomes for migrants, migrants' families, and the government. Internal migration is credited for promoting basic and advanced educational acquisition for both migrants and their dependents, thereby controlling out-of-school children and youth of SSA. In Ghana, migrants who have secured employment at destinations send money to their families back in rural areas for livelihoods. Through remittances, many rural households with migrant family members are able to raise children and keep them in school (Kabki et al., 2004; Lall, Timmins, & Shouyue, 2009; Teye, 2018). This is particularly true in Ashanti region in Ghana (Wong, 2006). This has also contributed to an enhancement of rural business enterprises and economy (Herman, 2006; Smith, 2007a, 2007b), housing (Poel, 2005), and overall community development (Mumuni, 2007). This implies that remittances emanating from internal migration play a significant role in Ghana's poverty alleviation and development discourse.

In Kenya, internal migration is perceived to a key contributor of educational outcomes, both directly and indirectly, attracting students nationally and internationally (National Coordination Mechanism on Migration, 2018b). Most young people migrate to urban areas in pursuit of college and university education which are almost non-existent in rural areas. Migration thus enables the young people to acquire requisite education and skill development needed for employment. Most public and private higher educational institutions are established in urban centres prompting all forms of internal migration – urban-rural, rural-urban, and urban-urban. For migrants with post-college and university education, access to formal employment has been tenable compared to those without such education or those who never migrated. The employed migrants, bound by familial ties, often send money back home for educational purposes for siblings and for other development projects in rural areas (International Organization for Migration, 2015b; Oucho et al., 2014). This implies that migration greatly contributes to the advancement of the country's educational attainment both directly and indirectly.

Nigeria's case does not deviate from the Ghanaian and Kenyan context. Most internal migrants in Nigeria have acquired high education and found decent jobs that enabled them grow in their careers and businesses (IOM, 2016; Okoronkwo, 2014). In an effort to support their dependents' educational prospects, migrants in Nigerian urban centres often remit monies home to help in furthering education of their children, siblings, and other family members both in rural areas as well as in other urban areas but pursuing education. For instance, in Abia, Bayelsa, Anambra, Lagos, Oyo, and Cross River, funds remitted to families in these regions by migrant families were used to support dependents' education as well as help recipient family members build schools, buy books, fund scholarships, and purchase other school materials like furniture (Oyeniyi, 2013; World Bank, 2012a, 2012b, 2011).

Internal migration has also enabled migrants and their dependents to go through foreign educational curricula. The Nigerian economy has attracted foreign nationals working in international companies and organizations. This led to the establishment of schools that suit such expatriates' educational needs. Consequently, British, American, and Turkish among other types of schools have been set up in Abuja, Lagos, and many other cities across the country. The same applies for universities since some foreign universities have been set up in Nigeria's major cities (International Organization for Migration, 2014b; Oyeniyi, 2013). Nigerians, most of whom are internal migrants with means, have enrolled their children in these schools, enabling their children to acquire foreign education as well as cultures that befit those of the school's parent county (International Organization for Migration, 2014a; Oyeniyi, 2013).

For instance, the large influx of internal migrants from rural areas as well as from city to city or from one urban area to another has resulted in increased students' enrolment beyond the capacities of existing institutions in major urban centres, particularly Greater Accra and Greater Kumasi (Teye, 2018). As a result, the ratio of students to teachers is imbalanced across all educational levels. Consequently, quality of educational outcomes for students has been found to be wanting, considering that students are getting the requisite time and attention from teachers. The situation further worsens the high youth unemployment in Ghana due to lack of and poor exhibition of employability skills (Lall, Selod, & Shalizi 2006; Lall et al., 2009;). In the same breath, the young migrants migrating in pursuit of better or higher educational attainments in polytechnics, colleges, and universities in Ghana contend with few educators because the majority of qualified educators have migrated to other countries [emigration] for better prospects. In fact, over 60% of faculty positions in polytechnics and 40% in public universities are vacant, lowering educational outcomes for learners (Awumbila, 2017; Duplantier et al., 2017).

Kenya and Nigeria contend with a similar predicament. This is because education is also stifled by migration in Kenya due to the imbalanced ratio of teachers to learners/students in most Kenyan institutions. For instance, a significant number of Kenyans have emigrated to other countries in pursuit of better opportunities – leaving few teachers to teach a high student population (International Organization for Migration, 2015b). This has a direct negative effect on educational outcomes of Kenyan students. In fact, in light of this predicament, most institutions, particularly private primary institutions in informal areas, resort to hiring unqualified teachers to meet the shortfall (International Organization for Migration, 2018d; Mberu et al., 2017), which has the possibility of compromising quality. This is partly because of the high costs involved in hiring a trained teacher, and also the willingness of the sought teacher to teach in informal settings. For Nigeria, rural-urban migration has led to increased enrolments in urban schools compared to rural schools, leading to increased resourcing of urban schools (Oyeniyi, 2013), which has had reduced investments in rural schools resulting in lower educational outcomes among learners in rural schools (International Organization for Migration, 2014a). It is thus evident that migration has both positive and negative outcomes on education.

iii) Family systems

Family is loosely and conventionally observed as a group co-residence, cooking from the same kitchen and pot, sharing of household prepared meals, and joint decision-making. However, as a result of internal migration, families and family structures have become more fluid in composition, size, and location (International Organization for Migration, 2017, 2015b; Ratha et al., 2011). Family as a unit is the core of shelter, relationship development, parenting, economic production, consumption, and inheritance, hence an essential component that warrants an in-depth look in light of migration.

It is undisputed that migration has contributed both positively and negatively in migrants' socio-economic status, reflected in their familial systems. In Ghana for instance, internal migrants immensely contribute to rural development. For instance, in a study of households in Nima and Old Fadama, migrants report mutual support to and from rural homes. For in-transfer (receipt of aid), only 24% confirmed receipt of rural support while 78% confirmed out-transfer (remittances) to rural areas to build houses and other development projects (Awumbila, Owusu, & Teye, 2014), which have contributed to migrants and the families closed-knit union and interdependence.

In Kenya, internal migration has been observed to have both direct and indirect consequences on family and household members, particularly in terms of the gender roles, expenditure, socialization processes, poverty and inequality, consumption patterns, migration decisions, and livelihood strategies (International Organization for Migration, 2018d). These have further been catalyzed by modernity and a mix of environmental, economic, and social factors leading to development of new types of households and family formations, structure, and composition (International Organization for Migration, 2015a). For instance, with migration of population from rural to urban, urban to other urban areas, rural area to another plantation-dominant rural area, or from urban area to a rural area (circular/oscillatory migration), families and households have become less nuclear and extended (Oucho & Oucho, 2010), but with observable developmental results. Migrants in urban areas in Kenya, particularly those in informal settlements, maintain close contacts with their rural homes perhaps as a source of safety nets for psychosocial and material support. For instance, a study revealed that 80% of slum-dwellers in Nairobi maintained contact with their families in their rural homes during any time in the course of the year. Family-specific factors like nuclear family members living in rural places play an integral part in contact maintenance between migrants and rural family members (Mberu et al., 2012). The reasons and patterns of linkages are in keeping with migrants' material and financial contributions to rural origins. This implies that internal migrants in urban areas are in fact not living in isolation but rather in a distant communal web with rural families. Migrants in urban areas keep such networks with rural residents as means of creating a sustained and trusted web of safeguards against rural development risks. A study of migrants in Western Kenya revealed that migrants keep contacts with rural residents, especially immediate families to help them advance development projects. Migrants were found to send material and financial resources for rural development projects, including construction of rural houses, care of elderly parents, purchase of livestock, school fees for children and siblings, and community fundraising (Ochieng & Onyatta, 2016; Oucho et al., 2014; Oucho, 2009).

This is similar to the Nigerian context wherein migration is linked to rural development since most migrants invest in rural development in various ways. For instance, studies of migrants from Eastern Nigeria reveal that Igbo migrants heavily invest in residential buildings in their rural homes to provide critical household and accommodation facilities. Such investments are aimed at enhancing migrants' social status at family and community level. In fact, in most Igbo communities, rich indigenes compete in building outstanding infrastructures at home to outdo the other. This has resulted in existence of modern facilities in this region including but not limited to boreholes fitted with taps, electricity generators, and satellite dishes which are extended to benefit local communities, including churches, hospitals, markets, roads, and community electrification (Mberu, 2015). Such rural investments have even had multiplier effects that have motivated other migrants from other rural communities to return and invest in rural homes (Chukwuezi, 2001).

On the negative side, internal migration has had adverse effects on familial relations, especially when children or a spouse is left behind. Since in most cases it is only one parent who migrates (at least in the initial stages), a pool of single parenthood has emerged (Contreras & Griffith, 2012). Evidence indicates that when mothers migrate, there is a high likelihood that their children (left behind) will drop out of school or become vulnerable to situations of incest, abuse, and neglect (International Labor Organization, 2004; Oucho & Oucho, 2015; International Labor Organization, 2018).

In Ghana, some internal migrants in cities tend to send their children to rural homes, dubbed 'postal babies' to be tended to by friends and relatives. Others are sent to boarding or hostel facilities in other towns or rural areas. In instances in which internal migration involves spousal separation, cases of extramarital affairs are common, resulting in marital tensions. The situation becomes even more complicated when sexually transmitted diseases like HIV and AIDS are reported (Deshingkar & Grimm, 2005; Lattof, Coast, Leone, & Nyarko, 2018). Evidence also indicates that internal migration leads to the re-shaping of the parent-child relationship inconsistencies in relation to mothers' role in caregiving. This is consistent with a study finding on Ghanaian migrant population which revealed that migration tend to reduce motherhood, especially where other relatives and family members are involved to offer childcare support to children in the absence of maternal mothers (Lattof, 2018).

In Kenya, there is a surge in the number of divorces and separations attributed to migration in which one spouse leaves the other behind. As a result, internal migration in Kenya is, to a great extent, blamed for the increased number of female-headed households, single-people households, and single-parent families. Such emerging family and household arrangements have had far-ranging effects on societal social relations. For instance, Kenya's children in single-parent-headed households exhibit and experience higher incidences of low access to basic necessities like healthcare and education as well as economic poverty than their counterparts with all parents (Regional Mixed Migration Secretariat, 2018; International Organization for Migration, 2018d). Equally, internal migration negatively affects the elderly left behind because they lack the essential family and household support from migrant family/household members. The diminished long-term care for the elderly from the family/household thus puts more pressure on the State, being the custodian of all the citizenry (International Organization for Migration, 2015b). Nevertheless, remittances from internal migrants also help in cushioning the family/household members left behind from the adverse effects of poverty. Families with migrants in urban centres report receipt of remittance from families in the cities/towns for educational support for siblings and children, farming, for purchase of livestock, for healthcare of sick family members, for construction of permanent houses, and for funeral expenses (International Organization for Migration, 2015b; Oucho et al., 2014; Ratha et al., 2011; Kiiru, 2010).

Equally, in Nigeria, internal migration is also linked to societal ills that upset social harmony, especially in rural areas. For instance, internal migration is blamed on increased incidences of prostitution, forced labour, and human trafficking and deemed to be a cause of waste management challenges and related environmental challenges, and urban un/under-employment (Oyeniyi, 2013; Melde & El Mouaatamid, 2011). Studies have shown that vulnerable populations – children from vulnerable households and women – in Nigeria's rural areas are often lured to migrate to urban areas by persons known and trusted by them and their family members for employment, educational attainments or for family reunions only to end up as victims of trafficking serving non-relatives at low or no pay (Akinyoade, 2012). For instance, due to internal migration practices, women and children (children of both genders) have been trafficked from Shaki in Oyo State, Cross River, Ebonyi, Imo, Kwara, Akwa Ibom, and Benue to cities like Ibadan, Lagos, Port-Harcourt, Abeokuta, Calabar, and Kano (UNICEF, 2012; Olagbegi, 2006; Olagbegi et al., 2006), to work in jobs different from those they agreed to when living their rural destinations leading to family and friendship disintegration and mistrust (Akinyoade, 2012; Olori, 2012). Consequently, internal migration is and has served as a catalyst for prostitution, human trafficking, and child abuse.

iv) Health

Internal migration, either in moderation or excesses, has critical ramifications on countries' healthcare systems. Migrants are able to access better healthcare that are not readily available at the source region. For instance, health services that may not be easily accessible for one reason or another in rural areas can be accessed easily in urban destinations.

In Ghana, rural restrictions on sexuality are more prohibitive for women than men who seek certain medical services, especially for unmarried women (Anglewicz, Van-Landingham, & Phuengsamran, 2014). For instance, access to certain maternal healthcare services where gender norms are less restrictive on violence against women is less likely (Adjiwanou & LeGrand, 2014; Maternowska et al., 2010). Such limited decision-making capabilities among women pertaining to their health, particularly sexual and reproductive health, motivates affected women to migrate to cities or urban areas to avoid discriminatory practices associated with private healthcare needs. This could explain observed high migration of women from the north, where such restrictions exist, to cities/urban areas in the south (Ayanore, Pavlova, Biesma, & Groot, 2017). Internal migration has thus enabled migrants (rural or urban migrants) in Ghana to have access to better healthcare services at destinations, mostly urban centres (Canning & Schultz, 2012). In Nigeria, internal migration has been central in enhancing the life expectancy of Nigerian migrants. For instance, migrants from rural areas where health facilities and services sought are either non-existent or inadequate, migration to other areas, preferably cities and major towns, has offered the alternative better healthcare access (Aliyu & Amadu, 2017). Consequently, internal migration has offered migrants the opportunities to access quality healthcare and related services from government/public or privately owned health facilities (Oyeniyi, 2013). This is also true in the Kenyan context since migrants are able to access better healthcare in health facilities situated in urban centres through an operable referral system (International Organization for Migration, 2011).

Internal migration could also lead to serious health-related complications. Excess population in urban centres/destinations pose serious environmental challenges, including poor and excessive garbage disposal mechanisms that may result in poor health for migrants. High migration to urban areas has stretched the capacities of existing healthcare providers in major Ghanaian towns and cities, thus leading inadequate and poor service provision to patients (Ortensi, 2015; Canning & Schultz, 2012).

Kenya's Nairobi City is a preferred destination for most internal migrants. As a result, the city has not been able to cope with the increasing migrant population (Mberu et al., 2017). In particular, health services have been overstretched, leaving a majority of the urban poor with no access to vital healthcare services. Most informal or crowded residential areas in Nairobi, for instance, are breeding grounds for diseases because they often harbour undocumented and/or illegal migrants who find it difficult to access healthcare services due to fear related to lack of documentation and language barriers for effective communication while in health facilities (International Organization for Migration, 2018d, 2011). This has especially contributed to the spread of diseases like malaria, tuberculosis (TB), and HIV and AIDS among other sexually transmitted infections (STIs) (International Organization for Migration, 2018d; Oucho, 2010) in the city. This has led to difficulties in containing the diseases, thus complicating the fight against the diseases. It is thus not surprising to find treatable diseases re-emerging even if the city has been declared free of the disease.

Nigeria's case is no different. For instance, evidence reveals that sexual initiation among Nigerian youth, internal migrants aged 15–24, largely indicates stronger associations compared to non-migrants, while rural-rural and urban-rural migrants demonstrate the sturdiest independent connection with premarital sexual initiation (Mberu & White, 2011). This shows that internal migration contributes to earlier sexual initiation among the non-married population, a situation that calls for enhanced migrant youth awareness in understanding and solving premarital sexual problems and related behaviour change. Also, Nigerian health professionals are the most mobile professionals both locally and internationally to other stations or cities for better opportunities with the deleterious impacts on healthcare delivery. This could partly explain the poor doctor-patient ratio of 1:3,500 compared with the World Health Organization (WHO) recommended ratio of 1:600 (International Organization for Migration, 2016; Adekola, 2016). This situation has been captured to be a salient contributor to Nigeria's poor healthcare provision in some part of the country, especially rural areas, resulting in high infant and child mortalities (International Organization for Migration, 2016; Onibokun & Faniran, 2015).

Conclusions

Internal migration is undoubtedly widespread and greatly influenced by similar and cross-cutting pull and push factors in SSA. Equally, the effects of internal migration on urbanization, education, health, and familial systems and structures are similar across Ghana, Kenya, and Nigeria. In these countries, internal migration plays an integral part in the gains and or setbacks in all spheres of socioeconomic development. It is for this reason that migration policy makers, practitioners, and development researchers should craft favourable and/or well-informed migration policies that will specifically address internal migration related challenges to attain an all-encompassing urban development that is oriented to specific urban development outcomes. Internal migration has great potential for any country's overall urban, education, health, and family systems' development and strengthening. This explains why the SSA countries especially should reinvent their migration and development related policies. SSA countries must reset their internal migration policies in line with their development prospects, be it urban, health, social relations and networks, education, or overall human development. Respective countries must recognize that the *status quo* is no longer effective and that the health, education, urban, and even the social networks are desperate for a proper management if a more prosperous with a promising sustainable future for SSA is to be attained.

The fact that cities and other urban areas and plantation zones remain key destinations for migrants implies that these areas receive the heaviest brunt of migration-related benefits and challenges. For this reason, 'reset' (reinvented migration policies) must take into account the prospects of cities, large towns, and plantation zones considering that they are integral part of the countries' domestic economies. Consequently, SSA governments and particularly Ghana, Kenya, and Nigeria should endeavour to ensure that their migration development initiatives radiate throughout the country and encourage well-coordinated rural-urban linkages. This result can only be effected when there are balanced development prospects for both rural and urban areas that lend to and/or reinforce each other. Devoid of this, both rural and urban areas will find themselves intertwined in a complex web of obstinate socioeconomic tension and poverty. Moreover, cities and towns have a unique capability and transformative power to offer new economic forms, exhibiting notable environmental sensitivity, social life, and culture, all of which are in one way or the other linked to inhabitants' health, education, and familial networks.

Governments should, therefore, enact internal migration policies in light of the urbanization, educational, health, and social/familial networks. Also, they should recognize that diverse internal migration has existed and is also evolving. Hence, they must be encouraged and supported to devise internal migration and related policies that take into account not only the present gains or challenges attributed to internal migration but also those that are sustainable for the future for their children and grandchildren's benefit.

Recommendations

The following recommendations thus suffice for a healthy and sustainable internal migration that will guarantee sustained gains in the urban, education, health, and social/familial spheres:

General

I Governments, not limited to the three countries' case studies, must recognize the important role of internal migration as a key instrument for countries' development – both rural and urban. For this reason, governments should and must capture internal-migration-specific data to enable them to advance their (governments') capacities to engage in evidence-informed policy-making on internal migration;

II In recognizing internal migration as a reliable tool for development, governments as well as other development stakeholders should develop strategies that will ensure that benefits arising from internal migration are fully attained, and should be infused into governments' development strategies. Consequently, countries ought to institutionalize frameworks that enhance migration that is beneficial to them, their families, and communities at points of destination and origin;

Data capture and disaggregation

III Data collected about internal migration should focus on the impact of migration on migrants' families left behind, particularly the children and the elderly who are most often left to work in farms in rural areas. This is because most research on internal migration often focusses on internal migrants' economic input in urban areas and challenges experienced in urban destinations. This could help bolster the grossly inadequate data on internal migration remittances that are remitted by internal migrants, and thus ascertain the actual contribution of internal migration to rural and national development;

IV Understanding the causes and profile of migration at the point of origin can help governments to know exactly the drivers and impacts of internal migration and thus formulate evidence-informed policy to address the push factors;

V It is important for governments as well as other development stakeholders to determine migrants' ages at migration and such migrants' final destinations to enable governments to craft targeted policies that respond to migrants' groups that need assistance the most;

VI It is also important to understand the effects and causes of internal migration by gender, considering that men and women encounter varied obstacles when internally migrating;

Policy

VII Benefits attributed to internal migration can be effectively and efficiently harnessed if governments create support systems and provide them to potential migrants before migration, at migration, and after migration (at destinations). Such support includes but is not limited to training on financial literacy, life skills, and marketable vocational and employment-relevant skills

References

Ackah, C., & Medvedev, D. (2010). *Internal migration in Ghana: Determinants and welfare impacts*. Washington, DC: World Bank. Retrieved from www.researchgate.net/profile/Denis_Medvedev/publication/46443918_Internal_migration_in_Ghana_Determinants_and_welfare_impacts/links/02e7e52c54f4344cab000000/Internal-migration-in-Ghana-Determinants-and-welfare-impacts.pdf?origin=publication_detail

Adekola, P. O. (2016). *Migration, urbanization and environmental problems in Nigeria*. Ota: Covenant University of Nigeria. Retrieved from www.researchgate.net/profile/Adekola_O/publication/318816836_Migration_Urbanization_and_Environmental_Problems_in_Nigeria/links/5980479d0f7e9b8802f0fd8f/Migration-Urbanization-and-Environmental-Problems-in-Nigeria.pdf?origin=publication_detail

Adjiwanou, V., & LeGrand, T. (2014). Gender inequality and the use of maternal healthcare services in rural sub-Saharan Africa. *Health & Place*, *29*(1), 67–78.

African Development Bank. (2018). *Annual Development Effectiveness Review 2018: Made in Africa – Industrialising the continent*. Abidjan: African Development Bank (AfDB). Retrieved from www.afdb.org/fileadmin/uploads/afdb/Documents/Development_Effectiveness_Review_2018/ADER_2018_EN.pdf

African Development Bank. (2019). *2019 Annual report*. African Development Bank. Retrieved from https://www.afdb.org/sites/default/files/documents/publications/afdb_annual_report_2019_eng.pdf

Africapolis, I. (2015). *Update: West African studies*. Paris: OECD Publishing.

Akinyoade, A. (2012). *Forced labour in Nigeria: A research report*. Rome: Department of Equal Opportunities (DEO).

Aliyu, A., & Amadu, L. (2017). Urbanization, cities, and health: The challenges to Nigeria – A Review. *Annals of African Medicine*, *16*(4), 149–158. Retrieved from www.ncbi.nlm.nih.gov/pmc/articles/PMC5676403/

Anarfi, J., Kwankye, S., Ababio, O. M., & Tiemoko, R. (2003). *Migration from and to Ghana: A background paper*. Brighton: University of Sussex. Retrieved from www.researchgate.net/publication/253408103_Migration_From_and_To_Ghana_A_Background_Paper

Angel, S. (2011). *Making room for a planet of cities: Policy Focus Report*. Cambridge, MA: Lincoln Institute of Land Policy. Retrieved from www.lincolninst.edu/sites/default/files/pubfiles/making-room-for-a-planet-of-cities-full_0.pdf

Anglewicz, P., Van-Landingham, M., & Phuengsamran, D. (2014). Rural-to-urban migration and sexual debut in Thailand. *Demography*, *51*(5), 1955–1976.

Avis, W. (2019). *Urban expansion in Nigeria*. Birmingham: University of Birmingham. Retrieved from https://opendocs.ids.ac.uk/opendocs/bitstream/handle/20.500.12413/14797/692_Urban_Expansion_of_Nigerian_Cities.pdf?sequence=3&isAllowed=y

Awumbila, M. (2017). *Drivers of migration and urbanization in Africa: Key trends and issues*. Legon: Centre for Migration Studies. Retrieved from https://pdfs.semanticscholar.org/36d3/22465721e1ae7ae4c596e287fe4a2ad414a1.pdf

Awumbila, M., Manuh, T., Quartey, P., Tagoe, C. A., & Bosiakoh, T. A. (2008). *Migration country paper (Ghana)*. Legon: Centre for Migration Studies, University of Ghana.

Awumbila, M., Owusu, G., & Teye, J. K. (2014). *Can rural-urban migration into slums reduce poverty? Evidence from Ghana*. Brighton: University of Sussex. Retrieved from www.migratingoutofpoverty.org/files/file.php?name=wp-13 – awumbila-owusu-teye-2014-can-rural-urban-migration-into-slums-reduce-poverty-final.pdf&site=354

Awumbila, M., Teye, J. K., & Yaro, J. A. (2016). Of silent maids, skilled gardeners and careful madams: Gendered dynamics and strategies of migrant domestic workers in Accra, Ghana. *Geojournal*, *82*, 957–970. https://doi.org/10.1007/s10708-016-9711-5

Ayanore, M. A., Pavlova, M., Biesma, R., & Groot, W. (2017). Stakeholder's experiences, expectations and decision making on reproductive care: An ethnographic study of three districts in northern Ghana. *PLoS One*, *12*(11), e0186908. doi:10.1371/journal.pone.0186908

BBC Monitoring. (2017, August 10). *Ghana country profile*. Retrieved from www.bbc.com/news/world-africa-13433790

Black, R., King, R., & Tiemoko, R. (2003). *Migration, return and small enterprise development in Ghana: A route out of poverty? Sussex Migration Working Paper*. Brighton: Centre for Migration Research, University of Sussex. Retrieved from www.researchgate.net/publication/239531975_Migration_return_and_small_enterprise_development_in_Ghana_A_route_out_of_poverty

Bloch, R., Fox, S., Monroy, J., & Ojo, A. (2015). *Urbanisation and urban expansion in Nigeria*. Urbanisation Research Nigeria (URN) Research Report. London: ICF International. Retrieved from https://assets.publishing.service.gov.uk/media/57a0897bed915d3cfd00027a/61250-URN_Theme_A_Urbanisation_Report_FINAL.pdf

Canning, D., & Schultz, T. P. (2012). The economic consequences of reproductive health and family planning. *Lancet, 380*(9837), 165–171.

Central Intelligence Agency. (2017, September 8). *The world fact-book: Ghana*. Central Intelligence Agency (CIA). Retrieved from www.cia.gov/library/publications/the-worldfactbook/geos/gh.html

Chapman, M., & Prothero, R. M. (1984). Themes on circulation in the third world. *International Migration Review, 17*(4), 597–632.

Chen, N., Valente, P., & Zlotnik, H. (1998). What do we know about recent trends in urbanization? In R. E. Bilsborrow (Ed.), *Migration, urbanization and development: New directions and issues* (pp. 531–560). Netherlands: Springer. Retrieved from www.springer.com/gp/book/9780792380320#aboutBook

Chukwuezi, B. (2001). Through thick and thin: Igbo rural-urban circularity, identity and investment. *Journal of Contemporary African Studies, 19*(1), 55–66.

The Cities Alliance. (2007). *Foundation for urban development in Africa: The legacy of Akin Mabogunje*. Brussels: The Cities Alliance. Retrieved from https://documents.worldbank.org/curated/en/482851468202163524/pdf/481540/WP0urban10Box338889B01PUBLIC1.pdf

Contreras, R., & Griffith, D. (2012). Managing migration, managing motherhood: The moral economy of gendered migration. *International Migration, 50*(4), 51–66.

De Haas, H. (2008). International migration, national development and the role of governments: The case of Nigeria (A. Adepoju, T.V. Naerssen, & A. Zoomers, Eds.). *International migration and national development in sub-Saharan Africa: Viewpoints and policy initiatives in the countries of origin: Afrika-Studiecentrum Series, 10*(1), 161–181.

Desgroppes, A., & Taupin, S. (2011). *Kibera: The biggest slum in Africa*? Nairobi: Institut Français de Recherche en Afrique (IFRA). Retrieved from https://journals.openedition.org/eastafrica/521

Deshingkar, P., & Grimm, S. (2005). *Internal migration and development: A global perspective* (No. 19). United Nations Publications. Retrieved from https://publications.International Organization for Migration.int/books/mrs-ndeg19-internal-migration-and-development-global-perspective

Dudwick, N. (2011). *From farm to firm: Rural-urban transition in developing countries*. Washington, DC: The World Bank.

Duplantier, A., Ksoll, C., Lehrer, K., & Seitz, W. (2017). *The internal migration choices of Ghanaian youths*. Quebec: University of Sherbrooke. Retrieved from www.wider.unu.edu/sites/default/files/DUPLANTIER%2C%20Anne_paper.pdf

Edwin, D. (2016). Factors responsible for youth migration to the city: The case of Ghana. *Journal of Social Sciences and Humanities, 2*(1), 10–22. Retrieved from www.researchgate.net/publication/322538243_Factors_Responsible_for_Youth_Migration_to_the_City_The_Case_of_Ghana

European Commission. (2004). *Technical mission to Libya on illegal migration*. Brussels: European Commission (EC).

Fafchamps, M., & Shilpi, F. (2013). Determinants of the choice of migration destination. *Oxford Bulletin of Economics and Statistics, 75*(3), 388–409.

Farrell, K. (2018a). An inquiry into the nature and causes of Nigeria's rapid urban transition. *Urban Forum, 29*(3), 277–298. Retrieved from https://link.springer.com/article/10.1007/s12132- 018-9335-6

Farrell, K. (2018b). An inquiry into the nature and causes of Nigeria's rapid urban transition. *Urban Forum, 39*(3), 277–298. Retrieved from https://link.spreinger.com/article/10.1007/s12132-018-9335-6.

Findlay, J. (2019). *Largest ethnic groups in Nigeria*. World Atlas. Retrieved from https://www.worldatlas.com/articles/largest-ethnic-groups-in-nigeria.html

Ghana Statistical Service. (2016). *Population and housing census – National Analytical Report*. Ghana Statistical Service (GSS). Retrieved from www.statsghana.gov.gh/docfiles/2010phc/National_Analytical_Report.pdf

Herman, E. (2006). Migration as a family business: The role of personal networks in the mobility phase of Migration. *International Migration, 44*(4), 191–230.

Honorati, M., & De-Silva, S. J. (2016). *Expanding job opportunities in Ghana*. Washington, DC: The World Bank.

Horwood, C. (2015). *Irregular migration flows in the Horn of Africa: Challenges and implications for source, transit and destination countries*. Occasional Paper Series, No. 18 |2015. Department of Immigration and Border Protection: Australian Government. Retrieved from https://trove.nla.gov.au/work/215552135?selectedversion=NBD58899435

International Labor Organization. (2004). *Towards a fair deal for migrant workers in the global economy*. Geneva: International Labor Organization. Retrieved from https://www.ilo.org/public/english/standards/relm/ilc/ilc92/pdf/rep-vi.pdf

International Labor Organization (2018). *ILO global estimates on international migrants and workers: Results and methodology* (2nd ed.). Geneva: International Labor Organization (ILO). Retrieved from www.ilo.org/wcmsp5/groups/public/ – dgreports/ – dcomm/ – publ/documents/publication/wcms_652001.pdf

International Organization for Migration. (2009a). *Migration in Ghana: A country profile 2009*. Accra: International Organization for Migration (IOM).

International Organization for Migration. (2009b). *Migration in Nigeria. A country profile 2009*. Abuja: International Organization for Migration (IOM). Retrieved from https://reliefweb.int/sites/reliefweb.int/files/resources/96194F75629D335BC1257769003746BD-Full_report.pdf

International Organization for Migration. (2011). *An analysis of migration health in Kenya: Healthy migrants in healthy communities*. Nairobi: International Organization for Migration (IOM).

International Organization for Migration. (2014a). *Migration in Nigeria: A country profile 2014*. Abuja: International Organization for Migration (IOM).

International Organization for Migration. (2014b). *Needs assessment in the Nigerian Education Sector*. Abuja: International Organization for Migration (IOM). Retrieved from https://publications.iom.int/system/files/pdf/needs_assessment_nigerianeducsector.pdf

International Organization for Migration. (2015a). *Migration Governance Framework*. International Organization for Migration (IOM). Retrieved from www.iom.int/sites/default/files/about-iom/migof_brochure_a4_en.pdf

International Organization for Migration. (2015b). *Migration in Kenya: A country profile*. Nairobi: International Organization for Migration. Retrieved from https://publications.iom.int/system/files/pdf/migration_profile_kenya.pdf

International Organization for Migration. (2016). *Measuring well governed migration; The 2016 Migration Governance Index: A study of the Economist Intelligence Unit*. Geneva: International Organization for Migration (IOM). Retrieved from https://publications.iom.int/books/measuring-well-governed-migration-2016-migration-governance-index

International Organization for Migration. (2017). *Migration, environment and climate change: Evidence for policy research project in Kenya*. Nairobi: International Organization for Migration (IOM).

International Organization for Migration. (2018a). *World migration report 2018*. Geneva: International Organization for Migration (IOM).

International Organization for Migration. (2018b). *Mapping and socio-economic profiling of communities of return in Ghana*. Geneva: International Organization for Migration (IOM). Retrieved from https://static1.squarespace.com/static/5cfe2c8927234e0001688343/t/5d1ddbdb345aa60001cf69c9/1562237920716/IOM+-+Ghana+-+Full+Report.pdf

International Organization for Migration. (2018c). *Migration in Kenya: A country profile 2018*. Geneva: International Organization for Migration (IOM).

International Organization for Migration. (2018d). *Improving the capacity of government of Kenya in counter human trafficking*. Geneva: International Organization for Migration (IOM). Retrieved from http://kenya.iom.int/project/improving-capacity-government-kenya-counter-human-trafficking

International Organization for Migration. (2019). *World migration report 2020*. Geneva: International Organization for Migration (International Organization for Migration).

International Organization for Migration (IOM) & International Centre for Migration Policy Development (ICMPD). (2015). *Survey on migration policies in West Africa*. Abuja: International Organization for Migration (IOM).

Kabki, M., Mazzucato, V., & Appiah, E. (2004). Wo benane a eye bebree: The Economic Impact of Remittances of Netherlands-Based Ghanaian Migrants on Rural Ashanti. *Population, Space and Place, 10*(2), 85–97.

Kenya National Bureau of Statistics. (2019). *2019 Kenya population and housing census: Volume I*. Kenya National Bureau of Statistics. Retrieved from https://www.knbs.or.ke/?wpdmpro=2019-kenya-population-and-housing-census-volume-i-population-by-county-and-sub-county

Kiiru, J. M. (2010). Remittances and poverty in Kenya. *OIDA International Journal of Sustainable Development, 1*(8), 33–41.

Knoema. (2019). *Nigeria – Urban population as a share of total population*. New York: Knoema. Retrieved from https://knoema.com/atlas/Nigeria/Urban-population

Lall, S. V., Selod, H., & Shalizi, Z. (2006). *Rural-urban migration in developing countries: A survey of theoretical predictions and empirical findings*. World Bank Policy Research.

Lall, S. V., Timmins, C., & Shouyue, Y. (2009). *Connecting lagging and leading regions: The role of labor mobility*. Policy Research Working Paper Series 4843. Washington, DC: The World Bank.

Lattof, S. R. (2018). Health insurance and care-seeking behaviours of female migrants in Accra, Ghana. *Health Policy and Planning, 33*(4), 505–515.

Lattof, S. R., Coast, E., Leone, T., & Nyarko, P. (2018). Contemporary female migration in Ghana: Analyses of the 2000 and 2010 censuses. *Demographic Research, 39*(44), 1181–1226.

Maastricht Graduate School of Governance. (2017). *Ghana migration profile: Study on migration routes in West and Central Africa*. Maastricht: Maastricht Graduate School of Governance (MGSoG). Retrieved from www.merit.unu.edu/publications/uploads/1518185722.pdf

Maternowska, C., Estrada, F., Campero, L., Herrera, C., Brindis, C. D., & Vostrejs, M. M. (2010). Gender, culture and reproductive decision-making among recent Mexican migrants in California. *Culture Health & Sexuality, 12*(1), 29–43.

Mberu, B., Beguy, D., & Ezeh, A. (2017). Internal migration, urbanization and slums in sub-Saharan Africa. In H. Groth & J. F. May (Eds.), *Africa's population: In search of a demographic dividend* (pp. 315–332). Springer. doi:10.1007/978-3-319-46889-1_20

Mberu, B. U. (2015). Migration circulation and rural development in sub-Saharan Africa: A multi-factor review of the case of Eastern Nigeria. In O. Wusu, N. E. Nwokocha, & L. Ntoimo (Eds.), *Demographic issues in Nigeria: Insights and implications*. Bloomington, IN: Author House.

Mberu, B. U., Ezeh, A. C., Langat, G. C., Oti, S., Kimani, J. K., & Beguy. D. (2012). Family ties and urban-rural linkages among older migrants in Nairobi informal settlements. *Population, Space and Place, 19*(3), 275–293. https://doi.org/10.1002/psp.1711

Mberu, B. U., & White, M. J. (2011). Internal migration and health: Premarital sexual initiation in Nigeria. *Social Science and Medicine, 72*(8), 1284–1293.

Melde, S., & El-Mouaatamid, B. (2011). *Global phenomenon, invisible cases: Human trafficking in sub-Saharan Africa, the Caribbean and the Pacific*. Brussels: ACP Observatory on Migration/IOM. Retrieved from www.acpmigration-obs.org/sites/default/files/Background%20Note%201_2011_ACP%20Obs_Trafficking%20in%20Persons%20Feb%202011_0.pdf

Methmann, C., & Oels, A. (2015). From 'fearing' to 'empowering' climate refugees: Governing climate induced migration in the name of resilience. *Security Dialogue, 46*(1), 51–68.

Mumuni, D. (2007). *To whom much is given, much is expected: Involving the migrant in community development: Case of the West Mamprusi District of Northern Ghana*. Amsterdam: International School for Humanities and Social Sciences, University of Amsterdam.

National Coordination Mechanism on Migration. (2018a). *Position report on global compact*. Paper presented in New York Stakeholders Workshop on Migration, New York.

National Coordination Mechanism on Migration. (2018b). *2018 Draft Kenya migration policy*. Nairobi: Government of Kenya.

National Population Commission. (2012). *Internal migration survey in Nigeria 2010*. National Population Commission (NPopC), Government of Nigeria.

Nigeria National Bureau of Statistics. (2013). *2012 and estimates for Q1 – Q3, 2013: Gross Domestic Product for Nigeria*. Abuja: Nigeria National Bureau of Statistics (NNBS).

Nigeria National Bureau of Statistics. (2014). *Job creation report, 2nd – 4th Quarter 2013 Job creation survey: A Collaborative Survey between the National Bureau of Statistics, the Office of the Chief Economic Adviser to the President, Federal Ministry of Labour and Productivity and National Directorate of Employment*. Abuja: Nigeria National Bureau of Statistics (NNBS).

Nyaoro, D., Schade, J., & Schmidt, K. (2016). *Assessing the evidence: Migration, environment and climate change in Kenya*. Nairobi: International Organization for Migration (IOM). Retrieved from https://publications.iom.int/system/files/assessing_the_evidence_kenya.pdf

Obour, P. B., Owusu, K., & Teye, J. K. (2017). From seasonal migrants to Settiers: Climate change and permanent migration to the Transitional Zone of Ghana. In S. Tonah, M. S. Boatemaa, & J. A. Arthur (Eds.), *Migration and development in Africa: Trends, challenges and policy implications*. Accra: Arthur Lexington Books. Retrieved from www.amazon.com/Migration-Development-Africa-Challenges-Implications/dp/1498516831

Ochieng, V., & Onyatta, K. (2016). Challenges and coping strategies for rural-urban migrants in Kibera informal settlements, Kenya. In J. O. Oucho (Eds.), *Rural-urban migration and urban-rural linkages:*

The Western Kenya Case. Nairobi: Friedrich Ebert Stiftung. Retrieved from www.amazon.com/Rural-Urban-Migration-Urban-Rural-Linkages-Western/dp/9966098313

OECD. (2016). *Urbanisation dynamics in West Africa 1950–2010*. Paris: OECD Publishing. Retrieved from http://oecdinsights.org/2016/03/21/africapolis-measuring-urbanisation-dynamics-in-west-africa/

Ofem, B. (2012). A review of the criteria for defining urban areas in Nigeria. *Journal of Urban Ecology*, *37*(3), 167–171. https://doi.org/10.1080/09709274.2012.11906461

Okoronkwo, E. (2014). *Patterns, determinants and consequences of migration among Igbo women in Lagos, Nigeria*. Ibadan: University of Ibadan.

Olagbegi, B. O. (2006). *Review of legislation on trafficking and forced labour in Nigeria*. Geneva: International Labour Organization (ILO).

Olagbegi, B. O., Aminu, L. S., Akiode, B. A., Zacharia, Y., Ezekwem, U., & Menkiti, M. C. (2006). Human trafficking in Nigeria: Root causes and recommendations. *Policy Paper Poverty Series*, *14*, 11–69.

Olori, T. (2012). *Labour: Nigeria, Benin join forces to fight child trafficking*. Retrieved from http://ipsnews.net/africa/interna.asp?idnews=20511

Onibokun, A., & Faniran, A. (2015). Urbanization and urban problems in Nigeria. *Urban Research in Nigeria*. Retrieved from www.books.openedition.org/ifra

Ortensi, L. E. (2015). Engendering the fertility-migration nexus: The role of women's migratory patterns in the analysis of fertility after migration. *Demographic Research*, *32*(53), 1435–1468.

Oucho, J. (2015). *Migration in East Africa: Practice and knowledge gaps for policy*. Report to Ford Foundation. New York: Ford Foundation

Oucho, J. O. (n.d). *Changing perspectives of internal migration in Eastern Africa*. Nairobi: African Migration and Development Policy Centre (AMADPOC). Retrieved from www.migratingoutofpoverty.org/files/file.php?name=oucho-changing-perspectives-of-internal-migration-in-eastern-africa.pdf&site=354

Oucho, J. O. (2009). Voluntary versus Forced Migration in sub-Saharan Africa. In C. Fischer & R. Vollmer (Eds.), *Brief 39: Migration and displacement in sub-Saharan Africa – The security-migration nexus II* (pp. 11–19). Bonn: Bonn International Centre for Conversion (BICC).

Oucho, J. O. (2010). Undercurrents of post-election violence in Kenya: Issues in the long term agenda. In K. Kanyinga & D. Okello. (Eds.), *Tensions and reversals in democratic transitions: The Kenya 2007 General Elections* (pp. 491–531). Nairobi: Society for International Development and Institute for Development Studies, University of Nairobi.

Oucho, J. O., & Oucho, L. A. (2010). *Migration, urbanisation and health challenges in sub-Saharan Africa*. African Migration and Development Policy Centre (AMADPOC). Retrieved from www.researchgate.net/profile/Linda_Oucho/publication/272486637_MIGRATION_URBANISATION_AND_HEALTH_CHALLENGES_IN_SUB-SAHARAN_AFRICA/links/54e5d1fd0cf2cd2e028b33c1/MIGRATION-URBANISATION-AND-HEALTH-CHALLENGES-IN-SUB-SAHARAN-AFRICA.pdf?origin=publication_detail

Oucho, J. O., & Oucho, L. A. (2015). *Migration, urbanisation and health challenges in sub-Saharan Africa*. Nairobi: African Migration and Development Policy Centre (AMADPOC). Retrieved from www.researchgate.net/publication/272486637_MIGRATION_URBANISATION_AND_HEALTH_CHALLENGES_IN_SUB-SAHARAN_AFRICA

Oucho, J. O., Oucho, L. A., & Ochieng, V. (2014). *Is migration the solution to poverty alleviation in Kenya? Rural-urban migration experiences of migrants from Western Kenya to Kisumu and Nairobi*. Working Paper 21. Brighton: Migrating out of Poverty, University of Sussex. Retrieved from www.migratingoutofpoverty.org/files/file.php?name=wp21-oucho-oucho-ochieng-2014-is-migration-the-solution-to-poverty-in-kenya.pdf&site=354

Oucho, L. A. (2019). *Cities of migration: Perspectives from Kenya*. Nairobi: African Migration and Development Policy Centre (AMADPOC). Retrieved from https://migrationpolicycentre.eu/docs/2019_MPC_Annual_Conference/Cities-of-Migration-Oucho.pdf

Owusu, A. B. (2018). An assessment of urban vegetation abundance in Accra Metropolitan Area, Ghana: A geospatial approach. *Journal of Environmental Geography*, *11*(1–2), 37–44.

Oyeniyi, B. A. (2013). *Internal migration in Nigeria: A positive contribution to human development*. Brussels: African, Caribbean and Pacific (ACP) Observatory on Migration.

Poel, P. E. F. (2005). *Informal institutions, transaction costs and trust: A case study on housing construction by migrants in Ashanti-Mampong, Ghana*. Amsterdam: The University of Amsterdam.

Quartey, P. (2006). *Migration and development: Challenges and opportunities for sending countries, Ghana Country Case Study*. German Marshal Fund of the USA. Retrieved from https://publications.iom.int/system/files/pdf/mrs_22.pdf

Ratha, D., Mohapatra, S., Özden, C., Plaza, S., Shaw, W., & Shimeles, A. (2011). *Leveraging migration in Africa: Remittances, skills, and investments*. Washington, DC: World Bank.

Regional Mixed Migration Secretariat. (2013). *Mixed migration in Kenya: The scale of movement and associated protection risks*. Nairobi: Regional Mixed Migration Secretariat (RMMS).

Regional Mixed Migration Secretariat. (2018). *Mixed migration in Kenya: The scale of movement and associated protection risks*. Nairobi: Regional Mixed Migration Secretariat (RMMS).

Smith, L. (2007a, July). *Through the transnational lens: The influence of migrants on the economy of Accra, Ghana*. Paper for the AEGIS European Conference on African Studies in Leiden.

Smith, L. (2007b). *Tied to migrants: Transnational influences on the economy of Accra, Ghana*. Accra: African Studies Centre.

Taiwo, I. (2013, January). *Growth and poverty in Nigeria: Trends and redistribution policies*. Paper presented at the NISER National Policy Dialogue, Abuja.

Teye, J. (2018). *Urbanisation and migration in Africa*. Accra: Centre for Migration Studies, University of Ghana.

UNCTAD. (2018). *Patterns and trends of migration*. Geneva: UNCTAD. Retrieved from https://unctad.org/en/PublicationChapters/edar2018_ch2_en.pdf

UNDESA. (2014). *Human development report 2014*. New York: UN DESA. Retrieved from https://sustainabledevelopment.un.org/content/documents/1789hdr14-report-en-1.pdf

UNDESA. (2015). *International migrant stock 2015*. New York: UN DESA. Retrieved from www.un.org/en/development/desa/population/migration/data/estimates2/estimates15.shtml.

UN DESA. (2017). *International migration 2017: Report (ST/ESA/SER.A/438)*. New York: United Nations, Department of Economic and Social Affairs, Population Division (UN DESA).

UN DESA. (2019a). *International migration 2019: Highlights*. New York: UN DESA.

UN DESA. (2019b). *World urbanization prospects 2018: Highlights*. New York: UN DESA. Retrieved from https://population.un.org/wup/Publications/Files?WUP2018-Highlights.pdf

UNESCO. (2019). *Global education monitoring report, 2019: Migration, displacement and education: building bridges, not walls*. UNESCO. Retrieved from https://unesdoc.unesco.org/ark:/48223/pf0000265866.page=33

UN-Habitat. (2013). *Kibera integrated water, sanitation and waste management project post-project intervention evaluation*. Nairobi: UN-Habitat. Retrieved from https://mirror.unhabitat.org/downloads/docs/Evaluation%20of%20Kibera%20Water,%20Sanitation%20and%20Waste%20water%20project.pdf

UN-HABITAT. (2014). *The state of African cities 2014: Re-imagining sustainable urban transitions*. Nairobi: UN-Habitat. Retrieved from www.gwp.org/globalassets/global/toolbox/references/the-state-of-african-cities-2014_re-imagining-sustainable-urban-transitions-un-habitat-2014.pdf

UN-Habitat. (2018). *Working a better urban future: Annual progress report 2018*. UN-Habitat. Retrieved from https://unhabitat.org/ sites/default/files/documents/2019-05/annual_progress_report_2018.pdf

UNICEF. (2012). *State of the world's children*. New York: UNICEF. Retrieved from www.unicef.org/sowc2012/pdfs/SOWC-2012-DEFINITIONS.pdf

United Nations Development Programme. (2016). *Human development report 2016*. New York: UNDP. Retrieved from http://hdr.undp.org/sites/default/files/2016_human_development_report.pdf

United Nations Development Programme. (2019). *Ghana: human development indicators*. New York: UNDP. Retrieved from http://hdr.undp.org/en/countries/profiles/GHA

Van der Geest, K. (2011). *The Dagara Farmer at home and away: Migration, environment and development in Ghana*. Leiden: African Studies Centre.

WHO. (2005). *A billion voices: Listening and responding to the health needs of slum dwellers and informal settlers in new urban settings*. WHO Kobe Centre. Retrieved from www.who.int/social_determinants/resources/urban_settings.pdf

Wong, M. (2006). The gendered politics of remittances in Ghanaian transnational Families. *Economic Geography*, *82*(4), 355–381. doi:10.1111/j.1944-8287.2006. tb00321.x.

World Bank. (1999). *World development indicators, 1999*. Washington, DC: World Bank.

World Bank. (2011). *Leveraging migration for Africa: Remittances, skills and investments*. Washington, DC: World Bank.

World Bank. (2012a). *Migration and remittances factbook 2011*. Washington, DC: World Bank.

World Bank. (2012b). *Migration and development brief* (Vol. 19). Washington, DC: World Bank.

World Bank. (2019). *GDP per capita (current US$) – Ghana*. Washington, DC: World Bank. Retrieved from https://data.worldbank.org/indicator/NY.GDP.PCAP.CD?locations=GH

World Population Review. (2020). *Nigerian Population 2020*. Walnut, CA: World Population Review. Retrieved from https://worldpopulationreview.com/countries/nigeria-population

30

CHANGING PERSPECTIVES OF INTERNAL MIGRATION IN EAST AFRICA REVISITED[1]

Alfred Agwanda, Mary Muyonga, Milton Adieri, and George Odipo

Introduction

Migration has been a way of life in Africa over the generations. People on the African continent have migrated in response to demographic, economic, political, and other factors, including environmental disasters and conflicts. The issue of migration has gained currency in the global and African Union (AU) policy agenda. Migration intensities are likely to increase because of continuing strong pressures for global integration, capitalism's demand for certain types of labour, and people's desire to improve their life-chances (AU, 2018).

This paper seeks to extend the discussion started off by Oucho (2014) on the nature and extent of the changing perspectives of internal migration within the East African region. We restrict to the regions encompassing three countries: Kenya, Tanzania, and Uganda respectively and those that focus on the contributions of African scholars. These countries, although diverse in geophysical environment, share some similar historical, political, demographic, and socio-economic backgrounds which are important to the understanding of migration processes and systems.

Oucho (2014) concluded that the internal migration in the region has been changing with voluntary migration continuing to increase in volumes alongside forced and irregular internal migration in virtually all the countries, precipitating diverse consequences for development. This paper is an update of the discourse initiated by Oucho (2014) and reviews the changing themes of inquiry. A notable gap in the paper by Oucho (2014) was the inadequate discussion on methodologies and methods in migration research including the various paradigms of migration (Berriane & de Haas, 2012).

The rationale for the focus on migration studies is derived from the increased policy interest in recent times. The African Union (2018) migration policy framework for Africa acknowledges that African countries have witnessed changing patterns of migration, a phenomenon that has become both dynamic and extremely complex in the process of social, economic, and political transitions. However, movement within national borders is by far the most significant form of migration especially for poor people, in terms of both the volume and potential impact (DfID, 2007). This forms the rationale for being specific to internal migration.

 DOI: 10.4324/9780429287213-36

Overview of migration studies in East Africa since independence

The early studies of migration in the East African region concluded that migration began as a result of colonial policies and practices. In particular, colonial tax systems required cash payments and therefore necessitated wage work. The colonialists also introduced cash crops but the white settlers monopolized their production (Black, Lyndsay, & Pooley, 2004). Workers from countries such as Burundi, Malawi, Mozambique, and Rwanda were recruited to Kenya, Tanzania, and Uganda for employment on agricultural estates and mines in Democratic Republic of Congo and Uganda (Black et al., 2004).

The immediate post-independence period in the three East African countries (Tanzania in 1961, Uganda in 1962, and Kenya in 1963) ushered in spontaneous out-migration to urban areas and to other more developed rural areas (Ominde, 1965; Oucho, 2014).[2] The period marks a significant change in internal migration, especially rural-urban migration that had been restricted by the colonial administration (Ominde, 1965).

The second main feature of migration within the East African region is circulation (Oucho, Oucho, & Ochieng, 2014). This process of temporary or semi-permanent migration from rural areas to another rural or an urban area for employment was also characterized by the strong links that were maintained with the area of origin. The circulation patterns have strong historical roots with schooling introduced during the colonial time in East Africa (Oucho, 1995a, 1995b). The migration flows have historical precedents in the post-colonial and colonial education systems and form an important part of historical mobility in and within Kenya, Tanzania, and Uganda. These patterns were maintained at least until the 1980s, despite greater availability of schools within daily commuting distance (Oucho, 1988). The system of education which was common across Kenya, Uganda, and Tanzania was meant to encourage the building of a national rather than ethnic identity. The migration for education also encouraged onward migration once schooling was completed, coupled with higher availability of formal-sector jobs in towns and higher wages available there (cf. Black et al., 2004).

These early studies were mainly descriptive using largely census data and focussed primarily on typologies of internal migration (Ominde, 1965, 1968; Dak, 1968; Oucho 1988, 2014; Moshi, 2010; Msigwa & Mbongo, 2013;. Banyikwa, 2017, Aikaeli, Mtui, & Tarp, 2021). However, these studies were also supplemented by anthropological and sociological cases studies seeking to understand the causes of the post-independence migration (Oucho, 2014).

The changing perspectives

The publication of Todaro study in Kenya in the 1970s saw a paradigm shift from mere description to modelling of migration movement based on individual decision-making (Todaro, 1969; Harris & Todaro, 1970). It formed the first fundamental shift in methodology and methods for migration analysis. However, early application of Todaro hypothesis to guide the theory and explanation of internal migration was initially done by non- African scholars in the 1970s. The main hypothesis was that the migrant bases his or her decision on the discounted present value of the difference between urban expected income (taking into account the probability of finding a job) and rural expected income, less the cost of moving. The major conclusion from these studies was that economic motivators are the primary determinant of the quantity and direction of migration flows. That is expected urban and/or rural incomes influence the migration of rural dwellers to urban areas (Agesa & Agesa, 1999; Agesa, 2000, 2001). Secondly, they centred on explaining rural to urban migration reflecting traditional two-sector models of development (Wineman & Thomas, 2017). Most studies, however, did not consider migration as a household decision (Agesa & Kim, 2001) nor did they consider migration from rural to other rural areas.

Despite criticisms, this paradigm of migration (neoclassical approach) has been the most influential explanation of the internal migration in East African migration (Agesa, 1996; Msigwa & Mbongo, 2013; Oyvat & Mwangi wa Gĩthĩnji, 2017). The popularity stems from its ability to combine the micro-perspective of individual decision-making and macro counterpart of structural determinants. Simply stated, migration results from the uneven geographical distribution of labour and capital. In some regions where labour is scarce relative to capital, its price – the wage level – is correspondingly high, while in other regions it is the opposite. As a result, workers tend to move from regions where labour is abundant and wages low to labour-scarce regions where wages are high. In so doing, they contribute to the redistribution of the factors of production and to the equalization of wages between countries in the long run, thereby redressing original inequalities. It can be concluded, thus, that in the neoclassical view, the origin of migration is to be sought in disparities in wage rates between regions, which in turn mirror income and welfare disparities (Arango, 2019).

The neoclassical model was often augmented by the 'push-pull' hypothesis which contends that some areas attract or pull migrants where the benefits are perceived to exceed costs, while other areas propel or push migrants out where costs are perceived to exceed the benefits. Researchers have identified a number of 'push-pull' factors relating to migration: these include geographic, socio-demographic, economic, climatic, and environmentally related (see Pirani, Marino, & Alessandra, 2019 for a more recent study for the case of Tanzania).

Other than the neoclassical approach motivated by Todaro models, there has been a shift from merely understanding the migration process to focussing on individual migrant agency. Such studies include the conscious reliance on social networks in influencing the decision to migrate (Muto, 2012) and also the application of human capital theory. The human capital theory approach argues that individual characteristics play a bigger role in determining the likelihood to move or not. These individual characteristics include education, skills, age, risk-taking capacity, capacity to face new situations, entrepreneurship, and ethnicity. These individual characteristics cut across different analytical traditions (Ginsburg et al., 2016).

The age-selective nature of migration in most studies and different contexts has led to the conclusion that young adults are the most mobile group in East Africa (Mwegallawa, 1984; Mercandalli & Losch, 2017). Awuor, Odipo, and Agwanda (2018) used census data to explore the age patterns of intra-provincial migration flows in Kenya and observed that the peak age at migration that occurred between age 18 and 24 was different by sex but similar to those observed in East Asian countries. The recognition of age as a factor in explaining the migration process and associated systems has led to a number of studies that focus on youth migration and associated impacts (Barratt, Mbonye, & Seeley, 2012; Nzabona, Asiimwe, Kakuba, Tuyiragize, & Mushomi, 2019).

Another important individual characteristic is educational attainment which is usually taken to represent an individual's human capital. Education is assumed to act as an enabler of migration by improving employment opportunities and the likelihood of securing work (Ginsburg et al., 2016). But human capital acquisition may be a driver or a consequence of movement and in the last decade, studies on migration and education linkages have produced results that are rather divergent (Ginsburg et al., 2016).

Some studies have used the household rather than the individual as a unit of study (Oniang'o, 1995). These studies have generally concluded that many households consider migration as a strategy to improve their livelihood, minimize their risks, and diversify their income sources (Mercandalli & Losch, 2017). Rural families tend to increase their livelihood security by splitting the locations of the family, most often by one member of the family migrating to an urban area. This observation was highlighted in marginal areas because of insufficient economic capital in these rural areas to diversify sources of income without migration (Oniang'o, 1995).

The changing nature of perspectives of migration has also seen attempts to establish new and more inclusive concepts aimed at describing the complexities of migration (Kuhnt, 2019). It has been observed that migration cannot be explained by the neoclassical approach alone or even with augmentation of push-pull theory. In the new perspectives, concepts such as 'determinants', 'drivers', and 'causes' of migration have emerged in literature. The use of these terms reflects different study approaches and disciplines. The term 'drivers' of migration has recently gained prominence alongside 'determinants' and 'causes' (Mercandalli et al., 2019). The recognition of environmental influences on migration has generated greater attention to the concept of drivers of migration because environmental change could shape migration in significant ways given the complex interactions with socio-economic diversity.

Within East African countries, the renewed focus on environmentally driven migration (Oucho, 2002; Borderon, Raya, Endale, Kebede, & Sporer, 2019) amid socio-economic factors has been motivated by the fact that for all the East African countries, the majority of the population relies on agriculture as a primary source of livelihood with very low levels of irrigation and technology in agricultural production and vulnerable to climate change.

A study supported by the World Bank noted that climate change is a growing driver of internal migration in this region (Rigaud et al., 2018), especially with increasing crop failure and water stress (Kubik & Mathilde, 2016; Rigaud et al., 2018). The significance of the studies on migration induced by climate change lies in the fact that there is an increase in the chances of migration under distress which creates the growing challenges for human development and planning (Borderon et al., 2019). Thus climate-induced migration has become not only of academic concern but also of increased policy discourse (Nyakaana, Sengendo, & Lwasa, 2007; Ocello, Petrucci, Testa, & Vignoli, 2015; Farley-Kiwanuka & Farley-Kiwanuka, 2020).

The issues on the determinants of migration are now being examined more broadly than before. Mercandalli and Losch (2017) consider any spatial movement of people from rural areas to urban or other rural areas, within or between countries, for social, economic, political, and environmental reasons, and implying or not a change of residence, on short-term or long-term bases as rural out-migration. The fact is that circumstances have changed from the past; there is a blurred demarcation between rural and urban and the growing importance of rural-urban linkages, with mixed lifestyles and socio-economic behaviours related to the intensifying rural-urban relations; thus, rethinking and modification of future research on internal migration areas are required (Mercandalli, Rapone, Bourgeois, & Khalil, 2017). In their conceptualization of rural out-migration, Mercandalli and Losch (2017) use the 'driver configuration' to identify five major dimensions (shown in Figure 30.1) that influence local migration, including global factor modifiers.

Earlier studies, especially Ominde (1968), noted that land utilization and acquisition may have been the key initial causes of migration immediately post-independence; however, in the 1980s, this issue was largely neglected. The significance and magnitudes of land inequality and per-capita land's impact on migration is gaining attention (Oyvat & Mwangi wa Gĩthĩnji, 2017; Wineman & Thomas, 2017). Oyvat and Mwangi wa Gĩthĩnji's (2017) study using the Kenya Household and Budget Survey of 2005 notes that unlike the previous studies on Kenya, both higher land inequality and lower per-capita land in the home districts of Kenyan households' heads increase the household heads' probability of migrating. But the significance and magnitudes of land inequality and per-capita land's impact on migration is different depending on destination and sex of the migrant (Oyvat & Mwangi wa Gĩthĩnji, 2017). They conclude that

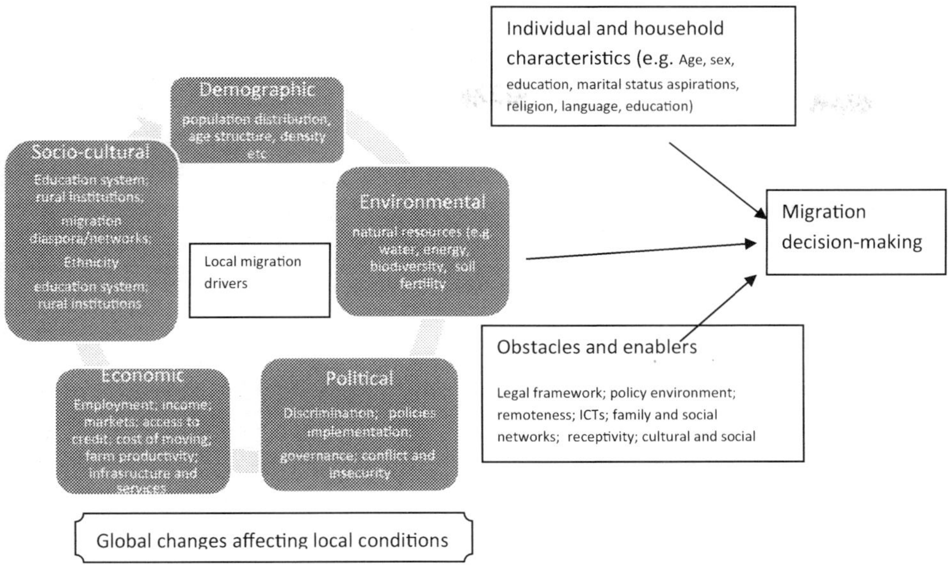

Figure 30.1 The multifaceted drivers of rural migration.

Source: Mercandalli et al., 2017

higher land inequality pushes rural dwellers to other rural areas and less-populated cities/towns. The rural out-migration intensity may be increasing but the drivers observed during the 1970s may differ from those drivers in the 2000s.

Mercandall and Losch (2017) have revisited circular migration which had been cited in earlier publications but not studied. In their study of temporary migration, short-term movements from smallholder farming areas is an important means of supplementing incomes and raising the productivity of subsistence agriculture through investments in capital, seeds, and irrigation. Circulation is in fact part of a household strategy to maintain or improve the traditional livelihood base such as farming. Wineman and Thomas (2017) investigate whether intra-rural migration enables migrants to access more land, higher quality land, or greater off-farm income generating opportunities that may, in turn, translate into improved well-being. They conclude that across all destinations in Tanzania, migrants are more likely to draw from off-farm and non-farm income sources, suggesting that even intra-rural migration represents a shift away from agriculture and this is likely the dominant channel through which migrants benefit.

The other perspective which was rarely examined in the past but is gaining prominence is the gendered nature of the migration process. Migration literature on sub-Saharan Africa has highlighted differential patterns of migration by sex and has emphasized the feminization of migration streams (Adepoju, 2008). Family-related migration especially for marriage reasons is also an important determinant of female migration (Oyvat & Mwangi wa Gĩthĩnji, 2017). Females move at younger ages in connection with marriage, while movements amongst males may be prompted by economic opportunities or employment (Agesa & R. U. Agesa, 1999). In Southern Tanzania, a research study by IIED suggests that male migration to save and invest in rural areas is common. In contrast, in Northern Tanzania, opportunities for migration appear to be important for marginalized women (cited in Black et al., 2006). The effects of education on the propensity to migrate for females have been mixed (Ginsburg et al., 2016).

Until recently there have been few studies that focus on the linkages between internal migration and poverty. The DfID supported the University of Sussex's research consortium in Kenya and other countries that link migration and poverty (Oucho et al., 2014). Another set of studies was reported in the World Bank staff-supported study across several countries in the developing world (Tanzania among the countries). In addition to linkage between migration and poverty, the linkage between migration and inequality has attracted a number of studies (see Muyonga, Odipo, & Agwanda, 2020 for extensive review). Using World Bank Remittances Survey data, several studies have assessed the impact of remittances on inequality (Bang, Mitra, & Wunnava, 2016 for Kenya; Mushomi, Ntozi, & Rutaremwa, 2017 for Uganda; Hansen, 2012 for Tanzania).

Research and policy implications of changing perspectives

The renewed research interest in migration can be said to have been driven by national and regional policy interests (AU, 2018). Current policy literature widely views migration[3] as having the potential to contribute to development and poverty alleviation (AU, 2018). Therefore, governments are being encouraged to seek ways to maximize the benefits of migration (AU, 2018). However, the policy concerns and direction need to be supported with evidence from research (see Oucho, 2014 for elaboration).

Scholars of migration ought to think of ways of framing migration research to account for an increased variety of movements together with their policy implications. Until recently, migration and development have been treated as very separate policy areas. Migration management has been focussed on policy measures that control movement of people and integrate regular migrants into national labour markets and wider society (DfID, 2007). To development practitioners, especially rural development and urban planners, migration has been viewed as a failure of development, since people leave their communities despite programmes and projects to help them improve their lives in their home areas (DfID, 2007).

Past studies viewed the link between migration and poverty more negatively (Black et al., 2006). In addition, studies relating migration and poverty had been rare (Oucho et al., 2014). The studies which claim that migration is a selective process often report that migrants are often not from the poorest regions, since remoteness may make migration more difficult, and usually not from the poorest households, because the cost of migration may be too high (Deshingkar & Start, 2003). Few studies that have examined migration and poverty conclude that the poor move shorter distances, perhaps to neighbouring regions because they lack social capital to move long distances (Awour et al., 2018). However, the counterclaim is that often researchers base their assumptions on poverty of the place and not poverty of people (De Haan & Yaqub, 2010). In addition, such studies may be lacking simultaneity of both origin and destination. De Haan and Yaqub (2010) conclude that different migrants have different motives, reflecting different opportunities. Secondly, there is a lack of estimates of the scale of internal migration and its impact on rural livelihoods (Black et al., 2004) in trying to understand migration, poverty, and development linkages.

The policy impetus requires in-depth understanding of the drivers of migration within each context that will help to clarify policy choices (UNECA, 2017). The most challenging tasks for exploring policy options are the need to establish circumstances in which some drivers of migration are more important than others, and which combinations of drivers are more potent than others. However, as long as people's changing lifestyle preferences and increasing material expectations cannot be met locally, this will typically translate in increasing aspirations to migrate (UNECA, 2017).

Researchers have particularly called for more in-depth study of rural-to-rural migration or more broadly, rural-out migration. For example, Wineman and Thomas (2017) conclude that intra-rural migration merits greater attention in the discourse on rural development and structural transformation. Rural-rural migrants are in the greatest need of support because they are often poorer, invisible to the official regulatory system, and much more vulnerable to abuse and hazardous living conditions (Deshingkar & Grimm, 2005). But little is known about those who do not move and the increasing invisible forms of movement such as child migration; volume and key factors that perpetuate the phenomena are still unknown.

While reasons for out-migration are relatively well understood, there is inadequate information on why people return to their rural origins, a phenomenon described as 'return migration' (Oucho, 2014; Deshingkar & Grimm, 2004). The temporary nature of this type of migration within East Africa manifests by the number of migrants who return to their rural homes because they may have failed to secure employment or to retire (Oucho, 1996). Further, Oucho (1996) notes that first-time migrants have a bias to return to their rural areas, but we do not know the experience of generation migrants and their choices. Return migrants embody a valuable resource for sending areas because they often bring back skills, funds, and different values which could help in, say, improving agricultural practices (Deshingkar & Grimm, 2004). Further studies are needed in understanding the constraints and opportunities faced by return migrants and what policy can do to help.

A recurring paradigm over the past years has been the 'feminization of migration'. The term feminization refers to the increasingly active participation of migrant women in the processes of mobility. The initial analyses of migration assumed that most migrants were young males, and that women would only move to reunite with their family members (associational migration); however, census data from these countries show that female migration is becoming more evident (see KNBS, 2012 for Kenya). The gender-sensitive migration studies are less prominent and further insights are needed to assess how gender relations are socially constituted (and therefore changeable), including gender as a social dimension that interacts with migration processes in many ways. Further, it is important to explore how migrant femininities and masculinities are transformed by (post-) migration processes.

In addition to under-researched areas of critical policy importance, the studies have generally under-acknowledged the role of migration in the structural transformation process until recently (Mercandalli & Losch, 2017). Rural-urban migration remains a prominent feature which coexists with rural-rural or urban-rural migration, either short- or long-term, as well as persistent and growing circular movements consisting in recurrent migration between a place of origin and one or more places of destination, both at internal and continental levels (Mercandalli & Losch, 2017).

Although remittances have been cited as an important aspect of the contribution of migration to development, the focus has largely been on international migration. However, data from Kenya have indicated that internal remittances may out-number cross-border transfers (Muliro, 2012; World Bank, 2013 cited in IOM, 2013). This reflects the magnitude of internal migration, a topic hardly studied or discussed despite larger poverty reduction potential than international remittances for an even larger number of people. While this is generally true, it is also true that semi-skilled and low-skilled workers move to areas where remittances come from (IOM, 2013). This is one factor driving rural- urban migration but there are few comprehensive studies to invalidate or support it. This calls for revisiting some of the under-researched areas in which scholars can demonstrate the different ways to address a range of empirical questions.

In this review a few caveats are warranted, given the growing complexity of the migration process, its spatial nature, and the need to understand the individual migrant agency and associated structural processes that drive migration. Firstly, methodological issues are generally studied by non-African scholars. Secondly, several disciplines contribute to understanding the nature of the process, its drivers, and its consequences. Therefore, an interdisciplinary approach to migration inquiry is inevitable. Thirdly, there are various innovations that have been adopted to improve the study of internal migration including use of mobile service data, use of GIS technology, and mixed methods that use qualitative and quantitative analyses to nuance the discourse. Furthermore, there is a need for advocacy for migration surveys just like demographic and health surveys with comparable methodologies across countries. Such options would greatly satisfy policy needs to shape and harness migration-related opportunities.

An overarching observation is that there are many studies done by African researchers especially at higher learning institutions (such as the PhD and master's thesis) which are largely invisible, giving a false impression that researchers in the region are not active in the discourse. However, what may be of concern is the inadequate dissemination of such useful works to broader audiences and inadequate use of digital platforms.

Conclusions

This review attempts to draw the attention of scholars and students of migration regarding the constellation of migration literature, which is heterogeneous with almost-different concerns, different conclusions, and possible flaws in explaining why migrations occur in the region. Internal migration is still the dominant form of migration, and labour circulation has persisted ever since independence. Studies generally conclude that many households consider migration a strategy to improve their livelihood, minimize their risks, and diversify their income sources. Thus, people in East Africa migrate to improve their livelihoods and in search of a better future, which includes the need to escape poverty, food insecurity, and lack of employment opportunities, as well as ethnic, gender, and other forms of discrimination and marginalization. The continued climate change adds further complexities, since the combination of climate events and socio-economic factors are causing more and more people to leave agriculture and rural areas (Oucho, 2002, 2007; Rigaud et al., 2018). But rural people also move for other reasons related to access to better and higher education, as well as other services, and often due to family matters (Mercandalli & Losch, 2017). At an individual level, the search for employment still dominates the desire for movement, but only for the youth. There has been an increase in the volume of female migrants, but analyses show that different factors influence male and female propensities to migrate.

Despite these conclusions, the prospects for identifying appropriate policy measures may be hampered by the limited understanding of some aspects of internal migration which has received scant research. The policy framework suggests that migration is important for development and poverty alleviation; but there are few nationwide studies about the poverty reduction potential of internal migration. While reasons for out-migration are relatively well understood, little is known about why people return (especially to their rural origins). Furthermore, intra-rural migration merits greater attention in the discourse on rural development and structural transformation (Mercandalli et al., 2019). Moreover, current public policies still fail to recognize the spatial and occupational complexity of rural and urban livelihoods (Mercandalli et al., 2017). Gender issues have been incorporated in the human development policy literature but gender-sensitive migration studies are, however, less prominent. In particular, further insights are needed to assess how gender relation is socially constructed and how its changing nature interacts with migration processes, including how they are transformed by (post-) migration processes.

Notes

1 This paper is dedicated to the late John Oyaro Oucho, Professor of Demography at the Population Studies and Research Institute, University of Nairobi, who spent his entire academic work on migration research, not only in Kenya but also many other African countries.

2 According to Oucho, early post-independence migration studies in East Africa can be traced to 1) Southall's (1961, 1969) anthropological work; 2) Monsted and Walji's (1978) study on rural-rural migration due to land shortage, environmental hazards, unemployment, migration selectivity, and family structure; 3) Hirst's (1969) study of net migration patterns in Tanzania; 4) Dak's (1968) spatial analysis of migrants in Uganda; and 5) Ominde's (1968) work on land and population movements in Kenya, which was concurrent with Soja's (1968) comprehensive study of Kenya's geography of modernization (J. O. Oucho, 2014; DfID, 2004 for details; Black et al., 2004, 2006).

3 See International Organization for Migration (IOM), 2013. Migration and development within the South: New evidence from African, Caribbean and Pacific countries. ACP Observatory on Migration. IOM Geneva

References

Adepoju, A. (2008). Perspectives on international migration and national development in sub-Saharan Africa. In *International migration and national development in sub-Saharan Africa* (pp. 21–48). Leiden: Brill.

African Union (AU). (2018, May). *Migration policy framework for Africa and plan of action (2018–2030)*. Addis Ababa: African Union Commission, AU Department for Social Affairs.

Agesa, R. U. (1996). *Migration and gender wage differences in Kenya*. Milwaukee: University of Wisconsin.

Agesa, R. U. (2000). The incentive for rural to urban migration: A re-examination of the Harris-Todaro model. *Applied Economics Letters*, 7(2), 107–110.

Agesa, R. U. (2001). Migration and the urban to rural earnings difference: A sample selection approach. *Economic Development and Cultural Change*, *49*(4), 847–865.

Agesa, J., & Agesa, R. U. (1999). Gender differences in the incidence of rural to urban migration: Evidence from Kenya. *Journal of Development Studies*, *35*(6), 36–59. doi:10.1080/00220389908422601

Agesa, R. U., & Kim, S. (2001). Rural to urban migration as a household decision: Evidence from Kenya. *Review of Development Economics*, *5*(1), 60–75.

Aikaeli, J., Mtui, J., & Tarp, F. (2021). Rural-urban migration, urbanisation and unemployment: The case of Tanzania Mainland. *African Journal of Economic Review*, *9*(1), 87–108.

Arango J. (2019). Explaining migration: A critical view. *International Social Science Journal*. special issue. First published: 19 March 2019 https://doi.org/10.1111/issj.12183. This article is reprinted from *International Social Science Journal*, 2000; *52*: 283–296.

Awuor, V., Odipo, G., & Agwanda, A. (2018). Age schedules of intra-provincial migration in Kenya. *African Population Studies*, *32*(2), 4356–4375.

Bang, J. T., Mitra, A., & Wunnava, P. V. (2016). Do remittances improve income inequality? An instrumental variable quantile analysis of the Kenyan case. *Economic Modelling*, *58*, 394–402.

Banyikwa, W. F. (2017). Outcomes of rural-urban migration in Tanzania. *Tanzania Journal for Population Studies and Development*, *16*(1). Retrieved from journals.udsm.ac.tz

Barratt, C., Mbonye, M., & Seeley, J. (2012). Between town and country: Shifting identity and migrant youth in Uganda. *The Journal of Modern African Studies*, 201–223.

Berriane, M., & De Haas, H. (2012). *African migrations research: Innovative methods and methodologies*. Trenton: Africa World Press.

Black, R., Crush, J., Pederby, S., Ammassari, S., Hilken, L., Mouillesseux, S., . . . Rajkotia, R. (2006). *Migration and development in Africa: An overview* (rep., pp. I–160). Waterloo, ON: Southern African Migration Programme. African Migration and Development Series No. 1.

Black, R., Lyndsay, M., & Pooley, C. (2004). *Migration and pro-poor policy in East Africa*. Working Paper C7. Sussex Centre for Migration Research.

Borderon, M., Raya, S., Endale, M., Kebede, R., & Sporer, P. (2019). Migration influenced by environmental change in Africa: A systematic review of empirical evidence. *Demographic Research*, *41*, 491–544, Article 18.

Bwambale, M. F., Bukuluki, P., Moyer, C. A., & Borne, B. H. V. D. (2021). Demographic and behavioural drivers of intra-urban mobility of migrant street children and youth in Kampala, Uganda. *PLoS One*, *16*(2), e0247156.

Dak, O. (1968). *A geographical analysis of the distribution of migrants in Uganda* (Unpublished Doctoral Dissertation). Makerere University, Kampala, Uganda.

De Haan, A., & Yaqub, S. (2010). Migration and poverty: Linkages, knowledge gaps and policy implications. In K. Hujo & N. Piper (Eds.), *South-south migration implications for social policy and development*. Social Policy in a Development Context Series. Basingstoke: Palgrave Macmillan.

Department for International Development (DfID). (2004, July). *Migration and pro-poor policy in sub-Saharan Africa*. Policy Briefing prepared by the Sussex Development Research Centre on Migration.

Department for International Development (DfID). (2007). *Moving out of poverty – Making migration work better for poor people*. Department for International Development. PRD 103. ISBN: 1 86192 875 1. Abercrombie House, Eaglesham Road, East Kilbride, Glasgow G75 8EA, United Kingdom

Deshingkar, P., & Grimm, S. (2004). *Voluntary internal migration: An update*. Paper commissioned by the Urban and Rural Change Team and the Migration Team. Policy Division, DFID. ODI.

Deshingkar, P., & Grimm, S. (2005). *Internal migration and development: A global perspective*. Geneva: IOM.

Deshingkar, P., & Start, D. (2003). *Seasonal migration for livelihoods, coping, accumulation and exclusion*. Working Paper No. 220. Overseas Development Institute, London.

Farley-Kiwanuka, A., & Farley-Kiwanuka, S. Y. (2020). *Migration as adaptation: Addressing rural-urban migration in Uganda*. Retrieved from www.africaportal.org/publications/migration-adaptation-addressing-rural-urban-migration-uganda/

Ginsburg, C., Béguy, D., Orvalho, A., Odhiambo, F., Abdramane, S., White, M. J., . . . Collinson, M. A. (2016). Human capital on the move: Education as a determinant of internal migration in selected INDEPTH surveillance populations in Africa. *Demographic Research*, *34*(30), 845–884. Retrieved from www.demographic-research.org/Volumes/Vol34/30

Hansen, P. (2012). Revisiting the remittance mantra: A study of migration – development policy formation in Tanzania. *International Migration*, *50*(3), 77–91.

Harris, J. R., & Todaro, M. P. (1970). Migration, unemployment and development: A two-sector analysis. *The American Economic Review*, *60*(1), 126–142.

Hirst, M.A. (1969). Net migration patterns over Tanzania. *East African Geographical Review*, 7, 25-36

International Organization for Migration (IOM). (2013). *Migration and development within the South: New evidence from African, Caribbean and Pacific countries*. Geneva: ACP Observatory on Migration, IOM.

Kenya National Bureau of Statistics (KNBS). (2012, March). *The 2009 Kenya population and housing census, analytical report on, migration* (Vol. VII). Kenya: Government Printer Nairobi.

Kubik, Z., & Mathilde, M. (2016). Weather shocks, agricultural production and migration: Evidence from Tanzania. *The Journal of Development Studies*, *52*(5), 665–680. doi:10.1080/00220388.2015.1107049

Kuhnt, J. (2019). *Literature review: Drivers of migration and why do people leave their homes? Is there an easy answer? A structured overview of migratory determinants*. Discussion Paper/Deutsches Institut für Entwicklungspolitik ISSN (Online), 2512.

Mercandalli, S., & Losch, B. (Eds). (2017). *Rural Africa in motion: Dynamics and drivers of migration South of the Sahara*. Rome: FAO and CIRAD (Food and Agriculture Organization of the United Nations and the Centre de Coopération Internationale en Recherche Agronomique pour le Développement), p. 60.

Mercandalli, S., Losch, B., Belebema, M., Bélières, J., Bourgeois, R., Dinbabo, M., . . . Nshimbi, C. (2019). *Rural migration in sub-Saharan Africa: Patterns, drivers and relation to structural transformation*. Rome: FAO and CIRAD. https://doi.org/10.4060/ca7404en

Mercandalli, S., Rapone, C., Bourgeois, R., & Khalil, C. (2017). *Rural migration and the new dynamics of structural transformation in sub-Saharan Africa*. Rome: Food and Agriculture Organization.

Monsted, M., & Walji, P. (1978). *A demographic analysis of East Africa*. Uppsala: The Scandinavian Institute of African Studies.

Moshi, H. P. (2010). Migration in Tanzania: Patterns, characteristics and impact. *Eastern Africa Social Science Research Review*, *26*(1), 91–109. doi:10.1353/eas.0.0013

Msigwa, R. E., &. Mbongo, J. (2013). Determinants of internal migration in Tanzania. *Journal of Economics and Sustainable Development*, *4*(9), 28–35.

Muliro, A. (2012, February 21). *The M-Pesa experience: Some reflections from Kenya*. Presentation given at the conference entitled Transfert d'argent des migrants: Réduction des coûts et produits financiers innovants (Migrant money transfers: Reduction of costs and innovative financial products), Paris.

Mushomi, J. A., Ntozi, J. P., & Rutaremwa, G. (2017). Migrant remittance behavior in Uganda: A household analysis. *African Population Studies*, *31*(2).

Muto, M. (2012). The impacts of mobile phones and personal networks on rural-to-urban migration: Evidence from Uganda. *Journal of African Economies, 21*(5), 787–807.
Muyonga, M., Odipo, G., & Agwanda, A. O. (2020). Interlinkages between migration and inequality in Africa: Review of contemporary studies. *African Human Mobility Review* (AHMR), 6.
Mwegallawa, P. S. (1984). *Internal migration in Tanzania: The factors influencing rural-urban youth migration: A case study of Gairo in Kilosa district of Morogoro* (Unpublished Doctoral Dissertation). University of Dar es Salaam.
Nyakaana, J. B., Sengendo, H., & Lwasa, S. (2007). *Population, urban development and the environment in Uganda: The case of Kampala city and its environs*. Kampala, Uganda: Faculty of Arts, Makerere University, pp. 1–24.
Nzabona, A., Asiimwe, J. B., Kakuba, C., Tuyiragize, R., & Mushomi, J. (2019). Correlates of youth internal migration and employment in Uganda. *African Population Studies, 33*(1), 4621–4630.
Ocello, C., Petrucci, A., Testa, M. R., & Vignoli, D. (2015). Environmental aspects of internal migration in Tanzania. *Population and Environment, 37*(1), 99–108.
Ominde, S. H. (1965). Population movements to the main urban areas of Kenya. *Cahiers d'Études africaines*, 593–617.
Ominde, S. H. (1968, February 22). *Geography and African development*. Inaugural Lecture, University College Nairobi. Retrieved from http://erepository.uonbi.ac.ke/bitstream/handle/11295/47557/scan0005.pdf
Oniang'o, R. (1995). The impact of out-migration on household livelihoods and on the management of natural resources: A Kenyan case study. *IDS Bulletin, 6*(1), 54–60.
Oucho, J. O. (1988). Spatial population change in Kenya: A district-level Analysis. In S. H. Ominde (Ed.), *Kenya's population and development to the year 2000 A.D.* (pp. 131–139). Nairobi: East African Educational Books.
Oucho, J. O. (1995a). Emigration dynamics of Eastern African countries. *International Migration* (Geneva, Switzerland), *33*(3–4), 391.
Oucho, J. O. (1995b). International migration and sustainable human development in Eastern and Southern Africa. *International Migration* (Geneva, Switzerland), *33*(1), 31.
Oucho, J. O. (1996). Recent internal migration processes in sub-Saharan Africa: Determinants, consequences and data adequacy issues. In R. E. Bilsborrow (Ed.), *Migration, urbanization, and development: New directions and issues* (pp. 89–120). New York: UNFPA and Kluwer Academic Publishers.
Oucho, J. O. (2002). *Undercurrents of ethnic conflict in Kenya*. Leiden and Boston: Brill Academic Publishers.
Oucho, J. O. (2007, November 15–16). Environmental impact of refugees and internally displaced persons in sub-Saharan Africa. Keynote Address, *African Migration Alliance Biennial Workshop on Climate Change, Environment and Migration*, East London, South Africa.
Oucho, J. O. (2014). *Changing perspectives of internal migration in Eastern Africa*. Nairobi, Kenya: Population Studies and Research Institute, and African Migration and Development Policy Centre (AMADPOC), Mimeo.
Oucho, J. O., Oucho, L. A., & Ochieng, V. (2014). *Rural-urban migration experiences of migrants from Western Kenya to Kisumu and Nairobi*. Migration Out of Poverty, Working Paper No. 21. Sussex Centre for Migration Research.
Oyvat, C., & Mwangi wa Gĩthĩnji. (2017). *Migration in Kenya: Beyond Harris-Todaro*. London: Greenwich Political Economy Research Centre.
Pirani, E. M., Marino, F., & Alessandra, P. (2019). Correlates of inter-districts migrations in Tanzania: A gravity-type modeling approach. *Statistica, 79*(2), 201–221. doi:10.6092/issn.1973-2201/8538 Corpus ID: 202132601. Retrieved from https://rivista-statistica.unibo.it/article/view/8538
Rigaud, K. K., Sherbinin, A. d, Bryan, J., Bergmann, J., Viviane, C., Kayly, O., . . . Amelia, M. (2018). *Groundswell: Preparing for internal climate migration*. Washington, DC: The World Bank.
Soja, E. W. (1968). *The geography of modernization in Kenya*. Syracuse, NY: Syracuse University Press.
Southall, A. W. (1961). Population movements in East Africa. In K. M. Barbour & R. M. Prothero (Eds.), *Essays on African population* (pp. 157–192). London: Routledge & Kegan Paul.
Southall, A. W. (1969). Orientations in political anthropology. *Canadian Journal of African Studies/La Revue canadienne des études africaines, 3*(1), 42–52.
Todaro, M. P. (1969). A model of labor migration and urban unemployment in less developed countries. *The American Economic Review, 59*(1), 138–148.
United Nations Economic Commission for Africa (UNECA). (2017, October). *African migration: Drivers of migration in Africa*. Prepared for Africa Regional Consultative Meeting on the Global Compact on Safe, Orderly and Regular Migration.

United Nations Development Programme (UNDP). (2010). *Mobility and migration: A guidance note for human development report teams*. New York: United Nations.

Wineman, A., & Thomas, S. J. (2017). *Intra-rural migration and pathways to greater well-being: Evidence from Tanzania*. Feed the Future Innovation Lab for Food Security Policy, Research Report No. 60. Department of Agricultural, Food, and Resource Economics, Michigan State University. Accessed 6 June 2020.

World Bank. (2013). *Remittance data inflows*. Washington, DC: World Bank. Retrieved from http://go.worldbank.org/092X1CHHD0

31

INTERNATIONAL MIGRATION AND DEVELOPMENT IN SUB-SAHARAN AFRICA

Aderanti Adepoju

Introduction

In sub-Saharan Africa (SSA), intra- and inter-country movements continue to be a central feature of life of the people. Much of this movement takes place in diverse political, economic, socio-ethnic and ecological settings but remains essentially intra-regional (Adepoju, 2010). Migrants from and within the region include temporary cross-border workers, unskilled and temporary cross-border workers, unskilled and temporary contract workers, traders, undocumented migrants, highly skilled professionals and refugees. Distinctive forms of migration characterize the different sub-regions: labour migration from Western and Central Africa to other locations within the region, as well as developed northern and oil-rich countries of the Middle East; refugee flows within Eastern, and increasingly in Western, Africa; labour migration from Eastern and Southern African countries to South Africa, and cross-border clandestine migration of nomads in West and East Africa. These configurations are, however, changing dynamically to the extent that no country remains unaffected by international migration flows with some serving concurrently as countries of origins, or transit or destination for migrants (Adepoju, 2005). These countries are also concurrently experiencing challenges and opportunities with respect to the emigration of skilled professionals, the diaspora's links with country of origin, and migrants' remittances from within and outside the region.

The issues raised in this paper relate specifically to sub-Saharan Africa: the root causes of emigration dynamics, migration configuration within and outside the region, emigration of skilled professionals, the diaspora and remittances. We then focus on the consequence of these dynamics for the region, ending with some suggestions on how migration's potential win-win-win can be attained.

The number of international migrants in Africa rose from 9 million in 1960 to 16 million in 2000; and Africa had more than double the number of international migrants than Latin American and the Caribbean since 1980, and about one half to one third of the number in Asia. This represents 14% and 9%, respectively, of the share of worldwide international migration. Among the sub-regions, Western and Eastern Africa have higher numbers of international migrants in general and increasingly also of female international migrants. Females have increased their share of international migrants between 1960 and 2000, overtaking Asia but still trailing other regions (Zlotnik, 2003). Unlike in other world regions, these migrations, better described as

 DOI: 10.4324/9780429287213-37

'circulations' involving more than 7 million economically active persons and an unspecified number of undocumented migrants (ILO, 2004a), are largely intraregional. These complex configurations are changing dynamically and are reflected in increasing female migration, diversification of migration destinations, transformation of labour flows into commercial migration and emigration of skilled health and other professionals. These, and trafficking human beings and the changing map of refugee flows, are the key migratory configurations.

The specificity of migration dynamics in Africa

In a region rooted in migrations, voluntary and compelled, intra-regional migration configurations are fostered by shared culture, language and colonial heritage, factors which also blur the distinction between internal and international migration and circulation, and between migration in regular and irregular situation in the region (Adepoju, 1998). The colonial systems reinforced the foundation of present-day stocks, flows and pattern of migration in the region. The complementary economies of neighbouring countries and cultural affinity facilitated movements across frontiers. Consequently, significant migration across long borders without distinct landmarks was largely undocumented since frontier workers commuted daily between home and place of work on adjacent sides of national borders (Adepoju, 1988). The fluidity of this phenomenon has prompted the discussion whether the term 'circulation' rather than migration would be more appropriate in the African context.

These migrations take place largely within the context of economic unions. Regional economic unions are often dominated by the economies of a single country, and movements of persons have been directed to a limited number of countries within these unions. Examples of these are Botswana and South Africa in Southern Africa, Gabon in Central Africa, Kenya in Eastern Africa and Côte d'Ivoire and Nigeria in West Africa. In reality, the prosperity of many of these countries was built by migrant labour on cocoa and coffee plantations in Ghana and Côte d'Ivoire, mines and agriculture in South Africa and forestry and oil in Gabon. Resource-rich but labour-short countries such as Botswana, Gabon and Côte d'Ivoire rely heavily on immigrant labour. Thus, for instance, 28% of the population of Côte d'Ivoire are foreign-born and one quarter of the workers in Gabon are foreigners from and outside Africa. An estimated two million immigrants reside in South Africa (Adepoju, 2000).

In **Western Africa,** intra-regional migration is essentially north-south, and the principal countries of emigration include Burkina Faso, Mali, Togo and in the early 1980s, Ghana. Since the beginning of the century, workers from Burkina Faso have been attracted to the plantation and construction industries in Côte d'Ivoire and (during the 1950s and 1960s) to cocoa farms in Ghana. Indeed, by 1975, 17% of Burkinabes were living abroad. Contract workers and clandestine migrants from south-east Nigeria worked in plantations of the then Fernando Po and Spanish Guinea (Zachariah & Cond'e, 1981). Senegal is a country of both immigration and emigration (estimated to be about half and half each). About half of its immigrants came from Guinea and Guinea Bissau, including refugees whose situation in Ghana gave rise to and sustained the exodus of both skilled and unskilled persons, both men and women. Academics and professional doctors, architects, teachers, engineers and pharmacists, frustrated by deteriorating research and training facilities, readily responded to the demand for their skills and were absorbed into Nigeria's hospitals and government parastatals. Ghana and Nigeria have thus experienced 'migration transition' from being 'receiving' countries to becoming 'sending' countries in recent decades. Today, Ghana is also experiencing some return migration of skilled professionals.

In **Eastern Africa**, people migrating between Kenya, Uganda and Tanzania took advantage of a common language, cultural affinity and shared colonial experience, as well as the defunct and recently resuscitated East African Economic Community. Migrants originated from and worked in the rural areas of a unified political and economic space. The sisal, tea and coffee plantations in Tanzania, Kenya sugar and tea estates, and the cotton plantations in Uganda all employed locals as well as foreign labourers from the hinterlands of Rwanda and Burundi, densely populated and resource-poor (both have joined the resuscitated East African Community). Oucho (1998) categorized the countries of the Eastern Africa sub-region into three groups with respect to migration dynamics: major emigration countries, namely Eritrea, Ethiopia, Djibouti, Somalia – all in the Horn – as well as Burundi, Rwanda and Mozambique; immigration countries Kenya, Tanzania Malawi and Zimbabwe; and countries of both emigration and immigration which are Uganda and Zambia, adding however, that the net migration status of all these countries changes over times. This is precisely the case of Zimbabwe which became a country of emigration in the wake of political crisis and the collapse of the country's economy, and of Zambia, following the slump in the copper price in the world market. Kenya today is a country divided, with 300,000 people displaced and over 1,000 murdered in the wake of post-election crisis (Ayiemba, 2011).

The major countries of immigration in **Central Africa** are mineral-rich Gabon, Equatorial Guinea and the Democratic Republic of Congo (DRC). The plantation and mining sectors in Gabon and Equatorial Guinea and the palm plantations in Cameroon offer employment opportunities to immigrant labourers from the Central African Republic, Congo and Nigeria, as well as traders and domestic and service workers from Senegal, Mali, Benin and Togo. A rich but small country, Gabon relies on contract labourers and immigrants from other African countries and from Europe, who constitute about a quarter of the wage earners. In the 1980s and earlier, thousands of immigrants had entered Gabon from Burundi, Rwanda, DRC and Congo in search of a better life and greater security. As urban unemployment soared to 20%, a presidential decree was issued in 1991 to safeguard jobs for nationals and 'Gabonize' the labour force, and in September 1994, the government enacted laws requiring foreigners to register and pay residence fees, or leave the country by mid-February 1995. By the deadline, about 55,000 foreign nationals were expelled, while 1,500 had legalized their residency (Le Courier, 1997).

In **Southern Africa**, during the apartheid era, labour migrants were recruited in droves from neighbouring countries, often from particular regions and villages to work in designated mines and farms. Undocumented migrants from Lesotho, Zimbabwe and Mozambique worked as seasonal labourers on the farms of Mpumalanga, Free State and Northern Province. What is new is perhaps the scale and diversity of the origin of present-day immigrants who brought their skills, enterprise, drive and their astute posture, visibility and eagerness to explore prospects in Africa's most buoyant economy. Motivated, adaptable and less scornful of menial jobs, immigrants not only do jobs most locals loathe, they also accept lower wages which locals scorn, prompting charges by labour unions that they depress wage levels (Oucho & Crush, 2001).

Changing migratory configurations also implies that the Republic of South Africa (RSA) is concurrently not only a recipient but a sender, perhaps also a transit country, exporting skilled migrants to Europe, North America and Australia. The thousands who emigrated from the country just before and soon after 1994 were mostly skilled whites, especially doctors and their families, sceptical of the prospects of black majority rule and frightened of rising crime in the country. The main migrant labour configuration was from peripheral countries, designed to meet South Africa's Apartheid-era labour requirement (Adepoju, 2003).

In recent years, Botswana has become a major country of immigration. A prosperous, politically stable country with a rapid and steady economic growth over the past two decades, it has attracted highly skilled professionals, who are in short supply, from Ghana, Zambia, Uganda, Zimbabwe, Nigeria and Kenya. Most of these people work in the private sector and at universities, taking advantage of the relaxed laws on residence and entry introduced in the early 1990s, now being replaced by the localization policy in favour of indigenes (Campbell, 2003).

Root causes and patterns of migration

In general, the major factors prompting emigration are the huge disparities in earning potential between poor and rich countries. These differences reflect prospect for better employment opportunities, training and skill development and, of course, higher incomes in more favourable socio-economic environments. In recent times, migration has been fuelled globally by access to information, declining costs of travel, demographics dynamics, labour demand and supply dynamics and the economic return to labour in high-income countries (UN, 2007; OECD, 2005).

In sub-Saharan Africa, emigration pressure is fuelled by unstable politics, ethno-religious conflicts, poverty and rapidly growing populations. Rapid population and labour force growth have combined with persistent economic decline, huge external debts, retrenchment of public-sector workers in response to structural adjustment measures, and environmental deterioration to shape trends and patterns of international migration.

Consequently, migration is not only growing in volume in all major sub-regions; most countries do not have a single migration configuration but a whole range of types at once. Sustained past high fertility (the demographics momentum) ensures rapid increases in persons of working ages. Growing at about 2.8 percent per year, the region requires about 7.5 million new jobs merely to stabilize the employment situation. Youth unemployment of 18–50%, and increasing among graduates ready to do any work, anywhere and at any wage, creates the pools of potential destitute and desperate migrants, whose numbers are set to double within 25 years.

Unlike Asia's 'Four Tigers' (Hong Kong, Singapore, South Korea and Taiwan), however, SSA countries have failed to take advantage of the demographic dividend of a virile young population for investment, economics growth and employment generation. Sub-Saharan Africa's unemployment rate of 9.8% in 2006 was lower than only that of the Middle East/North Africa region, and it has the highest figure for the working poor. Globally the number of the working poor at the US$1 level declined between 2001 and 2006 – but in SSA it increased by 14 million while the number of US$2-a-day workers reached a record high of 26 million in 2006 (ILO, 2007). The situation has since worsened as the ongoing global economic and financial crisis bites harder and more deeply. It is precisely the sizeable work deficit that prompts the emigration of youths, desperately seeking a more secure alternative and a future, to engage in dangerous and uncertain journeys in dare-devil ventures to enter Europe in irregular and undocumented situations (see the following).

In most countries, the public sector – the dominant employer – has not been able to provide viable employment opportunities to meet the demands of the rapidly-growing labour force, thus generating large numbers of unemployed youth. Mismanaged economies and human rights abuses, especially under military regimes across the sub-region, have spurred the exile of both skilled and unskilled persons. Conflicts and environmental degradation further aggravate the pressure for migration from poorer to relatively prosperous regions within, and increasingly outside, the region. In the Sahel in particular, desertification and cyclical famines have triggered waves of environmentally displaced persons across national frontiers within and outside the sub-region (Adepoju, 1998).

Stressful economic conditions, especially the absence of sustainable livelihood opportunities, the perception of a bleak future, coupled with widening disparities in incomes and living standards between the north and the south, have been compounded by political factors, especially poor governance and human rights abuses, fuelling the emigration of young educated persons. Africa's political and economic crises have triggered migratory flows to new destinations which have no prior historical, political or economic links to the countries of emigration. Moreover, as the various crises have intensified, migratory outflows have increased in both size and effect. Broader international trends of globalization, regional integration, network formation, political transformation and the entry of multinational corporations in search of cheap labour, coupled with domestic political and economic malaise, have resulted in many immigrant-receiving countries that were once emigrant-sending countries (Adepoju, 2006b). For more than a decade now, these traditional labour importing countries and attractive destinations for migrants have experienced endemic political and economic crises, which spur out-migration of their nationals and of migrants.

Irregular migration to Europe

The introduction of tougher rules regarding entry and residence of foreigners in Europe for regular migration has, since the mid-1990s, inadvertently pushed irregular African migrants to use complex routes via the Maghreb as a transit region to enter Europe clandestinely. African migrants have increasingly adopted more sophisticated, daring and evasive methods to enter northern countries, even as border controls are tightened. The Maghreb countries, apart from serving as a source of migrants to the European Union countries (especially Spain, France, the Netherlands and Belgium) and the Gulf States, have also become migrant transit and destination countries (Adepoju, 2006a). Indeed, the increasing migration through and pressure on transit countries of the Maghreb by irregular migrants from Africa in the hope of crossing to Europe via the Spanish Canary Islands and the Italian island of Lampedusa is one of the most dramatic migration configurations over the last ten years (GCIM, 2005). The numbers and especially the desperation of these youths are fuelled by distorted information on labour market conditions in EU countries and the increasing professionalism of traffickers, scams and bogus travel intermediaries with promises of passage to Europe, encouraged by the regularization of the status of irregular immigrants in Spain, among others.

Many die in rickety boats on the sea, or of dehydration along the desert routes. About 2,000 Africans are believed to drown in the Mediterranean each year while attempting to cross to Europe. The deaths of six irregular immigrants attempting to scale the wire fence in Ceuta to enter Spain in September 2005 prompted the Spanish government to double the height of this metal barricade and defend it with Spanish Legion soldiers and the Civil Guard. The government also stepped up its anti-immigrant collaboration with Moroccan security forces. Since the mid-1990s, intensified border patrolling at the Straits of Gibraltar has prompted migrants to cross from places further east on the Mediterranean coast, as well as exploring new crossing points from ports in Senegal and Mauritania (Adepoju, 2006a). For these young men and women, creating more productive jobs and decent work locally holds the promise of arresting the irregular migration of an increasing number of persons surreptitiously seeking entry to Europe.

Demand and supply of unskilled and skilled workers

Rich countries need immigrants to cope with prevailing economic and demographic imperatives: unskilled, sometimes undocumented, immigrants to do poorly paid, dirty and dangerous jobs which nationals scorn; and highly skilled professional IT specialists, engineers, doctors and nurses are in short supply. In many poor African countries, the best and brightest are migrating abroad, sometimes working in mental jobs – a loss of productivity to both sending and receiving countries and indeed the migrants whose skills are underutilized. This situation persists since globalization, which facilitates movement of capital information and technology, frowns on labour mobility.

Unskilled migrants are required for some kinds of economic activities and are vital to the thriving local economy. Without unskilled migrant workers to do the unglamorous jobs, which indigenes are increasingly reluctant to take up, some services in rich countries could not function. In virtually all developed regions, undocumented immigrants are exploited and vulnerable, compelled to accept jobs with unpleasant physical demands, low and irregular wages and long working hours. The irregular situation of migrants can and does mitigate the potential advantages of migration. Most irregular migrants work in the underground economy characterized by unstable jobs and low pay. Restricted to the Three D's – dirty, demeaning and dangerous jobs – they are vulnerable and exploited, they cannot unionize, and unscrupulous employers often refuse to pay, threatening them with deportation if brought to the attention of immigration officials. A growing number of migrants are in vulnerable situations, mainly because of their irregular status or the kind of work they do, and many face discriminations. Most irregular migrants are unskilled and frustrated, and have poor access to training opportunities, advancement and job carrier. Many African graduate engineers in EU countries clean train tracks, wash toilets, or drive cabs as a survival strategy to enter the restrictive labour market. Many spend years working to defray the huge cost of their irregular migration, and are unable to remit money home. Being vulnerable, exploitable and subject to uncertainty and insecurity, when they do remit money, they normally opt for informal and risky channels of remittances for fear of apprehension and deportation.

The greying of populations and labour shortages in rich countries may accelerate the demand for labour in many sectors. In SSA, high population growth accentuates the supply of manpower, creating a pool of potential emigrants with a mix of skills, ready to fill vacancies created by an ageing population in the north. The interplay, by promoting migration between these regions, transcends narrow demographic dynamics. Experience has shown that strict restriction on legal migration leads to illegal movements. Closed borders with zero immigration and open borders for unrestricted immigration are both unrealistic aims, prompting some EU countries to propose a strategy of conditional opening of borders to admit immigrants who satisfy specified criteria, to cope with prevailing economic and demographic imperatives. What seems obvious is that additional workers are required to make up for the expected shortfall in the domestic labour force of rich countries and to bolster economic growth (GCIM, 2005). This statistical reality is, however, clouded by xenophobic public opinion. Partial solutions include training local unskilled and unemployed persons, and attracting women to the labour market. Rich countries nevertheless need immigrants to do poorly paid, dirty and dangerous jobs which nationals scorn. They also need highly specialized professionals, especially software specialists, engineers, doctors and nurses, all of whom are in short supply.

Brain drain

Upon gaining independence, African countries invested heavily in education to train nationals to fill the gap created by the departing colonialists, education being regarded as the main vehicle for rapid development. Within a generation, these poor countries were able to produce professionals and, recently, IT specialists. Others were trained abroad, building on the foundation of science and mathematics courses, even as these countries were trapped in the immense demographic momentum in a situation of sluggish economic growth and employment generation.

However, education expanded faster than the absorptive capacity of these countries' economies. The small private and bloated public sectors absorbed only a few graduates, resulting in graduates' unemployment. Many students sponsored to do post-graduate studies in technology, science and engineering abroad stayed back at the end of their studies. Emigration of highly qualified professionals from Zimbabwe, Zambia, Senegal, Ghana and Uganda to South Africa and outside Africa in the 1970s intensified in the 1980s to Europe, North America and the oil-rich Middle East; between 1986 and 1990, for example, and estimated 50,000 to 60,000 middle- and high-level African managers emigrated as domestic socio-economic and political conditions deteriorated (Adepoju, 2000). Many more are believed to have emigrated in recent years. The global migration market allows developed countries to unilaterally and freely select who should be admitted, what skill combination and income profile is acceptable, when and for how long without recourse to the countries of origin that incurred the human capital investment in the migrants. The battle for brains, or talent hunt, is propelled by the dynamics of knowledge-based economies: the possibilities offered by technology and the globalization of economic activities since many industries now operate with an international network of operations, components and talents. In many developed economies, highly qualified labour for knowledge-intensive activities is being recruited from third-world and emerging-market-economy countries (Van Agtmael, 2007).

In the Netherlands, for example, the government's 'inviting policy' in 2004 simplified the admission of highly qualified professionals, required for dynamic knowledge-intensive economy of the twenty-first century, from developing countries using a points system based on personal talents, age, education and work experience. Germany's migration law, which came into effect in 2005, creates opportunities for admitting academics and specialists in the technology sector by offering them permanent residence. Their family members can work without restrictions and are not subject to integration requirements. The basic principle of France's new bill on immigration and integration is to secure a more 'elective' immigration for work, study and research, with a focus on migrants with specific talents who have the potential to contribute to the economic development of France.

Britain's point system, adopted in March 2006, for admitting students and labour migrants, offers highly skilled migrants a residence permit for a maximum of five years. It also allows them to change jobs without further verification. The system permits students to look for work for a year in England and two years in Scotland at the end of their studies (Adepoju, 2007a). If you visit a health facility, it is quite likely that the doctor will be Kenyan, the nurse Ghanaian, the anaesthetist Zimbabwean, the surgeon South African, the therapist Nigerian!

In the United States, the Department of Health and Human Services projected a shortfall of about 270,000 full-time registered nurses by 2010 and 800,000 by 2020 (Clearfield & Batalova, 2007). Already in 2005, 15% of all healthcare workers were foreign-born. Sub-Saharan African immigrants in the USA are dominated by West Africans. Of the 809,152 foreign-born SSA population in the USA captured by official statistics in 2002, 357,360 originated from West Africa.

These include 139,493 Nigerians, with South Africans constituting a majority of those from Southern Africa, 70,275 out of 71,883. Most of these immigrants have tertiary education, including students with doctoral degrees (Luca, 2005).

Highly skilled professionals, including doctors, paramedical personnel, nurses, teachers, engineers, scientists and technologists from Africa, were and continue to be attracted by relatively higher salaries and better living conditions in rich countries. For instance, after the collapse of Nigeria's oil-led economy in the mid-1980s, many Ghanaian professionals who had earlier worked in Nigeria moved in a step-wise pattern to South Africa, and then to Europe and North

America and the oil-rich Middle East. Many highly skilled people have emigrated to developed countries in response to the deteriorating domestic socio-economic and political conditions.

According to OECD estimates, of the nearly 4 million foreign-born population of sub-Saharan Africa residents in OECD countries, the USA (929,723), the UK (812,371), France (565,590), Portugal (348,263), Canada (271,095) and Australia (188,928) are the major recipient countries. Others with slightly more than 100000 sub-Sahara Africans include the Netherlands (116,349) and Belgium (107,716), trailed by Sweden (68,077), Spain (79,263) and Greece (56,859). More than 100,000 (2.5%) are professionals (OECD, 2007). This is, ironically, about the same as the number of expatriate professionals employed by aid agencies in sub-Saharan Africa as part of the overall aid package at a cost to the region of about $4 billion. This process denies the region the optimum utilization of the skills of its diaspora and of development goals by the outflow of homegrown scarce skilled manpower (United Nations, 2003). For Nigerians and Zambians in particular, highly skilled professionals constitute about half or more of expatriates living in OECD countries. Two in every five nationals of Benin, Tanzania, Zimbabwe, Cameroon, Lesotho, Malawi and South Africa are highly skilled professionals. The driving force is the wide differential in incomes: a trained nurse in Uganda earns US$38 per month and a doctor $67 per month while their colleagues in the USA could earn about $3,000 and $10,000 respectively. The region thereby pays the price of producing the human capital for use by the rich countries and is denied the realization of its development goals.

About 23,000 African university graduates and 50,000 executives leave the sub-Saharan region annually, and about 40,000 of them with PhD degrees now live outside Africa (Meyer, 2001). It is estimated that people of foreign origin represent 12% of the highly qualified component of the labour force in the USA, and this may well also be true of many European countries. Africans with professional, technical and managerial skills have used the USA's 'diversity visa' (or green card lottery) programme, which was designed to liberalize immigration by creating avenues for large numbers of immigrants from new sources to enter the USA. Between 1990 and 1998, these numbered 52,000, or 7% of the total of professional, technical and managerial immigrants to the USA (Lucas, 2005). Probably about a third of researchers and engineers from poor countries work in (developed) OECD countries, a significant number indeed and a huge human capital flow produced at great cost by poor countries (Adepoju, 2006b).

Specialists in new technologies, engineering, medicine and healthcare are a small proportion of the emigrants from sub-Saharan Africa, but they cost the region in a variety of ways and far beyond their numbers, not least because of the lost opportunity for the training of replacement cohort: tertiary educational institutions lack experienced leaders to train those required for a variety of development activities and to undertake research for development. The large exodus of doctors has negatively impacted the training of new doctors and on the quality of health services delivery in Nigeria (from where about 600 medical specialists work in Saudi Arabia and Kuwait, and up to 12,000 in the USA), in Ghana (where 60% of doctors trained in the 1980s have emigrated), South Africa (where many white doctors have emigrated to Canada, Australia, the USA and UK) and Zimbabwe (where about 60% of doctors' home country's economy has collapsed) (Adepoju, 2005). The driving force is the wide differential in incomes and working conditions.

The overall magnitude and impact of the brain drain from sub-Saharan Africa is captured in a report by the United Nations which estimates that 'over the next decade Africa will need to train an additional 1 million health care professionals. The leaders must find ways to retain more of the doctors, nurses, pharmacists and laboratory technicians (which) they currently produce' (United Nations, 2005, p. 18). Blaming the rich countries for contributing to the crisis by creating a fatal 'flow' of health professions from the region, the report points out that there are more Malawian doctors practising in Manchester, UK, than in Malawi itself, while 550 of the 600 Zambian doctors trained in medical school from 1978 to 1999 have emigrated abroad (ibid). The IOM reports, similarly, that more Ethiopian doctors are practicing in Chicago (USA) than in Ethiopia. More than half of nurses and doctors have emigrated from Malawi, and another quarter of the remaining health workers are probably infected with HIV/AIDS. If statistics are to be trusted, Ghana has lost 50% of its doctors to Canada, Britain and the USA. Three quarters of Zimbabwe's doctors have left the country since the early 1990s and half of social health workers have relocated abroad since 2001. In the last eight years more than 1,600 nurses and about 12,500 doctors from the region are currently registered to work in Britain (UKNMC, 2005).

Millennium development goals and other development agendas in the region are being compromised by the emigration of its scarce skilled manpower. A major challenge now facing the region is how to retain, attract back and effectively utilize the rare skills of nationals living mainly in the OECD countries for national development. Sub-Saharan African transnational communities rarely sever ties with home and this is manifested in their investment portfolios; some are active in political advocacy, charity and cultural exchange. The series of initiatives to identify and attract back skilled professional engineers, medical doctors, professors, scientists, information technologists and other highly skilled professionals and utilize their expertise for national development should be encouraged and supported by development partners and rich countries. Political leaders courting nationals to return home must also address the push factors that spurred the brain drain. Remittances do not compensate for the potential contribution of the skilled emigrants through training and transfer of expertise to younger cohorts at home.

Migration, especially of skilled professionals to engineer development, is a global issue, and is of concern to both poor and rich countries – albeit from opposite perspectives. Rich countries have been prompted to rethink and consolidate policies on who should be attracted and admitted to satisfy their skilled labour shortage. For poor countries especially in Africa and Asia the loss of specialists in IT, engineering and medicine, while a miniscule proportion of the workforce, has impacted far beyond the numbers involved. This migration process denies these poorer regions the optimum utilization of the skills of their diaspora. Many African countries today are churning out students without the requisite rigour of learning from older experts in their fields, or doing research for development and training, thereby stalling development activities and accelerating the collapse of institutions.

Brain circulation

In SSA, we are now witnessing the transformation of brain drain to brain circulation within the region, especially from parts of the Africa to Côte d'Ivoire, Gabon, Botswana and South Africa. As political and economic crises continue to adversely affect conditions in the traditional countries of immigration within the region, highly skilled professionals pressured to leave their countries by the uncertain economic conditions have found a new RSA, and the booming economy of Botswana, attractive alternatives to Europe, North America and the Gulf States transforming the erstwhile brain drain *from* into brain circulation *within* the region. Migration to RSA increased further since the demise of the Apartheid regime and the spectacular political transformation in the country. The migrants were mostly skilled professionals, professors, doctors, lawyers, nurses and engineers unlike the traditional immigrants from Lesotho, Swaziland, Botswana, Malawi and Mozambique whose nationals were mostly unskilled mine workers and farm labourers. Most migrants in Botswana are highly skilled professionals in industry, university and private sectors (Adepoju, 2003). There are about 300,000 unfilled posts in South Africa requiring skills which nationals do not possess, in a situation of about 40% unemployment rate even as white doctors, engineers, nurses and other professionals are emigrating to Australia, Canada and UK, attracted by higher incomes, scared of the rising domestic crime and oblivious to the progressive policies of the post-Apartheid era.

The diaspora

Migrants'-diaspora-return continuum and linkages are both strong and pervasive in Africa. During their sojourn abroad, migrants maintain contact by visiting and sending money home. African emigrants usually nurse the hope to return home at the nearest opportunity. Many sending countries (Ghana, Cape Verde, Nigeria, Burkina Faso) have expatriate populations spread over all parts of the world, as a result of emigration over generations. The number of African diaspora is clouded by the history of the slave trade, but an estimated 30 million Africans are working outside their countries of origin (Ratha, 2011). More recent emigrants, wherever they are, are rarely severing their ties with home (Adepoju, 2006c). Given favourable working conditions at home, skilled professionals in the diaspora would prefer to return there to contribute to the development of their countries. At the political level, the African Union has officially recognized the diaspora as Africa's sixth region (others being Western, Central, Northern, Southern and Eastern Africa).

Building networks of scientists with their colleagues at home, which enables the diaspora professionals to contribute to the development of home countries without residential relocation, should be encouraged; but the stiff immigration policies of rich countries deny many scientists the flexibility to relocate. But the challenges are daunting: many poor African countries lack the requisite infrastructure, even as poverty, corruption and mismanagement artificially increases. African diaspora are active in political advocacy, charity and cultural exchange. For example, Ghanaian diaspora in the UK have pressed and received concession from their government to participate in national elections and are also actively involved in modernizing the political process. African diasporic associations also help new arrivals adapt and enter into labour markets, reinforce cultural identity, and mobilize members' capital for community development projects at 'home' and contribute to charity and development programmes (Adepoju, 2007b). Nigerians in Diaspora Organizations (NIDO) have established and are actively involved in dialogue with governments at home.

Networking amongst professionals in the diaspora and their counterparts at home should be encouraged in training, technology transfer, information exchange and research projects, principally via the internet. The possibility for IT specialists in Africa to work for international corporations without physical dislocation should again be encouraged. African leaders are now exploring strategies to attract back their nationals to contribute to national development. Leaders of Nigeria, Kenya, Ghana and others have held series of meetings with their nationals in diaspora, encouraging them to run with offers of incentives to do so. About a dozen governments have established ministries or agencies of the diaspora to coordinate diaspora-related programmes. Many migrants who also nurse the hope to return home ultimately may have acquired skills and capital that can be productively invested back home but we should also recognize that the skills acquired by some may not match available job opportunities at home. We need more evidence-based research on lessons learnt from, for instance, IOM's Return and Registration of Qualified Nationals and similar programmes in Africa to facilitate return, retention and reintegration of nationals and to promote their potential for country of origin development.

Remittances and another diaspora resource

Diaspora resources include economic remittance, other contributions such as social capital (sources of ideas, behaviours, identities and social capital), technological capital (transfer of knowledge and skills) and political remittance (political support, identities and practices). In general, migration is a factor of economic development that can have both positive and negative consequences. Advantages of migration include migrants' remittances, lower unemployment, less population pressure and knowledge brought by returning migrants. Immigrants in general embody energy, determination and enterprise and can dynamize economies, social organization and interchange of experience. The major challenge is how to make migration work productively for, and to channel movements into, regular situations to benefit the three key actors – migrants, origin and destination countries, societies and families.

In addition to direct financial contributions, migration leads to formation of transnational communities, which boosts economic development. Migrant communities abroad, as well as returning migrants, become conduits for new ideas and investment. Migrants themselves form associations and networks abroad. Returning migrants bring back skills and work experiences from abroad. Emigrants can also transfer knowledge, technology and investments to countries of origin.

Remittances have been rising steeply and now parallel export earnings, official ODA, and in the case of Lesotho, accounts for one half of the GNP. Remittances are an important source of income for developing countries. Nationals of Egypt, Burkina Faso, Nigeria, Cape Verde, Lesotho, Eritrea and so on working abroad remit huge sums of money to their home countries. The sheer volume of remittances – over $40 billion a year – has kindled optimism about their positive contribution, and the role of the diaspora, to development in home countries. Remittances are expected to be additional sources of development financing in Africa by providing a lifeline, not only to communities and families to enable them to gain access to basic services such as housing, education and health, but also to national savings and investment via money and capital markets. However, the real impact of remittances on the economies of emigration countries in Africa is yet to be fully understood because, apart from their raising the level of national savings, remittances are essentially private transfers that do not determine their destination or their use. Nor are market forces able to channel remittance to the most productive sectors into the most innovative entrepreneurial hands to promote development (Ratha, 2007).

The use of remittances varies widely, including as lifelines to poor relations left behind to pay for basic services, healthcare in particular; education of siblings and children; to set up enterprises; and to enhance agricultural production through improved irrigation schemes and other agricultural inputs, as in Mali and Senegal. In Lesotho, remittances constitute the lifeline to the survival of impoverished rural households. Since migration in Africa is generally a household portfolio diversification strategy, pooling resources helps the poor overcome the poverty constraint to migration (Boswell & Crisp, 2004). Remittances sent to families at home could tremendously benefit recipients to supplement living conditions, investment in education of children and siblings, healthcare and improved housing, and to set up enterprises with multiple effects on local economies. Hometown associations' investment can improve basic infrastructural facilities that benefit all households, with local and often wider multiplier effects. In poor communities that lack basic services normally provided by the government, the pressing needs are for better housing, funds to pay school fees and buy textbooks and uniforms, and access to basic health services which migrants' remittances supplement or pay for. Many migrants harbour the ambition to return home ultimately and invest in petty trading, refurbished or new buildings, real estates which are highly yielding, and savings as fallback on return.

Another pertinent issue is that of reliability of remittances. Many families in Africa who depend on remittance from relatives in the United States and Europe for day-to-day support are being affected by the global economic meltdown and the crisis-induced retrenchment and unemployment in countries of immigration. This takes a heavy toll on the daily budget of recipients via reduced levels of remittances. Not all remittances are routed via official channels, in view of heavy transaction costs and risks. Transaction costs of money transfers are exorbitant and may be risky through informal channels. Irregular migrants normally opt for informal channels of remittance for fear of apprehension and deportation (Doorn, 2002). Senegalese emigrants have adapted the indigenous, trust-based traditional human courier system (Kara International Exchange) and network of traders, visiting relations and associates to send money home. This process is prompt, avoids exchange rate fluctuations and costly transfer charges, and overcomes the bottleneck of poor accessibility to remote rural areas. African governments are increasingly interested in promoting migrants' remittances for investment purposes, and are using their embassies to disseminate information on available investment opportunities to their national abroad, offering favourable (tax and related) incentive-based policy environment in the country as in Ghana. Kenya's government has expressed its readiness to explore matching funds or provide security for bank loans for its nationals in the diaspora willing to invest at home. The possibility of diaspora bonds has also been flagged. All stakeholders should work in concert in exploring the opportunities and minimizing the obstacles for remittances, and in particular in lobbying for low-cost transfer services and less stringent regulations in order to increase its productive use.

Trade and migration

The limited size of internal markets, and especially the disadvantageous position of sub-Saharan African countries in the new era of globalization, impact migration dynamics in various ways. Agricultural subsidies in OECD countries, especially the USA and Europe, have a negative effect on the income of farmers in the region. The subsidies on cotton in the USA which artificially spur the level of local production and depressed world prices, impoverishes millions of Africans. The US spends more on subsidizing 25,000 cotton farmers ($4 billion) than it does on its entire aid budget for Africa. The immediate impact was a loss of $301 million by African exporters, with Burkina Faso, Mali and Benin each losing about 2% of GDP growth. West and Central Africa produced 17% of world cotton exports in 2002 (up from 4% in 1980), but heavy subsidies to the small number of cotton growers in the USA have drastically affected the livelihoods of 10 million cotton growers and their families in Benin, Mali, Burkina Faso, Chad, Togo, Kenya and Ghana (OECD, 2005). Most of these people are now migrating to the cities in a desperate bid for survival. Also, the World Bank estimated that high tariffs and technical barriers to trade cost the region about US$20 billion yearly in lost exports, much needed revenue which could have been used for development and employment-generation (IOM, 2004). The clamour by African leaders to achieve mutually beneficial trade relations is understandable: deepening poverty has frustrated recent achievements in democratic and economic reform and efforts to improve living conditions of their people, stimulate economic growth and generate employment opportunities.

Cooperation and dialogue for policy coherence

Policy dialogue on migration is at a crossroads, not least because of the diversity of actors and stakeholders in poor and rich countries, and a variety of often-conflicting interest groups. The migration of skilled and unskilled persons is therefore of increasing concern to both rich and poor countries, but from different perspectives. In both blocks in poor and in rich countries, economic and demographic factors underline current debate and policy and there is little or no convergence on issues dealing with migration. In spite of the global financial and economic crisis that is reshaping the architecture of international migration, countries need migrants as contributors to development. Migration could and should be a win-win-win game, though admittedly, some lose; some gain. What is needed is a comprehensive perspective and policy coherence for the orderly and humane management of migration so that globalization wears a human face (Stiglitz, 2006).

Migration matters should no longer be handled bilaterally; a regional, or even global, approach that harmonizes migration policies is required. There is also need for dialogue and consultation among the various stakeholders to discuss common approaches to their migration concerns and interests, to share ideas and to enhance understanding and cooperation in migration management. Such a process could lead to the development of a coherent national, intra-regional, inter-regional and international policy framework for the management of migration. Indeed, migration and development policies might have a better chance of succeeding if both sides of the migratory space circumstance in the countries of origin and of destination were taken into account (Van Dalen & Esveldt, 2003). Indeed, a critical ingredient in the formulation of a coherent migration-friendly policy is an understanding of the dynamics and underlying factors of migration both at the origin and at the destination.

Discourses on migration, especially from the receiving end, are full of anxiety, misconceptions, myths and prejudices; and also fed on xenophobia. In that context, the positive aspects of migrants as agents of development in source and destination countries should be made explicit. Dialogue and consultations among the various stakeholders, to discuss common approaches to their migration concerns and interests, share ideas and enhance understanding and cooperation in migration management, could lead to the development of a coherent policy framework for the management of migration. In order to provide planners, politicians and policy-makers with comprehensive data on migration dynamics, cross-country collaborative research using innovative approaches to capture emerging and changing configurations is required on a number of themes. Foremost among these, we need information on the interlinked factors that drive traditional and changing migratory flows labour migration, brain drain/brain circulation in various contexts in the region. Of special policy concern is the independent migration of female professionals and its impact on gender roles, as well as on family, social and development policies. Since migration in sub-Saharan Africa is essentially intra-regional, policy research must also address the causes of the region's contagious conflicts. Peace and stability are prerequisites for investment, development and employment generation, and good governance can help curtail skills flight and the exiling of the intelligentsia. The lesson to be learnt from the collapse of the WTO Doha trade negotiations in 2006 is that political will must be mustered to open the markets of rich countries to exports from developing countries to remove tariffs on imports of labour-intensive, job-creating goods produced by poor countries, in order to enhance economic growth and generate employment. Unless economic and other opportunities are created in poor countries, pressures for international migration will intensify, further stalling domestic development. The outsourcing of the responsibility for policing of borders, and of halting irregular migrants from the EU to the Maghreb countries is both unrealistic and unsustainable for lack of the financial and logistical facilities essential in carrying out the defence of their borders against the surge of irregular immigrants from other parts of Africa, and beyond. The recognition that strict control does not produce the desired results, but instead inadvertently spurs trafficking, the EU countries have proposed investing in job creation, economic growth and poverty alleviation schemes in Africa, in order to stem the tide of irregular emigration. This strategy also includes some form of guest-worker scheme and circulatory migration that allows Africans to work in specified sectors of labour shortage in EU countries, the regular situations. Mali is serving as a pilot for the new strategy. African countries need to ensure that their specific interests and concerns are adequately reflected in any bilateral and multilateral migration negotiations. Issues relating to the treatment of their nationals living and working in regular situations in EU countries, the rights of irregular migrants to basic services, and the need to review the unfair trade regimes which impoverish millions of their nationals who are engaged in farming at home should assume centre stage in future migration agreements. Efforts should be made to revisit existing agreements in order to review and amend unfavourable conditions. Bilateral and multilateral agreements between countries sending and receiving migrants must also address the issue of depleting sub-Saharan Africa of its scarce skilled-manpower resources. It is important that residential laws of rich countries be made flexible, to give skilled professionals the opportunity of relocating without losing their residence rights in those countries (Adepoju, van Naerssen, & Zoomers, 2007).

The future of migration dynamics: a shared responsibility

African countries are facing daunting challenges with respect to most migratory configurations. Poverty eradication strategies should therefore be at the forefront of development assistance, aligned with domestic mechanisms for stable macro-economics environments favourable to growth, to generate employment opportunities and foster enterprise and self-sustaining livelihoods. Efforts by poor African countries to restructure their economies and open their markets to share in the global economy have been disappointing. Thus far, emphasis on economics and political aspects and policies has ignored the crucial demographic dimension that rapid population growth intensifies poverty and emigration pressure.

Rich countries have a moral responsibility to assist programmes for the orderly return and reintegration of migrants to their countries of origin, especially highly skilled professionals whose expertise is being productively utilized in these rich countries. Any long-term solution should emphasize economic growth and employment generation, the promotion of human rights, and security and related policy measures as well as the factors that generate emigration from poor countries in the first place. In a spirit of co-responsibility, rich countries have to help poor African countries foster local development. Compensation for the brain drain could take the form of supporting projects which involve professionals going back to their countries of origin for short periods, to work in special programmes and education (ILO, 2004b). Ethical recruitment of highly skilled professionals must be enforced, and bilateral agreements promoted to minimize the adverse consequences on the development of source countries. Such bilateral and multilateral agreements between developed and SSA countries should also address issues of haemorrhaging of its scarce skilled-manpower resources. It is important that residential rules in rich countries be made flexible to enable skilled professionals the opportunity for virtual relocation without losing their residence rights.

It seems apparent that success of restrictive migration policies depends on improving the economic situation in the immigrants' countries of origin. Such a strategy also has the potential to stimulate the return of skilled nationals needed for development in their own countries. The calls for cooperation between the poor sub-Saharan African labour-exporting countries and those of the north, beyond the rhetoric of co-development. Unless economic and other opportunities are created in these countries, pressures for international migration will intensify. And in spite of the sharp economic and demographic divide between rich and poor countries, international migration can, with determination, political will, the right policies and recognition of the potential positive contribution of migration to development, indeed be a win-win-win situation for countries and societies that send and receive migrants and indeed the migrants themselves.

References

Adepoju, A. (1988). International migration in Africa south of the Saharan. In R. Appleyard (Ed.), *International migration today: Trends and prospects* (Vol. 1). Paris: UNESCO.

Adepoju, A. (1998). *Links between internal and international migration: The African situation (first published 1984).* Selected articles to commemorate 50th anniversary of International Social Science Journal. Paris: UNESCO.

Adepoju, A. (2000). Regional integration, continuity and changing patterns of intra-regional migration in sub-Saharan Africa. In M. A. B. Siddique (Ed.), *International migration into the 21st century: Essays in honour of Reginald Appleyard.* Aldershot, UK: Edward Edgar Publishing.

Adepoju, A. (2003). Continuity and changing configurations of migration to and from the Republic of South Africa. *International Migration, 41*(1).

Adepoju, A. (2005, November 3–4). *Perspectives on migration within and from sub-Saharan Africa.* Background paper for the Conference on Policy Coherence for Development: The African Experience. Paris: Organisational for Economic cooperation and Development.

Adepoju, A. (2006a). *The challenge of labour migration flows between West Africa and the Maghreb.* Migration Research Papers. Geneva: International Labour Organisation.

Adepoju, A. (2006b, July 6–8). *Recent trends in international migration in and from Africa.* Background Papers No. 1, CeSPI and SID International Conference on Migration and Development: Opportunities and challenges for Euro-African Relations, Rome.

Adepoju, A. (2006c). Placing international migration in the context of the 3D's: Demography, development and democracy. *International Migration, 44*(4).

Adepoju, A. (2007a). Perspectives on international migration and national development in sub-Saharan Africa. In A. Adepoju, T. van Naerssen, & A. Zoomers (Eds.), *International migration and national development in sub-Saharan Africa.* Leiden: Afrika -Studiecentrum Series.

Adepoju, A. (2007b). *Migration in sub-Saharan Africa.* Uppsala: Nordic African Studies Centre.

Adepoju, A. (Ed.). (2010). *International migration within, to and from Africa in a globalise world.* Accra: Sub-Saharan Publishers.

Adepoju, A., van Naerssen, T., & Zoomers, A. (Eds.) (2007). *International migration and national development in sub-Saharan Africa.* Leiden: Afrika-Studiecentrum Series.

Ayiemba, E. (2011). Problems and opportunities of displacement for policy action: Lessons from the 2007 post-election violence and refugee camps in Kenya. In J. O. Oucho (Ed.), *Migration in the service of African development: A book written in honour of Professor Aderanti Adepoju.* Ibadan: Safari Publishers.

Azam, J. P., & Gubret, F. (2005, May 29). *Migrant remittances and economics development in Africa: A review of evidence.* Paper prepared for the African Economic Research Consortium Plenary Session, Nairobi. Retrieved on July 2007, from http://idei.fr/doc/wp/2005/remit.pdf

Boswell, C., & Crisp, J. (2004). *Poverty, international migration and Asylum.* WIDER Policy Brief 2004/008. Helsinki: UNU-WIDER.

Campbell, E. K. (2003). Attitudes of Botswana citizens towards immigrants: Signs of xenophobia? *International Migration, 41*(4), 71–109.

Clearfield, E., & Batalova, J. (2007, July). Foreign -born health-care workers in the United States. *Migration Information Source.* Retrieved on July 2007, from http://www.migrationinformation.org/development.cfm

Doorn, J. (2002). *Globalisation, remittances and development.* Geneva: International Labour Organization (ILO), Social Finance Unit.

GCIM (Global Commission on International Migration). (2005). *Migration in an inter-connected world: New directions for action.* Geneva: GCIM.

ILO. (2004a, September). *Declaration on employment and poverty alleviation in Africa.* Issues Paper, Extraordinary Summit of African Union Heads of State and Governments, Ouagadougou. ILO.

ILO. (2004b). *A fair globalization: Creating opportunities for all.* Report by the World Commission on the Social Dimension on Globalization. Geneva: ILO.

ILO. (2007). *Global employment trends brief 2007*. Geneva: ILO.

IOM. (2004). *Migration for development in Africa*. General Strategy Paper. Geneva: IOM.

Le Courier. (1997, September–October). Reportage: Gabon. *African Caribbean Pacific, 165*.

Lucas, R. E. B. (2005). International migration to the high-income countries: Some consequences for economic development in sending countries. In F. Bourguignon, B. Pleskovic, & A. Sapir (Eds.), *Are we on track to achieve the millennium development goals? World Bank and Oxford University Press Netherlands Government 2006: Towards a modern migration policy*. The Hague: Ministry of Justice.

Meyer, J. (2001). Network approach versus brain drain: Lessons from the diaspora. *International Migration, 39*(5), 91–110.

OECD (Organisation for Economic Cooperation and Development). (2005). *Trends in international migration: Annual Report 2007*. Paris: OECD.

OECD. (2007). *International migration outlook: Annual Report 2007*. Paris: OECD.

Oucho, J. O. (1998). Regional integration and labour mobility in Eastern and Southern Africa. In R. Appleyard (Ed.), *Emigration dynamic in developing countries: Vol. I. Sub-Saharan Africa*. Sydney: Ashgate Publishing.

Oucho, J. O., & Crush, J. (2001). Contra free movement: South Africa and SADC migration protocols. *Africa Today, 48*(3), 139–158.

Ratha, D. (2011). Leveraging remittances for development. *Migration Information Source*.

Ratha, D., & Shaw, W. (2007). *South-South migration and remittances*. World Bank Working Paper No. 102. Washington, DC: World Bank.

Stiglitz, J. (2006). *Making globalisation work*. New York: W. W. Norton.

UKNMC (UK Nursing and Midwifery Council). (2005). *Annual statistics 2004–2005*. London: UKNMC.

UN. (2003). Reversing Africa's 'brain drain': New initiatives tap skills of African expatriates. *Africa Recovery, 17*(2), I.

UN. (2005). Africa needs 1 million health professionals. *Africa Renewal, 18*(4), 4.

UN. (2007). *Trends in total migration stocks 2005 revision*. POP/DB/MIG/ Rev2005. New York: Population Division, Department of Economic and Social Affairs.

Van Agtmael, A. (2007). *The emerging markets century: How a new breed of world-class companies is overtaking the world*. New York: The Free Press.

Van Dalen, H. P., & Esveldt, I. (2003). Migration 'out of Africa'. *Maandschrift Economie, 67*(3).

Zachariah, K. C., & Condé, J. (1981). *Migration in West Africa: Demographic aspects*. London: Oxford University Press (with World Bank).

Zlotnik, H. (2003, March). The global dimensions of female migration. *Migration Information Source*.

PART 7

Demographic dividend

32

THE DEMOGRAPHY OF HUMAN CAPITAL FORMATION IN SUB-SAHARAN AFRICA, 1950–2100

Claudia Reiter, Anne Goujon, and Samir K.C.

Introduction

Education is widely regarded to be a key driver of socio-economic development. The literature is rich in showing the substantial impact that increased levels of education can have on economic development (Lutz, Crespo Cuaresma, & Sanderson, 2008), innovation capacity (Pelkonen & Teräväinen-Litardo, 2013), demographic behaviour (Lutz & Skirbekk, 2014), adaptive capacity to environmental change (Lutz, Muttarak, & Striessnig, 2014), conflict prevention (Østby & Urdal, 2011), women's autonomy (Jejeebhoy, 1995), etc. Given the overwhelming relevance of education on both the individual and the aggregate levels, it is essential to understand and grasp what have been the changes and trends in educational attainment – particularly, in countries which are still struggling to get the human capital boost that is necessary to bring large segments of the population out of poverty.

Sub-Saharan Africa (SSA) is the world region with the largest number of countries that have not yet attained universal primary education. When SSA countries gained independence from colonial rule around 1960, the region lagged far behind other parts of the world on nearly every education indicator. After substantial progress in the 1960s and 1970s, the economic crisis of the 1980s again severely impaired education in Africa: declining public resources and private economic hardship resulted in an erosion of quality and primary level participation rates (Verspoor, 2000). As of today, these setbacks could not be fully reversed: despite considerable educational expansion ever since, 20% of today's 15–19-year-olds in SSA have never attended any school (Wittgenstein Centre for Demography and Global Human Capital, 2018).

In addition and not unrelatedly, rapid population growth poses further challenges to the region. Besides putting pressure on food supplies and other resources, a continued rise in the number of children may strongly affect the potential of many SSA countries to achieve universal education as envisaged by the Sustainable Development Goal 4 – which is 'to ensure inclusive and equitable quality education and promote lifelong learning opportunities for all'. Ironically, population growth may also be decelerated through rising educational attainment: as empirical evidence shows, almost universally, better-educated women consistently want fewer children,

 DOI: 10.4324/9780429287213-39

have greater autonomy in reproductive decision-making, and more knowledge about and access to contraception (Bongaarts, 2010; Cleland & Rodriguez, 1988).

To better understand how human capital has evolved over time in SSA, this article analyzes changes in absolute and share of levels of educational attainment from 1950 to 2015, comparing across countries and regions, generations, and gender. In addition, we will explore the potential future of levels of education and its impact on population size and structure in SSA according to several scenarios that have been developed up to 2100. The remainder of this article is structured as follows. After the introduction, we shortly present the methodology used for estimating the data on educational attainment both for the past and the future in Section 2. This also includes definitions on educational attainment categories as well as short scenario descriptions. In the third section, we analyze in detail educational attainment in SSA from 1950 to 2015, discussing the results along the lines of three significant gaps in education that exist in terms of gender, generation, and geography. In the fourth section, we present scenarios of projection results to 2100 – both in terms of population size and educational attainment – according to several scenarios which we also compare to projections provided by the UN and IHME. Finally, we conclude this article with a discussion of the relevance on emphasizing education in the development plan of most SSA countries.

Data and methods

The data in this chapter are based on the reconstructions (1950–2015) and projections (2015–2100) that are documented in several books and articles (Lutz, Goujon, KC, & Sanderson, 2005; Lutz, Butz, & KC, 2014; Lutz, Goujon, KC, Stonawski, & Stilianakis, 2018; Goujon et al., 2016; Speringer, Goujon, Reiter, Jurasszovich, & Eder, 2019). The general methodology follows the cohort component method of multi-dimensional population projections. The reconstruction is based on the most recent available data on share of population by age, sex, and levels of educational attainment that were back-projected using historical available data to validate and inform the reconstruction, and the population as estimated by the United Nations (2017). The projections starting from 2015 to 2100 follow several scenarios of development for fertility, mortality, and migration patterns, as specified in Table 32.2.

Multi-state methods are particularly appropriate for modelling changes in educational attainment. They sub-divide the population into different states, i.e. educational attainment categories, which have their specific fertility, mortality, and migration patterns. To describe movements between states, age- and sex-specific transition rates are applied. Given that educational attainment is usually attained before the age of 30 and that people can only move up to higher attainment categories, transitions are concentrated at younger ages. In addition, fertility and mortality levels tend to vary greatly and systematically by level of education; hence, their explicit consideration greatly improves the model and makes a crucial difference (Lutz et al., 2018).

The result is the population by age (in five-year age groups), sex, and six educational attainment categories, which allows to study the diffusion of education during the 1950–2015 period (reconstruction) on the one hand and demographic and human capital scenarios up to 2100 on the other hand (projections). The education categories are listed in Table 32.1. Table 32.2 presents the pre-defined scenario descriptions used in the projections. Finally, it is important to note that we do not here measure the literacy of the population and that having no education is not the same as being illiterate (one can learn to read and write outside school), but also that having been to school does not necessarily entail literacy as has been shown more recently by the World Bank (World Bank, 2019).

Table 32.1 *Definition of Educational Attainment Categories*

Categories	*ISCED 2011 level*	*Allocation rules*
No education	No level or ISCED 0 Grade 1 of ISCED 1 not completed	Illiterates and persons who have never attended school; persons who were attending first grade of primary education at time of survey; persons attending adult literacy courses at time of survey; khalwa (first level of traditional Koranic schools)
Incomplete primary	Incomplete ISCED 1	Persons attending any ISCED 1 grade below last grade at time of survey; persons who indicated an unknown number of grades/years at ISCED 1 level; traditional Koranic schools above khalwa level
Primary	Completed ISCED 1 Incomplete ISCED 2	Completed last grade of ISCED 1 level or grades below the last grade of ISCED 2 level; persons attending last grade of ISCED 2 at time of survey; persons who indicated an unknown number of grades at ISCED 2 level
Lower secondary	Completed ISCED 2 Incomplete ISCED 3	Completed last grade of ISCED 2 level or grades below the last grade of ISCED 3 level; persons attending last grade of ISCED 3 at time of survey; persons who indicated an unknown number of grades at ISCED 3 level
Upper secondary	Completed ISCED 3 Incomplete ISCED 4, 5, or 6	Completed last grade of ISCED 3 level; completed number grades or years below the standard duration at ISCED 4, 5, or 6 level; persons who indicated an unknown number of grades at ISCED 4, 5, or 6 level
Post-secondary	Completed ISCED 4, 5, 6, 7, or 8	Persons who have completed number of years or grades corresponding to standard duration of ISCED 4 or ISCED 5 programmes; persons holding degrees corresponding to ISCED 4, ISCED 5, ISCED 6, ISCED 7, and ISCED 6 levels

Source: Adapted from Goujon et al., 2016.

Table 32.2 Scenario Definitions[1]

Scenario	*Definition*
Rapid Development (SSP1)	Population Component of Rapid Development (SSP1): This scenario assumes a future that is moving toward a more sustainable path, with educational and health investments accelerating the demographic transition, leading to a relatively low world population. The emphasis is on strengthening human wellbeing. This is associated with high education, low mortality and low fertility. Migration levels are assumed to be medium for all countries under this SSP.
Medium (SSP2)	Population Component of Medium (SSP2): This is the middle-of-the-road scenario that can also be seen as the most likely path for each country. It combines for all countries medium fertility with medium mortality, medium migration, and the Global Education Trend (GET) education scenario.
Stalled Development (SSP3)	Population Component of Stalled Development (SSP3): This scenario portrays a world separated into regions characterized by extreme poverty, pockets of moderate wealth, and many countries struggling to maintain living standards for rapidly growing populations. This is associated with low education, high mortality, and high fertility. Due to the emphasis on security and barriers to international exchange, migration is assumed to be low for all countries.

Source: Wittgenstein Centre for Demography and Global Human Capital, 2018.

Education progress from 1950 to 2015

Levels of educational attainment of the sub-Saharan African population and sub-regions

In 1950, most of SSA was still colonized by European powers to the exception of Ethiopia, Liberia, and South Africa, where the Apartheid had been institutionalized in 1948. Overall, levels of educational attainment were very low on the sub-continent in 1950 as shown on Figure 32.1, with about 85% of the population 15+ having received no education at all, and 9% who participated in primary education but did not complete. This reflects the situation in Eastern Africa (respectively 84% with no education and 12% with incomplete primary education) and middle Africa (80% and 13%). In Southern Africa, education was more widely spread with those shares being reduced to 57% and 17%. On the contrary, Western Africa was the region with the highest share of the 15+ population without any education (90% and 4% with an incomplete primary education).

How has this changed? The most spectacular change has to do with the increase in the population 15+ having received at least some years of education, about 68% in 2015, from 16% in 1950. The share of the population with no education declined by 4 percentage points on average every 5 years, slightly levelling off in the 1980s, which was a difficult economic period for SSA. This is an impressive increase in educational attainment, particularly considering that, over the same period, the SSA population more than quintupled from 180 to 970 million people, making school expansion an uphill battle. All sub-regions experienced a similar increase in education, however, at a different level and to a different extent (see Section 3.1).

The majority of the population who had received any kind of education had mostly received incomplete primary education until 1960. This was at least the case in eastern and middle Africa; in Western and Southern Africa, on the other hand, even in the early 1950s, those who managed to enter education usually ended up with at least a completed primary education degree. But also, higher educational attainment groups have become much more accessible over the last decades in SSA: while in 1950 not even 1% of the population 15+ had attained upper secondary education, this share increased to almost 14% in 2015. Post-secondary education, however, remains still an exception, with roughly 5% of today's SSA population 15+ holding such a degree. Differences again vary considerably between different regions on the sub-continent: while almost 7% of the adult population have attained post-secondary education in Southern Africa, the proportion is only 3.2% in Eastern Africa.

It is important to note that Figure 32.1 covers the whole population, thus uniting in one number several generations of youth, both with and without the possibility to go through education. Given the rapid educational expansion happening in SSA, a disaggregation by age (as presented in Section 3.4) is particularly relevant since younger cohorts are significantly better-educated than older ones.

In the next sections we will look in more detail at disparities within SSA, more specifically on geographical, gender, and generational gaps, as shown in Goujon et al. (2016).

Geographical gap

While Figure 32.1 provides already important insights into the development of the SSA population by educational attainment over the last decades, it reveals little about the heterogeneity

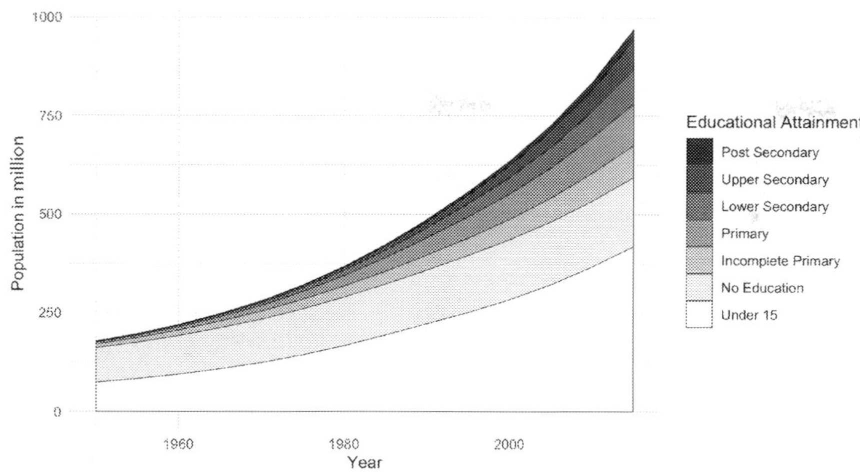

Figure 32.1 Population in sub-Saharan Africa by educational attainment, 1950–2015.

Source: Wittgenstein Centre for Demography and Global Human Capital, 2018.

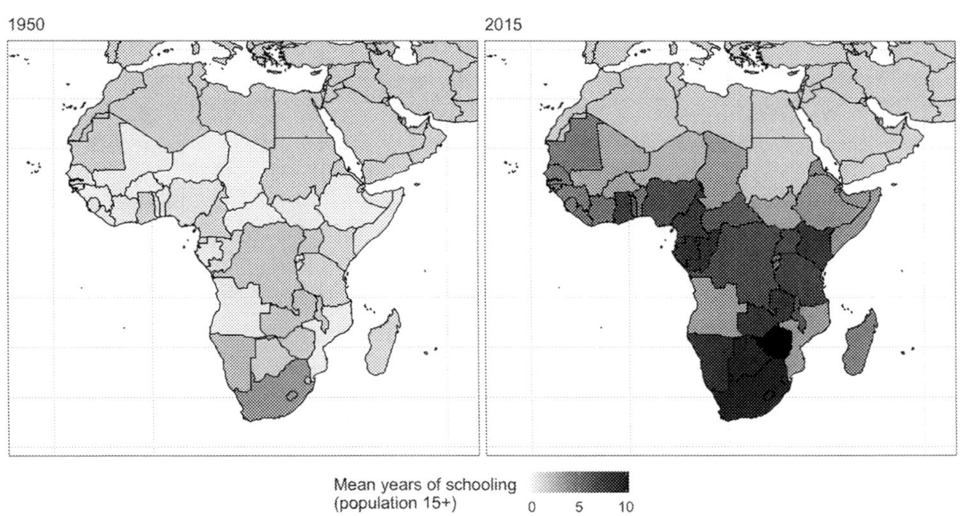

Figure 32.2 Mean years of schooling of the population 15+, 1950 and 2015.

Source: Wittgenstein Centre for Demography and Global Human Capital, 2018.

in terms of differences in human capital formation within SSA – a region which is quite diverse in terms of socio-economic development and political systems. To resolve this, Figure 32.2 shows two maps comparing the educational attainment by country – summarized by the mean years of schooling (MYS) of the population aged 15 years or older – for the years 1950 and 2015. While in 1950, populations in most countries had attained, on average, close to zero years of schooling, with South Africa taking clearly the lead despite its low value of 3.5 MYS, the situation is much more heterogeneous in 2015. Significant improvements in terms of educational attainment have happened in almost all countries – however, the extent and pace of these improvements differ substantially between countries. While some populations have managed to multiply their average schooling duration by a factor of up to 7 (e.g. Zimbabwe), other countries are still lagging behind with the average person experiencing less than 3 years of schooling. Today, Zimbabwe, the Seychelles, Mayotte, and South Africa are the countries with the highest mean years of schooling (approximately 10 years) in SSA, whereas Niger, Mali, Burkina Faso, and South Sudan bring up the rear. Consequently, not only countries have experienced a different path of development, but also diversity within the region has considerably increased – at least in terms of formal education: while the gap between the country with the highest MYS and the one with the lowest MYS was only 3.4 years in 1950, this has risen to the extent of 8.1 years in 2015. For more details, Appendix Table 32.1 provides the country population size as well as the country-specific educational attainment distribution for the population 15+ for all 50 SSA countries as well as for four sub-regions over time.

The heterogeneity in terms of educational attainment within sub-Saharan Africa becomes also evident when looking at Figure 32.3, depicting the share of the population who have attained at least lower secondary education by four geographic areas. While Southern Africa had already played a pioneering role in 1950 – at least compared to other SSA areas – its head start has further widened to about 35 percentage points, with currently more than 70% of the population 15+ having attained lower secondary education or higher. Eastern, middle, and Western Africa, on the other hand, have started at an equally low level. While Western and middle Africa managed to partly catch up, with considerable advances observable from the 1980s onwards, Eastern Africa has further fallen behind, only recently showing higher growth rates in the population share with lower secondary education or higher. Previous research suggests, however, that it needs broad segments of the population with at least a completed junior secondary education to give poor countries the necessary human capital boost to effectively fight poverty. Consequently, better education does not only empower people on the individual level, but is also a necessary (although not always sufficient) precondition for long-term socio-economic progress in these developing regions (Lutz et al., 2008).

Gender gap

In addition to geographical heterogeneity, there are also well-documented gender differences in educational attainment. While richer countries are currently experiencing the closing and reversal of the gender gap (De Hauw, Grow, & Van Bavel, 2017), women are still discriminated against in terms of access to education in many developing countries – with SSA being no exception. This not only hampers empowerment of women on the individual level (Jejeebhoy, 1995), but also has significant impact on societal and demographic developments. As mentioned previously, empirical evidence shows that better-educated women consistently want fewer children, are more autonomous in reproductive decision-making, and have better knowledge about and access to contraception (Bongaarts, 2010; Cleland & Rodriguez, 1988).

Figure 32.4 graphically depicts the gender gap in educational attainment by comparing the share of the SSA population aged 15 years or older with at least lower secondary education between males and females for the period 1950–2015. As can be seen on the graph, already in 1950, women were less likely to attain a junior high school degree than men, with this gap

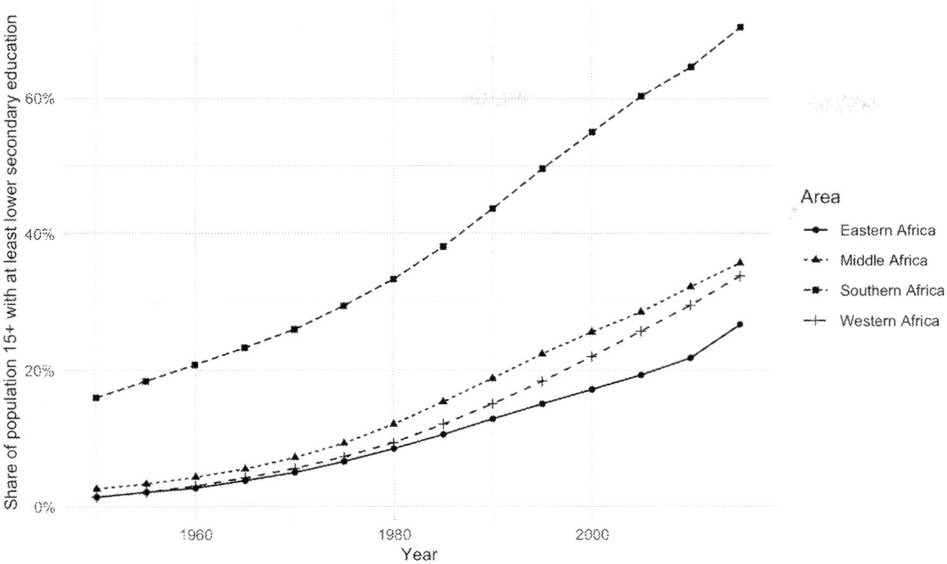

Figure 32.3 Share of population 15+ with at least lower secondary education by area, 1950–2015.

Source: Wittgenstein Centre for Demography and Global Human Capital, 2018.

further increasing over time. Starting from the early 1980s the gender gap in lower secondary or higher education remained more or less constant at a high level of about ten percentage points. Given that gender gaps in education are among the main factors that determine gender disparities in a broad set of socio-economic realms, including work, family, and public life, removing barriers that hamper the access to education for females is key to enhancing gender equality and women's empowerment (Bertocchi & Bozzano, 2020).

Looking more closely at country-specific gender differences in SSA reveals that the extent of gender discrimination varies considerably between countries. Figure 32.5 depicts the gender gap in mean years of schooling of the population 15+ by country for the year 2015. Interestingly, there are two countries, namely Lesotho and Namibia, where women, on average, attend even more years of schooling than men. Worthwhile emphasizing is Lesotho, where female MYS exceed male MYS by even 1.4 years. This is a result of concerted efforts from the Lesotho government since 2000 to encourage female education and nation-wide literacy, dedicating the highest percentage of their GDP to education of any country in the world. However, much of the progress in women's educational attainment in Lesotho can also be correlated to male emigration to South Africa, triggered by high unemployment and poverty (UNESCO, 2012). On the other end of the spectrum are countries such as Togo, the Democratic Republic of the Congo, and Liberia, where men, on average, went almost three years longer to school than women. As mentioned previously, education is a key component in preventing and eradicating poverty, further emphasizing the need for universal education in developing countries – not only for males but essentially also for females.

Figure 32.5 also highlights the fact that the level of educational attainment in SSA countries seems to be somehow correlated with the gender gap in MYS: with the exception of Lesotho,

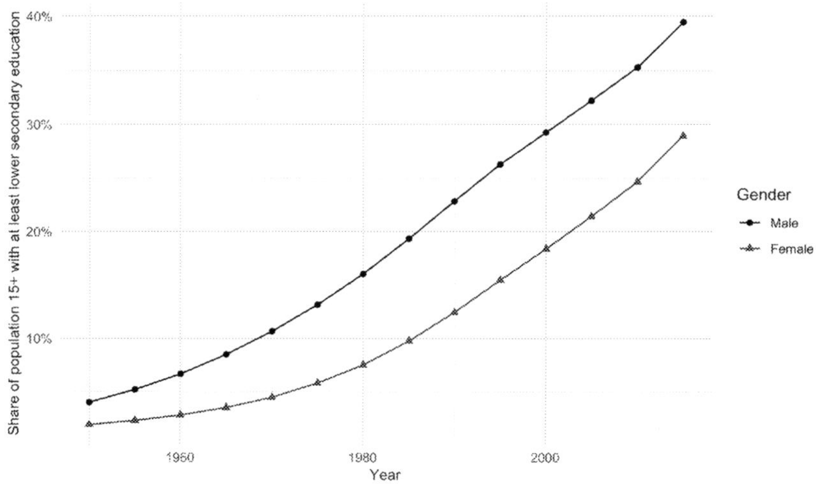

Figure 32.4 Share of population 15+ with at least lower secondary education by gender, SSA, 1950–2015.

Source: Wittgenstein Centre for Demography and Global Human Capital, 2018.

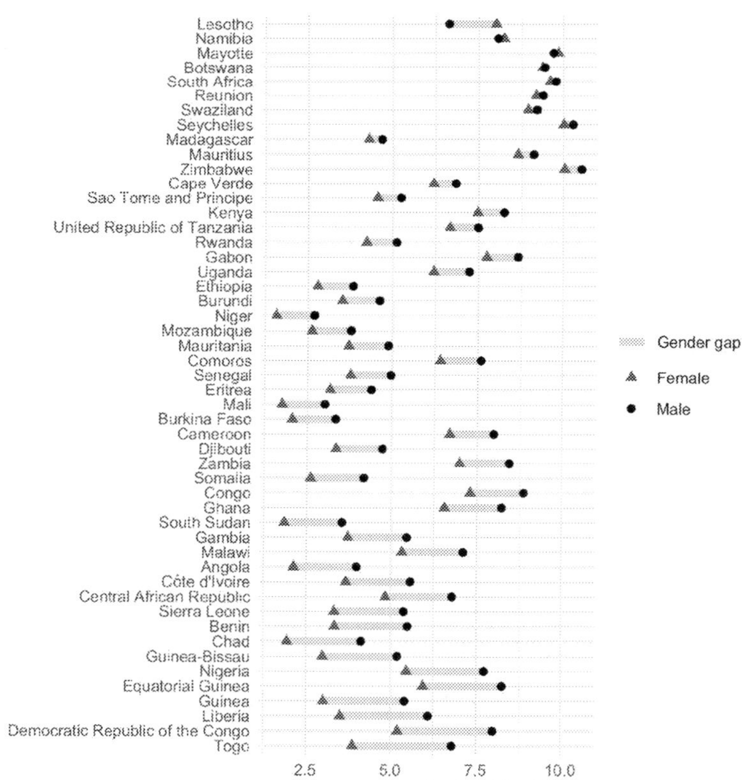

Figure 32.5 Gender gap in mean years of schooling (male MYS minus female MYS) of the population 15+ by country, SSA, 2015; countries are sorted by their gender gap.

Source: Wittgenstein Centre for Demography and Global Human Capital, 2018

countries with a smaller gender gap tend to have higher overall years of schooling (e.g. Namibia, Mayotte, Botswana, or South Africa), whereas countries with lower MYS tend to have a slightly higher gender gap. Having said that, there are also some notable exceptions, i.e. countries with both low mean years of schooling and a rather low gender gap (e.g. Madagascar or Sao Tome and Principe).

Generational gap

Finally, because this chapter focusses on the demography of human capital in SSA, we want to analyze educational attainment across generations. While using a summary measure of educational attainment, e.g. the mean years of schooling of the adult population above age 15, has the advantage of capturing the entire human capital of a population at one point in time in one single number, there is much to be gained from additionally breaking down this highly aggregate measure into different age groups, hence revealing inter-cohort changes that drive many of the socio-economic consequences that come from improving human capital (Lutz et al., 2018). This disaggregation is particularly relevant in countries that have recently gone through strong educational expansions – as virtually all SSA countries have – with younger cohorts being much better-educated than older ones. In these countries, the usage of mean years of schooling – by definition an average of age cohorts with very different levels of education – provides rather weak evidence for the effect of human capital on aggregate-level economic growth; by explicitly considering the age structure of human capital, however, it can be shown that economic growth is fastest when the better-educated young cohorts enter young adulthood (Lutz et al., 2008).

Figure 32.6 exemplifies that by depicting the share of the SSA population with at least secondary education from 1950 to 2015, disaggregated by three broad age groups: 20–39-year-olds, 40–64-year-olds, and the population 65+. As can be seen on the graphs, at each point in time, younger adults were consistently higher educated than older ones. This gap has considerably increased over time: currently, the share of 20–39-year-olds who have attained at least lower secondary education is almost 30 percentage points higher than the corresponding share among the population 65+. This reflects the massive educational expansion happening in SSA in the recent past – from which naturally only younger age groups could benefit.

A SSA country where the educational attainment distribution particularly differs between age groups is Africa's most populous country: Nigeria (see Figure 32.7). While in 2015 more than half of the population aged 20–24 have attained at least lower secondary education, almost 70% of the population 70+ have never attended any schools. This is a result of a cohort effect: the cohort of Nigerians aged 70–74 in 2015 were 5–9 years old in 1950 – at that time, Nigeria was much more underdeveloped than today with almost no children having access to basic formal education. The higher educational attainment in the oldest age group (100+) is clearly a selection effect: because those with higher education tend to live longer, it is not surprising that among this very specific group of centenarians, educational attainment is considerably higher compared to the average distribution of the generation. Further disaggregating the educational attainment distribution by gender (as depicted in the pyramid on the left plot of Figure 32.7) additionally reveals that gender discrimination in educational attainment is observable in all age groups in Nigeria; however, disadvantages for females are considerably stronger among older age groups.

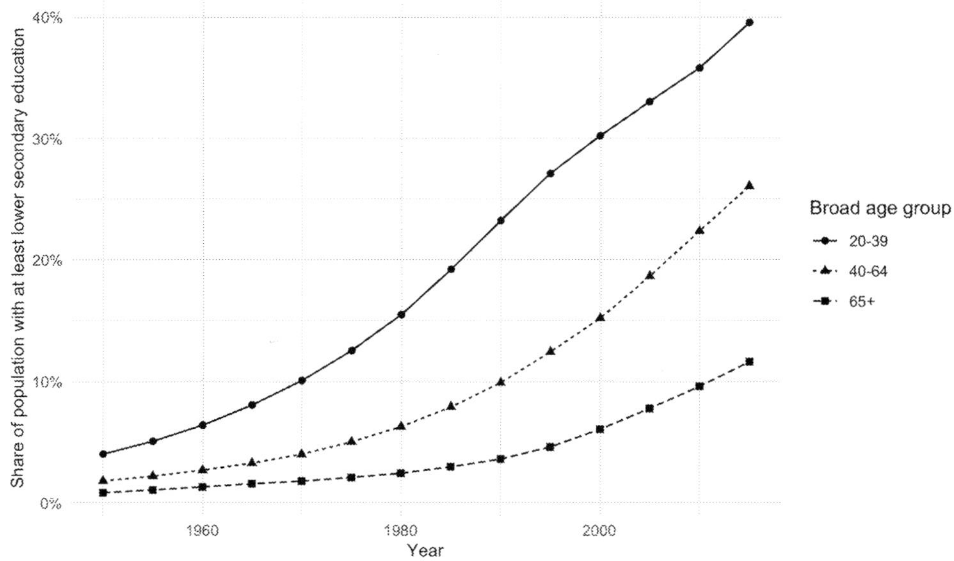

Figure 32.6 Share of population with at least lower secondary education by broad age groups, SSA, 1950–2015.

Source: Wittgenstein Centre for Demography and Global Human Capital, 2018.

Projections

Total population of SSA

The Wittgenstein Centre for Demography and Global Human Capital (WIC) has projected population for several scenarios; we choose to present here three scenarios spanning almost all possible futures featuring low, medium, and high population growth in the SSA region. These correspond to three Shared Socioeconomic Pathways (SSP) scenarios, SSP1, SSP2, and SSP3, respectively (see Section 2 for scenario descriptions). The trajectories for the demographic components were quantified based on trend extrapolation and experts' argument-based opinions (Lutz, Butz, et al., 2014) which were recently updated (Lutz et al., 2018).

According to the medium growth scenario, the population of SSA is expected to increase rapidly from 0.97 billion in 2015 to 1.93 billion by 2050 and stabilize at 2.58 billion by 2100 (see Figure 32.8). For the sake of comparison, we have included the results from two other projections, namely the UN's (UN Population Division, 2019) and IHME's (Institute for Health, Metrics and Evaluation (IHME), 2020). Both of them are between WIC's medium and high population growth scenario, with the UN expecting higher population growth than IHME. The shaded area in Figure 32.8 shows the UN's 95% and 80% uncertainty interval for the future projection, with the UN line representing the median. The likelihood of the WIC's medium scenario projection is closer to the lower boundary of the UN's 80% uncertainty interval.

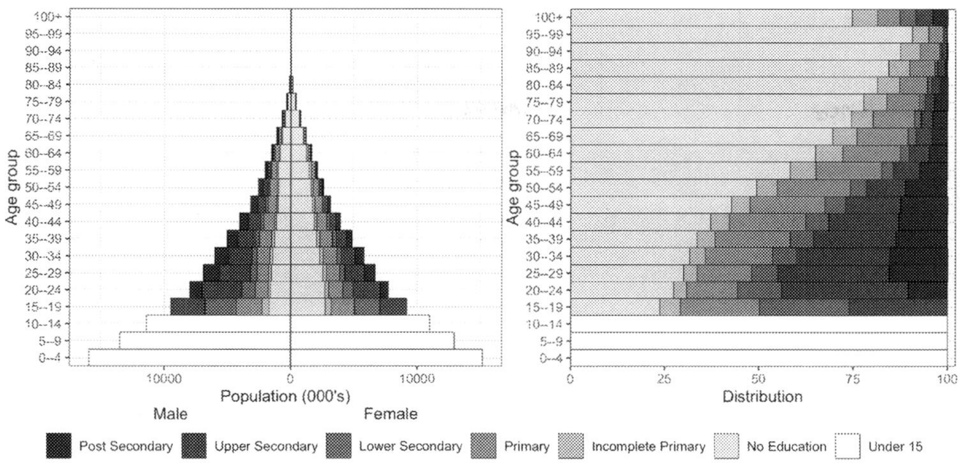

Figure 32.7 Population pyramid by education and educational attainment distribution, Nigeria, 2015.

Source: Wittgenstein Centre for Demography and Global Human Capital, 2018.

WIC's low and high growth scenarios range from 1.51 to 2.29 billion by 2050 and from 2.29 to 4.29 billion by 2100. This range of almost 780 million in 2050 is about 80% of the SSA population in 2015, indicating a very large uncertainty in the future population growth. Lower population size in the low growth scenario is due to a combination of scenario assumptions, i.e. rapid improvement in education (following SDG) along with a strong decline in fertility levels in all education groups (20% lower than the medium trajectory in 2030 and 25% by 2050). The expected fertility decline is because of the adoption of family planning measures at the individual level as well as community-level effects due to an increased level of education in the population (Fuchs & Goujon, 2014). The contribution of the lower fertility trajectory to the low population growth is much higher as compared to the contribution of a higher level of life expectancy which is also expected in the low population growth scenario, thus being the most optimistic scenario. Population growth peaks around 2070 at the level of 1.78 billion and then declines to 1.5 billion by 2100. According to the UN's probabilistic projection, the likelihood of the low population growth scenario is highly unlikely.

In contrast, in the high population growth scenario, today's population will be more than doubled in size by 2045. In this scenario, the improvement in education stalls, international migration comes to a halt, and the economic progress deteriorates as well. Also, the fertility rates by education are higher than in the medium trajectory (20% by 2030 and 25% by 2050). This results in an increase in overall fertility rates in some countries and low rates of fertility decline in all countries in SSA.

While population growth is inevitable in SSA, some countries are likely to have higher rates of increase than others due to their population structure and the level of fertility. According to WIC's medium projection, 29 out of 50 countries of SSA will experience doubling of their populations by the end of the century: Niger and Uganda by 2040, five more countries by 2045 (e.g. Tanzania), six more both by 2050 (including Nigeria and Congo) and 2055, and the remaining ones by 2075 (e.g. DR Congo by 2060 and Ethiopia by 2065). Detailed numbers on

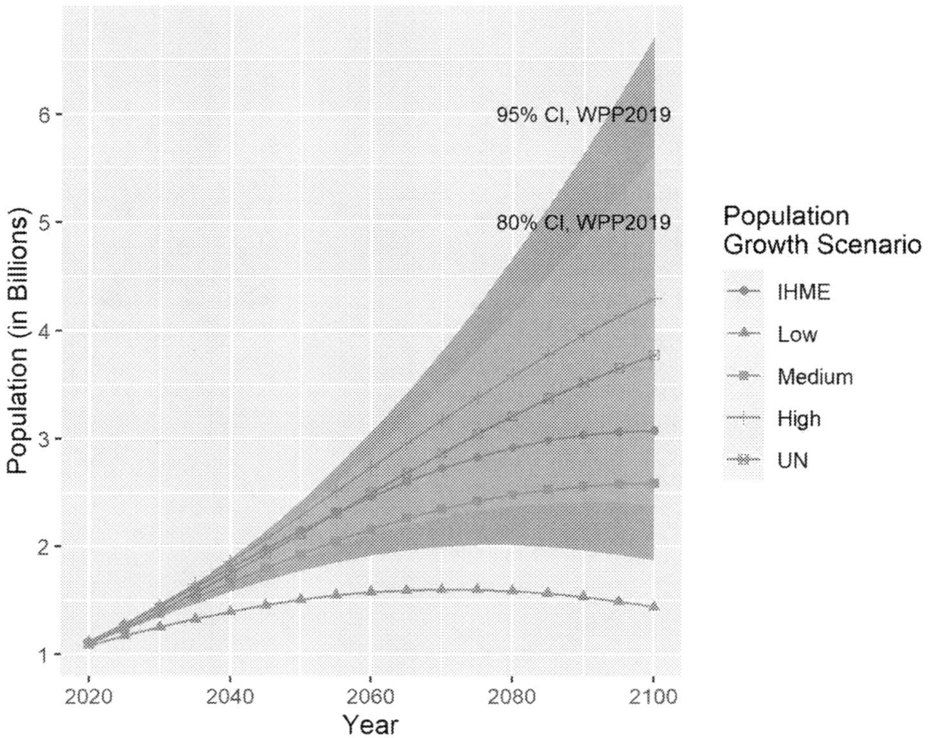

Figure 32.8 Total population projection in SSA, several scenarios.

Source: Wittgenstein Centre for Demography and Global Human Capital, 2018; UN Population Division, 2019; Institute for Health, Metrics and Evaluation (IHME), 2020.

expected population size according to SSP2 in quarter-century time steps for all countries can be found in Table A1.

By examining the results of the UN and WIC projection for each country in SSA, we find different sets of matches between the two sets of projections. By 2050, in more than 80% of the countries in SSA, WIC's medium projection is lower than the UN's medium variant. Eight countries have lower population by more than 20%, with lowest in Burundi (32% lower with 17.1 million population in WIC's medium) and in other medium-sized countries such as Angola (24%, 59.1 million), Cameroon (22%, 39.4 million), Mozambique (22%, 51.1 million), and Côte d'Ivoire (21%, 40.3 million). Twenty countries are in the range of 10–20% lower, including very large countries such as DR Congo (16%, 162.5 million) and Ethiopia (10%, 205 million). Fourteen countries are in the range of 0–10%, including the continent's most populous country Nigeria (5% lower, 382.5 million). There are eight countries wherein WIC's medium projection is higher than the UN's medium, including Zimbabwe (2% higher with 25 million), Uganda (12%, 101.4 million), and highest in South Sudan (38%, 27.6 million) and Eritrea (39%, 8.3 million).

In terms of the UN's uncertainty range, some countries in WIC's medium projection lie within the UN's uncertainty interval, such as Nigeria, South Africa, etc. For another set of countries, the medium projection is lower than the 95% uncertainty range, showing the discrepancy between the two projections. Interestingly, in many countries, the UN projection matches with the high population scenario (Guinea, Guinea-Bissau, Mali, Liberia, Niger), or is even higher than SSP3 (Mauritania).

Projection of human capital in SSA

WIC projects population by age, sex, and educational attainment. As mentioned earlier, there are two ways to study the level of education in a population: using educational attainment distributions or using mean years of schooling (MYS). While the former provides a much richer picture, also showing inequality of education, the latter is a simple average measure, having the advantage of capturing the entire human capital of a population at one point in time in one single number. As specified before, at present, the level of educational attainment in SSA is the lowest in the world with MYS among the population aged 15 years or older (MYS15+) of 5.85 years. Projections of MYS15+ estimate a considerable increase in the level of human capital to 9.02 years by 2050 (SSP2), with a slight reduction in the gender gap to 0.83 years (1.5 in 2015). Among 20–39-year-olds, MYS are expected to be slightly higher at the level of 9.97 years with a smaller gender gap of 0.65 years in 2050. Variation in MYS of 15+ between SSA countries is expected to remain very high, with a range of 5.17 years in Mali and 12.8 years in Zimbabwe. Among the younger population aged 20–39 years, MYS are estimated to range from 5.9 years in Mali to 14.1 years in the Seychelles.

To describe the future of the educational attainment distribution in SSA, we use the proportion with at least lower secondary educational attainment (higher education) and those with no education, that were, in 2015, 34% and 32% respectively among the population 15+, and 27% and 49% among 20–39-year-olds. According to the medium scenario, by 2050, the disparity is expected to decline with three fifths of the population aged 15+ with higher education and still 16% with no education. Among 20–39-year-olds, it is two thirds and 13% respectively. This indicates that the SDG's universal secondary attainment target will not be met under the trend scenario. It is interesting to observe that after 2045, the proportion with at least secondary education starts declining and the proportion with no education starts increasing reaching 58% and 17% respectively by 2100. This is due to the fact that the population in countries with lower level of human capital coupled with higher levels of fertility are increasing relatively more rapidly. Similar results have been shown for India (KC, Wurzer, Speringer, & Lutz, 2018). At the country level, in 2050 (SSP2), population aged 15+ with higher education is expected to range from 27.3% in Niger to 94.6% in South Africa and from 64.5% (Niger) to 99.6% (South Africa) by 2100. Among 20–39-year-olds, shares are expected to remain considerably larger as compared to the total population.

In the medium variant of the UN, the fertility level in countries of SSA is expected to decline from a range between 1.70 in Mauritius to 7.55 in Niger in 2010–2015 to 1.47 to 4.70 in the same countries by 2045–2050 (UN Population Division, 2019). Overall, the TFR in SSA is expected to decline from 5.4 in 2010–2015 to 3.36 (95% CI: 2.91–3.76) by 2045–2050.

Conclusion

Despite rapid educational expansion in the recent past, sub-Saharan Africa's human capital is still lagging behind the rest of the world. Given the enormous relevance of education both on the individual level and for the region's socio-economic development on the whole, we cannot emphasize enough the importance for SSA to invest in human capital and to place education in the centre of any development plan. While these investments are certainly associated with short-term costs, since it takes a long time to translate the education of children into better human capital of the adult labour force, in the long run, it is definitely one of the best investments societies can make in their future.

Realizing the potential of human capital requires that all young sub-Saharan-Africans have a solid foundation in basic education (at least lower secondary level) as well as accessible opportunities to continue beyond basic education. As pointed out in this article, SDG 4, 'to ensure inclusive and equitable quality education and promote lifelong learning opportunities for all' is likely to be not met by 2030 in many SSA countries, given that past trends of educational attainment and demographic developments will continue in the future. Moreover, existing gaps in human capital in terms of gender, generation, and geography need to be closed to make sure that education is indeed inclusive and equitable, thus leaving no one behind.

In addition to its empowering feature, education has been shown to strongly and systematically influence fertility. The rather low levels of education on the sub-continent are associated with very high levels of fertility. For example, the country with the highest total fertility rate in the world is Niger, where a woman, on average, gives birth to more than seven children; Niger, on the other hand, is also one of the top five countries as regards the highest share of population 15+ who never attended any school (66.5%). Increasing access to education, particularly for women, will not only enhance female autonomy, but can also contribute significantly to tackling the challenge of population growth and accompanying resource scarcity in SSA.

Finally, albeit this article has a clear focus on quantitative aspects of education, the issue may be raised whether the increase in schooling has not come at the expense of quality. Several local studies have shown that the increase in children in school was not followed by a similar increase in the number of teachers or classrooms (Association for the Development of Education in Africa, 2011). In Niger, for instance, many teachers had to be contracted and were not adequately trained, and in an evaluation performed in 2017, it was found that 66% of the teachers were scoring less than average (Education International, 2017). In Lutz et al. (2021), the authors estimated that the gap between mean years of schooling and skills in literacy adjusted mean years of schooling (SLAMYS) – a new measure of human capital that considers not only the quantity but also the quality of education – has increased. In other words, the partly impressive recent gains in the expansion of schooling in many developing countries did not lead to a corresponding increase in skills. As regards SSA, the region was estimated to have currently about the same SLAMYS level as eastern Asia in 1970. If skills are indeed a key driver of social and economic development, this result implies that SSA lags almost half a century behind eastern Asia (Lutz et al., 2021). Consequently, not only giving everyone the chance to be in school but ensuring that students actually learn skills and competencies essential for success in daily life is yet another goal policy-makers have to address when developing strategies for the future.

Note

1 Scenarios are based on the Shared Socioeconomic Pathways (SSP) scenarios related to the Intergovernmental Panel on Climate Change (IPCC). For further details see O'Neill et al. (2017) and Riahi et al. (2017).

References

Association for the Development of Education in Africa. (2011). *Policy frameworks on contract teachers.* ADEA. Retrieved from https://teachertaskforce.org/sites/default/files/migrate_default_content_files/adeapolicyframeworks.pdf

Bertocchi, G., & Bozzano, M. (2020). Gender gaps in education. In K. F. Zimmermann (Ed.), *Handbook of labor, human resources and population economics* (pp. 1–31). Cham, Switzerland: Springer.

Bongaarts, J. (2010). The causes of educational differences in fertility in sub-Saharan Africa. *Vienna Yearbook of Population Research, 8*, 31–50.

Cleland, J. G., & Rodriguez, G. (1988). The effect of parental education on marital fertility in developing countries. *Population Studies, 42*(3), 419–442. https://doi.org/10.1080/0032472031000143566

De Hauw, Y., Grow, A., & Van Bavel, J. (2017). The Reversed Gender Gap in education and assortative mating in Europe. *European Journal of Population, 33*(4), 445–474. https://doi.org/10.1007/s10680-016-9407-z

Education International. (2017). *Niger: Unions challenge the government's teacher evaluation.* Retrieved from www.ei-ie.org/en/detail/15347/niger-unions-challenge-the-government%E2%80%99s-teacher-evaluation

Fuchs, R., & Goujon, A. (2014). Future fertility in high fertility countries. In W. Lutz, W. P. Butz, & S. KC (Eds.), *World population and human capital in the 21st century* (pp. 147–225). Oxford: Oxford University Press. Retrieved from http://ukcatalogue.oup.com/product/9780198703167.do

Goujon, A., KC, S., Speringer, M., Barakat, B., Potancoková, M., Eder, J., . . . Lutz, W. (2016). A harmonized dataset on global educational attainment between 1970 and 2060 – An analytical window into recent trends and future prospects in human capital development. *Journal of Demographic Economics, 82*(3), 315–363. https://doi.org/10.1017/dem.2016.10

Institute for Health, Metrics and Evaluation (IHME). (2020). *Population forecasting.* Seattle, WA: University of Washington. Retrieved from https://vizhub.healthdata.org/population-forecast/

Jejeebhoy, S. (1995). *Women's education, autonomy and reproductive behaviour: Experience from developing countries.* Oxford: Clarendon Press.

KC, S., Wurzer, M., Speringer, M., & Lutz, W. (2018). Future population and human capital in heterogeneous India. *Proceedings of the National Academy of Sciences, 115*(33), 201722359. https://doi.org/10.1073/pnas.1722359115

Lutz, W., Butz, W. P., & KC, S. (2014). *World population and human capital in the twenty-first century.* Oxford: Oxford University Press.

Lutz, W., Crespo Cuaresma, J., & Sanderson, W. C. (2008). The demography of educational attainment and economic growth. *Science, 319*(5866), 1047–1048. https://doi.org/10.1126/science.1151753

Lutz, W., Goujon, A., KC, S., & Sanderson, W. (2005). Reconstruction of populations by age, sex and level of educational attainment for 120 countries for 1970–2000. *Vienna Yearbook of Population Research, 5*(1), 193–235. https://doi.org/10.1553/populationyearbook2007s193

Lutz, W., Goujon, A. V., KC, S., Stonawski, M., & Stilianakis, N. (2018). *Demographic and human capital scenarios for the 21st century: 2018 Assessment for 201 countries.* Publications Office of the European Union. https://doi.org/10.2760/41776

Lutz, W., Muttarak, R., & Striessnig, E. (2014). Universal education is key to enhanced climate adaptation. *Science, 346*(6213), 1061–1062. https://doi.org/10.1126/science.1257975

Lutz, W., Reiter, C., Özdemir, C., Yildiz, D., Guimaraes, R., & Goujon, A. (2021). Skills-adjusted human capital shows rising global gap. *Proceedings of the National Academy of Sciences, 118*(7). https://doi.org/10.1073/pnas.2015826118

Lutz, W., & Skirbekk, V. (2014). How education drives demography and knowledge informs projections. In W. Lutz, W. P. Butz, & S. KC (Eds.), *World population and human capital in the 21st century* (pp. 14–38). Oxford: Oxford University Press. Retrieved from http://ukcatalogue.oup.com/product/9780198703167.do

O'Neill, B. C., Kriegler, E., Ebi, K. L., Kemp-Benedict, E., Riahi, K., Rothman, D. S., . . . Solecki, W. (2017). The roads ahead: Narratives for shared socioeconomic pathways describing world futures in the 21st century. *Global Environmental Change, 42*, 169–180. https://doi.org/10.1016/j.gloenvcha.2015.01.004

Østby, G., & Urdal, H. (2011). *Education and conflict: What the evidence says.* CSCW Policy Brief. PRIO.

Pelkonen, A., & Teräväinen-Litardo, T. (2013). Convergence and divergence in research, higher education and innovation policies: An analysis of nine European countries. In T. Erkkilä (Ed.), *Global university rankings: Challenges for European higher education* (pp. 53–74). London: Palgrave Macmillan UK. https://doi.org/10.1057/9781137296870_4

Riahi, K., van Vuuren, D. P., Kriegler, E., Edmonds, J., O'Neill, B. C., Fujimori, S., . . . Tavoni, M. (2017). The shared socioeconomic pathways and their energy, land use, and greenhouse gas emissions implications: An overview. *Global Environmental Change, 42*, 153–168. https://doi.org/10.1016/j.gloenvcha.2016.05.009

Speringer, M., Goujon, A., Reiter, C., Jurasszovich, S., & Eder, J. (2019). *Global reconstruction of educational attainment, 1950 to 2015: Methodology and assessment*. Vienna Institute of Demography Working Papers, 02/2019.

UNESCO. (2012). *UNESCO global partnership for girls' and women's education – One year on*. Lesotho. Retrieved from www.unesco.org/new/fileadmin/MULTIMEDIA/HQ/ED/pdf/Lesotho.pdf

UN Population Division. (2019). *World population prospects 2019*. Retrieved from https://population.un.org/wpp/Download/Standard/Population/

Verspoor, A. (2000). *Sub-Saharan Africa: Overview, stalled progress in primary education, beyond primary education, unprecedented expansion of tertiary education, private education*. Retrieved from https://education.stateuniversity.com/pages/2466/Sub-Saharan-Africa.html

Wittgenstein Centre for Demography and Global Human Capital. (2018). *Wittgenstein Centre Data Explorer Version 2.0 (Beta)*. Retrieved from www.wittgensteincentre.org/dataexplorer

World Bank. (2019). *The education crisis: Being in school is not the same as learning*. Retrieved from www.worldbank.org/en/news/immersive-story/2019/01/22/pass-or-fail-how-can-the-world-do-its-homework

Appendix Table 32.1 Total Population and Educational Attainment Distribution, SSA Countries, 1950–2100 (SSP2)

Country	*Pop/Education*	*1950*	*1975*	*2000*	*2025*	*2050*	*2075*	*2100*
Angola	Total population	4,386	7,398	15,657	36,945	59,106	73,890	77,204
	- % Under 15	42	48	50	42	29	21	17
% pop15+	No education	89.5	75.3	55.9	35.5	18.3	7.7	2.2
by education	Incomplete primary	6.8	12.3	16	13.3	10.6	6.4	2.9
	Primary	3.1	10	19.3	26.7	27.3	22.1	13.8
	Lower secondary	0.5	1.8	6.1	14.9	23.5	28.9	29
	Upper secondary	0.1	0.6	2.7	9	18.9	32.2	47.3
	Post-secondary	0	0	0.1	0.6	1.4	2.6	4.8
Benin	Total	2,255	3,253	6,892	13,476	20,192	24,319	24,973
	Under 15	35	44	45	39	27	20	17
% pop15+	No education	93.5	81.2	61.9	35.7	20.5	10.3	4.1
by education	Incomplete primary	4.4	7.7	13.8	16.9	16.7	12.4	7.1
	Primary	1.9	7.3	13.6	21.6	20.9	18.1	13
	Lower secondary	0.2	2.3	6.6	13.2	17.9	20.7	20.6
	Upper secondary	0.1	1	2.9	9.3	18.1	28.9	40.6
	Post-secondary	0	0.4	1.2	3.3	6	9.6	14.5
Botswana	Total	413	825	1,724	2,575	3,134	3,144	2,845
	Under 15	41	47	38	29	20	17	15
% pop15+	No education	71.3	49	19.1	5.7	1.2	0.2	0.1
by education	Incomplete primary	24.3	23.1	11.6	4.1	1.1	0.2	0.1
	Primary	2.9	15.5	27.6	15	7.2	2.4	0.5
	Lower secondary	1.1	6.9	18.4	25.6	21.1	13.5	7.6
	Upper secondary	0.4	4.3	13.4	29.7	39.1	42.2	38.8
	Post-Secondary	0	1.3	9.9	19.9	30.2	41.5	53

(Continued)

Appendix Table 32.1 (Continued)

Country	*Pop/Education*	*1950*	*1975*	*2000*	*2025*	*2050*	*2075*	*2100*
Burkina Faso	Total	4,284	6,155	11,608	23,666	38,255	48,946	52,672
	Under 15	41	44	47	42	32	24	18
% pop15+	No education	98.8	93.6	81.1	55.2	31.4	15.3	6.2
by education	Incomplete primary	0.5	2.1	7.2	9.4	10.5	8.4	5.3
	Primary	0.5	2.6	5.2	9.5	12.4	12.2	9.4
	Lower secondary	0.2	1.2	4.2	16	25.2	29.5	28.9
	Upper secondary	0	0.3	1.5	7.7	16.5	27.7	39.2
	Post-secondary	0	0.1	0.8	2.1	4	6.9	11
Burundi	Total	2,309	3,671	6,620	12,698	17,117	18,555	16,915
	Under 15	41	45	48	41	27	20	16
% pop15+	No education	93.7	79.3	56.9	26.3	10.7	4.1	1.2
by education	Incomplete primary	5	13.3	20.7	20.9	13.9	7.5	2.9
	Primary	1.1	6.2	18.2	35.5	41.4	35.9	24.4
	Lower secondary	0.2	0.9	2.7	8.8	14.8	19.2	20.3
	Upper secondary	0	0.2	0.9	5.7	13.3	23.5	35.8
	Post-Secondary	0	0.1	0.6	2.9	5.9	9.9	15.5
Cameroon	Total	4,388	7,610	15,584	28,376	39,445	44,693	43,532
	Under 15	39	43	44	39	26	19	16
% pop15+	No education	80.1	54.4	34	13.8	4.9	1.3	0.2
by education	Incomplete primary	10.9	12	7.6	3.3	1.3	0.4	0.1
	Primary	7.9	26.6	36.2	29.5	18.9	10	3.7
	Lower secondary	0.7	5.2	13.4	28.7	32.5	29.3	21.8
	Upper secondary	0.4	1.4	5.9	15.5	25.9	34.6	40.8
	Post-secondary	0.1	0.5	2.9	9.2	16.5	24.3	33.3
Cape Verde	Total	178	273	435	587	652	607	488
	Under 15	33	48	43	27	19	14	11
% pop15+	No education	81.8	52.6	18.8	4.9	1.3	0.4	0.1
by education	Incomplete primary	13.2	30.8	41.5	32.1	21.6	12.5	6.3
	Primary	3.9	9.9	16	19.9	19.8	16.6	12.2
	Lower secondary	0.8	4.5	15.6	27.2	30.1	29.7	25.4
	Upper secondary	0.2	1.4	5.5	9.9	17.3	25.7	33.9
	Post-secondary	0.1	0.8	2.5	6.1	10	15.2	22
Central African Republic	Total	1,327	2,017	3,755	5,377	6,918	7,290	6,501
	Under 15	36	42	42	38	26	20	16
% pop15+	No education	97.9	76	42.6	11.2	2.5	0.4	0
by education	Incomplete primary	1.9	16.2	30.3	17.2	7.5	2.7	0.5
	Primary	0.2	6.1	15.7	28	23.7	15.1	7.1
	Lower secondary	0.1	1.2	8.4	31.5	42.2	43.5	37.5
	Upper secondary	0	0.4	2.2	9.4	18.9	29.8	41.5
	Post-secondary	0	0.1	0.9	2.6	5.2	8.5	13.3
Chad	Total	2,502	4,088	8,344	18,461	29,639	37,302	39,728
	Under 15	38	44	49	44	31	22	18
% pop15+	No education	99.1	91.1	73	43.2	19.6	7.5	1.9
by education	Incomplete primary	0.6	4.1	12.1	17.9	15.3	9.1	3.9
	Primary	0.2	3.4	9.1	17.3	23.4	21.5	14.6
	Lower secondary	0.1	0.9	3.7	11.9	21	27	28.2
	Upper secondary	0	0.3	1.3	6.8	15.3	25.9	37.3
	Post-secondary	0	0.2	0.8	2.8	5.4	9.1	14.1

(*Continued*)

Appendix Table 32.1 (Continued)

Country	*Pop/Education*	*1950*	*1975*	*2000*	*2025*	*2050*	*2075*	*2100*
Comoros	Total	158	256	545	959	1,323	1,480	1,411
	Under 15	38	45	44	37	26	19	16
% pop15+	No education	96.2	82.6	46.6	16.7	4.8	1	0.2
	Incomplete primary	2.4	4.1	11.1	10.8	6.1	2.5	0.7
by education	Primary	1	7.7	20.6	19.5	15.4	9.2	4.1
	Lower secondary	0.3	3.8	12.3	19.7	19.8	16.3	11.6
	Upper secondary	0.1	1.2	4.6	17.3	27.7	34.6	37
	Post-secondary	0	0.6	4.9	15.9	26.2	36.3	46.4
Congo	Total	814	1,570	3,155	6,309	9,225	10,902	10,983
	Under 15	41	45	42	38	26	20	16
% pop15+	No education	84.4	47.6	15.7	3.5	0.8	0.2	0.1
by education	Incomplete primary	8.8	17.9	16	7.6	2.7	0.7	0.1
	Primary	5.4	22.4	37.7	32.1	20.3	10.5	4.1
	Lower secondary	1.1	7.9	18.2	32.6	35.4	31	23.1
	Upper secondary	0.2	2.3	6.6	16.5	28.1	38.6	45.6
	Post-secondary	0.1	1.8	5.7	7.7	12.6	19	27.1
Cote d'Ivoire	Total	2,630	6,624	16,617	28,757	40,285	46,919	47,757
	Under 15	43	45	44	39	26	19	16
% pop15+	No education	94.3	80.8	58.4	31.3	14.1	5.5	1.6
by education	Incomplete primary	2.7	5.5	11.5	15.3	12.6	7.9	3.7
	Primary	2.1	8.8	16.8	20.3	20.6	16.6	10.6
	Lower secondary	0.5	3.5	8.3	15.8	21	22.9	21.2
	Upper secondary	0.2	1.1	3.3	10	18.3	27.2	35.3
	Post-secondary	0.1	0.3	1.8	7.2	13.3	19.8	27.5
DR Congo	Total	12,184	22,902	47,100	100,851	162,540	204,392	214,139
	Under 15	44	44	46	43	30	22	18
% pop15+	No education	69	47.4	24.4	9.2	2.7	0.7	0.1
by education	Incomplete primary	22.1	27.2	24.8	15.6	6.7	2.3	0.5
	Primary	3.9	11.3	14.8	15	10.6	5.7	2.3
	Lower secondary	3.5	10.7	23.1	34	36.2	30.6	21.8
	Upper secondary	0.4	2.6	10.2	20.4	33.4	44.3	51.5
	Post-secondary	1.1	0.8	2.8	5.7	10.3	16.4	23.8
Djibouti	Total	62	224	718	1,112	1,485	1,670	1,707
	Under 15	47	47	41	28	21	17	15
% pop15+	No education				39.5	21.3	9.2	3
by education	Incomplete primary				15.5	11	6.1	2.5
	Primary				10.3	12.3	10.9	7.3
	Lower secondary				13.7	17.5	17.9	15.4
	Upper secondary				14.9	25.8	35.7	42.5
	Post-secondary				6	12.1	20.2	29.3
Equatorial Guinea	Total	226	232	553	1,489	2,189	2,599	2,716
	Under 15	34	43	45	36	26	19	16
% pop15+	No education	81.2	47.4	14.2	3.5	1.2	0.4	0.1
by education	Incomplete primary	10.3	19.7	23.5	8.4	2.9	0.7	0.2
	Primary	7.4	26	40.7	32.6	20.3	10.1	4
	Lower secondary	1	5.5	15.6	34.2	40	37.7	29.7
	Upper secondary	0.1	1	3.4	14.8	24.7	34.3	42.1
	Post-Secondary	0	0.5	2.6	6.6	11	16.8	23.9

(*Continued*)

Appendix Table 32.1 (Continued)

Country	*Pop/Education*	*1950*	*1975*	*2000*	*2025*	*2050*	*2075*	*2100*
Eritrea	Total	1,142	2,076	3,393	5,944	8,323	9,426	9,095
	Under 15	45	44	45	37	26	19	15
% pop15+	No education				37.9	20.2	9.4	3.5
by education	Incomplete primary				15.7	10.9	6.3	2.9
	Primary				10.9	12.9	11.4	8
	Lower secondary				15.6	18.9	18.7	16.1
	Upper secondary				14.9	26.3	35.9	42.8
	Post-secondary				5	10.8	18.3	26.6
Ethiopia	Total	18,128	32,569	66,480	126,582	184,491	208,354	191,437
	Under 15	44	45	47	37	25	16	11
% pop15+	No education	95.4	88.2	69.7	42.3	24.1	12.4	5.2
by education	Incomplete primary	3.2	6.7	13.8	18.8	14.8	9.5	4.9
	Primary	1.1	3.7	11.2	16.7	20.2	19	14.5
	Lower secondary	0.2	0.7	2.1	9.2	14.5	16.6	16
	Upper secondary	0.1	0.5	2.3	11	22.3	35.4	48
	Post-secondary	0	0.2	0.9	2.1	4.1	7.1	11.4
Gabon	Total	473	650	1,232	2,352	3,157	3,552	3,538
	Under 15	29	37	41	33	22	17	14
% pop15+	No education	89.7	54	19.3	4.7	1.8	0.6	0.2
by education	Incomplete primary	7.1	17.5	16	7.5	2.8	0.8	0.2
	Primary	2.8	19.6	37.3	26.1	15.7	7.6	2.8
	Lower secondary	0.2	5.4	17.3	32.2	32.4	27.2	19.2
	Upper secondary	0.1	1.6	4.1	15.9	26.1	34.2	38.7
	Post-secondary	0	1.9	6.1	13.5	21.2	29.6	38.8
Gambia	Total	271	521	1,232	2,544	3,745	4,418	4,435
	Under 15	41	43	46	41	27	20	16
% pop15+	No education	96.2	91.9	71.9	38.9	19	8.3	2.9
by education	Incomplete primary	0.5	1	3.7	7	6.9	5	2.7
	Primary	1.1	2.9	8.1	11.5	12.2	9.8	6.1
	Lower secondary	1.2	2.8	8.9	19.4	22.1	21.8	18.7
	Upper secondary	1	1.4	5.9	17.8	30	40.1	48
	Post-secondary	0	0.2	1.6	5.3	9.8	15	21.6
Ghana	Total	4,981	9,831	18,939	33,825	48,386	57,899	60,763
	Under 15	45	46	42	36	27	20	16
% pop15+	No education	83	56.3	35.8	17.5	7.4	2.6	0.7
by education	Incomplete primary	4.5	6.9	8.2	7.6	4.5	2.1	0.8
	Primary	5.8	11.3	13.2	7.7	6	3.7	1.9
	Lower secondary	5.7	19.1	30.4	39.9	38.3	31.4	22.5
	Upper secondary	0.9	4.3	8.4	20.9	33.6	44.5	51.8
	Post-secondary	0.1	2	4	6.4	10.2	15.6	22.3
Guinea	Total	3,094	4,362	8,803	15,158	21,736	25,039	24,493
	Under 15	37	41	44	39	28	21	16
% pop15+	No education	98.2	87.3	70.2	41.5	22.6	11	4.2
by education	Incomplete primary	0.7	3.8	8.2	13.9	12.2	8.5	4.8
	Primary	0.7	4.1	9.9	9.6	10.7	9.4	6.7
	Lower secondary	0.3	2.4	5.4	15	19.8	20.6	18.4
	Upper secondary	0	1.6	3.2	12.7	22.2	31.9	39.9
	Post-secondary	0	0.9	3	7.3	12.5	18.6	26

(*Continued*)

Appendix Table 32.1 (Continued)

Country	*Pop/Education*	*1950*	*1975*	*2000*	*2025*	*2050*	*2075*	*2100*
Guinea-Bissau	Total	535	779	1,302	2,147	2,846	3,034	2,730
	Under 15	38	41	43	39	27	20	17
% pop15+	No education	96.6	84.2	58.9	29.2	13	4.9	1.5
by education	Incomplete primary	3.1	11.2	19.3	20.8	14.4	8.2	3.5
	Primary	0.2	2.6	10.5	15.8	17.2	13.8	8.5
	Lower secondary	0	1.2	4.5	14.6	20.1	21.4	19.1
	Upper secondary	0	0.8	5.6	17.6	31.5	45.4	57.3
	Post-secondary	0	0	1.2	2	3.6	6.3	10.2
Kenya	Total	6,077	13,487	31,489	59,894	90,650	109,913	113,617
	Under 15	40	50	45	37	27	20	16
% pop15+	No education	78.3	49.1	21.6	7.4	2.4	0.6	0.1
by education	Incomplete primary	15.2	20.7	15	6.7	2.6	0.7	0.2
	Primary	3.8	14.9	21.9	12.4	7.4	3.6	1.4
	Lower secondary	2	10.8	23	34.9	30.7	22	13.6
	Upper secondary	0.6	3.4	13.6	29.2	41.3	49.7	52.2
	Post-secondary	0.1	1	5	9.4	15.6	23.3	32.5
Lesotho	Total	734	1,150	1,862	2,404	2,677	2,559	2,168
	Under 15	41	45	41	34	25	20	17
% pop15+	No education	43.6	28.7	15.7	5.6	1.7	0.4	0.1
by education	Incomplete primary	49.7	52.7	37.3	20.3	8.2	2.6	0.5
	Primary	4.5	12.3	28.9	31.1	22.7	12	4.3
	Lower secondary	1.5	3.1	8.9	18.1	22.6	20.2	14.2
	Upper secondary	0.4	2.2	5.7	16	29	40.2	45.6
	Post-secondary	0.3	1	3.5	8.9	15.8	24.5	35.3
Liberia	Total	930	1,627	2,889	5,699	8,374	9,808	9,745
	Under 15	41	44	43	38	28	21	16
% pop15+	No education	92.9	80.3	59.6	33.1	15.8	6.5	2.2
by education	Incomplete primary	3	4	6.7	8.7	6.8	4.3	2.1
	Primary	3	7.7	11.2	12.2	12.1	9.2	5.6
	Lower secondary	0.7	4	9	19.3	22.5	21	17
	Upper secondary	0.4	3.5	11.9	23.8	37.6	50.7	60.2
	Post-secondary	0.1	0.5	1.7	3	5.2	8.3	12.8
Madagascar	Total	4,084	7,556	15,700	30,765	46,071	56,463	59,896
	Under 15	38	46	45	37	26	19	15
% pop15+	No education	69.5	47.3	26.8	12.3	5.4	2.2	0.7
by education	Incomplete primary	26.6	36.5	41.4	34.9	22.7	12.6	5.6
	Primary	2.8	10.8	18.5	28.5	30.6	26.2	18.6
	Lower secondary	0.9	3.5	8	15.1	22.4	26.3	26.1
	Upper secondary	0.2	1.6	3.5	6.9	14.9	26.2	38.4
	Post-secondary	0	0.4	1.8	2.3	3.9	6.6	10.7
Malawi	Total	2,954	5,293	11,273	23,689	42,577	59,153	67,287
	Under 15	46	47	47	42	34	24	18
% pop15+	No education	70.2	54.5	35.5	16.8	7.2	2.6	0.8
by education	Incomplete primary	21.8	24.8	24.5	18	9.4	4	1.3
	Primary	5	10.1	14.3	15.6	13.7	9.4	5.3
	Lower secondary	2.6	8.7	19.3	30.7	34.5	30.5	22.9
	Upper secondary	0.3	1.7	5.6	16.9	31.6	47	58.8
	Post-secondary	0	0.1	0.7	2	3.7	6.6	10.9

(Continued)

Appendix Table 32.1 (Continued)

Country	*Pop/Education*	*1950*	*1975*	*2000*	*2025*	*2050*	*2075*	*2100*
Mali	Total	4,708	6,482	11,017	22,885	36,468	44,999	46,343
	Under 15	39	43	46	44	31	23	18
% pop15+	No education	95.4	90.3	79.9	59.5	39.3	22.3	10.1
by education	Incomplete primary	2.6	4.2	8.4	13.3	15.1	13.2	9.1
	Primary	1.5	3.3	5.3	9.6	12.2	13.2	11.6
	Lower secondary	0.3	1.4	3.5	9.2	15.3	19.8	21.7
	Upper secondary	0.1	0.6	1.8	5.7	13.1	23.2	34.5
	Post-secondary	0	0.2	1	2.7	5	8.3	13
Mauritian	Total	661	1,329	2,709	5,204	7,341	8,528	8,623
	Under 15	44	46	43	36	25	19	15
% pop15+	No education				39.7	20.5	9.1	3.2
by education	Incomplete primary				9	8.4	6.1	3.4
	Primary				21.7	23.1	19.3	13.1
	Lower secondary				14.7	20.4	22.9	21.5
	Upper secondary				10.6	19.9	30.6	40.9
	Post-secondary				4.3	7.6	12.1	18
Mauritius	Total	493	892	1,185	1,253	1,125	932	752
	Under 15	45	40	26	16	14	13	12
% pop15+	No education	45.7	22.5	8	2.5	0.6	0.2	0.1
by education	Incomplete primary	45.2	35.2	26.6	16.1	8.6	2.8	0.9
	Primary	6.4	24	23.6	20.3	14.2	8	3.3
	Lower secondary	1.8	8.6	14.7	18.4	18.1	14.8	10.1
	Upper secondary	1	8.9	23.9	34.8	45.1	53.3	55.8
	Post-Secondary	0	0.8	3.1	7.9	13.4	20.9	29.8
Mayotte	Total	15	46	150	308	479	608	674
	Under 15	32	49	44	34	24	17	13
% pop15+	No education				1.6	0.7	0.3	0.1
by education	Incomplete primary				3.2	1.1	0.4	0.1
	Primary				14.3	7	3.1	1.3
	Lower secondary				21.6	15.3	10.3	6.8
	Upper secondary				40.8	47.6	48.4	45.3
	Post-secondary				18.5	28.4	37.5	46.3
Mozambique	Total	6,246	10,422	18,184	35,425	51,093	59,383	58,655
	Under 15	41	44	45	40	27	20	17
% pop15+	No education	94.7	85.2	69.8	45.2	25.3	12.4	4.5
by education	Incomplete primary	4	8.7	14.4	15.2	11.6	7.2	3.4
	Primary	0.9	3.3	4.5	9.6	12.5	11.6	8.1
	Lower secondary	0.3	2.2	8.4	19.1	27.5	30.2	27.2
	Upper secondary	0	0.5	2.6	9.9	21.1	34.9	50.2
	Post-secondary	0	0.1	0.4	1	2	3.8	6.7
Namibia	Total	485	906	1,899	2,926	3,798	4,094	3,856
	Under 15	39	44	41	34	23	18	15
% pop15+	No education	58.7	42.3	19.8	7.4	2.4	0.7	0.1
by education	Incomplete primary	29.2	33.2	24.7	11.6	4.2	1.1	0.2
	Primary	7.6	14.3	23.3	16.8	10.2	4.8	1.6
	Lower secondary	2.8	5.6	13	28.3	27.4	20.5	12.6
	Upper secondary	1.6	4	13.3	26.1	39.8	48.7	51.1
	Post-secondary	0.1	0.7	5.9	9.7	16	24.2	34.5

(*Continued*)

Appendix Table 32.1 (Continued)

Country	*Pop/Education*	*1950*	*1975*	*2000*	*2025*	*2050*	*2075*	*2100*
Niger	Total	2,560	5,207	11,315	28,296	58,617	92,007	114,481
	Under 15	49	48	48	48	39	28	21
% pop15+	No education	99.5	94.9	82.6	55.3	30.8	14.6	5.9
by education	Incomplete primary	0.3	2.4	8.5	18	21.7	17.7	11.3
	Primary	0.2	2	5.9	14.6	20.2	21.5	18.2
	Lower secondary	0	0.5	1.6	7.7	17	25.9	30.7
	Upper secondary	0	0.2	0.5	2.8	7.4	15	25
	Post-secondary	0	0.1	0.8	1.5	2.9	5.3	8.8
Nigeria	Total	37,860	63,522	122,768	230,833	382,510	521,007	603,378
	Under 15	42	43	43	42	34	25	20
% pop15+	No education	88.1	74.5	48	23.5	8.9	2.6	0.6
by education	Incomplete primary	5.2	6.2	5.3	4.3	2.9	1.5	0.6
	Primary	5.3	12.3	19.6	15.9	11.1	6.2	3
	Lower secondary	0.8	3.2	8.1	15.4	16.7	13.7	9.9
	Upper secondary	0.6	2.9	13.1	27.9	40.2	46.7	47.3
	Post-secondary	0	1	5.9	12.8	20.3	29.2	38.6
Reunion	Total	248	485	737	933	1,044	1,077	1,080
	Under 15	40	42	29	21	18	15	14
% pop15+	No education	68.8	29.7	9.5	3	1	0.5	0.2
by education	Incomplete primary	16.4	18.2	11.3	5.8	2.1	0.5	0.2
	Primary	11.7	29.6	30.2	20.3	10.6	3.9	1.5
	Lower secondary	2.2	10.8	14.8	17.6	15	10.8	7.2
	Upper secondary	0.6	8.1	22.9	35.5	44.7	47.9	45.2
	Post-secondary	0.3	3.6	11.3	17.7	26.6	36.4	45.7
Rwanda	Total	2,186	4,359	7,965	14,725	22,596	27,600	28,328
	Under 15	43	47	45	37	29	22	17
% pop15+	No education	82.7	58.3	30.8	11.6	4	1.2	0.3
by education	Incomplete primary	16.3	37.4	49.8	44.5	29.3	15.4	6.3
	Primary	0.8	2.8	12.5	20.7	23.5	20.1	13.7
	Lower secondary	0.2	1	3.4	10.2	16.7	19.5	18.3
	Upper secondary	0	0.4	2.7	10.3	21.6	35.7	48.4
	Post-secondary	0	0.1	0.8	2.7	4.9	8.1	13
Sao Tome and Principe	Total	60	83	139	233	293	299	253
	Under 15	33	48	45	37	24	18	15
% pop15+	No education	94	57.1	19.2	3.4	0.7	0.1	0
by education	Incomplete primary	5.9	33.2	46.1	28.8	13.4	5.1	1.2
	Primary	0.1	7.1	21.7	34.9	31.6	22.7	12.4
	Lower secondary	0	2.3	8.1	22.4	33.7	38.5	36.5
	Upper secondary	0	0.2	4.2	8.8	17.4	28.1	40.6
	Post-secondary	0	0	0.7	1.6	3.2	5.5	9.2
Senegal	Total	2,487	4,911	9,841	19,260	29,389	36,158	38,045
	Under 15	42	45	45	39	28	21	16
% pop15+	No education	94	82.4	66.3	38.8	19.7	8.8	3.1
by education	Incomplete primary	1.5	2.7	7	9.2	8.4	5.9	3.3
	Primary	3.3	8.7	15.8	22	23.2	19.1	13
	Lower secondary	0.9	3.7	6.1	15.2	21	23.3	21.7
	Upper secondary	0.3	1.4	2.7	10.7	20.2	31	41.1
	Post-secondary	0.1	1	2	4.2	7.4	11.9	17.7

(*Continued*)

Appendix Table 32.1 (Continued)

Country	*Pop/Education*	*1950*	*1975*	*2000*	*2025*	*2050*	*2075*	*2100*
Seychelles	Total	36	60	81	98	97	90	83
	Under 15	31	41	29	22	18	16	14
% pop15+	No education				2.6	1.1	0.6	0.3
by education	Incomplete primary				5.3	1.8	0.5	0.2
	Primary				20	9.8	3.4	1.3
	Lower secondary				17.8	15	10.5	7
	Upper secondary				36.1	45.1	47.7	44.4
	Post-secondary				18.2	27.2	37.2	46.8
Sierra Leone	Total	1,982	2,906	4,299	8,846	12,108	13,345	12,629
	Under 15	41	43	47	38	27	20	16
% pop15+ by	No education	93.5	84.8	68.5	41.3	22	10	3.4
education	Incomplete primary	2.2	3.7	8	11.2	9.7	6.6	3.5
	Primary	1.9	4.6	8.1	12.4	13.6	11.4	7.5
	Lower secondary	1.3	3.6	7.9	17.4	23.4	24.9	22.2
	Upper secondary	0.8	2.5	5.2	13.5	24.1	35.3	45.5
	Post-secondary	0.2	0.9	2.3	4.2	7.4	11.8	17.8
Somalia	Total	2,264	3,880	8,150	18,474	30,032	37,702	39,158
	Under 15	41	44	52	44	32	23	18
% pop15+	No education	79.2	72.8	61.1	39.5	21.2	9.8	3.5
by education	Incomplete primary	18.9	19.3	22.4	18.2	12.1	6.9	3.1
	Primary	0.6	2.4	3.3	10	13.7	12.1	8.2
	Lower secondary	0.9	3.1	7.5	18.4	25.7	27.4	24.2
	Upper secondary	0.4	2.1	4.2	11.1	22.1	35.4	47.9
	Post-secondary	0	0.3	1.5	2.8	5.1	8.4	13
South Africa	Total	13,616	25,760	44,612	61,674	71,386	72,371	68,081
	Under 15	38	42	34	27	21	17	15
% pop15+	No education	56.2	29.7	11.4	3.6	1	0.3	0.1
by education	Incomplete primary	14.1	20.8	13.8	5.8	1.6	0.3	0.1
	Primary	11.8	17.8	16.5	7	2.9	1	0.3
	Lower secondary	9.4	16.3	28.3	29	21.7	13	7.2
	Upper secondary	7.6	12.9	24.4	45.8	59	63.8	60.8
	Post-secondary	0.9	2.6	5.6	8.8	13.9	21.6	31.6
South Sudan	Total	2,583	4,117	6,696	16,130	27,621	36,603	40,738
	Under 15	44	44	45	39	29	22	18
% pop15+	No education	93.2	90.1	81.5	57.3	34.8	18.2	7.4
by education	Incomplete primary	0	0	0	0	0	0	0
	Primary	5.9	7.7	10.9	13.3	14.9	13.1	9.1
	Lower secondary	0	0	0	0	0	0	0
	Upper secondary	0.9	2	6.4	24.9	42.2	56.4	65.6
	Post-secondary	0	0.2	1.2	4.6	8.1	12.3	17.9
Swaziland	Total	273	517	1,061	1,528	1,853	1,874	1,671
	Under 15	43	48	44	34	25	19	16
% pop15+	No education	71.8	42.5	16.6	4.1	1	0.2	0
by education	Incomplete primary	23.5	28.4	22.6	7.6	2.3	0.4	0.1
	Primary	4.1	19.4	29.8	15.1	7.6	2.8	0.7
	Lower secondary	0.4	5.6	13.5	23.7	19.2	12.9	7.7
	Upper secondary	0.1	2.3	10.9	35.3	47.4	51.1	47.6
	Post-secondary	0.1	1.8	6.5	14.2	22.5	32.5	43.8

(*Continued*)

Appendix Table 32.1 (Continued)

Country	*Pop/Education*	*1950*	*1975*	*2000*	*2025*	*2050*	*2075*	*2100*
Tanzania	Total	7,650	15,980	34,125	71,576	118,667	154,255	168,819
	Under 15	46	46	45	42	30	22	17
% pop15+	No education	78.8	53	27.6	10.7	3.6	1	0.2
by education	Incomplete primary	14.7	17.9	11.8	5.2	2	0.7	0.2
	Primary	5.8	24.9	51.6	57.6	48.8	34.5	20.4
	Lower secondary	0.6	3.3	6.5	16.7	24.4	27.3	25.5
	Upper secondary	0.1	0.5	1.2	5.7	13.1	23.2	33.8
	Post-secondary	0	0.4	1.3	4.1	8	13.2	19.8
Togo	Total	1,396	2,410	4,870	9,128	12,610	14,244	13,994
	Under 15	41	46	44	37	25	19	16
% pop15+	No education	92.4	75.6	47	21.5	8.8	3.1	0.9
by education	Incomplete primary	4.8	10.4	19.1	20.5	16	9.8	4.6
	Primary	2.4	10	20.6	28.9	29.1	23.9	15.7
	Lower secondary	0.3	2.1	6.3	14	19.4	22.6	22.1
	Upper secondary	0.1	1.3	5.1	10.4	18.6	28.1	38.2
	Post-secondary	0	0.4	2	4.6	8.1	12.5	18.4
Uganda	Total	5,158	10,827	23,983	55,100	101,354	143,038	165,353
	Under 15	43	47	50	45	36	26	19
% pop15+	No education	70.7	47.8	24.4	8.9	2.9	0.9	0.2
by education	Incomplete primary	22.4	31.1	40.2	25.5	13	5.4	1.8
	Primary	4.5	14.3	25.2	33.4	31.2	22.1	12.9
	Lower secondary	2	5.4	7	19.2	26.3	27.7	23.6
	Upper secondary	0.2	0.7	1.6	8.9	19.1	31.2	42.4
	Post-secondary	0.2	0.8	1.7	4.1	7.5	12.7	19.1
Zambia	Total	2,310	4,969	10,552	21,624	37,073	48,944	53,472
	Under 15	45	48	46	43	33	24	18
% pop15+	No education	76.5	44.1	21.8	8.1	2.8	0.8	0.2
by education	Incomplete primary	11.2	20.6	22.3	15	7.2	2.8	0.8
	Primary	5.6	15.6	23.2	20.6	15.3	9	4.3
	Lower secondary	3.1	8.9	17.1	27.3	28.9	23.9	16.8
	Upper secondary	1.6	4.7	7.8	16.9	27.6	36.6	41.6
	Post-secondary	2	6	7.8	12.1	18.2	26.9	36.3
Zimbabwe	Total	2,747	6,150	12,388	19,148	25,040	26,523	24,071
	Under 15	42	48	42	37	24	18	15
% pop15+	No education	77.9	35.6	11.8	3.1	1	0.3	0.1
by education	Incomplete primary	11.9	22.4	11.5	3.6	1	0.3	0.1
	Primary	4.3	15.6	19	10.1	5.3	2.3	0.8
	Lower secondary	3.6	16.1	26	18	12.5	8.4	5.8
	Upper secondary	1.6	7.4	25.2	54.6	64.1	65.5	61.5
	Post-secondary	0.8	2.9	6.6	10.5	16.2	23.2	31.9
Eastern Africa	Total	66,796	127,294	261,125	516,463	808,299	1,001,820	1,042,600
	Under 15	43	46	46	39	29	21	16
% pop15+	No education	84.1	65.5	42.8	23.7	12	5.4	1.9
by education	Incomplete primary	11.5	17.3	19.7	16.3	10.3	5.5	2.3
	Primary	2.9	10.5	20.4	23.5	23.1	18.2	11.8
	Lower secondary	1	4.3	9.5	17.8	22.4	23	20.1
	Upper secondary	0.3	1.6	5.5	14.4	24.5	35.6	45.5
	Post-secondary	0.1	0.7	2.2	4.4	7.7	12.3	18.3

(*Continued*)

Appendix Table 32.1 (Continued)

Country	*Pop/Education*	*1950*	*1975*	*2000*	*2025*	*2050*	*2075*	*2100*
Middle Africa	Total	26,498	46,779	96,113	200,392	312,511	384,918	398,593
	Under 15	41	44	46	42	29	21	17
% pop15+	No education	80	58	35.2	17.5	7.4	2.7	0.7
by education	Incomplete primary	13.5	19.4	19.3	13.2	7.4	3.5	1.2
	Primary	3.9	13.3	19.9	20.8	16.8	11.3	6
	Lower secondary	1.8	6.9	16.3	27.6	32	30.1	24.2
	Upper secondary	0.3	1.8	7	15.8	27.3	38.4	47.6
	Post-secondary	0.5	0.6	2.3	5.2	9.1	14	20.3
Southern Africa	Total	15,666	29,696	52,857	71,109	82,851	84,045	78,623
	Under 15	38	42	34	28	21	17	15
% pop15+	No education	56.4	30.7	12.2	3.9	1.1	0.3	0.1
by education	Incomplete primary	16.6	22.5	15	6.4	1.9	0.4	0.1
	Primary	11	17.4	17.8	8.6	4.1	1.6	0.5
	Lower secondary	8.4	15.1	26.5	28.4	21.9	13.6	7.7
	Upper secondary	6.8	11.9	22.8	43.4	56.2	61.3	58.8
	Post-secondary	0.8	2.4	5.7	9.3	14.8	22.8	32.8
Western Africa	Total	70,902	120,173	235,513	450,314	723,519	951,284	1,065,556
	Under 15	42	44	44	41	32	24	19
% pop15+	No education	90.8	77.5	54.9	31.1	15.2	6.4	2.3
by education	Incomplete primary	3.9	5.6	7.3	8.5	7.5	5.3	3
	Primary	3.9	9.6	15.8	15.3	13.5	10.1	6.6
	Lower secondary	1	4.1	9.1	16.8	19.6	18.9	16.2
	Upper secondary	0.4	2.3	8.8	19.7	30.2	38.4	43.1
	Post-secondary	0	0.9	4.1	8.7	14.1	20.9	28.8

Source: Wittgenstein Centre for Demography and Global Human Capital 2018.

Notes: Total population is shown in thousands; for five countries (Djibouti, Eritrea, Mauritania, Mayotte, Seychelles) no data on educational attainment for the past (1950–2010) are available.

33

DEMOGRAPHIC TRANSITION AND DEVELOPMENT IN AFRICA

Patricia Agupusi

Introduction

This chapter poses two simple questions – what is the relationship between demography and development? How would countries of Africa avoid the Malthusian population theory outcome and reap demographic dividend? According to the United Nations, Africa started with a much higher total fertility rate of 6.7 in the 1960s, which fell below the rate of 6 children per woman only in the 1990s. In 2015, the total fertility rate in Africa was 4.7 children per woman, which is still far higher than in Europe and North America in the 1960s (Bloom, Kuhn, & Prettner, 2017). Except for a few countries, fertility rates and youth dependency rates in Africa are among the highest in the world. As a result, there is a renewed debate on the impact of demographic transition in Africa. With a population share of 46% for 15 years and younger, Africa is the youngest region in the world, according to the Population Reference Bureau (PRB) 2019 data. Fertility rates and youth dependency rates in Africa are among the highest in the world, exposing the region to higher poverty rates, lower labour productivity, high unemployment or underemployment, and the risk of political instability (Canning, Raja, & Yazbeck, 2015). On the other hand, some see Africa's young population as a potential for a developmental leap (Bloom, Mitgang, & Osher, 2016; Canning et al., 2015; Mubila, 2012). Consequently, demographic transition in Africa is attracting debate from both scholars and policymakers on the implications of Africa's growing young demography in the face of developmental challenges. Whether the current demographic structure would bring disaster, as predicted by some, or bring dividends to accelerate development, is dependent on various endogenous factors such as the health, education, and economic policies a country is formulating and implementing to improve its human capital.

This chapter draws from the demographic dividend framework to examine the pathways African countries are taking to transform their young demography for development. This chapter continues with a general overview of the relationship between demography and development starting with the major theories of the population to demographic transition in other regions. This is followed by a brief analysis of the relationship between human capital, institution, and development. Drawing from other regions that have gone through the demographic transition (Jemna, 2015; Doran, 2012), I outline four major interrelated factors that could lead

DOI: 10.4324/9780429287213-40

to a demographic dividend, while failing to meet them could lead to disaster. These major factors include 1) investment in education, 2) institutional arrangement, 3) economic policies, and 4) good governance.

Methodology

This is a critical analysis and interpretation study that draws from secondary data to examine how the principles of development and the demographic transition could be harnessed (Brecht, 2015; Bhattacherjee, 2012). As noted earlier, the core question I set out to address in this chapter is whether African countries could turn demographic transition into a catalyst for development, or if disaster will ensue. This is based on the assumption that the relationship between demographic transition and development is neutral and depends on how each country manages its demography. I triangulate data drawn from the World Bank, the United Nation Population Fund (UNFPA), the Population Reference Bureau (PRB), and scholarship to present a theoretical analysis of the relationship between demographic transition and development with the case of Africa. With the understanding that Africa is vast and very diverse, the focus is on universal principles of development and the role of human capital. According to Bloom and Canning (2011) a demographic dividend is a composite of accounting and behavioural forces. The accounting forces include expansion of the potential labour force as the young population reaches the working age; and the fact that the working ages coincide with the prime years for savings. As the authors observed, if these factors are key to the accumulation of physical and human capital and technological innovation, how a country harnesses these factors is important in determining whether a demographic dividend will be achieved. Given that primary principles of economic development include institutional arrangements, physical and human capital accumulation, and technological innovations (Agupusi, 2016), these are used as integrated factors to assess whether countries in Africa would reap the demographic dividend. First, a look at the relationship between demography and economic development and how the demographic transition could turn into a dividend, or disaster, in African countries.

Conceptual framework: relationship between development and demography

Development is centred on the improvement of human life and its environment. It is the degree of quality of the population that shapes the development process of a country. And, with an improved standard of living, literacy, and rise in the middle class, the demographic transition becomes advantageous. Three perspectives can be drawn from the decades-long debate on the relationship between population and economic development – that population growth restricts, promotes, or is independent of economic growth (Bloom, Canning, & Sevilla, 2003). As rightly noted by the authors, these explanations focus on population size and growth, instead of the demography (the way in which the population is distributed across different age groups,) which can change dramatically. As the population grows, the age structure also changes, and this trend is called demographic transition. The Demographic Transition Model (DTM) is based on historical population trends of two demographic characteristics – birth and death rates – to suggest that a country's total population growth rate cycles through stages as that country develops economically. According to this theory, every country passes through different stages of population growth. In the first stage, the birth rate and the death rate are high, and the growth rate of the population is low. In the second stage, the birth rate remains stable, but the death rate falls rapidly. In the third stage, the birth rate begins to fall and tends to equal the death rate. The growth rate of the population is very slow. In the fourth stage, birth and death rates are both low, stabilizing the population (Thompson, 1929). If we follow these definitions, one can safely argue that the average African demography is hovering between the second and third stages with younger demography dominating the population. Theoretically, young demography means potentially long lifespans to boost and sustain economic development. This is because when a country invests in the young population it translates to quality human capital, a large pool of productive working population that can create wealth for sustained development. So, with the right policies, a demographic dividend could be achieved.

However, population growth does not automatically lead to a demographic dividend. Demographic dividend refers to the growth in an economy that is the result of a change in the age structure of a country's population. It describes the interplay between changes in a population's age structure due to the demographic transition and rapid economic growth (Canning et al., 2015). The change in age structure is typically brought on by a decline in fertility and mortality rates. Given that people's economic behaviour varies at different stages of life, changes in a country's age structure can have significant effects on its economic performance (Bloom et al., 2016; Iqbal, Yasmin, & Yaseen, 2015; Jemna, 2015). Demographic change can influence the underlying growth rate of the economy, structural productivity growth, living standards, savings rates, consumption, and investment. It can also influence the long-run unemployment rate and equilibrium interest rate, housing market trends, and the demand for financial assets (Mesters, 2018, p. 2). Countries with declining populations – large numbers of children and the elderly – may not be able to sustain their economies due in large part to low productivity and more financial and material resources invested to support them. The same could be observed across Europe where fertility rates have been below the replacement level for some time.[1] In China, the growth rate of the working-age population has slowed since the late 1980s, and partly because of its previous one-child policy, China's (ibid) population is also rapidly aging (Peng, 2011). The median age in China has increased from around 19 years in 1970 to 37 years in 2015. In addition, China was able to benefit from its large population in the country's developmental leap in the last four decades.

While most developed countries are grappling with their aging populations, the opposite is the case with African countries. As noted earlier, the region has recorded the youngest demography with 15 years of age and encompassing 45% of the population. This trend gives many African countries the opportunity to generate a high-quality working population for development in the following decades. Generally, demographic transition correlates with development given that it is a process when a country moves from high fertility and high mortality rates to high fertility and low mortality rates that occur in relation to economic growth (Kirk, 1996; Caldwell, 2007; Dyson 2013). Incidentally, this period of demographic transition is associated with consistent economic growth over the past two decades. High demography could also lead to high unemployment, underemployment, political violence, and social crisis. Thus, the relationship between demography and development flows in both directions, creating a virtuous circle that can boost and sustain growth and development, or a disaster that could lead to a vicious circle. Whether a country can translate its young population to be a driver for a development process hinges on interrelated factors: these are an investment in education for human capital development, a quality institutional arrangement that creates a viable economic environment, and right economic policy and good governance. Given strong complementarities among these areas, coordinated policies will likely be most effective in generating the momentum needed to pull Africa's economies out of a development trap (Bloom et al., 2017).

The population debate and Malthusian theory in Africa

The relationship between development and demography continues to draw interest especially with the population growth in Africa. As noted earlier, there are three schools of thought on the relationship between demography and development – positive, negative, and neutral. However, pessimism dominates the discourse on Africa – viewing population growth as negative to development. Previously it was argued that Africa is sparsely populated and mitigates development (Bloom et al., 1998; Herbst, 1990). Less than two decades later, the argument is that a rapidly growing African population is mitigating development despite having a population lower than those of India and China. This pessimistic view is mostly influenced by the Malthus population theory. Given that many African countries have problems with food security and increasingly violent conflicts, it makes Malthus's population model relevant to this analysis. According to Malthus, due to a higher population than the availability of food, many people will die from a shortage of food. The Malthusian Trap (or 'Malthusian Population Trap') is the idea that higher levels of food production created by more advanced agricultural techniques create higher population levels, spatial problems, food shortages, and decline in income (Madsen, Robertson, & Ye, 2019).

The trap theory has continued to guide the study of demographic change and development suggesting that the ongoing failure for many countries to attain development is due to the Malthusian trap. By implications, population rise in Africa would lead to economic stagnation, food insecurity, a continuation of unemployment and under-employment, conflict, and wars. The question is whether there is a causal relationship between these problems in African countries and population growth. Or could a rise in population with high young demography be a catalyst for lifting many out of poverty and spur sustainable development? Moreover, there is a lack of evidence to suggest the Malthusian theory of population and economic stagnation (Persson, 2008; Allen, 2008). Rather, Madsen et al. (2019) in their study argue for the idea of a post-Malthusian era in which technological progress accelerate, and populations boom. They also suggest that overall, demographic factors were a critical source of past economic stagnation and, therefore, may also remain an essential source of contemporary underdevelopment (p. 37), depending on how population growth is managed. Thus, Malthusian theorists and proponents of a negative relationship between population rise and development are not entirely wrong in their analysis. Perhaps it should be viewed as an outcome of when a country does not strategically invest in its growing population. Thus, the Malthusian theory is not inevitable and could be avoided. So even if the Malthusian demography still applies, there is a way out. This transition from a Malthusian to a post-Malthusian era is key to gaining demographic dividend through improvements in technology, human capital, sound economic policies, and state capacity. Perhaps, it may also simply be that economic stagnation and poverty were a consequence of other factors such as poor institutions and governance (Acemoglu, Gallego, & Robinson, 2014); (Agupusi, 2016). As noted by Bloom et al. (2016, p. 5) a unified growth theory of an increase in education accompanies the decrease in fertility, leads to faster human capital accumulation, and accelerated technological progress would break the economic stagnation predicted by the Malthusian theory. This chapter's focus on human capital development argues that with the right institutional arrangements and human capital investments, African countries could achieve demographic dividend for development.

Human capital, institution, and development – the tripod relationship

If we follow Sen's Theory of Development as an expansion of capabilities, the purpose of development is to improve human lives by removing the obstacles such as poverty, illiteracy, ill health, lack of access to resources, or lack of civil and political freedoms (Sen, 2001). Therefore, a country that could invest in different stages of its population and provide an environment for freedom for people to reach their capacity is turning demographic transition into development and development into human well-being – demographic dividend. Thus, development in this discourse translates into economic growth and poverty reduction. A country needs a good proportion of the working population to enhance the economy. Quality human capital correlates to economic growth and well-being, which in turn equals development.

Therefore, the relationship between development and demography is to examine how a demographic transition could lead to sustained economic growth and a reduction in poverty.[2] According to the World Bank (see Figure 33.1) the fast-growing economies of China and India have lifted nearly 1 billion people out of extreme poverty.[3]

Incidentally, China and India alone account for more than 36% of the world population (2.7 billion). On the other hand, the entire region of the African population is over 1 billion. Despite a recent economic stagnation due to COVID-19 and internal crises in some African countries such as Nigeria and South Africa, many African countries have experienced sustained growth in the last two decades. The consistent economic rise coincides with demographic transition and stagnation of extreme poverty in the region. However, extreme poverty has shifted to Africa and is concentrated in countries[4] with low economic growth in the past decades (Roser &

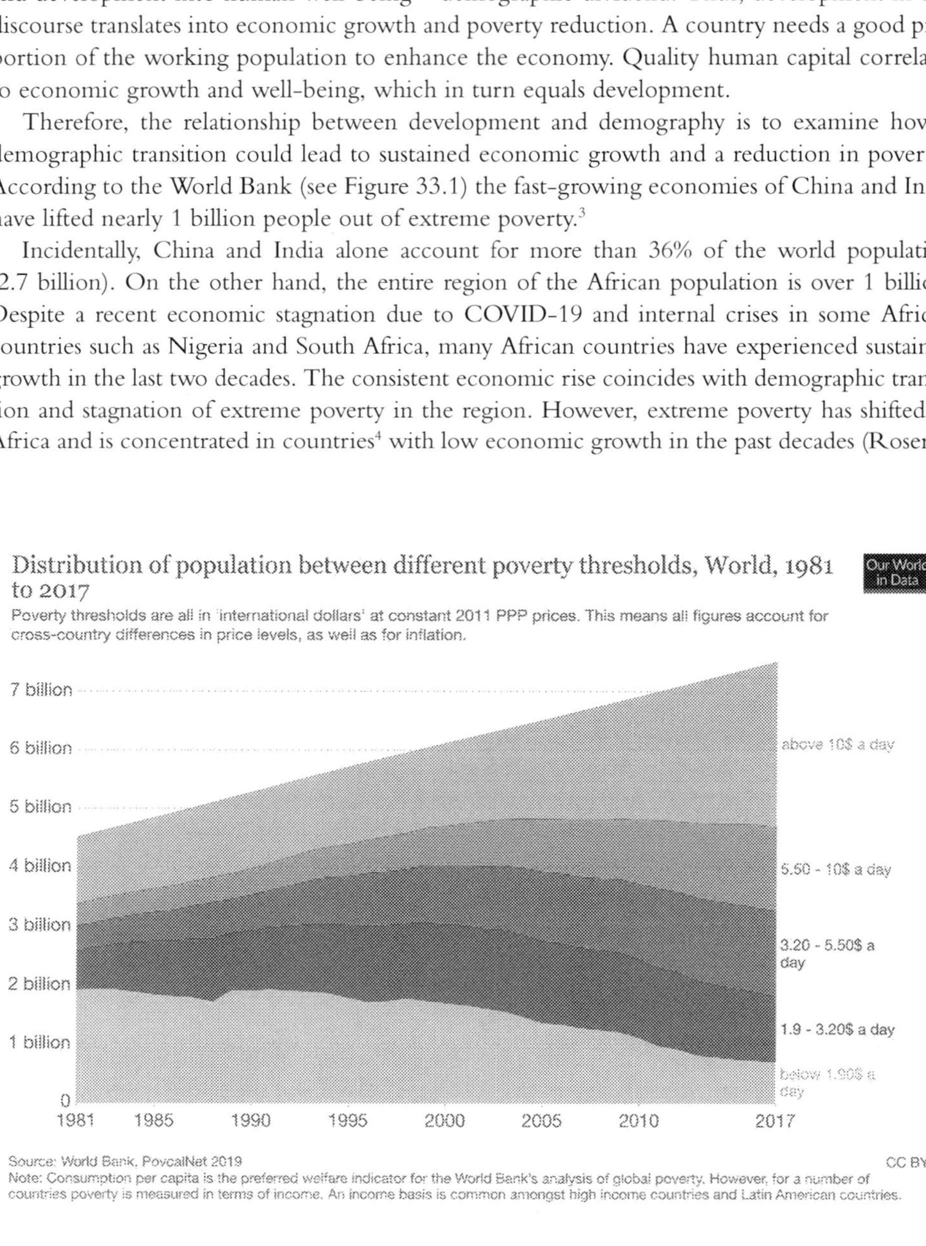

Figure 33.1 Distribution of population between different poverty thresholds, 1981–2015.

Ortiz-Ospina, 2019).[5] If one follows this logic, high growth eradicates extreme poverty and, more generally, alleviates poverty as a whole. The combination of high poverty and a population of young people leads to social malaise, conflict, and war – thereby turning the podium of demographic transition into a disaster and reaffirms Malthus's argument. A demographic dividend is not guaranteed in every country. If, for example, the birth rate is slow to decline, investments in education are less likely because families and countries will have fewer resources per child (Canning et al., 2015, p. 5). Also, if there is no economic diversification to create jobs, and not enough skilled labour to sustain a growing economy, a demographic transition becomes a disaster due to a lack of human capital. As both a means and an end, human capital remains pivotal to development. Demographic transition is thus likely to provide an opportunity to reduce poverty and yield a demographic dividend that will lead to economic success as it did in the Asian emerging markets where one third of East Asia's economic 'miracle' is attributed to demographic change (Bloom & Canning, 2011; Mubila, 2012, p. 1). All of this suggests that a country interested in taking full advantage of demographic transition must invest in human capital and institutional arrangements that would enable a productive and innovative population to develop. The question remains, to what extent are African countries investing in education, technical skills, and innovation?

Human capital development and the demographic dividend in Africa

Human capital theory has been influential in education policy both nationally and internationally. This is based on the assumption that human capital is an economic capital and investment in formal education enhances human capability and economic productivity (Agupusi, 2019). African countries have the potential to turn their young demography into an educated workforce (human capital) that would lead to greater innovation and technological advances, thereby increasing Total Factor Productivity (TFP). This could be achieved by investing in quality education and developing quality institutions. Human capital development is seen as a function of education, health, infrastructure, and institutional indicators (Shuaibu & Timothy, 2016). Human capital and institutions provide the theoretical framework for this chapter and are treated as endogenous in understanding the relationship between development and demographic transition. Institutions and human capital are predictors of development: institutions + human and physical capital = development (North & Thomas, 1973; cf. Acemoglu et al., 2014, p. 2). Human capital is assessed by the quality of education.

No country yet has been able to develop without investing in its human capital through education and organizing its core institutions to promote efficient entrepreneurship and technological innovation (Agupusi, 2016; Acemoglu & Robinson, 2012; North, 1990; Rodrik, Subramanian, & Trebbi, 2004; Glaeser, La Porta, Lopez-de-Silanes, & Shleifer, 2004). Over the past two decades, literacy rates have improved and African countries are striving to build their human capital so they can compete for jobs and attract foreign investment (Majgaard & Mingat, 2012). However, the gender gap in higher education is widening especially in countries like Benin, Cameroon, the Central African Republic, Chad, and Guinea-Bissau, which corresponds with high poverty and Low Total Fertility Rates (TFR) in these countries. According to the World Bank study of Ethiopia, Ghana, and Kenya, there is a causal relationship between female education and fertility decline. See Figure 33.2.

Other studies (Ashraf, Weil, & Wilde, 2013; Mason et al., 2016) show that declining fertility variants reduce TFR and increase annual GDP per capita by 0.225 percentage points. If this continues, it would correspond to the UN-projected average TFR of Africa from 5.71 in 2015 to 2.71 in 2065, and causally, increase annual economic growth by 0.9 percentage point for the span of 50 years (Bloom et al., 2016). Bridging the gender gap in education would increase

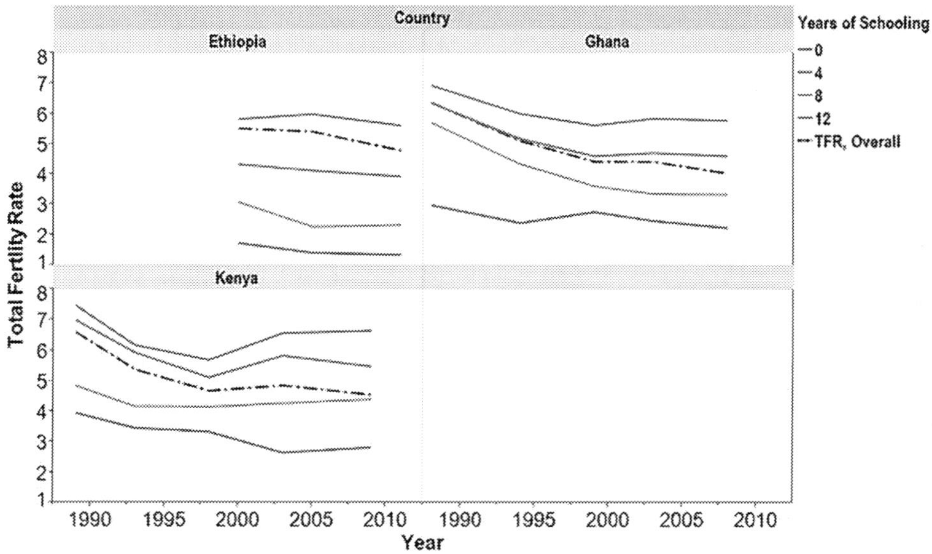

Figure 33.2 Relationship between female education and fertility: Ethiopia, Ghana, and Kenya.

Source: Data from Demographic and Health Surveys in Ethiopia, Ghana and Kenya [1988–2011] (Pradhan, World Bank, 2015)

the share of workers and income, and build a more productive population. For example, in the study of Nigeria, Ashra et al. (2013) projected that reducing Nigeria's TFR from the high-variant to a low-variant level would increase the country's per-capita income to over $13,000 by 2060, as compared to the high fertility scenario. For a country like Nigeria, an increase in per capita does not solely hinge on a reduction in TFR. Other factors such as the quality of education, good governance, and institutions would help to expand the economy in order to absorb labour as needed.

In addition to bridging the gender gap, improving the quality of education would enhance the demographic dividend for development. Meanwhile, while literacy rates have increased quantitatively over the past decade, education quality is lagging far behind. Quality of education is correlated to the level of public expenditures on education. According to the State of Education Report 2015, African countries devote an average of 5% of the total GDP ($1.5 trillion) to public education expenditures. In real terms, this is minimal compared to North America ($32 trillion [5%] of GDP per capita) and Europe ($24 trillion [5%] of GDP per capita), respectively. Some countries in Africa, however, invest even less than others in education. Nigeria and Guinea, for example, spend less than 1% of their GDP, in comparison to countries like South Africa, which spends 6.3% of its GDP on education, and Ghana, which spends 5.5% of its GDP (cf. Agupusi, 2019). Low investment in education also has an impact on school conditions, teacher salaries, and training. A World Bank report finds that the degree of randomness in the distribution of classrooms, textbooks, and school furniture is sometimes higher than that of the distribution of teachers (Majaard & Mingat, 2012). Studies by Ashraf et al. (2013) and Mason et al. (2016) show that investments in physical and human capital turned out to be the dominant drivers over the second stage of demographic transition and demographic dividend for development. Institutions play an important role in human capital development and creating an environment for people to enhance their capabilities, as well as productivity. An inclusive, effective, and efficient institution improves resources for quality education and equitable development.

Analysis

Let's examine the premises of this chapter. With the recognition that Africa is very diverse and population growth and structure varies from countries to countries, the region remains the youngest. i) Demographic transition with a high percentage of young population has a potential to boost development – demographic dividend or undermine development. ii) African countries are still developing and need a quality productive population for innovation, entrepreneurship, and economy of scale. iii) Development is about people achieving their capability to improve their well-being – demographic dividend. iv) To achieve this, an integrated framework that includes quality human capital and institutional arrangement, the right economic policies, and good governance is needed.

Institutions have been central to the discourse on social-economic development. 'Institution is the rule of the game. It is humanly devised constraints that structure human interaction', which became an inspiring frame for facilitating new ways of thinking about the role of institutions in determining economic outcomes (North, 1990). As previously noted, African countries are within stages two and three of the demographic transition, which means a high percentage of young populations. Consequently, there is a high youth dependency rate in Africa. Unemployment is growing with 1 in 5 African youth not employed, educated, or trained (NEET)[6] If this trend continues, African countries will fall into the negative projection of Malthusian theory, and the demographic transition will be stalled, leading to disaster. There is a rising internal political and social violence in different countries (such as Sudan, Mali, Ethiopia, DRC, and Nigeria). Food insecurity continues to rise, and massive migrations in search of opportunities are threatening social cohesion.

Despite the improvement in human capital, the effects of education on the labour market are not encouraging. The economy is growing but not creating enough jobs to absorb the labour force. The African Population Ratio (EPR) has declined slightly. Many African countries remain jobless due to the lack of economic diversification. There are poor infrastructure and ineffective institutions that create a negative economic environment for the young population to thrive and attract foreign direct investment. As a result, even though the average level of school has been increasing, 'the weighted average labour productivity for Sub-Saharan Africa, across all sectors, has remained at practically the same level since 1985' (Majgaard & Mingat, 2012, p. 10). If the economy cannot utilize human capital to its fullest potential, then demography will negate development.

The slow progress of demographic dividend in many African countries is a result of various factors dependent on a particular country's economic and development status. However, institutions and governance are the principal factors that could affect both human capital and economic development. Institutions create incentives for individual members of the economy to form organizations so that they can take advantage of the opportunities. Evidence has shown that countries with inclusive institutions make progress more than the rest (Acemoglu & Robinson, 2012; Agupusi, 2016). However, it has also shown that without good governance, the right policies and institutions will not be enforced.

Summary

Following the analysis, the argument in this chapter is that the relationship between development and population is neutral and dependent on the structure of the population and how a country invests in its demography at different stages to gain quality human capital. In recent years China, India, and other large countries have proven that Malthus's population projections and trap theory are highly avoidable. At the same time, many countries including those in Africa could also fall within the projected negative outcome of food insecurity, increasing poverty, conflicts, and war and underdevelopment. Without the right policies, institutions, and state capacity, demographic change will result in rising poverty. The high youth poverty rates in Africa are due to a lack of jobs and very low-earning jobs in the informal sector. A study by the ILO (2018) shows that the majority of youth both educated and non-educated are engaged in the informal economy. The World Bank study shows an increase in education at all levels. Nevertheless, in terms of labour market outcomes, the rise in the educational attainment of the labour force in the region appears to have had little impact on average labour productivity (Majgaard & Mingat, 2012, p. 10). The study went on to explain this as a mismatch due to shortages of highly skilled labour in science and technology. This explanation failed to recognize that while investment in education could improve human capital, a large working-age population requires a comparable large demand for labour to meet the supply (Canning et al., 2015). And the labour supply and demand can only work with an expanded economy that would demand the available labour and encourage interest in higher education. So, the major challenge African countries in their early stage of demographic transition are facing is in diversifying their economies while investing in human capital development. Without the appropriate social and economic policies, the extra labour supply can result in unemployment and underemployment, which can lead to political instability, elevated crime, and a deterioration of social capital (Urdal, 2006 cf. Canning et al., 2015). A demographic transition is a part of human history. There is little doubt that the relationship between demography and development is neutral. The rise in population and demographic transitions African countries are experiencing could become a development catalyst as seen in many Asian countries like China that anchored its development on its demographic transition. The outcome has been sustained economic development and the lifting of hundreds of millions of its population from poverty. It is important to note that demographic dividend is not only about investing in human capital, rather that it would also involve an integrated approach of human capital and economic development, through an institutional building, right economic policies, and governance.

Conclusion and future research agenda

While this chapter looks at Africa as a whole, it is with the understanding that there is heterogeneity across the region. There are also variations in the stages of demographic transition and development across the region. Except for a few countries in Southern Africa and some island nations, fertility rates and youth dependency rates in sub-Saharan Africa are among the highest in the world, exposing the region to higher poverty rates. There are also smaller investments in children, lower labour productivity, high unemployment and underemployment, and the risk of political instability. This trend could be changed. Africa's potential for enjoying a demographic dividend is large. Over the next few decades, the mortality rate is expected to fall substantially, and half of the population will be within the working age. To sustainably address the employment challenges Africa is facing, particularly for the youth, and to reap the demographic dividend, concerted efforts are required to implement appropriate and customized policies to expand the economy. The four integrated factors – quality human capital, inclusive institutions, sound economic policies, and governance are universal principles for development that could be used to harness the young population for development and a deterrent to falling into the Malthusian population trap.

Lack of robust and valid data is a challenge in African study and this chapter is not an exception. However, a major gap in this study is a research methodology that takes a macro-overview approach. However, this also opens multiple avenues for future research agenda that apply the integrated framework in examining the relationship between demographic changes and development in Africa. Firstly, it is important to conduct an empirical study that takes both qualitative and quantitative approaches to provide a more holistic understanding of the region's challenges in harnessing its demographic changes. Secondly, given the heterogeneity of African countries, examining this relationship in individual countries will address the problem of a one-size-fits-all solution dominant in addressing African developmental problems. The third issue for a further research agenda is the intersection between determinant of economic policy stringency and the negative relationship between higher school attendance and employment. The following questions need to be addressed: 'Why are higher education graduates less productive?' 'What are the right socio-economic policies that suit a particular country?' These would provide answer to the question of institutional arrangement and viable economic environment for the young population to thrive and contribute to the development processes.

Notes

1 See United Nations, Department of Economic and Social Affairs, Population Division (2017, p. XXVII).
2 Poverty is focused on multidimensional poverty.
3 https://blogs.worldbank.org/opendata/which-countries-reduced-poverty-rates-most China has eradicated extreme poverty.
4 Central African Republic, Burundi, Liberia, the Democratic Republic of Congo, Niger, Sierra Leone, Madagascar, Togo, Guinea-Bissau, and the Gambia.
5 See World Bank data https://ourworldindata.org/extreme-poverty-projections 8.
6 This is a conservative estimate due to the informal economy and poor data. ILO (2020) report.

References

Acemoglu, D., Gallego, F. A., & Robinson, J. A. (2014). Institutions, human capital, and development. *Annual Review of Economics*, *6*(1), 875–912.

Acemoglu, D., & Robinson, J. A. (2012). *Why nations fail: The origins of power, prosperity, and poverty*. New York: Crown Business.

Agupusi, P. (2016). Homegrown development initiatives in Africa: Illusion or reality? *Watson Institute for International and Public Affairs Research Paper*, 2016–29.

Agupusi, P. (2019). The effect of parents' education appreciation on intergenerational inequality. *International Journal of Educational Development*, *66*, 214–222.

Allen, R. C. (2008). A review of Gregory Clark's a farewell to alms: A brief economic history of the world. *Journal of Economic Literature*, *46*(4), 946–973.

Ashraf, Q. H., Weil, D. N., & Wilde, J. (2013). The effect of fertility reduction on economic growth. *Population and Development Review*, *39*, 97–130.

Bhattacherjee, A. (2012). *Social science research: Principles, methods, and practices. Textbooks collection*. 3 USF Tampa, Library Open Access. Retrieved from http://scholarcommons.usf.edu/oa_textbooks/3

Bloom, D. E., & Canning, D. (2011). *Demographics and development policy*. Programme on the Global Demography of Aging (PGDA), Working Paper Series, No. 66.

Bloom, D. E., Canning, D., & Sevilla, J. (2003). *The demographic dividend: A new perspective on the economic consequences of population change*. Carlifornia: Rand Corporation.

Bloom, D. E., Kuhn, M., & Prettner, K. (2017). Africa's prospects for enjoying a demographic dividend. *Journal of Demographic Economics*, *83*(1), 63–76.

Bloom, D. E., Mitgang, E., & Osher, B. (2016). *Demography of global ageing*. IZA Discussion Papers, No. 10164. Bonn: Institute of Labour Economics

Bloom, D. E., Sachs, J. D., Collier, P., & Udry, C. (1998). Geography, demography, and economic growth in Africa. *Brookings Papers on Economic Activity, 1998*(2), 207–295.
Brecht, A. (2015). *Political theory: The foundations of twentieth-century political thought* (Vol. 2311). Princeton, NJ: Princeton University Press.
Caldwell, J. C. (2007). *Demographic transition theory*. Netherland: Springer Science & Business Media.
Canning, D., Raja, S., & Yazbeck, A. S. (Eds.). (2015). *Africa's demographic transition: Dividend or disaster?* Washington, DC: The World Bank.
Doran, J. (2012). An analysis of the interdependence of demographic factors, labor effort and economic growth in Ireland. *International Journal of Social Economics, 39*(3), 221–237.
Dyson, T. (2013). *Population and development: The demographic transition*. London, New York: Zed Books Ltd.
Glaeser, E. L., La Porta, R., Lopez-de-Silanes, F., & Shleifer, A. (2004). Do institutions cause growth? *Journal of Economic Growth, 9*(3), 271–303.
Herbst, J. (1990). War and the state in Africa. *International Security, 14*(4), 117–139.
International Labour Organization (ILO) Report. (2018). Women and men in the informal economy: a statistical picture. Retrieved from https://www.ilo.org/wcmsp5/groups/public/---dgreports/---dcomm/documents/publication/wcms_626831.pdf
International Labour Organization (ILO). (2020). *Global employment trends for youth 2020: Africa*. Retrieved November 2020, from www.ilo.org/wcmsp5/groups/public/ – dgreports/ – dcomm/documents/briefingnote/w cms_737670.pdf
Iqbal, K., Yasmin, N., & Yaseen, M. R. (2015). Impact of demographic transition on economic growth of Pakistan. *Journal of Finance and Economics, 3*(2), 44–50.
Jemna, D. V. (2015). Causality relationship between economic development and fertility in Romania on regional level. *Procedia Economics and Finance, 20*, 334–341.
Kirk, D. (1996). Demographic transition theory. *Population Studies, 50*(3), 361–387.
Madsen, J. B., Robertson, P. E., & Ye, L. (2019). Malthus was right: Explaining a millennium of stagnation. *European Economic Review, 118*, 51–68.
Majgaard, K., & Mingat, A. (2012). *Education in sub-Saharan Africa: A comparative analysis*. Washington, DC: The World Bank.
Mason, A., Lee, R., & Xue Jiang, J. (2016). Demographic dividends, human capital, and saving. *The Journal of the Economics of Ageing*, 7, 106–122.
Maurice, M. (2012). *Africa's demographic trends* (Briefing Note 4). Abidjan Cote d'Ivoire: African Development Bank.
Mester, L. J. (2018). Demographics and their implications for the economy and policy. *Cato Journal, 38*, 399.
North, D. C. (1990). *Institutions, institutional change and economic performance*. New York: Cambridge University Press.
North, D. C., & Thomas, R. P. (1973). *The rise of the western world: A new economic history*. Cambridge, MA: Cambridge University Press.
Peng, X. (2011). China's demographic history and future challenges. *Science, 333*(6042), 581–587.
Persson, K. G. (2008). The Malthus delusion. *European Review of Economic History, 12*(2), 165–173.
Pradhan, E. (2015). *Female education and childbearing: A closer look at the data*. Retrieved February 15, 2021, from https://blogs.worldbank.org/health/female-education-and-childbearing-closer-look-data
Rodrik, D., Subramanian, A., & Trebbi, F. (2004). Institutions rule: The primacy of institutions over geography and integration in economic development. *Journal of Economic Growth, 9*(2), 131–165.
Roser, M., & Ortiz-Ospina, E. (2019). *Global extreme poverty. Our world in data*. Retrieved February 2021, from https://ourworldindata.org/extreme-poverty
Sen, A. (2001). *Development as freedom*. Oxford Paperbacks. New York: Anchor book, Random House.
Shuaibu, M., & Timothy, P. O. (2016). Human capital development dynamics in Africa: Evidence from panel cointegration and causality in 33 countries. *Applied Econometrics and International Development, 16*(1), 116–131.
Thompson, W. (1929). Population. *American Journal of Sociology*, 34, 959–975.
United Nations, Department of Economic and Social Affairs, Population Division. (2017). *World population prospects: The 2017 revision, Volume II: Demographic profiles, ST/ESA/SER.A/400*. Retrieved from https://esa.un.org/unpd/wpp/Publications/Files/WPP2017_Volume-II-Demographic-Profiles.pdf and https://esa.un.org/unpd/wpp/
Urdal, H. (2006). A clash of generations? Youth bulges and political violence. *International Studies Quarterly, 50*(3), 607-630

34

THE ECONOMIC LIFECYCLE AND AFRICA'S DEMOGRAPHIC DIVIDEND

Evidence from national transfer accounts

Morné Oosthuizen

Introduction

Declining fertility rates and burgeoning youth populations in countries across Africa have launched heightened interest in the prospect of the demographic dividend (DD). This has been compounded by the urgent need for all African countries to achieve the high and sustained economic growth rates required to improve living standards, reduce poverty, and invest for future growth. Even though fertility rates are falling, African countries can expect to see rapid growth of their youth populations for some time, with ever-increasing numbers of young people entering the labour market in search of jobs. The past decade, therefore, has seen an increased general awareness of and, importantly, significant political support for the realization of the DD.

The DD is defined slightly differently by different authors. Bloom et al. (2003) define it as 'the opportunity for economic growth . . . that [the demographic transition] offers to developing nations'. Weny et al. (2017) define it as 'the acceleration of sustainable development accomplished when declining fertility leads to a bulge in the population entering the labour force', while Groth and May (2017) describe it as 'the accelerated economic growth and increasing surplus resulting from an expansion of the working-age population with respect to the young dependent population'. What definitions of the DD have in common is the acknowledgement that growth of the working-age population relative to the total population has the potential to reduce the dependence on workers to support non-working individuals within the population, benefiting economic growth and development by making resources available to raise living standards and invest in human and other forms of capital.

Africa's population is projected to undergo significant change over the coming decades: the share of the continent's population under 15 years is expected to fall from 40.3% in 2020 to 29.4% by 2060; at the same time, the workingage population will grow from 56.1% to 63.6% of the population, while those aged 65 years and older will double their share to 7.0% (own calculations, United Nations, 2019). These types of shifts in the structure of the population, which later in the demographic transition include population ageing, 'set in motion a vast array of social and economic processes that [lead] to profound changes in society and to important growth in the economy' (Reher, 2012).

 DOI: 10.4324/9780429287213-41

One of the important reasons for these changes is the fact that economic behaviour – producing, consuming, sharing, and saving – varies across the life course. Children produce little if anything in the market, have not had time to save, and therefore their consumption is primarily financed through transfers from family or from government. The elderly may or may not be economically active and, if they are unable to finance their consumption through labour income, the cost must be covered through income from their assets, dissaving, or through transfers from family or from government. During the prime working ages, the average persons earn more from their labour than they consume; they are thus able to share this income directly with others or indirectly through the state, and accumulate assets to support themselves in old age. Together, childhood, productive adulthood, and old age represent the three broad phases of the economic lifecycle, and variations in the age distribution of the population across these three groups imply differing balances between aggregate consumption and aggregate production.

It is the flow of resources across and between generations that National Transfer Accounts (NTA) tries to measure.[1] By quantifying these flows, it becomes possible to analyze the economic lifecycle – the 'patterns of consumption and earnings across age that lead to a mismatch between material needs and the ability to satisfy those needs through own labour' (United Nations, 2013) – and the DD.

The scale of the projected changes in population age structure, and the pace with which African countries will need to create productive employment and expand investments in human capital in order to avoid a 'demographic disaster', necessitate ongoing research to better understand the DD. This is particularly important given the dividend's once-off and transitory nature.

This chapter has three key objectives. Firstly, it draws together findings from the African NTA literature to analyze the first DD. This literature is, however, relatively sparse and a substantial portion of it has been published in non-academic formats. Further, not all authors have been interested in the same metrics of the DD, complicating a coherent cross-country analysis. Therefore, this chapter will, secondly, directly employ the NTA profiles produced by African country teams and included within the NTA database (National Transfer Accounts Project, 2020) to analyze one of the most comprehensive sets of individual African country NTA estimates to date. The important contributions of each of the NTA country teams in establishing the evidence base that make this analysis possible is therefore recognized here. Finally, the chapter highlights some of the key issues that are emerging for future research in the region.

Methods and measures

National transfer accounts and the economic lifecycle

NTAs map resource flows across age groups as individuals 'produce, consume, share, and save resources' (Mason & Lee, 2011b). Together, these four flows reflect the economic lifecycle (Mason & Lee, 2011a) and are influenced by the particular social, economic, institutional, and cultural context.

The NTA framework is developed from the identity between inflows (labour income Y_l, asset income Y_A, and transfer inflows τ^+) and outflows (consumption C, transfers outflows τ^-, and saving S), which holds for individuals, households, and entire economies:

$$\underbrace{Y_l + Y_A + \tau^+}_{Inflows} = \underbrace{C + \tau^- + S}_{Outflows} \tag{1}$$

Through rearrangement, the NTA flow identity is derived, in which x is the age of a given cohort:

$$\underbrace{C(x)-Y_l(x)}_{Lifecycle\ Deficit}=\underbrace{\underbrace{\tau^+(x)-\tau^-(x)}_{Net\ Transfers}+\underbrace{Y_A(x)-S(x)}_{Asset-based\ Reallocations}}_{Age\ Reallocations} \tag{2}$$

In terms of this identity, the difference between consumption and labour income at each age is known as the lifecycle deficit. When the deficit is negative because labour income exceeds consumption, a lifecycle surplus exists. The lifecycle deficit is financed through age reallocations, consisting of net transfers and asset-based reallocations: cohorts with lifecycle deficits obtain resources necessary to cover these deficits through a combination of net transfer inflows – flowing through both private and public channels – asset income, and dissaving.

Each of the flows within the NTA flow identity is further disaggregated. Labour income consists of employment and self-employment income, while all other types of flows are separated into public and private flows. The distinction between public and private flows reflects the types of institutions that act as intermediaries between individuals (United Nations, 2013, p. 27). In addition, NTA distinguishes the rest of the world for certain types of flows.

Given the focus of this chapter, it is worth noting the components that compose consumption. As already noted, consumption is disaggregated into private consumption and public consumption. Within each of these, standard NTA disaggregates between consumption of education, consumption of health, and all other consumption. Consumption of education and health vary significantly and in very particular ways by age.

Broadly speaking, constructing a set of NTAs proceeds as follows. Firstly, using survey or administrative data, a given age profile is constructed to reflect the mean value across the entire population at each age. When an individual does not experience a particular flow – e.g. an unemployed person has no labour income – that individual is included within the calculation with a zero value. Where data is available at an individual level, the profile can be constructed directly from these values. Where data is available at a household level, as is the case for most consumption data, these values are allocated to individuals econometrically, through a standard rule, or using additional information relating to utilization.

The age profiles derived from survey data are often noisy. The second step is to smooth the profiles while ensuring that smoothing does not obscure real discontinuities. A key exception here is education, due to the very specific real patterns of participation and consumption that should not be smoothed away. Age profiles are finally adjusted multiplicatively so that the population-weighted age profiles yield aggregates that equal the corresponding aggregates observed in national accounts and government budgets.

To facilitate cross-country comparisons, each country's age profiles are standardized by dividing them by the mean labour income observed for 30–49-year-olds in that country, termed 'peak labour income' here. This mean labour income is calculated directly from the labour income profile and is unweighted.

The economic support ratio and the first demographic dividend

Using the NTA framework, it is possible to estimate the magnitude and timing of the first and second DDs (Mason et al., 2017). The first dividend arises once boom generations, formed as a bulge in the population pyramid due to falling fertility and mortality rates, begin entering the prime working ages. With fewer dependent children relative to the economically productive population, more resources are available for consumption, saving, and investment in human capital. The second DD arises later, as the boom generations begin to reach retirement age. Faced with extended retirement due to rising longevity, adults may choose to provide for their own retirement by accumulating savings. This coincides with increased investment in the human capital of younger generations as fertility continues to fall. Through this accumulation of both financial and human capital, incomes may be permanently raised. This is the second DD (Mason & Lee, 2006, p. 15). For the purposes of this chapter, only the estimation of the first DD is detailed.

Total consumption in an economy, C, is defined as the share of total income, Y, that is not saved. Thus,

$$C(t) = Y(t) \times [1 - s(t)] \tag{3}$$

where $s(t)$ is the savings rate in period t. To derive a measure of welfare, total consumption (or income) could be divided by the population to yield per-capita consumption (or income). However, as previously noted, both consumption and income vary by age. Based on the NTA concepts, it is possible to define the number of effective consumers N and the number of effective producers L as:

$$N(t) = \sum_{x=0}^{\omega} \phi(x) P(x,t) \tag{4}$$

and

$$L(t) = \sum_{x=0}^{\omega} \gamma(x) P(x,t) \tag{5}$$

Here ϕ and γ respectively represent 'age-specific, time-invariant vectors of coefficients measuring age variation in consumption and productivity' (Mason & Lee, 2007), while $P(x, t)$ is the population of age x in time t ranging from age zero to age ω (the oldest cohort). Put differently, ϕ is the consumption age profile and γ the labour income age profile from equation 2 and, once weighted by the population age structure, equal total consumption and total labour income.

From equation 3, consumption per effective consumer is the product of three factors, namely the savings rate, income per effective producer $Y(t)/L(t)$, and the ratio of effective producers to effective consumers $L(t)/N(t)$:

$$\frac{C(t)}{N(t)} = \frac{L(t)}{N(t)} \times \frac{Y(t)}{L(t)} \times [1 - s(t)] \tag{6}$$

The ratio of effective producers to effective consumers $L(t)/N(t)$ is also referred to as the economic support ratio or the 'NTA support ratio' (Prskawetz & Sambt, 2014). Assuming a constant ratio of labour income to total income over time, equation 6 can be restated in growth terms as:

$$gr\left[\frac{C(t)}{N(t)}\right] = gr\left[\frac{L(t)}{N(t)}\right] + gr\left[\frac{Y(t)}{L(t)}\right] + gr[1 - s(t)] \tag{7}$$

where gr[z] denotes the growth rate of z. The rate of change of the economic support ratio – the first term on the righthand side of equation 7 – provides an estimate of the first DD. A rising support ratio indicates that the number of effective producers is increasing relative to the number of effective consumers, and that consumption per effective consumer is rising, and vice versa. The second term, $gr\left[\frac{Y(t)}{L(t)}\right]$, is the growth rate of income per effective producer, or productivity growth, and is linked to the second DD.

Using estimates of per-capita consumption and labour income across the life course, it is therefore possible to estimate the first DD. It is important to note, however, that these consumption and labour income profiles are held constant over time, while it is only the population age structure that is allowed to change. This is an important constraint, as also noted by Dramani and Oga (2017), given that patterns of economic flows may change significantly over time. However, this approach makes it possible to isolate the impact of changing demography.

The economic lifecycle in African countries

Africa within a global context

Figure 34.1 provides an overview of the patterns of labour income and consumption observed in the 26 African countries for which there are estimates, and places them within the context of the patterns observed globally. The African consumption and labour income profiles are calculated as the median values at each age of the standardized national profiles for countries in the region. The global profiles are similarly constructed.

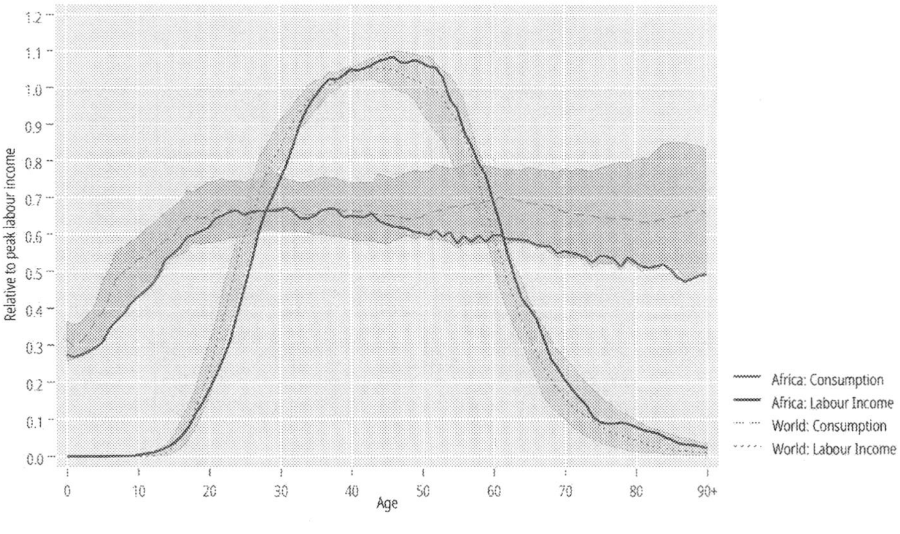

Figure 34.1 Consumption and labour income in Africa.

Source: Own calculations, National Transfer Accounts Project (2020) and Oosthuizen (2018c).

Note: Profiles are constructed as the median value at each age across the country-specific profiles within a given region. Shaded regions are the global interquartile ranges for the consumption and labour income profiles. African countries for which there are data are Benin (2007); Botswana (2010); Burkina Faso (2014); Cameroon (2014); Central African Republic (2008); Chad (2011); Côte d'Ivoire (2014); Eswatini (2011); Ethiopia (2005); Gabon (2005); Gambia (2015); Ghana (2005); Guinea (2012); Guinea-Bissau (2010); Kenya (2005); Mali (2015); Mauritania (2014); Mauritius (2003); Mozambique (2008); Namibia (2012); Niger (2014); Nigeria (2016); São Tomé and Príncipe (2012); Senegal (2011); Sierra Leone (2011); and South Africa (2005).

The African labour income profile follows the conventional pattern: labour income is zero or negligible amongst the very young and the very old, but much higher in the prime working ages. However, the African labour income profile differs from the global pattern in two important respects.

Firstly, per-capita labour income is significantly lower relative to peak labour income amongst African countries than is the case globally, with the African labour income profile lying at the lower bound of the global interquartile range. Between the ages of 22 and 27, per-capita labour income in African countries is 10–14 percentage points lower than is the case globally. Interestingly, the labour income gap emerges as the result of divergence in the labour income profiles before age 25. This gap is the result of a combination of Africa's high levels of youth unemployment and underemployment, and relatively low-productivity work by young people, which contribute to 'deeply ingrained decent work deficits' amongst African youth (International Labour Organisation, 2020).

Secondly, labour incomes tend to be higher amongst elderly African cohorts than amongst their counterparts globally. In absolute terms, the gap is largest between the ages of 58 and 70 years, ranging between 5% and 10% of peak labour income. However, between the ages of 66 and 72 years, per-capita labour income is roughly one third higher in African countries than globally. For cohorts in their eighties and above, African labour income is typically more than twice the global levels. Older Africans, many of whom would be considered of retirement age, clearly remain active in the labour market deeper into old age than their counterparts in other regions. This is indicative of weak provision for retirement, whether through the accumulation of retirement savings or through state old-age pensions. Indeed, just 22.7% of adults above the statutory pensionable age receive a pension in sub-Saharan Africa compared to 67.9% globally (International Labour Organisation, 2017b). This weak support for the elderly is also illustrated by the less precipitous decline in labour income just prior to age 60, indicating that African adults are less likely than their counterparts elsewhere to exit employment or self-employment completely in their late fifties.

The African labour income profile shows evidence of economic activity at very young ages. At age 6, this median profile first rises from zero and is estimated at 1% of peak labour income at age 12. While these values are small, it still means that half of the countries have higher values. Further, low values may obscure high rates of participation if the activities are sufficiently low productivity. Economic activity at such early ages has important implications for the process of human capital accumulation through education and health that is critical for the realization of the first DD.

The African consumption profile tends to be near the lower bound of the global interquartile range. Figure 34.1 shows that per-capita consumption in African countries rises from just under 30% of peak labour income amongst young children to 65% by age 22. It remains at roughly this level until age 43 and then gradually declines to below 60% at age 55. For the oldest cohorts, per-capita consumption is just 50% of peak labour income.

This pattern of labour income that peaks for adults in their twenties and thirties and declines across the remainder of the life course stands in stark contrast to the global pattern that, broadly speaking, sees consumption remain stable across adulthood. Consumption is also relatively low for children in Africa, with a gap ranging between 7% and 12% of peak labour income between the ages of 4 and 13 years, and it is only by the early twenties that the gap is closed.

These gaps are not driven by differences in absolute levels of consumption between richer and poorer countries. Instead, the gap observed at younger ages points to the larger number of children in African countries relative to the working population, implying greater demands placed on the labour incomes of working adults on the continent. The gap in per-capita consumption levels for older adult cohorts is the outcome of institutional contexts that are less supportive of maintaining consumption levels in Africa, whether through public transfers, private transfers, asset income, or dissaving.

Country-specific patterns of labour income and consumption

The median profiles presented obscure substantial cross-country variation. The extent of this variation is illustrated in Figure 34.2, which plots the consumption and labour income profiles

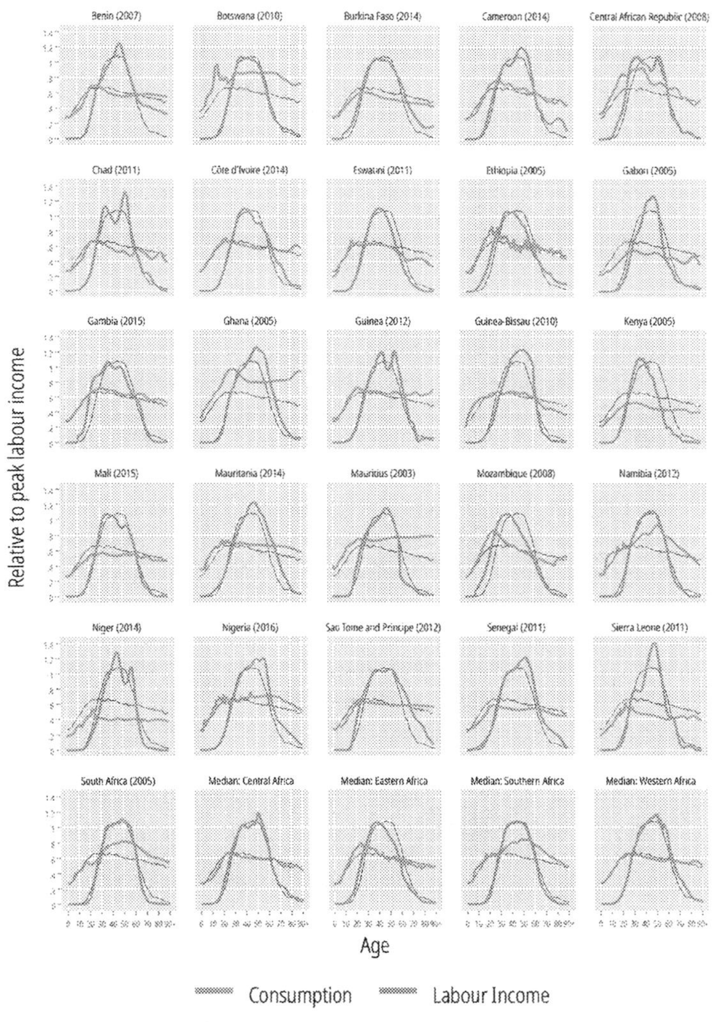

Figure 34.2 Consumption and labour income in African countries.

Source: Own calculations, National Transfer Accounts Project (2020) and Oosthuizen (2018c).

Note: Median consumption and labour income profiles for Africa are represented by solid black lines. Countries are grouped to construct regional aggregates based on the ILO regional classification as follows: Ethiopia, Kenya and Mozambique (Eastern Africa); Botswana, Eswatini, Namibia, and South Africa (Southern Africa); Cameroon, Central African Republic, Chad, Gabon, and São Tomé and Príncipe (Central Africa); and Benin, Burkina Faso, Côte d'Ivoire, Gambia, Ghana, Guinea, Guinea-Bissau, Mali, Mauritania, Niger, Nigeria, Senegal, and Sierra Leone (Western Africa).

for the 26 African countries with NTA estimates, as well as median profiles for Eastern, Southern, Central and Western Africa. Nevertheless, it is possible to identify particular features that characterize multiple countries.

Firstly, low labour income amongst youth cohorts compared to the continental median profile is observed in countries like Gabon, Namibia, Niger, and South Africa.

Secondly, relatively high labour income for young cohorts is observed in the Central African Republic, Ethiopia, the Gambia, Mozambique, and São Tomé and Príncipe.

Thirdly, in some countries, exit from the labour market at older ages is delayed or, for significant proportions of the elderly, does not occur at all, resulting in labour income profiles that do not fall quickly to zero at 'retirement age' or that remain significantly above zero even for the oldest cohorts. Delayed exit is observed in Burkina Faso, Côte d'Ivoire, Mauritania, Nigeria, São Tomé and Príncipe, and Senegal, while elderly cohorts earn significant labour income in countries such as Benin, Burkina Faso, Cameroon, Nigeria, São Tomé and Príncipe, and Senegal.

Conversely, in some countries, exit from the labour market at retirement age is relatively rapid with little labour income observed for elderly cohorts. Good examples are Guinea-Bissau, Kenya, Mali, Mauritius, Namibia, Niger, and South Africa. Mauritius and Guinea-Bissau, in particular, see precipitous declines in per-capita labour income around age 60, while the early decline observed in Kenya is linked to a younger retirement age of 55 years (Mwabu et al., 2011).

As a result, labour income profiles may appear to be shifted towards younger or towards older ages when compared with the African profile. Those that lean towards younger ages include Eswatini and Kenya (due to relatively early declines in per-capita labour income amongst older working-age cohorts), and Ethiopia and Mozambique (due to relatively early rises in per-capita labour income amongst youth). In contrast, labour income profiles lean towards older ages in Ghana, Guinea, Mauritania, Niger, Nigeria, and Senegal.

Various countries' consumption profiles reflect the general pattern of relatively constant per-capita consumption across adulthood; these countries include Guinea, Mali, Mauritania, and Mauritius, which actually see gradually rising consumption with age. In Botswana and Ghana, per-capita consumption is less stable, but still remains relatively constant. Most other countries see falling consumption for older cohorts. Two important exceptions are South Africa and Namibia, where per-capita consumption rises and peaks only in later adulthood before declining steeply for older cohorts.

The level of consumption relative to peak labour income also differs across countries. In Botswana, Central African Republic, Ghana, and South Africa, per-capita consumption is relatively high, while the opposite is true for Burkina Faso, Gabon, Niger, Senegal, and Sierra Leone.

Regionally, the Central African profiles are very similar to those for the continent as a whole, while for Western Africa the only real difference is relatively high labour income amongst older working age and elderly cohorts. In Eastern Africa, per-capita consumption amongst youth is high relative to the continent as a whole, while the labour income profile is clearly shifted to the left, towards younger ages. Southern Africa, on the other hand, has unusually high consumption levels amongst older working age cohorts, and lower labour income amongst youth and post-retirement cohorts.

The lifecycle surplus in African countries

The varying patterns of labour income and consumption observed in Figure 34.2 result in significant differences in the profiles of the lifecycle deficit (consumption less labour income).

These differences impact on the timing and duration of the period of lifecycle surplus, as well as the depth of the deficit or surplus.

Differences in the timing and duration of the lifecycle surplus are summarized in Figure 34.3.[2] Globally, based on median profiles for all countries with data, labour income first exceeds consumption on a per-capita basis at age 27. This period of lifecycle surplus lasts for 32 years, ending at age 58; at older ages, on average, labour income is once again insufficient on its own to finance consumption.

For most world regions, the duration of the lifecycle surplus is 32–33 years, the only exception being Latin America and the Caribbean (LAC) at 26 years. However, there are clear differences in timing: in Asia and the Pacific and Europe and central Asia, the transition to lifecycle surplus occurs at ages 25 and 26 respectively. In contrast, this transition occurs only at age 28 in LAC and at age 29 in Africa. These varying transition ages, combined with slightly different durations, mean that the transition to deficit occurs across a relatively wide age range.

Variation amongst African regions is even greater. At the one extreme are Western and Central Africa, where the duration of the lifecycle surplus is 35 and 36 years respectively; in Southern Africa, in contrast, it is just 27 years. This difference is primarily the result of adults generating lifecycle surpluses at older ages in the former regions. Southern Africa is hard hit by unemployment, particularly amongst youth. However, it is also rather unique on the continent in that countries in the region have relatively substantial formal sectors as well as social assistance systems with strong coverage of the elderly; together, this creates the context for relatively rapid exit from the labour market as cohorts reach retirement age.

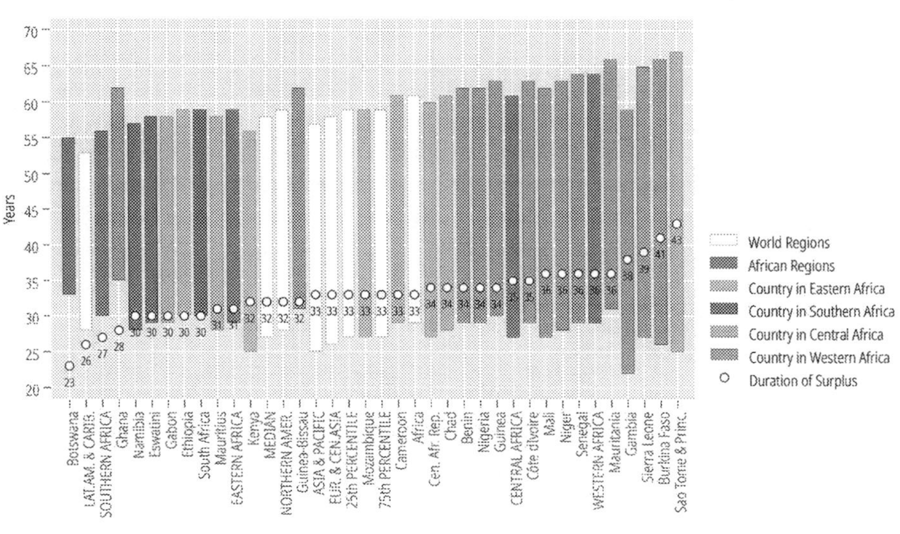

Figure 34.3 Lifecycle surpluses in African countries.

Source: Own calculations, National Transfer Accounts Project (2020) and Oosthuizen (2018c).

Note: Countries are grouped to construct regional aggregates based on the ILO regional classification as follows: Ethiopia, Kenya, and Mozambique (Eastern Africa); Botswana, Eswatini, Namibia, and South Africa (Southern Africa); Cameroon, Central African Republic, Chad, Gabon, and São Tomé and Príncipe (Central Africa); and Benin, Burkina Faso, Côte d'Ivoire, Gambia, Ghana, Guinea, Guinea-Bissau, Mali, Mauritania, Niger, Nigeria, Senegal, and Sierra Leone (Western Africa).

These regional differences are also clear in the positions of countries in the figure. Southern African countries are all located on the left, indicating shorter durations of the lifecycle surplus period. Eastern African countries also tend to be on the left, but not as far left as those in Southern Africa. Central and particularly Western African countries, in contrast, tend to be located on the right.

The analysis of the economic lifecycle raises several important points with respect to the DD. Firstly, even within regions, societies differ significantly in terms of the patterns of consumption and labour income, highlighting the need to construct estimates for more countries. Secondly, the shift between being dependent on non-labour sources of consumption financing and having more than enough labour income to finance consumption is gradual. Thirdly, contrary to common references to the working-age population (15–64-year-olds) as the productive population, the NTA results show much later transitions from economic dependence to independence. Olaniyan, Soyibo, and Lawanson (2012) note that '[child] dependency in Nigeria does not end until age 33'. Finally, apart from differing in terms of the duration of the surplus period and its timing, surpluses (and, indeed, deficits) differ in terms of their magnitude. This is clear from the lifecycle deficits presented in Figure 34.5 in the Appendix.

The demographic dividend

Estimates of the demographic dividend

The per-capita consumption and labour income profiles provide the basis for the estimation of the first DD and, as a result, most researchers have tended to present these estimates as a follow-up to their NTA profiles. Estimating the second DD is more complex and requires additional assumptions beyond the NTA profiles and, as a result, is less common, particularly for African countries.

Since NTAs have yet to be constructed for all countries, Mason, R. Lee, Abrigo, and S. H. Lee (2017) provide a set of regional estimates by modelling NTA profiles for 106 additional countries using the actual profiles for 60 countries, including estimates for African countries constructed by the various teams on the continent. These modelled profiles represent, as the authors freely admit, a second-best option, but are useful in providing a general picture of regional trends. On the basis of these profiles, Mason et al. (2017) calculate regional estimates of the first and second DDs, summarized in Table 34.1 as context to the estimates from African studies that are presented later.

Africa is a clear outlier, with its first DD only beginning in 1993, three decades after it started in Europe. The first dividend is, though, projected to last more than twice as long in Africa than in Europe. The average annual magnitude of the dividend is estimated to be largest in Asia (0.607% per annum), followed by the Americas. Africa's average of 0.373% is slightly higher than that of Europe and Oceania.

However, combining these averages with the duration of the dividend period reveals that Africa and Asia will have experienced the largest cumulative first DDs: in Africa, demographic change is projected to raise living standards by a total of 35.1%, with a similar effect expected in Asia (34.8%). At its peak, however, Africa's first DD is not particularly large – it is around three fifths of that observed in Asia (0.82% compared to 1.38% in Asia) – and the peak occurs 25 years after the start of the dividend period, later than any of the other regions.

The long duration of the first DD period in Africa means that, over the 100 years from its start, the first DD is estimated to average 0.32%, compared to 0.18% in Asia and -0.08% in Europe. However, the second dividend is projected to be twice as large over the same period

Table 34.1 Estimated Demographic Dividends by World Region

	Africa	*Americas*	*Asia*	*Europe*	*Oceania*
First Dividend					
Start year	1993	1975	1973	1962	1974
Duration	92	58	58	38	65
% per year	0.373	0.502	0.607	0.346	0.291
Cumulative %	35.1	30.6	34.8	15.0	20.6
Peak dividend (dividend year)					
First	0.82 (25)	0.84 (19)	1.38 (20)	0.68 (22)	0.66 (14)
Second	1.33 (51)	1.15 (43)	1.88 (42)	1.24 (37)	1.24 (38)
Combined	1.80 (48)	1.51 (33)	2.35 (34)	1.35 (28)	1.50 (28)
Average dividend, 100 years					
First	0.32	0.15	0.18	-0.08	0.09
Second	0.67	0.67	0.72	0.56	0.71
Combined	1.00	0.82	0.90	0.48	0.80

Source: Mason et al. (2017, pp. 25, 35).

Note: Country-level data is unweighted in constructing regional or global estimates. Years are counted from the year in which the first demographic dividend was first positive.

(0.67%) and, although it is slightly smaller than those of Asia, Oceania, and the Americas, it combines with the relatively large first dividend to create the largest combined dividend amongst all regions. At 1.00% per annum over the century, Africa's combined DD over the 100 years is more than 10% larger than that in Asia and more than twice that of Europe.

African authors have published estimates of the first DD for various African countries, although no published estimates of the second DD have been found. Table 32.2 summarizes estimates of the first DD for 12 African countries and three regional groupings.

There is wide variation in the timing of the first DD across African countries. This is not surprising given the different stages of the demographic transition in which African countries find themselves. At one extreme is Mauritius, whose first DD has already turned negative. In other countries, such as Botswana and South Africa, the DD period began prior to 1990 and is expected to end by the 2040s. Most countries, however, saw their first DDs turn positive during the 1990s or later, and these positive dividends will last beyond 2050.

Few authors report the magnitude of the first DD over the entire period during which it is positive, whether on an annual average or cumulative basis, although most either report the magnitude of the dividend at its peak or depict it graphically, enabling the approximate value to be read off the graph. The peak value of the dividend ranges from 1.5% per annum in Botswana at its 2008 peak to 0.5% per annum or less in countries such as Mozambique in the late 2020s and Senegal in the late 2010s.

Importantly, of the 12 countries presented in Table 34.2, only Niger has not yet entered the DD period. That said, Niger has seen prior short-lived spells in the 1950s, 1970s, and 1990s, during which demographic change is estimated to have had a positive impact on living standards.

In a study covering 16 African countries mainly in West Africa, Dramani and Oga (2017) analyze DDs using NTA estimates, focussing primarily on the support ratio and its rate of change (i.e. the first DD) for 2015–2016. Based on their estimates, the authors find that only in Niger was the support ratio not already rising by 2015–2016, with the rate of change as high as 0.73% in Ethiopia (Dramani & Oga, 2017).

Table 34.2 Estimated First Demographic Dividends in African Countries and Regions

Country	*Base Year*	*Duration*	*Peak Year*	*Peak Value*	*Source*
Botswana	2010	P1990– L2040s	2008	1.5%	AFIDEP (2018)
Burkina Faso	2014	1996–2050+	2033	0.58%	Republic of Burkina Faso (n.d.c)
Chad	2016	2009–2050+	2040s	0.78%	Republic of Chad (n.d.c)
Eswatini	2010	P1990–2060+	2019/20	1.13%	Kingdom of Swaziland (2017a)
Ghana	2005	1990–2050+	2031	± 0.65% *	Amporfu, Sakyi, and Frimpong (2014)
Mauritania	2014	1988–2050+	E2000s	± 0.55% *	Islamic Republic of Mauritania (n.d.a)
Mauritius	2003	P1990–2010	n.a.	over 1.0% *	Oosthuizen and Lilenstein (2018)
Mozambique	2008	2009–2050+	L2020s	± 0.5% *	Chipembe, Gaspar, Mariano, Maunze, and Munamoha (2013)
Namibia	2010	P1990–2060+	1997	0.87%	Republic of Namibia (2018)
Niger	2014	2028–2050+ (positive spells in 1950s, 1970s, and 1990s)	n.a.	n.a.	Republic of Niger (n.d.c)
Nigeria	2004	±2004–2050+	2030s	± 0.65% *	Soyibo, Olaniyan, and Lawanson (2013)
	2004	2003–2050+	2031	± 1.25% *	Olaniyan et al. (2012)
	2016	2000–2050+	2034	Just under 1.0%	Olaniyan et al. (2018a)
Senegal	2005	2000–2050+	E2020s	± 0.7% *	Dramani and Ndiaye (2012)
	2005	P2000–2050+	L2010s	± 0.4% *	Dramani, Ndiaye, and Ouarmé (2013)
South Africa	2005	M1970s – L2040s	E1990s	± 0.9% *	Oosthuizen (2013)
	2005	1975 – M2040s	M1990s	Just over 1.0%	Oosthuizen (2014b)
	2005	1977–2006; 2014–2050+	E1990s	Over 1.0%	Oosthuizen (2014a)
	2015	P1990 – ±2041	n.a.	Over 0.9%	Oosthuizen (2019)
SWEDD	unsp.	2012–2050+	n.a.	Over 0.6%	CREG (n.d.b)
Central Africa	unsp.	2007–2050+	±2030 *	n.a.	Dramani (2019)
Western Africa	unsp.	1997–2050+	n.a.	n.a.	Dramani (2019)

Note: Base year refers to the base year of the estimated NTA profiles. In the table, the following abbreviations are used: P = Pre; E = Early; M = Mid; L = Late. Not all figures are reported in each source: when this is the case, figures are estimated based on graphical representations of the first demographic dividend and are indicated by an asterisk (*). When first dividends are projected to last beyond 2050 or 2060, these are indicated by '2050+' or '2060+'. SWEDD countries are Burkina Faso, Chad, Côte d'Ivoire, Mali, Mauritania, and Niger. When figures are marked as not available (n.a.), the source does not report the value nor is it possible to determine an approximate value from graphical representations of the dividend.

The demographic dividend and the window of opportunity

Table 34.2 paints an unusual picture of the DD for those more familiar with analyses of the DD framed in terms of the 'window of opportunity' or 'demographic window', defined by United Nations (2004) as the period during which children under 15 years and those aged 65 years and older account for less than 30% and 15% of the population respectively.

In essence, the notion of the demographic window is one embedded in dependency ratios. This it has in common with a large part of the DD literature (e.g. Bloom, Canning, & Malaney, 2000). Thus, the window of opportunity views children under 15 years and older adults aged 65 years and above as economically dependent – a burden on society – supported by the population aged 15–64 years.

Despite being computationally simple, the approach has important drawbacks. Firstly, while the age cut-offs correspond to those of the working-age population, they are somewhat arbitrary (Mason & R. Lee, 2007) and consequently result in misclassification. Such fixed-age cut-offs 'do not take into account current demographic, economic and social circumstances' (Dramani & Oga, 2017), nor do they account for differences between countries or over time in societal patterns of consumption and income that exist due to various institutional and other factors (Prskawetz & Sambt, 2014). It is also entirely possible that the window of opportunity may be closed in one country but, in a second country with an identical dependency ratio, it may be open. These issues are resolved by NTAs, which allow for gradual shift between states of dependence and non-dependence.

Critically, though, the window-of-opportunity approach paints a very different picture of the DD and, in particular, its timing. To illustrate this, Figure 34.4 presents the projected first DD for the 26 countries over the 1970–2070 period, calculated using the per-capita consumption and labour income profiles and population projections from the *2019 Revision of the World Population Prospects* (United Nations, 2019). The shaded area in each plot represents the period during which the window of opportunity will be open; the year in the bottom righthand corner of each plot is the year in which the window opens for that country. It should be noted that in all but one country (namely Mauritius) the window of opportunity is projected to remain open beyond 2070; in the case of Niger, the window does not open at all before 2070.

The window of opportunity clearly puts the dividend period significantly further into the future than does the NTA approach. Indeed, the NTA estimates indicate that each of the 26 countries has already started enjoying a positive first dividend. The only exceptions are Niger, where the dividend is projected to begin in the mid-2020s, and Mauritius, where the first DD period has already passed. There are also important differences across regions. In the four Southern African countries presented, the peak of the first DD has already passed, with South Africa having the smallest remaining dividend in terms of both annual magnitude and duration. Amongst Western and Central African countries, most are in the early stages of the dividend period. Further, 14 of these 18 countries have not yet reached their peak dividends. In Eastern Africa, the picture is more diverse: Ethiopia and Mozambique are still approaching their peak dividend periods, Kenya is about to see rapid decline in the magnitude of its annual dividend, while Mauritius is already experiencing a negative first DD.

In contrast to NTA-based estimates of the DD, the window of opportunity is open in 2020 in only two countries, Mauritius and South Africa. In many instances, the window opens half a century or more after the first DD is projected to have turned positive. From a policy perspective, this is extremely problematic. In the vast majority of African countries, the window of opportunity presents a potential benefit that will arise decades into the future. Thus, while there is pressure for policymakers to make the appropriate choices, there is relatively little urgency

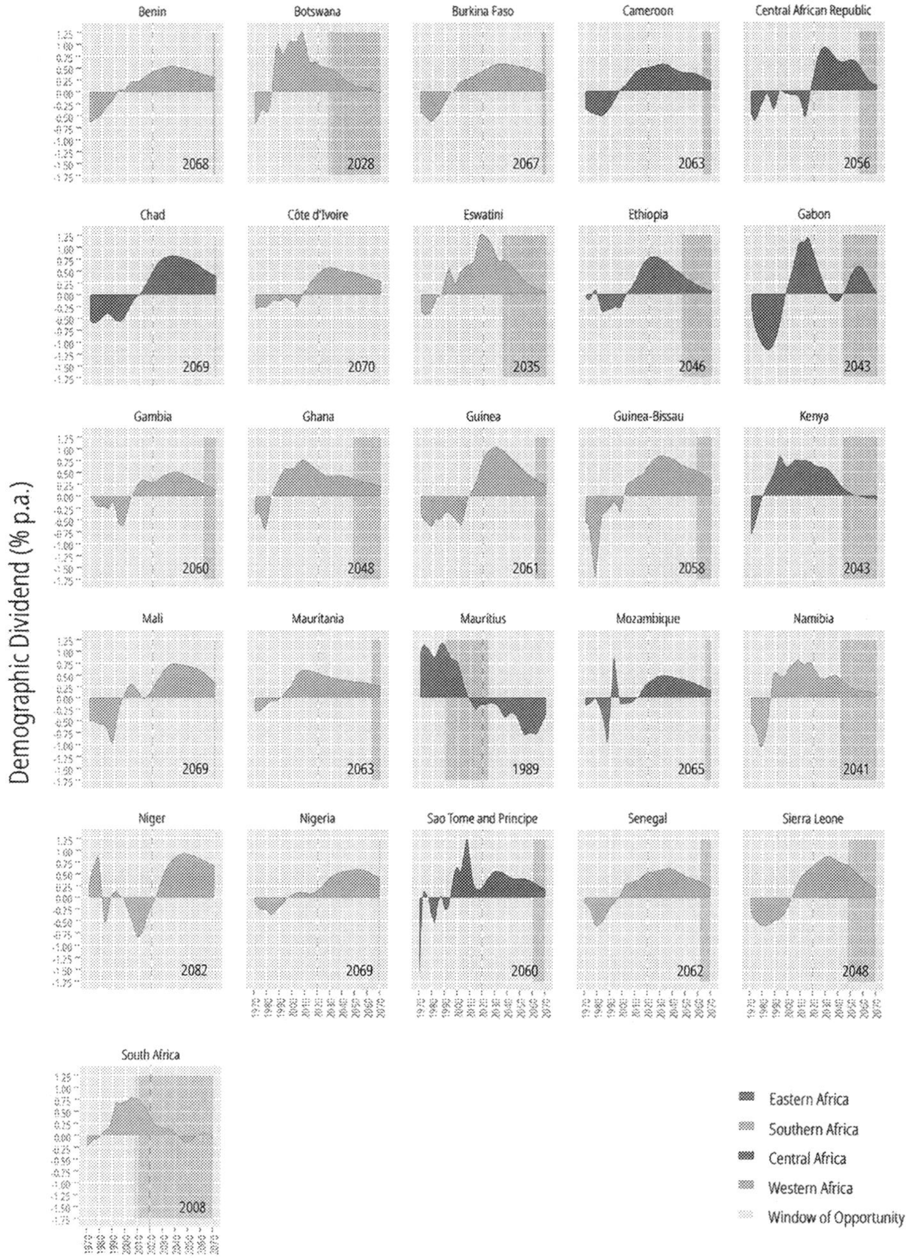

Figure 34.4 The first demographic dividend and the window of opportunity.

Source: Own calculations, using National Transfer Accounts Project (2020), United Nations (2019), and Oosthuizen (2018c).

Note: Demographic dividends are calculated using NTA profiles and the latest population projections from the United Nations (2019). Years in the bottom righthand corner of each graph indicate the year in which the window of opportunity – when the share of the population under the age of 15 years is below 30%, and the share aged 65 years and older is below 15% – is expected to open. The dotted vertical line indicates the year 2020.

and difficult policy choices can relatively easily be deferred beyond the next election. However, NTA estimates, which are based on a more nuanced measure of economic dependence, bring a much greater sense of immediacy and urgency.

Policy for a demographic dividend

Projections such as those presented in Figure 34.4 may convey a sense of inevitability that they will materialize at a specific time and at a particular magnitude. One of the challenges with the DD research is, therefore, ensuring that particularly policy audiences are clear that the dividend represents a potential benefit to the economy. This is despite the fact that the global literature on the DD has, since its inception, emphasized that harnessing the dividend is contingent on a supportive economic, policy, and institutional context (Bloom, Canning, & Sevilla, 2003; United Nations, 2004).

Poor policymaking may therefore mean that African countries might not be able to fully harness the DD. Conversely, good policymaking has the potential to reinforce the DD. The potential for stronger (or weaker) DDs lies in the fact that NTA-based estimates of the DD are grounded in profiles of consumption and labour income that reflect the economy at a particular point in time. Thus, to the extent that future patterns of production and consumption are 'better' or 'worse' than they were in the base year, a larger or smaller dividend may be realized.

Policy-focussed NTA research on the first DD tends to focus on four key areas, namely fertility, the labour market, human capital (education and health), and institutions and good governance. These policy areas are discussed in further detail below.

Fertility

The DD arises as societies proceed through the demographic transition and it should therefore come as no surprise that fertility is a key factor influencing the realization of the DD. Bloom et al. (2003) highlight health policy's centrality to the achievement of the DD in initiating the demographic transition itself: 'Improved sanitation, immunization programs, antibiotics, and contraceptives initiate the declines in mortality that lead to declines in fertility, which together cause changes in the age distribution and size of a population'. Indeed, that African countries have been slow to enter the first DD periods is linked to persistently high fertility rates that have slowed the demographic transition (Bloom & Canning, 2011; Shapiro & Hinde, 2017).

The slow pace of the demographic transition in many African countries further results in a lower peak for the first DD, even while extending the dividend period and dampening the dividend's impact once it turns negative (Mason et al., 2017). This relationship between the pace of the demographic transition and the magnitude of the DD is also highlighted by others (Canning, Raja, & Yazbeck, 2015; UNFPA, 2014) and implies a role for policymaking. Canning et al. (2015) identify scope for policy aimed at hastening the demographic transition by extending access to family planning services, lowering rates of child mortality, and improving educational outcomes for girls and women; the UNFPA and AFIDEP (2015) make policy recommendations along similar lines.

The impact of alternative fertility trajectories on the DD has been modelled for various African countries. For South Africa, Oosthuizen (2015) finds that lower fertility is associated with a shorter period of positive first DD but that the dividend tends to be larger in any given year. Chipembe et al. (2013) show that projections using the low fertility rather than the medium fertility variant 'show an annual boost to economic growth of 0.5 percent or more for 20 years from 2019 to 2039'. Similarly, CREG (n.d.b) project a substantially higher first dividend in the presence of lower fertility for the Sahel region. Positive effects are also found for Botswana (AFIDEP, 2018), Eswatini (Kingdom of Swaziland, 2017a), Kenya (Mwabu, Muriithi, & Mutegi, 2013), Mauritania (Islamic Republic of Mauritania, n.d.a), and Senegal (Dramani et al., 2013).

The magnitude of this effect is estimated in a number of countries. For example, while the cumulative effect of the first DD in Botswana between 2010 and 2060 under the medium-fertility assumption is a 19% increase in living standards, it is as high as 24% if the low-fertility projections are used and as low as 9% assuming constant fertility (AFIDEP, 2018). In Eswatini, the cumulative effect of the DD rises from 32% to 40% if the low rather than the medium fertility assumption is used (Kingdom of Swaziland, 2017a); for Namibia, the corresponding figures over the same period are 22% and 28% (Republic of Namibia, 2018).

In the higher fertility countries of Western and Central Africa, lower fertility is found to have substantial effects on the magnitude of the first DD. CREG (n.d.b) find that, by 2035, the DD under the low fertility assumption would be twice the size of that under the high fertility assumption for a combined group of six West African countries. This finding is borne out in the individual country estimates (Republic of Burkina Faso, n.d.c; Islamic Republic of Mauritania, n.d.d).

Labour markets

The labour market is key to harnessing the DDs. As Ahmed, Cruz, Go, Maliszewska, and Osorio-Rodarte (2014) note, harnessing the dividend is contingent on whether 'the burgeoning working age population can be gainfully employed and if the boost in savings (and thus investment) predicted by theory can be realised'. However, given the rate at which this cohort is expected to grow within Africa, ensuring that good quality jobs are created at the pace required to absorb new labour market entrants – and to maintain that pace over the course of decades – remains an immense challenge.

Depending on the country context, policy options may vary, although NTAs are generally silent on which specific policies to pursue. Bloom et al. (2003) highlight '[open] economies, flexible labor forces, and modern institutions' as key factors, noting that the establishment of social safety nets and interventions aimed at facilitating the movement of workers out of occupations and sectors in decline may be essential in making flexibility more palatable to workers. What is clear, however, is that without the requisite economic growth, these job opportunities will not materialize and investments in human capital will not yield their expected returns. Crucially, however, cohorts in the productive ages will be constrained in their ability to accumulate assets in preparation for their retirement, thwarting the realization of the second dividend before it has even started.

Current labour market conditions in many African countries, however, remain challenging. Formal sectors tend to be small, many workers are confined to low productivity activities, and underemployment is common. Relative to formal employment, informal and other low-productivity employment serves to depress per-capita labour income, while at the same time potentially constraining public consumption and investment through its effects on tax revenues (Amporfu et al., 2014).

Underemployment is highlighted as a key concern by Dramani and Ndiaye (2012) who note that Senegal's 10% unemployment rate hides the fact that 23% of the employed are underemployed with very low incomes. Concern regarding the constraints imposed on the DD by current labour market conditions is also raised in countries such as Ghana, where just 2% of new labour market entrants reportedly find employment in the formal sector (Amporfu et al., 2014).

Similarly, with 43% of Nigerian youth either unemployed or underemployed, Olaniyan et al. (2018b) argue that the realization of Nigeria's DD hinges on the creation of wage employment on a 'massive' scale. According to Bloom et al. (2010), the country would need to 'create around 50 million jobs over 2010–2030' to realize the dividend.

It is, though, important to remember that the current state of the labour market is already built into countries' labour income profiles. Thus, estimates of the DD assume that the current state remains unchanged and, while deteriorating labour market conditions would limit the magnitude of the dividend that is eventually achieved, improvements may reinforce the dividend.

This type of improvement in labour market conditions has been modelled for a number of countries on the continent. This has typically been done through gradually adjusting the labour income profile towards an 'ideal' profile and suggests potential to significantly boost the DD, even for countries in the late stages of their first dividend period. In Botswana, convergence of the labour income profile of youth cohorts to that of the median NTA country between 2015 and 2035 nearly doubles the cumulative effect of the DD over that period from 11.7% (no convergence) to 20.5% (AFIDEP, 2018). Similar results are found for Eswatini – convergence of the labour income profile for youth to that of the median NTA country is projected to raise the cumulative dividend for 2015–2060 from 33% to 41% (Kingdom of Swaziland, 2017a) – and Namibia, where the same convergence process yields a cumulative dividend of 31% over the 2010–2060 period, compared to the baseline of 22% (Republic of Namibia, 2018).

Human capital

Human capital – encompassing health and education – is a key channel through which the DD is harnessed. The role of health policy in driving the demographic transition has already been noted, but, beyond triggering and helping sustain the demographic transition, appropriate health policies are key to ensuring a healthy, productive population. As Bloom and Canning (2011) note, '[better] health means that students learn more quickly, workers produce more effectively, foreign investors are more likely to be attracted, and savings rise'.

Recent experience has shown that a lack of resourcing of the health system or an inadequate response to health crises can seriously jeopardize the DD, with the HIV/AIDS pandemic being a particularly pertinent example. Whiteside and Zebryck (2017), for example, argue that HIV/AIDS placed the DD 'under threat in parts of Africa', through its disproportionate impact on younger working-age adults. Without robust interventions, HIV/AIDS undermines a population's productive capacity by limiting labour market engagement by those living with the disease, and eventually negatively impacts the size of the working-age population when they die. Further, those required to care for sick family members may see their own ability to find and keep employment negatively impacted. Similarly, the effect on Africa's DD of the global COVID-19 pandemic will operate through a range of channels, including the labour market and human capital accumulation, and is likely to be significant.

Investment in education makes sense for the harnessing of the DD for several reasons. Better-educated workers are able to earn more in the labour market than those with less education, raising per-capita incomes and boosting both the first and second DDs. Further, there is evidence to suggest that more educated populations may benefit most from the DD (Drummond, Thakoor, & Yu, 2014). The key challenge for many African countries relates to the scale of education provision required. As Soyibo, Mwabu, Olaniyan, and Muriithi (2012) note, '[in] economies with high youth dependency ratios, families tend to be heavily burdened with health and education expenditures [and] because these human capital investments must be spread over a large number of children, spending per child is low'.

Investing in particularly girls' education has a number of effects that reinforce the DD. Since higher levels of education are associated with higher opportunity costs of not working, investing in education encourages greater labour force participation amongst women (International Labour Organisation, 2017a). More educated women are also less likely to hold strongly patriarchal values and have greater bargaining power within their households, both of which ease their participation in the labour force (Diwan & Vartanova, 2017). In turn, more education is associated with delayed marriage and childbearing, and possibly lower lifetime fertility although the effect, if any, is small (Chakravarty, Das, & Vaillant, 2017; Heath & Jayachandran, 2017).

Overall, there is evidence from NTA research of a quality-quantity trade-off in terms of human capital investment. R. Lee and Mason (2010) find, using NTA data for 19 countries, that 'human capital expenditures per child are substantially higher where fertility is lower, to the extent that the product of the total fertility rate and human capital spending per child is roughly a constant share of labor income across countries'. Thus, it appears that part of the proceeds from the first dividend may be allocated to human capital accumulation, 'reinforcing the economic benefits of fertility decline' and potentially '[reducing] or at least [postponing] the support problems brought on by population aging' (R. Lee & Mason, 2010). A similar pattern is found for 10 African countries with total fertility rates ranging between 4.5 and 8.0 by Dramani and Oga (2017): human capital spending per child is found to range from 103% to 379% of peak labour income, suggesting that lower fertility may free up significant amounts of resources for raising living standards or further investing in children's human capital.

Based on estimates from 34 countries, Mason and R. Lee (2012) find that a fall in the number of births per woman of 10% is associated with an 8% rise in per-capita spending on human capital accumulation. However, the authors find that this relationship is weakened in low-income countries, implying weaker second DDs than would normally have been expected given the experience of other countries.

Institutions

Given the policy complexities and long-time horizons over which various policies operate, the quality of institutions is critically important in harnessing the DD (Bloom et al., 2003; R. Lee, S. H. Lee, & Mason, 2006; UNFPA & AFIDEP, 2015). The term is used very broadly and encompasses aspects such as political freedoms and openness; levels of corruption; openness of trade; infrastructure quality (including education, healthcare, communications, and transport infrastructure); and appropriate labour market regulation (Bloom, Canning, Fink, & Finlay, 2007).

Institutional quality is fundamental to the attainment of the DD in two respects. Good quality institutions help to create the economic, social, legal, and policy context supportive of the DD process, while also helping balance the costs and benefits of policy interventions across generations. Critically for many developing countries, 'corruption and rent seeking by an extractive ruling elite could lead to a situation in which the gains from declining fertility are largely wasted and a DD does not emerge' (Bloom et al., 2007).

A multiplicity of interrelated factors influences the extent to which countries are able to harness the DD, limiting the effectiveness of isolated policy interventions. Instead, policymakers are required to be active across a range of areas, from population policy to education and skills development, to health, to economic policy that includes all sections of society within the growth process, and to the development and strengthening of institutions.

Taking the NTA demographic dividend research in Africa forwards

While the core NTA methodology has been firmly established, researchers have begun exploring new areas by adapting the methodology to address emerging research questions. Much of the research in Africa has focussed on describing the economic lifecycle and estimating the first DD, but it is clear that more nuanced research is required to inform policy that aims to fully harness the DD.

The NTA research effort on the continent is hampered by a number of factors. Perhaps foremost amongst these is the relatively low levels of capacity. Even though there are estimates for 26 countries on the continent, not all of these countries have teams and the broader pool of researchers is relatively small. A second constraint, also raised by Dramani and Oga (2017), relates to infrequent data collection. Given the cross-sectional nature of the NTA estimates, it is important that estimates are updated regularly. However, the required underlying household surveys are often not conducted according to a regular or relatively frequent schedule. As a result, in many African countries it is only possible to construct one or two sets of accounts within the last 20 years, which prevents the type of active monitoring and feedback needed to inform policymaking in this area.

While country priorities may vary, there are four key research areas that merit attention from African NTA researchers, namely gender, the urban-rural divide, education, and inequality. Common to all four of these areas is the fact that NTAs are national-level estimates, averaged over the entire population within each age cohort, and hence they obscure the extent of variation across different sub-groups.

Gender

Disaggregations of NTA profiles by gender reveal stark differences between males and females across a range of NTA flows. While the extent of the differences may vary, where it has been most apparent is in the labour income profile: males consistently outproduce women irrespective of the country. As a result, males tend to produce large lifecycle surpluses while women produce much smaller surpluses or even no surpluses in some countries. A key reason for this is NTA's link to national accounts, which explicitly excludes the unpaid care work predominantly performed by women and girls in households around the world. Thus, much of the productive activity of women and girls is invisible within the standard NTA framework.

At the same time, there are numerous reasons why it would be interesting to analyze males and females separately. The opportunities, constraints, available choices, traditional roles, societal norms, institutional rules, and rights that characterize the lived experience of women differ, in large and small ways, from those experienced by men. These factors influence production, consumption, sharing, and saving – and therefore the gender-specific economic lifecycle – in different ways.

These two factors have underpinned the development of the National Time Transfer Accounts (NTTA) methodology, which incorporates unpaid care work – both direct care for others and indirect care activities, such as cooking and cleaning – into estimates of the economic lifecycle (Donehower, 2018). This is achieved through quantifying the time spent on these activities, typically on the basis of time-use survey data, and imputing a wage used to value this time. This production is analogous to labour income, while the imputed consumption of this care work mirrors market consumption within the standard NTA framework. Together, these estimates of market and household production and consumption can be integrated to estimate a total lifecycle deficit that is more representative of total production and consumption.

Full NTTA estimates have been constructed for a number of African countries, although African time-use data is scarce. These include Ghana (Amporfu, Sakyi, Frimpong, Arthur, & Novignon, 2018), Mauritius (Oosthuizen & Lilenstein, 2018), Senegal (Dramani & Akpo, n.d.), and South Africa (Oosthuizen, 2018a, 2018b). Where time-use data does not exist, gender-disaggregated NTA profiles have been published for Burkina Faso (Republic of Burkina Faso, n.d.b), Chad (Republic of Chad, n.d.b), Mali (Republic of Mali, n.d.b), Mauritania (Islamic Republic of Mauritania, n.d.b), Niger (Republic of Niger, n.d.b), and for a group of six West African countries (CREG, n.d.a).

In each of these studies that report on this, males have been found to outproduce females in the market over most, if not all, of the life course. Relatively low levels of labour income amongst women mean that they generate much smaller lifecycle surpluses over shorter periods of time than do men (Burkina Faso, Chad, Mauritania, South Africa in 2010). In some countries, such as Ghana, Mali, Mauritius, and South Africa (in 2000), women are found to produce no surplus at all. In Niger, though, the surplus period is only slightly smaller for women than men and the difference in the magnitude of the surplus is relatively small. However, once care work is accounted for, women are often found to spend more time in productive activities than men over most of the life course.

The NTTA work raises two important issues related to the DD that are worth noting. Firstly, the key costs (as reflected by per-capita consumption) related to infants and small children are time costs. For example, Mauritian estimates suggest that including the value of the consumption of care by infants raised per-capita consumption by 160% (Oosthuizen & Lilenstein, 2018). Such costs are important to understand, particularly in the context of low-fertility countries such as those in Northern Africa.

Second, gender-disaggregated labour income profiles make it possible to assess the impact on the DD of reducing gender inequalities. Oosthuizen (2018b), for example, estimates the impact on the South African DD of narrowing the gender gap in the labour income profiles over a 40-year period from 2010 to 2050, and finds that narrowing the gap by 25% (by raising female labour income) leads to a doubling of the cumulative effect of the first DD over that period. Such calculations are useful but should be contextualized by the fact that women already spend as much as, if not more time in productive activities than men. Thus, efforts to close this gap should be about more than simply shifting women into the labour market in order to be effective: they should address inequalities in the distribution of care work, as well as inequalities in educational attainment, access to jobs, and remuneration.

The gender-related NTA work in Africa has not yet pushed further to assess the extent to which gender inequalities may be limiting the potential benefits from the DD. In doing so, the research should be careful not to portray women as an untapped source of additional labour, and should engage with the key issues relating to gender equity across the life course both in the market and at home.

Inequality, education, and the urban-rural divide

Inequality is an important challenge in many African countries and may become increasingly problematic as economies grow and develop. Most recent estimates suggest that eight of the ten most unequal countries as measured by the Gini coefficient are in Africa, with Southern Africa particularly unequal (World Bank, 2020). International comparisons of NTAs indicate that labour income and consumption profiles may differ systematically depending on, amongst other factors, the relative wealth of the country (Mason et al., 2017, for example). This suggests that differences may be observed between income groups within countries. Thus, ongoing societal changes in African countries may significantly influence the generational economy, and the DD more specifically, through effecting 'compositional' shifts within national populations. This raises the question of how these changes might impact the extent to which national level profiles remain representative over time.

Analysis of inequalities in the context of NTA has typically entailed the construction of separate accounts for different sub-populations. These sub-populations have been defined in a variety of ways in developing countries, including socio-economic status (Turra & Queiroz, 2005), educational attainment (Fernàndez-Varela & Mejía-Guevara, 2012), or by urban-rural location (Maliki, 2011; Shen & S. H. Lee, 2014).

Despite this growing global NTA literature related to inequality, relatively few African studies have taken this approach. The key exceptions are the urban-rural disaggregations that were conducted as part of the research in a number of West African countries (Republic of Burkina Faso, n.d.a; Republic of Mali, n.d.a; Islamic Republic of Mauritania, n.d.c; Republic of Niger, n.d.a; Republic of Chad, n.d.a), regional estimates for Senegal (CREFAT, n.d.), and race-disaggregated estimates for South Africa (Oosthuizen, 2019). Despite its relative paucity, this research provides important insights into the differences in the economic lifecycle between different groups within African societies.

In countries that expect to see significant rural-to-urban migration, these disaggregated estimates may prove useful in generating more nuanced estimates of the DD. The same is true for sub-populations defined by educational attainment in contexts wherein improvements in education are expected to be significant over the coming decades.

It is clear, though, that inequality has the potential to significantly 'distort' the national-level NTA profiles. According to Oosthuizen (2019), 'national-level profiles can be distorted by a combination of economic inequality and demographic differences'. Importantly, using sub-population consumption and labour income profiles, Oosthuizen (2019) also shows that estimates of the DDs using national-level profiles may be significantly impacted – in terms of magnitude and timing – in a high-inequality context where richer and poorer groups are at different points in the demographic transition.

Conclusion

Issues pertaining to the DD are likely to command considerable attention in African countries over the coming decades, as large cohorts of young people enter the labour market each year. While there are a number of approaches to considering the DD, the NTA methodology provides a useful framework for understanding patterns of resource flows across generations and for analyzing the effects of demographic change on national economies. With accounts being estimated for an increasing number of countries on the continent using a consistent approach, it has become possible to construct a broader view of the DD in Africa.

Much of the NTA research on the continent has been focussed on describing the economic lifecycle and estimating the first DD. The research has revealed the degree of heterogeneity amongst African countries in terms of both the timing of the first DD and its expected magnitude. In common with other research into the DD, NTA research emphasizes the fact that the dividend is not automatic and instead is dependent on governments providing the appropriate supportive economic and institutional context. As Dramani (2019) notes, the extent to which the dividends are achieved will be a function of government policymaking and follow-through. This reinforces the importance of institutions and good governance.

While the labour market is central to the realization of the first DD, it is also foundational for the second DD. The latter is dependent on cohorts in the productive ages being able to accumulate assets, and this is impossible without the availability of remunerative work. In the context of rapid technological change, automation, and the fourth industrial revolution, this suggests that attainment of the second DD will be a significant challenge for countries around the world, including in Africa.

In contrast to the conventional dependency ratio approach that signals the opening and closing of the demographic window, the NTA research clearly shows that the first DD is already being experienced by most African countries. This highlights the urgency with which policymakers need to respond. This urgency of policy intervention is highlighted in several national reports on the DD. In this context, a further complication is the long lead times for many of the required interventions, particularly relating to education, health, and fertility. Beyond necessitating a long-term view from policymakers, policy for maximizing the DD requires government commitment over multiple election cycles, something which is challenging in any democracy in the twenty-first century.

There is unanimity across the DD literature that the DD represents a potential benefit that can only be harnessed where governments are able to create the necessary supportive policy and institutional contexts. As African countries continue to move through this period of favourable demographic change, the findings from NTA and other research related to the DD will assist with monitoring trends and assessing the ways in which changing social, economic, and institutional contexts are unleashing or suppressing the dividend. Importantly, they will provide the evidence that will, hopefully, encourage policymakers to consistently make the necessary longer-term policy choices.

Notes

1 The NTA methodology has been developed as part of a global research effort led by Lee and Mason (2011) and has been formalized in a manual published by the United Nations (2013). As of mid-2020, the NTA network consists of 96 countries from all over the world; 9 African countries are full members of the network, while another 20 African countries have or are busy constructing NTA estimates. However, while there are NTA estimates for 26 African countries, a key data gap is Northern Africa, for which there are currently no NTA estimates.

2 Actual lifecycle deficit profiles are presented in Figure 34.5.

References

AFIDEP. (2018). *Opportunities and policy actions to maximise the demographic dividend in Botswana*. Gaborone: Republic of Botswana and UNFPA.

Ahmed, S. A., Cruz, M., Go, D. S., Maliszewska, M., & Osorio-Rodarte, I. (2014). *How significant is Africa's demographic dividend for its future growth and poverty reduction?* Policy Research Working Paper No. 7134. World Bank.

Amporfu, E., Sakyi, D., & Frimpong, P. B. (2014). *Demographic dividend of Ghana: The National Transfer Accounts approach*. NTA Working Paper No. 14–02. Retrieved from www.ntaccounts.org.

Amporfu, E., Sakyi, D., Frimpong, P. B., Arthur, E., & Novignon, J. (2018). *The distribution of paid and unpaid work among men and women in Ghana: The National Time Transfer Accounts approach*. CWW Working Paper WP3. Counting Women's Work. Retrieved from www.countingwomenswork.org.

Bloom, D. E., & Canning, D. (2011). *Demographics and development policy*. PGDA Working Paper No. 66. Program on the Global Demography of Aging, Harvard University. Retrieved from www.hsph.harvard.edu/pgda/working.html/.

Bloom, D. E., Canning, D., Fink, G., & Finlay, J. E. (2007). *Realizing the demographic dividend: Is Africa any different?* PGDA Working Paper No. 23. Program on the Global Demography of Aging, Harvard University. Retrieved from www.hsph.harvard.edu/pgda/working.html/

Bloom, D. E., Canning, D., & Malaney, P. N. (2000). Population dynamics and economic growth in Asia. *Population and Development Review*, *26*(Supplement: Population and Economic Change in East Asia), 257–290.

Bloom, D. E., Canning, D., & Sevilla, J. (2003). *The demographic dividend: A new perspective on the economic consequences of population change*. RAND Corporation. Retrieved from www.rand.org/pubs/monograph_reports/MR1274

Bloom, D. E., Finlay, J., Humair, S., Mason, A., Olaniyan, O., & Soyibo, A. (2010). *Prospects for economic growth in Nigeria: A demographic perspective*. NTA Working Paper No. 10–09. Retrieved from www.ntaccounts.org.

Canning, D., Raja, S., & Yazbeck, A. S. (2015). *Africa's demographic transition: Dividend or disaster?* Washington, DC: World Bank and Agence Francaise de Développement. Retrieved from https://openknowledge.worldbank.org/handle/10986/22036

Chakravarty, S., Das, S., & Vaillant, J. (2017). *Gender and youth employment in sub-Saharan Africa*. Policy Research Working Paper No. 8245. World Bank, Washington, DC.

Chipembe, C., Gaspar, M., Mariano, G., Maunze, X., & Munamoha, R. (2013). *Mozambique at the start of a demographic dividend*. NTA Country Brief, Mozambique. National Transfer Accounts, East-West Center, Honolulu. Retrieved from www.ntaccounts.org

CREFAT. (n.d.). *Développement economique local au Sénégal*. Policy Brief, CREG-CREFAT, UNDP, Ministère de l'Economie des Finances, and UNFPA. Retrieved from https://creg-center.org/country-briefs-senegal/

CREG. (n.d.a). *Gender in SWEDD countries*. Sahel Women Empowerment and Demographic Dividend (SWEDD) Policy Brief No. 3 (SWEDD-PR17-DPE). World Bank. Retrieved from https://creg-center.org/policy-swedd-2/

CREG. (n.d.b). *Sahel's countries window of opportunity*. Sahel Women Empowerment and Demographic Dividend (SWEDD) Policy Brief No. 1 (SWEDD-PR17-DPE). World Bank. Retrieved from https://creg-center.org/policy-swedd-2/

Diwan, I., & Vartanova, I. (2017). *The effect of patriarchal culture on women's labor force participation*. ERF Working Paper No. 1101. Economic Research Forum, Giza. Retrieved from www.erg.org.eg

Donehower, G. (2018). *Measuring the gendered economy: Counting Women's Work methodology*. CWW Working Paper WP4. Counting Women's Work. Retrieved from www.countingwomenswork.org

Dramani, L. (2019). Le dividende démographique en Afrique de l'Ouest et du Centre: définitions, mesures, résultats. *Sud/Nord*, 33–44.

Dramani, L., & Akpo, E. (n.d.). *Contribution des femmes Sénégalaises à la croissance économique*. Policy Brief. CREG-CREFAT, UNDP, Ministère de l'Economie des Finances, and UNFPA. https://creg-center.org/country-briefs-senegal/

Dramani, L., & Ndiaye, F. (2012). Estimating the first demographic dividend in Senegal: The National Transfers Account approach. *British Journal of Economics, Management and Trade*, *2*(2), 23–59.

Dramani, L., Ndiaye, F., & Ouarmé, A. (2013). *Will Senegal enjoy a demographic dividend?* NTA Country Brief, Senegal. National Transfer Accounts, East-West Center, Honolulu. Retrieved from www.ntaccounts.org

Dramani, L., & Oga, I. J. B. (2017). Understanding demographic dividends in Africa: The NTA approach. *Journal of Demographic Economics*, *83*(1), 85–101. doi:10.1017/dem.2016.30

Drummond, P., Thakoor, V., & Yu, S. (2014). *Africa rising: Harnessing the demographic dividend*. IMF Working Paper WP/14/143. International Monetary Fund, Washington, DC. Retrieved from www.imf.org/en/publications

Fernàndez-Varela, F., & Mejía-Guevara, I. (2012, June 13–16). *Socioeconomic differences in the distribution by age of public transfers in Mexico*. Paper prepared for the European Population Conference 2012, Stockholm, Sweden. Retrieved from http://epc2012.princeton.edu/papers/120958

Groth, H., & May, J. F. (2017b). Introduction. In H. Groth & J. F. May (Eds.), *Africa's population: In search of a demographic dividend* (pp. 1–8). Cham, Switzerland: Springer.

Heath, R., & Jayachandran, S. (2017). *The causes and consequences of increased female education and labor force participation in developing countries*. NBER Working Paper Series No. 22766. National Bureau of Economic Research, Cambridge, MA.

International Labour Organisation. (2017a). *World employment and social outlook: Trends for women 2017*. Geneva: International Labour Office.

International Labour Organisation. (2017b). *World social protection report 2017–2019: Universal social protection to achieve the Sustainable Development Goals*. Geneva: International Labour Organization.

International Labour Organisation. (2020). *World employment and social outlook: Trends 2020*. Geneva: International Labour Organization.

Islamic Republic of Mauritania. (n.d.a). *Dividende demographique en Mauritanie: Entre mythes et realites.* Policy Brief No. 2. Projet d'Autonomisation des Femmes et Dividende Démographique au Sahel Projet SWEDD-Mauritanie, World Bank, and UNFPA. Retrieved from https://creg-center.org/country-briefs-mauritanie/

Islamic Republic of Mauritania. (n.d.b). *Genre et dividende demographique au Mauritanie.* Policy Brief No. 3. Projet d'Autonomisation des Femmes et Dividende Démographique au Sahel Projet SWEDD-Mauritanie, World Bank, and UNFPA. Retrieved from https://creg-center.org/country-briefs-mauritanie/

Islamic Republic of Mauritania. (n.d.c). *Milieu residence en Mauritanie.* Policy Brief No. 4. Projet d'Autonomisation des Femmes et Dividende Démographique au Sahel Projet SWEDD-Mauritanie, World Bank, and UNFPA. Retrieved from https://creg-center.org/country-briefs-mauritanie/

Islamic Republic of Mauritania. (n.d.d). *Prospérité partagée en Mauritanie: Apport du dividend démographique.* Policy Brief No. 7. Projet d'Autonomisation des Femmes et Dividende Démographique au Sahel Projet SWEDD-Mauritanie, World Bank, and UNFPA. Retrieved from https://creg-center.org/country-briefs-mauritanie/

Kingdom of Swaziland. (2017a). *Towards maximising the demographic dividend in Swaziland.* Mbabane, Eswatini: Ministry of Economic Planning and Development.

Kingdom of Swaziland. (2017b, December). *Towards maximising the demographic dividend in Swaziland.* Policy Brief. Kingdom of Swaziland, AFIDEP, Development Policy Research Unit, and UNFPA.

Lee, R., Lee, S. H., & Mason, A. (2006). *Charting the economic life cycle.* NBER Working Paper Series No. 12379. National Bureau of Economic Research, Cambridge, MA. Retrieved from www.nber.org/papers/w12379/

Lee, R., & Mason, A. (2010). Fertility, human capital, and economic growth over the demographic transition. *European Journal of Population, 26*(2), 159–182.

Lee, R., & Mason, A. (2011). *Population aging and the generational economy: A global perspective.* Cheltenham, UK, and Ottawa, Canada: Edward Elgar and IDRC.

Maliki, M. (2011). The support system for Indonesian elders: Moving toward a sustainable national pension system. In R. Lee & A. Mason (Eds.), *Population aging and the generational economy: A global perspective* (pp. 513–527). Cheltenham, UK; and Ottawa, Canada: Edward Elgar and IDRC.

Mason, A., & Lee, R. (2006). Reform and support systems for the elderly in developing countries: Capturing the second demographic dividend. *GENUS, LXII*(2), 11–35.

Mason, A., & Lee, R. (2007). Transfers, capital and consumption over the demographic transition. In N. O. Robert Clark & A. Mason (Eds.), *Population aging, intergenerational transfers and the macroeconomy* (pp. 128–162). Cheltenham, UK: Edward Elgar.

Mason, A., & Lee, R. (2011a). Introducing age into national accounts. In R. Lee & A. Mason (Eds.), *Population aging and the generational economy: A global perspective* (pp. 55–78). Cheltenham, UK; and Ottawa, Canada: Edward Elgar Publishing, Inc. and the International Development Research Centre.

Mason, A., & Lee, R. (2011b). Population aging and the generational economy: Key findings. In R. Lee & A. Mason (Eds.), *Population aging and the generational economy: A global perspective* (pp. 3–31). Cheltenham, UK; and Ottawa, Canada: Edward Elgar Publishing, Inc. and the International Development Research Centre.

Mason, A., & Lee, R. (2012). *Demographic dividends and aging in lower-income countries.* National Transfer Accounts Working Paper No. 12–01. Center for the Economics and Demography of Aging, University of California, Berkeley, and the East-West Center, Honolulu. Retrieved from www.ntaccounts.org

Mason, A., Lee, R., Abrigo, M., & Lee, S. H. (2017). *Support ratios and demographic dividends: Estimates for the world.* Technical Paper No. 2017/1. United Nations Department of Economic and Social Affairs, Population Division, New York. Retrieved from www.un.org/en/development/desa/population/publications/pdf/technical/TP2017-1.pdf

Mwabu, G., Muriithi, M. K., & Mutegi, R. G. (2011). National Transfer Accounts for Kenya: The economic lifecycle in 1994. In R. Lee & A. Mason (Eds.), *Population aging and the generational economy: A global perspective* (pp. 367–378). Cheltenham, UK; and Ottawa, Canada: Edward Elgar Publishing, Inc., and the International Development Research Centre.

Mwabu, G., Muriithi, M. K., & Mutegi, R. (2013). *Boosting Kenya's demographic dividend.* NTA Country Brief, Kenya. National Transfer Accounts, East-West Center, Honolulu. Retrieved from www.ntaccounts.org

National Transfer Accounts Project. (2020). *National Transfer Accounts database.* Online database. National Transfer Accounts Project. Retrieved on July 6, 2020, from www.ntaccounts.org/

Olaniyan, O., Soyibo, A., & Lawanson, A. O. (2012). Demographic transition, demographic dividend and economic growth in Nigeria. *African Population Studies*, *26*(2), 159–176.

Olaniyan, O., Soyibo, A., Lawanson, A. O., Olasehinde, N., Odumosu, M., Orekoya, A., . . . Adeyemi, F. (2018a). *Harnessing the demographic dividend for the sustainable development of Nigeria: 2016 Demographic dividend report of Nigeria*. Published by Health Policy Training and Research Programme (HPTRP), University of Ibadan, Nigeria for the United Nations Population Fund (UNFPA), Nigeria.

Olaniyan, O., Soyibo, A., Lawanson, A. O., Olasehinde, N., Odumosu, M., Orekoya, A., . . . Adeyemi, F. (2018b). *Youth unemployment and demographic dividend*. Demographic Dividend Policy Brief No. 3. United Nations Population Fund, National Transfer Accounts, and Health Policy Training and Research Programme, University of Ibadan, Nigeria. Retrieved from www.ntaccounts.org

Oosthuizen, M. (2013). *Maximising South Africa's demographic dividend*. DPRU Working Paper No. 13/157, Development Policy Research Unit, University of Cape Town. Retrieved from www.dpru.uct.ac.za/

Oosthuizen, M. (2014a). Capturing South Africa's demographic dividend. In H. Bhorat, A. Hirsch, R. Kanbur, & M. Ncube (Eds.), *The Oxford companion to the economics of South Africa* (pp. 231–235). New York: Oxford University Press.

Oosthuizen, M. (2014b, December). The South African generational economy. In *Policy in focus*, *30*. Brasilia: International Policy Centre for Inclusive Growth, United Nations Development Programme. Retrieved from www.ipc-undp.org/publication/27558

Oosthuizen, M. (2015). Bonus or mirage? South Africa's demographic dividend. *Journal of the Economics of Ageing*, *5*, 14–22. doi:10.1016/j.jeoa.2014.08.007

Oosthuizen, M. (2018a). *Counting women's work in South Africa: Estimates of household production across the lifecycle in 2000*. CWW Working Paper WP6. Counting Women's Work. Retrieved from www.countingwomenswork.org/

Oosthuizen, M. (2018b). *Counting women's work in South Africa: Incorporating unpaid work into estimates of the economic lifecycle in 2010*. CWW Working Paper WP8. Counting Women's Work. Retrieved from www.countingwomenswork.org

Oosthuizen, M. (2018c, October). *National Transfer Accounts estimates for Mauritius, 2003*. Version 1. Unpublished database.

Oosthuizen, M. (2019). *Inequality and the generational economy: Race-disaggregated National Transfer Accounts for South Africa, 2015*. WIDER Working Paper 2019/24. UNU-WIDER, Helsinki. Retrieved from www.wider.unu.edu/publication/inequality-and-generational-economy

Oosthuizen, M., & Lilenstein, K. (2018). *Counting women's work in Mauritius: Household production across the lifecycle in 2003*. CWW Working Paper WP7. Counting Women's Work. Retrieved from www.countingwomenswork.org/

Prskawetz, A., & Sambt, J. (2014). Economic support ratios and the demographic dividend in Europe. *Demographic Research*, *30*(34), 963–1010. doi:10.4054/DemRes.2014.30.34

Reher, D. (2012). Population and the economy during the demographic transition. *Economic Affairs*, *32*(1), 10–16.

Republic of Burkina Faso. (n.d.a). *Disparites spatiales et dividende demographique au Burkina Faso*. Policy Brief No. 6. Projet d'Autonomisation des Femmes et Dividende Démographique au Sahel (PAFDDS)-SWEDD-Burkina Faso. Republic of Burkina Faso, World Bank and UNFPA. Retrieved from https://creg-center.org/country-briefs-burkina-faso/

Republic of Burkina Faso. (n.d.b). *Genre et dividende demographique au Burkina Faso*. Policy Brief No. 5. Women's Empowerment and Demographic Dividend in the Sahel (PAFDDS), SWEDD Burkina Faso. World Bank and UNFPA. Retrieved from https://creg-center.org/country-briefs-burkina-faso/

Republic of Burkina Faso. (n.d.c). *Le dividende demographique: Pour un développement inclusif au Burkina-Faso*. Policy Brief No. 1. Projet d'Autonomisation des Femmes et Dividende Démographique au Sahel (PAFDDS)-SWEDD-Burkina Faso. Republic of Burkina Faso, World Bank and UNFPA. Retrieved from https://creg-center.org/country-briefs-burkina-faso/

Republic of Chad. (n.d.a). *Disparites spatiales et dividende demographique au Chad*. Policy Brief No. 6. Projet d'Autonomisation des Femmes et Dividende Démographique au Sahel Projet SWEDD-Tchad, World Bank, and UNFPA. Retrieved from https://creg-center.org/country-briefs-tchad/

Republic of Chad. (n.d.b). *Genre et dividende demographique au Tchad*. Policy Brief No. 5. Projet d'Autonomisation des Femmes et Dividende Démographique au Sahel Projet SWEDD-Tchad, World Bank, and UNFPA. Retrieved from https://creg-center.org/country-briefs-tchad/

Republic of Chad. (n.d.c). *Synthese du profil du dividende demographique au Tchad.* Policy Brief No. 1. Projet d'Autonomisation des Femmes et Dividende Démographique au Sahel Projet SWEDD-Tchad, World Bank, and UNFPA. Retrieved from https://creg-center.org/country-briefs-tchad/

Republic of Mali. (n.d.a). *Disparites spatiales et dividende demographique au Mali.* Policy Brief No. 6. Ministère de la Population et de l'Aménagement du Territoire, World Bank, UNFPA, CREG, and CREFAT. Retrieved from https://creg-center.org/country-briefs-mali/

Republic of Mali. (n.d.b). *Genre et dividende demographique au Mali.* Policy Brief No. 5. Ministère de la Population et de l'Aménagement du Territoire, World Bank, UNFPA, CREG, and CREFAT. Retrieved from https://creg-center.org/country-briefs-mali/

Republic of Namibia. (2018). *Towards maximising the demographic dividend in Namibia.* Republic of Namibia and UNFPA. Retrieved from www.afidep.org/

Republic of Niger. (n.d.a). *Disparites regionales et dividende demographique au Niger.* Policy Brief No. 6. Projet d'Autonomisation des Femmes et Dividende Démographique au Sahel (PAFDDS-SWEDD)-Niger, World Bank and UNFPA. Retrieved from https://creg-center.org/country-briefs-niger/

Republic of Niger. (n.d.b). *Genre et dividende demographique au Niger.* Policy Brief No. 5. Projet d'Autonomisation des Femmes et Dividende Démographique au Sahel (PAFDDSSWEDD)-Niger, World Bank and UNFPA. Retrieved from https://creg-center.org/country-briefs-niger/

Republic of Niger. (n.d.c). *Le Niger a l'heure du bonus demographique.* Policy Brief No. 3. Projet d'Autonomisation des Femmes et Dividende Démographique au Sahel (PAFDDSSWEDD)-Niger, World Bank and UNFPA. Retrieved from https://creg-center.org/country-briefs-niger/

Shapiro, D., & Hinde, A. (2017). On the pace of fertility decline in sub-Saharan Africa. *Demographic Research, 37*, 1327–1338. doi:10.4054/demres.2017.37.40

Shen, K., & Lee, S. H. (2014). *Benefit incidence of public transfers: Evidence from the People's Republic of China.* ADB Economics Working Paper Series No. 413. Retrieved from www.adb.org/publications/papers

Soyibo, A., Mwabu, G., Olaniyan, O., & Muriithi, M. (2012, August). Comparative analysis of economic lifecycle deficits in Kenya and Nigeria: Some estimation results. *The African Statistical Journal, 15*, 25–39.

Soyibo, A., Olaniyan, O., & Lawanson, A. O. (2013). *Will Nigeria benefit from a demographic dividend?* NTA Country Brief, Nigeria. National Transfer Accounts, East-West Center, Honolulu. Retrieved from www.ntaccounts.org

Turra, C. M., & Queiroz, B. L. (2005, July 6–7). *Intergenerational transfers and socioeconomic inequality in Brazil: A first look.* Paper prepared for the Taller sobre Transformaciones Demograficas, Transferencias Intergeneracionales y Proteccion Social en America Latina, CELADE, Santiago, Chile. Retrieved from www.abep.nepo.unicamp.br/docs/PopPobreza/TurraQueiroz.pdf

UNFPA. (2014). *State of the world population 2014.* New York: UNFPA.

UNFPA and AFIDEP. (2015). *Synthesis report on the demographic dividend in Africa.* Johannesburg, South Africa: UNFPA East and Southern Africa Regional Office.

United Nations. (2004). *World population to 2300.* New York: United Nations, Department of Economic and Social Affairs, Population Division.

United Nations. (2013). *Measuring and analysing the generational economy: National Transfer Accounts manual.* New York: United Nations, Population Division, Economic and Social Affairs.

United Nations. (2019). *World population prospects: The 2019 revision.* New York: Department of Economic and Social Affairs, Population Division. Retrived from http://esa.un.org/unpd/wpp/

Weny, K., Snow, R., & Zhang, S. (2017). *The demographic dividend atlas for Africa: Tracking the potential for a demographic dividend.* UNFPA. Retrived from www.unfpa.org/

Whiteside, A., & Zebryck, N. (2017). New and re-emerging infectious diseases in sub-Saharan Africa. In H. Groth & J. F. May (Eds.), *Africa's population: In search of a demographic dividend* (pp. 299–314). Cham, Switzerland: Springer.

World Bank. (2020). *World data bank.* Online database. Retrieved from http://databank.worldbank.org/

Appendix

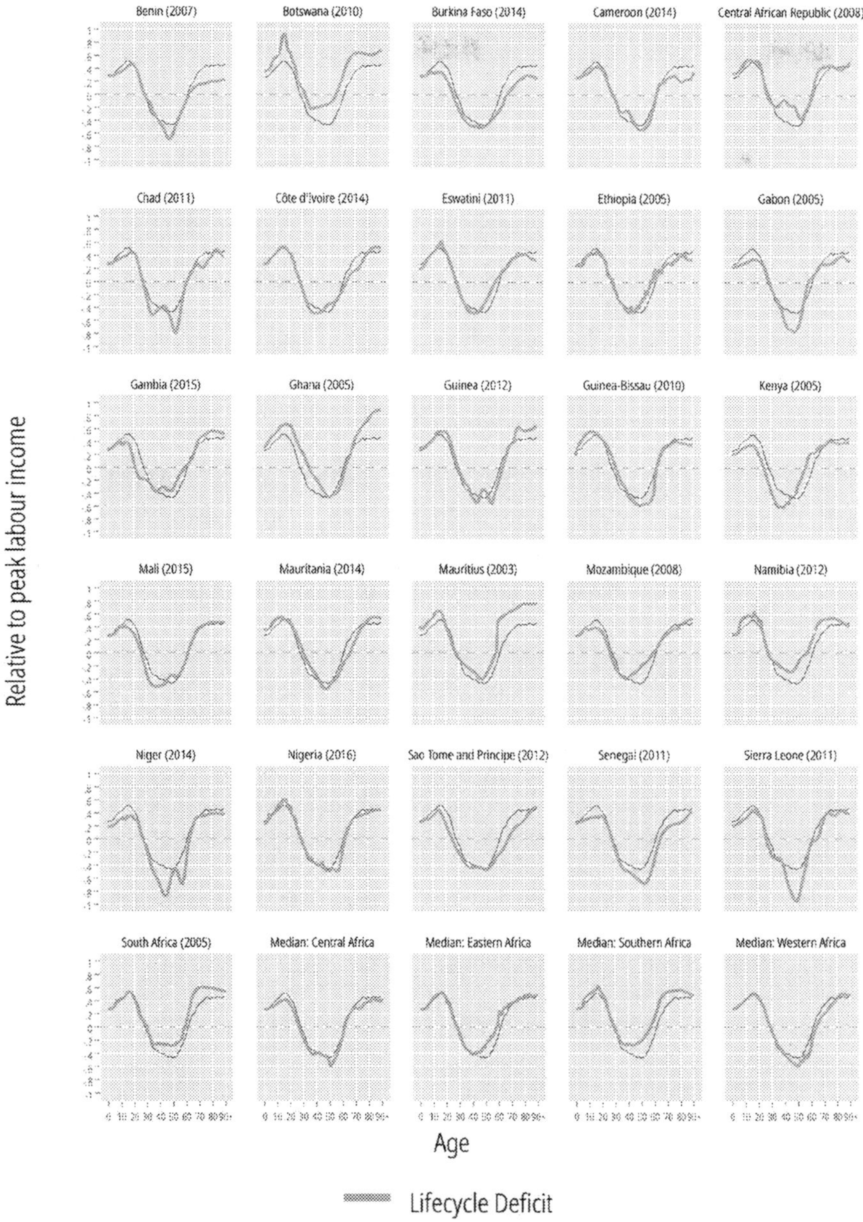

Figure 34.5 Lifecycle deficit in African countries.

Source: Own calculations, National Transfer Accounts Project (2020) and Oosthuizen (2018c).

Note: The lifecycle deficit based on the median consumption and labour income profiles for Africa are represented by solid black lines. Countries are grouped to construct regional aggregates based on the ILO regional classification as follows: Ethiopia, Kenya, and Mozambique (Eastern Africa); Botswana, Eswatini, Namibia, and South Africa (Southern Africa); Cameroon, Central African Republic, Chad, Gabon, and São Tomé and Príncipe (Central Africa); and Benin, Burkina Faso, Côte d'Ivoire, Gambia, Ghana, Guinea, Guinea-Bissau, Mali, Mauritania, Niger, Nigeria, Senegal, and Sierra Leone (Western Africa).

35

DEMOGRAPHIC DIVIDEND MONITORING INDEX CONCEPTUAL FRAMEWORK AND CASE STUDIES IN AFRICA

Latif Dramani, Edem Akpo, Jean Baptiste Oga, Camille Détondji Guidimé, Silvère Konan, Sam Agbahoungba, Dalomi Bahan, Cheikh Tidiane Ndiaye, and Crispin Mabika

Introduction

Formulated about the East Asian economic miracle of the 1960s to 1990s, the demographic dividend refers to the acceleration of economic growth resulting from changes in the age structure of the population accompanied by strategic investments in health, education, economic policy, and good governance. It is a key element in the framework of the African Common Position on the People-Centred Post-2015 Development Agenda. The inclusion of the demographic dividend in the Programme for Sustainable Development to 2030 was one of Africa's major contributions to the programme. For the African Union (2016), taking full advantage of the demographic dividend in Africa presents a strategic opportunity to realize the aspirations and goals of Agenda 2063 and Agenda 2030.

Although there is a consensus on the concept of the demographic dividend, unsolved challenges are its measurement on the one hand and its monitoring one the second hand. Based on the National Transfer Accounts (NTA) methodology, the United Nations quantifies the size of the first demographic dividend as 'the growth rate of the economic support ratio', that is the direct contribution of changes in the support ratio to economic growth. If the NTA approach provides a consensual solution to the measurement of demographic dividend (DD), its monitoring remains an issue. In another words, how to know whether a given country is progressing towards capturing and harnessing the DD remains challenging until recently.

In this regard, the Regional Centre for Generational Economics (CREG/CREFAT), with the collaboration of the West and Central Regional Office of UNFPA, has developed the so-called the Demographic Dividend Monitoring Index (DDMI) in 2017. In fact, the DDMI is a composite index composed of several socio-economic variables affecting the demographic potential and the well-being of people. These variables are drawn from the existing literature review surrounding the concept.

DOI: 10.4324/9780429287213-42

The DDMI is an indicator that enables a country or territory to assess its progress in capturing the demographic dividend and covers five (5) dimensions: (i) economic dependency, (ii) quality of the living environment, (iii) transitions in poverty, (iv) extended human development, and (v) networks and territories. Developed in the SWEDD (Sahel Women Empowerment and Demographic Dividend) project framework, the DDMI is adopted and in implementation in about ten (10) African countries including Benin, Burkina Faso, Cameroon, Chad, Côte d'Ivoire, Guinea, Mali, Mauritania, Niger, Senegal, and Togo.

The importance of taking gender specificities into account in the implementation of economic policies is no longer to be discussed.[1] Amid the range of the gender equality and/or inequality that exists,[2] to the best of our knowledge, none of them specifically gives a breakdown of men's and women's contributions in the DD capturing and harnessing. However, it is recognized that a double demographic dividend could be reaped when adequate policies that improve women's human capital and especially girls' education are set up and implemented. First, this dividend improves their quality of life, enabling them to become more productive. Second, it would result in a return on investment that would benefit children through improved education and health care.

So, to better orient policies for greater gender equality, this chapter also presents the results in capturing the demographic dividend by gender. The gender index of demographic dividend (GDDI) was developed by the CREG with the partnership of the United Nations Economic Commission for Africa (UNECA) in this regard.

The chapter is divided into four main sections. Firstly, a brief review of the literature is presented on the concept of the demographic dividend and its applications in Africa; then the methodology for calculating the indicator is presented followed by the presentation of results at the global level and by sex. The work ends with a discussion on the perspectives of this research.

The main objective of this chapter is twofold: firstly, it is to build a systematic review on the empirical evidence on the demographic dividend in Africa; secondly, it is to expose the methodological approach behind the DDMI; and thirdly, it is to showcase some results from this index for some African countries. The major innovation of DDMI lies in the fact that it makes it possible to apprehend the demographic dividend under several prisms (gender, spatial, and lifecycle) in line with the AU 2030 and 2063 programmes.

Selective literature review on the dividend and related constructions

Theoretical knowledge of the demographic dividend

The concept of the demographic dividend (DD) that emerged in the 1950s was used to justify certain population policies such as family planning. Subsequently, DD theory has focussed on integrating population dynamics into economic analysis (Bloom, Canning, & Sevilla, 2003; Mason & Lee, 2006). The demographic window of opportunity is a phenomenon that passes through the demographic transition (Dramani & Bahan, 2019). The potential effects that change in the age structure of the population, as opposed to population size and growth, has on the economic growth of countries have been of interest to researchers and practitioners. As a result, they have begun to reflect on the relationship between population and development (United Nations, 2013). DD is the acceleration of economic growth that would result from changes in the age structure of a population (Bloom & Canning, 2003; Mason, 2005; Lee & Mason, 2007; Mason & Lee, 2007). Population dynamics due to births, deaths, and migration (Guidime, Oga, & Ndoye, 2019) offer opportunities for determining a level of productivity and market to boost economic activity. It is understood that population dynamics do not obscure the potential for economic convergence of countries under certain conditions (Dramani et al., 2019; Eloundou-Enyegue, Giroux, & Tenikue, 2017). Thus, two dividends are distinguished (first dividend and second dividend). While the first is due to the massive activation of young people, the second focusses on the quality of employment that promotes savings, productivity, and reinvestment. Nested generation models have favoured the study of intergenerational flow exchanges (United Nations, 2013). The presence of many assumptions in nested models – difficult to rationalize in national economic systems – compromises the relevance of policy formulations (Lee, 1994). Becker and Murphy (1988) integrate investment in the education of children (under 14 years of age) into nested generation models to determine a level of growth through optimal labour productivity.

The demographic dividend becomes clearer in its measurement with the inclusion of average labour income of age and average consumption of age in the determination of relative effective labour productivity.

Empirical knowledge of the determination of the demographic dividend and its related applications for development in Africa

Empirically, a lot of work has been done in Africa. It is the case of Ukpolo's (2002) works in 'Population Growth and Economic Growth in Africa'. As a result of his work, he especially found a negative, long-run causal relationship between the two variables in Nigeria: population growth negatively affects economic growth in the long term. However, in Ivory Coast, the results show that population growth causes economic growth in the short run. Klasen and Lawson (2007), try in their paper to examine the link between population and per-capita economic growth, and poverty, using the interesting case study of Uganda. And they found both theoretical considerations and strong empirical evidence suggest that the currently high population growth puts a considerable break on per-capita growth prospects in Uganda. Moreover, it contributes significantly to low achievement in poverty reduction and is associated with households being persistently poor and moving into poverty.

Akintunde, Olomola, and Oladeji (2013), examine in their study, the effects of population dynamics on economic growth in sub-Saharan Africa from 1970 to 2005. And the results show that total fertility rate had a negative impact on economic growth while, life expectancy at birth had a positive influence on economic growth. The region needs to address the high population growth to have a sustainable economic development. More recently, Peter and Bakari (2018), in their study on the 'Impact of Population Growth on Economic Growth in Africa', despite the negative impact of fertility on economic growth of Africa, suggest that population growth exerts a positive impact on economic growth of Africa. Through population growth and dynamics, the demographic dividend can also contribute to the economic growth, provided that the economy is able to accumulate physical and human capital and to absorb the potentially active population into productive employment and according to place of residence (Dramani & Oga, 2017; Bahan & Dramani, 2016). Health, governance, the ratio of labour to skilled population, and employment are catalysts for the positive effect of population dynamics by age on economic growth. Convincing results for Western and Central African countries are increasingly known (Bahan & Dramani, 2016, 2020; Bahan & Dramani, 2019; Dramani, Akpo, & Agbahoungba 2019; Biao, Oga, & Guidimé, 2014).

The understanding of the demographic dividend in Africa has revealed itself more with methodological aspects (Dramani & Oga, 2017). We also have for illustrative purposes, the work of Olanrewaju et al. (2018), entitled 'Harnessing Demographic Dividend for Sustainable

Development of Nigeria'. This report examines and identifies the period and duration of the windows of opportunity that are expected to generate the demographic dividend of Nigeria. It also identifies the structure of existing policies and how they can be shaped to enable the citizens to harness and benefit from the dividends. Finally, the report can assist policy-makers to understand the nation's prospects and potentials for the demographic dividend and come up with appropriate policies and programmes to harness it.

Previously, Mwabu (2013) realized a work based on the demographic transition and demographic dividends in Kenya. The main conclusions of this work are that Kenya can take advantage of opportunity resulting from demographic transition to reap the first demographic dividend. Also, with growth in life expectancy, an incentive to save is being created because people expect to live beyond the labour income generation stage, thus creating potential for the second demographic dividend.

Using the National Transfer Accounts approach, Amporfu, Sakyi, and Frimpong (2014) estimate the lifecycle deficit and hence the first demographic dividend for Ghana in 2005. They found that Ghana started enjoying the first demographic dividend in 1990 and is expected to peak around 2031. In other words, the population structure of Ghana has been favourable to the economic growth since 1990 and the country is currently benefiting from this demographic potential. Questioning the effects of demographic transition on the size of the demographic dividend in sub-Saharan African countries, Eastwood and Lipton (2011) concluded that, even in the case of rapid decline in fertility rate, the demographic dividend will be lower in comparison with that of Asian countries. They based their analysis on UN projections about the decline in total fertility rate over the period 1985–2025. For them, apart from the transition dividends, low savings in most of Africa (in contrast to Asia) stem from unsustainable per person consumption as it depletes their capital, especially since the continent's demographics continue to grow. (Eastwood & Lipton, 2011). In the same vein, Basu and Basu (2014) analyzed the trend of key demographic features in Africa and found that, even though there is a huge demographic potential that would occur in Africa, there is a case for cautious optimism. According to them, two major factors must be considered: firstly, the demand for high fertility is probably stronger than predicted by the usual socio-economic correlates of fertility; secondly, the historical and cultural approval of women's participation in the labour force, which is not the same across African countries.

The effects of population dynamics on economic growth in Africa has prompted the development of the Demographic Dividend Tracking Index (DDTI) (Dramani, 2019; Dramani et al., 2019). A bijective relationship is found between the demographic dividend and economic structures such as economic dependency coverage, extended human capital, quality of life, poverty transition, and networks and territories. Dramani (2019) designed and set up National Observatories for Monitoring the Demographic Dividend. This tool is in line with the objectives of Agenda 2063 of the African States. Considering gender in the broad sense and sex strictly in the study of observed socio-economic disparities has favoured the construction of the gender index for monitoring the demographic dividend (Dramani et al., 2019).

Based on the work of the Counting Women's Work research network, the contribution of women to the social economy is determined empirically (Morné, 2018; Morné & Kezia, 2018). On the other hand, removing barriers to women's work could, in some countries, increase output by as much as 25%. Hakura, Hussain, Newiak, Thakoor, and Yang (2016) examine the impact of income and gender inequality on economic growth in sub-Saharan Africa. Income and gender inequality are negatively associated with GDP per capita growth. Reducing gender inequality could increase GDP per capita growth by 0.9 percentage points. Dramani and Oga (2017), applying the NTTA method to Senegalese data, find that domestic work time averages

7 hours per day for women and only 30 minutes per day for men. It finds that women work more and earn less than men over a period of 25 to 80 years.

Monitoring the demographic dividend and taking gender into account in the process of sustainable development is of interest to African countries. This index finds its source in the theory of economic and social well-being (Dramani & Bahan, 2019).

Methodology of the Demographic Dividend Monitoring Index with gender lens

Demographic Dividend Monitoring Index normative

The Demographic Dividend Monitoring Index (DDMI) is a composite index created by the CREG to assess and monitor the progress of African countries in achieving the demographic dividend (DD). It is based on five dimensions: coverage of economic dependence, quality of living environment, transitions to poverty, broad human development, and lastly networks and territories. While the demographic transition is its starting point, the achievement of DD is accompanied by change in many interacting areas. This makes it possible to optimize the demographic dividend through appropriate policies.

The DDMI is a unitless index with a value between 0 (worst) and 1 (excellent). It is obtained by averaging five indicators related to the aforementioned dimensions. These dimensional indices are the Economic Dependency Coverage Index (EDCI); the Living Environment Quality Index (LEQI); the Poverty Exit Synthetic Index (PESI); the Expanded Human Development Index (EHDI); and the Synthetic Network and Territory Index (SNTI). Each dimensional index covers from one to seven fields or sub-dimensions. In turn, the sub-dimensions are made up of several elementary indicators that are specific to them. The methods used to develop the dimensional index are described in the following paragraphs.

Economic Dependency Coverage Index (EDCI)

The Economic Dependency Coverage Index is based on the life-cycle deficit (LCD) and is defined as the ratio of the economic surplus of non-dependent people to the deficit of economically dependent people.

So, with this disaggregation of consumption ($C_{a,s}$) and labour income ($YL_{a,s}$) by age and sex, we can determine for each sex its surplus and its deficit from the formulas described here:

$$Surplus_s = -\sum_a (C_{a,s} - YL_{a,s}) \text{ under the condition } C_{a,s} \leq YL_{a,s}$$

$$De'ficit_s = \sum_a (C_{a,s} - YL_{a,s}) \text{ under the condition } C_{a,s} > YL_{a,s}$$

where the subscript ***s*** denotes the sex, and $C_{a,s}$ and $YL_{a,s}$ represent aggregated consumption and aggregated labour income, respectively, of individuals of age ***a*** and sex ***s***.

Thus, the EDCI for individuals of sex ***s*** is obtained as follows:

$$\boldsymbol{EDCI_s = \frac{Surplus_s}{Deficit_s}}$$

Most of data for the construction of country profiles comes mainly from different sources: socio-economic survey, national accounts, administrative registers, and population projections from international institutions (United Nations).

The composite Index of Living Environment Quality (LEQI)

The living environment is defined as the environment in which the individual lives and which can have an influence on his or her well-being. Based on the theories of well-being, the Living Environment Quality Index (LEQI) was developed by the OECD (2008) as part of the Better Life Initiative to provide countries with tools to measure quality of life. This project was prompted by the Stiglitz-Sen-Fitoussi Commission's 2009 report, which highlights the shortcomings of GDP as an indicator of wealth measurement.

In its basic formulation, it covers 11 criteria considered essential to well-being. However, in the framework of DD monitoring, only 7 of the 11 are retained in the quality of living environment dimension. Each criterion of well-being is measured by one to four indicators. Within each criterion, we calculate the average of the elementary indicators that constitute the sub-dimension after normalization.

Normalization is based on a classical formula that converts the original values of the indicators into numbers between 0 (the worst possible result) and 1 (the best possible result). The details of the methodology are explained by the CREG/CREFAT (2016) in the handbook on dimensions and monitoring indicators of the Demographic Dividend Observatory. The list of indicators is displayed in the following table.

Data for the indicators are available in international databases, household surveys, household perception surveys, and administrative sources. The table summarizes the sub-dimensions, the name and nature of the indicators, and the normalization formula for each indicator.

Finally, the LEQI index is calculated as follows:

$$LEQI = \frac{\mathbf{3} * CIV + \mathbf{3} * SOC + \mathbf{4} * ENV + \mathbf{4} * HOU + \mathbf{3} * SWB + \mathbf{3} * VPP + \mathbf{4} * SEC}{\mathbf{24}}$$

Table 35.1 Sub-Dimensions and Quality Indicators for Each Dimension of the Index

Sub-dimensions	*Indicators*	*Normalization Formulas*
Civic engagement and governance **(CIV)**	Electoral participation	N=x
	Stakeholder participation in the development of laws and regulations	N=x
Social network **(SOC)**	Quality of the social network	N=x
Environment (**ENV**)	Air pollution	N=1 – min(x,50)/50
	Quality of water	N=x
Housing conditions (**HOU**)	Number of rooms per person	N=min(x; 1)
	Access to basic sanitation facilities	N=x
	Cost of housing	N=1 – min(x,0.5)/0.5
Subjective well-being **(SWB)**	Satisfaction with life	N=x
Professional work and private life balance **VPP**	Number of hours of heavy work	N= 1 – x
	Time for leisure and self-care	N=1 – |x – 6| /16
Security (**SEC**)	Feeling of security when walking alone at night	N=x
	Homicide rate	N=1-min(x;20)/20

In addition, it is worth noting that the LEQI can be obtained for the population, but it is also disaggregated by sex. Among the basic indicators some are gender-specific and some are not. An example is air pollution or water quality. For these variables, we assign identical values to both sexes.

Poverty Exit Synthetic Index (PESI)

The measurement and analysis of poverty is of particular importance in the process of monitoring and evaluating the effectiveness of public policies, as well as in monitoring developments regarding the optimization of the demographic dividend. However, given the large inequalities in the distribution of wealth and the high vulnerability of households in developing countries, it seems even more important to better understand the phenomenon of poverty and to better target at-risk populations. Thus, work on poverty dynamics aims to identify individuals moving in and out of poverty over time and to analyze the main factors that play an important role in this mobility of poverty. The PESI is based on the approach of Dang and Lanjouw (2013). By considering two periods T1 and T2, four categories of individuals emerge: (i) P-P: the proportion of individuals who remained poor in periods T1 and T2 (chronic or permanent poverty or poverty trap); (ii) P-NP: the proportion of individuals who moved from a state of poverty to a state of non-poverty between T1 and T2 (exit from poverty); (iii) NP-P: the proportion of individuals who moved from a state of non-poor to a state of poverty between T1 and T2 (change in poverty); and (4) NP-NP: the proportion of individuals who remained non-poor in periods T1 and T2 (no poverty). The PESI makes it possible to determine the poverty escape rate among the vulnerable population, i.e. the people who move from a state of poverty to a state of non-poor and vice versa. It is formulated as follows:

$$PESI = \left(\frac{P \rightarrow NP}{P \rightarrow NP + NP \rightarrow P} \times \frac{NP \rightarrow NP}{NP \rightarrow NP + P \rightarrow P} \right)^{\frac{1}{2}}$$

The methodology of Dang and Lanjouw (2013) is also applicable to specific population sub-groups. Thus, we can determine the proportion of women or men living in chronic poverty or in non-poverty; the proportion of women or men who moved from poverty to non-poverty; and who moved from non-poverty to poverty. Thus, to analyze gender inequalities in terms of poverty dynamics, the ISSP is calculated for the sub-groups of women and men using the formula shown here:

$$PESI_s = \left(\frac{P \rightarrow NP_s}{P \rightarrow NP_s + NP \rightarrow P_s} \times \frac{NP \rightarrow NP_s}{NP \rightarrow NP_s + P \rightarrow P_s} \right)^{\frac{1}{2}}$$

The 's' index denotes sex, but it can also denote a gender sub-group.

Expanded Human Development Index (EHDI)

The Expanded Human Development Index (EHDI) is a composite measure of human development. It incorporates the dimensions and indicators of the HDI (human development index developed by UNDP) plus total fertility rate, with the possibility of disaggregation at the sub-national level. It covers three sub-dimensions: (i) health, measured by life expectancy at birth and the total fertility rate (TFR); (ii) education, measured by the average length of schooling for adults over 25 years of age and the expected length of schooling for school-age children; (iii) standard of living, measured by consumption expenditure per capita.

Listed here are the basics of each indicator:

- **Health** is represented by life expectancy at birth and the total fertility rate (TFR). Life expectancy at birth measures longevity and indirectly integrates the satisfaction of basic material needs such as access to healthy food, clean water, decent housing, good hygiene, and medical care. Regarding fertility, its inclusion in the HDI is justified by the fact that "high fertility poses health problems and presents risks for children and their mothers, harms investment in human capital, slows economic growth, and poses a 'potential threat'" (Dramani, 2016).

Based on relevant existing literature,[3] a reduction in fertility rates is considered beneficial for low-income countries because it is associated with better maternal and child health, women's empowerment, poverty, and the fight against hunger. It also contributes to the achievement of the DD.

- **Education** is measured by the average duration of schooling for adults over 25 and the expected duration of schooling for school-aged children. It reflects the satisfaction of intangible needs such as the ability to participate in decision-making at the workplace or in society. For the average duration of schooling for adults over 25 and the expected duration of schooling, the standardization formula is:

$$\frac{ACTUAL\ VALUE - MIN\ VALUE}{MAX\ VALUE - MIN\ VALUE}$$

Based on UNPD norms, 0 is the minimum value and 15 the maximum value for the average duration of schooling for adults (25 years and older). Concerning the school duration for school-age children, the minimum value is 0 and the maximum is 18.

- **The standard of living** is apprehended by the logarithm of per-capita consumption expenditure. In fact, the final consumption of individuals makes it possible to measure their decent standard of living or the level of their economic well-being.

For the standard of living, the standardization formula is:

$$\frac{LOG(ACTUAL\ VALUE) - LOG(MIN\ VALUE)}{LOG(MAX\ VALUE) - LOG(MIN\ VALUE)}$$

with a minimal value of \$67 and maximum value of \$20,723.

The EHDI represents the geometric mean of the normalized indices used to measure the levels reached in each sub-dimension (CREG/CREFAT, 2016). Maximum values are the highest values observed during the period considered (1980–2016). The minimum values are those that we are entitled to consider as subsistence values. For the TFR, a specific treatment is carried out so that the standardized index takes the value 1 when the TFR is 3 children per woman, and the value 0 when the ISF is equal to 0 (minimum) or 8 (maximum).

The standardized total fertility rate (TFRN) is given by the following expression:

$$\boldsymbol{TFRN(x) = \frac{x}{3} * 1_{[0;3]}(x) + \frac{(8-x)}{(8-3)} * 1_{]3;8]}(x)}$$

wherein x = TFR; $\mathbf{1}_{[0;3]}(x)$, and $\mathbf{1}_{]3;8]}(x)$ functions indicative of x.

A very high TFR presents barriers to DD achievement because it accelerates the growth rate of the young dependent population. But also, when it is very weak it causes a rapid aging of the population and makes renewal hypothetical. Thus, when it is very high or very low, the TFR has both economic and demographic disadvantages for the country. Under such conditions, demographers' recommendations lead to an optimal TFR of about 3 children per woman.

The construction of the EHDI is carried out in three stages. Firstly, indicators in different units are normalized to transform their value from 0 to 1. Secondly, (normalized) indicators belonging to the same sub-dimension are aggregated using a geometric mean to obtain the sub-dimensional indices. Finally, the HDI represents the geometric mean of the three sub-dimensional indices of health, education, and standard of living:

$$EHDI = \sqrt[3]{IH * IE * ICONT}$$

For the purpose of calculating the gender specific EHDI, the same value of the TFR will be assigned to men and women. Within each population category (men and women), the aggregation of the gender indicators and the TFR leads to a gender-differentiated estimation. Data for the indicators should come from a national education and health survey and a household survey.

Synthetic Network and Territory Index (SNTI)

The synthetic index of networks and territories (SNTI) provides information on territorial mobility by describing the attractiveness of territories, human migration, financial and goods flows, and the distribution of infrastructure within a national territory. The SNTI covers four sub-dimensions: (i) urbanization, (ii) migration, (iii) basic social and economic infrastructures, and (iv) financial flows and capacities. The indicators are standardized so that the values range from 0 (the lowest score) to 1 (the highest score). The sub-dimensional index is obtained by the geometric mean of the indicators which constitute the sub-dimension. Table 35.2 contains details of the SNTI indicators.

Table 35.2 Sub-Dimensions and Indicators of the Networks and Territories Dimension

Criteria or Sub-dimensions	*Indicators*	*Normalization*	*Type of indicators*
Urbanization	Population density	$\frac{x - \min(X)}{\max(X) - \min(X)}$	Gender-specific
	Average size of households	$\frac{x - \min(X)}{\max(X) - \min(X)}$	Gender-specific
	Urbanization rate	$N = x$	Gender-specific
	Ratio of renter households to owner households	$N = x$	Gender-specific
Migration	Entry index	$N = x$ Given by the ratio of the number of entries to the total population	Gender-specific

(*Continued*)

Criteria or Sub-dimensions	*Indicators*	*Normalization*	*Type of indicators*
	Exit index	$N = x$ Given by the ratio of the number of exits to the total population	Gender-specific
Infrastructure and basic social services	Index of access to infrastructure and basic social services	$N = x$	Gender-specific
	Quality index of infrastructures and basic social services	$N = x$	Gender-specific
Financial flows	Transfer index		Gender-specific
	Rate of access to formal transfer services	$N = x$	Gender-specific
	Consumption per capita		Gender-specific
	Cost of the basket of housewives in the region	$\frac{x - \min(X)}{\max(X) - \min(X)}$ Min=84,416 et Max=800,005,907	Gender-specific

Source: CREG, 2019

The index developed to monitor sustainable development by controlling the effects of population dynamics on the economy is centred on the NTA methodology.

Standardization is based on a classic formula that converts the original values of the indicators into numbers between 0 and 1.

For each sub-dimension, the sub-dimensional indicator is obtained by using a geometric average of the indicators which constitute it. The geometric mean method is preferred to the arithmetic mean in the sense that the latter does not consider the weight of the values of each variable in the overall indicator (compensation effects between values do not exist with the geometric mean method).

The formula used is shown here:

$$\boldsymbol{I_k} = \left(\prod_{d=1}^{n} \boldsymbol{ind_d} \right)^{\frac{1}{n}}$$

k=1, . . . ,4 and d=1, . . . ,n wherein n is the number of indicators monitored in the relevant sub-dimension.

The calculation of the Networks and Territories Synthetic Index is obtained here:

$$\boldsymbol{NSTI} = \left(\prod_{k=1}^{m} \boldsymbol{I_k} \right)^{\frac{1}{n}}$$

with m the number of sub-dimensions of the global dimension networks and territories (here m=4), I_k is the indicator calculated for each dimension k, k=1, . . . ,4.

It should be noted that among the variables used to determine the NTSI, some are sex-specific and others are not differentiable in terms of gender. The calculation of the SNTI by sex uses the described methodology, but with sex-differentiated values for the sex-specific variables and identical values for the non-gender-specific variables.

Demographic Dividend Monitoring Index conceptual framework normative

The index developed to monitor sustainable development by controlling the effects of population dynamics on the economy is centred on the NTA methodology. Generational economics is therefore at the heart of the scientific disciplines to contribute to inputs on the issue of sustainable development in countries.

Gap analysis

Methodology description

Gap Analysis compares a current situation to a desired state to determine what it would take to achieve the desired state. Therefore, the method has three essential components: (1) a measure

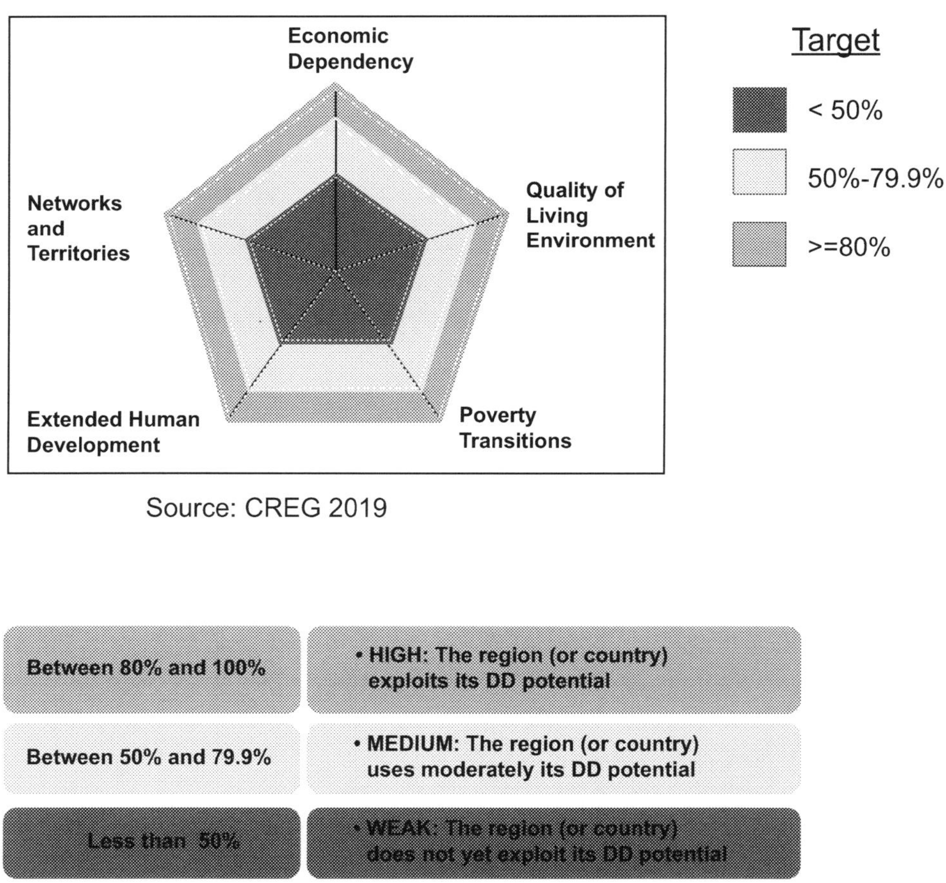

Figure 35.1 Demographic Dividend Monitoring Index: how to read the scale.

Source: Authors' calculation

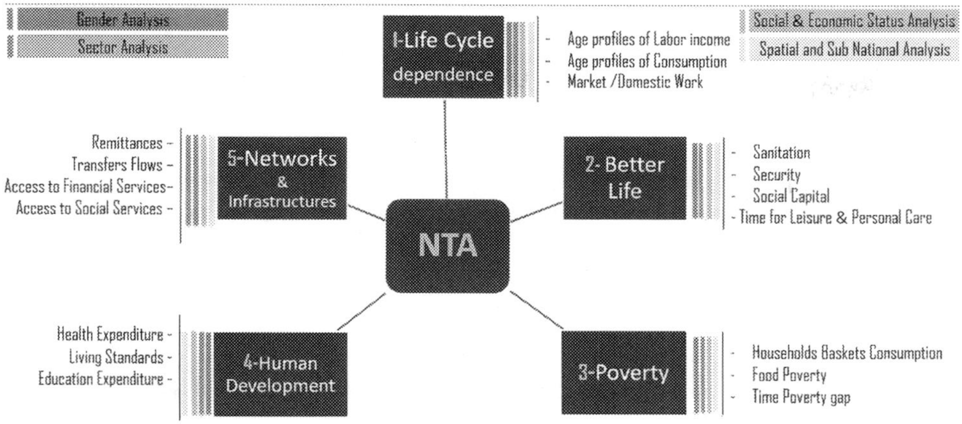

Figure 35.2 Integrated conceptual model of the Demographic Dividend Index.

Source: authors

to characterize the current situation; (2) a definition of the situation deemed desirable; and (3) a relatively simple measure to characterize the cost to be incurred, the steps to be taken to improve certain key indicators that should allow for a shift from (1) to (2).

In addition, an objective is defined, and the current situation (described by the sub-dimensions) is compared with this objective. The sub-dimensions below the objective are identified as well as the indicators on which to act to achieve the desired situation. However, the quantification of the gaps to be filled requires the definition of reference thresholds. Since the dimensions, sub-dimensions, and indicators have standardized values between 0 and 1, the desirable situation is that the value of each component is greater than R = 0.5. Thus, the threshold of R = 0.5 is taken as the reference that it at least reaches, for example. Therefore, any sub-dimension whose value is less than 0.5 is considered 'hypothetical'. Within the 'hypothetical' sub-dimensions, indicators below 0.5 are areas wherein changes are needed to bring the sub-dimension back to the desired state. The gap to be filled to reach the baseline for an indicator below this is given by:

$$\textbf{Gap to be filled} = \mathbf{R} - \mathbf{X}$$

wherein X is the indicator and R = 0.5 the reference or threshold to be reached. An initial estimate of DDMI and its sub-dimensions is made according to the methodology presented here. This presents the current situation in the country and gives an idea of the most important deviations from the target threshold.

Planning of interventions and determination of investment elasticities

After identifying the indicators below the baseline and their deviations from the baseline, the change to be made in the indicator to bring it back to the desired situation requires a few actions and costs. Specific actions for each identified indicator must be planned and executed for a change in the level of the indicator. In this sense, monetary calculations of the supply factors must be carried out to determine the amount of investment required to bring the indicator from its current state to the desired reference state. Thus, investment elasticities are calculated for each indicator whose value is to be transferred to a reference value. For an indicator X measured between two periods, the investment elasticity is obtained by the following formula:

$$e = \frac{\Delta X}{\Delta K} \times \frac{K}{X}$$

ΔX represent the variation of in indicator X between the two periods, and ΔK the variations in capital K of the projects or sectors related to indicator X.

This elasticity measures the percentage variation of the indicator (e%) following a variation in investment of 1%.

Results of monitoring the demographic dividend in selected African countries

This section presents the results of DD monitoring index in selected African countries. It is subdivided into two subsections. The first section presents and analyzes the results of the Demographic Dividend Monitoring Index (DDMI) and its components, while the second section analyzes the results of the Gender Demographic Dividend Index (GDDI).

Results for DDMI and its components

– Identification and data sources

As described earlier, the construction of the Demographic Dividend Monitoring Index (DDMI) required a huge number of variables, both quantitative and qualitative. These variables are sources from variable data sources. However, the main data source is surveys and national accounts. The survey used by each country is listed here:

1. Benin: Integrated modular survey on household living conditions (EMICoV)
2. Burkina Faso: continuous multisectoral survey (EMC)
3. Côte d'Ivoire: Survey on the Standard of Living of Households in Côte d'Ivoire (ENV)
4. Mali: Modular and Permanent Household Survey (EMOP)
5. Mauritania: Permanent Survey on Living Conditions of Households (EPCV)
6. Chad: Survey on Household Living Conditions and Poverty (ECOSIT)
7. Nigeria: Nigerian Living Standards Survey (NLSS)
8. Guinea: Light Survey for Poverty Assessment (ELEP)
9. Niger: National Survey of Household Living Conditions (QUIBB)
10. South Africa: Living Conditions of Households (LCS)

Other complementary sources are often mobilized in the DDMI construction. These include census, electoral commission data, World Development Indicators (WDI) of the World Bank, atmospheric survey centre, Global Peace Index (GPI), Demographic and Health Survey (DHS), and other administrative data. The use of international data is because of the frequent lack of important information at national levels. In cases in which a country possesses all necessary data, then national data is full privileged. The DDMI is based on national data and survey.

– Results of DDMI components in Africa

The Demographic Dividend Monitoring Index (DDMI) was primarily calibrated for the member countries of the SWEDD (Sahel's Women Empowerment and Demographic Dividend) project, which financed the construction and implementation of this index. The index was then adopted by several other African countries. Table 35.3 presents the results of the DDMI components for some African countries.

Very little coverage of economic dependency among countries

In the Sahel region, economic dependency affects on average individuals aged 0–27 and 64 and over. Their lifecycle deficit is estimated at US$79 billion. The non-dependent people are in the 28–63 age group. The economic surplus they generate amounts to US$33 billion and covers only 42% of the deficit of dependent people. The EDCI thus calculated reveals a 58% deviation from the average target of 50% economic dependency coverage in the Sahel zone. Out of the seven Sahel countries, only Niger, with an ECDI of 57.6%, manages to cover more than half of the deficit of dependent persons, while other countries such as Mali, Mauritania, and Burkina Faso are close to the 50% threshold, considerable efforts still need to be made by Sahelian countries such as Benin, Chad, and Côte d'Ivoire. Outside the Sahel, South Africa and Nigeria have relatively very low EDCI despite their economic power on the African continent. The situation is the same for Senegal and Guinea, with EDCI scores of 37.1% and 31.1% respectively.

Perceived quality of living environment satisfactory in most African countries

As regards the quality of the living environment, it is moderately satisfactory in the Sahel zone with an index of 53.7%. This performance is mainly explained by the subjective well-being (77%) and work/life balance (55%) sub-dimensions, for which the Sahel scores well. On the other hand, one deplores the insufficient level of housing conditions (46%) to improve individual well-being, the unsatisfactory quality of the environment (47%) and low civic engagement (48%) which have negatively impacted the quality of the living environment. In the zone,

Table 35.3 DDMI Dimensional Index Results for Africa

Country	*Reference Year*	*EDCI*	*LEQI*	*PESI*	*EHDI*	*NTSI*
Benin	2018	0,286	0,540	0,587	0,479	0,164
Burkina Faso	2018	0,468	0,431	0,614	0,389	0,162
Côte d'Ivoire	2018	0,382	0,590	0,537	0,549	0,247
Mali	2018	0,454	0,506	0,525	0,376	0,143
Mauritania	2018	0,446	0,589	0,722	0,571	0,198
Niger	2018	0,576	0,606	0,547	0,309	0,102
Chad	2018	0,384	0,524	0,554	0,357	0,061
South Africa	2019	0,216	0,563	0,700	0,803	0,374
Nigeria	2020	0,297	0,510	0,602	0,595	0,230
Guinea	2019	0,311	0,575	0,452	0,432	0,096
Senegal	2019	0,371	0,632	0,579	0,486	0,187

Source: Authors' calculation

Niger has the highest LEQI (60.6%), while Burkina Faso has the lowest index at 43.1%. The situation in Burkina Faso could be due to the low quality of the social network; subjective well-being is relatively low without neglecting the deterioration of the security situation linked to the repeated incursions of Boko Haram into Burkina Faso territory in recent years. In the other countries, although the quality of the living environment is appreciable, Senegal enjoys the best quality of living environment with a LEQI of 63.2%.

Towards a more accentuated transition from poverty to non-poverty

The countries of the Sahel are in a positive poverty dynamic. The Synthetic Index of Exit from Poverty (PESI) indicates that on average 56% of households have stabilized in pure non-poverty or have moved from poverty to non-poverty. Chronic poverty affects nearly a quarter of households in the Sahel (24%). However, the proportion of households that move out of poverty (23%) is higher than the proportion that move into poverty (20%). Moreover, one third of households remain in pure non-poverty on a sustainable basis. All the countries in the zone record appreciable PESIs above the minimum threshold of 50% with high performance for Mauritania (72%), Burkina Faso (61%), and Benin (59%).

In the zone outside the Sahel, the two African giants show the best performances in terms of poverty exit with PESIs of 70% for South Africa and 60.2% for Nigeria. Guinea has the lowest PESI (45.2%) while Senegal has a poverty exit index of 57.9%.

Human development is still a major challenge in African countries

In terms of broad human development, the performance of Sahelian countries remains relatively weak with an HDI index of 42%. The relatively low stock of human capital in this area is explained by the "Education" dimension, with a score of 26%, particularly the average duration of schooling, which hardly exceeds 3 years in the zone. The highest EHDIs were observed in Mauritania (57%) and Côte d'Ivoire (51%). Burkina Faso (38.9%), Mali (37.6%), Niger (30.9%), and Chad (35.7%) are the countries furthest behind in terms of widespread human development in the zone. Benin is 2 points away from the minimum threshold of 50%. In the other non-SWEDD countries, South Africa has a very high EHDI of 80.3% followed by Nigeria (59.5%); this reflects the massive and quality investments in education and health in these countries. Senegal (48.6%) and Guinea (43.2%) will need to make further efforts to reach the 50% threshold.

Weaknesses in the use of networks and weak interconnection between territories

The Sahel is characterized by low fluidity, low financial capacity, and low mobility. This is partly reflected in the NSTI's average score for the zone, which is clearly low (18%) and where the migration (10%) and financial flows (14%) sub-dimensions are poorly rated. A country-specific analysis shows that Côte d'Ivoire (30%) is ahead of the other countries although it is below the recommended minimum threshold. Urbanization and infrastructure are more developed in this country. The gap to be filled by the latter is smaller compared to other countries. On the other hand, the situation of networks and territories is very worrying in Chad (6.1%), Niger, and Mali where the gap to be filled exceeds 45%. South Africa has the highest NTSI (37.4%) although this is still insufficient to accelerate DD capture. The situation in terms of infrastructure coverage and territorial attractiveness in Nigeria (NSTI = 23%) is like that of Côte d'Ivoire. There are also strong similarities between the NSTI levels of Senegal (18.7%) and Mauritania

(19.8%), while the NSTI of Guinea (9.6%) is comparable to that of Chad (6.1%). These countries require huge structuring efforts to increase the contribution of territories to DD capture.

- DDMI results in Africa

This sub-section presents the results of DDMI for the Sahel countries as well as for four African countries, namely Guinea, Nigeria, Senegal, and South Africa. Table 35.4 presents the results of DDMI in these countries as well as the gap at the 50% threshold to be filled.

According to this table, the Sahel is not yet exploiting its demographic potential. Indeed, the DDMI of this zone stands at 39.1%, about 11% below the 50% threshold. The countries closest to the 50% threshold are Mauritania (46.4%) and Côte d'Ivoire (44%), which are 3.6% and 6% of the threshold. Benin (37.2%), Burkina Faso (37.9%), Mali (36.5%), and Niger (36%) are in an acceptable dynamic not far from the former. However, the case of Chad is worrying, with a DDMI score of 29.9%, i.e. a 20.1% deviation from the minimum threshold. Particular attention must be paid to DD issues in this country. Table 35.3 shows the contributions of each of the dimensions to the regional DDMI value for Sahelian countries.

As shown in the Table 35.3, the weakness of DDMI in the Sahel is the result of low scores in the dimensions of lifecycle deficit (41.9%), human development (42.2%), and networks and territories (18.5%). The dimensions of living environment quality and poverty transition have relatively acceptable scores of 53% and 55.7% respectively.

In countries outside the Sahel, South Africa leads the way with an estimated DDMI score of 48%, i.e. 2% of the 50% threshold, followed by Nigeria with a DDMI of 41.6%, i.e. a gap of 8.4% of the required threshold. Senegal has a DDMI score like that of Nigeria, while Guinea's DDMI score is 32%, which is relatively very low in view of the country's demographic challenges.

In summary, out of the 12 countries covered, none of them has a DDMI score of at least 50%. In other words, these countries are not exploiting their demographic potential although several studies show that the potential for DD exists in these countries. South Africa remains the leader with a DDMI of 48%. It is followed by countries such as Mauritania (46.4%), Côte d'Ivoire (44%), Nigeria (41.6%), and Senegal (41.5%). These countries are less than 10% of the 50% threshold required to trigger the capture and exploitation of DD. Chad has the lowest DDMI among these countries.

Table 35.4 DDMI Results and Gap to be Filled in Africa

	DDMI	*Deviation at 50%*
Benin	0,372	0,128
Burkina Faso	0,379	0,121
Côte d'Ivoire	0,440	0,060
Mali	0,365	0,135
Mauritania	0,464	0,036
Niger	0,360	0,140
Chad	0,299	0,201
South Africa	0,480	0,020
Nigeria	0,416	0,084
Guinea	0,320	0,180
Senegal	0,415	0,085

Source: Authors' calculation

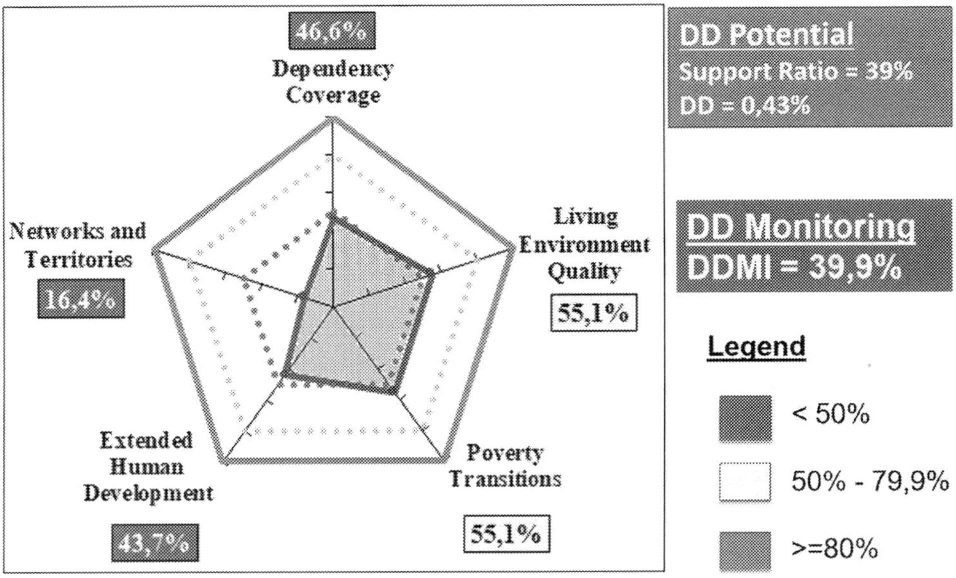

Figure 35.3 DDMI for Sahelian countries.

Source: Author's calculation

Gender Demographic Dividend Index (GDDI) results

The Gender Demographic Dividend Index (GDDI) is a disaggregation of the Demographic Dividend Tracking Index (DDMI) by gender. In this section, the GDDI index has been calibrated for three countries in Africa: two countries in West Africa, namely Niger and Senegal, and one country in Southern Africa, namely South Africa. Table 35.5 presents the results of the DDMI components disaggregated by gender for these countries.

The analysis in Table 35.5 shows that for the three countries under consideration, economic dependence is lower among women than among men. Except for South Africa, where the EDCI for men is below 50%, the coverage of economic dependency is above 65%, in contrast to the situation of women, whose EDCI remains below the minimum threshold of 50%. The quality of the living environment is, on the other hand, more favourable because the development of women's demographic potential remains higher than that of men for the countries under consideration. Indeed, women's LEQI is higher than that of men. However, it is important to note that, in terms of quality of the living environment, all three countries score well in terms of capturing DD. Regarding poverty dynamics, they are in favour of women, who experience more exits from poverty than men. Whatever the country, the poverty dynamics are favourable because, according to the PESI index scores, 52% or more of the population is out of poverty. This proportion is the same for South African men and women whose PESI index scores for men are equal to those for women. South Africa is the only country with a Human Development Index that is favourable to capturing the demographic dividend. By gender, women benefit more from broad human development than men who also have a relatively acceptable EHDI level in that country. This reflects the country's efforts to reduce inequalities in the priority areas of education and health in South Africa. The EHDI of others is low, with disparities in favour of women. Despite the considerable efforts made by these countries, certain socio-anthropological

Table 35.5 Gender Disaggregated DDMI Components for Selected Countries in Africa

	ICDE	*IQCV*	*ISSP*	*IDHE*	*ISRT*
Women					
South Africa	0,101	0,604	0,700	0,804	0,337
Niger	0,473	0,615	0,667	0,283	0,093
Senegal	0,037	0,649	0,643	0,463	0,163
Men					
South Africa	0,379	0,542	0,700	0,797	0,386
Niger	0,666	0,605	0,531	0,334	0,111
Senegal	0,913	0,609	0,529	0,511	0,204

Source: Authors' calculation

Table 35.6 GDDI Results for Selected Countries in Africa

	GDDI		*DDMI*
	Women	*Men*	
South Africa	0,410	0,536	0,480
Niger	0,348	0,380	0,361
Senegal	0,259	0,498	0,415

Source: Authors

realities could explain these gender inequalities in terms of human development (especially education and health) in these countries. Women's contribution to the attractiveness of territories and infrastructure networks for capturing the demographic dividend remains relatively very small compared to that of men in any country. This reflects the low participation of women compared to men in the development of territories in the sense of encouraging the exploitation of demographic potential for local development. However, in all three countries, the synthetic index for networks and territories is very low and below the 50% threshold.

Table 35.6 presents and allows an analysis of the real gender disparities incorporated in DDMI training according to the countries under consideration. In South Africa, while men display a DD index (53.6%) favourable to the exploitation of their demographic potential, this is not the case for women. Women have a GDDI of 41% below the threshold for capturing and exploiting DD. At the same time in the other countries (Niger and Senegal), although the level of GDDI is low in relation to the DD capture threshold, the contribution of men remains significantly higher than that of women. There is thus a noticeable disparity in the contribution of women and men to DD capture and exploitation efforts. This disparity is largely to the disadvantage of women. However, some countries such as South Africa are demonstrating efforts to reduce these inequalities for the full empowerment and participation of women in the exploitation of the demographic dividend.

Sensitivity of results

The study of the demographic dividend is part of a multi-disciplinary approach and its application in African countries faces the enormous challenge of designing a tool with a solid theoretical foundation while giving it the necessary flexibility and versatility to consider such varied analytical prisms as gender inequalities, spatial disparities, lifecycle, sectors of activity, and socio-economic status.

The design of DDMI fills the enormous gap that previously existed in the monitoring of DD in countries. The composite DDMI has the potential to address several challenges:

- the challenge of international comparison, in that the index allows the use of the same harmonized methodology for all countries.
- the challenge of local development, in that it provides countries with a robust indicator for monitoring all aspects of development at the sub-national level.
- the challenge of analyzing exogenous shocks. Based on harmonized indicators collected at the finest level in each country, DDMI provides decision-makers at national and local levels, as well as the research community, with rapid impact responses for most exogenous shocks. The most illustrative example is the COVID-19 impact analysis for which the results obtained in the very short term help policy-makers make rapid decisions in the context of economic recovery.

The demographic dividend is the economic growth resulting from transformations in the age pyramid of a country's population. A demographic dividend occurs when a decline in the birth rate leads to changes in the age distribution of a population; this means that less investment is needed to meet the needs of the youngest groups and that there are relatively more adults in the working population. This situation could be translated into opportunities for economic growth and human capital development if significant investments that promote economic development and family well-being are made.

Today, it is recognized that African countries are at different stages of the demographic transition. Most of these countries are still at the very beginning of the transition process, when the challenge is to initiate or accelerate fertility decline. Thus, it is widely recognized that some countries struggling to lift their populations out of poverty should make every effort to benefit from the boost that this dividend could provide.

It should be emphasized that the design and implementation of DDMI comes at a crucial time when countries in sub-Saharan Africa face enormous challenges related to their socio-economic development. This work contributes to an in-depth reflection that is fortunately developing in a context wherein capturing the demographic dividend is seen as an opportunity for achieving sustainable development.

In view of the results obtained across the diversity of countries in this article, it urges regional and national authorities to engage in a dynamic of structural transformation of the economy that cannot ignore the demographic challenges and endogenous specificities of each country's terroir. In this wake, the economic policies implemented should better guarantee the demographic transition at a local level. This would provide advantages that could facilitate the ultimate achievement of individual and collective well-being, which is the foundation of all development agendas.

Perspectives

The CREG's outlook or research agenda over at least 25 years is promising, although it depends on several factors. Firstly, NTA expertise and its corollary, generational economics, is increasingly in demand both in academia and in the administrations of almost all sub-Saharan African countries, given the limitations of conventional theoretical approaches. The pressing interest for this expertise requires the structuring of a university course with two objectives; the theorization of a new approach to economic growth based on the NTA methodology, and generational economics in public administration according to the respective demographic profiles. In academia, demography, economics, and related disciplines must be developed to remain within the international standard of scientific research and thereby develop competitiveness and international scientific collaborations. In this regard, the CREG intends to invest in the training of a considerable mass of young people in the generational economy at the university level as an opportunity to strengthen the capacities of public administrations and to push African states to take advantage of the demographic dividend.

Africa today faces a vast competition with regions of the world that have a high level of scientific knowledge and technology. This gap in knowledge levels must be bridged as soon as possible if the promises of 2063 are to be realized within the time frame set. The organization of a university course in the field of economics and demography could provide member countries with the right researchers and technicians to support locally the different administrations involved in accelerating inclusive economic growth in this march towards the development of the continent. The financing of this training, which will be done on a competitive basis, will come in part from the excellence scholarships granted by governments and various other donors.

Through the scientific evidence published for different countries by local research teams, different political and other actors should work in a collaborative synergy to contribute to the achievement of the continent's political agenda by 2063.

Agenda 2063 is the will expressed for the vision of the continent's development for the next 50 years by the heads of state, after taking stock and learning from the situation of the region during the previous 50 years. This opportunity enabled the continent's leaders to reaffirm the ambition to make the twenty-first century the century of Africa. This vision determines the direction of all countries' efforts to advance science, technology, and the well-being of their people in terms of development.

There is a clear resolve at the highest level of the continent's action to mobilize the populations and their ownership of development programmes, to improve resource mobilization and to enhance the leading role of the sub regional economic communities, which are called upon to use their expertise to give impetus to national plans for Africa's development. As was to be expected, several lessons must be drawn from past approaches which have not often helped either to better identify complex problems or, even less so, to provide adequate solutions. The excellence of the consortium responds to this concern to draw lessons from the past in order to use the NTA approach and generational economics theories to integrate this dimension into the particular structure of African demography, the level of economic dependence on long awaited economic performance.

It is up to the consortium to bring its expertise towards inclusive growth and sustainable development. The characteristics of the populations, their contributions in terms of production, and their challenges in terms of expenditure are all levers without which the same mistakes of the past are likely to be repeated. This demo-economic starting point varies from one country to another according to gender, networks, and territories, living environment, poverty and epidemiological transition, etc. These issues are the main subjects of scientific interest for the CREG in the coming years.

Notes

1 See Elson, 1995; Seguino, 2019, etc.
2 Global gender gap index; gender inequality index; gender development index; Social Institution and Gender Index, etc.
3 See Cleland et al. (2006); Canning and Schultz (2012) for more details.

References

Akintunde, T. S., Olomola, P. A., & Oladeji, S. I. (2013). Population dynamics and economic growth in sub-Saharan Africa. *Journal of Economics and Sustainable Development, 4*(13), ISSN 2222–1700 (Paper) ISSN 2222–2855.

Amporfu, E., Sakyi, D., & Frimpong, P. B. (2014). *Demographic dividend of Ghana: The National Transfer Accounts approach*. NTA Acounts Paper.

Bahan, D., & Dramani, L. (2016). Structure and dynamic of economy and its links with population well-being in Burkina Faso from 1990 to 2015. *Journal of Economics, Management and Trade, 12*(1),1–13.

Bahan, D., & Dramani, L. (2019). Socioeconomic status and fertility decline in Burkina Faso, 2003–2015. *Applied Economics and Finance, 6*(2), 56–70.

Bahan, D., & Dramani, L. (2020). Le bien-être social au Burkina Faso: Quelle est la place des structures familiales? *Journal of Economics, 8*(1), 53–67.

Basu, A. M., & Basu, K. (2014). *The prospects for an imminent demographic dividend in Africa: The case for cautious optimism*. WIDER Working Paper 2014/053.

Becker, G. S., & Murphy, K. M. (1988). The family and the state. *Journal of Law and Economics, 31*, 1–18.

Biao, B., Oga, IJ-B., & Guidimé, C. D. (2014). Demographic transition and economic growth in Benin . . . *British Journal of Economics. Management & Trade, 2*(2), 39–59.

Bloom, D., Canning, D., & Sevilla, J. (2003). *The demographic dividend: A new perspective on the economic consequences of population change*. Santa Monica, CA: RAND Corporation, MR – 1274.

Bloom, D. E., & Canning, D. (2003). How demographic change can bolster economic performance in developing countries. *World Economics-Henley on Thames, 4*(4), 1–14.

Canning, D., & Schultz, T. P. (2012). *The economic consequences of reproductive health and family planning. The Lancet*, 380(9837), 165–171. ISSN 0140-6736. https://doi.org/10.1016/S0140-6736(12)60827-7

Cleland, J., Bernstein, S., Ezeh, A., Faundes, A., Glasier, A, & Innis, J. (2006). Family planning: The unfinished agenda. *The Lancet, 368*(9549), 1810–1827. ISSN 0140-6736. https://doi.org/10.1016/S0140-6736(06)69480-4

Commission de l'Union Africaine. (2015). *Agenda 2063: l'Afrique que nous voulons*. Addis Ababa: African Union

CREG (2019). *Dividende Démographique et développement durable: fondements théoriques et modèles normatifs* (Vol. 01), Senegal: Edition l'Harmattan Sénégal.

CREG/CREFAT. (2016). *Manuel de formation sur les dimensions et indicateurs de suivi de l'Observatoire du Dividende Démographique*. Dakar : GREG/CREFAT

Dang, H-A., & Lanjouw, P. (2013). *Measuring poverty dynamics with* synthetic *panels based on cross-sections*. Policy Research Working Paper; No. 6504.Washington, DC: World Bank. © World Bank. Retrieved from https://openknowledge.worldbank.org/handle/10986/15863 License: CC BY 3.0 IGO.

Dramani, L. (2016). *Economie Générationnelle et Dividende démographique au Sénégal: Théorie et Applications* (Vol. 2). Senegal: Edition L'Harmattan Sénégal.

Dramani, L. (2019). *Dividende démographique en Afrique de l'Ouest et du Centre: Définitions, Mesures et Résultats*. Monographies Sud-Nord N°9, Panthéon Sorbonne.

Dramani, L., Agbahoungba, L. S. W., & Ndiaye, O. (2019). Genre et dividende démographique. In L. Dramani (Ed.), *Dividende démographique et développement durable: Fondements théoriques et modèles normatifs*. Tome 1. Edition L'Harmattan, ISBN: 978 2 343 17642 0; 225 pages.

Dramani, L., Akpo, E., & Agbahoungba, S. (2019). *Déficit du cycle de vie et capture du dividende démographique en Afrique Subsaharienne: Nécessité d'une autonomisation des femmes sénégalaises*. Retrieved from http://uaps2019.popconf.org/uploads/190771

Dramani, L., & Bahan, D. (2019a). Théorie et mesures du bien-être économique et social. In L. Dramani L. (Ed.), *Dividende démographique et développement durable: Fondements théoriques et modèles normatifs*. Tome 1. Edition L'Harmattan. ISBN: 978 2 343 17642 0, 225 pages.

Dramani, L., & Bahan, D. (2019b). Des théories explicatives de la transition démographique au dividende démographique. In L. Dramani (Ed.), *Dividende démographique et développement durable: Fondements théoriques et modèles normatifs*. Tome 1. Edition L'Harmattan. ISBN: 978 2 343 17642 0; 225 pages.

Dramani, L., & Oga, J. B. (2017). Understanding Demographic dividends in Africa: The NTA Approach. *Journal of Demographic Economics, 83*, 85–101.

Eastwood, R., & Lipton, M. (2011). Demographic transition in sub-Saharan Africa: How big will the economic dividend be? *Population Studies: A Journal of Demography, 65*(1), 9–35. doi:10.1080/00324728.2010.547946

Eloundou-Enyegue, P., Giroux, S., & Tenikue, M. (2017). African transitions and fertility inequality: A Demographic Kuznets Hypothesis. *Population and Development Review, 43*, 59–83. Retrieved on February 26, 2021, from www.jstor.org/stable/26622874

Elson, D. (1995). Gender awareness in modeling structural adjustment. *World Development, 23*(11), 1851–1868.

Guidime, C., Oga, J.-B., et Ndoye, E. M. Y. (2019). Migration et dividende démographique. In L. Dramani (Ed.), *Dividende démographique et développement durable: Fondements théoriques et modèles normatifs*. Tome 1. Edition L'Harmattan. ISBN: 978 2 343 17642 0; 225 pages.

Hakura, D., Hussain, M., Newiak, M., Thakoor, V., & Yang, F. (2016). *Inequality, gender gaps and economic growth: Comparative evidence for sub-Saharan Africa*. International Monetary Fund Working Paper 16/11, pp. 1–29.

Klasen, S., & Lawson, D. (2007). *The impact of population growth on economic growth and poverty reduction in Uganda*. Diskussionsbeiträge, No. 133, GeorgAugust-Universität Göttingen, Volkswirtschaftliches Seminar, Göttingen.

Lee, R. D. (1994). The formal demography of population aging, transfers, and the economic life cycle. In Martin, L & Preston, S. (eds) *Demography of Aging*, 8–49. Washington Dc: National Academy Press

Lee, R., & Mason, A. (2007). *Population ageing, wealth, and economic growth: Demographic dividends and public policy*. Background Paper for the World Economic and Social Survey, Department of Economic and Social Affairs, United Nations.

Mason, A. (2005). Demographic transition and demographic dividends in developed and developing countries. *United Nations Expert Group Meeting on Social and Economic Implications of Changing Population Age Structures*, Mexico City.

Mason, A., & Lee, R. (2006). Reform and support systems for the elderly in developing countries: Capturing the second demographic dividend. *Genus, 62*(2), 11–35.

Mason, A., & Lee, R. (2007). Transfers, capital, and consumption over the demographic transition. In R. Clark, A. Mason, & N. Ogawa (Eds.), *Population aging, intergenerational transfers and the macroeconomy* (pp. 128–162). Cheltenham, UK: Edward Elgar.

Morné, O. (2018). *Counting women's work in South Africa: Incorporating unpaid work into estimates of the economic lifecycle in 2010*. CWW Working Paper No. 8, South Africa.

Morné, O., & Kezia, L. (2018). *Counting women's work in Mauritius: Household production across the lifecycle in Mauritus in 2003*. CWW Working Paper No. 7, South Africa.

OECD. (2008). Handbook on constructing composite indicators. *Methodology and User Guide*. Retrieved from www.oecd.org/publishing/corrigenda

Olanrewaju, O., Soyibo, A., Lawanson, A. O., Olasehinde, N., Odumosu, M., Orekoya, A., . . . Adeyemi, F. (2018). *Harnessing the demographic dividend for the sustainable development of Nigeria: 2016 Demographic dividend report of Nigeria*. Published by Health Policy Training and Research Programme (HPTRP), University of Ibadan, Nigeria for the United Naons Populaons Fund (UNFPA), Nigeria.

Peter, A., & Bakary, I. H. (2018, October–December). Impact of population growth on economic growth in Africa: A dynamic panel data approach (1980–2015). *Pakistan Journal of Humanities and Social Sciences, 6*(4), 412–427.

Seguino, S. (2020). Engendering macroeconomic theory and policy. *Feminist Economics, 26*(2), 27–61. doi :10.1080/13545701.2019.1609691

Ukpolo, V. (2002). Population growth and economic growth in Africa. *Journal of Developing Societies, 18*(4), 315–329. https://doi.org/10.1177/0169796X0201800402

United Nations. (2013). *National Transfer Accounts manual: Measuring and analysing the generational economy*. Department of Economic and Social Affairs, Population Division.

PART 8

Ageing

36

AGEING IN SUB-SAHARAN AFRICA

Demographic and historical perspectives

Ayo S. Adebowale, Obiageli Onwusaka, Mobolaji M. Salawu, Segun Bello and David A. Adewole

Introduction

Population ageing is an increasing median age in a population due to declining fertility rates and rising life expectancy. This is partly due to progress achieved in public health programs and survival chances (UN, 2019). Populations around the world are ageing at a faster pace than in the past. Presently, there are more than 1 billion people aged 65 years or older, with most living in low- and middle-income countries (Figure 36.1). Trends of ageing population that emerged first in developed countries are now seen in virtually all developing countries including Africa. There were 703 million elderly persons worldwide in 2019. Eastern and Southeastern Asia carry the highest burden of the world's older population (260 million), followed by Europe and North America (over 200 million). The global number of elderly persons is projected to be more than double (about 1.5 billion) in 2050, which means 1 in 6 people in the world will be over age 65 (16%), an increase from 1 in 11 in 2019 (9%) (United Nations, 2019). In sub-Saharan Africa (SSA), the number of ageing population was 31.9 million in 2020, and this was projected to reach 101.4 million by 2050 (United Nations, 2019, 2020).

The projected increase in the ageing population in SSA has implications on health services needed for the elderly. Many elderly persons do not have access to even the basic resources necessary to live a comfortable life and some others confront multiple barriers that prevent them from full participation in societal activities. Non-communicable diseases such as heart disease, cancer and diabetes are among the factors that result in poor health outcomes among the elderly in SSA and older persons are at an increased risk of poor health (Aboderin & Beard, 2015; Audain, Carr, Dikmen, Zotor, & Ellahi, 2017). The contagious diseases, like HIV/AIDS, Lassa Fever, Dengue Fever and emerging diseases will constitute an additional challenge to the health of elderly persons in SSA. Unfortunately, the preventive care measures against these diseases are usually targeted at younger people while elderly are often neglected. Elderly persons in some situations are given little information on healthy ageing and will have to compete with other age segments of the population for services including health care access. Chronic poverty is endemic in SSA and is a fundamental risk factor for the well-being of the elderly (PRB, 2019). The COVID-19 pandemic poses additional health challenges to the survival of the elderly population. Researches have shown that the attack rate and the case fatality rate of COVID-19 are higher among the elderly population than other age segments of the population (Davis et al.,

 DOI: 10.4324/9780429287213-44

2020). Elderly care is a value which is entrenched in African culture, but there is an apparent shift in this tradition, mainly due to economic hardship and modernization. With the notable exceptions of a few countries in SSA, formal pensions (whether contributory or not) or other social welfare schemes are virtually missing and, where such exist, the payment of benefits tend to be minimal and covers only a fractional part of the elderly population (Dorfman, 2015).

Unlike other regions of the world, the ageing population poses a significant challenge to the sub-Saharan African region, due to its record of high levels of poverty, HIV/AIDS and emerging and re-emerging diseases. The increasing presence of older persons in the SSA will attract both opportunities and challenges for the countries in the region. Elderly people have the knowledge and skills that could be used to assist societies in dealing with numerous problems which they face. If their well-being and health conditions are improved, families, communities and nations may benefit from the wealth of experience of elderly individuals historically, socially and economically. Conversely, population ageing may pose some challenges like health, social support and economic challenges associated with elderly. The dependency ratio will increase, health facilities are likely to be overstretched and the need for psychosocial support will increase in most countries in SSA. Unfortunately, a compendium of information on the methods used for ageing research, ageing theories previously used, methodological issues on ageing that require further research, and ageing policies that are specific to countries in SSA are not readily available. It is against this background that the current research was put in place to document these themes mainly for reference purpose. The study outcomes will further strengthen the scientific basis for policy makers to meet the health challenges of elderly in SSA.

Literature review

The unique consequence of an ageing population and the growing number of elderly persons in different parts of the world has made ageing studies important in research. The deterioration in the elderly situation in SSA can be perceived in the context of the HIV/AIDS epidemic and other infectious diseases, population growth, changing socio-cultural norms and harsh macroeconomic trends in the countries across the region. Many studies have been conducted in the different dimensions of ageing in different parts of SSA. The main idea of these earlier studies

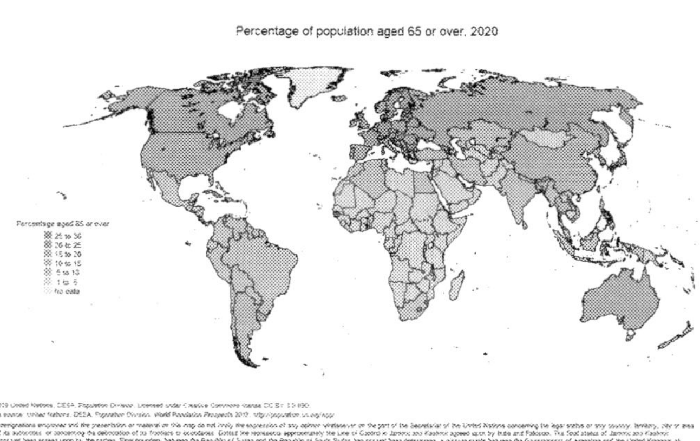

Figure 36.1 Percentage of the population aged 65 years and older.

Source: United Nations, DESA, Population Division. World Population Prospects 2019. http//population.un.org.

was to establish ways of improving the health of elderly population and increasing their survival chances. The results from previous studies on elderly health care access, disease conditions and their roles at family levels are similar and what is generally known is that old age presents itself with at least a health challenge. However, behavioural practices at younger ages or currently may predispose elderly to more complex health problems (National Research Council, 2001). Nevertheless, improvement in access to health care and family support (physical and financial) will advance the general health outcomes of elderly in SSA.

The ageing process predisposes elderly persons to higher risks of diseases and infections. At this period, the elderly population is at risk of nutritional deficiency, which may aggravate other health problems (Audain et al., 2019). In a study of 400 elderly individuals in urban areas in the northern region of Ghana, it was established that almost all the respondents were independent in performing all daily activities and that malnutrition is a burden among the elderly in the region (Aganiba, Owusu, Steiner-Asiedu, & Dittoh, 2015). A similar study in Kenya found high incidence of pneumonia among persons aged ≥65 years and that access to care influenced hospital utilization (Tornheim et al., 2007). A study conducted among elderly persons in Goma, DRC documented a high prevalence of type 2 diabetes mellitus (8.0%) (Mbamukonka, Agasa, Tonen-Wolyec, Mukonkole, & Tshilumba, 2017). A study conducted in South Africa to examine if proximity of the residence of elderly people to mine dumps is associated with chronic respiratory disease showed a high level of chronic respiratory symptoms and diseases among the elderly (Nkosi & Voyi, 2015). In this country, another study established an association between influenza vaccination and the hospitalization occurrence for acute respiratory or cardiovascular diseases, or all-cause death in an elderly population (van Vuuren, Rheeder, & Hak, 2009). Depression, loneliness, decreased physical activity and decreased social interaction are other common diseases among elderly (Fontal, Nonvignon, Aikins, Nwosu, & Aryeetey, 2017).

A five-year study by Ojagbemi et al. to describe factors associated with incidence of dementia and dementia mortality in a large community sample of elderly persons in Nigeria, confirmed low incidence of dementia and that the disease was significantly associated with higher mortality risk. Lower cognitive reserve was identified as one of the risk factors for incidence of dementia and high prevalence of hypertension was found among the elderly (Ojagbemi, Bello, & Gureje, 2016). A Nigerian study also showed that elderly patients with hypertension are habitually not aware of having the disease and those who received treatment for the disease have adequate control of blood pressure (Raji, Abiona, & Gureje, 2017). Involvement in any work activities and financial support from children were linked to better psychological well-being among elderly in a rural community in Nigeria (Ibitoye, Sanuade, Adebowale, & Ayeni, 2014). In Kendall and Anglewicz (2018) study conducted among older persons in rural Malawi revealed that better mental and physical well-being was found among elderly women who reside with offspring compared to those living only with grandchildren. However, in Kenyan studies, it was revealed that elderly caretakers faced major difficulties in caring for orphans and the presence of children in households headed by the elderly aggravates their economic challenge (Nyambedha, Wandibba, & Aagaard-Hansen, 2003; Muga & Onyango-Ouma, 2009).

The health-seeking practices of elderly has implication on their morbidity and mortality. Prevailing healthcare systems in a country combined with individual beliefs and philosophies about ageing and healthcare are often reported as determinants of access to health care among ageing population (Ibitoye et al., 2014). A study conducted in the DRC on the health care seeking behaviour of elderly during a time of conflict showed that very few supports were received from their own relatives and those of the same faith while supports were predominantly obtained through begging and unknown sources with government playing no role in the elderly care and support (Lutala, Kwalya, Kasagila, Watongoka, & Mupenda, 2010). It was recommended that creation of income-related activities for elderly will alleviate the search for money for health care provision when the need arises. In this country, another study showed that elderly reported that they suffer from numerous health ailments attributed to harsh living conditions and due to their inability to pay for health care services (Zihindula & Maharaj, 2013). In Kenya, Wairiuko, Cheboi, Ochieng and Oyore's (2017) study revealed that elderly people had poor perceptions of quality of health care services. Modifiable social and lifestyle factors predicted successful ageing among the elderly in a Nigerian study, signifying that health promotion aiming at behavioural change may lead to noticeable benefits for health and well-being in old age (Gureje, Oladimeji, & Abiona, 2014).

Health systems in some countries in SSA often lack the specialized personnel and infrastructure to provide adequate care for elderly persons. Social support for elderly populations in such resource-constrained settings and family caregivers are lacking. A study in Ghana and DRC showed that support/caregiving for elderly populations imposes economic burden on families, potentially affecting the economic situation of families with accompanied implications for equity and imminent family support (Nortey, Aryeetey, Aikins, Amendah, & Nonvignon, 2017; Zihindula & Maharaj, 2013).

Methods

This study was conducted in SSA and cuts across all the countries in the region. The male and female life expectancies in SSA were 59 and 62 years respectively; life expectancy at birth between 2020–2025 will be between 55 and 60 years. There are four regional blocks in SSA, namely Eastern Africa, Western Africa, Central Africa and Southern Africa. The death rate in SSA is 9 per 1,000 people with a 2.4% rate of natural increase while 3% and 43% of the population were aged ≥65 years and <15 years respectively. The GNI per capita PPP is INT-$3,828, although with striking variations across countries in the region (PRB, 2019).

A rigorous literature search was conducted from November 2019 to May 2020 (both electronic and manual) to identify all published peer-reviewed studies reporting ageing in SSA countries. The academic search engines used for this study were picked because of their wider coverage, ability to provide an immediate solution to all research-related needs for a scientific paper, and also to pave way for a personal and customized research materials' search on a specific topic of interest.

The electronic databases are:

1 Pubmed/Medline (https://pubmed.ncbi.nlm.nih.gov/),
2 Cochrane Library (www.cochranelibrary.com/),
3 Google Scholar (http://scholar.google.com/),
4 Bioline International (www.bioline.org.br/),
5 Directory of Open Access Journals (www.doaj.org/),
6 BioOne (www.bioone.org/),
7 ScienceDirect (www.sciencedirect.com/)
8 AJOL (www.ajol.info/index.php/ajol)

Literature search was done with the use of special keywords and search continued until the saturation point was reached. The identified relevant articles were independently screened on the basis of their title and abstract. A review of the complete text of potentially relevant articles was conducted and agreement was reached by the screening team. Summaries from these studies were cross-tabulated in terms of what is known and what should be known with respect to methodological, theoretical, practical, substantive issues, and research done by Africans/African scholars.

The review used three methods to collect data, including document search, database search and electronic/internet search. Existing documents and research papers on ageing were reviewed based on the research questions of this study. The researchers reached an agreement on the modus operandi (criteria) for literature search before the commencement of the exercise and these criteria were adopted as a guide for literature search. The inclusion criteria were specific to relevant original research, reviews, systematic reviews, reports and articles published in English. The review excluded articles that have no important findings relevant to the research questions of this study. Articles that have only abstract, those from the same authors which replicate findings and those that have identical findings within the same country were also excluded.

Publication titles from the initial search were revised and used to polish terms for the systematic search. The research questions and key words were used as search mechanisms in the electronic databases. A manual search was also conducted to identify possible literature that could have been omitted during the database search. We also searched relevant references from the identified literature. Studies were selected based on the application of inclusion and exclusion criteria by two independent researchers. The process began with review of abstracts and full articles were read subsequently once the abstract was deemed relevant to the study. Thereafter, the identified full articles were independently assessed and consensus was reached about the suitability of the paper for the study. Criteria were also developed to streamline articles through prioritization. The reports were aggregated based on the thematic analysis.

Results from literature search

The patterns, trends and projections of ageing population in sub-Saharan Africa

The projected percentage of the population aged 65 years and older from year 1950 to 2100 for the four regional blocks in SSA is presented in Figure 36.2. The global trend in the population aged 65 years and older was at variance with that exhibited by sub-Saharan Africa. The trend and projection in the percentage of elderly population in SSA was similar to that exhibited by Western Africa and Eastern Africa over the projection periods but differs from that of central and Southern Africa. Between the years 1950 and 2001, there was a decline in the percentage of elderly population across the regions, particularly Central Africa which experienced a sharp decline during the periods. However, there is evidence that all the regional blocks in SSA will consistently experience an increase in the population aged ≥65 years in the next 80 years.The mber of persons aged ≥65 years in 2019 in sub-Saharan Africa was 31.9 million and this was rojected to be 101.4 million by 2050, a 218% increase of elderly persons in the region between the projected periods. In 2019, Nigeria (5.5 million), Ethiopia (3.9 million), South Africa (3.2 million), Democratic Republic of Congo (2.6 million) and Tanzania (1.5 million) were the top five countries with high burden of elderly in sub-Saharan Africa. Nigeria, the most populous country in the region, had a share of about 17.2% of the total population of elderly in SSA (World Population Prospects, 2019).

About 3.0% of people in SSA were aged ≥65 years in 2019 and this will increase to 3.3% going by 2030 projection. In 2019 and for 2030 projection, Southern Africa (5.3%) has the highest proportion of its population being elderly persons while central (2.8%) and Western Africa (2.8%) have the least. The old-age dependency ratio and economic old-age dependency ratio of 6.8 and 7.3 in 2019 was projected to 7.1 and 7.6 by the end of year 2030 respectively. In

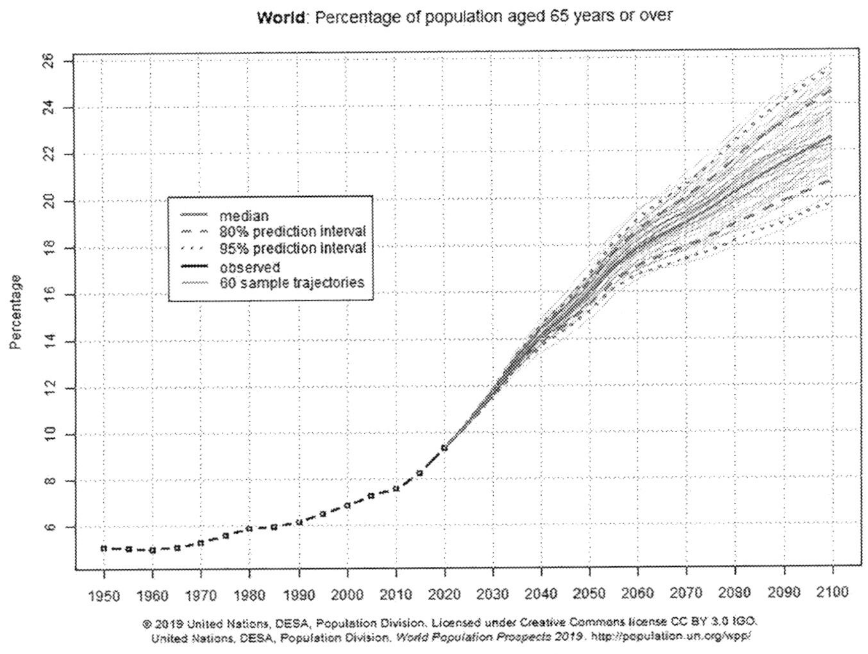

Figure 36.2a World percentage of population aged 65 years or over.

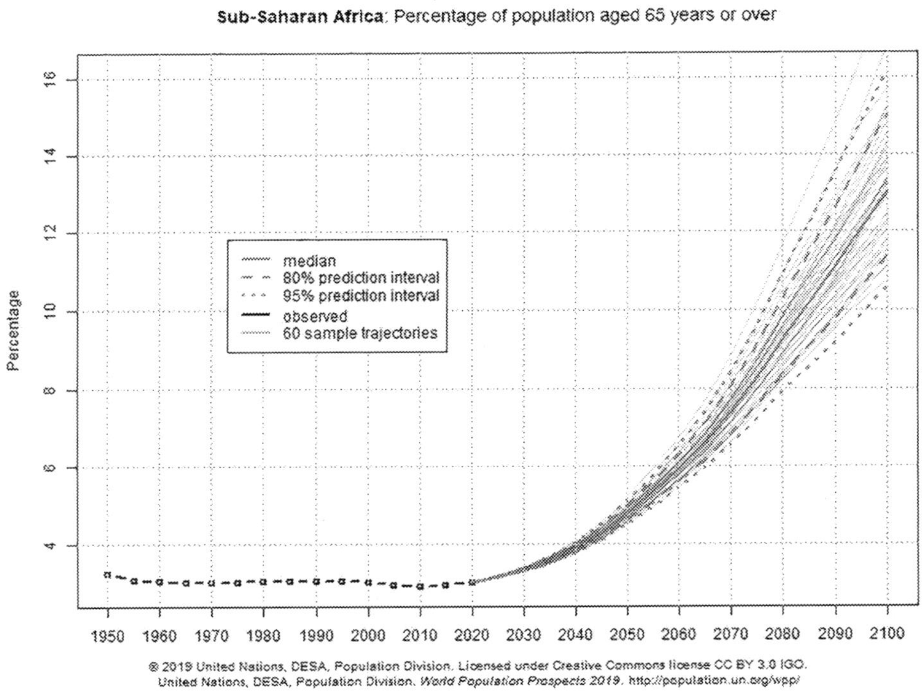

Figure 36.2b Sub-Saharan African percentage of population aged 65 years or over.

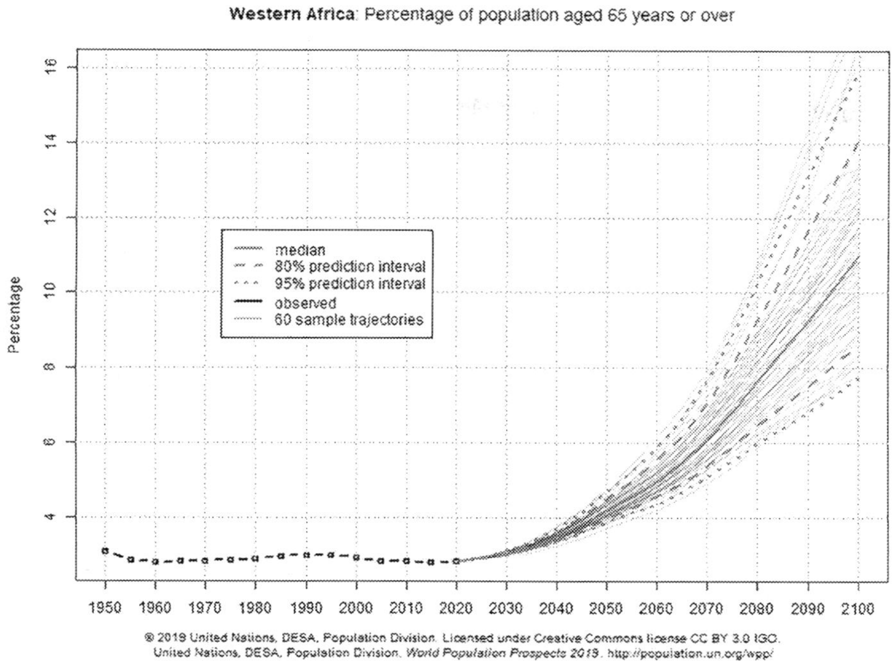

Figure 36.2c Western Africa percentage of population aged 65 years or over.

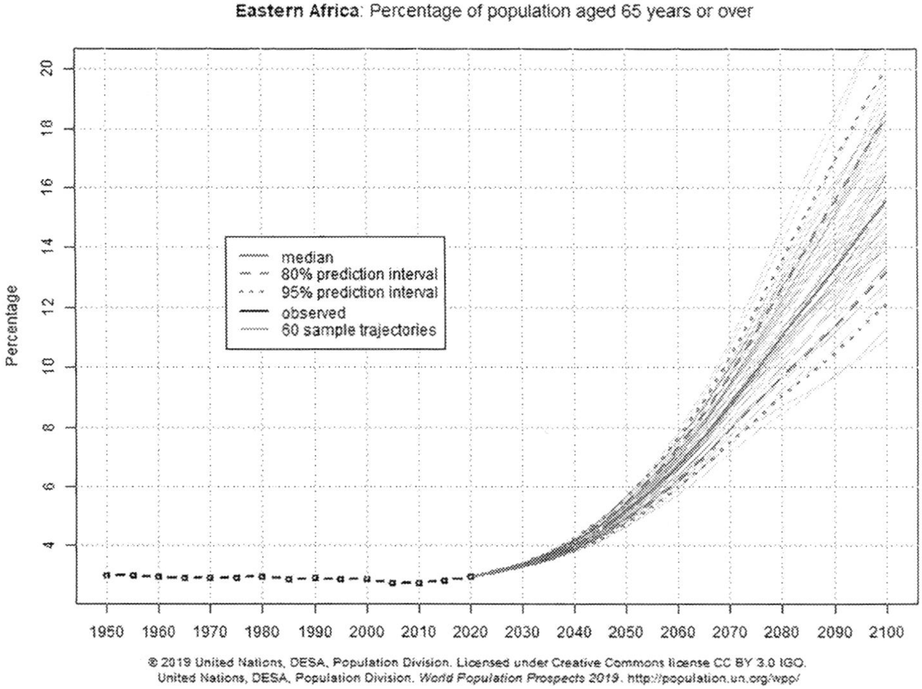

Figure 36.2d Eastern Africa percentage of population aged 65 years or over.

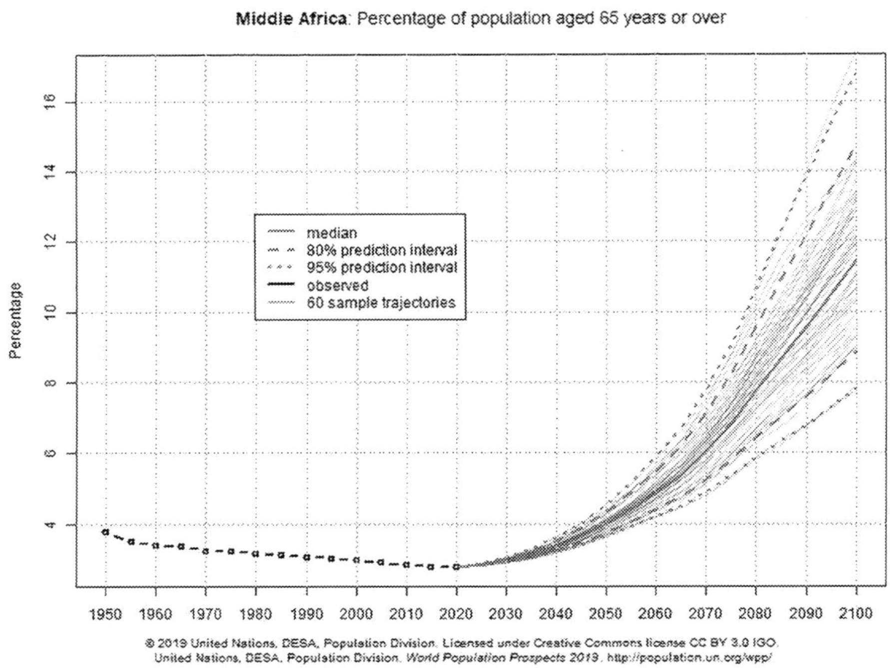

Figure 36.2e Central Africa percentage of population aged 65 years or over.

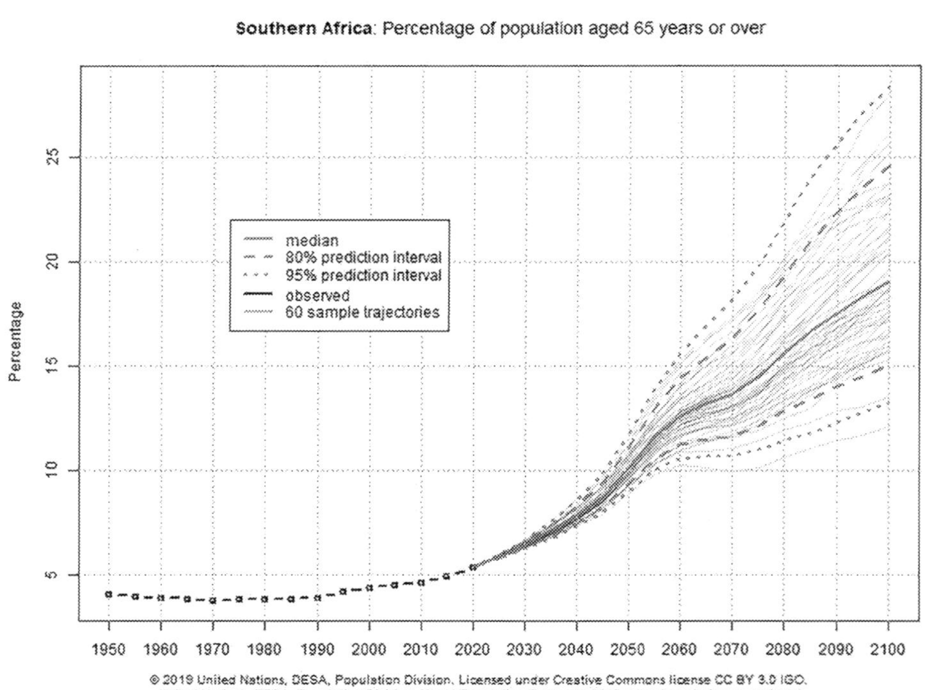

Figure 36.2f Southern Africa percentage of population aged 65 years or over.

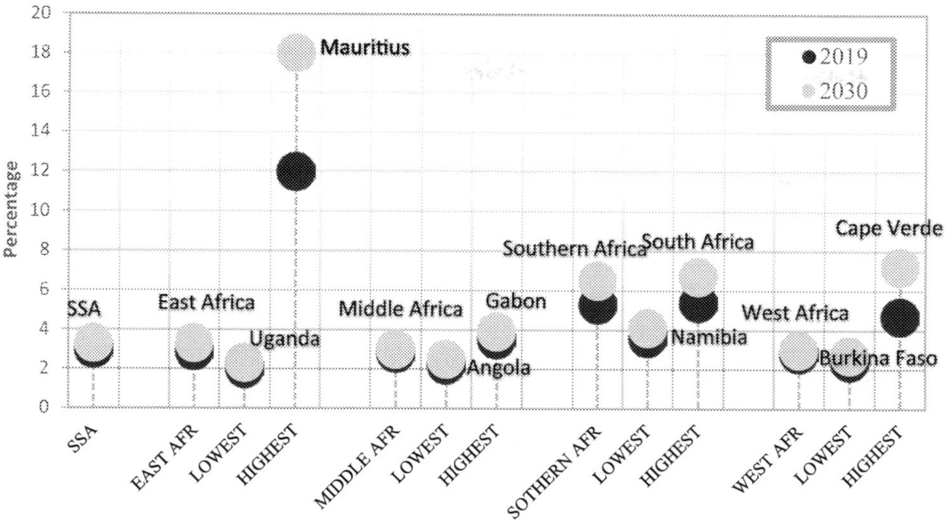

Figure 36.3 Percentage of the population aged 65+ in sub-Saharan Africa.

the Eastern Africa, between 2019 and 2030, the percentage of elderly persons in the population will increase from 2.9 to 3.3. In this region, Uganda (2019: 2.0%, 2030: 2.3%) and Mauritius (2019: 12.0%, 2030: 18.0%) had the least and highest percentage of elderly in the population respectively. In Central Africa, the population proportion of elderly in 2019 was least in Angola (2019: 2.2%, 2030: 2.3%) and highest in Gabon (2019: 3.5%, 2030: 3.9%) while Burkina Faso (2019: 2.4%, 2030: 2.7%) and Cape Verde (2019: 4.7%, 2020: 7.2%) had the least and highest in West Africa respectively. Mauritius, Cape Verde and South Africa were likely to record marked change in the population of elderly between 2019 and 2030 (Figure 36.3) (UN, 2019).

Existing theories used to explain the behavioural changes that drive ageing pattern in Africa

Ageing is an important aspect of human life. The propensity to contribute less and depend more on others as individuals advance in age creates a burden of ageing on the society. Nearly all physiological functions lose efficiency with ageing; there is also a relationship between ageing and an increased vulnerability to trauma, disease, weakening of the immune system and various forms of stress (Chaudieu et al., 2011; Nikolich-Žugich, 2018). Declining health and cognitive or physical functioning may necessitate that elderly move to supportive care environments that drain resources. Critical to all the issues associated with ageing is the formulation of ageing theories. Many theories exist about the age-related change process, and they are not intertwined, but they often contradict one another. These theories provide the basis at which better understanding of ageing can be accomplished (Jose et al., 2007).

Among the main theories of ageing widely known in the literature is the free radical theory (Harman, 1956). Harman theorized that free radicals derived from oxygen are responsible for damage caused by ageing. This results from the inability of antioxidant systems to continuously offset all the free radicals generated during the cell life cycle. This leads to oxidative damage in the cell and tissues (Stadtman, 1992; Sohal, Agarwal, Dubey, & Orr, 1993; Harman, 1978).

A free radical is any molecule that has a free electron which makes it react with healthy molecules in a destructive way. Diet, lifestyle, drugs and radiation, etc., are all known drivers of free radical production within human body (Harman, 1956). This theory was used in South Africa to investigate whether plasma vitamin C and E status is lowered in subjects with Alzheimer's Disease (AD) and dementia (Charlton, Rabinowitz, Geffen, & Dhansay, 2004). Miquel, Economos, Fleming and Johnson (1980) leveraged on the radical theory to propose the mitochondrial theory of free radicals in ageing which suggests that mitochondria from the post mitotic cells use oxygen at high speeds, to produce reactive oxygen species which cause oxidative stress as they overcome the antioxidant cellular defenses (Miquel & Fleming, 1986).

The ageing theory of wear and tear was based on the idea that ageing is a consequence of wearing out of vital parts in body cells and tissues (Pearl, 1928). The neuroendocrine theory is a form of wear-and-tear theory with a special focus on the neuroendocrine system which involves a complicated network of biochemicals that direct the release of hormones altered by the hypothalamus situated in the brain. As individuals grow older, the hypothalamus loses its efficiency in regulatory ability, and as a result, the receptors which uptake individual hormones become less sensitive to them (Vladimir Dilman & Ward Dean, 1992). Conversely, the programmed theory emphasized that ageing is a result of the changes in gene expression that affect the mechanisms responsible for maintenance, repair and defense responses. The theory contemplates that ageing results from a biological programme that intentionally causes weakening of the body organs and death in order to obtain a direct evolutionary advantage realized by restraining lifespan beyond a species-specific optimum lifespan. This theory relied on endocrine and immunological theories. While the endocrine theory opined that the biological clock acts through hormones to control the pace of ageing (Vladimir Dilman & Ward Dean, 1992), immunological theory emphasized that the immune system is programmed to deteriorate over time, leading to an increased susceptibility to infectious disease and consequently results in ageing and death (Walford, 1964).

The membrane theory of ageing however, argued that it is the age-related changes of the cell's ability to transfer chemicals, heat and electrical processes that impair it. As individuals grow older, the cell membrane becomes less lipid which causes an impediment to its efficiency in terms of conducting normal function and there is a toxic buildup in the system (Zs.-Nagy, 1978). Another one is the cross-linking theory which believes that it is the binding of glucose to protein that causes various health problems in the human system (Bjorksten, 1978). The occurrence of such binding impaires the protein and hampers its efficient performance. The accumulation of cross-linked proteins damages cells and tissues, slowing down bodily processes and thus resulting in ageing. Living a longer life will lead to the increased likelihood of oxygen meeting glucose and protein. The known cross-linking disorders include senile cataract and the appearance of tough, leathery and yellow skin (Bjorksten, 1978).

Disengagement theory formulated by Cumming and Henry (1961) is recognized as the first formal psychosocial theory that tried to elucidate the ageing process. This theory submitted that ageing is an unavoidable process in which many of the relationships between an individual and members of the society are withdrawn and those left behind are altered in quality. As people age, there is the tendency to keep more distance from the society and new forms of relationships with the society are established. The theory has attracted strong disapproval as innate, universal and unidirectional. The other two psychosocial theories are activity theory and the continuity theory. The activity theory opined that an individual's self-concept is associated with the roles he holds and suggests that successful ageing will occur when elderly persons stay active and maintain social interactions (Havighurst, 1961). New roles have to be substituted for the lost roles in order to uphold a positive sense of self. The theory was criticized because of its failure to consider the inequalities in health and economics that may deter the elderly's ability to partake in such activities. The continuity theory of ageing by Atchley (1971) states that elderly persons will typically maintain the same activities, behaviours and relationships as they did in their earlier years of life by adapting strategies that are related to their past experiences (American Society on Aging, 2007; Atchley, 1989).

Study design and data analysis methods used for ageing research in sub-Saharan Africa

Numerous ageing studies have been conducted across countries in SSA. The main focus of the reviewed studies is on assessment of health conditions of elderly persons, their health-seeking behaviour and their status with respect to socioeconomic stability and activities. For the implementation of the studies, different design approaches have been used but most studies were cross-sectional involving either quantitative or qualitative research or both and based on self-reported information. Very few adopted quasi-experimental, longitudinal, retrospective cohort, case-control and nested case-control approaches. A study that examined the association between influenza vaccination and the occurrence of hospitalization for acute respiratory or cardiovascular diseases, or all-cause death in an elderly population in South Africa, utilized a nested case-control design (van Vuuren, Rheeder, & Hak, 2009). While some of these studies were purely descriptive, others were analytical and to some extent, laboratory experiments were used to validate the health conditions of elderly. Some studies also used observational methods to assess the level of preparedness of the health facilities in terms of health care provision and response to the care for elderly. Primary data were used in most cases but some of the studies on the elderly conducted in SSA were also based on secondary data analysis mainly obtained from surveillance sites or hospital records or earlier conducted health survey.

Cross-sectional study design/quantitative research

This section discussed a few among several studies that had been conducted in SSA with the use of a cross-sectional descriptive design. A Burkina Faso study examined functional disability in activities of daily living and instrumental or domestic activities of daily living in the elderly living at home used a cross-sectional approach (Berthé et al., 2017). This study design was also applied in the description of clinical, electrocardiographic and echocardiographic aspects of arterial hypertension in elderly patients in Senegal (Sarr et al., 2016), examination of the type and severity of disability experienced by elderly patients in Uganda (Bachani et al., 2018), association of chronic respiratory disease and proximity to mine dumps among the elderly in Gauteng and North West Province, South Africa (Nkosi, Wichmann, & Voyi, 2015) and association between sociodemographic variables and successful ageing among elderly in Angola (Galiana, Gutiérrez, Sancho, Francisco, & Tmás, 2016; Gutiérrez, Tomás, Galiana, Sancho, & Cebrià, 2013). In Nigeria, some of the studies conducted among elderly, based on cross-sectional design, are investigation of health-related quality of life, profile and correlates of functional status of elderly, factors associated with falls, and extent of elder abuse and neglect (Ogunyemi, Odeyemi, Kanma-Okafor, & Ladi-Akinyemi, 2018; Fakoya et al., 2018; Ajayi, Adebusoye, Ogunbode, Akinyemi, & Adebayo, 2015; Bekibele & Gureje, 2010). In Kenya, the method was used to examine household composition and food security among the elderly caretakers, and factors influencing access to healthcare among elderly were identified using method-mix approach (Muga & Ounyago-Ouma, 2009; Wairiuko et al., 2017). The cross-sectional design was used in Ghana, DRC and Tanzania in ageing-related research (Nortey et al., 2017; Fonta et al., 2017; Lutala, Kwalya, Kasagila, Watongoka, & Mupenda, 2010; Zihindula & Mahara, 2013; Nagu et al., 2017). In Tanzania, this study design was, at different times, used to compare the disability levels for dementia, stroke and Parkinson's disease in a community-based study, examine the profile and degree of derangements of plasma lipids among elderly individuals, and determination of the nutritional status, functional ability and food habits of institutionalized and non-institutionalized elderly people (Kisoli et al., 2015; Mwangengwa et al., 2014; Nyaruhucha, Msuya, & Matrida, 2004).

Qualitative studies

Qualitative methods (QMs) were used in different ageing studies conducted in Burkina Faso (Ouedraogo, Attané, & Gyasi, 2019; Berthé-Sanou et al., 2013; Hien et al., 2015). A study in Senegal based on a collection of qualitative data assessed the real-life experiences, perception of ageing, challenges and coping strategies of elderly (Ka et al., 2018). In a Nigerian study, QM was used to identify factors that have contributed to the state of elderly in destitution (Fajemilehin, Ayandiran, & Salami, 2007). In Tanzania, the conceptualization of depression amongst older adults selected from rural villages in Kilimanjaro was examined using QM (Howorth et al., 2019). QMs were used to assess changing trends in accessing care and support for the elderly in Uganda (Amurwon, 2019), exploration of reasons why elderly people diagnosed with presbycusis and fitted with hearing aids stop using hearing aids post fitting in Johannesburg, South Africa (Moroe & Vazzana, 2019), in examining social participation and perceived depression among elderly population in South Africa (Hao et al., 2017). A study in Ghana that deals with ideas and practices of care of elderly people in a rural community was based on anthropological fieldwork, mainly conversations with 35 elderly people and observations in their daily lives (Van der Geest, 2002). In a Cameroonian study that explored the determinants of active and healthy ageing, a mixed method of data collection was used (Naah, Njong, & Kimengsi, 2020).

Longitudinal studies

The longitudinal method was used in some of the reviewed studies. To mention a few, Oshi, Oshi, Alobu and Ukwaja (2014) and Tobi, Ndokwu and Edomwonyi (2018) conducted a cohort study of adult TB patients in two large health facilities in Nigeria and examined the characteristics of critically ill elderly patients admitted to a tertiary intensive care unit in Nigeria respectively. A prospective analysis was conducted to examine pinch grafting of chronic leg ulcers in a series of elderly patients in rural Cameroon (Kadia et al., 2017). In rural Malawi, a study examined the relationship between household composition and health at older ages (Kendall & Anglewicz, 2018). Others that have utilized longitudinal data include frailty data from people elderly people living in the selected rural Hai District of northern Tanzania to identifying frailty and its outcomes within 3-year follow-up (Gray et al., 2017), determination of the predictors of subjective health, depression, and quality of life among elderly men and women living in the rural South Africa using data from a longitudinal study of an INDEPTH community in South Africa (Wang et al., 2019; Payne, Gómez-Olivé, Kahn, & Berkman, 2017).

Observational studies

An observational method was used to assess the level of health facilities preparedness and response to elderly care in some of the reviewed studies. In Uganda, as was the case for most of the studies that used this method, randomly selected health facilities were assessed for their availability of critical items deemed important for provision of geriatric-friendly services as derived from World Health Organization's Age-Friendly Primary Health Care Centres Toolkit (Ssensamba, Mukuru, Nakafeero, Ssenyonga, & Kiwanuka, 2019).

Secondary data

Some of the earlier studies conducted among elderly persons in SSA used secondary data. In Ghana, Ghanaian Living Standards Survey from 2012 to 2013 data was used to identify the determinants of NHIS enrolment for older individuals living in rural Ghana (Van der Wielen, Channon, & Falkingham, 2018). WHO Study on Global Ageing and Adult Health (SAGE) Wave 1 was used to compare the measurement and decomposition of socioeconomic inequality in single- and multi-morbidity in older adults in China and Ghana (Kunna, San, & Stewart, 2016) and this data source was employed in other studies to examine the risk factors for hypertension and predictors of self-reported health in Ghana (Tenkorang, Kuuire, Luginaah, & Banchani, 2017; Fonta et al., 2017). In Nigeria, Adisa (2015) conducted a study to identify determinants of catastrophic health spending among poorly insured elderly households in urban cities using data on out-of-pocket payments and self-reported health status sourced from the Nigerian General Household Panel Survey. Data extracted from 2013 Nigeria General Household Survey were used to examine factors associated with the healthcare-seeking behaviour of older people (Atchessi, Ridde, Abimbola, & Zunzunegui, 2018). Ageing studies have also been conducted based on the 2010 Uganda National Household Survey (Wandera, Ddumba, Akinyemi, Adedini, & Odimegwu, 2017), records of the Sinawe Centre from South Africa (Meel, 2017), and Ouagadougou Health and Demographic Surveillance System in Burkina Faso (Onadja, Atchessi, Soura, Rossier, & Zunzunegui, 2013). A study that evaluates the influence of local district conditions on subjective quality of life of older South African adults also used WHO-Study of Global Ageing and Adult Health survey data (Ralston, 2018). Hospital records were accessed to analyze type 2 diabetes mellitus among the elderly in Goma, Democratic Republic of the Congo (Mbamukonka, Agasa, Tonen-Wolyec, Mukonkole, & Tshilumba, 2017).

Data analysis method

The data analysis methods used in the reviewed studies are similar particularly when the study designs used are alike. In almost all the revised papers used in this study that were based on cross-sectional design and longitudinal design, regression class of models such as binary logistic regression (Onadja et al., 2013, Fakoya et al., 2018), multivariable regression (Jardim et al., 2018), probit regression (Adisa, 2015), poisson regression (Atchessi et al., 2018) and tobit regression (Naah et al., 2020) were used as statistical tools. Others include multilevel regression analysis (Van der Wielen et al., 2018), random-effects (Tenkorang et al., 2017) and C-log-log models (Wandera et al., 2017). Where studies are purely descriptive, the analysis stops at the level of univariate and to some extent, for some studies that have their outcome variable non-normal distribution or categorical variable, Chi-square (Yusuff & Okoh, 2015), Kruskal-Wallis and Dunn's post hoc tests (Ssensamba et al., 2019) were used. For the reviewed qualitative studies, the analysis was either based on content analysis, or thematic or narrative analytical frameworks (Ouedraogo et al., 2019; Berthé-Sanou et al., 2013).

Existing ageing policies in sub-Saharan Africa

Ageing policies are scarce in SSA countries (Aboderin & Ferreira, 2008). Although, a few countries in the region have policy on ageing while some others are either contemplating on having theirs or at the planning stage or implementation stage. The challenge of implementation is compounded with the fact that health interventions to enable access to health care among the elderly are discriminatory; and coupled with this is poor health system infrastructure in many of these countries (World Health Organization, 2004). In the same vein, mental health care is also lacking in the agenda of many of these policies except in countries like Kenya and South Africa that seem to have it in place. Policies and programmes to promote adequate nutritional intake of older persons have been integrated into national policies or strategies on ageing – in Kenya, Senegal and South Africa. In Mozambique and Senegal, there exist mainstreaming of older persons' nutritional needs or programmes into policies specifically for promoting adequate nutrition in later life. (United Nations Population Fund and Help Age International, 2011).

The calls for ageing policies in SSA countries are embedded in the UN Madrid Plan of Action on Ageing (MIPAA) (2002) and the African Union Policy Framework and Plan of Action on Ageing (AU PFPA, 2003) which place importance on three strategies: multidimensional health promotion to prevent disease and disability among the older people, implementation of policies to ensure unrestricted access to adequate rehabilitation and curative care, and adequate training of the healthcare workforce for the elderly care. Ghana, Mozambique, South Africa, Uganda and Tanzania have endorsed national policies on the ageing population, while a few like Nigeria, Cameroon and Rwanda have drafted policies, but these are yet to be passed into law. Despite weak progression of the implementation of ageing policies in most countries in SSA, the Gambia, Uganda and Ethiopia, are showing considerable progress.

In Nigeria, the social welfare department through the Social Development Act Decree 12 of 1974 and Social Development Policy 1989 is charged with the mandate to care for the elderly, and other segments of the population, particularly the vulnerable groups. The only policy on ageing in Nigeria was a draft developed in 2008. It is anticipated that the policy will be fully reviewed and endorsed by the government. However, the Ministry of Women's Affairs and Social Development has embarked on programmes to improve the welfare of elderly citizens, such as skills acquisition, income support for older persons and community-based care through material assistance (MWSD, 2008). Some states in Nigeria provide social security for the elderly, and give them some waivers on certain public services. In addition, government has revitalized the National Pension Commission and the Pension Transitional Arrangement Directorate to ensure that retirees receive their entitlements more quickly than usual. In Ghana, the Persons with Disabilities Act (2006), though not age-specific, provides relevant contextual information that should help improve the well-being of older people across the country. The government of Ghana developed the National Ageing Policy and its Implementation Action Plan in October 2010. Various health conditions affecting older people were identified and the need to maintain a healthy lifestyle in old age was clearly stated in the policy document. The implementation of the Ghana National Ageing Policy is still very weak (Government of Ghana, 2010; Ministry of Employment and Social Welfare, 2010).

The Cameroonian government has a guide to a healthy and active ageing. The Cameroon Constitution, penal code (28) and civil law (205) protect the rights of the elderly entirely and they are equally covered by Law No 69LF18 of 10 November 1969 and the degree of application 75/733 of 19 August 1975, in which their social security is guaranteed. The Ministry of Social Affairs (MINAS) in Cameroon has adopted the MIPAA (MINAS, 2012) as a framework to achieve the elderly concerns and needs. In order to position the actions of stakeholders and partners in favor of the elderly, five main areas were proposed: health and welfare, participation, a favourable and enabling environment, an improvement of living standards and research on ageing. In Cameroon, the National Reproductive Health Strategy/Policy (2005–2012) shows evidence of the mainstreaming of ageing. In Kenya, social protection programs were executed within the national policies and frameworks, including the country's constitution. The budget allocations for its social protection programs were under the control of government (Ministry of Labour Social Security and Services, 2014). Health ageing and the prevention of non-communicable diseases among older persons are included in the National Health Development Plan (2004–2008) of Senegal. Almost all the sub-themes of the existing policies in Senegal make provisions for older persons.

Ethiopia has legislations that are related to social security and pension which was introduced in 1961 in legal decree of 46/196, with the view to protecting welfare of government retirees and their dependents (Federal Negarit Gazeta, 1996). Mozambique is among the few countries in SSA to develop a country-specific policy and strategy to implement social protection programs which is an equivalent of the UN Social Protection Floor. The countries also have a food subsidy programme, which provides transfers to older persons and those with disabilities (Mozambique, 2002). Key policies and legislative instruments specific on ageing issues and rights of older persons in Mozambique include Social Policy on Ageing Issues (1998); National Plan of Ageing Issues (2005–2009; 2010–2014 and 2015–2019); Law of Promotion and Protection of rights of older people (2007 and 2014); Old Age Grant (2016); The Constitution – Article no. 95, rights at old age and provision of specific policies for realization of rights at Old Age; and National Strategy of Basic Social Security (Phase I, 2010–2014 & Phase II, 2016–2024). In terms of social pensions, the Lesotho government ratified the Pension Act, which made the distribution of pensions a legal right for elderly persons (Government of Lesotho, 2012).

The Department of Social Welfare, in collaboration with partners such as WHO, Age Care Association and Ageing with a Smile, over the years has provided key intervention strategies for elderly persons in the Gambia (National Report, 2012). The vital interventions instituted by this joint effort include building a home for the elderly poor, home care support for sick elderly persons, routine health checks, waiver of medical bills and rehabilitation services. The 1995 Constitution of Uganda identifies the rights of the elderly and provides the basis for the enactment of laws that protect and meet the needs of the elderly. The Ugandan government has been equally efficient in ensuring that its 2009 ageing policy, the National Council for Older Persons Bill, and National Plan of Action for Older Persons (2011/2016) are in tandem with the objectives of MIPAA (The Republic of Uganda, 2012) The central priority of these policies is health accessibility for older persons through modification of health services to provide for the elderly needs. This approach is distinct compared to other sub-Saharan Africa countries because it promotes research into elderly health needs, mainstreaming health issues, updating health workers on elderly issues and special outreach programs.

In Burkina Faso, there is a substantial allocation from the national budget to support the activities of older people's organizations. The Ministry of Social Action and National Solidarity, through its Department of the Elderly, has also been instrumental in setting up National Council of Elderly (CNPA) in 2002 (Burkina Faso, 2002). Niger does not have a policy on the elderly but there is existence of national legislation to fight against elder abuse. In Botswana and Côte d'Ivoire, policy on elderly persons is still in a draft form, yet to be approved and the implementation is subject to availability of funding. The South African Policy for Older Persons was developed in 2005 (South African National Department of Social Development, 2005) and the political declaration adopting the Madrid International Plan of Action on Ageing in 2002 was signed thereafter (United Nations, 2002). The South Africa Older Persons Policy and the Older

Persons Act address care and support for caregivers and alongside these, other programmes also facilitate informal care. In South Africa, the National Policy Guidelines for Victim Empowerment of 2009 mentions older persons as a priority target group and recognizes that they may need special assistance when accessing the juridical system.

Tanzania is the second country to have a policy on ageing in Africa, enacted in the year 2003 (Ministry of Labor, Youth Development and Sports, 2003). The main objective of the National Ageing Policy, 2003, is to ensure that older people are valued in society, provided with rights and services and accorded the opportunity to fully participate in the daily life of the community. The components of this policy also emerged from 1991 United Nation Declaration No. 67 which recognize elderly people's rights, freedom, participation, care and respect, self-fulfillment and dignity (Ministry of Labour Youth Development and Sports, 2003). Since 1976, the Mauritian government has been operating a non-contributory universal pension to people aged ≥60 years and they are also entitled to travel freely on public transport. Mauritius is the first African country to formulate an official plan of action for the elderly. The National Policy on Elderly was launched in 2001 with the theme 'Ageing with Dignity' (Government Gazette

Table 36.1 National Institutions Responsible for Ageing in Some Sub-Saharan African Countries

Country	*Institution*
Angola	Ministry of Social Action, Family and Women's Promotion
Botswana	Department of Social Protection of the Ministry of Local Government and Rural Development
Burkina Faso	The Ministry of Social Action and National Solidarity (MSANS or MASSN)
Burundi	Department of Economic and Social Affairs
Cameroon	Ministry of Social Affairs, Directorate for Social Protection of Handicapped People and Older People
Cape Verde	Ministry of Health and Social Security
Central Africa Republic	Ministry of Public Service, Administrative Reform, Labor, Employment and Social Protection
Chad	Ministry of Public Affairs, Employment, and Social Dialogue
Ethiopia	Ministry of Labour and Social Affairs, Elderly Affairs Body
Gabon	Ministry of Social Development and Family, Social Insurance and National Solidarity
Gambia	Social Security and Housing Finance Corporation
Ghana	Ministry of employment and social welfare; Ministry of Women's and Children's Affairs
Guinea	Ministry of Technical Education, Vocational Training, Employment, and Labor
Kenya	National Social Security Fund Board of Trustees
Lesotho	Ministry of Social Development and Help Age International Ministry of Social Development
Liberia	National Social Security and Welfare Corporation
Malawi	Ministry of Persons with Disabilities and the Elderly; Malawi Network for Older Persons Organizations
Mali	Ministry of Solidarity and Humanitarian Action; National Social Insurance Institute
Mauritania	Ministry of Civil Service, Labor, and Administration Modernization
Mauritius	The Ministry of Social Security and National Solidarity
Mozambique	Ministry of Women's Affairs and Social Action, Department of Older Persons

(*Continued*)

Country	*Institution*
Namibia	Ministry of Labour, Industrial Relations and Employment Creation; Social Security Commission; Ministry of Poverty Eradication and Social Welfare; Ministry of Veterans' Affairs
Niger	Ministry of Employment, Labour and Social Protection
Nigeria	Ministry of Women's Affairs and Social Development
Rwanda	Ministry of Finance and Economic Planning; Rwanda Social Security Board
Senegal	Ministry of Social Actions and National Solidarity, Division of Older Persons
South Africa	Department of Social Development, Directorate of Care and Services to Older Persons
Tanzania	Ministry of Labour, Employment, and Youth Development
Swaziland	Ministry of Labour and Social Security; Social Welfare Department
Togo	Ministry of Labor, Employment and Social Security
Uganda	Ministry of Gender, Labour and Social Development, Department for Persons with Disabilities and Older People
Zambia	Ministry of Labour and Social Security
Zimbabwe	Ministry of Public Service, Labour, and Social Welfare

of Mauritius, 2005). This policy affirms the principles guiding the Vienna Plan of Action on Ageing (1982) and the UN Principles for Older Persons (1991). There are legal frameworks that make provision for the rights of older persons in Malawi. The Constitution of the Republic of Malawi assures the right to development for all people and provides the statutory basis for enactment of laws and policy formulation and programme planning that address the concerns of older persons in Malawi. The Malawi National Policy for Older Persons takes into account the three priority areas recommended for action by the UMPAA (National Policy for Older Persons in Malawi).

Methodological issues on ageing that require further research

Ageing research is not different from other research; it simply emphasizes some characteristics that are often more difficult to investigate, such as problems/illnesses of age, rarionale for carrying out ageing research when this category of people has few years to live, non-specific manifestations of problems and the need for adequate sources of information (WHO, 2015). There has been an exponential increase in studies on ageing over the years; therefore, there are several specific methodological features that should be considered when carrying out ageing research in sub-Saharan Africa. In this regard, five major challenges to ageing research in sub-Saharan Africa have been previously identified. These include a lack of homogeneity in the definition of older persons with significant variation being observed both between and within countries, scarcity of empirical research and adequate data on ageing, the beliefs of older persons about ageing, considerable diversity in the indicator variables and the need to support local research capacity to facilitate research (National Research Council, 2006).

Researchers have expressed great concerns over the use of age to define older persons in sub-Saharan Africa. They observed that the conventional use of age ≥60 years or ≥65 years was mainly based on the creation of a state social welfare system for older workers in developed countries but used as the universally accepted standard definition of old age. The cultural and societal peculiarities between and within countries were not taken into consideration in this standard definition (Velkoff & Kowal, 2006). Different societies have several criteria for classification of an individual as 'old'. For instance, a Kenya study revealed that people attribute old age to physical features or appearance like gray hair, wrinkles, obvious frailty, by their life experiences or by their roles within the community (Velkoff & Kowal, 2006). Studies conducted in Ghana and South Africa have also indicated that old age is defined based on the ability to work, physical strength, health condition, social attributes, level of dependency on others due to advancement in years and leadership (Ahenkora, 1999; Mohatle & Agyarko, 1999). Consequently, appropriate mechanisms should be geared towards the establishment of common definitions of age that will facilitate unique data collection on ageing across countries.

Most countries in sub-Saharan Africa have a young population with a broad-based population pyramid and very few aged persons at the top due to high mortality. In this uneven distribution of population, priority attention is focussed on the younger segment, to the detriment of the older persons, because the younger population as the largest part of the workforce contributes most to economic growth and development. Conflicting results in the projection of the number of older persons in sub-Saharan African countries by different organizations on the account of limited data constitutes a great challenge to the planning and implementation of programmes and research on ageing in the African sub-region. For instance, comparing the Census Bureau and UN projections for 2030, there was substantial difference in the magnitude of the estimate in Ethiopia, Nigeria, Swaziland, South Africa, Ghana, Senegal, Uganda and Tanzania among others (U.S. Census Bureau, 2019; United Nations, 2019). Collaborations between international organizations by harmonizing their methodologies to derive a unique method for demographic parameters, estimations and projections in sub-Saharan Africa will expunge this challenge.

Lack of adequate vital registration systems which could be used as the base data for population projection is an important issue that is yet to be addressed by several countries in sub-Saharan Africa. The available modes of data collection in sub-Saharan Africa such as demographic and health surveys, census, and those from demographic surveillance sites have their peculiar limitations. The demographic surveillance field sites potentially provide high-quality data but the data are not typically nationally representative. In addition to limitation in data, questions posed in ageing research generally do not completely agree with those from the empirical investigation because that would require observation of the whole populations over a generation. Moreover, there are several challenges to measuring health status in a cross-sectional survey. The field assessment of an individual's health conditions can be hectic, expensive and, at times, subject to spiky ethical issues. In such cases, researchers resort to utilization of self-reported responses to questions about health status which are in most situations sensitive to the cultural environment, and the perceived way the individual societies measure illness and disease. Anchored vignettes have been used to enhance the relative comparability of self-reported health indices (Murray et al., 2003).

Study design remains one of the methodological issues in ageing research in sub-Saharan Africa. Prevalence studies are not always possible among the aged due to lack of uniformity in the frequency of health problems or illnesses across the old age spectrum. For reliable prevalence research outcomes among older persons, besides the time and place, stratification of individuals into specific age groups is essential. It is also necessary to increase the use of randomization and longitudinal surveys rather than the cross-sectional approach in ageing research in sub-Saharan Africa in order to enhance causality of association and inference.

Discussion

In the reviewed papers and materials for this study, there was a declination in the number of elderly persons in SSA between 1950 and 2001, Central Africa in particular. However, clear evidence suggests that the number of elderly populations in the SSA countries has consistently increased in the past two decades and this trend will be observed in many years ahead (UN, 2019). The projection pattern observed in SSA was very similar to that of Western and Eastern Africa but at variance with the projection pattern exhibited by central and Southern African regions (UN, 2019). The reflection of similar projection patterns of elderly in West and East Africa is an indication that the pattern of increase in elderly populations in these regions in the years ahead will shape the experience of a projected number of elderly populations in SSA as an entity. The short-term projection revealed that between 2019 and 2030, Southern Africa as a region is expected to have the highest proportion of elderly persons in its population, among the four regional blocks in SSA (UN, 2019).

Theories are often articulated to elucidate, predict and comprehend a particular phenomenon. In some situations, theories are used to test and extend an existing body of knowledge within the limits of some specific assumptions. The body mechanisms continually undergo many biochemical reactions irrespective of the inherited gene type of an individual. Habitually, some of these reactions do cause damage to the body cells and tissues, eventually ageing the body. Most of the theories of ageing reviewed in this paper attest to these assumptions. The free radicals, wear and tear, programmed theory, endocrine, membrane and cross-linking are theories of ageing which specify that changes in biological processes of the body and gene expressions as a result of their deterioration and toxic buildup in the system lead to ageing (Harman, 1956; Pearl, 1928). The psychosocial theory which includes disengagement, continuity and activity theories opined that ageing occurs when people are disengaged from or less active in their usual activities and fail to maintain social interactions (Cumming & Henry, 1961). Explicitly, the continuity theory was of the view that adaptation of past experiences will enable the elderly to maintain their routine activities as observed in their early years (Atchley, 1989).

Different methods have been used in the past to conduct ageing research in SSA. Nevertheless, the majority of these studies used a cross-sectional design (Nkosi et al., 2015; Fakoya et al., 2018). Longitudinal and quasi-experimental designs were also often used (Oshi et al., 2014; Tobi et al., 2018; Kadia et al., 2017; Kendall & Anglewicz, 2018). The case control and nested case control approaches were rarely used for ageing studies in the SSA countries. Some of these studies were based on either primary or secondary data or both. The secondary data were usually based on hospital records and/or national or organizations' database and surveillance sites (Tenkorang et al., 2017; Fonta et al., 2017; Wandera et al., 2017). The qualitative mode of research was done in some of these studies but at times complemented with a quantitative approach. For confirmatory purposes, in situations wherein research may involve identification of some health conditions like hypertension, heart disease, cancer, diabetes etc., laboratory tests were conducted in line with best practices available anywhere in the world. The quantitative data analysis tools were basically a regression class of models (Onadja et al., 2013, Fakoya et al., 2018) and for some studies in which the outcome variable is skewed or does not follow a specific pattern of distribution, the non-parametric statistics like Chi-square or Kruskal-Wallis were used, while content analysis, or thematic or narrative approach was mainly used for qualitative studies. However, a gap exists in the study design and data analysis methods previously used for ageing research in SSA compared to what is obtainable in some similar research conducted in developed countries.

Systematic reviews and meta-analyses on ageing research are scarce in sub-Saharan Africa despite their importance in health care planning, decision-making, and health policy. They also play an important role in evidence-based clinical practice guidelines. There is a high number of quantitative research on ageing in sub-Saharan Africa. This is a welcome development because qualitative research has the propensity to address the shortcomings of quantitative research by enriching the understanding of ageing with exhaustive data, exclusive methods and clear values. It is thus essential to link qualitative research to the contemporary technological advancement in information systems and communication in order to inform contemporary ageing programmes and policies.

Literatures have also highlighted the dearth of trained health workforce in the area of geriatric and gerontology, except for countries like Kenya and South Africa. However, countries like Cameroon, Nigeria, South Africa and Kenya have plans to improve the training of health care personnel for ageing (Saka, Oosthuizen, & Nlooto, 2019).

Conclusion

An increase in the number of elderly persons is currently observed in many countries in SSA and projections show that all the regional blocks in SSA will consistently experience increase in the population aged ≥65 years in the next 80 years. Nigeria, Ethiopia, South Africa, Democratic Republic of Congo and Tanzania are the top five countries with a high burden of elderly in SSA. Unless changes occur in the pattern of age distribution, the future ageing of the population in SSA will make the burden of caring for older persons an increasingly prominent issue in the region. As the population ages in SSA, there will be an increase in the proportion of elderly persons who will seek medical care. Therefore, there is the need for the governments in the region to initiate or enhance programmes that provide social and health insurance support for the elderly. The framework for ageing policies in countries across SSA will need an integration of strong advocacy and research on ageing in order to improve the elderly health and social conditions in the region.

References

Aboderin, I. A. G., & Beardm, J. R. (2015). Older people's health in sub-Saharan Africa. *Lancet, 385*(9968), e9–e11.

Aboderin, I. A. G., & Ferreira, M. (2008). Linking ageing to development agendas in sub-Saharan Africa: Challenges and approaches. *Journal of Population Ageing, 1*(1), 51–73.

Adisa, O. (2015). Investigating determinants of catastrophic health spending among poorly insured elderly households in urban Nigeria [published correction appears in *International Journal for Equity in Health, 14*, 104]. *International Journal for Equity in Health, 14*, 79.

African Union Policy Framework and Plan of Action on Ageing (AU PFPA). (2003). *Protocol to the African charter on human and peoples' rights on the rights of older persons in Africa*. Retrieved from https://au.int/sites

Aganiba, B. A., Owusu, W. B., Steiner-Asiedu, M., & Dittoh, S. (2015). Association between lifestyle and health variables with nutritional status of the elderly in the northern region of Ghana. *African Journal of Food, Agriculture, Nutrition and Development, 15*(4).

Ahenkora, K. (1999). The contribution of older people to development: The Ghana study. *Help Age International, and Help Age Ghana, 15.*

Ajayi, S. A., Adebusoye, L. A., Ogunbode, A. M., Akinyemi, J. O., & Adebayo, A. M. (2015). Profile and correlates of functional status in elderly patients presenting at a primary care clinic in Nigeria. *African Journal of Primary Health Care & Family Medicine,* 7(1), 810.

American Society on Aging. (2007). *Continuity theory: How elders find wisdom in spite of it all.* Archived from the original on 2008-01-11. Retrieved December 16, 2007, from https://www.asaging.org/at/at-214/continuity.html

Amurwon, J. (2019). "It's like I never had a child of my own": Care and support for the elderly in a changing socioeconomic context in rural Uganda. *The Journals of Gerontology, Series B: Psychological Sciences and Social Sciences, 74*(8), 1483–1491.

Atchessi, N., Ridde, V., Abimbola, S., & Zunzunegui, M. V. (2018). Factors associated with the healthcare-seeking behaviour of older people in Nigeria. *Archives of Gerontology and Geriatrics, 79*, 1–7.

Atchley, R. C. (1989). A continuity theory of normal aging. *The Gerontologist, 29*(2), 183–190.

Audain, K., Carr, M., Dikmen, D., Zotor, F., & Ellahi, B. (2017). Exploring the health status of older persons in sub-Saharan Africa. *Proceedings of the Nutrition Society, 76*(4), 574–579.

Bachani, A. M., Bentley, J. A., Zia, N., Galiwango, E., Lum, J., Tuli, G., & Ho, S. E. (2018). Caregiving for Uganda's elders with disability: Using cross-sectional surveillance data to identify healthcare service gaps in low- and middle-income settings. *Disability and Health Journal, 11*(3), 456–460.

Bekibele, C. O., & Gureje, O. (2010). Fall incidence in a population of elderly persons in Nigeria. *Gerontology, 56*(3), 278–283. https://dx.doi.org/10.1159/000236327

Berthé, A., Somda, M. A., Berthé-Sanou, L., Konaté, B., Hien, H., Bayala, E., . . . Macq, J. (2017). Advantages and disadvantages of using the PRISMA7 to determine the elderly subjects for whom the SMAF is useful for assessing functional status in Bobo-Dioulasso, Burkina Faso. *Médecine et Santé Tropicales, 27*(1), 71–76.

Berthé-Sanou, L., Berthé, A., Drabo, M., Badini-Kinda, F., Somé, M., Ouedraogo, D., & Macq, J. (2013). Analysis of the Burkinabe National Health Program for the Elderly (BNPEH) 2008–2012. *Sante Publique, 25*(4), 517–526.

Bjorksten, J. (1978). The cross linkage theory of aging. *Journal of the American Getriaric Society, 16*(4), 408–427.

Burkina Faso. (2002). *The ministry of social action and national solidarity.* Retrieved from https://www.action-sociale.gov.bf/accueil

Charlton, K. E., Rabinowitz, T. L., Geffen, L. N., & Dhansay, M. A. (2004). Lowered plasma vitamin C, but not vitamin E, concentrations in dementia patients. *The Journal of Nutrition, Health and Aging, 8*(2), 99–107.

Chaudieu, I., Norton, J., Ritchie, K., Birmes, P., Vaiva, G., & Ancelin, M. L. (2011). Late-life health consequences of exposure to trauma in a general elderly population: The mediating role of re-experiencing posttraumatic symptoms. *The Journal of Clinical Psychiatry, 72*(7), 929–935.

Cumming, E., & Henry, W. (1961). *Growing old.* New York, NY: Basic Books.

Davies, N. G., Klepac, P., Liu, Y., Prem, K., & Jit, M. (2020). Age-dependent effects in the transmission and control of COVID-19 epidemics. *Nature Medicine, 26*, 1205–1211.

Dorfman, M. (2015). *Pension patterns in sub-Saharan Africa* (Social protection and labor discussion paper no. 1503, World Bank Group). Washington, DC: World Bank. Retrieved from https://openknowledge.worldbank.org/handle

Fajemilehin, B. R., Ayandiran, E. O., & Salami, K. K. (2007). Elderly destitution in Ile-Ife community of Osun State, Nigeria. *International Journal of Nursing Practice, 13*(3), 161–165.

Fakoya, O. O., Abioye-Kuteyi, E. A., Bello, I. S., Oyegbade, O. O., Olowookere, S. A., & Ezeoma, I. T. (2018). Determinants of quality of life of elderly patients attending a general practice clinic in Southwest Nigeria. *International Quarterly of Community Health Education, 39*(1), 3–7.

Federal Negarit Gazeta. (1996). Ethiopia – social security (general standards) (Law, Act. Social Security Authority Establishment Proclamation No. 38/1996 [date of entry into force: 1996-07-02 | ETH-1996-L-47324]). *Federal Negarit Gazeta, 2*, 190–194.

Fontal, C. L., Nonvignon, J., Aikins, M., Nwosu, E., & Aryeetey, G. C. (2017). Predictors of self- reported health among the elderly in Ghana: A cross sectional study. *BMC Geriatrics, 17*(1), 171.

Galiana, L., Gutiérrez, M., Sancho, P., Francisco, E. H., & Tmás, J. M. (2016) Socio-demographic variables and successful aging of the Angolan elderly. *Scientifica (Cairo), 2016*, 5306756. doi:10.1155/2016/5306756.

Government Gazette of Mauritius. (2005). *Legal supplement to the government Gazette of Mauritius no. 44 of 7 May 2005: The protection of elderly persons ACT 2005.* Retrieved from www.ilo.org/dyn/natlex/docs

Government of Ghana. (2010). *National ageing policy: Ageing with security and dignity.* Ghana: Ministry of Gender, Children and Social Protection Republic of Accra. Retrieved from https://www.mogcsp.gov.gh

Government of Lesotho. (2012). *National Strategic Development Plan 2012/3–2016/17.* Maseru, Lesotho: Lesotho Government Ministry of Development Planning. Retrieved from https://hivstar.lshtm.ac.uk

Gray, W. K., Orega, G., Kisoli, A., Rogathi, J., Paddick, S., Longdon, A.R., Walker, R.W., Dewhurst, F., Dewhurst, M., Chaote, P. & Dotchin, C. (2017). Identifying frailty and its outcomes in older people in rural Tanzania. *Experimental Aging Research, 43*(3), 257–273.

Gureje, O., Oladimeji, B. D., & Abiona, T. (2014). Profile and determinants of successful aging in the Ibadan study of ageing. *Journal of the American Geriatrics Society, 62*(5), 836–842.

Gutiérrez, M., Tomás, J. M., Galiana, L., Sancho, P., & Cebrià, M. A. (2013). Predicting life satisfaction of the Angolan elderly: A structural model. *Aging & Mental Health, 17*(1), 94–101.

Hao, G., Bishwajit, G., Tang, S., Nie, C., Ji, L., & Huang, R. (2017). Social participation and perceived depression among elderly population in South Africa. *Clinical Interventions in Aging, 12*, 971–976.

Harman, D. (1956). Aging: A theory based on free radical and radiation chemistry. *The Journals of Gerontology, 11*, 298–300.

Harman, D. (1978). Free radical theory of aging: Nutritional implications. *Age, 1*, 145–152.

Havighurst, R. J. (1961). Successful aging. *The Gerontologist, 1*(1), 8–13.

Hien, H., Berthé, A., Konaté B., Drabo, M. K., Tou, F., Somda, D., . . . Macq, J. (2015). Healthcare journey of the elderly in Bobo-Dioulasso, Burkina Faso: A cross-sectional survey. *The Pan African Medical Journal, 20*, 128.

Howorth, K., Paddick, S. M., Rogathi, J., Walker, R., Gray, W., Oates, L. L., . . . Dotchin, C. (2019). Conceptualization of depression amongst older adults in rural Tanzania: A qualitative study. *International Psychogeriatrics, 31*(10), 1473–1481.

Ibitoye, O. A., Sanuade, O. A., Adebowale, A. S., & Ayeni, O. (2014). The determinants of health care utilization among the elderly in a rural community in Northern Nigeria. *Journal of Humanities and Social Science, 19*(7), 154–159.

Jardim, T. V., Witham, M. D., Abrahams-Gessel, S., Gómez-Olivé, F. X., Tollman, S., Berkman, L., & Gaziano, T. A. (2018). Cardiovascular disease profile of the oldest adults in rural South Africa: Data from the HAALSI study (Health and Aging in Africa: Longitudinal Studies of INDEPTH Communities). *Journal of the American Geriatrics Society, 66*(11), 2151–2157.

Ka, O., Seck, I., Coumé, M., Thiongane, B., Mbaye, E. H., & Dia, A. T. (2018). Analysis of public policies in favor of the elderly people in Senegal: State of legal protection. *Geriatrie et Psychologie Neuropsychiatrie du Vieillissement, 16*(1), 23–30.

Kadia, B. M., Dimala, C. A., Aroke, D., Ekabe, C. J., Kadia, R. S., & Mefire, A. C. (2017). A prospective analysis of pinch grafting of chronic leg ulcers in a series of elderly patients in rural Cameroon. *BMC Dermatology, 17*(1), 4.

Kendall, J., & Anglewicz, P. (2018). Living arrangements and health at older ages in rural Malawi. *Ageing & Society, 38*(5), 1018–1040.

Kisoli, A., Gray, W. K., Dotchin, C. L., Orega, G., Dewhurst, F., Paddick, S. M., . . . Walker, R. W. (2015). Levels of functional disability in elderly people in Tanzania with dementia, stroke and Parkinson's disease. *Acta Neuropsychiatrica, 27*(4), 206–212.

Kunna, R., San, S. M., & Stewart, W. J. (2016). Measurement and decomposition of socioeconomic inequality in single and multimorbidity in older adults in China and Ghana: Results from the WHO study on global AGEing and adult health (SAGE). *International Journal for Equity in Health, 16*(1), 79.

Lutala, M. P., Kwalya, T. M., Kasagila, E. K., Watongoka, L. H., & Mupenda, B. W. (2010). Health care seeking and financial behaviours of the elderly during wartime in Goma, democratic republic of Congo. *African Journal of Primary Health Care & Family Medicine, 2*(1), 108. doi:10.4102/phcfm.v2i1.108

Mbamukonka, P. K., Agasa, S. B., Tonen-Wolyec, S., Mukonkole, J. P., & Tshilumba, C. K. (2017). Type 2 diabetes mellitus among the elderly in Goma, democratic republic of the Congo: Prevalence, clinical features and complications. *African Journal of Health Issues, 1*(1), 5–16.

Meel, B. L. (2017). An epidemiology of sexual assault among elderly women in the Mthatha area of South Africa. *Medicine, Science and the Law, 57*(2), 69–74.

MINAS. (2012). *National policy document on the protection and welfare of older persons (draft)*. Yaounde, Cameroon: MINAS Ministère des Affaires Sociales du Cameroun. Retrieved from http://www.minas.gov.cm

Ministry of Employment and Social Welfare. (2010). *National ageing policy. Ageing with security and dignity*. Retrieved from https://s3.amazonaws

Ministry of Labour Social Security and Services. (2014). *National policy on older people and ageing* (Rev.). Republic of Kenya. Retrieved from http://www.partners-popdev.org/ageing

Ministry of Labour Youth Development and Sports. (2003). *National ageing policy*. United Republic of Tanzania. Retrieved from http://interactions.eldis

Ministry of Labour, Youth Development and Sports September. (2003). *National ageing policy: United Republic of Tanzania*. Retrieved from http://interactions.eldis.org/sites/interactions.eldis.org/

Miquel, J., & Fleming, J. E. (1986). Theoretical and experimental support for an oxygen radical-mitochondrial damage hypothesis of cell aging. In J. E. Johnson Jr., D. Harman, R. Walford, & J. Miquel (Eds.), *Free radicals, aging and degenerative diseases* (pp. 51–74). New York, NY: Alan R. Liss.

Miquel, J., Economos, A. C., Fleming, J., & Johnson, J. E., Jr. (1980). Mitochondrial role in cell aging. *Experimental Gerontology, 15*, 575–591.

Mohatle, T., & Agyarko, R. (1999). Contributions of older persons to development: The South African study. *HelpAge International, 1999*, 22.

Moroe, N., & Vazzana, N. (2019). The disuse of hearing aids in elderly people diagnosed with a presbycusis at an old age home, in Johannesburg, South Africa: A pilot study. *African Health Sciences, 19*(2), 2183–2188.

Mozambique (2002). National policy for older people. Maputo: Government Press.

Muga, G. O., & Onyango-Ouma, W. (2009). Changing household composition and food security among the elderly caretakers in rural western Kenya. *Journal of Cross-Cultural Gerontology, 24*(3), 259–272.

Murray, C. J. L., Özaltin, E., Tandon, A., Salomon, J. A., Sadana, R., & Chatterji, S. (2003). Empirical evaluation of the anchoring vignette approach in health systems. In C. L. J. Murray & D. R. Evans (Eds.), *Health systems performance assessment: Debates, methods, and empiricism* (pp. 369–399). Geneva, Switzerland: World Health Organization.

Mwangengwa, L. M., John, J., Elfuraha, B., Werema, C.J., Mushi, J., Mohamed, A.H., Ngarashi, D. & Mpanduji, D.G. (2014). Profile of plasma lipids and degree of derangements among the elderly of Morogoro region, Tanzania. *Tanzania Journal of Health Research, 16*(4), 261–268.

MWSD. (2008). *Ministry of Women Affairs and Social Development*. Retrieved from www.womenaffairs

Naah, F. L., Njong, A. M., & Kimengsi, J. N. (2020). Determinants of active and healthy ageing in sub-Saharan Africa: Evidence from Cameroon. *International Journal of Environmental Research and Public Health, 17*(9), 3038.

Nagu, T., Ray, R., Munseri, P., Moshiro, C., Shayo, G., Kazema, R., Mugusi, F., Pallangyo, K. (2017). Tuberculosis among the elderly in Tanzania: Disease presentation and initial response to treatment. *The International Journal of Tuberculosis and Lung Disease, 21*(12), 1251–1257.

National Report. (2012). National report of the Republic of the Gambia. Banjul: Government Press

National Research Council. (2001). The health of aging populations. In *(US) Panel on a research agenda and new data for an aging world* (Preparing for an Aging World: The Case for Cross-National Research). Washington, DC: National Academies Press. Retrieved from www.ncbi.nlm.nih.gov/books/NBK98373/

National Research Council. (2006). Aging in sub-Saharan Africa: Recommendations for furthering research. In B. Cohen & J. Menken (Eds.), *Panel on policy research and data needs to meet the challenge of aging in Africa* (Committee on Population, Division of Behavioral and Social Sciences and Education). Washington, DC: The National Academies Press.

Nikolich-Žugich, J. (2018). The twilight of immunity: Emerging concepts in aging of the immune system [published correction appears in Nat Immunol]. *Nature Immunology, 19*(1), 10–19.

Nkosi, V., Wichmann, J., & Voyi, K. (2015). Chronic respiratory disease among the elderly in South Africa: Any association with proximity to mine dumps? *Environmental Health, 14*, 33.

Nortey, S. T., Aryeetey, G. C., Aikins, M., Amendah, D., & Nonvignon, J. (2017). Economic burden of family caregiving for elderly population in southern Ghana: The case of a peri-urban district. *International Journal for Equity in Health, 16*, 16. https://doi.org/10.1186/s12939-016-0511-9

Nyambedha, E. O., Wandibba, S., & Aagaard-Hansen, J. (2003). "Retirement lost"-the new role of the elderly as caretakers for orphans in Western Kenya. *Journal of Cross-Cultural Gerontology, 18*(1), 33–52.

Nyaruhucha, C. N., Msuya, J. M., & Matrida, E. (2004). Nutritional status, functional ability and food habits of institutionalised and non-institutionalised elderly people in Morogoro Region, Tanzania. *East African Medical Journal, 81*(5), 248–253.

Ogunyemi, A. O., Odeyemi, K. A., Kanma-Okafor, O. J., & Ladi-Akinyemi, T. W. (2018). Health-related quality of life of the elderly in institutional care and non-institutional care in Southwestern Nigeria: A comparative study. *West African Journal of Medicine, 35*(1), 25–32.

Ojagbemi, A., Bello, T., & Gureje, O. (2016). Cognitive reserve, incident dementia, and associated mortality in the Ibadan study of ageing. *Journal of the American Geriatrics Society, 64*(3), 590–595.

Onadja, Y., Atchessi, N., Soura, B. A., Rossier, C., & Zunzunegui, M. V. (2013). Gender differences in cognitive impairment and mobility disability in old age: A cross-sectional study in Ouagadougou, Burkina Faso. *Archives of Gerontology and Geriatrics, 57*(3), 311–318.

Oshi, D. C., Oshi, S. N., Alobu, I., & Ukwaja, K. N. (2014). Profile and treatment outcomes of tuberculosis in the elderly in southeastern Nigeria, 2011–2012. *PLoS One, 9*(11), e111910.

Ouedraogo, R., Attané, A., & Gyasi, R. M. (2019). Aging in the context of HIV/AIDS: Spaces for renegotiation and recomposition of mutual solidarity in Burkina Faso. *Journal of the International Association of Providers of AIDS Care, 18*.

Payne, C. F., Gómez-Olivé, F. X., Kahn, K., & Berkman, L. (2017). Physical function in an aging population in rural South Africa: Findings from HAALSI and cross-national comparisons with HRS sister studies. *The Journals of Gerontology, Series B: Psychological Sciences and Social Sciences, 72*(4), 665–679.

Pearl, R. (1928). *The rate of living*. London: University of London Press.

PRB. (2019). *World population data sheet*. Population Reference Bureau. Retrieved on January 7, 2020, from www.prb.org/worldpopdata

Raji, Y. R., Abiona, T., & Gureje, O. (2017). Awareness of hypertension and its impact on blood pressure control among elderly Nigerians: Report from the Ibadan study of aging. *The Pan African Medical Journal, 27*, 190.

Ralston, M. (2018). The role of older persons' environment in aging well: Quality of life, illness, and community context in South Africa. *The Gerontologist, 58*(1), 111–120.

Saka, S., Oosthuizen, F., & Nlooto, M. (2019). National policies and older people's healthcare in sub-Saharan Africa: A scoping review. *Annals of Global Health, 85*(1), 91.

Sarr, S. A., Babaka, K., Mboup, M. C., Fall, P. D., Dia, K., Bodian, M., . . . Ba, S. A. (2016). Aspects cliniques, électrocardiographiques et échocardiographiques de l'hypertendu âgé au Sénégal [Clinical, electrocardiographic and echocardiographic aspects in elderly hypertensive patients in Senegal]. *The Pan African Medical Journal, 25*, 77.

Sohal, R. S., Agarwal, S., Dubey, A., & Orr, W. C. (1993). Protein oxidative damage is associated with life expectancy of houseflies. *Proceedings of the National Academy of Sciences of the United States of America, 90*, 7255–7259.

South African National Department of Social Development. (2005). *South African policy for older persons*. Pretoria, South Africa: NDSD. Retrieved from www.westerncape.gov.za/assets/departments/social-development/south_african_policy_for_older_persons_2005.pdf

Ssensamba, J. T., Mukuru, M., Nakafeero, M., Ssenyonga, R., & Kiwanuka, S. N. (2019). Health systems readiness to provide geriatric friendly care services in Uganda: A cross-sectional study. *BMC Geriatrics, 19*(1), 256.

Stadtman, E. R. (1992). Protein oxidation and aging. *Science, 257*(5074), 1220–1224.

Tenkorang, E. Y., Kuuire, V., Luginaah, I., & Banchani, E. (2017). Examining risk factors for hypertension in Ghana: Evidence from the study on global ageing and adult health. *Global Health Promotion, 24*(1), 14–26.

The Republic of Uganda. (2012). National plan of action for older people 2012/2013-2016/2017. In *Ageing with security and dignity*. Retrieved from http://www.mglsd.go.ug/Plans/NATIONAL

Tobi, K. U., Ndokwu, E. O., & Edomwonyi, N. P. (2018). Characteristics of critically ill elderly patients admitted to a tertiary intensive care unit in Nigeria and outcome of management. *West African Journal of Medicine, 35*(2), 75–78.

Tornheim, J. A., Manya, A. S., Oyando, N., Kabaka, S., Breiman, R. F., & Feikin, D. R. (2007). The epidemiology of hospitalized pneumonia in rural Kenya: The potential of surveillance data in setting public health priorities. *International Journal of Infectious Diseases, 11*(6), 536–543.

United Nations. (2002). *Madrid International Plan of Action on Ageing (MIPAA) and Political Declaration*. Madrid, Spain: Second World Assembly on Ageing. Retrieved from www.un.org/en/events/pastevents/pdfs/Madrid_plan.pdf

United Nations. (2019). *World population prospects 2019: Department of economic and social affairs, population division* Data Booket. (Highlights [ST/ESA/SER.A/423]).

United Nations. (2020). *World population prospects 2019: Department of economic and social affairs, population division*. Data Booket. (Highlights [ST/ESA/SER.A/423]).

United Nations Population Fund and Help Age International. (2011). *Overview of available policies and legislation, data and research, and institutional arrangements relating to older persons – progress since Madrid*. Report compiled in preparation for *The State of the World's Older Persons 2012*. New York. Retrieved from https://www.unfpa.org/

U.S. Census Bureau. (2019). *United States Census Bureau*. Suitland, United States of America. Retrieved from https://www.census.gov/

Van der Geest, S. (2002). Respect and reciprocity: Care of elderly people in rural Ghana. *Journal of Cross-Cultural Gerontology, 17*, 3–31. https://doi.org/10.1023/A:1014843 004627

Van der Wielen, N., Channon, A. A., & Falkingham, J. (2018). Universal health coverage in the context of population ageing: What determines health insurance enrolment in rural Ghana? *BMC Public Health, 18*(1), 657.

van Vuuren, A., Rheeder, P., & Hak, E. (2009). Effectiveness of influenza vaccination in the elderly in South Africa. *Epidemiology & Infection, 137*(7), 994–1002.

Velkoff, V. A., & Kowal, P. R. (2006). Aging in sub-Saharan Africa: The changing Demography of the region. In National Research Council (US) Committee on Population, B. Cohen, & J. Menken (Eds.), *Aging in sub-Saharan Africa: Recommendation for furthering research*. Washington, DC: National Academies Press. Retrieved from www.ncbi.nlm.nih.gov/books/NBK20301/#

Viña, J., Borrás, C., & Jaime, M. (2007). Theories of ageing. *IUBMB Life, 59*(4–5), 249–254.

Vladimir, D., & Ward, D. (1992). *The neuroendocrine theory of aging*. Pensacola, FL: The Center for Bio-Gerontology.

Wairiuko, J. M., Cheboi, S. K., Ochieng, G. O., & Oyore, J. P. (2017). Access to healthcare services in informal settlement: Perspective of the elderly in Kibera Slum Nairobi-Kenya. *Annals of Medical and Health Science Research, 7*, 5–9.

Walford, R. L. (1964). The immunologic theory of aging. *The Gerontologist, 4*(4), 195–197. https://doi.org/10.1093/geront/4.4.195

Wandera, S. O., Ddumba, I., Akinyemi, J. O., Adedini, S. A., & Odimegwu, C. (2017). Living Alone among older persons in Uganda: Prevalence and associated factors. *Ageing International, 42*(4), 429–446.

Wang, C., Pu, R., Li, Z., Ji, L., Li, X., Ghose, B., . . . Tang, S. (2019). Subjective health and quality of life among elderly people living with chronic multi-morbidity and difficulty in activities of daily living in rural South Africa. *Clinical Interventions in Aging, 14*, 1285–1296.

World Health Organization. (2004). *Report on a WHO workshop: Minimum data set on ageing in sub-Saharan Africa. Pretoria, South Africa. February 12–14, 2003*. Geneva: WHO, Evidence and Information for Policy.

World Health Organization. (2015). *World report on ageing and health*. World Health Organization. Retrieved from https://apps.who.int/iris/handle/10665/186463

Yusuff, K. B., & Okoh, C. N. (2015). Frequency, types and factors associated with potentially harmful drug interactions in ambulatory elderly patients in Nigeria. *International Journal of Pharmacy Practice, 23*(5), 353–356.

Zihindula, G., & Maharaj, P. (2013). Health and health seeking behaviour in the democratic republic of the Congo: Perspectives of the elderly. In P. Maharaj (Ed.), *Aging and health in Africa. International perspectives on aging* (Vol. 4). Boston, MA: Springer. https://doi.org/10.1007/978-1-4419-8357-2_4

Zs-Nagy, I. (1978). A membrane hypothesis of aging. *Journal of Theoretical Biology, 75*, 189–195.

37

INTERGENERATIONAL FAMILY SUPPORT AND THE HEALTH AND WELL-BEING OF OLDER ADULTS IN SUB-SAHARAN AFRICA

A systematic review

Mark A. Aviisah, Hinke H. Haisma, and Tobias C. Vogt

Introduction

Population ageing is occurring globally and sub-Saharan Africa (SSA) is no exception. Sub-Saharan Africa's population aged 60 and older was estimated at 52 million as of 2019 and is projected to increase three-fold to 158 million by 2050 (UNDESA, 2019). This means that this share of SSA's population will increase from 4.8% to 7.4% in the next three decades. Compared to all United Nations Sustainable Development Regions, SSA witnesses the largest gains in life expectancy at birth since 2000 and will remain the leader in life expectancy gains until 2040 (UNDESA, 2019). Despite these improvements, significant disparities in life expectancy at birth and age 60 exist, both for gender and across the sub-region (UNDESA, 2019). For instance, average life expectancy at birth in the Central African Republic stood at 53 years in 2019 as opposed to 75 in Mauritius (UNDESA, 2019). In spite of the fact that older adults in SSA are still an important source of support for the younger generation, an increasing number of people who survive beyond 60 years and advance in age will experience dependency (Aboderin & Hoffman, 2015; Ardington et al., 2010; Uwakwe et al., 2009). An increasing number of studies indicating an increasing prevalence of chronic conditions and functional disabilities among older people in SSA may deepen this dependency (Mugisha et al., 2016; Wandera, Ntozi, & Kwagala, 2014). This will inevitably lead to an increased need for support by older adults to survive, and to continue to participate physically and socially in society.

Older adults in African families are regarded as essential partners in the generational support system, where they provide and receive support, normally in settings of considerable economic and infrastructural limitations (Hoffman & Pype, 2016; Lloyd-Sherlock, 2010; Therborn, 2006). Despite this pivotal role played by older adults in families, public support for the welfare of the younger generation (e.g. educational subsidies and youth employment programmes) takes precedence over support for the older generation in SSA (Aboderin,

DOI: 10.4324/9780429287213-45

2010; Adamchak, 1989). Given that public support in terms of pensions and health insurance is largely non-existent for the majority of older people in SSA, family support remains the main (if not the only) source of support for many older persons across the region (Hoffman & Pype, 2016; Unanka, 2002). Families may help older family members by providing different forms of support – instrumental, emotional, and structural (Rossi & Rossi, 1990; Seeman & Berkman, 1988). Typically, instrumental support includes practical forms of support such as providing financial or material support, help with household chores, and personal care, as well as informational support (Rossi & Rossi, 1990; Shumaker & Brownell, 1984). In contrast, emotional support involves providing love, affection, care, companionship, identity, and belonging (Rossi & Rossi, 1990; Vaux, 1988). However, the distinction (whether instrumental or emotional support) between some support behaviours may not always be straightforward since some may accomplish multiple functions simultaneously (Shumaker & Brownell, 1984). Structural forms of support encompass the social network of individuals available who may provide support such as frequency of contact, size of social network, and proximity of relations and friends (Seeman & Berkman, 1988; Barrera, 1986). Intergenerational family support principally refers to the provision of either instrumental or emotional support by the older to the younger generation (downwards); but also includes support by the younger to older generation (upwards) within the family (Attias-Donfut, Ogg, & Wolff, 2005; Litwin, 2004). These forms of support are mostly reflected in parent-child or grandparent-grandchild relations (Merz, Consedine, Schulze, & Schuengel, 2009; Grundy & Henretta, 2006).

Family support provided to older people has been associated with the health and well-being outcomes of older people in different countries (Bélanger et al., 2016; Nyirenda et al., 2015; Teerawichitchainan, Pothisiri, & Long, 2015; Chen & Silverstein, 2000). Previous research on associations between family support received in later life and indicators of health and well-being has produced mixed findings (Mao, Chi, & Wu, 2019; Teerawichitchainan et al., 2015; Zunzunegui, Béland, & Otero, 2001; Silverstein & Bengtson, 1994). While some studies suggest beneficial effects of family support received on the well-being of older people (Teerawichitchainan et al., 2015; Silverstein, Chen, & Heller, 1996), others suggest family support received has little or a negative influence on well-being in later life (Merz & Consedine, 2009; Lowenstein, Katz, & Gur-Yaish, 2007). Different aspects of family support like support intensity, normative expectations, and attachment security have different effects on health and well-being in later life and may explain the contrary findings reported (Merz & Consedine, 2009; Chen & Silverstein, 2000). Despite these contradictory findings, the majority of studies suggest beneficial effects of family support depending on the type of support provided and the health and well-being outcomes examined (Teerawichitchainan et al., 2015; Cong & Silverstein, 2008).

The effect of various types of family support received by older adults have been associated with reduced depressive symptoms (Bélanger et al., 2016; Cong & Silverstein, 2008), self-rated health (Mao et al., 2019; Bélanger et al., 2016; Zunzunegui et al., 2001), mental health (Davey & Eggebeen, 1998), and functional health status (Liu, Liang, & Gu, 1995) of older adults. For instance, Cong and Silverstein (2008) found that assistance with household chores and personal care from daughters-in-law reduced depressive symptoms of rural older Chinese adults. Likewise, other studies have also found the receipt of instrumental family support by older people to be positively associated with better mental health in later life (Silverstein et al., 1996; Silverstein & Bengtson, 1994). Other researchers, however, have found instrumental family support received by older adults associated with deterioration in subjective health among older adults (Zunzunegui et al., 2001; Seeman, Bruce, & McAvay, 1996). The provision of instrumental support has been shown to accompany feelings of dependence, subsequently inducing poor subjective health status of older adults (Zunzunegui et al., 2001; Seeman et al., 1996). Emotional and financial support received from family members have been found to be positively related to improved self-rated health, lower levels of depression, and better psychological health in later life (Bélanger et al., 2016; Teerawichitchainan et al., 2015; Guo, 2014; Silverstein, Cong, & Li, 2006; Zunzunegui et al., 2001). For example, financial transfers from adult children improved psychological health among Thai, Vietnamese, and Myanmarese older adults (Teerawichitchainan et al., 2015). Financial support is more likely to directly act as a resource for health service use and indirectly reduce stress for optimal cognitive health (Lee, Lyu, Lee, & Burr, 2013). Social family support has been found to be associated with the recipient's health-related behaviours and health status (Thoits, 2011; Cohen, 1988). It is argued that lack of social support and social isolation is related to an increased risk of cognitive decline (Green, Rebok, & Lyketsos, 2008). Emotional and financial support provided by family to older adults have been positively linked with higher levels of subjective well-being in older adults (Bélanger et al., 2016; Lee et al., 2013; Merz & Consedine, 2009; Chen & Silverstein, 2000). In contrast, other researchers have found that older adults who were only recipients of support from adult children and did not provide any support in return reported lower life satisfaction than their counterparts who provided some support (Merz et al., 2009; Lowenstein et al., 2007). Studies indicate that receiving support in old age can have negative consequences on well-being due to the desire of older persons to maintain self-esteem and to stay autonomous (Lee et al., 1995; Lieberman and Tobin 1983;). Chen and Feeley (2014) argue that social support from children indirectly improved subjective well-being through the absence of loneliness. Social support received may help one to de-stress and reduce loneliness thereby indirectly leading to improved well-being (Choi, Park, Cho, Chun, & Park, 2016). Generally, studies from very different cultural and socioeconomic backgrounds suggest that family support to older people has mainly positive effects for the health and well-being of the elderly.

There has been a steady growth of research on the effect of support provided by older people to the younger generation in the past two decades in SSA, particularly in the context of HIV/AIDS, labour migration, and poverty (Ardington et al., 2010; Ferreira, 2006; Posel, Fairburn, & Lund, 2006). In comparison to these studies, relatively little attention has been paid to studies on family support from younger to older people in SSA and its effects on their health and well-being as opposed to support from older to younger people. What forms of support do older people in SSA receive from their family and wider network of relatives and how does it affect their health and well-being? Are there any inconsistencies in the health and well-being effects of the support older people receive? Therefore, the aim of this systematic review is to provide an overview of intergenerational family support provided to older adults in SSA and summarize its effects on their health and well-being. Given the rapid population ageing occurring in SSA, there is the need to systematically analyze existing work on family support provided to older people living in SSA and its association with their health and well-being. Bringing these to the fore will fill a gap by highlighting the health and well-being effects of family support in later life in this context. Also, it may drive the urgently needed policy change and public discourse on family support for older people, triggering appropriate policy and programmatic action. At the population level, the impact of this systematic review on policy and interventions may contribute towards an improved health and well-being, and the general welfare of the older adult population of SSA.

Methods

Study design and review framework

This systematic literature review was conducted according to the recommendations outlined in the Preferred Reporting Items for Systematic Reviews and Meta-Analyses (PRISMA) statement (Moher, Liberati, Tetzlaff, Altman, & Group, 2009).

Search strategy and screening

A three-stage search strategy was used in this review. A limited search in Web of Science and Scopus databases was initially conducted to identify key words and indexing terms used in the titles and abstracts of relevant articles. Thereafter, a second search using all identified key words and indexing terms was undertaken across all selected databases. The databases searched were MEDLINE (EBSCO), PsycINFO (EBSCO), SocINDEX (EBSCO), Web of Science core collection, Scopus, PubMed, ProQuest Social Services Abstracts, and African Journals Online. Medical Subject Headings (MeSH) term categories were applied across all index terms in the PubMed search to ensure that all relevant publications were identified. Some of the main keywords and MeSH terms and their combinations used were 'family support', 'social support', 'social capital', 'intergenerational relations', 'intergenerational transfers', 'financial support', 'activities of daily living', 'caregiving', 'older adults', 'elderly', and 'sub-Saharan Africa'. **Box 37.1** shows the complete list of the main key words and index terms applied across all databases in the review.

A search for unpublished studies and reports was undertaken in the World Health Organization library (WHOLIS), World Bank electronic library, ProQuest Dissertations and Theses Global, and HelpAge International. Searches were also conducted to retrieve unpublished works such as government reports, government white papers, reports of ministries of health, and reports of seminars and conference proceedings. All records identified were imported into Endnote and exported into an Excel file. Two authors (MAA, TCV) initially screened the titles and abstracts of all identified publications and thereafter independently carried out full-text assessment for eligibility and inclusion. Disagreements over eligibility and inclusion were resolved by a third author (HH). Finally, the reference lists of eligible publications were hand-searched for additional publications. Figure 37.1 shows the PRISMA flow diagram illustrating screening of studies for inclusion in the review.

Inclusion and exclusion criteria

Studies published in English and conducted among community-residing (or non-institutionalized) older people living in SSA between January 2000 and May 2020 were included. All sub-Saharan African countries were included in the database searches. Studies of any design and methodology examining the association between intergenerational family support received by older adults on measures of their health and well-being were included: primary empirical quantitative, qualitative and mixed methods, theoretical studies, working papers, and reports. Studies that exclusively focussed on family support provided to older adults or received by older adults in the context of HIV/AIDS were excluded.

Definition of concepts

Intergenerational family support in this review was conceptualized as the provision of instrumental, emotional, and structural forms of support to older adults by family or kin. SSA

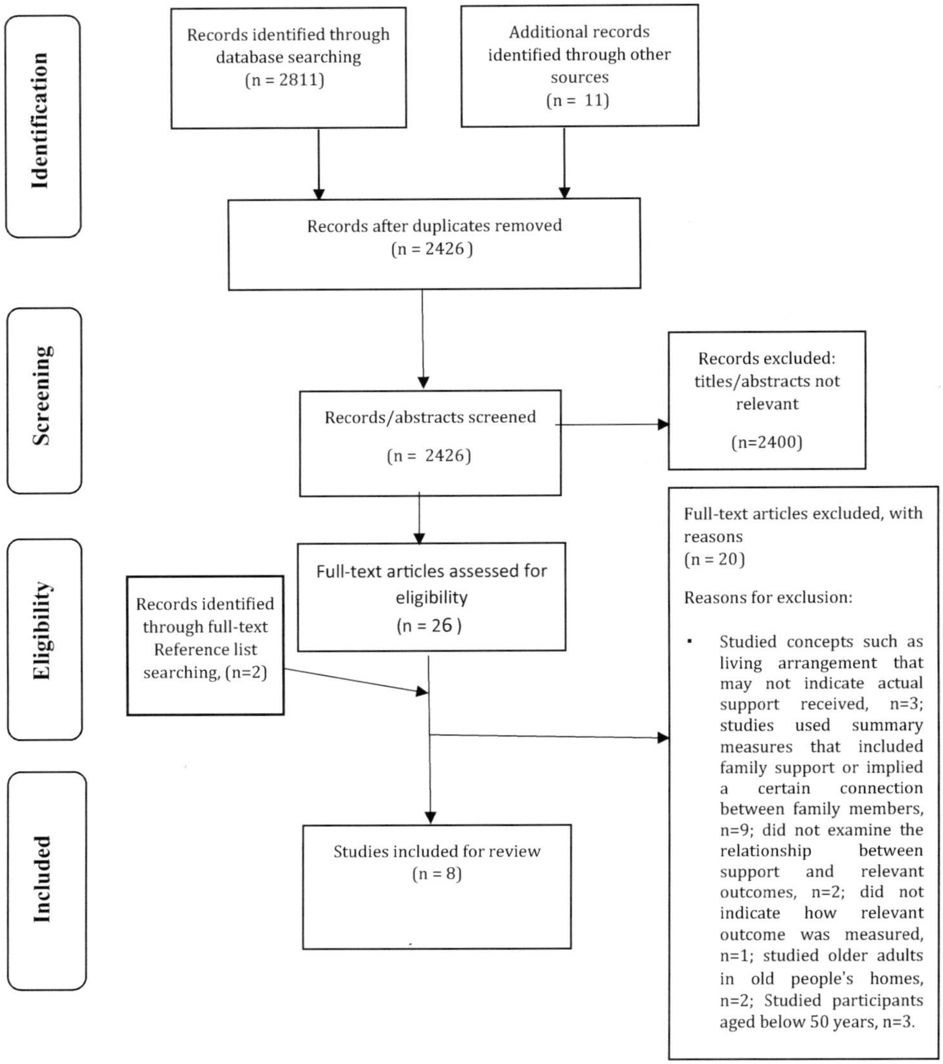

Figure 37.1 PRISMA flow diagram illustrating screening of studies for inclusion in the review.

region refers to countries south of the Sahara based on the United Nations' classification of countries (UNDESA, 2019). Although older people in sub-Saharan Africa are defined as persons aged 60 years and older in line with the United Nations' recommended cut-off for defining an older person globally, this review considers persons aged 50 and older as older people given the relatively short remaining life expectancy at age 50 (23 years) in the sub region (UNDESA, 2019; McIntyre, 2005). Moreover, most ageing studies in Africa but also other countries or regions focus on individuals aged 50 and older (Kunna, San Sebastian, & Stewart Williams, 2017). Therefore, focussing on studies that investigated older adults aged 50 and older was considered appropriate and ensured more studies met the eligibility criteria for the review.

Box 37.1 Complete list of the main key words and index terms applied across all databases in the review

Family OR relative OR relations OR kin AND support OR social support OR emotional support OR material support OR monetary support OR financial support OR personal support OR instrumental support OR practical support OR health support OR activities of daily living OR instrumental activities of daily living OR intergenerational support OR intergenerational transfers OR financial transfer OR cash transfer OR intergenerational relation OR intergenerational reciprocity OR family support OR family network OR kin networks OR kin support OR social capital OR social networks OR caregiving OR care OR needs AND older people OR older adult OR older person OR seniors OR elderly person OR elderly OR geriatric OR later years OR later life AND Africa OR sub-Saharan Africa OR African country OR Western Africa OR Eastern Africa OR Central Africa OR Southern Africa

*UN-listed SSA countries: Burundi, Comoros, Djibouti, Eritrea, Ethiopia, Madagascar, Malawi, Mauritius, Mozambique, Rwanda, Seychelles, South Sudan, Somalia, Uganda, Tanzania, Zambia, Zimbabwe, Angola, Cameroon, Central African Republic, Chad, Congo, DRC, Equatorial Guinea, Gabon, Sao Tome and Principe, Botswana, Swaziland, Lesotho, Namibia, South Africa, Benin, Burkina Faso, Cape Verde, Côte d'Ivoire, Gambia, Ghana, Guinea, Guinea-Bissau, Liberia, Mali, Mauritania, Niger, Nigeria, Senegal, Sierra Leone, Togo.

Data extraction

Data from eligible studies was extracted on authors, publication year, study country, study title, study design and population, research methods, support provided, findings on support received and association with indicators of health and well-being, and study limitations.

Quality assessment

Assessment of the methodological quality of included studies was conducted based on the National Institute of Health (NIH) Quality Assessment Tool for Observational Cohort and Cross-Sectional Studies (NIH, 2014). This is an instrument that has 14 criteria and is used to critically appraise the internal validity of quantitative studies. The 14 criteria include: research question, study population, sample recruitment and eligibility criteria, sample size justification, exposure and outcome assessment, follow-up rate, and statistical analysis. Each criterion was rated 'yes', 'no', 'cannot determine', 'not applicable', or 'not reported'. Using these criteria, we provide an overall quality rating (Good, Fair, Poor) for each study assessed. None of the studies that met all selection criteria used qualitative methods.

Synthesis of findings

A narrative synthesis was used to summarize the findings of the included studies. It is the preferred method of quantitative data synthesis when statistical synthesis is not possible as was the case in our review given the heterogeneity of concepts and variables. A narrative synthesis is a textual approach to synthesizing findings from included studies (Popay et al., 2006). Two authors (TCV, HH) cross-validated the synthesized findings.

Results

Study characteristics

A total of 2,811 records were identified through database searching, while an additional 11 were identified through other sources. Extending the search time frame before year 2000 did not result in more suitable publications. After duplicates were removed, 2,426 records were screened, and 2,400 that had titles or abstracts not relevant to the review aim were excluded. Consequently, 26 full-text articles were retrieved and assessed for eligibility. Two records were identified through hand-searching the reference list of full-text articles retrieved. Twenty (20) studies were excluded based on reasons such as studies using summary measures that included family support or implied a certain connection between family members but not support (9), examining the effect of living arrangement (3), assessing the effects of family support on participants aged below 50 years (3), and others (5). Finally, eight studies met all eligibility criteria and were included in the review. Three of the quantitative studies included in the review were from cross sectional surveys, while the remaining five were from longitudinal surveys. Four studies were conducted in Nigeria and two each from Kenya and Ghana. Study participants were mainly recruited from the general population residing in both urban and rural areas. The sample sizes of the studies ranged from 350 to 2,608. Table 37.1 shows characteristics of included studies.

Effect of family support on health and well-being of older adults in SSA

Findings on the effect of family support provided to older adults on their health and well-being are presented in Table 37.2. Four studies examined frequency of contact with family members (Gyasi, Yeboah, Mensah, Ouedraogo, & Addae, 2019; Ojagbemi, Bello, & Gureje, 2018; Gureje, Kola, Afolabi, & Olley, 2008; Gureje, Oladeji, & Abiona, 2011), three assessed the effect of financial support (Gyasi, Phillips, & Abass, 2018; Kodzi, Gyimah, Emina, & Ezeh, 2010, 2011), while one study analyzed the effect of social support from family members (Olagunju, 2015). Six studies examined the association between family support provided to older adults and indicators of their health. Five studies found a positive relationship between the health of older adults and family support provided to or received by the elderly, while one reported a non-significant association. Two studies from Ghana suggest that older adults' psychological well-being benefited from their frequent contact with family and receiving regular remittances from distant adult children (Gyasi et al., 2018, 2019). Compared to having no contact, frequent contact with family reduced psychological distress by almost 3 ($\beta = -2.975$, $SE = 1.024$, $p < 0.005$) among lonely older adults (Gyasi et al., 2019), while regular remittances from distant adult children increased good psychological well-being ($\beta = 0.484$, $p < 0.005$) of older adults (Gyasi et al., 2018). Similarly, two studies from Nigeria suggest social support and frequent contact with family members was associated with lower risk of depression in later life (Ojagbemi et al., 2018; Olagunju, Olutoki, Ogunnubi, & Adeyemi, 2015). For instance, Ojagbemi et al. (2018) found that older women ($HR = 2.2$, 95% $CI = 1.0–4.7$)) with no regular contact with family had a two-times higher risk of the onset of major depressive disorder than older women with regular contact. Older adults receiving material or financial support from extended family members reported better self-rated health in a study in Kenya (Kodzi et al., 2010). In this

Table 37.1 Characteristics of Included Studies

Author(s)/Year/ Study country	*Study title*	*Design and Methods*	*Sample Size (Male; Female %)*	*Study population and setting*	*Overall Quality Rating*
Ojagbemi et al., 2018; Nigeria	Gender differential in social and economic predictors of incident major depressive disorder in the Ibadan Study of Ageing	Design: longitudinal study, Ibadan Study of Ageing (ISA), 2003–2009. Methods: multi-stage cluster probability sampling, Kish table selection method, sample weighting, Chi-square test, actuarial adjustment approach, Kaplan– Meier Analyses, and Cox regression models.	1,394 (M 51.6%; F 48.4%)	People aged 65 years and older. Setting: 8 states in southwest and north-central regions of Nigeria (Ondo, Ekiti, Osun, Lagos, Ogun, Oyo, Kogi, and Kwara) in urban and rural areas. Mean age: 74.6 years	Good
Olagunju et al., 2015; Nigeria	Late-life depression: Burden, severity, and relationship with social support dimensions in a West African community.	Design: Descriptive cross-sectional Methods: multi-stage random sampling, Kish method, Chi-square test.	350 (M 47.1%; F 52.9%)	People aged 60+ years. Setting: Ethnically diverse densely populated urban area (Mushin [a]LGA, Lagos). 65% of participants aged below 70 years	Poor
Gureje et al., 2011; Nigeria	Incidence and risk factors for late-life depression in the Ibadan Study of Ageing.	Design: longitudinal study (ISA), 2003–2007. Methods: multi-stage cluster probability sampling, Kish table selection method, sample weighting, Chi-square test, t-test, Cox proportional hazards regression, logistic regressions.	1,408 (M 59.6%; F 40.4%)	People aged 65 years and older. Setting: 8 states in southwest and north-central regions of Nigeria (Ondo, Ekiti, Osun, Lagos, Ogun, Oyo, Kogi, and Kwara) in urban and rural areas. Mean age: 72.4 years	Fair

(*Continued*)

Table 37.1 (Continued)

Author(s)/Year/ Study country	*Study title*	*Design and Methods*	*Sample Size (Male; Female %)*	*Study population and setting*	*Overall Quality Rating*
Gureje et al., 2008; Nigeria	Determinants of quality of life of elderly Nigerians: results from the Ibadan Study of Ageing.	Design: longitudinal study (ISA), 2003–2004. Methods: multi-stage stratified area probability sampling, linear regression modelling.	2,152 (not stated)	People aged 65 years and older. Setting: 8 states in southwest and north-central regions of Nigeria (Ondo, Ekiti, Osun, Lagos, Ogun, Oyo, Kogi, and Kwara) in urban and rural areas. Mean age: not stated	Fair
Gyasi et al., 2019; Ghana.	Neighbourhood, social isolation, and mental health outcome among older people in Ghana.	Design: Cross-sectional study, Aging, Health, Psychological Well-being, and Health-seeking Behaviour project, 2016–2017. Methods: Multi-stage stratified area probability sampling with over sampling of older adults, Pearson correlations, Ordinary Least Square (OLS) regression modelling.	1,200 (M 36.8%; F 63.2%)	Adults aged 50+ years. Setting: study population stratified by geographical, sociocultural, and rural-urban settlements in the Ashanti Region of Ghana. Mean age: 66.2 years	Good
Gyasi et al., 2018; Ghana	Social support networks and psychological well-being in community-dwelling older Ghanaian cohorts.	Design: Cross-sectional study, Aging, Health, Psychological Well-being, and Health-seeking Behaviour project, 2016–2017. Methods: multi-stage stratified area probability sampling with an oversample of older adults, Pearson correlations, multivariate logit regression models.	1,200 (M 36.8; F 63.2)	Adults aged 50+ years. Setting: study population stratified by geographical, sociocultural, and rural-urban settlements in the Ashanti Region of Ghana. Mean age: 66.2 years	Good

Kodzi et al., 2011; Kenya	Understanding ageing in sub-Saharan Africa: exploring the contributions of religious and secular social involvement to life satisfaction.	Design: longitudinal study, Nairobi Urban Health and Demographic Surveillance System (NUHDSS), 2006/2007. Methods: census, OLS regression models.	2,608 (M 66.1%; F 33.9%)	Adults aged 50+ years. Setting: two informal settlements (slum) communities in Nairobi, Kenya. Mean age: 59 years	Good
Kodzi et al., 2010; Kenya	Religious Involvement, Social Engagement, and Subjective Health Status of Older Residents of Informal Neighbourhoods of Nairobi.	Design: longitudinal study, Nairobi Urban Health and Demographic Surveillance System (NUHDSS), 2006/2007. Methods: census, Ordinal Logistic Regression models.	2,608 (M 66.1%; F 33.9%)	Adults aged 50+ years. Setting: two informal settlements (slum) communities in Nairobi, Kenya. Mean age: 59 years	Good

Note: [a]Local Government Area

Table 37.2 The Effect of Family Support Provided to Older Adults in SSA on Their Health and Well-Being Indicators

Studies	*Family support provided*	*Indicator for measuring support*	*Health/well-being measure (s) studied*	*Main findings on association with health/well-being*	*Study limitations*
Ojagbemi et al., 2018	Frequency of contact with family members not residing with respondent.	Regular contacts with family, assessed based on World Mental Health (WMH) survey version of the World Health Organization's (WHO) Composite International Diagnostic Interview (CIDI) (Kessler & Ustun, 2004). Response options were: 1 = nearly every day, 2 = 3–4 days per week, 3 = 1–2 days per week, 4 = 1–3 days a month, 5 = less than once in a month, 6 = never; dichotomized into contacts less than once and more than once in a month.	Major Depressive Disorder (MDD), assessed based on WHO's Composite International Diagnostic Interview (CIDI) (Kessler & Ustun, 2004) and Diagnostic and Statistical Manual of Mental Disorders (DSM)-IV criteria (APA, 1994). Control variables: socio-demographic characteristics (e.g. age, sex, etc.)	Lack of regular contact with family members is a risk factor for the onset of MDD for older women ([a]HR = 2.2, 95% [b]CI = 1.0–4.7) and not for older men.	51.5% attrition. Participants who dropped out of study were more likely to belong to lower economic standing, and more women than men belonged to this category.
Olagunju et al., 2015	Social support from family.	Multidimensional Scale for Perceived Social Support (MSPSS) (Zimet, Dahlem, Zimet, & Farley, 1988); MSPSS scores below the mean score of 4.95 ± 0.96 was considered as low social support.	Depression based on the Geriatric Depression screening (GDS) scale (Yesavage et al., 1982); presence of depression considered as mild based on an 11–20 score and sever at 21–30 score.	High social support from family members (Chi = 4.434, p = 0.035) was protective against depression among older adults and vice versa.	Inability to control for bidirectional relationship between social support and depression due to cross-sectional design. Lack of control of effects confounding variables. Prevalence of depression may be higher because of the use of GDS instead of clinically defined standard diagnostic criteria.

Gureje et al., 2011	Frequency of contact with family members not residing with respondent.	Frequency of contact assessed based on WMH WHO CIDI (Kessler & Ustun, 2004). Response options dichotomized into no contact at all and contact once per month to daily.	Major Depressive Disorder (MDD) assessed based on the WMH survey version of the WHO Composite International Diagnostic Interview (CIDI) (Kessler & Ustun, 2004) and diagnosis based on DSM-IV criteria (APA, 1994). Control variables: socio-demographic (e.g. age, sex).	Regular contact with family was not significantly associated with new onset of MDD among older people.	Self-reporting may be associated with recall bias that could affect rate of depression. Rate of depression may have been underestimated due to assessment method.
Gureje et al., 2008	Frequency of contact with family members not residing with older adult.	Frequency of contacts assessed based on WMH WHO CIDI (Kessler & Ustun, 2004). Response options dichotomized into less than once in 6 months vs. more than once.	Quality of life assessed based on the WHO Quality of Life (WHOQOL-BREF); which contains 4 domains (physical, psychological, environmental, and social) (WHOQOL-Group, 1998). Control variables: socio-demographic, health-related factors.	Contact with family members was significantly related to quality of life in the psychological ($^c\beta = -14.20$; $p = 0.003$), physical ($\beta = -12.70$; $p = 0.009$) and environmental ($\beta = -15.52$; $p = 0.001$) domains but not the social ($\beta = -2.98$; $p = 0.612$) domain among older persons.	Eliciting information by self-reporting (e.g. chronic health conditions) could lead to misreporting. Causal inference cannot be made due to cross-sectional design. The accuracy of information from older adults with mental health problems could be affected.

(*Continued*)

Table 37.2 (Continued)

Studies	*Family support provided*	*Indicator for measuring support*	*Health/well-being measure (s) studied*	*Main findings on association with health/well-being*	*Study limitations*
Gyasi et al., 2019; Ghana	Social connectedness.	Social connectedness, made up of frequency of family contact, social engagements (responses rated on a 5-point scale: 1= never, 2=less frequently, 3=frequently, 4=very frequently, and 5=every day; dichotomized into 1= frequently [frequently/ very frequently/every day] and 0=not frequently [never/less frequently]), and emotional bonds with at least one person (responses coded as 1=yes, 0=no).	Psychological Distress (PD) assessed based on Kessler Psychological Distress Scale (KPDS-K10) (Kessler et al., 2002). Question: In the last 4 weeks did you feel (a) tired out for no good reason? (b) nervous or uneasy? (c) so nervous that nothing could calm you down? (d) hopeless or lonely? (e) restless or fidget? (f) so restless you could not sit still? (g) depressed? (h) that everything was an effort? (i) so sad or bored that nothing could cheer you up? and (j) worthless or having no value? (five response categories: 1 = none of the time, 2 = a little of the time, 3 = some of the time, 4 = most of the time, 5 = all of the time) Scores ranged from 10–50; a cut-off score ≥ 20 was used to denote PD. Control variables: socio-demographic and health-related variables.	Frequent contact with family ($\beta = -2.975$, [d]SE = 1.024, $p < 0.005$) significantly decreased psychological distress among lonely older adults. Similar effects were found for frequent family contact ($\beta = -0.118$, SE = 1.129, $p < 0.05$) among older adults who lived alone.	No causal or directional inferences can be made as a result of the cross-sectional nature of the study. Self-reporting of data can be prone to measurement bias and can affect the reliability of findings.

Gyasi et al., 2018	Regular remittances from distant adult children.	Regular remittances (responses coded as: 1= remittances received and 0= no remittances)	Psychological well-being (composite 10-item questions adapted from Kessler Psychological Distress Scale [KPDS-K10]) (Kessler et al., 2002). [same items and scale as Gyasi et al., 2019] Control variables: socio-demographic, socio-economic, and health-related covariates.	Remittances received by older adults was positively associated with good psychological well-being ($\beta = 0.484$, $p < 0.005$) even in the presence of other relevant factors, particularly among urban residents.	Self-reporting of data is prone to under or overestimation of measures. The effect of changing support patterns on psychological well-being could not be estimated.
Kodzi et al., 2011	Social engagement, composed of number of close friends (sociability), support from relatives other than children (material or financial), and social participation index.	Receiving support (material or financial) from relatives (response options: 1=yes, 0 =no).	General life satisfaction index, derived from three questions: (1) taking all things together, how satisfied are you with life as a whole these days? (2) How would you rate your overall quality of life? (Responses rated on a 5-point scale: 1= very dissatisfied, 2= dissatisfied, 3= neither satisfied or dissatisfied, 4= satisfied, 5=very satisfied) (3) Taking all things together, how happy would you say you are these days? (Responses rated on a 5-point scale: 1=very unhappy, 2=unhappy, 3=neutral, 4= happy, 5=very happy) Control variables: socio-demographic, socio-economic, and health-related variables.	Receiving material support from extended family members exerted strong positive effects ($\beta = 0.081$; $p < 0.001$) on general life satisfaction in later life even amidst other important factors such as health status.	Social desirability may result in over estimation of positive life satisfaction in face-to-face interviews. Self-reporting prone to recall bias. Quality of social relationships, support, and personal religious devotion which could affect life satisfaction were not estimated.

(*Continued*)

Table 37.2 (Continued)

Studies	*Family support provided*	*Indicator for measuring support*	*Health/well-being measure (s) studied*	*Main findings on association with health/ well-being*	*Study limitations*
Kodzi et al., 2010	Social engagement, composed of number of close friends (sociability), support from relatives other than children (material or financial), and social participation index.	Receiving support (material or financial) from relatives (response options: 1=yes, 0 =no).	Self-rated health, measured based on a single question: (1) In general, how would you rate your health today? (Responses rated on a 5-point likert scale: very good, good, moderate, bad, or very bad) Control variables: socio-demographic, socio-economic, and health-related variables.	Receiving material or financial support from relatives independently contributed (OR = 1.36; $p < 0.05$) to better self-rated health of older adults.	Social desirability may result in overestimation of positive life satisfaction in face-to-face interviews. Self-reporting prone to recall bias. Quality of social relationships, support, and personal religious devotion which could affect health status were not estimated.

Note: [a] HR=Hazard Ratio; [b] CI=Confidence Interval; [c] β=unstandardized regression coefficient; [d] SE=Standard Error

study, the odds of older adults who received material support from family experiencing better self-rated health was 36% (OR = 1.36; $p < 0.05$) higher than those who did not. The findings of the studies included in our review show that family support has a positive effect on subjective well-being. The studies found that having less than once in six months contact with family members strongly decreased quality of life among older Nigerians by up to 15.52 ($\beta = -15.52$; $p = 0.001$), while material or financial support ($\beta = 0.081$; $p < 0.001$) from extended family members independently contributed to high satisfaction with life among older Kenyans (Gureje et al., 2008; Kodzi et al., 2011).

The effect of other related support concepts on health and well-being of older adults in SSA

While our review solely focused on the effect of support provided by only family or kinsmen to older adults, we identified other studies that examined other support related concepts or sources of support in SSA such as social capital, social relations, social support network, and living arrangement and their effects on health and well-being of older persons (e.g. Gyasi, 2019; Ralston, Schatz, Madhavan, Gómez-Olivé, & Collinson, 2019; Macia, Duboz, Montepare, & Gueye, 2015; Ramlagan, Peltzer, & Phaswana-Mafuya, 2013). Also, we were unable to disentangle the effect of family support components from some studies because summary measures were used. For example, social connectedness in Gyasi et al. (2019) was derived from combining variables such as frequency of contact with family, social engagements, and having an emotional bond with at least one person. These studies did not meet our inclusion criteria. Nonetheless, we found that higher social capital (Ramlagan et al., 2013), social support networks (Gyasi, 2019), social relations (Macia et al., 2015), and residing in two-generation linear-linked multigenerational households (Ralston et al., 2019) were generally positively related to better health and well-being in later life.

Quality of included studies

According to the NIH quality assessment tool, five of the eight eligible studies included were rated to be of good or high quality. They clearly described the recruitment process for participants, provided detailed description of the study design and methods used, described processes and justification for required sample size, statistically adjusted key potential confounding variables for their effect on the outcome variables, and presented findings clearly. Studies that were rated to be of fair or poor quality (n=3) failed to account for the effect of key confounding variables on the outcome variable. These weaknesses are likely to increase the risk of bias and affect the internal validity of the studies. Table 37.3 shows quality assessment of included studies.

Discussion

Our review sought to provide an overview of the studies on family support provided to older adults in SSA and to summarize the effects on health and well-being in later life, considering the increasing number of older adults in SSA. We identified only eight studies that met all eligibility criteria and were included in the review. The few studies identified is a clear indication of a gap in the literature that needs to be filled. We found that instrumental (i.e. financial support), emotional (i.e. social support), and structural (frequent contact with non-coresident family) support provided to older adults were beneficial to their health and well-being. Specifically, social support and frequent contact with non-coresident family members

Table 37.3 Quality Assessment of Included Studies

National Institute of Health (NIH) Quality Assessment Tool for Observational Cohort and Cross-Sectional Studies/Studies included in review	*Olagunju et al., 2015*	*Gureje et al., 2008*	*Kodzi et al., 2010*	*Ojagbemi et al., 2018.*	*Kodzi et al., 2011*	*Gureje et al., 2011*	*Gyasi et al., 2018.*	*Gyasi et al., 2019*		
1 Was the research question or objective in this paper clearly stated?	Y	Y	Y	Y	Y	Y	Y	Y		
2 Was the study population clearly specified and defined?	Y	Y	Y	Y	Y	Y	Y	Y		
3 Was the participation rate of eligible persons at least 50%?	Y	Y	Y	Y	Y	Y	Y	Y	**Key**	
4 Were all the subjects selected or recruited from the same or similar populations (including the same time period)? Were inclusion and exclusion criteria for being in the study prespecified and applied uniformly to all participants?	Y	Y	Y	Y	Y	Y	Y	Y	**Y**	***Yes***
5 Was a sample size justification, power description, or variance and effect estimates provided?	Y	N	N	N	N	N	Y	Y	**N**	***No***
6 For the analyses in this paper, were the exposure(s) of interest measured prior to the outcome(s) being measured?	N	N	N	Y	N	Y	N	N	**NA**	***Not Applicable***
7 Was the timeframe sufficient so that one could reasonably expect to see an association between exposure and outcome if it existed?	N	N	N	Y	N	Y	N	N	**NR**	***Not Reported***
8 For exposures that can vary in amount or level, did the study examine different levels of the exposure as related to the outcome (e.g., categories of exposure, or exposure measured as continuous variable)?	NA	NA	NA	NA	NA	NA	NA	NA	**CD**	***Cannot Determine***
9 Were the exposure measures (independent variables) clearly defined, valid, reliable, and implemented consistently across all study participants?	Y	Y	Y	Y	Y	Y	Y	Y		
10 Was the exposure(s) assessed more than once over time?	NA	NA	NA	Y	NA	N	NA	NA		
11 Were the outcome measures (dependent variables) clearly defined, valid, reliable, and implemented consistently across all study participants?	Y	Y	Y	Y	Y	Y	Y	Y		
12 Were the outcome assessors blinded to the exposure status of participants?	NA	NA	NA	NA	NA	NA	NA	NA		
13 Was loss to follow-up after baseline 20% or less?	NA	NA	NA	N	NA	N	NA	NA		
14 Were key potential confounding variables measured and adjusted statistically for their impact on the relationship between exposure(s) and outcome(s)?	N	Y	Y	Y	Y	Y	Y	Y		
OVERALL RATING (GOOD, FAIR, POOR)	**POOR**	**FAIR**	**GOOD**	**GOOD**	**GOOD**	**FAIR**	**GOOD**	**GOOD**		

were protective against poor psychological health and protective of general well-being and quality of life of older adults (Gyasi et al., 2019; Ojagbemi et al., 2018; Olagunju et al., 2015 Gureje et al., 2008). These findings corroborate previous observations on the buffering effects of social support networks and social relationships of older adults against poor mental health outcomes in low- and middle-income countries (Miao, Wu, & Sun, 2019; Teerawichitchainan et al., 2015) and high-income countries (Roh et al., 2015; Thompson & Heller, 1990). Our review suggests that very little is known about family support provided to older adults and the effects on health and well-being in later life compared to other regions of the world. Social support is considered to act as a resource for coping with adverse mental health events (Cohen & Wills, 1985). For example, frequent in-person meetings and phone contact with non-coresident adult children was associated with a reduced risk of depression among older adults in Korea (Roh et al., 2015), while Thompson and Heller (1990) observed social support from family members improved the psychological well-being of older women in the USA. Since studies suggest that the family is the main source of social support for older adults in SSA, this finding is not unexpected (Unanka, 2002; Van der Geest, 2016). In many societies in SSA, families tend to reside in proximity in order to share resources between generations within multigenerational households and to support one another through difficult times. This encourages intergenerational family interdependence in the face of limited economic security and social services, typical of most low-resource settings (Pelcastre-Villafuerte, Treviño-Siller, González-Vázquez, & Márquez-Serrano, 2011; Peil, 1991). This social integration into the extended family system widens one's social network and increases the chances of receiving social support from kinsmen.

Our review found financial support from non-coresident adult children and extended family members positively related to better psychological, self-rated health and subjective well-being among recipient older adults. This finding is in line with other studies in similar non-Western contexts such as Thailand, Vietnam, and Brazil (Bélanger et al., 2016; Guo, 2014; Teerawichitchainan et al., 2015). In this context, where public support for older adults is hardly available, financial support from family members especially adult children may help older parents utilize health services and cope with financial stress for better health outcomes and well-being. Additionally, receiving financial support from one's adult children can be culturally desirable, because it is often interpreted as being 'successful' in life, and may boost one's social status in society, which could lead to an older adult experiencing greater life satisfaction (Teerawichitchainan et al., 2015). Furthermore, society considers providing support to older parents by adult children their moral duty and it also fits into the assertion that children are old-age economic security in SSA (Aboderin, 2004; Apt, 2002). It should be noted however that in this context, financial support from adult children to older parents is usually motivated by the needs (e.g. health care costs) of older parents (Hogan, Eggebeen, & Clogg, 1993). In contrast, while beneficial effects of financial support from adult children to older parents have been reported in Western contexts (Zunzunegui et al., 2001; Silverstein & Bengtson, 1994), some other studies associate financial support from adult children with poor psychological well-being of older parents (Lowenstein et al., 2007). It is argued that older persons who receive financial support in Western contexts normally prefer to remain functionally independent and may feel dependent on adult children, causing distress and subsequently deterioration in well-being (Pyke & Bengtson, 1996). The differences in the effect of receiving financial assistance from adult children in the two scenarios above may be explained by the socio-cultural perspective.

Review contribution and strengths

We believe that our review contributes to the ageing literature in SSA in two different ways. Firstly, a considerable number of research studies have been conducted on support provided by older adults in SSA (reflecting the role of the elderly in African families) and the effects on health and well-being, but limited research on support provided to older adults and the effects on their health and well-being. It is worth iterating that there is quite some evidence for support provision to older people and its effect on health and well-being in later life in other world regions, including low- and middle-income countries, but it's not really clear how much we know about SSA (Teerawichitchainan et al., 2015; Lowenstein et al., 2007; Lee, Netzer, & Coward, 1995). Our review therefore highlights the positive effects of family support on the health and well-being of older sub-Saharan Africans. To the extent that the family plays a central role in the social protection of majority of older people in SSA, and given that the population is rapidly ageing, coupled with the high cost of establishing and running social welfare programmes for the elderly, for now, countries in SSA may be better off implementing programmes that motivate families to continue their support functions.

Secondly, while our findings suggest the need for more research on the topic in SSA, it also draws scholarly attention on the need to differentiate the forms (instrumental or emotional) and source of family support in research as these are known to exhibit distinct effects on the health and well-being of older people (Merz & Consedine, 2009; Silverstein et al., 2006; Cong & Silverstein, 2008). In the study by Olagunju et al. (2015) the relationship of the provider and specific social support provided (e.g. emotional or instrumental) was not indicated, while in the case of Kodzi et al. (2011) the researchers failed to indicate the relationship of the provider. For instance, the provision of instrumental support (e.g. help with household chores) by daughters and daughters-in-law and financial support by sons and sons-in-law to older parents is considered customarily appropriate in African society, hence may exert different effects on health and well-being than a support relationship viewed as customarily inappropriate as found in other low-resource settings (Okoyė, 2012; Coe, 2011; Cong & Silverstein, 2008). For example, a study in China reported help with household chores from daughters-in-law resulted in reduced depressive symptoms of older parents compared to their counterparts who received support from sons (Cong & Silverstein, 2008). This suggests that future research should be mindful of this in order to detect a more nuanced picture of the relationship between family support received and the health and well-being of older persons.

This review presents evidence regarding the effect of various types of family support provided to older adults in SSA on their health and well-being. To the best of our knowledge, this is the first systematic review on the topic in SSA. The evidence presented is based on a systematic search of eight databases, including searches in other sources for unpublished works.

Review limitations

It was not feasible to conduct a meta-analysis as a result of the different types of family support and varied measures used to assess support (e.g. different response scales were used in assessing frequency of contact with family) and health or well-being in this review. This review may miss evidence from French-speaking SSA countries. But, if there were many of them at all, we would have identified them through the bibliography of other articles. Also, this review could not account for the extent to which socio-demographic, socio-cultural, health-related, and country-level factors influenced the effect of family support on the health and well-being outcomes of older adults within and between countries, since these are known to moderate support effects.

Conclusions

As our review shows, currently, the evidence indicates a beneficial relation between family support (i.e. frequent contact, social support, financial support) provided and the health and well-being of recipient older adults in SSA. We found frequent social contact with family and social support provided to older adults positively associated with better psychological well-being and quality of life among older adults. In addition, this review evinces that financial support from non-coresident adult children and extended family members to older adults relates to their better psychological well-being, self-rated health, and greater satisfaction with life. Despite our findings, so far, not much empirical work has been done on this topic in SSA. The findings are based on eight studies and suggest that more research, both quantitative and qualitative, needs to be undertaken to examine the relationship between family support provided and the health and well-being of older sub-Saharan Africans. In light of an ageing SSA population and poor resource context, sub-Saharan African governments must recognize the enormous support burden on families, raise awareness on the importance of family support, and promote interventions that motivate families to meet the support needs of older persons. One way to achieve this is to pay allowances or grant tax reliefs to poor families who maintain an older person. Another way may involve using campaigns to promote family support towards older adults. For instance, campaigns that aim to encourage families to stay socially connected and to use social events such as festivals, marriage ceremonies, and naming ceremonies to 'honour' and to engage older members may benefit their well-being.

Acknowledgements

MAA wishes to acknowledge funding for his doctoral studies from the Faculty of Spatial Sciences, University of Groningen, the Netherlands, through the PhD Scholarship Programme and the University of Health and Allied Sciences, Ghana. The authors are grateful to Dr. Stephen Adaawen, Population Research Centre, Faculty of Spatial Sciences, University of Groningen, for proofreading the manuscript.

Author contributions

MAA, HH, and TCV conceptualized the study. MAA undertook the literature search. MAA and TCV screened publications and assessed full text for eligibility and inclusion. MAA extracted the data and synthesized the findings. TCV and HH cross-validated synthesized findings. MAA drafted the manuscript. HH and TCV provided supervisory support in drafting and revising the manuscript. All authors read and approved the final manuscript.

References

Aboderin, I. (2004). Decline in material family support for older people in Urban Ghana, Africa: Understanding processes and causes of change. *The Journals of Gerontology, Series B: Psychological Sciences and Social Sciences*, *59*(3), S128–S137. https://doi.org/10.1093/geronb/59.3.s128

Aboderin, I. (2010). Understanding and advancing the health of older populations in sub-Saharan Africa: Policy perspectives and evidence needs. *Public Health Reviews*, *32*(2), 357–376. https://doi.org/10.1007/bf03391607

Aboderin, I., & Hoffman, J. (2015). Families, intergenerational bonds, and aging in sub-Saharan Africa. *Canadian Journal on Aging/La Revue canadienne du vieillissement*, *34*(3), 282–289. https://doi.org/10.1017/s0714980815000239

Adamchak, D. J. (1989). Population aging in sub-Saharan Africa: The effects of development on the elderly. *Population and Environment*, *10*(3), 162–176. https://doi.org/10.1007/bf01257902

American Psychiatric Association. (1994). *Diagnostic and statistical manual of mental disorders. Fourth edition (DSM-IV)* (4th ed.). Washington, DC: American Psychiatric Association.

Apt, N. A. (2002). Ageing and the changing role of the family and the community: An African perspective. *International Social Security Review*, *55*(1), 39–47. https://doi.org/10.1111/1468-246x.00113

Ardington, C., Case, A., Islam, M., Lam, D., Leibbrandt, M., Menendez, A., & Olgiati, A. (2010). The impact of AIDS on intergenerational support in South Africa: Evidence from the Cape Area Panel Study. *Research on Aging*, *32*(1), 97–121. https://doi.org/10.1177/0164027509348143

Attias-Donfut, C., Ogg, J., & Wolff, F.-C. (2005). European patterns of intergenerational financial and time transfers. *European Journal of Ageing*, *2*(3), 161–173. https://doi.org/10.1007/s10433-005-0008-7

Barrera, M. (1986). Distinctions between social support concepts, measures, and models. *American Journal of Community Psychology*, *14*(4), 413–445. Retrieved from https://onlinelibrary-wiley-com.proxy-ub.rug.nl/doi/pdfdirect/10.1007/BF00922627

Bélanger, E., Ahmed, T., Vafaei, A., Curcio, C. L., Phillips, S. P., & Zunzunegui, M. V. (2016). Sources of social support associated with health and quality of life: A cross-sectional study among Canadian and Latin American older adults. *BMJ Open*, *6*(6), e011503. https://doi.org/10.1136/bmjopen-2016-011503

Chen, X., & Silverstein, M. (2000). Intergenerational social support and the psychological well-being of older parents in China. *Research on Aging*, *22*(1), 43–65. https://doi.org/10.1177/0164027500221003

Chen, Y., & Feeley, T. H. (2014). Social support, social strain, loneliness, and well-being among older adults. *Journal of Social and Personal Relationships*, *31*(2), 141–161. https://doi.org/10.1177/0265407513488728

Choi, Y., Park, S., Cho, K. H., Chun, S.-Y., & Park, E.-C. (2016). A change in social activity affect cognitive function in middle-aged and older Koreans: Analysis of a Korean longitudinal study on aging (2006–2012). *International Journal of Geriatric Psychiatry*, *31*(8), 912–919. https://doi.org/10.1002/gps.4408

Coe, C. (2011). What is the impact of transnational migration on family life? Women's comparisons of internal and international migration in a small town in Ghana. *American Ethnologist*, *38*(1), 148–163. https://doi.org/10.1111/j.1548-1425.2010.01298.x

Cohen, S. (1988). Psychosocial models of the role of social support in the etiology of physical disease. *Health Psychology*, 7(3), 269–297. https://doi.org/10.1037/0278-6133.7.3.269

Cohen, S., & Wills, T. A. (1985). Stress, social support, and the buffering hypothesis. *Psychological Bulletin*, *98*(2), 310. https://doi.org/10.1037/0033-2909.98.2.310

Cong, Z., & Silverstein, M. (2008). Intergenerational support and depression among elders in rural China: Do daughters-in-law matter? *Journal of Marriage and Family*, *70*(3), 599–612. https://doi.org/10.1111/j.1741-3737.2008.00508.x

Davey, A., & Eggebeen, D. J. (1998). Patterns of intergenerational exchange and mental health. *The Journals of Gerontology, Series B: Psychological Sciences and Social Sciences*, *53B*(2), P86–P95. https://doi.org/10.1093/geronb/53b.2.p86

Ferreira, M. (2006). The differential impact of social-pension income on household poverty alleviation in three South African ethnic groups. *Ageing and Society*, *26*(3), 337–354. https://doi.org/10.1017/s0144686x0600482x

Green, A. F., Rebok, G., & Lyketsos, C. G. (2008). Influence of social network characteristics on cognition and functional status with aging. *International Journal of Geriatric Psychiatry: A Journal of the Psychiatry of Late Life and Allied Sciences*, *23*(9), 972–978. https://doi.org/10.1002/gps.2023

Grundy, E., & Henretta, J. C. (2006). Between elderly parents and adult children: A new look at the intergenerational care provided by the 'sandwich generation'. *Ageing and Society*, *26*(5), 707–722. https://doi.org/10.1017/s0144686x06004934

Guo, M. (2014). Parental status and late-life well-being in rural China: The benefits of having multiple children. *Aging & Mental Health*, *18*(1), 19–29. https://doi.org/10.1080/13607863.2013.799117

Gureje, O., Kola, L., Afolabi, E., & Olley, B. O. (2008). Determinants of quality of life of elderly Nigerians: Results from the Ibadan study of ageing. *African Journal of Medicine and Medical Sciences, 37*(3), 239. Retrieved from https://pubmed.ncbi.nlm.nih.gov/18982816/

Gureje, O., Oladeji, B., & Abiona, T. (2011). Incidence and risk factors for late-life depression in the Ibadan study of ageing. *Psychological Medicine, 41*(9), 1897. http://doi.org/10.1017/S0033291710002643

Gyasi, R. M. (2019). Social support, physical activity and psychological distress among community-dwelling older Ghanaians. *Archives of Gerontology and Geriatrics, 81*, 142–148. https://doi.org/10.1016/j.archger.2018.11.016

Gyasi, R. M., Phillips, D. R., & Abass, K. (2018). Social support networks and psychological wellbeing in community-dwelling older Ghanaian cohorts. *International Psychogeriatrics, 31*(7), 1047–1057. https://doi.org/10.1017/S1041610218001539

Gyasi, R. M., Yeboah, A. A., Mensah, C. M., Ouedraogo, R., & Addae, E. A. (2019). Neighborhood, social isolation and mental health outcome among older people in Ghana. *Journal of Affective Disorders, 259*, 154–163. https://doi.org/10.1016/j.jad.2019.08.024

Hoffman, J., & Pype, K. (2016). Introduction: Spaces and practices of care for older people in Sub-Saharan Africa. In J. Hoffman & K. Pype (Eds), *Ageing in sub-Saharan Africa* (pp. 1–20). London: Policy Press Policy Press.

Hogan, D. P., Eggebeen, D. J., & Clogg, C. C. (1993). The structure of intergenerational exchanges in American families. *American Journal of Sociology, 98*(6), 1428–1458. https://doi.org/10.1086/230194

Kessler, R. C., Andrews, G., Colpe, L. J., Hiripi, E., Mroczek, D. K., Normand, S. L. T., . . . Zaslavsky, A. M. (2002). Short screening scales to monitor population prevalences and trends in non-specific psychological distress. *Psychological Medicine, 32*(6), 959–976. doi:10.1017/S0033291702006074

Kessler, R. C., & Ustün, T. B. (2004). The World Mental Health (WMH) survey initiative version of the World Health Organization (WHO) Composite International Diagnostic Interview (CIDI). *International Journal of Methods in Psychiatric Research, 13*(2), 93–121. https://doi.org/10.1002/mpr.168

Kodzi, I. A., Gyimah, S. O., Emina, J. B., & Ezeh, A. C. (2010). Religious involvement, social engagement, and subjective health status of older residents of informal neighborhoods of Nairobi. *Journal of Urban Health, 88*(2), 370–380. https://doi.org/10.1007/s11524-010-9482-0

Kodzi, I. A., Gyimah, S. O., Emina, J. B., & Ezeh, A. C. (2011). Understanding aging in sub-Saharan Africa: Exploring the contributions of religious and secular social involvement to life satisfaction. *Ageing and Society, 31*(3), 455. https://doi.org/10.1017/S0144686X10001005

Kunna, R., San Sebastian, M., & Stewart Williams, J. (2017). Measurement and decomposition of socioeconomic inequality in single and multimorbidity in older adults in China and Ghana: Results from the WHO study on global AGEing and adult health (SAGE). *International Journal for Equity in Health, 16*(1), 79–79. https://doi.org/10.1186/s12939-017-0578-y

Lee, G. R., Netzer, J. K., & Coward, R. T. (1995). Depression among older parents: The role of intergenerational exchange. *Journal of Marriage and the Family, 57*(3), 823. https://doi.org/10.2307/353935

Lee, H. J., Lyu, J., Lee, C. M., & Burr, J. A. (2013). Intergenerational financial exchange and the psychological well-being of older adults in the Republic of Korea. *Aging & Mental Health, 18*(1), 30–39. https://doi.org/10.1080/13607863.2013.784955

Lieberman, M., & Tobin, S. (1983). *The experience of old age: Stress, coping and survival*. New York, NY: Basic Books.

Litwin, H. (2004). Intergenerational exchange patterns and their correlates in an aging Israeli cohort. *Research on Aging, 26*(2), 202–223. https://doi.org/10.1177/0164027503260631

Liu, X., Liang, J., & Gu, S. (1995). Flows of social support and health status among older persons in China. *Social Science & Medicine, 41*(8), 1175–1184. https://doi.org/10.1016/0277-9536(94)00427-u

Lloyd-Sherlock, P. (2010). *Population ageing and international development*: Bristol: Bristol University Press.

Lowenstein, A., Katz, R., & Gur-Yaish, N. (2007). Reciprocity in parent-child exchange and life satisfaction among the elderly: A cross-national perspective. *Journal of Social Issues, 63*(4), 865–883. https://doi.org/10.1111/j.1540-4560.2007.00541.x

Macia, E., Duboz, P., Montepare, J. M., & Gueye, L. (2015). Exploring life satisfaction among older adults in Dakar. *Journal of Cross-Cultural Gerontology, 30*(4), 377–391. https://doi.org/10.1007/s10823-015-9275-8

Mao, W., Chi, I., & Wu, S. (2019). Multidimensional intergenerational instrumental support and self-rated health among older adults in rural China: Trajectories and correlated change over 11 years. *Research on Aging, 41*(2), 115–138. https://doi.org/10.1177/0164027518783512

McIntyre, D. (2005). Health policy and older people in Africa. In P. Lloyd-Sherlock (Ed.), *Living longer: Ageing, development and social protection* (pp. 160–183). Geneva: United Nations Research Institute for Social Development.

Merz, E.-M., & Consedine, N. S. (2009). The association of family support and wellbeing in later life depends on adult attachment style. *Attachment & Human Development, 11*(2), 203–221. https://doi.org/10.1080/14616730802625185

Merz, E.-M., Consedine, N. S., Schulze, H.-J., & Schuengel, C. (2009). Wellbeing of adult children and ageing parents: Associations with intergenerational support and relationship quality. *Ageing and Society, 29*(5), 783–802. https://doi.org/10.1017/s0144686x09008514

Miao, J., Wu, X., & Sun, X. (2019). Neighborhood, social cohesion, and the elderly's depression in Shanghai. *Social Science & Medicine, 229*, 134–143. https://doi.org/10.1016/j.socscimed.2018.08.022

Moher, D., Liberati, A., Tetzlaff, J., Altman, D. G., & Group, P. (2009). Preferred reporting items for systematic reviews and meta-analyses: The PRISMA statement. *PLoS Medicine, 6*(7), e1000097. https://doi.org/10.1371/journal.pmed.1000097

Mugisha, J. O., Schatz, E. J., Randell, M., Kuteesa, M., Kowal, P., Negin, J., & Seeley, J. (2016). Chronic disease, risk factors and disability in adults aged 50 and above living with and without HIV: Findings from the wellbeing of older people study in Uganda. *Global Health Action, 9*(1). https://doi.org/10.3402/gha.v9.31098

Nyirenda, M., Evandrou, M., Mutevedzi, P., Hosegood, V., Falkingham, J., & Newell, M.-L. (2015). Who cares? Implications of care-giving and-receiving by HIV-infected or-affected older people on functional disability and emotional wellbeing. *Ageing & Society, 35*(1), 169–202. https://doi.org/10.1017/S0144686X13000615

National Institutes of Health. (2014). *Quality assessment tool for observational cohort and cross-sectional studies* [cited 2020 May 15]. Retrieved from https://www.nhlbi.nih.gov/health-pro/guidelines/in-develop/cardiovascular-risk-reduction/tools/cohort

Ojagbemi, A., Bello, T., & Gureje, O. (2018). Gender differential in social and economic predictors of incident major depressive disorder in the Ibadan Study of Ageing. *Social Psychiatry and Psychiatric Epidemiology, 53*(4), 351–361. https://doi.org/10.1007/s00127-018-1500-7

Okoye, U. O. (2012). Family care-giving for ageing parents in Nigeria: Gender differences, cultural imperatives and the role of education. *International Journal of Education and Ageing, 2*(2), 139–154.

Olagunju, A. T., Olutoki, M. O., Ogunnubi, O. P., & Adeyemi, J. D. (2015). Late-life depression: Burden, severity and relationship with social support dimensions in a West African community. *Archives of Gerontology and Geriatrics, 61*(2), 240–246. https://doi.org/10.1016/j.archger.2015.05.002

Peil, M. (1991). Family support for the Nigerian elderly. *Journal of Comparative Family Studies, 22*(1), 85–100. https://doi.org/10.3138/jcfs.22.1.85

Pelcastre-Villafuerte, B. E., Treviño-Siller, S., González-Vázquez, T., & Márquez-Serrano, M. (2011). Social support and living conditions in poor elderly people in urban Mexico. *Cadernos de Saúde Pública, 27*(3), 460–470. https://doi.org/10.1590/s0102-311x2011000300007

Popay, J., Roberts, H., Sowden, A., Petticrew, M. Arai, L., Rodger, M., . . . Duffy, S. (2006). *Guidance on the conduct of narrative synthesis in systematic reviews. A product from the ESRC methods programme Version, 1*, b92. Retrieved May 14, 2020, from www.lancaster.ac.uk/media/lancaster-university/contentassets/documents/fhm/dhr/chir/NSsynthesisguidanceVersion1-April2006.pdf

Posel, D., Fairburn, J. A., & Lund, F. (2006). Labour migration and households: A reconsideration of the effects of the social pension on labour supply in South Africa. *Economic Modelling, 23*(5), 836–853. https://doi.org/10.1016/j.econmod.2005.10.010

Pyke, K. D., & Bengtson, V. L. (1996). Caring more or less: Individualistic and collectivist systems of family eldercare. *Journal of Marriage and the Family*, 379–392. https://doi.org/10.2307/353503

Ralston, M., Schatz, E., Madhavan, S., Gómez-Olivé, F. X., & Collinson, M. A. (2019). Perceived quality of life and living arrangements among older rural South Africans: Do all households fare the same? *Ageing & Society, 39*(12), 2735–2755. https://doi.org/10.1017/S0144686X18001198

Ramlagan, S., Peltzer, K., & Phaswana-Mafuya, N. (2013). Social capital and health among older adults in South Africa. *BMC Geriatrics, 13*(1), 100. Retrieved from www.biomedcentral.com/1471-2318/13/100

Roh, H. W., Lee, Y., Lee, K. S., Chang, K. J., Kim, J., Lee, S. J., . . . Son, S. J. (2015). Frequency of contact with non-cohabitating adult children and risk of depression in elderly: A community-based three-year longitudinal study in Korea. *Archives of Gerontology and Geriatrics, 60*(1), 183–189. https://doi.org/10.1016/j.archger.2014.09.007

Rossi, A. S., & Rossi, P. H. (1990). *Of human bonding: Parent-children relationship across the life course*. Hawthorne, NY: Aldine.

Seeman, T. E., & Berkman, L. F. (1988). Structural characteristics of social networks and their relationship with social support in the elderly: Who provides support. *Social Science & Medicine, 26*(7), 737–749. https://doi.org/10.1016/0277-9536(88)90065-2

Seeman, T. E., Bruce, M. L., & McAvay, G. J. (1996). Social network characteristics and onset of ADL disability: MacArthur studies of successful aging. *The Journals of Gerontology, Series B: Psychological Sciences and Social Sciences, 51B*(4), S191–S200. https://doi.org/10.1093/geronb/51b.4.s191

Shumaker, S. A., & Brownell, A. (1984). Toward a theory of social support: Closing conceptual gaps. *Journal of Social Issues, 40*(4), 11–36. https://doi.org/10.1111/j.1540-4560.1984.tb01105.x

Silverstein, M., & Bengtson, V. L. (1994). Does intergenerational social support influence the psychological well-being of older parents? The contingencies of declining health and widowhood. *Social Science & Medicine, 38*(7), 943–957. https://doi.org/10.1016/0277-9536(94)90427-8

Silverstein, M., Chen, X., & Heller, K. (1996). Too much of a good thing? Intergenerational social support and the psychological well-being of older parents. *Journal of Marriage and the Family, 58*(4), 970. https://doi.org/10.2307/353984

Silverstein, M., Cong, Z., & Li, S. (2006). Intergenerational transfers and living arrangements of older people in rural China: Consequences for psychological well-being. *The Journals of Gerontology, Series B: Psychological Sciences and Social Sciences, 61*(5), S256–S266. https://doi.org/10.1093/geronb/61.5.S256

Teerawichitchainan, B., Pothisiri, W., & Long, G. T. (2015). How do living arrangements and intergenerational support matter for psychological health of elderly parents? Evidence from Myanmar, Vietnam, and Thailand. *Social Science & Medicine, 136–137*, 106–116. https://doi.org/10.1016/j.socscimed.2015.05.019

The WHOQOL Group. (1998). Development of the World Health Organization WHOQOL-BREF Quality of Life Assessment. *Psychological Medicine, 28*(3), 551–558. https://doi.org/10.1017/s0033291798006667

Therborn, G. (2006). *African families in a global context* (research report no. 131). Uppsala, Sweden: Nordiska African Institute.

Thoits, P. A. (2011). Mechanisms linking social ties and support to physical and mental health. *Journal of Health and Social Behavior, 52*(2), 145–161. https://doi.org/10.1177/0022146510395592

Thompson, M. G., & Heller, K. (1990). Facets of support related to well-being: Quantitative social isolation and perceived family support in a sample of elderly women. *Psychology and Aging, 5*(4), 535–544. https://doi.org/10.1037/0882-7974.5.4.535

Unanka, G. O. (2002). Family support and health status of the elderly in Imo State of Nigeria. *Journal of Social Issues, 58*(4), 681–695. https://doi.org/10.1111/1540-4560.00040

United Nations, Department of Economic and Social Affairs, Population Division. (2019). *World Population Prospects 2019, custom data acquired via website*. Retrieved on March 20, 2020, from https://population.un.org/wpp/Download/Standard/Population/

Uwakwe, R., Ibeh, C. C., Modebe, A. I., Bo, E., Ezeama, N., Njelita, I., . . . Prince, M. J. (2009). The epidemiology of dependence in older people in Nigeria: Prevalence, determinants, informal care, and health service utilization. A 10/66 Dementia Research Group Cross-Sectional Survey. *Journal of the American Geriatrics Society, 57*(9), 1620–1627. https://doi.org/10.1111/j.1532-5415.2009.02397.x

Van der Geest, S. (2016). Will families in Ghana continue to care for older people? Logic and contradiction in policy. In J. Hoffman & K. Pype (Eds.), *Ageing in Sub-Saharan Africa: Spaces and Practices of Care* (pp. 21–41). London: Policy Press.

Vaux, A. (1988). *Social support: Theory, research, and intervention*. Westport, CT: Praeger Publishers.

Wandera, S. O., Ntozi, J., & Kwagala, B. (2014). Prevalence and correlates of disability among older Ugandans: Evidence from the Uganda National Household Survey. *Global Health Action*, 7, 25686. https://doi.org/10.3402/gha.v7.25686.

Yesavage, J. A., Brink, T. L., Rose, T. L., Lum, O., Huang, V., Adey, M., & Leirer, V. O. (1982). Development and validation of a geriatric depression screening scale: A preliminary report. *Journal of Psychiatric Research, 17*(1), 37–49. doi:10.1016/0022-3956(82)90033-4

Zimet, G. D., Dahlem, N. W., Zimet, S. G., & Farley, G. K. (1988). The Multidimensional Scale of Perceived Social Support. *Journal of Personality Assessment, 52*(1), 30–41. doi:10.1207/s15327752jpa5201_2

Zunzunegui, M. V., Béland, F., & Otero, A. (2001). Support from children, living arrangements, self-rated health and depressive symptoms of older people in Spain. *International Journal of Epidemiology, 30*(5), 1090–1099. https://doi.org/10.1093/ije/30.5.1090

PART 9

Mortality

38

CAUSES OF DEATH AND THE DOUBLE BURDEN OF DISEASE IN AFRICA

Evidence from the sub-Saharan Africa

N.N. Wekwete and K. Mangombe

Introduction

Context

Sub-Saharan Africa is experiencing a rapid epidemiological transition characterized by a shift from a burden of communicable diseases (CDs) to an increase of non-communicable diseases (NCDs) (IHME, 2018). Double burden of disease means the co-existence of communicable and non-communicable diseases (Hussein, 2014). Sub-Saharan African countries are experiencing a burden of communicable diseases such as HIV/AIDS, malaria, tuberculosis (TB), and of late the coronavirus disease (COVID-19)(Gouda et al., 2019; IHME, 2018) while, at the same time, experiencing an increase in NCDs, such as cancers, diabetes, chronic respiratory diseases, chronic kidney disease, high blood pressure, cardiovascular diseases and mental health disease due to alcohol and drug abuse and smoking (IHME, 2018; Meghji et al., 2016). Road injuries are also top contributors to health loss (IHME, 2018).

Unhealthy eating habits and reckless lifestyles have increasingly become the risk factors of non-communicable diseases, including tobacco consumption, harmful alcohol use, unhealthy diet, physical inactivity, obesity or high blood pressure (WHO Africa Region, 2016). The problem is that sub-Saharan countries are not economically developed and lack the advanced health systems that developed countries have, to manage non-communicable diseases or delay death. Thus, without significant investment in a health care system and not addressing the root causes of the diseases, sub-Saharan Africa will continue to experience not only an increase in the burden of the diseases, but also an unmanageable health situation. Therefore, understanding the burden of disease and its components is fundamental to health planning, health decision-making and health care delivery in the African context (Househam, 2010). However, not much attention has been paid to the extent to which communicable diseases contribute to the burden of non-communicable diseases and to the potential for common intervention strategies. The study aims to document the double burden of the diseases and the risk factors contributing to this double burden in the sub-Saharan African countries from African researchers, diasporic Africans and scholars in Africa in order inform health systems responses to these changes.

 DOI: 10.4324/9780429287213-47

Conceptual definitions

Table 38.1 presents definitions of key indicators and some concepts.

Theoretical and conceptual issues

Causes of death have changed from communicable to non-communicable diseases in adults in developed countries. Omran's (1971) Epidemiological Transition Theory proposed that countries would experience changes in patterns of health and diseases from infectious diseases to man-made and degenerative diseases (Omran, 1971). The theory proposes that, as countries develop, they move from infectious diseases to man-made diseases which include non-communicable diseases. The theory focuses on the complex changes in patterns of health and diseases, their demographic, socio-economic, biological determinants and their consequences on population and groups. Omran proposed three 'stages' which all societies have to go through in the process of modernization. The first stage, which is the 'Age of Pestilence and Famine',

Table 38.1 Definition of Key Indicators

Indicator/Concept	*Definition*
Life expectancy at birth (e^0)	The average number of years of life expected by a hypothetical cohort of individuals who would be subject throughout their lives to the age-specific mortality rates of a given year or period.
Adult mortality	The probability that an individual alive at exact age 15 will die before exact age 60, given the mortality conditions of a given year or period. It is expressed as deaths per 1,000 persons reaching age 15.
Maternal mortality	Death of a woman while pregnant or within 42 days of termination of pregnancy, irrespective of the duration and site of the pregnancy, from any cause related to or aggravated by the pregnancy or its management but not from accidental or incidental causes.
Maternal mortality ratio (MMR)	The number of maternal deaths per 100,000 live births in a given period.
Under-five mortality (5q0):	The probability that a child born in a specific year or period will die before reaching the age of 5 years, if subject to the age-specific mortality rates of that period. It is expressed as deaths per 1,000 live births.
Neo-natal mortality	The probability of dying within the first month of life.
Group I deaths	Deaths caused by communicable (infectious) diseases, as well as maternal, perinatal (new-born) and nutritional conditions.
Group II deaths	Deaths caused by non-communicable diseases.
Group III deaths	Deaths caused by injuries.
Metabolic Equivalent (MET)	The ratio of a person's working metabolic rate relative to the resting metabolic rate. METs are commonly used to express the intensity of physical activity, and are also used to analyze STEPs data.
Type 1 Diabetes	A chronic disease caused because the pancreas does not produce enough insulin (CDC, 2020). Previously called insulin-dependent or juvenile diabetes, it is usually diagnosed in children, teens and young adults, but it can develop at any age.
Type 2 Diabetes	Type 2 diabetes is the body's inability to effectively use the insulin it produces. It most often develops in people over age 45, but more and more children, teens and young adults are also developing it.

is characterized by a direct regime of high and fluctuating death rates and the prevalence of infectious diseases, such as measles, smallpox and typhoid. The second stage, the 'Age of Receding Pandemics', is characterized by an increase in life expectancy as the epidemics recede and the impact of infectious diseases on death rates declines (Agyei-Mensah & Aikins, 2010). The third stage, the 'Age of Degenerative and Man-made Diseases', is when the infectious diseases have been replaced by man-made and degenerative diseases; infectious diseases have receded, and their place has been taken by chronic, degenerative diseases, such as cardiovascular disease, stroke and cancers. Such diseases are associated with ageing populations. Two more stages were added to the model, stages 4 and 5. Stage 4 is the 'Age of Delayed Degenerative Diseases', when there is a decline in degenerative diseases because of delayed onset or better diagnosis and treatment. In this stage, degenerative diseases still remain important as major causes of death, but life expectancy is lengthened due to changes in medical technology (Agyei-Mensah & Aikins, 2010). Stage 5 is the 'Age of Emergent and Re-Emergent Infections', which is characterized by the resurgence of both old and new infections and parasitic diseases.

The ETT model has been criticized for its assumption that the shift in diseases is sequential, moving from infectious to communicable diseases. This does not apply to most of the developing countries, particularly sub-Saharan Africa, because it is now experiencing the double burden of communicable and non-communicable diseases and yet not fully developed. The protracted polarized model, which had 'two key elements: (i) the "prolonged or protracted" element and (ii) the "epidemiological polarized" element' was used to conceptualize Africa's 'double burden of disease' (Frenk, Bobadilla, Sepulveda, & Lpez, 1989, p. 881). The model recognizes the coexistence of communicable diseases such as malaria and tuberculosis, and chronic NCDs such as hypertension, stroke and diabetes (Cooper, Rotimi, Kaufman, Muna, & Mensah, 1998) similar to the added fifth stage of the ETT. 'The prolonged or protracted element' described partial changes in morbidity and mortality patterns that resulted in the coexistence of infectious disease (both a resurgence of the old and the emergence of the new) and chronic NCDs; while the epidemiological polarized element described the relationship between social class inequalities and higher morbidity and mortality rates among poor populations who experience higher rates of infectious and nutrition-related diseases (Frenk et al., 1989, p. 881). Thus, the model is relevant when looking at the 'double burden of disease' in the SSA region because it recognizes the co-existence of communicable diseases and non-communicable diseases (Agyei-Mensah & Aikins, 2010). The sub-Saharan countries are experiencing the burden of infectious diseases, such as HIV and AIDS, tuberculosis (TB), malaria and of late the COVID-19 pandemic, as well as non-communicable diseases, such as cancer and diabetes (Gouda et al., 2019; Hussein, 2014; Mocumbi, 2012).

In order to understand this double burden of diseases, there is a need to understand the risk factors of these diseases among SSA countries. The disease burden was conceptualized from the Mosley and Chen framework which looks at both the proximate and underlying causes of morbidity and mortality. The framework takes into account the immediate or direct causes that include the health behavioural, nutrition, injuries and environmental contamination factors, as well as the distal factors that include the socio-economic and cultural factors. The disease burden has wide-ranging effects on the population, the economy, health systems and other factors (Narayan & Donnenfeld, 2016). Risk factors include proximate determinants and socio-economic underlying factors. Proximate determinants directly affect the diseases: although communicable diseases have traditionally been leading causes of disease and mortality in sub-Saharan Africa, rapid urbanization, changes in dietary patterns, behavioural and biological factors and major improvements in the prevention and treatment of communicable diseases, particularly AIDS, that are helping raise life expectancy, are all contributing to a shift in disease patterns (Patricio Marquez & Farringdon, 2012). Thus, proximate determinants include: (i) Personal behaviours (alcohol and tobacco use, healthy diet, hygiene, sexual behaviour); (ii) Injuries (accidental and intentional interpersonal injuries); (iii) Personal illness control (physical activity, ignorance or lack of resources); (iv) Nutrition (malnutrition or obesity); and (v) environmental (water and sanitation, urbanization). The underlying socio-economic causes include education, income, traditional and cultural beliefs.

Methods and measures

The study used extensive desktop review and analysis of reports and studies by African researchers and Western scholars in Africa. Key documents that were used in this study include reports from the various the Demographic and Health Surveys (DHSs) in Africa, United Nations Department of Economic and Social Affairs (UNDESA) (2019), World Health Organization (WHO) African Region, the African Union (AU) and Africa Centres for Disease Control and Prevention (CDC, 2020), and other sources on the health and mortality in sub-Saharan Africa. On statistics on COVID-19, sources included WHO and AU Member States for proving data on the number of confirmed cases, deaths and recoveries. In addition, an extensive literature review of previous studies on the burden of diseases in sub-Saharan Africa conducted by African researchers was done. On the burden of HIV and AIDS, for HIV estimates, we utilized literature on HIV mostly from Gona et al. (2020) on their analysis on the mortality and morbidity due to HIV and AIDS in 16 SADC countries between 1990 and 2017. The authors used estimates from the Global Burden of Diseases, Injuries and Risk Factor (GBD) study, a 'systematic, scientific effort by the Institute for Health Metrics and Evaluation (IHME) to quantify the comparative magnitude of health loss due to diseases, injuries, and risk factors by age, sex, and geographies for specific points in time' (Gona et al., 2020). In sub-Saharan Africa, country-level data on traffic injury is very limited. Even South Africa, which has available data, also does not have complete vital registration and injury statistics, and had to make assumptions. The data from the cause-of-death profile of the urban-based National Injury Mortality Surveillance System (NIMSS) were extrapolated to all areas. Thus, there is a need to understand the determinants of road injuries and deaths in the region and to evaluate interventions to reduce the burden.

The study utilized Omran's (1971) Epidemiological Transition Theory (ETT) that proposes that countries would experience changes in patterns of health and diseases from infectious diseases to man-made and degenerative diseases (Omran, 1971). The next subsections briefly discuss causes of death with reference to communicable and non-communicable diseases, as well as the risk factors associated with mortality and mortality. The future research agenda in the context of double burden diseases projections within Africa is covered. Finally, the conclusion remarks are presented.

Empirical findings

The key concerns of this work are the shift of the causes of death from CDs to NCDs which will affect the weak health systems in the region. Also, areas of concern included are the risk factors of deaths, especially the NCD risk factors, and weak health systems. These are presented in this section.

The double burden of diseases

The disease pattern occurrence in the sub-Saharan Africa region is experiencing a double burden of diseases, with NCDs on the increase (Mudie et al., 2019). Communicable diseases account for two thirds of the total disease burden (WHO, 2014; Nyirenda, 2016). The communicable diseases seen as a burden in Africa include lower respiratory infections, HIV/AIDS, tuberculosis (TB), malaria, measles, cholera and of late, COVID-19 pandemic, which has caused lots of deaths worldwide. Although the burden of infectious diseases is still high and outweighs that of NCDs in SSA, non-communicable diseases, which include cardiovascular diseases, ischemic heart diseases, diabetes, respiratory conditions, cancers, neurological disorders and hypertension, have become major sources of morbidity and mortality and the 'burden will overtake that of infectious diseases by 2035 (Nyirenda, 2016, p. 157).

Figure 38.1 presents the leading causes of death in Africa in 2000 and 2018. The top five leading causes of death in Africa in 2018 were lower respiratory infections (10.9%), HIV/AIDS (8.3%), diarrhoeal diseases (7%), stroke (4.9%) and ischaemic heart diseases (4.9%) (WHO, 2020). This shows that Africa, although dominated by CDs, is experiencing the burden of NCDs.

Acute lower respiratory tract infections (ALRIs), which affect people's airways and lungs, have maintained the leading position since 2010. In 2018, the sub-Saharan region accounted for 50% of the global 5.8 million deaths due to ALRI (Seidu et al., 2019). HIV/AIDS, which is the second leading cause of death in Africa, has been declining over the years, especially in countries that have up-scaled HIV prevention strategies to behaviour change and anti-retroviral therapy (ART) (WHO, 2014). The five leading countries with the highest proportion of HIV/AIDS-related deaths were Botswana (28.7%), South Africa (28.5%), Lesotho (25.1%), Eswatini (24.8%) and Mozambique (24.2%) (Gona et al., 2020). While ART has extended life for most people living with HIV, it is important that people living with HIV should strictly adhere to treatment because failure to follow up from care and defaulting, especially for first-line treatment, significantly affects survivability. Ideally, when one defaults on the first line, the next step

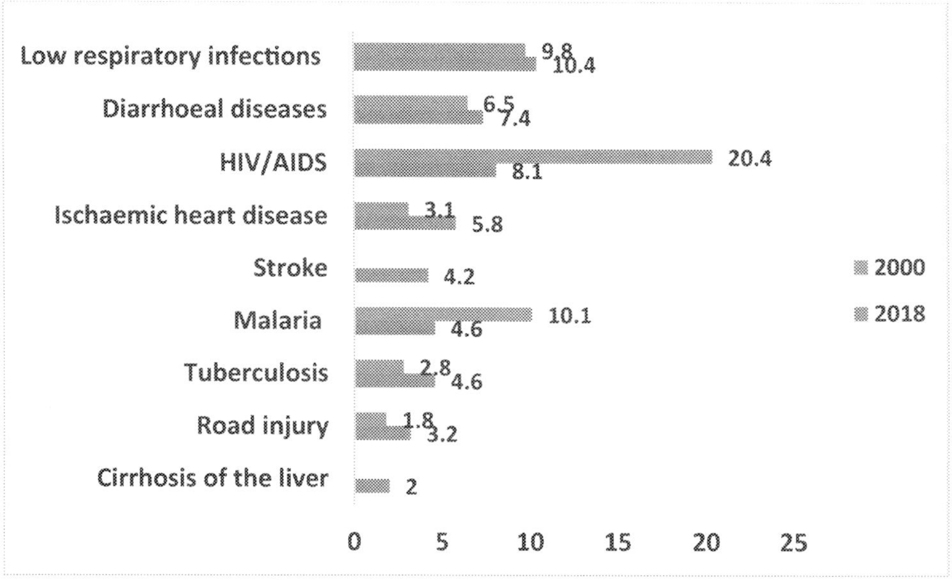

Figure 38.1 Leading causes of death in Africa, 2000, 2018, percentage.

Source: (WHO, 2020)

would be initiation into the second line, which because of cost, is out of reach for most rural communities, thereby compromising survival of patients (Gona et al., 2020).

Tuberculosis (TB) incidence in SSA is most prevalent in Southern Africa where the HIV/AIDS burden is highest. In 2018, the highest TB incidences were in Lesotho (611/100,000), Mozambique (551), South Africa (520), Namibia (524) and, in Central Africa, in Gabon (525) and Central Africa Republic (540) whilst the least were in island countries, i.e. Mauritius (13) and Seychelles (18) (WHO, 2020). The HIV/AIDS-TB co-infection is an added burden to the region (Hussein, 2014). As seen in Figure 38.1, TB is the fourth to HIV/AIDS as the greatest killer worldwide due to a single infectious agent. The success in control of TB in the region has been due to the improved coverage of major interventions such as the 'expansion of Directly Observed Treatment (DOTS), improved diagnostics, resulting in improved case detection in adults and children; and better access to HIV testing and treatment for tuberculosis patients' (WHO, 2014).

Diarrhoeal diseases, the third top cause of deaths, are the major killer among under-five children in Africa. Death is caused by dehydration, poor absorption of nutrients or infectious complications, such as a compromised intestinal wall, with malnutrition increasing the risk (WHO Africa Region, 2016). However, deaths due to diarrhoeal diseases have been on the decline from 725,000 in 2010 to 643,000 in 2015. Cholera, a diarrhoeal disease that is often fatal and can kill within hours if left untreated, remains a persistent public health problem in SSA (WHO, 2014; Lessler et al., 2018; Clark et al., 2018). A study on cholera incidence in SSA, excluding Djibouti and Eretria, between 2010 and 2016, found that more than 200 million people were living in areas with at least some cholera incidence (Lessler et al., 2018). Cholera risk among the people exposed to cholera cases was 5–11 times higher than that among those not exposed to cholera (Ali et al., 2016). However, the distribution of cholera cases varies among the countries and within the country. Some countries are more prone to cholera and have high number of cases every year, such as the eastern part of DRC while in other areas it is concentrated in large outbreaks but separated by many years of low activity (Lessler et al., 2018). Although cholera outbreaks in the region are largely due to lack of access to safe water and appropriate sanitation, and can be prevented by the new oral vaccination which can effectively prevent cholera for at least 3 years after administration, the provision of vaccination can be hampered by the limited financial resources faced by the health systems (Lessler et al., 2018; Ali et al., 2016).

Malaria incidence is prevalent in Western and Central Africa, with the highest experienced in Rwanda (486.5 per 1,000 population at risk), Burkina Faso (398.7), Mali (386.8), Benin (386.2), Liberia (361.5), Niger (356.6), Central Africa Republic (347.3), Côte d'Ivoire (330.6), Sierra Leone (320.4) and the Democratic Republic of Congo (319.8) (WHO, 2020). Lowest incidences were recorded in South Africa (1.7), Eswatini (0.8) and Botswana (0.6) (WHO, 2020). However, malaria rates have declined by 50% in the region due to 'improved availability and use of insecticide-treated nets, diagnosis-based treatment with artemisinin-based combination therapy, engagement of communities in malaria control, and strengthening capacity in vector control for malaria' (WHO, 2014).

The novel coronavirus SARS-CoV2 (COVID-19), which originated in China in December 2019, has become the major cause of death worldwide. Since the World Health Organization declared the coronavirus a pandemic on 11 March 2020, it has spread at an alarming rate, with more than half of countries in the region experiencing community transmission (WHO, 2020). As of 15 March 2021, a total of 4,041,835 COVID-19 cases, 108,064 deaths (case fatality rate [CFR] of 2.7%) and 3,630,060 recoveries were reported in 55 African Union (AU) Member States (African Union & Africa CDC, 2021). See Table 38.2. This is 5% of all cases

Table 38.2 Distribution of COVID-19 Confirmed Cases, Deaths and Recoveries by Region in Africa, 15 March 2021

Region	*Number of Confirmed Cases*	*Number of Deaths*	*Number of Recoveries*
Southern Africa	1,873,691	58,284	1,755,949
Northern Africa	1,201,672	34,372	1,062,497
Eastern Africa	440,548	8,128	338,207
Western Africa	413,088	5,392	375,178
Central Africa	112,836	1,888	98,229
Africa	**4,041,835**	**108,064**	**3,630,060**

Source: African Union & Africa CDC (2021)

Table 38.3 Top Ten Countries of COVID-19 Cases in Sub-Saharan Africa

Country	*Number of Confirmed Cases*	*Number of Deaths*
South Africa	1,517,666	50,462
Nigeria	157,671	1,951
Ethiopia	162,954	2,394
Kenya	107,329	1,870
Ghana	86,092	629
Zambia	80,687	1,109
Mozambique	61,170	674
Uganda	40,452	334
Namibia	39,466	436
Cameroon	38,988	551
Zimbabwe	36,223	1,483
Senegal	35,247	898
Côte d'Ivoire	33,976	196
Malawi	32,283	1,058
Sudan	30,540	1,895
Democratic Republic of Congo	26,405	711

Source: Africa CDC (2021) Outbreak Brief #60: Coronavirus Disease 2019 (COVID-19) Pandemic

reported globally. Southern Africa was the worst-affected, registering the highest percentage, 46%, of confirmed cases and 54% of the deaths in Africa.

As of 9 March 2021, South Africa had 373,628 confirmed cases, followed by Nigeria (37,255), Ghana (28,430), Cameroon (16,157) and Côte d'Ivoire (14,312). See Table 38.3. In this episode of the COVID-19 pandemic, people living with HIV and not on effective treatment or virally suppressed may be at greater risk of getting infected with COVID-19. The lockdowns imposed in most countries have resulted in extraordinary and stringent measures to contain, slow the pace of, or reduce the impact of the virus, putting PLHIV at a greater risk because some of them are not able to get their treatment drugs.

Countries in SSA are undergoing a demographic transition from CDs as cause of poor health and deaths to an increase in prevalence of NCDs (Gouda et al., 2019). The shift is largely due to the decline in CDs which results in increase in life expectancy, thereby shifting the risk of mortality to NCDs which occur mostly among the older people (Narayan & Donnenfeld, 2016). Richer communities tend to experience more NCDs while the poor tend to experience more of the CDs and the double burden of NCDs (Marquez & Farringdon, 2012). In some countries like Mauritius and the Seychelles, NCDs are the main cause of morbidity and mortality (Marquez & Farringdon, 2012).

Ischaemic heart disease was the fifth leading cause of death in Africa. The region is experiencing an increase in cardiovascular diseases due to major improvements in the prevention and treatment of communicable diseases, particularly HIV and AIDS, that are helping raise life expectancy in the region (Gouda et al., 2019; WHO, 2014). Strokes are the leading cause of death among the cardiovascular diseases, with the prevalence varying between African countries and ethnic groups, possibly due to their differing stages in the epidemiologic transition, lifestyle factors and health care access (Dalal et al., 2011). Hypertension, which is a predictor of stroke, has become a burden in the region, registering the world's highest prevalence (38.1% among males, 35.5% among females), with some countries such as Cape Verde, Mozambique, Niger, and Sao Tome and Principe reporting prevalence rates of 50% or higher (WHO, 2014; Dalal et al., 2011; Addo, Smeeth, & Leon, 2007). Awareness and treatment for hypertension is low in the region (Addo et al., 2007). Research in cardiovascular diseases in the region has been hampered by financial resources (Mocumbi, 2012).

Cancer is on the rise in Africa, with breast, cervix, liver and prostate cancers having the highest incidence (Dalal et al., 2011). Estimates from 2008 show that cancer was responsible for 5% of deaths in the region; ranging from 2% in countries such as Burkina Faso, the Democratic Republic of Congo, Mali, Niger, Sierra Leone and Zimbabwe, to 7% in Algeria (Dalal et al., 2011). The most common cancers among women are breast, cervical, stomach, lung and colorectal cancer while the most common among men are prostate and liver cancers (Dalal et al., 2011). The majority of women with breast cancer in Africa (80%) present at advanced stages compared to 15% of women in high-income countries (Sitas et al., 2008; Barton, Frommer, & Shafiq, 2006). Major causes of cancer in Africa are infectious agents, increasing tobacco and alcohol use, unhealthy diets, physical inactivity and environmental pollution (Parkin et al., 2008).

Diabetes has been on the increase in the region, especially type 2 diabetes (Gouda et al., 2019; Hall, Thomsen, Henriksen, & Lohse, 2011). The increase in diabetes is largely due to the imported dietary practices and globalization in the developing world (Hussein, 2014). According to the STEPS community studies, prevalence of diabetes in Africa ranged from 2.5% in the Seychelles to 16% in the Democratic Republic of Congo (Dalal et al., 2011). However, prevalence of diabetes in the rural areas was very low, ranging from 0% in Togo or Sierra Leone to 8.1% in Uganda (Dalal et al., 2011).

Road traffic injuries constitute a major health and development problem the world over, especially in Africa (WHO, 2020). The SSA region contributes 16% to global road accidents, yet it has the least number of cars (2%) with the highest mortality rates due to accidents occurring in Nigeria and South Africa, 33.7 and 31.9 deaths per 100,000 population per year, respectively (WHO, 2014). Pedestrians are more vulnerable since they constituted more than half of the road traffic deaths (Norman, Matzopoulos, & Bradshaw, 2014), yet most of the countries in the region lack policies for protecting vulnerable road users (WHO, 2014).

The double burden of diseases could have a devastating impact on the region which already has significant resource constraints (Nyirenda, 2016). Thus, there is need for understanding of the local drivers of NCDs in SSA from researchers in the region to come up with appropriate intervention strategies that effectively address these changing health needs (Nyirenda, 2016).

Risk factors of the burden of diseases

Sub-Saharan Africa has seen an increase in the burden of NCDs, while maintaining the CDs, though on the decline. Most of the NCDs are due to risk factors such as unhealthy diet, physical inactivity, tobacco and alcohol use, which may lead to cardiovascular disease, diabetes and cancer (WHO, 2014; Gouda et al., 2019; Househam, 2010).

Unhealthy diet, an important risk factor of NCDs, includes high intake of saturated and trans fats, salt, sugar and calories, and insufficient consumption of fruit and vegetables (Gouda et al., 2019; Hussein, 2014; WHO, 2014). Data from the WHO STEPwise approach to Surveillance (STEPS) and other surveys carried out in the African region as a continent show low consumption of fruits and vegetables in most countries (WHO, 2014). High dietary salt/sodium intake is a major risk factor of hypertension and increases the risk of heart disease and stroke (Muthuri, Oti, Lilford, & Oyebode, 2016; WHO, 2012). High salt intake is common in the SSA region, with a sodium intake in many adults of above the WHO recommended 2 grams/day, with urban populations likely to consume more than the rural populations (Oyebode, Oti, Chen, & Lilford, 2016). Salt is used not only to preserve food, but also to make food tastier and is also added to already-prepared food by the consumer, since processed food is rare (WHO, 2014). High blood glucose and cholesterol levels may be caused by diets rich in sugars and fats and poor in fruits, vegetables and nutrients, and by physical inactivity (WHO, 2014). In countries where STEPS survey data on fasting blood glucose are available, between 5% and 15% of the population has been found to have diabetes (WHO, 2014). Of the few studies carried out, sugar intake in 6–9-year-olds in South Africa ranged from 22 grams in the Eastern Cape to 57 grams in the Western Cape Province (Steyn & Temple, 2012). Sugar intake is on the increase because of the sugar-sweetened soft drinks and beverages, especially in the urban areas. Several governments are putting measures in place to reduce excessive levels of sugar and salt in foods (WHO, 2014). For example, Mauritius has banned the sale of sugar-sweetened soft drinks and juices and unhealthy snacks high in calories, salt, fats and sugar in schools and introduced a tax on sugar found in sugar-sweetened beverages, while South Africa regulates salt in processed foods (WHO, 2014). Such unhealthy diet can lead to high cholesterol, overweight, obesity, diabetes and hypertension. In several countries in SSA, overweight and obesity levels have reached epidemic proportions, especially among women (WHO, 2014). The STEPs data show that around half of the women were overweight or obese, with 58.2% in Lesotho (WHO, 2014). Community studies conducted earlier have found that obesity ranged from 0.4% in Tanzania to 43% in South Africa, with women more likely to be obese compared to their male counterparts and that approximately a third of adult women more likely to be obese (Dalal et al., 2011). Living in an urban area is associated with raised blood pressure, blood sugar and body mass index (BMI) (Hussein, 2014).

Physical inactivity is a risk factor of NCDs that is a growing but largely unrecognized problem in the region (WHO, 2014). With Africa going through increasing urbanization and occupations changing from manual to more sedentary, office-based activities, physical inactivity becomes an increasingly risky factor (WHO, 2014). In a study of 22 African countries, physical activity was higher in men (83.8%) than women (75.7%) (Guthold et al., 2011). Similarly, in a study conducted in a mainly rural population in northern Tanzania, work-related physical activity was sufficient (96%) for both males and females, noted to be higher in males (97.3%) compared to females (94%) (John et al., 2017). In contrast, the prevalence of physical inactivity was higher among women compared to men in Swaziland and Namibia (WHO, 2014). Most physical activity in Africa is associated with occupation (WHO, 2014). The study in northern

Tanzania found that farmers had a higher odds of sufficient physical activity than those in professional jobs in both males and females (John et al., 2017). In a study of urbanization, physical activity and metabolic health among adults in urban and rural Cameroon, urban dwellers had a significantly lower physical activity energy expenditure than rural dwellers (Assah, Ekelund, Brage, & Mbanya, 2011). Similar findings were found in a mostly rural area in Tanzania among men, where the odds of sufficient physical activity in males were lower in rural areas compared to urban areas, but in females, were higher in rural areas compared to urban areas (John et al., 2017). Regular physical activity promotes psychological well-being and reduces blood pressure among people with hypertension. Studies have shown that physically active people live longer and are less likely to suffer from diabetes, heart diseases and cancer (WHO, 2014). Thus, monitoring the level of exposure to physical inactivity is important for policy-makers and public health programme planners.

Tobacco and alcohol use are also risk factors for NCDs (Hussein, 2014). Tobacco use is the leading cause of lung cancer, heart disease, chronic respiratory diseases and chronic lung disease (Naik & Kaneda, 2015). According to the WHO STEPs data, the prevalence of tobacco use in sub-Saharan Africa ranged from 4.6% in Niger to 31.4% in South Africa (WHO, 2020). Men generally tend to smoke more than women. In South Africa, smoking prevalence ranged from 28% to 71% among men compared to 7% to 40% among women (Dalal et al., 2011). Adolescents in Africa are starting to smoke at younger ages (about one in ten), thereby increasingly exposing themselves to the risk of NCDs (Naik & Kaneda, 2015). For example, in South Africa, 24% of boys and 19% of girls aged 13–15 years use tobacco while in Zambia, about 25% of both boys and girls use tobacco (Naik & Kaneda, 2015). Disease burden caused by harmful use of alcohol is rising in the SSA region. Alcohol use was ranked the number-one risk factor in Southern Africa, fifth in both Eastern and Western Africa and sixth in Central Africa (Marquez & Farrington, 2013). A greater proportion of men who smoked also consumed alcohol (WHO, 2020). Alcohol abuse increases the risk of road traffic accidents leading to traffic injuries and deaths, unprotected sex, intentional and unintentional injuries, poor mental health, and gender-based violence (Naik & Kaneda, 2015; Norman et al., 2014).

Research agenda

Sub-Saharan African countries are undergoing epidemiological transition to NCDs, but at the same time experiencing more of the CDs, which are expected to disappear as the prevalence of NCDs increases. A wide range of data shows that in the last decade, the overall health of the people living in the region has improved considerably, in spite of the region experiencing a double burden of communicable and non-communicable diseases. Understanding the changing demography of SSA is important in drawing solutions to causes of death and burden of diseases. The region is still characterized by rapid population growth, large-scale environmental disruptions due to increasing population and urbanization which has shifted most people towards sedentary lifestyles, unhealthy diets and tobacco use, which are associated with overweight and obesity, a pre-condition of developing NCDs (Mwanazambi, 2010). On the other hand, communicable diseases like HIV/AIDS and tuberculosis are still prevalent in the region, which also need care and treatment, just like the NCDs. As a result, cross fertilization of care approaches is 'growing between CDs and NCDs in both chronic care models and palliative or end of life care' (Marquez & Farrington, 2013, p. 26). Care models from HIV/AIDS and tuberculosis are being extended/adapted to chronic conditions and comorbidities (Marquez & Farrington, 2013). For example, in Malawi, the directly observed therapy, short course (DOTS) framework for tuberculosis has been applied to the management of people with diabetes mellitus (Allain et al.,

2011). There are also models for collaboration with TB control programmes in primary care to benefit patients with non-infectious respiratory disease such as asthma. For instance, in Zambia, the availability of cervical cancer screening and treatment, especially for high-risk HIV-positive women and the promotion of breast cancer education, are being expanded by leveraging existing HIV/AIDS platforms and investments (Marquez & Farringdon, 2012, p. 26). Thus, there is a need for cost-effective strategies to combat the double burden of diseases in SSA (Marquez & Farrington, 2013). Therefore, future research should be targeted at care and management of the double burden of diseases in order to come up with innovative ways to deliver a better level of health care. There is a need to understand the NCD risk factors because NCDs tend to greatly affect the health systems, most of which are already weak. Thus, the region should focus on health research and development efforts which will assist in providing evidence-based solutions (Ijsselmuiden, Marais, Becerra-Posada, & Ghannem, 2012). Gaps need to be identified early and accurately to help identify interventions that meet the health needs of the people of the region. The region, because of poor health systems and limited resources, is more likely to be affected, thereby undermining development and sustainable interventions. Since the region consists of the majority of low-income countries and limited financial and human resources, they are not able to delay deaths due to NCDs. Thus, health research focusing on health financing, health service delivery, health technology development and socio-environment health concern are important. There are several current initiatives through donors that have greatly contributed to capacity strengthening of health research in sub-Saharan Africa (Whitworth et al., 2008). These external funders help in a collaborative role in financing health research capacity strengthening activities in sub-Saharan Africa (Morel, Maher, Nyirenda, & Olesen, 2018).

Conclusion

Sub-Saharan Africa is facing a burden of communicable and non-communicable diseases. This is contrary to Omran's Epidemiological Transition Theory which proposed that, as countries develop, they shift from high mortality and infectious diseases to low mortality and man-made and degenerative diseases. The region has seen an increase in NCDs, yet maintaining the infectious diseases, both as the major causes of death. The shift to NCDs is not due to development of the countries, but rather due to globalization and urbanization, again contrary to what the ETT proposed. The double burden of communicable and non-communicable diseases presents a myriad of complex medical, psychosocial, economic and political challenges in the region. While the region has seen an increase in the burden of non-communicable diseases such as stroke, heart disease, diabetes, cancers and road traffic accidents, communicable diseases such as lower respiratory infections, HIV/AIDS, diarrhoeal diseases, tuberculosis, malaria and cholera are still the major causes of death. However, NCDs are more likely to be the main cause of morbidity and mortality among the richer countries and some populations while the poor tend to experience more of the communicable diseases, thus the double burden of diseases.

The increase in the burden of NCDs is largely due to changes in lifestyle, unhealthy diets, physical inactivity and alcohol and tobacco use, as a result of globalization. The problem of air pollution, both indoor and outdoor, has also contributed to the burden of diseases in the region. However, use of solid fuels poses NCD health risks. The provision of affordable, reliable and clean cooking fuels and technologies would reduce air pollution indoors and outdoors for the majority of the households. The majority of the population do not have access to safely-managed drinking water and have poor sanitation. However, provision of safe water and appropriate sanitation, coupled with the oral vaccination, will protect the people from water-borne diseases such as cholera. However, the provision of vaccination can be hampered by the inadequate financial resources. The situation is exacerbated by the limited hand-washing facilities with soap and water in schools and public places, which is critical in prevention of COVID-19 and water-borne diseases such as cholera. Thus, improvement of infrastructure at household, community and public levels would definitely reduce the burden of disease caused by these risk factors. Interventions and strategies to reduce the double burden of CDs and NCDs are highly appreciated. The NCD risk factors can be reduced by adopting the WHO Global Strategies on healthy diet, physical activity and smoke-free initiatives. There is a need for advocacy to promote education and awareness of the NCD risk factors in schools and workplaces and through all forms of media. NCDs are causing challenges in health systems of the countries in the region and these need to be addressed. Unfortunately, comparable data is not available on some of the risk factors in some countries. Thus, there is a need for collection of data on the risk factors that is comparable in all the countries in the region in order to come up with efficient interventions.

References

Addo, J., Smeeth, L., & Leon, D. A. (2007). Global health – hypertension in sub-Saharan Africa hypertension in sub-Saharan Africa: A systematic review. *Hypertension*, *50*, 1012–1018. https://doi.org/10.1161/HYPERTENSIONAHA.107.093336

African Union, & Africa CDC. (2021). *Outbreak break #60: Coronavirus disease 2019 (COVID-19) pandemic*. Addis Ababa: Ethiopia.

Agyei-Mensah, S., & Aikins, A. (2010). Epidemiological transition and the double burden of disease in Accra, Ghana. *Journal of Urban Health*, *87*(5), 879–897. https://doi.org/10.1007/s11524-010-9492-y

Ali, M., Debes, A. K., Luquero, F. J., Kim, D. R., Park, J. Y., Digilio, L., . . . Sack, D. A. (2016). Potential for controlling cholera using a ring vaccination strategy: Re-analysis of data from a cluster-randomized clinical trial. *PLoS Medicine*, *13*(9), 1–16. https://doi.org/10.1371/journal.pmed.1002120

Allain, T. J., van Oosterhout, J. J., Douglas, G. P., Joukes, S., Gadabu, O. J., Darts, C., . . . Harries, A. D. (2011). Applying lessons learnt from the "DOTS" Tuberculosis Model to monitoring and evaluating persons with diabetes mellitus in Blantyre, Malawi. *Tropical Medicine and International Health*, *16*(9), 1077–1084. https://doi.org/10.1111/j.1365-3156.2011.02808.x

Assah, F. K., Ekelund, U., Brage, S., & Mbanya, J. C. N. (2011). Urbanization, physical activity, and metabolic health in sub-Saharan Africa. *Diabetes Care*, *34*(June 2014), 491–496. https://doi.org/10.2337/dc10-0990

Barton, M. B., Frommer, M., & Shafiq, J. (2006). Role of radiotherapy in cancer control in low-income and middle-income countries. *Lancet Oncology*, 7(7), 584–595. https://doi.org/10.1016/S1470-2045(06)70759-8

Clark, C. J., Ferguson, G., Shrestha, B., Shrestha, P. N., Oakes, J. M., Gupta, J., . . . Yount, K. M. (2018). Social norms and women's risk of intimate partner violence in Nepal. *Social Science and Medicine*, *202*(June 2017), 162–169. https://doi.org/10.1016/j.socscimed.2018.02.017

Cooper, R. S., Rotimi, C. N., Kaufman, J. S., Muna, W. F. T., & Mensah, G. A. (1998). Hypertension treatment and control in sub-Saharan Africa: The epidemiological basis for policy. *BMJ*, *316*, 614–617.

Dalal, S., Beunza, J. J., Volmink, J., Adebamowo, C., Bajunirwe, F., Njelekela, M., . . . Holmes, M. D. (2011). Non-communicable diseases in sub-Saharan Africa: What we know now. *International Journal of Epidemiology*, *40*(4), 885–901. https://doi.org/10.1093/ije/dyr050

Frenk, J., Bobadilla, J. L., Sepulveda, J., & Lpez, M. (1989). Health transition in middle-income countries. *New Challenges for Health Care*, *4*(1), 29–39. https://doi.org/10.1093/heapol/4.1.29

Gona, P. N., Gona, C. M., Ballout, S., Rao, S. R., Kimokoti, R., Mapoma, C. C., & Mokdad, A. H. (2020). Burden and changes in HIV/AIDS morbidity and mortality in Southern Africa Development Community Countries, 1990–2017. *BMC Public Health*, *20*(867), 1–14.

Gouda, H. N., Charlson, F., Sorsdahl, K., Ahmadzada, S., Ferrari, A. J., Erskine, H., . . . Whiteford, H. (2019). Burden of non-communicable diseases in sub-Saharan Africa, 1990–2017: Results from the Global Burden of Disease Study 2017. *The Lancet Global Health*, 7(10), e1375–e1387. https://doi.org/10.1016/S2214-109X(19)30374-2

Guthold, R., Louazani, S. A., Riley, L. M., Cowan, M. J., Bovet, P., Damasceno, A., . . . Armstrong, T. P. (2011). Physical activity in 22 African Countries: Results from the World Health Organization

STEPwise approach to chronic disease risk factor surveillance. *American Journal of Preventive Medicine, 41*(1), 52–60. https://doi.org/10.1016/j.amepre.2011.03.008

Hall, V., Thomsen, R. W., Henriksen, O., & Lohse, N. (2011). Diabetes in Sub Saharan Africa 1999–2011: Epidemiology and public health implications. A systematic review. *BMC Public Health, 11*(564), 1–2.

Househam, K. C. (2010). Africa's burden of disease: The University of Cape Town sub-Saharan Africa Centre for Chronic Disease. *South African Medical Journal, 100*(2), 94–95. https://doi.org/10.7196/samj.3977

Hussein, A. A. (2014). The "epidemiological transmission" and "double-burden of disease": A focus on Africa. *Majmaah Journal of Health Sceince, 2*(2), 3–11.

IHME. (2018). *Global burden of disease study 2017*. Retrieved from http://ghdx.healthdata.org/gbd-2017

Ijsselmuiden, C., Marais, D. L., Becerra-Posada, F., & Ghannem, H. (2012). Africa's neglected area of human resources for health research – The way forward. *South African Medical Journal, 102*(4), 228–233. https://doi.org/10.7196/SAMJ.5377

John, B., Todd, J., Mboya, I., Mosha, M., Urassa, M., & Mtuy, T. (2017). Physical activity and associated factors from a cross-sectional survey among adults in northern Tanzania. *BMC Public Health, 17*(588), 1–8. https://doi.org/10.1186/s12889-017-4512-4

Lessler, J., Moore, S. M., Luquero, F. J., McKay, H. S., Grais, R., Henkens, M., . . . Azman, A. S. (2018). Mapping the burden of cholera in sub-Saharan Africa and implications for control: An analysis of data across geographical scales. *The Lancet, 391*(10133), 1908–1915. https://doi.org/10.1016/S0140-6736(17)33050-7

Marquez, P. V., & Farringdon, J. L. (2012). Africa's next burden: Non-infectious disease. *BMJ (Overseas and Retired Doctors Ed.), 345*(7873), 24–27.

Marquez, P. V., & Farrington, J. L. (2013). *The challenge of non-communicable diseases and road traffic injuries in sub-Saharan Africa*. Brazzaville: World Health Organisation.

Meghji, J., Nadeau, G., Davis, K. J., Wang, D., Nyirenda, M. J., Gordon, S. B., & Mortimer, K. (2016). Noncommunicable lung disease in sub-Saharan Africa a community-based cross-sectional study of adults in urban Malawi. *American Journal of Respiratory and Critical Care Medicine, 194*(1), 67–76. https://doi.org/10.1164/rccm.201509-1807OC

Mocumbi, A. O. (2012). Lack of focus on cardiovascular disease in sub-Saharan Africa. *Cardiovascular Diagnosis and Therapy, 2*(1), 74–747. https://doi.org/10.3978/j.issn.2223-3652.2012.01.03

Morel, T., Maher, D., Nyirenda, T., & Olesen, O. F. (2018). Strengthening health research capacity in sub-Saharan Africa: Mapping the 2012–2017 landscape of externally funded international postgraduate training at institutions in the region. *Globalization and Health, 14*(1), 1–10. https://doi.org/10.1186/s12992-018-0395-0

Mudie, K., Mei Jin Tan, M., Kendall, L., Addo, J., dos-Santos-Silva, I., Quint, J., . . . Perel, P. (2019). Non-communicable diseases in sub-saharan Africa: A scoping review of large cohort studies. *Journal of Global Health, 9*(2). https://doi.org/10.7189/jogh.09.020409

Muthuri, S. K., Oti, S. O., Lilford, R. J., & Oyebode, O. (2016). Salt reduction interventions in sub-Saharan Africa: A systematic review. *PLoS One, 11*(3), 1–11. https://doi.org/10.1371/journal.pone.0149680

Mwanazambi, K. (2010). Environmental problems in Africa: A theological response. *Ethiopian Journal of Environmental Studies and Management, 3*(2), 54–64.

Naik, R., & Kaneda, T. (2015). Noncommunicable diseases in Africa: Youth are the key to curbing the epidemic and achieveing sustainable development. In *Population reference Bureau* (Vol. 2014, Issue April). Retrieved from www.prb.org/pdf15/ncds-africa-policybrief.pdf

Narayan, K., & Donnenfeld, Z. (2016). Envisioning a healthy future: Africa's shifting burden of disease. *African Futures Paper, 18*. https://doi.org/10.2139/ssrn.2860539

Norman, R., Matzopoulos, R., & Bradshaw, D. (2014). *The high burden of injuries in South Africa*. https://doi.org/10.2471/BLT

Nyirenda, M. J. (2016). Non-communicable diseases in sub-Saharan Africa : Understanding the drivers of the epidemic to inform intervention strategies. *International Health, 8*, 157–158. https://doi.org/10.1093/inthealth/ihw021

Omran. (1971). *The epidemiologic transition : A theory of the epidemiology of population change author (s): Abdel R. Omran centennial : Selected articles from the "Milbank Quarterly". 83(4), 731–757 (2005)*. Wiley on behalf of Milbank Memorial Fund.

Oyebode, O., Oti, S., Chen, Y. F., & Lilford, R. J. (2016). Salt intakes in sub-Saharan Africa: A systematic review and meta-regression. *Population Health Metrics, 14*(1). https://doi.org/10.1186/s12963-015-0068-7

Parkin, D. M., Sitas, F., Chirenje, M., Stein, L., Abratt, R., & Wabinga, H. (2008). Part I: Cancer in indigenous Africans-burden, distribution, and trends. *The Lancet Oncology*, *9*(7), 683–692. https://doi.org/10.1016/S1470-2045(08)70175-X

Seidu, A. A., Dickson, K. S., Ahinkorah, B. O., Amu, H., Darteh, E. K. M., & Kumi-Kyereme, A. (2019). Prevalence and determinants of Acute Lower Respiratory Infections among children under-five years in sub – Saharan Africa: Evidence from demographic and health surveys. *SSM – Population Health*, *8*, 100443. https://doi.org/10.1016/j.ssmph.2019.100443

Sitas, F., Parkin, D. M., Chirenje, M., Stein, L., Abratt, R., & Wabinga, H. (2008). Cancer in Indigenous Africans – causes and control. *Lancet Oncology*, *9*(8), 786–795. Retrieved from www.thelancet.com/oncology

Steyn, N. P., & Temple, N. J. (2012). Evidence to support a food-based dietary guideline on sugar consumption in South Africa. *BMC Public Health*, *12*(1), 1. https://doi.org/10.1186/1471-2458-12-502

Whitworth, J. A., Kokwaro, G., Kinyanjui, S., Snewin, V. A., Tanner, M., Walport, M., & Sewankambo, N. (2008). Strengthening capacity for health research in Africa. *The Lancet*, *372*(9649), 1590–1593. https://doi.org/10.1016/S0140-6736(08)61660-8

WHO. (2012). *Guideline: Sodium intake for adults and children*. Geneva: World Health Organization.

WHO. (2014). The health of the people: What works. In *African Regional Health Report 2014*. https://doi.org/2014

WHO. (2020). *World Health Statistics 2020: Monitoring health for the SDGs*. Geneva: World Health Organization.

WHO Africa Region. (2016). *Report on the status of major health risk factors for noncommunicable diseases: WHO African Region, 2015*. Brazzaville: World Health Organization.

39

DYNAMICS OF ADULT MORTALITY IN SUB-SAHARAN AFRICA

Are there prospects for decline?

Ayo S. Adebowale, Adeniyi F. Fagbamigbe, Tubosun Olowolafe and Rotimi F. Afolabi

Introduction

Adult mortality, although much higher in less-developed countries than the developed countries, has reduced globally, from 380 per 1,000 alive at age 15 years in 1950, to 140 per 1,000 between 2015–2020. In Asia, Europe, Latin America/Caribbean, North America and Oceania, adult mortality was 467/1,000, 196/1,000, 332/1,000, 196/1,000 and 265/1,000 respectively between 1950 and 1955. Six decades (2015–2020) after this period, the adult mortality has greatly reduced in these world sub-regions and ranges from 93 per 1,000 in Oceania to 136 per 1,000 in Latin America/Caribbean. In Africa, adult mortality reduced from 462 per 1,000 in 1950–1955 to 249 per 1,000 in 2015–2020 (United Nations, 2019). These estimates are similar to the estimates in South Asia where the adult mortality male/female was 290/284 per 1,000. Coincidentally, the two sub-regions have the poorest health indicators in the world. These patterns in the dynamics of adult mortality statistics which had been confirmed by other data sources showed that Africa has the current highest adult mortality rate compared to other continents (Figure 39.1). Although differences exist in the level of adult mortality between and within the five regional blocks in Africa, except for few countries, the adult mortality rate remains high across countries in the region (United Nations, 2019).

Adult mortality is one of the main demographic parameters and an important public health issue that has received little attention in sub-Saharan Africa. The neglect is often attributed to the paucity of empirical data on adult deaths as a result of the poor vital registration system and inadequate surveillance system in most countries in the region (Moultrie et al., 2013). The problems involved in measuring adult mortality in sub-Saharan African countries have been established by demographers and adult-mortality researchers (Moultrie et al., 2013; Adebowale & Adedini, 2014). In this perspective, nearly all of the estimates of adult mortality made for sub-Saharan Africa were based on data from either census or surveys and few from hospital records, including other inquiries put in place by the national statistical organizations. The inescapable lack of vital registration data makes it indispensable to derive adult mortality estimates using indirect demographic techniques. However, the methodological limitations of the available methods often used to provide a retrospective estimate of adult mortality constitute a great

 DOI: 10.4324/9780429287213-48

challenge. Sub-Saharan Africa is ranked as a high adult mortality region worldwide (United Nations, 2019). The high adult mortality rate experienced in the region is aggravated by HIV/AIDS epidemic, malaria, tuberculosis, cancer, emerging and re-emerging diseases like dengue fever, Lassa fever, Ebola, COVID-19 etc. (United Nations, 2019; Chisumpa, Odimegwu, & Saikia, 2019; Davies, 2020). The poor health service delivery and harsh economic condition are impediments to the survival of people in sub-Saharan Africa. Unfortunately, most of the available health facilities, particularly the private hospitals which enjoy the patronage of the majority of the people in the region, are not adequately equipped to provide services for the adult.

Compared to other world sub-regions, adult mortality is high in sub-Saharan Africa. Unemployment, decaying public health institutions, avoidable environmental pollutants, poverty, hunger, stress and exposures to lack of safety precautionary measures at work are part of numerous factors that predispose adults to an untimely death in sub-Saharan Africa. The lackadaisical stance of most government/people in the position of authorities and lack of strong political will on the part of leaders in this African sub-region constitute a further threat to healthy life among adults. The people in the age group 15–60 years belong to the working class; the absolute reliance on this set of people by the huge number of individuals in the other age groups in the face of poor and harsh economic conditions is an additional challenge to adult survival in sub-Saharan Africa.

Adult mortality rate has reduced in many countries in sub-Saharan Africa; however, this world sub-region remains a high risk for adult deaths (Moultrie et al., 2013; United Nations, 2019). Unfortunately, little information is known about the documentation of methodological, theoretical, practical and substantive issues on adult mortality in sub-Saharan Africa. Against this background, this study attempts to provide a comprehensive descriptive account of what is known in the past five decades and what should be known in the next decades about adult mortality in sub-Saharan Africa. The specific objectives of the study are to document information on the following: the past, present and projected levels of adult mortality across countries in sub-Saharan Africa; methods utilized for the estimation of adult mortality; existing suggested methods for adult mortality estimates; projection techniques already used for adult mortality estimation in sub-Saharan Africa. Others include methods used in advanced countries for adult mortality estimation that could be adopted for future estimation of adult mortality in sub-Saharan Africa, demography and population studies programmes in African tertiary institutions that have and teach methods of estimating adult mortality in sub-Saharan Africa. For instance, the widowhood method has proved to be reliable in the developed countries but may be less reliable in the SSA because it can produce biased results in polygamous societies which is not uncommon in the SSA. The methods often ignore the deaths of subsequent – the younger – wives. Also, men that have many wives are over-reported and husbands may intentionally omit or misreport deaths that are associated with sensitive issues (Odimegwu, Chisumpa, & Somefun, 2018). Besides, vital registration and census are very irregular in the SSA, and less reliable where it exists. This has made the multi-round demographic surveys, conducted in several sub-Saharan countries, the only available sources of data for computation of adult mortality.

In many countries across the world, public-health efforts within country and global interventional programmes have been channeled mainly to improve child survival and reproductive health. Contrarily, little importance has been placed on adult mortality especially in the developing world sub-regions like sub-Saharan Africa. Planning, monitoring and evaluation of the effectiveness of public health programmes will require accurate information on the past, present and future level of adult mortality in sub-Saharan Africa. SSA countries have not implemented any significant public-health policies and programmes to address adult mortality but studies have shown that strengthening of HIV/AIDS-related health programmes could significantly

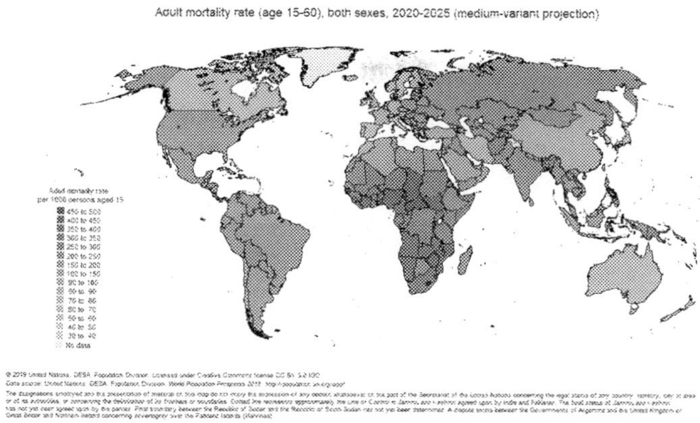

Figure 39.1 Adult mortality rate (age 15–60), both sexes, 2020–2025 (medium-variant projection).

Source: 2019 by United Nations, DESA, Population Division, World Population Prospects, 2019. http://population.un.org/licenses/wpp/

contribute to the reduction of adult mortality in countries such as Zambia (Chisumpa, Odimegwu, & Saikia, 2019). Investigation of adult mortality in Africa will also provide a perfect basis for the population estimates and projections that are pertinent to planning in any population subdivisions.

Method

The study was conducted in sub-Saharan Africa (Figure 39.2) and cuts across all the countries in this African sub-region. There are four regional blocks in sub-Saharan Africa: West Africa, Southern Africa, East Africa and Central Africa.

The world and sub-Saharan African population by broad age group is presented in Figure 39.3 below. Worldwide and in sub-Saharan Africa, the age range 25–64 years constituted the majority, and this trend has been sustained over the years, although the rise in the population of people in the age group 25–64 years above other age groups in recent times in sub-Saharan Africa has been observed worldwide several decades ago. The 2050 projection also indicates that the population of people in the age group 25–64 years will consistently increase in the years ahead.

A literature search was conducted to identify all published peer-reviewed studies reporting adult mortality in sub-Saharan Africa. However, the search was limited to five decades and included only articles published in the English language. The limit to five decades was necessitated as a compliance with the tenets of this book's call for submission. Authors can neither write nor interpret French language, so papers that were written in French were also excluded. Adult mortalities studies from advanced countries were also reviewed to borrow from their experience on their applied methodologies. The following electronic databases were used to conduct the literature search: PubMed/Medline, Cochrane Library, Web of Science core collections and Google Scholar using the key search terms. Studies included for final review had to report one or more of estimation methods, data source, trends and projections of adult mortality in sub-Saharan Africa. The database searches were stored in EndNote X7. The developed review protocol purposely for this study was used to review and report the identified relevant

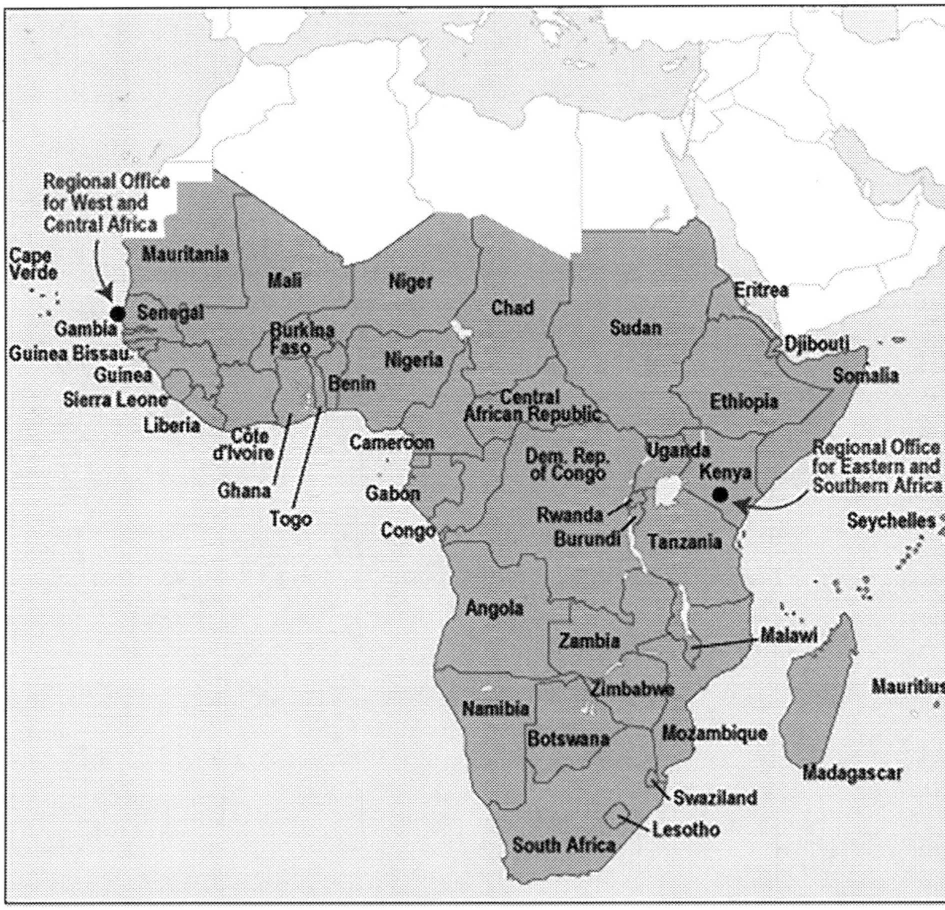

Figure 39.2 Map of sub-Saharan Africa.

Source: WebQuest: Sub-Saharan Africa Safari! www.pinterest.com

adult mortality studies conducted in sub-Saharan Africa. A flow chart illustrating the article selection and screening process is illustrated here (Figure 39.4).

Questions were framed in line with the objectives of this study. An extensive search for adult mortality studies was conducted using multiple resources (both computerized and printed). We ensured that the article selection criteria flowed directly from the questions. The relevance and qualities of the studies were assessed based on the selection criteria using general critical appraisal guides and design-based quality checklists. Independent screening of all the relevant articles identified was done by the authors based on the title and abstract. The authors ensured that discrepancies and disagreements in the selection process were resolved through constructive discussions. Thereafter, all the relevant papers/articles were retrieved and their main contents further reviewed. The information obtained from the reviewed articles was synthesized. The search was based on available information on adult mortality in any of the countries in sub-Saharan Africa.

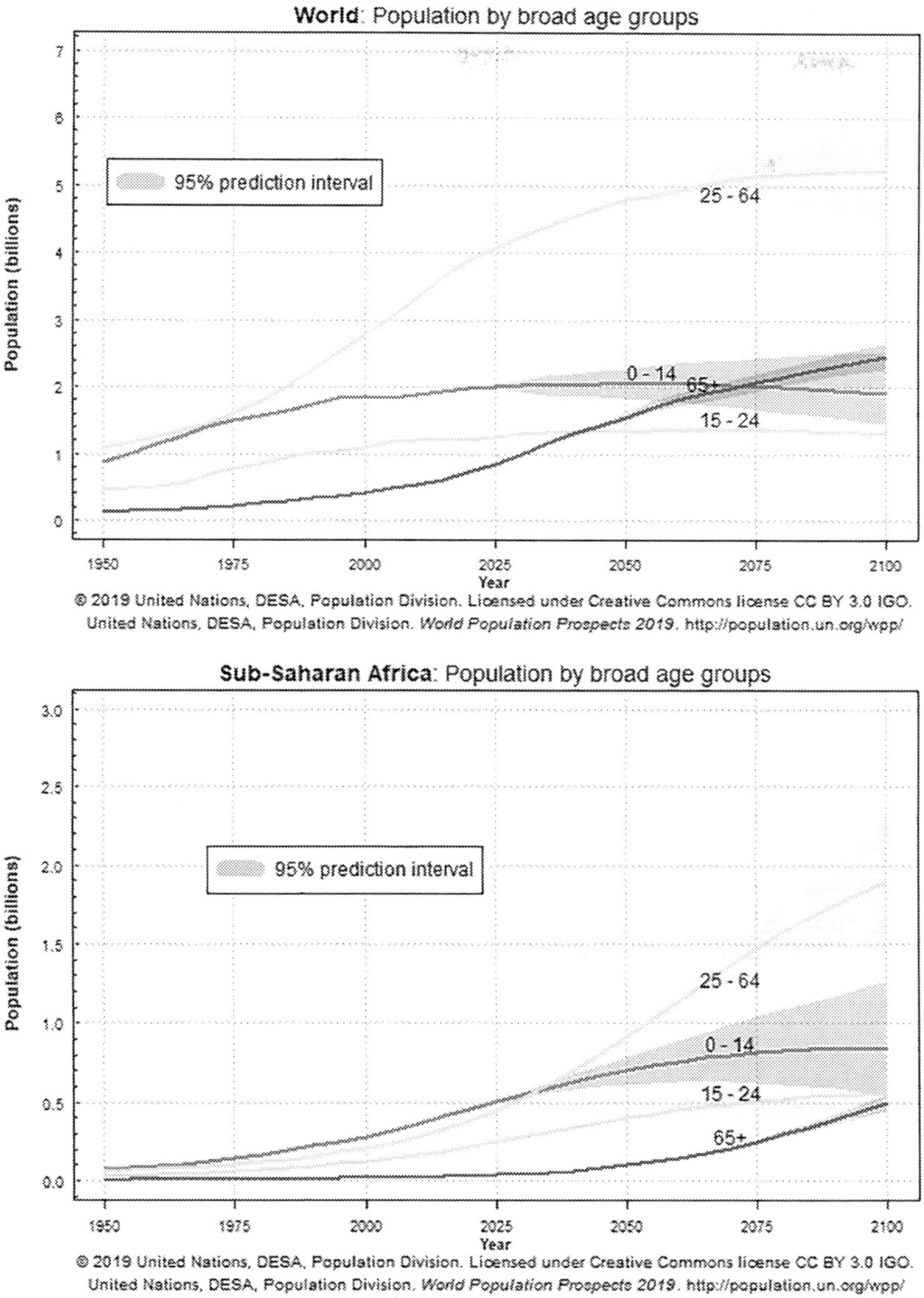

Figure 39.3 Population by broad age group.

Source: 2019 by United Nations, DESA, Population Division, World Population Prospects, 2019. http://population.un.org/licenses/wpp/

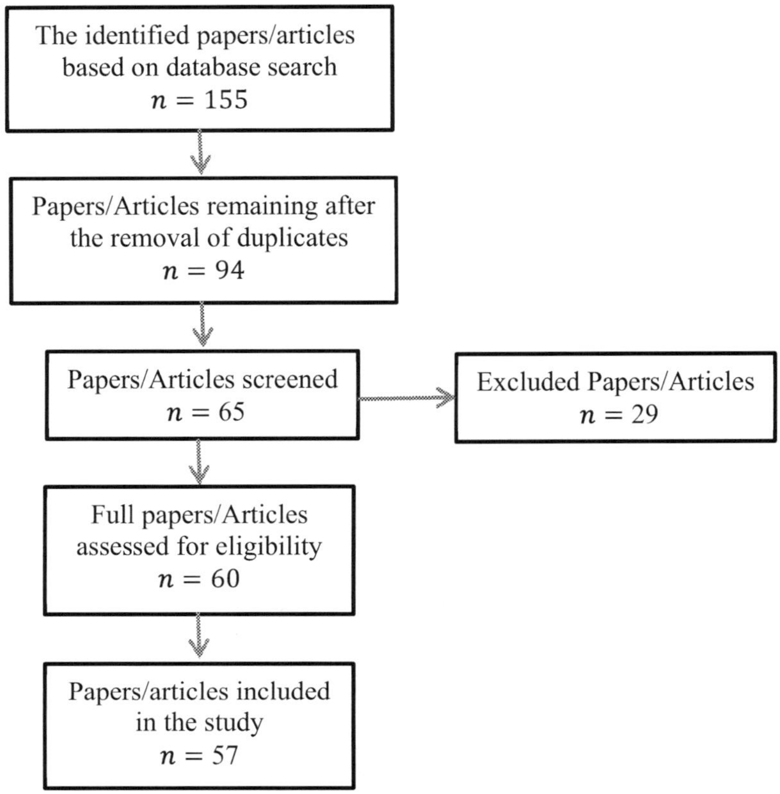

Figure 39.4 Flow chart of the articles' selectfgcon and screening process.

Sixty-five (65) articles were identified to be qualified out of the 94 initially articles screened for duplication. We could only have full access to 60 articles out of which 3 were further excluded because of the papers' poor quality of presentations.

Search results

Past, present and projected levels of adult mortality across countries in sub-Saharan Africa

Trends and projected level of life expectancies at birth in sub-Saharan Africa

The estimates of the past, present and projected males' and females' life expectancies at birth $\left(e_0^x\right)$ in sub-Saharan Africa are displayed in Figure 39.5. The pattern of e_0^x is the same for males and females in this African sub-region but there is evidence of higher survival chances to a particular age x among females than males across years. The e_0^x increased sharply and steadily between 1950 and 1990 after which it was stagnated for about 15 years and then rose again uniformly until 2020. The e_0^x as projected from 2020 to 2100 is expected to increase consistently throughout the period but at a slower pace than the past increase rate. In 2030, the e_0^x for males

World (both sexes)

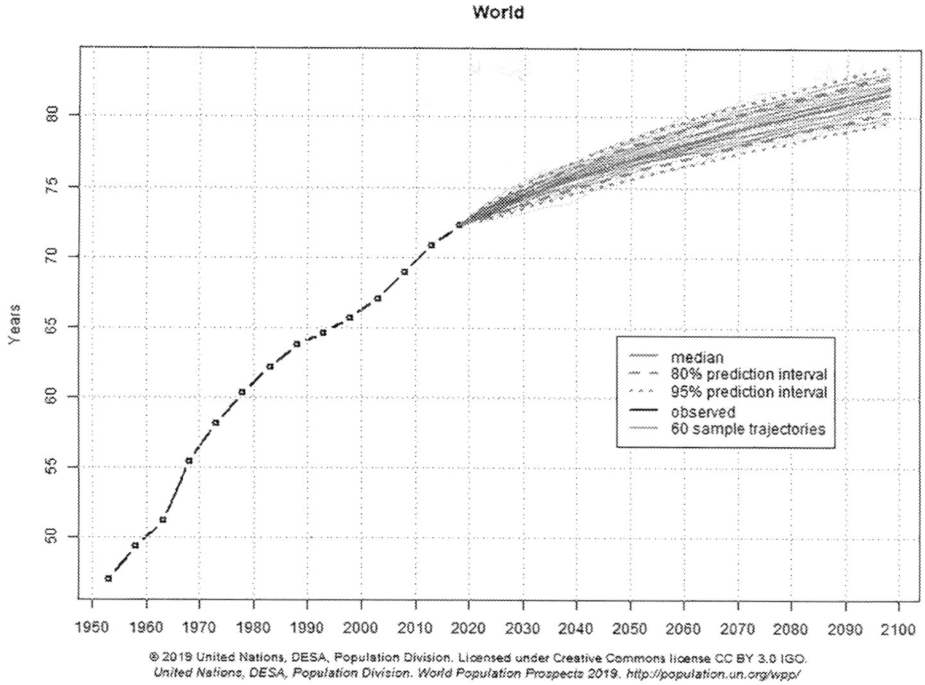

Sub-Saharan Africa (both sexes)

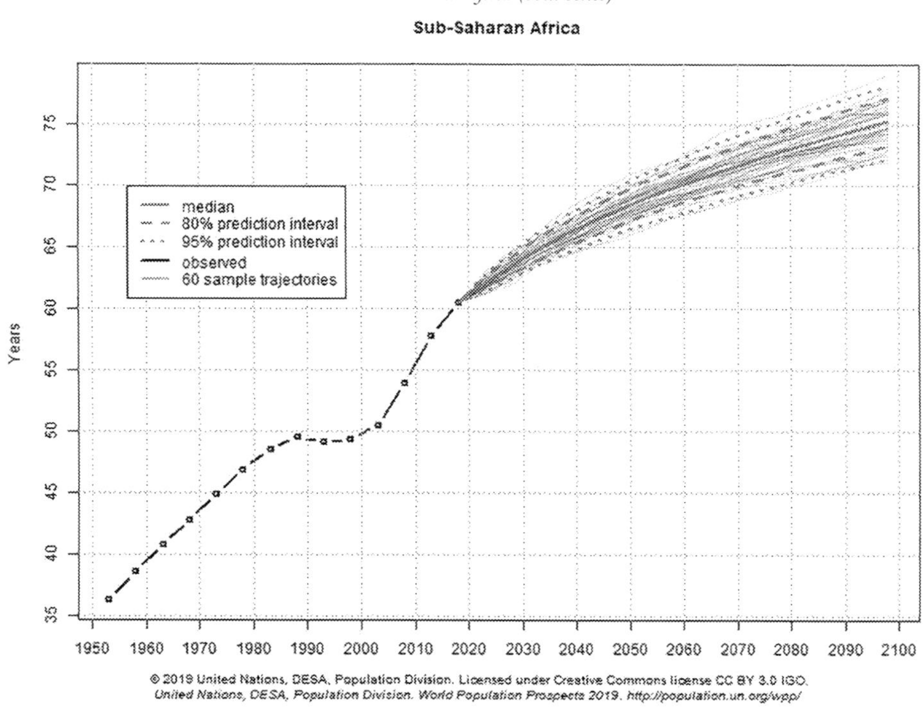

Figure 39.5 Life expectancy at birth for males and females in sub-Saharan Africa.v*Source:* 2019 by United Nations, DESA, Population Division, World Population Prospects, 2019. http://population.un.org/licenses/wpp/

Sub-Saharan Africa (males)

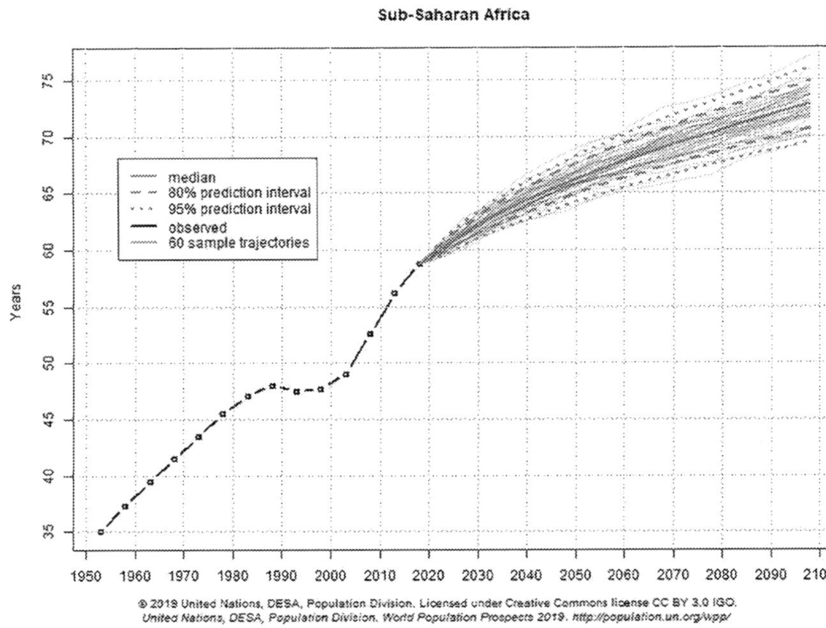

Sub-Saharan Africa (females)

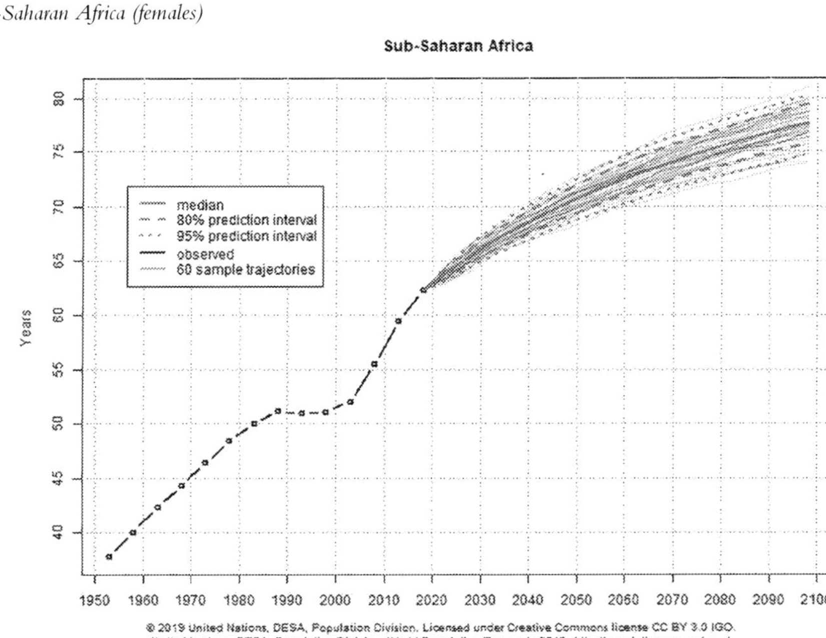

Figure 39.5 (Continued)

and females is expected to be 59 and 63 years respectfully. By the year 2100, the e_0^x is likely to fall in the range 70–75 years for males and 75–80 years for females (United Nations, 2019).

Trends in adult mortality (45q15) in sub-Saharan Africa regions (1950–2050)

The trends and projections in adult mortality rate per 1,000 in the regions of sub-Saharan Africa from 1950 to 2050 are displayed in Figure 39.6. The data show that adult mortality falls consistently between 1950 and 1990 but increases between 1990 and 2005 after which the adult mortality is expected to reduce again throughout the rest of the projection period (2005–2050). The pattern observed for sub-Saharan Africa as a unit is seen across all the four regional blocks in this African sub-region. However, the adult mortality rate was found to be lowest in Southern Africa compared to the other three regions in sub-Saharan Africa between 1950 and 2000, but remains highest from 2005 through 2050. It appeared that apartheid did not have any negative effects on life expectancies during that period. Moreover, the upsurge in adult mortality after 2000 coincided with the discovery of HIV/AIDS. Southern Africa remains the HIV/AIDS worst-hit sub-region. East Africa had the least adult mortality among all the regions in sub-Saharan Africa between 2015 and 2020. In the years ahead (from 2020 to 2050), the adult mortality in West Africa and Southern Africa perfectly align with each other while that of middle Africa will be a reflection of the expected pattern in the whole sub-Saharan Africa (United Nations, 2019).

The data as displayed in Table 39.1 show that in each of the countries in sub-Saharan Africa, adult mortality is expected to reduce consistently in the years ahead. However, by the year 2050, the least adult mortality is expected to be found in Réunion (54 per 1,000), a country from Eastern Africa, and highest in Lesotho (311 per 1,000). Data further showed that among the countries in the Eastern Africa region, South Sudan (600 per 1,000) experienced the highest adult mortality between 1950 and 1955 while the Seychelles had least (228 per 1,000). By the

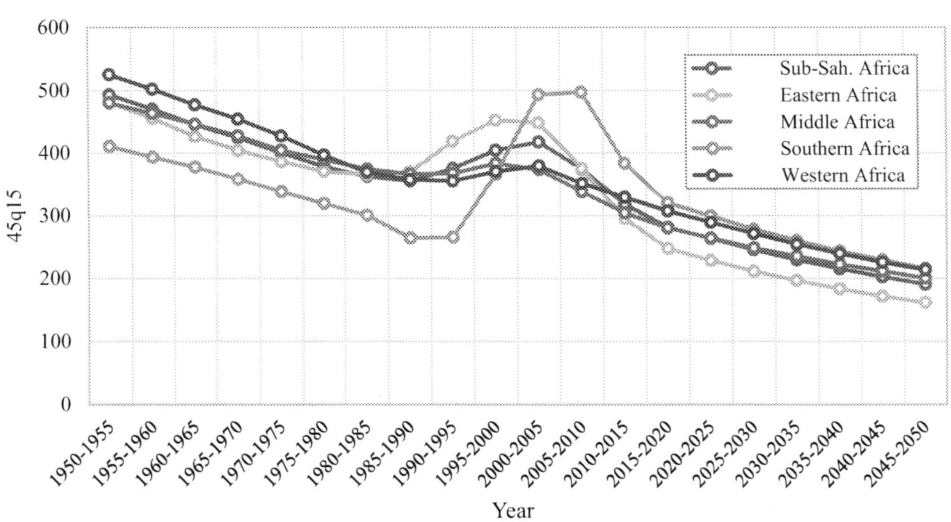

Figure 39.6 Trends and projections in adult mortality (*45q15*) per 1,000 in sub-Saharan Africa regions (1950–2050).

period 2015–2020, Réunion with the adult mortality of 82 per 1,000 had the least while Zimbabwe (358 per 1,000) is expected to have the highest adult mortality in East Africa. In middle Africa, Central African Republic (300 per 1,000) is expected to have the highest adult mortality and Sao Tome and Principe (113 per 1,000) the least by the end of the projection period (2050). Botswana (157 per 1,000) and Lesotho (311 per 1,000) are expected to have the least and highest adult mortality across countries in the Southern African region respectively. In West Africa, the countries with the highest projected estimate of adult mortality by the year 2050 are Côte d'Ivoire (254 per 1,000) and Sierra Leone (254 per 1,000) while the lowest level of adult mortality will be found in Cabo Verde (91 per 1,000) (United Nations, 2019).

Data sources and analysis methods utilized for adult mortality estimates across countries in sub-Saharan Africa

The Vital Registration System and Records are inadequate in almost all the countries in Sub-Saharan Africa (SSA). Consequently, estimates of adult mortality rates are often based on reported deaths from census and survey data. Unfortunately, such data sources are fraught with inconsistencies in terms of underreporting of deaths and age at deaths. Advanced demographic methods have been developed to account for or limit such errors especially for comparison between countries and sub-national groups. In SSA, applications of these demographic methods are still insufficient compared to their utilizations in other world sub-regions. A summary of the data sources and analysis methods used for the estimation of adult mortality or adult mortality studies in SSA is provided in this section.

In the year 2000, the WHO used its mortality database to generate set of life table estimates for 191 countries including a new family of model life tables through the Brass Logit system extension (Murray et al., 2003). The major concern about these life tables for African use is that only data from Zimbabwe, South Africa and Tanzania were used and as a result may not be a true representation of the African system. The WHO estimated adult mortality for other countries through extrapolation from childhood mortality estimates by modelling the link between the child and adult mortality in its database of more than 1,800 life tables, using its modified logit life table system. Unfortunately, this database includes few life tables from countries in SSA and other parts of the world with high child mortality levels recognized as typical of this African sub-region. Thus, there is no assurance that the estimates will be more accurate for Africa than those generated by the UN Population Division using model life tables computed from the historical data on high-mortality Western populations.

Timaeus, in his comparative research on the measurement of adult mortality in less-developed countries conducted in the year 1991, found that different authors have previously estimated adult survivorship probability based on the orphanhood method in countries like Benin, Sierra Leone, Zimbabwe, Gambia, Kenya, Swaziland and Ghana whereas information on recent deaths combined with the orphanhood method was used in Mali, Mauritania, Cameroon, Congo, Tanzania and Lesotho. The multi-round survey has been used in Côte d'Ivoire, Liberia, Senegal and recent deaths method used in Togo, Madagascar, Rwanda and Botswana while the widowhood method was used in northern Sudan (Timaeus, 1991).

A study by Timaeus (1993) which provided a descriptive account of levels, trends and patterns of adult mortality in sub-Saharan Africa also examined the extent of the public health problem that such mortality poses. Data from national censuses, Population Growth Estimation surveys of the early 1970s, the World Fertility Surveys (WFS), Demographic and Health Surveys (DHS) and statistical institutions in the respective countries in SSA were used in the analyses. Direct estimates of adult mortality in some countries were based on retrospective questions

Table 39.1 Trends in adult mortality ($_{45}q_{15}$)* in countries in sub-Saharan Africa (1950–2050).

Country	*1950–1955*	*2015–2020*	*2025–2030*	*2045–2050*	*Country*	*1950–1955*	*2015–2020*	*2025–2030*	*2045–2050*
Sub-Saharan Africa	**493**	**281**	**245**	**190**	DRC	463	252	226	187
Eastern Africa	**481**	**247**	**211**	**161**	Equatorial Guinea	518	321	282	225
Burundi	464	285	244	185	Gabon	489	214	194	160
Comoros	502	222	201	168	Sao T. & Principe	393	158	142	113
Djibouti	442	210	184	146	**Southern Africa**	410	320	278	215
Eritrea	522	244	204	154	Botswana	424	204	188	157
Ethiopia	522	214	181	138	Eswatini	470	408	345	258
Kenya	430	233	203	159	Lesotho	414	488	428	311
Madagascar	495	211	176	130	Namibia	466	302	251	187
Malawi	443	274	219	154	South Africa	406	317	276	215
Mauritius	397	144	128	96	**Western Africa**	525	307	271	213
Mayotte	407	100	86	60	Benin	511	238	210	176
Mozambique	507	331	274	196	Burkina Faso	558	247	207	157
Réunion	393	82	72	54	Cabo Verde	393	136	123	91
Rwanda	453	192	161	119	Côte d'Ivoire	489	348	309	254
Seychelles	228	154	142	108	Gambia	572	256	218	174
Somalia	524	300	271	223	Ghana	430	238	208	166
South Sudan	600	329	298	245	Guinea	537	247	214	172
Uganda	455	271	231	174	Guinea-Bissau	505	340	298	231
Tanzania	440	225	193	146	Liberia	556	230	203	166
Zambia	431	275	238	183	Mali	607	257	223	183
Zimbabwe	364	358	313	238	Mauritania	471	199	183	160
Middle Africa	480	280	248	200	Niger	516	241	205	160
Angola	497	279	239	186	Nigeria	525	348	313	245
Cameroon	471	303	266	207	Senegal	508	180	155	122
Central Afr. Rep.	531	415	378	300	Sierra Leone	531	377	334	254
Chad	499	359	331	269	Togo	509	264	230	185
Congo	505	263	235	191	***per 1,000**				

Data Source: © 2019, United Nations, made available under a Creative Commons license CC BY 3.0 IGO: http://creativecommons.org

about recent deaths in the households included in the censuses, single-round surveys and multi-round demographic surveys. Other sources included data on retrospective questions about the mother's and father's survival (Brass & Hill, 1973), and spouses (Hill, 1977). The variant of the method proposed by Timaeus (1992) was used to determine the basic orphanhood estimates. The time reference of these estimates was based on Brass and Bamgboye's (1981) method. Udjo (1991) determined the levels and trends in male and female adult mortality among the Kanuri in northeast Nigeria using the orphanhood and widowhood methods. Adult mortality in Burundi was estimated using data from the 1987 Demographic and Health Survey. In the study, estimates from the traditional indirect methods were compared with those from the inter-survey method using data on the number of years since the respondent's parent died (Makinson, 1993). Using data from Demographic and Health Surveys (DHS) of six countries and one in-depth DHS, Bicego examined the use of sibling histories to directly estimate rates of adult mortality in selected countries in SSA. The estimated adult mortality rates were presented at the national level and compared with estimates obtained from other available published sources. There was consistency in the results from the study and that of the external sources. The study's findings establish that DHS-type sibling histories remain unexploited sources of data that will add to knowledge on adult mortality dynamics in Africa (Bicego, 1997).

Timaeus and Jasseh (2004) report the levels, trends and age patterns of adult mortality in 23 SSA countries, based on the sibling histories and orphanhood data collected by the countries' Demographic and Health Surveys. The authors found that adult mortality has risen sharply since HIV became prevalent, but the size and speed of the mortality increase vary greatly among countries. The contribution that AIDS makes to adult mortality in rural South Africa was quantified by Hosegood, Vanneste and Timaeus (2004) study using data from demographic surveillance of the population in a rural area of northern KwaZulu Natal province. Verbal autopsy interviews were conducted among the caregivers of those who died to identify the causes of adult deaths, and this was validated with the available hospital notes. The authors calculated the death rates and other mortality indices using both direct and orphanhood methods. It was concluded that adult mortality will continue to be on the increase if effective treatment interventions are not found.

A study was based on large representative rural household surveys summarized and synthesized across the results of a set of country studies on the effects of prime-age adult mortality on rural households in Kenya, Malawi, Mozambique, Rwanda, and Zambia (Mather et al., 2004). A similar study that reported the levels, trends and age patterns of adult mortality in 23 SSA countries was based on the analysis of data on sibling histories and orphanhood as collected by Demographic and Health Surveys. The study revealed that an increase in adult mortality has been observed since the onset of HIV in Africa, but variations existed in the pace of the mortality increase across the countries investigated (Timaeus & Jasseh, 2004). Chisumpa and Dorrington (2011) derived estimates of the level of and trend in adult mortality in Zambia. In this study, the standard orphanhood method was applied to the data on survivorship of parents from various Zambia Demographic and Health and Living Conditions Monitoring Surveys to estimate adult mortality. The orphanhood method was found to have captured some of the trends but failed to provide definitive mortality estimates, but the adult mortality rate was found to be comparable to estimates from other sources.

Reniers, Masquelier and Gerland (2011) compared trends in UN estimates of adult mortality with those derived from reports of sibling survival in the Demographic and Health Surveys. The discussion on the distribution of causes of death was based on verbal autopsy data obtained from a number of demographic surveillance sites. A few general patterns of adult mortality trends were found to be similar across most sources. A study that aimed at determining whether the U.S. President's Emergency Plan for AIDS Relief (PEPFAR) was associated with relative changes in adult mortality in SSA countries and districts where it most intensively operated was conducted by Bendavid, Holmes, Bhattacharya and Miller (2012). Person-level data from the Demographic and Health Surveys were used to conduct cross-country and within-country analyses of adult mortality and PEPFAR's activities. Adult mortality was compared in nine African focus countries (Ethiopia, Kenya, Mozambique, Namibia, Nigeria, Rwanda, Tanzania, Uganda and Zambia) with 18 African non-focus countries from 1998 to 2008. Subnational analyses were performed using the information on PEPFAR's programmatic intensity in Tanzania and Rwanda. Between 2004 and 2008, all-cause adult mortality declined more in PEPFAR focus countries relative to non-focus countries. It was not possible to determine whether PEPFAR was associated with mortality effects separate from reductions in HIV-specific deaths.

Chukwu and Oladipupo (2012) in their study used the Lee-Carter method to model adult mortality in Nigeria. Using the age-specific mortality rates for Nigerians aged 15–84 years, an evaluation of trends in the general pattern of adult mortality, the pace of change in mortality by age, and projection of mortality index, and rates were determined. The model's parameters were estimated based on the Lee-Carter proposed model and singular value decomposition technique, while the mortality index was predicted using the Li and Lee (2005) approach.

Masquelier and colleagues used data on the survival of the children and siblings obtained in Demographic and Health Surveys to estimate adult mortality in SSA. The finding from this study showed that adult mortality in many East and Southern African countries increased noticeably in the past two decades, resonating the effect of the high prevalence of HIV/AIDS in the regions. However, declination was observed in adult mortality in these regions in recent years (Masquelier, Eaton, Gerland, Pelletier, & Mutai, 2014). In a study conducted in SSA, the authors assessed the level of adult mortality using data from five countries (Kenya, Rwanda, Senegal, Tanzania and South Africa) from the regional blocks in SSA. Data were analyzed using census survival method, INDEPTH life tables, and Coale-Demeny model life tables. The estimated adult mortality by census survival method was consistently higher than the values obtained from the use of INDEPTH method in 4 of the 5 analyzed countries (Adebowale & Adedini, 2014). The differences are due to the differences in the assumptions and parameters of the two methods.

The completeness and accuracy of data on survival of a respondent's siblings were evaluated through a record linkage study conducted in Senegal. The retrospective siblings' survival histories were linked at the individual level to prospective mortality data and genealogies obtained from a health and demographic surveillance system (Helleringer et al., 2014). A study explored the rural-urban differences in adult mortality across countries in sub-Saharan Africa based on Demographic and Health Survey datasets from 30 countries between 1991 and 2014. The indirect orphanhood method was used to determine the conditional probabilities of dying between ages 15 and 60 years (Menashe-Oren & Stecklov, 2018).

A study by Masquelier, Reniers and Pison (2017) designed to compare the estimates of adult mortality in SSA to empirical estimates used the age-specific mortality rates for adults aged 15–59 years obtained from nationally representative sibling survival data (Demographic and Health Surveys), recent household deaths and vital registration data having adjusted for under-reporting errors. Comparisons were directly made with adult mortality by UNAIDS estimates which utilized orphanhood method. The results showed that UNAIDS estimates were higher than sibling mortality estimates, except among men in countries with very high HIV prevalence. Doctor and Udo (2017) used data from Demographic and Health Surveys conducted between 1990 and 2014 in 25 countries in SSA, to examine the trends in all-cause prime adult mortality (measured by the probability of dying between exact ages 15 and 50) and sex differences in adult mortality by region.

Akinyemi and Olowolafe (2017) provided an estimate of adult mortality in Nigeria with the use of siblinghood method. In the study, a model life table was used to derive survivorship probabilities from estimates of child and adult mortality for Nigeria and the results were compared with INDEPTH model life tables, Brass African LT, Coale-Demeny Regional MLT and Log-Quadratic method. Indirect orphanhood method was applied to 90 DHS datasets (1991–2014) from 30 countries in sub-Saharan Africa to examine the adult mortality differences by rural-urban residence Menashe-Oren and Stecklov (2018). Findings from this study showed a higher adult mortality rate among men than women. A similar study used orphanhood, widowhood and siblinghood methods for the estimation of levels of adult mortality in ten countries in sub-Saharan Africa (Cameroon, Kenya, Liberia, Mali, Sierra Leone, South Africa, South Sudan, Sudan, Tanzania and Uganda) using both census and survey data that were collected between 2001 and 2009 (Odimegwu, Chisumpa, & Somefun, 2018). Among the three methods used for this study, the widowhood provided the least estimates. However, the disparity was observed in adult mortality estimates derived from the direct and indirect siblinghood methods.

Another study which provided estimates of adult mortality across geopolitical zones in Nigeria used the 2013 Nigeria Demographic and Health Survey. The Brass Logit system, siblings' survival method and Heligman-Pollard model were used to generate estimates of adult mortality (Afam, Olowolafe, Gbadebo, & Adebowale, 2018). Data extracted from the 2010–2012 Zambia sample vital registration and verbal autopsy survey were used to examine causes of adult death in Zambia. Death associated with HIV/AIDS, injury and accidents were the main identified causes of adult deaths in the country. It was found that if HIV/AIDS is excluded as a cause of death in Zambia, life expectancy at age 15 years may increase by 5.7 years for males and 6.4 years for females (Chisumpa et al., 2019). Bangha et al. (2017) compare adult mortality estimates from 16 HDSSs in nine countries in SSA using INDEPTHStats data. The authors used life table techniques to examine the differences in adult mortality trends and identification of mortality clusters in SSA. Disparities in adult mortality trends were found across the three regions in SSA with the Southern and Eastern African regions having relatively higher mortality than the West African region. Trends in older adult mortality in SSA countries were examined using five-year aggregated information about the child (${}_5q_0$) and adult mortality (${}_{45}q_{15}$) from the United Nations World Population Prospects. Data analysis was conducted from 1990 to 2014. Indirect model life table systems indexed by child and adult mortality approach was used to know if M varies in the recent decades or it is shifting and compressing as found in developed countries (Ouedraogo, Ouellette, & Duthe, 2019).

In a Rwandan study, the network survival method was used for adult death rates estimation. The method was based on data from Rwanda, without reliance on the use of model life tables or pooling of data from other countries. The estimates obtained from the use of this method was found to be similar to estimates from other methods and thus recommended for use in countries where reliable estimates of adult death rates are greatly needed (Feehan, Mahy, & Salganik, 2017).

Projection techniques already used for adult mortality in sub-Saharan Africa and elsewhere around the World

Adult mortality projections provide indispensable statistics on population ageing, protect the future of public health and assess the possible effects on health care systems with the view to informing policy planning. The current increase in life expectancy beyond previously held bounds has brought to the forefront the critical prominence of the adult mortality projection. The theory and practice of adult mortality projection have progressed swiftly in recent decades and several approaches to adult mortality forecasts have been suggested (Booth & Tickle, 2008). Short-run or small-interval projections classically depend on simple extrapolation of historical trends in mortality rates, in life expectancy or in model parameters, but for longer periods, say more than a decade, simple extrapolation can lead to spurious results. The choice of methods for the estimation of long-term mortality levels or trends, therefore, depends on the experts' opinion. Unfortunately, such methods are conservative or subjective because explanation may be restricted to certain death causes with known bases. The observed age patterns of adult mortality with the use of mathematical models have been widely and extensively discussed in the literature. The quantity and complexity of mortality models have increased speedily since the first proposition of the mortality law by Gompertz (1825). Specialized demographic software for adult mortality estimation (e.g MORTPAK, ModMatch, Spectrum, Spectrum 44; Bayes Life HIV R package) have been developed and applied.

The literature search shows that numerous studies aimed at generating adult mortality estimates at national or sub-national level have been conducted in SSA (Bradshaw & Timaeus, 2006), but adult mortality projections at country level by independent African researchers are scarce. Most of the available projections are conducted by international organizations and scholars outside Africa. Projections that involved countries in SSA are often used to either test or validate the output from new models or compare the adult mortality levels from selected African countries with those of countries from other world regions. Therefore, in this section of the paper, available existing or proposed methods of projecting adult mortality and general mortality based on the search coverage are documented.

In 1825, a simple parametric model was proposed for mortality estimation by Gompertz (Gompertz, 1825). This model was improved upon by Makeham in 1860 through the addition of a constant to address the deviation at lower ages observed in Gompertz model (Makeham, 1860). The Makeham model signifies a clear enhancement of the Gompertz model at younger ages; nevertheless, it overestimates mortality at the oldest ages. Brass (1971) used the logit transformation of the observed and standard survival functions to estimate adult mortality. The limitation of this model in terms of lack of fit at the young and old ages was addressed by Zaba (1979) who proposed a four-parameter extension that includes two deviations' pattern from the standard. An alternative extension proposed by other researchers utilized different power transformations at young and old ages, converging to the logit as the powers approach zero. A small revision of the standard below age 15 years was also suggested. Ewbank, Gomez de Leon and Stoto (1983) observed that the two extensions are non-linear in the additional parameters and thus cumbersome to fit, but they suggested an alternative estimation procedure to circumvent these challenges (Ewbank et al., 1983). An attempt to address the limitation of the Brass 1971 model was also made by Murray et al. (2003) by the proposition of a modified system that in addition to the logit transformation uses two additional sets of age-specific coefficients which adjust for survivorship at under-five and adult.

The Lee-Carter age-period-cohort model is one of the prominent methods used for projecting mortality (Lee & Carter, 1992). This method was used by the US Census Bureau to forecast as a benchmark for their long-run forecast of life expectancy. Basellini and Camarda (2019) in their study used a deaths distribution to model and forecast adult mortality. In this study, they introduced a relational model that relates a fixed 'standard' to a series of observed distributions through the age-axis transformation. Their model used only three parameters, and it captures and splits mortality developments in terms of shifting and compression dynamics. Comparison between this model and the Lee-Carter model showed that it perfectly fits the observed mortality pattern and that its forecasts are more exact and optimistic than the Lee-Carter variants (Basellini & Camarda, 2019). Conventionally, a commonly-used method targets life expectancy when a value is assumed for a future date with a specified trajectory (Pollard, 1987). The expected life expectancy forecasts from such an approach are generally considered to be too low (Tuljapurkar, Li, & Boe, 2000; Bongaarts, 2005). The logistic model has been used for the pattern of change over time in age-specific adult mortality rates and more complex logistic models that included more parameters have also been offered by researchers (Horiuchi & Wilmoth,

1998). The logistic regression was modified by Bongaarts (2005) when he proposed a variant to the model called the shifting logistic model.

Linear extrapolation is another technique that has been used for mortality projection. The assumption that past mortality and current mortality trends will be sustained throughout the projection period makes extrapolation method the fundamental of most mortality forecasting methods (Denton, Feaver, & Spencer, 2005). The independent linear extrapolation of the logarithms of age-specific rates, comparable to the assumption that constant age-specific mortality reduction factors, has often been applied (Pollard, 1987). The non-linear extrapolation can be used too if the appropriate functional form is assumed. The extrapolative forecasting methods often rely on time series models (Box, Jenkins, & Reinsel, 1994). The time series models are advantageous because of their stochastic tendency and they allow the computation of the probabilistic prediction interval for the estimated value but the approach is more suitable for short time projection (Denton et al., 2005; Bell, 1997). The autoregressive model has also been used to model life expectancy at specific ages in some countries.

In the countries with a high burden of HIV/AIDS, mortality has been projected by modelling explicitly the epidemic's course and making projections based on HIV infection on a yearly basis (United Nations, 2017). The life expectancy at birth was projected for countries using Bayesian probabilistic life expectancy projection methods. The method was extended to account for trends in HIV prevalence and adult antiretroviral therapy coverage (Godwin & Raftery, 2017; United Nations, 2017). In Zimbabwe, the 1992 census data was used to estimate the number of non-HIV-related deaths, and provide a short-term projection model to estimate the number of deaths attributed to HIV infection in 1995 and the year 2000. The authors concluded that even if all HIV transmission is put to a halt after 1995, the projection suggested that three fifths of adult deaths would be attributed to HIV in the year 2000 (Robinson & Marindo, 1999). For 40 high-HIV/AIDS epidemic countries, the United Nations projects mortality using the Spectrum/Estimation and Projection Package (EPP) model, a complex, multistate model designed for short-term projections of policy-relevant quantities for the epidemic. A simpler approach that avoided the multistate modelling and compatible with existing UN projection methods for other countries was proposed by Sharrow, Godwin, He, Clark and Raftery (2018) through the projection of changes in life expectancy stochastically using a simple time series regression model. Using model life tables designed specifically for countries with HIV/AIDS epidemics, the projected changes in life expectancy were later converted to age- and sex-specific mortality rates. These are then input to the cohort component method, as for other countries.

Parameterization function is another method widely used for mortality graduation; the method smooths the forecast rates across age (Forfar, McCutcheon, & Wilkie, 1988) but their use in mortality forecast is imperfect. It involves repeated fitting of the mortality curve to yearly data, thereby obtaining a time series for each parameter in the model. A Bayesian log-bilinear poisson regression model was used to forecast mortality. Markov Chain Monte Carlo methods were used for the computations and comparisons made with other existing methods (Czado, Delwarde, & Denuit, 2005). A multi-country study was conducted to forecast national age-specific mortality and life expectancy, using an approach that accounted for the uncertainty linked to the choice of the forecasting model. A collection of 21 forecasting models was developed during the study, and these models were integrated into the final projection. The method was used for age-specific mortality (ASM) projection in 35 industrialized countries with credible vital statistics and the projected ASM data were used to calculate life expectancy at birth and probability of dying before age 70 years (Kontis et al., 2017). The adult mortality estimation procedures for the intercensal interval were developed and applied in a study conducted by Black and colleagues. The method yields estimates of the completeness of adult mortality registration by comparing this outcome with that of recently developed methods of estimating adult mortality in which accurate data are lacking (Black, Hsu, Sanders, & Taylor, 2017).

In projecting future levels of mortality, the probabilistic methods are often used by the United Nations because they reflect the uncertainty of the projections based on the historical variability of changes in each variable. The method accounts for the past mortality experience of each country, while also reflecting uncertainty about future changes based on the experience of other countries under similar conditions (United Nations, 2019). Regression-based models (Czado et al., 2005; Bongaarts, 2005; Sharrow et al., 2018) have also been used to project adult mortality, but their use has been less successful, due to nonlinearities in time. Some other techniques previously used for mortality modelling and projection as found in the literature include Keyfitz (1991), Pollard (1987), Murphy (1990), Tuljapurkar and Boe (1998), Pitacco (2004), Wong-Fupuy and Haberman (2004), Bengtsson and Keilman (2003), Keilman (2005) and Booth (2006).

Demography and population studies programmes in African tertiary institutions that teach methods of estimating adult mortality

The training of population specialists in SSA could be traced to the early 1960s. Methods of demographic estimation and advanced demographic techniques have always been included in the curriculum of demography and population studies programmes at both undergraduate and postgraduate levels. All the population studies and demography programmes accessed online in the current review (Table 39.2) included adult mortality estimation and projection in their curriculum either as a course or as part of the synopsis of a course. The curriculum of these programmes has undergone several reviews in some of the institutions and as such strongly considered the new approaches to the estimation and projection of adult mortality. Most courses that have adult mortality issues are either made compulsory or required in the curriculum of the demographic and population studies assessed and as such are taught to students.

Discussion

Over the past two decades, life expectancy has increased consistently in SSA (United Nations, 2019). Much of this rise is attributable to slight reductions in adult mortality and improvement in public health interventional programmes. However, in order to sustain a further increase in life expectancy in the future, additional reductions in adult mortality are needed in the countries across SSA. Adult mortality remains poorly measured in SSA countries. Death registration is often incomplete and age-related information is usually inaccurate. Unfortunately, there is much uncertainty pertaining to the quality of census data which are needed as the denominators for the computation of standard rates. This study examines the trends and prospects of adult mortality in SSA. A concise description of past adult mortality trends will provide the basis for projections.

Data on mortality are very scarce in SSA and the available ones are fraught with errors and gross inadequacies. Very few countries in sub-Saharan Africa have a civil registration system with a satisfactory number of reported deaths that could be used to estimate adult mortality at the national level. Most adult mortality estimates in countries in SSA were based on census data and surveys (Adebowale & Adedini, 2014; Afam et al., 2018; Chisumpa et al., 2019). The Demographic and Health Survey's rounds have been widely used. Measuring adult mortality using censuses and cross-sectional surveys requires indirect techniques (Moultrie et al., 2013) which are disposed to common bias and errors. However, the growing number of health and

Table 39.2 List of Population Studies and Demography Programmes in the SSA Accessed Online in the Current Review

S/N	*Name of the programme/institution*	*Country*	*Website*	*Year Established*
1	Centre for Actuarial Research, University of Cape Town	South Africa	www.care.uct.ac.za/	2011
2	Center for Population Studies, University of Zimbabwe	Zimbabwe	www.euni.de/tools/	1982
3	Demography and population Studies, University of Witwatersrand	South Africa	www.wits.ac.za/ socialsciencesdemography-and-population-studies/	2003
4	Demographic Training and Research Centre, University of Addis Ababa	Ethiopia	www.abyssiniagateway.net/ethiopia/ aau/demography.html	1986
5	Demographic Unit, University of Dares-Salaam	Tanzania	www.google.co.ug/	NA
6	Department of Demography and Social Statistics, Federal University, Oye Ekiti	Nigeria	http://dss.fuoye.edu.ng/	2011
7	Department of Demography and Social Statistics, Obafemi Awolowo University, Ile-Ife	Nigeria	http://oauife.edu.ng/faculties/soc _sciences/demography/underg.htm	1976
8	Department of Population and Health, University of Cape Coast	Ghana	https://ucc.edu.gh/departments/ department-population-and-health	2007
9	Department of Population Studies, University of Botswana	Botswana	www.ub.bw/learning_faculties. cfm?pid=611	1983
10	Department of Population Studies, University of Malawi, Chancellor College	Malawi	www.cc.ac.mw/ department/population-studies	1984
11	Department of Population Studies, Makerere	Uganda	http://statistics.mak.ac.ug/popstaff html and http://statistics.mak.ac.ug/	NA
12	Department of Population Studies, University of Zambia	Zambia	www.unza.zm/schools/ humanities/departments/population	2011
13	Department of statistics and population studies, University of Western Cape	South Africa	www.uwc.ac.za/Faculties /NS/ Population_Studies	NA
14	Higher Institute of Population Sciences (ISSP) at the Joseph Ki-Zerbo University	Burkina Faso	www.issp.bf/index.php/fr/	1974
15	Institut de Formation et de Recherche Démographiques (IFORD)	Cameroon	www.iford-cm.org/ index.php/component	1971
16	Medical Demography Unit, Department of Epid. & Medical Stat., University of Ibadan	Nigeria	http://com.ui.edu.ng/department	2005

(*Continued*)

S/N	Name of the programme/institution	Country	Website	Year Established
17	Population and Development Studies Programme, University of Kinshasa	Democratic Rep. of Congo	https://unikin.academia.edu/Departments/Population_and_development	NA
18	Population Studies and Research institute, University of Nairobi	Kenya	https://psri.uonbi.ac.ke/	1976
19	Development studies and Population Studies Programme, School of Built Environment, University of Kwazulu Natal	South Africa	http://sds.ukzn.ac.za/Homepage.aspx	1954
20	Regional Institute for Population Studies (RIPS) at the University of Ghana	Ghana	www.rips-ug.edu.gh/index. php/academics/programmes	1972
21	Population Training and Research, North-West University, Mafikeng, South Africa	South Africa	www.nwu.ac.za/content/nwu Mafikeng Campus	NA

Important Note: Contained in this list are only the demography and population studies programmes in the universities within SSA that the authors were able to access online during the period of literature search. Therefore, there could be other universities in SSA that currently run the programme within, not captured here.

demographic surveillance systems offer a remedy to the scarcity of information regarding estimates of adult mortality in SSA. Census schedules in most cases in SSA countries do not include relevant questions that could be used to generate direct estimates of adult mortality, and as such, there is over-reliance on the use of age distribution from two consecutive censuses or intercensal cohort survival or age-specific growth. Consequently, adult mortality scholars have suggested inclusion of questions about recent deaths in households and parental survival of household members in the national census schedule as a way of obtaining adult mortality data (Timæus & Jasseh, 2004). A few countries in SSA often ask either of the two questions in their censuses.

A handful of studies on adult mortality in SSA relies on data from demographic surveillance sites for many years. These studies provide a framework for adult mortality estimates in the region. The huge magnitude of HIV in Africa attracts many more of such surveillance systems in which vital events are collected, monitored and evaluated at regular intervals (Hosegood, Vanneste, & Timaeus, 2004). The major challenge with the use of data from these sites for demographic estimation is low coverage and specificity to only small and selected populations. Consequently, their use for the adult mortality's estimation at the national level is limited due to not being statistically representative of the population of the whole country. The non-availability or scarcity of reliable empirical estimates has prompted the international agencies like United Nations, US Census Bureau and technical demographers to use estimates of child mortality and assumptions about the age pattern of mortality taken from a particular family of model life tables for the computation of adult mortality and life expectancies in SSA countries (United Nations, 2004, 2019).

The estimate of the conventional life table indices can be obtained from the parental survival data using the orphanhood method through which the mortality trend can be generated. The ratio resulting from matching age groups in the second population to the first population provides a summary measure of adult mortality with the assumption that the population is closed to migration and that the two censuses are the same in terms of coverage (Bradshaw & Timaeus, 2006). Aside the limitations posed by inadequate or non-existence of vital registration system on the estimates of adult mortality in SSA, not many countries took into consideration adult mortality attributed to AIDS and other emerging/re-emerging diseases or other causes in their census schedule and survey questionnaires. Thus, the non-inclusion of such questions further demeans the quality of adult mortality estimates from these data sources. The peculiarity of the aforementioned challenges to most developing nations across the world makes the adult mortality estimates in SSA countries comparable to others.

The available studies on adult mortality in SSA as identified in the current study mainly used the orphanhood, widowhood method, siblings' history, siblings' survival and Lee-Carter methods and survival of the children and siblings (Udjo, 1991; Hosegood et al., 2004; Reniers et al., 2011; Chukwu & Oladipupo, 2012; Odimegwu et al., 2018). Others are census survival method, INDEPTH life tables, Coale-Demeny model life tables, Log-Quadratic method and the Heligman-Pollard model (Adebowale & Adedini, 2014; Akinyemi & Olowolafe, 2017, Afam et al., 2018). These demographic techniques which were designed to account for the poor data quality or used in proxy for the generation of adult mortality estimates had their origination from the data integrated from other countries with either none or very few countries included from SSA. One can argue that the consistent reporting of high adult mortality estimates in sub-Saharan African countries by international agencies and scholars could be attributed to the use of such data in their estimation methodologies. Adult mortality research needs in SSA include further comparative evaluations of methods in terms of the accuracy of the point forecast and its uncertainty, encompassing a wide range of mortality situations.

The searched literature on adult mortality suggests that adult mortality is declining in SSA and across its four regional blocks (United Nations, 2017, 2019). The decline is modest; based on the projections, there is a possibility of continuous reduction in adult mortality rates in the decades ahead if the present mortality schedule is sustained. However, within the past seven decades (1950–2020), several countries in SSA, particularly those from Southern and Eastern Africa which are highly affected by HIV, have experienced reversal in adult mortality. In these countries where HIV/AIDS is endemic, adult mortality has declined and will continue to decline as a result of availability of antiretroviral therapy (United Nations, 2019). The emerging disease like Ebola, COVID-19, Lassa fever, and others may pose a serious threat to the sustenance of adult mortality reduction in some SSA countries if appropriate mechanisms to mitigate the spread or reoccurrence of these deadly diseases are not instituted.

Despite the teaching of adult mortality estimation and projection methods in population training centres in SSA, the existing research in this technical aspect of demography is still very scanty. Only very few African demographers have demonstrated skills on the use of these methods as evidenced in the available publications on adult mortality research in SSA. The lack of interest in this aspect of demography may be due to poor support for training of technical demographers, shortage of competent trainers, inadequate training infrastructure and shift in the focus of graduates to other lucrative areas of demography. The crucial role of demographers, especially the technical demographers, in national building calls for more focussed investment in training and re-training of demographers in the SSA. Bankrolling of technical demography programmes and advanced demographic research training by governments and international agencies in SSA is therefore recommended.

Policy implication

Understanding the descriptive study of the level, patterns, trends and prospects of adult mortality in SSA has implications for consolidating the scientific basis for policy makers to meeting the health challenges of the working population (15–64 years) who bear the burden of providing the needs and support for other age segments of the population. The findings from this study have implications for the design of efforts to alleviate adult mortality rates in sub-Saharan Africa, and for key development policies and priorities for programmes of action. It will also aid policy on improvement of the health systems' responses to the care of the adult population in SSA. In addition, findings from this study will be relevant to the transformation and advancement of adult mortality teaching and research in sub-Saharan Africa.

Conclusion

This paper provides a basis for tracking progress in adult mortality reduction with the goal of sustaining the trend. Adult mortality rate is high in SSA but the rate has reduced over time, and according to demographic projections, this trend will continue in the years ahead. Most estimates of adult mortality were based on census and survey data sources; however, the orphanhood and sibling survival methods are the most commonly used techniques for the generation of adult mortality estimates in SSA. The origination of these applied methods to African data was based on data from other world sub-regions and therefore, the estimates produced with them may be unreliable. Adult mortality researchers who are Africans either by birth or citizenship are few in number and there is a possibility of having no replacement for these researchers if they retire from the active service. Thus, extinction of adult mortality research by Africans, estimates in particular, is imminent in SSA. Virtually all demography and population institutions in SSA have adult mortality in their respective curricula as part of course synopses and the methodologies of its estimates are taught but yet to fully transform into real-life practical applications.

The governments across countries in SSA should initiate plans to revamp their vital registration system and those who already have a good structure in place should enhance it. Implementation of this agenda will augment demographic data source and quality on adult deaths for the generation of good, reliable and robust estimate of adult mortality in SSA. This is likely to be a long-term programme because of logistic, funding and cultural challenges. Therefore, training and motivation of young demographers and population researchers on the use of advanced skills needed to apply the available and emerging indirect methods are urgently required in sub-Saharan Africa. Although the current report highlighted the basis for tracking progress in adult mortality, and the capacity and investment in qualified demographers to adequately estimate adult mortality as a means of monitoring a country's well-being in the region, there are needs for future research in the depth of the gaps and capacities of the demographers.

References

Adebowale, A. S., & Adedini, S. A. (2014). Chapter 5: Indirect estimation of levels of adult mortality in sub-Saharan Africa. In C. O. Odimegwu & J. Kekovole (Eds.), *Continuity and change in sub-Saharan African demography* (pp. 83–103). New York: Routledge. ISBN: 978-0-415-71194-4 (United States of America).

Afam, B. O., Olowolafe, T. A., Gbadebo, B. M., & Adebowale, A. S. (2018). Modelling regional differentials in childhood and adult mortality in Nigeria. *African Population Studies, 32*(1).

Akinyemi, J. O., & Olowolafe, T. A. (2017). Survivorship probabilities in Nigeria: Comparison of four model life table system. *Journal of Demography and Social Statistics, 4*(1), 1–20.

Bangha, M., Wak, G., Jasseh, M., Pison, G., Newton, R., Gomez-Olive, X. F., . . . Sankoh, O. (2017). Assessing levels and trends of adult mortality in Sub Saharan Africa using INDEPTH health and demographic surveillance systems. *International Journal for Population, Development and Reproductive Health*, 43–52.

Basellini, U., & Camarda, C. G. (2019). Modelling and forecasting adult age-at-death distributions. *Population Studies*, *73*(1), 119–138.

Bell, W. (1997). Comparing and assessing time series methods for forecasting age-specific fertility and mortality rates. *Journal of Official Statistics, 13*(3), 279–303.

Bendavid, E., Holmes, C. B., Bhattacharya, J., & Miller, G. (2012). HIV development assistance and adult mortality in Africa. *JAMA, 307*(19), 2060–2067. https://doi.org/10.1001/jama.2012.2001

Bengtsson, T., & Keilman, N. (Eds.) (2003). *Perspectives on mortality forecasting* (Vol. I. Current practice). Stockholm: Swedish National Social Insurance Board.

Bicego, G. (1997). Estimating adult mortality rates in the context of the AIDS epidemic in sub-Saharan Africa: Analysis of DHS sibling histories. *Health Transition Review,* 7(2), 7–22.

Black, D. A., Hsu, Y.-C., Sanders, S. G., & Taylor, L. J. (2017). Combining forward and backward mortality estimation. *Population Studies, 71*(3), 281–292.

Bongaarts, J. (2005). Long-range trends in adult mortality: Models and projection methods. *Demography, 42*, 23–49.

Booth, H. (2006). Demographic forecasting: 1980 to 2005 in review. *International Journal of Forecasting, 22*, 547–581.

Booth, H., & Tickle, L. (2008). Mortality modelling and forecasting: A review of methods. *AAS, 3*(I/II), 3–43.

Box, G., Jenkins, G. M., & Reinsel, G. C. (1994). Time series analysis: Forecasting and control (3rd ed.). Englewood, NJ: Prentice Hall.

Bradshaw, D., & Timaeus, I. M. (2006). Levels and trends of Adult mortality. In D. T. Jamison, R. G. Feachem, M. W. Makgoba, et al. (Eds.). *Disease and mortality in sub-Saharan Africa* (2nd ed.). Washington, DC: The International Bank for Reconstruction and Development/The World Bank. Retrieved from www.ncbi.nlm.nih.gov/books/NBK2297/

Brass, W. (1971). On the scale of mortality. In W. Brass (Ed.), *Biological aspects of demography* (pp. 69–110). London: Taylor and Francis.

Brass, W., & Bamgboye, E. A. (1981). *The time location of reports of survivorship: Estimates for maternal and paternal orphanhood and the ever-widowed* (Centre for Population Studies Working Paper 81–1). London: London School of Hygiene and Tropical Medicine.

Brass, W., & Hill, K. H. (1973). Estimating adult mortality from orphanhood. In *International Population Conference, Liège, 1973* (Vol. 3). Liège: International Union for the Scientific Study of Population.

Chisumpa, V. H., & Dorrington, R. (2011). Estimating adult mortality in Zambia using information on survival of parents from surveys. *African Population Studies*, 25(1).

Chisumpa, V. H., Odimegwu, O. C., & Saikia, N. (2019). Adult mortality in sub-Saharan Africa: Cross-sectional study of causes of death in Zambia. *Tropical Medicine and International Health, 24*(10), 1208–1220. https://doi.org/10.1111/tmi.13302

Chukwu, A. U., & Oladipupo, E. O. (2012). Modelling adult mortality in Nigeria: Analysis based on the Lee-Carter model. *Studies in Mathematical Sciences,* 5(2).

Czado, C., Delwarde, A., & Denuit, M. (2005). Bayesian Poisson log-bilinear mortality projections. *Insurance: Mathematics and Economics, 36*(24), 260–284.

Davies, M. A. (2020). HIV and risk of COVID-19 death: A population cohort study from the Western Cape Province, South Africa. *medRxiv: The Preprint Server for Health Sciences.* https://doi.org/10.1101/2020.07.02.20145185

Denton, F., Feaver, C., & Spencer, B. (2005). Time series analysis and stochastic forecasting: An econometric study of mortality and life expectancy. *Journal of Population Economics, 18*(2), 203–227.

Doctor, H. V., & Udo, I. E. (2017). Prime-age adult mortality in sub-Saharan Africa: Examining trends in demographic and health surveys conducted between 1990 and 2014. *Journal of Population Research, 34*(4), 373–386.

Ewbank, D. C., Gomez de Leon, J. C., & Stoto, M. A. (1983). A reducible four-parameter system of model life tables. *Population Studies, 37*(1), 105–127.

Feehan, D. M., Mahy, M., & Salganik, M. J. (2017). The network survival method for estimating adult mortality: Evidence from a survey experiment in Rwanda. *Demography, 54*(4), 1503–1528. https://doi.org/10.1007/s13524-017-0594-y

Forfar, D. O., McCutcheon, J. J., & Wilkie, A. D. (1988). On graduation by mathematical formula. *Journal of the Institute of Actuaries, 115*(1), 97–245.

Godwin, J., & Raftery, A. E. (2017). Bayesian projection of life expectancy accounting for the HIV/AIDS epidemic. *Demographic Research, 37*, 1549–1610. https://doi.org/10.4054/DemRes.2017.37.48

Gompertz, B. (1825). On the nature of the function expressive of the law of human mortality, and on a new mode of determining the value of life contingencies. *Philosophical Transactions of the Royal Society of London, 115*, 513–583.

Helleringer, S., Pison, G., Kanté, A. M., Almamy, M., Kanté, G. D., & Armelle, A. (2014). Reporting Errors In Siblings' Survival Histories And Their Impact On Adult Mortality Estimates: Results from a record linkage study in Senegal. *Demography, 51*, 387–411.

Hill, K., & Trussell, T. J. (1977). Further developments in indirect mortality estimation. *Population Studies, 31*, 75–84.

Horiuchi, S., & Wilmoth, J. R. (1998). Deceleration in the age pattern of mortality at older ages. *Demography, 35*, 391–412. https://doi.org/10.2307/3004009

Hosegood, V., Vanneste, A., & Timæus, I. M. (2004). Levels and causes of adult mortality in rural South Africa: The impact of AIDS. *AIDS, 18*(4), 663–671.

Keilman, N. (Ed.). (2005). *Perspectives on mortality forecasting* (Vol. II. Probabilistic models). Stockholm: Swedish Social Insurance Agency.

Keyfitz, N. (1991). Experiments in the projection of mortality. *Canadian Studies in Population, 18*(2), 1–17.

Kontis, V., Bennett, J. E., Mathers, C. D., Li, G., Foreman, K., & Ezzat, M. (2017). Future life expectancy in 35 industrialized countries: Projections with a Bayesian model ensemble. *Lancet, 389*(1), 1323–1335.

Lee, R. D., & Carter, L. R. (1992). Modelling and forecasting U.S. mortality. *Journal of the American Statistical Association, 87*(419), 659–671.

Li, N., & Lee, R. (2005). Coherent mortality forecasts for a group of populations: An extension of the lee-carter method. *Demography, 42*, 575–594. https://doi.org/10.1353/dem.2005.0021

Makeham, W. (1860). On the law of mortality and the construction of annuity tables. *The Assurance Magazine, and Journal of the Institute of Actuaries, 8*(6), 301–310. Retrieved on August 31, 2020, from www.jstor.org/stable/41134925

Makinson, C. (1993). Estimates of adult mortality in Burundi. *Journal of Biosocial Sciences, 25*(2), 169–186.

Masquelier, B., Eaton, J. W., Gerland, P., Pelletier, F., & Mutai, K. K. (2017). Age patterns and sex ratios of adult mortality in countries with high HIV prevalence. *AIDS, 31*(1), 77–85. https://doi.org/10.1097/QAD.0000000000001332

Masquelier, B., Reniers, G., & Pison, G. (2014). Divergences in trends in child and adult mortality in sub-Saharan Africa: Survey evidence on the survival of children and siblings. *Population Studies, 68*(2), 161–177. https://doi.org/10.1080/00324728.2013.856458

Mather, D., Donovan, C., Jayne, T. S., Weber, M., Chapoto, A., Mazhangara, E., . . . Mghenyi, E. (2004). *A cross-country analysis of household responses to adult mortality in rural sub-Saharan Africa: Implications for HIV/AIDS mitigation and rural development policies*. No 54571, Food Security International Development Working Papers from Michigan State University. Retrieved from https://econpapers.repec.org/

Menashe-Oren, A., & Stecklov, G. (2018). Urban – rural disparities in adult mortality in sub-Saharan Africa. *Demographic Research, 39*(5), 136–176.

Moultrie, T. A., Dorrington, R. E., Hill, A. G., Hill, K., Timæus, I., & Zaba, B. (2013). *Tools for demographic estimation*. Paris: International Union for the Scientific Study of Population. demographicestimation.iussp.org

Murray, C. J. L., Ferguson, B. D., Lopez, A. D., Guillot, M., Salomon, J. A., & Ahmad, O. (2003). Modified logit life table system: principles, empirical validation, and application. *Population Studies, 57*, 165–182.

Murphy, M. J. (1990). Methods of forecasting mortality for population projections. In *Population projections: Trends, methods and uses* (pp. 87–102). Occasional Paper 38. London: OPCS.

Odimegwu, C., Chisumpa, V. H., & Somefun, O. D. (2018). Adult mortality in sub-Saharan Africa using 2001–2009 census data: Does estimation method matter? *Genus, 74*(1), 10. https://doi.org/10.1186/s41118-017-0025-3

Ouedraogo, S., Ouellette, N., & Duthe, G. (2019). *Recent trends in older adult mortality in sub-Saharan Africa: An analysis of the modal age at death in late life*. Paper presented at Population Association of America Meeting 2019. Retrieved from http://paa2019.populationassociation.org/abstracts/193611

Pitacco, E. (2004). Survival models in a dynamic context: A survey. *Mathematics and Economics, 35*, 279–298.

Pollard, J. H. (1987). Projection of age-specific mortality rates. Population Bulletin of the United Nations, 21–22, 55–69.

Reniers, G., Masquelier, B., & Gerland, P. (2011). Adult mortality in Africa. In R. Rogers & E. Crimmins (Eds.), *International handbook of adult mortality: International handbooks of population, 2*. https://doi.org/10.1007/978-90-481-9996-9_7

Robinson, N. J., & Marindo, R. (1999). Current estimates of and future projections for adult deaths attributed to HIV infection in Zimbabwe. *Journal of Acquired Immune Deficiency Syndromes and Human Retrovirology: Official Publication of the International Retrovirology Association, 20*(2), 187–194. https://doi.org/10.1097/00042560-199902010-00012

Sharrow, D. J., Godwin, J., He, Y., Clark, S. J., & Raftery, A. E. (2018). Probabilistic population projections for countries with generalized HIV/AIDS epidemics. *Population Studies, 72*(1), 1–15.

Timaeus, I. M. (1991). Measurement of adult mortality in less developed countries: A comparative review. *Population Index, 57*(4), 552–568.

Timaeus, I. M. (1992). Estimation of adult mortality from paternal orphanhood: A reassessment and a new approach. *Population Bulletin of the United Nations, 33*, 47–63.

Timaeus, I. M. (1993). *Adult mortality. "Demographic change in sub-Saharan Africa". National Research Council*. Washington, DC: The National Academies Press. https://doi.org/10.17226/2207

Timaeus, I. M., & Jasseh, M. (2004). Adult mortality in sub-Saharan Africa: Evidence from demographic and health surveys. *Demography, 41*, 757–772. https://doi.org/10.1353/dem

Tuljapurkar, S., & Boe, C. (1998). Mortality change and forecasting: How much and how little do we know? *North American Actuarial Journal, 2*(4), 13–47.

Tuljapurkar, S., Li, N., & Boe, C. (2000). A universal pattern of mortality decline in the G7 countries. *Nature, 405*, 789–792.

Udjo, E. O. (1991). Adult mortality from information on orphanhood and widowhood among the Kanuri of Nigeria. *Journal of Biosocial Sciences, 23*(2), 155–165.

United Nations. (2004). *World population to 2300*. New York, NY: Author.

United Nations. (2017). Mortality. *Department of Economic and Social Affairs*. Retrieved from www.un.org/en/development/desa/population/theme/mortality/index.asp

United Nations. (2019). Department of Economic and Social Affairs, Population Division. *World Population Prospects*. custom data acquired via website. Retrieved from http://creativecommons.org/licenses/by/3.0/igo/

Wong-Fupuy, C., & Haberman, S. (2004). Projecting mortality trends: Recent developments in the United Kingdom and the United States. *North American Actuarial Journal, 8*(2), 56–83.

Zaba, B. (1979). The four-parameter logit life table system. *Population Studies, 33*(1), 79–100.

40

MATERNAL MORTALITY IN SUB-SAHARAN AFRICA

A systematic review of measurement, levels and determinants

Dorothy N. Ononokpono, Bernard Baffour, Nsidibe Usoro, and Olukemi Adebola

Introduction

Maternal mortality refers to the deaths of women due to complications during pregnancy, childbirth, or the neonatal period up to six weeks (42 days) after childbirth, and it is a challenge to achieving long and healthy lives for women. According to the World Health Organization (WHO), roughly 303,000 women died in 2015 following pregnancy and childbirth (WHO, 2016). Of all these deaths which could have been prevented, 99% occurred in developing countries and more than half (66%) occurred in sub-Saharan Africa (SSA) (WHO, 2016). Based on an estimated maternal mortality ratio (MMR) of 546 per 100,000 live births in the sub-Saharan African region, WHO reported that the leading cause of gender differences in life expectancy at birth between men and women was (inadequate) maternal conditions which contribute to increased mortality for women of reproductive age (World Health Statistics, 2019). Although considerable progress has been made in the reduction of maternal deaths globally, high maternal mortality remains the biggest health challenge in sub-Saharan Africa.

Notably, between 1990 and 2010, Africa recorded a remarkable reduction in maternal deaths by 41%, and a decline of 49% over two decades, from 990 deaths per 100,000 live births in 1990 to 510 per 100,000 in 2013 (UNFPA, 2019). Despite the progress made, the African continent contributes 57% of all maternal mortality ratios worldwide, and the rate is still 78 times higher than those of Australia and New Zealand which have the lowest ratio of any region (United Nations, Department of Economics and Social Affairs, 2019; UNFPA, 2013). However, it is worthwhile to mention that this average figure masks the heterogeneity in maternal mortality across different sub-Saharan African countries. For instance, the maternal mortality in the Seychelles is low, and comparable to some developed countries, at 53 deaths per 100,000 live births, whereas the maternal mortality in Sierra Leone is almost 25 times higher at 1,120 deaths per 100,000 live births (WHO, 2016).

Similarly, the WHO (2014) estimated that in 2013, some 289,000 women died during or immediately following pregnancy and childbirth and that the maternal mortality ratio in developing countries was 230 per 100,000 live births, while it is 16 per 100,000 in the developed countries. The World Bank (2016) asserted that by the end of the Millennium Development

 DOI: 10.4324/9780429287213-49

Goals (MDGs) in the year 2015, the majority of the sub-Saharan African countries did not achieve the improved maternal health target of reducing maternal mortality ratio by three quarters, between 1990 and 2015. Furthermore, the WHO report indicated that while it is good to have targets for maternal mortality reduction, it may be difficult to achieve because accurate measurement of maternal mortality remains challenging and many maternal deaths go uncounted in sub-Saharan African countries (WHO, 2019).

Maternal mortality has been measured using various indices such as direct and indirect sisterhood or sibling methods and reproductive age mortality studies, as well as birth and death (vital) registration. Of these, it is noteworthy to mention that when accurate and timely data are available, direct methods of estimation are preferable because of their ability to provide complete coverage of the population. However, Boerma (1988) noted that vital registration systems in Africa are incomplete and unlikely to play a role in assessing maternal mortality; and besides, data from studies on maternal mortality in Africa give widely varying results on levels, medical causes, and differentials. Although population-based surveys of different kinds including censuses are increasingly being used to assess the magnitude of maternal mortality globally, Boerma argued that such studies within the sub-Saharan region are scarce, of varying quality, and lacking in universal coverage of the population.

Besides the aforementioned argument, many countries still lack well-functioning civil registration and vital statistics (CRVS) systems; and where such systems do exist, reporting errors continue to pose a challenge to data accuracy. More recently, Damian, Njau, Lisasi, Msuya, and Boulle (2019) reported that most studies have shown a tendency to be biased downwards, and therefore underestimate the mortality risk. Furthermore, the estimates derived from different reporting institutions provided conflicting results. There is, therefore, a need to apply additional estimation techniques which utilize available multiple data sources to correct for underreporting. Understanding more efficient methods of estimating maternal mortality will be useful in obtaining accurate data on maternal mortality in the continent. Besides this, population-based surveys of different kinds including censuses are increasingly being used to assess the magnitude of maternal mortality, but such studies are scarce in Africa (Boerma, 1988).

Several studies have linked maternal mortality to both clinical and non-clinical factors. For instance, Olonade, Olawande, Alabi, and Imhonopi (2019) noted in their study that apart from medical-related causes which can be direct or indirect, certain socio-cultural and socioeconomic factors influence the outcome of pregnancies. According to the WHO (2019), poverty, distance to health facilities, lack of information, inadequate and poor-quality services, and cultural belief practices are major determinants of the high rate of maternal mortality in sub-Saharan Africa.

While attempts have been made by extant studies to examine the magnitude, measurement, and determinants of maternal mortality in sub-Saharan Africa, a systematic review on the levels, measurement and determinants of maternal mortality have received little attention. To the best of our knowledge, there are few or no single studies involving a review of the three indicators. Besides, the Sustainable Development Goal (SDG) Target 3.1 seeks to reduce the global maternal mortality ratio to less than 70 per 100,000 live births by 2030, and for this to be achievable, there is a need for a more elaborate review of studies for a better understanding of the magnitude, efficient methods of estimation, and determinants of maternal mortality. Our review tends to highlight the underlying challenges of understanding the issues around maternal mortality in Sub-Saharan Africa, which would be useful for informing policies and improving maternal health.

This paper, through a systematic review of past studies, examined methods of measurement, levels, and determinants of maternal mortality in sub-Saharan Africa to identify new approaches in the measurement of maternal mortality and obtain accurate information on maternal mortality data between the period 1990–2020.

Methodology

Published peer-reviewed journal articles and relevant grey literature were reviewed to identify primary research articles focussing on the levels, measurement, and determinants of maternal mortality in Africa or sub-Saharan African countries. We use the United Nations definition of sub-Saharan Africa to refer to the geographical and ethnographic area of the African continent that lies south of the Sahara Desert and includes 46 of Africa's 54 countries (excluding Algeria, Djibouti, Egypt, Libya, Morocco, Somalia, Sudan, and Tunisia). An electronic search was conducted using online databases such as Scopus, PubMed, Medline, Google Scholar, Research Gate, and publications of Elsevier and *The Lancet*. Also, the Google search engine was used to identify grey literature not published in peer-reviewed journals and the references of all identified literature were manually screened. A combination of keywords was used, including sub-Saharan Africa and each of the individual countries in the region. Also, key terms for mortality and maternal mortality were included in the search. We focussed on research on maternal mortality primarily conducted in the African continent by African scholars, and then the search was widened to include scholars from other countries. Preference was given to publications and literature dating 1990 to 2020 except when the paper was particularly relevant. The reason was to capture a wide range of methods used in measuring maternal mortality and identify factors that are mostly associated with maternal mortality over the decades. Moreover, since Africa recorded a remarkable reduction in maternal mortality during the period 1990, it is therefore important to understand how much progress sub-Saharan Africa has made in the reduction of maternal mortality in the last thirty years. We defined maternal mortality based on the WHO (ICD-10) definition of death as 'the death of a woman while pregnant or within 42 days (six weeks) of the termination of pregnancy; irrespective of the duration and site of the pregnancy, from any cause related to or aggravated by the pregnancy or its management but not from accidental or incidental causes' (WHO, 2004).

Since the aim of this study was to identify the levels, measurement, and determinants of maternal mortality, original quantitative, qualitative, and analytical studies that met these criteria were included in the review. Specifically, studies that provided estimates of levels and measurements of maternal mortality derived directly or from surveys were included. Other grey literature such as publications of the World Health Organization, UNICEF, UNFPA, World Bank, and relevant working papers were included in the study. However, commentaries, and experimental studies and unpublished papers were excluded from the review. Also, studies were excluded if they were not undertaken in Africa or without a specific focus on the sub-Saharan African region.

Search strategies and inclusion criteria

Medical subject heading (MeSH) terms were used to search for relevant information; these included 'maternal mortality', 'maternal mortality in sub-Saharan Africa', 'estimates of maternal mortality', 'measurements and determinants of maternal mortality in Africa'. After removing duplicates and abstracts which did not include the search terms, 56 journal articles and grey literature that analyzed the levels, measurements and determinants of maternal mortality in Africa were systematically reviewed.

Definitions

It is important to establish some definitions since many sources have differing definitions. For instance, the maternal mortality ratio and maternal mortality rate are used interchangeably in the literature to mean the number of maternal deaths per 100,000 live births. However, the WHO distinguishes between the two. On the one hand, maternal mortality ratio is the true measure of the risk of death associated with a woman once she has become pregnant and is defined as the number of maternal deaths per 100,000 live births. On the other hand, the maternal mortality rate is the number of maternal deaths in a given period per 100,000 women of reproductive age during the same period.

For our study, we have defined the maternal mortality rate as the number of maternal deaths (direct and indirect) in a given period per 100,000 women of reproductive age (generally 15–49 years) during the same time period. By focussing on women of reproductive age, it captures the likelihood of both becoming pregnant and dying during pregnancy.

There is a third measure, the lifetime risk (LTR), or probability, of maternal death. Whereas the maternal mortality ratio and maternal mortality rate are respectively measures of the frequency of maternal deaths in relation to the number of live births, or to the female population of reproductive age, the lifetime risk of maternal mortality describes the cumulative loss of life due to maternal death over the female life course, and it provides a better summary measure of the impact of maternal mortality: it is usually expressed as the probability that a 15-year-old girl will eventually die from maternal and childbirth-related causes (Wilmoth, 2009). Other measures are pregnancy-related mortality ratio and pregnancy-related mortality rate. Pregnancy-related mortality ratio (PRMR) is the number of pregnancy-related deaths per 100,000 live births. In other words, PRMR is calculated by dividing the total pregnancy-related mortality rate by the general fertility rate for the same period and is expressed per 100,000 live births. On the other hand, pregnancy-related mortality rate is the number of resident deaths of individuals within 42 days of pregnancy termination due to any cause in a specified geographic area (country, state, county, etc.) divided by total resident live births for the same geographic area for a specified time period, usually a calendar year, and multiplied by 100,000. The PRMR captures pregnancy related deaths, and therefore a more specific measure than pregnancy-related mortality rate which includes mortality from both pregnancy and non-pregnancy related cause.

Generally, there are challenges associated with these measurement indicators due to lack of accurate data and no single data collection method is adequate for investigating all aspects of maternal mortality. Besides, most countries in sub-Saharan Africa do not have vital registration systems to provide reliable data; hence, population based surveys are the primary source of information for measuring maternal mortality.

Findings

Measures (indicators) of maternal mortality

The new global target as reflected in the Sustainable Development Goal 3 is to reduce maternal death to 70 by 2030. However, measuring maternal mortality remains a major challenge in sub-Saharan Africa as indicated by most of the studies reviewed. The most common measure of maternal mortality is the maternal mortality ratio (MMR). MMR is defined as the number of maternal deaths per 100,000 live births. MMR was used in measuring maternal mortality in almost all the studies except for one study in sub-Saharan Africa that used age-standardized maternal mortality rates (MMRates) and proportions of maternal death (Merdad & Ali, 2018).

Table 40.1 Methods for Measuring Maternal Mortality and Data Source

References	*Region/Country*	*Maternal mortality estimation methods*	*Measures of maternal mortality*	*Data source*
Bomela, 2020	South Africa	Direct estimation	MMR	Statistics South Africa, vital registration
Ohunene et al., 2019	Nigeria	Sisterhood method	MMR	Community study
WHO/UNICEF/UNFPA/The World Bank, 2019	Sub-Saharan Africa	Sisterhood method, sibling- history	MMR, MMRates, LTR	Surveys, health services reports, civil registration, censuses, and disease surveillance systems
Gulumbe, Alabi, Omisakin, & Omolek, 2018	Nigeria	Sisterhood method	LTR, MMR	Community Survey
Merdad and Ali, 2018	Sub-Saharan Africa	Sibling-history	Age-standardized MMRates and proportions	Demographic Health Survey (DHS)
Sharma, Brown, Kainuwa, Leight, & Nyqvist, 2017	Nigeria	Sisterhood method	MMR	Community Survey, civil registration
Mgawadere, Unkels, Adegoke, & van den Broek, 2016	Malawi	Direct estimation	MMR	RAMOS, Health facility and population data
Pierre-Marie et al., 2015	Cameroon	Direct estimation	Mean MMR	Hospital register
Udjo et al., 2014	South Africa	Growth Balance Method, relational Gompertz model	MMR	Census, Community Survey and death registrations
Montoya, Calvert, & Filippi, 2014	Sub-Saharan Africa	Meta-analysis	MMR	Hospital-based studies
DerSarkissian, Thompson, & Arah, 2013	Africa	Statistical model-based	Mean MMR, Standard deviation	Global agencies
Doctor et al., 2012	Nigeria	Sisterhood method, Sibling history	MMR, LTR	Household survey
Mojekwu and Ibekwe, 2012	Nigeria	Statistical model-based	MMR, MMRates, LTR	Bureau of Statistics
Garenne, McCaa, & Nacro, 2011	South Africa	Direct estimation	MMR	Community Survey
Oye-Adeniran et al., 2011	Nigeria	Sisterhood method	MMR	Population-based
Garenne, McCaa, & Nacro, 2008	South Africa	Direct estimation	MMR	Census

(*Continued*)

Table 40.1 (Continued)

References	*Region/Country*	*Maternal mortality estimation methods*	*Measures of maternal mortality*	*Data source*
Olapade and Lawoyin, 2008	Nigeria	Direct estimation	MMR	Hospital records
Hill et al., 2007	Sub-Saharan Africa	Direct estimation	MMR	All available data
Rogo, Oucho, & Philip Mwalali, 2006	Sub-Saharan Africa	Sisterhood method, sibling-history and household deaths	MMR, MMRates, LTR	WHO, UNICEF Population-based data, vital registration
Ujah et al., 2005	Nigeria	Direct estimation	MMR	Hospital records
Mbaruku, Vork, Vyagusa, Mwakipiti, & van Roosmalen, 2003	Tanzania	Sisterhood method	MMR	Community survey
Etard, Kodio, & Traoré, 1999	Mali	Direct estimation	MMR, late maternal mortality	Prospective cohort study Community inquiries, the maternity units and the reference hospital
Garenne et al., 1997	Burkina Faso	Direct and Sisterhood method	MMR	Retrospective study
Oosterbaan, 1995	Guinea-Bissau	Direct estimation	MMR	Verbal autopsies, hospital and health centre records.
Martey, Djan, Twum, Browne, & Opoku, 1994	Ghana	Sisterhood method	MMR	Community-based survey

Note: *MMR = Maternal mortality ratio, MMRates = Maternal mortality rates, LTR = Lifetime risk.

Data sources and estimation methods

As previously mentioned, there are varieties of data sources for estimating maternal mortality, with the gold standard being data collected through a vital registration system. However, nationally representative, accurate, and complete registration of deaths is routinely unavailable in most sub-Saharan countries. Because of this, censuses, population-based household surveys (for instance the Demographic and Health Surveys), reproductive-age mortality studies, hospital records, and other confidential enquiries into maternal deaths are used as alternative data sources for obtaining maternal mortality information at the national level.

From our systematic review, the most widely used method for estimating maternal mortality was the sisterhood and sibling history method, reported in 10 (40%) of the studies reviewed. Notably, most of these studies utilized data from large surveys such as the Demographic and Health Survey, retrospective studies, and community-based surveys. In these surveys, women respondents were asked to list all their siblings, and for each sibling, information about their survival is explored. For female siblings who have died at age 12 or older, the interviewer inquires about their years since death, and whether or not the sister's death was associated with pregnancy, childbirth, or in the two months following delivery (Ahmed, Li, Scrafford, & Pullum, 2014).

Another nine studies employed the direct estimation method using maternal death records from various sources such as hospital registers or vital registration, censuses, prospective cohort study, reproductive-age mortality studies (RAMOS), and verbal autopsy. Of these, reproductive-age mortality studies are considered the best approach in the absence of vital registration. In this case, all deaths among women of reproductive age are identified using a variety of sources including health facility records, reports of community deaths, and census data. If these deaths were pregnancy- or childbirth-related, then they are identified as maternal deaths and then are subsequently reviewed to determine the underlying cause of death and contributing conditions.

Statistical models are now being increasingly used for estimating maternal mortality in developing countries lacking functional vital registration systems using covariates such as the general fertility, access to maternal healthcare, socio-economic factors, and geographic characteristics amongst others to explain the variation in maternal mortality at a sub-national level. Our review also identified three studies – one in South Africa (Udjo et al., 2014), one in Nigeria (Mojekwu & Ibekwe, 2012), and another one in the Central, Southern, East, and West African region (DerSarkissian, 2013), which used innovative statistical techniques to model the risk factors (both observed and unobserved) associated with maternal death. A study by Montoya and colleagues used meta-analysis to examine the patterns of hospital-based maternal mortality of 64 hospitals located in 16 countries in sub-Saharan Africa (Montoya et al., 2014). With meta-analysis, different results from multiple scientific studies can be combined and pooled together to provide evidence, while taking into account the heterogeneity of the various studies. Hospital-based studies are often more reliable as a form of direct estimation because information about the maternal cause of death is routinely collected, and in most cases is a statutory requirement for death certification. Notably, five out of the nine studies that used direct estimation were hospital-based, while two studies in South Africa used vital registration and census data (Bomela, 2020; Garenne et al., 2008). Meanwhile, one study in Burkina Faso employed direct and sisterhood methods (Garenne et al., 1997).

Levels and trends

There are large variations between countries in the magnitude of maternal mortality, with a few countries having extremely high maternal mortality ratios (MMR) of 1,000 or more per

Table 40.2 Levels of Maternal Mmortality in Selected Sub-Saharan African Countries

Region/Country	*MMR/100,000 live births*	*(UI)*	*Lifetime risk of maternal deaths*	*Period of report*
Sub-Saharan Africa	534	490–636	36	2000–2017
South Sudan	1,150	789–1,710	18	2000–2017
Chad	1,140	847–1,590	15	2000–2017
Sierra Leone	1,120	808–1,620	20	2000–2017
Nigeria	917	658–1,320	21	2000–2017
Central African Republic	829	463–1,470	25	2000–2017
Somalia	829	385–1,590	20	2000–2017
Mauritania	776	528–1,140	28	2000–2017
Guinea Bissau	667	457–995	32	2000–2017
Liberia	661	481–943	32	2000–2017
Côte d'Ivoire	617	426–896	34	2000–2017
Gambia	597	440–808	31	2000–2017
Guinea	576	437–779	35	2000–2017
Mali	562	419–784	29	2000–2017
Burundi	548	413–728	33	2000–2017
Lesotho	544	391–788	58	2000–2017
Cameroon	529	376–760	40	2000–2017
United Republic of Tanzania	524	399–712	36	2000–2017
Niger	509	368–724	27	2000–2017
Eritrea	480	327–718	46	
Democratic Republic of Congo	473	341–693	34	2000–2017
Zimbabwe	458	360–577	55	2000–2017
Eswatini	437	255–792	72	2000–2017
Ethiopia	401	298–573	55	2000–2017
Equatorial Guinea	301	181–504	67	2000–2017
Ghana	308	223–420	82	2000–2017
Senegal	315	237–434	65	2000–2017
Burkina Faso	320	220–454	57	2000–2017
Madagascar	335	229–484	66	2000–2017
Kenya	342	253–476	76	2000–2017
Malawi	349	244–507	60	2000–2017
Uganda	375	278–523	49	2000–2017
Congo	378	271–523	58	2000–2017
Togo	396	270–557	56	2000–2017
Benin	397	291–570	49	2000–2017
Mauritius	61	46–85	1,200	2000–2017
Cape Verde	58	45–75	670	2000–2017
Seychelles	53	26–109	790	2000–2017

Source: WHO, UNICEF, World Bank Group, and the United Nations Population Division (2019)

*Only countries categorized as having extremely high (>1,000), very high (500–999), high (300–499), and very low (<100) MMR were included in the table.

Notes:

(a) The 80% uncertainty intervals (UI) computed for all the estimates provide the 10th and 90th percentiles of the posterior distributions. These intervals of precision are chosen rather than the more standard 95% UIs because of the substantial uncertainty inherent in maternal mortality outcomes.

(b) The adult lifetime risk of maternal death for women in the population is defined as the probability that a 15-year-old girl in the year of the estimate will eventually die from a maternal cause of death. Because it is a probability, it is interpreted as 1 in displayed value in the table. For instance, sub-Saharan lifetime risk is 1 in 36.

100,000 live births; and there are large disparities within countries and between people with high and low income per 100,000 live births (WHO, 2014). Similarly, a recent UNICEF report revealed that the majority of maternal death recorded among women of reproductive age in sub-Saharan Africa is among young adolescents aged 10–14 years (UNICEF, 2019).

Results in Table 40.2 show estimates of the maternal mortality ratio and lifetime risk of maternal deaths in the sub-Saharan African region and countries from the year 2000 to 2017 (WHO, UNICEF, World Bank Group, & United Nations Population Division, 2019). All the maternal mortality indicators derived from the WHO also include a point estimate and an 80% uncertainty interval arranged in descending order as depicted by the five major groups into which countries are categorized (extremely high, very high, high, low, very low) depending on the severity of their maternal mortality ratio or otherwise. Countries in the first category are those with a extremely high maternal mortality ratio, i.e. countries with over 1,000 maternal deaths per 100,000 live births. These countries are Chad, Sierra Leone, and South Sudan. Nigeria, apart from recording the highest estimated number of maternal deaths accounting for about 23% of the global estimate in 2017, also took the lead among the fifteen countries in sub-Saharan Africa reported having been in the second group of countries with a very high maternal mortality ratio in 2017 (i.e. estimates ranging between 500 and 999). Only three countries in sub-Saharan Africa are in the group with a very low maternal mortality ratio, namely: Mauritius (61), Cape Verde (58), and the Seychelles (53). Notably, Chad and Mauritius have extremely high and low lifetime risks of maternal deaths of 15 and 1,200 respectively.

Determinants

The relationship between maternal mortality and several factors was identified in almost 50% of the studies included in this review. These factors were grouped into three themes (socio-economic and demographic; cultural practices; behavioural, health; and water, sanitation, and hygiene-related), and the results and their references are summarized in Table 40.3. Of the 28 studies on the determinants of maternal mortality, 6 were conducted in sub-Saharan Africa, 10 in Nigeria, 2 in Ethiopia, 3 in South Africa, and 1 each in Zimbabwe, Burkina Faso, Malawi, Cameroon, and Guinea Bissau; and 2 studies were carried out for the whole of Africa.

Socio-economic determinants

Socio-economic determinants were reported in 17 studies and the most widely reported socio-economic factors influencing maternal mortality that were cited in 12 out of the 17 studies were educational level and illiteracy. A study conducted in Nigeria and South Africa indicated that maternal education was the primary determinant of maternal mortality. Women with no schooling or illiterate women were associated with a very high maternal mortality ratio (Garenne et al., 2007; Ujah et al., 2005). Another common factor associated with maternal mortality was economic status; this was cited by 7 studies. One study in Nigeria found that community wealth was significantly associated with maternal mortality in the south (Azuh et al., 2017), and the likelihood of maternal death decreased with increasing community wealth (Meh et al., 2019). Besides, Harrison (1997) in his study attributed maternal mortality to mass poverty. Conversely, in another study, no significant relationship was observed between other economic indicators with maternal mortality except the gross national income per capita, the per-capita government expenditure on health, and the out-of-pocket expenditure on health (Alvarez et al., 2009).

Table 40.3 Description of Factors Associated with Maternal Mortality and Countries or Research

Authors	*Region /Country*	*Socio-economic/Demographic*	*Cultural practices*	*Behavioural/health and WaSH-related (Water and Sanitary Hygiene)*
Bomela, 2020	South Africa	Maternal age, education, marital status, occupation	-	-
Batist, 2019	Sub-Saharan Africa	Educational disparities, economic inequalities, insufficient access to financial resources, health expenditure per capita	Sociocultural gender inequities	Access to adequate nutrition, health, and hygiene
Crago, 2019	LMICS (including Africa)	-	-	Access to clean water; inadequate sanitary practices; exposure to dirty, stagnant water
Meh, Thind, Ryan, & Terry, 2019	Nigeria	Media exposure, education, residence type and wealth index, age	Prevalence of polygamy, religion, female agency	-
Olonade et al, 2019	Nigeria	Socio-economic development and poverty, urbanity/rurality, geographic isolation	Female agency, belief systems around pregnancy and childbirth	-
Sharma et al., 2017	Nigeria	Age, time of death, age of deceased sister, age at marriage	-	Effectiveness of health system in provision of maternal and child services
Mgawadere et al., 2016	Malawi	Age, illiteracy, teenage mother, marital status	-	Pregnancy-related infections, health-seeking behaviour, poor health facility, skilled birth attendants
Songa, Macline, & Rakuom, 2015	Sub-Saharan Africa	socio-economic status, inequity of health provision	-	Poor health management, water quality and quantity, distance to water source, menstrual hygiene, clean cord-cutting, antenatal care and water in medical facility, staff training, hygiene and cleanliness
Pierre-Marie et al., 2015	Cameroon			Lack of antenatal care
Yaya, Data, & Llndtjorn, 2015	Ethiopia	No road access, illiterate male partner	-	-

Ogunjimi, Ibe, & Ikorok, 2012	Nigeria	Maternal age, educational attainment, economic status, poor socio-economic development	Early marriage, female genital mutilation	Antenatal attendance, weak health care system
Ijadunola, Ijadunola, Esimai, & Abiona, 2010	Nigeria	-	-	Lack of access to emergency obstetric care, poor staff training, lack of knowledge among health staff
Alvarez, Gil, Hernandez, & Gil, 2009	Sub-Saharan Africa	Educational disparity, socio-economic status	-	Poor healthcare services, lack of skilled personnel, sanitary condition, lack of access to improved water source.
Ethiopian Society of Population Studies, 2008	Ethiopia	Age and sex of sibling, time of death relative to pregnancy, childbirth poverty	Harmful traditional practices	Lack of access to health care services, low utilization of health services, health-care-seeking behaviour, health status, postpartum period, high fertility, malnutrition
Okonofua, 2008	Africa	Socio-economic disempowerment, poverty, illiteracy, ignorance	Harmful traditional practices	Quality of healthcare, poor health infrastructure.
Garenne et.al., 2008	South Africa	Education, socio-economic status	-	-
Rogo et al., 2006	Sub-Saharan Africa	Social status, education, age, parity, income	-	Availability of health services and water sanitation, nutrition status
Oladapo, Lamina, & Fakoya, 2006	Nigeria	-	-	Booking status (previous birth history, complications), deficiency in health care facilities, poor quality of maternal care
Grieco and Turner, 2005	Africa	Constraints on mobility, socio-economic status	-	Poor accessibility to health facilities.
Ujah et al., 2005	Nigeria	Educational disparity, socio-economic status, high prevalence of illiteracy	Ethnic status	Booking status (previous birth history, complications)
Buor and Bream, 2004	Sub-Saharan Africa	Life expectancy at birth, socio-economic status	-	Lack of adequate health care services, poor staff training
Okaro et al., 2001	Nigeria	-	-	Effective measures for tackling obstetric complications

(Continued)

Table 40.3 (Continued)

Authors	*Region /Country*	*Socio-economic/Demographic*	*Cultural practices*	*Behavioural/health and WaSH-related (Water and Sanitary Hygiene)*
Shen and Williamson, 1999	Sub-Saharan Africa	Education, economic status, age of pregnant woman	social customs and traditions, sex discrimination, teenage (mother) marriage	Health-care-seeking, behaviour, malnutrition
Wall, 1998	Nigeria	Poverty, education	Islamic culture that undervalues status of women	Poor access to health care
Fawcus, Mbizvo, Lindmark, & Nystrom, 1996	Zimbabwe	Socio-economic status, lack of transportation, geographic isolation	-	Lack of appropriately trained personnel, suboptimal clinic and hospital management, delayed or prevented access to health care facilities
Garenne et al., 1997	Burkina Faso	Age, socio-economic status	-	Lack of adequate health care services
Harrison, 1997	Nigeria	Poverty, illiteracy, Socio-economic status.	-	Unbooked emergencies
Oosterbaan, 1995	Guinea Bissau	Distance to hospital	Home delivery, ethnicity, religion	No antenatal care, delivery assistance by Traditional Birth Attendants

Demographic determinants

Demographic factors were cited in 10 studies. Of all the demographic factors, maternal age was the most common (cited in 9 out of 10 studies). A community study in Malawi using a Reproductive Age Mortality Survey (RAMOS) indicated that young maternal age was associated with high maternal mortality (Mgawadere et al., 2016). The study revealed that the proportion of adolescent maternal death (15–19 years) was 15.2 % (23 out of 151 deaths) while 6% (9 out of 151) maternal deaths were for women aged 40 years and older. Three out of 10 studies cited marital status as an important determinant of maternal mortality. In particular, a study in South Africa showed that unmarried women had the highest number of maternal deaths (Bomela, 2020).

Cultural practices associated with maternal mortality

Nine of the studies cited some cultural and traditional practices associated with maternal mortality, such as socio-cultural gender inequalities or discrimination, religious and cultural practices that undervalue women, early marriage, female genital mutilation, and other social customs and traditions. One study posited that maternal mortality needs to be framed as a human rights issue, and indicated a high correlation between maternal mortality ratios and gender inequalities as it relates to the systemic accessibility of health services (Batist, 2019). The study further explained that gender inequalities were embedded within the fabric of many sub-Saharan African countries, including Nigeria, Tanzania, and Kenya, where patriarchy or male-dominated social ideals and norms persist and continue to silence and marginalize African women. Another study, this time situated in northern Nigeria, reported that Hausa women were not valued, subjected to assume a subordinate and servile position in life by their (Islamic) religion, and forced into early marriage (Wall, 1998). This subordination prevents them from accessing life-saving health care when they are pregnant and often led to complications during childbirth and maternal mortality. A similar study in Nigeria indicated that early marriage accounted for about 23% of maternal mortality in 2012 (Ogunjimi et al., 2012). It is well established that there are geographical and socio-cultural determinants of early marriage; and early marriage makes young girls liable to pregnancy, maternal morbidity and mortality (Amoako, Abu, & Utazi, 2019). Besides, Olonade, Olawande, Alabi, and Imhonopi (2019) noted that apart from medical-related causes which can be direct or indirect, certain socio-cultural factors influence maternal mortality. The authors indicated that some cultures forbid pregnant women from eating eggs and snails which are needed for the supply of nutrients to the mother and baby during pregnancy, and this may lead to incidences of high iron deficiency or anaemia that consequently leads to death if not well managed.

Behavioural determinants

In two of the studies conducted in Guinea Bissau and Cameroon, the lack of antenatal care attendance and delivery assisted by traditional birth attendants (TBAs) were reported as important determinants of maternal mortality (Oosterbaan, 1995; Pierre-Marie, 2015).

Health and health care system determinants

Health and health care system-related determinants were reported in 19 studies. In one study conducted in Zimbabwe, lack of appropriately trained personnel, suboptimal clinic and hospital management, and delayed or prevented access to health care facilities were cited as the major determinants of maternal mortality (Fawcus et al., 1996). Another study in Nigeria reported that maternal mortality was associated with lack of access to emergency obstetric care, poor staff training, and lack of knowledge among health staff (Ijadunola et al., 2010). Alvarez and colleagues reported significant correlation of maternal mortality rate in sub-Saharan Africa with prenatal care coverage and births assisted by skilled health personnel (Alvarez et al., 2009). Of the 19 studies that reported health and health care system determinants, three papers cited malnutrition as important determinants of maternal mortality.

Water, sanitation, and hygiene (WASH)

Of the 28 papers selected, 4 reported that water, sanitation, and hygiene were associated with maternal mortality. Our systematic review yielded a study by Songa and colleagues who studied the link between water, sanitation, and hygiene and maternal health, and identified that other extant factors were associated with poorer maternal outcomes – for example, personal and menstrual hygiene, and birth attendant hygiene during and after delivery (Songa et al., 2015). The study also found that increased access to improved water sources and improved sanitation is significantly associated with decreased maternal mortality ratios. These results were confirmed by another study using meta-analyzed data from studies undertaken between 1997 and 2006 and found that decreasing maternal mortality was significantly correlated with increasing access to improved water sources such as piped water, public tap, borehole or pump, or protected well (Alvarez et al., 2009). Yet another study by Crago (2019) indicated that an estimated 8% of maternal deaths (and up to 15% in lower-middle-income countries [LMICs] including Africa) could be directly linked to unhygienic conditions during labour, birth, and poor post-natal hygiene.

Discussion

The results included in this study are based on 56 original studies with various designs which have examined either levels and determinants or methods of maternal mortality estimation in sub-Saharan Africa. These studies were found by systematically searching eight electronic databases. Based on this, we find that maternal mortality in sub-Saharan Africa is estimated at 533 per 100,000 live births – the comparative figure for Europe is 8 per 100,000. While this highlights the growing disparity in maternal health outcomes between the developing and developed countries, our systematic review found that even within sub-Saharan Africa, there was also heterogeneity in maternal mortality ratios. The figure varied between a low MMR of 53 deaths per 100,000 live births in the Seychelles and a high of 1,140 deaths per 100,000 births in Chad.

However, these national estimates of maternal mortality in most of sub-Saharan Africa are based on limited or incomplete data. This problem is exacerbated in high-mortality countries where firstly the majority of births are not in a health facility, and subsequently, the majority of deaths go unregistered. The lack of data was revealed in the methods used for estimating maternal mortality because the majority of the studies reviewed used the indirect sisterhood method. The WHO report also confirmed that accurate measurement of MM levels remains an immense challenge in SSA and hundreds of thousands of women are still dying due to complications of pregnancy and/or childbirth (WHO, 2015). The African Panel reported in 2010 that one of the major obstacles countries face among others to improve maternal health is insufficient data which prevents ministries from implementing programmes most effectively (African Progress Panel, 2010).

In the absence of complete civil registration and vital statistics (CRVS), countries in sub-Saharan Africa are using specialized studies on mortality such as surveillance systems, national registries, Demographic and Health Surveys, censuses, and reproductive age studies to directly or indirectly measure maternal mortality. Finally, maternal mortality is impacted and influenced by several medical, socio-economic, demographic, behavioural, and cultural factors, and these are particularly evidenced in sub-Saharan Africa. The differences between those countries with low and high maternal mortality were government investment on health and education, access to health care, training and supervision of traditional birth attendants, gender equity, water, sanitation and hygiene practices, and poverty.

Limitations

The literature survey identified a vast number of articles on maternal health but in regard to the specific topic of the levels, measurement, and determinants of maternal mortality in sub-Saharan Africa, this was distinctly lacking. Much of the literature reviewed is of relatively small studies which are location-specific and do not allow us to make large-scale evidence-based generalizations over the whole of the sub-Saharan African region. Furthermore, issues such as the impact of HIV/AIDS, political systems, and the impact of environmental factors such as climate change have not been discussed. Nonetheless, this review provides a stepping stone for other researchers to undertake more rigorous studies on these issues vis-à-vis maternal mortality.

Conclusion

Understanding the levels, measurement, and determinants of maternal mortality in sub-Saharan Africa is critically important for addressing the inequities in maternal health outcomes in developing and developed countries, and working towards the SDG target 3.1 which seeks to reduce all preventable maternal mortality by 2030. However, it is impossible to develop policy and interventions to reduce maternal deaths without ameliorating the barriers due to the systemic factors that plague sub-Saharan Africa. This review has demonstrated that a proper assessment of the levels, measurement, and determinants of maternal death in sub-Saharan Africa remains difficult due to the lack of complete and accurate data, and without dramatic investment in data collection (through a country-specific complete civil registration and vital statistics) there is likely to be no improvement envisaged soon.

Agenda for future research

Future research on maternal mortality in Africa could address the issue of reliable data sources, use of routing health information, censuses, and refinement of estimation methods, particularly the indirect sisterhood method which is the most commonly used. In addition, future agendas could focus on the role of health systems, governance, and community engagement in the fight for maternal survival.

References

Africa Progress Panel. (2010, September). *Maternal health: Investing in the lifeline of healthy societies and economies* [Policy brief]. Geneva: Africa Progress Panel.

Ahmed, S., Li, Q., Scrafford, C., & Pullum, T. W. (2014). *DHS methodological reports number 13: An assessment of DHS maternal mortality data and estimates*. Rockville, MD: ICF International.

Alvarez, J. L., Gil, G., Hernandez, V., & Gil, A. (2009). Factors associated with maternal mortality in sub-Saharan Africa: An ecological study. *BMC Public Health, 9*, 462. https://doi.org/10.1186/1471-2458-9-462

Amoako, J. F., Abu, M., & Utazi, C. E. (2019). Geospatial correlates of early marriage and union formation in Ghana. *PLoS One, 14*(10), e0223296. https://doi.org/10.1371/journal.pone.0223296

Azuh, D. E., Azuh, A. E., Iweala, E. J., Adeloye, D., Akanbi, M., & Mordi, R. (2017). Factors influencing maternal mortality among rural communities in South-Western Nigeria. *International Journal of Women's Health, 9*, 179–188. http://doi.org/10.2147/IJWH.SI20184

Batist, J. (2019). An intersectional analysis of maternal mortality in sub-Saharan Africa: A human right issue. *Journal of Global Health, 9*(1). http://doi.org/10.7189/jogh.09.010320

Boerma, J. T. (1988). Maternal mortality in sub-Saharan Africa: Levels, causes and interventions. *Annual IFORD, 12*(1), 49–68.

Bomela, N. J. (2020). Maternal mortality by socio-demographic characteristics and cause of death in South Africa: 2007–2015. *BMC Public Health, 20*, 157.

Buor, D., & Bream, K. (2004). An analysis of the determinants of maternal mortality in sub-Saharan Africa. *Journal of Women's Health, 13*(8), 926–938.

Crago, J. (2019). *Poor WASH leaves women behind*. FIGO (The International Federation of Gynecology and Obstetrics). Retrieved from www.figo.org/

Damian, J. D., Njau, B., Lisasi, E., Msuya, S. E., & Boulle, A. (2019). Trends in maternal and neonatal mortality in South Africa: A systematic review. *BMC Systematic Reviews, 8*, 76.

DerSarkissian, M., Thompson, C. A., & Arah, O. A. (2013). Time series analysis of maternal mortality in Africa from 1990 to 2005. *Journal of Epidemiology and Community Health, 67*(12). http://doi.org/10.1136/jech-2013-202565

Doctor, H. V., Olatunji, A., Findley, S. E., Afenyadu, G. Y., Abdulwahab, A., & Jumare, A. (2012). Maternal mortality in northern Nigeria: Findings of a health and demographic surveillance system in Zamfara State, Nigeria. *Tropical Doctor, 42*(3), 140–143. http://doi.org/10.1258/td.2012.120062

Etard, J. F., Kodio, B., & Traoré, S. (1999). Assessment of maternal mortality and late maternal mortality among a cohort of pregnant women in Bamako, Mali. *British Journal of Obstetrics and Gynaecology, 106*(1), 60–65. http://doi.org/10.1111/j.1471–0528.1999.tb08086.x

Ethiopian Society of Population Studies. (2008, October). *Maternal Mortality Findings from EDHS2005*. Addis Ababa: Ethiopian Society of Population Studies.

Fawcus, S., Mbizvo, M., Lindmark, G., & Nystrom, L. (1996). A community – based Investigation of avoidable factors for maternal mortality in Zimbabwe. *Studies in Family Planning, 27*(6), 319–327.

Garenne, M., McCan, R., & Nacro, K. (2007, 10–14 December). *Maternal mortality in South Africa in 2001: From census to epidemiology*. A paper Prepared for the UAPS Conference, Arush.

Garenne, M., McCaa, R., & Nacro, K. (2008). Maternal mortality in South Africa in 2001: From demographic census to epidemiological investigation. *Population Health Metrics, 21*(6), 4. http://doi.org/10.1186/1478–7954–64

Garenne, M., McCaa, R., & Nacro, K. (2011). Maternal mortality in South Africa: An update from the 2007 Community Survey. *Population Research, 8*(1), 89–101. http://doi.org/10.1007/s12546–010-9037-y

Garenne, M., Sauerborn, R., Nougtara, A., Borchert, M., Benzler, J., & Diesfeld, J. (1997). Direct and indirect estimates of maternal mortality in rural Burkina Faso. *Studies in Family Planning, 28*(1), 54–61.

Grieco, M., & Turner, J. (2005). *Maternal Mortality: Africa's Burden. Toolkit on Gender, transport and maternal mortality*. Retrieved from www.people.cornell.edu./pages/mg294/maternal mortlity.html

Gulumbe, S., Alabi, O., Omisakin, O. A., & Omolek, S. (2018). Maternal mortality ratio in selected rural communities in Kebbi State, Northwest Nigeria. *BMC Pregnancy and Childbirth, 18*, 503.

Harrison, K. A. (1997). Maternal mortality in Nigeria: The real issues. *African Journal of Reproductive Health, 1*(1), 7–13.

Hill, K., Thomas, K., Abouzahr, C., Walker, N., Say, L., Inoue, M., & Suzuki, E. (2007). Estimates of maternal mortality worldwide between 1990 and 2005: An assessment of available data. *The Lancet, 370(9595*), 1311–1319.

Ijadunola, K. T., Ijadunola, M. Y., Esimai, O. A., & Abiona, T. C. (2010). New paradigm old thinking: The case for emergency obstetric care in the prevention of maternal mortality in Nigeria. *BMC Women Health, 10,* 6. Retrieved from www.biomedcentral.com/1472-6874/10/6

Martey, J. O., Djan, J. O., Twum, S., Browne, E. N., & Opoku, S. A. (1994). Maternal mortality and related factors in Ejisu District, Ghana. *East African Medical Journal, 71*(10), 656–660.

Mbaruku, G., Vork, F., Vyagusa, D., Mwakipiti, R., & van Roosmalen, J. (2003). Estimates of maternal mortality in western Tanzania by the sisterhood method. *African Journal of Reproductive Health, 7*(3), 84–91.

Meh, C., Thind, A., Ryan, B., & Terry, A. (2019). Levels and determinants of maternal mortality in northern and southern Nigeria. *BMC Pregnancy and Childbirth, 19*, 417.

Merdad, L., & Ali, M. M. (2018). Timing of maternal death: Levels, trends and ecological correlates using sibling data from 34 Sub-Saharan African countries. *PLoS One, 13*(1), e0189416.

Mgawadere, F., Kana, T., & van den Broek, N. (2017). Measuring maternal mortality: A systematic review of methods used to obtain estimates of the maternal mortality ratio (MMR) in low-and middle-income countries. *British Medical Bulletin, 121*, 121–134. http://doi.org/10.1093/bmb/ldw056

Mgawadere, F., Unkels, R., Adegoke, A., & van den Broek, N. (2016). Measuring maternal mortality using a Reproductive Age Mortality Study (RAMOS). *BMC Pregnancy Childbirth, 16*, 291. https://doi.org/10.1186/s12884-016-1084-8

Mojekwu, J. N., & Ibekwe, U. (2012). Maternal mortality in Nigeria: Examination of intervention methods. *International Journal of Humanities and Social Science, 2*(20), 135–149.

Montoya, A., Calvert, C., & Filippi, V. (2014). Explaining differences in maternal mortality levels in sub-Saharan African hospitals: A systematic review and meta-analysis. *International Health, 6*, 1–11. http://doi.org/10.1093/inthealth/iht03

Ogunjimi, L. O., Ibe, R. T., & Ikorok, M. M. (2012). Curbing maternal and child mortality: The Nigerian experience. *International Journal of Nursing and Midwifery, 4*(3), 33–39. http://doi.org/10.5897/IJNM//.030

Okaro, J. M., Umezulike, A. C., Onah, H. E., Chukwuwali, L. I., Ezugwu, O. F., & Nweke, P. C. (2001). Maternal mortality at the University of Nigeria Teaching Hospital, Enugu, before and after Kenya. *African Journal of Reproductive Health, 5*(2), 50–97.

Okonofua, F. E. (2008). Maternal mortality prevention in Africa-need to focus on access and quality of care. *African Journal of Reproductive Health, 12*(3), 9–12.

Oladapo, O. T., Lamina, M. A., & Fakoya, T. A. (2006). Maternal deaths in Sagamu in the new millennium: A facility – based retrospective analysis. *BMC Pregnancy and Childbirth, 6*, 6. http://doi.org/10.1186/1471-2393-6-6

Olapade, F. E., & Lawoyin, T. O. (2008). Maternal mortality in a Nigerian maternity hospital. *African Journal of Biomedical Research, 11*, 267–273.

Olonade, O., Olawande, T. I., Alabi, O. J., & Imhonopi, D. (2019). Maternal mortality and maternal healthcare in Nigeria: Implications for socio-economic development. *Open Access Macedonian Journal of Medical Sciences,* 7(5), 849–855. https://doi/org/10.3889/oamjms.2019.041

Oosterbaan, M. M. (1995). Guinea-Bissau: Maternal mortality assessment. *World Health Statistics Quarterly, 48*(1), 34–38.

Oye-Adeniran, B. A., Odeyemi, K. A., Gbadegesin, A., Ekanem, E. E., Osilaja, O. K., Akin-Adenekan, O., & Umoh, A. V. (2011). The use of the sisterhood method for estimating maternal mortality ratio in Lagos state, Nigeria. *Journal of Obstetrics and Gynaecology, 31*(4), 315–319. https://doi/org/10.3109/01443615.2011.561381

Pierre-Marie, T., Gregory, H. E., Maxwell, D. I., Robinson, E. M., Yvette, M., & Nelson, F. J. (2015). Maternal mortality in Cameroon: A university teaching hospital report. *Pan African Medical Journal, 21*, 16. https://doi/org/10.11604/pamj.2015.21.16.3912

Rogo, K. O., Oucho, J., & Philip Mwalali, P. (2006). Maternal mortality. In D. T. Jamison, R. G. Feachem, M. W. Makgoba, et al. (Eds.), *Disease and mortality in sub-Saharan Africa* (2nd ed.). Washington, DC: The International Bank for Reconstruction and Development/The World Bank.

Sharma, V., Brown, W., Kainuwa, M. A., Leight, J., & Nyqvist, M. B. (2017). High maternal mortality in Jigawa State, Northern Nigeria estimated using the sisterhood method. *BMC Pregnancy and Childbirth, 17*, 163. https://doi/org/10.1186/s12884-017-1341-5

Shen, C., & Williamson, J. B. (1999). Maternal mortality, women's status and economic dependency in less developed countries: A cross-national analysis. *Social Science &Medicine, 49*, 197–214.

Songa, I., Macline, M., & Rakuom, C. (2015). Maternal child health through water, sanitation and hygiene. *Sky Journal of Medicine and Medical Science, 3*(7), 94–104.

Udjo, E. O., & Lalthapersad-Pillay, P. (2014). Estimating maternal mortality and causes in South Africa: National and provincial levels. *Midwifery, 30*(5), 512–518. https://doi/org/10.1016/j.midw.2013.05.011

Ujah, I. O. A., Aisierr, J. T., Mutihir, D. J., Vandergagt, R. H., Glew, R. H., & Uguru, V. E. (2005). Factors contributing to maternal mortality in North-central Nigeria: A seventeenth – year review. *African Journal of Reproductive Health, 9*(3), 27–40.
UNFPA. (2013). *Maternal health in Africa*. Factsheet prepared for the summit of Campaign on Accelerated Reduction of Maternal, Newborn and Child Mortality in Africa (CARMMA). Retrieved from www.unfpa.org
UNFPA. (2019). *Maternal health. East and Southern Africa*. Retrieved from https://esaro.unfpa.org/en/topics/maternal-health
UNICEF. (2019). *Level and trend in child and maternal mortality*. New York, NY: UNICEF's Approach. Retrieved from www.who.int/news-room/fact-sheets/detail/maternal-mortality
United Nations, Department of Economic and Social Affairs, Population Division (2019). *World Mortality 2019: Highlights (ST/ESA/SER.A/432)*. London: United Nations.
Usman, N. O., Abdullahi, H. M., Nmadu, A. G., Omole, V. N., & Ango, J. T. Estimation of maternal mortality by sisterhood method in two rural communities in Kaduna State, Nigeria. *Journal of Tropical Medicine, 21*, 62–66.
Wall, L. L. (1998). Dead mothers and injured wives: The social context of maternal mortality and mortality among the Hausa of Northern Nigeria. *Studies in Family Planning, 29*(4), 341–359.
WHO. (2015). *Trends in maternal mortality: 1990–2015: Estimates by WHO, UNICEF, World Bank and the United Nations Population Division*. Washington, DC: World Health Organization.
Wilmoth, J. (2009). The lifetime risk of maternal mortality: concept and measurement. *Bulletin of the World Health Organization, 87*, 256–262. https://doi/org/10.2471/BLT.07.048280
World Health Organization. (2004). *International statistical classification of diseases and related health problems: Instruction manual*. Geneva, Switzerland: World Health Organization.
World Health Organization. (2014). *Maternal mortality and morbidity. Maternal mortality factsheet*. No.348. Geneva: World Health Organization
World Health Organization. (2016). *Maternal mortality: Fact sheet*. Geneva, Switzerland: World Health Organization.
World Health Organization. (2019). *Maternal mortality*. Geneva, Switzerland: World Health Organization.
World Health Organization, UNICEF, World Bank Group, & United Nations Population Division. (2019). *Trends in maternal mortality: 2000 to 2017*. Geneva, Switzerland: World Health Organization.
World Health Statistics. (2019). *Monitoring health for the SDGs, sustainable development goals*. Geneva: World Health Organization.
Yaya, Y., Data, T., & Llndtjorn, B. (2015). Maternal mortality in rural south Ethiopia: Outcomes of community-based birth registration by health extension workers. *PLoS One, 10*(3), e0119321.

41

ESTIMATING MATERNAL MORTALITY

Surveillance methods and agenda for improvement

Oluwatosin Ariyo and Henry Victor Doctor

Introduction

Maternal mortality, as defined by the World Health Organization (WHO), is the death of a woman while pregnant or within 42 days of pregnancy termination, regardless of the duration and site of the pregnancy, from any cause related to or aggravated by the pregnancy or its management but not from accidental or incidental causes (World Health Organization, 2019). Due to its association with women's socioeconomic status, availability of high-quality health services, and the subsequent utilization, maternal mortality is an indicator of a society's overall health status (Sajedinejad, Majdzadeh, Vedadhir, Tabatabaei, & Mohammad, 2015). Maternal deaths are often a result of complications during pregnancy and after delivery (Doctor et al., 2012a). About 75% of these complications are related to severe bleeding, infections, and high blood pressure (before and during pregnancy) and are largely preventable through adequate medical care during the antenatal period. Despite being preventable, about 800 women die from pregnancy or childbirth, daily. With two thirds of the global burden of death (196,000 maternal deaths) in 2017 occurring in sub-Saharan Africa (SSA), and an estimated maternal mortality ratio (MMR) of 542 [95% CI: 498–649] deaths per 100,000 live births, reducing maternal deaths remains a priority for sub-Saharan African countries (World Health Organization, 2019).

While there has been a global downward trend in the number of maternal deaths, the rates have been slow and disparate, especially in countries with insufficient and/or inaccurate data. Adequate data about causes, mediating, and moderating factors associated with maternal deaths are essential to reduce these death rates. Valid and accurate data are needed to estimate the true magnitude of maternal deaths; inform the development and delivery of programs and policies to eliminate maternal deaths; and assess the effectiveness of interventions and monitor progress towards elimination (World Health Organization, 2019). However, in many SSA countries, routine data monitoring systems are inadequate or unavailable, with less than 12% of countries meeting the criteria for reasonable completion of cause of death data (Amanhi Study Group, 2016).

In addition to insufficient surveillance systems, estimating maternal mortality in SSA may be challenging due to its comparatively low occurrence in the population, as well as factors within the health care system (such as weak hospital record systems, misclassification of maternal deaths) and the community context (such as under-reporting of abortion-related deaths,

 DOI: 10.4324/9780429287213-50

exclusion of deaths that occur outside a medical facility, and undisclosed pregnancy status at the time of death). Without the availability of data that adequately captures the rates of maternal mortality, the picture of maternal death is incomplete. These gaps make it difficult to implement efficient and effective programs and policies that prioritize leverage points for action. Problems that are not monitored cannot be measured, and if not measured cannot be improved.

In acknowledgment of this negative health indicator, the paucity of information, and the Sustainable Development Goal target 3.1 to reduce the global MMR to less than 70 deaths per 100,000 live births by 2030, the WHO's Ending Preventable Maternal Mortality Strategy delineates 'improving metrics, measurement, and data quality' as one of two central objectives for action (World Health Organization, 2015). To assess the current status of efforts to improve the measurement of MMR, this chapter is a synthesis of the existing body of knowledge to document methodologies that have been employed to investigate maternal mortality in sub-Saharan Africa since the early 1970s. The chapter specifically focusses on the age-related mortality, sisterhood method, verbal autopsy (VA), and other demographic approaches for estimating maternal mortality. The chapter concludes with a discussion on further areas of research, policy, and practice to identify and address the needs of girls and women in sub-Saharan Africa within the context of the global agenda for sustainable development.

Theoretical and conceptual issues in studies of maternal mortality in sub-Saharan Africa

MMR is the generally accepted measure for estimating maternal deaths. It measures a pregnant woman's risk of dying from pregnancy-related causes within a given period, usually one year. Other indicators of maternal mortality in use are:

- *Maternal Mortality Rate* (MMRate): the number of maternal deaths divided by person-years lived by women of reproductive age in a population. The MMRate captures both the risk of maternal death per pregnancy or per birth (whether live birth or stillbirth) and the level of fertility in the population.
- *Proportion ·of Maternal Deaths*: the proportion of maternal mortality among all deaths of reproductive-age females.
- *Adult Lifetime Risk of Maternal Death*: measures the probability that a female will die from maternal causes over the period of her 35-year reproductive life-course, thus considering the probability that each occurrence of pregnancy leads to a pregnancy-related death.

Data to estimate maternal mortality come from various sources, including civil registration and vital statistics (CRVS) systems, which are the preferred data sources or the gold standard for collecting mortality data. CRVS systems capture all deaths occurring in a country and use standardized coding systems to systematically categorize medically certified deaths by cause. Other sources of data used to estimate maternal mortality include population-based household surveys using the sisterhood method; reproductive-age mortality studies (RAMOS); confidential inquiries into maternal deaths; VAs; censuses and other specialized maternal mortality studies conducted at the national level (World Health Organization, 2019). Irrespective of the source used to generate national-level estimates, the essential factor in estimating maternal mortality is to ensure the availability of robust, accurate, nationally-representative data sources with a clear and detailed description of data collection and quality assurance mechanisms.

In SSA, population-based surveys are the primary source of information for calculating MMRs due to non-existent or dysfunctional CRVS systems. These surveys include RAMOS, population surveys, or censuses that collect data and enable direct estimation or use of sisterhood method techniques.

RAMOS is a surveillance of all deaths of reproductive-aged females. This method can be either prospective or retrospective. It is usually a combination of passive and active data collection, such as cross-sectional household surveys, continuous population surveillance, hospital and health centre records, and key informant interviews.

Direct Estimation uses data derived from household surveys or censuses in which residents are asked questions about maternal deaths that recently occurred in the household within a given period, often 1–2 years.

The Sisterhood Method utilizes data from a set of questions in a survey of adults on the aggregate number of their living and dead sisters, with two variations, the ***direct*** and ***indirect*** method (Graham, Brass, & Snow, 1989). The indirect method was the first validated method; it asks four questions limited to a 10-to-12-year period before the survey. The latter validated direct method asks eight to eleven questions in a shorter period of 3–4 years before the survey.

These methods provide information that have propagated efforts to reduce maternal deaths. However, they are often characterized by fragmented and uncoordinated collections from multiple sources. Although RAMOS and direct estimation methods provide accurate estimates, they require large sample sizes to obtain single-point estimates with sufficiently narrow confidence intervals to enable monitoring of time trends and are thus time-consuming and expensive. The sisterhood method, although also expensive and time-consuming, if the direct method is used, attempts to counter challenges of large sample size requirements by interviewing adult respondents about the survival of all their sisters.

In SSA, data to estimate maternal mortality have recently started coming from health and demographic surveillance systems (HDSS) which offer an opportunity to understand mortality patterns in localized settings with the potential for generalization in similar settings (Baiden, Hodgson, & Binka, 2006). In SSA, as is the case in other regions, HDSS sites are governed by standards set by a global network (INDEPTH Network) of HDSSs that provide a more complete picture of the health status of communities. Since its inception in 1998, the network has collected robust data that are uniquely positioned to answer the most pressing questions on health, population dynamics, and development. As of 2018, INDEPTH membership composed of 42 member health research centres that observed through 49 HDSS field sites the life events of over 3.8 million people in 19 low- and middle-income countries in Africa, Asia, and Oceania (INDEPTH Network, 2020).

Drawing on the aforementioned sources, the United Nations Maternal Mortality Estimation Inter-Agency Group (UN MMEIG), collaborates with technical experts on new rounds of country-level estimates of MMR globally with the most recent estimates at the time of writing this chapter available between 2000 and 2017.

Methods

A comprehensive literature review with variation of the following keywords 'estimating maternal mortality' was conducted in several academic databases including MEDLINE, African Index, PubMed, African Journals Online, Web of Science, Google Scholar, African Index Medicus, and CINAHL. The search was limited to work in sub-Saharan Africa written in English by African scholars, Africans in the diaspora, and Western scholars in Africa and published between January 1970 and December 2019. In a snowball approach, the reference list of articles meeting the search criteria was searched for additional articles.

The keywords used in the search were variations of the terms 'estimating', 'estimation of', 'maternal mortality', and 'maternal deaths'. The databases allowed for MeSH-enabled (medical subject headings) queries and the use of Boolean operators (AND, OR) to string the keywords and enable precision and efficiency of the search.

The titles and abstracts of the articles were independently reviewed by the two authors. The full texts of articles that met the criteria based on the initial review were further reviewed for eligibility for inclusion in this review.

Findings

Of the 50 studies identified for initial review, 34 studies met the criteria for further review and are synthesized in this chapter. These 34 studies utilized six different surveillance methods. Vital registration (11 studies) and the indirect sisterhood method (9 studies) were the most prevalently utilized methods (Table 41.1). The six surveillance methods utilized by the 34 studies are described here.

Table 41.1 Methods Utilized to Estimate Maternal Mortality in Sub-Saharan Africa

Surveillance Method	*Number of Studies*	*Countries*
Reproductive Age Mortality Studies (RAMOS)	4	Guinea-Bissau, Ghana, Ethiopia, Malawi
Direct Sisterhood Method	4	Benin, Burkina Faso, Burundi, Central African Republic, Cameroon, Chad, Comoros, Côte d'Ivoire, Democratic Republic of Congo, Ethiopia, Gabon, Guinea, Kenya, Lesotho, Liberia, Madagascar, Malawi, Mali, Mozambique, Namibia, Niger, Nigeria, Rwanda, Sao Tome and Principe, Senegal, Sierra Leone, South Africa, Swaziland, Togo, Tanzania, Uganda, Zambia, Zimbabwe
Indirect Sisterhood Method	9	Liberia, Mali, Nigeria, Swaziland, Tanzania, Uganda
Verbal Autopsy (VA)	4	Burkina Faso, Democratic Republic of Congo, Ghana, Ivory Coast, Kenya, Mali, Mauritania, Niger, Senegal, Tanzania, Zambia
Vital Registration	11	Angola, Benin, Botswana, Burundi, Burkina Faso, Cameroon, Cape Verde, Chad, Central African Republic, Comoros, Congo, Côte d'Ivoire, Djibouti, Democratic Republic of Congo, Equatorial Guinea, Eritrea, Ethiopia, Gabon, Gambia, Ghana, Guinea, Guinea-Bissau, Kenya, Lesotho, Liberia, Madagascar, Malawi, Mali, Mauritania, Mauritius, Mozambique, Namibia, Niger, Nigeria, Rwanda, Senegal, Sierra Leone, Somalia, South Africa, Sudan, Swaziland, Tanzania, Togo, Uganda, Zambia, Zimbabwe
Maternal and Perinatal Death Surveillance and Response (MPDSR)	2	Nigeria

Reproductive age mortality studies

In a RAMOS approach, the deaths of women of reproductive age (usually 15 to 49 years) are identified from different sources including vital statistics registries, population surveys, and census data. After deaths are identified from these sources, VAs are used to triangulate identified cases and confirm pregnancy-related factors as the cause of death. Four studies in Ghana, Guinea-Bissau, Ethiopia, and Malawi used RAMOS as the surveillance method to estimate MMR. Two were prospective studies (Høj, Da Silva, Hedegaard, Sandström, & Aaby, 2002; Mgawadere, Unkels, Adegoke, & van den Broek, 2016), and the other two were retrospective studies (Godefay, Byass, Kinsman, & Mulugeta, 2015; Zakariah et al., 2009).

The prospective study in Guinea-Bissau used a survey in a longitudinal, cluster sample to estimate the number of maternal deaths in a six-year period. In Malawi, the prospective RAMOS was conducted in three phases over a one-year period. In the first phase, the deaths of reproductive-age women were identified; next, maternal deaths among deaths of reproductive-age women were identified; and in the last phase, reviews of VA and health facilities were conducted to confirm contributors and cause of death. In this study, the researchers identified deaths at both the health facility and community level by engaging interdisciplinary teams and stakeholders to identify and report incidents of mortality. The investigation conducted in Ghana also employed RAMOS in a retrospective review of data from multiple medical records to identify deaths of reproductive-aged women, characterized as women between the ages of 10 to 50 years. Although the investigations in Malawi and Guinea-Bissau also used VAs in the identification of maternal deaths, VA was the primary mode of data collection in the retrospective cross-sectional study conducted in Ethiopia.

Sisterhood method

The sisterhood method is an indirect method to estimate maternal mortality derived from similar demographic measures that have been used to measure child and adult mortality and adapted to estimate maternal mortality. In the sisterhood method, data are retrospectively collected by asking adult respondents about the deaths of all their adult sisters. This method can be conducted using one of two approaches: the ***direct*** or ***indirect*** sisterhood method. In the ***indirect sisterhood*** method, respondents are asked four questions about how many of their sisters reached adulthood, how many died, and if those who died were pregnant around the time of death (Table 41.2).

In the latter approach, the ***direct sisterhood method,*** often used in the Demographic and Health Survey (DHS), respondents are asked more detailed information about their sisters. Respondents are asked up to 11 questions, including the numbers who reached adulthood, how many have died, the age at death, the year in which the death occurred, and the number of years since the death. Twelve studies in Ethiopia, Liberia, Mali, Nigeria, Swaziland, Tanzania, and Uganda used the sisterhood method to estimate maternal deaths in the respective countries. One study was conducted at a multi-national level and included analysis of data from 34 sub-Saharan African countries.

Most studies in this review used the indirect sisterhood methods and were conducted at the country (Lech & Zwane, 2002), state (Doctor et al., 2012b; Oye-Adeniran et al., 2011), regional (Aa, Grove, Haugsjå, & Hinderaker, 2011; Mbaruku, Vork, Vyagusa, Mwakipiti, & van Roosmalen, 2003), and district (Adegoke, Campbell, Ogundeji, Lawoyin, & Thomson, 2013; Font et al., 2000; Olsen et al., 2000; Orach, 2000) levels. Sample sizes of 2,100 to 3,200 adult respondents are recommended to estimate MMR with 80% power and 95% confidence

Table 41.2 Survey Questions for Sisterhood Methods of Estimating Maternal Mortality (WHO/UNICEF, 1997)

Indirect Sisterhood Method	1 How many sisters (born to the same mother) have you ever had who were ever married (including those who are now dead)? 2 How many of these ever-married sisters are alive now? 3 How many of these ever-married sisters are dead? 4 How many of these dead sisters died while they were pregnant, or during childbirth, or during the six weeks after the end of pregnancy?
Direct Sisterhood Method	1 How many children did your mother give birth to? 2 How many of these births did your mother have before you were born? 3 What was the name given to your oldest (next oldest) brother or sister? 4 Is (NAME) male or female? 5 Is (NAME) still alive? 6 How old is (NAME)? 7 In what year did (NAME) die? OR How many years ago did (NAME) die? 8 How old was (NAME) when she died? *For dead sisters only:* 9 Was (NAME) pregnant when she died? 10 Did (NAME) die during childbirth? 11 Did (NAME) die within two months after the end of pregnancy or childbirth?

level, where MMR is expected to be between 500 and 750, and 8,000 to 13,000 respondents is recommended to achieve 90% power (Hanley, Hagen, & Shiferaw, 1996).

To calculate sample size for each population, a random sampling method can be employed using the WHO's formula (WHO/UNICEF, 1997):

$$\mathbf{n = 4P(1 - P) / e^2}$$

in which
n is the number of respondents;
P is the average number of adult sisters per respondent divided by estimated lifetime risk of maternal death;
e is the maximum error that will be tolerated in the proportion, generally 10%.

Sample sizes in these nine studies ranged from 721 (in a district-level investigation) to 17,087 (in a state-level investigation) respondents. Four studies used the direct sisterhood method and were conducted at the county (Moseson et al., 2014) and national (Ariyo, Ozodiegwu, & Doctor, 2017; Gebremedhin, 2018), and multi-national (Merdad & Ali, 2018) levels. The study in Liberia was a population-based survey of a randomly selected cluster sample in a selected county, with a sample size of 1,985 (82.7% of the 2,400 target sample). The study in Nigeria was conducted at the national level using data from the Nigeria DHS. The study in Ethiopia also analyzed data from the DHS and included three additional DHS-sponsored surveys, including National Family Health and specialized maternal mortality surveys. A total of 248 surveys from 80 different countries were included in the analytical model and about half (n = 127) were from sub-Saharan African countries. The multi-national level study based its estimation only on DHS data. This analysis used data from the maternal mortality modules of 84 DHS surveys from 34 sub-Saharan African countries (Table 41.1) in a 15-year period (1990 to 2014).

Verbal autopsy

Verbal autopsies have been used to estimate infant and childhood mortality and were updated by the WHO to also estimate maternal deaths. VAs are used to determine cause of death in communities with unreliable vital registration systems and where most people die at home without previous contact with health facilities. This method of surveillance conducts interviews with knowledgeable ties (e.g. relatives, caregivers, or neighbours) of the deceased using a standardized questionnaire that elicits information about signs, symptoms, medical history, and circumstances surrounding the death in order to reach a medically acceptable diagnosis (World Health Organization, 2016). Four studies used VA as the sole method to estimate maternal mortality at the national (Etard, Kodio, & Traoré, 1999), sub-national (Desai et al., 2013), and regional (Ahmed et al., 2018; Bouvier-Colle et al., 2001) levels.

Three of the four studies used prospective designs to assess maternal deaths and collected varying sociodemographic information, such as marital status, age, and education, about the deceased. The sub-national study in western Kenya (Desai et al., 2013) conducted a retrospective investigation using data from HDSS sites.

Vital registration

Vital registration systems are used in most countries as a continuous, compulsory, and standardized record of the incidence and characteristics of vital events relevant to the country, and are backed by their legislative regulations (Mgawadere, Kana, & Van Den Broek, 2017; Phillips et al., 2015). These systems collect essential population-level data on life events including births and deaths and if collected completely, accurately, and timely, are ideal data to estimate maternal deaths. However, in recording incidents of death, many countries do not adequately collect cause-of-death data. Most of the studies in this review used vital registration to estimate MMR. Seven studies were conducted in Nigeria, and the other four studies were each conducted in Ghana, Gambia, South Africa, and Tanzania.

All the studies conducted retrospective analyses, and all but one study, conducted in Nigeria, used data from health facility records. Six studies in Nigeria (Agan, Monjok, Akpan, Omoronyia, & Ekabua, 2018; Ezegwui et al., 2013; Kullima, Kawuwa, Audu, Geidam, & Mairiga, 2009; Obiechina et al., 2013; Okaro et al., 2001; Oladapo, Lamina, & Fakoya, 2006) extracted data on maternal deaths and varying sociodemographic factors (such as age, parity education) from state university teaching hospital records. Another study (Adamu, Salihu, Sathiakumar, & Alexander, 2003) in Nigeria used data from the state's ministry of health records which included health facility and community level data. The studies in Ghana (Geelhoed et al., 2003), Gambia (Hoestermann, Ogbaselassie, Wacker, & Bastert, 1996), and Tanzania (Mapunda et al., 2016) also collected data on maternal deaths from hospital records while the study in South Africa (Bomela, 2020) conducted a national estimation of maternal mortality using data from the country's department of home affairs.

Maternal and perinatal death surveillance and response

Maternal and Perinatal Death Surveillance and Response (MPDSR) is a recently recommended approach to estimating maternal mortality. MPDSR builds on existing maternal death review systems where each maternal death is reviewed by a local committee that examines the medical and non-medical factors associated with the maternal death. This surveillance method allows countries to link their health information system and maternal death data to quality-of-care improvement processes at both local and national levels. MPDSR relies on active surveillance and reporting, emphasizing 'zero reporting' in the instances when there are no deaths to be reported, and focusses on the response portion of the surveillance. To be effectively implemented, this method requires policy-enforced pathways for routine identification and timely reporting of maternal deaths, systematic review of identified deaths, synthesis and interpretation of data, and implementation of recommendations for improvement (WHO et al., 2004) (Table 41.3).

We identified two studies that reported implementation of the MPDSR in two different states in Nigeria. One study conducted used the national protocol to conduct monthly MPDSR, over a two-year period, in three hospitals in one state (Okonofua et al., 2017). The other study also used the national protocol but conducted surveillance in one hospital (Aikpitanyi et al., 2019). The study included the MMR, primary, and associated medical causes of death, and recommendations for prevention at the health facility level. Evidence of this surveillance system was also found in Ethiopia (Ayele et al., 2019), where the country has established a national policy that enforces reporting of maternal, perinatal, and neonatal death by health facilities and communities to their respective health systems. However, the located article is an evaluation of the surveillance system and does not include details about implementation.

Table 41.3 Essential Components of a National Maternal and Perinatal Death Surveillance and Response System

Policy indicators	• National policy requiring notification of all maternal deaths • National policy requiring review of all maternal deaths • Requirement of a national maternal death review committee in place • Requirement of a subnational maternal death review committee in place • Requirement of both national and subnational maternal death review committees in place • Requirement of a national maternal death review committee that meets at least biannually
Guiding principles for operation	• Notification and investigation of all suspected maternal deaths in women of reproductive age (15–45 years) • Notification within 24 hours of maternal deaths in facilities (or within 48 hours when a woman dies in the community) • Zero reporting when no suspected maternal deaths have occurred • Timely review of all probable maternal deaths • Immediate recommendations, where possible, to help facilities and communities prevent similar deaths, ensuring that key messages reach people who can make a difference • Timely review and analysis at district and national levels to identify trends and patterns • Timely publication of findings and recommendations at national level • Continuous monitoring of the MDSR system and of how recommendations are implemented

Discussion

Globally, maternal mortality remains a widely acknowledged indicator of the overall health of a population, the status of women in the society, and the efficiency of its health system. Ensuring that countries, especially under-resourced countries, collect reliable, high-quality data to measure maternal mortality remains a daunting challenge. Findings from this review suggest that vital registrations systems are currently the most utilized method of maternal death surveillance in SSA. However, CRVS systems remain dysfunctional in sub-Saharan African countries, and interventions to address maternal mortality challenges cannot be accurately evaluated if countries are not able to generate data of high quality. Efforts to address these challenges are on-going but the progress remains slow. The total cost of scaling up CRVS systems was estimated to be US$3.82 billion in 73 countries globally or an average US$199 million financing gap per year for the period 2015–2024 (World Bank & World Health Organization, 2014). The key to enhancing and sustaining CRVS systems is strong national leadership overseeing a country-led plan. This remains the greatest challenge, yet to be achieved, at least for the foreseeable future.

Addressing existing data gaps to measure maternal mortality in SSA remains one of the top priorities for the global public health community. Several approaches such as the implementation of RAMOS, verbal autopsies, and enhancing CRVS systems have been employed to bridge these gaps. Global comparable estimates adjusted to correct for underreporting and misclassification are available. However, most global comparisons and associated summary indices are insensitive to national policy changes and local context, and thus compromise efforts to strengthen national health information systems. Health information systems (HIS) that respond to national needs are urgently needed to provide data that can be used to measure MMRs and monitor progress towards the SDGs (Rashidian, 2019). Without improvements in national HIS, including CRVS systems, measurement of maternal mortality will be problematic, particularly in countries with limited resources. The need to improve CRVS remains a priority at the global level and SSA, in particular.

For example, the Third Conference of African Ministers Responsible for Civil Registration held in Côte d'Ivoire in 2015 called upon the WHO, in collaboration with panAfrican organizations and other partners, to intensify their efforts in developing real-time death registration and cause-of-death information systems at country level (Yamoussoukro Declaration, 2015). While some countries are implementing interventions to improve CRVS systems, the resources and time required to address existing gaps are enormous and require key strategic enablers such as a network of global experts to advance CRVS systems, established frameworks and coordination, political commitment, continuous country CRVS assessments to identify gaps, and adoption of relevant technologies to enhance processing and utilization of cause-of-death data.

Further, to effectively and sustainably address maternal mortality, surveillance methods should also include identification of the social, cultural, and economic factors that cause and exacerbate maternal morbidity and mortality. Maternal deaths do not occur in isolation but are largely influenced by women's socioecological environments. Evidence suggests that economic empowerment and gender equality have potential implications for maternal death rates. Women's agency and economic status significantly impact their health as individuals, and especially as mothers. Women with higher agency and socioeconomic status have better access to opportunities and resources, including quality health care, and therefore have better health status and outcomes. Striving for gender equality across all spheres and utilizing a life-course approach to impact the health, education, and agency of girls and women should be the core of strategies to improve maternal health.

While most of the studies we reviewed included assessments of the association between medical care and maternal deaths, few studies (most using DHS data) considered the sociocultural context in which the deaths occurred. Although DHS assesses respondents' socioeconomic status (economic empowerment, participation in decision making, self-agency) these variables can only be used to estimate the siblings' status by proxy. This proximal association is not reliable because it cannot be assumed that a sibling's experience always mirrors that of her dead sister. Considering its capacity to prospectively monitor pregnancy-related death, MPDSR holds the greatest potential for collecting linked sociodemographic data of pregnant women.

Variables that accurately measure indices of women's empowerment, both qualitatively and quantitatively, are necessary to adequately investigate their association with maternal mortality. However, there are currently no widely validated measures to assess these constructs. Conditions can only be improved if they are measured and they can only be measured if they are identified and monitored. Future studies can build on existing research to develop and empirically evaluate measures and theoretical models which assess and further investigate the association between women's empowerment and maternal health status and outcomes. These measures can then be incorporated into surveillance methods to identify and prevent maternal deaths.

Conclusion: agenda for improvement

Findings from this review suggest that vital registration systems are currently the most utilized method of maternal death surveillance in SSA. However, these systems are inadequate for effective surveillance in sub-Saharan African countries. Strong national leadership overseeing a country-led plan is crucial to improving and sustaining the existing CRVS systems. Equally crucial is the need to implement responsive national HIS to generate contextually relevant data that can be used to measure MMRs. Further, to effectively and sustainably reduce maternal mortality, improvement strategies must consider the sociocultural context in which these deaths occur. Developing and implementing surveillance methods to investigate the social, cultural, and economic factors that cause and influence maternal morbidity and mortality, including through use of qualitative instruments to gather contextual data, is an essential agenda for improvement in measuring and reducing maternal deaths in SSA.

References

Aa, I., Grove, M. A., Haugsjå, A. H., & Hinderaker, S. G. (2011). High maternal mortality estimated by the sisterhood method in a rural area of Mali. *BMC Pregnancy and Childbirth, 11*(1), 1–6.

Adamu, Y. M., Salihu, H. M., Sathiakumar, N., & Alexander, G. R. (2003). Maternal mortality in Northern Nigeria: A population-based study. *European Journal of Obstetrics and Gynecology and Reproductive Biology, 109*(2), 153–159. https://doi.org/10.1016/S0301-2115(03)00009-5

Adegoke, A. A., Campbell, M., Ogundeji, M. O., Lawoyin, T. O., & Thomson, A. M. (2013). Community study of maternal mortality in South West Nigeria: How applicable is the sisterhood method. *Maternal and Child Health Journal, 17*(2), 319–329.

Agan, T. U., Monjok, E., Akpan, U. B., Omoronyia, O. E., & Ekabua, J. E. (2018). Trend and causes of maternal mortality in a nigerian tertiary hospital: A 5-year retrospective study (2010–2014) at the university of calabar teaching hospital, Calabar, Nigeria. *Open Access Macedonian Journal of Medical Sciences, 6*(6), 1153–1158. https://doi.org/10.3889/oamjms.2018.220

Ahmed, I., Ali, S. M., Amenga-Etego, S., Ariff, S., Bahl, R., Baqui, A. H., . . . Zaidi, A. (2018). Population-based rates, timing, and causes of maternal deaths, stillbirths, and neonatal deaths in south Asia and sub-Saharan Africa: A multi-country prospective cohort study. *The Lancet Global Health, 6*(12), e1297–e1308. https://doi.org/10.1016/S2214-109X(18)30385-1

Aikpitanyi, J., Ohenhen, V., Ugbodaga, P., Ojemhen, B., Omo-Omorodion, B. I., Ntoimo, L. F. C., . . . Okonofua, F. E. (2019). Maternal death review and surveillance: The case of Central Hospital, Benin City, Nigeria. *PLoS One*, *14*(12), 1–13. https://doi.org/10.1371/journal.pone.0226075

Amanhi Study Group. (2016). Burden, timing and causes of maternal and neonatal deaths and stillbirths in sub-Saharan Africa and South Asia: Protocol for a prospective cohort study. *Journal of Global Health*, *6*(2), 020602. https://doi.org/10.7189/jogh.06.020602

Ariyo, O., Ozodiegwu, I. D., & Doctor, H. V. (2017). The influence of the social and cultural environment on maternal mortality in Nigeria: Evidence from the 2013 demographic and health survey. *PLoS One*, *12*(12). https://doi.org/10.1371/journal.pone.0190285

Ayele, B., Gebretnsae, H., Hadgu, T., Negash, D., Gsilassie, F., Alemu, T., . . . Godefay, H. (2019). Maternal and perinatal death surveillance and response in Ethiopia: Achievements, challenges and prospects. *PLoS One*, *14*(10), 1–24. https://doi.org/10.1371/journal.pone.0223540

Baiden, F., Hodgson, A., & Binka, F. N. (2006). Demographic surveillance sites and emerging challenges in international health. *Bulletin of the World Health Organization*, *84*(3), 161–256.

Bomela, N. J. (2020). Maternal mortality by socio-demographic characteristics and cause of death in South Africa: 2007–2015. *BMC Public Health*, *20*(1), 1–20. https://doi.org/10.1186/s12889-020-8179-x

Bouvier-Colle, M.-H., Ouedraogo, C., Dumont, A., Vangeenderhuysen, C., Salanave, B., & Decam, C. (2001). Maternal mortality in West Africa. *Acta Obstetricia et Gynecologica Scandinavica*, *80*(2), 113–113. https://doi.org/10.1080/j.1600-0412.2001.080002113.x

Desai, M., Phillips-Howard, P. A., Odhiambo, F. O., Katana, A., Ouma, P., Hamel, M. J., . . . Laserson, K. F. (2013). An analysis of pregnancy-related mortality in the KEMRI/CDC health and demographic surveillance system in Western Kenya. *PLoS One*, *8*(7). https://doi.org/10.1371/journal.pone.0068733

Doctor, H. V., Findley, S. E., Ager, A., Cometto, G., Afenyadu, G. Y., Adamu, F., & Green, C. (2012a). Using community-based research to shape the design and delivery of maternal health services in Northern Nigeria. *Reproductive Health Matters*, *20*(39), 104–112. https://doi.org/10.1016/S0968-8080(12)39615-8

Doctor, H. V., Olatunji, A., Findley, S. E., Afenyadu, G. Y., Abdulwahad, A., & Jumare, A. (2012b). Maternal mortality in northern Nigeria : Findings. *Tropical Doctor*, 140–143.

Etard, J. F., Kodio, B., & Traoré, S. (1999). Assessment of maternal mortality and late maternal mortality among a cohort of pregnant women in bamako, mali. *BJOG: An International Journal of Obstetrics and Gynaecology*, *106*(1), 60–65. https://doi.org/10.1111/j.1471-0528.1999.tb08086.x

Ezegwui, H., Onoh, R., Ikeako, L., Onyebuchi, A., Umeorah, J., Ezeonu, P., & Ibekwe, P. (2013). Investigating maternal mortality in a Public Teaching Hospital, Abakaliki, Ebonyi State, Nigeria. *Annals of Medical and Health Sciences Research*, *3*(1), 75. https://doi.org/10.4103/2141-9248.109511

Font, F., Alonso González, M., Nathan, R., Lwilla, F., Kimario, J., Tanner, M., & Alonso, P. L. (2000). Maternal mortality in a rural district of southeastern Tanzania: An application of the sisterhood method. *International Journal of Epidemiology*, *29*(1), 107–112. https://doi.org/10.1093/ije/29.1.107

Gebremedhin, S. (2018). Development of a new model for estimating maternal mortality ratio at national and subnational levels and its application for describing sub-national variations of maternal death in Ethiopia. *PLoS One*, *13*(8), 1–18. https://doi.org/10.1371/journal.pone.0201990

Geelhoed, D. W., Visser, L. E., Asare, K., Schagen Van Leeuwen, J. H., & Van Roosmalen, J. (2003). Trends in maternal mortality: A 13-year hospital-based study in rural Ghana. *European Journal of Obstetrics and Gynecology and Reproductive Biology*, *107*(2), 135–139. https://doi.org/10.1016/S0301-2115(02)00224-5

Godefay, H., Byass, P., Kinsman, J., & Mulugeta, A. (2015). Understanding maternal mortality from top – Down and bottom – Up perspectives: Case of Tigray Region, Ethiopia. *Journal of Global Health*, *5*(1), 1–8. https://doi.org/10.7189/jogh.05.010404

Graham, W., Brass, W., & Snow, R. W. (1989). Estimating maternal mortality: The sisterhood method. *Studies in Family Planning*, *20*(3), 125–135.

Hanley, J. A., Hagen, C. A., & Shiferaw, T. (1996). Confidence intervals and sample-size calculations for the sisterhood method of estimating maternal mortality. *Studies in Family Planning*, 220–227. https://doi.org/10.2307/2137955

Hoestermann, C. F. L., Ogbaselassie, G., Wacker, J., & Bastert, G. (1996). Maternal mortality in the main referral hospital in The Gambia, West Africa. *Tropical Medicine & International Health*, *1*(5), 710–717. https://doi.org/10.1111/j.1365-3156.1996.tb00099.x

Høj, L., Da Silva, D., Hedegaard, K., Sandström, A., & Aaby, P. (2002). Factors associated with maternal mortality in rural Guinea-Bissau. A longitudinal population-based study. *BJOG: An International Journal of Obstetrics and Gynaecology*, *109*(7), 792–799. https://doi.org/10.1016/S1470-0328(02)01259-4

INDEPTH Network. (2020). *About us*. Retrieved on July 23, 2020, from www.indepth-network.org/about-us

Kullima, A. A., Kawuwa, M. B., Audu, B. M., Geidam, A. D., & Mairiga, A. G. (2009). Trends in maternal mortality in a tertiary institution in northern Nigeria. *Annals of African Medicine*, *8*(4), 221–224. https://doi.org/10.4103/1596-3519.59575

Lech, M. M., & Zwane, A. (2002). Survey on maternal mortality in Swaziland using the sisterhood method. *Paediatric and Perinatal Epidemiology*, *16*(2), 101–107. https://doi.org/10.1046/j.1365-3016.2002.00411.x

Mapunda, O. E., Msuya, S. E., Kapologwe, N., John, B., Damian, D. J., & Mahande, M. J. (2016). Assessment of maternal mortality and its associated causes at Shinyanga Regional Hospital in Tanzania. *Women's Health Bulletin*, *4*(2). https://doi.org/10.17795/whb-38976

Mbaruku, G., Vork, F., Vyagusa, D., Mwakipiti, R., & van Roosmalen, J. (2003). Estimates of maternal mortality in western Tanzania by the sisterhood method. *African Journal of Reproductive Health*, 7(3), 84–91. https://doi.org/10.2307/3583293

Merdad, L., & Ali, M. M. (2018). Timing of maternal death: Levels, trends, and ecological correlates using sibling data from 34 sub-Saharan African countries. *PLoS One*, *13*(1), 1–13. https://doi.org/10.1371/journal.pone.0189416

Mgawadere, F., Kana, T., & Van Den Broek, N. (2017). Measuring maternal mortality: A systematic review of methods used to obtain estimates of the Maternal Mortality Ratio (MMR) in low- and middle-income countries. *British Medical Bulletin*, *121*(1), 121–134. https://doi.org/10.1093/bmb/ldw056

Mgawadere, F., Unkels, R., Adegoke, A., & van den Broek, N. (2016). Measuring maternal mortality using a Reproductive Age Mortality Study (RAMOS). *BMC Pregnancy and Childbirth*, *16*(1), 1–9. https://doi.org/10.1186/s12884-016-1084-8

Moseson, H., Massaquoi, M., Bawo, L., Birch, L., Dahn, B., Zolia, Y., . . . Gerdts, C. (2014). Estimation of maternal and neonatal mortality at the subnational level in Liberia. *International Journal of Gynecology and Obstetrics*, *127*(2), 194–200. https://doi.org/10.1016/j.ijgo.2014.05.007

Obiechina, N. J., Okolie, V. E., Okechukwu, Z. C., Oguejiofor, C. F., Udegbunam, O. I., Nwajiaku, L. S. A., . . . Egeonu, R. (2013). Maternal mortality at nnamdi azikiwe University Teaching Hospital, Southeast Nigeria: A 10-year review (2003–2012). *International Journal of Women's Health*, *5*(1), 431–436. https://doi.org/10.2147/IJWH.S46988

Okaro, J. M., Umezulike, A. C., Onah, H. E., Chukwuali, L. I., Ezugwu, O. F., & Nweke, P. C. (2001). Maternal mortality at the University of Nigeria Teaching Hospital, Enugu, before and after Kenya. *African Journal of Reproductive Health*, *5*(2), 90–97. https://doi.org/10.2307/3583434

Okonofua, F., Imosemi, D., Igboin, B., Adeyemi, A., Chibuko, C., Idowu, A., & Imongan, W. (2017). Maternal death review and outcomes: An assessment in Lagos State, Nigeria. *PLoS One*, *12*(12), 1–11. https://doi.org/10.1371/journal.pone.0188392

Oladapo, O. T., Lamina, M. A., & Fakoya, T. A. (2006). Maternal deaths in Sagamu in the new millenium: A facility-based retrospective analysis. *BMC Pregnancy and Childbirth*, *6*, 1–7. https://doi.org/10.1186/1471-2393-6-6

Olsen, B. E., Hinderaker, S. G., Kazaura, M., Lie, R. T., Bergsjø, P., Gasheka, P., & Kvåle, G. (2000). Estimates of maternal mortality by the sisterhood method in rural northern Tanzania: A household sample and an antenatal clinic sample. *British Journal of Obstetrics and Gynaecology*, *107*(10), 1290–1297. https://doi.org/10.1111/j.1471-0528.2000.tb11622.x

Orach, C. G. (2000). Maternal mortality estimated using the Sisterhood method in Gulu district, Uganda. *Tropical Doctor*, *30*(2), 72–74.

Oye-Adeniran, B. A., Odeyemi, K. A., Gbadegesin, A., Ekanem, E. E., Osilaja, O. K., Akin-Adenekan, O., & Umoh, A. V. (2011). The use of the sisterhood method for estimating maternal mortality ratio in Lagos state, Nigeria. *Journal of Obstetrics and Gynaecology*, *31*(4), 315–319. https://doi.org/10.3109/01443615.2011.561381

Phillips, D. E., AbouZahr, C., Lopez, A. D., Mikkelsen, L., De Savigny, D., Lozano, R., . . . Setel, P. W. (2015). Are well functioning civil registration and vital statistics systems associated with better health outcomes? *The Lancet*, *386*(10001), 1386–1394. https://doi.org/10.1016/S0140-6736(15)60172-6

Rashidian, A. (2019). Effective health information systems for delivering the Sustainable Development Goals and the universal health coverage agenda. *East Mediterranean Health Journal*, *25*(12), 849–851. https://doi.org/10.18356/ea6aec90-en

Sajedinejad, S., Majdzadeh, R., Vedadhir, A. A., Tabatabaei, M. G., & Mohammad, K. (2015). Maternal mortality: A cross-sectional study in global health. *Globalization and Health, 11*(1), 1–13. https://doi.org/10.1186/s12992-015-0087-y

World Bank & World Health Organization. (2014). *Global civil registration and vital statistics: Scaling up investment plan 2015–2024.* Retrieved from www.worldbank.org/content/dam/Worldbank/document/HDN/Health/CRVS Scaling-up plan final 5–28–14web.pdf

World Health Organization. (2015). *Strategies toward ending preventable maternal mortality (EPMM)* (Vol. 6736, Issue 2015). Geneva: WHO.

World Health Organization. (2016). *Verbal autopsy standards: The 2016 WHO verbal autopsy instrument.* 1–143. Retrieved from www.who.int/healthinfo/statistics/verbalautopsystandards/en/

World Health Organization. (2019). *Trends in maternal mortality 2000 to 2017: Estimates by WHO, UNICEF, UNFPA, World Bank Group and the United Nations Population Division.* Geneva: WHO.

World Health Organization, UNFPA, & CDC. (2004). *Maternal death surveillance and response techincal guidance.* 38. Geneva: WHO.

World Health Organization & UNICEF. (1997). The sisterhood method for estimating maternal mortality: Guidance notes for potential users. *Division of Reproductive Health*, 1–22. Retrieved from http://apps.who.int/iris/bitstream/handle/10665/64007/WHO_RHT_97.28.pdf;jsessionid=80925206DD9BD07CBA120B3227E20FDB?sequence=1

Yamoussoukro Declaration. (2015). *The third conference of African Ministers responsible for civil registration.* Retrieved from https://unstats.un.org/unsd/demographic/crvs/Global_CRVS_Docs/news/Third-Conf_resolutions.pdf

Zakariah, A. Y., Alexander, S., Van Roosmalen, J., Buekens, P., Kwawukume, E. Y., & Frimpong, P. (2009). Reproductive age mortality survey (RAMOS) in Accra, Ghana. *Reproductive Health, 6*(1), 1–6. https://doi.org/10.1186/1742-4755-6-7

42

INFANT AND CHILD MORTALITY IN SUB-SAHARAN AFRICA

An overview of levels, determinants, interventions and updates on estimation techniques

Sunday A. Adedini and Joshua O. Akinyemi

Introduction

Despite global reduction, infant and child mortality remains high in sub-Saharan Africa (SSA). Although SSA has witnessed declines, variation in under-five mortality rate between the developed regions and SSA remains almost 20-fold (Adedini, Akinyemi, & Wandera, 2019; Alabi, Oyedokun, Doctor, & Adedini, 2017; UNICEF et al., 2018). The region bears a high burden of global under-five deaths because children in SSA are 15 times more likely to die before age 5 compared to those in the developed countries. Besides, SSA is home to five of the six countries in the world with under-five mortality rate above 100 deaths per 1,000 live births (WHO, 2018).

Historically and for many years, lack of relevant data such as civil registration and vital statistics limited the ability to monitor progress in child mortality reduction in SSA. However, recent years have witnessed tremendous progress in demographic data collection and analysis, using different robust direct and indirect estimation techniques. This has led to the provision of more timely information for socio-economic and public health planning aimed at improving child health and well-being. As a result, evidence-based public health programmes and interventions have been introduced in many countries to prevent avoidable morbidity and mortality among children (Adedini et al., 2019; Black et al., 2008; Ukwuani, Cornwel, & Suchindran, 2002; UNICEF, 2012). Examples of such initiatives include the Polio Eradication Initiative, Expanded Programme on Immunization, and Child Health and Mortality Prevention Surveillance being implemented across selected SSA countries (Cunningham et al., 2019; Salzberg et al., 2019), as well as country-specific intervention programmes such as the Save One Million Lives Programme and National Emergency Action Plan in Nigeria and National Food and Nutrition Security Plan in South Africa.

Millennium Development Goal 4 (which aimed at reducing child mortality by two thirds between 1990 and 2015) could not be achieved in many SSA countries, but the new international development framework – the Sustainable Development Goal (SDG) 3 which seeks to

DOI: 10.4324/9780429287213-51

end preventable deaths of children, among other targets, provides a unique opportunity for the region to change the narratives. Meanwhile, provision of timely evidence on levels and trends in child health and survival will be important for monitoring progress on the SDG target 3.2 (reducing child mortality to 25 deaths per 1,000 live births in SSA) and other country-specific programmes. This chapter provides synthesized data from different sources to furnish key evidence on child health and survival in sub-Saharan Africa.

Objectives

Objectives of this book chapter are to:

1 review updates on direct and indirect childhood estimation techniques;
2 collate and analyze evidence on the levels, trends, patterns and determinants of infant and child mortality in SSA; and
3 synthesize and analyze evidence on programmes and interventions implemented towards improving child health and survival across SSA countries.

Definition of concepts and terms

Under-five mortality rate is the probability per 1,000 that a newborn baby will die before reaching age five, if subject to age-specific mortality rates of the specified year.

Infant mortality rate is the number of infants dying before reaching one year of age, per 1,000 live births in a given year.

Neonatal mortality rate is the number of neonates dying before reaching 28 days of age, per 1,000 live births in a given year.

Data and information sources

The data source for this chapter is mainly published and unpublished materials. We collated, analyzed, and synthesized available evidence to address the objectives. We reviewed evidence from the major databases – Scopus, Hinari, National Library of Medicine, Web of Science and PubMed. In addition, the websites of relevant agencies of United Nations such as UNICEF, UNDP and the WHO as well as the websites of national statistical organizations of SSA countries were searched for relevant materials and data. The search terms included child health, infant mortality, child mortality, under-five mortality, estimation techniques for child mortality, sub-Saharan Africa, etc. The review period for the chapter mainly covered the period 2000 to 2020.

The common sources of data for monitoring the levels of infant and child mortality include vital registration systems (VRS), household surveys, censuses, health and demographic surveillance systems and health facility-based data. These data sources are described in many standard texts and online resources (Mather & Cortes, 2007; Rowland, 2003). The contemporary status of each of these data sources in Africa is briefly described with their main strengths and weaknesses.

(i) Vital Registration System

All things being equal, continuous registration of births and deaths is the richest source of data for child mortality measurement (Rajaratnam, Tran, Lopez, & Murray, 2010). With complete

VRS data, the infant and child mortality rate can be calculated with numerators coming from the VRS while the denominator is derived from population census figures. Assuming VRS is fully functional with good level of completeness, it has two shortcomings as a basis for measuring childhood mortality. The first is the limited amount of socio-economic data that can realistically be collected, thereby limiting the depth of potential analysis. The second is that only infant mortality, rather than broader childhood, mortality can be readily measured (Hill, 1991). To estimate childhood mortality, additional data on exposure to risk in later childhood are needed. Perhaps the greatest downside of VRS in Africa and many other developing regions is that they are often weak with very poor levels of completeness. A global assessment of the Vital Statistics Performance Index (VPSI) showed that majority of the countries in the African region were low performers (Mikkelsen et al., 2015). VSPI is very low in most countries in the sub-Sahara region (except South Africa) because civil registration systems are non-existent or so dysfunctional that no data were ever reported from them. There are several initiatives spearheaded by the African Union to improve VRS (African Centre for Statistics and Economic Commission for Africa, 2017) but individual countries need to address the problem of poor coverage of VRS.

(ii) Censuses

Population census is defined as 'the total process of collecting, evaluating, analyzing, and publishing or otherwise disseminating demographic, economic and social data pertaining, at a specified time, to all persons in a country or in a well-delimited part of a country' (United Nations Statistical Division, 2014). Its essential features include individual enumeration, universality within a defined territory, simultaneity and defined periodicity. Censuses provide the denominators required for calculation of vital rates and ratios. In other words, censuses provide the 'population at risk'. All things being equal, censuses are conducted on decennial basis. However, some African countries are not able to maintain this due to their inability to raise the enormous technical and financial resources that are required. It is important to note some of the weakness of population censuses as far as vital statistics is concerned. Non-sampling errors such as overcounting and undercounting are common. Censuses do not include detailed information about socio-economic profile, population health and nutrition. Census data are also subject to recall bias, age misstatements and reference-period problems. There are standard demographic techniques to detect and correct some of these demographic errors. Another challenge associated with censuses is the frequency at which they are conducted (every 10 years). This does not permit regular update of data needed to monitor population health and development. To overcome this limitation, censuses are often supplemented with population-based household sample surveys.

To fill the mortality data gap, some censuses include retrospective data collection of household deaths by age and sex during some reference period, typically 12 or 24 months, prior to the census (Hill, 1991). In theory, such information could provide levels and age patterns of childhood mortality for the year or two years before the census. However, this method could not provide information on trends except by repetition and would not, in a large-scale enquiry, be very useful as a way of identifying deaths for cause-of-death investigation through the application of verbal autopsies (Hill, 1991). The method was applied to the child survivorship data from the 1991 Nigeria census post-enumeration survey but it performed very poorly and was jettisoned (NPC, 1998). There isn't much data about experience from other countries, probably because household surveys are conducted regularly from which mortality levels are readily estimated.

(iii) Household Surveys

Household surveys are the most common source of data for monitoring the levels of child mortality in most African countries. Unlike population censuses for which household heads are the main respondents, other household members such as women and children are often captured during surveys. Survey sample sizes are smaller than censuses and are selected to be nationally representative of the larger population. The two types of household sample surveys are single-round and multi-round surveys (Akinyemi, 2019). Single-round surveys are cross-sectional surveys in which respondents are interviewed only once. Prominent examples of these are the defunct World Fertility Surveys (WFS) conducted in the 1970s and early 1980s in more than 40 countries; Demographic and Health Surveys (DHS) which took over after the WFS; and Multiple Indicator Cluster Surveys (MICS) anchored by UNICEF to study child health and related topics. These popular surveys are conducted on quinquennial basis in most countries. However, a few countries such as Senegal conduct DHS every year on a continuous basis. Though the objectives of the surveys often vary, the underlying principles for their design and implementation are very similar.

In multi-round surveys, after the initial interview, follow-up visits are made and respondents interviewed more than once using a longitudinal design. Repeated interviews permit correction of inconsistent data from earlier rounds. In addition, such design allows changes in household composition, births, deaths, migration and the associated characteristics to be explored in depth. The main challenge for this type of survey is that it is costly and complex to administer. While longitudinal surveys are common in US and Europe, experience from a few developing countries showed that the quality of data does deteriorate over time. Perhaps this explains why multi-round surveys are not common in developing countries.

To estimate child mortality levels from surveys, data are collected on summary birth history (SBH) or full birth history (FBH) of women. The ensuing child survivorship data are translated to estimates of infant and childhood mortality either by direct technique using the synthetic cohort life table method for FBH or by the indirect techniques devised and developed by Brass and others for SBH (Rajaratnam et al., 2010).

Household surveys also have their own limitations. They suffer from problems such as age misstatement, recall errors and sampling errors. Due to limited sample size, estimates are provided only for national and large sub-national levels. Small or local area estimates are rarely provided and therefore it is difficult to use survey data to evaluate programmes at these lower administrative levels of the population. Advances in small area estimation may be employed to overcome this limitation in the nearest future.

(iv) Surveillance Systems

This is a close relative of the multi-round survey, whereby a geographically defined population is kept under detailed study for an extended time period. The oldest known example of a surveillance system is the International Centre for Diarrhoeal Disease Research study at Matlab-thana in Bangladesh (Koenig, Faveau, & Wojtyniak, 1991), but similar systems also exist in African countries such as Senegal, the Gambia, Ghana, Kenya, South Africa, Burkina Faso and Tanzania among others (Baiden, Hodgson, & Binka, 2006). The key characteristic of a surveillance system is a defined geographical area, the population of which is visited at frequent intervals, even as often as once a month, to inquire about demographic events, morbid episodes, contraceptive use or any other focus of a particular study.

Health and demographic surveillance systems (HDSS) monitor births, deaths, causes of death, migration and other health indices within a defined population over time. HDSS have grown to become a good source of data for vital statistics in developing countries. HDSS across the developing world formed a network known as INDEPTH (International Network for Demographic Evaluation of Population and Their Health). Using the INDEPTH platform (www.indepth-network.org/), HDSS data have been pooled from several sites in Africa and used to provide useful information on demographic characteristics for the continent.

The surveillance system can generate excellent measures of levels, age patterns and differentials of childhood mortality for the study population. Trends can also be measured over the life of the system, but they may be affected by other activities, such as health intervention trials in the study area. Information on cause of death can be obtained by verbal autopsy methods, and only resource availability limits the amount of other information that can be collected. In the absence of usable vital registration data, a surveillance system may be the only source of data that can reveal sharp discontinuities in childhood mortality (Baiden et al., 2006). Surveillance systems provide opportunities for nesting several prevention and intervention projects. A case study of such possibilities is the Child Health and Mortality Prevention Surveillance (CHAMPS) network which aims to deploy innovative methods to generate data on causes of childhood death and thereby inform prevention policies (Salzberg et al., 2019). Most of the sites in the CHAMPS network have existing HDSS which have hosted many other health interventions in the past (Cunningham et al., 2019).

Multi-round surveys and surveillance systems are excellent approaches to detailed research activities that provide reliable results on childhood mortality levels, trends and causes. However, both are extremely expensive and their longitudinal nature makes them susceptible to political or economic instability. Besides, they are unable to provide quick measures because time is needed to build up sufficient events and exposure to risk to calculate stable rates. Furthermore, a surveillance system is unable to produce national estimates because of its limited geographic coverage and the risk of its becoming less and less representative with time. This is the main reason for exclusion of surveillance data from the periodical trend analysis conducted by the United Nations Inter-Agency Group for Child Mortality Estimation (IGME, 2019).

(v) Health facilities

Health facilities play two key roles as sources of data for monitoring childhood mortality (Akinyemi, 2019). Firstly, health facilities function as an informant for occurrence of births and deaths. Secondly, they are primarily responsible for certification of causes of death. The first role is dependent on the extent of health service utilization in a country. In settings wherein most births and deaths take place at health facilities, it is possible to compile the required information and transmit to the relevant agency in charge of vital events registration. For many developing countries where these vital events take place outside health facilities and there is no compliance with civil registration laws, completeness of recording is very poor. The ultimate consequence is that civil registration systems in such settings are grossly inadequate.

As per the second role of health facilities, certification of cause of death is a statutory responsibility. Information from the death certificate is also useful for determining the leading cause of death in a population so that public health interventions can be designed. Death certification is supposed to be done by a medical practitioner; with death certificate issued in compliance with international standards such as those stipulated for the International Statistical Classification of Diseases and Related Health Problems (ICD). The ICD-10 was designed to enhance systematic recording, analysis, interpretation and comparison of mortality and morbidity data collected over time and across countries. Its usefulness is dependent on correct documentation using appropriate terms and terminologies. The extent of compliance with this standard is unknown for many countries in sub-Saharan Africa. Generally, mortality data in Africa have some flaws, including inconsistencies and underreporting of information as well as underestimation of the impact of HIV/AIDS in some regions on the continent, thus necessitating the use of indirect estimation techniques for determining the levels and pattern of mortality.

Overview of childhood mortality estimation techniques

Reliable estimates of childhood mortality are important for socio-economic and public health planning. While traditional sources of demographic data such as civil registration and vital statistics (CRVS) can furnish the required data for estimating the level of infant and child mortality, CRVSs are largely incomplete in most SSA countries (Adedini & Odimegwu, 2011; Salzberg et al., 2019). As a result, demographers have widely employed a branch of demography called 'technical demography', using indirect estimation techniques to obtain the best attainable infant and child mortality rates from censuses and surveys (Adedini, 2013; United Nations, 1988a, 1988b). These methods are regarded as indirect estimation techniques because they rely on information that is only indirectly related to mortality (United Nations, 1988a). Such information may include number of children ever born (CEB) and children surviving and can be obtained through censuses and surveys. Although there has been improvement in the quality of censuses and surveys across SSA, the quality of basic demographic data such as age and sex, as well as birth and death reporting remains poor (Njoku, Okunlola, & Adedini, 2018), and does not often permit direct estimation of demographic parameters. Therefore, demographers and other population scientists rely on indirect estimation techniques to obtain vital rates from censuses and surveys.

Largely, the indirect methods for childhood mortality estimation originated from the popular 'Brass technique' in which life table measures of child mortality were derived from data on children born and surviving to women of reproductive ages (Brass & Coale, 1968). The method has gone through extensive refinements and has had a wide applicability in African demography (Blacker & Brass, 2005; Hill & Figuerora, 2001; Palloni & Heligman, 1985; Trussell, 1975). A later classification of these indirect techniques was done in terms of the data source – household surveys or those from health facilities (Hill, 2013b). For household surveys, such as Demographic and Health Survey (DHS), childhood mortality could be estimated from the summary birth history (total number of children ever born and children dead or still alive) using the original Brass technique. Alternatively, a full birth history dataset may be collected and subjected to 'life table analysis' to determine childhood mortality rates (Hill, 2013a). Another method based on survey data uses data on survival of the recent birth to women. For data from health facilities, the 'preceding birth technique' is employed (Brass & Macrae, 1985; Hill & Aguirre, 1990). Many of these methods are not free from challenges of selection and other types of biases. As a remedy, there have been suggestions on how to correct the biases in the indirect methods (Collumbien & Sloggett, 2001; Ward & Zaba, 2008). Following the HIV pandemic which affected many SSA countries, several attempts have been made to assess the effects on direct and indirect childhood mortality estimation with a view to deriving correction factors (Quattrochi, Salomon, Hill, & Castro, 2019; Walker, Hill, & Zhao, 2012). A prominent indirect method of estimating child mortality is based on the use of INDEPTH life table. The INDEPTH life table accounts for the effects of HIV/AIDS on child survival in sub-Saharan Africa (INDEPTH, 2004). Lately, the UN Inter-agency Group for Child Mortality Estimation employs more complex statistical techniques to derive childhood mortality estimates from combination of data from several sources and varying qualities. Bayesian inference techniques are employed to estimate the level of uncertainties (Alkema, New, Pedersen, & You, 2014). Recently, techniques for small area estimation methods have also been developed to provide childhood mortality levels at sub-national or lower administrative units in developing countries (Li et al., 2019; Wakefield et al., 2019). In summary, the techniques for childhood mortality estimation are perhaps more developed and less controversial than maternal and other adult mortality. Future areas of development will be necessary in regard to use of routine health information so that the reliance on quinquennial surveys can be overcome.

Overview of child mortality frameworks as used in African studies and appraisal of their applicability to the contemporary African situations

The decision on which factors to include in an analytical model is usually based on a conceptual framework describing the relationships between the variables concerned (Victora, Huttly, Fuchs, & Olinto, 1997). Building such a framework requires knowledge about the determinants of the specific outcome of interest. The Mosley-Chen framework is the most-employed framework for studies on childhood mortality. The centre point of the framework was that *all socio-economic variables operate through a limited set of 'proximate' determinants (intermediate variables) that directly influence the risk of disease and the outcome (morbidity) of disease conditions (mortality).* Specifically, the determinants of childhood mortality were grouped into proximate and socio-economic factors. Proximate or intermediate/intervening factors are those that directly affect the risk of childhood death. Examples are maternal factors (age, parity and birth interval), environmental contamination (sanitation and safe drinking water), nutrition, injuries and personal illness control. The socio-economic (distal) determinants are factors that influence the health status of a population by operating through the intermediate variables.

Prior to the development of the Mosley-Chen framework, most child survival studies followed either social science or medical science approaches. Many of the analyses were based on multivariate techniques using different types of models: linear models, logit models or hazard models, multilevel models and structural equation models. During the modelling process, variables are entered in blocks or in a sequential manner. Though these analytical models gave insight into the determinants of childhood mortality, however, many of them were not built on a clear theoretical or conceptual framework. Consequent upon the development of the analytical framework by Mosley and Chen in the early 1980s, many studies have applied it in analysis of childhood mortality determinants.

Hill identified three modelling strategies (with their strengths and limitations) that have evolved after the Mosley-Chen framework (Hill, 2000). The first strategy is the analysis of links between background (socio-economic) factors and proximate determinants (e.g. analysis of factors associated with child immunization or birth intervals). This approach provides insight on how to improve health systems but it gives no direct indication of the health gain. Besides, some proximate determinants are difficult to measure objectively. The second strategy used models incorporating childhood mortality with proximate determinants and background variables (in a stepwise manner starting with background variables). This can give insight into how the background variables operate through the proximate determinants but interpretation is not straight-forward because not all proximate factors are measurable. The third modelling strategy is the development of reduced-form models for net associations of background variables and childhood mortality. This approach helps to quantify the net influence of background factors but it will not be able to identify what health systems should focus on in order to improve child survival. In contrast to the use of one approach, Lay and Robilliard (2009) combined the three approaches in a systematic manner to investigate complementarities between childhood mortality and two other MDGs (universal primary education and gender equality).

The statistical modelling approach best suited for any proposed analyses is determined by the objective(s). Therefore, it is difficult to argue for the superiority of one modelling strategy over the other. Rather than advocating a specific approach, it is better for statistical modelling to be guided by a clear analytical/conceptual framework. Unfortunately, many studies deviate from this pragmatic approach. Masuy-Stroobant (2001) observed that in many studies, the Mosley-Chen model is rarely employed in the design or the statistical modelling process but often invoked in the interpretation and discussion of results.

The Mosley-Chen analytical framework has been instrumental to many programmatic interventions that have helped to reduce the level of infant and child mortality in Africa (Hill, 2000). However, Macassa et al. argued that it failed to adequately cater for the complex social dimension of health (Macassa, Hallqvist, & Lynch, 2011). Although many authors have investigated the contextual determinants of childhood mortality especially in Africa (Adedini, Odimegwu, Imasiku, Ononokpono, & Ibisomi, 2014; Akinyemi, Adedini, & Odimegwu, 2017; Antai & Antai, 2008; Boco, 2010), they often adapt and expand the Mosley-Chen framework. To fill the void observed in the framework, Macassa and colleagues proposed what they termed 'a socio-epidemiological' framework to investigate inequalities in child survival (Macassa et al., 2011). The key feature of the framework was a more elaborate expatiation about the mechanism by which social context and social position affect proximate and distal factors to escalate child survival inequalities. They also identify policy entry points to reduce inequities in child survival. A major challenge to operationalizing this framework is the mix of data required, which cut across several levels and are very difficult to gather empirically. Not many empirical studies have applied the framework since it was published in 2011.

Further, prior research has established the usefulness of the theories of demographic, epidemiological and health transitions for the study of population changes, including childhood mortality in Africa (Defo, 2014; Kabudula et al., 2017; Tollman et al., 2008). These theories have particularly been employed to explain the decline in infant and child mortality and gains achieved in life expectancy over four decades between the 1950s and 1990s.

It is necessary to make a remark on the empirical application of these frameworks in regard to data availability. The most common data sources for investigating childhood mortality determinants often do not have all relevant variables, especially those related to morbidity and injury. These data are difficult to collect in cross-sectional surveys which are the most common data source for analysis of mortality determinants in Africa. Perhaps recent and future initiatives on child mortality surveillance can fill this lacuna.

Levels, trends and patterns of infant and child mortality in sub-Saharan Africa

Reducing mortality among children and newborns is an important component of the Sustainable Development Goal (SDG) 3 (WHO, 2020). A review of recent data shows that under-five mortality has declined by nearly 60% globally, from an estimated rate of 93 deaths (per 1,000 livebirths) in 1990 to 39 in 2018. This indicates that 1 in 26 children died before age five in 2018 compared to 1 in 11 in 1990 (UNICEF, WHO, & World Bank, 2020, WHO, 2020).

Despite the significant reduction in the global rates of under-five mortality, a review of trend data, as presented in Figures 42.1 and 42.2, shows that SSA continues to bear an increasing burden of global under-five deaths. SSA's under-five mortality rate of 78 deaths per 1,000 live

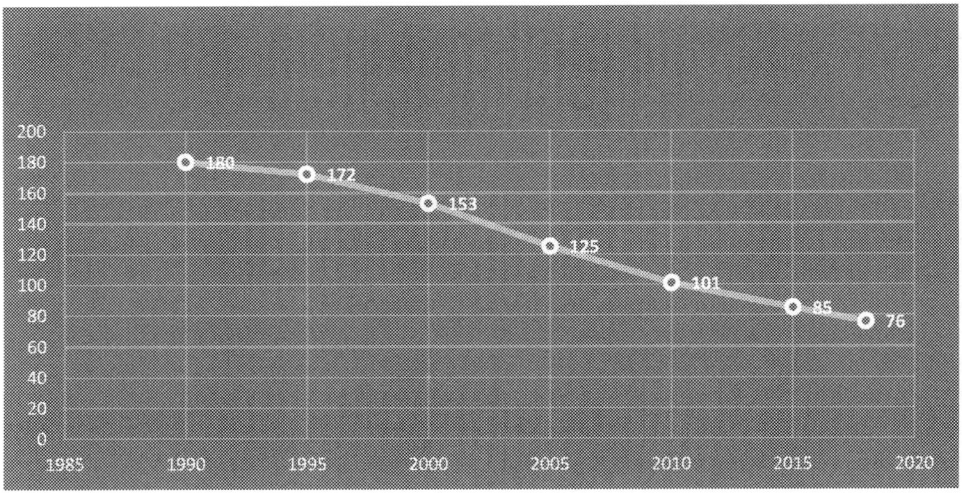

Figure 42.1 Trend in under-five mortality rate in sub-Saharan Africa (1990 to 2018).

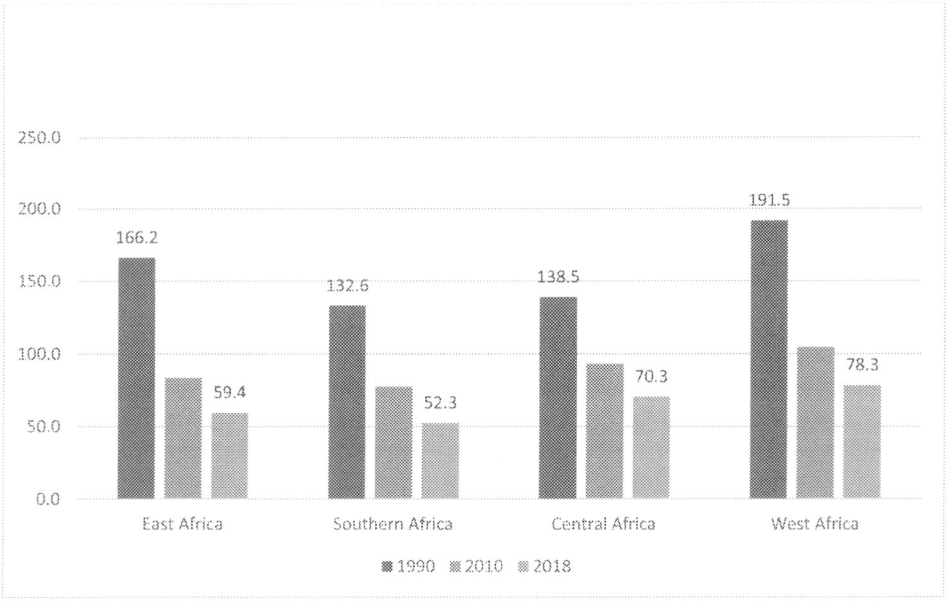

Figure 42.2 Sub-regional variation in under-five mortality in sub-Saharan Africa (1990 to 2018).

births is higher than the global average rate of 39 and is 8 times higher than the Europe average rate of 9 deaths per 1,000 live births (WHO, 2020, UNICEF et al., 2020; World Bank, 2010). In line with the SDG 3, 120 countries have already met the target of reducing under-five mortality to at least 25 deaths per 1,000 live births, while 21 countries are on course to meeting the target by 2030, if the current progress is sustained (WHO, 2020).

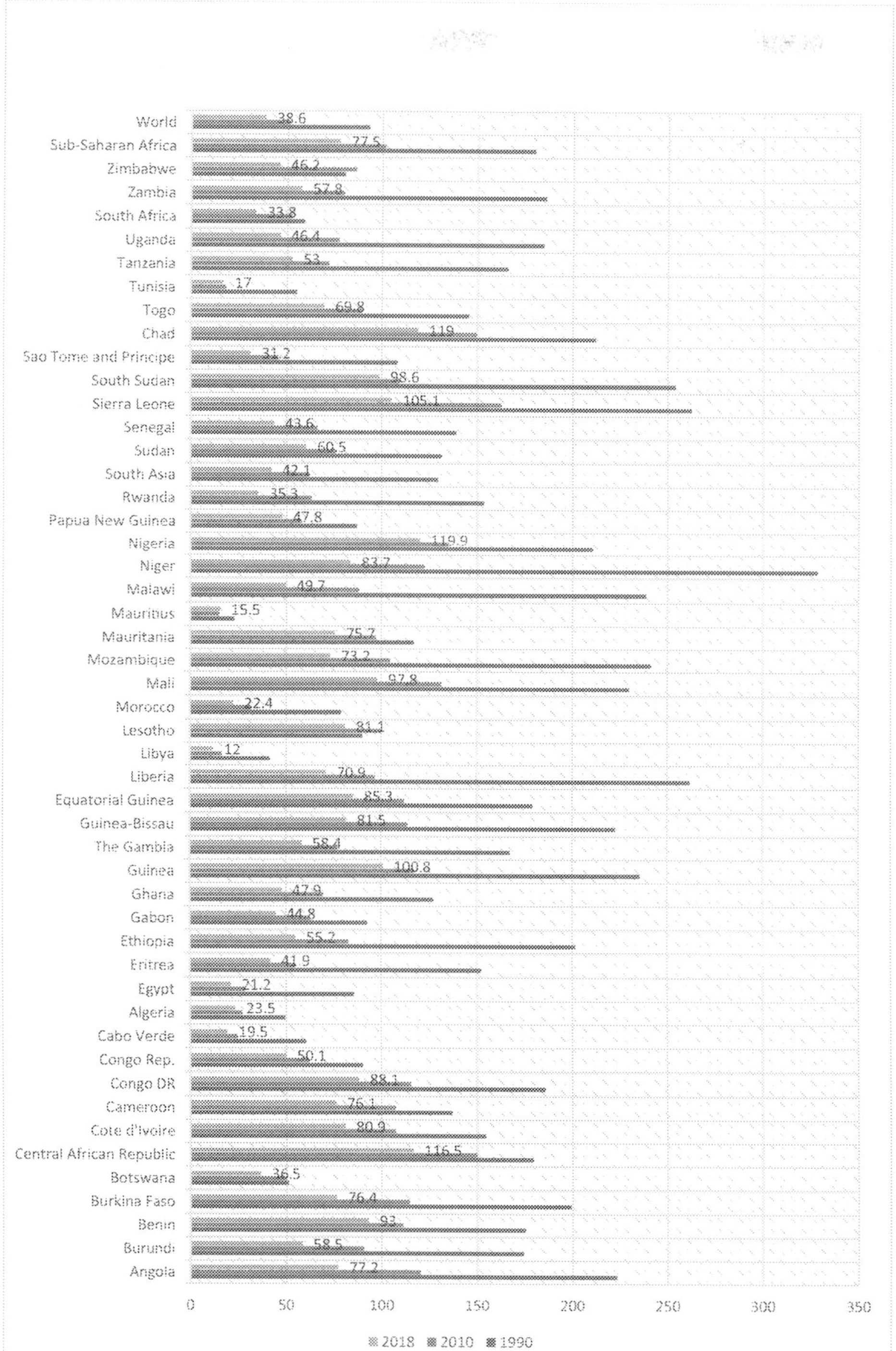

Figure 42.3 Trends in under-five mortality rate (per 1,000 live births) in Africa and the world (1990–2018).

Reviewed data shows that progress in child health and survival is not homogeneous across SSA. While some countries and sub-regions within the region (Figures 42.2 and 42.3) have made satisfactory progress in child mortality reduction, others recorded a somewhat tardy progress. The reviewed literature and data show that the decline in under-five mortality rate (per 1,000 livebirths) was highest in Southern Africa (from 133 in 1990 to 52 in 2018) and lowest in West Africa (from 192 in 1990 to 78 in 2018) (Akinyemi, Bamgboye, & Ayeni, 2015; Oestergaard et al., 2011; UNICEF et al., 2018).

Overview of interventions implemented across SSA towards improving child health

Most deaths of children below the age of five have been attributable to six diseases (Adedini & Alaba, 2019; UNICEF et al., 2018). Table 42.3 presents findings from a review of evidence on the six major childkiller diseases in SSA and the world. These conditions killed almost 5 million under-five children in 2000. The successes recorded by a number of health programmes across SSA and South Asia have led to a significant reduction in the number of deaths due to these diseases, from over 4.6 million in 2000 to around 2 million in 2015. Some of the implemented programmes that led to remarkable progress in child survival in SSA include improved access to healthcare, safe drinking water and effective vaccination programmes. Table 42.4 shows

Table 42.1 Key Reproductive Health Factors Affecting Child Survival in Sub-Saharan Africa (SSA)

Before or during pregnancy	*During childbirth*	*After childbirth*	*References*
Antenatal care use (ANC) – % of mothers (age 15–49) who attended ANC by any provider at least four times during pregnancy ranged from 43% in Ethiopia (2019) and Mali (2018) to 78% in South Africa (2016) and Gambia (2018), compared to 100% in most developed countries.	*Early child-bearing/births to too-young mothers* – % of women age 20–24 who gave birth before age 18 in SSA ranged from 6% in Rwanda (2015) to 51% in Chad (2015), compared to 1% in Tunisia (North Africa).	*Annual under-five death* – Roughly half of 5.3 million deaths of under-five children that died in 2018 occurred in SSA.	(UNICEF, 2008; UINCEF et al., 2020)
Demand for family planning (FP) satisfied with modern methods – % of women (age 15–49) who have their need for FP satisfied with modern methods in SSA ranged from 20% in Chad (2015) to 81% in Zimbabwe (2014).	*Institutional deliveries* – Percentage of deliveries in a health facility among women aged 15–49 years in SSA ranged from 12 in South Sudan (2010), to 46 in Angola (2016), to 100 in Botswana (2015).	*Postnatal care for newborns* – % of newborns who have postnatal contact with a health provider within 2 days of delivery stood at 5% in Chad (2015), 12% in Nigeria (2017), 91% in Ghana (2018) and Zimbabwe (2019).	(UNICEF et al., 2020)

(*Continued*)

Before or during pregnancy	*During childbirth*	*After childbirth*	*References*
High rate of too-close pregnancies in SSA – Birth interval of 3 or more years is associated with lesser risk of childhood death/ malnutrition as well as lower risk of maternal death.	*Skilled birth attendant* – % of deliveries attended by skilled health personnel ranged from 20% in Chad (2015), to 97% in South Africa (2016) and 100% in Mauritius (2016).	*Vaccination* – 76% (DPT) and 74% (measles) of children 12–23 months were immunized in 2018 in SSA compared to 95% in developed countries.	(UNICEF, 2008; UINCEF et al., 2020; Rutstein, 2008)
		Low birth weight – In 2015, proportion of low-birth-weight newborns ranged from 7% in Sao Tome and Principe to 24% in Comoros; compared to 2% in Sweden.	(UNICEF, WHO, World Bank, and United Nations, 2019)

Note*:* SSA – sub-Saharan Africa; ANC – antenatal care, WB – World Bank

Table 42.2 Risk Factors/Drivers of Child Mortality

Analytical level	*Risk factors/drivers of child mortality*	*References*
Individual level	Childhood malnutrition, child's low birth weight, low or no education of mothers, mother's poor healthcare knowledge and practices, child's sex and discriminatory feeding and medical practices, mother's non-use of family planning, negative dietary beliefs and practices, non-breastfeeding of children	(Fotso, 2007; Uthman, 2009) (Adedini & Odimegwu, 2017; Antai, 2011; Imdad, Yakoob, & Bhutta, 2011)
Household level	Poor household wealth, poor housing or overcrowded condition, poor financial access to care, unsafe drinking water and food, poor hygiene practices, lack of social support	(Collison, Dey, Hannah, & Stevenson, 2007; Fuchs, Pamuk, & Lutz, 2010)
Community level	Ecological setting, place of residence, social norms and practices, high fertility norms	(Adedini, Odimegwu, Imasiku, Ononokpono, & Ibisomi, 2015; World Bank, 2010)
Policy/health system level	Healthcare system/context, political economy, high or under-five mortality context, disease control policy context	

the various intervention programmes implemented by government and development partners across sub-Saharan Africa.

Considering that the Millennium Development Goal 4 of reducing under-five mortality by two thirds between 1990 and 2015 was not achieved, there is a lot that needs to be done in SAA

Table 42.3 Major Global Childhood Killer Diseases

The disease ranking in terms of fatality	*Diseases*	*Cause(s) of the disease*	*Symptoms of the disease*	*Risk factors of the disease*	*Proportion of children that died from the disease in the world in 2015*	*Preventable or treatable condition*	*References*
1	Pneumonia	Bacterial infection	Fever, coughing, difficulty breathing, chest pain	Malnutrition, low birth weight, overcrowding	920,000 (16% of all global under-five deaths)	Treatable with antibiotics; preventable using pneumococcal vaccines	(WHO, 2020; UNICEF et al., 2019)
2	Diarrhoea	Infection of intestinal track by pathogens – rotavirus, E. coli bacterium being spread through contaminated water and food or person to person; only rotavirus currently has a vaccine	Stooling, dehydration	Contamination of water and food	526,000 (70% of diarrheal deaths occur in children <2 years)	Preventable through good sanitation, hygiene and access to clean water.	(WHO, 2020; UNICEF et al., 2019)
3	Malaria	Parasite transmitted by mosquito bites, mainly in the tropical regions	High temperature, headaches, pains, sweats and chills	Living in malaria-endemic area	306,000	Treatable with antimalarial drugs	(UNICEF et al., 2019)
4	Meningitis	Infection of meninges (lining of brains and spinal cord)	High fever, stiff neck, headaches, vomiting; can kill within 24–48 hours	Living in meningitis endemic area, climate; overcrowding	116,000	Bacterial infection can be treated with antibiotics; vaccines are also available for prevention	(WHO, 2020)
5	HIV	Can be transmitted to babies during pregnancy, childbirth or breastfeeding.	HIV weakens the immune system and can lead to AIDS and other infections	Mother-to-child-transmission – the biggest in under-fives	87,000	HIV has no cure, but antiretroviral drugs can stop the virus.	(UNICEF et al., 2019, WHO, 2020)
6	Measles	Caused by a virus which is transmittable through direct contact or through the air	High fever, cough, runny nose, red and watery eyes, body rash	Children in poor countries, particularly those malnourished have a high risk of dying from measles	74,000	Vaccination programmes against the disease have been effective in SSA	WHO, CDC

Source: WHO: World Health Organization, CDC: Centre for Disease Control; SSA: sub-Saharan Africa; UNICEF: United Nations Children's Fund

Table 42.4 Child Mortality Prevention Intervention Programmes in Sub-Saharan Africa

S/N	*Programme*	*Focus of the programme*	*Year introduced*	*Countries where it was implemented*	*Strengths/Weakness of the programme*
1	Disease control	Mainly malaria disease control	First half of twentieth century	Implemented by colonial governments across malaria endemic countries	Largely fragmented. Malaria still accounts for the majority of global childhood deaths
		Reduction/eradication of specific diseases – smallpox, Guinea worm, leprosy, trachoma, elephantiasis	1950s–1970s	SSA	Highly successful – notably, smallpox was eradicated from Africa in 1977
		Ongoing disease control	Ongoing	SSA	91% reduction in measles deaths in Africa between 2000 and 2006
2	comprehensive primary health care	Community health and integrated approaches to health service delivery and intersectoral collaboration	1950s	SSA	
3	Expanded Programme on Immunization, launched in 1974	Initiated by the World Health Organization, EPI seeks to make vaccines available to all children	1974	SSA and other parts of the world	EPI campaign led to the eradication of smallpox; a 99% decline in global polio infections and 78% decrease in global measles deaths. With the eradication of polio in Nigeria in 2020, the African continent has been declared polio-free by the WHO
4	Selective primary health care	Due to economic constraints in SSA, the programme focussed on selected key diseases/conditions through relatively inexpensive medical technologies called GOBI	1980s	SSA	GOBI and EPI made a great contribution to reduction in global child deaths in the 1980s

(*Continued*)

Table 42.4 (Continued)

S/N	*Programme*	*Focus of the programme*	*Year introduced*	*Countries where it was implemented*	*Strengths/Weakness of the programme*
5	Integrated approaches	Focussed on increasing access to PHC in SSA through community participation and provision of cost-effective solutions to address health challenges.	1990s	SSA	The 1990s and the early years of the current decade have seen a renewed focus on integrated approaches to health-service delivery
		IMC, which employed a cross-cutting approach to case management of childhood illness, admitting that there is usually more than one contributing cause of child death	1992	SSA	Positive outcomes for IMCI were reported across many SSA countries
		ACSD programme – introduced the Canadian International Development Agency, UNICEF and national governments to reduce under-five mortality through behavioural changes on issues – such as breastfeeding, use of insecticide-treated nets in malaria-endemic areas	2002	West and Central Africa	ACSD has grown and is focusing on more than 16 million people in 11 West and Central Africa countries with high under-five mortality rates
		Integrated management of childhood disease (IMCI) aims to reduce death, illness and disability, and to promote improved growth and development among children under five years of age. IMCI includes both preventive and curative elements that are implemented by families and communities as well as by health facilities			
6.	Child Health and Mortality Prevention Surveillance	CHAMPS tracks the causes of under-five mortality and stillbirths using minimally invasive tissue sampling (MITS), post-mortem laboratory and pathology testing, verbal autopsy and clinical and demographic data in comprehensive mortality surveillance	2015	Implemented in selected SSA countries – Ethiopia, Kenya, Mali Mozambique, Sierra Leone, South Africa; and Bangladesh in South Asia	CHAMPS has established facility- and community-based mortality notification systems, with the aim of reporting and determining cause of under-five deaths and stillbirths in selected areas. Data on cause of death is available to local, national and global stakeholders to inform strategies to reduce child mortality in SAA and South Asia. The major limitation of CHAMPS programme is that its data may not be generalizable to all the countries of SSA

Note: GOBI – growth monitoring for undernutrition, oral rehydration therapy; EPI: Expanded Programme on Immunization; PHC: primary health care; SSA: sub-Saharan Africa; IMC: integrated management of childhood illness; ACSD: Accelerated Child Survival and Development

if the SDG target of reducing child mortality to 25 deaths per 1,000 live births will be achieved across the region by 2030.

To address the high level of child mortality in SSA, several programmes and interventions have been implemented by governments of various countries and development partners and donors. These range from initiatives targeting the common childhood killer diseases, such as malaria, pneumonia, meningitis, diarrhoea; or condition such as undernutrition; to the provision of a continuum of healthcare services, including targeted antenatal care, institutional delivery care, and postnatal care. Table 42.4 presents the major programmes implemented across SSA countries to address child mortality in the region.

The various intervention programmes implemented across SSA led to significant reductions in child mortality in the region. This was achieved through the implementation of various interventions which led to a number of achievements such as rapid progress in child survival, advances in malaria prevention and treatment, expanded distribution and use of micronutrient supplementation, reduction in measles deaths, increased access to antiretroviral treatment for HIV-positive mothers and children and increase in the rate of exclusive breastfeeding,

Future research agenda

With the benefit of hindsight, there has been an impressive advancement in child survival in the past two decades. Looking forward into the future, there have been several innovative attempts to set priorities for child health and survival especially in the area of implementation research (Were et al., 2015). Top issues in some of these agenda settings deal mostly with getting proven child health interventions to those most in need – the vulnerable and disadvantaged groups. There are aspirations to develop new interventions to promote neonatal survival. It is a matter of research priority to identify novel techniques and innovations that would lead to prevention of stillbirths and newborn death. There is also the need to improve data collection on child morbidity and child health care utilization as well as registration of birth and child's death (Adedini, Odimegwu, Imasiku, Ononokpono, & Ibisomi, 2020).

Beyond these empirical child health priorities, there are future opportunities to be explored in the area of methodological approaches to monitoring of child mortality levels, trends and determinants. The volume of data for monitoring child health outcomes is increasing by the day. New techniques to integrate data from multiple sources would definitely be needed. For example, innovative approaches would be needed to combine data from surveys, surveillance systems, health facilities and routine health information systems to fill existing and emerging knowledge gaps.

Further, there are new advances in the area of precision public health which aims to promote clear identification of sub-populations that need urgent child survival interventions. This is made possible by developments in geospatial statistical methodologies and the fast-pace of computing power. Advancement in computational possibilities is opening up more opportunities for deployment of data science tools and techniques to promote maternal, newborn and child health outcomes. This will continue to be relevant for better understanding of the extent to which child health outcomes have longer-term health outlooks. Another area with promising future is genomics. Genes and environment have been demonstrated to affect health outcomes in adult population. This may also be relevant to children's health outcomes in the near future.

Lastly, the entire globe is presently confronted with a public health challenge in COVID-19 and other health emergencies such as Ebola and Lassa fever. COVID-19 especially has disrupted many health programmes. Early modelling studies are suggesting that these could have grave consequences for children's health and survival (Pérez-Escamilla,

Cunningham, & Moran, 2020; Roberton et al., 2020). Besides, experiences from some West African countries ravaged by Ebola between 2014 and 2016 also showed that maternal and child health services were severely disrupted (Barden-O'Fallon, Barry, Brodish, & Hazerjian, 2015; Brolin Ribacke, Saulnier, Eriksson, & von Schreeb, 2016; Kamara et al., 2017). A lot of work would need to be done in documenting the short-, medium- and long-term effects of COVID-19 and its preventive measures on different aspect of child health services. Operational research will also be needed to inform development of creative strategies to sustain child health interventions and survival programmes in pandemics and other health emergencies.

References

Adedini, S. A. (2013). *Contexual determinants of infant and child mortality in Nigeria* (PhD Thesis). University of the Witwatersrand.

Adedini, S. A., & Alaba, O. (2019). *An in-depth exploration of community perspectives and responses to major childhood killer diseases in Nigeria.* Paper presented at the Population Association of America, USA.

Adedini, S. A., & Odimegwu, C. O. (2011). Assessing knowledge, attitude and practice of vital registration system in South-west Nigeria. *Ife Psychologia, 19*(1), 456–471.

Adedini, S. A., & Odimegwu, C. O. (2017). Polygynous family system, neighbourhood contexts and under-five mortality in sub-Saharan Africa. *Development Southern Africa,* 1–17.

Adedini, S. A., Akinyemi, J., & Wandera, S. (2019). Women's position in the household as a determinant of neonatal mortality in sub-Saharan Africa. *South African Journal of Child Health, 13*(1), 17–22.

Adedini, S. A., Odimegwu, C., Imasiku, E. N., Ononokpono, D. N., & Ibisomi, L. (2014). Regional variations in infant and child mortality in Nigeria: A multilevel analysis. *Journal of Biosocial Science, 47*(2), 165–187. https://doi.org/10.1017/s0021932013000734

Adedini, S. A., Odimegwu, C., Imasiku, E. N., Ononokpono, D. N., & Ibisomi, L. (2015). Regional variations in infant and child mortality in Nigeria: A multilevel analysis. *Journal of Biosocial Science, 47*(2), 165–187.

Adedini, S. A., Sello, M., Thaele, D., & Madhi, S. A. (2020). Patterns of healthcare utilisation and barriers affecting access to child healthcare services in low-income urban South African settings. *South African Journal of Child Health, 14*(1), 34–39.

African Centre for Statistics and Economic Commission for Africa. (2017). *Practical guide on the improvement of death registration and causes of death processes within a civil registration and vital statistics system.* Retrieved from Addis Ababa.

Akinyemi, J. O. (2019). Vital statistics. In A. S. Adebowale & J. O. Akinyemi (Eds.), *Selected topics in medical statistics* (pp. 41–64). Ile Ife: ANDKOLAD.

Akinyemi, J. O., Adedini, S., & Odimegwu, C. (2017). Individual v. community-level measures of women's decision-making involvement and child survival in Nigeria. *South African Journal of Child Health, 11*(1), 26–32.

Akinyemi, J. O., Bamgboye, E. A., & Ayeni, O. (2015). Trends in neonatal mortality in Nigeria and effects of bio-demographic and maternal characteristics. *BMC Pediatrics, 15,* 36. https://doi.org/10.1186/s12887-015-0349-0

Alabi, O., Oyedokun, O. A., Doctor, H. V., & Adedini, S. A. (2017). Determinants of under-five mortality clustering in a health and demographic surveillance system in Zamfara State, northern Nigeria. *African Population Studies, 31*(1).

Alkema, L., New, J. R., Pedersen, J., & You, D. (2014). Child mortality estimation 2013: An overview of updates in estimation methods by the United Nations Inter-agency Group for Child Mortality Estimation. *PLoS One, 9*(7), e101112.

Antai, D. (2011). Inequalities in under-5 mortality in Nigeria: Do ethnicity and socioeconomic position matter? *Journal of Epidemiology, 21*(1), 13–20.

Antai, D., & Antai, J. (2008). Individual- and contextual-level determinants of social inequities in under-five mortality in Nigeria: Differentials by religious affiliation of the mother. *World Health and Population, 10*(4), 38–52.

Baiden, F., Hodgson, A., & Binka, F. N. (2006). Demographic surveillance sites and emerging challenges in international health. *Bulletin of the World Health Organization, 84*(3), 163–164.

Barden-O'Fallon, J., Barry, M. A., Brodish, P., & Hazerjian, J. (2015). Rapid assessment of Ebola-related implications for reproductive, maternal, newborn and child health service delivery and utilization in Guinea. *PLoS Currents*, 7. https://doi.org/10.1371/currents.outbreaks.0b0ba06009dd091bc39ddb3c6d7b0826

Barthélémy Kuate Defo. (2014) Demographic, epidemiological, and health transitions: are they relevant to population health patterns in Africa? *Global Health Action*, 7, 1. https://doi.org/10.3402/gha.v7.22443

Black, R. E., Allen, L. H., Bhutta, Z. A., Caulfield, L. E., de Onis, M., Ezzati, M., . . . Rivera, J. (2008). Maternal and child undernutrition: global and regional exposures and health consequences. *The Lancet*, *371*(9608), 243–260. https://doi.org/10.1016/s0140-6736(07)61690-0

Blacker, J., & Brass, W. (2005). The estimation of infant mortality from proportions dying among births in the past 24 months. *Southern African Journal of Demography*, 25–42.

Boco, A. G. (2010). *Individual and community level effects on child mortality: An analysis of 28 demographic and health surveys in Sub-Saharan Africa*. Calverton, MD: ICF Macro.

Brass, W., & Coale, A. J. (1968). Methods of analysis and estimation In W. Brass, A. J. Coale, P. Demeny, F. Hiesel, F. Lorimer, A. Romaniuk, & E. Van dan Walle (Eds.), *The demography of tropica Africa* (pp. 88–139). Princeton, NJ: Princeton University Press.

Brass, W., & Macrae, S. (1985). *Childhood mortality estimated from reports on previous births given by mothers at the time of a maternity: II. Adapted multiplying factor technique*. Paper presented at the Asian and Pacific Census Forum.

Brolin Ribacke, K. J., Saulnier, D. D., Eriksson, A., & von Schreeb, J. (2016). Effects of the West Africa Ebola virus disease on health-care utilization – A systematic review. *Frontiers in Public Health, 4*, 222. https://doi.org/10.3389/fpubh.2016.00222

Collison, D., Dey, C., Hannah, G., & Stevenson, L. (2007). Income inequality and child mortality in wealth nations. *Journal of Public Health, 29*(2), 114–117.

Collumbien, M., & Sloggett, A. (2001). Adjustment methods for bias in the indirect childhood mortality estimates. In B. Zaba & J. Blacker (Eds.), *Brass tacks: Essays in medical demography* (pp. 20–42). London: Athlone Press.

Cunningham, S. A., Shaikh, N. I., Nhacolo, A., Raghunathan, P. L., Kotloff, K., Naser, A. M., . . . Onuwchekwa, U. U. (2019). Health and demographic surveillance systems within the child health and mortality prevention surveillance network. *Clinical Infectious Diseases*, *69*(Supplement 4), S274–S279.

Fotso, J. C. (2007). Urban-rural differentials in child malnutrition: Trends and socioeconomic correlates in sub-Saharan Africa. *Health and Place, 13*. https://doi.org/10.1016/j.healthplace.2006.01.004

Fuchs, R., Pamuk, E., & Lutz, W. (2010). Education or wealth: Which matters more for reducing child mortality in developing countries? *Vienna Yearbook of Population Research*, *8*, 175–199. https://doi.org/10.2307/23025514

Hill, A. G., & Aguirre, A. (1990). Childhood mortality estimates using the preceding birth technique: some applications and extensions. *Population Studies*, *44*(2), 317–340.

Hill, K. (1991). Approaches to the measurement of childhood mortality: A comparative review. *Population Index*, *57*(3), 368–382.

Hill, K. (2000). Frameworks for studying the determinants of child survival. *Bulletin of the World Health Organization*, *81*(2), 138–139.

Hill, K. (2013a). Direct estimation of child mortality from birth histories. In T. Moultrie, R. Dorrington, A. Hill, K. Hill, I. M. Timaeus, & B. Zaba (Eds.), *Tools for demographic estimation*. Paris: International Union for the Scientific Study of Population.

Hill, K. (2013b). Introduction to child mortality analysis. In T. Moultrie, R. Dorrington, A. Hill, K. Hill, I. M. Timaeus, & B. Zaba (Eds.), *Tools for demographic estimation*. Paris: International Union for the Scientific Study of Population.

Hill, K., & Figuerora, M.-E. (2001). Child mortality estimation by time since first birth. In B. Zaba & J. Blacker (Eds.), *Brass tacks: Essays in medical demography* (pp. 9–19). London: Athlone.

IGME. (2019). *Explanatory Notes: Child mortality trend series to 2018*. UNICEF, the WHO, the UN Population Division and the World Bank Group.

Imdad, A., Yakoob, M. Y., & Bhutta, Z. A. (2011). Impact of maternal education about complementary feeding and provision of complementary foods on child growth in developing countries. *BMC Public Health*, *11*(3). https://doi.org/1471–2458/11/S3/S25

INDEPTH. (2004). *INDEPTH model life tables for sub-Saharan Africa*. Aldershot: Ashgate.

Kabudula, C. W., Houle, B., Collinson, M. A., Kahn, K., Gómez-Olivé, F. X., Clark, S. J., & Tollman, S. (2017). Progression of the epidemiological transition in a rural South African setting: findings from population surveillance in Agincourt, 1993–2013. *BMC Public Health, 17*(1), 1–15. https://doi.org/10.1186/s12889-017-4312-x

Kamara, M. H., Najjemba, R., van Griensven, J., Yorpoi, D., Jimissa, A. S., Chan, A. K., & Mishra, S. (2017). Increase in acute malnutrition in children following the 2014–2015 Ebola outbreak in rural Sierra Leone. *Public Health Action*, 7(Suppl 1), S27–S33. https://doi.org/10.5588/pha.16.0084

Koenig, M. V., Faveau, V., & Wojtyniak, B. (1991). Mortality reductions from health interventions: The case of immunization in Bangladesh. *Population and Development Review, 17*(1).

Lay, J., & Robilliard, A.-S. (2009). *The complementarity of MDG achievements: The case of child mortality in Sub-Sahara Africa.* Washington, DC: The World Bank.

Li, Z., Hsiao, Y., Godwin, J., Martin, B. D., Wakefield, J., Clark, S. J., . . . Group, I. T. A. (2019). Changes in the spatial distribution of the under-five mortality rate: Small-area analysis of 122 DHS surveys in 262 subregions of 35 countries in Africa. *PLoS One, 14*(1), e0210645.

Macassa, G., Hallqvist, J., & Lynch, J. W. (2011). Inequalities in child mortality in sub-Saharan Africa: A social epidemiologic framework. *African Journal of Health Sciences, 18*(1–2), 14–26.

Masuy-Stroobant, G. (2001). Determinants of infant mortality: How far are conceptual frameworks really modelled? *Texte publie sous la responsabilite de lauteur. Document de Travail no 13.*

Mather, M., & Cortes, R. (2007). Demographic data: Censuses, registers, surveys. *The Blackwell Encyclopedia of Sociology*, 1–4.

Mikkelsen, L., Phillips, D. E., AbouZahr, C., Setel, P. W., de Savigny, D., Lozano, R., & Lopez, A. D. (2015). A global assessment of civil registration and vital statistics systems: Monitoring data quality and progress. *The Lancet, 386*(10001), 1395–1406. https://doi.org/10.1016/s0140-6736(15)60171-4

National Population Commission [Nigeria]. (1998). *Population census of the Federal Republic of Nigeria: Analytical report at the national level.* Abuja, Nigeria: National Population Commission.

Njoku, E., Okunlola, D. O., & Adedini, S. A. (2018). Demographic assessment and adjustment of census age distribution in selected West African Countries. *African Population Studies, 32*(3).

Oestergaard, M. Z., Inoue, M., Yoshida, S., Mahanani, W. R., Gore, F. M., Cousens, S., . . . Mathers, C. D. (2011). Neonatal mortality levels for 193 countries in 2009 with trends since 1990: A systematic analysis of progress, projections, and priorities. *PLoS Medicine, 8*(8), e1001080.

Palloni, A., & Heligman, L. (1985). Re-estimation of structural parameters to obtain estimates of mortality in developing countries. *Population Bulletin of the United Nations, 18*, 10.

Pérez-Escamilla, R., Cunningham, K., & Moran, V. H. (2020). COVID-19 and maternal and child food and nutrition insecurity: A complex syndemic. *Maternal & Child Nutrition, 16*(3), e13036. https://doi.org/10.1111/mcn.13036

Quattrochi, J., Salomon, J. A., Hill, K., & Castro, M. C. (2019). Measuring and correcting bias in indirect estimates of under-5 mortality in populations affected by HIV/AIDS: A simulation study. *BMC Public Health, 19*(1), 1516.

Rajaratnam, J. K., Tran, L. N., Lopez, A. D., & Murray, C. J. (2010). Measuring under-five mortality: Validation of new low-cost methods. *PLoS Medicine*, 7(4), 1–24. doi:10.1371/journal.pmed.1000253

Roberton, T., Carter, E. D., Chou, V. B., Stegmuller, A. R., Jackson, B. D., Tam, Y., . . . Walker, N. (2020). Early estimates of the indirect effects of the COVID-19 pandemic on maternal and child mortality in low-income and middle-income countries: A modelling study. *Lancet Glob Health, 8*(7), e901–e908. https://doi.org/10.1016/s2214-109x(20)30229-1

Rowland, D. T. (2003). *Demographic methods and concepts.* Oxford: OUP.

Rutstein, S. O. (2008). *Further evidence of the effects of preceding birth intervals on neonatal, infant, and under-five-years mortality and nutritional status in developing countries: evidence from the demographic and health surveys.* Calverton, MD: Macro International Incorporated.

Salzberg, N. T., Sivalogan, K., Bassat, Q., Taylor, A. W., Adedini, S., El Arifeen, S., . . . Cain, C. J. (2019). Mortality surveillance methods to identify and characterize deaths in child health and mortality prevention surveillance network sites. *Clinical Infectious Diseases, 69*(Supplement 4), S262–S273. https://doi.org/10.1093/cid/ciz599

Tollman, S. M., Kahn, K., Sartorius, B., Collinson, M. A., Clark, S. J., & Garenne, M. L. (2008). Implications of mortality transition for primary health care in rural South Africa: A population-based surveillance study. *The Lancet, 372*(9642), 893–901.

Trussell, T. J. (1975). A re-estimation of the multiplying factors of the Brass technique for determining childhood survivorship rates. *Population Studies, XXIX*(1), 97–108.

Ukwuani, F. A., Cornwel, G. T., & Suchindran, C. M. (2002). Polygyny and child survival in Nigeria: Age-dependent effects. *Journal of Population Research, 19*(1), 155–171.

UNICEF. (2008): *The state of Africa's children*. Geneva: United Nations

UNICEF, WHO, World Bank, & UN DESA Population Division. (2018). *Under-five mortality estimates by the UN Inter-agency Group for Child Mortality Estimation*. Retrieved from https://data.worldbank.org/indicator/SH.DTH.MORT

UNICEF, WHO, World Bank, & United Nations. (2019). *Under-five mortality estimates by the UN Inter-agency Group for Child Mortality Estimation*. Geneva: United Nations

UNICEF, WHO, & World Bank. (2020). *Under-five mortality estimates by the UN Inter-agency Group for Child Mortality Estimation*. https://www.unicef.org/media/79371/file/UN-IGME-child-mortality-report-2020.pdf.pdf

United Nations. (1988a). *A guide on indirect estimation techniques*. New York: United Nations.

United Nations. (1988b). *Mortpark-Lite: The United Nations software package and manual for mortality measurement*. New York: United Nations.

United Nations Statistical Division. (2014). *Principles and recommendations for a vital statistics system: Revision 3* (Vol. 836). New York, NY: United Nations Publications.

Uthman, A. O. (2009). A multilevel analysis of individual and community effect on chronic childhood malnutrition in rural Nigeria. *Journal of Tropical Pediatrics, 55*(2), 109–115.

Victora, C. G., Huttly, S. R., Fuchs, S. C., & Olinto, M. T. A. (1997). The role of conceptual frameworks in epidemiological analysis: A hierarchical approach. *International Journal of Epidemiology, 26*(1), 224–227.

Wakefield, J., Fuglstad, G.-A., Riebler, A., Godwin, J., Wilson, K., & Clark, S. J. (2019). Estimating under-five mortality in space and time in a developing world context. *Statistical Methods in Medical Research, 28*(9), 2614–2634.

Walker, N., Hill, K., & Zhao, F. (2012). Child mortality estimation: methods used to adjust for bias due to AIDS in estimating trends in under-five mortality. *PLoS Medicine, 9*(8), e1001298.

Ward, P., & Zaba, B. (2008). The effect of HIV on estimation of child mortality using the children surviving/children born technique. *Southern African Journal of Demography, 11*(1), 39–73.

Were, W. M., Daelmans, B., Bhutta, Z., Duke, T., Bahl, R., Boschi-Pinto, C., . . . Bhan, M. K. (2015). Children's health priorities and interventions. *BMJ: British Medical Journal, 351*, h4300. https://doi.org/10.1136/bmj.h4300

WHO. (2018). *Global Health Observatory data repository: Probability of dying per 1000 live births Data by WHO region*. Retrieved from http://apps.who.int/gho/data/view.main.CM1300R?lang=en

World Bank. (2010). *Determinants and consequences of high fertility: A synopsis of the evidence*. Retrieved from www.worldbank.org

WHO. (2020). *Children: Improving survival and well-being*. Retrieved October 15, 2021, from https://www.who.int/news-room/fact-sheets/detail/children-reducing-mortality

PART 10

Concluding matters

43
ANTHROPOLOGICAL DEMOGRAPHY IN AFRICA

Daniel Jordan Smith

Introduction

Over the last three decades, anthropology and demography have collaborated to create the relatively new subfield of anthropological demography. Africa has been central to this scholarly project, both in its origins and in contemporary research. Earlier generations of anthropologists explored numerous population-related issues. Their interests were unabashedly demographic. Further, pathbreaking African and Africa-focused demographers recognized decades ago the importance of social context in shaping demographic behaviour and outcomes. But it took a long time before these pursuits coalesced into a coherent enterprise. Although anthropological demography is still relatively new and developing, by now, many Africanist demographers have embraced the need to understand culture.

Anthropology's contribution to the study of population in Africa grew out of the discipline's abiding curiosity about kinship and marriage as foundational elements in human social organization. A focus on kinship and marriage continues to characterize ongoing work in African anthropological demography, but along the way anthropologists have also contributed significantly to demographically oriented scholarship examining fertility transition and contraceptive use, migration, urbanization, and – to a lesser extent – mortality.

While anthropology and demography have become intertwined in the study of multiple population-related topics in Africa, the emergence of the AIDS epidemic in the late twentieth century undoubtedly catalyzed energy and funding for research that examined the cultural and social-contextual dimensions of human demographic and health behaviour – particularly regarding gender and sexuality. AIDS in Africa led to a veritable explosion of research and scholarship at the intersection of anthropology and demography, even as many of the practitioners may not have identified themselves explicitly as anthropological demographers.

This chapter briefly reviews the history and contributions of anthropological demography in Africa, suggests that the results of an often-de facto partnership between anthropology and demography have been productive but not always optimal, provides one extended example of the kind of research that emerged in response to Africa's AIDS epidemic, and argues that a larger cadre and network of African researchers formally trained in anthropological demography would generate much-needed in-depth scholarship that is necessary to understand and address the continent's demographic, health, and development challenges.

 DOI: 10.4324/9780429287213-53

Anthropology's historical interest in population issues

While the 'armchair' anthropologists of the nineteenth century considered population-related issues in their writings about distant peoples and cultures, it was the advent in the early twentieth century of long-term ethnographic field research as the basis for anthropological understanding that was the real precursor to contemporary anthropological demography (Kertzer & Fricke, 1997). Studies of African societies constituted a central part of this more empirically grounded, first-hand research. Although some anthropologists during this period worked directly for colonial governments and their findings were sometimes used to advance or protect imperialist aims, the insights provided by up-close, community-based ethnographic studies proved as useful to the critics of colonial (and postcolonial) projects as to their architects.

As early as the 1930s, British and U.K.-based anthropologists working in Africa, such as Meyer Fortes, E.E. Evans-Pritchard, Daryll Forde, and A.R. Radcliffe-Brown, had developed a keen interest in marriage, and in kinship systems more generally (Fortes, 2018 [1949]; Evans-Pritchard, 1951; Radcliffe-Brown & Forde, 1950). As part of his detailed study of kinship among the Tallensi (in what is now Ghana), Fortes (2018 [1949]), for example, conducted demographically detailed household surveys and examined fertility-related behaviour and outcomes. By the mid-twentieth century, other social anthropologists doing research in Africa, such as Max Gluckman (1940), J. Clyde Mitchell (1965), Arnold Epstein (1958), and Hortense Powdermaker (1962), investigated the social consequences of urbanization and related patterns of rural-to-urban (and circular) migration.

Many of the most influential Africanist anthropologists who studied demographic processes in the second half of the twentieth century, such as Elizabeth Colson beginning in the 1950s (Colson, 1958), Abner Cohen beginning in the 1960s (Cohen, 1969), and Caroline Bledsoe beginning in the 1980s (Bledsoe, 1980), drew explicitly on the scholarly legacies and orientations of earlier British social anthropology. Much of contemporary anthropological demography in Africa has its roots, even if not always explicitly, in scholarly traditions that focused on social organization.

Demography looks to anthropology

While Africanist anthropology's interest in population processes was inspired by empirical and theoretical questions about the nature of political and social organization and about the consequences of social change, Africanist demographers' attraction to anthropology was, arguably, more methodological than theoretical. As David Kertzer notes in a recent overview of the field of anthropological demography, 'By the 1970s the sample survey had become demography's dominant methodology. But while it offered the prospect of gaining nationally representative data, and furnishing straightforward means for cross-national comparison, the limitations of the approach soon became apparent' (2019, p. 621). Australian demographer John Caldwell led the call for more nuanced qualitative studies to supplement what could be learned from surveys. Caldwell and his collaborators had conducted intensive village-based research (what he called 'micro' studies), including in the Yoruba-speaking western region of Nigeria (Caldwell, Hill, & Hull, 1988). This, along with an extensive reading of ethnographic literature, convinced him of the value of more anthropological approaches.

Caldwell and like-minded demographers were keen to learn from anthropological methods. He lamented: 'Most demographers work on large data sets, often with little contact with the people whom the statistics describe' (1982, p. 4). A number of Nigerian demographers were directly involved in Caldwell's turn to anthropology. The importance of cultural context was integral to much of the work of these scholars who either collaborated directly with Caldwell, influenced him, or were influenced by him. Prominent examples include P.O. Olusanya's work on family planning (1969) and marriage (1970, 1971); I.O. Orubuloye's studies of male and female sexuality (1993a, 1997), sexual networking (1991), and the role of religious leaders in relation to the AIDS epidemic (1993b); and Uche Isiugo-Abanihe's publications about child fostering (1985) and the cultural context of high fertility (1994). One can see the ongoing influence of the turn to anthropological methods among demographers working on and from other African countries as well; for example, in Francis Dodoo's work on gender and reproductive behaviour (1998) and Parfait Eloundou-Enyegue's scholarship about the relationship between inequality and fertility transition (2012, 2017).

But while Caldwell led the way in advocating for and incorporating more anthropological approaches in African demography, and while many Africanist demographers (and demographers more generally) have embraced qualitative methods and the need to understand social context, anthropologists have not always been satisfied with the way demography has used theory and conceptualized culture. From the beginnings of the shared enterprise, some anthropologists – including many of those committed to anthropological demography as a subfield – have worried that demographers have adopted antiquated or inadequate theory.

Anthropologists' unease with demographers' appropriation of anthropological methods without incorporating corresponding theory can be boiled down to what Kertzer calls, in his aforementioned overview of anthropological demography, the 'problem of culture' (2019, p. 622). For much of the last 50 years, anthropology has been preoccupied with complicating – and in some quarters attempting to do away with – its own core concept of culture. To its critics, and also to many who would prefer to preserve the discipline's founding conceptual preoccupation, the idea of 'culture' is misleading when it hides power dynamics, disregards history, ignores the role of human agency in its production and ever-changing nature, and obscures the multiplicity of practices and perspectives that exist in any society. While championing the move to pay more attention to social context in demographic analysis, anthropologists sometimes worry that demographers oversimplify culture as a falsely tidy and too-conveniently efficient way to account for context.

Specifically, critics have disparaged the attempt to reduce culture to a set of discrete variables that can be measured. Even anthropologists sympathetic to demography have decried its depiction of culture as static rather than historically dynamic (Hammel, 1990). Further, salient theoretical ideas about human agency and about the effects of power are perceived by some anthropologists to be absent, or at least underappreciated, in demographic analysis (Carter, 1995). Caldwell himself provoked withering criticism from many anthropologists who reacted negatively to his analysis of the cultural context of AIDS in Africa (Caldwell et al., 1989). Being demography's foremost champion of anthropology did not protect him from scathing scrutiny. As alluded to earlier, much of this anthropological angst about cultural theory is a reflection of debates and discontents within anthropology itself. But the discipline's self-targeted critiques do not automatically render similar appraisals of others misplaced or mistaken.

Africa's fertility transition

The global concern about overpopulation, which took hold of the world's imagination in the 1960s, proved to be a research and funding boon for demography. Population scientists could present themselves as, and were perceived to be, the experts who could help solve the problem (Connelly, 2009). While most regions of the world experienced dramatic fertility declines in the twentieth century, by the 1980s demographers were worried about – and continue to be puzzled by – Africa's seemingly 'stalled' or 'lagging' demographic transition (Bongaarts, 2017; Bongaarts & Casterline, 2013; Caldwell & Caldwell, 1987; Caldwell et al., 1992). While anthropological demography was emerging as a subfield during this period, a number of anthropologists conducted research that either explicitly or implicitly helped to explain the social context of continued high fertility on the continent.

For example, Elisha Renne and Daniel Jordan Smith, anthropologists working in the southwestern and southeastern regions of Nigeria, respectively, carried out studies that illuminated the political, economic, and social circumstances that made it rational for Nigerians to continue to desire relatively large families (Renne, 1995, 2003; Smith, 1999, 2004). In this work they built on earlier anthropological insights about the cultural importance of parenthood (Fortes, 1978), the utility of kinship ties in navigating local political economies (Berry, 1985, 1989), and the related and central significance of 'wealth in people' (Guyer, 1993, 1995) in African social and economic life. While Smith showed how Igbos in southeastern Nigeria accessed modern opportunities and resources by 'having people' (with the kin group being first and foremost among one's people), Renne illustrated the effects of government land tenure policy on fertility among the Yoruba. Uncertainty regarding land rights led some people to seek security through having many children. Renne elaborated the more general point: 'Ideas about the reproduction of family houses and names, like ideas about land tenure and children, are intimately linked, thus underscoring the inappropriateness of analyzing fertility levels in abstraction from this broader social context' (1995, p. 123). Pamela Feldman-Savelsberg's (1999) work in northwest Cameroon is another example of rich ethnography that situates the continued value of relatively high fertility in a broad cultural context.

Anthropological demographers who did not directly address the conundrum of Africa's persistent high fertility offered other findings and insights relevant to understanding fertility-related behaviour. For example, Bledsoe's work (some with demographer Allan Hill) debunks the conventional notion of 'natural fertility', showing, based on her research in the Gambia, that women in so-called natural fertility regimes in fact exert extensive agency vis-à-vis their fertility. The Gambian women she studied used contraception to restore bodily health, but with the aim of enabling high fertility rather than reducing it (Bledsoe & Hill, 1998; Bledsoe, Hill, D'Allessandro, & Langerock, 1994; Bledsoe, 2002). Other scholarship with a feminist orientation has also contributed to theoretical understandings of fertility decision-making, moving away from rational choice theory toward a conception of human agency that accounts for both complex social constraints and the contingent opportunities afforded by uncertainties. Jennifer Johnson-Hanks' (2006) work on young women's educational, sexual, and fertility trajectories in Cameroon, leading to her development of the concept of 'vital conjunctures', is an influential example.

While anthropological demography has employed and extended lessons from feminist anthropology to complicate and enrich the understanding of women's positions, interests, decisions, and actions vis-à-vis their fertility, Africa-focused scholars have also undertaken research to better account for men and masculinity in fertility-related processes and outcomes. Demographers have recognized the need for more attention to men since at least the 1990s (Dodoo, 1998; Frost & Dodoo, 2009; Derose & Ezeh, 2005) and anthropologists have equally begun to deliver relevant research (Bledsoe, Guyer, & Lerner, 2000; Orobatan, 2000; Townsend, 2000; Smith, 2017, 2020). Contrary to assumptions that African men are by and large highly pro-natal because of their desire to perpetuate patriarchal privilege, at least some ethnographic evidence suggests that men in contemporary African societies have good reasons to delay marriage and parenthood, and to support the decision to have fewer children (Hunter, 2010a; Smith, 2020).

Anthropological demographers have also investigated the relationship between migration and fertility in Africa. For example, Bruce Whitehouse (2009, 2012) shows how migrants from Mali living in the Republic of Congo use childbearing strategically to strengthen their transnational networks by placing children with kin back home. Bledsoe and Sow (2011, 2013; Bledsoe, Houle, & Sow, 2007) explore similar issues, studying and analyzing the behaviour of migrants from high-fertility African societies who have settled in low-fertility European societies. This strategic use of fertility and the circulation of children occurs in contexts of internal migration as well, as Smith's (2011) study of Igbo rural-urban connections in Nigeria illustrates. In each instance, these anthropologists not only flesh out the social context that helps explain demographic behaviour, they also offer empirically grounded theoretical perspectives regarding the complex interplay of individual agency and social-structural constraints.

Finally, a few anthropologists interested in fertility have recognized that for many men and women, their biggest problem is not too much fertility, but the inability to have children at all. Given that in many African societies, 'Parenthood is regarded as a *sine qua non* for the attainment of the full development of the complete person to which all aspire' (Fortes, 1978, p. 125), it is surprising how little attention demography has paid to the problem of infertility. Marcia Inhorn's (1994, 1996) pioneering work on infertility in Egypt and Marida Hollos' (2003; Hollos & Larsen, 2008; Hollos, Larsen, Obono, & Whitehouse, 2009) studies in Nigeria and Tanzania stand out as noteworthy anthropological contributions on the topic, pulling back the curtain on a problem that brings people stigma and shame.

The definition and meaning(s) of marriage

For demographers, marital status is a key variable in data collection and analysis. Proper measurement is central to the assessment of many aspects of population dynamics. In demographic surveys, 'married or not' is frequently posed as a dichotomous 'yes or no' question. While anthropologists have been equally interested in marriage, their findings have emphasized its diverse, fluid, and processual character – defying the easy categorization assumed in binary survey responses. Demographers have increasingly come to recognize the complexity and ambiguity of marital status and have borrowed from anthropology ideas to try to better measure and assess the definition, meanings, and social realities of marriage.

In addition to pointing out its fluidity, anthropological demographers have been interested in a number of aspects of marriage in Africa, including its function in solidifying social ties, its facilitation of the reproduction of gender roles and associated inequalities, and the effects of significant social changes such as increases in formal education, the global circulation of values about gender equality, and the rise of love and choice as relationship ideals (challenging older practices of so-called arranged marriage). Recent anthropological studies of marriage in Africa have also looked at issues such as extramarital sexuality, the effects of transnational migration on spousal relations, and the growing trend, especially in Southern Africa, of people choosing to eschew marriage altogether. The anthropological literature on marriage in Africa is too vast to review here, but I offer a few illustrative examples.

Regarding the decline in formal marriage in Southern Africa, Mark Hunter (2010a) has provided compelling ethnography to account for the reasons why South Africans – especially men – find the prospect of marriage daunting. Much of it has to do with the near impossibility of fulfilling expectations for 'provider love' – a term for specifically masculine cultural-economic norms about how to demonstrate caring and love. Julia Pauli's (2019) work on Namibia offers perhaps the most comprehensive anthropological findings documenting and explaining the decline in marriage in Southern Africa, while still emphasizing the key point that, despite its formal decline, marriage remains an important touchstone in social life. Even in other African societies where marriage remains nearly universal, the economic challenges of marrying are widely felt and commonly expressed (Masquelier, 2005; Smith, 2020).

The relationship between love and marriage has been a frequent topic in Africanist anthropology in recent years (Cole & Thomas, 2009; Hunter, 2010a; Hannaford & Foley, 2015). Building on the well-documented idea that in African societies socioeconomic and emotional care are deeply intertwined, much of this literature examines the changing contours of marriage, and specifically their gendered dimensions and consequences. Expectations regarding love (and fidelity) in marriage become emotional and social resources that both men and women can deploy to bolster their gendered interests (Parikh, 2009, 2016; Cole, 2010; Smith, 2009, 2010a).

In the context of Africa's HIV epidemic, some of the anthropological research on modern marriage has turned to examining extramarital sexuality (Parikh, 2007, 2009; Smith, 2007). Much of this works suggests that extramarital sexual behaviour is about more than just sex; it is about social class, reputation, and the performance of gender (Spronk, 2012; Mojola, 2014; Smith, 2017). Findings also suggest that, paradoxically, practices of extramarital sex do not automatically imply a diminution in the cultural value of marriage, or even a disregard for the ideal of love in marriage.

Finally, the growing prevalence of transnational migration has led anthropologists to explore its multidimensional impact on marriage. Whether in Cameroon (Johnson-Hanks, 2007), Madagascar (Cole, 2014a, 2014b), Senegal (Hannaford, 2017), or elsewhere, African marriages increasingly involve a transnational dimension. Hannaford, for example, shows that as Senegalese men and women experience both rising expectations for wealth and consumption and increasing economic challenges, transnational marriage has emerged as an important life strategy. In her study, she focuses primarily on Senegalese men who have migrated to Europe and the wives they leave behind in West Africa. Among the key findings is that transnational marriages are geared to build a future in Senegal, not in Italy, France, or other northern destinations. She further shows that husbands and wives often have both convergent and conflicting interests. On the one hand, both genders are interested in making families, building houses, supporting kin, and forging reputations as good people. Husbands and wives separated by thousands of miles are mutually invested in having their marriage appear – and be – successful. On the other hand, men and women sometimes engage in acts of deception to protect their individual gendered interests; for example, men withhold information about their financial struggles in Europe and women try to evade their husbands' sometimes overbearing surveillance from afar.

Migration: Africans on the move

The examples of transnational migration and its intertwining with marriage (Hannaford, 2017) and of the circulation of children among migrants and their families in place of origin as a kind of socio-political strategy (Whitehouse, 2009, 2012) are just a couple of the many instances and aspects of anthropological demographers' focus on migration in Africa. Anthropological studies have also complicated overly economic explanations regarding who moves (Cliggett, 2000), examined how migration affects ethnic conflict (Smith, 2006), and investigated the causes and effects of forced migration for the resulting internally displaced and international refugee populations (Malkki, 1995; Lubkemann, 2010). In the wake of the rising HIV epidemic, anthropologists have contributed significantly to understanding the role of mobility and migration in exacerbating the risk of infection (Setel, 1999; Thornton, 2008).

Many anthropological accounts of African migration augment the economics-centric interpretations of migrants' motives that dominate most demographic analyses by also accounting for migration's social and cultural dimensions. Few anthropologists would discount the centrality of economic needs and aspirations in shaping people's decisions to migrate, nor would they dismiss the importance of economic wherewithal as a factor in the capacity to move. But as Caroline Melly (2011, 2017) shows for aspiring and actual international migrants in/from Senegal, the need for money is itself underpinned by larger social-reproductive projects related to family, community, the performance of gender, and pressure to be seen as a moral person. Anthropology's emphasis on migration's social and moral economies has helped flesh out the understanding of this basic demographic phenomenon.

Migration is also frequently spurred by people's desire to escape conflict and violence. Anthropologists have drawn significant attention to forced migration in Africa, shedding light on a population-related problem that has been relatively understudied in demography. Ethnographers have documented and theorized about the dynamics of forced migration in the context of war and other violent conflicts (Lubkemann, 2008, 2010) and examined refugee camps and their populations (Malkki, 1995). In a different twist on the relationship between migration and conflict, Smith (2006) shows how in Nigeria the movement of people not only results from violence, but also contributes to the hardening of ethnic identities and animosities that in turn spur more conflict.

Mobility was early on implicated in the spread of HIV in Africa. Anthropologists have undertaken research to deepen the understanding of the relationship between mobility, sexuality, and AIDS (Setel, 1999; Thornton, 2008; Thomas et al., 2010). Much of the research in Africa has focused on the nexus of labour migration and sexual behaviour (Hunter, 2010b; Ondimu, 2010; van Blerk, 2010). Other work has examined even more specifically the gendered dimensions of how mobility intersects with sexual behaviour and HIV risk (Harrison, Cleland, & Frohlich, 2008; Smith, 2010b; Hampshire, Porter, Mashiri, Maponya, & Dube, 2011).

AIDS and anthropological demography in Africa

As noted at the beginning of this essay, Africa's AIDS epidemic resulted in a dramatic upsurge in anthropological research at the intersection of public health and demography. Relatively quickly, epidemiologists, demographers, and government policymakers recognized that understanding and preventing (and, eventually, treating) HIV required research that situated behaviour in its fullest social and cultural contexts. As a disease that is primarily transmitted through sexual relations, AIDS called for social scientific analysis that placed sexuality at the complex intersections of gender and power, intimacy and inequality, and political and moral economies. Anthropology was uniquely positioned to take up these challenges. Perhaps similar to how the alarm regarding the perceived threats of overpopulation resulted in a heyday for demography, AIDS triggered a florescence of government and foundation-funded anthropological research. This work has generated a huge body of scholarship, far too voluminous to review here, even cursorily. Instead of offering superficial snippets of various scholars' work on HIV/AIDS in Africa, in this final section I provide an extended example from my own anthropological-demographic work on youth, gender, rural-to-urban migration, and HIV risk in Nigeria as an illustration of this kind of research.

Gender, sex, migration, and the morality of risk during Nigeria's HIV epidemic

In Africa, and arguably more widely, the AIDS epidemic heightened the stakes of normative gendered practice and sexual intimacy. As the spread of the disease magnified the risk of infection, sickness, and death, the moral discourses HIV generated made behaviours related to gender and sexuality – whether it was how people dressed, with whom they had sex, or how they negotiated relationships with their partners – the object of increased social scrutiny. Even as changes associated with modern, urban social life in Africa provided people – perhaps especially women – with new liberties and opportunities, gender inequality was reproduced in novel and powerful ways. In this section, I summarize the findings from a study I conducted examining how unmarried young women in Africa's most populous country, Nigeria, navigated the complicated landscape of migration, work, sex, and social relationships in the era of AIDS, including how their strategies to survive and to improve their lives were often judged through moral lenses shaped by the epidemic.

Sometimes unwittingly, scholarship about African gender and sexuality and AIDS has fed into pernicious stereotypes about promiscuous African sexual traditions (Caldwell et al., 1989). As the findings I present here show, it is more accurate to explain risky sexual behaviour in the context of the contradictions created by conservative sexual moralities combined with situations of profound material deprivation and growing economic aspirations than to attribute such behaviour to some sort of misguided notion of an essential African cultural promiscuity. Understanding morally driven and highly-gendered interpretations and responses to social inequality is central to making sense of patterns of risky behaviour and infection.

A significant body of scholarship aimed at understanding heterosexual transmission in Africa has focused particularly on the complex relationship between women's vulnerability and women's agency. Scholars have rightly pointed out that for many African women, the combination of poverty, migration, and gender inequality is often deadly, because women have been put in positions in which risky sexual relations are one of the only means of survival (Schoepf, 1992; Ulin, 1992). The concept of 'survival sex' as articulated by Preston-Whyte, Varga, Oosthuizen, Roberts, and Blose (2000) and others (Wojcicki, 2002) emphasizes the extent to which women are structurally constrained and therefore often forced to rely on risky sexual liaisons to support themselves and their families.

Without discounting the extent to which many women rely on prostitution and other forms of transactional sex to survive, a compelling literature has shown that women use sexual relationships with men not simply to survive, but also to advance their aspirations for consumption, to achieve educational and employment goals well beyond mere survival, and to enable them to help fulfil obligations to kin and community (Hunter, 2002; Leclerc-Madlala, 2003; Johnson-Hanks, 2006; Cole, 2010). Acknowledging women's agency and the aspirations beyond survival that motivate various kinds of transactional relationships need not contradict the fundamental point that economic hardships and gender inequalities create contexts that put women in vulnerable positions, increasing the likelihood that they will become infected with HIV and infect others. But attention to women's agency and to the panoply of socially mediated expectations and desires that frame and motivate sexual behaviours offers a more nuanced perspective on the relationship between economics, gender, sexuality, and HIV risk.

Female migration, urban sexual economies, and HIV

AIDS in Africa has been widely linked to gendered patterns of migration (Herdt, 1997; Lurie et al., 2003; Lurie, 2006). In recent decades, demographers and other social scientists have drawn attention to the growing proportion of rural-to-urban migrants in sub-Saharan Africa who are female, young, and unmarried (Adepoju, 2003; Gugler & Ludwar-Ene, 1995; Makinwa-Adebusoye, 1990; Mberu, 2005). This trend represents a relatively new pattern, since previous rural-to-urban migration streams had been predominantly male, and women tended to move in more significant numbers as the married partners of male migrants than as single and independent agents in their own right. Nowadays in Nigeria, as in much of sub-Saharan Africa, a combination of increasing aspirations and opportunities, challenging economic circumstances, and sometimes-burdensome kinship obligations compel large numbers of young single women to migrate from rural to urban areas. Many young female migrants adapt to the challenges of the city by engaging in sexual relationships with men who can provide resources for them.

The findings presented here are the result of a two-year study in 2001 and 2002 of unmarried Igbo rural-to-urban migrants from southeastern Nigeria between 15 and 24 years old who were residing in the northern Nigerian city of Kano (Smith, 2003, 2014). The study included a survey of 431 male and female migrants, intensive interviews with 20 young women from the larger sample, and several months of participant observation. In analysing the strategies that enabled young women to adapt to city life, it became clear that female migrants inevitably navigated the local sexual economy as they strived to survive and succeed in their new environment. For most young women, sexual relationships with men proved to be a major means of garnering economic support, albeit in ways that spanned a wide range of forms with regard to the explicitness of the economic basis for the relationship, the intimacy and duration of ties, and the moral valence for the women, their partners, and the larger community. The experiences of the young female migrants who were the subject of this study show that the moral dimensions of this sexual economy can have equal or greater consequences for the risk of HIV infection associated with gender inequality as do the more material aspects.

The findings point to three positions in the spectrum of relationships in Kano's migrant community's sexual economy, each with implications for young women's risk of HIV infection. The three types of relationships were 1) commercial sex, mostly associated with brothels; 2) sexual relationships that originated from connections that were established in the plethora of local bars, taverns, and eateries that served alcohol in Kano's migrant quarter; and 3) longer-term relationships that were less explicitly economic and often included a notion of romance and commitment. Of course, many kinds of relationships did not fit neatly in any category, some relationships evolved over time from one type to another, and many women experienced more than one type of relationship, either over time or concurrently. The conventional view is that the more overtly economic a sexual relationship is, the more likely a woman has been compelled to participate because of poverty, the more pernicious it is for the perpetuation of gender inequality, and the higher the risk of HIV infection. But the picture looks more complicated if the social and moral aspects of gender inequality are figured in with the economic aspects.

Work, sex, morality, and HIV

When the survey team, made up mostly of young Igbos from the major university in Kano, spanned out across the city to interview migrants, one of the supervisors, a middle-aged university lecturer from the Igbo Southeast, expressed considerable surprise at the number of young migrant women working as commercial sex workers in brothels. He characterized his palpable dismay in a phrase that was repeated frequently by members of the research team over the study period. He lamented that he would never again react the same when, back home in the southeast, the parent of a young female migrant announced proudly, 'My daughter is working in Kano.' Little did their parents suspect, he suggested, what sort of work their daughters were doing.

Interviews with young women working in brothels confirmed that most of them resorted to sex work in response to economic needs in circumstances in which they felt they had no other viable options. Data from the larger survey sample indicated that women who were sex workers had few (and often no) kin in Kano who could help them. In the larger overall migrant population, more than half of the young female migrants had kin in the city, and many of them boarded with a relative. The lack of kinship ties increased young women's economic desperation, but it also freed them somewhat from the moral gaze of extended family who would have considered sex work extremely stigmatizing.

Commercial sex work was viewed as morally unacceptable in the wider Igbo migrant community as well. Indeed, its unacceptability was exacerbated by the fact that many of the migrant sex workers' clients were local men, who differed from Igbo migrants in ethnicity and religion (Igbo migrants are predominantly Christian; the local population in Kano is mostly Hausa-speaking and Muslim). In addition to stigma, some sex workers faced exploitation and mistreatment from clients and from the men who owned and ran the hotels where they worked. But paradoxically, young Igbo migrant women who engaged in professional sex work also seemed to escape some of the moral restrictions that constrain the behaviour of most Igbo women. They had certain freedoms compared to women who were more tightly bound to their kin and to particular men. For example, commercial sex workers in the study drank and smoked much more commonly and openly than other migrant women. They talked to men with much greater liberty, arguing with them, laughing at them, and cursing them in ways that most other women would find difficult and even dangerous. Significantly, commercial sex workers also said that they regularly used condoms and usually did not hesitate to try to get their clients to wear them. They did not always succeed, but, compared with other women in the study, they discussed condoms much more openly, they often showed them to interviewers, and they seemed much less constrained by condoms' association with sexual immorality, which inhibited use by many young migrants.

I do not mean to suggest that female sex work was a path to female liberation. Commercial sex work was highly stigmatized not only in the Igbo migrant community in Kano, but also in Nigeria generally. But because sex work put women 'beyond the pale' morally, their source of economic livelihood offered them considerable liberties that were unavailable to women who were more observant of social and moral norms. My point is not to celebrate sex work, but rather to compare and contrast it to other ways that young migrant women navigated Kano's urban sexual economy. For many young migrant women who work in other sectors of Kano's economy, shared notions of morality and perceptions that social change was undermining traditional norms intersected with their livelihoods and their sexual behaviour. Morality reinforced gender inequality as much as economics did.

While full-fledged commercial sex work was undertaken by a relatively small fraction of young unmarried Igbo migrants, many more young women worked in jobs at bars, taverns, eateries, and a range of other entertainment establishments. At these venues, male clientele commonly bantered playfully with female cooks, servers, and other employees. In many cases (but certainly not most), these encounters evolved into sexual relationships. The spectrum of entertainment establishments, the intentions and behaviours of young women, and the kinds of relationships that unfolded were highly diverse. In some cases, the line between sex work and tavern work was blurry; in others, young women only slept with a man when the relationship could be understood as romantically inclined or emotionally committed. But in almost all instances neither the man nor the woman viewed these relationships as commercial sex. Yet it was equally the case that the man was always expected to provide some form of economic support to his sexual partner.

In these contexts, young women had to be careful not to behave too much like sex workers, because their physical attraction, emotional appeal, and moral authenticity depended on obscuring or euphemizing the economic aspect of a sexual relationship. This makes it even more noteworthy that in-depth interviews and informal discussions with many men and women revealed that the actual level of economic support that men provided in any sexual relationship was not smaller when the encounter was perceived in less overtly economic terms. In fact, often the less explicitly transactional the relationship, the greater was the level of a man's monetary support. But these more morally acceptable (and economically beneficial) relationships came with other 'costs' for women. In certain respects, the decorum required for a young female migrant to distinguish herself from a prostitute entailed behaviour that reinforced gendered stereotypes that kept women subservient to men. Perhaps the most significant and potentially deleterious example of this – at least vis-à-vis the HIV/AIDS epidemic – was with regard to the use of condoms. Many young women reported that it was difficult and awkward for them to suggest using condoms with their lovers, partly because such a suggestion made them appear, as several men and women put it, 'too professional'.

'No finance without romance'

Young unmarried women in cities in Nigeria must steer their way through entrenched forms of gender inequality, traversing a complex sexual economy as they try to survive and succeed in urban environments. My findings in Kano, which emphasize the moral as well as the material dimensions of social systems, do not suggest that the economic foundations and consequences of gender inequality are any less significant. But by examining the complex terrain of the Kano migrant community's sexual economy, the intertwining of the material and the moral becomes apparent, producing circumstances, strategies, and consequences for HIV risk behaviour that are multifaceted and sometimes contradictory. The realities of the sexual economy in Kano suggest that young migrant women frequently must navigate uneven moral and material terrains, trading currencies across domains, risking failure in one realm for success in the other, trying to keep their reputations intact even as they secure their livelihoods, and reinforcing some aspects of gender inequality even as they challenge others.

While relatively few women end up as commercial sex workers, most young female migrants must find their way through the complex intersection of monetary, moral, and sexual economies as they struggle to pursue their aspirations and work to preserve their reputations. The pressures that bar girls and others in the entertainment sector faced to conceal – or at least euphemize – their economic motives also affected young women who were neither commercial sex workers nor service industry employees. While my findings suggested that sex workers and service workers tended to be more economically and socially vulnerable than many other migrant women (since they generally had less income, poorer housing, and fewer Kano-based kin), many young migrant women who fit neither category also had precarious livelihoods and relied on men with whom they had sexual relationships for economic support. For such women, the importance of assuring the perceived morality of the relationship was paramount, since men were much more likely to spend significantly on women who they believed were sexually exclusive and emotionally bound to them – even in cases in which the men were already married to someone else.

Young women commonly expressed self-awareness about the economic motivations for sexual relationships with men using the phrase 'there is no romance without finance'. While this expression suggests women's strategic economic use of their sexuality, it is equally revealing to invert the phrase and note that for women to succeed in securing the most valuable male support – that which is not only the most financially lucrative, but also the most socially acceptable – they must behave in ways that privilege other aspects of the relationship above bald material exchange. In this sense, for women seeking to avoid the stigma of prostitution, 'there is no finance without romance'.

Most young women interviewed in Kano wholeheartedly preferred relationships in which they received financial support in the context of emotionally supportive and socially and morally sanctioned relationships. But it was clear that in this gender-unequal society, in order to please men, women had to behave in ways that reinforced their dependence upon them. Men expected significant degrees of acquiescence to male needs and priorities in order to reward women with both money and moral approval.

For most young women in Nigeria, it is a continuous challenge to balance economic exigencies, their social reputations, and their own emotional and physical desires. As the country changes so rapidly – with increases in rural-to-urban migration, higher levels of formal education, ever-growing exposure to globally circulating ideas, practices, and things, and a huge young population that is increasingly likely to stay unmarried for up to a decade after reaching sexual maturity – the sexual and moral lives of young women and the country's AIDS epidemic are interconnected in a collective imagination that is deeply ambivalent about all these transformations.

Nigerians' collective anxiety about the AIDS epidemic has focused significantly on the lives of young people. The younger generations are viewed as personifying new aspirations and lifestyles that reflect trends in the country's political economy that many Nigerians find both appealing and troubling. The troubling changes include rises in inequality, greed, materialism, and individualism, all of which are seen as threatening values of sharing and reciprocal obligation associated with kinship and community, but also as opening the door for HIV. The popular concern with young people is also a product of the fact that the social lives and cultural practices of the next generations embody the outcome of current processes of social reproduction. These worries about social reproduction are frequently voiced through narratives about young people's sexual behaviour, expressing a widely shared understanding of AIDS as the consequence of collective moral failings. Condemnation of youthful sexual morality is focused especially on young women because of gender double standards, but also because their virtue and its failures stand symbolically for the moral state of society more generally.

Conclusion

Anthropological demography has enriched the understanding of population-related processes, behaviours, and outcomes in Africa, not least in relation to pressing public health problems. In this essay, I have only been able to skim the surface with regard to the breadth and depth of Africanist anthropological research relevant to population studies. Despite longstanding and ongoing interests that many anthropologists have in demographic phenomena, it remains the case that many ethnographers who work on population-related topics do not self-identify as anthropological demographers. This is true primarily for two reasons. Firstly, the subfield of medical anthropology has become so popular and prestigious that it subsumes much of the work that could also be accurately described as anthropological demography. Given the overlap in topics and the current professional benefits of being a medical anthropologist, this trend is likely to persist. Secondly, in contemporary sociocultural anthropology many scholars have a kneejerk negative reaction to quantification and its presumed association with positivism, making some people disinclined to embrace the 'demographer' label, even when modified by 'anthropological'. This is unfortunate because, as so much of the literature reviewed here attests, the vast majority of anthropological-demographic research is highly ethnographic and theoretically far from positivism.

In addition to the general aversion of many anthropologists to quantification and demography, there is a dearth of Africans trained in anthropology overall, much less in anthropological demography. Significant efforts have been launched over the past couple of decades to train African demographers at institutions on the continent, including notable programs like the Consortium for Advanced Research Training in Africa (CARTA) and the l'Institut de Formation et de Recherche Démographiques (IFORD). But these laudable efforts offer little or no training in anthropological demography. In general, anthropology has been shunned as a discipline at African universities because of its historical association with colonialism. This is understandable. But anthropology has moved forward from its colonial entanglements. In contemporary population studies there is, arguably, no better way to assure that African voices and contexts are fully accounted for in all their ethnographic depth and complexity than to train a large cadre of African anthropologists and anthropological demographers. Training programs like CARTA and IFORD would do well to work with African universities to make this happen. African anthropologists and anthropological demographers are needed not only in Africa, but all over the world.

References

Adepoju, A. (2003). Migration in West Africa. *Development, 46*(3), 37–41.

Berry, S. (1985). *Fathers work for their sons: Accumulation, mobility, and class formation in an extended Yorùbá community*. Berkeley, CA: University of California Press.

Berry, S. (1989). Social institutions and access to resources. *Africa, 59*(1), 41–55.

Bledsoe, C. (1980). *Women and marriage in Kpelle society*. Stanford, CA: Stanford University Press.

Bledsoe, C. (2002). *Contingent lives: Fertility, time, and aging in West Africa*. Chicago: University of Chicago Press.

Bledsoe, C., & Hill, A. (1998). Social norms, natural fertility, and the resumption of postpartum 'contact' in the Gambia. In A. M. Basu & P. Aaby (Eds.), *The methods and uses of anthropological demography* (pp. 268–297). Oxford: Oxford University Press.

Bledsoe, C., Hill, A., D'Allessandro, U., & Langerock, P. (1994). Constructing natural fertility: The use of western contraceptive technologies in rural Gambia. *Population and Development Review, 20*(1), 81–113.

Bledsoe, C., Guyer, J., & Lerner, S. (Eds.). (2000). *Fertility and the male life cycle in the era of fertility decline*. Oxford: Oxford University Press.

Bledsoe, C., Houle, R., & Sow, P. (2007). High fertility Gambians in low fertility Spain: The dynamics of child accumulation across transnational space. *Demographic Research, 16*(12), 375–412.

Bledsoe, C., & Sow, P. (2011). Family reunification ideals and the practice of transnational reproductive life among Africans in Europe. In C. Browner & C. Sargent (Eds.), *Reproduction, globalism, and the state* (pp. 175–191). Durham, NC: Duke University Press.

Bledsoe, C., & Sow, P. (2013). Back to Africa: Second chances for the children of West African immigrants. In L. Oso & N. Ribas-Mateos (Eds.), *The international handbook on gender, migration and transnationalism: Global and development perspectives* (pp. 185–207). Cheltenham, UK: Elgar Press.

Bongaarts, J. (2017). Africa's unique fertility transition. *Population and Development Review, 43*, 39–58.

Bongaarts, J., & Casterline, J. (2013). Fertility transition: Is sub-Saharan Africa different? *Population and Development Review, 38*, 153–168.

Caldwell, J. (1982). *Theory of fertility decline*. Cambridge, MA: Academic Press.

Caldwell, J., & Caldwell, P. (1987). The cultural context of high fertility in sub-Saharan Africa. *Population and Development Review, 13*(3), 409–437.

Caldwell, J., Caldwell, P., & Quiggin, P. (1989). The social context of AIDS in sub-Saharan Africa. *Population and Development Review, 15*(2), 185–234.

Caldwell, J., Hill, A., & Hull, V. (Eds.). (1988). *Micro-approaches to demographic research*. London: Taylor & Francis.

Caldwell, J., Orubuloye, I. O., & Caldwell, P. (1992). Fertility decline in Africa: A new type of transition? *Population and Development Review, 18*(2), 211–242.

Carter, A. (1995). Agency and fertility: For an ethnography of practice. In S. Greenhalgh (Ed.), *Situating fertility: Anthropology and demographic inquiry* (pp. 55–85). Cambridge: Cambridge University Press.

Cliggett, L. (2000). Social components of migration: Experiences from Southern Province, Zambia. *Human Organization, 59*, 125–35.

Cohen, A. (1969). *Custom and politics in urban Africa: A study of Hausa migrants in Yoruba towns*. London: Routledge.

Cole, J. (2010). *Sex and salvation: Imagining the future in Madagascar*. Chicago, IL: University of Chicago Press.

Cole, J. (2014a). The telephone Malgache: Transnational gossip and social transformation among Malagasy marriage migrants in France. *American Ethnologist, 41*(2), 276–289.

Cole, J. (2014b). Producing value among Malagasy marriage migrants in France: Managing horizons of expectation. *Current Anthropology, 55*(S9), S85–S94.

Cole, J., & Thomas, L. (Eds.). (2009). *Love in Africa*. Chicago: University of Chicago Press.

Colson, E. (1958). *Marriage and the family among the Plateau Tonga of Northern Rhodesia*. Manchester: Manchester University Press.

Connelly, M. (2009). *Fatal misconception: The struggle to control world population*. Cambridge, MA: Harvard University Press.

DeRose, L., & Ezeh, A. (2005). Men's influence on the onset and progress of fertility decline in Ghana, 1988–98. *Population Studies, 59*(2), 197–210.

Dodoo, F. (1998). Men matter: Additive and interactive gendered preferences and reproductive behavior in Kenya. *Demography, 35*(2), 229–242.

Eloundou-Enyegue, P., & Giroux, S. (2012). Demographic change and rural-urban inequality in sub-Saharan Africa: Theory and trends. In *International handbook of rural demography* (pp. 125–135). New York: Springer.

Eloundou-Enyegue, P., Giroux, S., & Tenikue, M. (2017). African transitions and fertility inequality: A demographic Kuznets hypothesis. *Population and Development Review, 43*, 59–83.

Epstein, A. (1958). *Politics in an urban African community*. Manchester: Manchester University Press.

Evans-Pritchard, E. E. (1951). *Kinship and marriage among the Nuer*. Oxford: Clarendon Press.

Feldman-Savelsberg, P. (1999). *Plundered kitchens, empty wombs: Threatened reproduction and identity in the Cameroon Grassfields*. Ann Arbor, MI: University of Michigan Press.

Fortes, M. (1978). Parenthood, marriage and fertility in West Africa. *Journal of Development Studies, 14*(4), 121–148.

Fortes, M. (2018) [1949]. *The web of kinship among the Tallensi: The second part of an analysis of the social structure of a trans-Volta tribe*. London: Routledge.

Frost, A., & Dodoo, F. (2009). Men are missing from African family planning. *Contexts, 8*(1), 44–49.

Gluckman, M. (1940). Analysis of a social situation in modern Zululand. *Bantu Studies, 14*(1), 1–30.

Gugler, J., & Ludwar-Ene, G. (1995). Gender and migration in Africa south of the Sahara. In J. Baker & T. Aina (Eds.), *Migration experiences in Africa* (pp. 257–268). Uppsala: Nordiska Afrikainstitutet.

Guyer, J. (1993). Wealth in people and self-realization in Equatorial Africa. *Man, 28*(2), 243–265.

Guyer, J. (1995). Wealth in people, wealth in things – Introduction. *The Journal of African History, 36*(1), 83–90.

Hammel, E. (1990). A theory of culture for demography. *Population and Development Review, 16*(3), 455–485.

Hampshire, K., Porter, G., Mashiri, M., Maponya, G., & Dube, S. (2011). Proposing love on the way to school: Mobility, sexuality and youth transitions in South Africa. *Culture, Health & Sexuality, 13*(2), 217–231.

Hannaford, D. (2017). *Marriage without borders: Transnational spouses in neoliberal Senegal*. Philadelphia, PA: University of Pennsylvania Press.

Hannaford, D., & Foley, E. (2015). Negotiating love and marriage in contemporary Senegal: A good man is hard to find. *African Studies Review, 58*(2), 205–225.

Harrison, A., Cleland, J., & Frohlich, J. (2008). Young people's sexual partnerships in KwaZulu-Natal, South Africa: Patterns, contextual influences, and HIV risk. *Studies in Family Planning, 39*(4), 295–308.

Herdt, G. (Ed.). (1997). *Sexual cultures and migration in the era of AIDS: Anthropological and demographic perspectives*. Oxford: Oxford University Press.
Hollos, M. (2003). Profiles of infertility in southern Nigeria: Women's voices from Amakiri. *African Journal of Reproductive Health, 7*(2), 46–56.
Hollos, M., & Larsen, U. (2008). Motherhood in sub-Saharan Africa: The social consequences of infertility in an urban population in northern Tanzania. *Culture, Health & Sexuality, 10*(2), 159–173.
Hollos, M., Larsen, U., Obono, O., & Whitehouse, B. (2009). The problem of infertility in high fertility populations: Meanings, consequences and coping mechanisms in two Nigerian communities. *Social Science & Medicine, 68*(11), 2061–2068.
Hunter, M. (2002). The materiality of everyday sex: Thinking beyond 'prostitution'. *African Studies, 61*(1), 99–120.
Hunter, M. (2010a). *Love in the time of AIDS: Inequality, gender, and rights in South Africa*. Bloomington, IN: Indiana University Press.
Hunter, M. (2010b). From migrating men to moving women: Trends in South Africa's changing political economy and geography of intimacy. In F. Thomas, M. Haour-Knipe, & P. Aggleton (Eds.), *Mobility, sexuality and AIDS* (pp. 159–169). London: Routledge.
Inhorn, M. (1994). *Quest for conception: Gender, infertility and Egyptian medical traditions*. Philadelphia, PA: University of Pennsylvania Press.
Inhorn, M. (1996). *Infertility and patriarchy: The cultural politics of gender and family life in Egypt*. Philadelphia, PA: University of Pennsylvania Press.
Isiugo-Abanihe, U. (1985). Child fosterage in West Africa. *Population and Development Review, 11*(1), 53–73.
Isiugo-Abanihe, U. (1994). The socio-cultural context of high fertility among Igbo women. *International Sociology, 9*(2), 237–258.
Johnson-Hanks, J. (2006). *Uncertain honor: Modern motherhood in an African crisis*. Chicago, IL: University of Chicago Press.
Johnson-Hanks, J. (2007). Women on the market: Marriage, consumption, and the internet in urban Cameroon. *American Ethnologist, 34*(4), 642–658.
Kertzer, D. (2019). Anthropological demography. In D. Polston (Ed.), *Handbook of population* (2nd ed., pp. 619–641). New York: Springer.
Kertzer, D., & Fricke, T. (Eds). (1997). *Anthropological demography: Toward a new synthesis*. Chicago, IL: University of Chicago Press.
Leclerc-Madlala, S. (2003). Transactional sex and the pursuit of modernity. *Social Dynamics, 29*(2), 213–233.
Lubkemann, S. (2008). Involuntary immobility: On a theoretical invisibility in forced migration studies. *Journal of Refugee Studies, 21*(4), 454–475.
Lubkemann, S. (2010). *Culture in chaos: An anthropology of the social condition in war*. Chicago, IL: University of Chicago Press.
Lurie, M. (2006). The epidemiology of migration and HIV/AIDS in South Africa. *Journal of Ethnic and Migration Studies, 32*(4), 649–666.
Lurie, M., Williams, B., Zuma, K., Mkaya-Mwamburi, D., Garnett, G., Sweat, M., . . . Salim, K. (2003). Who infects whom? HIV-1 concordance and discordance among migrant and non-migrant couples in South Africa. *AIDS, 17*(15), 2245–2252.
Makinwa-Adebusoye, P. (1990). Female migration in Africa. In *Conference on the role of migration in African development: Issues and policies for the '90s vol. I commissioned papers* (pp. 198–211). Dakar: Union for African Population Studies.
Malkki, L. (1995). *Purity and exile: Violence, memory, and national cosmology among Hutu refugees in Tanzania*. Chicago, IL: University of Chicago Press.
Masquelier, A. (2005). The scorpion's sting: Youth, marriage and the struggle for social maturity in Niger. *Journal of the Royal Anthropological Institute, 11*(1), 59–83.
Mberu, B. (2005). Who moves and who stays? Rural out-migration in Nigeria. *Journal of Population Research, 22*(2), 141–161.
Melly, C. (2011). Titanic tales of missing men: Reconfigurations of national identity and gendered presence in Dakar, Senegal. *American Ethnologist, 38*(2), 361–376.
Melly, C. (2017). *Bottleneck: Moving, building, and belonging in an African city*. Chicago, IL: University of Chicago Press.
Mitchell, J. C. (1965). Differential fertility amongst urban Africans in Zambia. *Rhodes-Livingstone Journal, 37*, 1–25.

Mojola, S. (2014). *Love, money, and HIV: Becoming a modern African woman in the age of AIDS*. Berkeley, CA: University of California Press.

Ondimu, K. (2010). Labour migration and risky sexual behaviour: Tea plantation workers in Kericho District, Kenya. In F. Thomas, M. Haour-Knipe, & P. Aggleton (Eds.), *Mobility, sexuality and AIDS* (pp. 170–183). London: Routledge.

Olusanya, P. O. (1969). Nigeria: Cultural barriers to family planning among the Yorubas. *Studies in Family Planning, 1*(37), 13–16.

Olusanya, P. O. (1970). A note on some factors affecting the stability of marriage among the Yoruba of western Nigeria. *Journal of Marriage and the Family, 32*(1), 150–155.

Olusanya, P. O. (1971). The problem of multiple causation in population analysis, with particular reference to the polygamy-fertility hypothesis. *The Sociological Review, 19*(2), 165–178.

Orobaton, N. (2000). Dimensions of sexuality among Nigerian men: Implications for fertility and reproductive health. In C. Bledsoe, S. Lerner, & J. Guyer (Eds.), *Fertility and the male life cycle in the era of fertility decline* (pp. 207–230). Oxford: Oxford University Press.

Orubuloye, I. O., Caldwell, J., & Caldwell, P. (1991). Sexual networking in the Ekiti District of Nigeria. *Studies in Family Planning, 22*(2), 61–73.

Orubuloye, I. O., Caldwell, J., & Caldwell, P. (1993a). African women's control over their sexuality in an era of AIDS: A study of the Yoruba of Nigeria. *Social Science & Medicine, 37*(7), 859–872.

Orubuloye, I. O., Caldwell, J., & Caldwell, P. (1993b). The role of religious leaders in changing sexual behaviour in southwest Nigeria in an era of AIDS. *Health Transition Review, 3*(S), 93–104.

Orubuloye, I. O., Caldwell, J., & Caldwell, P. (1997). Perceived male sexual needs and male sexual behaviour in southwest Nigeria. *Social Science & Medicine, 44*(8), 1195–1207.

Parikh, S. (2007). The political economy of marriage and HIV: The ABC approach, 'safe' infidelity, and managing moral risk in Uganda. *American Journal of Public Health, 97*(7), 1198–1208.

Parikh, S. (2009). Going public: Modern wives, men's infidelity, and marriage in east-central Uganda. In *The Secret: Love, marriage, and HIV* (pp. 168–196). Nashville, TN: Vanderbilt University Press.

Parikh, S. (2016). *Regulating romance: Youth love letters, moral anxiety, and intervention in Uganda's time of AIDS*. Nashville, TN: Vanderbilt University Press.

Pauli, J. (2019). *The decline of marriage in Namibia: Kinship and social class in a rural community*. Bielefeld: Verlag.

Powdermaker, H. (1962). *Copper town: Changing Africa: The human situation on the Rhodesian Copperbelt*. Manhattan, NY: Harper & Row.

Preston-Whyte, E., Varga, C., Oosthuizen, H., Roberts, R., & Blose, F. (2000). Survival sex and HIV/AIDS in an African city. In R. Parker, R. Barbosa, & P. Aggleton (Eds.), *Framing the sexual subject: The politics of gender, sexuality, and power* (pp. 165–190). Berkeley, CA: University of California Press.

Radcliffe-Brown, A. R., & Forde, D. (2015) [1950]. *African systems of kinship and marriage*. London: Routledge.

Renne, E. (1995). Houses, fertility, and the Nigerian land use act. *Population and Development Review, 21*(1), 113–126.

Renne, E. (2003). *Population and progress in a Yoruba town*. Ann Arbor, MI: University of Michigan Press.

Schoepf, B. (1992). Women at risk: Case studies from Zaire. In G. Herdt & S. Lindenbaum (Eds.), *The time of AIDS: Social analysis, theory, and method* (pp. 259–286). New York: Sage Publications.

Setel, P. (1999). *A plague of paradoxes: AIDS, culture, and demography in northern Tanzania*. Chicago, IL: University of Chicago Press.

Smith, D. J. (1999). *Having people: Family, fertility and modernity in Igbo-speaking Nigeria* (PhD dissertation). Atlanta, GA: Emory University.

Smith, D. J. (2003). Imagining HIV/AIDS: Morality and perceptions of personal risk in Nigeria. *Medical Anthropology, 22*(4), 343–372.

Smith, D. J. (2004). Contradictions in Nigeria's fertility transition: The burdens and benefits of having people. *Population and Development Review, 30*(2), 221–238.

Smith, D. J. (2006). Internal migration and the escalation of ethnic and religious violence in urban Nigeria. In M. Murray & G. Meyers (Eds.), *Cities in contemporary Africa* (pp. 53–69). Palgrave Macmillan.

Smith, D. J. (2007). Modern marriage, men's extramarital sex, and HIV risk in southeastern Nigeria. *American Journal of Public Health, 97*(6), 997–1005.

Smith, D. J. (2009). Managing men, marriage, and modern love: Women's perspectives on intimacy and male infidelity in southeastern Nigeria. In J. Cole & L. Thomas (Eds.), *Love in Africa* (pp. 157–180). Chicago, IL: University of Chicago Press.

Smith, D. J. (2010a). Promiscuous girls, good wives, and cheating husbands: Gender inequality, transitions to marriage, and infidelity in southeastern Nigeria. *Anthropological Quarterly, 83*(1), 123–152.

Smith, D. J. (2010b). Migration, men's extramarital sex and the risk of HIV infection in Nigeria. In F. Thomas, M. Haour-Knipe, & P. Aggleton (Eds.), *Mobility, sexuality and AIDS* (pp. 203–214). London: Routledge.

Smith, D. J. (2011). Rural-to-urban migration, kinship networks, and fertility among the Igbo in Nigeria. *African Population Studies, 25*(2), 320–336.

Smith, D. J. (2014). *AIDS doesn't show its face: Inequality, morality, and social change in Nigeria*. Chicago, IL: University of Chicago Press.

Smith, D. J. (2017). *To be a man is not a one-day job: Masculinity, money, and intimacy in Nigeria*. Chicago, IL: University of Chicago Press.

Smith, D. J. (2020). Masculinity, money, and the postponement of parenthood in Nigeria. *Population and Development Review, 46*(1), 101–120.

Spronk, R. (2012). *Ambiguous pleasures: Sexuality and middleclass self-perceptions in Nairobi*. New York, NY: Berghahn Books.

Thomas, F., Haour-Knipe, M., & Aggleton, P. (Eds.). (2010). *Mobility, sexuality and AIDS*. London: Routledge.

Thornton, R. (2008). *Unimagined community: Sex, networks, and AIDS in Uganda and South Africa*. Berkeley, CA: University of California Press.

Townsend, N. (2000). Male fertility as a lifetime of relationships: Contextualizing men's biological reproduction in Botswana. In C. Bledsoe, S. Lerner, & J. Guyer (Eds.), *Fertility and the male life cycle in the era of fertility decline* (pp. 343–364). Oxford: Oxford University Press.

Ulin, P. (1992). African women and AIDS: Negotiating behavior change. *Social Science & Medicine, 34*(1), 63–73.

van Blerk, L. (2010). Young sex workers in Ethiopia: Linking migration, sex work and AIDS. In F. Thomas, M. Haour-Knipe, & P. Aggleton (Eds.), *Mobility, sexuality and AIDS* (pp. 184–191). London: Routledge.

Whitehouse, B. (2009). Transnational childrearing and the preservation of transnational identity in Brazzaville, Congo. *Global Networks, 9*(1), 82–99.

Whitehouse, B. (2012). *Migrants and strangers in an African city*. Bloomington, IN: Indiana University Press.

Wojcicki, J. (2002). 'She drank his money': Survival sex and the problem of violence in taverns in Gauteng Province, South Africa. *Medical Anthropology Quarterly, 16*(3), 267–293.

44

THE ROLE OF QUALITY DATA IN CHANGING HIV/AIDS TRAJECTORY AND NARRATIVES IN SUB-SAHARAN AFRICA[1]

Jacob A. Adetunji

Introduction

Africa, especially sub-Saharan Africa (SSA), has been severely affected by the Human Immunodeficiency Virus (HIV) and its sequelae, the Acquired Immune Deficiency Syndrome (AIDS). Although there was only a negligible number of HIV cases in SSA in the 1980s, by the year 2000, about 17.6 million (or about 70.7%) of the 24.9 million people living with HIV/AIDS globally were in the region. UNAIDS estimates the prevalence of HIV among adults in SSA as 9% in 2000, compared to 1.2% globally (UNAIDS, 2000, 2004). By 2010, the proportion of the 31.7 million people living with HIV globally that was in SSA was 67.8% (or 21.5 million), and by 2018, 25.7 million (or 68%) of the 37.8 million living with HIV globally were in SSA. In other words, although SSA has only about 14% of the world's population, it has 68% of the people living with HIV/AIDS globally. Several efforts have been made to contain the epidemic in SSA, including the US President's Emergency Program for AIDS Relief (PEPFAR).

SSA is also the region with perhaps the weakest health data infrastructure in the world. There was a paucity of population-based data at national levels that were needed to reliably quantify and track the HIV/AIDS epidemic in sub-Saharan Africa in the 1990s and early 2000s. The types of data available were usually small-scale studies that covered fairly limited geographic locations. Many of these data came from HIV/AIDS research studies, surveillance sites, and longitudinal studies. Their results and data therefore tend to have limited generalizability. In fact, epidemiologist James Chin is reported to have described the production of HIV/AIDS estimates of the 1990s more as an art rather than science (Lamptey, Wigley, Carr, & Collymore, 2002, p. 7).

The objective of this paper is to describe how this inadequate availability of quality data negatively impacted the results of model-based estimates of HIV prevalence and AIDS deaths in sub-Saharan Africa and how availability of quality population-based sero-data led to an improved understanding of the epidemic and increased political commitment, which in turn led to a gradual decrease in HIV prevalence in the region. We paid specific attention to quality, population-based sero-prevalence data from the Demographic and Health Surveys (DHS) Program.

DOI: 10.4324/9780429287213-54

The general lack of quality HIV prevalence data

When HIV began to spread in SSA in the 1980s and 1990s, there was a general dearth of quality data that could be used to estimate its prevalence rates and socio-demographic and geographic patterns. Most of the initial sources of data on HIV/AIDS in SSA were specialized and academic studies, sentinel surveillance in antenatal clinics (ANC), and longitudinal study sites. These information sources were scattered all over SSA and were typically not planned to provide representative data for the countries in which they were located or for the whole sub-region. However, in the absence of good data, scholars were willing to do the best they could with these imperfect or unrepresentative data. In fact, beginning from the early 1990s, the International Programs Center of the US Census Bureau received funding support to compile a database for these research and surveillance data (Stanecki & Way, 1997; US Census Bureau, 1994, 1999).

One rationale for such an exercise was that the geographical locations of various HIV/AIDS studies would increase and thus enhance the representativeness of their data over time. Increased representativeness would give researchers a better understanding of the variations in the nature of the epidemic and improve their models. However, we know that it would take an awfully long time before the geographical distribution of these studies, which are often chosen for the convenience of researchers, will begin to mirror the realities of the countries (or the subcontinent) in which they are located. Described here is a set of factors that militated against the representativeness of the database approach.

Firstly, although data from special longitudinal study sites and randomized controlled trials may be the best for establishing causation and assessing true effects of treatments, their results are usually not generalizable and over time, there are Hawthorne effects (resulting from a prolonged exposure to being studied or observed) that may make the population of these studies unrepresentative of the ordinary people who were not subjected to a prolonged observation. Secondly, hospital-based studies tend to rely on clinical records of self-selected clients/patients, and therefore are not representative of the general population. For example, it is usually difficult to get accurate data on the denominator for the cases in a hospital. Thirdly, while data from sentinel surveillance sites, often based in ANCs, are the closest to population-based HIV estimates, they are susceptible to non-representativeness biases mainly due to self-selection effects. In many cases, clinics that serve as sentinel sites for HIV testing were often purposively selected because of their accessibility to the main road, or easy to access. Hence, remote clinics are less likely to be included.

Besides, many of these clinics were ANCs, which poses a few representativeness challenges. For example, we know that clients of ANCs are also self-selected – pregnant or postpartum women are the primary clients. Their data do not include men. And pregnant women's HIV prevalence rates might differ from those of men for various reasons. Pregnant women tend to have had a higher frequency of unprotected sexual exposure than the general population that includes single men and women, many of whom may be sexually inactive. Even when single men and women are sexually active, they tend to use condoms at a higher rate than the general population. Moreover, pregnancy may lower the immunity of the women and thus increase their risk of HIV acquisition. In other words, pregnant women have higher exposure to risk of HIV acquisition than the regular adult population (CSO and ORC Macro, 2003, p. 240). Even then, ANC attendance tends to vary by age, socioeconomic status, education level, parity, ethnic group, and religion (Glynn et al., 2001). The pattern of bias in high-fertility settings has been found to differ from those in low-fertility settings (Gregson et al., 2002). Therefore, national level estimates of HIV prevalence that are based on test results from ANCs are often not representative of the whole population. Nevertheless, HIV surveillance surveys based on ANCs remained the most common source of HIV data in the 1990s and early 2000 (Glynn, 2001). The conclusion that can be drawn from this situation is that HIV/AIDS data from were beset by various biases and quality issues. Eze (2009) provides a detailed illustration of the problems of data quality in Nigeria and consequent absence of serious efforts to combat the HIV/AIDS epidemic until after 1999.

Consequences of poor HIV prevalence data

There were several consequences of not having good quality HIV prevalence data in sub-Saharan Africa.

1 *Reliance on statistical models:* Firstly, in the absence of good data, modellers were kings. Much of what was known about the prevalence of HIV in the region was based on models. In fact, it could be argued that there was over-reliance on models. An overview of these early HIV models is available in Stoto (1993). Gregson et al. (2007) also present a critical assessment of the early models of the demographic impact of HIV/AIDS in the region. Here, an overview of two of the models that were used to estimate HIV prevalence in the 1990s is presented:

   - The iwgAIDS model, which was developed by an inter-agency working group (iwg) on AIDS models and methods (hence, the name iwgAIDS). It was sponsored by the US State Department (Way & Stanecki, 1991). Its goal was to show the demographic impact of the epidemic, particularly in Africa. It was data-intensive and very demanding in terms of its input requirements. The input requirements include the proportion promiscuous (male/female, urban/rural), the number of sexual contacts per partner per month, STD acquisition rate per sexual contact, and use of condoms. Because it was difficult to find reliable data for these inputs, analysts and experts had to 'guesstimate' them. For example, a high-risk single female age 25–29 was assumed to have an average of 22.5 sexual contacts per month, and four contacts for a male with similar characteristics. The rate of HIV transmission per contact was estimated at 0.003 for females and 0.015 for males. The age pattern of HIV infection in the model was based on the findings of a 1987–88 sero-survey from Uganda (Way & Stanecki, 1991, p. 50). Thus, the possibility existed for multiple layers of biases. The model result indicated that urban HIV prevalence was 6.7% in 1990 and would increase to 16.7% in 2015. Rural prevalence rate was estimated at 0.5% in 1990 and would increase to 5.3% in 2015.
   - The Bulatao and Bos model was developed at the World Bank with the purpose of assessing the demographic impact of the AIDS epidemic. It had a lot of data input requirements, including male-female and female-male HIV transmission rate, the proportion of sexual acts protected with a condom, number of single-men contacts with prostitute, promiscuous contacts with non-prostitutes, etc. (Bulatao & Bos, 1992).

   It is a known fact that these models (in fact, all models) come with their specific assumptions; and the assumptions may not accurately reflect the exact realities of the population that they model. Hence, the estimates that come from them are prone to errors of varying magnitude. When the data input into the models are also prone to errors, then there is a compounding of inaccuracies that vitiate the outputs of the models. For example, there were AIDS impact projections in the 1990s indicating that by 2010, life expectancies at birth would be 50% of what it could have been without HIV/AIDS (33 years instead of

66 years) in Zambia, 43% less in Zimbabwe (40 years instead of 70 years), 41% less in Kenya (40 years instead of 68 years), and 47% less in Uganda – or 31 years instead of 59 years (Cohen & Trussell, 1996, p. 2; Stanecki & Way, 1997, p. 27; US Census, 1999). Of course, none of these projections came true for various reasons – life expectancy in Uganda in 2010 was 52 years, 57 years in Kenya and 42 years in Zambia (Population Reference Bureau, 2010).

2 *Reliance on indirect clinical case definition of AIDS*: Not only were the HIV prevalence rates based on models in SSA, there were problems with AIDS definition in the region also. The initial clinical case definition of AIDS for the region relied on algorithms, which had its challenges. Before 1986, the CDC diagnostic protocol was adopted by the WHO for clinical case definition for surveillance purposes for AIDS in SSA. It was difficult to use in countries with low diagnostic resources. Therefore, the WHO came up with a clinical case definition for AIDS that did not rely on serological testing. This WHO clinical case definition of AIDS for surveillance purposes indicates that any adolescent or adult who has at least 2 major signs and presents with at least 1 of the minor signs was considered to have AIDS if those conditions are not known to result from a condition unrelated to HIV infection.

The major signs are weight loss greater than 10%, chronic diarrhoea lasting for more than 1 month, and prolonged fever for more than 1 month. The minor signs are persistent cough for more than 1 month, generalized pruritic dermatitis, recurrent herpes zoster, oropharyngeal candidiasis, chronic disseminated herpes simplex, and generalized lymphadenopathy. The presence of Kaposi's sarcoma or cryptococcal meningitis is sufficient for the diagnosis of AIDS (De Cock et al., 1988, Adetunji, 1999). This 1985 clinical case definition of AIDS was adopted at a conference in Bangui. Various studies have found that the sensitivity of this approach is extremely low. Keou, Bélec, Esunge, Cancre, and Gresenguet (1992) found a sensitivity of 35% in Zaire. Another study tested the sensitivity of this clinical definition and found it to be 52%, with a specificity of 78%, i.e., its positive predictive value was 50% and its negative predictive value was 80% (De Cock et al., 1988).

3 *A drag on effective policy response:* Another consequence of relying on model estimates and clinical case definitions for HIV/AIDS was that health policy makers in SSA often did not believe the numbers that they produced – they were referred to as fictitious or cooked. Many African scholars did not believe the numbers about HIV/AIDS coming out of UNAIDS and the World Bank either. This lack of buy-in to the HIV/AIDS numbers impeded commitment to preventive action. The air of incredulity was fuelled by the belief that the West was trying to blame Africa for a problem that began among homosexuals in the US. Besides, Africa was being portrayed as sexually reckless and egregiously promiscuous. The lack of faith in the numbers delayed the implementation of preventive policy actions, while the virus was spreading. Uganda provided an early model of effective preventive policy action through its 'zero grazing' campaign, i.e., abstinence (A), being faithful to one partner (B), or condom use if either abstinence or being faithful was not possible (C). This was called the ABC approach.

4 *Increasing call for population-based HIV data:* Because of these consequences of relying on poor-quality data, program managers, policy makers and researchers began to call for investment in quality population-based data (Adetunji, 1999). For example, the Panel on Data and Research Priorities for Arresting AIDS in SSA that was set up by the US National Research Council in the 1990s made this plea as one of the recommendations: it asked that more data be collected on the prevalence and incidence of STD and HIV in SSA (Cohen & Trussell, 1996, p. 104). Initially, these calls for a population-based sero-survey

for HIV were not heeded by donors who worked in the HIV/AIDS space. The cost of collecting population-based sero data was thought to unreasonable and some argued that it was perhaps unethical to divert funds that could have been used to treat those HIV-infected persons who were facing imminent risk of death into data collection. After much persuasion, technical managers of the DHS program secured the concurrence of senior managers and the funding to collect biomarker HIV data in Mali, but with the proviso that it is accompanied by a few wrap-around studies – including a qualitative study – to investigate whether respondents understood the meaning of the informed consent form. Consequently, DHS initiated the collection of HIV biomarkers in the 2001 Mali DHS. Since then, the DHS Program has provided technical assistance in the implementation of about 90 surveys with HIV testing in about 45 countries

The DHS program and its HIV sero-survey approach

The DHS Program was launched in 1984 by the US Agency for International Development with the objectives of providing technical assistance to participating countries in the design and implementation of quality health surveys that provide data for evidence-based decision-making. The program also aimed to expand the international population and health database and advance survey methodology. To date, it has provided technical assistance in the implementation of about 400 surveys in more than 90 countries in the developing world. The approach to HIV testing that was adopted by DHS in most participating countries is the dried blood samples (DBS) of capillary blood taken by finger prick and collected on special filter papers on which are pre-printed circles. Each of these circles is filled with drops of blood from respondent's fingers, and the filter papers with DBS are stored in a drying box filled with desiccants and allowed to dry overnight (Mishra, Medley, Hong, Gu, & Robey, 2009).

A rigorous protocol for properly handling the DBS was developed and was followed until they were shipped to the laboratory for testing. The laboratories that are selected for testing the samples must have been inspected beforehand, their equipment and protocols updated if needed, and their laboratory scientists trained to follow approved standards. In the laboratories, a carefully written algorithm that maximizes the sensitivity and specificity of the HIV test results is followed for testing. There are also rigorous quality assurance plans that must be followed in the laboratories. The DBS approach is preferred over venous blood draw because it offers a few advantages: firstly, it is less invasive than venous blood samples, and secondly, it is easier to store and to transport (see Mishra et al., 2009, p. 6).

The DHS approach followed the WHO protocols. They were based on blood samples collected by trained nationals of participating countries, and followed the same rigorous quality assurance protocols that are hallmarks of the DHS household surveys; the testing was done in the best laboratories in the countries, under the close supervision of highly qualified scientists from participating countries using updated equipment, and protocols. In many countries, the protocols were reviewed by CDC. In all cases, the protocols were also approved by the institutional review boards of the host countries to ensure that the highest ethical processes were followed. Details of the ethical standards of the DHS processes are described in Adetunji and Shelton (2011). HIV prevalence results were vetted by a team of expert/technical coordinating committees set up by the host-country governments with participation from relevant international NGOs. At the end of the day, whatever HIV prevalence came out of these rigorous scientific standards were the best results representing the situation in the country at that point in time.

Initially, the HIV results were not linked to variables in the household survey beyond age, sex, rural-urban residence, and region. However, beginning in 2003 with the Kenya DHS, the anonymous linking methodology was adopted – it allows the linking of HIV test results to respondents' characteristics after all identifying information in the HIV results has been scrambled to preserve anonymity and respondents' privacy. Between 2001 and 2018, at least 32 sub-Saharan African countries completed an HIV sero-survey under the DHS program. Of these, 22 have conducted at least two rounds while 11 countries have conducted three or more. The list of countries with completed DHS with HIV testing is presented in the Appendix (Table A1).

How quality sero-survey data changed the trajectory

There are several ways through which the sero-prevalence data from the DHS changed the trajectory of the HIV epidemic in Africa, and indeed across the world. One was through their quality. They produce reliable and quality population-based assessment of HIV that is nationally representative, and by age, sex, rural-urban residence, and region. The results were therefore accepted by the host-country government and were used for program and policy planning. The international donor community also accepted the results. This acceptance and confidence in the HIV test results as close to the true picture of the epidemic in their domain was a game changer: it paved the way for policies to be developed for prevention, care, and treatment. Some of the countries started asking for specific tabulations and formats of presentation of the results that suited their purposes. For example, Tanzania asked for an 'Atlas' of the epidemic – i.e., for a visual representation of the geographic distribution of HIV prevalence rates overlaid on other geo-data of interest (TACAIDS et al., 2006). Uganda issued a policy document on HIV/AIDS from the results of the 2004–2005 sero-survey (Uganda Ministry of Health, 2007). Zambia asked for information on syphilis as part of the HIV sero-survey.[2] The flexibility and richness of the DHS sero-data motivated some countries to start requesting that HIV testing be included in their DHS. In fact, some countries started doing stand-alone HIV sero-surveys, which were called the HIV/AIDS Indicator Surveys (AIS). These requests for AIS increased because of PEPFAR also.

The availability of anonymously-linked HIV prevalence data beginning from 2003 in Kenya also dramatically improved our understanding of the impact of risk behaviour and socioeconomic status on the HIV/AIDS epidemic. Stakeholders in HIV programming and policies began to see patterns in the population-based sero-prevalence survey data from DHS that showed the biases in earlier model-based estimates. Perhaps the most important effect of the DHS results was that they produced lower HIV prevalence rates. In almost every country, DHS sero-surveys produced prevalence rates that were much lower than the model-based estimates of HIV prevalence rates from UNAIDS and other sources. For example, the DHS estimate of HIV prevalence in Mali in 2001 was 1.7% compared with 2.3%–2.4% (i.e., UNAIDS's estimate was 25% higher than the DHS estimate). In Zambia in 2002, DHS found a national HIV prevalence rate of 16%, which was about 20% less than the estimates based on ANC surveillance sites that were being used by the government (CSO and ORC Macro, 2003, p. 239). UNAIDS's (2000) estimate of adult HIV prevalence for Kenya in 1997 was 11.6% compared to 6.7% in DHS for 2003. WHO (1996) estimates of adult HIV prevalence rate for 1994 was 8.5% for Togo (DHS found it to be 2.5% in 2013), 14.5% for Uganda (DHS found 6.4% in 2004), and 7.2% for Rwanda (DHS found 3% in 2005). Although various factors might be adduced for the differences, including interventions to reduce the prevalence, it is likely that WHO estimates for 1994 were higher than actual prevalence in many of these countries. The biggest decline in global HIV prevalence and in the estimated number of people living with HIV/AIDS came after India completed an HIV sero-survey through the DHS program in 2005/06 and the national HIV prevalence rate was below 1%. The quality and consistently lower results from DHS eventually led to UNAIDS modifying its assumptions and lowering the trajectory of HIV prevalence rates, including the number of people living with HIV/AIDS for the whole world.

Through DHS sero-survey data, HIV prevalence rates could be produced for regions and rural-urban residence. As a result, governments in several SSA countries as well as bilateral donors were able to reassess whether the geographical distribution of health facilities and treatment efforts aligned with the need for HIV treatment and the location of health facilities; they have been able to identify which groups (or sub-national areas) have higher prevalence rates, etc. Examples of publications that mapped HIV prevalence rates by geographical location include Tanzania and Uganda (TACAIDS et al., 2006, Ministry of Health Kampala and Macro, 2007). This realignment of needs and resources led to programming efficiencies and bigger impact.

In fact, countries that have more than one DHS sero-survey have been able to see declining trends in prevalence among risk groups and geographical areas (see Appendix Table A1). The table also shows not only that HIV prevalence has declined over time in most countries, but the decline has also been witnessed in countries with high, medium, or low prevalence. For example, Zambia has four data points between 2001–2002 and 2018 and its prevalence rate declined from 15.6% to 11.1% (a 29% decline). Zimbabwe's prevalence declined by about a quarter from 18% in 2005 to 13.6% in 2015, and Cameroon's prevalence declined by a half from 5.4% in 2004 to 2.7% in 2018. The prevalence rates remained unchanged over time in countries such as Rwanda, Senegal, Sierra Leone, and Guinea. Some countries such as Lesotho, Mozambique, and Uganda saw modest increases in HIV prevalence rates.

DHS data and changes in HIV/AIDS narratives

Availability of reliable, nationally representative and cross-nationally comparable sero-prevalence data through the DHS program changed the narrative about HIV in several ways. First, one of the initial beliefs about HIV/AIDS was that poverty was a major risk factor for infection (UNAIDS, 2004, p. 16). Some people in Africa jokingly said that AIDS is an acronym that truly stands for Acquired Income Deficiency Syndrome or the American Idea for Discouraging Sex (Eze, 2009, p. 1; Awofala & Ogundele, 2018). One of the earliest papers to call this belief to question was by Shelton, Cassell and Adetunji (2005). The article was based on an analysis of DHS anonymously-linked HIV sero-prevalence data from the 2003–2004 Tanzania DHS. The results show a positive correlation between wealth quintiles, which is a proxy for household economic status, and HIV prevalence rates. HIV prevalence rates were found to be lower among men and women in poorer households than among those in richer households (see Figure 44.1). For example, HIV prevalence among women in the richest quintile was four times that among women in the poorest quintile. This sounded counter-intuitive and was contrary to popular opinion that poverty and lack of economic opportunity are major drivers of the AIDS epidemic in Africa. Since then, many other analyses have found support for our results (Mishra et al., 2007).

Secondly, the assumption that unfaithful men were bringing HIV to their faithful wives at home was prevalent in many circles (McGrath et al., 1992; Schoepf, Walu, Rukarangira, Payanzo, & Schoepf, 1991; Blanc, 2001; O'Leary, 2000). However, that assumption started to change as data when DHS sero-surveys began to show a pattern that did not support those earlier assumptions. For example, Adetunji (2005) analyzed DHS data from Kenya, Mali, and

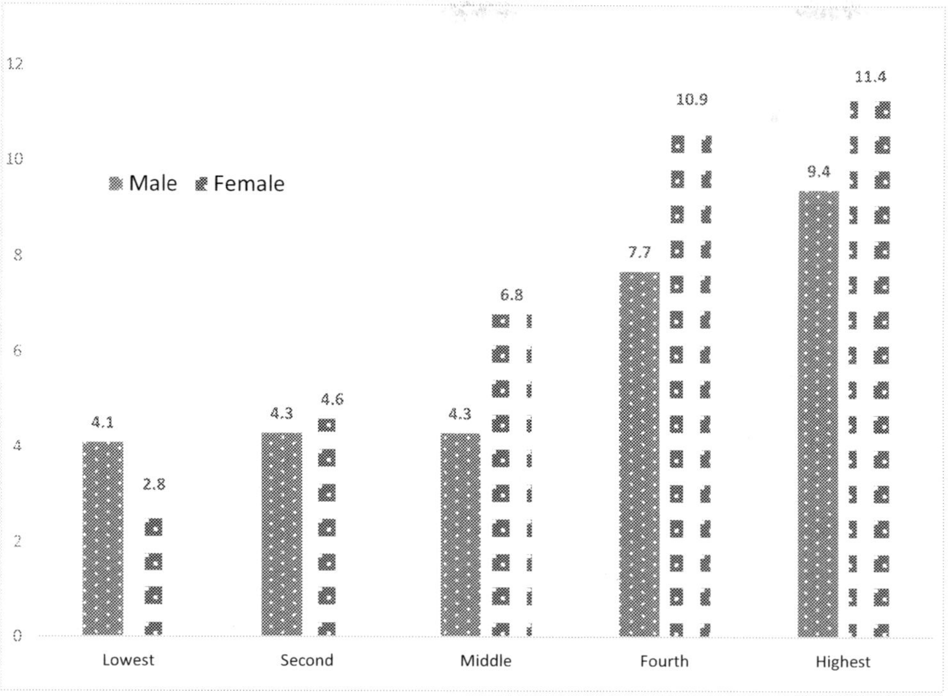

Figure 44.1 Sex differences in HIV prevalence rates by wealth quintiles (Tanzania, 2003–2004).
Source: Chart was first presented in Shelton, Cassell and Adetunji (2005).

Zambia and found that there were more HIV-positive women at almost every age until ages 40 and over (Table 44.1).

An analysis of DHS matched couples' data from six countries in sub-Saharan Africa (Adetunji, 2007) found significant proportions of HIV-positive wives who were married to HIV negative husbands (Tables 44.2 and 44.3). For example, in both rural and urban areas of Cameroon, the wives were more likely to be the infected partner among sero-discordant couples: the wives were the infected partner in 53% of the cases. Similarly in Kenya, in 61% of sero-discordant couples, the wives were the infected partners, while the husbands were HIV-negative. In other SSA countries with couples' HIV data, there are significant proportions of sero-discordant couples in which the women were the HIV-positive partners.Table 44.2 shows hat in most HIV-discordant couples in urban areas, women were more likely to be the infected partners in three of the six countries, and in two of the six countries women were more likely to be the infected partner irrespective of place of residence. At the time of writing, of the 56 DHS datasets with HIV data for matched couples in SSA, women were more likely to be the HIV-positive partner among HIV sero-discordant couples in 24 surveys; wives were as likely to be the infected partner as their husbands in 3 countries, and husbands were more likely to be the HIV positive partners in the remaining 29 surveys. Overall, the results of the sero-discordant study (Adetunji, 2007) confirm that HIV sero-discordance is a significant problem in SSA. This indicates a high unmet need for targeted preventive intervention among couples. Unless that need is met, the potential exists that a large proportion (if not all) of sero-negative partners in a discordant partnership will sero-convert. Previous studies have suggested that it takes some time

Table 44.1 HIV Prevalence Rates by Age and Sex in Kenya, Mali, and Zambia

Age	*Kenya*			*Mali*			*Zambia*		
	Male	*Female*	*F/M Ratio*	*Male*	*Female*	*F/M Ratio*	*Male*	*Female*	*F/M Ratio*
15–19	0.5	3.5	7.0	0.3	1.1	3.7	1.6	6.6	4.1
20–24	2.4	8.7	3.6	0.3	1.6	5.3	4.4	16.3	3.7
25–29	6.5	12.0	1.8	0.7	3.2	4.4	15.0	25.1	1.7
30–34	6.1	11.6	1.9	3.8	3.3	0.9	20.5	29.4	1.5
35–39	8.6	11.8	1.4	1.1	2.8	2.5	22.4	22.6	1.0
40–44	8.6	10.3	1.2	1.8	1.2	0.7	20.5	17.3	0.8
45–49	6.0	4.7	0.8	2.6	1.0	0.4	20.2	13.6	0.7
Total	**4.5**	**8.7**	**1.9**	**1.3**	**2.0**	**1.54**	**12.9**	**17.8**	**1.4**

Source: Demographic and Health Surveys sero-prevalence data for Kenya (2003) Mali (2001) and Zambia (2002).

Table 44.2 Prevalence of Sero-Discordant Couples in Urban and Rural Areas and Distribution by Sex of the Infected Partner

	Urban			*Rural*		
	Prevalence among discordant couples (%)	*Percent of couples in which the man is the infected partner*	*Percent of couples with HIV+ woman and HIV- man*	*Prevalence among discordant couples (%)*	*Percent of couples in which the man is the infected partner*	*Percent of couples with HIV+ woman and HIV- man*
Cameroon	7.3	47.3	52.7	3.2	46.9	53.1
Uganda	7.9	49.4	50.6	4.3	62.8	37.2
Kenya	10.3	37.9	62.1	6.7	38.8	61.2
Tanzania	12.2	50.8	49.2	6.7	58.2	41.8
Malawi	18.3	75.4	24.6	8.6	54.7	45.3
Lesotho	9.2	60.9	39.1	14.6	67.1	32.9

Source: Adetunji (2007).

for sero-conversion to take place in sero-discordant heterosexual couples. Quinn et al. (2000) estimated an incidence rate of 12 per 100 person years of exposure. Therefore, there is a window of opportunity for prevention. Available evidence suggests that when discordant couples are identified and counselled, their adoption of preventive behaviour increases rapidly (Allen et al., 1992). This is particularly encouraging. Without such pertinent preventive interventions, sero-conversion among discordant couples is much higher than in sero-concordant negative couples by a ratio of about 58:1 (Hugonnet et al., 2002).

Adetunji (2007) also discussed potentially effective intervention among sero-discordant couples, with a particular focus on voluntary counselling and testing (VCT). He argues that a VCT intervention that targets individuals alone may not work for various reasons, one of which is fear of disclosure of HIV-positive status. A South African study of about 1,050 HIV-positive men and women who know their status revealed that they were reluctant to reveal their HIV status to sexual partners (Simbayi et al., 2007). A qualitative study in Uganda found that married men and women who know that they are HIV-positive are reluctant to disclose their HIV status to their spouses for fear of stigma, of not knowing the HIV status of their spouses, and reluctance

Table 44.3 Percentage of Matched Couples that are Sero-Concordant or Sero-Discordant in Sub-Saharan Africa

Country	*Survey*	*Both HIV+*	*Man HIV+ woman HIV-*	*Woman HIV+ man HIV-*	*Both HIV-*	
Angola	2015–16 DHS	0.3	0.8	1.1	97.8	w
Burkina Faso	2010 DHS	0.2	0.5	0.7	98.6	w
Burkina Faso	2003 DHS	0.5	1.7	1.0	96.9	
Burundi	2016–17 DHS	0.5	0.6	0.4	98.6	
Burundi	2010 DHS	1.1	0.4	0.6	97.8	w
Cameroon	2018 DHS	0.8	1.7	1.6	95.9	
Cameroon	2011 DHS	1.5	2.8	3.1	92.6	w
Cameroon	2004 DHS	2.3	2.4	2.7	92.6	w
Chad	2014–15 DHS	0.3	0.9	1.0	97.8	w
Congo DR	2013–14 DHS	0.2	0.5	0.9	98.4	w
Congo DR	2007 DHS	0.2	0.6	1.1	98.1	w
Côte d'Ivoire	2011–12 DHS	1.9	2.8	2.6	92.7	
Eswatini	2006–07 DHS	28.8	7.7	8.7	54.8	w
Ethiopia	2016 DHS	0.3	0.4	0.4	98.9	=
Ethiopia	2011 DHS	0.6	0.4	0.7	98.3	w
Ethiopia	2005 DHS	0.3	0.8	1.0	97.9	w
Gabon	2012 DHS	1.3	2.0	5.9	90.8	w
Gambia	2013 DHS	0.8	1.6	0.9	96.7	
Ghana	2014 DHS	0.8	0.8	1.7	96.7	w
Ghana	2003 DHS	1.0	1.7	1.5	95.8	
Guinea	2018 DHS	0.2	1.6	1.2	97	
Guinea	2012 DHS	0.8	1.0	1.3	96.8	w
Guinea	2005 DHS	0.4	0.9	0.6	98	
Kenya	2008–09 DHS	3.1	2.8	3.2	91	w
Kenya	2003 DHS	3.6	2.9	4.6	88.9	w
Lesotho	2014 DHS	19.9	8.2	6.9	65	
Lesotho	2009 DHS	18.9	9.5	7.6	64	
Lesotho	2004 DHS	19.5	9.0	4.6	66.9	
Liberia	2013 DHS	0.5	1.7	1.1	96.7	
Liberia	2007 DHS	0.3	0.8	1.3	97.7	w
Malawi	2015–16 DHS	5.6	4.5	3.9	86	
Malawi	2010 DHS	6.3	4.7	3.8	85.3	
Malawi	2004 DHS	7.0	5.7	4.0	83.3	
Mali	2012–13 DHS	0.2	0.8	0.9	98.1	w
Mali	2006 DHS	0.4	0.4	0.9	98.3	w
Mozambique	2015 AIS	7.1	4.8	4.8	83.3	=
Namibia	2013 DHS	11.7	8.4	5.8	74.1	
Niger	2012 DHS	0.2	0.2	0.1	99.6	
Niger	2006 DHS	0.2	0.6	0.4	98.8	
Rwanda	2014–15 DHS	2.1	1.5	1.3	95.1	
Rwanda	2010 DHS	2.4	1.3	0.9	95.4	
Rwanda	2005 DHS	1.7	1.4	0.8	96.1	
Sao Tome and Principe	2008–09 DHS	0.5	2.0	0.4	97	
Senegal	2017 DHS	0.2	0.4	0.4	99	=

(*Continued*)

Country	Survey	Both HIV+	Man HIV+ woman HIV-	Woman HIV+ man HIV-	Both HIV-	
Senegal	2010–11 DHS	0.4	0.6	0.7	98.3	w
Senegal	2005 DHS	0.4	0.4	0.3	98.8	
Sierra Leone	2013 DHS	0.2	1.4	1.2	97.3	
Sierra Leone	2008 DHS	0.5	0.7	1.0	97.8	w
South Africa	2016 DHS	14.7	5.1	10.6	69.7	w
Togo	2013–14 DHS	1.2	1.0	1.4	96.3	w
Zambia	2018 DHS	7.8	3.1	4.5	84.6	w
Zambia	2013–14 DHS	8.2	6.1	5.2	80.5	
Zambia	2007 DHS	8.0	6.6	4.6	80.9	
Zimbabwe	2015 DHS	10.9	5.0	3.8	80.3	
Zimbabwe	2010–11 DHS	10.3	6.7	4.5	78.5	
Zimbabwe	2005–06 DHS	14.7	8.1	5.2	72.1	

Source: DHS STATCompiler. In the last column, "w" means that the percentage of serodicordant couples in which the woman is the HIV-positive partner is higher than those in which the man is the infected partner.

to break the heart of their spouses (Yoder et al., 2007). Some are simply afraid that they would be blamed for bringing HIV to the family. In the Uganda study, 50% of women and 36% of men who tested positive did not disclose their HIV status to their spouses. Those likely to disclose their status to their partners are those who were extremely sick and needed care, and those who had come with their spouses.

Adetunji (2007) also argues that interventions that focus on women in antenatal clinics will not be sufficient if they focus on providing testing and counselling to pregnant women without testing their husbands. They will be missing a significant number of women who test HIV-negative, but live with HIV-positive male partners. For example, in urban areas of Malawi where 33% of co-resident couples are HIV-positive, only 15 percentage points (or 15 out of 33%) are in sero-concordant relationships. Thus, about 60% of women who are HIV-positive and in co-resident couple relationships have the potential to be tested in antenatal clinic (about 96% of urban women receive antenatal care from trained medical personnel). About 40% will be in relationships in which only the men are HIV-positive. In urban Tanzania, about 37% of women in HIV-positive couple relationships can potentially be tested in an antenatal clinic. However, in urban areas of Lesotho, where almost all HIV-positive couples live in sero-concordant relationships, 87% of HIV-positive women in co-resident relationships can be seen in an antenatal clinic (about 90% of women in Lesotho receive antenatal care from medical personnel). The lowest proportion of women who have the potential to be seen in an antenatal clinic for VCT is in rural Tanzania: only 56%. The remaining 44% are in male-positive sero-discordant relationships. Only about 75% of women with recent births in rural Tanzania received antenatal care from a nurse/midwife/doctor.

An argument exists therefore that supports the adoption of couple counselling to alleviate or eliminate the negative consequences of HIV status (Padian, O'Brien, Chang, Glass, & Francis, 1993; Painter, 2001; Hochgesang et al., 2005). Couple counselling as an approach looks at couples as a unit and seeks to equip HIV-positive couples with the skills and information that they need to cope with their HIV status. The approach has been more successful among those planning to marry than among those who are already married. Part of the reason for lack of appreciable success among married or cohabiting couples is the way the VCT is set up and the way counsellors are trained: many counsellors do not have the requisite training to handle couples' counselling. Most have been trained to do individual counselling and guidelines for couples' counselling are not widely available. However, couples' counselling is a promising area and has worked well when tried as an intervention. Those who have used it as an approach attest to its usefulness in helping discordant couples understand that HIV status is not necessary a result of marital unfaithfulness since infection could pre-date marriage.

Finally, the contribution of a paper published by Adetunji (2000) is that it allays the fear that HIV/AIDS prevalence could wipe away or reverse the gains in child survival that had been made through interventions over the previous decades (Valleroy, Harris, & Way, 1996). The analysis was based on DHS data from 25 countries found that major negative impact of HIV prevalence on child survival was observed only in countries with high HIV prevalence rates – defined as adult HIV prevalence rate of 5% or higher. The most severe impact was in Zimbabwe where 61% of the under-five mortality rate in 1994 was explained by high HIV prevalence. This was followed by Kenya were 28% of under-five mortality rate was due to high HIV prevalence, and Zambia where HIV prevalence explained 27% of under-five mortality rate. However, in a vast majority of countries with a moderate (1–5%) HIV prevalence or low HIV prevalence (below 1%), the effect on child survival was not of the magnitude that could reverse the downward trends in under-five mortality. The study concluded that the direct effects of HIV/AIDS prevalence among adults were not as large as scholars had assumed. Although the study called for further research and better data before any firm conclusions can be reached, the results suggest that HIV/AIDS alone might not be a sufficient explanation for reversals in mortality gains among under-five-year-olds, except in extremely high HIV-prevalence countries with low mortality rates.

Conclusions

The main objective of this paper is to highlight how weak data and predominant reliance on model estimates of HIV prevalence in sub-Saharan Africa seemed to have dampened the motivation of many African health policy leaders to take effective actions and how the availability of reliable population-based sero-prevalence data from the region changed that. We paid special attention to the role of the DHS program, beginning from 2001. The sero-data became widely available especially with the arrival of PEPFAR and showed in almost all cases that model-based estimates of HIV prevalence were higher than those from nationally representative household surveys. Although UNAIDS was initially reluctant to accept the DHS sero-data results, by 2005, it had changed its mind about their quality because the DHS program produced consistent results, matched the results from sentinel surveillance estimates when results of DHS were limited to clusters around the sentinel surveillance sites, and it was also able to dispel other criticisms such as bias that could come from non-coverage of the institutional and the homeless populations. Today, the difference between UNAIDS estimates and DHS results are minimal. Effective program interventions and policy actions have led to declines in HIV prevalence rates in almost every country in SSA (see Appendix Table A1). Similarly, some unfounded beliefs and narratives about HIV/AIDS, such as the assumption that unfaithful husbands were always bringing HIV infection to their spouses, have also been revised because of data on couple sero-discordance. The number of national high-quality HIV/AIDS datasets and sources has increased in SSA and so has occurrence of evidence-based programming and policies.

The general conclusion is that more emphasis needs to be placed on collecting quality population-based data that build a strong host-country buy-in and confidence. This is especially important for countries like Nigeria where HIV prevalence and incidence data are still weak

(Eze, 2009, Awofala & Ogundele, 2018). Investments in quality data should also include support for training and expertise in data collection, quality assurance, analysis, and communication for policy and program decisions. The world of data has changed somewhat from what it was in the 1980s and 1990s. Better surveillance data are now available and are being used to monitor epidemics and pandemics – including the coronavirus.

Notes

1 Views and opinions expressed in this paper belong to the author. They do not necessarily represent the views and opinions of the US Agency for International Development.
2 Details of the ethical challenges presented by this request in Zambia are described in Adetunji and Shelton (2011).

References

Adetunji, J. A. (1999). HIV infection and AIDS-related deaths in Arica. In *Health and Mortality: Issues of Global Concern* (pp. 442–467, ST/ESA/SER.R/152). New York, NY: United Nations.

Adetunji, J. A. (2000). Trends in under-five mortality rates and the HIV/AIS epidemic. *Bulletin of the World Health Organization, 78*, 1200–1206.

Adetunji, J. A. (2005, March 31–April 2). *Gender imbalance in the HIV prevalence in sub-Saharan Africa.* A poster paper presented at the annual meeting of the Population Association of America, Philadelphia, PA.

Adetunji, J. A. (2007, March 29–31). *HIV Sero-discordance among heterosexual couples in sub-Saharan Africa.* Paper presented at the annual meeting of the Population Association of America, New York.

Adetunji, J. A., & Shelton, J. D. (2011, December 5–9). *Ethical issues in the collection, analysis and dissemination of DHS data in sub-Saharan Africa.* Paper presented at the 6th African Population Conference, Ouagadougou.

Allen, S., Trice, J., Van de Perre, P., Serufilira, A., Hudes, E., Nsengumuremyi, F., . . . Hulley S. (1992). Effect of serotesting with counseling on condom use and seroconversion among HIV discordant couples in Africa. *British Medical Journal, 304*, 1605–1609.

Awofala, A. A., & Ogundele, O. E. (2018). HIV epidemiology in Nigeria. *Saudi Journal of Biological Sciences, 25*(4), 667–670.

Blanc, A. K. (2001). The effect of power in sexual relationships on sexual and reproductive health: an examination of the evidence. *Studies in Family Planning, 32*(3), 189–213.

Bulatao, R. A., & Bos, E. R. (1992). *Projecting the demographic impact of AIDS.* Policy Research Working Papers, Vol. 941. Washington, DC: World Bank.

Cohen, B., & Trussell, J. (1996). *Preventing and mitigating AIDS in sub-Saharan Africa: Research priorities for the social and behavioral sciences.* Washington, DC: National Academy Press.

CSO and ORC Macro. (2003). *2001–02 Zambia demographic and health survey.* Calverton: ORC Macro.

De Cock, K. M., Colebunders, R., Francis, H., Nzilambi, N., Laga, M., Ryder, R. W., . . . Piot, P. (1988). Evaluation of the WHO clinical case definition for AIDS in rural Zaire. *AIDS, 2*(3), 219–221.

Eze, J. I. (2009). *Modeling HIV/AIDS epidemic in Nigeria* (Unpublished Doctoral Dissertation). Submitted to the University of Glasgow, March. Retrieved from http://theses.gla.ac.uk/642/1/2009EzePhD.pdf

Glynn, J. R., Buvé, A., Caraël, M., Musonda, R. D., Kahindo, M., Macauley, I., . . . the Study Group on Heterogeneity of HIV Epidemics in African Cities. (2001). Factors influencing the difference in HIV prevalence between antenatal clinic and general population in sub-Saharan Africa. *AIDS, 15*(13), 1717–1725.

Gregson, S., Nyamukapa, C., Lopman, B., Mushati, P., Garnett, G. P., Chandiwana, S. K., & Anderson, R. M. (2007). Critique of early models of the demographic impact of HIV/AIDS in sub-Saharan Africa based on contemporary empirical data from Zimbabwe. *Proceedings of the National Academy of Sciences USA, 104*(37), 1458–1459.

Gregson, S., Terceira, N., Kakowa, M., Mason, P. R., Anderson, R. M., Chandiwana, S. K., & Caraël, M. (2002). Study of bias in antenatal clinic HIV-1 surveillance data in a high contraceptive prevalence population in sub-Saharan Africa. *AIDS, 16*(4), 643–652.

Hochgesang, M. S., Killam, W. P., Aberle-Grasse, J., Newman, D., Limbe, W., & Davis, M. K. (2005). HIV sero-discordance in couples seeking VCT services in Malawi. *Malawi Medical Journal, 17*(4), 132–158.

Hugonnet, S., Mosha, F., Todd, J., Mugeye, K., Klokke, A., Ndeki, L., . . . Hayes, R. (2002). Incidence of HIV infection in stable sexual partnerships: A retrospective cohort study of 1802 couples in Mwanza region, Tanzania. *Journal of Acquired Immune Deficiency Syndrome, 30*(1), 73–80.

Keou, F. X., Bélec, L., Esunge, P. M., Cancre, N., & Gresenguet, G. (1992). World Health Organization clinical case definition for AIDS in Africa: An analysis of evaluations. *East African Medical Journal, 69*(10), 550–553.

Lamptey, P., Wigley, M., Carr, D., & Collymore, Y. (2002). Facing the HIV/AIDS pandemic. *Population Bulletin, 57*(3).

McGrath, J. W., Schumann, D. A., Pearson-Marks, J., Rwabukwali C. B., Mukasa R., Namande, B., & Nakayiwa, S. (1992). Cultural determinants of sexual risk behavior for AIDS among Baganda women. *Medical Anthropology Quarterly*. 6 (2), 153–161.

Ministry of Health Kampala and Macro International Inc. (2007). *Uganda atlas of HIV/AIDS indicators 2004–05*. Calverton and Kampala: Ministry of Health and Macro International.

Mishra, V, Bignami, S., Greener, R., Vaessen, M., Hong, R., Ghys, P., . . . Rutstein, S. (2007). *A study of the association of HIV infection with wealth in sub-Saharan Africa*. DHS Working Paper. No. 31. Calverton, MD: Macro International.

Mishra, V., Medley, A., Hong, R., Gu, Y., & Robey, B. (2009). *Levels and spread of HIV seroprevalence and associated factors: evidence from national household surveys* (DHS Comparative Report No. 22). Calverton: Macro International.

O'Leary, A. (2000). Women at risk for HIV from a primary partner: Balancing risk and intimacy. *Annual Review of Sex Research, 11*, 191–234.

Padian, N. S., O'Brien, T. R., Chang, Y., Glass, S., & Francis, D. P. (1993). Prevention of heterosexual transmission of human immunodeficiency virus through couple counseling. *Journal of Acquired Immune Deficiency Syndrome, 6*(9), 1043–1048.

Painter, T. M. (2001). Voluntary counseling and testing for couples: A high-leverage intervention for HIV prevention in sub-Saharan Africa. *Social Science and Medicine, 53*(11), 1397–1411.

Population Reference Bureau. (2010). *2010 World Population Data Sheet*. Washington, DC: Population Reference Bureau.

Quinn, T. C., Wawer, M. J., Sewankambo, N., Serwadda, D., Li, C., Wabwire-Mangen, F., . . . Gray, R. H. for the Rakai Project Study Group. (2000). Viral load and heterosexual transmission of Human Immunodeficiency Virus Type 1. *New England Journal of Medicine, 342*, 921–929.

Schoepf, B. G., Walu, E., Rukarangira, N., Payanzo, N., & Schoepf, C. (1991). Gender, power, and risk of AIDS and Zaire. In M. Turshen (Ed.), *Women and health in Africa* (pp. 187–203). Trenton, NJ: Africa World Press.

Shelton, J. D., Cassell, M. M., & Adetunji, J. (2005). Is poverty or wealth at the root of HIV? *The Lancet, 366*(9491), 1057–1058.

Simbayi, L. C., Kalichman, S. C., Strebel, A., Cloete, A., Henda, N., & Mqeketo, A. (2007). Disclosure of HIV status to sex partners and sexual risk behaviours among HIV-positive men and women, Cape Town, South Africa. *Sexually Transmitted Infections, 83*, 29–34.

Stanecki, K. A., & Way, P. O. (1997). The demographic impact of HIV/AIDS: Perspectives from the world population profile: 1996 (IPC Staff Paper No. 86). Washington, DC: US Census Bureau.

Stoto, M. A. (1993). Models of the demographic effect of AIDS. In K. Foote, K. Hill, & L. Martin (Eds.), *Demographic change in sub-Saharan Africa* (pp. 350–379). Washington, DC: National Academy of Sciences.

TACAIDS (Tanzania Commission for AIDS), National Bureau of Statistics (NBS), National AIDS Control Programme (NACP), and ORC Macro. (2006). *Tanzania atlas of HIV/AIDS indicators*. Dar es Salaam and Calverton: TACAIDS and ORC Macro.

Uganda Ministry of Health. (2007). *Policy recommendations based on the major findings of the 2004–05 Uganda HIV/AIDS sero-behavioural survey*. Kampala: Ministry of Health.

UNAIDS. (2000). *HIV prevalence estimates for countries and regions*. Geneva: United Nations Joint Program on HIV/AIDS.

UNAIDS (Joint United Nations Programme on HIV/AIDS). (2004). *2004 Report on the global AIDS epidemics*. Geneva: UNAIDS.

US Bureau of the Census. (1994). *Recent HIV seroprevalence levels by country: December 1994* (Research Note No. 15). Washington, DC: Center for International Research, Census Bureau.

US Census Bureau. (1999). *Recent HIV seroprevalence levels by country: February 1999* (Research Note 26). Washington, DC: International Program Center, Census Bureau.

Valleroy, L. A., Harris, J. R., & Way, P. O. (1996). The impact of HIV-1 infection on child survival in the developing world. *AIDS, 4*, 667–672.

Way, P., & Stanecki, K. (1991). *The demographic impact of an AIDS epidemic on an African country: Application of the IWG AIDS model* (CIR Staff Paper No. 58). Washington, DC: US Census Bureau.

World Health Organization. (1996). *The current global situation of AIDS: 30 June 1996*. Geneva: WHO and UNAIDS.

Yoder, S. (2007). VCT process and patterns of HIV disclosure in UPHOLD project, Uganda (Unpublished manuscript). ORC Macro/UPHOLD.

Appendix

Table A1 HIV Prevalence Rates from DHS Sero-Surveys in Sub-Saharan Africa (2001–2018)

Country	*Survey Year*	*Women*	*Men*	*Total*	*Women*	*Men*	*Total*
Angola	2015–16	2.6	1.2	2	6387	5144	11531
Burkina Faso	2010	1.2	0.8	1	8298	6317	14615
Burkina Faso	2003	1.6	1.5	1.5	4086	3065	7151
Burundi	2016–17	1.2	0.6	0.9	8496	6558	15055
Burundi	2010	1.7	1	1.4	4533	3554	8087
Cameroon	2018	3.4	1.9	2.7	6416	5830	12246
Cameroon	2011	5.6	2.9	4.3	7221	6282	13503
Cameroon	2004	6.6	4.1	5.4	5128	4619	9746
Chad	2014–15	1.8	1.3	1.6	5656	4558	10214
Congo	2009	4.1	2.1	3.2	6438	5671	12110
Congo DR	2013–14	1.6	0.6	1.2	9264	7504	16768
Congo DR	2007	1.6	0.9	1.3	4492	4012	8504
Côte d'Ivoire	2011–12	4.6	2.7	3.7	4509	4051	8560
Côte d'Ivoire	2005	6.4	2.9	4.7	4413	4023	8436
Eswatini	2006–07	31.1	19.7	25.9	4424	3763	8187
Ethiopia	2016	1.2	0.6	0.9	13297	11381	24679
Ethiopia	2011	1.9	1	1.5	14695	12581	27276
Ethiopia	2005	1.9	0.9	1.4	5736	4803	10539
Gabon	2012	5.8	2.2	4.1	5459	4986	10445
Gambia	2013	2.1	1.7	1.9	4089	3450	7539
Ghana	2014	2.8	1.1	2	4444	3883	8326
Ghana	2003	2.4	1.4	2	5089	4045	9134
Guinea	2018	1.6	1.3	1.5	5062	3505	8567
Guinea	2012	2.1	1.2	1.7	4622	3327	7949
Guinea	2005	1.9	0.9	1.5	3742	2577	6319
Kenya	2008–09	8.0	4.3	6.3	3641	3066	6707
Kenya	2003	8.7	4.6	6.7	3151	2851	6001
Lesotho	2014	29.7	18.6	24.6	3175	2646	5821
Lesotho	2009	26.7	18	23	3778	2856	6634
Lesotho	2004	26.3	19	23.4	3030	2015	5045
Liberia	2013	2.0	1.7	1.9	4397	3785	8182
Liberia	2007	1.8	1.2	1.5	6381	5351	11733
Malawi	2015–16	10.8	6.4	8.8	7737	6720	14457
Malawi	2010	12.9	8.1	10.6	7091	6497	13588

(*Continued*)

Table A1 (Continued)

Country	*Survey Year*	*Women*	*Men*	*Total*	*Women*	*Men*	*Total*
Malawi	2004	13.3	10.2	11.8	2686	2465	5150
Mali	2012–13	1.3	0.8	1.1	4806	3503	8310
Mali	2006	1.4	0.9	1.2	4528	3614	8141
Mali	2001	2.1	1.3	1.8	3842	2595	6438
Mozambique	2015	15.4	10.1	13.2	5807	4228	10035
Mozambique	2009	13.1	9.2	11.5	5229	3832	9061
Namibia	2013	16.9	10.9	14	4051	3680	7731
Niger	2012	0.4	0.4	0.4	5000	3125	8124
Niger	2006	0.7	0.7	0.7	4406	2856	7262
Rwanda	2014–15	3.6	2.2	3	6752	5551	12302
Rwanda	2010	3.7	2.2	3	6917	5690	12607
Rwanda	2005	3.6	2.3	3	5641	4348	9988
Sao Tome	2008–09	1.3	1.7	1.5	2378	2110	4488
Senegal	2017	0.5	0.4	0.5	7618	6083	13701
Senegal	2010–11	0.6	0.4	0.5	5326	4104	9430
Senegal	2005	0.7	0.4	0.5	4229	3183	7412
Sierra Leone	2013	1.7	1.3	1.5	7695	6261	13956
Sierra Leone	2008	1.7	1.2	1.5	3448	2726	6174
South Africa	2016	27.3	14.4	21.2	2485	2199	4685
Tanzania	2011–12	6.2	3.8	5.1	9756	7989	17745
Tanzania	2007–08	6.6	4.6	5.7	8179	6865	15044
Tanzania	2003–04	7.7	6.3	7	5749	4994	10743
Togo	2013–14	3.1	1.7	2.5	4737	3984	8721
Uganda	2011	8.3	6.1	7.3	10883	8673	19557
Uganda	2004–05	7.5	5	6.4	9350	7477	16827
Zambia	2018	14.2	7.5	11.1	12817	10950	23767
Zambia	2013–14	15.1	11.3	13.3	14719	13140	27859
Zambia	2007	16.1	12.3	14.3	5502	4942	10444
Zambia	2001–02	17.8	12.9	15.6	2073	1734	3807
Zimbabwe	2015	16.7	10.5	13.8	8667	7475	16142
Zimbabwe	2010–11	17.7	12.3	15.2	7313	6250	13563
Zimbabwe	2005–06	21.1	14.5	18.1	6947	5848	12796

Source: DHS STATcompiler

45

THE STATE OF THE AFRICAN DEMOGRAPHIC TRANSITION, 1990–2016

Lungile F. Motsa and Clifford O. Odimegwu

Introduction: conceptual definitions and context

Virtually, human populations are dynamic as entrenched in the classic demographic model. The universally underway demographic transitions that account for dramatic reductions in fertility and mortality rates provide sufficient evidence, including in the African continent. In Africa, the unfolding demographic transition is not only deemed as incomparable by several scholars (Madsen, 2013; Bongaarts & Casterline, 2013; Machiyama, 2010), but recent world population projections have also underscored a rapid growth of the continent's population. According to the United Nations Department of Economic and Social Affairs, Population Division (UN DESA, 2017, 2019), Africa is the second most densely populated continent after Asia, characterized by an increase from an estimated 1.1 billion inhabitants in mid-2017 to 1.3 billion inhabitants in mid-2019. As asserted in the UN DESA's report (2019), the continent comprised nearly 17 percent of the 7.7 billion estimated global population and yielded approximately 100 million additional inhabitants annually. Noteworthy, these demographic trends are demonstrative of the distinctive multi-layered population dynamics ascribed to the unique political, environmental, and socio-economic challenges that are prevalent in Africa. For instance, the African continent is perpetually fraught with civil wars, high prevalence of diseases such as malaria and HIV/AIDS, extreme poverty due to poorly performing economies, low educational attainments, and bad climatic conditions.

Therefore, the demographic transition also remains an important demographic phenomenon in Africa despite its longstanding and contemporary criticism. Its significance has been underscored by researchers including Kebede, Goujon, and Lutz (2019) who argued that all human populations across the globe have commenced the demographic transition process. Additionally, an early progress towards a demographic transition is directly linked to the attainment of the Sustainable Development Goals (SDGs) because it could enable the formulation of appropriate policies to create a conducive environment for improved living standards, enhanced human development, and sustained opportunities, especially in underprivileged countries, communities, and households (Samman & Watkins, 2017). Thus, its importance for Africa cannot be overemphasized as the continent seeks to achieve the SDGs by the year 2030.

As widely known, the classic demographic transition is a brainchild of Frank W. Notestein (1945) that was initially formulated to describe and understand population change in European

DOI: 10.4324/9780429287213-55

countries. It is defined as a process in which countries evolve from experiencing high birth and death rates due to poor socio-economic development and public health conditions to experiencing low birth and death rates due to both advanced socio-economic development and improved public health conditions (Williams, Manfredi, & Melegaro, 2018; Livi-Bacci, 2017; Notestein, 1945). During the transition, populations initially experience plummeting death rates resulting in rapid population growth and young age structure and later followed by a decline in birth rates, which after some time leads to rapid population ageing (Williams et al., 2018). As stated by Caldwell (1976), it was through the demographic transition framework that intense debates were triggered concerning the causal factors of population growth and the consequential means to control population during the 1960s and 1980s and continues to be influential to date (Defo, 2014). Subsequently, several scholars (Williams et al., 2018; Bongaarts, 2016; Defo, 2014; Cleland, 2012; Askew, Maggwa, & Obare, 2010) have endeavoured to examine the demographic transition, specifically how it has unfolded in other regions over the past decades, including the African region.

The demographic transition has its roots in the developed world and congruently described the population scenarios in industrialized countries (Defo, 2014). However, there exists substantial evidence of the underway fertility and mortality transitions in sub-Saharan Africa, albeit the pace of the transitions has been found to sharply differ across regions and within countries (Canning et al., 2015; Nugent & Seligman, 2013; Caldwell, Orubuloye, O., & Caldwell, 1992; Caldwell, 2006; Kalipeni, 1995). Historically, sub-Saharan Africa lagged behind all the world regions in commencing the demographic transition. The region only experienced a fall in fertility in the 1970s and 1980s whereas its onset in Europe was at the end of the nineteenth century and it spread globally including Asia in the 1950s and 1960s (Willekens, 2015; Kebede et al., 2019).

Since the fertility transition began in Africa, available evidence shows that the transition is slow-paced; with high fertility rates still observed in most countries while it has stalled in other countries, especially those in West Africa (Kebede et al., 2019; Sippel, Kiziak. Woellert, & Klingholz, 2011; Bongaarts & Casterline, 2013; Bongaarts, 2016; Madsen, 2013; Sneeringer, 2009). As of mid-2019, the continent's total fertility rate stood at 4.4 children per woman, more than double the level of replacement fertility (UN DESA, 2019). Accordingly, numerous studies have attributed the high fertility in sub-Sahara Africa to the widespread poor socio-economic development alongside low levels of urbanization, persistent low contraceptive use, and high desired family size (Bongaarts & Casterline, 2013; Ndahindwa et al., 2014) while other studies linked the fertility stalls to female education disruptions (Kebede et al., 2019) as well as changes in contraceptive use, age at marriage, income, and labour-force participation (Garenne, 2009). Conversely, the factors explaining the underway fertility decline in sub-Saharan Africa have been examined. For example, a macro-level study of 48 sub-Saharan African countries ascribed a considerable decline in fertility to income per capita, infant mortality, and the role of technology through education across the continent (Chisadza & Bittencourt, 2016). Further, fertility decline was linked to women's education, household wealth, and delayed start of sexual activities among married/cohabiting and never-married women in Rwanda (Ndahindwa et al., 2014).

Consistently with the demographic transition principle, the mortality transition preceded the fertility transition in Africa. However, the mortality transition did not progress on a continuous downward trajectory as postulated in the demographic transition theory. In sub-Saharan Africa, unprecedented civil wars and diseases including the HIV/AIDS pandemic and rising cases of non-communicable diseases (NCDs) have interrupted the mortality transition since the 1980s (Gouda et al., 2019; Canning et al., 2015; Houle, Clark, Go´mez-Olive, Kahn, & Tollman, 2014; Akachi & Canning, 2008). Great variations in the underway mortality transitions both between and within countries have been predominantly witnessed in Africa compared to other regions in the developing world. The divergence of the demographic transitions occurring within African countries was also underscored by Madsen (2013). Available evidence shows that sub-Saharan Africa's demographic transition suffers a high communicable disease burden due to hepatitis B in the Senegal-Gambia region (Williams et al., 2018) whilst the Southern African region suffered an overwhelming prevalence of the HIV/AIDS pandemic (Canning et al., 2015). For example, the health transition in South Africa was marked by three characteristically different transition typologies; a 'counter transition' in which mortality spiked among children and young adults, an 'epidemiologic polarization' in which vulnerable groups experienced a higher burden of mortality, and a 'protracted transition' in which a double burden of emergent HIV/AIDS combined with an increase in NCDs among older adults (Kahn, Garenne, Collinson, & Tollman, 2007). Further, Menashe-Oren and Stecklov (2018) uncovered existence of rural-urban disparities in adult mortality characterized by surplus adult mortality that shifts from the urban to rural setting as countries develop in sub-Saharan Africa.

Likewise, sub-Saharan Africa experiences an exceptional under-five mortality transition. The continent accounts for the world's highest under-five mortality rate estimated at 81 deaths per 1,000 live births compared to 43 deaths per 1,000 live births on global average, with factors including fertility rate, water quality, total expenditure on health per capita, sanitation access, and female employment rate being the major driving forces (Acheampong et al., 2018). Evidence also depicts that significant within-country variations in under-five mortality characterize the mortality transition in sub-Saharan Africa. Accordingly, Burke, Heft-Neal, and Bendavid (2016) found that sub-national determinants explained a larger proportion of under-five mortality than do country-level attributes in 28 African countries. Consequently, sub-Saharan Africa has the lowest life expectancy in the world, estimated at 61.1 years in 2019, regardless of the considerable approximately 12-year average gain in survival attained since 1990 (UN DESA, 2019).

Thus, notwithstanding the accumulated body of literature on demographic trends in Africa, research that has examined concurrently the changes in fertility and mortality across the continent remain relatively inadequate. This is despite the existing evidence showing marked fertility and mortality declines in countries such as Rwanda and Mauritius, fluctuations in trends and patterns of both fertility and mortality rates due to fertility stalls, re-emergence of infectious diseases such as malaria and tuberculosis, the advent of HIV/AIDS, and an upsurge in non-communicable diseases like diabetes and cancer in certain parts of the continent which have altered the demographic transitions (Machiyama, 2010; Otieno, Agwanda, & Khasakhala, 2020; Sneeringer, 2009; Chisumpa, Odimegwu, & Saikia, 2019; Golding et al., 2017; Kuate-Defo, 2002; Menashe-Oren & Stecklov, 2018; Teller, Hailemariam, Gebreselassie, & Seifu, 2011; Willekens, 2015; Cleland, 2012). Available studies that investigated fertility and mortality changes date too far back in time, and in most cases, analyses were country- or region-specific and often focussed on a single analysis of either fertility or mortality transition over a period of time (Williams et al., 2018; Defo, 2014; Askew et al., 2010; Bongaarts, 2016; Ndahindwa et al., 2014; Akachi & Canning, 2008; Kahn et al., 2007; Kahn, 2006; Notkola, Timaeus, & Siiskonen, 2000). Hence, similarities and variations in both fertility and mortality transitions between regions and within individual countries have not been unmasked in Africa. It is therefore against this backdrop that it is important to have holistic and recent analyses of the various resemblances and departures regarding the African fertility and mortality transitions.

Moreover, as an important population process, the demographic transition has transformed and impacted global populations over the years and continues to do so to date. Globally, demographic changes due to the demographic transition have had deep effects on human society and impacted poverty, economic growth, health, and overall human development (Canning et al., 2015; Lee & Reher, 2011). Conversely, other global phenomena which are on par with the demographic transition such as the spread of democratic government, industrial revolution, urbanization increase, and the continuous rise in the human population's educational levels are deemed to have originated and evolved during the demographic transition (Lee & Reher, 2011). Thus, the analysis and constant update of population dynamics cannot be overemphasized because populations alongside their changes remain central parts of development (Mubila, 2012), shaping development trajectories in multiple countries by bringing both opportunities and challenges (World Bank, 2016). Specifically, not only do the current population trends in Africa have a critical influence on the future trajectories of population sizes in the continent, but they also have a direct link with the required resources to improve social and economic well-being, human capital, youth social resilience, and the steep rise in population growth (Madsen, 2013).

Therefore, utilizing data sourced from the World Bank database, this chapter presents a descriptive analysis of the demographic transition in 54 African countries in the period spanning 26 years, 1990–2016. The analysis took a closer look at the overall progression of the demographic transitions with regard to their patterns and speed by examining two demographic components: fertility (crude birth rates) and mortality (crude death rates) in five African regions. The regions comprised Eastern Africa, Central Africa, Northern Africa, Southern Africa, and Western Africa. Specifically, average levels of both fertility and mortality decline were calculated and further ranked for detailed comparisons between and within regions. Lastly, the research agenda and conclusion were presented to respectively draw attention to research, ramifications, and some policy implications of the mortality and fertility changes in Africa.

Theoretical and conceptual issues as used in African studies

The demographic transition is not a new concept in demographic discourse and African studies in general. According to Edmonston (2014), the classic demographic transition initially occurred among European countries in the 1600s and 1700s, when mortality rates began their steady decline, causing continued population growth due to predominant moderately high fertility rates which only began to fall in the late 1800s and 1900s. It is further documented that around the mid-1900s, the fertility rates of European populations fell to replacement levels and have since progressed to well below replacement levels (Edmonston, 2014).

Subsequently, the concept of the demographic transition was developed by scholars in Europe including Aldophe Landry and Warren Thompson, who first described the regular patterns of population change and later Kingsley Davis and Frank Notestein, who connected population change patterns to trends in socio-economic development in the second quarter of the twentieth century (Blue & Espenshade, 2011; Nam, 1994). Embedded in its foundations, the demographic transition that historically and gradually began in some parts of Europe and spread to North America and Australia was inferred to be a universal principle that populations in the middle and low-income countries are expected to experience (Defo, 2014). However, researchers have found that its occurrence in developing countries has been more rapid and characterized by divergent patterns. Further, the issue of a lack of an agreement among researchers on an all-inclusive theory of the causes of demographic transition despite empirical evidence showing both common patterns of demographic trajectories across populations and variations across regions was raised by Blue and Espenshade (2011). Specifically, investigations revealed that the timing of the transition and the level of the socio-economic development that triggers the transition as well as the cultural and religious beliefs under which decisions on fertility are made differ across populations (Bongaarts & Watkins, 1996; Watkins, 1986; Caldwell, 2006).

Therefore, as a descriptive concept, the demographic transition is a generalized depiction of a long-run population trend shown in five stages employed by Blue and Espenshade (2011) as follows:

Stage 1: This is the pre-transition stage, characterized by both high and fluctuating crude birth and death rates with resultant low natural increase rates.

Stage 2: This is an early transition stage, characterized by crude death rates that start plummeting while the crude birth rates remain high, resulting in moderate natural increase rates.

Stage 3: This stage is marked by crude birth rates that begin to fall alongside the crude death rates although the crude birth rates fall, greatly exceeding the crude death rates, thus fuelling rapid population growth.

Stage 4: At this stage, crude death rates are low and the crude birth rates continue falling even slightly above or nearly at replacement fertility, leading to population ageing.

Stage 5: This is the stage characterized by low crude birth and death rates resulting in below-replacement fertility. It illustrates the current population situation in developed countries such as Germany and Italy.

Noteworthy, this chapter adopted the five-stage demographic transition as a benchmark model to analyze and compare the evolution of the crude birth and death rates between 1990 and 2016 in African countries.

Methods and measures used

The data used for this chapter's analysis were downloaded from the World Bank database and spanned a 26-year period, 1990–2016, for 54 African countries. Estimates of fertility and mortality were compiled for the 54 countries to illustrate how the demographic transition has unfolded in Africa. To depict both the patterns and speed of the mortality and fertility transitions, the crude death and birth rates per 1,000 population corresponding to each country were respectively utilized in the analysis.

The focus was on vital statistics, specifically the crude birth and death rates because they are readily available without the need for additional information. Crude birth and death rates are measured in a more reliable manner using accurate counts of births and deaths in a population. Moreover, the availability of these vital statistics for long periods of time enables a comparative analysis across different countries and regions.

Thus, to demonstrate how the countries have undergone their demographic transitions in this analysis, a two-fold analysis was done as follows:

1. A comparative analysis of the regions in terms of the average crude death and birth rates in 1990–2016 were first calculated. Then, percentage declines or inclines in fertility and mortality were calculated for all the regions by subtracting the 2016 crude birth and death rates from those obtained in 1990. Lastly, graphs depicting the patterns of the crude birth and death rates between 1990 and 2016 were drawn for each region.
2. A second comparative analysis of the various countries in each region was done by calculating the percentage declines or inclines in the crude birth and death rates during the 26-year period. To ascertain how each country performed in the demographic transition in relation

to other countries in the region, they were then ranked according to the attained percentage declines or inclines in crude birth and death rates during the observation period.

Empirical findings

Demographic transition by African regions

The demographic transition has been underway in Africa since the 1990s. This has been revealed by an analysis of 54 African countries, namely Eastern Africa, Central Africa, Northern Africa, Southern Africa, and Western Africa from 1990 to 2016. Thus, Figure 45.1 shows the levels of mortality and fertility declines among African regions between 1990 and 2016.

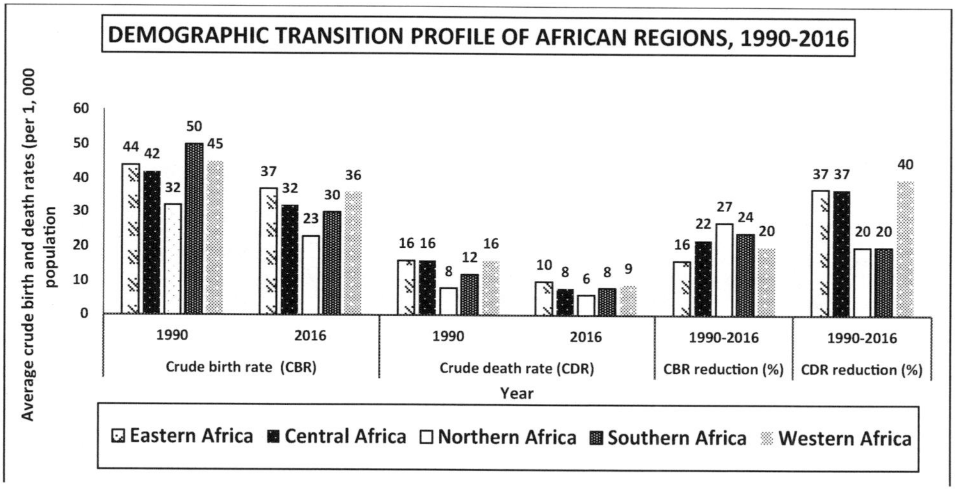

Figure 45.1 The demographic transition profile of African regions, 1990-2016.

Central Africa

The empirical evidence points to an underway demographic transition in Central Africa, albeit the pace of progress has been erratic in the 26-year observation period. Between 1990 and 2016, the region achieved a 16% average decline in fertility, attaining the lowest fertility reduction (fifth position) in Africa shown in Figure 45.1. The crude birth rate reduced from an average of 44 to 37 births per 1,000 population from 1990 to 2016. Conversely, the crude death rate decreased from an average of 16 to 10 deaths per 1,000 population from 1990 to 2016, depicting a 37% average decline in mortality. The mortality transition pattern indicates that the region had considerable population survival gain between 1990 and 2016, placing it in the second position in Africa for its mortality reduction achievement as demonstrated in Figure 45.1.

In 2016, Angola, Democratic Republic of Congo (DRC), and Chad were characterized by crude birth rates that were above the regional average estimated at 37 births per 1,000 population whilst African Central Republic together with Chad exhibited crude death rates that were above the regional average crude birth rate estimated at 10 deaths per 1,000 population. Generally, the fertility transition in the region has been the slowest in Africa. Within the region, Figure 45.2 shows that Gabon experienced the lowest crude birth rate throughout 1990–2016 (37 and 30 births per 1,000 population in 1990 and 2016, respectively) whereas Chad experienced the highest crude birth rate since 1994, having recorded 43 births per 1,000 population in 2016. Additionally, a common pattern of stalled fertility transition in the region can be observed in Figure 45.2. Regarding the mortality transition pattern, Sao Tome and Principe consistently displayed lower crude death rates whilst Congo Republic, DRC, Gabon, Cameroon, and Central African Republic indicated different stages at which they experienced an upsurge in mortality in the middle of the transition, probably due to civil wars or disease outbreaks as depicted in Figure 45.3.

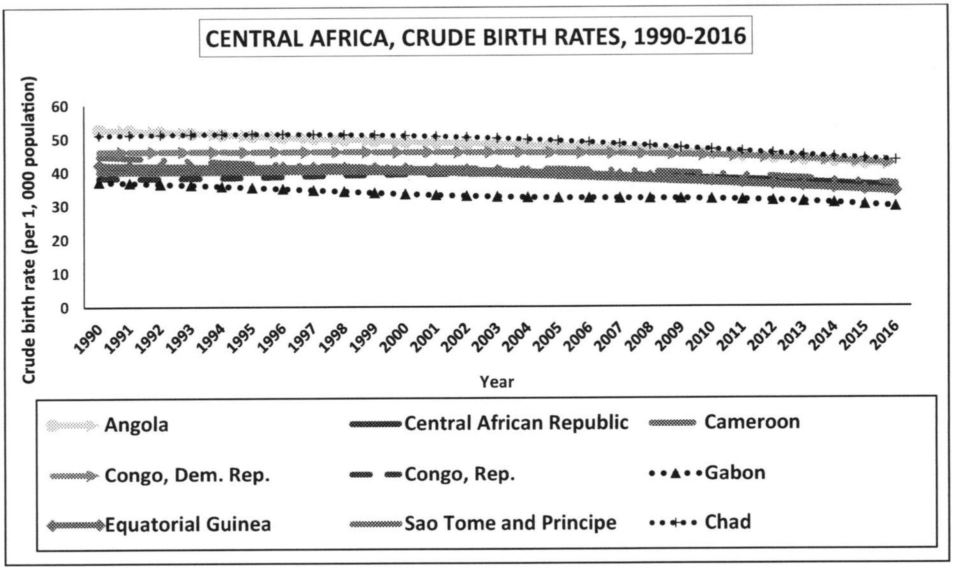

Figure 45.2 The fertility transition profile of Central Africa.

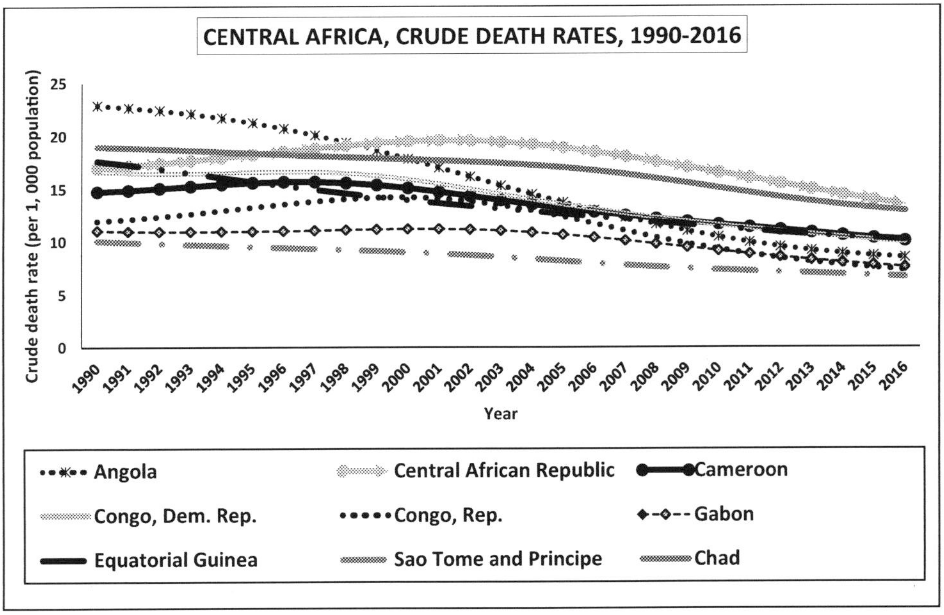

Figure 45.3 The mortality transition profile of Central Africa.

Eastern Africa

In the Eastern African region, signs of the underway demographic transition in 1990–2016 are evident. On average, the crude birth rate reduced from 42 to 32 births per 1,000 population from 1990 to 2016. The evidence highlighted a 22% average decrease in 26 years, the third-highest reduction in Africa as illustrated in Figure 45.1. Conversely, the fall in the average crude death rate has been 13% higher than the fall in crude birth rate, earning the region another third position in Africa for its mortality reduction feat. The mortality reduction achievement was demonstrated by a 35% average decline in crude death rate between 1990 and 2016. It is observed in Figure 45.1 that the crude death rate reduced from an average of 16 to 8 deaths per 1,000 population between 1990 and 2016. Within Eastern Africa, variations in the patterns of crude birth and death rates exist among countries as shown in Figures 45.4 and 45.5.

In 2016, Burundi, Somalia, South Somalia, Mozambique, Uganda, and Tanzania exhibited crude birth rates that were higher than the regional average of 32 birth per 1,000 population. On the contrary, Mauritius and the Seychelles depicted the lowest crude birth rates of less than 20 births per 1,000 population in the same year. In relation to the mortality pattern shown in Figure 45.5, Rwanda's mortality transition remarkably depicted the lowest crude death rate of 6 deaths per 1,000 together with Kenya despite suffering the region's highest crude death rates in the period 1990–1997, partly ascribed to the 1994 genocide. Additionally, multiple stalls marred the demographic transition in the Seychelles, Kenya, Mauritius, and Eritrea. Overall, the mortality transition is much faster than the fertility transition in Eastern Africa. Therefore, more efforts are still needed to reduce fertility levels in the region.

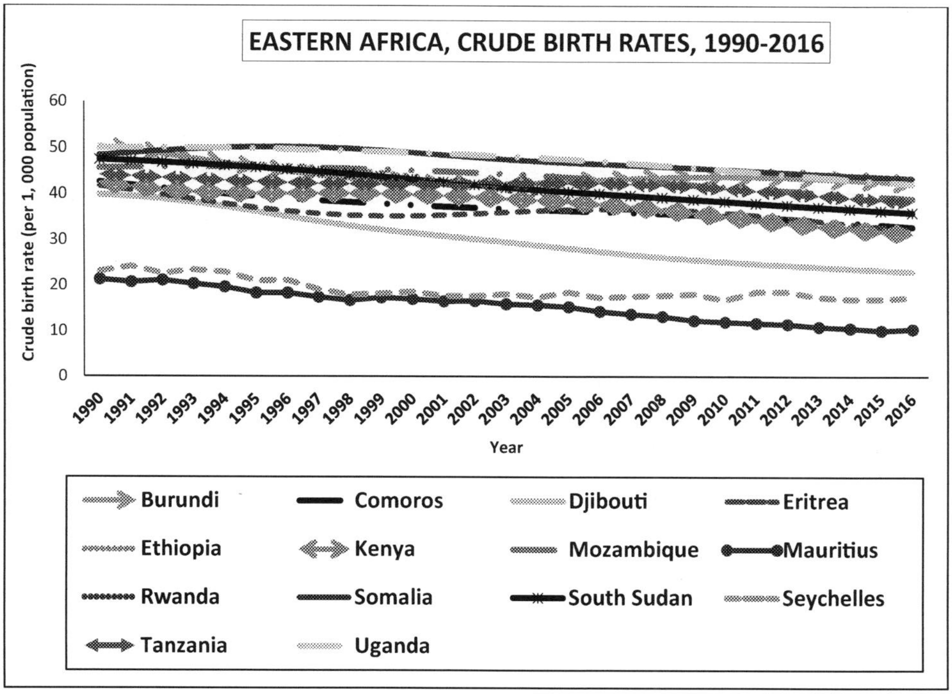

Figure 45.4 The fertility transition profile of Eastern Africa.

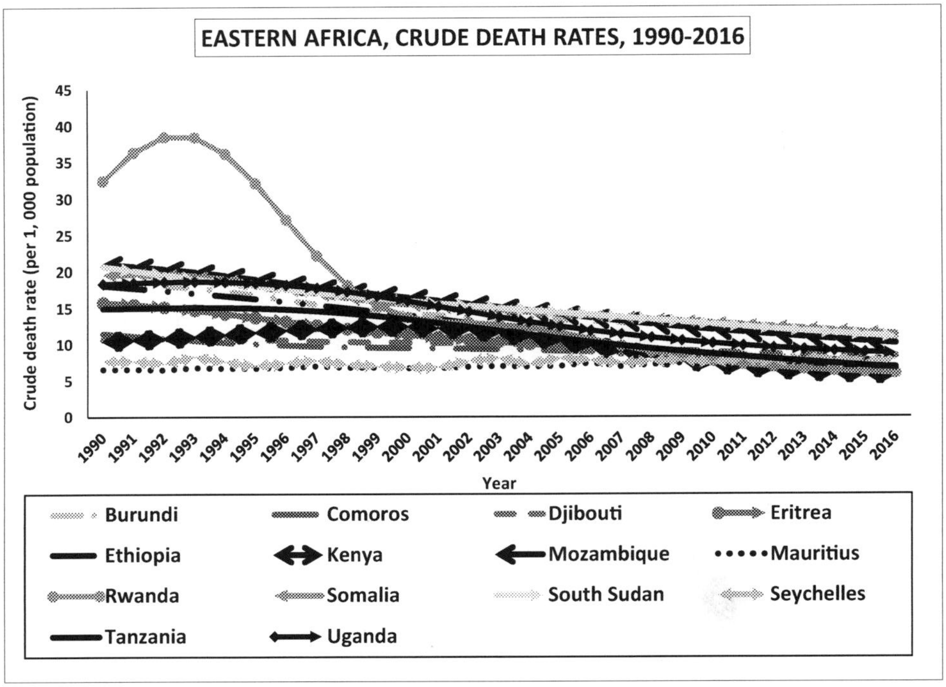

Figure 45.5 The mortality transition profile of Eastern Africa.

Northern Africa

Northern Africa also experienced a one-sided pace of progress in the demographic transition in 1990–2016. Whilst the region achieved the highest average fertility decline in Africa, however, its average mortality decline was the lowest together with that of Southern Africa as depicted in Figure 45.1. Noteworthy, the low level of mortality decline characterizing the region could also be attributed to the fact that almost all Northern African countries, except for Sudan, were already exhibiting crude death rates that were below 10 deaths per 1,000 population in 1990. This contrasts with the mortality situation in other African countries whose crude death rates in 1990 were more than 10 deaths per 1,000 population such as Rwanda and Sierra Leone. Therefore, these findings must be interpreted with caution.

With respect to the fertility transition, the crude birth rate in Northern Africa reduced from an average of 32 to 24 births per 1,000 population between 1990 and 2016. This subsequently translated to a 27% average fertility decline, earning the first position in Africa for exceptionally attaining the highest average fertility decline. Conversely, the crude death rate fell from an average of 8 to 6 deaths per 1,000 population from 1990 to 2016, hence achieving the lowest gain in population survival in Africa as illustrated by the 20% mortality decline in Figure 45.1. In relation to the fertility pattern, Figure 45.6 shows that Sudan and Egypt had the highest crude birth rates, above the regional average of 23 births per 1,000 population in 2016. Additionally, Sudan and Tunisia consistently maintained the highest and lowest crude birth rates in the region throughout 1990–2016, respectively.

The mortality transition pattern presented in Figure 45.7 shows that Sudan also exhibited the highest crude death rates throughout the observation period. Noteworthy, the mortality pattern further reveals that from 1990 up to 2008, Libya exhibited the lowest crude death rates and

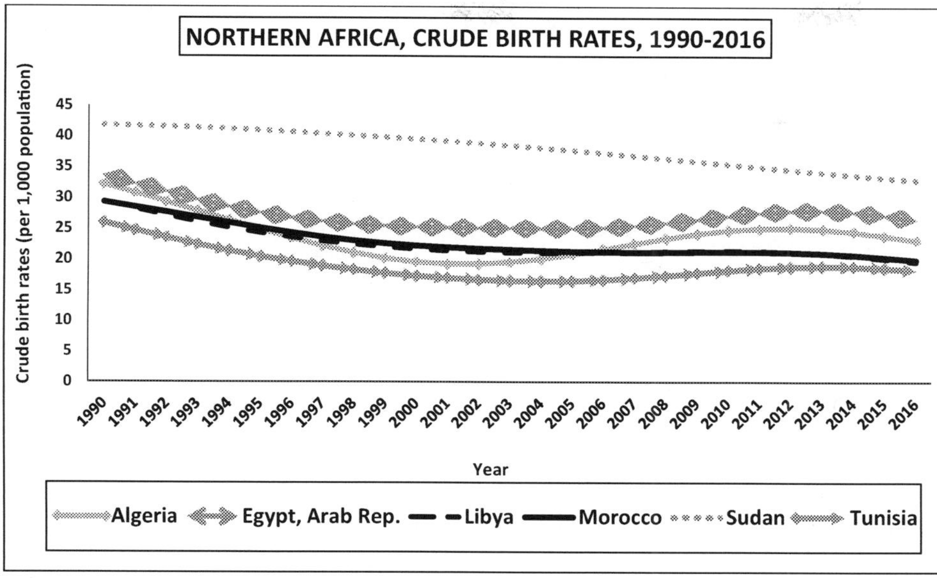

Figure 45.6 The fertility transition profile of Northern Africa.

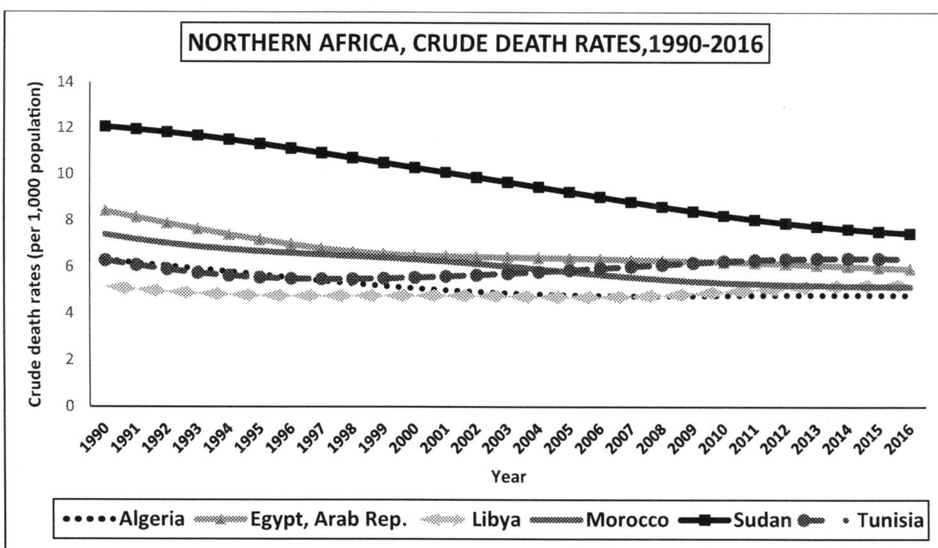

Figure 45.7 The mortality transition profile of Northern Africa.

thereafter Algeria led with the lowest crude death rates. Moreover, the mortality setback suffered by Libya after 2008 might have been caused by the political unrest that occurred after the assassination of the then leader Colonel Muammar Gaddafi in 2011. Other remarkable features of the demographic transition pattern in Northern Africa are the apparent stalling fertility rates, particularly in Algeria, Egypt, and Tunisia from the mid-2000s as well as the nearly stationary mortality rates experienced since the mid-1990s in Egypt, Libya, and Tunisia.

Southern Africa

Southern Africa's demographic transition is partially on course despite the drawbacks caused by the highest prevalence of the HIV/AIDS pandemic. The region came after Northern Africa by attaining the second-highest average decline in fertility in Africa as demonstrated by the 24% in Figure 45.1. This is resultant from an average crude birth rate decrease from 50 to 30 births per 1,000 population between 1990 and 2016. On the contrary, mortality levels in Southern Africa dropped by 20% as the average crude death rate reduced from 12 to 8 deaths per 1,000 population between 1990 and 2016, making it a high-mortality zone in Africa as shown in Figure 45.1. In 2016, Madagascar, Malawi, Zambia, and Zimbabwe exhibited above the regional average crude birth rate of 30 births per 1,000 population. Throughout 1990–2016, Malawi and Zambia alternately experienced the highest crude birth rates whilst South Africa consistently experienced the lowest crude birth rates, with Botswana placed second-lowest as illustrated in Figure 45.8. Notably, Zimbabwe experienced an upsurge in crude birth rates from 2001 up to 2014.

The pattern of the mortality transition in Figure 45.9 indicates that Lesotho followed by South Africa and Eswatini experienced crude death rates that were above the regional average of 8 deaths per 1,000 population in 2016. Interestingly, both Malawi and Zambia's crude death rates dramatically reduced between 2001 and 2016 despite being characterized by the highest rates of death between 1990 and 2000. Also, Madagascar's crude death rate gradually reduced during 1990–2016, attaining the lowest crude death rate. Lastly, the distinctive evidence of the negative impact of the HIV/AIDS pandemic in Southern Africa is apparent in the upsurges in crude death rates experienced from the early 1990s to the late 2000s in Lesotho, South Africa, Eswatini, Namibia, Botswana, and Zimbabwe as shown in Figure 45.9. Further, the huge dent caused by the HIV/AIDS pandemic on the mortality transition manifested in the 2016 crude death rates which matched those experienced in the 1990s by most countries in the region.

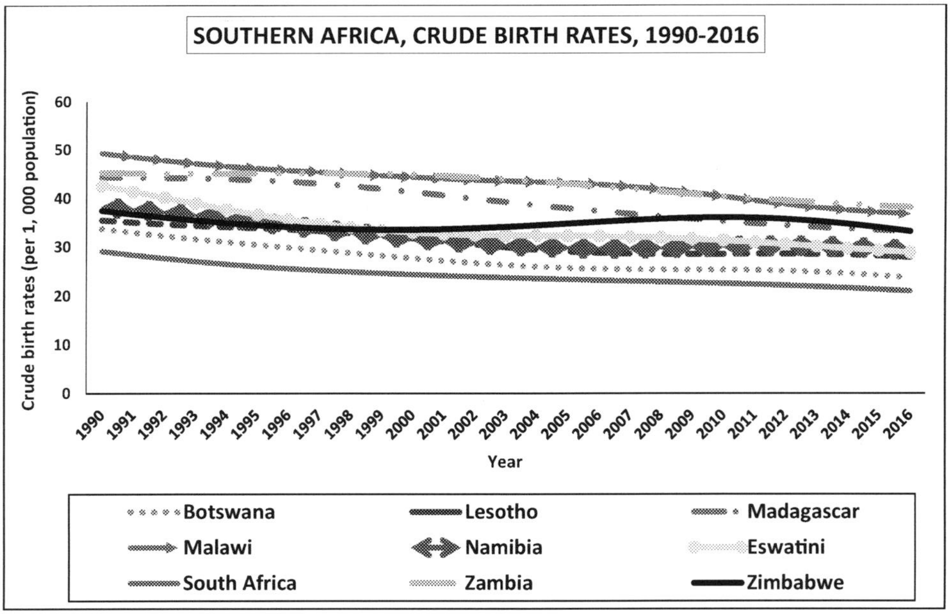

Figure 45.8 The fertility transition profile of Southern Africa.

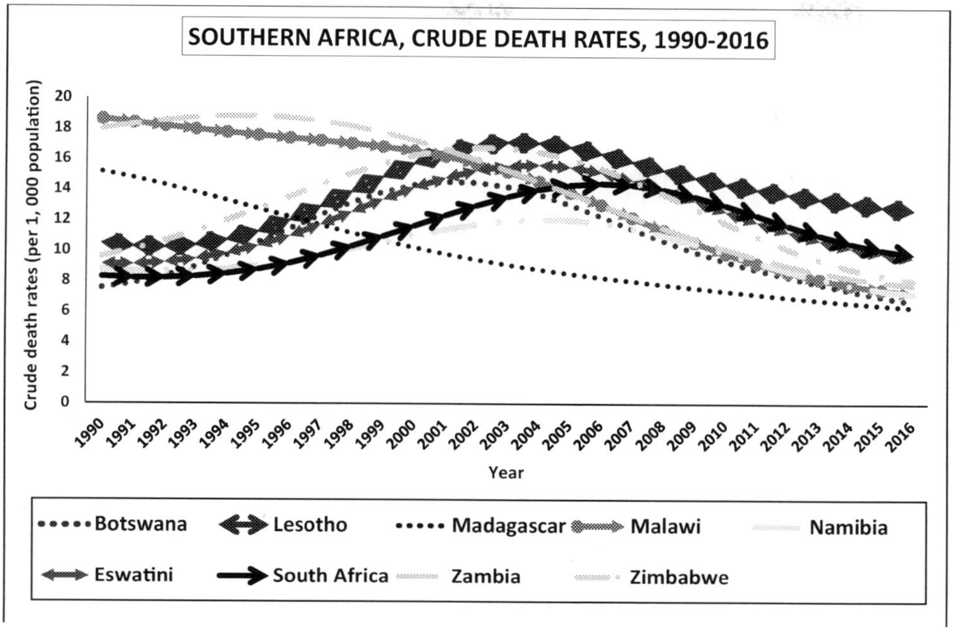

Figure 45.9 The mortality transition of Southern Africa.

Western Africa

Western Africa was marked by an uneven demographic transition from 1990 to 2016. Figure 45.1 indicates that the average crude birth rate declined from 45 to 36 births per 1,000 population, translating to a 20% average reduction in the 26-year period. This places the region fourth in Africa in terms of its fertility reduction campaign. Conversely, the region demonstrated a 40% average crude death rate decrease between 1990 and 2016, the highest average mortality reduction accomplishment in Africa as shown in Figure 45.1. In the region, Figure 45.10 illustrates Benin, Burkina Faso, Côte d'Ivoire, the Gambia, Mali, Niger, and Guinea-Bissau were characterized by crude death rates that were higher than the regional average of 36 births per 1,000 population in 2016.

Throughout 1990–2016, Niger, closely followed by Guinea-Bissau, consistently exhibited the highest crude birth rates whilst Cabo Verde followed by Ghana consistently maintained the lowest crude birth rates. Apart from Cabo Verde, the pace of crude birth-rate decline among Western African countries is somewhat slow or has stalled as revealed by the almost horizontal fertility trends during the observation period. Despite the region having made better progress in reducing mortality than fertility, countries consisting of Côte d'Ivoire, Guinea-Bissau, Niger, Mali, Nigeria, and Sierra Leone still recorded well above the regional average crude death rate of 9 deaths per 1,000 population in 2016 as shown in Figure 45.11. Strikingly, the mortality pattern of Côte d'Ivoire shows that the country experienced an upsurge in crude death rates between 1990 and 2008. Figure 45.11 also reveals that Sierra Leone was consistently marked by the highest crude death rates whereas Cabo Verde was characterized by the lowest crude death rates throughout 1990–2016. Notably, Senegal's crude death rate was also closely tied to that of Cabo Verde in 2016 as one of the countries with better population survival in Western Africa.

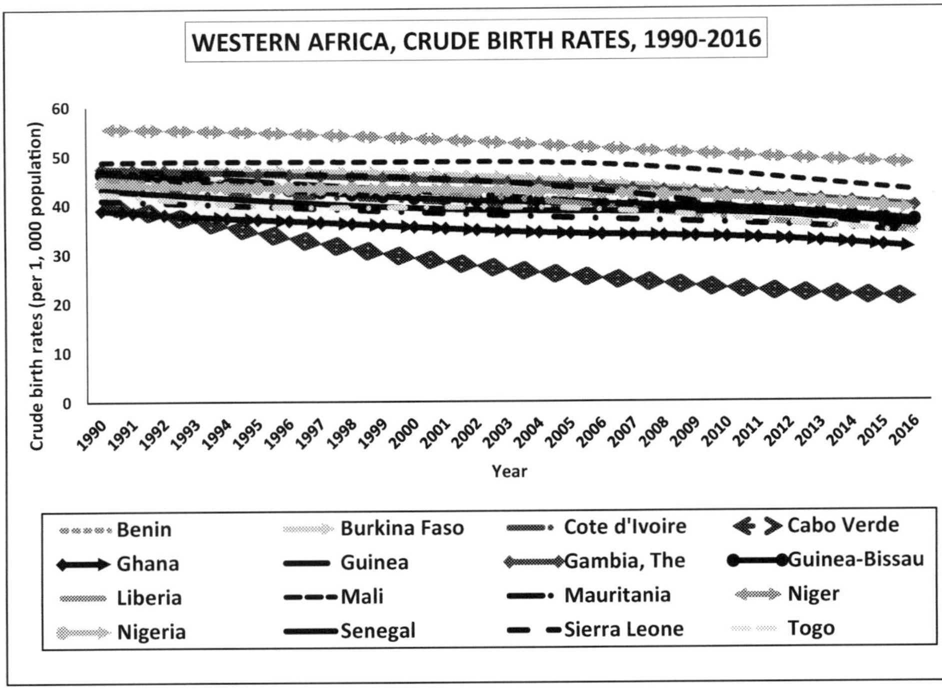

Figure 45.10 The fertility transition profile of Western Africa.

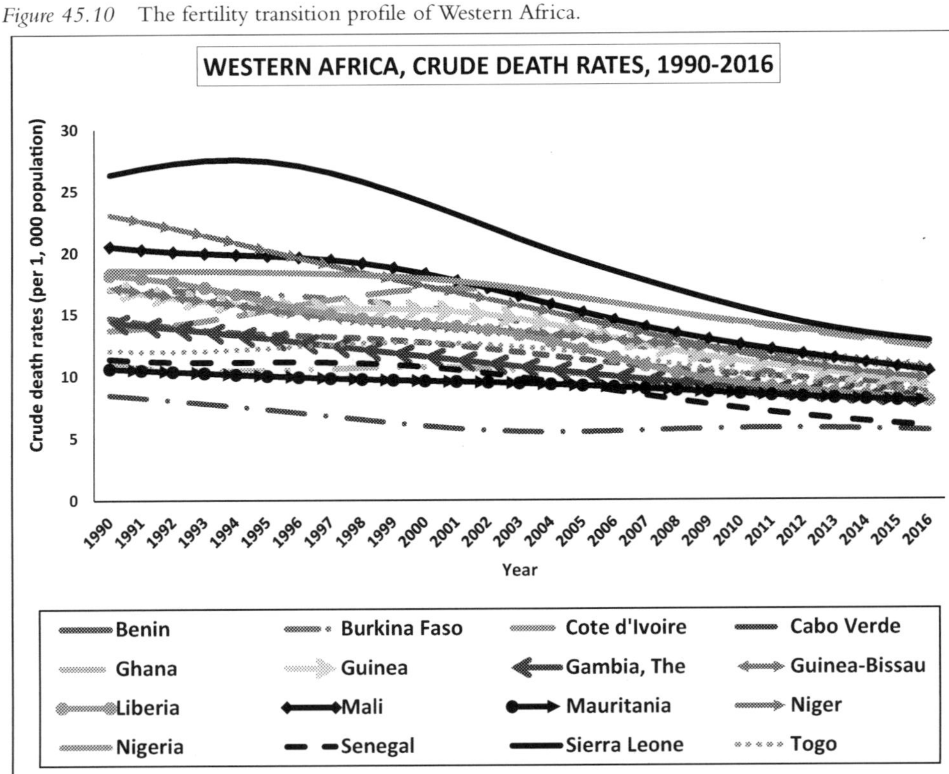

Figure 45.11 The mortality transition profile of Western Africa.

The demographic transition by Central African countries

Progress on the demographic transition was tracked for 9 countries in Central Africa between 1990 and 2016. These countries included Angola, Cameroon, Central Africa Republic, Chad, Democratic Republic of Congo (DRC), Congo Republic, Equatorial Guinea, Gabon, and Sao Tome and Principe. The results in Figure 45.12 show how each country performed regarding the reductions of both fertility and mortality in 1990–2016. It is highlighted in the evidence that Angola out-paced all the countries by attaining the highest reductions in both fertility (21%) and mortality (63%) during the 26-year observation period. With regard to the fertility decline, Gabon also made remarkable progress by matching Angola's achievement. On the other hand, DRC demonstrated the lowest fertility decline (8%) whilst Central African Republic accomplished the lowest mortality decline (20%).

Overall, the results revealed that most countries in Central Africa still depict characteristics for both stage 2 and 3 of the Demographic Transition Model. Even though fertility rates have started plummeting in most countries, however, they have not exceeded mortality rates as can be seen in the estimated levels of fertility and declines shown in Figure 45.12. Consequently, moderate and rapid population growth is experienced among these countries and will continue to be sustained by the resultant population momentum for several decades to come.

The demographic transition by Eastern African countries

The analysis of the pace of progress on the demographic transition in Eastern Africa encompassed 14 countries. These were Burundi, Comoros, Djibouti, Eritrea, Ethiopia, Kenya, Mozambique, Mauritius, Rwanda, Somalia, South Sudan, the Seychelles, Tanzania, and Uganda. Table 45.1 presents the findings on the progress made by individual countries. The

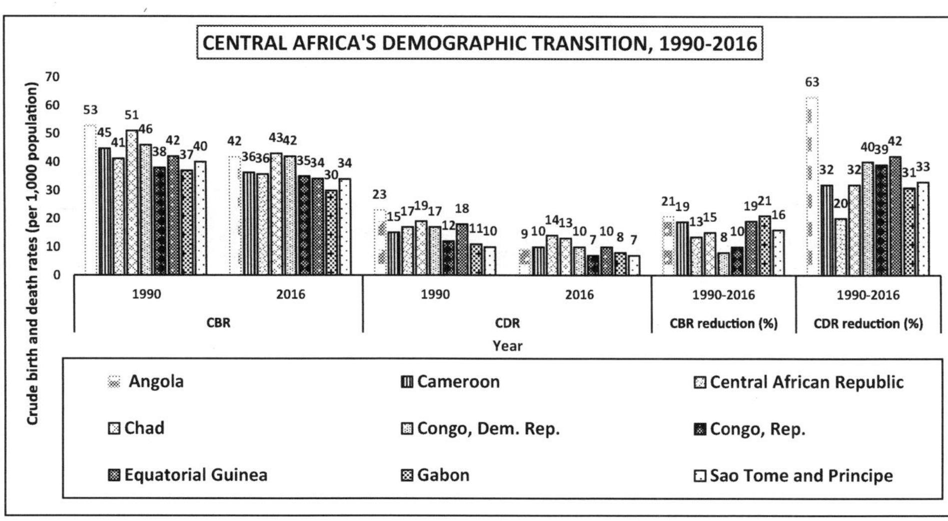

Figure 45.12 The demographic transition profile of Central Africa.

findings revealed that Mauritius experienced the highest fertility decline (51%) whereas the least decline in fertility (10%) characterized Somalia. It is also shown that Rwanda outpaced all the countries in Eastern Africa by attaining the highest mortality reduction (82%) while Mauritius reversed its population survival gains during the observation period by -23% and the Seychelles made no progress on mortality decline as demonstrated by the estimated 0%. Like Central Africa, most of the countries are still stuck between stage 2 and stage 3 of the Demographic Transition Model. Noteworthy, Djibouti is nearing stage 4 whilst Mauritius is already showing stage 4 characteristics of the Demographic Transition Model. Moreover, the negative percentage decline in mortality for Mauritius is indicative of a country that is already experiencing an ageing population, hence the rise in mortality.

The demographic transition by Northern African countries

In Northern Africa, a total of six countries were assessed on the progress they have made towards the completion of the demographic transition: Algeria, Egypt, Libya, Morocco, Sudan, and Tunisia. Each individual country's pace of progress on the demographic transition between 1990 and 2016 is shown in Figure 45.13. The findings established that Libya had the highest fertility decline (33%) whilst Egypt and Sudan matched by exhibiting the lowest reduction in fertility (21%). Conversely, Sudan was characterized by the highest mortality decline (38%) whereas Libya and Tunisia were marred by similar increases in mortality estimated at -1% as opposed to mortality declines. A closer look at the demographic transition profiles by each country revealed that fertility stalled in most of the countries, especially around the 2000s onwards. On the other hand, it was observed that mortality was generally low throughout the observation period in the Northern African region. Overall, except for Sudan, the unfolding demographic transitions in most countries appear not to conform to the precepts of the classic demographic model. This is due to the characteristic fertility stalls and increasing mortality in some countries, further causing population fluctuation, and presenting difficulties in placing these countries on one particular stage of the Demographic Transition Model.

Table 45.1: Eastern African Countries' Percentage Fertility (CBR) and Mortality (CDR) Declines by Descending Order, 1990–2016

Rank	*Country*	*Fertility Decline (%)*	*Country*	*Mortality Decline (%)*
1	Mauritius	51	Rwanda	82
2	Djibouti	42	Ethiopia	62
3	Rwanda	34	Eritrea	57
4	Ethiopia	33	Tanzania	55
5	Kenya	26	Uganda	53
6	Seychelles	25	Mozambique	52
7	South Sudan	24	South Sudan	47
8	Comoros and Eritrea	23	Kenya	45
9	Burundi and Uganda	16	Somalia	42
10	Mozambique	15	Burundi	40
11	Tanzania	13	Comoros	36
12	Somalia	10	Djibouti	22
13			Seychelles	0
14			Mauritius	-23

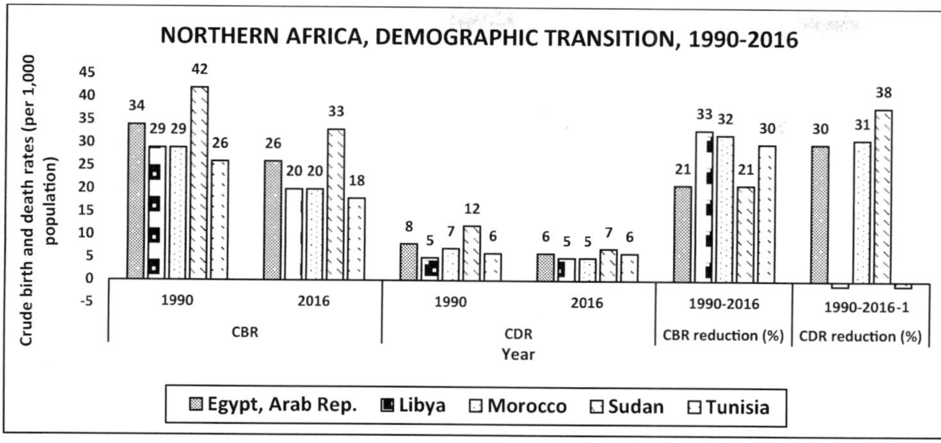

Figure 45.13 The demographic transition profile of Northern Africa.

The demographic transition by Southern African countries

The Southern African region consisted of nine countries whose progress on the demographic transition was analyzed. These were Botswana, Lesotho, Madagascar, Malawi, Namibia, Eswatini, South Africa, Zambia, and Zimbabwe. Figure 45.14 reveals that Eswatini outperformed all the countries by achieving the highest fertility decline (32%) whereas Zimbabwe had the least fertility reduction estimated at 11%. Conversely, Malawi made exceptional progress in its mortality reduction quest by attaining a 61% decline in 1990–2016. Further, the results showed the alarming negative effects of the HIV/AIDS pandemic in the region which

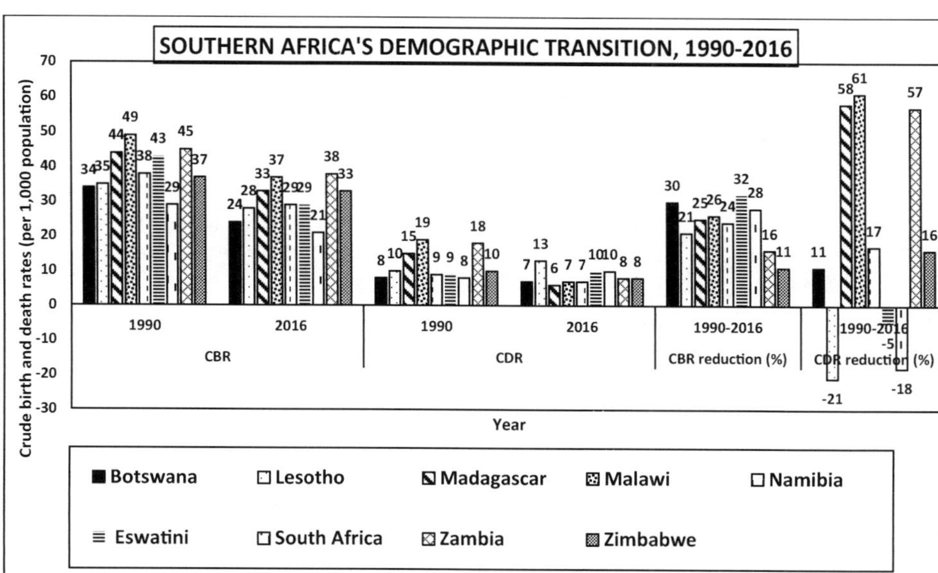

Figure 45.14 The demographic transition profile of Southern Africa.

saw Eswatini, South Africa, and Lesotho reversing their population survival gains by -5%, -18%, and -21% in 1990–2016, respectively. Other countries including Namibia, Zimbabwe, and Botswana were also hardest hit by the pandemic since they were marked by higher fertility than mortality decline, a rare feature among African countries because the opposite has largely been the portrayed picture in this analysis. Similarly to other regions, Southern African countries depicted characteristics that were found in different stages of the Demographic Transition Model due to the HIV/AIDS pandemic and predominantly stalled fertility, hence the difficulty in placing individual countries on one distinct stage of the model.

Demographic transition by Western African countries

In Western Africa, a total of 16 countries were included in the analysis: Benin, Burkina Faso, Côte d'Ivoire, Cabo Verde, Ghana, Guinea, the Gambia, Guinea-Bissau, Liberia, Mali, Mauritania, Niger, Nigeria, Senegal, Sierra Leone, and Togo. The analysis in Table 45.2 indicates that Cabo Verde was marked by the highest fertility decline (48%) whilst Nigeria exhibited the least fertility decline (12%) between 1990 and 2016. In relation to mortality reduction, Niger was characterized by the highest mortality reduction estimated at 58% whereas Côte D'Ivoire experienced the least gain in population survival as evident in the 11% mortality decline attained by the country in 1990–2016. Overall, most of the countries in Western Africa seem to be still stuck on stage 2 and stage 3 of the Demographic Transition Model, except for Cabo Verde which depicts all characteristics of stage 3 and bordering on stage 4 of the model. Consequently, high population growth characterizes this region as fertility rates remain high with only insignificant downward shifts being observed in countries like Niger, Mali, and Nigeria despite the substantial fall in death rates achieved in the region. Additionally, it appears that countries in this region might still take a longer period in stage 3 because of the imminent population momentum that will be generated by the currently bulging populations.

Table 45.2: Western African Countries' Percentage Fertility (CBR) and Mortality (CDR) Declines by Descending Order, 1990–2016

Rank	*Country*	*Fertility Decline (%)*	*Country*	*Mortality Decline (%)*
1	Cabo Verde	48	Niger	58
2	Sierra Leone	25	Liberia	57
3	Liberia	24	Sierra Leone	52
4	Guinea	23	Mali and Burkina Faso	50
5	Guinea-Bissau	21	Senegal	48
6	Benin, Ghana and Togo	20	Guinea	46
7	Burkina Faso	18	The Gambia	44
8	The Gambia, Mauritania and Senegal	17	Guinea-Bissau	39
9	Cote D'Ivoire	15	Benin	38
10	Mali and Niger	13	Cabo Verde	34
11	Nigeria	12	Nigeria	33
12			Togo	28
13			Mauritania and Ghana	25
14			Cote D'Ivoire	11

Research agenda

It has been brought to light through the analysis that Africa's demographic transition is proceeding at a slow pace, unpredictable and to a certain extent incomparable across the five regions. Not only have the African countries depicted continued rapid population growth due to lower crude birth rate decline than crude death rate decline, but the underway demographic transitions have varied from one region to another and from one country to the next, hence being inconsistent with the principles of the classic demographic transition. For instance, the findings illustrated that three regions (Central, Eastern, and Western Africa) attained higher mortality declines whereas the remaining two regions (Northern and Southern Africa) exhibited higher fertility reductions in Africa between 1990 and 2016.

The results also suggested that most countries are still between stages 2 and 3 of the classic demographic model. Primarily, African countries attained higher mortality declines than fertility declines which is an attribute of stage 2 of the classic demographic transition model. Conversely, the underway fertility transition in Africa, a characteristic of stage 3 of the classic demographic transition model, has not yet yielded levels of fertility decline that exceed the levels of mortality decline as hypothesized in the model. These findings suggest that a longer period will be required by most African countries to pass through stage 3 of the demographic transition model. In addition, though the onset and progression of the mortality transitions were somewhat on course for many African countries, unprecedented civil wars, disease outbreaks, and re-emergence of infectious diseases have disrupted the mortality transitions in some parts of the continent. Therefore, the irregularities in African demographic transitions will undoubtedly continue to sustain the unique population problems the continent is grappling with such as having young population age structures, high dependency ratios, and low life expectancies.

To address the current demographic transition situation, there is a need for more country-specific research and evidence-based population policies and programmes in African countries. For instance, countries in Central, Eastern, and Western Africa need to channel their research and intervention programmes towards improving the efficiency of family planning programmes and empowerment of women through education and labour-force participation to help lower the fertility rates. Women's education has been identified by demographers as the main determinant of contraceptive use, age at marriage, and infant and under-five mortality. Therefore, huge investments in national voluntary family planning programmes in terms of financial and human resources, accessibility, and political support as well as the education of women can cause dramatic positive shifts in both the mortality and fertility transitions in Africa. Empirical evidence on the reasons for fertility stalls in African countries can help guide population policies and reproductive health programmes in addressing challenges related to family planning. On the other hand, more research to help improve child health in Africa, especially in regions like Southern Africa that exhibited lower mortality declines is needed. In addition, investments in child survival and health programmes, reproductive health programmes, public health programmes, and prioritization of girls' education would substantially lower both fertility and mortality rates in the continent, thus helping the continent attain its demographic dividend in tandem with the demographic transition.

Conclusion

In view of the analysis, it is apparent that the unfolding demographic transition in Africa is to a great extent inconsistent with the theoretical underpinnings of the classic demographic transition. This is in conformity with the model's longstanding criticism of its inapplicability in developing countries, especially the African continent. According to the demographic transition principle, the fall in mortality rates marks the onset of the demographic transition which is later followed by a fall in fertility rates until they are both stable and fluctuate at lower levels. However, except for Mauritius, the Seychelles, Cabo Verde, and Djibouti, most countries in Africa depicted unique fertility and mortality transitions that were largely divergent from the precepts of the classic demographic transition model.

With respect to the fertility transition, the few aforementioned African countries have thus far managed to follow the mould of the original demographic transition while about 50 countries in the continent continued to grapple with simultaneously high, barely reducing, and fluctuating fertility rates. Comparatively, the analysis showed that the mortality transition has by far been the most successful transition in Africa. This was portrayed by the considerable mortality declines attained by most countries which were approximately double the level of fertility declines in 1990–2016. This is despite the increase in mortality rates due to the HIV/AIDS pandemic and political unrest especially in Southern and Northern Africa which caused a deviation from the expected gradual mortality decline envisaged in the classic demographic transition model, respectively.

Therefore, the analysis has proven that the demographic transition model as a European concept is not entirely relevant in the African context, albeit it remains an important framework to describe the fertility and mortality scenarios in the continent. Although both the fertility and mortality transitions have been underway, their progression was flawed by inherent fertility stalls and unprecedented upsurges in mortality rates, respectively. The fact that African countries constantly face adverse challenges including ailing economies, poverty, urbanization without equivalent industrial development or employment, high illiteracy rates, and heavy disease burdens is a threat to the possible emulation of the demographic transition in the continent.

In Africa, it appears that the large fertility reductions experienced by developed countries primarily through scaled-up family planning programmes would somewhat take a longer period to be achieved due to poor access to key developmental factors such as education and employment which play significant roles in determining the fertility trajectory of the populace. Additionally, early marriages and sexual debuts, large desired family sizes, and high under-five-mortality rates are some of the underlying factors that continue to have a negative effect on the fertility transition as demonstrated by the prevalent fertility stalls and slow downward fertility shift in Africa. The exceptional pro-natalist culture even when economic modernization exists has also been blamed for the maintained high fertility in Africa by some scholars. Hence, it would still take most African countries several decades to reach replacement and below-replacement fertility. Conversely, health-related issues such as poor access to preventive measures, safe drinking water and basic sanitation, unhealthy diets, maternal complications, and infectious diseases are some of the inherent problems that compromise the mortality transition in Africa. For instance, the likelihood of an emergence of new major infectious diseases such as the prevalent novel coronavirus poses a threat that might further alter the mortality transitions in Africa.

Therefore, the slow and stalling fertility transition combined with the fast-paced mortality transition in Africa will continue to sustain high population growth for several decades due to population momentum caused by the current young population age structures. This means that more investments in education, health, job creation, family planning, and environmental conservation must be made to accommodate the future bulge in populations and help fast-track the reduction of both fertility and mortality rates.

References

Acheampong, M., Ejiofor, C., Salinas-Miranda, A., Jaward, F. M., Eduful, M., & Yu, Q. (2018). Bridging the under-five mortality gap for Africa in the era of sustainable development goals: An Ordinary Least Squares (OLS) analysis. *Annals of Global Health, 84*(1), 110–120. https://doi.org/10.29024/aogh.9

Akachi, Y., & Canning, D. (2008). *The mortality and morbidity transitions in sub-Saharan Africa: Evidence from adult heights*. PGDA Working Paper No. 33. Cambridge, MA: Harvard Initiative for Global Health, Harvard University.

Askew, I., Maggwa, N., & Obare, F. (2010). *Fertility transitions in Ghana and Kenya: Trends, determinants, and implications for policy and programs*. London: UKaid, Department for International Development (DfID), Research Programme Consortium.

Blue, L., & Espenshade, T. J. (2011). Population momentum across the demographic transition. *Population Development Review, 37*(4), 721–774.

Bongaarts, J. (2016). *Africa's unique fertility transition*. New York, NY: Population Council.

Bongaarts, J., & Casterline, J. (2013). Fertility transition: Is sub Saharan Africa different? *Population and Development Review, 38*(s1), 153–168. Retrieved from www.ncbi.nlm.nih.gov/pmc/articles/PMC4011385/

Bongaarts, J., & Watkins, S. C. (1996). Social interactions and contemporary fertility transitions. *Population and Development Review, 22*(4), 639–682.

Burke, M., Heft-Neal, S., & Bendavid, E. (2016). Sources of variation in under-5 mortality across sub-Saharan Africa: A spatial analysis. *Lancet Global Health, 4*, e936–e945.

Caldwell, J. C. (1976). Toward a restatement of demographic transition theory. *Population Development Review, 2*, 32166.

Caldwell, J. C. (2006). *Demographic transition theory*. Amsterdam: Springer.

Caldwell, J. C., Orubuloye, O., & Caldwell, P. (1992). Fertility decline in Africa: A new type of transition? *Population and Development Review, 18*(2), 211–242.

Canning, D., Raja, S., & Yazbeck, A. S. (Eds.). (2015) *Africa's demographic transition: Dividend or disaster?* Washington, DC: World Bank.

Chisadza, C., & Bittencourt, M. (2016). *The fertility transition: Panel evidence from sub-Saharan Africa*. Economic Research Southern Africa. National Treasury of South Africa. Retrieved from https://www.econrsa.org/system/files/publications/working_papers/working_paper_620.pdf

Chisumpa, V. H., Odimegwu, C. O., & Saikia, N. (2019). *Mortality in sub-Saharan Africa: What is killing adults aged 15–59 years in Zambia?* Vienna Institute of Demography Working Papers No. 04/2019. Vienna: Austrian Academy of Sciences (ÖAW), Vienna Institute of Demography (VID).

Cleland, J. (2012). *Will Africa benefit from the demographic dividend*. The Health & Education Advice & Resource Team (HEART). United Kingdom. Retrieved from https://assets.publishing.service.gov.uk/media/57a08aafe5274a31e0000706/Demographic-Dividend-November-2012.pdf

Defo, B. K. (2014). Demographic, epidemiological, and health transitions: Are they relevant to population health patterns in Africa? *Global Health Action*, 7, 22443. http://doi.org/10.3402/gha.v7.22443

Edmonston, B. (2014). Two centuries of demographic change in Canada. *Canadian Studies in Population, 41*(1–2), 1–37.

Garenne, M. (2009). Situations of fertility stall in sub-Saharan Africa. *African Population Studies, 23*(2).

Golding, N., Burstein, R., Longbottom, J., Browne, A. J., Fullman, N., Osgood-Zimmerman, A., . . . Hay, S. I. (2017). Mapping under-5 and neonatal mortality in Africa, 2000–15: A baseline analysis for the Sustainable Development Goals. *The Lancet, 390*, 211–282.

Gouda, H. N., Charlson, F., Sorsdahl, K. Ahmadzada, S., Ferrari, A. J., Erskine, H., . . . Whiteford, H. (2019). Burden of non-communicable diseases in sub-Saharan Africa, 1990–2017: Results from the Global Burden of Disease Study 2017. *The Lancet Global Health*, 7, e1375–e1387.

Houle, B., Clark, S. J., Go´mez-Olive, F. X., Kahn, K., & Tollman, S. M. (2014). The unfolding counter-transition in rural South Africa: Mortality and cause of death, 1994–2009. *PLoS One, 9*(6), e100420. https://doi.org/10.1371/journal.pone.0100420

Kahn, K., Garenne, M. L., Collinson, M. A., & Tollman, S. M. (2007). Mortality trends in a new South Africa: Hard to make a fresh start. *Scandinavian Journal of Public Health, 35*(Suppl. 69), 26–34.

Kalipeni, E. (1995). The fertility transition in Africa. *American Geographical Society, 85*(3), 286–300.

Kebede, E., Goujon, A., & Lutz, W. (2019). Stalls in Africa's fertility decline partly result from disruptions in female education. *PNAS, 116*(8).

Kuate-Defo, B. (2002). *Mortality and health transition in Africa: Explaining the reversal trend in childhood mortality*. IUSSP Paper. Rostock: Germany.

Lee, R. D., & Reher, D. S. (2011). Introduction: Landscape of demographic transition and its aftermath. *Population Development and Review, 37*(s1), 1–7.

Livi-Bacci, M. (2017). *A concise history of world population growth* (6th ed.). Oxford: Blackwell.

Machiyama, K. (2010). *A re-examination of recent fertility declines in Sub-Saharan Africa* (DHS Working Papers No. 68). Calverton, MD: ICF Macro.

Madsen, E. L. (2013). *Why has the demographic transition stalled in sub-Saharan Africa*. Environmental Change and Security Program, Woodrow Wilson International Center for Scholars, Washington, DC. https://www.newsecuritybeat.org/2013/08/demographic-transition-stalled-sub-saharan-africa/

Menashe-Oren, A., & Stecklov, G. (2018). Urban-rural disparities in adult mortality in sub-Saharan Africa. *Demographic Research, 139*(5), 36–176. https://doi.org/10.4054/DemRes.2018.39.5

Mubila, M. (2012). *Briefing Note 4: Africa's demographic trends*. African Development Bank Group. https://www.afdb.org/fileadmin/uploads/afdb/Documents/Policy-Documents/FINAL%20Briefing%20Note%204%20Africas%20Demographic%20Trends.pdf

Nam, C. (1994). *Understanding population change*. Itasca, IL: FE Peacock Publishers; Organisation for Economic Co-operation and Development.

Ndahindwa, V., Kamanzi, C., Semakula, M., Abalikumwen, F., Hedt-Gauthier, B., & Thomson, D. R. (2014). Determinants of fertility in Rwanda in the context of a fertility transition: A secondary analysis of the 2010 Demographic and Health Survey. *Reproductive Health, 11*, 87.

Notestein, F. W. (1945). Population*the long view. In: T. W. Schultz (Ed.), *Food for the world* (pp. 36–57). Chicago, IL: University of Chicago Press.

Notkola, V., Timaeus, I. M., & Siiskonen, H. (2000). Mortality transition in the Ovamboland Region of Namibia, 1930–1990. *A Journal of Demography, 54*(2), 153–167.

Nugent, R., & Seligman, B. (2013). *Demographics and development in the 21st century: Initiative technical background paper: How demographic change affects development*. Washington, DC: Center for Global Development. Retrieved from https://www.cgdev.org/sites/default/files/archive/doc/Demographic_and_Development/DD_background_12_10_08.PDF

Otieno, V., Agwanda, A., & Khasakhala, A. (2020). Fertility transition in selected sub-Saharan African countries: The role of family planning programs [version 2; peer review: 1 approved, 1 approved with reservations], *F1000 Research, 8*, 1748. https://doi.org/10.12688/f1000research.20585.2

Samman, E., & Watkins, K. (2017). *Africa's opportunity: Reaping the early harvest of the demographic transition and ensuring no one is left behind*. London: Overseas Development Institute. Retrieved from https://cdn.odi.org/media/documents/11812.pdf

Sippel, L., Kiziak. T., Woellert, F., & Klingholz, R. (2011). *Africa's demographic challenges: How a young population can make development possible*. Berlin: Berlin Institute of Population and Development.

Sneeringer, S. E. (2009). *Fertility transition in sub-Saharan Africa: A comparative analysis of cohort trends in 30 Countries* (DHS Comparative Reports No. 23). Calverton, MD: ICF Macro.

Teller, C. H., Hailemariam, A., Gebreselassie, T., & Seifu, Y. (2011). The uniqueness of the Ethiopian demographic transition within sub-Saharan Africa: multiple responses to population pressure, and preconditions for the rural fertility decline and capturing the demographic dividend. *African Population Studies, 25*(2).

United Nations, Department of Economic and Social Affairs, Population Division. (2017). *World population prospects 2017 revision. Data booklet*. New York, NY: United Nations.

United Nations, Department of Economic and Social Affairs, Population Division. (2019). *World population prospects 2019. Data booklet*. New York, NY: United Nations.

Watkins, S. C. (1986). Conclusions. In Ansley J. Coale & S. C. Watkins (Eds.), *The decline of fertility in Europe*. Princeton, NJ: Princeton University Press.

Willekens, F. (2015). *Demographic transitions in Europe and the World*. London and New York: Routledge.

Williams, J. R., Manfredi, P., & Melegaro, A. (2018). The potential impact of the demographic transition in the Senegal-Gambia region of sub-Saharan Africa on the burden of infectious disease and its potential synergies with control programmes: The case of hepatitis *B. BMC Medicine, 16*, 118. https://doi.org/10.1186/s12916-018-1100-0

World Bank Group. (2016). *Global Monitoring Report 2015/2016*. Retrieved from pubdocs.worldbank.org

INDEX

Note: Page numbers in *italic* indicate a figure and page numbers in **bold** indicate a table on the corresponding page.

Printed in the United States
by Baker & Taylor Publisher Services